POLITICS IN AMERICA
THIRD EDITION

TEXAS EDITION

THOMAS R. DYE
Florida State University

with L. TUCKER GIBSON, JR.
Trinity University

and CLAY ROBISON
Houston Chronicle

PRENTICE HALL, Upper Saddle River, New Jersey 07458

Library of Congress Cataloging-in-Publication Data

The Library of Congress has catalogued the national edition of this work as follows:
Dye, Thomas R.
    Politics in America / Thomas R. Dye. — 3rd ed.
        p.   cm.
    Includes bibliographical references and index.
    ISBN 0-13-095689-9
    1. United States—Politics and government.   2. Texas—Politics and
government   I. Title.
JK271.D94   1998   98-27686
320.473—dc21   CIP

Editorial Director: Charlyce Jones Owen
Editor-in-Chief: Nancy Roberts
Senior Acquisitions Editor: Beth Gillett
Development Supervisor: David Chodoff
AVP, Director of Production and Manufacturing: Barbara Kittle
Production Editor: Barbara Reilly
Copy Editor: Anne Lesser
Editorial Assistants: Kathryn Sheehan, Darren Rich, Brian Prybella
Production Assistants: Kathleen Sleys, Claire Rottino, Nicole Tellem
Director of Marketing: Gina Sluss
Marketing Manager: Christopher DeJohn
Manufacturing Manager: Nick Sklitsis
Prepress and Manufacturing Buyer: Bob Anderson
Creative Design Director: Leslie Osher
Interior and Cover Design: Susan Walrath
Line Art Coordinator: Guy Ruggiero
Electronic Art Creation: Maria Piper
Supervisor of Production Services: John Jordan
Electronic Page Layout: Joh Lisa, Scott Garrison
Director, Image Resource Center: Lori Morris-Nantz
Photo Research Supervisor: Melinda Lee Reo
Image Permissions Supervisor: Kay Dellosa
Photo Research: Eloise Marion Donnelly
Permissions Coordinator: Anthony Arabia
Cover Coordinator: Karen Sanatar
Cover Photo: Doug Amand / Tony Stone Images

This book was set in 12/13 Perpetua by Prentice Hall Production Services
and was printed and bound by Courier Companies, Inc.
The cover was printed by Phoenix Color Corp.

10 9 8 7 6 5 4 3

ISBN 0-13-095511-6

PRENTICE-HALL INTERNATIONAL (UK) LIMITED, *London*
PRENTICE-HALL OF AUSTRALIA PTY. LIMITED, *Sydney*
PRENTICE-HALL CANADA INC., *Toronto*
PRENTICE-HALL HISPANOAMERICANA, S.A., *Mexico*
PRENTICE-HALL OF INDIA PRIVATE LIMITED, *New Delhi*
PRENTICE-HALL OF JAPAN, INC., *Tokyo*
PRENTICE-HALL ASIA PTE. LTD., *Singapore*
EDITORA PRENTICE-HALL DO BRASIL, LTD., *Rio de Janeiro*

BRIEF CONTENTS

CONTENTS

PART II ☆ CONSTITUTION

The ascendancy of any elite depends upon the success of the practices it adopts. . . .
The Constitution, written and unwritten, embodies the practices which are deemed
most fundamental to the governmental and social order.

Harold Lasswell

THE CONSTITUTION: LIMITING GOVERNMENTAL POWER   61

FEDERALISM: DIVIDING GOVERNMENTAL POWER   97

PART III ☆ PARTICIPANTS

People strive for power—to get the most of what there is to get.
Harold Lasswell

 ## OPINION AND PARTICIPATION: THINKING AND ACTING IN POLITICS 127

 ## MASS MEDIA: SETTING THE POLITICAL AGENDA 165

7 POLITICAL PARTIES: ORGANIZING POLITICS   195

8 CAMPAIGNS AND ELECTIONS: DECIDING WHO GOVERNS   237

9 INTEREST GROUPS: GETTING THEIR SHARE AND MORE   283

PART IV ☆ INSTITUTIONS

Authority is the expected and legitimate possession of power.
Harold Lasswell

10 CONGRESS: POLITICS ON CAPITOL HILL 321

11 THE PRESIDENT: WHITE HOUSE POLITICS 377

12 THE BUREAUCRACY: BUREAUCRATIC POLITICS 423

13 COURTS: JUDICIAL POLITICS 465

PART V ☆ OUTCOMES

*That political science concentrates upon the influential does not imply the
neglect of the total distribution of values throughout the community. . . .
The emphasis upon the probability that the few (elite) will get the most does not
imply that the many (mass) do not profit from some political changes.*

Harold Lasswell

14 POLITICS AND PERSONAL LIBERTY 505

15 POLITICS AND CIVIL RIGHTS 545

PART VI ☆ TEXAS POLITICS

 ## THE SOCIAL AND ECONOMIC MILIEU OF TEXAS POLITICS   677

 ## THE TEXAS CONSTITUTION   711

 ## INTEREST GROUPS, POLITICAL PARTIES, AND ELECTIONS IN TEXAS   737

THE TEXAS LEGISLATURE 769

THE TEXAS EXECUTIVE AND BUREAUCRACY 805

PREFACE

Politics is the activity by which people try to get more of whatever there is to get. It is about the struggle over the allocation of values in society. It is, in Howard Lasswell's classic phrase, about "who gets what, when, and how."

Politics consists of all of the activities—reasonable discussion, impassioned oratory, campaigning, balloting, fund raising, advertising, lobbying, demonstrating, rioting, street fighting, and waging war—by which conflict is carried on. Managing conflict is the principle function of the political system, and power—to decide who gets what, when, and how—is its ultimate goal.

Using Lasswell's definition of politics as its unifying framework, *Politics in America, Third Edition,* introduces students to the American political system by examining the struggle for power—the participants, the stakes, the processes, and the institutional arenas.

WHY *POLITICS IN AMERICA?*

Recent market research indicates that 76 percent of instructors teaching the Introductory American Government course find engaging their students to be their most difficult task. *Politics in America, Third Edition,* is written to be lively and absorbing, reflecting the teaching philosophy that stimulating students' interest in politics and public affairs is the most important goal of an introductory course. Interesting examples and controversial debates spark students' interest and keep them connected to the material. The struggle for power in society is not a dull topic, and textbooks should not make it so.

Politics in America, Third Edition, strives for a balanced presentation, but "balanced" does not mean boring. It does not mean the avoidance of controversy. Liberal and conservative arguments are set forth clearly and forcefully. Race and gender are given particular attention, not because it is currently fashionable to do so, but because American politics has long been driven by these factors. As in previous editions, the trademark of this book continues to be its desire to pull students into the American political debate.

ORGANIZATION

Part I, "Politics," begins with Lasswell's classic definition of politics and proceeds to describe the nature and functions of government and the meaning of democracy. It poses the question: How democratic is the American political system? It describes the American political culture: its contradictions between liberty and conformity, political equality and economic inequality, equality of opportunity and equality of results, thus laying the groundwork for understanding the struggle over who gets what.

Part II, "Constitution," describes the politics of constitution making—deciding how to decide. It describes how the struggle over the U.S. Constitution reflected the distribution of power in the new nation. It focuses on the classic arguments of the Founders for limiting and dividing governmental power and the structural arrangements designed to accomplish this end.

Part III, "Participants," begins by examining individual participation in politics—the way people acquire and hold political opinions and act on them. It examines the influences of family, school, gender, race, and the role of media in shaping political opinion. It describes how organization concentrates power—to win public office in the case of party organizations, and to influence policy in the case of interest groups. It assesses the role of personal ambition and the role of money in politics.

Part IV, "Institutions," describes the various governmental arenas in which the struggle for power takes place—the Congress, the presidency, the bureaucracy, the courts. More important, it evaluates the power that comes with control of each of these institutions.

Part V, "Outcomes," deals with public policies, the result of the struggle over the allocation of values. It is especially concerned with the two fundamental values of American society, liberty and equality. Each is examined in separate chapters, as are economic policies, welfare policies, and national security policies.

INSTRUCTIONAL FEATURES

Chapter Opening Poll Each chapter of *Politics in America, Third Edition,* opens with a brief poll, called "Ask Yourself about Politics," that alerts students to the crucial issues the chapter covers and the impact of those issues on their lives. This tool can be used to get students reading and thinking about how and why politics is important to them as individuals and as members of a community. In the third edition, we are excited to offer this survey as an interactive exercise on the book's accompanying Web page (www.prenhall.com/dye). Now students can compare their answers to these questions with those of students from across the country.

Text and Features The body of each chapter is divided into *text* and *features*. The text provides the framework for understanding American politics. Each chapter begins with a brief discussion of power in relation to the subject matter of the chapter: for example, limiting governmental power (Chapter 3, "The Constitution"), dividing governmental power (Chapter 4, "Federalism") and the power of the media (Chapter 6, "Mass Media"). By focusing the beginning of each chapter on questions of power, students can more easily set the chapter content in the context of Lasswell's definition of politics.

The features in each chapter provide timeliness, relevance, stimulation, and perspective.

- **"What Do You Think?"** These features pose controversial questions to students and provide national opinion survey data on them. They cover a wide range of topics designed to stimulate classroom discussion. Examples include: "Can You Trust Government?" "Should the Media Report on the Private Lives of Public Officials?" "Should We Mix Politics and Religion?" "Do We Need Special Prosecutors to Investigate Presidents?" "What Constitutes Sexual Harassment?" "Should We Enact a Flat Tax?"

- **"A Conflicting View"** These features challenge students to rethink conventional notions about American politics. They are designed to be controversial. "Politics as Violence," for example, briefly summarizes the view that much of American political development has been accompanied by violence. Other "Conflicting View" features include: "An Economic Interpretation of the Constitution," "Objections to the Constitution by an Anti-Federalist," "Let the People Vote on National Issues," "The War on Drugs as a Threat to Liberty," "The Constitution Should Be Color-Blind," and "Government Programs as a Cause of Poverty."

- **"Compared to What?"** These features provide students with global context by comparing the United States with other nations. Examples include "Freedom and Democracy around the World" and "Authoritarianism and Totalitarianism," in addition to topics such as voter turnout, television culture, and crime and punishment.

- **"People in Politics"** These features are designed to personalize politics for students, to show them that the participants in the struggle for power are real people. They discuss where prominent people in politics went to school, how they got started in politics, how their careers developed, and how much power they came to possess. They focus on both historical figures like Thomas Hobbes, John Locke, James Madison, and current figures such as Newt Gingrich, Richard Gephardt, Al Gore, Colin Powell, and Christine Todd Whitman.

- **"Up Close"** These features illustrate the struggle over who gets what. They range over a wide variety of current political conflicts, such as: "Sex, Lies, Partisanship and Impeachment," "The President Shakes the Money Tree," "Campaign 2000, Off and Running," "Ideology on Campus: Students versus Professors," "AARP, The Nation's Most Powerful Interest Group," and "The Christian Coalition: Organizing the Faithful." A special feature, "How to Run for Office," provides practical advice on how to get into electoral politics.

- **"Across the USA"** These features provide maps that summarize important statistical and demographic information relevant to American politics.

- **"Politics in Cyberspace"** As technology becomes a daily part of our lives, the political arena becomes more and more accessible. These new features encourage students to go beyond the textbook and explore the abundance of political information available on the World Wide Web. They direct students not just to widely used sites like those maintained by the major news organizations or major government offices, but also to party, ideological, think tank, and interest group sites such as those maintained by the Democratic National Committee, Republican National Committee, Americans for Democratic Action, the Brookings Institution, the Heritage Foundation, the Center for Reponsive Politics, the National Association for the Advancement of Colored People, and the American Civil Liberties Union. Students are encouraged to engage in original research by examining such sites as those maintained by the Federal Elections Commission, the Office of Management and Budget, the Federal Reserve Board, the Library of Congress, the National Bureau of Economic Research, the Equal Employment Opportunity Commission, and the Cornell University Law School.

Pedagogical aids Each chapter includes an opening outline, a running marginal glossary that helps students master important concepts, a summary, and a list of suggested readings.

Currency Although the Introduction to American Government course is not a course on current events, students are most interested in what is going on around them. *Politics in America, Third Edition,* features up-to-date coverage of critical political issues—from the 1998 Congressional elections to Clinton's battles with the independent counsel—giving students a context into which to put today's headlines.

SUPPLEMENTS AVAILABLE FOR THE INSTRUCTOR

- **Companion Web Site - Course Manager Edition** (www.prenhall.com/dye) Containing a wealth of additional resources, this free Web site includes the original text of more than 150 primary source documents mentioned in the text, an update section with the latest news and suggestions on how to tie it to lectures, teaching strategies for the new instructor, and additional Web links. The Course Management functions allow instructors to send e-mails to one student or a whole class, monitor grades, organize and post course syllabuses, and perform many other classroom management tasks. In addition, the page offers interactive practice tests, writing instruction, career information, and the interactive survey for your students.

- **Instructor's Manual** (0-13-095898-0) For each chapter, a summary, review of concepts, lecture suggestions and topic outlines, and additional resource materials—including a guide to media resources—are provided.

- **Test Item File** (0-13-095899-9) Thoroughly reviewed and revised to ensure the highest level of quality and accuracy, this file offers over 1800 questions in multiple-choice, true/false, and essay format with page references to the text.

- **Prentice Hall Custom Test** A computerized test bank contains the items from the Test Item File. The program allows full editing of questions and the addition of instructor-generated items. Available in DOS, Windows, and Macintosh versions.

- **Telephone Test Preparation Service** With one call to our toll-free 800 number, you can have Prentice Hall prepare tests with up to 200 questions chosen from the Test Item File. Within 48 hours of your request, you will receive a personalized exam with answer key.

- **American Government Transparencies, Series V** This set of 75 to 100 four-color transparency acetates reproduces illustrations, charts, and maps from the text as well as from additional sources. An Instructor's Guide is also available.

- **ABCNEWS ABC News/Prentice Hall Video Library Images in American Government** (0-13-364498-7) Issues in American Government (0-13-304023-2); Election '96 (0-13-79369-3). Prentice Hall and ABC News bring chapter concepts to life by illustrating them with newsworthy topics and pressing issues. The library consists of feature segments from such award-winning programs as *Nightline, 20/20, World News Tonight/The American Agenda,* and *This Week.* An Instructor's Guide providing synopses and questions is also available.

- **Strategies for Teaching American Government: A Guide for the New Instructor** (0-13-339003-9) This unique guide offers a wealth of practical advice and information to help new instructors face the challenges of teaching American government.

SUPPLEMENTS AVAILABLE FOR THE STUDENT

- **Companion Web Site** (www.prenhall.com/dye) Students can now take full advantage of the World Wide Web to enrich the study of American Government through the *Politics in America* Web site. Created by Dave Garson of North Carolina State University, the site features interactive practice tests, chapter objectives and overviews, additional graphs and charts, and more than 150 primary source documents that are covered in the text. Interactive Web exercises guide students to do research with a series of questions and links. Students can also tap into information on the 2000 presidential election, writing in political science, career opportunities, and internship information.

- **Study Guide** (0-13-958927-9)   Includes chapter outlines, study notes, a glossary, and practice tests designed to reinforce information in the text and help students develop a greater understanding of American government and politics.

- **The Write Stuff: Writing as a Performing and Political Art, Second Edition** (0-13-364746-3) by Thomas E. Cronin   This brief, humorous booklet provides ideas and suggestions on writing in political science and is available free to students using *Politics in America, Third Edition.*

-  **The New York Times/ Prentice Hall Themes of the Times** Prentice Hall joins forces with the premier news publication, *The New York Times*, to provide a student newspaper supplement containing recent articles pertinent to American government. These articles augment the text material and provide real-world examples. The publication is updated twice a year.

- **Political Science on the Internet, 1998–1999 Edition** (0-13-978768-2)   This brief guide introduces students to the origin and innovations behind the Internet and provides clear strategies for navigating the complexity of the Internet and World Wide Web. Exercises within and at the end of the chapters allow students to practice searching for the myriad resources available to the student of political science. This 48-page supplementary book is free to students when purchased as a package with *Politics in America, Third Edition.*

ACKNOWLEDGMENTS

Politics in America, Third Edition, reflects the influence of many splendid teachers, students, and colleagues who have helped me over the years. I am grateful for the early guidance of Frank Sorauf, my undergraduate student adviser at Pennsylvania State College, and James G. Coke, my Ph.D. dissertation director at the University of Pennsylvania. Georgia Parthemos at the University of Georgia and Malcolm Parsons at Florida State University gave me my first teaching posts. But my students over the years contributed most to my education—notably Susan MacManus, Kent Penney, Ed Benton, James Ammons, and especially John Robey. And I am deeply grateful to Harriet Crawford of the Policy Sciences Center, who turned my scratchings into a manuscript.

At Prentice Hall I am indebted to Beth Gillett, Nancy Roberts, and Charlyce Jones Owen for their confidence in the project. David Chodoff at Prentice Hall provided invaluable editorial guidance, and Barbara Reilly guided the book smoothly through production with professional competence.

Finally, I would like to thank the many reviewers who evaluated the text and contributed invaluable advice:

Danny Adkinson, Oklahoma State University
Weston Agor, University of Texas at El Paso
Angela Burger, UWC-Marathon Company
Mel Cohen, Miami University, Middletown
Frank Colon, Lehigh University
Roy Dawes, University of Southwestern Louisiana
John Ellis, San Antonio College
Larry Elowitz, University of Southwestern Louisiana
Edward Fox, Eastern Washington University
Marilyn A. W. Garr, Johnson County Community College
John Green, University of Akron
Dale Herspring, Kansas State University
Fred Kramer, University of Massachusetts at Amherst
Dale Krane, University of Nebraska at Omaha
Nancy McGlen, Niagara University
John McGlennon, College of William and Mary
James Meader, Augustana College
Jo Anne Myers, Marist College
Max Neiman, University of California-Riverside
Christopher Petras, Central Michigan University
Sandra L. Quinn-Musgrove, Our Lady of the Lake University
Bruce Rogers, American River College
Bill Rutherford, Odessa University
John Shea, West Chester University
Robert Small, Massosoit County College
Henry Steck, SUNY-Cortland
Gerald Strom, University of Illinois at Chicago
Morris M. Wilhelm, Indiana University Southeast
Al Waite, Central Texas College
John Whitney, Lincoln Land Community College

PREFACE TO THE TEXAS EDITION

Texas government and politics are shaped by the complex relationships within the federal system as well as by the state's unique political history and cultural heritage. Texas has much in common with the other forty-nine states, including its form of government, which is structured around general principles of popular sovereignty, limited goverment, separation of powers, and checks and balances, to name a few. The political culture of the state draws from the dominant themes that characterize the national political culture, and the legal system has basically been shaped by Anglo-Saxon legal traditions. From party politics to interest group activities to mass political behavior, Texans behave much like their fellow citizens in other states.

From one perspective, our analysis of Texas government and politics is an introduction to state and local government, using Texas as a case study. There are many generalizations and conclusions that can be drawn from our analysis of Texas and applied to other states. Conversely, there are elements of our analysis that speak to the unique aspects of the Texas political experience. Those who have developed a deep attachment to the state, as well as visitors and newcomers, tend to feel that there is something unique, if not special, about the Lone Star State and its people. For some, this "uniqueness" is in the pride (some would say arrogance) that Texans take in their state. For others, it is the tradition of the frontier, the myths of rugged individualism and self-reliance that translate into the state's conservatism and "style of politics."

For more than 25 years, we have both been fascinated by the politics of the state, and while many aspects of state government have remained the same, it is the continuous process of change that elicits our greatest interest. We have attempted to provide a historical perspective that lays the groundwork for the changes that have taken place and will take place as we move into the twenty-first century.

Our special thanks go to the staff at Prentice Hall. Beth Gillett, David Chodoff, Barbara Reilly, Eloise Marion Donnelly, and others of the editorial staff have provided invaluable support to us throughout this project.

L. Tucker Gibson, Jr.
Clay Robison

ASK YOURSELF ABOUT POLITICS

1. Can you trust the government to do what is right most of the time?
Yes ☐ No ☐

2. Should any group other than the government have the right to use force?
Yes ☐ No ☐

3. Is violence ever justified as a means of bringing about political change?
Yes ☐ No ☐

4. Is it ever right to disobey the law?
Yes ☐ No ☐

5. Should important decisions in a democracy be submitted to voters rather than decided by Congress?
Yes ☐ No ☐

6. Has government in the United States grown too big?
Yes ☐ No ☐

7. In a democracy should "majority rule" be able to limit the rights of members of an unpopular or dangerous minority?
Yes ☐ No ☐

8. Is government trying to do too many things that should be left to individuals?
Yes ☐ No ☐

Chapter 1

POLITICS
WHO GETS WHAT, WHEN, AND HOW

CHAPTER OUTLINE

FEATURES

Who has power and how they use it are the basis of all these questions. Issues of power underlie everything we call politics and the study of political science.

POLITICS AND POLITICAL SCIENCE

Politics is deciding "who gets what, when, and how." It is an activity by which people try to get more of whatever there is to get—money, prestige, jobs, respect, sex, even power itself. Politics occurs in many different settings. We talk about office politics, student politics, union politics, church politics, and so forth. But political science usually limits its attention to *politics in government*.

Conflict exists in all political activities as participants struggle over who gets what, when, and how. From the streets to the Congress to the White House, participants in the political process compete to further their goals and ambitions.

Political science is the study of politics, or the study of who gets what, when, and how. The *who* are the participants in politics—voters, special-interest groups, political parties, television and the press, corporations and labor unions, lawyers and lobbyists, foundations and think tanks, and both elected and appointed government officials, including members of Congress, the president and vice-president, judges, prosecutors, and bureaucrats. The *what* of politics are public policies—the decisions that governments make concerning social welfare, health care, education, national defense, law enforcement, the environment, taxation, and thousands of other issues that come before governments. The *when* and *how* are the political process—campaigns and elections, political reporting in the news media, television debates, fund raising, lobbying, decision making in the White House and executive agencies, and decision making in the courts.

Political science is generally concerned with three questions: *Who governs? For what ends? By what means?* Throughout this book, we are concerned with who participates in politics, how government decisions are made, who benefits most from those decisions, and who bears their greatest costs (see Figure 1-1).

Politics would be simple if everyone agreed on who should govern, who should get what, who should pay for it, and how and when it should be done. But conflict

politics Deciding who gets what, when, and how.

political science The study of politics: who governs, for what ends, and by what means.

Who Governs: Participants

Governmental

President and White House staff
Executive Office of the President, including Office of Management and Budget
Cabinet officers and executive agency heads
Bureaucrats

Congress members
Congressional staff

Supreme Court justices
Federal appellate and district judges

Nongovernmental

Voters
Campaign contributors
Interest-group leaders and members
Party leaders and party identifiers in the electorate
Corporate and union leaders
Media leaders, including press and television anchors and reporters
Lawyers and lobbyists
Think tanks and foundation personnel

When and How: Institutions and Processes

Institutions

Constitution
  Separation of powers
  Checks and balances
  Federalism
  Judicial review
  Amendment procedures
  Electoral system

Presidency
Congress
  Senate
  House of Representatives

Courts
  Supreme Court
  Appellate Court
  District Court

Parties
  National committees
  Conventions
  State and local organizations

Press and television

Processes

Socialization and learning
Opinion formation
Party identification
Voting
Contributing
Joining organizations
Talking politics

Running for office
Campaigning
Polling
Fund raising
Parading and demonstrating
Nonviolent direct action
Violence

Agenda setting
Lobbying
Logrolling
Deciding
Budgeting
Implementing and evaluating
Adjudicating

What Outcomes: Public Policies

Civil liberties
Civil rights
Equality
Criminal justice
Welfare
Social Security
Health
Education

Energy
Environmental protection
Economic development
Economic stability
Taxation
Government spending and deficits
National defense
Foreign affairs

FIGURE 1-1 Who Gets What, When, and How

Political science is the study of politics. The study of politics includes the questions "Who governs?" (that is, who are the participants in politics, both within and outside of government?); "When and how are political decisions made?" (that is, how do the institutions and processes of politics function?); and "What outcomes are produced?" (that is, what public policies are adopted?). Shown here are some of the topics of concern to political science.

arises from disagreements over these questions, and sometimes the question of confidence in the government itself underlies the conflict (see *What Do You Think?* "Can You Trust the Government?"). Politics arises out of conflict, and it consists of all the activities—reasonable discussion, impassioned oratory, balloting, campaigning, lobbying, parading, rioting, street fighting, and waging war—by which conflict is carried on.

Can You Trust the Government?

Americans are suspicious of big government. Many do not trust the government in Washington to "do what is right." Although commentators often bemoan Americans' lack of confidence in government, this attitude may be a blessing in disguise. After all, if people are too trusting of government, always ready to believe that what the government does is right, they are vulnerable to bad government. A little suspicion of government may be good protection for a free people.

Confidence in government has varied over the years, as measured by polls asking, "How much of the time do you think you can trust the government in Washington to do what is right? Just about always? Most of the time? Some of the time? None of the time?" During the early years of the Johnson Administration (and even earlier, during the Kennedy and Eisenhower presidencies), public confidence in government was high. But defeat and humiliation in Vietnam appeared to diminish public confidence. On the heels of the Vietnam experience came the Watergate scandal and President Richard Nixon's forced resignation—the first resignation of a president in U.S. history—which caused public confidence in government to fall further. Presidents Gerald Ford and Jimmy Carter were unable to halt the downward slump, and the Iranian hostage crisis in 1980 caused public confidence in government to slide even lower.

Throughout the long years of decline in public confidence in government, television has broadcast many negative images of government and public policy. Television producers seldom consider good news as "news" but instead focus on violence, scandal, corruption, and incompetence. Bad news drives out the good on television. People heavily exposed to negative television reporting gradually lose their trust in government. So the explanation for the decline in public confidence in government in the past three decades may be a product of (1) a series of disturbing events (the Vietnam War, the Watergate scandal, and the Iranian hostage crisis) and/or (2) television reporting of these events and negative television reporting in general.

Public confidence in government grew during the Reagan presidency. Ronald Reagan himself, paradoxically, was publicly critical of government. In his Inaugural Address in 1981, he said, "Government is not the solution to our problem. Government is the problem." Perhaps President Reagan's personal popularity was part of the reason that popular confidence in government rose.

Economic recessions erode public confidence in government. People expect the president and Congress to lead them out of "hard times." The recession of 1990–92 was not particularly deep by historical standards, but it was one of the nation's longest periods of slowed economic progress. George Bush's Gulf War success raised public confidence only temporarily; the perceived failure of his

POLITICS AND GOVERNMENT

What distinguishes governmental politics from politics in other institutions in society? After all, parents, teachers, unions, banks, corporations, and many other organizations make decisions about who gets what in society. The answer is that only **government** decisions can *extend to the whole society*, and only government can *legitimately use force*. Other institutions encompass only a part of society: for example, students and faculty in a college, members of a church or union, employees or customers of a corporation. And individuals have a legal right to voluntarily withdraw from nongovernmental organizations. But governments make decisions affecting everyone, and no one can voluntarily withdraw from government's authority (without leaving the country, and thus becoming subject to some other government's authority). Some individuals and organizations—muggers, gangs, crime families—occasionally use physical force to get what they want. In fact, the

government Organization extending to the whole society that can legitimately use force to carry out its decisions.

Public Confidence That the Federal Government Can Be Trusted to "Do the Right Thing"

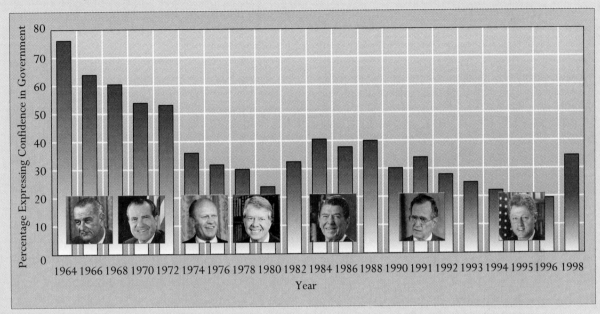

Source: Gallup Opinion Polls; see also Arthur H. Miller, "Confidence in Government during the 1980's," *American Politics Quarterly* 19 (April 1991):147–73.

administration to act decisively to restore the nation's economic health helped to send public confidence in government back down to historic lows. Public trust in government fell to a new low early in the Clinton presidency. Indeed, Clinton attributed the failure of Congress to enact a national health care program to popular distrust of government. But sustained growth in the economy under President Clinton improved public trust in government somewhat.

history of the United States has been punctuated by examples of violence used for political ends (see *A Conflicting View:* "American Politics as Violence"). But only governments can use force legitimately—that is, people generally believe it is acceptable for the government to use force if necessary to uphold its laws, but they do not extend this right to other institutions or individuals.

Most people would say that they obey the law in order to avoid fines and stay out of prison. But if large numbers of people all decided to disobey the law at the same time, the government would not have enough police or jails to hold them all. The government can rely on force only against relatively small numbers of offenders. Most of us, most of the time, obey laws out of habit—the habit of compliance. We have been taught to believe that law and order are necessary and that government is right to punish those who disobey its laws.

Government thus enjoys **legitimacy**, or rightfulness, in its use of force.[1] A democratic government has a special claim to legitimacy because it is based on the

legitimacy Widespread acceptance of something as necessary, rightful, and legally binding.

A Conflicting View

American Politics as Violence

We think of one of the central functions of government, especially democratic government, as the peaceful management of conflict in society and the protection of individual safety. Yet political violence has played a prominent role in American history. The United States was founded in armed revolution, and violence has been both a source of power and a stimulus to social change ever since. Despite their pious pronouncements against it, Americans have frequently employed violence, even in their most idealistic endeavors.

The longest and most brutal violence in American history—that between whites and Native Americans—began when the first settlers arrived in 1607. The "Indian Wars" continued with only temporary truces for nearly 300 years, until the final battle at Wounded Knee, South Dakota, in 1890. Early colonial experience in a rugged frontier country gave rise to the tradition of an armed civilian militia, which was used successfully in the Revolutionary War against British rule.

After the Revolutionary War, many armed farmers and debtors resorted to violence to assert their economic interests. The most serious rebellion broke out in 1786 in Massachusetts, when a band of insurgents, composed of farmers and laborers and led by Bunker Hill veteran Daniel Shays, captured several courthouses. Shays's Rebellion was put down by a small mercenary army paid for by well-to-do citizens who feared that a wholesale attack on property rights was imminent. The growing violence in the states contributed to the momentum leading to the Constitutional Convention of 1787, where a new central government was established with the power to "insure domestic Tranquility."

Ratification of the Constitution did not stop violence, however. Vigilantism (taking the law into one's own hands) arose in response to a perennial American problem: the absence of effective law and order in the frontier region. Practically every state and territory west of the Appalachians had at one time or another a well-organized vigilante movement, frequently backed by prominent citizens.

The ultimate turning of citizen on citizen—the Civil War—was the bloodiest war Americans ever fought. Total battle deaths of the northern and southern armies exceeded American battle deaths in World War II, even though the U.S. population at the time of the Civil War was only one-quarter that of the World War II period. Violence was also a prime ingredient of the early labor movement in the United States. Both management and workers resorted to violence in the struggles accompanying the Industrial Revolution. The last great spasm of violence in the history of American labor came in the 1930s, with the strikes and plant takeovers that accompanied the successful drive to unionize the automobile, steel, and other mass-production industries.

A long history of racial violence continues to plague the United States. Slavery itself was accompanied by untold violence. An estimated one-third to one-half of the Africans captured in slave raids never survived the ordeal of initiation into slavery. After the Civil War, racial strife and Ku Klux Klan activity became routine in the old Confederacy, and the white supremacy movement employed violence to reestablish white rule in the southern social system. Racial violence directed against blacks—whipping, torture, and lynching—was fairly common from the 1870s to the 1930s. During World War II, serious racial violence erupted in Detroit, where black and white mobs battled each other in 1943. More than 150 major riots involving race were reported in American cities from 1965 to 1968, and the rioting, burning, and looting in south-central Los Angeles in 1992 reminded the nation that racial violence—and the conditions that foment it—are continuing threats to society.

Today self-styled citizen "militias" in various parts of the country believe that they must be armed and trained in military tactics in order to ensure that federal agencies, or perhaps even the United Nations, do not threaten American freedom. More than seventy people died near Waco, Texas, in 1992, when federal agents attempted to disarm one such group. And Timothy McVeigh was convicted of the nation's single most destructive act of domestic violence in the Oklahoma City federal office building bombing in 1994 that killed 265 people.

Americans think of democratic politics as stable, with the authority to govern transferred peacefully from one administration to the next according to the preferences of the electorate. Yet political assassinations have taken the lives of four presidents: Abraham Lincoln in 1865, James A. Garfield in 1881, William McKinley in 1901, and John F. Kennedy in 1963. Several other presidents have been the targets of assassination attempts, and the assassination of Dr. Martin Luther King, Jr., in 1968 ended an era of progress in civil rights in America.

consent of its people, who participate in the selection of its leaders and the making of its laws. Those who disagree with a law have the option of working for its change by speaking out, petitioning, demonstrating, forming interest groups or parties, voting against unpopular leaders, or running for office themselves. Since people living in a democracy can effect change by "working within the system," they have a greater moral obligation to obey the law than people living under regimes in which they have no voice. However, there may be some occasions when "civil disobedience" even in a democracy may be morally justified (see *A Conflicting View:* "Sometimes It's Right to Disobey the Law").

THE PURPOSES OF GOVERNMENT

All governments tax, penalize, punish, restrict, and regulate their people. Governments in the United States—the federal government in Washington, the 50 state governments, and the more than 86,000 local governments—take nearly 40 cents out of every dollar Americans earn. Each year, the Congress enacts about 500 laws; federal bureaucracies publish about 19,000 rules and regulations; the state legislatures enact about 25,000 laws; and cities, counties, school districts, and other local governments enact countless local ordinances. Each of these laws restricts our freedom in some way. Each dollar taken out of our wages or profits reduces our freedom to choose what to do with our money.

Why do people put up with governments? An answer to this question can be found in the words of the Preamble to the Constitution of the United States:

> We the people of the United States, in Order to form a more perfect Union, establish Justice, insure domestic Tranquility, provide for the common defense, promote the general Welfare, and secure the Blessings of Liberty to ourselves and our Posterity, do ordain and establish this Constitution for the United States of America.

To Establish Justice and Insure Domestic Tranquility Government manages conflict and maintains order. We might think of government as a **social contract** among people who agree to allow themselves to be regulated and taxed in exchange for protection of their lives and property. No society can allow individuals or groups to settle their conflicts by street fighting, murder, kidnapping, rioting, bombing, or terrorism. Whenever government fails to control such violence, we describe it as "a breakdown in law and order." Without the protection of government, human lives and property are endangered, and only those skilled with fists and weapons have much of a chance of survival. The seventeenth-century English political philosopher Thomas Hobbes described life without government as "a war where every man is

social contract Idea that government originates as an implied contract among individuals who agree to obey laws in exchange for protection of their rights.

PEANUTS reprinted by permission of UFS, Inc.

Sometimes It's Right to Disobey the Law

Civil disobedience is the nonviolent violation of laws that people believe to be unjust. Civil disobedience denies the *legitimacy*, or rightfulness, of a law and implies that a higher moral authority takes precedence over unjust laws. It is frequently a political tactic of minorities. (Majorities can more easily change laws through conventional political activity.) Civil disobedience is also an attractive tactic for groups that wish to change the status quo.

Why resort to civil disobedience in a democracy? Why not work within the democratic system to change unjust laws? In 1963 a group of Alabama clergy posed these questions to Martin Luther King, Jr., and asked him to call off mass demonstrations in Birmingham, Alabama. King, who had been arrested in the demonstrations, replied in his now-famous "Letter from Birmingham City Jail":

> You may well ask, "Why direct action? Why sit-ins, marches, etc.?" . . . Nonviolent direct action seeks to create such a crisis and establish such creative tension that a community that has constantly refused to negotiate is forced to confront the issue. It seeks to so dramatize the issue that it can no longer be ignored. . . . One may well ask, "How can you advocate breaking some laws and obeying others?" The answer is found in the fact that there are unjust laws. I would be the first to advocate obeying just laws. One has not only a legal but a moral responsibility to obey just laws. Conversely, one has a moral responsibility to disobey unjust laws.

King argued that *nonviolent direct action* was a vital aspect of democratic politics. The political purpose of civil disobedience is to call attention or "to bear witness" to the existence of injustices. Only laws regarded as unjust are broken, and they are broken openly, without hatred or violence. Punishment is actively sought rather than avoided, since punishment will further emphasize the injustice of the laws.

The objective of nonviolent civil disobedience is to stir the conscience of an apathetic majority and to win support for measures that will eliminate the injustices. By accepting punishment for

© Flip Schulke

Dr. Martin Luther King, Jr., shown here marching in Mississippi with his wife, Coretta Scott King, and others, used civil disobedience to advance the rights of African Americans during the 1950s and 1960s.

the violation of an unjust law, persons practicing civil disobedience demonstrate their sincerity. They hope to shame the majority and to make it ask itself how far it is willing to go to protect the status quo. Thus, according to King's teachings, civil disobedience is clearly differentiated from hatred and violence:

> In no sense do I advocate evading or defying the law as the rabid segregationist would do. This would lead to anarchy. One who breaks an unjust law must do it openly, lovingly (not hatefully as the white mothers did in New Orleans when they were seen on television screaming "nigger, nigger, nigger") and with a willingness to accept the penalty. I submit that an individual who breaks a law that conscience tells him is unjust, and willingly accepts the penalty by staying in jail to arouse the conscience of the community over its injustice, is in reality expressing the very highest respect for law.

In 1964 Martin Luther King, Jr., received the Nobel Peace Prize in recognition of his extraordinary contributions to the development of nonviolent methods of social change.

Source: Martin Luther King, Jr., "Letter from Birmingham City Jail," April 16, 1963.

Thomas Hobbes and the Need for Leviathan

The notion of life without government holds a certain romantic appeal, since all governments restrict personal freedom. *Anarchism* is a term describing opposition to government in any form. But what would life really be like without any government at all?

The English political philosopher Thomas Hobbes (1588–1679) warned that the true state of nature (without any government or social organization at all) would be a "war of everyone against everyone" in which life would be "solitary, poor, nasty, brutish, and short." Hobbes's beliefs about the cruelty and violence of human nature led him to conclude that a strong and powerful government, which he called Leviathan after a biblical sea monster, was essential to the preservation of life, property, justice, and freedom. "Where there is no common power, there is no law; where no law, no justice. Force and fraud [become] the two cardinal virtues."

Hobbes fled England during that nation's civil war, whose violence, brutality, and waste of life and property inspired his most important work, *Leviathan* (1651). In it, Hobbes argued that government derived its power from the consent of the people. But in Hobbes's view the social contract was a one-sided bargain; fear drove people to agree to surrender their liberty in exchange for protection from others. The government's power had to be absolute, Hobbes believed, because only such a Leviathan government could successfully control the violent propensities of humankind.

The Hobbesian view of human nature and life without government is very pessimistic. Yet today, when we observe the total breakdown of law and order in societies from Somalia to Bosnia to riot-torn cities at home, we are reminded of the aptness of Hobbes's warnings.

---

enemy to every man," where people live in "continual fear and danger of violent death"[2] (see *People in Politics:* "Thomas Hobbes and the Need for Leviathan").

To Provide for the Common Defense Many anthropologists link the origins of government to warfare—to the need of early communities to protect themselves from raids by outsiders and to organize raids against others. Since the Revolutionary War, the U.S. government has been responsible for the country's defense, but today, with a diminished threat to national security from the states of the former Soviet Union, national defense absorbs less than 15 percent of the *federal* government's budget and less than 8 percent of *all* government spending—federal, state, and local combined. Nevertheless, national defense remains a primary responsibility of the U.S. government.

To Promote the General Welfare Government promotes the general welfare in a number of ways. It provides **public goods**—goods and services that private markets cannot readily furnish either because they are too expensive for individuals to buy for themselves (for example, a national park, a highway, or a sewage disposal plant) or because if one person bought them, everyone else would "free-ride," or use them without paying (for example, clean air, police protection, or national defense). Nevertheless, Americans acquire most of their goods and services on the **free market**, through voluntary exchange among individuals, firms, and corporations. The **gross domestic product (GDP)**—the dollar sum of all the goods and services produced in the United States in a year—amounts to over $8 trillion.

public goods Goods and services that cannot readily be provided by markets, either because they are too expensive for a single individual to buy or because if one person bought them, everyone else would use them without paying.

free market Free competition for voluntary exchange among individuals, firms, and corporations.

gross domestic product (GDP) The dollar sum of all the goods and services produced in a nation in a year.

Up Close

How Big Is Government and What Does It Do?

Government in the United States has grown enormously throughout the twentieth century, both in absolute terms and in relation to the size of the national economy. The size of the economy is usually measured by the gross domestic product (GDP), the dollar sum of all the goods and services produced in the United States in a year. Governments accounted for only about 8 percent of the GDP at the beginning of the century, and most governmental activities were carried out by state and local governments. Two world wars, the New Deal programs devised during the Great Depression of the 1930s, and the growth of the Great Society programs of the 1960s and 1970s all greatly expanded the size of government, particularly the federal government. The rise in government growth relative to the economy leveled off during the Reagan presidency (1981–89). Today, federal expenditures amount to about 21 percent of GDP, and total governmental expenditures are about 34 percent of GDP (see Graph A).

Not everything that government does is reflected in governmental expenditures. *Regulatory activity*, for example, especially environmental regulations, imposes significant costs on individuals and businesses; these costs are not shown in government budgets. Nevertheless, government spending is a common indicator of governmental functions and priorities. For example,

(A) What Government Spends

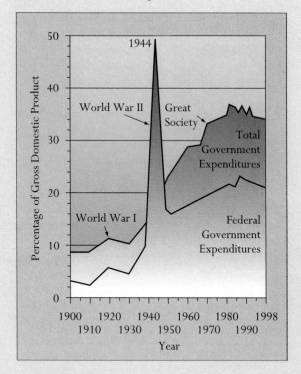

Source: *Budget of the United States Government, 1998.*

Graph B indicates that the *federal government* spends more on senior citizens—in Social Security and Medicare outlays—than on any *other* function, including national defense. The national debt is now so large

---

Government spending in the United States—federal, state, and local governments combined—amounts to about $2.7 trillion, or about 34 percent of the gross domestic product (see *Up Close:* "How Big Is Government and What Does It Do?").

Governments also regulate society. Free markets cannot function effectively if individuals and firms engage in fraud, deception, or unfair competition, or if contracts cannot be enforced. Moreover, many economic activities impose costs on persons who are not direct participants in these activities. Economists refer to such costs as **externalities**. A factory that produces air pollution or wastewater imposes external costs on community residents who would otherwise enjoy cleaner air or water. A junkyard that creates an eyesore makes life less pleasant for neighbors and passersby. Many government regulations are designed to reduce these external costs.

To promote general welfare, governments also use **income transfers** from taxpayers to people who are regarded as deserving. Government agencies and

externalities Costs imposed on people who are not direct participants in an activity.

income transfers Government transfers of income from taxpayers to persons regarded as deserving.

(B) What the Federal Government Does

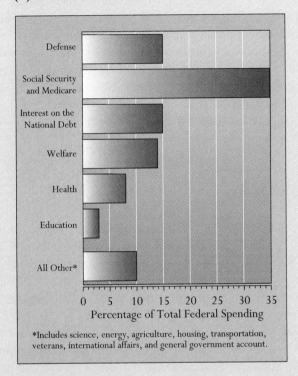

Percentage of Total Federal Spending

*Includes science, energy, agriculture, housing, transportation, veterans, international affairs, and general government account.

Source: Budget of the United States Government, 1998.

(C) What State and Local Governments Do

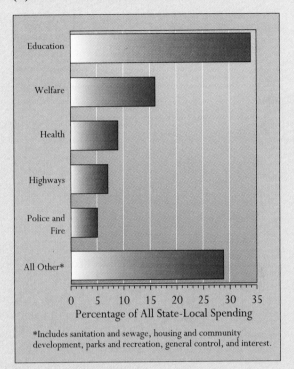

Percentage of All State-Local Spending

*Includes sanitation and sewage, housing and community development, parks and recreation, general control, and interest.

Source: Statistical Abstract of the United States, 1996.

that interest payments on it consume 15 percent of all federal spending. Federal welfare and health programs account for substantial budget outlays, but federal financial support of education is very modest.

State and local governments in the United States bear the major burden of public education. Welfare and health functions consume larger shares of their budgets than highways and law enforcement do (see Graph C).

programs provide support and care for individuals who cannot supply these things for themselves through the private job market, for example, ill, elderly, and disabled people, and dependent children who cannot usually be expected to find productive employment. However, it is important to realize that payments to the poor are less than one-fifth of all government transfer payments to individuals. The largest income transfer programs are Social Security and Medicare, which are paid to the elderly regardless of their personal wealth. Other large transfer payments go to farmers, veterans, and the unemployed, as well as to a wide variety of businesses. As we shall see, the struggle of individuals and groups to obtain direct government payments is a major motivator of political activity.

To Secure the Blessings of Liberty   All governments must maintain order, protect national security, provide public goods, regulate society, and care for those unable to fend for themselves. But *democratic* governments have a special added responsibility—to protect individual liberty by ensuring that all people are treated equally before the law. No one is above the law. The president must obey the Constitution and laws of the United States, and so must members of Congress, governors, judges, and the police. A democratic government must protect people's freedom to speak and write what they please, to practice their religion, to petition, to form groups and parties, to enjoy personal privacy, and to exercise their rights if accused of a crime.

The concentration of government power can be a threat to freedom. If a democratic government acquires great power in order to maintain order, protect national security, or provide many collective goods and services, it runs the risk of becoming too powerful for the preservation of freedom. The question is how to keep government from becoming so pervasive it threatens the individual liberty it was established to protect (see *What Do You Think?* "What Should Be the Role of Government in American Society?").

THE MEANING OF DEMOCRACY

Throughout the centuries, thinkers in many different cultures contributed to the development of democratic government. Early Greek philosophers contributed the word **democracy**, which means "rule by the many." But there is no single definition of *democracy*, nor is there a tightly organized system of democratic thought. It is better, perhaps, to speak of democratic traditions than of a single democratic ideology.

Unfortunately, the looseness of the term *democracy* allows it to be perverted by *anti*democratic governments. Hardly a nation in the world exists that does not *claim* to be "democratic." Governments that outlaw political opposition, suppress dissent, discourage religion, and deny fundamental freedoms of speech and press still claim to be "democracies," "democratic republics," or "people's republics" (for example, the Democratic People's Republic of Korea is the official name of Communist North Korea). These governments defend their use of the term *democracy* by claiming that their policies reflect the true interests of their people. But they are unwilling to allow political freedoms or to hold free elections in order to find out whether their people really agree with their policies. In effect, they use the term as a political slogan rather than a true description of their government.[3]

The actual existence of **democratic ideals** varies considerably from country to country, regardless of their names (see *Compared to What?* "Freedom and Democracy in the World"). A meaningful definition of democracy must include the following ideals: recognition of the dignity of every individual; equal protection under the law for every individual; opportunity for everyone to participate in public decisions; and decision making by majority rule, with one person having one vote.

Individual Dignity   The underlying value of democracy is the dignity of the individual. Human beings are entitled to life and liberty, personal property, and equal protection under the law. These liberties are *not* granted by governments; they belong to every person born into the world. The English political philosopher John Locke (1632–1704) argued that a higher "natural law" guaranteed liberty to every person and that this natural law was morally superior to all human laws and governments. Each individual possesses "certain inalienable Rights, among these are Life, Liberty, and Property"[4] (see *People in Politics:* "John Locke and the Justification of Revolution").

democracy   Governing system in which the people govern themselves; from the Greek term meaning "rule by the many."

democratic ideals   Individual dignity, equality before the law, widespread participation in public decisions, and public decisions by majority rule, with one person having one vote.

What Do You Think?

What Should Be the Role of Government in American Society?

How many responsibilities should the government undertake in a democratic society? If the government tries to do too much—to solve all or most of the problems confronting individuals, families, businesses, the environment, and so on—will it undermine personal responsibility, individual effort, family, church, and community? In the next chapter we examine the tension between current "liberal" ideas about the value of an active, involved government versus "conservative" notions favoring a minimal government role in society (see "Ideologies: Liberalism and Conservatism" in Chapter 2).

Overall, Americans appear to be ambivalent on the question of government's role in a democratic society. On the one hand, they generally believe that their government is "trying to do too many things that should be left to individuals and businesses." When asked about the role of government in their lives, 58 percent of those surveyed said that they felt the government was "doing too much" to solve the country's problems (see Graph A). Similarly, more people believe that government has a negative than a positive impact on their lives (see Graph B). Yet on the other hand, when asked about the major responsibilities that government currently undertakes—Social Security, Medicare, national defense, law enforcement, public education, and so on—most Americans said that they support them as a "good use" of their tax dollars (see Graph C).

(A) Government Involvement in Solving Problems

Question: *Some people think the government is trying to do too many things that should be left to individuals and businesses. Others think that government should do more to solve our country's problems. Which comes closer to your own view?*

"Doing too much"	58%
"Should do more"	33%
Mixed/No opinion	9%

(B) Government's Impact on People's Lives

Question: *These days, what kind of impact do you think the government has on most people's lives: a positive impact, a negative impact, or doesn't the government have much impact on most people's lives?*

"Positive"	28%
"Negative"	41%
"Not much"	22%
"Don't know"	9%

(C) Support for Federal Programs

Question: *For each of the following federal programs, I would like to know how much you personally support this as a good use of your tax dollars. Do you support [name of program] a great deal, a fair amount, just a little, or not at all?*

Percentage Expressing "a Great Deal" of Support

Social Security	69%
Armed services	64%
Medicare	64%
Workplace safety	63%
Discrimination	61%
Public schools	61%
Food, drug safety	60%
College loans	56%
Minimum wage	56%
Environment	55%
Law enforcement	45%
Family leave	40%
NASA	34%
Affirmative action	29%
Welfare	24%

Sources: Gallup/CNN/USA Today Poll, 1997, reported in *The Polling Report*, February 10, 1997; Harris Poll, 1997, reported in *The Polling Report*, February 24, 1997.

Freedom and Democracy around the World

Worldwide progress toward freedom and democracy has been evident over the past decade, not only in the collapse of communism in Eastern Europe and the Soviet Union but also in the movements toward democracy in such nations as South Africa, South Korea, Taiwan, and Nicaragua. Nevertheless, more than half the world's people live under governments that can hardly be called democracies.

One way to assess the degree of democracy in a governmental system is to consider its record in ensuring political freedoms—enabling citizens to participate meaningfully in government—and individual liberties. A checklist for political freedoms might include whether the chief executive and national legislature are elected; whether elections are generally fair, with open campaigning and honest tabulation of votes; and whether multiple candidates and parties participate. A checklist for individual liberties might include whether the press and broadcasting are free and independent of the government; whether people are free to assemble, protest, and form opposition parties; whether religious institutions, labor unions, business organizations, and other groups are free and independent of the government; and whether individuals are free to own property, travel, and move their residence.

The Freedom House, a New York–based think tank that regularly surveys political conditions around the world, ranks nations according to the amount of political freedom and individual liberty they allow. The categories are "Free," "Partly Free," and "Not Free," based on each nation's combined average score on political freedom and individual liberty.

The Map of Freedom

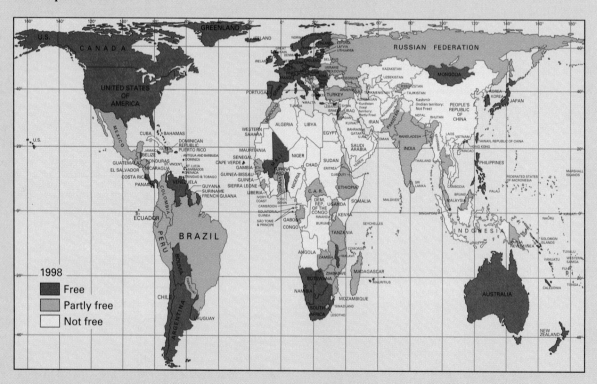

Source: Freedom House, 1998.

Individual dignity requires personal freedom. People who are directed by governments in every aspect of their lives, people who are "collectivized" and made into workers for the state, people who are enslaved—all are denied the personal dignity to which all human beings are entitled. Democratic governments try to minimize the role of government in the lives of citizens.

Equality   True democracy requires equal protection of the law for every individual. Democratic governments cannot discriminate between blacks and whites, or men and women, or rich and poor, or any groups of people in applying the law. Not only must a democratic government refrain from discrimination itself, but it must also work to prevent discrimination in society generally. Today our notion of equality extends to equality of opportunity—the obligation of government to ensure that all Americans have an opportunity to develop their full potential.

Participation in Decision Making   Democracy means individual participation in the decisions that affect individuals' lives. People should be free to choose for themselves how they want to live. Individual participation in government is necessary for individual dignity. People in a democracy should not have decisions made *for* them but *by* them. Even if they make mistakes, it is better that they be permitted to do so than to take away their rights to make their own decisions. The true democrat would reject even a wise and benevolent dictatorship because it would threaten the individual's character, self-reliance, and dignity. The argument for democracy is not that the people will always choose wise policies for themselves but that people who cannot choose for themselves are not really free.

Majority Rule: One Person, One Vote   Collective decision making in democracies must be by majority rule with each person having one vote. That is, each person's vote must be equal to every other person's, regardless of status, money, or fame. Whenever any individual is denied political equality because of race, sex, or wealth, then the government is not truly democratic. Majorities are not always right. But majority *rule* means that all persons have an equal say in decisions affecting them. If people are truly equal, their votes must count equally, and a majority vote must decide the issue, even if the majority decides foolishly.

THE PARADOX OF DEMOCRACY

What if a *majority* of the people decide to attack the rights of some unpopular individuals or minority groups? What if hate, prejudice, or racism infects a majority of people and they vote for leaders who promise to "get rid of the Jews" or "put blacks in their place" or "bash a few gays"? What if a majority of people vote to take away the property of wealthy people and distribute it among themselves? Do we abide by the principle of majority rule and allow the majority to do what it wants? Or do we defend the principle of individual liberty and limit the majority's power? If we enshrine the principle of majority rule, we are placing all our confidence in the wisdom and righteousness of the majority of the people. Yet we know that democracy means more than majority rule, that it also means freedom and dignity for the individual. How do we resolve this **paradox of democracy**—the potential for conflict between majority rule and individual freedom?

paradox of democracy
Potential for conflict between individual freedom and majority rule.

Limiting the Power of Majorities   The Founders of the American nation were not sure that freedom would be safe in the hands of the majority. In *The Federalist Papers*

John Locke and the Justification of Revolution

The most important single voice influencing the thought of the nation's Founders was that of English philosopher John Locke (1632–1704). Locke's writings, especially his *Second Treatise on Government* (1690), inspired the American Revolution, the Declaration of Independence, and the Constitution of the United States.

Like Thomas Hobbes, Locke was an aristocrat who was forced to flee during England's civil war. Yet despite living in fear of political persecution, he never adopted Hobbes's pessimistic view of human nature. Rather, he held that people are basically decent, orderly, social minded, and capable of self-government.

In his *Treatise on Civil Government* (1688), Locke argued that "all men are by nature free, equal, and independent" and all enjoy "the rights to life, liberty, and property." These laws of nature are "self-evident" to those who "make use of reason." People "consent" to enter into a social contract and "accept the bonds of government" in order to better protect their rights. People "unite in a commonwealth" especially for "the preservation of their property." Government is based on the consent of the people. An "absolute monarch" is "inconsistent with civil society" because people retain the ability to judge for themselves whether their rights are truly being protected by government. The only justification for government is its ability to protect life, liberty, and property.

It follows that any government that "transgresses" on these rights, "either by ambition, fear, folly, or corruption," breaches the social contract and "forfeits the power the people had put into its hands." The people then have the right to "resume their original

liberty," dissolve their bonds with the government, and create a new government "such as they think fit." Thus Locke endorsed the right of revolution—the moral right of a people to dissolve a government that violates their fundamental rights. But he advised that people should not undertake such an action unless confronted with a long list of serious grievances and many "fruitless attempts" to redress them. And he reassured rulers that a good government has nothing to fear from acceptance of his theory of the right of revolution.

When Thomas Jefferson wrote his eloquent defense of the American Revolution in the Declaration of Independence for the Continental Congress in Philadelphia in 1776, he borrowed heavily from Locke (perhaps even to the point of plagiarism):

> We hold these Truths to be self-evident, that all Men are created equal, that they are endowed by their Creator with certain unalienable Rights, that among these are Life, Liberty, and the Pursuit of Happiness—That to secure these Rights, Governments are instituted among Men, deriving their just Powers from the Consent of the Governed, that whenever any Form of Government becomes destructive of these Ends, it is the Right of the People to alter or to abolish it . . . . But when a long Train of Abuses and Usurpations, pursuing invariably the same Object, evinces a Design to reduce them under absolute Despotism, it is their Right, it is their Duty, to throw off such Government. . . . The History of the present King of Great Britain is a History of repeated Injuries and Usurpations, all having in direct Object the Establishment of an absolute Tyranny over these States. . . .
>
> We, therefore, the Representatives of the UNITED STATES OF AMERICA, in General Congress, Assembled, appealing to the Supreme Judge of the World for the Rectitude of our Intentions, do, in the Name, and by Authority of the good People of these Colonies, solemnly Publish and Declare, That these United Colonies are, and of Right ought to be, Free and Independent States.

The paradox of democracy balances the principle of majority rule against the principle of individual liberty. When the German people voted Adolf Hitler and the Nazi Party into power, did majority rule give the Nazis free rein to restrict the individual liberties of the people? Or did those who abhorred the trespasses of their government have the right to fight against its power?

in 1787, James Madison warned against a direct democracy: "Pure democracy . . . can admit of no cure for the mischiefs of faction. . . . There is nothing to check the inducements to sacrifice the weaker party, or an obnoxious individual."[5] So the Founders wrote a Constitution and adopted a Bill of Rights that limited the power of government over the individual, that placed some personal liberties beyond the reach of majorities. They established the principle of **limited government**—a government that is itself restrained by law. Under a limited government, even if a majority of voters wanted to, they could not prohibit communists or atheists or racists from speaking or writing. Nor could they ban certain religions, set aside the rights of criminal defendants to a fair trial, or prohibit people from moving or quitting their jobs. These rights belong to individuals, not to majorities or governments.

Totalitarianism: Unlimited Government Power   No government can be truly democratic if it directs every aspect of its citizens' lives. Individuals must be free to shape their own lives, free from the dictates of governments or even majorities of their fellow citizens. Indeed, we call a government with *un*limited power over its citizens totalitarian. Under **totalitarianism**, the individual possesses no personal liberty. Totalitarian governments decide what people can say or write; what unions, churches, or parties they can join, if any; where people must live; what work they must do; what goods they can find in stores and what they will be allowed to buy and sell; whether citizens will be allowed to travel outside of their country; and so on. Under a totalitarian government, the total life of the individual is subject to government control.

Constitutional Government   Constitutions, written or unwritten, are the principal means by which governmental powers are limited. Constitutions set forth the liberties of individuals and restrain governments from interfering with these liberties. Consider, for example, the opening words of the First Amendment to the

limited government   Principle that government power over the individual is limited, that there are some personal liberties that even a majority cannot regulate, and that government itself is restrained by law.

totalitarianism   Rule by an elite that exercises unlimited power over individuals in all aspects of life.

constitution   Written or unwritten rules by which government operates, including limits on governmental power.

Political sociologists have observed that the military in totalitarian societies has a distinct body language. Soldiers in Nazi Germany and, as seen here, the former Soviet Union used a "goose step" when on parade—a march in which the knee is unbent and the foot, encased in a heavy boot, is stamped on the ground, providing a powerful image of authority and force. In democratic societies, the goose step is not employed; indeed, it is regarded as somewhat ridiculous.

U.S. Constitution: "Congress shall make no law respecting an establishment of religion, or prohibiting the free exercise thereof." This amendment places religious belief beyond the reach of the government. The government itself is restrained by law. It cannot, even by majority vote, interfere with the personal liberty to worship as one chooses. In addition, armed with the power of judicial review, the courts can declare unconstitutional laws passed by majority vote of Congress or state legislatures (see "Judicial Power" in Chapter 13).

Throughout this book we examine how well limited constitutional government succeeds in preserving individual liberty in the United States. We examine free speech and press, the mass media, religious freedom, the freedom to protest and demonstrate, and the freedom to support political candidates and interest groups of all kinds. We examine how well the U.S. Constitution protects individuals from discrimination and inequality. And we examine how far government can go in regulating work, homes, business, and the marketplace without destroying individual liberty.

DIRECT VERSUS REPRESENTATIVE DEMOCRACY

In the Gettysburg Address, Abraham Lincoln spoke about "a government of the people, by the people, for the people," and his ringing phrase remains an American ideal. But can we take this phrase literally? More than 265 million Americans are spread over 4 million square miles. If we brought everyone together, standing shoulder to shoulder, they would occupy 66 square miles. One round of five-minute speeches by everyone would take 5,000 years. "People could be born, grow old, and die while they waited for the assembly to make one decision."[6]

Direct democracy (also called pure or participatory democracy), where everyone actively participates in every decision, is rare. The closest approximation to direct democracy in American government may be the traditional New England town meeting, where all of the citizens come together face to face to decide about town affairs. But today most New England towns vest authority in a board of officials elected by the townspeople to make policy decisions between town meetings, and professional administrators are appointed to supervise the day-to-day town services. The town meeting is rapidly vanishing because citizens cannot spend so much of their time and energy in community decision making.

Representative democracy recognizes that it is impossible to expect millions of people to come together and decide every issue. Instead, representatives of the people are elected by the people to decide issues on behalf of the people. Elections must be open to competition so that the people can choose representatives who reflect their own views. And elections must take place in an environment of free speech and press, so that both candidates and voters can freely express their views. Finally, elections must be held periodically so that representatives can be thrown out of office if they no longer reflect the views of the majority of the people.

No government can claim to be a representative democracy, then, unless

1. Representatives are selected by vote of all the people.
2. Elections are open to competition.
3. Candidates and voters can freely express themselves.
4. Representatives are selected periodically.

So when we hear of "elections" in which only one party is permitted to run candidates, candidates are not free to express their views, or leaders are elected "for life," then we know that these governments are *not* really democracies, regardless of what they may call themselves.

Throughout this book, as we examine how well representative democracy works in the United States, we consider such issues as participation in elections—why some people vote and others do not —whether parties and candidates offer the voters real alternatives, whether modern political campaigning informs voters or only confuses them, and whether elected representatives are responsive to the wishes of voters. These are the kinds of issues that concern political science.

direct democracy   Governing system in which every person participates actively in every public decision, rather than delegating decision making to representatives.

representative democracy   Governing system in which public decision making is delegated to representatives of the people chosen by popular vote in free, open, and periodic election.

WHO REALLY GOVERNS?

Democracy is an inspiring ideal. But is democratic government really possible? Is it possible for millions of people to govern themselves, with every voice having equal influence? Or will a small number of people inevitably acquire more power than others? To what extent is democracy attainable in *any* society, and how democratic is the American political system? That is, who really governs?

The Elitist Perspective   "Government is always government by the few, whether in the name of the few, the one, or the many."[7] This quotation from political scientists Harold Lasswell and Daniel Lerner expresses the basic idea of **elitism**. All societies, including democracies, divide themselves into the few who have power and the many who do not. In every society, there is a division of labor. Only a few people are directly involved in governing a nation; most people are content to let others undertake the tasks of government. The *elite* are the few who have power; the *masses* are the many who do not. This theory holds that an elite is inevitable in *any* social organization. We cannot form a club, a church, a business, or a government without selecting some people to provide leadership. And leaders will always have a perspective on the organization different from that of its members.

In any large, complex society, then, whether or not it is a democracy, decisions are made by tiny minorities. Out of more than 265 million Americans, only a few thousand individuals at most participate directly in decisions about war and peace, wages and prices, employment and production, law and justice, taxes and benefits, health and welfare.

Elitism does *not* mean that leaders always exploit or oppress members. On the contrary, elites may be very concerned for the welfare of the masses. Elite status may be open to ambitious, talented, or educated individuals from the masses or may be closed to all except the wealthy. Elites may be very responsive to public opinion, or they may ignore the usually apathetic and ill-informed masses. But whether elites are self-seeking or public spirited, open or closed, responsive or unresponsive, it is they and not the masses who actually make the decisions.

Contemporary elite theory argues that power in America is concentrated in a small *institutional* elite. Sociologist C. Wright Mills popularized the term *power elite* in arguing that leaders of corporations, the military establishment, and the national government come together at the top of a giant pyramid of power.[8] Other social scientists have found that more than half of the nation's total assets are concentrated in the 100 largest corporations and 50 largest banks; that the officers and directors of these corporations and banks interact frequently with leaders of government, the mass media, foundations, and universities; and that these leaders are drawn disproportionately from wealthy, educated, upper-class, white, male, Anglo-Saxon Protestant groups in American society.[9]

Most people do not regularly concern themselves with decision making in Washington. They are more concerned with their jobs, family, sports, and recreation than they are with politics. They are not well informed about tax laws, foreign policy, or even who represents them in Congress. Since the "masses" are largely apathetic and ill informed about policy questions, their views are likely

elitism   Theory that all societies, even democracies, are divided into the few who govern and the many who do not.

to be influenced more by what they see and hear on television than by their own experience. Most communication flows downward from elites to masses. Elitism argues that the masses have at best only an indirect influence on the decisions of elites.

The Pluralist Perspective   No one seriously argues that all Americans participate in *all* of the decisions that shape their lives; that majority preferences *always* prevail; that the values of life, liberty, and property are *never* sacrificed; or that *every* American enjoys equality of opportunity. Nevertheless, most American political scientists argue that the American system of government, which they describe as "pluralist," is the best possible approximation of the democratic ideal in a large, complex society. Pluralism is designed to make the theory of democracy "more realistic."[10]

Pluralism is the belief that democracy can be achieved in a large, complex society by competition, bargaining, and compromise among organized groups and that individuals can participate in decision making through membership in these groups and by choosing among parties and candidates in elections.

Pluralists recognize that the individual acting alone is no match for giant government bureaucracies, big corporations and banks, the television networks, labor unions, or other powerful interest groups. Instead, pluralists rely on *competition* among these organizations to protect the interests of individuals. They hope that countervailing centers of power—big business, big labor, big government—will check one another and prevent any single group from abusing its power and oppressing individual Americans.

Individuals in a pluralist democracy may not participate directly in decision making, but they can join and support *interest groups* whose leaders bargain on their behalf in the political arena. People are more effective in organized groups—for example, the Sierra Club for environmentalists, the American Civil Liberties Union (ACLU) for civil rights advocates, the National Association for the Advancement of Colored People (NAACP) or the Urban League for African Americans, the American Legion or Veterans of Foreign Wars for veterans, and the National Rifle Association (NRA) for opponents of gun control.

According to the pluralist view, the Democratic and Republican parties are really coalitions of groups: the national Democratic Party is a coalition of union members, big-city residents, blacks, Catholics, Jews, and, until recently, southerners; the national Republican Party is a coalition of business and professional people, suburbanites, farmers, and white Protestants. When voters choose candidates and parties, they are helping to determine which interest groups will enjoy a better reception in government.

Pluralists contend that there are multiple leadership groups in society (hence the term *pluralism*). They contend that power is widely dispersed among these groups; that no one group, not even the wealthy upper class, dominates decision making; and that groups which are influential in one area of decision making are not necessarily the same groups that are influential in other areas of decision making. Different groups of leaders make decisions in different issue areas.

Pluralism recognizes that public policy does not always coincide with majority preferences. Instead, public policy is the "equilibrium" reached in the conflict among group interests. It is the balance of competing interest groups,

pluralism   Theory that democracy can be achieved through competition among multiple organized groups and that individuals can participate in politics through group memberships and elections.

Up Close

Sources of Facts about American Government

America Votes Richard M. Scammon and Alice V. McGillivray, eds. Published biennially by Congressional Quarterly, Inc., 1414 22d St. NW, Washington, D.C., 20037, and available in most university libraries.

This work contains statistics on voting for president, governor, senator, and Congress member by state, congressional district, and county for primary and general elections.

Statistical Abstract of the United States Published annually by the U.S. Department of Commerce. Available in most libraries and through the Government Printing Office, Washington, D.C., 20402.

This volume presents summary statistics on the political, social, and economic organization of the United States. It serves not only as a source for statistics of national importance but also as a guide to further information, since references are given to the sources of all tables.

Budget of the United States Government Office of Management and Budget, Executive Office of the President. Available in government document libraries and through the Government Printing Office, Washington, D.C., 20402.

In addition to the annual budget message of the president, it contains a detailed department-by-department account of proposed budget items, giving the previous year's actual figures, the present year's estimated expenditures, and the coming year's proposed amounts. It also contains tables of estimates for trust funds and supplemental figures, including historical comparisons of budget receipts and expenditures.

Congressional Quarterly Weekly Report Available in most university libraries and from Congressional Quarterly, Inc., 1414 22d St. NW, Washington, D.C., 20037.

A reliable, useful, and timely news service, offering weekly summary sections: Nation Report, Political Report, Executive Branch, and Lobby Report, as well as congressional activity in committees and on the floor. Includes all the key votes taken each week in the House and Senate.

Congressional Quarterly Almanac Available in most university libraries and from Congressional Quarterly, Inc., 1414 22d St. NW, Washington, D.C., 20037.

Each volume offers a survey of legislation for each session of Congress. Major congressional action is summarized in sections dealing with categories of legislation (for example, agriculture, labor, appropriations, crime) subdivided according to specific

and therefore, say the pluralists, it is a reasonable approximation of society's preferences.

DEMOCRACY IN AMERICA

Is democracy alive and well in America today? Elitism raises serious questions about the possibility of achieving true democracy in any large, complex society. Pluralism is more comforting; it offers a way of reaffirming democratic values and providing some practical solutions to the problem of individual participation in a modern society.

There is no doubt about the strength of democratic ideals in American society. These ideals—individual dignity, equality, popular participation in government,

topics. Includes voting information on individual measures.

Congressional Directory Published by the Office of Congressional Directory, U.S. Congress, and available in most libraries and from the Government Printing Office, Washington, D.C., 20037.

Lists members of Congress, committee assignments, telephone numbers, and maps of congressional districts.

Congressional Record Published by the U.S. Congress and available in research libraries and from the Government Printing Office, Washington, D.C., 20037.

Issued daily while Congress is in session. Contains the president's messages, congressional speeches, debates in full, and a record of votes.

United States Government Organizational Manual Published by the National Archives and Records Administration. Available in most university libraries and from the Government Printing Office, Washington, D.C., 20037.

The official organization handbook of the federal government, giving information on the organization, activities, and current officials of the various departments, bureaus, offices, commissions, and so forth, with descriptions of quasi-official agencies and selected international organizations. Includes organizational charts.

United States Statutes at Large Published by the National Archives and Records Administration. Available in most university libraries and from the Government Printing Office, Washington, D.C., 20037.

Laws passed by Congress and signed by the president organized chronologically.

United States Code Available in law libraries and many university libraries and published by the Government Printing Office, Washington, D.C., 20037.

All general and permanent laws of the United States, arranged under titles—that is, by subject matter.

United States Reports Available in law libraries and many university libraries and published by the Government Printing Office, Washington, D.C., 20037.

Official text of all opinions of the Supreme Court in bound form plus comprehensive tables of cases reported, cases cited, and statutes cited. Includes subject index; approximately two to five volumes per term.

Federal Register Published by the National Archives and Records Administration. Available in most university libraries and from the Government Printing Office, Washington, D.C., 20037.

Official text of presidential documents, executive agency regulations (with their legal effects), proposed rules and regulations, and legal notices.

and majority rule—are the standards by which we judge the performance of the American political system. But we are still faced with the task of describing the reality of American politics.

This book explores who gets what, when, and how in the American political system; who participates in politics; what policies are decided upon; and when and how these decisions are made (see also *Up Close:* "Sources of Facts about American Government"). In so doing, it raises many controversial questions about the realities of democracy, elitism, and pluralism in American life. But this book does not supply the answers; as a responsible citizen, you have to provide your own answers. At the completion of your studies, you will have to decide for yourself whether the American political system is truly democratic. Your studies will help inform your judgment, but, in the end, you yourself must make that judgment. That is the burden of freedom.

Politics in Cyberspace

Getting into Politics

As the Internet grows, so does access to information about politics, government, and public affairs. The Politics in Cyberspace feature that appears in each chapter of this book lists and describes a selection of interesting or informative World Wide Web sites relevant to the chapter's subject. Highlighted here are some sites that provide a general background on American politics.

Keep in mind that internet addresses can change or dissappear without notice. If you get an error message, try deleting the part of the URL (the Universal Resource Locator, or web address) past the host name. Also, there are many online search engines that you can use to find an address or topic.

Current political news

http://www.allpolitics.com

News organizations are teaming up to produce Web sites dedicated to covering political information. This site, a joint effort by CNN and *Time* magazine, is one of the best places to begin looking for current political news.

The Federal Government

http://www.whitehouse.gov

This is a good starting point for general information on the executive branch of government, the White House, the president, and the vice president, as well as current press releases, speeches, and major policy documents.

Policy Research

http://www.freedomhouse.org

Many public organizations and "think tanks" have home pages, some providing the full text of reports or briefing papers on various issues. Freedom House is a resource for information on democracy around the world.

SUMMARY NOTES

- Politics is deciding who gets what, when, and how. It occurs in many different settings, but political science focuses on politics in government.
- Political science focuses on three central questions:
    - Who governs?
    - For what ends?
    - By what means?
- Government is distinguished from other social organizations in that it
    - Extends to the whole society
    - Can legitimately use force
- The purposes of government are to
    - Maintain order in society
    - Provide for national defense
    - Provide "public goods"
    - Regulate society
    - Transfer income
    - Protect individual liberty

- The ideals of democracy include
    - Recognition of individual dignity and personal freedom
    - Equality before the law
    - Widespread participation in decision making
    - Majority rule, with one person equaling one vote
- The principles of democracy pose a paradox: How can we resolve conflicts between our belief in majority rule and our belief in individual freedom?
- Limited government places individual liberty beyond the reach of majorities. Constitutions are the principal means of limiting government power.
- Direct democracy, in which everyone participates in every public decision, is very rare. Representative democracy means that public decisions are made by representatives elected by the people, in elections held periodically and open to competition, in which candidates and voters freely express themselves.

- Who really governs? The elitist perspective on American democracy focuses on the small number of leaders who actually decide national issues, compared to the mass of citizens who are apathetic and ill informed about politics. A pluralist perspective focuses on competition among organized groups in society, with indi- viduals participating through group membership and voting for parties and candidates in elections.

- How democratic is American government today? Democratic ideals are widely shared in our society. But you must make your own informed judgment about the realities of American politics.

SELECTED READINGS

CRONIN, THOMAS J. *Direct Democracy*. Cambridge, Mass.: Harvard University Press, 1989. A thoughtful discussion of direct versus representative democracy, as well as a review of initiative, referendum, and recall devices.

DAHL, ROBERT A. *Democracy and Its Critics*. New Haven, Conn.: Yale University Press, 1989. A defense of modern democracy from the pluralist perspective.

DYE, THOMAS R., AND HARMON ZEIGLER. *The Irony of Democracy*. 10th ed. Belmont, Calif.: Wadsworth, 1996. An interpretation of American politics from the elitist perspective.

FUKUYAMA, FRANCIS. *Trust*. New York: Free Press, 1995. Argues that the breakdown of trust in America—not only in the government but at a person-to-person level—is burdening the nation with formal rules and regulations, lengthy contracts, bureaucracy, lawyers, and lawsuits.

LASSWELL, HAROLD. *Politics: Who Gets What, When, and How*. New York: McGraw-Hill, 1936. Classic description of the nature of politics and the study of political science by America's foremost political scientist of the twentieth century.

MILLS, C. WRIGHT. *The Power Elite*. New York: Oxford University Press, 1956. Classic Marxist critique of elitism in American society, setting forth the argument that "corporate chieftains," "military warlords," and a "political directorate" come together to form the nation's power elite.

O'ROURKE, P. J. *Parliament of Whores*. New York: Atlantic Monthly Press, 1991. A humorist undertakes to explain American government as not only "huge, stupid, greedy" and making "nosy, officious, and dangerous intrusions into the smallest corners of life," but, worse, "boring."

PAGE, BENJAMIN I., AND ROBERT Y. SHAPIRO. *The Rational Public*. Chicago: University of Chicago Press, 1992. An examination of fifty years of public opinion polls convinces these authors that American government is generally responsive to the views of the majority.

WALTON, HANES, JR., *African American Power and Politics*. New York: Columbia University Press, 1997. A description of African American politics during the Reagan, Bush, and Clinton presidencies.

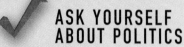

ASK YOURSELF ABOUT POLITICS

1 Do you consider yourself politically conservative, moderate, or liberal?
Conservative ☐ Moderate ☐
Liberal ☐

2 Are income differences in America widening?
Yes ☐ No ☐

3 Is it the government's responsibility to reduce income differences between people?
Yes ☐ No ☐

4 If incomes were made more equal, would people still be motivated to work hard?
Yes ☐ No ☐

5 Do Americans today still have the opportunity to significantly improve their condition in life?
Yes ☐ No ☐

6 Should the U.S. government curtail immigration to America?
Yes ☐ No ☐

7 Should illegal immigrants be denied welfare benefits?
Yes ☐ No ☐

8 Is American culture racist and sexist?
Yes ☐ No ☐

Ask yourself if your answers to these question are widely shared by most citizens of the United States. Your answers probably reflect not only your own beliefs and values but also those of the political culture to which you belong.

POLITICAL CULTURE

Ideas have power. We are all influenced by ideas—beliefs, values, symbols—more than we realize. Ideas provide us with rationalizations for ways of life, with guides for determining right and wrong, and with emotional impulses to action. Political institutions are shaped by ideas, and political leaders are constrained by them.

The term **political culture** refers to widely shared ideas about who should govern, for what ends, and by what means. **Values** are shared ideas about what is good and desirable. Values provide standards for judging what is right or wrong. **Beliefs** are shared ideas about what is true. Values and beliefs are often related. For example, if we believe that human beings are endowed by God with rights to life, liberty, and property, then we will value the protection of these rights. Thus beliefs can justify values.

Cultural descriptions are generalizations about the values and beliefs of many people in society, but these generalizations do not apply to everyone. Important variations in values and beliefs may exist within a society; these variations are frequently referred to as **subcultures** and may arise from such diverse bases as religion, racial or ethnic identity, or political group membership.

Because conflict is dramatic, it tends to capture our attention and lead us to overlook the many shared values and beliefs that constitute the American political culture. The media often focus on controversy, confrontation, and violence as supposedly more newsworthy than broad agreement on fundamental values. Yet in America, for example, no one expects that officeholders defeated in elections will try to retain power by calling out the military. No one believes it is right for public officials to accept bribes or sell government offices or inherit their positions. In many political cultures, past and present, however, such events have been and are still widely accepted.

Contradictions between Values and Conditions　Agreement over values in a political culture is no guarantee that there will not be contradictions between these values and actual conditions. People both in and out of politics frequently act contrary to their professed values. No doubt the most grievous contradiction between professed national beliefs and actual conditions in America is found in the long history of slavery, segregation, and racial discrimination. The contradiction between the words of the Declaration of Independence that "all men are created equal" and the practices of slavery and segregation became the "American dilemma."[1] But this contradiction does not mean that professed values are worthless; the very existence of the gap between values and behavior becomes a motivation for change. The history of the civil rights movement might be viewed as an effort to "bear witness" to the contradiction between the belief in equality and the existence of segregation and discrimination.[2] Whatever the obstacles to racial equality in America, these obstacles would be even greater if the nation's political culture did *not* include a professed belief in equality.

Inconsistent Applications　A political culture does not mean that shared principles are always applied in every circumstance. For example, people may truly believe in the principle of "free speech for all, no matter what their views might be," and yet when asked whether racists should be allowed to speak on a college campus, many people will say no. Thus general agreement with abstract principles of freedom of speech, freedom of the press, and academic freedom does not always ensure their application to specific individuals or groups.[3] Americans are frequently willing to restrict the freedoms of particularly obnoxious groups. A generation ago it was alleged communists and atheists whose freedoms were questioned. Over time these groups have become less threatening, but today people are still willing

political culture Widely shared views about who should govern, for what ends, and by what means.

values Shared ideas about what is good and desirable.

beliefs Shared ideas about what is true.

subcultures Variations on the prevailing values and beliefs in a society.

Proposition187, a ballot initiative in California denying state services to illegal immigrants, exposed a clash of cultures in Los Angeles.

to restrict the liberties of racists, pro-abortion or anti-abortion groups, homo-sexuals, and neo-Nazis.

Conflict   The idea of political culture does not mean an absence of conflict over values and beliefs. Indeed, much of politics involves conflict over very fundamental values. The American nation has experienced a bloody civil war, political assassinations, rioting and burning of cities, the forced resignation of a president, and other direct challenges to its political foundations. Indeed, much of this book deals with serious political conflict. Yet Americans do share many common ways of thinking about politics.

THE LIBERAL TRADITION IN AMERICA

No political value has been more widely held in the United States than individual liberty. The very beginnings of our history as a nation were shaped by **classical liberalism**, which asserted the worth and dignity of the individual. This political philosophy emphasized the rational ability of human beings to determine their own destinies, and it rejected ideas, practices, and institutions that submerged individuals into a larger whole and thus deprived them of their dignity. The only restriction on the individual was not to interfere with the liberties of others.

Political Liberty   Classical liberalism grew out of the eighteenth-century Enlightenment, the Age of Reason in which great philosophers such as Voltaire, John Locke, Jean-Jacques Rousseau, Adam Smith, and Thomas Jefferson affirmed their faith in reason, virtue, and common sense. Classical liberalism originated as an attack on the hereditary prerogatives and distinctions of a feudal society, the monarchy, the privileged aristocracy, and the state-established church.

Classical liberalism motivated America's Founders to declare their independence from England, to write the U.S. Constitution, and to establish the Republic. It

classical liberalism   Political philosophy asserting the worth and dignity of the individual and emphasizing the rational ability of human beings to determine their own destinies.

rationalized their actions and provided ideological legitimacy for the new nation. Locke, as we saw in Chapter 1, argued that a natural law, or moral principle, guaranteed every person "certain inalienable Rights," among them "Life, Liberty, and Property," and that human beings form a social contract with one another to establish a government to help protect their rights. Implicit in the social contract and the liberal notion of freedom is the belief that governmental activity and restrictions on the individual should be kept to a minimum.

Economic Freedom   Classical liberalism as a *political* idea is closely related to capitalism as an *economic* idea. **Capitalism** asserts the individual's right to own private property and to buy, sell, rent, and trade that property in a free market. The economic version of freedom is the freedom to make contracts, to bargain for one's services, to move from job to job, to join labor unions, to start one's own business. Capitalism stresses individual rationality in economic matters—freedom of choice in working, producing, buying, and selling—and limited governmental intervention in economic affairs. Classical liberalism emphasizes individual rationality in voter choice—freedom of speech, press, and political activity—and limitations on governmental power over individual liberty. In classical liberal politics, individuals are free to speak out, to form political parties, and to vote as they please—to pursue their political interests as they think best. In classical liberal economics, individuals are free to find work, to start businesses, and to spend their money as they please—to pursue their economic interests as they think best. The role of government is restricted to protecting private property, enforcing contracts, and performing only those functions and services that cannot be performed by the private market.

The value of liberty in these political and economic spheres has been paramount throughout our history. Only equality competes with liberty as the most honored value in the American political culture.

DILEMMAS OF EQUALITY

Since the bold assertion of the Declaration of Independence that "all men are created equal," Americans have generally believed that no person has greater worth than any other person. The principle of equal worth and dignity was a radical idea in 1776, when much of the world was dominated by hereditary monarchies, titled nobilities, and rigid caste and class systems. Belief in equality drove the expansion of voting rights in the early 1800s and ultimately destroyed the institution of slavery. Abraham Lincoln understood that equality was not so much a description of reality as an ideal to be aspired to: "a standard maxim for a free society which should be familiar to all, and revered by all; constantly looked to, constantly labored for, and even though never perfectly attained, constantly approximated and thereby augmenting the happiness and value of life to all people of all colors everywhere."[4] The millions who immigrated to the United States viewed this country as a land not only of opportunity but of *equal* opportunity, where everyone, regardless of birth, could rise in wealth and status based on hard work, natural talents, and perhaps good luck.

Today, most Americans agree that no one is intrinsically "better" than anyone else. This belief in equality, then, is fundamental to Americans, but a closer examination shows that throughout our history it has been tested, as beliefs and values so often are, by political realities.

capitalism   Economic system asserting the individual's right to own private property and to buy, sell, rent, and trade that property in a free market.

Political Equality   The nation's Founders shared the belief that the law should apply equally to all—that birth, status, or wealth do not justify differential application of the laws. But *legal equality* did not necessarily mean **political equality**, at least not in 1787 when the U.S. Constitution was written. The Constitution left the issue of voter qualifications to the states to decide for themselves. At that time, all states imposed either property or taxpayer qualifications for voting. Neither women nor slaves could vote anywhere. The expansion of voting rights to universal suffrage required many bitter battles over the course of two centuries. The long history of the struggle over voting rights illustrates the contradictions between values and practices (see "Securing the Right to Vote" in Chapter 5). Yet in the absence of the *value* of equality, voting rights might have remained restricted.

Equality of Opportunity   The American ideal of equality extends to **equality of opportunity**—the elimination of artificial barriers to success in life. The term *equality of opportunity* refers to the ability to make of oneself what one can, to develop one's talents and abilities, and to be rewarded for one's work, initiative, and achievement. Equality of opportunity means that everyone comes to the same starting line in life, with the same chance of success, and that whatever differences develop over time do so as a result of abilities, talents, initiative, hard work, and perhaps good luck.

Americans do not generally resent the fact that physicians, engineers, airline pilots, and others who have spent time and energy acquiring particular skills make more money than those whose jobs require fewer skills and less training. Neither do most Americans resent the fact that people who risk their own time and money to build a business, bring new or better products to market, and create jobs for others make more money than their employees. Nor do many Americans begrudge multimillion-dollar incomes to sports figures, rock stars, and movie stars whose talents entertain the public. And few Americans object when someone wins a million-dollar lottery, as long as everyone who entered the lottery had an equal chance at winning. Americans are generally willing to have government act to ensure equality of opportunity—to ensure that everyone has an equal chance at getting an education, landing a job, and buying a home, and that no barriers of race, sex, religion, or ethnicity bar individual advancement. Differences arise over whether special efforts such as *affirmative action* should be undertaken to overcome the effects of past discriminatory barriers (see "Affirmative Action in the Courts" in Chapter 15). But the ideal of equality of opportunity is widely shared.

Equality of Results   **Equality of results** refers to the equal sharing of income and material rewards. Equality of results means that everyone starts *and finishes* the race together, regardless of ability, talent, initiative, or work. Those who argue on behalf of this notion of equality say that if individuals are truly equal, then everyone should enjoy generally equal conditions in life. According to this belief, we should appreciate an individual's skills, work, knowledge, and contributions to society without creating inequalities of wealth and income. Government should act to *transfer* wealth and income from the rich to the poor to increase the total happiness of all members of society.

But equality of results, or absolute equality, is not a widely shared value in the United States. This notion of equality was referred to as "leveling" by Thomas Jefferson and generally has been denounced by the nation's political leadership—and by most Americans—then and now:

political equality   Belief that the law should apply equally to all and that every person's vote counts equally.

equality of opportunity
Elimination of artificial barriers to success in life and the opportunity for everyone to strive for success.

equality of results   Equal sharing of income and material goods regardless of one's efforts in life.

To take from one, because it is thought his own industry and that of his fathers has acquired too much, in order to spare to others who have not exercised equal industry and skill, is to violate arbitrarily . . . the guarantee to everyone the free exercise of his industry and the fruits acquired by it.[5]

The taking of private property from those who acquired it legitimately, for no other reason than to equalize wealth or income, is widely viewed as morally wrong. Moreover, many people believe that society generally would suffer if incomes were equalized. Absolute equality, in this view, would remove incentives for people to work, save, or produce. Everyone would slack off, production would decline, goods would be in short supply, and everyone would end up poorer than ever. So some inequality may be essential for the well-being of society.

Thus Americans believe strongly in equality of opportunity but not necessarily equality of results (see Figure 2-1). Americans seek fairness rather than equality of wealth and income.

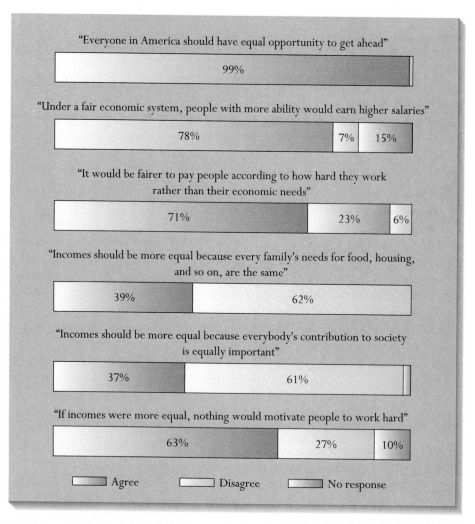

FIGURE 2-1 **Beliefs about Equality**

Source: Questions 1–3 based on Herbert McClosky and John Zaller, *The American Ethos: Public Attitudes toward Capitalism and Democracy* (Cambridge, Mass.: Harvard University Press, 1984), pp. 83–84; questions 4–6 based on James R. Kluegel and Eliot R. Smith, *Beliefs about Inequality: Americans' Views of What Is and What Ought to Be* (New York: Aldine de Gruyter, 1986).

Fairness   Americans value "fairness" even though they do not always agree on what is fair. Most Americans support a "floor" on income and material well-being—a level that no one, regardless of his or her condition, should be permitted to fall below—even though they differ over how high that floor should be. Indeed, the belief in a floor is consistent with the belief in equality of opportunity; extreme poverty would deny people, especially children, the opportunity to compete in life.[6] But very few Americans want to place a "ceiling" on income or wealth. This unwillingness to limit top income extends to nearly all groups in the United States, the poor as well as the rich. Generally, Americans want people who cannot provide for themselves to be well cared for, especially children, the elderly, the ill, and the disabled. They are often willing to "soak the rich" when searching for new tax sources, believing that the rich can easily afford to bear the burdens of government. But, unlike citizens in other Western democracies, Americans generally do *not* believe that government should equalize incomes (see *Compared to What?* "Should Government Equalize Incomes?").

Equality in Politics versus Economics   Americans make a clear distinction between the *private economic* sphere of life and the *public political* sphere.[7] In the

Compared to What?

Should Government Equalize Incomes?

Whereas American political culture emphasizes equality of *opportunity*, the political culture in the Western Europe democracies is much more inclined toward equality of *results*. Americans generally believe that government should provide a "floor," or safety net, to protect people against true hardship; but they are generally unwilling to place a "ceiling" on incomes, or to give government the task of equalizing income differences among people. In contrast, majorities in most other Western democracies agree with this statement: "It is government's responsibility to reduce income differences between people."

"It is the government's responsibility to reduce income differences between people."

Italy
Hungary
Netherlands
Britain
All
Germany
Australia
United States

0 10 20 30 40 50 60 70 80 90
Percent Agreeing

Source: U.S. News and World Report, August 7, 1989, p. 25, reporting data gathered by Gallup International Research Institute, International Research Associates, National Opinion Research Center, and International Social Survey Program, 1987–88.

private economic sphere, they value the principle of "earned desserts," meaning that individuals are entitled to what they achieve through hard work, skill, talent, risk, and even good luck. They are willing to tolerate inequalities of result in economics. Self-interested behavior in the marketplace is seen as appropriate and even beneficial, if properly constrained by rules that apply equally to everyone. But in the public political sphere, Americans value absolute equality—one person, one vote. They condemn disparities of power and influence among individuals. Self-interested behavior in politics is seen as corrupt.

As long as the economic and political spheres of life are perceived as separate, then economic inequalities and political equalities can exist side by side in a society.

INEQUALITY OF INCOME AND WEALTH

Conflict in society is generated more often by inequalities among people than by hardship or deprivation. Material well-being and standards of living are usually expressed in aggregate measures for a whole society—for example, gross domestic product per capita, income per capita, average life expectancy, infant mortality rate. These measures of societal well-being are vitally important to a nation and its people, but *political* conflict is more likely to occur over the *distribution* of well-being *within* a society. Unequal distributions can generate conflict even in a very affluent society with high levels of income and a high standard of living.

Inequality of Income Let us examine inequality of income in the United States systematically. Figure 2-2 divides all American families into five groups, or *quintiles*—from the lowest one-fifth in personal income to the highest one-fifth—and shows the percentage of total family personal income received by each of these groups over the years. (If perfect income equality existed, each fifth of American families would receive 20 percent of all family personal income.) The poorest one-fifth received only 3.5 percent of all family personal income in 1929; today, this group does a little better, at 4.2 percent of family personal income. The highest

As income and wealth differences between the "haves" and the "have-nots" increased in America during the 1980s and the early 1990s, more people fell through the cracks in the system and joined the ranks of the impoverished and homeless.

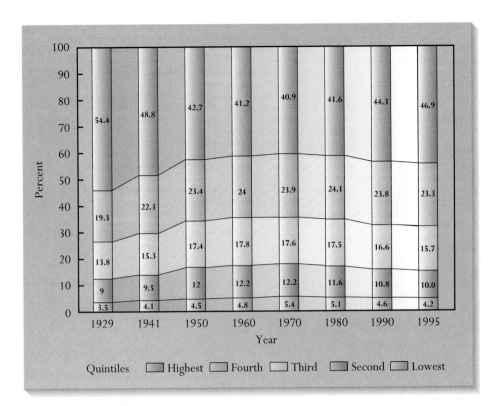

FIGURE 2-2 **The Distribution of Family Personal Income in the United States**

Source: *Statistical Abstract of the United States, 1997.*

one-fifth received 54.4 percent of all family personal income in 1929; today, its percentage stands at 46.2. This was the only income group to lose in relation to other income groups.

However, while income differences in the United States have declined over the long run, inequality has actually *increased* in recent years. The income of the poorest quintile declined from 5.4 to 4.2 percent of total income between 1970 and 1995; the income of the highest quintile rose from 40.9 to 46.9 percent of total income. This reversal of historical trends has generated both political rhetoric and serious scholarly inquiry about its causes.

Explaining Recent Increases in Income Inequality   Recent increases in income inequality in the United States are a product of several social and economic trends: (1) the decline of the manufacturing sector of the economy (and the loss of many relatively high-paying blue-collar jobs) and the ascendancy of the communications, information, and service sectors of the economy (with a combination of high-paying and low-paying jobs); (2) the rise in the number of two-wage families, making single-wage, female-headed households relatively less affluent; (3) demographic trends, which include larger proportions of aged and larger proportions of female-headed families; and (4) global competition, which restrains wages in unskilled and semiskilled jobs while rewarding people in high-technology, high-productivity occupations.

Inequality of Wealth   Inequalities of wealth in the United States are even greater than inequalities of income. *Wealth* is the total value of a family's assets—bank accounts, stocks, bonds, mutual funds, business equity, houses, cars, and major appliances—minus outstanding debts, such as credit card balances, mortgages, and

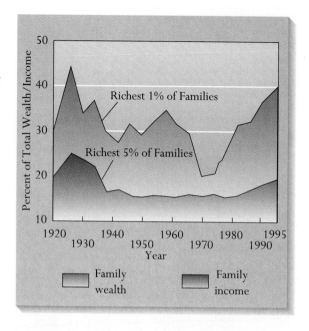

FIGURE 2-3 Inequality of Wealth and Income

Source: U.S. Bureau of the Census, *Current Population Reports, 1995*; see also Edward N. Wolff, *Top Heavy* (New York: Twentieth Century Fund, 1995), p. 28.

other loans. The top 1 percent of families in the United States owns almost 40 percent of all family wealth (see Figure 2-3). Inequality of wealth appeared to be diminishing until the mid-1970s, but in recent years it has surged sharply. Not surprisingly, age is the key determinant of family wealth; persons age fifty to sixty-five are by far the wealthiest, with persons over sixty-five close behind; young families generally have less than one-third of the assets of retirees.

SOCIAL MOBILITY

Political conflict over inequality might be greater in the United States if it were not for the prospect of **social mobility**. All societies are stratified, or layered, but societies differ greatly in the extent to which people move upward or downward in income and status over a lifetime or over generations. When there is social mobility, people have a good opportunity to get ahead if they study or work long and hard, save and invest wisely, or display initiative and enterprise in business affairs (however, see *A Conflicting View:* "Success Is Determined by the Bell Curve"). Fairly steep inequalities may be tolerated politically if people have a reasonable expectation of moving up over time, or at least of seeing their children do so.

How Much Mobility?   The United States describes itself as the land of opportunity. The really important political question may be how much real opportunity exists for individual Americans to improve their conditions in life relative to others. The impression given by Figure 2-2 is one of a static distribution system, with families permanently placed in upper or lower fifths of income earners. But there is considerable evidence of both upward and downward movement by people among income groupings.[8] About a third of the families in the poorest one-fifth will move upward within a decade, and about a third of families in the richest one-fifth will fall out of this top category. However, there appears to have been some slowing of this mobility in recent years; one's chances of escaping the bottom have diminished somewhat. Thus the nation is currently experiencing not only an increase in inequality but also a slowing of social mobility.

social mobility Extent to which people move upward or downward in income and status over a lifetime or generations.

Success Is Determined by the Bell Curve

Most Americans believe in social mobility—the idea that anyone who studies or works hard, saves and invests wisely, and makes good use of his or her talents, initiative, and enterprise can get ahead. But a controversial book, *The Bell Curve* by Richard J. Herrnstein and Charles Murray, sets forth the argument that general intelligence largely determines success in life. General intelligence, the authors contend, is distributed among the population in a bell-shaped curve, with most people clustered around the median, smaller numbers with higher intelligence (a "cognitive elite") at one end, and an unfortunate few trailing behind at the other end (see graph). Over time, say Herrnstein and Murray, intelligence is becoming ever more necessary for the performance of key jobs in the "information society." The result will be the continuing enhancement of the power and wealth of the cognitive elite and the further erosion of the lifestyle of the less intelligent.

Even more controversial than the authors' claim that general intelligence determines success is their contention that general intelligence is mostly (60 percent) genetic. Because intelligence is mostly inherited, programs to assist the underprivileged are useless or even counterproductive.

The cognitive elite, the authors predict, will continue to distance themselves from the masses in knowledge, skills, technical competence, income, and power while social problems will be concentrated among the "dullest." Indeed, they amass statistics showing that educational deficiencies, emotional problems, welfare reliance, early childbirth, and even criminal behavior are disproportionately concentrated in low-intelligence groups (see table).

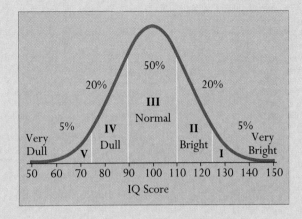

Population Distribution of IQ Scores

Source: Adapted with permission of The Free Press, a division of Simon & Schuster, from *The Bell Curve: Intelligence and Class Structure in American Life* by Richard J. Herrnstein and Charles Murray. Copyright © 1994 by Richard J. Herrnstein and Charles Murray.

But critics of *The Bell Curve* point out the lack of consensus on the role of genetics in intelligence. Indeed, recent research on infant development indicates that brain activity and the interconnections among brain cells are greatly affected by early human interaction. Infants in a stimulating environment—who are frequently coddled, spoken to, and sung to, for example—exhibit more brain activity than those with little environmental stimuli. Moreover, the implication of the bell curve thesis is that social classes and elitism are both natural and inevitable—and therefore that most efforts to ensure equality of opportunity are useless. This thesis might be seen as a justification for widening inequality in society. Finally, a racial dimension Herrnstein and Murray add to their argument is unnecessary to their thesis. Although they claim that the differences between African Americans, whites, and Asians on IQ tests should not matter if every individual were judged separately on IQ, clearly their argument reinforces racial stereotypes.

	Cognitive Class	High School Dropout	Women on Welfare Assistance	Mean Age at First Childbearing	Criminal Convictions (young white males)
I	Very Bright	0%	0%	27.2 years	3%
II	Bright	0	2	25.5	7
III	Normal	6	8	23.4	15
IV	Dull	35	17	21.0	21
V	Very Dull	55	31	19.8	14

Source: Table adapted from various chapters in Herrnstein and Murray, *The Bell Curve* (1994)

FIGURE 2-4 "Middle-Class"ifying Ourselves

Percentage of people in each group by annual household income and how they classify themselves. Source: *New York Times*/CBS News poll, reported in *New York Times*, February 15, 1993. Copyright © 1993 by *The New York Times* Company. Reprinted by permission.

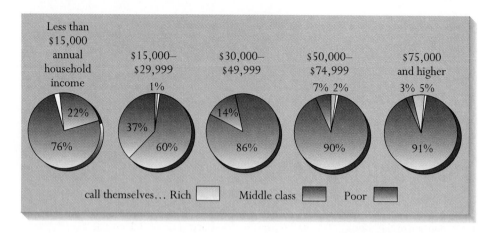

Mobility, Class Conflict, and Class Consciousness   Social mobility and the expectation of mobility, over a lifetime or over generations, may be the key to understanding why **class conflict**—conflict over wealth and power among social classes—is not as widespread or as intense in America as it is in many other nations. The *belief* in social mobility reduces the potential for class conflict because it diminishes **class consciousness**, the awareness of one's class position and the feeling of political solidarity with others in the same class in opposition to other classes. If class lines were impermeable and no one had any reasonable expectation of moving up or seeing his or her children move up, then class consciousness would rise and political conflict among classes would intensify.

Most Americans describe themselves as "middle class" rather than "rich" or "poor" or "lower class" or "upper class." There are no widely accepted income definitions of "middle class." The federal government officially defines a "poverty level" each year based on the annual cash income required to maintain a decent standard of living ($15,500 in 1996 for a family of four). Roughly 14 percent of the U.S. population lives with annual cash incomes below this poverty line. (For more discussion, see "Poverty in the United States" in Chapter 17.) This is the only income group in which a majority of people describe themselves as poor (see Figure 2-4). Large majorities in every other income group identify themselves as middle class. So it is no surprise that presidents, politicians, and political parties regularly claim to be defenders of America's "middle class"!

A NATION OF IMMIGRANTS

The United States is a nation of immigrants, from the first "boat people" (Pilgrims) to the latest Haitian refugees and Cuban *balseros* ("rafters"). Historically, most of the people who came to settle in this country did so because they believed their lives would be better here, and American political culture today has been greatly affected by the beliefs and values they brought with them. Americans are proud of their immigrant heritage and the freedom and opportunity the nation has extended to generations of "huddled masses yearning to be free"—words emblazoned on the Statue of Liberty in New York's harbor. Today about 8 percent of the U.S. population is foreign-born.

The United States accepts more immigrants than all other nations of the world combined. The vast majority of immigrants in recent years come from less-developed nations of Asia and Latin America (see Figure 2-5). Most immigrants come

class conflict   Conflict between upper and lower social classes over wealth and power.

class consciousness   Awareness of one's class position and a feeling of political solidarity with others within the same class in opposition to other classes.

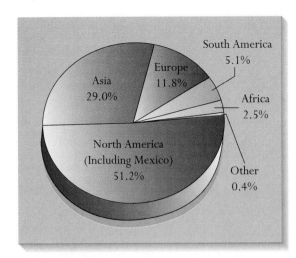

FIGURE 2-5 Origins of Legal Immigrants, 1991–94

Source: Statistical Abstract of the United States, 1996, p. 11.

to the United States for economic opportunity and personify the traits we typically think of as American: opportunism, ambition, perseverance, initiative, and a willingness to work hard. As immigrants have always done, they frequently take dirty, low-paying, thankless jobs that other Americans shun. When they open their own businesses, they often do so in blighted, crime-ridden neighborhoods long since abandoned by other entrepreneurs.

National Immigration Policy   Immigration policy is a responsibility of the national government. It was not until 1882 that Congress passed the first legislation restricting entry into the United States of persons alleged to be "undesirable" and virtually all Asians. After World War I, Congress passed the comprehensive Immigration Act of 1921, which established maximum numbers of new immigrants each year and set a quota for immigrants for each foreign country at 3 percent of the number of that nation's foreign-born who were living in the United States in

Haitian refugees risk their lives seeking opportunity in America.

FIGURE 2-6 **Immigration to the United States by Decades**

Source: Statistical Abstract of the United States, 1995, p. 10.

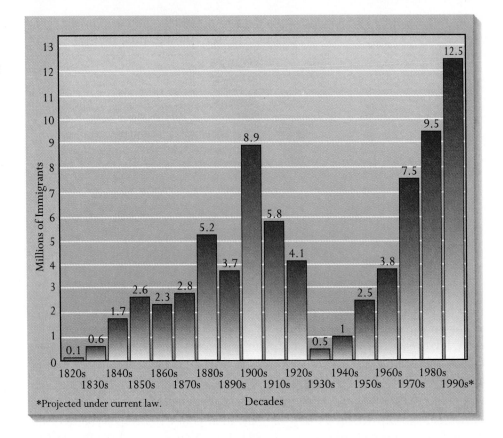

*Projected under current law.

1910, later reduced to 2 percent of the number living here in 1890. These restrictions reflected anti-immigration feelings that were generally directed at the large wave of Southern and Eastern European Catholic and Jewish immigrants (from Poland, Russia, Hungary, Italy, and Greece) entering the United States prior to World War I (see Figure 2-6). The law did *not* set any quotas for immigrants from the Western Hemisphere, and consequently immigration from Mexico sharply increased. It was not until the Immigration and Nationality Act of 1965 that national origin quotas were abolished, replaced by preference categories for close relatives of U.S. citizens or permanent resident aliens, professionals, and skilled workers.

Immigration "reform" was the announced goal of Congress in the Immigration Reform and Control Act of 1986, also known as the Simpson-Mazzoli Act. It sought to control immigration by placing principal responsibility on employers; it set fines for knowingly hiring an illegal alien, with prison terms for repeat offenders. However, it allowed employers to accept many different forms of easily forged documentation and at the same time subjected them to penalties for discriminating against legal foreign-born residents. To win political support, the act granted amnesty to illegal aliens who had lived in the United States since 1982. But the act failed to reduce the flow of either legal or illegal immigrants.

Today, roughly a million people per year are admitted *legally* to the United States as "lawful permanent residents" (persons who have needed job skills or who have relatives who are U.S. citizens) or as "political refugees" (persons with "a well-founded fear of persecution" in their country of origin). In addition, each year more than 25 million people are awarded temporary visas to enter the United States for study, business, or pleasure.

Illegal Immigration   The United States is a free and prosperous society with more than 5,000 miles of borders (2,000 with Mexico) and hundreds of international air and sea ports. In theory, a sovereign nation should be able to maintain secure borders, but in practice the United States has been unwilling and unable to do so. Estimates of illegal immigration vary widely, from the official U.S. Immigration and Naturalization Service (INS) estimate of 400,000 per year (about 45 percent of the legal immigration) to unofficial estimates ranging up to 3 million per year. The INS estimates that about 4 million illegal immigrants currently reside in the United States; unofficial estimates range up to 10 million or more. Many illegal immigrants slip across U.S. borders or enter ports with false documentation; many more overstay tourist, worker, or student visas (and are not counted by the INS as illegal immigrants).[9]

As a free society, the United States is not prepared to undertake massive roundups and summary deportations of millions of illegal residents. The Fifth and Fourteenth Amendments to the U.S. Constitution require that every *person* (not just citizen) be afforded "due process of law." The INS may turn back persons at the border or even hold them in detention camps. The Coast Guard may intercept boats at sea and return persons to their country of origin.[10] Aliens have no constitutional right to come to the United States. However, once in the United States, whether legally or illegally, every person is entitled to due process of law and equal protection of the laws. People are thus entitled to a fair hearing prior to any government attempt to deport them. Aliens are entitled to apply for asylum and present evidence at a hearing of their "well-founded fear of prosecution" if returned to their country. Experience has shown that the only way to reduce the flow of illegal immigration is to control it at the border, an expensive and difficult but not impossible task. Localized experiments in border enforcement have indicated that, with significant increases in INS personnel and technology, illegal immigration can be reduced by half or more.

Cultural Conflict   The politics of immigration centers on both cultural and economic conflicts. Although most Americans are themselves the descendants of immigrants (Native Americans constitute about 1 percent of the population), there is a widespread belief that today's immigrants are different from earlier waves. Population projections based on current immigration and fertility (birth) rates suggest that the ethnic character of the nation will shift dramatically over time because so many immigrants today are from Asia and Latin America rather than Europe.

The United States has always been an ethnically pluralist society, but all immigrants were expected to adopt American political culture—including a commitment to liberty, economic freedom, political equality, and equality of opportunity—and to learn American history and traditions, as well as the English language (See *What Do You Think?:* "Could You Pass the Citizenship Test?"). The nation's motto has been *E Pluribus Unum* (From Many, One) since 1782, but opponents of large-scale immigration fear that immigration currently represents a threat to cultural and political unity.[11] There have long been Italian, Irish, Polish, Chinese, and other ethnic neighborhoods in big cities, but the children of immigrants, if not the immigrants themselves, quickly became "Americanized." In contrast, today policy makers are divided over whether to protect and preserve language and cultural differences, for example through bilingual

What Do You Think?

Could You Pass the Citizenship Test?

People who have been lawfully admitted into the United States and granted permanent residence, and who have resided in the United States for at least five years and in their home state for the last six months, are eligible for naturalization as U.S. citizens. Federal district courts as well as offices of the U.S. Immigration and Naturalization Service (INS) may grant applications for citizenship. By law, the applicant must be over age eighteen, be able to read, write, and speak English, possess good moral character, and understand and demonstrate an attachment to the history, principles, and form of government of the United States. To ensure that new citizens "understand" the history, principles, and form of government of the United States, the INS administers a citizenship test. Could you pass it today?

Answer correctly at least 18 of 30 questions to pass:

1. How many stars are there on our flag?
2. What do the stars on the flag mean?
3. What color are the stripes?
4. What do the stripes on the flag mean?
5. What is the date of Independence Day?
6. Independence from whom?
7. What do we call a change to the Constitution?
8. How many branches are there in our government?
9. How many full terms can a president serve?
10. Who nominates judges of the Supreme Court?
11. How many Supreme Court justices are there?
12. Who was the main writer of the Declaration of Independence?
13. What holiday was celebrated for the first time by American colonists?
14. Who wrote the Star-Spangled Banner?
15. What is the minimum voting age in the U.S.?
16. Who was president during the Civil War?
17. Which president is called the "Father of our Country"?
18. What is the 50th state of the Union?
19. What is the name of the ship that brought the Pilgrims to America?
20. Who has the power to declare war?
21. What were the 13 original states of the U.S. called?
22. In what year was the Constitution written?
23. What is the introduction to the Constitution called?
24. Which president was the first Commander-in-Chief of the U.S. Army and Navy?
25. In what month do we vote for the president?
26. How many times may a senator be re-elected?
27. Who signs bills into law?
28. Who elects the president of the U.S.?
29. How many states are there in the U.S.?
30. Who becomes president if both the president and V.P. die?

Answers: 1. 50; 2. One for each state in the Union; 3. Red and white; 4. They represent the 13 original states; 5. July 4; 6. England; 7. Amendments; 8. 3; 9. 2; 10. The president; 11. 9; 12. Thomas Jefferson; 13. Thanksgiving; 14. Francis Scott Key; 15. 18; 16. Abraham Lincoln; 17. George Washington; 18. Hawaii; 19. The *Mayflower*; 20. The Congress; 21. Colonies; 22. 1787; 23. The Preamble; 24. George Washington; 25. November; 26. There is no limit at the present time; 27. The president; 28. The Electoral College; 29. 50; 30. Speaker of the House of Representatives.

Source: U.S. Immigration and Naturalization Service.

education, bilingual language ballots, and "language minority" voting districts (all currently required by amendments and interpretations of the Civil Rights Act of 1964 and the Voting Rights Act of 1965; see Chapter 14).

Economists differ over the economic impact of immigration—whether it creates jobs and new business or instead creates a surplus of labor and thus reduces wages. It is not clear whether the taxes paid by immigrants add more to the revenues of federal, state, and local governments than the services they use cost those governments—or vice versa.[12] Currently neither the states nor the federal government accurately tracks the immigration status of welfare recipients or public school pupils, two subjects of widespread debate in this country.

Political opposition to increased border enforcement and reduced immigration comes from a variety of sources. Large numbers of Americans identify with the aspirations of people striving to come to the United States, whether legally or illegally. Many Americans still have family and relatives living abroad who may wish to immigrate. Hispanic groups have been especially concerned about immigration enforcement efforts that may lead to discrimination against all Hispanic Americans. Powerful industry groups that benefit from the availability of illegal immigrants—such as agriculture, restaurants, clothing manufacturers, and hospitals—lobby in Washington to weaken enforcement efforts. Some employers prefer hiring illegal immigrants because they are willing to work at hard jobs for low pay and few if any benefits. Foreign governments, especially Mexico, have also protested U.S. enforcement policies.

IDEOLOGIES: LIBERALISM AND CONSERVATISM

An **ideology** is a consistent and integrated system of ideas, values, and beliefs. A political ideology tells us who *should* get what, when, and how; that is, it tells us who *ought* to govern and what goals they *ought* to pursue. When we use ideological terms such as *liberalism* and *conservatism*, we imply reasonably integrated sets of values and beliefs. And when we pin ideological labels on people, we imply that those people are fairly consistent in the application of these values and beliefs in public affairs. In reality, neither political leaders nor citizens always display integrated or consistent opinions; many hold conservative views on some issues and liberal views on others.[13] Many Americans avoid ideological labeling, either by describing themselves as "moderate" or "middle-of-the-road" or by simply declining to place themselves on an ideological scale. But as Figure 2-7

ideology Consistent and integrated system of ideas, values, and beliefs.

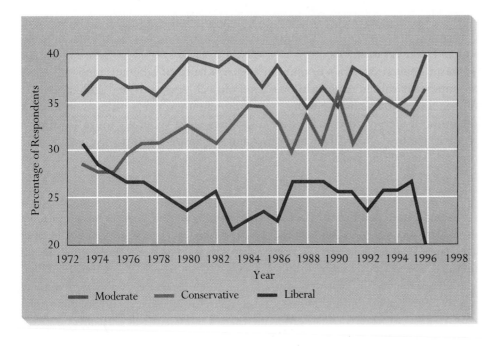

FIGURE 2-7 Americans: Liberal, Moderate, Conservative

Source: National Election Studies, University of Michigan.

Liberalism and Conservatism

States might be classified in terms of their voters' self-identification in opinion surveys as liberal, moderate, or conservative. The most conservative state is Utah (45 percent conservative, 37 percent moderate, 13 percent liberal), followed by Indiana (42 percent conservative, 39 percent moderate, 13 percent liberal). The most liberal states are Massachusetts (26 percent conservative, 42 percent moderate, 26 percent liberal); New York (29 percent conservative, 39 percent moderate, 26 percent liberal); and New Jersey (28 percent conservative, 40 percent moderate, 26 percent liberal).

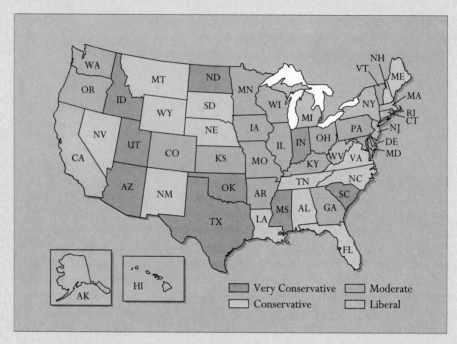

Source: Gerald C. Wright, Robert S. Erikson, and John P. McIver, "Public Opinion and Policy Liberalism in the American States," *American Journal of Political Science* 31 (November 1987): 980–1001. Reprinted by permission of the University of Wisconsin Press.

shows, among those who choose an ideological label to describe their politics, conservatives consistently outnumber liberals. (See also *Across the USA:* "Liberalism and Conservatism.")

Despite inconsistencies in opinion and avoidance of labeling, ideology plays an important role in American politics. Political *elites*—elected and appointed officeholders; journalists, editors, and commentators; party officials and interest-group leaders; and others active in politics—are generally more consistent in their political views than nonelites and are more likely to use ideological terms in describing politics.[14]

Modern Conservatism: Individualism plus Traditional Values Modern **conservatism** combines a belief in free markets, limited government, and individual self-reliance in economic affairs with a belief in the value of tradition, law, and morality in social affairs. Conservatives wish to retain our historical commitments to individual freedom from governmental controls; reliance on individual initiative and effort for self-development; a free-enterprise economy with a minimum of governmental intervention; and rewards for initiative, skill, risk, and hard work. These views are consistent with the early classical liberalism of Locke,

conservatism Belief in the value of free markets, limited government, and individual self-reliance in economic affairs, combined with a belief in the value of tradition, law, and morality in social affairs.

P. J. O'Rourke, Conservative with a Sense of Humor

"Giving money and power to government is like giving whiskey and car keys to teenage boys," according to political humorist P. J. O'Rourke. Two of his books—*Parliament of Whores: A Lone Humorist Attempts to Explain the Entire U.S. Government* (1991), dealing with the American political system, and *Give War a Chance: Eyewitness Accounts of Mankind's Struggle against Tyranny, Injustice, and Alcohol-Free Beer* (1992), describing international politics—have topped the best-seller lists. Describing himself as a "cigar-smoking conservative," O'Rourke actually bashes Republicans as well as Democrats:

> When you look at the Republicans you see the scum off the top of business. When you look at the Democrats you see the scum off the top of politics. Personally, I prefer business. A businessman will steal from you directly instead of getting the IRS to do it for him. And when Republicans ruin the environment, destroy the supply of affordable housing, and wreck the industrial infrastructure, at least they make a buck off it. The Democrats just do these things for fun.

O'Rourke describes his life as a youth growing up in Toledo, Ohio:

> My own family was poor when I was a kid, though I didn't know it; I just thought we were broke. My father died, and my mother married a drunken bum who shortly thereafter died himself. . . . But I honestly didn't know we were poor until just now, when I was researching poverty levels.

He counts himself lucky, because no one coddled him or sympathized with his family's distress. His mother never went on welfare. In the "bad old days," he was simply expected to shut up, behave, and work hard. O'Rourke started out as a Republican but joined the counterculture of the 1960s. Yet he says he was never a Democrat: "I went from being a Republican, to being a Maoist, then back to being a Republican again." He won a scholarship to Miami University of Ohio and later Johns Hopkins. In 1972 he went to work for *National Lampoon*, and on the strength of his irreverent articles he was elevated to editor-in-chief in 1978. Later he moved to Hollywood to write movie scripts, including Rodney Dangerfield films, then returned to New York to become an editor of *Rolling Stone*.

A frequent speaker on university campuses, O'Rourke reflects a distinctly conservative view of government: "A little government and a little luck are necessary in life but only a fool trusts either of them. . . . The whole idea of government is: if enough people get together and act in concert, they can take something and not pay for it." His latest book, *Age and Guile Beat Youth, Innocence, and a Bad Haircut: Twenty-five Years of P. J. O'Rourke* (1995), describes his ideological journey from youthful radicalism to his current mature (?) conservatism: "I was once younger than anyone ever has been. And on drugs. At least I hope I was on drugs. I'd hate to think that those were my sober and well-considered thoughts."

Source: P. J. O'Rourke, *Parliament of Whores: A Lone Humorist Attempts to Explain the Entire U.S. Government* (New York: Atlantic Monthly Press, 1991); and *Age and Guile Beat Youth, Innocence, and a Bad Haircut: Twenty-five Years of P. J. O'Rourke* (New York: Atlantic Monthly Press, 1995).

Jefferson, and the nation's Founders, discussed at the beginning of this chapter. The result is a confusion of ideological labels: modern conservatives claim to be the true inheritors of the (classical) liberal tradition.

Modern conservatism does indeed incorporate many classical liberal ideals, but it also has a distinct ideological tradition of its own. Conservatism is less optimistic about human nature (see *People in Politics:* "P. J. O'Rourke, Conservative with a Sense of Humor"). Traditionally, conservatives have recognized that human nature includes elements of irrationality, ignorance, hatred, and violence. Thus they have been more likely to place their faith in *law* and *traditional values* than in popular fads, trends, or emotions. To conservatives, the absence of law does not mean freedom but, rather, exposure to the tyranny of terrorism and violence. They believe that without the guidance of traditional values, people would soon come to grief through the unruliness of their passions, destroying both themselves and others. Conservatives argue that strong institutions—family, church, and community—are needed to control individuals' selfish and immoral impulses and to foster civilized ways of life.

liberalism Belief in the value of strong government to provide economic security and protection for civil rights, combined with a belief in personal freedom from government intervention in social conduct.

Modern Liberalism: Governmental Power to "Do Good" Modern **liberalism** combines a belief in a strong government to provide economic security and protection for civil rights with a belief in freedom from government intervention in social conduct. Modern liberalism retains the classical liberalism commitment to individual dignity, but it also emphasizes the importance of social and economic security for the whole population as a prerequisite to individual self-develop-

People in Politics

Barbara Boxer, Defending Liberalism

Perhaps no one has been more successful in defending liberal causes in Congress than California's outspoken U.S. senator, Barbara Boxer. Her political résumé boasts awards and honors from such organizations as Planned Parenthood (family planning, reproductive health, and abortion rights), the Sierra Club (environmental causes), Mobilization against AIDS, Anti-Defamation League (civil rights), and Public Citizen (consumer affairs).

A graduate of Brooklyn College with a B.A. in economics, Boxer worked briefly as a stockbroker before moving to San Francisco, where she became a journalist and later a campaign aide to a local congressional representative. Her political career is based in Marin County, a trendy, upper-class, liberal community north of San Francisco, where she first won elected office as member of the County Board of Supervisors. She was elected to the U.S. House of Representatives from her Marin County district in 1982 and quickly won a reputation as one of the most liberal members of the House. Appointed to the

House Armed Services Committee, she became a leading critic of defense spending and virtually every weapon requested by the military.

When her state's liberal Democratic senator, Alan Cranston, announced he would not seek reelection to the Senate in the wake of his censure in the Keating Five affair, Boxer sought the open seat. Her opponent, conservative Republican radio and TV commentator Bruce Herschensohn, hammered at Boxer's 143 overdrafts at the House bank, her frequent absenteeism, and her extensive use of congressional perks. But with the help of Clinton's 1992 landslide (47 to 32 percent) victory over George Bush in California, Boxer eked out a 48 to 45 percent victory over Herschensohn. Her victory, together with that of Dianne Feinstein, gave California a historical first—two women U.S. senators.

Boxer quickly emerged as a powerful force in the U.S. Senate on behalf of abortion rights. She led the Senate fight for a federal law protecting abortion clinics from obstruction by demonstrators. On the Environmental and Public Works Committee she helped block efforts to relax federal environmental regulations. She led the movement to oust Republican senator Bob Packwood from the Senate on charges of sexually harassing staff members. And she helped lead the fight for the Family Medical Leave Act, passed in the early days of the Clinton administration.

ment. Classical liberalism looked with suspicion on government as a potential source of "interference" with personal freedom, but modern liberalism looks on the power of government as a positive force for eliminating social and economic conditions that adversely affect people's lives and impede their self-development. The modern liberal approves of the use of governmental power to ensure the general welfare and to correct the perceived ills of society (see *People in Politics:* "Barbara Boxer, Defending Liberalism").

Today's liberals believe that government can change people's lives by working to end racial and sexual discrimination, abolish poverty, eliminate slums, create jobs, uplift the poor, provide medical care for all, educate the masses, protect the environment, and instill humanitarian values in everyone. The prevailing impulse is to "do good," to perform public services, and to assist the least fortunate in society, particularly the poor and minorities. Modern liberalism is impatient with what it sees as the slow progress of individual initiative and private enterprise toward solving socioeconomic problems, so it seeks to use the power of the national government to find solutions to society's troubles.

Modern liberalism continues to recognize the individual's right to own private property, but it imposes on the property owner social and economic obligations that are designed to reduce capitalism's hardships. It assumes that businesses will be privately owned but subject to considerable governmental regulation. Modern liberals are committed to a significant enlargement of the public (governmental) sector of society in education, welfare, housing, environmental protection, transportation, urban renewal, health care, employment, child care, and other areas. Modern liberalism envisions a larger role for government in the future: setting new goals, managing the economy, and redirecting national resources away from private wants toward public needs.

Modern liberalism defines equality somewhat differently from the way classical liberalism does. Classical liberalism stresses the value of equality of opportunity. Individuals should be free to make the most of their talents and skills, but differences in wealth or power that are a product of differences in talent, initiative, risk taking, and skill are accepted as natural. In contrast, modern liberalism contends that individual dignity and equality of opportunity depend in some measure on *reduction of absolute inequality* in society. Modern liberals believe that true equality of opportunity cannot be achieved where significant numbers of people are suffering from homelessness, hunger, treatable illness, or poverty. Thus modern liberalism supports government efforts to reduce inequalities in society.

Neo-Conservatism and Neo-Liberalism   Ideologies continually evolve. Both liberalism and conservatism in the United States have thus changed to meet new challenges and altered conditions. For example, in the 1960s and 1970s many liberals became disillusioned with large-scale, costly bureaucratic government programs. They were still concerned with poverty, discrimination, crime, ignorance, and pollution, but they came to believe that many government programs were ineffective or were making things worse. As they saw it, government was overloaded with tasks that should be left to the individual, the family, the church, or the free-market system. These liberals won the label **neo-conservatives** (new conservatives) in recognition of their changing views toward less government intervention in society. Most neo-conservatives ended up in the Republican Party.

neo-conservativism Traditional liberal concerns about the nation's social problems, but disillusionment with large-scale, costly bureaucratic government programs as solutions.

What Do You Think?

Are You a Liberal or a Conservative?

Not everyone consistently takes a liberal or a conservative position on every issue. But if you find that you agree with more positions under one of the following "liberal" or "conservative" lists, you are probably ready to label yourself ideologically.

	You Are **Liberal** if You Agree That	You Are **Conservative** if You Agree That
Economic policy	Government should regulate business to protect the public interest. The rich should pay higher taxes to support public services for all. Government spending for social welfare is a good investment in people.	Free-market competition is better at protecting the public than government regulation. Taxes should be kept as low as possible. Government welfare programs destroy incentives to work.
Crime	Government should place primary emphasis on alleviating the social conditions (such as poverty and joblessness) that cause crime.	Government should place primary emphasis on providing more police and prisons and stop courts from coddling criminals.
Social policy	Government should protect the right of women to choose abortion and fund abortions for poor women. Government should pursue affirmative action programs on behalf of minorities and women in employment, education, and so on. Government should keep religious prayers and ceremonies out of schools and public places.	Government should restrict abortion and not use taxpayer money for abortions. Government should not grant preferences to anyone based on race or sex. Government should allow prayers and religious observances in schools and public places.
National security policy	Government should support "human rights" throughout the world. Military spending should be reduced now that the cold war is over.	Government should pursue the "national interest" of the United States. Military spending must reflect a variety of new dangers in this post–cold war period.
You generally describe yourself as	"caring" "compassionate" "progressive"	"responsible" "moderate" "sensible"
and you describe your political opponents as	"extremists" "right-wing radicals" "reactionaries"	"knee jerks" "bleeding hearts" "left-wing radicals"

Other traditional liberals retained their faith in the power of government to solve social problems, but they sought new programs to restore the nation's economic health. Unlike old liberals, who placed social issues first on their agenda, these new liberals were convinced that little progress on social problems could be expected unless the economy was healthy. Thus they argued that government must take an active role in promoting and directing the nation's industrial growth. These **neo-liberals** were also generally critical of traditional liberals because they believed they were beholden to special-interest groups, such as labor unions, protection-seeking industries, and government employees, among others. They worried that traditional liberals would sacrifice American growth, productivity, and competitive edge in world markets to satisfy the demands of these groups. During the 1980s neo-liberals helped form the Democratic Leadership Council (with Governor Bill Clinton of Arkansas as chair) to push their "new" centrist agenda within the Democratic Party. During Clinton's presidency the neo-liberals tried to steer their leader away from programs to expand government, for example Clinton's massive health care program that failed to win congressional approval. Rather, the neo-liberals supported welfare reform, including time limits on benefits, as well as efforts to reduce the size of the federal government's annual budget deficits (see *People in Politics:* "Bill Clinton: The Ambivalent President" in Chapter 11).

IDEOLOGICAL BATTLEGROUNDS: FOUR PERSPECTIVES

If Americans aligned themselves along a single liberal-conservative dimension, politics in the United States would be easier to describe but far less interesting (see *What Do You Think?* "Are You a Liberal or a Conservative?"). We might define the liberal-conservative dimension as generally referring to the role of

neo-liberalism Continued faith in the power of government to solve social problems, but with priority given to stimulating economic growth over traditional liberal welfare programs.

Liberals' concern about efforts to curtail social welfare programs reflects their support of strong government, whereas conservatives' demands for tax cuts reflect their preference for government that encourages self-reliance and individual initiative.

Up Close

Think Tanks: The Battle of Ideas

Ideas have power, and the nation's think tanks battle to control the flow of ideas. Think tanks are private organizations, independent of government, that seek to influence policy making through books, articles, editorials, media interviews, and direct communication with government officials. Think tanks recruit scholars, writers, and former government officials to study policy questions and develop policy recommendations, which are then circulated among the press and television, special-interest groups, congressional committees and their staff, and executive agencies.

Think tanks are financed by private foundations, corporations, and wealthy individuals, as well as by the sale of the books and magazines they produce. They are usually governed by a board of trustees chosen in large measure for their ability to raise funds. Individual think tanks, even those that claim to provide unbiased, expert policy advice, tend to develop ideological identifications.

Among the most influential national think tanks are the Brookings Institution, the American Enterprise Institute, the Heritage Foundation, the Cato Foundation, and the Progressive Policy Institute. These five think tanks are active in a broad range of policy questions. Other think tanks may be equally influential in a specialized policy arena—for example, the Council on Foreign Relations, the Urban Institute, and Resources for the Future.

Brookings Institution   The Brookings Institution is the oldest and perhaps the most influential think tank in Washington, despite the growing influence of competing think tanks over the years. Brookings staffers dislike the institution's reputation as a "liberal think tank" and deny that Brookings can set national priorities. Yet the Harvard historian writing team of Leonard and Mark Silk describe Brookings as the central locus of the Washington "policy network." The Brookings Institution was started early in the twentieth century with grants from Robert Brookings, a wealthy St. Louis merchant; Andrew Carnegie, founder of U.S. Steel (now USX); John D. Rockefeller, founder of the Standard Oil Company (now Exxon); and Robert Eastman, founder of Kodak Corporation. Its recommendations for economy and efficiency in government led to the Budget and Accounting Act of 1921, which established the annual unified federal budget. (Before 1921, each department submitted separate budget requests to Congress.) In the 1960s the Brookings Institution, with grants from the Ford Foundation, helped design the War on Poverty (see "The Great Society" in Chapter 19). Today Brookings continues to influence federal tax and spending policies and social programs. Its journal, the *Brookings Review*, is read by a small but influential circle in Washington.

Enterprise Institute   For many years, Republicans dreamed of a "Brookings Institution for Republicans" that would help offset the liberal bias of Brookings. Beginning in the late 1970s, that role

government in society, with liberals favoring an active, powerful government and conservatives favoring a more limited, noninterventionist government. But many Americans make a distinction between *social conduct* and *economic affairs* in their views of the proper role of government. So it is possible to map ideology in the United States in a two-dimensional framework based (1) on whether people prefer more or less government (2) in either social or economic affairs. The result is the identification of four possible ideological types: liberals, conservatives, populists, and libertarians (see Figure 2-8 on page 52). Interestingly, in the battle over ideas, public policy think tanks have arisen that mirror these ideological types in their approach to government policy (see *Up Close:* "Think Tanks: The Battle of Ideas").

was assumed by the American Enterprise Institute (AEI). AEI attracted many distinguished neo-conservative scholars who were beginning to have doubts about big government. AEI publishes a journal, the *American Enterprise*, which regularly reports on American public opinion and comments on policy questions.

Heritage Foundation Conservative business-people, who once shunned Washington circles, gradually came to understand that without an institutional base in the capital they could never establish a strong and continuing influence in the policy network. The result of their efforts to build "a solid institutional base" and establish "a reputation for reliable scholarship and creative problem-solving" is the Heritage Foundation. The initial funding came from Colorado business executive/brewer Joseph Coors, who was later joined by two drugstore magnates, Jack Eckerd of Florida and Lewis I. Lehrman of New York. Heritage boasts that it accepts no government grants or contracts and has a larger number of individual contributors than any other think tank. It prides itself on being "on the top of the news" with quick "backgrounders"—reports and memoranda ready at the drop of a press release. Despite the emphasis on current, topical, and brief analyses, its flagship publication, *Policy Review*, has gained respect in academic circles. Heritage has also encouraged the formation of a loose network of state and regional think tanks.

Cato Institute The Cato Institute is a small think tank committed to libertarian ideas. It came to Washington in 1981 as an offspring of the Libertarian Party but gradually entered mainstream policy debates with free-market, limited-government, and antiregulatory recommendations. Conservatives generally applaud Cato's efforts to free the economy from government intervention and reduce the size of government but cringe at its call to legalize drugs. Cato also opposes spending for defense and foreign aid, and it urges a general withdrawal of the United States from world politics. It publishes *Cato Policy Review* as well as the more scholarly *Cato Journal*.

Progressive Policy Institute The Progressive Policy Institute was founded in 1989 to serve as an institutional base for efforts to move the Democratic Party and the nation toward growth-oriented economic policies. The institute is an outgrowth of the Democratic Leadership Council, formerly chaired by then-governor Bill Clinton of Arkansas. It advocates policies "designed to reverse America's slide, stimulate broad upward mobility and foster a more inclusive, more democratic capitalism." It seeks to renew the public sector by redesigning government along more entrepreneurial and less bureaucratic lines. Ideas generated by people affiliated with the Progressive Policy Institute often find their way into *Washington Monthly*, a lively magazine that generally reflects neo-liberal politics.

Liberals Liberals generally prefer an active, powerful government in economic affairs—a government that provides a broad range of public services; regulates business; protects civil rights; protects consumers and the environment; provides generous unemployment, welfare, and Social Security benefits; and reduces economic inequality. But many of these same liberals would limit the government's power to regulate social conduct. They oppose restrictions on abortion; oppose school prayer; favor "decriminalizing" marijuana use and "victimless" offenses like public intoxication and vagrancy; support gay rights and tolerance toward alternative lifestyles; oppose government restrictions on speech, press, and protest; oppose the death penalty; and strive to protect the rights of criminal defendants. Liberalism is the prevailing ideology among college professors, whereas most

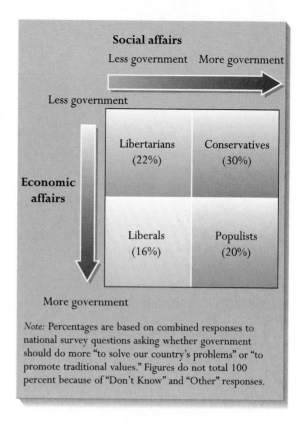

FIGURE 2-8 Mapping Ideologies: Opinions on the Role of Government

Source: American Enterprise 5 (May/June 1994): 91.

Social affairs

Less government   More government

Less government

Economic affairs

| Libertarians (22%) | Conservatives (30%) |
| Liberals (16%) | Populists (20%) |

More government

Note: Percentages are based on combined responses to national survey questions asking whether government should do more "to solve our country's problems" or "to promote traditional values." Figures do not total 100 percent because of "Don't Know" and "Other" responses.

college students think of themselves as "middle-of-the-road" (see *Up Close:* "Ideology on the Campus: Students versus Professors").

Conservatives In contrast, conservatives generally prefer limited noninterventionist government in economic affairs—a government that relies on free markets to provide and distribute goods and services; minimizes its regulatory activity; limits social welfare programs to the "truly needy"; keeps taxes low; and rejects schemes to equalize income or wealth. On the other hand, conservatives would strengthen government's power to regulate social conduct. They support restrictions on abortion; endorse school prayer; favor a war on drugs and pornography; oppose the legitimizing of homosexuality; support the death penalty; and advocate tougher criminal penalties.

Thus neither liberals nor conservatives in the United States take a consistent view toward the role of government. Most liberals today would expand government power in economic affairs and civil rights yet limit its power to regulate many areas of social conduct. Most conservatives would restrict government power in economic affairs and civil rights yet expand its power to regulate social conduct.

Populists The term **populism** is frequently used to describe the philosophy of people who are liberal on economic affairs but conservative on social matters. These people are really very consistent in their view toward the role of government. They favor a strong government to regulate business and provide economic security, and they also favor a strong government to control social conduct. They believe strongly in tradition, law, and morality in social affairs. Occasionally the term *populist* is also used to describe people who are generally resentful of government and national leadership. Although few people use the

populism Belief in the value of strong government to control business, provide economic security, and regulate social conduct, combined with a belief in tradition, law, and morality in social affairs.

Ideology on the Campus: Students versus Professors

Today most college students think of themselves as "middle-of-the-road." Among those who choose an ideological label, liberals slightly outnumber conservatives. A generation ago, students were much more likely to be liberal. In the early 1970s the war in Vietnam still raged, the military draft loomed large in young people's lives, political activism in the form of protests and demonstrations was common on campus, and drugs and nonconforming lifestyles were more in evidence. In this environment, liberals outnumbered conservatives among students by 2 to 1. Students of the 1980s confronted a different world: the Vietnam War and the military draft were history; competition for jobs was greater and a college education no longer guaranteed a middle-class life; affirmative action programs assisted minorities in education and employment; and political activism seemed to be a distraction from the more important task of career preparation. In this environment, fewer students described themselves as liberals, and conservatives gained near parity. In recent years, liberals and conservatives have been almost evenly matched on campus.

In contrast, professors' politics are decidedly liberal—more liberal than the general population's and more liberal than their students'. In a national sample of college professors, 51 percent described themselves as liberal, 17 percent as middle-of-the-road, and 28 percent as conservative. But distinct differences are apparent among faculty groups. Faculty in the humanities and social sciences are overwhelmingly political liberals. Liberals outnumber conservatives in the physical and biological sciences by

2 or 3 to 1. In engineering, liberals and conservatives are nearly equal; in law and business, conservatives outnumber liberals.

Political ideology of entering freshmen

Year	Liberal	Middle of the road	Conservative
1970	37%	45%	18%
1976	28%	56%	16%
1982	21%	60%	19%
1987	21%	59%	20%
1990	23%	55%	21%
1997	25%	55%	20%

Political ideology of professors

	Liberal	Middle of the road	Conservative
All	51%	17%	28%
Humanities	76%	9%	15%
Social Sciences	72%	14%	14%
Biological Sciences	61%	17%	23%
Physical Sciences	54%	19%	26%
Engineering	40%	22%	38%
Law	36%	22%	42%
Business	31%	17%	52%

☐ Liberal ☐ Middle of the road ☐ Conservative

Source: American Council on Education, *The American Freshman* (Los Angeles: Higher Education Research Institute, University of California at Los Angeles, published annually); and Carnegie Foundation for the Advancement of Teaching, reported in *American Enterprise* 2 (July/August 1991): 86–87.

term to describe themselves, populists may actually make up a large portion of the electorate. Liberal politicians can appeal for their votes by stressing economic issues, and conservative politicians can appeal to them by stressing social issues. And all politicians can appeal to their antigovernment bias by attacking "the fat cats," "the elitist snobs," or "the Washington power-holders."

Libertarians   People who are adherents of **libertarianism** are sometimes described as economic conservatives and social liberals, yet they are really very

libertarianism   Preference for minimal government intervention in both economic and social affairs.

consistent in their preference for minimal government intervention in both economic and social affairs. They oppose government interference both in the marketplace and in the private lives of citizens. Libertarians are against most environmental regulations, consumer protection laws, antidrug laws, and government restrictions on abortion. They favor a small government with limited functions, privatization of many government services, minimal welfare benefits, and low taxes. Libertarians also oppose defense spending, foreign aid, and U.S. involvement in world affairs.

DISSENT IN THE UNITED STATES

Dissent from the principal elements of American political culture—individualism, free enterprise, democracy, and equality of opportunity—has arisen over the years from both the *left* and the *right*. The **left** generally refers to socialists and communists, but it is sometimes used to brand liberals. The **right** generally refers to fascists and extreme nationalists, although it is sometimes used to stamp conservatives. Despite their professed hostility toward each other, **radicals** on the left and right share many characteristics. Both are **extremist**. They reject democratic politics, compromise, and coalition building as immoral, and they assert the supremacy of the "people" over laws, institutions, and individual rights. Extremists view politics with hostility, although they may make cynical use of democratic politics as a short-term tactical means to their goals.

Conspiracy theories are popular among extremists. For example, the left sees a conspiracy among high government, corporate, and military chieftains to profit from war; the right sees a conspiracy among communists, intellectuals, the United Nations, and Wall Street bankers to subordinate the United States to a world government. The historian Richard Hofstadter has referred to this tendency as "the paranoid style of politics."[15] Both the left and right are intolerant of the opinions of others and are willing to disrupt and intimidate those with whom they disagree. Whether shouting down speakers or disrupting meetings or burning crosses and parading in hoods, the impulse to violence is often present in those who subscribe to radical politics.

Antidemocratic Ideologies   Dissent in the United States has historical roots in antidemocratic movements that originated primarily outside its borders. These movements have spanned the political spectrum from the far right to the far left.

At the far-right end of this spectrum lies **fascism**, an ideology that asserts the supremacy of the state or race over individuals. The goal of fascism is unity of people, nation, and leadership—in the words of Adolf Hitler: *"Ein Volk, Ein Reich, Ein Füehrer"* (One People, One Nation, One Leader). Every individual, every interest, and every class are to be submerged for the good of the nation. Against the rights of liberty or equality, fascism asserts the duties of service, devotion, and discipline. Its goal is to develop a superior type of human being, with qualities of bravery, courage, genius, and strength. The World War II defeat of the two leading fascist regimes in history—Adolf Hitler's Nazi Germany and Benito Mussolini's fascist Italy—did not extinguish fascist ideas. Elements of fascist thought are found today in extremist movements in both the United States and Europe.

left   A reference to the liberal, progressive, and/or socialist side of the political spectrum.

right   A reference to the conservative, traditional, anti-communist side of the political spectrum.

radicalism   Advocacy of immediate and drastic changes in society, including the complete restructuring of institutions, values, and beliefs. Radicals may exist on either the extreme left or extreme right.

extremism   Rejection of democratic politics and the assertion of the supremacy of the "people" over laws, institutions, and individual rights.

fascism   Political ideology in which the state and/or race is assumed to be supreme over individuals.

Marxism   The theories of Karl Marx, among them that capitalists oppress workers and that worldwide revolution and the emergence of a classless society are inevitable.

Political extremists of the left and right often have more in common than they would like to admit. Although decidedly different in their political philosophies, both members of right-wing American neo-Nazi groups and members of left-wing communist groups reject democratic politics and assert the supremacy of the "people" over laws, institutions, and individual rights.

Marxism arose out of the turmoil of the Industrial Revolution as a protest against social evils and economic inequalities. Karl Marx (1818–83), its founder, was not an impoverished worker but rather an upper-middle-class intellectual unable to find an academic position. Benefiting from the financial support of his wealthy colleague Frederick Engels (1820–95), Marx spent years writing *Das Kapital* (1867), a lengthy work describing the evils of capitalism, especially the oppression of factory workers (the proletariat) and the inevitability of revolution. The two men collaborated on a popular pamphlet entitled *The Communist Manifesto* (1848), which called for a workers' revolution: "Workers of the world, unite. You have nothing to lose but your chains."

It fell to Vladimir Lenin (1870–1924) to implement Marx and Engels's revolutionary ideology in the Russian Revolution in 1917. According to **Leninism**, the key to a successful revolution is the organization of small, disciplined, hard-core groups of professional revolutionaries into a centralized totalitarian party. To explain why Marx's predictions about the ever-worsening conditions of the masses under capitalism proved untrue (workers' standards of living in Western democracies rose rapidly in the twentieth century), Lenin devised the theory of imperialism: advanced capitalist countries turned to war and colonialism, exploiting the Third World, in order to make their own workers relatively prosperous.

Communism is the outgrowth of Marxist-Leninist ideas about the necessity of class warfare, the inevitability of a worldwide proletarian revolution, and the concentration of all power in the "vanguard of the proletariat"—the Communist Party. Communism justifies violence as a means to attain power by arguing that the bourgeoisie (the capitalistic middle class) will never voluntarily give up its control

Leninism The theories of Vladimir Lenin, among them that advanced capitalist countries turned toward war and colonialism to make their own workers relatively prosperous.

communism System of government in which a single totalitarian party controls all means of production and distribution of goods and services.

over "the means of production" (the economy). Democracy is only "window dressing" to disguise capitalist exploitation. The Communist Party justifies authoritarian single-party rule as the "dictatorship of the proletariat." In theory, after a period of rule by the Communist Party, all property will be owned by the government, and a "classless" society of true communism will emerge.

Socialism **Socialism** shares with communism a condemnation of capitalist profit making as exploitative of the working classes. Communists and socialists agree on the "evils" of industrial capitalism: the concentration of wealth, the insensitivity of the profit motive to human needs, the insecurities and suffering brought on by the business cycle, the conflict of class interests, and the tendency of capitalist nations to involve themselves in imperialist wars. However, socialists are committed to the democratic process as a means of replacing capitalism with collective ownership of economic enterprise. Socialists generally reject the notion of violent revolution as a way to replace capitalism and instead advocate peaceful, constitutional roads to bring about change. Moreover, many socialists are prepared to govern in a free society under democratic principles, including freedom of speech and press and the right to organize political parties and oppose government policy. Socialism is egalitarian, seeking to reduce or eliminate inequalities in the distribution of wealth. It attempts to achieve equality of results, rather than mere equality of opportunity.

The End of History? Much of the history of the twentieth century has been the struggle between democratic capitalism and totalitarian communism. Thus the collapse of communism in Eastern Europe and the Soviet Union, symbolized by the tearing down of the Berlin Wall in 1989, as well as the worldwide movement toward free markets and democracy at the end of the twentieth century, has been labeled the **end of history**.[16] Democratic revolutions were largely inspired by the realization that free-market capitalism provided much higher standards of living than communism. The economies of Eastern Europe were falling further and further behind the economies of the capitalist nations of the West. Similar comparative observations of the successful economies of the Asian capitalist "Four Tigers"—South Korea, Taiwan, Singapore, and Hong Kong—even inspired China's communist leadership to experiment with market reforms. Communism destroyed the individual's incentive to work, produce, innovate, save, and invest in the future. Under communism, production for government goals (principally a strong military) came first; production for individual needs came last. The result was long lines at stores, shoddy products, and frequent bribery of bureaucrats to obtain necessary consumer items. More important, perhaps, the concentration of both economic and political power in the hands of a central bureaucracy proved to be incompatible with democracy. Communism relies on central direction, force, and repression. Communist systems curtail individual freedom and prohibit the development of separate parties and interest groups outside of government.

Capitalism does not *ensure* democracy; some capitalist nations are authoritarian. But economic freedom inspires demands for political freedom. Thus market reforms, initiated by communist leaders to increase productivity, led to democracy movements, and those movements eventually dismantled the communist system in Eastern Europe and the old Soviet Union.

socialism System of government involving collective or government ownership of economic enterprise, with the goal being equality of results, not merely equality of opportunity.

end of history The collapse of communism and the worldwide movement toward free markets and political democracy.

Politics in Cyberspace

Culture and Ideology

The nation's leading think tanks are important sources of information on political culture. All major think tanks maintain Web sites. So also do many ideological-based organizations, including the Americans for Democratic Action (liberal) and the American Conservative Union (conservative).

Americans for Democratic Action
http://www.adaction.org

"The voice of liberal activists," ADA describes itself as an independent liberal political organization founded in 1947 and dedicated to promoting individual liberty and economic justice for all Americans.

American Conservative Union
http://www.washtimes-weekly.com/conservative

"Your conservative voice in Washington" describes itself as pro-family, anti-crime, pro–free enterprise, anti–big government, pro–tax cut.

Brookings Institution
http://www.brook.edu

A private independent nonprofit research organization, Brookings seeks to improve the performance of American institutions, the effectiveness of government programs, and the quality of U.S. public policies.

American Enterprise Institute
http://www.aei.org

The American Enterprise Institute for Public Policy Research is dedicated to preserving and strengthening the foundation of freedom—limiting government, private enterprise, and vital cultural and political institutions, and a strong foreign policy and national defense—through scholarly research.

Heritage Foundation
http://www.heritage.org

Founded in 1973 the Heritage Foundation is a research and education institute—a think tank—whose misssion is to formulate and promote conservative public policies based on the principles of free enterprise, limited government, individual freedom, traditional American values and a strong national defese.

Progressive Policy Institute
http://www.dlcppi.org

The mission of the Progressive Policy Institute is to define and promote a new progressive politics for America in the twenty-first century. Through its research, policies, and perspectives, the Institute is fashioning a new governing philosphy and an agenda for public innovation geared to the Information Age.

Cato Institute
http://www.cato.org

Founded in 1977 the Cato Institute is a nonpartisan public policy research foundation headquartered in Washington D.C. The institute is named for *Cato's Letters,* libertarian pamphlets that helped lay the philosophical foundation for the American Revolution.

Academic Radicalism   Marxism survives on campuses today largely as an academic critique of the functioning of capitalism.[17] It provides some disaffected academics with ideas and language to attack everything that disturbs them about the United States—from poverty, racism, and environmental hazards to junk food, athletic scholarships, and obnoxious television advertising—conveniently blaming the "profit motive" for many of the ills of American society.

Contemporary radicals argue that the institutions of capitalism have conditioned people to be materialistic, competitive, and even violent. The individual has been transformed into a one-dimensional person in whom genuine humanistic values are repressed.[18] Profitability, rather than humanistic values, remains the primary criterion for decision making in the capitalist economy, and thus profitability is the reason for poverty and misery despite material abundance. Without capitalist institutions, life would be giving, cooperative, and compassionate. Only a *radical restructuring* of social and economic institutions will succeed in liberating people from these institutions to lead humanistic, cooperative lives.

To American radicals, the problem of social change is truly monumental, because capitalist values and institutions are deeply rooted in this country. Since most people are not aware that they are oppressed and victimized, the first step toward social change is consciousness raising—that is, making people aware of their misery.

The agenda of academic radicalism has been labeled **politically correct (PC)** thinking. Politically correct thinking views American society as racist, sexist, and homophobic. Overt bigotry is not the real issue, but rather Western institutions, language, and culture, which systematically oppress and victimize women, people of color, gays, and others.

Academic radicalism "includes the assumption that Western values are inherently oppressive, that the chief purpose of education is political transformation, and that all standards are arbitrary."[19] In PC thinking, "everything is political." Therefore curriculum, courses, and lectures—even language and demeanor—are judged according to whether they are politically correct or not. Universities have always been centers for the critical examination of institutions, values, and culture, but PC thinking does not really tolerate open discussion or debate. Opposition is denounced as "insensitive," racist, sexist, or worse, and intimidation is not infrequent (see "Political Correctness versus Free Speech on Campus" in Chapter 14).

politically correct (PC)
Repression of attitudes, speech, and writings that are deemed racist, sexist, homophobic (anti-homosexual), or otherwise "insensitive."

SUMMARY NOTES

- Ideas are sources of power. They provide people with guides for determining right and wrong and with rationales for political action. Political institutions are shaped by the values and beliefs of the political culture, and political leaders are restrained in their exercise of power by these ideas.

- The American political culture is a set of widely shared values and beliefs about who should govern, for what ends, and by what means.

- Americans share many common ways of thinking about politics. Nevertheless, there are often contradictions between professed values and actual conditions, problems in applying abstract beliefs to concrete situations, and even occasional conflict over fundamental values.

- Individual liberty is a fundamental value in American life. The classical liberal tradition that inspired the nation's Founders included both political liberties and economic freedoms.

- Equality is another fundamental American value. The nation's Founders believed in equality before the law; yet political equality, in the form of universal voting rights, required nearly two centuries to bring about.

- Equality of opportunity is a widely shared value; most Americans are opposed to artificial barriers of race, sex, religion, or ethnicity barring individual advancement. But equality of results is not a widely shared value; most Americans support a "floor" on income and well-being for their fellow citizens but oppose placing a "ceiling" on income or wealth.

- Income inequality has increased in recent years primarily as a result of economic and demographic changes. Most Americans believe that opportunities for individual advancement are still available, and this belief diminishes the potential for class conflict.

- Liberal and conservative ideologies in American politics present somewhat different sets of values and beliefs, even though they share a common commitment to individual dignity and private property. Generally, liberals favor an active, powerful government to provide economic security and protection for civil rights but oppose government restrictions on social conduct. Generally, conservatives favor minimal government intervention in economic affairs and civil rights but support many government restrictions on social conduct.

- Many Americans who identify themselves as liberals or conservatives are not always consistent in applying their professed views. Populists are liberal on economic issues but conservative in their views on social issues. Libertarians are conservative on economic issues but liberal in their social views.

- Liberal and conservative ideas evolve over time in response to new challenges and changing conditions. Neo-conservatives share the historical classical liberal concerns about the nation's social problems but no longer believe that solutions can be found in large-scale, costly bureaucratic government programs. Neo-liberals retain their faith in the power of government but focus their attention on efforts to promote economic growth as a prerequisite to solving social problems.

- The collapse of communism in Eastern Europe and the former Soviet Union and the worldwide movement toward free markets and democracy have undermined support for socialism throughout the world. Yet Marxism survives in academic circles as a critique of the functioning of capitalism.

SELECTED READINGS

EBENSTEIN, WILLIAM, AND EDWIN FOGELMAN. *Today's Isms: Communism, Fascism, Capitalism, Socialism.* 10th ed. Englewood Cliffs, N.J.: Prentice Hall, 1994. A concise description and history of the major isms.

GREYER, GEORGIE ANNE. *Americans No More.* New York: Atlantic Monthly Press, 1996. An argument that unchecked immigration, combined with emphases on multiculturalism and multilingualism, is undermining national unity.

HENRY, WILLIAM A., III. *In Defense of Elitism.* New York: Doubleday, 1994. A humorous as well as persuasive attack on the "myths" that everyone is alike (or should be), that a just society will produce equal success for everyone, and that "the common man" is always right.

HERRNSTEIN, RICHARD J., AND CHARLES MURRAY. *The Bell Curve: Intelligence and Class Structure in American Life.* New York: Free Press, 1994. A controversial argument that success in life is mainly a result of inherited intelligence and that a very bright "cognitive elite" will continue to distance themselves from the duller masses.

HUNTINGTON, SAMUEL P. *American Politics: The Promise of Disharmony.* Cambridge, Mass.: Harvard University Press, 1981. An examination of the gaps between the promise of the American ideals of liberty and equality and the performance of the American political system.

SMITH, JAMES A. *The Idea Brokers.* New York: Free Press, 1991. A description of the rise of think tanks and "the new policy elite" that inhabit them.

VERBA, SIDNEY, AND GARY R. ORREN. *Equality in America: The View from the Top.* Cambridge, Mass.: Harvard University Press, 1985. An examination of the attitudes of leaders of various sectors of American society toward equality of opportunity and equality of results.

WATTENBERG, BEN J. *Values Matter Most.* New York: Free Press, 1995. An argument that sound values rather than economic concerns will drive American politics in the future.

WOLFF, EDWARD N. *Top Heavy.* New York: Twentieth Century Fund, 1995. A fact-filled report on the increasing inequality of wealth in America, together with a proposal to tax wealth as well as income.

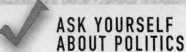 ## ASK YOURSELF ABOUT POLITICS

1. Was the original Constitution of 1787 a truly democratic document?
   Yes ☐ No ☐

2. Should citizens have the opportunity to vote directly on national government policies such as prayer in public schools or doctor-assisted suicides?
   Yes ☐ No ☐

3. Should a large state such as California, with 32 million people, elect more U.S. senators than a small state such as Wyoming, with only half a million people?
   Yes ☐ No ☐

4. Should federal laws always supersede state laws?
   Yes ☐ No ☐

5. Should the president be able to act independently to send U.S. troops into military action in places like Somalia and Bosnia if there is no formal declaration of war?
   Yes ☐ No ☐

6. Should the Constitution be amended to require Congress to pass only balanced budgets?
   Yes ☐ No ☐

7. Should the Constitution be amended to guarantee that equality of rights shall not be denied on account of sex?
   Yes ☐ No ☐

Chapter

3

THE CONSTITUTION
LIMITING GOVERNMENTAL POWER

In a democracy "of the people, by the people, and for the people," who really has the power to govern? Are strong national government and personal liberty compatible? Can majorities limit individual rights? America's Founders struggled with such questions, and in resolving them established the oldest existing constitutional government.

CHAPTER OUTLINE

FEATURES

CONSTITUTIONAL GOVERNMENT

Constitutions govern government. **Constitutionalism**—a government of laws, not of people—means that those who exercise governmental power are restricted in their use of it by a higher law. To place individual freedoms beyond the reach of government and beyond the reach of majorities, a constitution must truly limit and control the exercise of authority by government. It does so by setting forth individual liberties that the government—even with majority support—cannot violate.

A **constitution** legally establishes government authority. It sets up governmental bodies (such as the House of Representatives, the Senate, the presidency, and the Supreme Court in the United States). It grants them powers. It determines how their members are to be chosen. And it prescribes the rules by which they make decisions.

Constitutional decision making is deciding how to decide; that is, it is deciding on the rules for policy making. It is not policy making itself. Policies will be decided later, according to the rules set forth in the constitution.

A constitution cannot be changed by the ordinary acts of governmental bodies; change can come only through a process of general popular consent.[1] The U.S. Constitution, then, is superior to ordinary laws of Congress, orders of the president, decisions of the courts, acts of the state legislatures, and regulations of the bureaucracies. Indeed, the Constitution is "the supreme law of the land."

To be effective in protecting the individual from government, a constitution must be respected—by both the people and the government. Government officials must believe that they are in fact limited by the constitution, and private citizens must believe that they are in fact protected by it. The constitution must be taken seriously if it is to be effective in limiting government and protecting the liberties of individuals.

THE CONSTITUTIONAL TRADITION

Americans are strongly committed to the idea of a written constitution to establish government and limit its powers. In fact, the Constitutional Convention of 1787 had many important antecedents.

The Magna Carta, 1215 English lords, traditionally required to finance the kings' wars, forced King John to sign the Magna Carta, a document guaranteeing their feudal rights and setting the precedent of a limited government and monarchy.

The Mayflower Compact, 1620 Puritan colonists, while still aboard the *Mayflower*, signed a compact establishing a "civil body politic . . . to enact just and equal laws . . . for the general good of the colony; unto which we promise all due submission and obedience." After the Puritans landed at Plymouth, in what is today Massachusetts, they formed a colony based on the Mayflower Compact, thus setting a precedent of a government established by contract with the governed.

The Colonial Charters, 1630–1732 The charters that authorized settlement of the colonies in America were granted by royal action. For some of the colonies, the British king granted official proprietary rights to an individual, as in Maryland (granted to Lord Baltimore), Pennsylvania (to William Penn), and Delaware (also to Penn). For other colonies, the king granted royal commissions to companies to establish governments, as in Virginia, Massachusetts, New Hampshire, New York,

constitutionalism A government of laws, not people, operating on the principle that governmental power must be limited and government officials should be restrained in their exercise of power over individuals.

constitution The legal structure of a political system, establishing governmental bodies, granting their powers, determining how their members are selected, and prescribing the rules by which they make their decisions. Considered basic or fundamental, a constitution cannot be changed by ordinary acts of governmental bodies.

New Jersey, Georgia, and North and South Carolina. Royal charters were granted directly to the colonists themselves only in Connecticut and Rhode Island. These colonists drew up their charters and presented them to the king, setting a precedent in America for written contracts defining governmental power.

The "Charter Oak Affair" of 1685–88 began when King James II became displeased with his Connecticut subjects and issued an order for the repeal of the Connecticut Charter. In 1687 Sir Edmund Andros went to Hartford, dissolved the colonial government, and demanded that the charter be returned. But Captain John Wadsworth hid it in an oak tree. After the so-called Glorious Revolution in England in 1688, the charter was taken out and used again as the fundamental law of the colony. Subsequent British monarchs silently acquiesced in this restoration of rights, and the affair strengthened the notion of loyalty to the constitution rather than to the king.

The Declaration of Independence, 1776 The First Continental Congress, a convention of delegates from twelve of the thirteen original colonies, came together in 1774 to protest British interference in American affairs. But the Revolutionary War did not begin until April 19, 1775. The evening before, British regular troops marched out from Boston to seize arms stored by citizens in Lexington and Concord, Massachusetts. At dawn the next morning, the Minutemen—armed citizens organized for the protection of their towns—engaged the British regulars in brief battles, then harassed them all the way back to Boston. In June of that year, the Second Continental Congress appointed George Washington Commander-in-Chief of American forces and sent him to Boston to take command of the American militia surrounding the city. Still, popular support for the Revolution remained limited, and even many members of the Continental Congress hoped only to force changes—not to split off from Britain.

As this hope died, however, members of the Continental Congress came to view a formal Declaration of Independence as necessary to give legitimacy to their cause

After numerous drafts by Thomas Jefferson, including such changes as the deletion of a clause condemning slavery that offended North Carolina and Georgia, the Declaration of Independence was accepted by the majority of the Continental Congress on July 4, 1776. The document then became "the unanimous declaration of the thirteen United States of America" on July 19, and was signed by all members of the Continental Congress on August 2. Shown in this painting are (left to right) Benjamin Franklin, Thomas Jefferson, Robert Livingston, John Adams, and Roger Sherman.

and establish the basis for a new nation. Accordingly, on July 2, 1776, the Continental Congress "Resolved, that these United Colonies are, and, of right, ought to be free and independent States." Thomas Jefferson had been commissioned to write a justification for the action, which he presented to the Congress on July 4, 1776. In writing the Declaration of Independence, Jefferson lifted several phrases directly from the English political philosopher John Locke (see Chapter 1) asserting the rights of individuals, the contract theory of government, and the right of revolution. The declaration was signed first by the president of the Continental Congress, John Hancock.

The Revolutionary War ended when British General Charles Cornwallis surrendered at Yorktown, Virginia, in October 1781. But even as the war was being waged, the new nation was creating the framework of its government.

The Articles of Confederation, 1781–89   Although Richard Henry Lee, a Virginia delegate to the Continental Congress, first proposed that the newly independent states form a confederation on July 6, 1776, the Continental Congress did not approve the Articles of Confederation until November 15, 1777, and the last state to sign them, Maryland, did not do so until March 1, 1781. Under the Articles, Congress was a single house in which each state had two to seven members but only one vote. Congress itself created and appointed executives, judges, and military officers. It also had the power to make war and peace, conduct foreign affairs, and borrow and print money. But Congress could *not* collect taxes or enforce laws directly; it had to rely on the states to provide money and enforce its laws. The United States under the Articles was really a confederation of nations. Within this "firm league of friendship" (Article III of the Articles of Confederation), the national government was thought of as an alliance of independent states, not as a government "of the people."

TROUBLES CONFRONTING A NEW NATION

Two hundred years ago the United States was struggling to achieve nationhood. The new U.S. government achieved enormous successes under the Articles of Confederation: it won independence from Great Britain, the world's most powerful colonial nation at the time; it defeated vastly superior forces in a prolonged war for independence; it established a viable peace and won powerful allies (such as France) in the international community; it created an effective army and navy, established a postal system, and laid the foundations for national unity. But despite these successes in war and diplomacy, the political arrangements under the Articles were unsatisfactory to many influential groups—notably, bankers and investors who held U.S. government bonds, plantation owners, real estate developers, and merchants and shippers.

Financial Difficulties   Under the Articles of Confederation, Congress had no power to tax the people directly. Instead, Congress had to ask the states for money to pay its expenses, particularly the expenses of fighting the long and costly War of Independence with Great Britain. There was no way to force the states to make their payments to the national government. In fact, about 90 percent of the funds requisitioned by Congress from the states was never paid, so Congress had to borrow money from wealthy patriot investors to fight the war. Without the power to tax, however, Congress could not pay off these debts. Indeed, the value of U.S. governmental bonds fell to about 10 cents for every dollar's worth because few people believed the bonds would ever be paid off. Congress even stopped making interest payments on these bonds.

Commercial Obstacles   Under the Articles of Confederation, states were free to tax the goods of other states. Without the power to regulate interstate commerce, the national government was unable to protect merchants from heavy tariffs imposed on shipments from state to state. Southern planters could not ship their agricultural products to northern cities without paying state-imposed tariffs, and northern merchants could not ship manufactured products from state to state without interference. Merchants, manufacturers, shippers, and planters all wanted to develop national markets and prevent the states from imposing tariffs or restrictions on interstate trade. States competed with one another by passing low tariffs on foreign goods (to encourage the shipment of goods through their own ports) and high tariffs against one another's goods (to protect their own markets). The result was a great deal of confusion and bad feeling—as well as a great deal of smuggling.

Currency Problems   Under the Articles, the states themselves had the power to issue their own currency, regulate its value, and require that it be accepted in payment of debts. States had their own "legal tender" laws, which required creditors to accept state money if "tendered" in payment of debt. As a result, many forms of money were circulating: Virginia dollars, Rhode Island dollars, Pennsylvania dollars, and so on. Some states (Rhode Island, for example) printed a great deal of money, creating inflation in their currency and alienating banks and investors whose loans were being paid off in this cheap currency. If creditors refused payment in a particular state's currency, the debt could be abolished in that state. So finances throughout the states were very unstable, and banks and creditors were threatened by cheap paper money.

Civil Disorder   In several states, debtors openly revolted against tax collectors and sheriffs attempting to repossess farms on behalf of creditors who held unpaid mortgages. The most serious rebellion broke out in the summer of 1786 in western Massachusetts, where a band of 2,000 insurgent farmers captured the

In an attempt to prevent the foreclosure of farms by creditors, Revolutionary War veteran Daniel Shays led an armed mass of citizens in a march on a western Massachusetts courthouse. This uprising, which came to be known as Shays's Rebellion, exposed the Confederation's military weakness and increased support for a strong central government.

courthouses in several counties and briefly held the city of Springfield. Led by Daniel Shays, a veteran of the Revolutionary War battle at Bunker Hill, the insurgent army posed a direct threat to investors, bankers, creditors, and tax collectors by burning deeds, mortgages, and tax records to wipe out proof of the farmers' debts. Shays's Rebellion, as it was called, was finally put down by a small mercenary army, paid for by well-to-do citizens of Boston.

Reports of Shays's Rebellion filled the newspapers of the large eastern cities. George Washington, Alexander Hamilton, James Madison, and many other prominent Americans wrote their friends about it. The event galvanized property owners to support the creation of a strong central government capable of dealing with "radicalism." Only a strong central government, they wrote one another, could "insure domestic tranquility," guarantee "a republican form of government," and protect property "against domestic violence." It is no accident that all of these phrases appear in the Constitution of 1787.

The Road to the Constitutional Convention   In the spring of 1785, some wealthy merchants from Virginia and Maryland met at Alexandria, Virginia, to try to resolve a conflict between the two states over commerce and navigation on the Potomac River and Chesapeake Bay. George Washington, the new nation's most prominent citizen, took a personal interest in the meeting. As a wealthy plantation owner and a land speculator who owned more than 30,000 acres of land upstream on the Potomac, Washington was keenly interested in commercial problems under the Articles of Confederation. He lent his great prestige to the Alexandria meeting by inviting the participants to his house at Mount Vernon. Out of this conference came the idea for a general economic conference for all of the states, to be held in Annapolis, Maryland, in September 1786.

The Annapolis Convention turned out to be a key stepping-stone to the Constitutional Convention of 1787. Instead of concentrating on commerce and navigation between the states, the delegates at Annapolis, including Alexander Hamilton and James Madison, called for a general constitutional convention to suggest remedies to what they saw as defects in the Articles of Confederation.

On February 21, 1787, the Congress called for a convention to meet in Philadelphia for the "sole and express purpose" of revising the Articles of Confederation and reporting to the Congress and the state legislatures "such alterations and provisions therein as shall, when agreed to in Congress and confirmed by the states, render the federal Constitution adequate to the exigencies of government and the preservation of the union." Notice that Congress did not authorize the convention to write a new constitution or to call constitutional conventions in the states to ratify a new constitution. State legislatures sent delegates to Philadelphia expecting that their task would be limited to *revising* the Articles and that revisions would be sent back to Congress and state legislatures for their approval. But that is not what happened.

THE NATION'S FOUNDERS

The fifty-five delegates to the Constitutional Convention, which met in Philadelphia in the summer of 1787, quickly discarded the congressional mandate to merely "revise" the Articles of Confederation. The Virginia delegation, led by James Madison, arrived before a quorum of seven states had assembled and used the time to draw up an entirely new constitutional document. After the first formal session opened on May 25 and George Washington was elected president of the convention, the

Virginia Plan became the basis of discussion. Thus, at the very beginning of the convention, the decision was made to scrap the Articles of Confederation altogether, write a new constitution, and form a new national government.[2]

The Founders were very confident of their powers and abilities. They had been selected by their state legislatures (only Rhode Island, dominated by small farmers, refused to send a delegation). When Thomas Jefferson, then serving in the critical post of ambassador to France (the nation's military ally in the Revolutionary War), first saw the list of delegates, he exclaimed, "It is really an assembly of demigods." Indeed, among the nation's notables, only Jefferson and John Adams (then serving as ambassador to England) were absent. The eventual success of the convention, and the ratification of the new Constitution, resulted in part from the enormous prestige, experience, and achievements of the delegates themselves.

George Washington was the new nation's most popular and prestigious citizen (see *People in Politics:* "George Washington, Founder of a Nation"). Not only preeminent as a military leader and respected hero, he was also one of the richest people in the United States. In addition to his large estate on the Potomac, he possessed many thousands of acres of undeveloped land in western Virginia, Maryland, Pennsylvania, Kentucky, and the Northwest Territory. He owned major shares in the Potomac Company, the James River Company, the Bank of Columbia, and the Bank of Alexandria. And he held large amounts in U.S. bonds and securities. Thus he was personally concerned about obstacles to interstate commerce, unstable currencies, and the inability of Congress to pay its debts.

The Founders were extraordinarily well educated. At a time when very few men on the North American continent had gone to college, the Founders were conspicuous for their educational attainment. More than half the delegates had been educated at Harvard (founded in 1636), William and Mary (1693), Yale (1701), the University of Pennsylvania (1740), Columbia (1754), Princeton (1746), or in England. The tradition of legal training for political decision makers, which has continued in the United States to the present, was already evident. About a dozen delegates were active lawyers in 1787, and about three dozen had legal training.

The Founders also had extensive experience in governing. Many had participated in all the key events of the previous years, from the First Continental Congress in 1774 to the Declaration of Independence, the Articles of Confederation, and the successful conclusion of the Revolutionary War. Eight of the fifty-five delegates had signed the Declaration of Independence. Eleven delegates had served as officers in Washington's army in the Revolutionary War. Forty-two Founders had already served in the Congress. More than forty held high offices in state governments, including three who were state governors.

Above all, the delegates at Philadelphia were cosmopolitan. They approached political, economic, and military issues from a "continental" point of view. Unlike most Americans in 1787, their loyalties extended beyond their states. They were truly nationalists.[3]

CONSENSUS IN PHILADELPHIA

The Founders shared many ideas about government. We often focus our attention on *conflict* in the Convention of 1787 and the compromises reached by the participants, but the really important story of the Constitution is the *consensus* that was shared by these men of influence.

George Washington, Founder of a Nation

From the time he took command of the American Revolutionary forces in 1775 until he gave his Farewell Address to the nation in 1796 and returned to his Mount Vernon plantation, George Washington (1732–99) was, indeed, "First in war, first in peace, first in the hearts of his countrymen." His military success, combined with his diplomacy and practical political acumen, gave him overwhelming moral authority, which he used to inspire the Constitutional Convention, to secure the ratification of the Constitution, and then to guide the new nation through its first years.

Washington was raised on a Virginia plantation and inherited substantial landholdings, including his Mount Vernon plantation on the Potomac River. He began his career as a surveyor. His work took him deep into the wilderness of America's frontier. This experience later served him well when, at age twenty-one, he was commissioned by the governor of Virginia to explore "the Forks of the Ohio" (now Pittsburgh, Pennsylvania) and extend British claims against French interests west of the Allegheny Mountains. In 1753 Washington's application for a regular commission in the British army was rejected, but he was appointed a major and later promoted to lieutenant colonel in the Virginia militia.

In 1754 he led a small force toward the French Fort Duquesne, but after a brief battle at makeshift "Fort Necessity," he was obliged to retreat. In 1755 British Major General Edward Braddock asked the young militia officer to accompany his heavy regiments on a campaign to dislodge the French from Fort Duquesne. Braddock disregarded Washington's warnings about concealed ways of fighting in the New World; Braddock's parading redcoat forces were ambushed by the French and Indians near Pittsburgh, and the general was killed. Washington rallied what remained of the British forces and led them in a successful retreat back to Virginia.

Washington was viewed by Virginians as a hero, and at age twenty-two he was appointed by the Virginia Assembly "Colonel of the Virginia Regiment and Commander in Chief of all Virginia Forces." But regular British officers ridiculed the militia forces and asserted their authority over Washington. British General John Forbes occupied Fort Duquesne, renamed it Fort Pitt, and gave Washington's men the task of garrisoning it.

In 1759, having completed his service in the French and Indian Wars, Washington left his military post and returned to plantation life. He married a wealthy widow, Martha Custis, expanded his plantation holdings, and prospered in western land speculation.

The Virginia legislature elected Washington to attend the First Continental Congress in September 1774. Washington was the most celebrated veteran of the French and Indian Wars who was still young enough (forty-two) to lead military forces in a new struggle. John Adams of Massachusetts was anxious to unite the continent in the coming contest, and he persuaded the Second Continental Congress to give the Virginian command of the American revolutionary forces surrounding the British army in Boston.

Liberty and Property   The Founders had read John Locke and absorbed his idea that the purpose of government is to protect individual liberty and property. They believed in a natural law, superior to any human-made laws, that endowed each person with certain inalienable rights—the rights to life, liberty, and property. They believed that all people were equally entitled to these rights. Most of them, including slave owners George Washington and Thomas Jefferson, understood that the belief in personal liberty conflicted with the practice of slavery and found the inconsistency troubling.

Social Contract   The Founders believed that government originated in an implied contract among people. People agreed to establish government, obey laws,

Upon accepting command in 1775, Washington declined a salary and modestly suggested that his experience "may not be equal to the task."

Washington faced what appeared to be insurmountable odds in his campaigns against the British army. His ragtag soldiers were no match for the well-trained and better equipped British troops. In addition, America's citizen-soldiers were only obligated to brief periods of enlistment, which, combined with a high rate of desertion, nearly resulted in the collapse of Washington's army on several occasions. Through it all Washington persevered by employing many of the tactics later defined as the principles of guerrilla warfare. By retreating deep into Pennsylvania's Valley Forge, Washington avoided defeat and saved his army. His bold Christmas night attack against Hessian troops at Trenton, New Jersey, encouraged French intervention on America's behalf. Slowly Washington was able to wear down the British resolve to fight. In the end, he succeeded in trapping a British army at Yorktown, Virginia. Assisted by a French naval blockade, he accepted the surrender of Lord Cornwallis and 8,000 of his men on October 19, 1781. As a result, peace negotiations were opened in Paris.

Perhaps Washington's greatest contribution to democratic government occurred in 1783 in Newburgh, New York, near West Point, where the veterans of his Continental Army were encamped. Despite their hardships and ultimate victory in the Revolutionary War, these soldiers remained unpaid by Congress. Indeed, Congress ignored a series of letters, known as the Newburgh Addresses, that threatened military force if Congress continued to deny benefits to the veterans. Washington was invited to Newburgh by officers who hoped he would agree to lead a military coup against the Congress. But when Washington mounted the platform he denounced the use of force and the "infamous propositions" contained in their earlier addresses to Congress. There is little doubt that he could have chosen to march on the Congress with his veteran army and install himself as military dictator. World history is filled with revolutionary army leaders who did so. But Washington chose to preserve representative government.

One of the few noncontroversial decisions of the Constitutional Convention in 1787 was the selection of George Washington to preside over the meetings. He took little part in the debates; however, his enormous prestige helped to hold the convention together and later to win support for the new Constitution.

When the first Electoral College voted on the presidential candidates, Washington received all sixty-nine votes. John Adams was elected vice president. Washington steered a steady course for the new nation by maintaining a strict neutrality toward warring Europe; in his Farewell Address, he warned against foreign entanglements as well as the formation of political parties and party spirit, which, he said, "agitates the community with ill-founded jealousies."

George Washington died on December 14, 1799, in his home at Mount Vernon. During Washington's war service, the highest rank granted him by Congress was that of lieutenant-general. In 1976 Congress granted Washington the nation's highest military rank, General of the Armies, and confirmed him forever as the senior officer on U.S. Army rolls.

Source: George Washington, Farewell Address, September 17, 1796, in *Documents of American History* (10th ed.), eds. Henry Steele Commager and Milton Cantor (Englewood Cliffs, N.J.: Prentice Hall, 1988), 1:172.

and pay taxes in exchange for protection of their natural rights. This social contract gave government its legitimacy—a legitimacy that rested on the consent of the governed, not with gods or kings or force. If a government violated individual liberty, it broke the social contract and thus lost its legitimacy.

Representative Government   Although most of the world's governments in 1787 were hereditary monarchies, the Founders believed the people should have a voice in choosing their own representatives in government. They opposed hereditary aristocracy and titled nobility. Instead, they sought to forge a republic. **Republicanism** meant government by representatives of the people. The Founders expected the masses to consent to be governed by their leaders—men

republicanism Government by representatives of the people rather than directly by the people themselves.

of principle and property with ability, education, and a stake in the preservation of liberty. The Founders believed the people should have only a limited role in directly selecting their representatives: they should vote for members of the House of Representatives but senators, the president, and members of the Supreme Court should be selected by others more qualified to judge their ability.

Limited Government   The Founders believed unlimited power was corrupting and a concentration of power was dangerous. They believed in a written constitution that limited the scope of governmental power. They also believed in dividing power within government by creating separate bodies able to check and balance one another's powers.

Nationalism   Most important, the Founders shared a belief in **nationalism**—a strong and independent national (federal) government with power to govern directly, rather than through state governments. They sought to establish a government that would be recognized around the world as representing "We the people of the United States." Not everyone in America shared this enthusiasm for a strong federal government; indeed, opposition forces, calling themselves Anti-Federalists, almost succeeded in defeating the new Constitution. But the leaders meeting in Philadelphia in the summer of 1787 were convinced of the need for a strong central government that would share power with the states.

CONFLICT IN PHILADELPHIA

Consensus on basic principles of government was essential to the success of the Philadelphia convention. But conflict over the implementation of these principles not only tied up the convention for an entire summer but later threatened to prevent the states from ratifying, or voting to approve, the document the convention produced.

Representation   Representation was the most controversial issue in Philadelphia. Following the election of George Washington as president of the convention, Governor Edmund Randolph of Virginia rose to present a draft of a new constitution. This Virginia Plan called for a legislature with two houses: a lower house chosen by the people of the states, with representation according to population; and an upper house to be chosen by the lower house (see Table 3-1). Congress was to have the broad power to "legislate in all cases in which the separate states are incompetent, or in which the harmony of the United States may be interrupted." Congress was to have the power to nullify state laws that it believed violated the Constitution, thus ensuring the national government's supremacy over the states. The Virginia Plan also proposed a *parliamentary* form of government, in which the legislature (Congress) chose the principal executive officers of the government as well as federal judges. Finally, the Virginia Plan included a curious "council of revision," with the power to veto acts of Congress.

nationalism   Belief that shared cultural, historical, linguistic, and social characteristics of a people justify the creation of a government encompassing all of them; the resulting nation-state should be independent and legally equal to all other nation-states.

Delegates from New Jersey and Delaware objected strongly to the great power given to the national government in the Virginia Plan, the larger representation it proposed for the more populous states, and the plan's failure to recognize the role of the states in the composition of the new government. After several weeks of debate, William Paterson of New Jersey submitted a counterproposal. The New Jersey Plan called for a single-chamber Congress in which each state, regardless

| TABLE 3-1 | Constitutional Compromise |

The Virginia Plan	The New Jersey Plan	The Connecticut Compromise The Constitution of 1787
Two-house legislature, with the lower house directly elected based on state population and the upper house elected by the lower.	One-house legislature, with equal state representation, regardless of population.	Two-house legislature, with the House directly elected based on state population and the Senate selected by the state legislatures; two senators per state, regardless of population.
Legislature with broad power, including veto power over laws passed by the state legislatures.	Legislature with the same power as under the Articles of Confederation, plus the power to levy some taxes and to regulate commerce.	Legislature with broad power, including the power to tax and to regulate commerce.
President and cabinet elected by the legislature.	Separate multiperson executive, elected by the legislature, removable by petition from a majority of the state governors.	President chosen by an Electoral College.
National judiciary elected by the legislature.	National Judiciary appointed by the executive.	National judiciary appointed by the president and confirmed by the Senate.
"Council of Revision" with the power to veto laws of the legislature.	National Supremacy Clause similar to that found in Article VI of the 1787 Constitution.	National Supremacy Clause: the Constitution is "the supreme Law of the Land."

of its population, had one vote, just as under the Articles of Confederation. But unlike the Articles, the New Jersey Plan proposed separate executive and judicial branches of government and the expansion of the powers of Congress to include levying taxes and regulating commerce. Moreover, the New Jersey Plan included a National Supremacy Clause, declaring that the Constitution and federal laws would supersede state constitutions and laws.

Debate over representation in Congress raged into July 1787. At one point, the convention actually voted for the Virginia Plan, 7 votes to 3, but without New York, New Jersey, and Delaware, the new nation would not have been viable. Eventually, Roger Sherman of Connecticut came forward with a compromise. This Connecticut Compromise—sometimes called the Great Compromise—established two houses of Congress: in the upper house, the Senate, each state would have two members regardless of its size; in the lower body, the House of Representatives, each state would be represented according to population. Members of the House would be directly elected by the people; members of the Senate would be selected by their state legislaures. Legislation would have to pass both houses to be enacted. This compromise was approved by the convention on July 16.

Slavery Another conflict absorbing the attention of the delegates was slavery. In 1787 slavery was legal everywhere except in Massachusetts. Nevertheless, the delegates were too embarrassed to use the word *slave* or *slavery* in their debates or in the Constitution itself. Instead, they referred to "other persons" and "persons held to service or labour."

Delegates from the southern states, where slaves were a large proportion of the population, believed slaves should be counted in representation afforded the states, especially if taxes were to be levied on a population basis (which meant counting slaves as persons). Delegates from the northern states, with small slave populations, believed that "the people" counted for representation purposes should include only free persons. The Connecticut Plan included the now-infamous Three-fifths Compromise: three-fifths of the slaves of each state would be counted for purposes both of representation in the House of Representatives and for apportionment for direct taxes.

Slave owners also sought protection for their human "property" in the Constitution itself. They were particularly concerned about slaves running away to other states and claiming their freedom. So they succeeded in writing into the Constitution (Article IV, Section 2) a specific guarantee: "No persons held to Service or Labour in one State . . . escaping into another, shall . . . be discharged from such Service or Labour, but shall be delivered up on Claim of the Party to whom such Service or Labour may be due."

Yet another compromise dealt with the slave trade. The capture, transportation, and "breaking in" of African slaves was considered a nasty business, even by southern planters. Many wealthy Maryland and Virginia plantations were already well supplied with slaves and thus could afford the luxury of conscience to call for an end to slave importation. But other planters from the less-developed southern states, particularly South Carolina and Georgia, wanted additional slave labor. The final compromise prohibited the slave trade—but not before the year 1808, thereby giving the planters twenty years to import all the slaves they needed before the slave trade ended.

Voter Qualifications   Another important conflict centered on qualifications for voting and holding office in the new government. Most of the delegates believed that voters as well as officeholders should be men of property. (Only Benjamin Franklin went so far as to propose universal *male* suffrage.) But delegates argued over the specific wording of property qualifications, their views on the subject reflecting the source of their own wealth. Merchants, bankers, and manufacturers objected to making the ownership of a certain amount of land a qualification for

Although hotly debated, the issue of slave-holding was not resolved by the Founders in either the Declaration of Independence or the Constitution. As a result, the practice of buying and selling slaves—and the debate over this practice—continued for years to come, until political conflict exploded in the Civil War.

officeholding. James Madison, a plantation owner himself, was forced to admit that "landed possessions were no certain evidence of real wealth. Many enjoyed them who were more in debt than they were worth."

After much debate, the convention approved a constitution without any expressed property qualifications for voting or holding office, except those that the states might impose themselves: "The Electors in each State shall have the Qualifications requisite for Electors of the most numerous Branch of the State Legislature." At the time, every state had property qualifications for voting, and women were not permitted to vote or hold office. (The New Jersey Constitution of 1776 enfranchised women as well as men who owned property, but in 1787, a new state law limited the vote to "free white male citizens.")

RESOLVING THE ECONOMIC ISSUES

The Founders were just as concerned with "who gets what, when, and how" as today's politicians are. Important economic interests were at stake in the Constitution. Historian Charles A. Beard pointed out that the delegates to the Constitutional Convention were men of wealth: planters, slaveholders, merchants, manufacturers, shippers, bankers and investors, and land speculators. Moreover, most of the delegates owned Revolutionary War bonds that were now worthless and would remain so unless the national government could obtain the tax revenues to pay them off[4] (see *A Conflicting View*: "An Economic Interpretation of the Constitution"). But it is certainly not true that the Founders acted only out of personal interest. Wealthy delegates were found on both sides of constitutional debates, arguing principles as well as economic interests.[5]

Levying Taxes   A central purpose of the Constitution was to enable the national government to levy its own **taxes**, so that it could end its dependence on state contributions and achieve financial credibility. The very first power given to Congress in Article I, Section 8, is the power to tax: "The Congress shall have Power To lay and collect Taxes, Duties, Imposts and Excises, to pay the Debts and provide for the common Defence and general Welfare."

The financial credit of the United States and the interests of Revolutionary War bondholders were guaranteed by Article VI in the Constitution, which specifically declared that the new government would be obligated to pay the debts of the old government. Indeed, the nation's first secretary of the treasury, Alexander Hamilton, made repayment of the national debt the first priority of the Washington Administration.

The original Constitution placed most of the tax burden on consumers in the form of **tariffs** on goods imported into the United States. For more than a century, these tariffs provided the national government with its principal source of revenue. Tariffs were generally favored by American manufacturers, who wished to raise the price paid for foreign goods to make their home-produced goods more competitive. No taxes were permitted on *exports*, a protection for southern planters, who exported most of their tobacco and, later, cotton. Direct taxes on individuals were prohibited (Article I, Section 2) except in proportion to *population*. This provision prevented the national government from levying direct taxes in proportion to *income* until the Sixteenth Amendment (income tax) was ratified in 1913.

The power to tax and spend was given to Congress, not to the president or executive agencies. Instead, the Constitution was very specific: "No Money shall

taxes   Compulsory payments to the government.

tariff   Tax imposed on imported products (also called a custom's duty).

An Economic Interpretation of the Constitution

Charles Beard, historian and political scientist, provided the most controversial historical interpretation of the origin of American national government in his landmark book *An Economic Interpretation of the Constitution* (1913). Not all historians agree with Beard's economic interpretation, but all concede that it is a milestone in understanding the U.S. Constitution. Beard closely studied unpublished financial records of the U.S. Treasury Department and the personal letters and financial accounts of the fifty-five delegates to the Philadelphia convention. He concluded that they represented the following five economic interest groups, each of which benefited from specific provisions of the Constitution:

- **Public security interests** (persons holding U.S. bonds from the Revolutionary War: 37 of the 55 delegates). The taxing power was of great benefit to the holders of public securities, particularly when it was combined with the provision in Article VI that "all Debts contracted and Engagements entered into, before the Adoption of this Constitution, shall be as valid against the United States under this Constitution, as under the Confederation." That is, the national government would be obliged to pay off all those investors who held U.S. bonds, and the taxing power would give the national government the ability to do so on its own.

- **Merchants and manufacturers** (persons engaged in shipping and trade: 11 of the 55 delegates). The Interstate Commerce Clause, which eliminated state control over commerce, and the provision in Article I, Section 9, which prohibited the states from taxing exports, created a free-trade area, or "common market," among the thirteen states.

- **Bankers and investors** (24 of 55 delegates). Congress was given the power to make bankruptcy laws, to coin money and regulate its value, to fix standards of weights and measures, to punish counterfeiting, to establish post offices and post roads, to pass copyright and patent laws to protect authors and inventors, and to punish piracies and felonies committed on the high seas. Each of these powers is a specific asset to bankers and investors as well as merchants, authors, inventors, and shippers.

- **Western land speculators** (persons who purchased large tracts of land west of the Appalachian Mountains: 14 of the 55 delegates). If western settlers were to be protected from the Indians, and if the British were to be persuaded to give up their forts in Ohio and open the way to American westward expansion, the national government could not rely on state militias but must have an army of its own. Western land speculators welcomed the creation of a natioal army that would be employed primarily as an Indian-fighting force over the next century.

- **Slave owners** (15 of the 55 delegates). Protection against domestic insurrection also appealed to the southern slaveholders' deep-seated fear of a slave revolt. The Constitution permitted Congress to outlaw the *import of slaves* after the year 1808. But most southern planters were more interested in protecting their existing property and slaves than they were in extending the slave trade, and the Constitution provided an explicit advantage to slaveholders in Article IV, Section 2 (later revoked by the Thirteenth Amendment, which abolished slavery) by specifically requiring the forced return of slaves who might escape to free states.

Beard argued that the members of the Philadelphia convention who drafted the Constitution were, with a few exceptions, immediately, directly, and personally interested in, and derived economic advantages from, the establishment of the new system. But many historians disagree with Beard's emphasis on the economic motives of the Founders. The Constitution, they point out, was adopted in a society that was fundamentally democratic, and it was adopted by people who were primarily middle-class property owners, especially farmers, rather than owners of businesses. The Constitution was not just an economic document, although economic factors were certainly important. Since most of the people were middle class and owned private property, practically all Americans were interested in the protection of property.

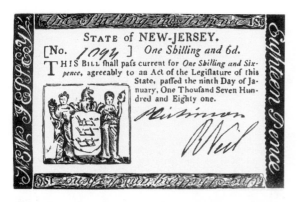

Under the Articles of Confederation, each state issued its own currency. Differences in currency regulation from state to state led to financial uncertainty and inflation. By creating a national currency and putting the national government in charge of the money supply, the Founders hoped to restore stability and control inflation.

be drawn from the Treasury, but in Consequence of Appropriations made by Law." This is the constitutional basis of Congress's "power of the purse."

Regulating Commerce   The new Constitution gave Congress the power to "regulate Commerce with foreign Nations, and among the several States" (Article I, Section 8), and it prohibited the states from imposing tariffs on goods shipped across state lines (Article I, Section 10). This power created what we call today a **common market**; it protected merchants against state-imposed tariffs and stimulated trade among the states. States were also prohibited from "impairing the Obligation of Contracts"—that is, passing any laws that would allow debtors to avoid their obligations to banks and other lenders.

Protecting Money   The Constitution also ensured that the new national government would control the money supply. Congress was given the power to coin money and regulate its value. More important, the states were prohibited from issuing their own paper money, thus protecting bankers and creditors from the repayment of debts in cheap state currencies. (No one wanted to be paid for goods or labor in Rhode Island's inflated dollars.) If only the national government could issue money, the Founders hoped, inflation could be minimized.

PROTECTING NATIONAL SECURITY

At the start of the Revolutionary War, the Continental Congress had given George Washington command of a small regular army—"Continentals"—paid for by Congress and also had authorized him to take command of state militia units. During the entire war, most of Washington's troops had been state militia. (The "militia" in those days was composed of every free adult male; each was expected to bring his own gun.) Washington himself had frequently decried the militia units as undisciplined, untrained, and unwilling to follow his orders. He wanted the new United States to have a *regular* army and navy, paid for by the Congress with its new taxing power, to back up the state militia units.

War and the Military Forces   Congress was authorized to "declare War," to raise and support a regular army and navy, and to make rules regulating these forces. It was also authorized to call up the militia, as it had done in the Revolution, in order to "execute the Laws of the Union, suppress Insurrections and repel Invasions." When the militia are called into national service, they come under the rule of Congress and the command of the president.

common market   Unified trade area in which all goods and services can be sold or exchanged free from customs or tariffs.

President Bill Clinton greets troops at a base in Bosnia on a Christmas visit in 1997. The president ordered troops to Bosnia in 1995 to help implement the Dayton accords to bring peace to that war-torn country. The Constitution makes the president the Commander-in-Chief of the armed forces.

The United States relied primarily on militia—citizen-soldiers organized in state units—until World War I. The regular U.S. Army, stationed in coastal and frontier forts, directed most of its actions against Native Americans. The major actions in America's nineteenth-century wars—the War of 1812 against the British, the Mexican War of 1846–48, the Civil War in 1861–65, and the Spanish-American War in 1898—were fought largely by citizen-soldiers from these state units.

Commander-in-Chief   Following the precedent set in the Revolutionary War, the new president, who everyone expected to be George Washington, was made "Commander-in-Chief of the Army and Navy of the United States, and of the Militia of the several States, when called into the actual Service of the United States." Clearly, there is some overlap in responsibility for national defense: Congress has the power to declare war, but the president is Commander-in-Chief. During the next two centuries, the president would order U.S. forces into 200 or more military actions, but Congress would declare war only five times. Conflict between the president and Congress over war-making powers continues to this day (see "Commander-in-Chief" in Chapter 11).

Foreign Affairs   The national government also assumed full power over foreign affairs and prohibited the states from entering into any "Treaty, Alliance, or Confederation." The Constitution gave the president, not Congress, the power to "make Treaties" and "appoint Ambassadors." However, the Constitution stipulated that the president could do these things only "by and with the Advice and Consent of the Senate," indicating an unwillingness to allow the president to act autonomously in these matters. The Senate's power to "advise and consent" to treaties and appointments, together with the congressional power over appropriations, gives the Congress important influence in foreign affairs. Nevertheless, the president remains the dominant figure in this arena.

THE STRUCTURE OF THE GOVERNMENT

The Constitution that emerged from the Philadelphia convention on September 17, 1787, founded a new government with a unique structure. That structure was designed to implement the Founders' beliefs in nationalism, limited government, republicanism, the social contract, and the protection of liberty and property. The Founders were realists; they did not have any romantic notions about the wisdom and virtue of "the people." James Madison wrote, "A dependence on the people is, no doubt, the primary control on the government; but experience has taught mankind the necessity of auxiliary precautions." The key structural arrangements in the Constitution—national supremacy, federalism, republicanism, separation of powers, checks and balances, and judicial review—all reflect the Founders' desire to create a strong national government while at the same time ensuring that it would not become a threat to liberty or property.

National Supremacy   The heart of the Constitution is the National Supremacy Clause of Article VI:

> This Constitution, and the Laws of the United States which shall be made in Pursuance thereof; and all Treaties made, or which shall be made, under the Authority of the United States, shall be the supreme Law of the Land; and the Judges in every State shall be bound thereby, any Thing in the Constitution or Laws of any State to the Contrary notwithstanding.

This sentence ensures that the Constitution itself is the supreme law of the land and that laws passed by Congress supersede state laws. This National Supremacy Clause establishes the authority of the Constitution and the U.S. government.

Federalism   The Constitution *divides power* between the nation and the states (see Chapter 4). It recognizes that both the national government and the state governments have independent legal authority over their own citizens: both can pass their own laws, levy their own taxes, and maintain their own courts. The states have an important role in the selection of national officeholders—in the apportionment of congressional seats and in the allocation of electoral votes for president. Most important, perhaps, both the Congress and three-quarters of the states must consent to changes in the Constitution itself.

Republicanism   To the Founders, a *republican* government meant the delegation of powers by the people to a small number of gifted individuals "whose wisdom may best discern the true interest of their country, and whose patriotism and love of justice, will be least likely to sacrifice it to temporary or partial considerations."[6] The Founders believed that enlightened leaders of principle and property with ability, education, and a stake in the preservation of liberty could govern the people better than the people could govern themselves. So they gave the voters only a limited voice in the selection of government leaders.

The Constitution of 1787 created *four* decision-making bodies, each with separate numbers, terms of office, and selection processes (see Table 3-2). Note that in the *original* Constitution only one of these four bodies—the House of Representatives—was to be directly elected by the people. The other three were removed from direct popular control: state legislatures selected U.S. senators; "electors" (chosen at the discretion of the state legislatures) selected the president; the president appointed Supreme Court and other federal judges.

Democracy?   The Founders believed that government rests ultimately on "the consent of the governed." But their notion of republicanism envisioned decision making by *representatives* of the people, not the people themselves (see

TABLE 3-2

Decision-Making Bodies in the Constitution of 1787

House of Representatives	Senate	President	Supreme Court
Members alloted to each state "according to their respective numbers," but each state guaranteed at least one member.	"Two senators from each state."	Single executive.	No size specified in the Constitution, but by recent tradition, nine.
Two-year term.	Six-year term.	Four-year term (later limited to two terms by the Twenty-second Amendment in 1951).	Life term.
Directly elected by "the People of the several States."	Selected by the state legislatures (later changed to direct election by the Seventeenth Amendment in 1913).	Selected by "Electors," appointed in each state "in such Manner as the Legislature thereof may direct" and equal to the total number of U.S. senators and House members to which the state is entitled in Congress.	Appointed by the president, "by and with the Advice and Consent of the Senate."

A Conflicting View: "Let the People Vote on National Issues"). The U.S. Constitution does not provide for *direct* voting by the people on national questions; that is, unlike many state constitutions today, it does not provide for national **referenda**. Moreover, as noted earlier, only the House of Representatives (sometimes referred to even today as "the people's house") was to be elected directly by voters in the states.

These republican arrangements may appear "undemocratic" from our perspective today, but in 1787 the U.S. Constitution was more democratic than any other governing system in the world. Although other nations were governed by monarchs, emperors, chieftains, and hereditary aristocracies, the Founders recognized that government depended on the *consent of the governed*. Later democratic impulses in America greatly altered the original Constitution (see "Constitutional Change" later in this chapter) and reshaped it into a much more democratic document.

SEPARATION OF POWERS AND CHECKS AND BALANCES

The Founders believed that unlimited power was corrupting and that the concentration of power was dangerous. James Madison wrote, "Ambition must be made to counteract ambition." The **separation of powers** within the national government—the creation of separate legislative, executive, and judicial branches in Articles I, II, and III of the Constitution—was designed to place internal controls on governmental power. Power is not only apportioned among three branches of govern-

referenda Proposed laws or constitutional amendments submitted to the voters for their direct approval or rejection; found in state constitutions but not in the U.S. Constitution.

separation of powers Constitutional division of powers among the three branches of the national government—legislative, executive, and judicial.

ment, but, perhaps more important, each branch is given important **checks and balances** over the actions of the others (see Figure 3-1). According to Madison, "The constant aim is to divide and arrange the several offices in such a manner as that each may be a check on the other." No bill can become a law without the approval of both the House and the Senate. The president shares legislative power through the power to sign or to veto laws of Congress, although Congress may override a presidential veto with a two-thirds vote in each house. The president may also suggest legislation, "give to the Congress Information of the State of the Union, and recommend to their Consideration such Measures as he shall judge necessary and expedient." The president may also convene special sessions of Congress.

However, the president's power of appointment is shared by the Senate, which confirms cabinet and ambassadorial appointments. The president must also secure the advice and consent of the Senate for any treaty. The president must execute the laws, but it is Congress that provides the money to do so. The president and the rest of the executive branch may not spend money that has not been appropriated by Congress. Congress must also authorize the creation of executive departments and agencies. Finally, Congress may impeach and remove the president from office for "Treason, Bribery, or other High Crimes and Misdemeanors."

Members of the Supreme Court are appointed by the president and confirmed by the Senate. Traditionally, this court has nine members, but Congress may determine the number of justices. More important, Congress must create lower federal district courts as well as courts of appeal. Congress must also determine the number of these judgeships and determine the jurisdiction of federal courts. But the most important check of all is the Supreme Court's power of judicial review.

Judicial review, which is not specifically mentioned in the Constitution itself, is the power of the judiciary to overturn laws of Congress and the states and actions of the president that the courts believe violate the Constitution (see "Judicial Power" in Chapter 13). Judicial review, in short, ensures compliance with the Constitution.

Many Federalists, including Alexander Hamilton, believed the Constitution of 1787 clearly implied that the Supreme Court could invalidate any laws of Congress or presidential actions it believed to be unconstitutional. Hamilton wrote in 1787, "Limited government . . . can be preserved in no other way than through the medium of courts of justice, whose duty it is to declare all acts contrary to the manifest tenor of the Constitution void."[7] But it was not until *Marbury v. Madison* in 1803 that Chief Justice John Marshall asserted a Supreme Court ruling that the Supreme Court possessed the power of judicial review over laws of Congress. (See *People in Politics:* "John Marshall and Early Supreme Court Politics" in Chapter 13.)

CONFLICT OVER RATIFICATION

Today the U.S. Constitution is a revered document, but in the winter of 1787–88, the Founders had real doubts about whether they could get it accepted as "the supreme Law of the Land." Indeed, the Constitution was ratified by only the narrowest of margins in the key states of Massachusetts, Virginia, and New York.

The Founders adopted a **ratification** procedure that was designed to enhance chances for acceptance of the Constitution. The ratification procedure

checks and balances
Constitutional provisions giving each branch of the national government certain checks over the actions of other branches.

judicial review Power of the U.S. Supreme Court and federal judiciary to declare laws of Congress and the states and actions of the president unconstitutional and therefore legally invalid.

ratification Power of a legislature to approve or reject decisions made by other bodies. State legislators or state conventions must ratify constitutional amendments submitted by Congress. The U.S. Senate must ratify treaties made by the president.

A Conflicting View

Let the People Vote on National Issues

"Direct democracy" means that the people themselves can initiate and decide policy questions by popular vote. The Founders were profoundly skeptical of this form of democracy. They had read about direct democracy in the ancient Greek city-state of Athens, and they believed the "follies" of direct democracy far outweighed any virtues it might possess. It was not until more than 100 years after the U.S. Constitution was written that widespread support developed in the American states for direct voter participation in policy making. Direct democracy developed in states and communities, and it is to be found today *only* in state and local government.

Why not extend our notion of democracy to include nationwide referenda voting on key public issues? Perhaps Congress should be authorized to place particularly controversial issues on a national ballot. Perhaps a petition signed by at least 1 million voters should also result in a question being placed on a national ballot.

Proponents of direct voting on national issues argue that national referenda would

- Enhance government responsiveness and accountability to the people.
- Stimulate national debate over policy questions.
- Increase voter interest and turnout on election day.

- Increase trust in government and diminish feelings of alienation from Washington.
- Give voters a direct role in policy making.

Opponents of direct democracy, from our nation's Founders to the present, argue that national referenda voting would

- Encourage majorities to sacrifice the rights of individuals and minorities.
- Lead to the adoption of unwise and unsound policies because voters are not sufficiently informed to cast intelligent ballots on many complex issues.
- Prevent consideration of alternative policies or modifications or amendments to the proposition set forth on the ballot. (In contrast, legislators devote a great deal of attention to writing, rewriting, and amending bills, as well as seeking out compromises among interests.)
- Enable special interests to mount expensive referendum campaigns; the outcomes of referenda would be heavily influenced by paid television advertising.

How would voters' decisions in national referenda differ from current government policies? A national poll on twenty-seven key policy issues produced the results shown here. The asterisks indicate issues in which *current public policy differs from popular preference*—almost half of the issues polled.

written into the new Constitution was a complete departure from what was then supposed to be the law of the land, the Articles of Confederation, in two major ways. First, the Articles of Confederation required that amendments be approved by *all* of the states. But since Rhode Island was firmly in the hands of small farmers, the Founders knew that unanimous approval was unlikely. So they simply wrote into their new Constitution that approval required only nine of the states. Second, the Founders called for special ratifying conventions in the states rather than risk submitting the Constitution to the state legislatures. Because the Constitution placed many prohibitions on

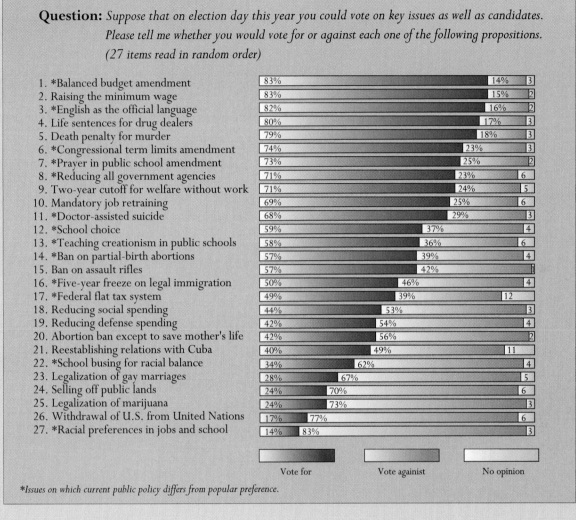

Question: *Suppose that on election day this year you could vote on key issues as well as candidates. Please tell me whether you would vote for or against each one of the following propositions. (27 items read in random order)*

	Vote for	Vote against	No opinion
1. *Balanced budget amendment	83%	14%	3
2. Raising the minimum wage	83%	15%	2
3. *English as the official language	82%	16%	2
4. Life sentences for drug dealers	80%	17%	3
5. Death penalty for murder	79%	18%	3
6. *Congressional term limits amendment	74%	23%	3
7. *Prayer in public school amendment	73%	25%	2
8. *Reducing all government agencies	71%	23%	6
9. Two-year cutoff for welfare without work	71%	24%	5
10. Mandatory job retraining	69%	25%	6
11. *Doctor-assisted suicide	68%	29%	3
12. *School choice	59%	37%	4
13. *Teaching creationism in public schools	58%	36%	6
14. *Ban on partial-birth abortions	57%	39%	4
15. Ban on assault rifles	57%	42%	1
16. *Five-year freeze on legal immigration	50%	46%	4
17. *Federal flat tax system	49%	39%	12
18. Reducing social spending	44%	53%	3
19. Reducing defense spending	42%	54%	4
20. Abortion ban except to save mother's life	42%	56%	2
21. Reestablishing relations with Cuba	40%	49%	11
22. *School busing for racial balance	34%	62%	4
23. Legalization of gay marriages	28%	67%	5
24. Selling off public lands	24%	70%	6
25. Legalization of marijuana	24%	73%	3
26. Withdrawal of U.S. from United Nations	17%	77%	6
27. *Racial preferences in jobs and school	14%	83%	3

Issues on which current public policy differs from popular preference.

Source: *The Gallup Poll Monthly*, May 1996.

the powers of states, the Founders believed that special constitutional ratifying conventions would be more likely to approve the document than would state legislatures.

The Founders enjoyed some important tactical advantages over the opposition. First, the Constitutional Convention was held in secret; potential opponents did not know what was coming out of it. Second, the Founders called for ratifying conventions to be held as quickly as possible so that the opposition could not get itself organized. Many state conventions met during the winter months, so it was difficult for some rural

FIGURE 3-1 The Separation of Powers and Checks and Balances

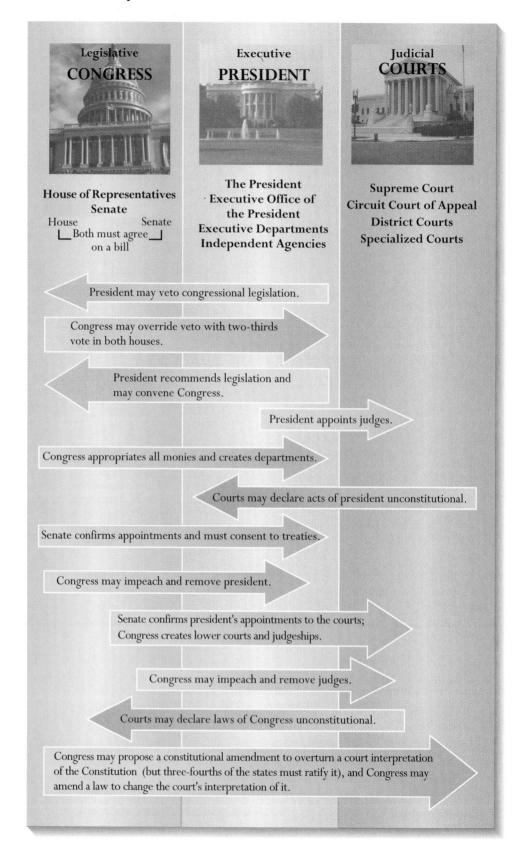

Legislative
CONGRESS

Executive
PRESIDENT

Judicial
COURTS

House of Representatives
Senate

House   Senate
⌐ Both must agree ⌐
on a bill

The President
Executive Office of
the President
Executive Departments
Independent Agencies

Supreme Court
Circuit Court of Appeal
District Courts
Specialized Courts

President may veto congressional legislation.

Congress may override veto with two-thirds vote in both houses.

President recommends legislation and may convene Congress.

President appoints judges.

Congress appropriates all monies and creates departments.

Courts may declare acts of president unconstitutional.

Senate confirms appointments and must consent to treaties.

Congress may impeach and remove president.

Senate confirms president's appointments to the courts; Congress creates lower courts and judgeships.

Congress may impeach and remove judges.

Courts may declare laws of Congress unconstitutional.

Congress may propose a constitutional amendment to overturn a court interpretation of the Constitution (but three-fourths of the states must ratify it), and Congress may amend a law to change the court's interpretation of it.

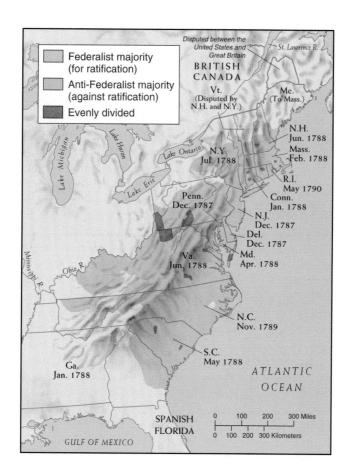

FIGURE 3-2 The Fight over Ratification

Source: Richard B. Morris, ed., *Encyclopedia of American History* (New York: Harper & Row, 1965), p. 118.

opponents of the Constitution to get to their county seats in order to vote (see Figure 3-2).

The Founders also waged a very professional (for 1787–88) media campaign in support of the Constitution. James Madison, Alexander Hamilton, and John Jay issued a series of eighty-five press releases, signed simply "Publius," on behalf of the Constitution. Major newspapers ran these essays, which were later collected and published as *The Federalist Papers.* The essays provide an excellent description and explanation of the Constitution by three of its writers and even today serve as a principal reference for political scientists and judges faced with constitutional ambiguities (see *People in Politics:* "James Madison and the Control of 'Faction'"). Two of the most important *Federalist Papers* are reprinted in the Appendix to this textbook.

Nevertheless, opponents of the Constitution—the Anti-Federalists—almost succeeded in defeating the document in New York and Virginia. They charged that the new Constitution would create an "aristocratic tyranny" and pose a threat to the "spirit of republicanism." They argued that the new Senate would be an aristocratic upper house and the new president a ruling monarch. They complained that neither the Senate nor the president were directly elected by the people. They also argued that the new national government would trample state governments and deny the people of the states the opportunity to handle their own political and economic affairs. Virginia patriot Patrick Henry urged the defeat of the Constitution "to preserve the poor Commonwealth of Virginia." Finally, their most effective argument was that the new Constitution

People in Politics

James Madison and the Control of "Faction"

The most important contributions to American democracy by James Madison (1751–1836) were his work in helping to write the Constitution and his insightful and scholarly defense of it during the ratification struggle. Indeed, Madison is more highly regarded by political scientists and historians as a *political theorist* than as the fourth president of the United States.

Madison's family owned a large plantation, Montpelier, near present-day Orange, Virginia. Private tutors and preparatory schools provided him with a thorough background in history, science, philosophy, and law. He graduated from the College of New Jersey (now Princeton University) at eighteen and assumed a number of elected and appointed positions in Virginia's colonial govern-

ment. In 1776 Madison drafted a new Virginia Constitution. While serving in Virginia's Revolutionary assembly, he met Thomas Jefferson; the two became lifetime political allies and friends. In 1787 Madison represented Virginia at the Constitutional Convention and took a leading role in its debates over the form of a new federal government. Many of the ideas in his Virginia Plan were incorporated into the Constitution.

Madison's political insights are revealed in *The Federalist Papers*, a series of eighty-five essays published in major newspapers in 1787–88, all signed simply "Publius." Alexander Hamilton and John Jay contributed some of them, but Madison wrote the two most important essays: Number 10, which explains the nature of political conflict (faction) and how it can be "controlled"; and Number 51, which explains the system of separation of powers and checks and balances (both reprinted in the Appendix of this textbook). According to Madison, "controlling faction" was the principal task of government.

What creates faction? According to Madison, conflict is part of human nature. In all societies, we find "a zeal for different opinions concerning religion,

---

lacked a bill of rights to protect individual liberty from government abuse (see *A Conflicting View:* "Objections to the Constitution by an Anti-Federalist" on page 86).

A BILL OF RIGHTS

It may be hard to imagine today, but the original Constitution had no **bill of rights**. This was a particularly glaring deficiency because many of the new state constitutions proudly displayed these written guarantees of individual liberty.

The Founders certainly believed in limited government and individual liberty, and they did write a few liberties into the body of the Constitution, including protection against ex post facto laws, a limited definition of treason, a guarantee of the writ of habeas corpus, and a guarantee of trial by jury (see Chapter 14).

The Federalists argued that there was really no need for a bill of rights because (1) the national government was one of **enumerated powers** only, meaning it

Bill of Rights   Written guarantees of basic individual liberties; the first ten amendments to the U.S. Constitution.

enumerated powers   Powers specifically mentioned in the Constitution as belonging to the national government.

concerning government, and many other points," as well as "an attachment to different leaders ambitiously contending for preeminence and power." Even when there are no serious differences among people, these "frivolous and fanciful distinctions" will inspire "unfriendly passions" and "violent conflicts."

Clearly, Madison believed conflict could arise over just about any matter. Yet "the most common and durable source of factions, has been the various and unequal distribution of property." That is, economic conflicts between rich and poor and between people with different kinds of wealth and sources of income are the most serious conflicts confronting society.

Madison argued that factions could best be controlled in a republican government extending over a large society with a "variety of parties and interests." He defended republicanism (representative democracy) over "pure democracy," which he believed "incompatible with personal security, or the rights of property." And he argued that protection against "factious combinations" can be achieved by including a great variety of competing interests in the political system so that no one interest will be able to "outnumber and oppress the rest." Modern pluralist political theory (see Chapter 1) claims Madison as a forerunner.

Madison served in the House of Representatives from 1789 to 1797 and was largely responsible for writing the first ten amendments to the Constitution—the Bill of Rights. While in the House, Madison became concerned over the expanding power of the national government led by Hamilton and his Federalist Party. Once a proponent of a strong central government, Madison shifted to a more moderate position and split with the Federalists. Frustrated with politics, he retired to his estate in 1797 until Thomas Jefferson appointed him secretary of state in 1801. He negotiated the Louisiana Purchase and was Jefferson's hand-picked successor to the presidency in 1809.

As president, Madison unfortunately allowed the nation to become embroiled in Europe's Napoleonic Wars. Conflict with the British over shipping rights and the impressment of American sailors led to a declaration of war against Great Britain in 1812. The war went badly for the United States; in 1814 Madison and the government were forced to flee Washington as the British burned the Capitol. After achieving an uneasy peace with Britain in 1815, Madison retired from politics, again following the footsteps of Thomas Jefferson by becoming president of the University of Virginia in 1826. Madison died at Montpelier on June 28, 1836.

could not exercise any power not expressly enumerated, or granted, in the Constitution; (2) the power to limit free speech or press, establish a religion, or otherwise restrain individual liberty was not among the enumerated powers; (3) therefore it was not necessary to specifically deny these powers to the new government. But the Anti-Federalists were unwilling to rest fundamental freedoms on a thin thread of logical inference from the notion of enumerated powers. They wanted specific written guarantees that the new national government would not interfere with the rights of individuals or the powers of the states. So Federalists at the New York, Massachusetts, and Virginia ratifying conventions promised to support the addition of a bill of rights to the Constitution in the very first Congress.

A young member of the new House of Representatives, James Madison, rose in 1789 and presented a bill of rights that he had drawn up after reviewing more than 200 recommendations sent from the states. Interestingly, the new Congress was so busy debating new tax laws that Madison had a difficult time attracting attention to his bill. Eventually, in September 1789, Congress approved a Bill of Rights as ten **amendments**, or formal changes, to the Constitution and sent them to the states. (Congress actually passed twelve amendments. One was never

amendment Formal change in a bill, law, or constitution.

 A Conflicting View

Objections to the Constitution by an Anti-Federalist

Virginia's George Mason was a delegate to the Constitutional Convention of 1787, but he refused to sign the final document and became a leading opponent of the new Constitution. Mason was a wealthy plantation owner and a heavy speculator in western (Ohio) lands. He was a friend of George Washington's, but he considered most other political figures of his day to be "babblers" and he generally avoided public office. However, in 1776 he authored Virginia's Declaration of Rights, which was widely copied in other state constitutions and later became the basis for the Bill of Rights. Although an ardent supporter of states' rights, he attended the Constitutional Convention of 1787 and, according to James Madison's notes on the proceedings, was an influential force in shaping the new national government. His refusal to sign the Constitution and his subsequent leadership of the opposition to its ratification made him the recognized early leader of the Anti-Federalists.

Mason's first objection to the Constitution was that it included no Bill of Rights. But he also objected to the powers given to the Senate, which was not directly elected by the people in the original document; to the federal courts; and to the president. He was wary of the Necessary and Proper Clause, which granted Congress the power to "make all laws which shall be necessary and proper" for carrying out the enumerated powers—those specifically mentioned in the Constitution. Mason correctly predicting that this clause would be used to preempt the powers of the states.

In his "objections to the Constitution" Mason wrote,

There is no declaration of rights; and the laws of the general government being paramount to the laws and constitutions of the several States, the declaration of rights in the separate States are no security.

The Senate has the power of altering all money-bills, and of originating appropriations of money, and the salaries of the officers of their own appointment in conjunction with the President of the United States; although they are not the representatives of the people, or amenable to them.

The judiciary of the United States is so constructed and extended as to absorb and destroy the judiciaries of the several States; thereby rendering law as tedious, intricate and expensive, and justice as unattainable by a great part of the community, as in England, and enabling the rich to oppress and ruin the poor.

By declaring all treaties supreme laws of the land, the Executive and the Senate have, in many cases, an exclusive power of legislation; which might have been avoided by proper distinctions with respect to treaties, and requiring the assent of the House of Representatives, where it could be done with safety.

Under their own construction of the general clause at the end of the enumerated powers, the Congress may grant monopolies in trade and commerce, constitute new crimes, inflict unusual and severe punishments, and extend their power as far as they shall think proper; so that the State Legislatures have no security for the powers now presumed to remain to them; or the people for their rights.

Note that virtually all of Mason's objections to the original Constitution had to be remedied at a later date. The Bill of Rights was added as the first ten amendments. Eventually (1913) the Seventeenth Amendment provided for the direct election of U.S. senators. The president by custom and law came to rely on a cabinet and later the National Security Council to provide "proper information and advice." And Mason correctly predicted that the federal judiciary would eventually render the law "tedious, intricate, and expensive" and that the Necessary and Proper Clause, which he refers to as "the general clause at the end of the enumerated powers," would be used to expand congressional powers at the expense of the states.

TABLE 3–3 | The Bill of Rights

Guaranteeing Freedom of Expression

First Amendment prohibits the government from abridging freedom of speech, press, assembly, and petition.

Guaranteeing Religious Freedom

First Amendment prohibits the government from establishing a religion or interfering with the free exercise of religion.

Affirming the Right to Bear Arms and Protecting Citizens from Quartering Troops

Second Amendment guarantees the right to bear arms.

Third Amendment prohibits troops from occupying citizens' home in peacetime.

Protecting the Rights of Accused Persons

Fourth Amendment protects against unreasonable searches and seizures.

Fifth Amendment requires an indictment by a grand jury for serious crimes; prohibits the government from trying a person twice for the same crime; prohibits the government from taking life, liberty, or property without due process of law; and prohibits the government from taking private property for public use without fair compensation to the owner.

Sixth Amendment guarantees a speedy and public jury trial, the right to confront witnesses in court, and the right to legal counsel for defense.

Seventh Amendment guarantees the right to a jury trial in civil cases.

Eighth Amendment prohibits the government from setting excessive bail or fines or inflicting cruel and unusual punishment.

Protecting the Rights of People and States

Ninth Amendment protects all other unspecified rights of the people.

Tenth Amendment reserves to the states or to the people those powers neither granted to the federal government nor prohibited to the states in the Constitution.

ratified; another, dealing with pay raises for Congress, was not ratified by the necessary three-quarters of the states until 1992.) The states promptly ratified the first ten amendments to the Constitution (see Table 3-3), and these changes took effect in 1791.

The Bill of Rights was originally designed to limit the powers of the new *national* government. The Bill of Rights begins with the command "Congress shall make no law. . . ." It was not until after the Civil War that the Constitution was amended to also prohibit states from violating individual liberties. The Fourteenth Amendment, ratified in 1868, includes the command "No State shall. . . ." It prohibits the states from depriving any person of "life, liberty or property, without due process of law," or abridging "the privileges or immunities of citizens of the United States," or denying any person "equal protection of the laws." Today virtually all of the liberties guaranteed in the Constitution protect individuals not only from the national government but also from state governments.

Compared to What?

Written Constitutions around the World

In 1787 the idea of a written constitution establishing a national government and limiting its power was unprecedented. Today most nations boast of a written constitution defining government institutions and setting forth "rights" of the people. Nations sometimes refer to their constitutions as "Basic Laws" or "Fundamental Laws." But few constitutions actually limit government power.

Many of today's nations achieved independence after World War II, and most national constitutions have been written since 1948. Many constitutions are symbolic. Like the Preamble to the U.S. Constitution—which declares national goals in general terms but is not enforceable in court—these documents set forth ideals but no specific procedures for their realization or enforcement. Many constitutions reflect the Universal Declaration of Human Rights adopted by the United Nations in 1948, and, like it, they confuse rights as legally enforceable protections against government with "rights" as desirable social and economic conditions.

The Declaration's many rights include

- "Rights to life, liberty, and security of person."
- Freedom from "torture or cruel, inhuman, or degrading treatment or punishments."
- Freedom from "arbitrary arrest, detention, or exile."
- Freedom from "arbitrary interference with privacy, family, home, or correspondence or attacks upon honor and reputation."
- "Right to leave any country and return."
- "Right to marry and form a family."
- "Rights to own property."
- "Freedom of thought, conscience, and religion."
- "Freedom of opinion and expression."
- "Freedom of peaceful assembly and association."
- "Right to social security."
- "Right to work . . . and to protection against unemployment."
- "Right to equality for equal work."
- "Right to just and feasible remuneration."
- "Rights to form and to join trade unions."
- "Right to rest and leisure."

- "Right to an adequate standard of living."
- "Right to education . . . , [which] shall be free at least in the elementary and fundamental stages."
- "Right to freely participate in the cultural life of the community, to enjoy the arts, and to share in scientific advancement and its benefits."

A survey of the constitutions of 142 nations calculated the percentage with provisions dealing with human rights and economic rights.

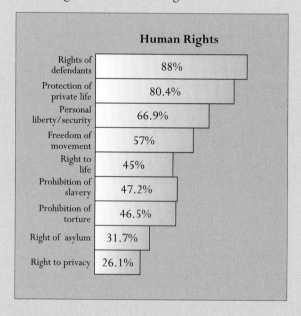

Human Rights

Rights of defendants	88%
Protection of private life	80.4%
Personal liberty/security	66.9%
Freedom of movement	57%
Right to life	45%
Prohibition of slavery	47.2%
Prohibition of torture	46.5%
Right of asylum	31.7%
Right to privacy	26.1%

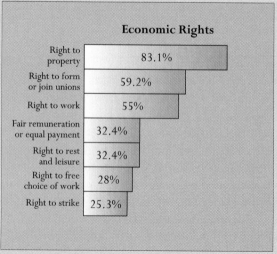

Economic Rights

Right to property	83.1%
Right to form or join unions	59.2%
Right to work	55%
Fair remuneration or equal payment	32.4%
Right to rest and leisure	32.4%
Right to free choice of work	28%
Right to strike	25.3%

Source: United Nations General Assembly, *Universal Declaration of Human Rights*, December 6, 1948, 2d sess., Doc. A/811; Hene van Maarseveen and Ger van der Tang, *Written Constitutions: A Computerized Comparative Study* (Dobbs Ferry, N.Y.: Oceans Publications, 1978).

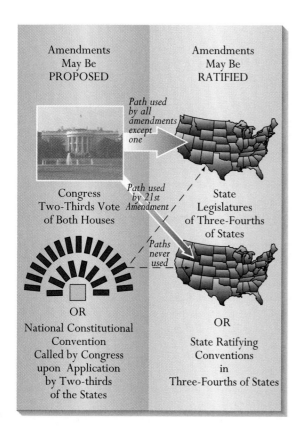

FIGURE 3-3 **Constitutional Amendment Process**

The Constitution set up two alternative routes for proposing amendments and two for ratifying them. One of the four possible combinations has actually been used for all except one (the Twenty-first) amendment. However, in our time there have been persistent calls for a constitutional convention to propose new amendments permitting school prayer, making abortion illegal, and requiring a balanced national budget.

CONSTITUTIONAL CHANGE

The purpose of a constitution is to govern government—to place limits on governmental power (see *Compared to What?* "Written Constitutions around the World"). Thus government itself must not be able to alter or amend a constitution easily. Yet the U.S. Constitution has changed over time, sometimes by formal amendment and other times by judicial interpretation, presidential and congressional action, and general custom and practice.

Amendments   A constitutional amendment must first be proposed, and then it must be ratified. The Constitution allows two methods of *proposing* a constitutional amendment: (1) by passage in the House and the Senate with a two-thirds vote, or (2) by passage in a national convention called by Congress in response to petitions by two-thirds of the state legislatures. Congress then chooses the method of *ratification*, which can be either (1) by vote in the legislatures of three-fourths of the states, or (2) by vote in conventions called for that purpose in three-fourths of the states (see Figure 3-3; see also *What Do You Think?* "Should We Amend the Constitution to Require a Balanced Budget?").

   Of the four possible combinations of proposal and ratification, the method involving proposal by a two-thirds vote of Congress and ratification by three-quarters of the legislatures has been used for all the amendments except one. Only for the Twenty-first Amendment's repeal of Prohibition did Congress call for state ratifying conventions (principally because Congress feared that southern Bible Belt state legislatures would vote against repeal). The method of proposal by national convention has never been used.

Should We Amend the Constitution to Require a Balanced Budget?

The United States government is now more than $5.5 *trillion* in debt, a figure equal to $20,000 for every man, woman, and child in the nation. This debt is owed to banks, insurance companies, investment firms, and anyone else who buys U.S. government bonds. The debt need not ever be paid off, but future generations of American taxpayers must continue to pay the annual interest costs.

Democrats and Republicans, liberals and conservatives, have all contributed to government deficits; they differ only in where they place the blame. Conservatives blame "runaway" government entitlement programs, such as Social Security and Medicare, as well as large-scale spending programs for welfare, education, job training, and agriculture. Liberals claim that the nation's high deficits result largely from cutting the taxes of the wealthy during the Reagan Administration. Democrats point out that the nation's largest annual deficits occurred in the Reagan and Bush Administrations. Republicans argue that Democrats in the Congress are responsible for these deficits because they failed to cut domestic spending as Republican presidents wished.

Regardless of who is to blame, the implications of the debt are serious. The painful legacy of these annual deficits will linger for generations. Interest payments on the debt consume about 15 cents out of every one dollar of federal expenditures. This means that taxpayers can receive at most only $.85 of public goods and services for every $1.00 paid to the federal government.

The robust growth of the economy in the 1990's, and the increased tax revenues this growth has produced for the federal government, allowed President Clinton to present a balanced budget to Congress in 1998, the first in thirty years. Indeed, today policymakers confront the question of what to do with the (projected) surpluses: Should we use this money to reduce the national debt; or to strengthen the Social Security and Medicare programs to serve increased numbers of older Americans; or to initiate new and expanded federal programs in education, health care, and child care, or to cut federal taxes?

The temptation to fritter away surpluses and return to deficit spending may overwhelm presidents and Congresses in the future. Deficit spending allows politicians to indulge current voters with more benefits and less taxes, while shifting the costs to younger generations, who are either too young to vote or who vote less often than older people do. New spending programs, unwise tax cuts, more generous retirement benefits, or even a slowing of the nation's economic growth may quickly plunge the federal budget back into red ink. Should we prevent this from occurring by amending the Constitution to require an annual balanced budget?

In 1995 the House of Representatives (by a vote of 300 to 132) passed an amendment to the Constitution which included the following command:

> "Total outlays for any fiscal year shall not exceed total receipts for the fiscal year, unless three-fifths of the whole number of each House of Congress shall provide by law for a specific excess of outlays over receipts by a roll-call vote."

But, by a single vote in the U.S. Senate, this amendment failed to get the necessary two-thirds majority that would have sent it to the states for ratification.

Public opinion polls regularly show strong support (70 to 80 percent or more) among the American people for a balanced budget amendment. But amending the Constitution requires a broad political consensus, and President Clinton and a majority of Democrats in the U.S. Senate oppose passage of the amendment. They argue that it might prevent the federal government from responding effectively to economic recessions or to wars or other national emergencies (although the proposed version permits federal deficits when approved by three-fifths of each house of Congress or when Congress has adopted a declaration of war). They also argue that enforcement would shift the power of the purse to the courts. One of the strongest lobbying groups opposing the amendment is the American Association of Retired Persons (AARP), which fears that a balanced budget might mean less generous Social Security benefits (see *Up Close:* "AARP: The Nation's Most Powerful Interest Group" in Chapter 9). More importantly, the nation's currently soaring economy, and the surpluses it is projected to produce, have taken the steam out of the balanced budget movement. (For more on economic policymaking, see Chapter 16.)

TABLE 3-4	Amendments to the Constitution since the Bill of Rights

Perfecting Constitutional Processes

Eleventh Amendment (1798) forbids federal lawsuits against a state by citizens of another state or nation.

Twelfth Amendment (1804) provides separate ballots for president and vice president in the Electoral College to prevent confusion.

Twentieth Amendment (1933) determines the dates for the beginning of the terms of Congress (January 3) and the president (January 20).

Twenty-second Amendment (1951) limits the president to two terms.

Twenty-fifth Amendment (1967) provides for presidential disability.

Twenty-seventh Amendment (1992) prevents Congress from raising its own pay in a single session.

The Experiment with Prohibition

Eighteenth Amendment (1919) prohibits the manufacture, sale, or transportation of intoxicating liquors.

Twenty-first Amendment (1933) repeals the Eighteenth Amendment.

The Income Tax

Sixteenth Amendment (1913) allows Congress to tax incomes.

Expanding Liberty

Thirteenth Amendment (1865) abolishes slavery.

Fourteenth Amendment (1868) protects life, liberty, and property and the privileges and immunities of citizenship and provides equal protection of the law.

Expanding Voting Rights

Fifteenth Amendment (1870) guarantees that the right to vote shall not be denied because of race.

Seventeenth Amendment (1913) provides for the election of senators by the people of each state.

Nineteenth Amendment (1920) guarantees that the right to vote shall not be denied because of sex.

Twenty-third Amendment (1961) gives the District of Columbia electoral votes for presidential elections.

Twenty-fourth Amendment (1964) guarantees that the right to vote shall not be denied because of failure to pay a poll tax or other tax.

Twenty-sixth Amendment (1971) guarantees that the right to vote shall not be denied to persons eighteen years of age or older.

In addition to the Bill of Rights, most of the constitutional amendments ratified over the nation's 200 years have expanded our notion of democracy. Today the Constitution includes 27 amendments, which means that only 17 (out of more than 10,000) proposed amendments have been ratified since the passage of the Bill of Rights. It is possible to classify the amendments that have been ratified into the broad categories of constitutional processes, Prohibition, income tax, individual liberty, and voting rights (see Table 3-4).

Amending the U.S. Constitution requires not only a two-thirds vote in both houses of Congress, reflecting *national* support, but also ratification by three-fourths of the states, reflecting widespread support within the *states*. The fate of the **Equal Rights Amendment**, popularly known as the ERA, illustrates the need for nationwide consensus in order to amend the Constitution. The Equal

Equal Rights Amendment (ERA) Proposed amendment to the Constitution guaranteeing that equal rights under the law shall not be denied or abridged on account of sex. Passed by Congress in 1972, the amendment failed to win ratification by three of the necessary three-fourths of the states.

Rights Amendment is a simple statement to which the vast majority of Americans agree, according to public opinion polls: "Equality of rights under the law shall not be denied or abridged by the United States or any state on account of sex." Congress passed the ERA in 1972 with far more than the necessary two-thirds vote; both Republicans and Democrats supported the ERA, and it was endorsed by Presidents Nixon, Ford, and Carter as well as most other national political leaders and organizations. By 1978, thirty-five state legislatures had ratified the amendment—three states short of the necessary thirty-eight (three-quarters). (Five states subsequently voted to rescind, or cancel, their earlier ratification. However, because there is no language in the Constitution regarding rescission, there is some disagreement about the constitutionality of this action.) Promising that the "ERA won't go away," proponents of the amendment have continued to press their case. But to date Congress has not acted to resubmit the ERA to the states.

Judicial Interpretations   Some of the greatest changes in the Constitution have come about not by formal amendment but by interpretations of the document by courts, Congresses, and presidents.

Through judicial review, the U.S. Supreme Court has come to play the major role in interpreting the meaning of the Constitution. This power is itself largely an interpretation of the Constitution (see "Judicial Power" in Chapter 13) because it is not specifically mentioned in the document. Over the years, the federal courts have been much more likely to strike down laws of the states than laws of Congress.

Supreme Court interpretations of the Constitution have given specific meaning to many of our most important constitutional phrases. Among the most important examples of constitutional change through judicial interpretation are the important meanings given to the Fourteenth Amendment, particularly its provisions that "No State shall . . . deprive any person of life, liberty, or property, without due process of law; nor deny to any person within its jurisdiction the equal protection of the laws":

- Deciding that "equal protection of the laws" requires an end to segregation of the races (*Brown v. Board of Education of Topeka*, 1954, and subsequent decisions).
- Deciding that "liberty" includes a woman's right to choose an abortion, and that the term *person* does not include the unborn fetus (*Roe v. Wade*, 1973, and subsequent decisions).
- Deciding that "equal protection of the laws" requires that every person's vote should be weighed equally in apportionment and districting plans for the House of Representatives, state legislatures, city councils, and so on (*Baker v. Carr*, 1964, and subsequent decisions).

Presidential and Congressional Action   Congress and the president have also undertaken to interpret the Constitution. Nearly every president, for example, has argued that the phrase "executive Power" in Article II includes more than the specific powers mentioned afterward. Thomas Jefferson purchased the Louisiana Territory from France in 1803 even though there is no constitutional authorization for the president, or even the national government, to acquire new territory. Presidents from George Washington to Richard Nixon have argued that Congress cannot force the executive branch to turn over documents it does not wish to disclose (see Chapter 11).

Congress by law has tried to restrict the president's power as commander-in-chief of the armed forces by requiring the president to notify Congress when U.S. troops are sent to "situations where imminent involvement in hostilities is clearly indicated" and limiting their stay to sixty days unless Congress authorizes an extension. This War Powers Act (1973), passed by Congress over President Richard Nixon's veto in the immediate aftermath of the Vietnam War, has been ignored by every president to date (see Chapter 11). Yet it indicates that Congress has its own ideas about interpreting the Constitution.

Custom and Practice   Finally, the Constitution changes over time as a result of generally accepted customs and practice. It is interesting to note, for example, that the Constitution never mentions political parties. (Many of the Founders disapproved of parties because they caused "faction" among the people.) But soon after Thomas Jefferson resigned as President Washington's first secretary of state (in part because he resented the influence of Secretary of the Treasury Alexander Hamilton), the Virginian attracted the support of Anti-Federalists, who believed the national government was too strong. When Washington retired from office, most Federalists supported John Adams as his successor. But many Anti-Federalists ran for posts as presidential electors, promising to be "Jefferson's men." Adams won the presidential election of 1796, but the Anti-Federalists organized themselves into a political party, the Democratic-Republicans, to oppose Adams in the election of 1800. The party secured pledges from candidates for presidential elector

Politics in Cyberspace

The Constitution

The sites listed here are a few of the many with information on the U.S. Constitution and constitutional issues.

The Carrier Library at James Madison University

http://library.jmu.edu/library/guides/ polisci/uscons.htm

This site has an extensive bibliography of works on the United States Constitution.

The University of Oklahoma Law Center Chronology of U.S. Historical Documents

http://www.law.ou.edu/ushist.html

This site provides the texts of important documents in U.S. history from colonial times to the present. As well as the Constitution, it includes the Declaration of Independence and the Articles of Confederation.

The U.S. House of Representatives Internet Law Library

http://law.house.gov/

This site provides a variety of links to the texts of important documents of the early Republic, including the Federalist Papers, as well as the Constitution and the Declaration of Independence.

National Archives and Records Administration

http://www.nara.gov

The National Archives posts photographs of original historical documents, including the U.S. Constitution and Magna Carta.

The Alderman Library at the University of Virginia

http://www.virginia.edu/pjm/home.html

The Alderman Library provides online access to the papers of James Madison.

to cast their electoral vote for Jefferson if they won their post; then the party helped win support for its slate of electors. In this way the Electoral College was transformed from a deliberative body where leading citizens from each state came together to decide for themselves who should be president into a ceremonial body where pledged electors simply cast their presidential vote for the candidate who had carried their state in the presidential election. (For a full discussion of the current operation of the Electoral College, see *Up Close:* "Understanding the Electoral College" in Chapter 8.)

SUMMARY NOTES

- The true meaning of constitutionalism is the limitation of governmental power. Constitutions govern governments; they are designed to restrict those who exercise governmental power. Constitutions not only establish governmental bodies and prescribe the rules by which they make their decisions, but, more important, they also limit the powers of government.

- The American tradition of written constitutions extends back through the Articles of Confederation, the colonial charters, and the Mayflower Compact to the thirteenth-century English Magna Carta. The Second Continental Congress in 1776 adopted a written Declaration of Independence to justify the colonies' separation from Great Britain. All of these documents strengthened the idea of a written contract defining governmental power.

- The movement for a Constitutional Convention in 1787 was inspired by the new government's inability to levy taxes under the Articles of Confederation, its inability to fund the Revolutionary War debt, obstacles to interstate commerce, monetary problems, and civil disorders, including Shays's Rebellion.

- The nation's Founders—fifty-five delegates to the Constitutional Convention in Philadelphia in 1787—shared a broad consensus on liberty and property, the social contract, republicanism, limited government, and the need for a national government.

- The Founders compromised their differences over representation by creating two co-equal houses in the Congress: the House of Representatives, with members apportioned to the states on the basis of population and directly elected by the people for two-year terms, and the Senate, with two members allotted to each state regardless of its population and

originally selected by state legislatures for six-year terms.

- The infamous slavery provisions in the Constitution—counting each slave as three-fifths of a person for purposes of taxation and representation, guaranteeing the return of escaped slaves, and postponing the end of the slave trade for twenty years—were also compromises. Voter qualifications in national elections were left to the states to determine.

- The structure of the national government reflects the Founders' beliefs in national supremacy, federalism, republicanism, separation of powers, checks and balances, and judicial review.

- The original Constitution gave the people very little influence on their government: only members of the House of Representatives were directly elected; senators were elected by state legislatures; the president was elected indirectly by "electors" chosen in each state; and members of the Supreme Court and federal judiciary were appointed for life by the president and confirmed by the Senate. Over time, the national government became more democratic through the expansion of voting rights, the direct election of senators, the emergence of political parties, and the practice of voting for presidential electors pledged to cast their vote for the candidates of one party.

- The separation of powers and checks and balances written into the Constitution was designed, in Madison's words, "to divide and arrange the several offices in such a manner as that each may be a check on the other." Judicial review was not specifically described in the original Constitution, but the Supreme Court soon asserted its power to overturn laws of Congress and the states, as well as presidential actions, that the Court determined to be in conflict with the Constitution.

- Opposition to the new Constitution was strong. Anti-Federalists argued that it created a national government that was aristocratic, undemocratic, and a threat to the rights of the states and the people. Their concerns resulted in the Bill of Rights: ten amendments added to the original Constitution, all designed to limit the power of the national government and protect the rights of individuals and states.

- Over time, constitutional changes have come about as a result of formal amendments, judicial interpretations, presidential and congressional actions, and changes in custom and practice. The most common method of constitutional amendment has been proposal by two-thirds vote of both houses of Congress followed by ratification by three-fourths of the state legislatures.

SELECTED READINGS

BEARD, CHARLES. *An Economic Interpretation of the Constitution.* New York: Macmillan, 1913. A classic work setting forth the argument that economic self-interest inspired the Founders in writing the Constitution.

MADISON, JAMES, ALEXANDER HAMILTON, AND JOHN JAY. *The Federalist Papers.* New York: Modern Library, 1937. These eighty-five collected essays written in 1787–88 in support of ratification of the Constitution remain the most important commentary on that document. Numbers 10 and 51 (reprinted in the Appendix) ought to be required reading for all students of American government.

MANSBRIDGE, JANE J. *Why We Lost the ERA.* Chicago: University of Chicago Press, 1986. An account of the politics of the lost ratification battle for the Equal Rights Amendment. Public opinion polls demonstrated strong national support for the ERA, but the constitutional requirement for ratification by three-fourths of the states allowed a minority to exercise a veto.

MCDONALD, FORREST B. *Novus Ordo Seculorum.* Lawrence: University Press of Kansas, 1986. A description of the intellectual origins of the Constitution and the "new secular order" that it represented.

PELTASON, J. W. *Understanding the Constitution.* 13th ed. New York: Harcourt Brace, 1994. Of the many books that explain the Constitution, this is one of the best. It contains explanations of the Declaration of Independence, the Articles of Confederation, and the Constitution. The book is written clearly and well suited for undergraduates.

ROSSITER, CLINTON L. *1787, The Grand Convention.* New York: Macmillan, 1960. A very readable account of the people and events surrounding the Constitutional Convention in 1787, with many insights into the conflicts and compromises that took place there.

STORING, HERBERT J. *What the Anti-Federalists Were For.* Chicago: University of Chicago Press, 1981. An examination of the arguments of the Anti-Federalists in opposition to the ratification of the Constitution.

TRIBE, LAURENCE H., AND MICHAEL C. DORF. *On Reading the Constitution.* Cambridge, Mass.: Harvard University Press, 1991. An argument that the Constitution was a compromise charter that incorporated contending visions of government. Therefore, no single interpretation can explain the document; its meaning must emerge from continuous debate among citizens and leaders.

WOOD, GORDON S. *The Creation of the American Republic, 1776–1787.* New York: Norton, 1993. A study of the political conflicts in the new nation that led to the Constitutional Convention.

The Constitution
of the
United States

THE PREAMBLE

We the People of the United States, in Order to form a more perfect Union, establish Justice, insure domestic Tranquility, provide for the common defense, promote the general Welfare, and secure the Blessings of Liberty to ourselves and our Posterity, do ordain and establish this Constitution for the United States of America.

ARTICLE I—THE LEGISLATIVE ARTICLE

Legislative Power

Section 1 All legislative Powers herein granted shall be vested in a Congress of the United States, which shall consist of a Senate and House of Representatives.

House of Representatives: Composition; Qualifications; Apportionment; Impeachment Power

Section 2 The House of Representatives shall be composed of Members chosen every second Year by the People of the several States, and the Electors in each State shall have the Qualifications requisite for Electors of the most numerous Branch of the State Legislature.

No Person shall be a Representative who shall not have attained to the Age of twenty five Years, and been seven Years a Citizen of the United States, and who shall not, when elected, be an Inhabitant of that State in which he shall be chosen.

Representatives and direct Taxes[1] shall be apportioned among the several States which may be included within this Union, according to their respective Numbers, *which shall be determined by adding to the whole Number of free Persons, including those bound to Service for a Term of Years, and excluding Indians not taxed, three fifths of all other Persons.*[2] The actual Enumeration shall be made within three Years after the first Meeting of the Congress of the United States, and within every subsequent Term of ten Years, in such Manner as they shall by Law direct. The Number of Representatives shall not exceed one for every thirty Thousand, but each State shall have at least one Representative; and until each enumeration shall be made, the State of New Hampshire shall be entitled to chuse three, Massachusetts eight, Rhode-Island and Providence Plantations one, Connecticut five, New-York six, New Jersey four, Pennsylvania eight, Delaware one, Maryland six, Virginia ten, North Carolina five, South Carolina five, and Georgia three.

When vacancies happen in the Representation from any State, the Executive Authority thereof shall issue Writs of Election to fill such Vacancies.

The House of Representatives shall chuse their Speaker and other Officers; and shall have the sole Power of Impeachment.

Senate Composition: Qualifications, Impeachment Trials

Section 3 The Senate of the United States shall be composed of two Senators from each State, *chosen by the Legislature thereof,*[3] for six Years; and each Senator shall have one Vote.

Immediately after they shall be assembled in Consequence of the first Election, they shall be divided as equally as may be into three Classes. The Seats of the Senators of the first Class shall be vacated at the Expiration of the second Year, of the second Class at the Expiration of the fourth Year, and of the third Class at the Expiration of the sixth Year, so that one third may be chosen every second Year; *and if Vacancies happen by Resignation, or otherwise, during the Recess of the Legislature of any State, the Executive thereof may make temporary Appointments until the next Meeting of the Legislature, which shall then fill such Vacancies.*[4]

No person shall be a Senator who shall not have attained to the Age of thirty Years, and been nine Years a Citizen of the United States, and who shall not, when elected, be an inhabitant of that State for which he shall be chosen.

The Vice President of the United States shall be President of the Senate, but shall have no Vote, unless they be equally divided.

The Senate shall chuse their other Officers, and also a President pro tempore, in the Absence of the Vice President, or when he shall exercise the Office of President of the United States.

The Senate shall have the sole Power to try all Impeachments. When sitting for that Purpose, they shall be on Oath or Affirmation. When the President of the United States is tried, the Chief Justice shall preside: And no Person shall be convicted without the Concurrence of two thirds of the Members present.

Judgment in Cases of Impeachment shall not extend further than to removal from Office, and disqualification to hold and enjoy any Office of honor, Trust or Profit under the United States; but the Party convicted shall nevertheless be liable and subject to Indictment, Trial, Judgment and Punishment, according to law.

Congressional Elections: Times, Places, Manner

Section 4 The Times, Places and Manner of holding Elections for Senators and Representatives, shall be prescribed in each State by the Legislature thereof; but the Congress may at any time by Law make or alter such Regulations, except as to the Places of chusing Senators.

---

[1]Modified by the 16th Amendment
[2]Replaced by Section 2, 14th Amendment

[3]Repealed by the 17th Amendment
[4]Modified by the 17th Amendment

The Congress shall assemble at least once in every Year, *and such Meeting shall be on the first Monday in December, unless they shall by Law appoint a different Day.*[5]

Powers and Duties of the Houses

Section 5   Each House shall be the Judge of the Elections, Returns and Qualifications of its own Members, and a Majority of each shall constitute a Quorum to do Business; but a smaller Number may adjourn from day to day, and may be authorized to compel the Attendance of absent Members, in such Manner, and under the Penalties as each House may provide.

Each House may determine the Rules of its Proceedings, punish its Members for disorderly Behaviour, and, with the Concurrence of two thirds, expel a Member.

Each House shall keep a Journal of its Proceedings, and from time to time publish the same, excepting such Parts as may in their Judgment require Secrecy; and the Yeas and Nays of the Members of either House on any question shall, at the Desire of one fifth of those Present, be entered on the Journal.

Neither House, during the Session of Congress, shall, without the Consent of the other, adjourn for more than three days, nor to any other place than that in which the two Houses shall be sitting.

Rights of Members

Section 6   The Senators and Representatives shall receive a Compensation for their Services, to be ascertained by Law, and paid out of the Treasury of the United States. They shall in all Cases, except Treason, Felony and Breach of the Peace, be privileged from Arrest during their Attendance at the Session of their respective Houses, and in going to and returning from the same; and for any Speech or Debate in either House, they shall not be questioned in any other Place.

No Senator or Representative, shall, during the time for which he was elected, be appointed to any civil Office under the authority of the United States, which shall have been created, or the Emoluments whereof shall have been encreased during such time; and no Person holding any Office under the United States, shall be a Member of either House during his Continuance in Office.

Legislative Powers: Bills and Resolutions

Section 7   All Bills for raising Revenue shall originate in the House of Representatives; but the Senate may propose or concur with Amendments as on other Bills.

Every Bill which shall have passed the House of Representatives and the Senate, shall, before it becomes a Law, be presented to the President of the United States; if he approve he shall sign it, but if not he shall return it, with his Objections to that House in which it shall have originated, who shall enter the Objections at large on their Journal, and proceed to reconsider it. If after such Reconsideration two thirds of that House shall agree to pass the Bill, it shall be sent, together with the Objections, to the other House, by which it shall likewise be reconsidered, and if approved by two thirds of that House, it shall become a Law. But in all such Cases the Votes of both Houses shall be determined by Yeas and Nays, and the Names of the Persons voting for and against the Bill shall be entered on the Journal of each House respectively. If any Bill shall not be returned by the President within ten Days (Sundays excepted) after it shall have been presented to him, the Same shall be a Law, in like Manner as if he had signed it, unless the Congress by their Adjournment prevent its Return, in which Case it shall not be a Law.

Every Order, Resolution, or Vote to which the Concurrence of the Senate and House of Representatives may be necessary (except on a question of Adjournment) shall be presented to the President of the United States; and before the Same shall take Effect, shall be approved by him, or being disapproved by him, shall be repassed by two thirds of the Senate and House of Representatives, according to the Rules and Limitations prescribed in the Case of a Bill.

Powers of Congress

Section 8   The Congress shall have Power To lay and collect Taxes, Duties, Imposts and Excises, to pay the Debts and provide for the common Defence and general Welfare of the United States; but all Duties, Imposts and Excises shall be uniform throughout the United States.

To borrow Money on the Credit of the United States;

To regulate Commerce with foreign Nations, and among the several States, and with the Indian Tribes;

To establish an uniform Rule of Naturalization, and uniform Laws on the subject of Bankruptcies throughout the United States;

To coin Money, regulate the Value thereof, and of foreign Coin, and fix the Standard of Weights and Measures;

To provide for the Punishment of counterfeiting the Securities and current Coin of the United States;

To establish Post Offices and post Roads;

To promote the Progress of Science and useful Arts, by securing for limited Times to Authors and Inventors the exclusive Right to their respective Writings and Discoveries,

To constitute Tribunals inferior to the supreme Court,

To define and punish Piracies and Felonies committed on the high Seas, and Offences against the Law of Nations;

To declare War, grant Letters of Marque and Reprisal, and make Rules concerning Captures on Land and Water;

To raise and support Armies, but no Appropriation of Money to that Use shall be for a longer Term than two Years;

To provide and maintain a Navy;

To make Rules for the Government and Regulation of the land and naval Forces;

To provide for calling for the Militia to execute the Laws of the Union, suppress Insurrections and repel Invasions;

To provide for organizing, arming, and disciplining, the Militia, and for governing such Part of them as may be employed in the Service of the United States, reserving to the States respectively, the Appointment of the Officers, and the Authority of training the Militia according to the discipline prescribed by Congress;

To exercise exclusive Legislation in all Cases whatsoever, over such District (not exceeding ten Miles square) as may, by Cession of particular States, and the Acceptance of Congress, become the Seat of the Government of the United States, and to exercise like Authority over all Places purchased by the Consent of the Legislature of the State in which the Same shall be, for the Erection of Forts, Magazines, Arsenals, dock-Yards, and other needful Buildings;—And

To make all Laws which shall be necessary and proper for carrying into Execution the foregoing Powers, and all other Powers vested by this Constitution in the Government of the United States, or in any Department or Officer thereof.

Powers Denied to Congress

Section 9   The Migration of Importation of such Persons as any of the States now existing shall think proper to admit, shall not be prohibited by the Congress prior to the Year one thousand eight hundred and eight, but a Tax or Duty may be imposed on such Importation, not exceeding ten dollars for each Person.

---

[5]Changed by the 20th Amendment

The privilege of the Writ of Habeas Corpus shall not be suspended, unless when in Cases of Rebellion or Invasion the public Safety may require it.

No Bill of Attainder or ex post facto Laws shall be passed.

No Capitation, or other direct, Tax shall be laid, unless in Proportion to the Census or Enumeration herein before directed to be taken.[6]

No Tax or Duty shall be laid on Articles exported from any State.

No Preference shall be given by any Regulation of Commerce or Revenue to the Ports of one State over those of another; nor shall Vessels bound to, or from, one State, be obliged to enter, clear, or pay Duties in another.

No Money shall be drawn from the Treasury, but in Consequence of Appropriations made by Law; and a regular Statement and Account of the Receipts and Expenditures of all public Money shall be published from time to time.

No Title of Nobility shall be granted by the United States; And no Person holding any Office of Profit or Trust under them, shall, without the Consent of Congress, accept of any present, Emolument, Office, or Title, of any kind whatever, from any King, Prince, or foreign State.

Powers Denied to the States

Section 10 No State shall enter into any Treaty, Alliance, or Confederation; grant Letters of Marque and Reprisal; coin Money; emit Bills of Credit; make any Thing but gold and silver Coin a Tender in Payment of Debts; pass any Bill of Attainder, ex post facto Law, or Law impairing the Obligation of Contracts, or grant any Title of Nobility.

No State shall, without the Consent of the Congress, lay any Imposts or Duties on Imports or Exports, except what may be absolutely necessary for executing its inspection Laws: and the net Produce of all Duties and Imposts, laid by any State on Imports or Exports, shall be for the Use of the Treasury of the United States; and all such Laws shall be subject to the Revision and Controul of the Congress.

No State shall, without the Consent of Congress, lay any Duty of Tonnage, keep Troops, or Ships of War in time of Peace, enter into any Agreement or Compact with another State, or with a foreign Power, or engage in War, unless actually invaded, or in such imminent Danger as will not admit of Delay.

Article II—THE EXECUTIVE ARTICLE

Nature and Scope of Presidential Power

Section 1 The executive Power shall be vested in a President of the United States of America. He shall hold his Office during the Term of four Years and, together with the Vice President, chosen for the same Term, be elected as follows:

Each State shall appoint, in such Manner as the Legislature thereof may direct, a Number of Electors, equal to the whole Number of Senators and Representatives to which the State may be entitled in the Congress: but no Senator or Representative, or Person holding an Office of Trust or Profit under the United States, shall be appointed an Elector.

The Electors shall meet in their respective States, and vote by Ballot for two Persons, of whom one at least shall not be an Inhabitant of the same State with themselves. And they shall make a List of all the Persons voted for, and of the Number of Votes for each; which List they shall sign and certify, and transmit sealed to the Seat of the Government of the United States, directed to the President of the Senate. The President of the Senate shall, in the Presence of the Senate and House of Representatives, open all the Certificates, and the Votes shall then be counted. The Person having the greatest Number of Votes shall be the President, if such Number be a Majority of the whole Number of Electors appointed; and if there be more than

one who have such Majority and have an equal Number of Votes, then the House of Representatives shall immediately chuse by Ballot one of them for President; and if no person have a Majority, then from the five highest on the List the said House shall in like Manner chuse the President. But in chusing the President, the Votes shall be taken by States, the Representation from each State having one Vote; A quorum for this Purpose shall consist of a Member or Members from two thirds of the States, and a Majority of all the States shall be necessary to a Choice. In every Case, after the Choice of the President, the person having the greatest Number of Votes of the Electors shall be the Vice President. But if there should remain two or more who have equal Vote, the Senate shall chuse from them by Ballot the Vice President.[7]

The Congress may determine the Time of chusing the Electors, and the Day on which they shall give their Votes; which Day shall be the same throughout the United States.

No Person except a natural born Citizen, or a Citizen of the United States, at the time of the Adoption of this Constitution, shall be eligible to the Office of President; neither shall any Person be eligible to that Office who shall not have attained to the Age of thirty five Years, and been fourteen Years a Resident within the United States.

In Case of the Removal of the President from Office, or of his Death, Resignation, or Inability to discharge the Powers and Duties of the said Office, the same shall devolve on the Vice President, and the Congress may by Law provide for the Case of Removal, Death, Resignation, or Inability, both of the President and Vice President, declaring what Officer shall then act as President, and such Officer shall act accordingly, until the Disability be removed, or a President shall be elected.[8]

The President shall, at stated Times, receive for his Services, a Compensation, which shall neither be encreased nor diminished during the Period of which he shall have been elected, and he shall not receive within that Period any other Emolument from the United States, or any of them.

Before he enter on the Execution of his Office, he shall take the following Oath or Affirmation:—"I do solemnly swear (or affirm) that I will faithfully execute the Office of President of the United States, and will to the best of my Ability, preserve, protect and defend the Constitution of the United States."

Powers and Duties of the President

Section 2 The President shall be the Commander in Chief of the Army and Navy of the United States, and of the Militia of the several States, when called into the actual Service of the United States, he may require the Opinion, in writing, of the principal Officer in each of the executive Departments, upon any Subject relating to the Duties of their respective Offices, and he shall have the Power to grant Reprieves and Pardons for Offences against the United States, except in Cases of Impeachment.

He shall have Power, by and with the Advice and Consent of the Senate to make Treaties, provided two thirds of the Senators present concur; and he shall nominate, and by and with the Advice and Consent of the Senate, shall appoint Ambassadors, other public Ministers and Consuls, Judges of the supreme Court, and all other Officers of the United States, whose Appointments are not herein otherwise provided for, and which shall be established by Law: but the Congress may by Law vest the Appointment of such inferior Officers, as they think proper, in the President alone, in the Courts of Law, or in the Heads of Departments.

The President shall have Power to fill up all Vacancies that may happen during the Recess of the Senate, by granting Commissions which shall expire at the End of their next Session.

Section 3 He shall from time to time give to the Congress Information of the State of the Union, and recommend to their Consideration such

---

[6]Modified by the 16th Amendment

[7]Changed by the 12th and 20th Amendments
[8]Modified by the 25th Amendment

Measures as he shall judge necessary and expedient; he may, on extraordinary Occasions, convene both Houses, or either of them, and in Case of Disagreement between them, with Respect to the Time of Adjournment, he may adjourn them to such Time as he shall think proper; he shall receive Ambassadors and other public Ministers; he shall take Care that the Laws be faithfully executed, and shall Commission all the Officers of the United States.

Section 4   The President, Vice President and all civil Officers of the United States, shall be removed from Office on Impeachment for, and Conviction of, Treason, Bribery, or other High Crimes and Misdemeanors.

ARTICLE III—THE JUDICIAL ARTICLE

Judicial Power, Courts, Judges

Section 1   The judicial Power of the United States, shall be vested in one supreme Court, and in such inferior Courts as the Congress may from time to time ordain and establish. The Judges, both the supreme and inferior Courts, shall hold their Offices during good Behaviour, and shall, at stated Times, receive for their Services, a Compensation, which shall not be diminished during their Continuance in Office.

Jurisdiction

Section 2   The judicial Power shall extend to all Cases, in Law and Equity, arising under this Constitution, the Laws of the United States, and Treaties made, or which shall be made, under their Authority;—to all Cases affecting Ambassadors, other public Ministers and Consuls;—to all Cases of admiralty and maritime Jurisdiction;—to Controversies to which the United States shall be a Party;—to Controversies between two or more States;— *between a State and Citizens of another State;*[9]—between Citizens of different States;—between Citizens of the same State claiming Lands under Grants of different States, and between a State, or the Citizens thereof, and foreign States, Citizens, or Subjects.

In all Cases affecting Ambassadors, other public Ministers and Consuls, and those in which a State shall be Party, the supreme Court shall have original Jurisdiction. In all the other Cases before mentioned, the supreme Court shall have appellate Jurisdiction, both as to Law and Fact, with such Exceptions, and under such Regulations as Congress shall make.

The Trial of all Crimes, except in Cases of Impeachment, shall be by Jury; and such Trial shall be held in the State where the said Crimes shall have been committed; but when not committed within any State, the Trial shall be at such Place or Places as the Congress may by Law have directed.

Treason

Section 3   Treason against the United States, shall consist only in levying War against them, or in adhering to their Enemies, giving them Aid and Comfort. No Persons shall be convicted of Treason unless on the Testimony of two Witnesses to the same overt Act, or on Confession in open Court.

The Congress shall have Power to declare the Punishment of Treason, but no Attainder of Treason shall work Corruption of Blood, or Forfeiture except during the Life of the Person attainted.

ARTICLE IV—INTERSTATE RELATIONS

Full Faith and Credit Clause

Section 1   Full Faith and Credit shall be given in each State to the public Acts, Records, and judicial Proceedings of every other State. And the Congress may by general Laws prescribe the Manner in which such Acts, Records and Proceedings shall be proved, and the Effect thereof.

Privileges and Immunities; Interstate Extradition

Section 2   The Citizens of each State shall be entitled to all Privileges and Immunities of Citizens in the several States.

A person charged in any State with Treason, Felony or other Crime, who shall flee from Justice, and be found in another State, shall on Demand of the executive Authority of the State from which he fled, be delivered up to be removed to the State having jurisdiction of the Crime.

No person held to Service or Labour in one State, under the Laws thereof, escaping into another, shall, in Consequence of any Law or Regulation therein, be discharged from such Service or Labour, but shall be delivered up on Claim of the Party to whom such Service or Labour may be due.[10]

Admission of States

Section 3   New States may be admitted by the Congress into this Union; but no new State shall be formed or erected within the Jurisdiction of any other State; nor any State to be formed by the Junction of two or more States, or Parts of States, without the Consent of the Legislatures of the States concerned as well as of the Congress.

The Congress shall have Power to dispose of and make all needful Rules and Regulations respecting the Territory or other Property belonging to the United States; and nothing in this Constitution shall be so construed as to Prejudice any Claims of the United States, or of any particular State.

Republican Form of Government

Section 4   The United States shall guarantee to every State in this Union a Republican Form of Government, and shall protect each of them against Invasion; and on Application of the Legislature, or of the Executive (when the Legislature cannot be convened) against domestic Violence.

ARTICLE V—THE AMENDING POWER

The Congress, whenever two thirds of both Houses shall deem it necessary, shall propose Amendments to this Constitution, or, on the Application of the Legislatures of two thirds of several States, shall call a Convention for proposing Amendments, which, in either Case, shall be valid to all Intents and Purposes, as Part of this Constitution, when ratified by the Legislatures of three fourths of the several States, or by Conventions in three fourths thereof, as the one or the other Mode of Ratification may be proposed by the Congress; Provided that no Amendment which may be made prior to the Year One thousand eight hundred and eight shall in any Manner affect the first and fourth Clauses in the Ninth Section of the first Article; and that no State, without its Consent, shall be deprived of its equal Suffrage in the Senate.

ARTICLE VI—THE SUPREMACY ACT

All Debts contracted and Engagements entered into, before the Adoption of this Constitution, shall be as valid against the United States under the Constitution, as under the Confederation.

This Constitution, and the Laws of the United States which shall be made in Pursuance thereof; and all Treaties made, or which shall be made, under the Authority of the United States, shall be the supreme Law of the Land; and the Judges in every State shall be bound thereby, any Thing in the Constitution or Laws of any State to the Contrary notwithstanding.

The Senators and Representative before mentioned, and the Members of the several State Legislatures, and all executive and judicial Officers, both of the United States and of the several States, shall be bound by Oath or

---

[9]Modified by the 11th Amendment

[10]Repealed by the 13th Amendment

Affirmation, to support this Constitution; but no religious Test shall ever be required as a Qualification to any Office or public Trust under the United States.

ARTICLE VII—RATIFICATION

The Ratification of the Conventions of nine States, shall be sufficient for the Establishment of this Constitution between the States so ratifying the Same.

Done in Convention by the Unanimous Consent of the States present the Seventeenth Day of September in the Year of our Lord one thousand seven hundred and Eighty seven and of the Independence of the United States of America the Twelfth. *In Witness whereof We have hereunto subscribed our Names.*

AMENDMENTS

[The first ten amendments were ratified on December 15, 1791, and form what is known as the "Bill of Rights."]

AMENDMENT 1—RELIGION, SPEECH, ASSEMBLY, AND POLITICS

Congress shall make no law respecting an establishment of religion, or prohibiting the free exercise thereof; or abridging the freedom of speech, or of the press; or the right of the people peaceably to assemble, and to petition the government for a redress of grievances.

AMENDMENT 2—MILITIA AND THE RIGHT TO BEAR ARMS

A well regulated Milita, being necessary to the security of a free State, the right of the people to keep and bear Arms, shall not be infringed.

AMENDMENT 3—QUARTERING OF SOLDIERS

No Soldier shall, in time of peace be quartered in any house, without the consent of the Owner, nor in time of war, but in manner to be prescribed by law.

AMENDMENT 4—SEARCHES AND SEIZURES

The right of the people to be secure in their persons, houses, papers, and effects, against unreasonable searches and seizures, shall not be violated, and no Warrants shall issue, but upon probable cause, supported by Oath or affirmation, and particularly describing the place to be searched, and the persons or things to be seized.

AMENDMENT 5—GRAND JURIES, SELF-INCRIMINATION, DOUBLE JEOPARDY, DUE PROCESS, AND EMINENT DOMAIN

No person shall be held to answer for a capital, or otherwise infamous crime, unless on a presentment or indictment of a Grand jury, except in cases arising in the land or naval forces, or in the Milita, when in actual service in time of War or public danger; nor shall any person be subject for the same offence to be twice put in jeopardy of life or limb; nor shall be compelled in any criminal case to be a witness against himself, nor be deprived of life, liberty, or property, without due process of law; nor shall private property be taken for public use, without just compensation.

AMENDMENT 6—CRIMINAL COURT PROCEDURES

In all criminal prosecutions, the accused shall enjoy the right to a speedy and public trial, by an impartial jury of the State and district wherein the crime shall have been committed, which district shall have been previously ascertained by law, and to be informed of the nature and cause of the accusation; to be confronted with the witnesses against him; to have compulsory process for obtaining Witnesses in his favor, and to have the Assistance of Counsel for his defense.

AMENDMENT 7—TRIAL BY JURY IN COMMON LAW CASES

In Suits at common law, where the value in controversy shall exceed twenty dollars, the right of trial by jury shall be preserved, and no fact tried by a jury shall be otherwise re-examined in any Court of the United States, than according to the rules of the common law.

AMENDMENT 8—BAIL, CRUEL AND UNUSUAL PUNISHMENT

Excessive bail shall not be required, nor excessive fines imposed, nor cruel and unusual punishments inflicted.

AMENDMENT 9—RIGHTS RETAINED BY THE PEOPLE

The enumeration in the Constitution, of certain rights, shall not be construed to deny or disparage others retained by the people.

AMENDMENT 10—RESERVED POWERS OF THE STATES

The powers not delegated to the United States by the Constitution, nor prohibited by it to the States, are reserved to the States respectively, or to the people.

AMENDMENT 11—SUITS AGAINST THE STATES

[Ratified February 7, 1795]

The Judicial power of the United States shall not be construed to extend to any suit in law or equity, commenced or prosecuted against one of the United States by Citizens of another State, or by Citizens or Subjects of any Foreign State.

AMENDMENT 12—ELECTION OF THE PRESIDENT

[Ratified July 27, 1804]

The Electors shall meet in their respective states, and vote by ballot for President and Vice-President, one of whom, at least, shall not be an inhabitant of the same state with themselves; they shall name in their ballots the person voted for as President, and in distinct ballots the person voted for as Vice-President, and they shall make distinct lists of all persons voted for as President, and of all persons voted for as Vice-President, and of the number of votes for each, which lists they shall sign and certify, and transmit sealed to the seat of the government of the United States, directed to the President of the Senate;—The President of the Senate shall, in presence of the Senate and House of Representatives, open all the certificates and the votes shall then be counted;—The person having the greatest number of votes for President, shall be the President, if such number be a majority of the whole number of Electors appointed; and if no person have such majority, then from the persons having the highest numbers not exceeding three on the list of those voted for as President, the House of Representatives shall choose immediately, by ballot, the President. But in choosing the President, the votes shall be taken by states, the representation from each state having one vote; a quorum for this purpose shall consist of a member or members from two-thirds of the states, and a majority of all states shall be necessary to a choice. And if the House of Representatives shall not choose a President whenever the right of choice shall devolve upon them, *before the fourth day of March next following*, then the Vice-President shall act as President, as in the case of the death or other constitutional disability of the President.[11] The person having the greatest number of votes as Vice-President, shall be the Vice-President, if such a number be a majority of the whole numbers of Electors appointed, and if no person have a majority, then from the two highest numbers on the list, the Senate shall choose the Vice-President; a quorum for the purpose shall consist of two-thirds of the whole number of Senators, and a majority of the whole number shall be necessary to a choice. But no person constitutionally ineligible to the office of President shall be eligible to that of Vice-President of the United States.

AMENDMENT 13—PROHIBITION OF SLAVERY

[Ratified December 6, 1865]

Section 1   Neither slavery nor involuntary servitude, except as a punishment for crime whereof the party shall have been duly convicted, shall exist within the United States, or any place subject to their jurisdiction.

Section 2   Congress shall have power to enforce this article by appropriate legislation.

AMENDMENT 14—CITIZENSHIP, DUE PROCESS, AND EQUAL PROTECTION OF THE LAWS

[Ratified July 9, 1868]

Section 1   All persons born or naturalized in the United States, and subject to the jurisdiction thereof, are citizens of the United States and of the State wherein they reside. No State shall make or enforce any law which shall abridge the privileges or immunities of citizens of the United States; nor shall any State deprive any person of life, liberty, or property, without due process of law; nor deny to any person within its jurisdiction the equal protection of the laws.

Section 2   Representatives shall be apportioned among the several States according to their respective numbers, counting the whole number of persons in each State, excluding Indians not taxed. But when the right to vote at any election for the choice of electors for President and Vice President of the United States, Representatives in Congress, the Executive and Judicial officers of a State, or the members of the Legislature thereof, is denied to any of the male inhabitants of such State, being twenty-one[12] years of age, and citizens of the United States, or in any way abridged, except for participation in rebellion, or other crime, the basis of representation therein shall be reduced in the proportion which the number of such male citizens shall bear to the whole number of male citizens twenty-one years of age in such State.

Section 3   No person shall be a Senator or Representative in Congress, or elector of President and Vice President, or hold any office, civil or military, under the United States, or under any State, who, having previously taken an oath, as a member of Congress, or as an officer of the United States, or as a member of any State legislature, or as an executive or judicial officer of any State, to support the Constitution of the United States, shall have engaged in insurrection or rebellion against the same, or given aid or comfort to the enemies thereof. But Congress may by a vote of two-thirds of each House, remove such disability.

Section 4   The validity of the public debt of the United States, authorized by law, including debts incurred for payment of pensions and bounties for services in suppressing insurrection or rebellion, shall not be questioned. But neither the United States nor any State shall assume or pay any debt or obligation incurred in aid of insurrection or rebellion against the United States, or any claim for the loss or emancipation of any slave; but all such debts, obligations and claims shall be held illegal and void.

Section 5   The Congress shall have power to enforce, by appropriate legislation, the provisions of this article.

AMENDMENT 15—THE RIGHT TO VOTE

[Ratified February 3, 1870]

Section 1   The right of citizens of the United States to vote shall not be denied or abridged by the United States or by any State on account of race, color, or previous condition of servitude.

Section 2   The Congress shall have power to enforce this article by appropriate legislation.

AMENDMENT 16—INCOME TAXES

[Ratified February 3, 1913]

The Congress shall have power to lay and collect taxes on incomes, from whatever source derived, without apportionment among the several States, and without regard to any census or enumeration.

AMENDMENT 17—DIRECT ELECTION OF SENATORS

[Ratified April 8, 1913]

The Senate of the United States shall be composed of two Senators from each State, elected by the people thereof, for six years; and each Senator shall have one vote. The electors in each State shall have the qualifications requisite for electors of the most numerous branch of the State legislatures.

When vacancies happen in the representation of any State in the Senate, the executive authority of such State shall issue writs of election to fill such vacancies: *Provided*, That the Legislature of any State may empower the executive thereof to make temporary appointment until the people fill the vacancies by election as the legislature may direct.

This amendment shall not be so construed as to affect the election or term of any Senator chosen before it becomes valid as part of the Constitution.

AMENDMENT 18—PROHIBITION

[Ratified January 16, 1919 Repealed December 5, 1933 by Amendment 21]

Section 1   After one year from the ratification of this article the manufacture, sale, or transportation of intoxicating liquors within, the importation thereof into, or the exportation thereof from the United States and all territory subject to the jurisdiction thereof for beverage purposes is hereby prohibited.

Section 2   The Congress and the several states shall have concurrent power to enforce this article by appropriate legislation.

Section 3   This article shall be inoperative unless it shall have been ratified as an amendment to the Constitution by the legislatures of the several states, as provided in the Constitution, within seven years from the date of the submission hereof to the States by the Congress.[13]

---

[11]Changed by the 20th Amendment
[12]Changed by the 26th Amendment

[13]Repealed by the 21st Amendment

AMENDMENT 19—FOR WOMEN'S SUFFRAGE

[Ratified August 18, 1920]

The right of the citizens of the United States to vote shall not be denied or abridged by the United States or by any State on account of sex.

Congress shall have power, by appropriate legislation, to enforce the provision of this article.

AMENDMENT 20—THE LAME DUCK AMENDMENT

[Ratified January 23, 1933]

Section 1   The terms of the President and Vice President shall end at noon on the 20th day of January, and the terms of the Senators and Representatives at noon on the 3rd day of January, of the years in which such terms would have ended if this article had not been ratified; and the terms of their successors shall then begin.

Section 2   The Congress shall assemble at least once in every year, and such meeting shall begin at noon on the 3rd day of January, unless they shall by law appoint a different day.

Section 3   If, at the time fixed for the beginning of the term of the President, the President elect shall have died, the Vice President elect shall become President. If a President shall not have been chosen before the time fixed for the beginning of his term, or if the President elect shall have failed to qualify, then the Vice President elect shall act as President until a President shall have qualified; and the Congress may by law provide for the case wherein neither a President elect nor a Vice President elect shall have qualified, declaring who shall then act as President, or the manner in which one who is to act shall be selected, and such person shall act accordingly until a President or Vice President shall have qualified.

Section 4   The Congress may by law provide for the case of the death of any of the persons from whom the House of Representatives may choose a President whenever the right of choice shall have developed upon them, and for the case of the death of any of the persons from whom the Senate may choose a Vice President whenever the right of choice shall have devolved upon them.

Section 5   Sections 1 and 2 shall take effect on the 15th day of October following the ratification of this article.

Section 6   This article shall be inoperative unless it shall have been ratified as an amendment to the Constitution by the legislatures of three-fourths of the several States within seven years from the date of its submission.

AMENDMENT 21—REPEAL OF PROHIBITION

[Ratified December 5, 1933]

Section 1   The eighteenth article of amendment to the Constitution of the United States is hereby repealed.

Section 2   The transportation or importation into any State, Territory, or Possession of the United States for delivery or use therein of intoxicating liquors, in violation of the laws thereof, is hereby prohibited.

Section 3   This article shall be inoperative unless it shall have been ratified as an amendment to the Constitution by conventions in the several States, as provided in the Constitution, within seven years from the date of the submission hereof to the States by the Congress.

AMENDMENT 22—NUMBER OF PRESIDENTIAL TERMS

[Ratified February 27, 1951]

Section 1   No person shall be elected to the office of the President more than twice, and no person who has held the office of President, or acted as Pres-

ident, for more than two years of a term to which some other person was elected President shall be elected to the Office of the President more than once. But this Article shall not apply to any person holding the office of President when this article was proposed by the Congress, and shall not prevent any person who may be holding the office of President, or acting as President, during the term within which this Article becomes operative from holding the office of President or acting as President during the remainder of such term.

Section 2   This Article shall be inoperative unless it shall have been ratified as an amendment to the Constitution by the legislatures of three-fourths of the several states within seven years from the date of its submission to the States by the Congress.

AMENDMENT 23—PRESIDENTIAL ELECTORS FOR THE DISTRICT OF COLUMBIA

[Ratified March 29, 1961]

Section 1   The District constituting the seat of Government of the United States shall appoint in such manner as the Congress may direct:

A number of electors of President and Vice President equal to the whole number of Senators and Representatives in Congress to which the District would be entitled if it were a State, but in no event more than the least populous State; they shall be in addition to those appointed by the States, but they shall be considered, for the purposes of the election of President and Vice President, to be electors appointed by a State; and they shall meet in the District and perform such duties as provided by the twelfth article of amendment.

Section 2   The Congress shall have power to enforce this article by appropriate legislation.

AMENDMENT 24—THE ANTI-POLL TAX AMENDMENT

[Ratified January 23, 1964]

Section 1   The right of citizens of the United States to vote in any primary or other election for President or Vice President, for electors for President or Vice President, or for Senator or Representative in Congress, shall not be denied or abridged by the United States or any State by reason of failure to pay any poll tax or other tax.

Section 2   The Congress shall have power to enforce this article by appropriate legislation.

AMENDMENT 25—PRESIDENTIAL DISABILITY, VICE PRESIDENTIAL VACANCIES

[Ratified February 10, 1967]

Section 1   In case of the removal of the President from office or his death or resignation, the Vice President shall become President.

Section 2   Whenever there is a vacancy in the office of the Vice President, the President shall nominate a Vice President who shall take the office upon confirmation by a majority vote of both houses of Congress.

Section 3   Whenever the President transmits to the President pro tempore of the Senate and the Speaker of the House of Representatives his written declaration that he is unable to discharge the powers and duties of his office, and until he transmits to them a written declaration to the contrary, such powers and duties shall be discharged by the Vice President as Acting President.

Section 4   Whenever the Vice-President and a majority of either the principal officers of the executive departments, or of such other body as Congress may by law provide, transmit to the President pro tempore of the Senate and the Speaker of the House of Representatives their written declaration that the President is unable to discharge the powers and duties of his office, the Vice President shall immediately assume the powers and duties of the office as Acting President.

Thereafter, when the President transmits to the President pro tempore of the Senate and the Speaker of the House of Representatives his written declaration that no inability exists, he shall resume the powers and duties of his office unless the Vice President and a majority of either the principal officers of the executive departments, or of such other body as Congress may by law provide, transmit within four days to the President pro tempore of the Senate and the Speaker of the House of Representatives their written declaration that the President is unable to discharge the powers and duties of his office. Thereupon Congress shall decide the issue, assembling within 48 hours for that purpose if not in session. If the Congress, within 21 days after receipt of the latter written declaration, or, if Congress is not in session, within 21 days after Congress is required to assemble, determines by two-thirds vote of both houses that the President is unable to discharge the powers and duties of his office, the Vice President shall continue to discharge the same as Acting President; otherwise, the President shall resume the powers and duties of his office.

Amendment 26—Eighteen-Year-Old Vote

[Ratified July 1, 1971]

Section 1   The right of citizens of the United States, who are eighteen years of age, or older, to vote shall not be denied or abridged by the United States or by any State on account of age.

Section 2   The Congress shall have power to enforce this article by appropriate legislation.

Amendment 27—Congressional Salaries

[Ratified May 7, 1992]

No law, varying the compensation for the services of the Senators and Representatives, shall take effect, until an election of Representative shall be intervened.

✓ ASK YOURSELF ABOUT POLITICS

1 Should a state be able to prevent enforcement of a federal law that the state believes to be unconstitutional?
Yes ☐ No ☐

2 Should the national government always have the final say in disputes with individual states?
Yes ☐ No ☐

3 Should the national government be able to prosecute a high school student for bringing a gun to school?
Yes ☐ No ☐

4 Should welfare benefits be the same in all states?
Yes ☐ No ☐

5 Should each state determine its own minimum age for drinking alcoholic beverages?
Yes ☐ No ☐

6 Should each state determine its own maximum highway speed limit?
Yes ☐ No ☐

7 Which level of government does the best job of dealing with the problems it faces?
Federal ☐ State ☐
Local ☐

8 Which level of government do you have the most confidence in?
Federal ☐ State ☐
Local ☐

CHAPTER 4

FEDERALISM
DIVIDING GOVERNMENTAL POWER

CHAPTER OUTLINE

Indestructible Union, Indestructible States

Why Federalism? The Argument for a "Compound Republic"

The Original Design of Federalism

The Evolution of American Federalism

Key Developments in American Federalism

Money and Power Flow to Washington

Coercive Federalism: Preemptions and Mandates

A Devolution Revolution?

FEATURES

Compared to What? Governmental Unions around the World

Up Close: The States versus the Tobacco Companies

A Conflicting View: The Dark Side of Federalism

What Do You Think? Which Government Does the Best Job?

Up Close: Can the Federal Government Outlaw Guns in Schools?

Up Close: How Congress Set a National Drinking Age

A Conflicting View: Liberals, Conservatives, and Federalism

People in Politics: Christine Todd Whitman, On the Cutting Edge of Change in the States

Politics in Cyberspace: Federalism

Just what should be the relationship between the national government and the states? Questions like these lie at the heart of the issue of who gets what, when, and how. They affect employment, transportation, health, education, the very air we breathe. And when there has been disagreement on them, the nation has been plunged into conflict at best, and the bloodiest war in its history at worst.

INDESTRUCTIBLE UNION, INDESTRUCTIBLE STATES

In December 1860 South Carolina seceded from the Union and in April 1861 authorized its state militia to expel U.S. troops from Fort Sumter in Charleston harbor. Although there is no provision in the Constitution for states leaving the Union, eleven southern states—South Carolina, Mississippi, Florida, Alabama, Georgia, Louisiana, Texas, Virginia,

97

Arkansas, Tennessee, and North Carolina, in that order—argued that the Union was a voluntary association and they were entitled to withdraw.[1] President Abraham Lincoln declared these states to be in armed rebellion and sent federal troops to crush the "rebels." The result was the nation's bloodiest war: more than 250,000 battle deaths and another 250,000 deaths from disease and privation, out of a total population of less than 30 million.

Following the Civil War, Chief Justice Salmon P. Chase confirmed what had been decided on the battlefield: "The Constitution, in all of its provisions, looks to an indestructible union, composed of indestructible states."[2]

Federalism divides power between two separate authorities—the nation and the states—each of which enforces its own laws directly on its citizens. Both the nation and the states pass laws, impose taxes, spend money, and maintain their own courts. Neither the nation nor the states can dissolve the Union or amend the Constitution without the consent of the other. The Constitution itself is the only legal source of authority for both the states and the nation; the states do not get their power from the national government, and the national government does not get its power from the states. Both national and state governments derive their power directly from the people.

American federalism differs from a **unitary system** of government, in which formal authority rests with the national government, and whatever powers are exercised by states, provinces, or subdivisions are given to those governments by the national government. Most of the world's governments—including France and Britain—are unitary. Federalism also differs from a **confederation** of states, in which the national government relies on the states for its authority, not the people (see Figure 4-1). Under the Articles of Confederation of 1781, the United States was a confederation. The national government could not even levy taxes; it had to ask the states for revenue. Like the United States, a number of other countries were confederations before establishing federal systems, and today new types of confederations with limited functions are being formed (see *Compared to What?* "Governmental Unions around the World").

People in the United States often think of the *federal government* when the word *government* comes up. In fact, today there are more than 85,000 American governments. These state and local governments are as important in American life as the federal government, for they provide such essential day-to-day services as schools, water, and police and fire departments (see Table 4-1). However, the U.S. Constitution, the supreme law of the land, recognizes the existence of only the national government and the states. Local governments have no guarantees of power—or even existence—under the U.S. Constitution. Whatever powers they have are given to them by the state government. States can create or abolish local governments, grant or withhold their powers, or change their boundaries without their consent. Some local governments have powers guaranteed in *state* constitutions, and some are even given **home rule**—the power to pass laws affecting local affairs, so long as those laws do not conflict with state or federal laws. About 60,000 of these 85,000 governments have the power to levy taxes to support activities authorized by state law.

In short, the American federal system is large and complex, with three levels of government—national, state, and local—sharing power. Indeed, the numbers and complexity of governments in the United States make **intergovernmental relations**—all of the interactions among these governments and their officials— a major concern of political scientists and policy makers.

federalism A constitutional arrangement whereby power is divided between national and subnational governments, each of which enforces its own laws directly on its citizens and neither of which can alter the arrangement without the consent of the other.

unitary system Constitutional arrangement whereby authority rests with the national government; subnational governments have only those powers given to them by the national government.

confederation Constitutional arrangement whereby the national government is created by and relies on subnational governments for its authority.

home rule Power of local government to pass laws affecting local affairs, so long as those laws do not conflict with state or federal laws.

intergovernmental relations Network of political, financial, and administrative relationships between units of the federal government and those of state and local governments.

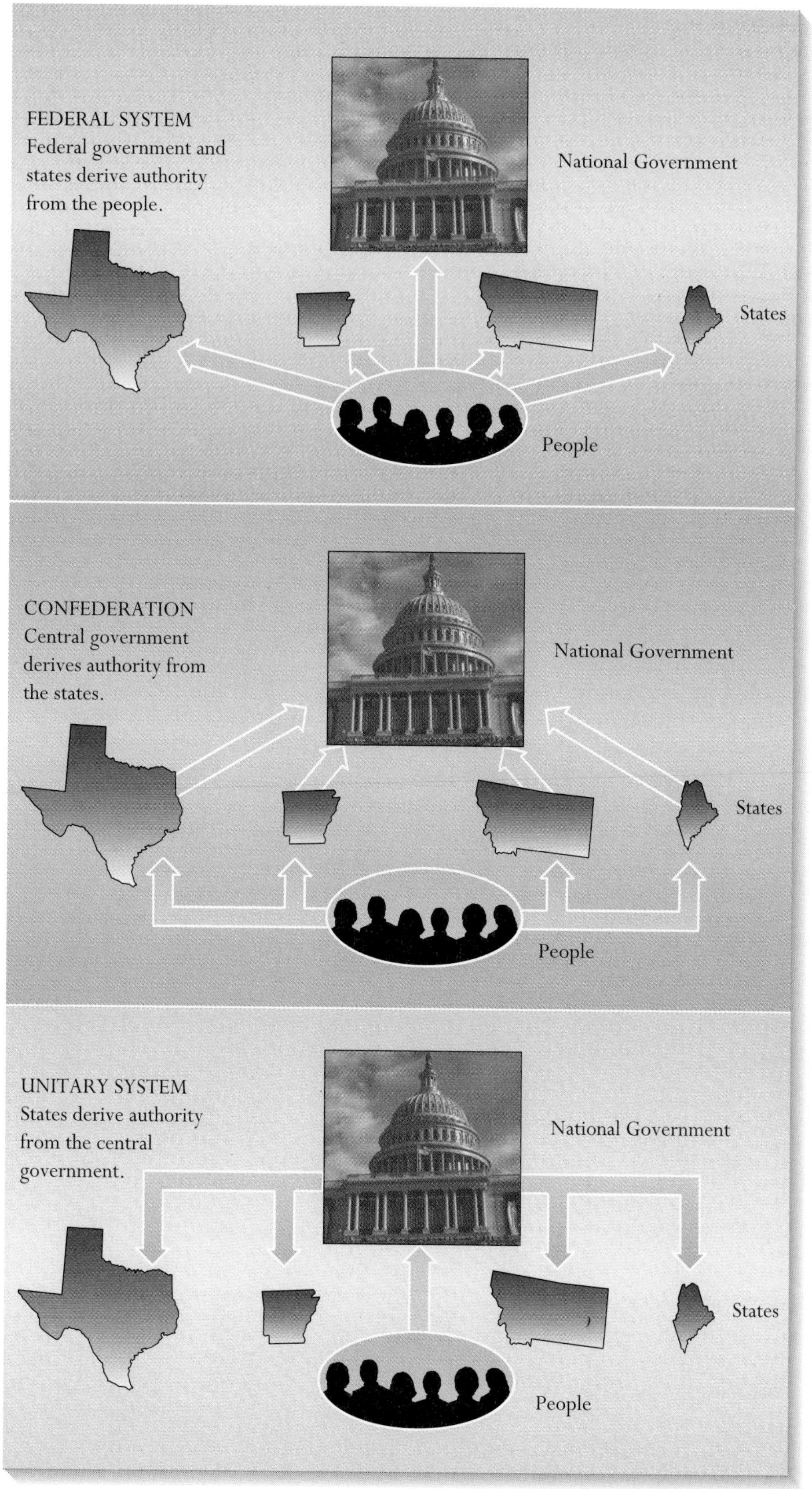

FEDERAL SYSTEM
Federal government and states derive authority from the people.
National Government
States
People
CONFEDERATION
Central government derives authority from the states.
National Government
States
People
UNITARY SYSTEM
States derive authority from the central government.
National Government
States
People

FIGURE 4-1 The Federal, Confederation, and Unitary Systems of Government

Governmental Unions around the World

Confederations have played important historical roles as societies moved toward nationhood. The case of the United States, in which the Articles of Confederation preceded the creation of a truly national government, is not unique. For example, the eighteenth-century German confederation predated the modern German nation, and the Helvetic confederation was transformed into the modern federal system of Switzerland.

The European Union   Today the most important political confederation is the European Union. The EU includes fifteen member nations—Austria, Belgium, Denmark, Finland, France, Germany, Greece, Ireland, Italy, Luxembourg, Netherlands, Portugal, Spain, Sweden, and the United Kingdom—and embraces well over 300 million people. The EU is a union with very specific functions granted by its members. It has a European Parliament; a Council of Ministers of member nations: a European Commission that serves as a bureaucracy to administer policy decisions, with a president rotating among the nations; and a European Court of Justice to adjudicate disputes among members.

The Commonwealth of Independent States   Currently, republics of the former Union of Soviet Socialist Republics—Armenia, Azerbaijan, Byelorussia, Estonia, Georgia, Kazakhstan, Kyrgyzstan, Latvia, Lithuania, Moldavia, Russia, Tajikistan, Turkmenistan, Ukraine, and Uzbekistan—are struggling to find an acceptable form of union. The central government of the USSR ceased to exist after December 31, 1991. The president of the new Russian Federated Republic, Boris Yeltsin, opened negotiations with other republics to create a Commonwealth of Independent States along lines that would resemble a confederacy. The Russian Federated Republic is itself a formal federation, and some of its states have demanded independence from Moscow. Rebellion in Chechnya was countered by a bloody military campaign in which Russian troops inflicted heavy damages on the capital city, Grozny. But eventually Moscow withdrew its troops and granted considerable autonomy to Chechnya.

Federal Systems   The formal constitutions of many governments describe a federal form of government. These include Argentina, Australia, Brazil, Canada, the Federal Republic of Germany, India, Malaysia, Mexico, Nigeria, Pakistan, Switzerland, the United Arab Emirates, the United States, and Venezuela. Yugoslavia was a federal system prior to its civil war and disintegration into ethnic enclaves of Serbia, Croatia, Macedonia, Montenegro, and war-torn Bosnia. Czechoslovakia was also a federal system with two republics prior to its peaceful division into two nations: Slovakia and the Czech Republic. However, despite a federal constitution, many of these governments are highly centralized, with the national government exercising a dominant role in the economic, social, and political life of the nation.

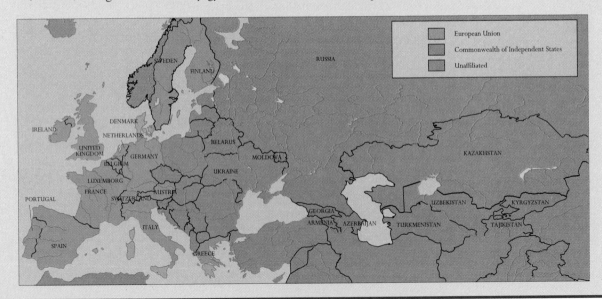

TABLE 4-1	How Many American Governments?	
	U.S. government	1
	States	50
	Counties	3,043
	Municipalities	19,279
	Townships	16,656
	Special districts	31,555
	School districts	14,422
	All governments	**85,006**

Source: *Statistical Abstract of the United States, 1997,* p. 297.

WHY FEDERALISM? THE ARGUMENT FOR A "COMPOUND REPUBLIC"

The nation's Founders believed that "republican principles" would help make government responsible to the people, but they also argued that "auxiliary precautions" were necessary to protect the liberties of minorities and individuals. They believed that majority rule in a democratic government made it particularly important to devise ways to protect minorities and individuals from "unjust" and "interested" *majorities*. They believed a federation would better protect liberty, disperse power, and manage conflict.

Protecting Liberty Constitutional guarantees of individual liberty do not enforce themselves. The Founders argued that to guarantee liberty, government should be structured to encourage "opposite and rival" centers of power *within* and *among* governments. So they settled on both federalism—dividing powers between the national and state governments—and *separation of powers*—the dispersal of power among branches within the national government.

> In the compound republic of America, the power surrendered by the people is first divided between two distinct governments, and then the portion allotted to each is subdivided among distinct and separate departments. Hence a double security arises to the rights of the people. The different governments will control each other, at the same time that each will be controlled by itself.[3]

Thus the Founders deliberately tried to create *competition* within and among governmental units as a means of protecting liberty. Rather than rely on the "better motives" of leaders, the Founders sought to construct a system in which governments and government officials would be constrained by competition with other governments and other government officials:

> Ambition must be made to counteract ambition. The interest of the man must be connected with the constitutional rights of the place. It may be a reflection on human nature that such devices should be necessary to control the abuses of government. But what is government itself but the greatest of all reflections on human natures?[4]

Dispersing Power Federalism distributes power widely among different sets of leaders, national as well as state and local officeholders. The Founders believed that multiple leadership groups offered more protection against tyranny than a

Up Close

The States versus the Tobacco Companies

It has long been recognized that cigarette smoking is the leading preventable cause of death in the United States. The federal government's efforts to reduce smoking long centered on educating the public to the health dangers involved. In 1964 the U.S. Surgeon General first reported (what most people suspected anyway) that smoking was related to cancer, heart disease, and emphysema. In 1965 Congress required health warnings on every pack of cigarettes sold. In 1970 Congress banned cigarette advertising from radio and television. Over time the percentage of the adult population that smoked fell from more than 50 percent in 1965 to about 25 percent by 1995.

As smoking declined, antismoking forces gained political strength in both Washington and the states. Various bans on smoking were enacted for domestic air travel, public buildings, areas of restaurants, and so on. Taxes on cigarettes were gradually increased; states added anywhere from 5 cents (North Carolina) to 82.5 cents (Washington) to the federal tax of 25 cents per pack. But Congress failed to act directly

on the national health care costs incurred by smoking. The states assumed the leadership in the tobacco fight.

Traditionally tobacco companies were very successful in defending themselves against product liability suits. It was difficult for individual smokers to prove in court that their particular illness (cancer, emphysema, heart disease) was produced directly from their smoking. Moreover, the tobacco companies argued that smokers understood the health dangers of smoking and therefore assumed the risk themselves. Indeed, they often pointed to the warning labels on each pack of cigarettes.

But in 1994 Mississippi and Florida filed civil lawsuits against the major tobacco companies, demanding reimbursement for their states' share of Medicaid costs incurred through smoking-related diseases. Florida passed a new state law, a Medicaid Third Party Liability Act, allowing statistical evidence of illnesses among large numbers of people to be used as evidence of causation. This meant that Florida could recover damages without necessarily showing that a product (cigarettes) actually caused injury to particular defendants (smokers). More importantly, the law declared that product manufacturers (the tobacco companies) cannot escape liability by showing that users of their product knowingly assumed all

single set of all-powerful leaders. State and local government offices also provide a political base for the opposition party when it has lost a national election. In this way, state and local governments contribute to party competition in the United States by helping to tide over the losing party after electoral defeat at the national level so that it can remain strong enough to challenge incumbents at the next election. And finally, state and local governments often provide a training ground for national political leaders. National leaders can be drawn from a pool of leaders experienced in state and local government.

Increasing Participation   Federalism allows more people to participate in the political system. With more than 85,000 governments in the United States—state, county, municipality, township, special district, and school district—nearly a million people hold some kind of public office.

Improving Efficiency   Federalism also makes government more manageable and efficient. Imagine the bureaucracy, red tape, and confusion if every governmental activity—police, schools, roads, fire fighting, garbage collection, sewage disposal, and so forth—in every local community in the nation were controlled by

or part of the risk of using it. In other words, the tobacco companies were denied the legal defense of showing that many individuals deliberately chose to smoke despite their awareness of the health risks.

With Mississippi and Florida leading the way, over forty states filed lawsuits against the tobacco companies for recovery of Medicaid costs associated with smoking-related diseases. The states argued,

> Cigarette-related disease has killed and continues to kill untold millions of Americans. In the name of profits, cigarette manufacturers choose to ignore and suppress the truth about the hazard of smoking. As a result Medicaid recipients have contracted smoking-related diseases including cancer, emphysema, and heart disease. The care of these Medicaid recipients has placed a significant burden on the State. This burden should rightfully be borne by the cigarette manufacturers. [*]

In pretrial negotiations with the states, led by Mississippi Attorney General Michael Moore, the tobacco companies, notably Phillip Morris, R. J. Reynolds, and Brown and Williamson, offered a nationwide settlement package. In exchange for dismissing the state cases and limiting the size of damages awards individuals could receive in smoking-related cases, the tobacco companies agreed to total payments of more than $368 billion to the states and to a national fund for children's health. The companies also agreed to end billboard and sports advertising and to other actions designed to reduce teen smoking over the years. The FDA would be given authority to reduce and eventually eliminate the nicotine content of cigarettes. Florida Attorney General Bob Butterworth boasted, "The Marlboro Man will be riding into the sunset on Joe Camel." [†] Mississippi's Michael Moore claimed that the agreement was "the most historic public health achievement in history." [‡]

But clearly tobacco sales constitute "interstate commerce," and thus Congress has the final word on any settlement negotiated by the states. President Clinton and many Congress members, responding to complaints from various sectors of the public health lobby, have been wary of endorsing the agreement. Mississippi and Florida settled their cases against the tobacco companies in 1997. But pending congressional legislation implementing the national agreement, the other states must continue to pursue their lawsuits.

---

[*] *State of Florida, et al. v. The American Tobacco Company, et al.* Civil Action No 95-1466 AH, Fifteenth Judicial Circuit, Palm Beach County (1996).

[†] *Newsweek*, June 30, 1997.

[‡] *New York Times*, June 21, 1997.

a centralized administration in Washington. Government can become arbitrary when a bureaucracy far from the scene directs local officials. Thus decentralization often softens the rigidity of law.

Ensuring Policy Responsiveness   Federalism encourages policy responsiveness (see *Up Close:* "The States versus the Tobacco Companies"). Multiple competing governments are more sensitive to citizens' views than a single "monopoly" government. The existence of multiple governments offering different packages of benefits and costs allows a better match between citizen preferences and public policy. Americans are very mobile. People and businesses can "vote with their feet" by relocating to those states and communities that most closely conform to their own policy preferences. This mobility not only facilitates a better match between citizen preferences and public policy but also encourages competition between states and communities to offer improved services at lower costs. [5]

Encouraging Policy Innovation   The Founders hoped that federalism would encourage policy experimentation and innovation. Today federalism may seem like a "conservative" idea, but it was once the instrument of liberal reformers. Federal programs as diverse as the income tax, unemployment compensation, Social Security, wage and hour legislation, bank deposit insurance, and food stamps were all state programs before becoming national undertakings. Today much of the current "liberal" policy agenda—mandatory health insurance for workers, child-care programs, notification of plant closings, government support of industrial research and development—has been embraced by various states. The phrase *laboratories of democracies* is generally attributed to the great progressive jurist Supreme Court Justice Louis D. Brandeis, who used it in defense of state experimentation with new solutions to social and economic problems.[6]

Managing Conflict   Federalism allows different peoples to come together in a nation without engendering irresolvable conflict. Conflicts between geographically separate groups in America are resolved by allowing each to pursue its own policies within its separate state or community instead of battling over a single national policy to be applied uniformly throughout the land.

Some Important Reservations   Despite the strengths of federalism, it has its problems. First of all, federalism can obstruct action on national issues. Although decentralization may reduce conflict at the national level, it may do so at the price of "sweeping under the rug" very serious national injustices (see *A Conflicting View:* "The Dark Side of Federalism"). Federalism also permits local leaders and citizens to frustrate national policy, to sacrifice national interest to local interests. Decentralized government provides an opportunity for local NIMBYs (people who subscribe to the motto "*N*ot *I*n *M*y *B*ack *Y*ard") to obstruct airports, highways, waste disposal plants, public housing, drug rehabilitation centers, and many other projects that would be in the national interest.

Finally, federalism permits the benefits and costs of government to be spread unevenly across the nation. For example, some states spend more than twice as much on the education of each child in the public schools as other states do. Taxes in some states are more than twice as high per capita as they are in other states. Welfare benefits in some states are more than twice as high as in other states. Competition among states may keep welfare benefits low in states that want to discourage poor people from moving there. Thus federalism obstructs uniformity in policy.

THE ORIGINAL DESIGN OF FEDERALISM

The U.S. Constitution *originally* defined American federalism in terms of (1) the powers expressly delegated to the national government plus the powers implied by those that are specifically granted, (2) the concurrent powers exercised by both states and the national government, (3) the powers reserved to the states, (4) the powers denied by the Constitution to both the national government and the states, and (5) the constitutional provisions giving the states a role in the composition of the national government (see Figure 4-2).

delegated, or **enumerated, powers**   Powers specifically mentioned in the Constitution as belonging to the national government.

Delegated Powers   The U.S. Constitution lists seventeen specific grants of power to Congress, in Article I, Section 8. These are usually referred to as the **delegated**, or **enumerated, powers**. They include authority over war and foreign affairs, authority over the economy ("interstate commerce"), control over the money supply, and the power to tax and spend "to pay the debts and provide for the

A Conflicting View

The Dark Side of Federalism

Segregationists once regularly used the argument of "states' rights" to deny equal protection of the law to African Americans. Indeed, *states' rights* become a code word for opposition to federal civil rights laws. In 1963 Governor George Wallace invoked the states' rights argument when he stood in the doorway at the University of Alabama to prevent the execution of a federal court order that the university admit two African American students and integrate. U.S. assistant attorney general Nicholas Katzenbach and federal marshals were on hand to enforce the order, and Wallace only temporarily delayed them. Shortly after his dramatic stand in front of the television cameras, he retreated to his office. Later in his career, Wallace sought African American votes, declaring, "I was wrong. Those days are over."

Federalism in America remains tainted by its historical association with slavery, segregation, and discrimination. In the Virginia and Kentucky Resolutions of 1798, Thomas Jefferson and James Madison asserted the doctrine of "nullification," claiming that states could nullify unconstitutional laws of Congress. Although the original intent of this doctrine was to counter congressional attacks on a free press under the Alien and Sedition Acts of 1798, it was later revived to defend slavery. John C. Calhoun of South Carolina argued forcefully in the years before the Civil War that slavery was an issue for the states to decide and the Constitution gave Congress no power to interfere with slavery in the southern states or in the new western territories.

In the years immediately following the Civil War, the issues of slavery, racial inequality, and African American voting rights were *nationalized*. Nationalizing these issues meant removing them from the jurisdiction of the states and placing them in the hands of the national government. The Thirteenth, Fourteenth, and Fifteenth Amendments to the Constitution were enforced by federal troops in the southern states during the post–Civil War Reconstruction era. But after the Compromise of 1876 led to the withdrawal of federal troops from the southern states, legal and social segregation of African Americans became a "way of life" in the region. Segregation was *denationalized*, which reduced national conflict over race but exacted a high price from the nation's African American population. Segregationists asserted the states' rights argument so often in defense of racial discrimination that it became a code phrase for racism. Not until the 1950s and 1960s were questions of segregation and equality again made into national issues. The civil rights movement asserted the supremacy of national law and in 1954 won a landmark decision in the case of *Brown v. Board of Education of Topeka*, when the U.S. Supreme Court ruled that segregation enforced by state (or local) officials violated the Fourteenth Amendment's guarantee that no state could deny any person the equal protection of the law. Later the *national* Civil Rights Act of 1964 outlawed discrimination in private employment and businesses serving the public.

Only now that national constitutional and legal guarantees of equal protection of the law are in place is it possible to reassess the true worth of federalism. Having established that federalism will not mean racial inequality, Americans are now free to explore the values of decentralized government.

In an attempt to block the admission of two African American students to the University of Alabama in 1963, Governor George Wallace barred the door with his body in the face of U.S. federal marshals. The tactic did not succeed, and the two students were admitted.

FIGURE 4-2 Original Constitutional Distribution of Powers

Under the Constitution of 1787, certain powers were delegated to the national government, other powers were shared by the national and state governments, and still other powers were reserved for state governments alone. Similarly, certain powers were denied by the Constitution to the national government, other powers were denied to both the national and state governments, and still other powers were denied only to state governments. Later amendments especially protected individual liberties.

POWERS GRANTED BY THE CONSTITUTION

NATIONAL GOVERNMENT Delegated Powers	NATIONAL AND STATE GOVERNMENTS Concurrent Powers	STATE GOVERNMENTS Reserved to the States
Military Affairs and Defense • Provide for the common defense (I-8). • Declare war (I-8). • Raise and support armies(I-8). • Provide and maintain a navy (I-8). • Define and punish piracies (I-8). • Define and punish offenses against the law of nations (I-8). • Provide for calling forth the militia to execute laws, suppress insurrections, and repel invasions (I-8). • Provide for organizing, arming, and disciplining the militia (I-8). • Declare the punishment of treason (III-3). **Economic Affairs** • Regulate commerce with foreign nations, among the several states, and with Indian tribes (I-8). • Establish uniform laws on bankruptcy (I-8). • Coin money and regulate its value (I-8). • Fix standards of weights and measures (I-8). • Provide for patents and copyrights (I-8). • Establish post offices and post roads (I-8). **Governmental Organization** • Constitute tribunals inferior to the Supreme Court (I-8, III-1). • Exercise exclusive legislative power over the seat of government and over certain military installations (I-8). • Admit new states (IV-3). • Dispose of and regulate territory or property of the United States (IV-3).	• Levy taxes (I-8). • Borrow money (I-8). • Contract and pay debts (I-8). • Charter banks and corporations (I-8). • Make and enforce laws (I-8). • Establish courts (I-8). • Provide for the general welfare (I-8).	• Regulate intrastate commerce. • Conduct elections. • Provide for public health, safety, and morals. • Establish local government. • Maintain the militia (National Guard). • Ratify amendments to the federal Constitution (V). • Determine voter qualifications (I-2).
"Implied" Powers • Make laws necessary and proper for carrying the expressed powers into execution (I-8).		**"Reserved" Powers** • Powers not delegated to national government nor denied to the States by the Constitution (X).

POWERS DENIED BY THE CONSTITUTION

NATIONAL GOVERNMENT	NATIONAL AND STATE GOVERNMENTS	STATE GOVERNMENTS
• Give preference to the ports of any state (I-9). • Impose a tax or duty on articles exported from any state (I-9). • Directly tax except by apportionment among the states on a population basis (I-9), now superseded as to income tax (Amendment XVI). • Draw money from the Treasury except by appropriation (I-9).	• Grant titles of nobility (I-9). • Limit the suspension of habeas corpus (I-9). • Issue bills of attainder (I-10). • Make ex post facto laws (I-10). • Establish a religion or prohibit the free exercise of religion (Amendment I). • Abridge freedom of speech, press, assembly, or right of petition (Amendment I). • Deny the right to bear arms protected (Amendment II). • Restrict quartering of soldiers in private homes (Amendment III). • Conduct unreasonable searches or seizures. (Amendment IV). • Deny guarantees of fair trials (Amendment V, Amendment VI, and Amendment VII). • Impose excessive bail or unusual punishments (Amendment VII). • Take life, liberty, or property without due process (Amendment V). • Permit slavery (Amendment XIII). • Deny life, liberty, or property without due process of law (Amendment XIV). • Deny voting because of race, color, previous servitude (Amendment XV), sex (Amendment XIX), or age if 18 or over (Amendment XXVI). • Deny voting because of nonpayment of any tax (Amendment XXIV).	**Economic Affairs** • Use legal tender other than gold or silver coin (I-10). • Issue separate state coinage (I-10). • Impair the obligation of contracts (I-10). • Emit bills of credit (I-10). • Levy import or export duties, except reasonable inspection fees, without the consent of Congress (I-10). • Abridge the privileges and immunities of national citizenship (Amendment XIV) • Make any law that violates federal law (Amendment VI). • Pay for rebellion against the United States or for emancipated slaves (Amendment XIV) **Foreign Affairs** • Enter into treaties, alliances, or confederations (I-10). • Make compact with a foreign state, except by congressional consent (I-10). **Military Affairs** • Issue letters of marque and reprisal (I-10). • Maintain standing military forces in peace without congressional consent (I-10). • Engage in war, without congressional consent, except in imminent danger or when invaded (I-10).

common defence and general welfare." After these specific grants of power comes the power "to make all laws which shall be necessary and proper for carrying into execution the foregoing powers, and all other powers vested by this Constitution in the government of the United States or in any department or officer thereof." This statement is generally known as the **Necessary and Proper Clause**, and it is the principal source of the national government's **implied powers**—powers not specifically listed in the Constitution but inferred from those that are.

National Supremacy   The delegated and implied powers, when coupled with the assertion of "national supremacy" (in Article VI), ensure a powerful national government. The **National Supremacy Clause** is very specific in asserting the supremacy of federal laws over state and local laws:

> This Constitution, and the laws of the United States which shall be made in pursuance thereof; and all treaties made, or which shall be made, under the authority of the United States, shall be the supreme law of the land; and the Judges in every state shall be bound thereby, any thing in the constitution or laws of any state to the contrary notwithstanding.

Concurrent and Reserved Powers   Despite broad grants of power to the national government, from the beginning of the Republic the states have retained considerable governing power. **Concurrent powers** are those recognized in the Constitution as belonging to *both* the national and state governments, including the power to tax and spend, make and enforce laws, and establish courts of justice. The Tenth Amendment reassured the states that "the powers not delegated to the United States . . . are reserved to the States respectively, or to the people." Through these **reserved powers**, the states generally retain control over property and contract law; criminal law; marriage and divorce; and the provision of education, highways, and social welfare activities. The states control the organization and powers of their own local governments. Finally, the states, like the federal government, retain the power to tax and spend for the general welfare.

Powers Denied to the States   The Constitution denies the states some powers in order to safeguard national unity. States are specifically denied the power to coin money, enter into treaties with foreign nations, interfere with the "obligation of contracts," levy taxes on imports or exports, or engage in war.

Powers Denied to the Nation and the States   The Constitution denies some powers to both national and state government—namely, the powers to abridge individual rights. The Bill of Rights originally applied only to the national government, but the Fourteenth Amendment, passed by Congress in 1866 and ratified by 1868, provided that the states must also adhere to fundamental guarantees of individual liberty.

State Role in National Government   The states are basic units in the organizational scheme of the national government. The House of Representatives apportions members to the states by population, and state legislatures draw up the districts that elect representatives. Every state has at least one member in the House of Representatives, regardless of its population. Each state elects two U.S. senators, regardless of its population. The president is chosen by the electoral votes of the states, with each state having as many electoral votes as it has senators and representatives combined. Finally, three-fourths of the states must ratify amendments to the U.S. Constitution.

Necessary and Proper Clause   Clause in Article I, Section 8, of the U.S. Constitution granting Congress the power to enact all laws that are "necessary and proper" for carrying out those responsibilities specifically delegated to it. Also referred to as the Implied Powers Clause.

implied powers   Powers not mentioned specifically in the Constitution as belonging to Congress but inferred as necessary and proper for carrying out the enumerated powers.

National Supremacy Clause   Clause in Article VI of the U.S. Constitution declaring the constitution and laws of the national government "the supreme law of the law" superior to the constitutions and laws of the states.

concurrent powers   Powers exercised by both the national government and state governments in the American federal system.

reserved powers   Powers not granted to the national government or specifically denied to the states in the Constitution that are recognized by the Tenth Amendment as belonging to the state governments. This guarantee, known as the Reserved Powers Clause, embodies the principle of American federalism.

"Look, the American people don't want to be bossed around by federal bureaucrats. They want to be bossed around by state bureaucrats."

THE EVOLUTION OF AMERICAN FEDERALISM

American federalism has evolved over 200 years from a state-centered division of power to a national-centered system of government. Although the original constitutional wordings have remained in place, power has flowed toward the national government since the earliest days of the Republic. American federalism has been forged in the fires of political conflicts between states and nation, conflicts that have usually been resolved in favor of the national government. Generalizing about the evolution of American federalism is no easy task. But let us try to describe broadly some major periods in the evolution of federalism, then look at five specific historical developments that had far-reaching impact on that evolution.

State-Centered Federalism, 1787–1868   From the adoption of the Constitution of 1787 to the end of the Civil War, the states were the most important units in the American federal system. It is true that during this period the legal foundation for the expansion of national power was being laid, but people looked to the states for resolving most policy questions and providing most public services. Even the issue of slavery was decided by state governments. The supremacy of the national government was frequently questioned, first by the Anti-Federalists (including Thomas Jefferson) and later by John C. Calhoun and other defenders of slavery.

Dual Federalism, 1868–1913   The supremacy of the national government was decided on the battlefields of the Civil War. Yet for nearly a half-century after that conflict, the national government narrowly interpreted its delegated powers, and the states continued to decide most domestic policy issues. The resulting pattern has been described as **dual federalism**. Under this pattern, the states and the nation divided most governmental functions. The national government concentrated its attention on the "delegated" powers—national defense, foreign affairs, tariffs, interstate commerce, the coinage of money, standard weights and measures, post office and post roads, and the admission of new states. State governments decided the important domestic policy issues—education, welfare, health, and criminal justice. The separation of policy responsibilities was once compared to a layer cake, with local governments at the base, state governments in the middle, and the national government at the top.[7]

Cooperative Federalism, 1913–1964   The distinction between national and state responsibilities gradually eroded in the first half of the twentieth century. American federalism was transformed by the Industrial Revolution and the development of a national economy; by the federal income tax in 1913, which shifted financial resources to the national government; and by the challenges of two world wars and the Great Depression. In response to the Great Depression of the 1930s, state governors welcomed massive federal public works projects under President Franklin D. Roosevelt's New Deal program. In addition, the federal government intervened directly in economic affairs, labor relations, business practices, and agriculture. Through its grants of money, the national government cooperated with the states in public assistance, employment services, child welfare, public housing, urban renewal, highway building, and vocational education.

This new pattern of federal-state relations was labeled **cooperative federalism**. Both the nation and the states exercised responsibilities for welfare, health, highways, education, and criminal justice. This merging of policy responsibilities

dual federalism   Early concept of federalism in which national and state powers were clearly distinguished and functionally separate.

cooperative federalism   Model of federalism in which national, state, and local governments work together exercising common policy responsibilities.

was compared to a marble cake: "As the colors are mixed in a marble cake, so functions are mixed in the American federal system."[8] Yet even in this period of shared national-state responsibility, the national government emphasized cooperation in achieving common national and state goals. Congress generally acknowledged that it had no direct constitutional authority to regulate public health, safety, or welfare. Instead, it relied primarily on its powers to tax and spend for the general welfare, providing financial assistance to state and local governments to achieve shared goals. Congress did not usually legislate directly on local matters.

Centralized Federalism, 1964–1980 Over the years, it became increasingly difficult to maintain the fiction that the national government was merely assisting the states to perform their domestic responsibilities. By the time President Lyndon B. Johnson launched the Great Society program in 1964, the federal government clearly had its own *national* goals. Virtually all problems confronting American society—from solid-waste disposal and water and air pollution to consumer safety, home insulation, noise abatement, and even "highway beautification"—were declared to be national problems. Congress legislated directly on any matter it chose, without regard to its *enumerated powers* and without pretending to render only financial assistance. The Supreme Court no longer concerned itself with the *reserved powers* of the states, and the Tenth Amendment lost most of its meaning. The pattern of national-state relations became **centralized federalism**. As for the cake analogies, one commentator observed, "The frosting had moved to the top, something like a pineapple upside-down cake."[9]

New Federalism, 1980–1985 **New federalism** was a phrase frequently applied to efforts to reverse the flow of power to Washington and to return responsibilities to states and communities. (The phrase originated in the administration of Richard M. Nixon, 1969–74, who used it to describe general revenue sharing—making federal grants to state and local governments with few strings attached.) New Federalism was popular early in the administration of President Ronald Reagan, who tried to reduce federal involvement in domestic programs and encourage states and cities to undertake greater policy responsibilities themselves. The result was that state and local governments were forced to rely more on their own sources of revenue and less on federal money. Still, centralizing tendencies in the American federal system continued.

centralized federalism
Model of federalism in which the national government assumes primary responsibility for determining national goals in all major policy areas and directs state and local government activity through conditions attached to money grants.

new federalism Attempts to return power and responsibility to the states and reduce the role of the national government in domestic affairs.

During the Great Depression of the 1930s, the massive public works projects sponsored by the federal government under President Franklin Roosevelt's New Deal reflected the emergence of cooperative federalism. Programs of the Work Progress Administration, like the one shown here, were responsible for the construction of buildings, bridges, highways, and airports throughout the country.

The Head Start program, part of Lyndon Johnson's Great Society program, was intended to help prepare poor preschool children for school. The Great Society legislation marked the beginning of the era of centralized federalism.

While the general public usually gave better marks to state and local governments than to the federal government, paradoxically that same public also favored greater federal involvement in policy areas traditionally thought to be state or local responsibilities (see *What Do You Think?* "Which Government Does the Best Job?").

Representational Federalism, 1985– Despite centralizing tendencies, it was still widely assumed prior to 1985 that the Congress could not directly legislate how state and local governments should go about performing their traditional functions. However, in its 1985 *Garcia v. San Antonio Metropolitan Transit Authority* decision, the U.S. Supreme Court appeared to remove all barriers to direct congressional legislation in matters traditionally reserved to the states. The case arose after Congress directly ordered state and local governments to pay minimum wages to their employees. The Court dismissed arguments that the nature of American federalism and the Reserved Powers Clause of the Tenth Amendment prevented Congress from directly legislating in state affairs. It said that the only protection for state powers was to be found in the states' role in electing U.S. senators, members of the U.S. House of Representatives, and the president. The court's ruling asserts a concept known as **representational federalism**.

No constitutional division of powers between states and nation is the idea behind representational federalism. Federalism is defined by the role of the states in electing members of Congress and the president. The United States is said to retain a federal system because its national officials are selected from subunits of government—the president through the allocation of Electoral College votes to the states and the Congress through the allocation of two Senate seats per state and the apportionment of representatives based on state population. Whatever protection exists for state power and independence must be found in the national political process, in the influence of state and district voters on their senators and representatives. In a strongly worded dissenting opinion in *Garcia*, Justice Lewis Powell argued that if federalism is to be retained, the Constitution—not Congress—should divide powers. "The states' role in our system of government is a matter of constitutional law, not legislative grace. . . . [This decision] today rejects almost 200 years of the understanding of the constitutional status of federalism."[10]

representational federalism
Assertion that no constitutional division of powers exists between the nation and the states but the states retain their constitutional role merely by selecting the president and members of Congress.

What Do You Think?

Which Government Does the Best Job?

Americans generally favor governments closer to home. Most surveys show that Americans have greater confidence in their state and local governments than in the federal government. But Americans are divided over whether they want the federal government or state and local governments to run programs in many *specific* policy areas.

CONFIDENCE
How much confidence do you have in these institutions?

THE FEDERAL GOVERNMENT

A great deal	4%
Quite a lot	11%
Some	47%
Very little	37%

YOUR STATE GOVERNMENT

A great deal	6%
Quite a lot	17%
Some	53%
Very little	23%

YOUR LOCAL GOVERNMENT

A great deal	11%
Quite a lot	20%
Some	46%
Very little	21%

POWER
Where should power be concentrated?

State government	64%
Federal government	26%

BEST JOB
Which level of government does the best job of dealing with the problems it faces?

Federal	14%
State	34%
Local	41%

NATIONAL INVOLVEMENT
Which level of government should run the following programs?

Service to immigrants

Federal	60%
State	15%
Local	6%

Welfare

Federal	40%
State	38%
Local	17%

Health care for the disabled, poor, and elderly

Federal	36%
State	28%
Local	18%

Opportunity for minorities

Federal	35%
State	30%
Local	28%

Air/water quality

Federal	35%
State	40%
Local	22%

Public education

Federal	21%
State	47%
Local	30%

Child care

Federal	16%
State	34%
Local	29%

Employment and job training

Federal	15%
State	59%
Local	24%

Law enforcement

Federal	15%
State	36%
Local	45%

Note: All figures are percentages of the U.S. public in national opinion surveys. Responses of "No opinion" and "Don't know" are not shown.

Source: General responses on confidence, power, and the running of specific programs from Hart and Teeter for the Council for Excellence in Government, *State Legislatures* (July/August 1995); responses on best job from Gallup/CNN/*USA Today* Poll reported in *The Polling Report* (February 10, 1997).

KEY DEVELOPMENTS IN AMERICAN FEDERALISM

Since the Constitution included nothing about the establishment of a national bank, controversy raged over Hamilton's proposal to establish one in 1790. Although this suggestion was acted on by Congress in 1791 and the first Bank of the United States was founded in Philadelphia, it took the Supreme Court's ruling in McCulloch v. Maryland *in 1819 to establish that Congress has certain implied powers and that national policies take precedence over state policies.*

McCulloch v. Maryland

Supreme Court decision (1819) broadly interpreting national power under the Necessary and Proper Clause of the Constitution and recognizing the supremacy of federal laws over state laws under the National Supremacy Clause.

During U.S. history, perhaps the most important developments in the evolution of federalism have been (1) the broad interpretation of the Necessary and Proper Clause by the Supreme Court, (2) the victory of the national government in the Civil War, (3) the establishment of a national system of civil rights based on the Fourteenth Amendment, (4) the growth of national power under the Interstate Commerce Clause, and (5) the growth of federal revenues as a result of the Sixteenth Amendment's authorization of the income tax.

McCulloch v. Maryland *and the Necessary and Proper Clause* Political conflict over the scope of national power is as old as the nation itself. In 1790 Secretary of the Treasury Alexander Hamilton proposed the establishment of a national bank. Congress acted on Hamilton's suggestion in 1791, establishing a national bank to serve as a depository for federal money and to aid the federal government in borrowing funds. Jeffersonians believed the national bank was a dangerous centralization of government. They objected that the power to establish the bank was nowhere to be found in the enumerated powers of Congress. Jefferson argued that Congress had no constitutional authority to establish a bank because a bank was not "indispensably necessary" to carrying out Congress's delegated functions.

Hamilton replied that Congress could derive the power to establish a bank from grants of authority in the Constitution relating to money, in combination with the clause authorizing Congress "to make all laws which shall be necessary and proper for carrying into execution the foregoing powers." Jefferson interpreted the word *necessary* to mean "indispensable," but Hamilton argued that the national government had the right to choose the manner and means of performing its delegated functions and was not restricted to employing only those means considered indispensable in the performance of its functions.

The question finally reached the Supreme Court in 1819, when the State of Maryland levied a tax on the national bank and the bank refused to pay it. In the case of ***McCulloch v. Maryland***, Chief Justice Marshall accepted the broader Hamiltonian version of the Necessary and Proper Clause: "Let the end be legitimate, let it be within the scope of the Constitution, and all means which are appropriate, which are plainly adopted to that end, which are not prohibited but consistent with the letter and the spirit of the Constitution, are constitutional."[11]

The *McCulloch* case firmly established the principle that the Necessary and Proper Clause gives Congress the right to choose its means in carrying out the enumerated powers of the national government. Because of this broad interpretation of the Necessary and Proper Clause, today Congress can devise programs, create agencies, and establish national laws on the basis of long chains of reasoning from the most meager phrases of the constitutional text. Hence many pundits have dubbed this clause the "Elastic Clause," since it seems to stretch to cover just about anything.

McCulloch also made a major contribution to the interpretation of the National Supremacy Clause. Chief Justice Marshall held that Maryland's tax on the national bank was unconstitutional because it interfered with a national activity being carried out under the Constitution and laws "made in pursuance thereof." In this case, Maryland's law conflicted with the federal law establishing the national bank.

In a long bloody war to establish national supremacy, the North's ultimate victory served to prove once and for all that the federal union cannot be dissolved.

From Marshall's time to the present, the National Supremacy Clause has been interpreted to mean that states cannot interfere with the operation of federal laws.

Secession and Civil War   The Civil War was the greatest crisis of the American federal system. Did a state have the right to oppose national law to the point of **secession**? In the years preceding the war, South Carolina's John C. Calhoun argued that the Constitution was a compact made by the *states* in their sovereign capacity rather than by the *people* in their national capacity. He contended that the federal government was an agent of the states, the states retained their sovereignty in this compact, and the federal government must not violate the compact, under the penalty of state **nullification** or even secession.

The question of secession was decided on Civil War battlefields between 1861 and 1865. Yet the states' rights doctrine and political disputes over the character of American federalism did not disappear with General Robert E. Lee's surrender at Appomattox. In addition to establishing that states cannot secede from the federal union, the Civil War led to three constitutional amendments clearly aimed at limiting state power in the interests of individual freedom. The Thirteenth Amendment eliminated slavery in the states; the Fifteenth Amendment prevented states from denying the vote on the basis of race, color, or previous enslavement; and the Fourteenth Amendment declared,

> No State shall make or enforce any law which shall abridge the privileges or immunities of citizens of the United States; nor shall any state deprive any person of life, liberty, or property, without due process of law; nor deny to any person within its jurisdiction the equal protection of the laws.

These amendments delegate to Congress the power to secure their enforcement. During the post–Civil War Reconstruction era (1866–76), Congress passed several

secession   Withdrawal of states or provinces from a larger political union; specifically, the unsuccessful attempt by eleven southern states to break away from the federal Union, an action that resulted in the Civil War.

nullification   Rejected interpretation of the Constitution that held that states could nullify within their borders an act of Congress that the states believed to be unconstitutional.

laws designed to enforce these amendments—laws guaranteeing the right to vote, providing remedies for the denial of rights by any person acting under "the color of law" (any public official), and prohibiting discrimination in public accommodation.[12] But after 1877, Congress gave up its efforts to reconstruct southern society, and the Supreme Court held important provisions of these laws unconstitutional.[13]

National Guarantees of Civil Rights   After World War I, the Supreme Court began to build a national system of civil rights based on the Fourteenth Amendment. The Court held that the Fourteenth Amendment prevented *states* from interfering with free speech, free press, or religious practices. Not until 1954, however, in the desegregation decision in *Brown v. Board of Education of Topeka*, did the Court begin to call for the full assertion of national authority on behalf of civil rights. When it decided that the Fourteenth Amendment prohibited the states from segregating the races in public schools, the Court was asserting national authority over longstanding practices in many of the states.

Despite the clear mandate of the Supreme Court, the southern states succeeded in avoiding all but token integration for more than ten years. Yet only occasionally did resistance take the form of **interposition**, that is, a state actively preventing the enforcement of a national law. Governor Orval Faubus called out the Arkansas National Guard to prevent a federal court from desegregating Little Rock Central High School in 1957. But this interposition ended quickly when President Dwight D. Eisenhower ordered the National Guard removed and sent units of the U.S. Army to enforce national authority. In 1962 President John F. Kennedy took a similar action when Governor Ross Barnett of Mississippi personally barred the entry of an African American student to the University of Mississippi despite a federal court order requiring his admission. These presidential actions reinforced the principle of national supremacy in the American political system.

The Expansion of Interstate Commerce   The growth of national power under the Interstate Commerce Clause of the Constitution is another important development in the evolution of American federalism. For many years, the U.S. Supreme Court narrowly defined *interstate commerce* to mean only the movement of goods and services across state lines. Until the late 1930s, it insisted that agriculture, mining, manufacturing, and labor relations were outside the reach of the delegated powers of the national government. However, when confronted with the Great Depression of the 1930s and Franklin Roosevelt's threat to add enough members to the Supreme Court to win favorable rulings, the Court yielded. It redefined *interstate commerce* to include any activity that "substantially affects" the national economy.[14] Indeed, the Court frequently approved of congressional restrictions on economic activities that had only very indirect effects on interstate commerce[15] (see *Up Close:* "Can the Federal Government Outlaw Guns in Schools?").

The Income Tax and Federal Grants   Even in the earliest days of the Republic, the national government was involved in public activities not specifically delegated to it by the Constitution. In the famous Northwest Ordinance of 1787, which provided for the governing of the territories west of the Appalachian Mountains, Congress made grants of land for the establishment of public schools. Then in the Morrill Land Grant Act of 1862, Congress provided grants of land to the states to promote higher education, especially agricultural and mechanical studies. Federal support for "A and M" or "land grant" universities continues today.

interposition   Argument, long rejected by the Supreme Court, that a state may place itself between its citizens and the national government to prevent the enforcement of a national law believed by the state to be unconstitutional.

Can the Federal Government Outlaw Guns in Schools?

Are there any limits at all to Congress's enumerated powers? Are there any areas of power truly *reserved* for the states only?

When a student, Alfonso Lopez, was apprehended at his Texas high school carrying a .38 caliber handgun, federal agents charged him with violating the federal Gun-Free School Zones Act of 1990. He was convicted and sentenced to six months in prison. His attorney appealed on the ground that it was beyond the constitutionally delegated powers of Congress to police local school zones; the Fifth Circuit Court agreed, and the case was appealed by the U.S. government to the Supreme Court in 1995.

On April 26, 1995, the U.S. Supreme Court issued its first opinion in more than sixty years that recognized a limit to Congress's power over interstate commerce and reaffirmed the Founders' notion that the federal government has only the powers enumerated in the U.S. Constitution. Chief Justice William H. Rehnquist, writing for the majority in the 5 to 4 decision, *U.S. v. Lopez*, even cited James Madison with approval: "The powers delegated by the proposed Constitution to the federal government are few and defined. Those which are to remain in the State governments are numerous and indefinite" (*Federalist Papers*, No. 45).

After reviewing virtually all of the key Commerce Clause cases in its history, the Court determined that an activity must *substantially affect* interstate commerce in order to be regulated by Congress. "The Court has never declared that Congress may use a relatively trivial impact on commerce as an excuse for broad general resolution of state and private activities." The U.S. government argued that the Gun-Free School Zones Act was a constitutional exercise of its interstate commerce power:

> [P]ossession of a firearm in a school zone may result in violent crime and that violent crime can be expected to affect the functioning of the national economy in two ways. First, the costs of violent crime are substantial and, through the mechanism of insurance, those costs are spread throughout the population. Second, violent crime reduces the willingness of individuals to travel to areas within the country that are perceived to be unsafe.

The Court rejected these arguments, holding that such tenuous reasoning would remove virtually all limits to federal power. "If we were to accept the Government's arguments, we are hard-pressed to posit any activity by an individual that Congress is without power to regulate." Moreover, "To uphold the Government's contentions here, we would have to pile inference upon inference in a manner that would bid fair to convert congressional activity under the Commerce Clause to a general police power of the sort retained by the states."

Voting with the majority were Justices Rehnquist (appointed to the Court by President Richard Nixon in 1971 and made Chief Justice by Reagan in 1986), Anthony M. Kennedy (Reagan, 1988), Sandra Day O'Connor (Reagan, 1981), Antonin Scalia (Reagan, 1986), and Clarence Thomas (Bush, 1991). Justice Stephen G. Breyer (Clinton, 1994) wrote a dissenting opinion and was joined by Justices John Paul Stevens (Ford, 1975), David Souter (Bush, 1990), and Ruth Bader Ginsburg (Clinton, 1993). Justice Breyer's dissent argued that the Court need only find that Congress has "a rational basis for finding a substantial connection between gun-related school violence and interstate commerce." He reasoned that "guns in schools significantly undermine the quality of education in our nation's classrooms" and that "education, although far more than a matter of economics, has long been inextricably intertwined with the nation's economy."

It is too early to judge the impact of this decision—whether it represents a return to traditional notions of enumerated powers of Congress and reserved powers of the state. The closeness of the vote, together with the decision's stark contrast to more than a half-century of case law on the Commerce Clause, provide no more than a hope that in the future the Supreme Court may move in the direction of strengthening federalism.

Source: U.S. v. Lopez, 63 L.W. 4343 (1995).

How Congress Set a National Drinking Age

Traditionally the *reserved* powers of the states included protection of the health, safety, and well-being of their citizens. The *enumerated* powers of Congress in the Constitution did *not* include regulating the sale and consumption of alcoholic beverages. Every state determined its own minimum age for drinking.

When the Twenty-sixth Amendment to the Constitution was passed in 1971, guaranteeing eighteen-year-olds the right to vote, most states lowered their minimum drinking age to eighteen. But by the early 1980s, some states had raised their minimums back to twenty-one in response to reports of teenage drinking and driving. Indeed, the National Transportation Safety Board reported that teenagers were statistically more likely to be involved in alcohol-related deaths than nonteenagers. The National Student Association, restaurant owners, and the beverage industry claimed that the selection of *all* teenagers for restriction was age discrimination. Whatever the merits of the argument, the issue was widely considered to be a *state* concern.

But the minimum drinking age became a national issue as a result of emotional appeals by groups such as Mothers Against Drunk Driving (MADD). Tragic stories told at televised committee hearings by grieving relatives of dead teenagers swept away federalism arguments. A few Congress members tried to argue that a national drinking age infringed on the powers of the state in a matter traditionally under state control. However, the new law did not directly mandate a national drinking age. Instead, it ordered the withholding of 10 percent of all federal highway funds from any state that failed to raise its minimum drinking age to twenty-one. States retained the rights to ignore the national minimum and give up a portion of their highway funds. (Congress used this same approach in 1974 in establishing a national 55-mile-per-hour speed limit.) Opponents of this device labeled it federal blackmail and a federal intrusion into state responsibilities. For some state officials, then, the issue was not teen drinking but rather the preemption of state authority.

Proponents of the legislation cited the *national* interest in setting a uniform minimum drinking age. They argued that protecting the lives of young people outweighed the states' interest in preserving their authority. Moreover, teens were crossing state lines to drink in states with lower drinking ages. New York, for example, with a minimum drinking age of nineteen, was attracting teenagers from Pennsylvania and New Jersey, where the drinking age was twenty-one. Reports of "bloody borders" were used to justify national action to establish a uniform drinking age. Although the Reagan White House had pledged to return responsibility to the states, it did not wish to offend the nation's mothers on such an emotional issue. Despite initial reservations, President Ronald Reagan supported the bill and signed it into law in 1984.

From a purely constitutional perspective, Congress simply exercised its power to spend money for the general welfare; it did not *directly* legislate in an area *reserved* to the states. Technically, states remain free to set their own minimum drinking age. Despite heated arguments in many state legislatures, all of the states adopted the twenty-one-year-old minimum national drinking age by 1990.

Appeals by groups such as Mothers Against Drunk Driving (MADD) helped overcome concerns that legislation effectively setting a national drinking age would infringe on state authority.

With the money provided to Washington by the passage of the Sixteenth (income tax) Amendment in 1913, Congress embarked on cash grants to the states. Among the earliest cash grant programs were the Federal Highway Act of 1916 and the Smith-Hughes Act of 1917 (vocational education). With federal money came federal direction. For example, states that wanted federal money for highways after 1916 had to create state highway departments and submit their highway plans for approval to the U.S. Bureau of Roads (now the Federal Highway Administration in the U.S. Department of Transportation). The federal government established uniform standards of construction and even a uniform road-numbering system (U.S. 1, U.S. 30, and so on).

Shortly after these programs began, the U.S. Supreme Court considered the claim that these federal grants were unconstitutional intrusions into areas "reserved" for the states. But the Court upheld grants as a legitimate exercise of Congress's power to tax and spend for the general welfare.[16]

MONEY AND POWER FLOW TO WASHINGTON

Over the years, power in the federal system has flowed to Washington because tax money has flowed to Washington. With its financial resources, the federal government has been able to offer assistance to state and local governments and thereby involve itself in just about every governmental function performed by these governments. Today the federal government is no longer one of *enumerated* or *delegated* powers. No activities are really *reserved* to the states. Through its power to tax and spend for the *general welfare*, the national government is now deeply involved in welfare, education, transportation, police protection, housing, hospitals, urban development, and other activities that were once the exclusive domain of state and local government (see *Up Close:* "How Congress Set a National Drinking Age").

Today grant-in-aid programs are the single most important source of federal influence over state and local activity. A **grant-in-aid** is defined as "payment of funds by one level of government (national or state) to be expended by another level (state or local) for a specified purpose, usually on a matching-funds basis (the federal government puts up only as much as the state or locality) and in accordance with prescribed standards of requirements."[17] No state or local government is *required* to accept grants-in-aid. Participation in grant-in-aid programs is voluntary. So in theory, if conditions attached to the grant money are too oppressive, state and local governments can simply decline to participate and pass up these funds.

More than one-fifth of all state and local government revenues currently come from federal grants. Federal grants are available in nearly every major category of state and local government activity. So numerous and diverse are these grants that there is often a lack of information about their availability, purpose, and requirements. In fact, federal grants can be obtained to preserve historic buildings, develop minority-owned businesses, aid foreign refugees, drain abandoned mines, control riots, and subsidize school milk programs. However, welfare (including cash benefits and food stamps), health (including Medicaid for the poor), and highways account for more than three-fourths of federal aid money (see Figure 4-3).

Thus many of the special projects and ongoing programs carried out today by state and local governments are funded by grants from the federal government. These funds have generally been dispersed as categorical grants, block grants, and general revenue-sharing grants:

grants-in-aid Payments of funds from the national government to state or local governments or from a state government to local governments for specific purposes.

- *Categorical Grant:* A grant for a specific, narrow project. The project must be approved by a federal administrative agency. Most federal aid money is distributed in the form of categorical grants. Categorical grants can be distributed on a project basis or a formula basis. Grants made on a project basis are distributed by federal administrative agencies to state or local governments that compete for project funds in their applications. Federal agencies have a great deal of discretion in selecting specific projects for support, and they can exercise direct control over the projects. Most categorical grants are distributed to state or local governments according to a fixed formula set by Congress.

- *Block Grant:* A grant for a general governmental function, such as health, social services, law enforcement, education, or community development. State and local governments have fairly wide discretion in deciding how to spend federal block grant money within a functional area. For example, cities receiving "community development" block grants can decide for themselves about specific neighborhood development projects, housing projects, community facilities, and so on. All block grants are distributed on a formula basis set by Congress. Federal administrative agencies may require reports and adherence to rules and guidelines, but they do not choose which specific projects to fund.

- *General Revenue Sharing (GRS):* Formerly a money grant for state or local governments to use as they saw fit, GRS gave state and local officials wide discretion in spending federal revenues. The program began in 1972 under President Richard M. Nixon's notion of New Federalism. GRS funds were allocated to state and local governments by a complex formula based on population, tax effort, and the income level of the population. General revenue sharing was ended in 1986 as the Reagan Administration (1981–89) sought to reduce the role of the federal government in domestic policy and reduce state and local government reliance on federal money.

Two modest steps toward decentralization took place under Reagan's New Federalism. First of all, general revenue sharing was ended. Although the original

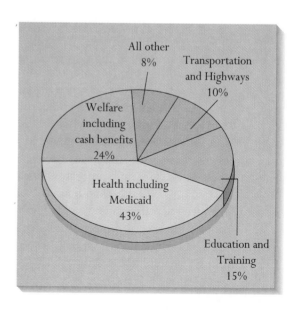

FIGURE 4-3 **Purposes of Federal Grants to State and Local Governments**

Over one-fifth of all state and local government revenues are derived from federal grants. Federal grants-in-aid to state and local governments are especially vital in the areas of health and welfare.

Source: *Budget of United States Government, 1998.*

FIGURE 4-4 State and Local Government Reliance on Federal Money

Under the New Federalism of the 1980s, federal money as a percentage of state and local revenue fell significantly. State and local governments had to rely more heavily on their own sources of revenue than on federal funds. In recent years, however, state and local reliance on federal money has begun to creep upward again.

idea behind GRS was to expand local powers by replacing many project grants with general revenues—and thus give local officials more policy discretion—the Reagan Administration argued that most GRS funds went to traditional local government functions that local taxpayers should fund themselves. Local officials did not spend so-called free money from Washington with the same care that they exercised when spending money extracted from their own voter-taxpayers. State and local officials lobbied long and hard in Congress to retain GRS, but the pressure of the federal deficit finally ended the program in 1986.

Second, block grants replaced many categorical grant programs, notably in health services, social services, community development, alcohol and drug abuse and mental health programs, and education. Actually, the struggle in Congress between those who favored categorical grants (mostly liberals and Democrats) and those who wanted to consolidate them into block grants (Reagan and the Republicans) ended in a draw, with many categorical grant programs remaining independent. Finally, the Reagan Administration was successful in slowing the overall growth of federal aid programs and thus reducing the dependence of state and local governments on federal money. During the 1980s the percentage of state-local revenue coming from the federal government actually declined (see Figure 4-4), only to begin its upward movement again in the 1990s.

COERCIVE FEDERALISM: PREEMPTIONS AND MANDATES

Traditionally, Congress avoided issuing direct orders to state and local governments. Instead, it sought to influence them by offering grants of money with federal rules, regulations, or "guidelines" attached. In theory at least, states and communities were free to forgo the money and ignore the strings attached to it. But increasingly Congress has undertaken direct regulation of areas traditionally reserved to the states and restricted state authority to regulate these areas. And it has issued direct orders to state and local governments to perform various services and comply with federal law in the performance of these services.

Federal Preemptions The supremacy of federal laws over those of the states, spelled out in the National Supremacy Clause of the Constitution, permits Congress to decide whether or not there is **preemption** of state laws in a particular field by federal law. In **total preemption**, the federal government assumes all regulatory powers in a particular field—for example, copyrights, bankruptcy, railroads, and airlines. No state regulations in a totally preempted field are permitted. **Partial preemption** stipulates that a state law on the same subject is valid as long as it does not conflict with the federal law in the same area. For example, the Occupational Safety and Health Act of 1970 specifically permits state regulation of any occupational safety or health issue on which the federal Occupational Safety and Health Administration (OSHA) has *not* developed a standard; but once OSHA enacts a standard, all state standards are nullified. A specific form of partial preemption called **standard partial preemption** permits states to regulate activities in a field already regulated by the federal government, as long as state regulatory standards are at least as stringent as those of the federal government. Usually states must submit their regulations to the responsible federal agency for approval; the federal agency may revoke a state's regulating power if that state fails to enforce the approved standards. For example, the federal Environmental Protection Agency (EPA) permits state environmental regulations that meet or exceed EPA standards.

Federal Mandates Federal **mandates** are direct orders to state and local governments to perform a particular activity or service or to comply with federal laws in the performance of their functions. Federal mandates occur in a wide variety of areas, from civil rights to minimum-wage regulations. Their range is reflected in some recent examples of federal mandates to state and local governments:

- *Age Discrimination Act, 1986:* Outlaws mandatory retirement ages for public as well as private employees, including police, fire fighters, and state college and university faculty.

- *Asbestos Hazard Emergency Act, 1986:* Orders school districts to inspect for asbestos hazards and remove asbestos from school buildings when necessary.

- *Safe Drinking Water Act, 1986:* Establishes national requirements for municipal water supplies; regulates municipal waste treatment plants.

- *Clean Air Act, 1990:* Bans municipal incinerators and requires auto emission inspections in certain urban areas.

- *Americans with Disabilities Act, 1990:* Requires all state and local government buildings to promote handicapped access.

- *National Voter Registration Act, 1993:* Requires states to register voters at driver's license, welfare, and unemployment compensation offices.

State and local governments frequently complain that the costs imposed on them by complying with such federal mandates are seldom reimbursed by Washington.

"Unfunded" Mandates Federal mandates often impose heavy costs on states and communities. When no federal monies are provided to cover these costs, the mandates are said to be **unfunded mandates**. Governors, mayors, and

---

preemption Total or partial federal assumption of power in a particular field, restricting the authority of the states.

total preemption Federal government's assumption of all regulatory powers in a particular field.

partial preemption Federal government's assumption of some regulatory powers in a particular field, with the stipulation that a state law on the same subject as a federal law is valid if it does not conflict with the federal law in the same area.

standard partial preemption Form of partial preemption in which the states are permitted to regulate activities already regulated by the federal government if the state regulatory standards are at least as stringent as the federal government's.

mandates Direct federal orders to state and local governments requiring them to perform a service or to obey federal laws in the performance of their functions.

unfunded mandates Mandates that impose costs on state and local governments (and private industry) without reimbursement from the federal government.

Liberals, Conservatives, and Federalism

From the earliest days of the Republic, American leaders and scholars have argued over federalism. Political interests that constitute a majority at the national level and control the national government generally praise the virtue of national supremacy. Political interests that do not control the national government but exercise controlling influence in one or more states generally see great merit in preserving the powers of the states.

In recent years, political conflict over federalism—over the division between national versus state and local responsibilities and finances—has tended to follow traditional "liberal" and "conservative" political cleavages. Generally, liberals seek to enhance the power of the *national* government because they believe people's lives can be changed—and bettered—by the exercise of national governmental power. The government in Washington has more power and resources than do state and local governments, which many liberals regard as too slow, cumbersome, weak, and unresponsive. Thus liberalism and centralization are closely related in American politics. The liberal argument for national authority can be summarized as follows:

- There is insufficient concern about social problems by state and local governments. The federal government must take the lead in civil rights, equal employment opportunities, care for the poor and aged, the provision of adequate medical care for all Americans, and the elimination of urban poverty and blight.

- It is difficult to achieve change when reform-minded citizens must deal with 50 state governments and more than 85,000 local governments. Change is more likely to be accomplished by a strong central government.

- State and local governments contribute to inequality in society by setting different levels of services in education, welfare, health, and other public functions. A strong national government can ensure uniformity of standards throughout the nation.

- A strong national government can unify the nation behind principles and ideals of social justice and economic progress. Extreme decentralization may favor local or regional "special" interests at the expense of the general "public" interest.

In contrast, conservatives generally seek to return power to *state and local* governments. Conservatives are skeptical about the "good" that government can do and believe that adding to the power of the national government is not an effective way of resolving society's problems. On the contrary, they argue that "government is the problem, not the solution." Excessive government regulation, burdensome taxation, and inflationary government spending combine to restrict individual freedom, penalize work and savings, and destroy incentives for economic growth. Government should be kept small, controllable, and close to the people. The conservative argument for state and local autonomy can be summarized as follows:

- Grass-roots government promotes a sense of self-responsibility and self-reliance.

- State and local governments can better adapt public programs to local needs and conditions.

- State and local governments promote participation in politics and civic responsibility by allowing more people to become involved in public questions.

- Competition between states and cities can result in improved public programs and services.

- The existence of multiple state and local governments encourages experimentation and innovation in public policy, from which the whole nation may gain.

There is no way to settle the argument over federalism once and for all. Debates about federalism are part of the fabric of American politics.

other state and local officials (including Bill Clinton, when he served as governor of Arkansas) have often urged Congress to stop imposing unfunded mandates on states and communities. Private industries have long voiced the same complaint. Regulations and mandates allow Congress to address problems while pushing the costs of doing so onto others. In 1995 Congress finally responded to these complaints by requiring that any bill imposing unfunded costs of $50 million or more on state and local governments (as determined by the Congressional Budget Office) would be subject to an additional procedural vote; a majority must vote to waive a prohibition against unfunded mandates before such a bill can come to the House or Senate floor. But this modest restraint is not likely to be very effective.

A DEVOLUTION REVOLUTION?

Controversy over federalism—what level of government should do what and who should pay for it—is as old as the nation itself (see *A Conflicting View:* "Liberals, Conservatives, and Federalism" on page 121). Beginning in 1995, with a new Republican majority in both houses of Congress and Republicans holding a majority of state governorships, debates over federalism were renewed. The new phrase was **devolution**—the passing down of responsibilities from the national government to the states (see *People in Politics:* "Christine Todd Whitman, On the Cutting Edge of Change in the States").

Reliance on Block Grants   Devolution may take the form of consolidating and transforming categorical grant-in-aid programs into block grants and giving the states greater flexibility in deciding how to spend these funds. This block grant approach is an extension of the Reagan era New Federalism, but Reagan never succeeded in getting more than 10 percent of total federal aid money transformed into block grants. In recent years Congress has debated the issue of transforming the two largest federal aid programs—welfare and Medicaid (health care for the poor)—into block grants.

Welfare Reform and Federalism   Welfare reform turned out to be the key to devolution. Bill Clinton once promised "to end welfare as we know it," but it was a Republican Congress in 1996 that did so. After President Clinton had twice vetoed welfare reform bills, he and Congress finally agreed to merge welfare reform with devolution by

- Establishing block grants with lump-sum allocations to the states for cash welfare payments.
- Granting the states broad flexibility in determining eligibility and benefit levels for persons receiving such aid.
- Allowing states to increase welfare spending if they choose to do so but penalizing states that reduce their spending for cash aid below 75 percent of their 1996 levels.
- Allowing states to deny additional cash payments for children born to women already receiving welfare assistance and allowing states to deny cash payments to parents under eighteen who do not live with an adult and attend school.
- Denying federal benefits to illegal aliens and allowing states to deny cash assistance, Medicaid, and social services to legal immigrants.

devolution   Passing down of responsibilities from the national government to the states.

Christine Todd Whitman, On the Cutting Edge of Change in the States

According to New Jersey's energetic governor, Christine Todd Whitman, "Time after time, Republicans and Democrats have found that things work better when states and communities set their *own* priorities, rather than being bossed around by bureaucrats in Washington." In her view, Washington should follow the lead of active Republican governors like herself—"toward less government, lower taxes, and less spending."

Christine Todd was raised in a political family; her father was Republican state chair in New Jersey. After earning a B.A. in political science from Wheaton College in Massachusetts in 1968, she worked on the staff of the Republican National Committee in Washington, where her job was to improve GOP contacts with students and minorities. Later she returned to New Jersey, married, and devoted much of her time to raising two daughters—"my greatest accomplishment."

In 1982 Christine Todd Whitman ran for and won her first elected office, to the Somerset County, New Jersey, Board of Chosen Freeholders (county commission). In 1988 the state's Republican governor appointed her president of the New Jersey Board of Public Utilities, where she developed a statewide reputation as a consumer advocate. In 1990 the state GOP needed a sacrificial lamb to fill the ballot space opposite the popular Democratic senator, Bill Bradley. But Whitman surprised both supporters and opponents by becoming a lion on the campaign trail and nearly upsetting the long-term incumbent. Indeed, Bill Bradley's close call in 1990 (Whitman won 49 percent of the vote) helped convince him to stay out of the presidential race in 1992 and allow Bill Clinton to win the Democratic nomination.

New Jersey's voters were upset by heavy tax increases imposed on them by Governor James Florio. Whitman pounded the tax-raising Democrat in newspaper columns and a radio talk show she hosted. When Florio came up for reelection in 1993, Whitman was well positioned to oust him with a hard-hitting campaign that featured an unlikely promise to reduce state income taxes by 30 percent.

Whitman's tax pledge was widely regarded as a political gimmick. But to the surprise of many observers, she delivered on her ambitious pledge, taking advantage of the state's economic recovery, privatizing several state functions, fighting the state's public employee unions, and making state government "smaller and smarter." Critics responded that many of her spending cuts were one-shot accounting ploys, that many state costs were shifted to local governments, that spending cuts hurt the poor, and that a state fiscal crisis would eventually develop. In the meantime, Whitman's success made her a national Republican star. But by 1997, New Jersey voters had shifted their attention from taxes to high auto insurance costs. Whitman was slow to respond to the new issue, and her support of abortion rights alienated some Republican voters. She was reelected by only a narrow margin, dimming her prospects of winning the vice presidential spot on the GOP ticket in 2000.

The Beginning of the End to Federal Entitlements? Since Franklin Delano Roosevelt's New Deal, with its federal guarantee of cash Aid to Families with Dependent Children (AFDC), low-income mothers and children had enjoyed a legal "entitlement" to welfare payments. But welfare reform, with its devolution of responsibility for determining eligibility to the states, ends this sixty-year federal entitlement. Today cash welfare benefit programs in the states receive federal funds (now labeled Temporary Assistance to Needy Families), but administration is left to the states. This major change in federal social welfare policy may become a model for future shedding of federal entitlement programs (see Chapter 17).

Politics in Cyberspace

Federalism

Many organizations and think tanks devote themselves to questions related to federalism. In addition, most states now maintain their own home pages with links to departments and agencies of state government.

The National Center of State Legislatures
http://www.ncsl.org

The National Center for State Legislatures provides links to the home pages of individual states as well as more general issues relating to federalism such as state-federal relations and devolution.

The Council of State Governements
http://www.csg.org

The Council of State Governments is another general source about state government and state-federal issues.

The Federalist Digest
http://www.federalistdigest.com

The *Federalist Digest*, a conservative online journal, provides links to the texts of many historical documents related to federalism, including the *Federalist Papers* and John Locke's second Treatise on Government.

The home pages of most states can be reached directly with the following URL format:

http://www.state.[state's postal code].US

To link to Alaska's home page, for example, you would enter www.state.AK.US; to Florida's home page, www.state.FL.US, and so forth.

SUMMARY NOTES

- The struggle for power between the national government and the states over two centuries has shaped American federalism today.

- Federalism is the division of power between two separate authorities, the nation and the state, each of which enforces its own laws directly on its citizens and neither of which can change the division of power without the consent of the other.

- American federalism was designed by the Founders as an additional protection for individual liberty by providing for the division and dispersal of power among multiple units of government.

- Federalism has also been defended as a means of increasing opportunities to hold public office, improving governmental efficiency, ensuring policy responsiveness, encouraging policy innovation, and managing conflict.

- However, federalism can also obstruct and frustrate national action. Narrow state interests can sometimes prevail over national interests or the interests of minorities within states. Segregation was long protected by theories of states' rights. Federalism

also results in uneven levels of public services through the nation.

- Power has flowed to the national government over time, as the original state-centered division of power has evolved into a national-centered system of government. Among the most important historical influences on this shift in power toward Washington have been the Supreme Court's broad interpretation of national power, the national government's victory over the secessionist states in the Civil War, the establishment of a national system of civil rights based on the Fourteenth Amendment, the growth of a national economy governed by Congress under its interstate commerce power, and the national government's accumulation of power through its greater financial resources.

- Federal grants to state and local governments have greatly expanded the national government's powers in areas previously regarded as *reserved* to the states. State and local governments have become increasingly dependent on federal money. President Ronald Reagan's New Federalism temporarily slowed the growth of federal aid.

- Federal grants are available for most state and local government activities, but welfare, health, and highways account for about three-fourths of these grants.

- Although Congress has generally refrained from directly legislating in areas traditionally *reserved* to the states, federal power in local affairs has grown as a result of federal rules, regulations, and guidelines established as conditions for the receipt of federal funds.

- The Supreme Court in its *Garcia* decision in 1985 removed all constitutional barriers to direct congressional legislation in matters traditionally reserved to the states. Establishing the principle of representational federalism, the Court said that states could defend their own interests through their representation in the national government.

- Representational federalism focuses on the role of the states in electing national officials—the president through the allocation of Electoral College votes to the states, the Senate through the allocation of two seats for each state, and the House through the appointment of representatives based on the state's population.

- Recent efforts at the "devolution" of federal responsibilities for welfare center on transforming federally determined individual entitlements to aid into block grants to the states.

SELECTED READINGS

BEER, SAMUEL H. *To Make a Nation: The Rediscovery of American Federalism.* Cambridge, Mass.: Harvard University Press, 1993. A historical account of the development of both federalism and nationalism in American political philosophy.

DYE, THOMAS R. *American Federalism: Competition among Governments.* Lexington, Mass.: Lexington Books, 1990. A theory of "competitive federalism" arguing that rivalries among governments improve public services while lowering taxes, restrain the growth of government, promote innovation and experimentation in public policies, inspire greater responsiveness to the preferences of citizen-taxpayers, and encourage economic growth.

ELAZAR, DANIEL J. *The American Partnership.* Chicago: University of Chicago Press, 1962. A study of the historical evolution of federalism, stressing the nation-state sharing of policy concerns and financing, from the early days of the Republic, and the politics behind the gradual growth of national power.

OSTRUM, VINCENT. *The Meaning of American Federalism.* San Francisco: ICS Press, 1991. A theoretical examination of federalism, setting forth the conditions for a self-governing rather than a state-governed society and arguing that multiple, overlapping units of government, with various checks on one another's power, provide a viable democratic system of conflict resolution.

PETERSON, PAUL E. *The Price of Federalism.* Washington, D.C.: Brookings Institution, 1995. Historical, theoretical, and empirical perspectives merged into a new, timely model of federalism that would allocate social welfare functions to the national government and education and economic development to states and communities.

PETERSON, PAUL E., BARRY C. RABE, and KENNETH K. WONG. *When Federalism Works.* Washington, D.C.: Brookings Institution, 1986. A well-developed argument that the national government is more effective in managing and financing "redistributional" policies and programs, whereas state and local governments are more effective in providing "developmental" policies and programs.

RIVLIN, ALICE M. *Reviving the American Dream.* Washington, D.C.: Brookings Institution, 1992. A comprehensive plan to restructure responsibilities between the national government and the states. The federal government would turn over to the states most of its programs in education, highways, economic development, and job training, along with common shared taxes to finance state and local efforts to revitalize the economy. The federal government would focus on welfare, Social Security, and health care, as well as international relations.

VAN HORN, CARL E. *The State of the States.* 3rd ed. Washington, D.C.: C.Q. Books, 1996. An assessment of the challenges facing state governments as a result of the devolution revolution.

✓ ASK YOURSELF ABOUT POLITICS

1 Should political leaders pay attention to public opinion polls when making decisions for the country?
Yes ⬭ No ⬭

2 Do you believe that your representative in Congress cares about your personal opinion on important issues?
Yes ⬭ No ⬭

3 Can you name the two U.S. senators from your state?
Yes ⬭ No ⬭

4 Is our government really legitimate when only about half the people vote in presidential elections?
Yes ⬭ No ⬭

5 Do you identify yourself with the same political party as your family?
Yes ⬭ No ⬭

6 Is it appropriate for religious leaders to try to influence how people vote?
Yes ⬭ No ⬭

7 Have you ever personally called or written to your representative in Congress?
Yes ⬭ No ⬭

8 Do you think you will ever run for public office yourself?
Yes ⬭ No ⬭

CHAPTER 5

OPINION AND PARTICIPATION
THINKING AND ACTING IN POLITICS

By thinking about politics and acting on your political opinions—voting, talking to friends, writing letters, joining organizations, attending meetings and rallies, contributing money, marching in demonstrations, or running for office yourself—you are participating in politics.

CHAPTER OUTLINE

Politics and Public Opinion

Socialization: The Origins of Political Opinions

Ideology and Opinion

Gender and Opinion

Race and Opinion

Policy and Opinion

Individual Participation in Politics

Securing the Right to Vote

Why Vote?

The Politics of Voter Turnout

Voters and Nonvoters

Nonvoting: What Difference Does It Make?

Protest as Political Participation

FEATURES

Up Close: Can We Believe the Polls?

Up Close: Abortion: The "Hot-Button" Issue

Compared to What? How "Exceptional" Is Opinion in America?

What Do You Think? College Students' Opinions

What Do You Think? Should We Mix Politics and Religion?

Compared to What? Voter Turnout in Western Democracies

Up Close: How to Run for Office

Politics in Cyberspace: Public Opinion

127

POLITICS AND PUBLIC OPINION

For most Americans, politics is *not* as interesting as football or basketball, or the sex lives of celebrities, or prime-time television entertainment. Although politicians, pollsters, and commentators frequently assume that Americans have formed opinions on major public issues, in fact, most have not given them very much thought. Nevertheless, **public opinion** commands the attention of politicians, the news media, and political scientists.

Public opinion is given a lot of attention in democracies because democratic government rests on the consent of the governed. The question of whether public opinion *should* direct government policy has confounded political philosophers for centuries. Edmund Burke, writing in 1790, argued that democratic representatives should serve the *interests* of the people, but not necessarily conform to their *will,* in deciding questions of public policy. In contrast, other political philosophers have evaluated the success of democratic institutions by whether or not they produce policies that conform to popular opinion.

Major shifts in public opinion in the United States generally translate into policy change. Both the president and Congress appear to respond over time to *general* public preferences for "more" or "less" government regulation, "more" or "less" government spending, "getting tough on crime," "reforming welfare," and so on.[1]

public opinion Aggregate of attitudes and opinions of individuals on a significant issue.

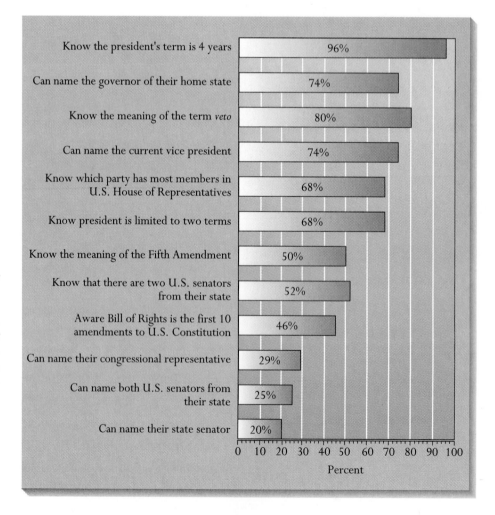

FIGURE 5-1 What Do Americans Know about Politics?

Politics is not the major interest of most Americans, and as a result, knowledge about the political system is limited. Less than one-third of the general public know the names of their representatives in Congress or their U.S. senators, and knowledge of specific foreign and domestic matters is even more limited.

Source: Data reported in Michael X. DelliCarpini and Scott Keeter, "The U.S. Public's Knowledge of Politics," *Public Opinion Quarterly 55* (May 1991): 583–612. Reprinted by permission of University of Chicago Press.

Statement	Percent
Know the president's term is 4 years	96%
Can name the governor of their home state	74%
Know the meaning of the term *veto*	80%
Can name the current vice president	74%
Know which party has most members in U.S. House of Representatives	68%
Know president is limited to two terms	68%
Know the meaning of the Fifth Amendment	50%
Know that there are two U.S. senators from their state	52%
Aware Bill of Rights is the first 10 amendments to U.S. Constitution	46%
Can name their congressional representative	29%
Can name both U.S. senators from their state	25%
Can name their state senator	20%

But as we see in this chapter, public opinion is often weak, unstable, ill informed, or nonexistent on *specific* policy issues. Consequently, elected officials have greater flexibility in dealing with these issues—but, at the same time, there is an increase in the influence of lobbyists, interest groups, reporters, commentators, and others who have direct access to policy makers. Moreover, the absence of well-formed public opinion on an issue provides interest groups and the media with the opportunity to influence policy indirectly by shaping popular opinion.

Politicians read the opinion polls. And even though many elected representatives claim that they exercise independent judgment about what is best for the nation in their decision making, we can be reasonably sure their "independent judgment" is influenced at least in part by what they think their constituents want. Public opinion commands the attention of politicians because even if only a small number of voters cast their ballots on the basis of the candidates' policy positions, those votes are still important. The cynical stereotype of the politician who reads the opinion polls before taking stands on the issues is often embarrassingly accurate.

All this attention to public opinion has created a thriving industry in public opinion polling and **survey research**. Polls have become a fixture of American political life (see *Up Close:* "Can We Believe the Polls?" on pages 130–31). But how much do Americans really think about politics? How informed, stable, and consistent is public opinion?

Knowledge Levels   Most Americans do not follow politics closely enough to develop well-informed opinions on many public issues (see Figure 5-1). Low levels of knowledge about government and public affairs make it difficult for people to form opinions on specific issues or policy proposals. Many opinion surveys ask questions about topics that people had not considered before being interviewed. Few respondents are willing to admit that they know nothing about the topic or have "no opinion." Respondents believe they should provide some sort of answer, even if their opinion was nonexistent before the question was asked. The result is that the polls themselves "create" opinions.[2]

The "Halo Effect"   Many respondents give "good citizen" or socially respectable answers, whether they are truthful or not, even to an anonymous interviewer. This **halo effect** leads to an *underestimation* of the true extent of prejudice, hatred, and bigotry. A very common example of the halo effect is the fact that people do not like to admit that they do not vote. Surveys regularly report higher percentages of people *saying* they voted in an election than the *actual* number of ballots cast (see Figure 5-2). Moreover, postelection surveys almost always produce higher percentages of people who say they voted for the winner than the actual vote tally for the winner. Apparently respondents do like to admit that they backed the loser.

survey research   Gathering of information about public opinion by questioning a representative sample of the population.

halo effect   Tendency of survey respondents to provide socially acceptable answers to questions.

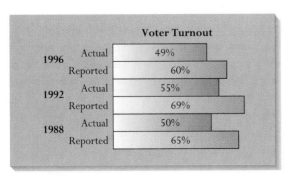

FIGURE 5-2   Halo Effects in Reported Presidential Voting

The halo effect in survey research—the tendency of respondents to give answers that are socially acceptable—is easily observable in voter surveys. Many more people claim to have voted than actually did so.

Sources: *General Social Surveys, 1994, 1996 (Chicago: National Opinion Research Center).*

Up Close

Can We Believe the Polls?

Survey research is a flourishing commercial enterprise. It is common in product marketing as well as in politics. There are national surveys, statewide surveys, and local market-area surveys. The national news media—notably CBS, NBC, ABC, and CNN television networks, the *New York Times* and the *Washington Post,* and *Time* and *Newsweek* magazines—regularly sponsor independent national surveys, especially during election campaigns. Major survey organizations—the American Institute of Public Opinion (Gallup), Louis Harris and Associates, National Opinion Research Center (NORC), the Roper Organization, National Election Studies (University of Michigan)—have been in business for a long time and have files of survey results going back many years. Political candidates also contract with private marketing and opinion research firms to conduct surveys in conjunction with their campaigns.

Public opinion surveys depend on the selection of a *random sample* of persons chosen in a way which ensures that every person in the *universe* of people about whom information is desired has an equal chance of being selected for interviewing. National samples, representative of all adults or all voters, usually include only about 1,000 persons. First, geographical areas (for example, counties or telephone area codes) that are representative of all such areas in the nation are chosen. Then residential telephone numbers are randomly selected within these areas. Once the numbers have been selected at random, the poll taker does not make substitutions but calls back several times if necessary to make contact so as not to bias the sample toward people who stay at home.

Even when random-selection procedures are closely followed, the sample may not be truly representative of the universe. But survey researchers can estimate the *sampling error* through the mathematics of probability. The sampling error is usually expressed as a percentage range—for example, plus or minus 3 percent—above and below the sample response within which there is a 95 percent likelihood that the universe response would be found if the entire universe were questioned. For example, if 65 percent of the survey respondents favor the death penalty and the sampling error is calculated at plus or minus 3 percent, then we can say there is a 95 percent probability that a survey of the whole population (the universe) would produce a response of between 62 and 68 percent in favor of the death penalty.

The wording and sequence of the questions asked in any format are more an art than a science and can often determine the outcome of the poll. Indeed, "loaded" or "leading" questions are often used by *un*professional pollsters simply to produce results favorable to their side of an argument. Professional pollsters strive for questions that are clear and precise, easily understood by the respondents, and as neutral and unbiased as possible. Nevertheless, because all questions have a potential bias, it is often better to examine *changes over time* in response to identically worded questions. Perhaps the best-known continuing question in public opinion polling is the presidential approval rating: "Do you approve or disapprove of the way _____ is handling his job as president?" Changes over time in public response to this question alert scholars, commentators, and presidents themselves to their public standing (see Chapter 11).

Weakly held opinions are more likely to change than strongly held opinions. Political commentators sometimes say that a particular candidate's support is "soft," meaning his or her supporters are not very

Inconsistencies Because so many people hold no real opinion on political issues, the wording of a question frequently determines their response. People respond positively to positive phrases (for example, "helping poor people," "improving education," "cleaning up the environment") and negatively to negative phrases (for example, "raising taxes," "expanding governmental power," "restricting choice").

The wording of questions, combined with weak or nonexistent opinion, often produces inconsistent responses. For example, when asked whether they agreed or disagreed with the statement that "people should have the right to purchase a sexu-

intense in their commitment, and, therefore, the polls could swing quickly away from the candidate.

Finally, widely reported news events may change public opinion very rapidly. A survey can only measure opinions at the time it is taken. A few days later public opinion may change, especially if major events are receiving heavy television coverage. Some political pollsters conduct continuous surveys until election night in order to catch last-minute opinion changes.

A common test of the accuracy of survey research is the comparison of the actual vote in presidential elec-tions to the predictions made by the major polls (see figure). Discrepancies between the actual and predicted vote percentages are sometimes used as rough measures of the validity of surveys. Most forecasts have been fairly accurate. The larger-than-usual errors in 1996 election predictions have been attributed to the failure of the major polls to accurately identify respon-dents who would actually vote on election day. It turned out that Clinton supporters were somewhat less likely to vote than Dole supporters. Hence the polls overestimated Clinton's vote percentage.

Forecasting Errors by Major Polls in Presidential Elections

	Predicted Winner	Actual Winner	Margin of Error
1996	CLINTON	CLINTON	**1996**
USA Today/CNN	52%	49%	3%
CBS/NY Times	53%		4%
1992	CLINTON	CLINTON	**1992**
USA Today/CNN	44%	43%	1%
Gallup	44%		1%
1988	BUSH	BUSH	**1988**
USA Today/CNN	55%	54%	1%
CBS/NY Times	53%		1%
1984	REAGAN	REAGAN	**1984**
Gallup	59.3%	59%	0.3%
CBS/NY Times	60.9%		1.9%
ABC/Washington Post	59.3%		0.3%

60 50 40 30 20 10 0   0 10 20 30 40 50 60

Percent

ally explicit book, magazine, or movie, if that's what they want to do," an over-whelming 80 percent endorsed the statement. However, when the same respondents were also asked whether they agreed with the opposite statement that "community authorities should be able to prohibit the selling of magazines or movies they consider to be pornographic," 65 percent approved of this view as well.[3]

Instability   Many people answer survey questions impulsively without very seri-ous consideration. They may hold fairly fixed attitudes—liberal or conservative, for

Abortion: The "Hot-Button" Issue

Although public opinion may be weak or nonexistent on many policy questions, there are a few "hot-button" issues in politics—issues on which virtually everyone has an opinion and many people feel very intensely about.

Abortion is one such highly sensitive issue. Both *pro-choice* proponents of legalized abortion and *pro-life* opponents claim to have public opinion on their side. *Interpretation* of the poll results becomes a political activity itself. Consider, for example, responses to the *general* question posed in the graph pictured here.

Pro-choice forces interpret these results as over-whelming support for legalized abortion; pro-life

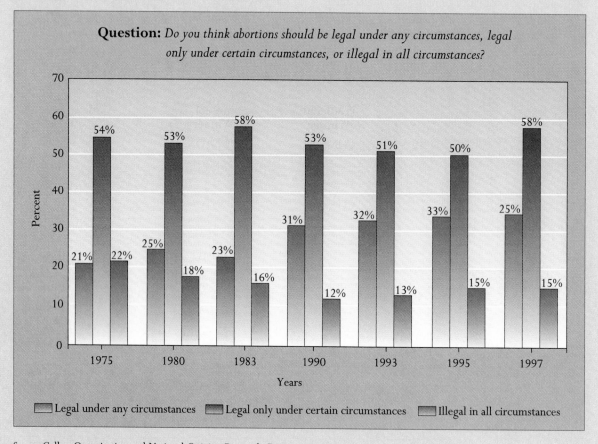

Question: *Do you think abortions should be legal under any circumstances, legal only under certain circumstances, or illegal in all circumstances?*

Legal under any circumstances ■ Legal only under certain circumstances ■ Illegal in all circumstances

Source: Gallup Organization and National Opinion Research Center

example—but they do not bother to mentally consult their attitude when responding to a question. This lack of thought often results in an apparent instability of opinions—people giving contradictory responses to the same question when asked it at different times.[4]

salient issues Issues about which most people have an opinion.

Salience People are likely to think about issues that receive a great deal of attention in the mass media—television, newspapers, magazines. **Salient issues** are those that people think about most—issues on which they hold stronger and more

commentators interpret these results as majority support for restricting abortion. Indeed, when the question sets forth *specific restrictions on* abortion, public opinion appears divided (see graph below).

In short, most Americans appear to want to keep some abortions legal but they believe that government should place certain restrictions on the practice.

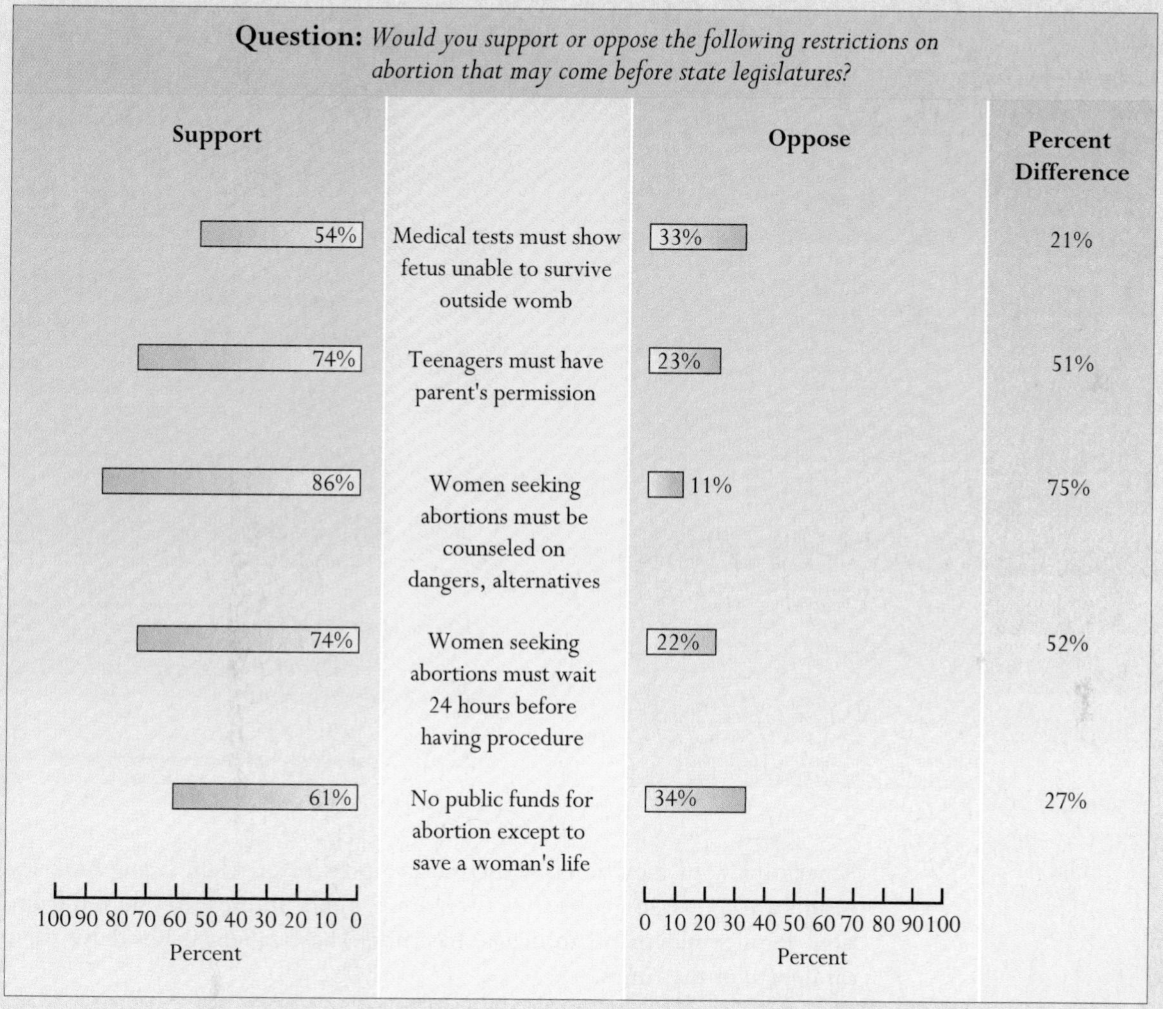

Question: *Would you support or oppose the following restrictions on abortion that may come before state legislatures?*

Support		Oppose	Percent Difference
54%	Medical tests must show fetus unable to survive outside womb	33%	21%
74%	Teenagers must have parent's permission	23%	51%
86%	Women seeking abortions must be counseled on dangers, alternatives	11%	75%
74%	Women seeking abortions must wait 24 hours before having procedure	22%	52%
61%	No public funds for abortion except to save a woman's life	34%	27%

100 90 80 70 60 50 40 30 20 10 0
Percent

0 10 20 30 40 50 60 70 80 90 100
Percent

stable opinions. These are issues that people feel relate directly to their own lives, such as abortion (see *Up Close:* "Abortion: The 'Hot-Button' Issue"). Salient issues are, therefore, more important in politics.

Salient issues change over time. In general, during recessions the most salient issue is "Jobs, Jobs, Jobs!"—that is, unemployment and the economy. During inflationary periods, the issue is "the high cost of living." During wartime, the war itself becomes the public's principal concern. A gasoline shortage can turn public concern toward energy issues. The Gallup Opinion Organization regularly asks

FIGURE 5-3 What's to Worry About?

Public concerns shift over time, as indicated by changing responses to the question, "What is the most important problem facing America?" In recent years, Americans have been alternately concerned about the economy, unemployment, drugs, and crime.

Source: Gallup opinion polls.

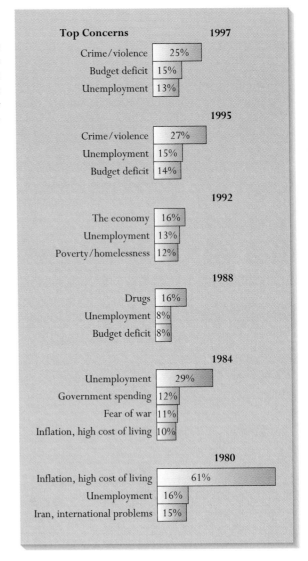

Americans what they think is "the most important problem facing America." The results are shown in Figure 5-3. Over time, public interest has shifted from inflation, to unemployment, to drugs, to crime. These salient issues drive the political debate of the times.

SOCIALIZATION: THE ORIGINS OF POLITICAL OPINIONS

Where do people acquire their political opinions? Political **socialization** is the learning of political values, beliefs, and opinions (see *Compared to What?* "How 'Exceptional' Is Opinion in America?" for a look at the results of different socialization patterns in other lands). It begins early in life when a child acquires images and attitudes toward public authority. Preschool children see "police officer" and "president" as powerful yet benevolent "helpers." These figures—police officer and president—are usually the first recognized sources of authority above

socialization Learning of values, beliefs, and opinions.

the parents who must be obeyed. They are usually positive images of authority at these early ages:

Q: What does the policeman do?

A: He catches bad people.[5]

Even the American flag is recognized by most U.S. preschoolers, who pick it out when asked, "Which flag is your favorite?" These early positive perceptions about political figures and symbols may later provide *diffuse support* for the political system—a reservoir of goodwill toward governmental authority that lends legitimacy to the political order.

Family   The family is the first agent of socialization, and some family influences appear to stay with people over a lifetime. Children in the early school grades (3 to 5) begin to identify themselves as Republicans or Democrats. These childhood party identifications are almost always the same as those of the parents. Indeed, parent-child correspondence in party identification may last a lifetime; in one study, 66 percent of adult children who identified themselves as Democrats had parents who were Democrats, and 51 percent of the Republicans had parents with the same political identification.[6] Even the children who abandoned the party of their parents tended to become independents rather than identify with the opposition party. When parents disagree on party (one a Democrat, the other a Republican), the child is more likely to adopt the mother's party identification, although many cross-pressured children become independents. However, party identification appears to be more easily passed on from parent to child than specific opinions on policy questions. Perhaps the reason is that parental party identifications are known to children, but few families conduct specific discussions of policy questions.

School   Political revolutionaries once believed that the school was the key to molding political values and beliefs. After the communist revolutions in Russia in 1917 and China in 1949, the schools became the focus of political indoctrination of the population. Indeed, after World War II, U.S. military occupation forces "de-Nazified" schools in Germany and also introduced democratic principles into Japanese schools. Today political battles rage over textbooks, teaching methods, prayer in schools, and other manifestations of politics in the classroom. But no strong evidence indicates a causal relationship between what is taught in the schools and the political attitudes of students.

Certainly the schools provide the factual basis for understanding government— how the president is chosen, the three branches of government, how a law is passed.

PEANUTS reprinted by permission of UFS, Inc.

Compared to What?

How "Exceptional" Is Opinion in America?

Do Americans differ much from Europeans in their social and political values? The American political culture places great value on individual liberty, limited government intervention in people's personal lives, equality of opportunity, and individual responsibility for one's own fate in life (see Chapter 2). The strong American commitment to these values has been labeled American "exceptionalism," suggesting that people in other nations, including the Western European democracies, are not as strongly committed to these values as are people in the United States.

The values of the political culture influence opinion on many specific issues. If the American political culture is truly "exceptional," Americans should differ significantly from Europeans on questions dealing with individual liberty, social mobility, and the role of government in society. And, indeed, cross-national survey research results do show significant differences between Americans and Europeans on these issues (see table).

Americans believe strongly in an "opportunity" society where people get ahead by their own efforts. Other peoples are more committed to a "security" society where the government assumes principal responsibility for their well-being. For example, Americans are much less likely to agree that the role of government is to reduce income differences between people or to "provide everyone with a guaranteed basic income." Americans are less likely than others (with the possible exception of the independent-minded Australians) to believe that government "should provide a job for everyone who wants one." Americans are not even sure they want the government to protect them by requiring seat belts or prohibiting smoking, another indication of our preference for letting individuals determine their own fate in life. Finally, Americans, more than other free peoples, believe in the possibility of upward social mobility—"improving our standard of living."

	"Government should reduce differences between high and low incomes"	"Government should provide everyone with a guaranteed basic income"	"Government should provide a job for everyone who wants one"	"Wearing seat belts should be required by law"	"In my country, people like me have a good chance of improving our standard of living"
United States	29%	21%	45%	49%	72%
Australia	44	38	40	92	61
Switzerland	43	43	50	NA*	59
Great Britain	64	61	59	80	37
Netherlands	65	50	75	NA	26
Germany	61	56	77	82	40
Austria	81	57	80	81	47
Italy	82	67	82	81	45
Hungary	80	79	92	NA	33

*NA = not asked

Source: Surveys for the International Social Survey Program by National Opinion Research Center (United States); by Social and Community Planning Research, London (Great Britain); by Zentrum for Umfragen, Methoden, und Analysen, Mannheim (West Germany); by Ricerca Sociale e di Marketing, Milan (Italy); by Institute für Soziologie, Graz University (Austria); by Australian National Research School of Social Sciences. Reported in *American Enterprise* 1 (March/April 1990): 115–17.

But even this elemental knowledge is likely to fade if not reinforced by additional education or exposure to the news media or discussion with family or peers.

The schools *try* to inculcate "good citizenship" values, including support for democratic rules, tolerance toward others, the importance of voting, and the legitimacy (rightfulness) of government authority. Patriotic symbols and ritu-

TABLE 5-1

Education and Tolerance

	Percentage Responding "Yes" (by highest degree completed)				
	No High School	High School	Junior College	College Degree	Total
If such a person wanted to make a speech in your community, should he be allowed to speak?					
Atheist	52%	73%	78%	86%	73%
Racist	47	61	60	73	61
Homosexual	59	79	84	91	79
Should a book that . . . be allowed to remain in a public library?					
. . . was against churches and religion . . .	47%	69%	75%	81%	69
. . . said black people are inferior . . .	49	65	67	75	66
. . . favored homosexuality . . .	45	69	72	83	68
Should such a person be allowed to teach in a college or university?					
Atheist	31%	50%	54%	68%	52%
Racist	33	41	45	52	42
Homosexual	47	71	79	83	71

Source: General Social Survey, 1996 (Chicago: National Opinion Research Center, 1997).

als abound in the classroom—the flag, the Pledge of Allegiance—and students are taught to respect the institutions of government. Generally the younger the student, the more positive the attitudes expressed toward political authority.[7] Yet despite the efforts of the schools to inspire support for the political system, distrust and cynicism creep in during the high school years. Although American youth retain a generally positive view of the political system, they share with adults increasing skepticism toward specific institutions and practices. During high school, students acquire some ability to think along liberal-conservative dimensions. The college experience appears to produce a "liberalizing" effect: College seniors tend to be more liberal than entering freshmen (see *What Do You Think?* "College Students' Opinions" on pages 138–39). But over the years following graduation, liberal views tend to moderate.

Why aren't the schools more effective in socializing students to democratic values? One explanation focuses on "the hidden curriculum," the decidedly authoritarian structure of the classroom and the school itself. The school may teach individual participation in decision making, majority rule, respect for the rights of others, and political equality, yet the school itself is hierarchically organized, students do not elect their teachers or decide the curriculum, and they are not equal in power to the teacher or principal. Hence it is argued that this hidden curriculum undermines democratic values. Students are aware of the difference between what is taught and what is practiced.

Although no direct evidence indicates that the schools can inculcate democratic values, people with more education tend to be more tolerant than those with less education and to be generally more supportive of the political system (see Table 5-1). This pattern suggests that the effects of schooling are gradual and subtle.

Church Religious beliefs and values may also shape political opinion. *Which* religion an individual identifies with (for example, Protestant, Catholic, Jewish)

College Students' Opinions

College students' opinions today appear to be somewhat more conservative than they were a generation ago, although student opinion varies with the nature of the issue. Students today take a tougher line toward crime and drugs: They support the death penalty, believe the courts are too lenient with criminals, and oppose legalization of marijuana. The students of the 1970s confronted an unpopular war in Vietnam, faced a military draft, and were more likely to experiment with drugs and alternative lifestyles. Today's students confront greater economic competition and increased educational requirements for employment. They are more concerned with their financial future than students were a generation ago and are less interested in "developing a meaningful philosophy of life" (see graph).

However, college students remain somewhat more liberal than the general population. Moreover, college seniors and graduate students are more liberal than first-year students; students at prestigious Ivy League universities are more liberal than students at state universities and community colleges; and students in humanities and social sciences are more liberal than students in engineering, physical sciences, and business. Over the years following graduation, many of these liberal predispositions tend to moderate.

The "liberalizing" effect of college may come about because of exposure to liberal professors (see *Up Close*: "Ideology on the Campus: Students versus Professors" in Chapter 2). It may also be the result of greater exposure to the political culture. College students read more newspapers and magazines than nonstudents, watch more television news, and see and hear more political activity on campus. They become aware of various reform movements—for example, civil rights, the women's movement, environmentalism—that noncollege people of the same age have little knowledge of. This "enlightenment" may directly promote liberal views: Even students who do not identify themselves with these movements learn what is socially acceptable and currently fashionable in educated circles.

affects public opinion. So does *how important* religion is in the individual's life. It is difficult to explain exactly how religion affects political values, but we can observe differences in the opinions expressed by Protestants, Catholics, and Jews; by people who say their religious beliefs are strong versus those who say they are not; and between fundamentalists (those who believe in a literal interpretation of the Bible) and nonfundamentalists. Religion shapes political attitudes on a variety of issues, including abortion, drugs, the death penalty, homosexuality, and prayer in public schools[8] (see Table 5-2). Religion also plays a measurable role in political ideology (see *What Do You Think?* "Should We Mix Politics and Religion?").

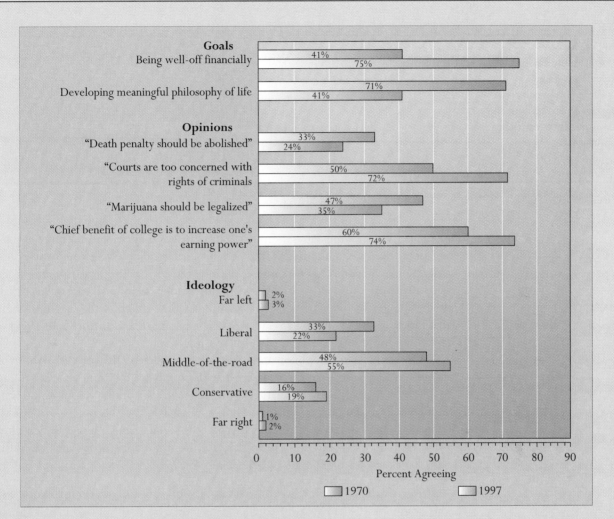

Goals
Being well-off financially — 41% / 75%

Developing meaningful philosophy of life — 71% / 41%

Opinions
"Death penalty should be abolished" — 33% / 24%

"Courts are too concerned with rights of criminals" — 50% / 72%

"Marijuana should be legalized" — 47% / 35%

"Chief benefit of college is to increase one's earning power" — 60% / 74%

Ideology
Far left — 2% / 3%

Liberal — 33% / 22%

Middle-of-the-road — 48% / 55%

Conservative — 16% / 19%

Far right — 1% / 2%

Percent Agreeing

0 10 20 30 40 50 60 70 80 90

☐ 1970   ☐ 1997

Source: The American Freshman: National Norms for Fall 1972, 1997 (American Council on Education & UCLA), as reported in the *Chronicle of Higher Education,* January 1998.

Generational and Life-Cycle Effects Age group differences in opinion occur on some important issues. This generation gap may be a product of **generational effects**—historical events that affect the views of those who lived through them. For example, the "Depression generation"—those persons who grew up during the Great Depression of the 1930s—may give greater support to government income-security programs because of this experience. The "baby boomers"—those persons who were born in the high-birthrate years following World War II (1946–64)—experienced the civil rights movement, the war in Vietnam, and changes in sexual morality, all of which may affect their views on many social issues.

generational effects Historical events that affect the views of those who lived through them.

TABLE 5-2

Religion and Public Opinion

Opinion	Affiliation			Faith		Belief That the Bible Is		
	Protestant	Catholic	Jew	Strong	Not Very Strong	Literal Word of God	Inspired by God	Book of Fables
Abortion for any reason should be legal	40%	33%	94%	28%	55%	29%	44%	74%
Legalize marijuana	19	21	41	13	29	12	22	43
Support death penalty	75	76	70	68	80	69	79	72
Remove book that favored homosexuality from library	34	22	6	36	23	43	20	17
Support prayer in public school	67	55	14	70	53	77	55	33

Source: General Social Survey, 1996 (Chicago: National Opinion Research Center, 1997).

The large size of the baby-boom generation makes their views especially important in politics. On some issues it is possible to identify a distinctive baby-boom generational viewpoint. For example, with regard to abortion, baby boomers are generally more supportive of legal abortion under various circumstances than either younger or older persons. However, over time much of the distinctiveness of the baby-boom generation has faded. As baby boomers have matured, their views have fitted more into common patterns of opinion.

A generation gap in opinion may also be a product of **life-cycle effects**— changes in life circumstances associated with age that affect one's views. Young people are expected to be idealistic. As they age and take on the responsibilities of raising children, holding a job, and paying a mortgage, they become more practical in outlook. The elderly are less amenable to social change, especially changes in morals. There is some limited evidence of life-cycle effects, but they are difficult to sort out from generational effects.[9]

Media Influence   Television is the major source of political information for Americans. More than two-thirds report that they receive "all or most" of their news from television, making newspapers, magazines, books, and radio secondary to television as a source of political information (see Chapter 6). Moreover, Americans rate television the "most believable" channel of communication.

But the effect of television on opinion is not really in persuading people to take one side of an issue or another. Instead, the principal effect is in *setting the agenda* for thinking and talking about politics. Television does not tell people *what* to think, but it does tell them what to think *about* (see Chapter 6, "Mass Media: Setting the Political Agenda"). Television coverage determines matters of general public concern. Without coverage, the general public would not know about, think about, or discuss most events, personalities, and issues. Media attention creates issues, and the amount of attention given an issue determines its importance.

The media can create new opinions more easily than they can change existing ones. The media can often suggest how we feel about new events or issues—those about which we have no prior feelings or experiences. And the media can reinforce values and attitudes we already hold. But there is very little evidence to indicate that the media can change existing values. (We return to the discussion of media power in Chapter 6.)

life-cycle effects   Changes in life circumstances associated with age that affect one's views.

What Do You Think?

Should We Mix Politics and Religion?

The United States is one of the most religious societies in the world, in terms of the proportion of the people who say they believe in God (96 percent), who say God has guided them in making decisions in their life (77 percent), who say they belong to an organized religion (70 percent), who say that religion is "very important" in their own life (60 percent), and who say they attend church at least once a month (58 percent). Most Americans believe religion should play an important role in addressing "all or most of today's problems" (64 percent), and they lament that religion is "losing its influence" in American life (69 percent).

At the same time, however, most Americans are concerned about religious leaders exercising influence in political life. Most respondents say it is "not appropriate for religious leaders to talk about their political beliefs as part of their religious activities (61 percent), "religious leaders should not try to influence how people vote in elections" (64 percent), and "religious groups should *not* advance their beliefs by being involved in politics and working to affect policy" (54 percent).

Approximately 40 percent of Americans describe themselves as "born-again or evangelical Christians." They are much more likely than those who do not describe themselves in these terms (54 percent) to be Republican and conservative in their politics. Indeed, fundamentalist Christians, sometimes labeled as the "Christian right," "Christian conservatives," or "religious right," have become an important core constituency of the Republican Party. Their political strength centers on their grass-roots activism—their willingness to work hard as campaign workers, organizers, and fund raisers. Perhaps their most effective tactic in recent elections has been to produce and distribute nonpartisan "voter guides" that compare the candidates on issues of interest to them, such as abortion, prayer in public schools, and homosexuality. These guides do not endorse any candidates by name, but readers can easily determine who best represents the views of religious conservatives. Often these guides are distributed in churches on the Sunday before Election Day.

But the political influence of Christian conservatives is limited by the American public's widespread view that religion and politics should not be mixed. Many church-goers as well as non–church-goers resent religious messages that appear in the political arena. Religious broadcaster Pat Robertson fared badly as a candidate in the Republican presidential primaries in 1988. Moreover, it is difficult for "true believers" to reach out and form political alliances with groups that do not fully share their views. Fundamentalist Protestant groups have largely failed to unite with black fundamentalists or with Orthodox Catholics or Orthodox Jews. Social conservatives often find themselves at odds with economic conservatives, who often do not share their social issue agenda. Nevertheless, fundamentalist Christian groups have exercised some influence in state elections.

Conservative

Born-again	57%
All others	24%

Liberal

Born-again	8%
All others	23%

Moderate

Born-again	35%
All others	52%

Source: Percentages from various Gallup opinion polls, reported in *American Enterprise* 5 (September/October 1994): 90–93, and in *Gallup Poll Monthly,* February 1995; voter research surveys, 1992, reported in *American Enterprise* 5 (September/October 1994): 95; case studies in South Carolina, Oklahoma, Virginia, Iowa, and Minnesota, reported in John C. Green, "The Christian Right in the 1994 Elections: A View from the States," *P.S.: Political Science and Politics* 28 (March 1995): 5–23.

IDEOLOGY AND OPINION

Ideology helps to shape opinion. Many people, especially politically interested and active people, approach policy questions with a fairly consistent and integrated set of principles—that is, an *ideology* (see Chapter 2). Liberal and conservative ideas about the proper role of government in the economy, about the regulation of social conduct, about equality and the distribution of income, and about civil rights influence people's views on specific policy questions.

To what extent do self-described liberals and conservatives differ over specific issues? Can we predict people's stances on particular issues by knowing whether they call themselves liberal or conservative? Generally speaking, self-described liberals and conservatives *do* differ in their responses to specific policy questions, although some take policy positions inconsistent with their proclaimed ideology (see Table 5-3). People who describe themselves as liberal generally favor governmental efforts to reduce income inequalities and to improve the positions of African Americans, other minorities, and women. Overall, it appears that ideology and opinion are fairly well linked—that the liberal-conservative dimension is related to opinions on specific policy questions.[10]

Yet it is also true that substantial percentages of self-described conservatives take liberal policy positions, and self-described liberals take conservative positions. These inconsistencies may show that significant portions of the population do not consistently apply ideological principles when determining their position on specific issues. The consistent application of ideology to policy issues may be more characteristic of the interested and active few than of the mass of citizens. Or these apparent inconsistencies may arise because people are focusing on different dimensions of liberalism and conservatism when they label themselves. That is, some people who label themselves conservatives may hold traditional social

TABLE 5-3	**Ideology and Opinion**			
	Percentage Agreeing			
	Liberals	*Moderates*	*Conservatives*	*Total*
Equality				
"Government should reduce income differences"	51%	41%	29%	39%
"Government should not concern itself with income differences"	31	32	51	38
Courts' treatment of criminals				
"Too harsh"	5	4	2	3
"Not harsh enough"	76	83	89	82
"About right"	13	8	6	9
Social issues				
Favor legalizing marijuana	34	22	15	23
Favor school prayer	43	60	67	58
Oppose busing for racial balance in public schools	52	63	71	63

Source: *General Social Survey, 1996* (Chicago: National Opinion Research Center, 1997).

views about abortion, homosexuality, prayer in the schools, crime, and pornography, but they want government to guarantee economic security. The term *populist* is sometimes applied to these social conservatives–economic liberals (see Chapter 2). Or these same people may label themselves liberal based on their view of the role of government in the economy, even though they hold traditional views about social conduct. In short, a single liberal-conservative dimension may be inadequate for describing the ideology of Americans, and this inadequacy explains the apparent inconsistencies.

GENDER AND OPINION

A **gender gap** in public opinion—a difference of opinion between men and women—occurs on only a few issues. Interestingly, a gender gap does *not* appear on women's issues: abortion, the role of women in business and politics, whether one would vote for a qualified woman for president, or whether men are better suited for political office. On these issues, men and women do not differ significantly (see Figure 5-4).

Instead, gender differences are more likely to appear on issues related to the use of force—for example, on gun control or the death penalty. Although majorities of both men and women support both gun control and the death penalty, men appear to give less support to gun control and more support to the death penalty than women do. The greater propensity of men to endorse the use of force has also been observed in international affairs. Small differences between men and women have also been reported on so-called compassion issues, with women more likely to favor protection for the vulnerable members of society, including children and aged, ill, and disabled people.

Politically, the most important gender gap is in party identification. Women are more likely to identify themselves as Democrats, and men more likely to identify themselves as Republicans. This difference emerged in the 1980s, when men were more likely than women to support Republican president Ronald Reagan. (Group differences in party identification are discussed at length in Chapter 7.)

RACE AND OPINION

Opinion over the extent of discrimination in the United States and over the causes of and remedies for racial inequality differs sharply across racial lines. Most whites believe there is very little discrimination toward African Americans in jobs, housing, or education and that differences between whites and blacks in society occur as a result of a lack of motivation among black people. Most African Americans strongly disagree with these views and believe that discrimination continues in employment, housing, and education and that differences between whites and blacks in standards of living are "mainly due to discrimination" (see Figure 5-5 on page 145).

African Americans generally support a more positive role for government in reducing inequality in society. Approximately two out of every three believe that government should do more to reduce income differences between rich and poor. Blacks favor busing to achieve racial balance in public schools, a view not shared by many whites. Given these preferences for a strong role for government, it is not

gender gap Aggregate differences in political opinions of men and women.

FIGURE 5-4 Searching for the Gender Gap

Men and women do not differ significantly on gender-related issues such as abortion, but they do tend to hold different opinions on other issues and in party affiliation, suggesting the influence of gender (or at least of gender socialization) on political opinion.

Source: General Social Survey, 1996 (Chicago: National Opinion Research Center, 1997).

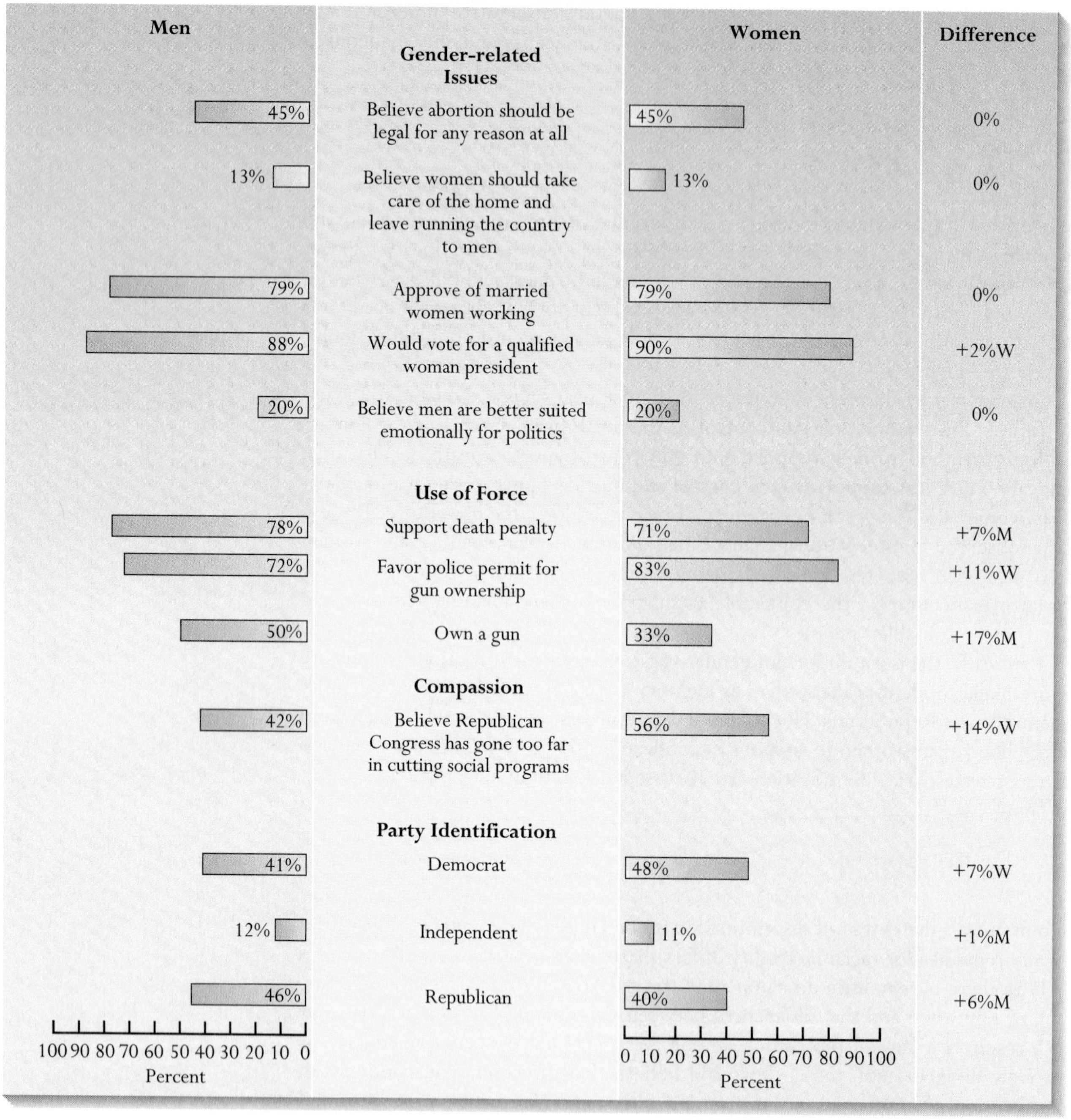

Men	Gender-related Issues	Women	Difference
45%	Believe abortion should be legal for any reason at all	45%	0%
13%	Believe women should take care of the home and leave running the country to men	13%	0%
79%	Approve of married women working	79%	0%
88%	Would vote for a qualified woman president	90%	+2%W
20%	Believe men are better suited emotionally for politics	20%	0%
	Use of Force		
78%	Support death penalty	71%	+7%M
72%	Favor police permit for gun ownership	83%	+11%W
50%	Own a gun	33%	+17%M
	Compassion		
42%	Believe Republican Congress has gone too far in cutting social programs	56%	+14%W
	Party Identification		
41%	Democrat	48%	+7%W
12%	Independent	11%	+1%M
46%	Republican	40%	+6%M

100 90 80 70 60 50 40 30 20 10 0
Percent

0 10 20 30 40 50 60 70 80 90 100
Percent

surprising that more blacks than whites identify themselves as liberals. Note, however, that about one-quarter of black people identify themselves as conservative. And indeed, on certain social issues—crime, drugs, school prayers—majorities of black people take conservative positions. However, black support for the death penalty is significantly less than white support.

FIGURE 5-5 Black and White Opinions

Black people and white people differ over the extent of discrimination in the United States as well as over its causes and remedies.

Source: Views on discrimination derived from data reported in *American Enterprise* 1 (January/February 1990): 96, 103; opinions on affirmative action derived from *American Enterprise* 2 (September/October 1991): 82–83; other questions from the *General Social Survey, 1996* (Chicago: National Opinion Research Center, 1997).

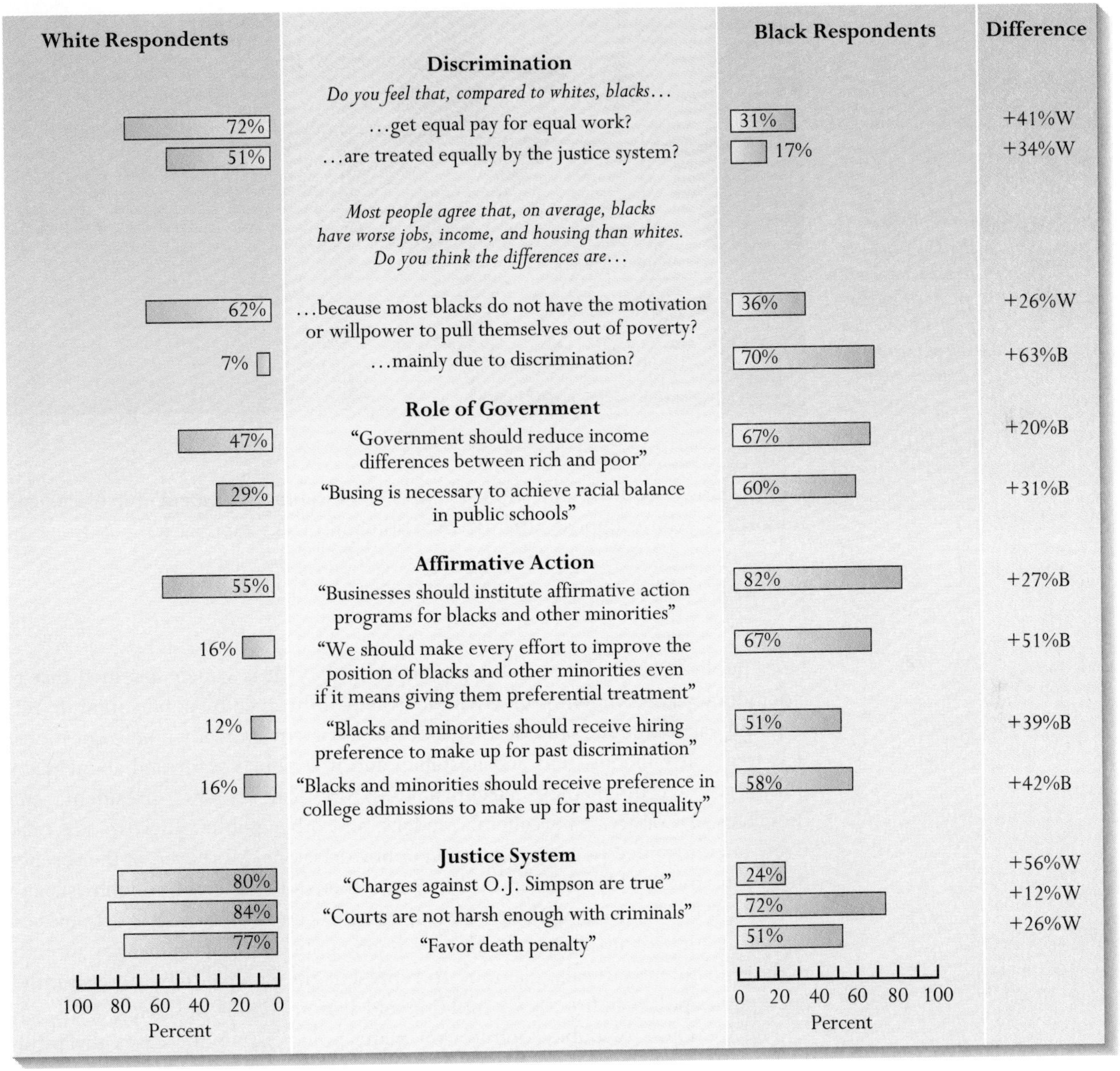

White Respondents		Black Respondents	Difference
	Discrimination *Do you feel that, compared to whites, blacks…*		
72%	…get equal pay for equal work?	31%	+41%W
51%	…are treated equally by the justice system?	17%	+34%W
	Most people agree that, on average, blacks have worse jobs, income, and housing than whites. Do you think the differences are…		
62%	…because most blacks do not have the motivation or willpower to pull themselves out of poverty?	36%	+26%W
7%	…mainly due to discrimination?	70%	+63%B
	Role of Government		
47%	"Government should reduce income differences between rich and poor"	67%	+20%B
29%	"Busing is necessary to achieve racial balance in public schools"	60%	+31%B
	Affirmative Action		
55%	"Businesses should institute affirmative action programs for blacks and other minorities"	82%	+27%B
16%	"We should make every effort to improve the position of blacks and other minorities even if it means giving them preferential treatment"	67%	+51%B
12%	"Blacks and minorities should receive hiring preference to make up for past discrimination"	51%	+39%B
16%	"Blacks and minorities should receive preference in college admissions to make up for past inequality"	58%	+42%B
	Justice System		
80%	"Charges against O.J. Simpson are true"	24%	+56%W
84%	"Courts are not harsh enough with criminals"	72%	+12%W
77%	"Favor death penalty"	51%	+26%W

100 80 60 40 20 0
Percent

0 20 40 60 80 100
Percent

African Americans are much more likely than whites to support governmental actions and programs to improve the position of black people and other minorities. Levels of support for affirmative action depend on the wording of the question, but regardless of wording, blacks are more likely to support racial and minority preferences than whites. For example, both blacks and whites say they "favor affirmative action programs in business," with blacks more likely to do so than

Students at Augustana College react to the verdict in the O.J. Simpson case. The verdict focused national attention on the great differences between the beliefs of whites and African Americans about the role of racism in the criminal justice system.

whites. However, if the question specifies "preferential treatment" for blacks and minorities, whites oppose affirmative action and blacks support it.

POLICY AND OPINION

Does public opinion determine government policy? It is widely assumed that in a democracy government policy will be heavily influenced by public opinion. Yet, as noted earlier, public opinion is weak or nonexistent on many policy questions; it is frequently inconsistent and unstable; and it is poorly informed about many policy issues. Under these circumstances, political leaders—presidents and members of Congress, bureaucrats, judges, and other public officials—are relatively unconstrained by mass opinion in policy decisions. Moreover, in the absence of well-formed public opinion on an issue, other political actors—lobbyists and lawyers, interest group spokespersons, journalists and commentators, television reporters and executives—can influence public policy by communicating directly with government officials, claiming to represent the public. They can also influence public policy indirectly by molding and shaping public opinion.

The weakness of public opinion on many policy issues increases the influence of elites, that small group of people who are interested and active in public affairs; who call or write their elected representatives; who join organizations and contribute money to causes and candidates; who attend meetings, rallies, and demonstrations; and who hold strong opinions on a wide variety of public issues. According to political scientist V. O. Key, Jr., the linkage between ordinary citizens and democratic government depends heavily on "that thin stratum of persons referred to variously as the political elite, the political activists, the leadership echelons, or the influentials."[11] Thus political *participation* appears to be the essential link between opinion and policy.

INDIVIDUAL PARTICIPATION IN POLITICS

Democracies provide a variety of ways for individuals to participate in politics. People may run for, and win, public office; take part in marches, demonstrations, and protests; make financial contributions to political candidates or causes; attend political meetings, speeches, and rallies; write letters to public officials or to newspapers; wear a political button or place a bumper sticker on their car; belong to organizations that support or oppose particular candidates or take stands on public issues; attempt to influence friends while discussing candidates or issues; and vote in elections. Individuals may also participate in politics passively, by simply following political issues and campaigns in the media, acquiring knowledge, forming opinions about public affairs, and expressing their views to others. These forms of political participation can be ranked according to their order of frequency (see Figure 5-6). Only a little more than half of the voting-age population vote in presidential elections, and far fewer vote in state and local elections.

SECURING THE RIGHT TO VOTE

Popular participation in government is part of the very definition of democracy. The long history of struggle to secure the right to vote—**suffrage**—reflects the democratizing of the American political system.

The Elimination of Property Qualifications, 1800–1840 The Constitution of 1787 left it to the states to determine voter qualifications. The Founders

suffrage Legal right to vote.

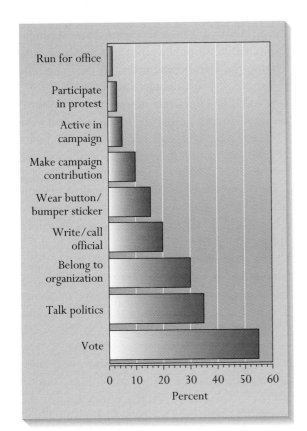

FIGURE 5-6 Political Participation

Only a small percentage of the American people are actively engaged in the political process, yet they receive most of the media attention. Less than 1 percent of the population runs for office at any level of government, and only about half of all voting-age Americans bother to go to the polls.

generally believed that only men of property had a sufficient "stake in society" to exercise their vote in a "responsible" fashion. However, the Founders could not agree on the wording of property qualifications for insertion into the Constitution, so they left the issue to the states, feeling safe in the knowledge that at the time every state had property qualifications for voting. Yet over time, Jeffersonian and Jacksonian principles of democracy, including confidence in the judgment of ordinary citizens, spread rapidly in the new Republic. The states themselves eliminated most property qualifications by 1840. Thus before the Civil War (1861–65), the vote had been extended to virtually all *white males* over twenty-one years of age.

The Fifteenth Amendment, 1870   The first important limitation on state powers over voting came with the ratification of the Fifteenth Amendment: "The right of citizens of the United States to vote shall not be denied or abridged by the United States or by any state on account of race, color, or previous condition of servitude." The object of this amendment, passed by the Reconstruction Congress after the Civil War and ratified in 1870, was to extend the vote to former black slaves and prohibit voter discrimination on the basis of race. The Fifteenth Amendment also gave Congress the power to enforce black voting rights "by appropriate legislation." The states retain their right to determine voter qualifications, *as long as they do not practice racial discrimination,* and Congress has the power to pass legislation ensuring black voting rights.

Continued Denial of Voting Rights, 1870–1964   For almost 100 years after the adoption of the Fifteenth Amendment, white politicians in the southern states were able to defeat its purposes. Social and economic pressures and threats of violence were used to intimidate many thousands of would-be black voters.

There were also many "legal" methods of disenfranchisement, including a technique known as the **white primary**. So strong was the Democratic Party throughout the South that the Democratic nomination for public office was tantamount to election. Thus *primary elections* to choose the Democratic nominee were the only elections in which real choices were made. If black people were prevented from voting in Democratic primaries, they could be effectively disenfranchised. Therefore, southern state legislatures resorted to the simple device of declaring the Democratic Party in southern states a private club and ruling that only white people could participate in its elections—that is, in primary elections. Blacks were free to vote in "official" general elections, but all whites tacitly agreed to support the Democratic, or "white man's," Party in general elections, regardless of their differences in the primary. Not until 1944, in *Smith v. Allwright,* did the Supreme Court declare the white primary unconstitutional and bring primary elections under the purview of the Fifteenth Amendment.

From an estimated 5 percent of voting-age black people registered in southern states in the 1940s, black registration rose to an estimated 20 percent in 1952, 25 percent in 1956, 28 percent in 1960, and 39 percent in 1964. But this last figure was still only about half of the comparable figure for white registration in the South. Despite the Fifteenth Amendment, many local registrars in the South succeeded in barring black registration by an endless variety of obstacles, delays, and frustrations. Application forms for registration were lengthy and complicated; even a minor error, like underlining rather than circling in the "Mr.——Mrs.——Miss" set of choices, as instructed, would lead to rejection. **Literacy tests** were the most common form of disenfranchisement. Many a black college graduate failed

white primary   Democratic Party primary elections in many southern counties in the early part of the twentieth century that excluded black people from voting.

literacy test   Examination of a person's ability to read and write as a prerequisite to voter registration; outlawed by Voting Rights Act (1965) as discriminatory.

Passage of the Voting Rights Act of 1965 opened the voting booth to millions of black voters formerly kept from the polls by a variety of discriminatory regulations in the South. Here African Americans in rural Alabama in 1966 line up at a local store to cast their votes in a primary that focused on an issue central to their existence—segregation.

to interpret "properly" the complex legal documents that were part of the test. White applicants for voter registration were seldom asked to go through these lengthy procedures.

The Civil Rights Act, the Twenty-fourth Amendment, and the Voting Rights Act, 1964–65   The Civil Rights Act of 1964 made it unlawful for registrars to apply unequal standards in registration procedures or to reject applications because of immaterial errors. It required that literacy tests be in writing and made a sixth-grade education a presumption of literacy. In 1970 Congress outlawed literacy tests altogether.

The Twenty-fourth Amendment to the Constitution, ratified in 1964, made **poll taxes**—taxes required of all voters—unconstitutional as a requirement for voting in national elections. In 1966 the Supreme Court declared poll taxes unconstitutional in state and local elections as well.[12]

In early 1965 civil rights organizations led by Martin Luther King, Jr., effectively demonstrated against local registrars in Selma, Alabama, who were still keeping large numbers of black people off the voting rolls. Registrars there closed their offices for all but a few hours every month, placed limits on the number of applications processed, went out to lunch when black applicants appeared, delayed months before processing black applications, and used a variety of other methods to keep blacks disenfranchised. In response to the Selma march, Congress enacted the strong Voting Rights Act in 1965. The U.S. attorney general, upon evidence of voter discrimination, was empowered to replace local registrars with federal registrars, abolish literacy tests, and register voters under simplified federal procedures. Southern counties that had previously discriminated in voting registration hurried to sign up black voters just to avoid the imposition of federal registrars. The Voting Rights Act of 1965 proved to be very effective, and Congress has voted to extend it over the years.

The Nineteenth Amendment, 1920   Following the Civil War, many of the women who had been active in the abolitionist movement to end slavery turned

poll taxes   Taxes imposed as a prerequisite to voting; prohibited by the Twenty-fourth Amendment.

The turn of the century saw the acceleration of the women's suffrage movement. Although Woodrow Wilson expressed support for granting the vote to women even before he took office in 1912, it took the activities of women "manning the homefront" during World War I to persuade the male electorate to pass the Nineteenth Amendment and give women access to the ballot box throughout the nation.

their attention to the condition of women in the United States. As abolitionists, they had learned to organize, conduct petition campaigns, and parade and demonstrate. Now they sought to improve the legal and political rights of women. In 1869 the Wyoming territory adopted women's suffrage; later, several other western states followed suit. But it was not until the Nineteenth Amendment was added to the U.S. Constitution in 1920 that women's right to vote in all elections was constitutionally guaranteed.

The Twenty-Sixth Amendment, 1971   The movement for eighteen-year-old voting received its original impetus during World War II. It was argued successfully in Georgia in 1944 that because eighteen-year-olds were being called upon to fight and die for their country, they deserved to have a voice in the conduct of government. However, this argument failed to convince adult voters in other states; qualifications for military service were not regarded as the same as qualifications for rational decision making in elections. In state after state, voters rejected state constitutional amendments designed to extend the vote to eighteen-year-olds.

Congress intervened on behalf of eighteen-year-old voting with the passage of the Twenty-sixth Amendment to the Constitution.[13] The states quickly ratified this amendment in 1971 during a period of national turbulence over the Vietnam War. Many supporters of the amendment believed that protests on the campuses and streets would be reduced if youthful protesters were given the vote.

The National Voter Registration Act, 1993   The National Voter Registration Act of 1993 mandates that the states offer people the opportunity to register to vote when they apply for driver's licenses or apply for welfare services. States must also offer registration by mail, and they must accept a simplified registration form prepared by the Federal Elections Commission. Finally, it bars states from removing the names of people from registration lists for failure to vote. Turnout gains from the act, however, proved to be modest at best.[14]

WHY VOTE?

Deciding whether to cast a vote in an election is just as important as deciding which candidate to vote for. *About half of the voting-age population in the United States typically fails to vote even in presidential elections.* Voter **turnout**—the number of actual voters in relation to the number of people eligible to register and vote—is even lower in off-year congressional and state elections, when presidential elections are not held. Turnout in local elections (for example, city, county, school board) is even lower when these elections are held separately from national elections. Voter turnout in presidential elections steadily declined for several decades (see Figure 5-7). Only the three-way presidential race in 1992 temporarily reversed the downward trend. In the Clinton-Dole presidential contest in 1996, turnout fell below 50 percent for the first time in over a century.

turnout Number of voters who actually cast ballots in an election, as a percentage of people eligible to register and vote.

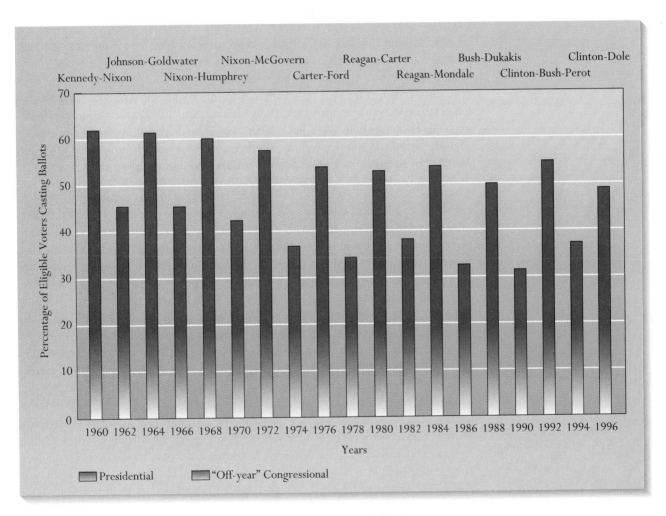

FIGURE 5-7 **Voter Turnout in Presidential and Congressional Elections**

Voter turnout is always lower in years without a presidential election. In addition, voter turnout has generally declined since 1960, even in presidential election years. The exception came in 1992, when intense interest in the contest between George Bush and Bill Clinton—spiced by the entry of independent Ross Perot—led to a higher-than-normal turnout. In 1996 fewer than half of voting-age Americans bothered to cast ballots.

Why vote? Usually, this question is asked in the negative: Why do so many people fail to register and vote? But greater insight into the question of voter participation can be obtained if we try to understand what motivates the people who do go to the polls.

The Rational Voter   From a purely "rational" perspective, an individual should vote only if the costs of voting (time spent in registering, informing oneself about the candidates, and going to the polls) are *less* than the expected value of having the preferred candidate win (the personal benefits gained from having one's candidate win), multiplied by the probability that one's own vote will be the deciding vote. Why vote when registering, following the political news, and getting to the polls take away time from work, family, or leisure activity? Why vote when the winner will not really change one's life for the better, or even do things much differently from what the loser would have done? Most important, why vote when the chance that one individual vote will determine who wins is very small? Thought of in this fashion, the wonder is that millions of Americans continue to vote.

The "rational" model can explain voter turnout only by adding "the intrinsic rewards of voting" to the equation. These rewards include the ethic of voting, patriotism, a sense of duty, and allegiance to democracy. People exercise their right to vote out of respect for that right rather than for any personal tangible benefit they expect to receive. They can look at the voting returns on television later in the evening, knowing they were part of an important national event. These psychological rewards do not depend on whether a single vote determines the outcome. Millions of people vote out of a sense of duty and commitment to democracy.

The Burden of Registration   Voter **registration** is a major obstacle to voting. Not only must citizens care enough to go to the polls on election day; they must also expend time and energy, weeks before the election, to register. Registration usually occurs at a time when interest in the campaign is far from its peak. It may involve a trip to the county courthouse and a procedure more complicated than voting itself. The registration requirement reduces voter turnout significantly. Approximately 85 percent of *registered voters* turn out for a presidential election, but this figure represents only about 50 percent of the *voting-age population*. This discrepancy suggests that registration is a significant barrier to participation.

Registration is supposed to prevent fraud. Voters must identify themselves on Election Day and show they have previously registered in their districts as voters; once they have voted, their names are checked off and they cannot vote again. Registration was adopted by most states in the early twentieth century as a reform designed to reduce the fraudulent voting that was often encouraged and organized by political machines. "Vote early and vote often" was the rallying cry of many party bosses, who sent their legions to the polls for repeated voting. (Registration did not end all voting fraud; some enterprising old party bosses continued to cast votes for registered persons who had died—"the tombstone vote"—or moved away.) But the trade-off for reducing fraud was to create an additional burden on the voter: registration.

THE POLITICS OF VOTER TURNOUT

Politics drives the debate over easing voter registration requirements. Democrats generally favor minimal requirements—for example, same-day registration, registration by mail, and registration at welfare and motor vehicle licensing offices. They

registration   Requirement that prospective voters establish their identity and place of residence prior to an election in order to be eligible to vote.

know that nonvoters are heavily drawn from groups that typically support the Democratic Party, including the less-educated, lower-income, and minority groups. Republicans are often less enthusiastic about easing voting requirements, but it is politically embarrassing to appear to oppose increased participation. It is not surprising that the National Voter Registration Act of 1993, popularly known as the "Motor-Voter Act," was a product of a Democratic Congress and a Democratic president.

The Stimulus of Competition   The more lively the competition between parties or between candidates, the greater the interest of citizens and the larger the voter turnout. When parties and candidates compete vigorously, they make news and are given large play by the mass media. Consequently, a setting of competitive politics generates more political stimuli than does a setting with weak competition. People are also more likely to perceive that their votes count in a close contest, and thus they are more likely to cast them. Moreover, when parties or candidates are fighting in a close contest, their supporters tend to spend more time and energy campaigning and getting out the vote.

Political Alienation   People who feel politics is irrelevant to their life—or who feel they cannot personally affect public affairs—are less likely to vote than people who feel they themselves can affect political outcomes and that these outcomes affect their life. Given the level of **political alienation** (two-thirds of respondents agree with the statement, "Most public officials are not really interested in the problems of people like me"),[15] it is surprising that so many people vote. Alienation is high among voters, and it is even higher among nonvoters.

Intensity   Finally, as we might expect, people who feel strongly about politics and who hold strong opinions about political issues are more likely to vote than people who do not. For example, people who describe themselves as *extreme* liberals or *extreme* conservatives are more likely to vote than people who describe themselves as moderates.

political alienation   Belief that politics is irrelevant to one's life and that one cannot personally affect public affairs.

People with strongly held views, like religious conservatives, are more likely to vote than others. This phenomenon gives them, and organizations like the Christian Coalition that mobilize them, increased political influence.

Explaining Turnouts   The general decline in U.S. voter turnout over the last several decades has generated a variety of explanations. This decline has occurred despite an easing of registration requirements and procedures over time. It may be a product of increasing distrust of government (see *What Do You Think?* "Can You Trust the Government?" in Chapter 1), which is related to political alienation. People who distrust the government are likely to feel they have little influence in politics. They are therefore less likely to go to the trouble of registering and voting. The focus of the media, particularly television, on corruption in government, sex scandals involving politicians, conflicts of interest, waste and inefficiency, and negative campaign advertising may add to popular feelings of alienation.

Another explanation focuses on the expansion of the electorate to include young people eighteen to twenty-one years of age. Young people do not vote in the same proportions as older people (see Figure 5-8). After the electorate was expanded by the Twenty-sixth Amendment to include persons eighteen years of age and over, voter turnout actually dropped, from 60.9 percent in the 1968 presidential election to 55.2 percent in the 1972 presidential election, the largest turnout decline in successive presidential elections.

Still another explanation focuses on the declining role of party organizations in the political system. Strong party organizations, or machines, that canvassed neighborhoods, took citizens to the courthouse to register them, contacted them personally during campaigns, and saw to it that they got to the polls on election day have largely disappeared (see Chapter 7).

Regardless of the explanations offered, it is interesting to note that most European democracies report higher voter turnout rates than the United States (see *Compared to What?* "Voter Turnout in Western Democracies").

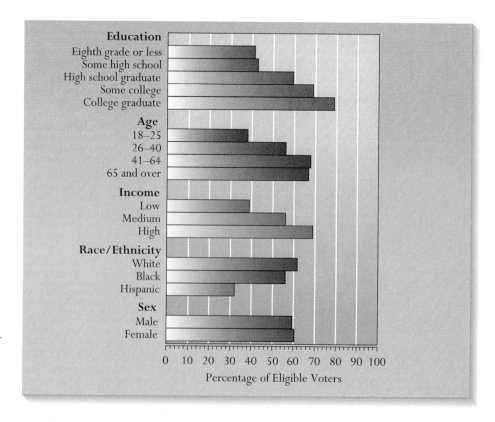

FIGURE 5-8 Voter Turnout by Social Groups

Although there is virtually no gender gap in who goes to the polls, voter turnout increases with education, age, and income. Major efforts to "get out the vote" in the African American community have raised voter turnout to nearly that of whites, but turnout among Hispanics continues to lag.

Source: U.S. Bureau of the Census, *Census Population Reports*, Series P-20.

Voter Turnout in Western Democracies

Other Western democracies regularly report higher voter turnout rates than the United States (see figure). Yet in an apparent paradox, Americans seem to be more supportive of their political institutions, less alienated from their political system, and even more patriotic than citizens of Western European nations. Why, then, are voter turnouts in the United States so much lower than in these other democracies?

The answer to this question lies primarily in the legal and institutional differences between the United States and the other democracies. First of all, in Austria, Australia, Belgium, and Italy, voting is *mandatory*. Penalties and the level of enforcement vary within and across these countries. Moreover, registration laws in the United States make voting more difficult than in other countries. In Western Europe, all citizens are required to register with the government and obtain identification cards. These cards are then used for admission to the polls. In contrast, voter registration is entirely voluntary in the United States, and voters must reregister if they change residences. Nearly 50 percent of the U.S. population changes residence at least once in a five-year period, thus necessitating reregistration.

Parties in the United States are more loosely organized, less disciplined, and less able to mobilize voters than are European parties. Moreover, many elections in the United States, notably elections for Congress, are not very competitive. The United States organizes congressional elections by district with winner-take-all rules, whereas many European parliaments are selected by proportional representation, with seats allocated to parties based on national vote totals. Proportional representation means every vote counts toward seats in the legislative body. Thus greater competition and proportional representation may encourage higher voter turnout in European democracies.

But cultural differences may also contribute to differences in turnout. The American political culture, with its tradition of individualism and self-reliance and its reluctance to empower government

(see Chapter 2), encourages Americans to resolve their problems through their own efforts rather than looking to government for solutions. Government is not as central to Americans as it is to Europeans, and therefore getting to the polls on election day is not seen as so important.

Voter turnout is substantially higher in most of the industrialized world than in the United States. In particular, nations such as Australia, where voting is mandatory, have very high turnouts. Ease of voter registration in most other nations also contributes to higher turnouts there.

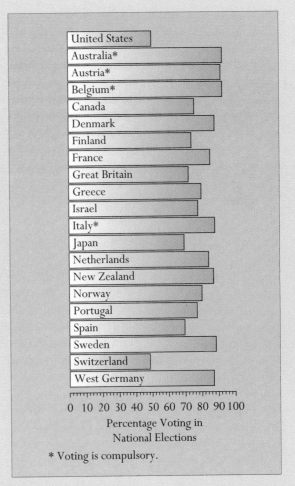

United States
Australia*
Austria*
Belgium*
Canada
Denmark
Finland
France
Great Britain
Greece
Israel
Italy*
Japan
Netherlands
New Zealand
Norway
Portugal
Spain
Sweden
Switzerland
West Germany

0 10 20 30 40 50 60 70 80 90 100

Percentage Voting in
National Elections

* Voting is compulsory.

Source: Congressional Research Service, reported in *Congressional Quarterly Weekly Report*, April 2, 1988, p. 863.

VOTERS AND NONVOTERS

Who votes and who doesn't? The perceived benefits and costs of voting apparently do not fall evenly across all social groups. Nonvoting would generate less concern if voters were a representative cross section of nonvoters. But voters differ from nonvoters in politically important ways.

Voters are better educated than nonvoters. Education appears to be the most important determinant of voter turnout[16] (see Figure 5-8). It may be that schooling promotes an interest in politics, instills the ethic of citizen participation, or gives people a better awareness of public affairs and an understanding of the role of elections in a democracy. Education is associated with a sense of confidence and political *efficacy*, the feeling that one can indeed have a personal impact on public affairs.

Age is another factor affecting voter participation. Perhaps because young people have more distractions, more demands on their time in school, work, or new family responsibilities, nonvoting is greatest among eighteen- to twenty-one-year-olds. In contrast, older Americans are politically influential in part because candidates know they turn out at the polls.

High-income people are more likely to vote than are low-income people. Most of this difference stems from the fact that high-income people are more likely to be well educated and older. But poor people may also feel alienated from the political system—they may lack a sense of political efficacy; they may feel they have little control over their own lives, let alone over public affairs. Or poor people may simply be so absorbed in the problems of life that they have little time or energy to spend on registering and voting.[17]

Income and education differences between participants and nonparticipants are even greater when other forms of political participation are considered. Higher-income, better-educated people are much more likely to be among those who make campaign contributions, who write or call their elected representatives, and who join and work in active political organizations.[18]

Historically, race was a major determinant of nonvoting. Black voter turnout, especially in the South, was markedly lower than white voter turnout. Black people continue today to have a slightly lower overall voter turnout than whites, but most of the remaining difference is attributable to differences between blacks and whites in educational and income levels. Blacks and whites at the same educational and income levels register and vote with the same frequency. Indeed, in cities where black people are well organized politically, black voter turnout may exceed white voter turnout.[19]

The greatest racial disparity in voter turnout is between Hispanics and others. Low voter participation by Hispanics may be a product of language differences, lack of cultural assimilation, or noncitizenship status.

NONVOTING: WHAT DIFFERENCE DOES IT MAKE?

How concerned should we be about low levels of participation in American politics? Certainly the democratic ideal envisions an active, participating citizenry. Democratic government, asserts the Declaration of Independence, derives its "just powers from the consent of the governed." The legitimacy of democratic government can be more easily questioned when half of the people fail to vote. That is, it is easier to question whether the government truly represents "the people" when only half of the people vote even in a presidential election. Voting is an expression of good citizenship, and it reinforces attachment to the nation and to democratic government. Nonvoting suggests alienation from the political system.

However, the *right* to vote is more important to democratic government than voter turnout. The nineteenth-century English political philosopher John Stuart Mill wrote, "Men, as well as women, do not need political rights in order that they might govern, but in order that they not be misgoverned."[20] As long as all adult Americans possess the right to vote, politicians must consider their interests. "Rulers in ruling classes are under a necessity of considering the interests of those who have the suffrage."[21] Democratic governments cannot really ignore the interests of anyone who can vote. People who have the right to vote, but who have voluntarily chosen not to exercise it in the past, can always change their minds, go to the polls, and "throw the rascals out."

Indeed, a huge army of nonvoters "hangs over the democratic process like a bomb ready to explode and change the course of history."[22] Some commentators view this latent "bomb" with alarm, but others view it as a potential resource in hard times. The last major surge in voting turnout occurred in 1932 in the midst of the Depression, when voters went to the polls in droves to oust incumbent Herbert Hoover and elect Franklin D. Roosevelt, who changed the role of government in the economy.

Voluntary nonvoting is not the same as being denied the suffrage. Politicians can indeed ignore the interests of people denied the vote by restrictive laws or practices or by intimidation or force. But when people *choose* not to exercise their right to vote, they may be saying that they do not believe their interests are really affected by government. The late Senator Sam Ervin is widely quoted on the topic of nonvoters:

> I'm not going to shed any crocodile tears if people don't care enough to vote. I don't believe in making it easy for apathetic lazy people. I'd be extremely happy if nobody in the United States voted except for the people who thought about the issues and made up their own minds and wanted to vote.[23]

But the class bias in voting presents another concern. It is frequently argued that greater overall turnout by better-educated, higher-income, older whites tilts the political system toward the interests of upper socioeconomic classes at the expense of poorer, less-educated, younger, black, and Hispanic people.[24] Thus the people we would expect to be most in need of government help are least represented among voters. This underrepresentation not only harms their policy interests but also contributes even further to their feelings of political alienation.

However, it is difficult to predict that major changes would occur in specific public policies if all socioeconomic groups voted with the same frequency. As we have already observed, rich and poor, black and white, often share the same opinions on policy issues or differ only in degree. The likely policy consequences of increased voter participation may be overestimated by scholars and commentators.[25]

PROTEST AS POLITICAL PARTICIPATION

Protests, marches, and demonstrations are important forms of political participation. Indeed, the First Amendment guarantees the right "peaceably to assemble, and to petition the government for redress of grievances." A march to the steps of Congress, a demonstration in Lafayette Park across the street from the White House, a mass assembly of people on the Washington Mall with speakers, sign waving, and songs, and the presentation of petitions to government officials are all forms of participation protected by the First Amendment.

Protests **Protests** are generally designed to call attention to an issue and to motivate others to apply pressure on public officials. In fact, protests are usually directed at the news media rather than at public officials themselves. If protesters could persuade public officials directly in the fashion of lobbyists and interest groups, they would not need to protest. Protests are intended to generate attention and support among previously uncommitted people—enough so the ultimate targets of the protest, public officials, will be pressured to act to redress grievances.

Coverage by the news media, especially television, is vital to the success of protest activity. The media not only carry the protesters' message to the mass public but also inform public officials about what is taking place. Protests provide the media with "good visuals"—pictorial dramatizations of political issues. The media welcome opportunities to present political issues in a confrontational fashion because confrontation helps capture larger audiences. Thus protesters and the media use each other to advance their separate goals.

Protests are most commonly employed by groups that have little influence in electoral politics. They were a key device of the civil rights movement at a time when many African Americans were barred from voting. In the absence of protest, the majority white population—and the public officials they elected—were at best unconcerned with the plight of black people in a segregated society. Protests, including a dramatic march on Washington in 1963 at which Martin Luther King, Jr., delivered his inspirational "I Have a Dream" speech, called attention to the injustices of segregation and placed civil rights on the agenda of decision makers.

Protests can be effectively employed by groups that are relatively small in number but whose members feel very intensely about the issue. Often the protest is a means by which these groups can obtain bargaining power with decision makers. Protests may threaten to tarnish the reputations of government officials or private corporations, or may threaten to disrupt their daily activities or reduce their business through boycotts or pressure on customers. If the protest is successful, protest leaders can then offer to end the protest in exchange for concessions from their targets.

Civil Disobedience **Civil disobedience** is a form of protest that involves breaking what are perceived as "unjust" laws. The purpose is to call attention to the existence of injustice. In the words of Martin Luther King, Jr., civil disobedience "seeks to dramatize the issue so that it can no longer be ignored"[26] (see *A Conflicting View:* "Sometimes It's Right to Disobey the Law" in Chapter 1). Those truly engaging in civil disobedience do not attempt to evade punishment for breaking the law but instead willingly accept the penalty. By doing so, they demonstrate not only their sincerity and commitment but also the injustice of the law. Cruelty or violence directed at the protesters by police or others contributes further to the drama of injustice. Like other protest activity, the success of civil disobedience depends on the willingness of the mass media to carry the message to both the general public and the political leadership.

Violence Violence can also be a form of political participation. Indeed, political violence—for example, assassinations, rioting, burning, looting—has been uncomfortably frequent in American politics over the years (see *A Conflicting View:* "American Politics as Violence" in Chapter 1). It is important to distinguish violence from protest. Peaceful protest is constitutionally protected. Often, organized

protests Public marches or demonstrations designed to call attention to an issue and motivate others to apply pressure on public officials.

civil disobedience Form of public protest involving the breaking of laws believed to be unjust.

If a law violates the civil rights of a group of individuals, don't they have not only a right but also a duty to disobey it? That was the argument advanced by the group of African American college students who sat down and asked to be served at a lunch counter in a Greensboro, North Carolina, Woolworth's store in 1960. Although jailed for their action, which violated segregation laws at the time, the young men's actions fueled the civil rights movement and helped bring about the end of segregation in America.

protest activity harnesses frustrations and hostilities, directs them into constitutionally acceptable activities, and thus avoids violence. Likewise, civil disobedience should be distinguished from violence. Civil disobedience breaks only "unjust" laws, without violence, and willingly accepts punishment without trying to escape.

Effectiveness How effective are protests? Protests can be effective in achieving some goals under some conditions. But protests are useless or even counterproductive in pursuit of other goals under other conditions. Here are some generalizations about the effectiveness of protests:

- Protests are more likely to be effective when directed at specific problems or laws rather than at general conditions that cannot readily be remedied by governmental action.
- Protests are more likely to be effective when targeted toward public officials who are capable of granting the desired concession or resolving the specific problem. Protests with no specific targets and protests directed at officials who have no power to change things are generally unproductive.
- Protests are more likely to succeed when the goal is limited to gaining access or representation in decision making or to placing an issue on the agenda of decision makers.
- Protests are not always effective in actually getting laws changed and are even less effective in ensuring that the impact of the changes will really improve the conditions that led to the protest.

Public officials can defuse protest activity in a variety of ways. They may greet protesters with smiles and reassurances that they agree with their goals. They may disperse symbolic satisfaction without any tangible results. They may grant token concessions with great publicity, perhaps remedying a specific case of injustice while doing little to affect general conditions. Or public officials may claim to be constrained either legally or financially from doing anything—the "I-would-like-to-

Up Close

How to Run for Office

Many rewards come with elected office—the opportunity to help shape public policy, public attention and name recognition, and many business, professional, and social contacts. But there are many drawbacks as well—the absence of privacy, a microscopic review of one's past, constant calls, meetings, interviews and handshaking, and perhaps most onerous of all, the continual need to solicit campaign funds.

Before You Run—Getting Involved Get involved in various organizations in your community:

- Neighborhood associations.
- Chambers of commerce, business associations.
- Churches and synagogues (become an usher, if possible, for visibility).
- Political groups (Democratic or Republican clubs, League of Women Voters, and so on).
- Parent-Teacher Associations (PTAs).
- Service clubs (Rotary, Kiwanis, Civitan, Toastmasters).
- Recreation organizations (Little League, flag football, soccer leagues, running and walking clubs, for example, as participant, coach, or umpire).

Deciding to Run—Know What You're Doing In deciding to run, and choosing the office for which you wish to run, you should become thoroughly familiar with the issues, duties, and responsibilities.

- Attend council or commission meetings, state legislative sessions, and/or committee hearings.
- Become familiar with current issues and officeholders, and obtain a copy of and read the budget.
- Learn the demographics of your district (racial, ethnic, and age composition; occupational mix; average income; neighborhood differences). If you do not fit the prevailing racial, ethnic, or age composition, think about moving to another district.
- Memorize a brief (preferably less than seven seconds) answer to the question, "Why are you running?"

Getting in the Race Contact your county elections department to obtain the following:

- Qualifying forms and information.
- Campaign financing forms and regulations.

- District and street maps for your district.
- Recent election results in your district.
- Election-law book or pamphlet.
- Voter registration lists (usually sold as lists, or labels, or tapes).
- Contact your party's county chairperson for advice; convince the party's leaders that you can win. Ask for a list of their regular campaign contributors.

Raising Money The easiest way to finance a campaign is to be rich enough to provide your own funds. Failing that, you must:

- Establish a campaign fund, according to the laws of your state.
- Find a treasurer/campaign-finance chairperson who knows many wealthy, politically involved people.
- Invite wealthy, politically involved people to small coffees, cocktail parties, dinners; give a brief campaign speech and then have your finance chairperson solicit contributions.
- Follow up fund-raising events and meetings with personal phone calls.
- Be prepared to continue fund-raising activities throughout your campaign; file accurate financial disclosure statements as required by state law.

Getting Organized Professional campaign managers and management firms almost always outperform volunteers. If you cannot afford professional management, you must rely on yourself or trusted friends to perform the following:

- Draw up a budget based on reasonable expectations of campaign funding.
- Interview and select a professional campaign-management firm, or appoint a trusted campaign manager.
- Ask trusted friends from various clubs, activities, neighborhoods, churches, and so on, to meet and serve as a campaign committee. If your district is racially or ethnically diverse, make sure all groups are represented on your committee.
- Decide on a campaign theme; research issues important to your community; develop brief, well-articulated positions on these issues.
- Open a campaign headquarters with desks and telephones. Buy a cell phone; use call forwarding; stay in contact. Use your garage if you can't afford an office.

- Arrange to meet with newspaper editors, editorial boards, TV station executives, and political reporters. Be prepared for tough questions.
- Hire a media consultant or advertising agency, or appoint a volunteer media director who knows television, radio, and newspaper advertising.
- Arrange a press conference to announce your candidacy. Notify all media well in advance. Arrange for overflow crowd of supporters to cheer and applaud.
- Produce eyecatching, inspirational 15--or 30-second television and radio ads that present a favorable image of you and stress your campaign theme.
- Prepare and print attractive campaign brochures, signs, and bumper stickers.
- Hire a local survey-research firm to conduct telephone surveys of voters in your district, asking what they think are the most important issues, how they stand on them, whether they recognize your name and your theme, and how they plan to vote. Be prepared to change your theme and your position on issues if surveys show strong opposition to your views.

On the Campaign Trail Campaigns themselves may be primarily *media centered* or primarily *door-to-door* ("retail") or some combination of both.

- Buy media time as early as possible from television and radio stations; insist on prime-time slots before, during, and after popular shows.
- Buy newspaper ads; insist on their placement in popular, well-read sections of the paper.
- Attend every community gathering possible, just to be seen, even if you do not give a speech. Keep all speeches *short*. Focus on one or two issues that your polls show are important to voters.
- Recruit paid or unpaid volunteers to hand out literature door-to-door. Record names and addresses of voters who say they support you.
- Canvass door-to-door with a brief (seven-second) self-introduction and statement of your reasons for running. Use registration lists to identify members of your own party, and try to address them by name. Also canvass offices, factories, coffee shops, shopping malls—anywhere you find a crowd.
- Organize a phone bank, either professional or volunteer. Prepare *brief* introduction and phone statements. Record names of people who say they support you.

- Know your opponent: Research his or her past affiliations, indiscretions if any, previous voting record, and public positions on issues.
- Be prepared to "define" your opponent in negative terms. Negative advertising works. But be fair: Base your comments on your opponent's public record. Emphasize his or her positions that clearly deviate from your district voters' known preferences.

Primary versus General Elections Remember that you will usually have to campaign in two elections—your party's primary and the general election.

- Before the primary, dentify potential opposition in your own party, try to dissuade them from running.
- Allocate your budget first to win the primary election. If you lose the primary, you won't need any funds for the general election.
- In general elections, you must broaden your appeal without distancing your own party supporters. Deemphasize your party affiliation unless your district regularly elects members of your party. In a close district or a district that regularly votes for the opposition party, stress your independence and your commitment to the *district's* interests.

On Election Day Turning out *your* voters is the key to success. Election day is the busiest day of the campaign for you and your staff.

- Use your phone bank to place as many calls as possible to party members in your district (especially those who have indicated in previous calls and visits that they support you). Remind them to vote; make sure your phone workers can tell each voter where to go to cast his or her vote.
- Solicit volunteers to drive people to the polls.
- Assign workers to as many polling places as possible. Most state laws require that they stay a specified distance from the voting booths. But they should be in evidence with your signs and literature to buttonhole voters before they go into the booths.
- Show up at city or county election office on election night with prepared victory statement thanking supporters and pledging your service to the district. (Also draft a courteous concession statement pledging your support to the winner, in case you lose.)
- Attend victory party with your supporters; meet many "new" friends.

help-you-but-I-can't" strategy. Or public officials can directly confront the protesters by charging that they are unrepresentative of the groups they are trying to help.

Perhaps the most challenging and sometimes the most effective kind of protest is to run for public office (see *Up Close*: "How to Run for Office"). Whether at the local level, such as the school board, or at the state or national level, the participation of one individual as a candidate—even when not elected—can make a difference in public affairs.

 Politics in Cyberspace

Public Opinion

Many news and polling organizations, including the Gallup organization, CNN, *USA Today*, The Harris Poll, Yankelovich Partners, ABC News Poll, NBC News, and CBS News/*New York Times* Poll track public opinion on current issues. The Web sites of major news organizations often include polling data from one of more of these organizations.

Major news organizations with polling information:

CNN and *Time*
http://www.Allpolitics.com

ABC News
http://www.abc.net.au/news

CBS News
http://www.cbs.com/navbar/news.html

NBC News
http://www.nbc.com/news
http://www.msnbc.com

The New York Times
http://www.nytimes.com

The Gallup Organization
http://www.gallup.com

The Gallup polling organization, with poll data going back to 1935, is the oldest continuous source of public opinion data. Its Web site posts special reports and surveys and provides access to its archives back to 1996.

SUMMARY NOTES

- Public opinion commands the attention of elected public officials in a democracy, yet many Americans are poorly informed and unconcerned about politics; their opinions on public issues are often changeable and inconsistent. Only a few highly salient issues generate strong and stable opinions.

- Political socialization—the learning of political values, beliefs, and opinions—starts at an early age. It is influenced by family, school, church, age group, and the media.

- Ideology also shapes opinion, especially among politically interested and active people who employ fairly consistent liberal or conservative ideas in forming their opinions on specific issues.

- Race and gender also influence public opinion. Blacks and whites differ over the extent of discrimination in the United States, as well as over its causes and remedies. Men and women tend to differ over issues involving the use of force. In recent years, women have tended to give greater support to the Democratic Party than men have.

- Individuals can exercise power in a democratic political system in a variety of ways. They can run for public office, take part in demonstrations and protests, make financial contributions to candidates, attend political events, write letters to newspapers or public officials, belong to political organizations, vote in elections, or simply hold and express opinions on public issues.

- Securing the right to vote for all Americans required nearly 200 years of political struggle. Key victories included the elimination of property qualifications by 1840, the Fifteenth Amendment in 1870 (eliminating restrictions based on race), the Nineteenth Amendment in 1920 (eliminating restrictions based on gender), the Civil Rights Act of 1964 and Voting Rights Act of 1965 (eliminating racial obstacles), the Twenty-fourth Amendment in 1964 (eliminating poll taxes), and the Twenty-sixth Amendment in 1971 (extending the right to vote to eighteen-year-olds).

- About half of the voting-age population fails to vote even in presidential elections. Voter turnout has steadily declined in recent decades. Voter registration is a major obstacle to voting. Turnout is affected by competition as well as by feelings of political alienation and distrust of government. Young people have the poorest record of voter turnout of any age group.

- Voluntary nonvoting is not as serious a threat to democracy as denial of the right to vote. Nevertheless, the class bias in voting may tilt the political system toward the interests of higher-income, better-educated, older whites at the expense of lower-income, less-educated, younger minorities.

- Protest is an important form of participation in politics. Protests are more commonly employed by groups with little direct influence over public officials. The object is to generate attention and support from previously uncommitted people in order to bring new pressure on public officials to redress grievances. Media coverage is vital to the success of protests.

SELECTED READINGS

ASHER, HERBERT. *Polling and the Public: What Every Citizen Should Know.* 4th ed. Washington, D.C.: Congressional Quarterly Press, 1998. Explains methods of polling and how results can be influenced by wording, sampling, and interviewing techniques; also covers how polls are used by the media and in campaigns.

BARKER, LUCIUS J., MACK H. JONES and KATHERINE TATE, *African Americans and the American Political System.* 4th ed. Englewood Cliffs, N.J.: Prentice Hall, 1998. An overview of African American political participation and the responsiveness of the presidency, Congress, courts, parties, and interest groups.

BRACE, PAUL, and BARBARA HINCKLEY. *Follow the Leader: Opinion Polls and the Modern Presidency.* New York: Basic Books, 1992. An assessment of how presidential actions affect public opinion polls, and how presidents in turn are influenced by the polls.

CONWAY, M. MARGARET. *Political Participation in the United States.* 2nd ed. Washington, D.C.: Congressional Quarterly Press, 1991. A comprehensive summary of who participates in politics and why.

CONWAY, M. MARGARET, GERTRUDE A. STEVERNAGEL, and DAVID AHERN. *Women and Political Participation.* Washington, D.C.: Congressional Quarterly Press, 1997. An examination of cultural change and women's participation in politics, including treatment of the gender gap in political attitudes and the impact of women's membership in the political elite.

ERIKSON, ROBERT S. and KENT L. TEDIN. *American Public Opinion.* 5th ed. Needham, Mass.: Allyn and Bacon, 1995. A comprehensive review of the forces influencing public opinion and an assessment of the influence of public opinion in American politics.

GREENSTEIN, FRED I. *Children and Politics.* New Haven, Conn.: Yale University Press, 1985. Early research on what children know about politics and how they learned it.

PAGE, BENJAMIN I., and ROBERT Y. SHAPIRO. *The Rational Public: Fifty Years of Trends in Americans' Policy Preferences.* Chicago: University of Chicago Press, 1992. An argument that government policies generally reflect public opinion.

STIMSON, JAMES A. *Public Opinion in America: Moods, Cycles, and Swings.* 2nd ed. Boulder, Colo.: Westview Press, 1998. A systematic analysis of swings and cycles in "policy moods" that roughly correspond to liberal and conservative views concerning the effectiveness of government in dealing with perceived problems.

WALD, KENNETH D. *Religion and Politics in the United States.* 3rd ed. Washington, D.C.: Congressional Quarterly Press, 1996. An explanation of the impact of religion on American political culture, the policy process, and voting behavior.

ZALLER, JOHN R. *The Nature and Origins of Mass Opinion.* New York: Cambridge University Press, 1992. An effort to develop and test a conceptual model of how people form political preferences, how political views and arguments diffuse through the population, and how people evaluate this information and convert their reactions into public opinion.

ASK YOURSELF ABOUT POLITICS

1 Are media professionals—news reporters, editors, anchors—the true voice of the people in public affairs?
Yes ___ No ___

2 Do the media mirror what is really news, rather than deciding themselves what's important and then making it news?
Yes ___ No ___

3 Is television your most important source of news?
Yes ___ No ___

4 Should the media report on all aspects of the private lives of public officials?
Yes ___ No ___

5 Do the media report equally fairly on Democratic and Republican candidates for office?
Yes ___ No ___

6 Should the media be legally required to be fair and accurate in reporting political news?
Yes ___ No ___

7 Are you more alienated than attracted by the media's coverage of politics?
Yes ___ No ___

8 Is your choice of candidates in elections affected by their advertising?
Yes ___ No ___

MASS MEDIA
SETTING
THE POLITICAL
AGENDA

Ask yourself how much of your knowledge about politics in America comes from television and newspapers and the radio. What you know about politics and how you participate are, in fact, largely determined by the power of the media to decide what they want you to know.

THE POWER OF THE MEDIA

Politics—the struggle over who gets what, when, and how—is largely carried out in the **mass media**. The arenas of political conflict are the various media of mass communication—television, newspapers, magazines, radio, books, recordings, motion pictures, the Internet (see *Up Close: "Media* Is a Plural Noun"). What we know about politics comes to us largely through these media. Unless we ourselves are admitted to the White House Oval Office or the committee rooms of Congress or dinner parties at foreign embassies, or unless we ourselves attend political rallies and demonstrations or travel to distant battlefields, we must rely on the mass media to tell us about politics. Furthermore, few of us ever have the opportunity to personally evaluate the character of presidential candidates or cabinet members or members of Congress, or to learn their views on public issues by talking with them face to face. Instead, we must learn about people as well as events from the mass media.

Great power derives from the control of information. *Who knows what* helps to determine *who gets what*. The media not only provide an arena for politics; they are themselves players in that arena. The media not only report on the struggles for power in society; they are themselves participants in those struggles. The media have long been referred to as America's "fourth branch" of government, and for good reason.

National News Media   Media power is concentrated in the leading television networks (ABC, CBS, NBC, and CNN), the nation's leading newspapers (*New York Times, Washington Post, Wall Street Journal*), and broad-circulation newsmagazines (*Newsweek, Time,* and *U.S. News and World Report*) (see Figure 6-1). The reporters, anchors, editors, and producers of these prestige news organizations constitute a relatively small group of people in whose hands rests the power to decide what we will know about people, events, and issues.

mass media   All means of communication with the general public, including television, newspapers, magazines, radio, books, recordings, motion pictures, and the Internet.

FIGURE 6-1 The National News Media

A handful of media outlets in the United States serve as the major sources of news information for the American public. Television is by far the most influential source today, with most Americans getting their news primarily from TV. The growth of cable television in recent years has accelerated this trend, with CNN becoming the "crisis network," the place to turn to see a war, an earthquake, or any other major event.

Source: Television viewers reported by A. C. Nielsen and Company for 1996; newspaper circulation for 1995 as reported in *Editor and Publisher,* June 1996.

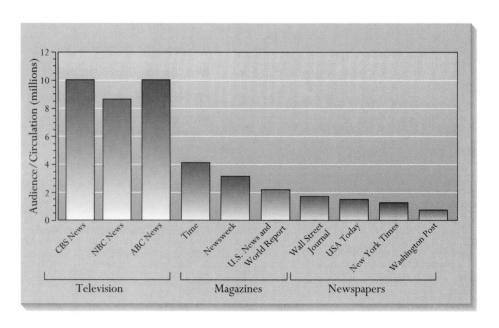

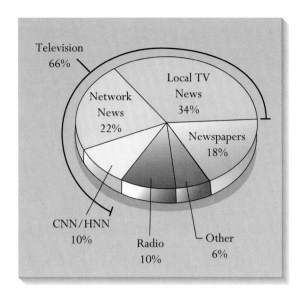

FIGURE 6-2 **Most Important News Source**
Source: Data from *Media Monitor*, May/June 1997, Center for Media and Public Affairs, Washington, D.C.

The Power of Television   Television is the most powerful medium of communication. It is the first true *mass* communication medium. Virtually every home in the United States has a television set, and the average home has the set turned on for about *seven* hours a day. Television is regularly chosen over other news media by Americans as "the most important" news source (see Figure 6-2). Nevertheless, there are differences among age groups in how they get their news (see *Up Close:* "How Young and Old Get Their News" on page 170). The national network evening news shows (*NBC Nightly News*, *ABC World News Tonight*, *CBS Evening News*) have lost viewship in recent years (down from a combined average of 40 million in 1980 to 28 million today). But viewship of cable CNN and its headline companion HNN has risen, and viewship of local television news has remained strong. Indeed, today more people watch local news than national network news. Television weekly news and magazines, notably CBS's *60 Minutes* and ABC's *20/20*, are regularly listed among the most popular shows on television; and television "tabloids" (such as *Hardcopy* and *Inside Edition*) are also gaining viewers. The power of television derives not only from its large audiences but also from its ability to communicate emotions as well as information. Television's power is found in its visuals—angry faces in a rioting mob, police beating an African American motorist, wounded soldiers being unloaded from a helicopter—scenes that convey an emotional message. Moreover, television focuses on the faces of individuals as well as on their words, portraying honesty or deception, humility or arrogance, compassion or indifference, humor or meanness, and a host of other personal characteristics. Skillful politicians understand that *what* one says may not be as important as *how* one says it. Image triumphs over substance on television.

The Myth of the Mirror   Media people themselves often deny that they exercise great power. They sometimes claim that they only "mirror" reality. They like to think of themselves as unbiased reporters who simply narrate happenings and transmit videotaped portrayals of people and events as they really are. Occasionally, editors or reporters or anchors will acknowledge that they make

Media Is a Plural Noun

For most of us, politics is a *mediated* experience. What we know about our political world comes to us not from personal experience but through the mass media. We can broaden our political knowledge by regularly monitoring all types of media.

Television For many years, national television was dominated by three networks: American Broadcasting Company (ABC), Columbia Broadcasting System (CBS), and National Broadcasting Company (NBC). As late as 1970, they captured more than 90 percent of the television audience. Today most of the nation's 1,000 local commercial TV stations remain affiliated with one or another of the networks. Local stations usually restrict themselves to local news coverage and then broadcast the network "feeds" of the "evening news" for national coverage. But technological developments, notably cable television and satellite broadcasting, destroyed the comfortable oligopoly of ABC, CBS, and NBC.

Today, more than two-thirds of the nation's homes have cable TV. Cable News Network (CNN), begun by independent entrepreneur Ted Turner, is a major competitor in news broadcasting; with its around-the-clock coverage, it dominates crisis reporting, as it did during the Gulf War. C-SPAN regularly broadcasts congressional proceedings and other Washington events. Other cable channels offer viewers a wide choice of sports broadcasting (ESPN), music (MTV), satellite "superstations" (Ted Turner's TNT), and pay television (HBO and Showtime).

Radio The nation's 10,000 radio stations are about evenly divided between AM and FM band broadcasting. Most programming features music, but *talk radio* is growing in both listeners and political importance. Talk-show hosts take telephone calls that often signal popular concerns and emotions. Often the hosts themselves are highly opinionated (for example, conservative Rush Limbaugh) and enjoy a national following.

Newspapers More than 70 percent of the adult population read one or another of the nation's 1,600 daily newspapers. The nation's *prestige* newspapers—the *New York Times, Washington Post,* and *Wall Street Journal*—are regularly read by government officials, corporate chiefs, interest-group leaders, and other media people.

Magazines The leading weekly newsmagazines—*Time* (4.1 million), *Newsweek* (3.2 million), and *U.S. News and World Report* (2.2 million)—reach a smaller but more politically attentive audience than do newspapers. Magazines of political commentary—for example, the *Nation* (liberal), *New Republic* (liberal), *National Review* (conservative), *American Spectator* (conservative), *Public Interest* (neo-conservative), and *Washington Monthly* (neo-liberal, anti-establishment)—reach very small but politically active audiences. The newer *George,* edited by John F. Kennedy, Jr., offers light, breezy, people-oriented coverage of current politics.

Motion Pictures Most of the 250 or so feature films produced and distributed in the United States each year are commercial ventures designed to attract theater-going (younger) audiences. Controversy over the effects of the sex and violence shown on the screen are almost as old as the movie industry itself. A system of industry self-regulation, with its *G, PG, R,* and *NC-17* (formerly *X*) ratings, was designed to deflect criticism and avoid government intervention.

A generation ago, the movie industry generally avoided movies with a social or political "message." As one wit at a major studio quipped, "If I want to send a message, I use Western Union." But independent producers broke the major studio monopoly, and today Hollywood regularly produces movies with liberal social and political themes.

Books and Recordings About half of all Americans claim to have read a book in the past year. About half of the 50,000 books published each year are textbooks for elementary or secondary schools or colleges and universities. Most of the trade books marketed in shopping mall bookstores across the country have little political content. However, a few books each year capture the attention of politically minded readers and help shape debate among opinion leaders.

The White House home page on the World Wide Web.

Most of the 700 million recordings (tapes, CD's, etc.) sold each year, mainly to young people, feature romantic themes. But some popular recordings incorporate a political message. Folk music has a tradition of social protest; rap music often voices racial concerns; country music often reflects populist and patriotic themes.

The Internet   The newest of the media now in play in politics is the Internet. Its use is recent enough that formal studies of its effectiveness are just beginning. But people in public life—from the president, to members of Congress, to interest groups, to local party organizers—have taken advantage of its presence to establish Web home pages and bulletin boards, and all the major online services have chat groups for political exchange. Several large media companies have ventured onto the Internet with politically oriented Web sites. Time Inc. and Cable News Network have a site called *All Politics* (http://www.allpolitics.com), and ABC News, *The Washington Post*, *Newsweek,* and *The National Journal* have joined forces to produce *Politics Now* (http://www.politics.now.com).

Source: U.S. Bureau of the Census, *Statistical Abstract of the United States,* 1995, p. 572. Data for 1995–98 are projections.

Up Close

How Young and Old Get Their News

Young people differ somewhat from older people in how they get their information about politics and public affairs. All age groups watch local news on television more than national news. And all age groups get most of their news from television rather than newspapers. But young people devote less time to watching or reading about the news than older people do.

Regular News Sources	Age Group			
	18–29 (%)	30–49 (%)	50–64 (%)	65+ (%)
Television				
Local news about your viewing area	50.8	62.6	74.3	77.5
National nightly network news on CBS, ABC, or NBC	21.8	34.5	60.3	64.0
Cable News Network (CNN)	18.7	24.0	33.1	32.2
C-SPAN	3.6	5.7	7.3	6.3
News magazine shows (such as *60 Minutes* or *20/20*)	19.6	33.0	47.5	52.2
TV shows (such as *A Current Affair*, *Hard Copy*, or *Inside Edition*)	14.7	16.8	25.1	23.5
Daytime talk shows (such as *Ricki Lake*, *Jerry Springer*, *Jenny Jones*)	17.2	8.2	7.6	7.0
Radio				
National Public Radio (NPR)	9.2	15.8	12.8	12.0
Rush Limbaugh's radio show	5.3	5.8	8.3	8.4
Newspapers				
Daily newspaper	60.0	71.1	74.3	84.0
Magazines				
News (such as *Time*, *U.S. News and World Report*, or *Newsweek*)	13.1	12.2	19.6	20.2

Note: Respondents were asked: "I'd like to know how often, if ever, you read certain types of publications, listen to the radio, or watch certain types of TV shows. For each that I read, tell me if you do it regularly, sometimes, hardly ever, or never. How often do you [X]?"

Source: The Pew Research Center for The People & The Press, 1993.

important decisions about what stories, people, events, or issues will be covered in the news, how much time or space they will be given, what visuals will be used, and what sources will be quoted. They may also occasionally acknowledge that they provide interpretations of the news and that their personal politics affect these interpretations. A few media people may even recognize that they can set the agenda for political decision making by focusing special attention on particular issues. But whether or not the editors, reporters, producers, or anchors acknowledge their own power, it is clear that they do more than passively mirror reality.

Members of the media enjoy far greater access than most Americans to politicians, particularly national figures such as the president. Thus the media's presentation of these figures significantly shapes the political knowledge and opinions of average citizens.

SOURCES OF MEDIA POWER

Government and the media are natural adversaries. (Thomas Jefferson once wrote that he would prefer newspapers without government to a government without newspapers. But after serving as president, he wrote that people who never read newspapers are better informed than those who do, because ignorance is closer to the truth than the falsehoods spread by newspapers.) Public officials have long been frustrated by the media. But the U.S. Constitution's First Amendment guarantee of a free press anticipates this conflict between government and the media. It prohibits government from resolving this conflict by silencing its critics.

Media professionals—television and newspaper reporters, editors, anchors, and producers—are not neutral observers of American politics but rather are active participants. They not only report events but also discover events to report, assign them political meaning, and predict their consequences (see *People in Politics:* "Stars of the Network News: Rather, Jennings, and Brokaw"). They seek to challenge government officials, debate political candidates, and define the problems of society. They see their profession as a "sacred trust" and themselves as the true voice of the people in public affairs.

Newsmaking Deciding what is "news" and who is "newsworthy"—**newsmaking**—is the most important source of media power. It is only through the media that the general public comes to know about events, personalities, and issues. Media attention makes topics public, creates issues, and elevates personalities from obscurity to celebrity. Each day, editors, producers, and reporters must select from millions of events, topics, and people those that will be videotaped, written about, and talked about. The media can never be a "picture of the world" because the whole world cannot be squeezed into the picture. The media must decide what is and is not "news."

Decisions about what will be news both influence popular discussion and cue public officials about topics they must turn their attention to. Politicians cannot

newsmaking Deciding what events, topics, presentations, and issues will be given coverage in the news.

People in Politics

Stars of the Network News: Rather, Jennings, and Brokaw

From left to right: Network news anchors Peter Jennings, Tom Brokaw, and Dan Rather.

Television news strives for credibility. Anchors are chosen not only for their personal appearance but also for the credibility they can lend to the news. The recognized all-time champion of credibility was CBS's Walter Cronkite, who for many years was "the most trusted man in America," according to all of the national polls.

Each night about 28 million Americans watch one of three men: Dan Rather, Peter Jennings, or Tom Brokaw. No other individuals—not presidents, movie stars, or popes—have had such extensive contact with so many people. These network celebrities are recognized and heard by more people than anyone else on the planet. The networks demand that an anchor be the network's premier journalist, principal showman, top editor, star, symbol of news excellence, and single most important living logo.

Anchors, then, are both celebrities and newspeople. They are chosen for their mass appeal, but they must also bring journalistic expertise to their jobs. The anchors help select from thousands of hours of videotapes and hundreds of separate stories that will be squeezed into the twenty-two minutes of nightly network news (eight minutes are reserved for commercials). Each minute represents approximately 160 spoken words; the total number of words on the entire newscast is less than found on a single news-

paper page. These inherent restrictions of the medium give great power to the anchors and their executive producers through their selection of what Americans will see and hear about the world each night.

All three network anchors are middle-aged, Anglo-Saxon, male Protestants. All share liberal and reformist social values and political beliefs.

Dan Rather, who deliberately projects an image of emotional intensity, has created both strong attachments and heated animosities among his audiences. He is most despised by conservatives because of his undisguised and passionate liberal views. Rather worked his way up through the ranks of CBS news following graduation from Sam Houston State College. He was a reporter and news director for the CBS affiliate station in Houston, then chief of the CBS London Bureau, and later Vietnam correspondent. He came to national prominence in 1966 as a CBS White House correspondent and took over the anchor position from Walter Cronkite in 1981.

The Canadian-born Peter Jennings projects an image of thoughtful, urbane sophistication. He is widely traveled (his father was a journalist), but his formal education ended in the tenth grade. ABC's *World News Tonight with Peter Jennings* devotes slightly more time to international news than do its rival news shows.

Tom Brokaw offers a calm, unemotional delivery with occasional touches of wry humor. Brokaw graduated from the University of South Dakota and started his career at an Omaha television station. He anchored local news in Atlanta and Los Angeles before moving up to the post of NBC White House correspondent in 1973. He hosted the NBC *Today* show from 1976 to 1982, and his show biz and talk-show-host experience has served him well as anchor of the *NBC Nightly News* since then. He is less ideological than Rather or Jennings and can appear relaxed and friendly with Republicans as well as Democrats.

The ratings race among the anchors is very close. Indeed, the closeness of those ratings may be driving the shows toward even more sensational themes, violent confrontations, and dramatic hype. Although all current shows have commentators, they are used less often; and it is now almost mandatory to end the show with a crowd-pleasing human interest story.

respond to reporters' questions by saying, "I don't know," or "That's not important," or "No comment." Media attention to a topic requires public officials to respond to it. Moreover, the media decide how important an issue or person or event is by their allocation of time and space. Topics early placement on the newscast and several minutes of airtime or that receive front-page newspaper coverage with headlines and pictures are believed to be important by viewers and readers.

Politicians have a love-hate relationship with the media. They need media attention to promote themselves, their message, and their programs. They crave the exposure, the name recognition, and the celebrity status that the media can confer. At the same time, they fear attack by the media. They know the media are active players in the political game, not just passive spectators. The media seek sensational stories of sin, sexuality, corruption, and scandal in government to attract viewers and readers, and thus the media pose a constant danger to politicians. Politicians understand the power of the media to make or break their careers.

"Making the news"—attracting media attention—has become a well-practiced art form in politics. The media jealously guard their power to grant or withhold public attention, but politicians, aspiring "celebrities," publicists, public relations firms, and interest groups all regularly try to influence the news. The result is an overflow of "media events"—activities arranged primarily to attract media coverage. Generally, the more bizarre, dramatic, and sensational the event, the more likely it is to make the news. It may be a march, a demonstration, a dramatic confrontation, or an emotional illustration of some injustice. Or it may be a press conference to which television and newspaper reporters are invited—whether or not there is any real news to announce. Or it may be a politician's visit to a factory or coal mine, or a walk through an inner-city neighborhood, or an inspection of a fire or other disaster site. During political campaigns, each day is a scramble to get just a few seconds on the network news, a *sound bite* of the candidate pronouncing a particularly striking phrase.

Agenda Setting   **Agenda setting** is the power to decide what will be decided. It is the power to define society's "problems," to create political issues, and to set forth alternative solutions. Deciding which issues will be addressed by government may be even more important than deciding how the issues will be resolved. The distinguished political scientist E. E. Schattschneider once wrote, "He who determines what politics is about runs the country."[1]

The real power of the media lies in their ability to set the political agenda for the nation. This power grows out of their ability to decide what is news. Media coverage determines what both citizens and public officials regard as "crises" or "problems" or "issues" to be resolved. Conditions ignored by the media seldom get on the agenda of political leaders. Media attention forces public officials to speak on the topic, take positions, and respond to questions. Media inattention allows problems to be ignored by government. "TV is the Great Legitimator. TV confers reality. Nothing happens in America, practically everyone seems to agree, until it happens on television."[2]

Political issues do not just "happen." The media are crucial to their development. Organized interest groups, professional public relations firms, government bureaucracies, political candidates, and elected officials all try to solicit the assistance of the media in shaping the political agenda. Creating an issue, publicizing it, dramatizing it, turning it into a "crisis," getting people to talk about it, and ultimately

agenda setting Deciding what will be decided; defining the problems and issues to be addressed by decision makers.

Groups hoping for free media coverage of their cause can improve their chances by framing their protests in dramatic form. Here, members of an animal-rights group attract the press by getting arrested during a protest against the fur industry, in which they painted themselves with red paint and wore leghold traps.

forcing government to do something about it, are the tactics of agenda setting. The participation of the mass media is vital to their success.[3]

Interpreting   The media not only decide what will be news, they also interpret the news for us. Editors, reporters, and anchors provide each story with an *angle*, an interpretation that places the story in a context and speculates about its meaning and consequences. The interpretation tells us what to think about the news.

Interpretation of television news begins with the *lead-in*, usually a statement about the importance of the news item or its relationship to other events. The selection of *visuals* is crucial to the interpretation, because people remember a picture better than words. The *voice-over* tells us what the visuals mean. A *recap* statement may summarize the meaning of the story.

News is presented in "stories." Reporters do not report facts; they tell stories. The story structure gives meaning to various pieces of information. Some common angles or themes of news stories are these:

- *Good guys versus bad guys:* for example, corrupt officials, foreign dictators, corporate polluters, and other assorted villains versus honest citizens, exploited workers, endangered children, or other innocents.
- *Little guys versus big guys:* for example, big corporations, the military, or insensitive bureaucracies versus consumers, taxpayers, poor people, or the elderly.
- *Appearance versus reality:* for example, the public statements of government officials or corporate executives versus whatever contradicting facts hardworking investigative reporters can find.

News is also "pictures." A story without visuals is not likely to be selected as television news in the first place. The use of visuals reinforces the angle. A close-up shot can reveal hostility, insincerity, or anxiety on the face of villains or can show fear, concern, sincerity, or compassion on the face of innocents. To emphasize elements of a story, an editor can stop the action, use slow motion, zoom the lens, add graphics, cut back and forth between antagonists, cut away for audience reaction, and so on. Videotaped interviews can be spliced to make the interviewees appear knowledgeable, informed, and sincere or, alternatively, ignorant, insensitive, and meanspirited. The media jealously guard the right to edit interviews themselves, rejecting virtually all attempts by interviewees to review and edit their own interviews.

Interpretation also occurs in the selection of *sources*, people who are presented as experienced and knowledgeable. The media select sources who express the media's views about an issue. Even when the media present both sides of a controversy, the choice of spokespersons can tilt the debate. If the media support a cause, they can select spokespersons who are personally appealing, articulate, and attractive. If they oppose a cause, they can select people who are unattractive, bumbling, confused, or obnoxious.

Socializing   The media have power to socialize audiences to the political culture. News, entertainment, and advertising all contribute to **socialization**— to the learning of political values. Socialization through television and motion pictures begins in early childhood and continues throughout life. Most of the political information people learn comes to them through television—specific facts as well as general values. Election coverage, for example, shows "how democracy works," encourages political participation, and legitimizes the winner's control of government. Advertising shows Americans desirable middle-class standards of

socialization   The learning of a culture and its values.

living even while it encourages people to buy automobiles, detergent, and beer, and entertainment programming socializes them to "acceptable" ways of life. Political values such as racial tolerance, sexual equality, and support for law enforcement are reinforced in movies, situation comedies, and police shows (see *Up Close:* "The Hollywood Liberals"). Realistic "docudramas" seize on specific political themes, from abortion, to homosexuality, to drug use, to child abuse, to AIDS. Entertainment news programming such as the highly popular *60 Minutes* is now regular prime-time fare. Thirty years ago, movies and television avoided political controversy. Today they thrive on it.

Persuading   The media, in both paid advertising and news and entertainment programming, engage in direct efforts to change our attitudes, opinions, and behavior. Newspaper editorials have traditionally been employed for direct persuasion. A great deal of the political commentary on television news and interview programs is aimed at persuading people to adopt the views of the commentators. Even many entertainment programs and movies are intended to promote specific political viewpoints. But most direct persuasion efforts come to us through paid advertising.

Corporations may use their advertising dollars not only to promote sales of their product but also to convey the message that they are good citizens—sensitive to the environment, concerned with worker and consumer safety, devoted to providing more and better jobs, goods, and services to America.

Political campaigning is now largely a media battle, with paid political advertisements as the weapons. Candidates rely on professional campaign-management firms, with their pollsters, public relations specialists, advertising-production people, and media consultants, to carry on the fight.

Governments and political leaders must rely on persuasion through the mass media to carry out their programs. Presidents can take their message directly to people in televised speeches, news conferences, and the yearly State of the Union message. Presidents by custom are accorded television time whenever they request it. In this way, they can go over the heads of Congress and even the media executives and reporters themselves to communicate directly with the people.

In short, persuasion is central to politics, and the media are the key to persuasion.

THE POLITICS OF THE MEDIA

The politics of the media are shaped by (1) their *economic interest,* (2) their *professional environment,* and (3) their *ideological leanings.* The economic interests of the media are primarily to attract and hold readers and viewers. Television networks and commercial stations charge advertisers on the basis of audience estimates made by the rating services. One rating service, A. C. Nielsen and Company, places electronic boxes in a national sample of television homes and calculates the proportion of these homes that watch a program (the rating), as well as the proportion of homes with their sets turned on that watch a particular program (the share). Newspapers' advertising revenue is based primarily on circulation figures. In short, the business of the media is to gather mass audiences to sell to advertisers.

Sensationalism   The economic interest of the media—the need to capture and hold audience attention—creates a bias toward "hype" in the selection of news, its presentation, and its interpretation. To attract viewers and readers, the media bias

The Hollywood Liberals

The motion picture and television industry centered in Hollywood has a profound effect on the nation's political culture. Much of the commercial product of Hollywood—both television entertainment programming and motion pictures—is directed toward young people. They are the heaviest watchers of television and the largest buyers of movie tickets. Thus Hollywood plays an important role in socializing young Americans to their political world.

With a few exceptions, Hollywood producers, directors, writers, studio executives, and actors are decidedly liberal in their political views, especially when compared with the general public. Of the Hollywood elite, more than 60 percent describe themselves as liberal and only 14 percent as conser-

vative, whereas in the general public, self-described conservatives outnumber liberals by a significant margin. Hollywood leaders are five times more likely to be Democrats than Republicans, although many claim to be independents. And on both economic and social issues, the Hollywood elite is significantly more liberal than the nation's general public or college-educated public (see figure).

The question remains, however, how much political influence Hollywood exercises over its audiences. Many television shows and motion pictures have little political content; they are designed almost exclusively to entertain, to gather the largest audiences for advertisers, and to sell theater tickets. Even shows or movies with political themes or pronounced political biases may not influence audiences as much as Hollywood would wish.

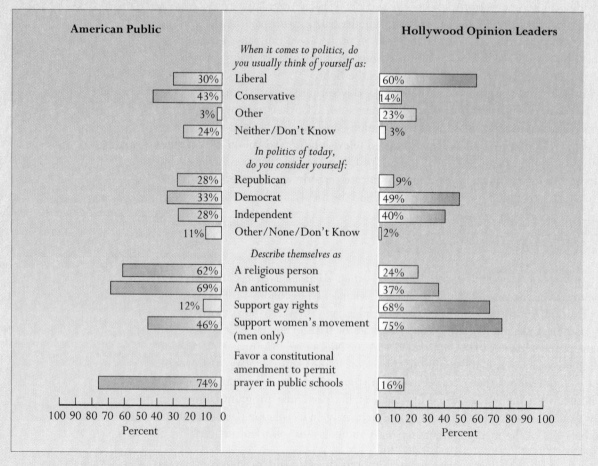

Source: David Prindle, "Hollywood Liberalism," *Social Science Quarterly* 74:1 (March 1993): 121. By permission of the author and the University of Texas Press. All rights retained by the University of Texas Press.

the news toward violence, conflict, scandal, corruption, sex, scares of various sorts, and the personal lives of politicians and celebrities. News is selected primarily for its emotional impact on audiences; its social, economic, or political significance is secondary to the need to capture attention.

News must "touch" audiences personally, arouse emotions, and hold the interest of people with short attention spans. Scare stories—street crime, drug use, AIDS, nuclear power plant accidents, global warming, and a host of health alarms—make "good" news, for they cause viewers to fear for their personal safety. The sex lives of politicians, once by custom off-limits to the press, are now public "affairs." Scandal and corruption among politicians, as well as selfishness and greed among business executives, are regular media themes.

Negativism   The media are biased toward bad news. Bad news attracts larger audiences than good news. Television news displays a pervasive bias toward the negative in American life—in government, business, the military, politics, education, and everywhere else. Bad-news stories on television outnumber good-news stories by at least 3 to 1.[4]

Good news gets little attention. For example, television news watchers are not likely to know that illegal drug use is declining in the United States; that both the air and water are measurably cleaner today than in past decades; that the nuclear power industry has the best safety record of any major industry in the United States; and that the aged in America are wealthier and enjoy higher incomes than the nonaged. Television has generally failed to report these stories or, even worse, has implied that the opposite is true.[5] Good news—stories about improved health statistics, longer life spans, better safety records, higher educational levels, for example—seldom provides the dramatic element needed to capture audience attention. The result is an overwhelming bad-news bias, especially on television.

Muckraking   The professional environment of reporters and editors predisposes them toward an activist style of journalism once dubbed **muckraking**. Reporters today view themselves as "watchdogs" of the public trust. They see themselves in noble terms—enemies of corruption, crusaders for justice, defenders of the disadvantaged. "The watchdog function, once considered remedial and subsidiary . . . [is now] paramount: the primary duty of the journalists is to focus attention on problems and deficits, failures and threats."[6] Their professional models are the crusading "investigative reporters" who expose wrongdoing in government, business, the military, and every other institution in society—except the media.

Many reporters go beyond the watchdog role and view themselves as adversaries of government. They feel that their first obligation is to attack wrongdoing—to expose greed, lawlessness, and evil in high places—so that citizens will force their government to reform. The working hypothesis almost universally shared among correspondents is that politicians are suspect: their public images are probably false, their public statements disingenuous, their moral pronouncements hypocritical, and their motives self-serving. Correspondents see it as their job to expose politicians by unmasking their disguises, debunking their claims, and piercing their rhetoric. In short, until proven otherwise, political figures of any party or persuasion are presumed to be opponents. Even on entertainment shows, politicians are usually depicted as corrupt, hypocritical, and self-seeking, and business executives as crooked, greedy, and insensitive. Reporters are particularly proud of their work when it results in official investigations.

"Bad news" is far more likely to make the news than "good news." Viewers sit up and take notice of disasters like the crash of TWA flight 800.

muckraking   Journalistic exposés of corruption, wrong-doing, or mismanagement in government, business, and other institutions of society.

What Do You Think?

Are the Media Biased?

Are the media biased, and if so in what direction—liberal or conservative? Arguments over media bias have grown in intensity as the media have come to play a central role in American politics.

Nearly three out of four Americans (74 percent) see "a fair amount" or "a great deal" of media bias in news coverage (see table below). And of those who see a bias, over twice as many see a liberal bias rather than a conservative bias. Indeed, even liberals see a liberal bias in the news; it is not a perception limited to conservatives, although they are more likely to see it. The liberal bias is much more likely to be seen by college graduates than by people who did not finish high school. It is also more likely to be seen by political activists than by those who engage in little or no political activity. However, African Americans are likely to see a conservative bias in the news, in contrast to the liberal bias perceived more often by whites.

Political bias is not Americans' only complaint about the national news media. Indeed, the most common complaint is that the media "ignore people's privacy" (80 percent). And majorities also complain about "one-sided coverage" (63 percent), "too negative" (61 percent), and "too much influence" (58 percent)—and they believe the media "abuse freedom of the press" (52 percent).

At the same time, Americans have high expectations of the role of the media in society: they expect the media to protect them from "abuse of power" by government, to hold public officials accountable, and to point out and help solve the problems of society.

Perceptions of Media Bias

	How Much Bias? "A Great Deal" or "Fair Amount" (%)	Direction of Bias	
		Liberal (%)	Conservative (%)
ALL	74	43	19
Race			
White	75	46	15
Black	64	24	40
Education			
Less than high school	56	29	33
High school graduate	75	42	19
College graduate	81	57	19
Ideology			
Liberal	70	41	22
Moderate	70	30	16
Conservative	81	57	19
Political Activism			
High	82	54	14
Low	76	42	22
None	65	34	22

Source: Data from *Media Monitor*, May/June, 1997, Center for Media and Public Affairs, Washington, D.C.

The activist role that the media have taken upon themselves means that the personal values of reporters, editors, producers, and anchors are a very important element of American politics. If the media limited themselves to a neutral observer role, then the political views of these people might have less of an impact on politics. Most newspeople argue that they do not allow their personal values to affect the news. But newspeople—like all of us—rely on their personal values in making decisions, including decisions about what is "newsworthy."

Liberalism   The political values of the media are decidedly liberal and reformist. Political scientist Doris A. Graber writes about the politics of the media: "Economic and social liberalism prevails, as does a preference for an internationalist foreign policy, caution about military intervention, and some suspicion about the ethics of established large institutions, particularly government."[7] Most Americans agree that media news coverage is biased and the bias is in a liberal direction (see *What Do You Think?* "Are the Media Biased?").

The media elite—the executives, producers, reporters, editors, and anchors—are clearly liberal or left-leaning in their political news. One study of news executives reported that 63 percent described themselves as "left-leaning," only 27 percent as "middle-of-the-road," and 10 percent as "right-leaning." Newsmakers describe themselves as either "independent" (45 percent) or Democratic (44 percent); very few (9 percent) admit to being Republican.[8]

A few conservative commentators are added to the liberal stew in order to add spice. Since controversy holds viewer attention, conservatives such as George Will, William F. Buckley, and Patrick Buchanan regularly play a confrontational role on news and talk shows. Talk *radio* is the one medium where conservatism prevails, among both hosts and call-ins (see *People in Politics:* "Rush Limbaugh, Bashing Liberals").

MEDIATED ELECTIONS

Political campaigning is largely a media activity, and the media, especially television, shape the nation's electoral politics.

The Media and Candidate-Voter Linkage   The media are the principal link between candidates and the voters. At one time, political party organizations performed this function, with city, ward, and precinct workers knocking on doors, distributing campaign literature, organizing rallies and candidate appearances, and getting out the vote on election day. But television has largely replaced party organizations and personal contact as the means by which candidates communicate with voters. Candidates come directly into the living room via television—on the nightly news, in broadcast debates and interviews, and in paid advertising (see Figure 6-3).

Media campaigning requires candidates to possess great skill in communications. Candidates must be able to project a favorable media *image*. The image is a composite of the candidate's words, mannerisms, appearance, personality, warmth, friendliness, humor, and ease in front of a camera. Policy positions have less to do with image than the candidate's ability to project personal qualities—leadership, compassion, strength, and character.

Television places an especially important emphasis on personal communication skills. Print media—newspapers and magazines—communicate only what is said. But *television communicates not only what is said but also how it is said.* For example,

Rush Limbaugh, Bashing Liberals

Welcome to the *Rush Limbaugh Show,* featuring "the number-one talk-show host in America," according to Rush himself. Limbaugh believes politics should be fun, but what is fun for him enrages liberal groups, who have been variously labeled by Limbaugh as "environmental wackos," "croissant people," and "femi-Nazis." Whether his popularity is due to his politics or to his show-manship, he does have the most popular radio talk show in the country.

Limbaugh hails from Cape Girardeau, Missouri. His father was a successful attorney, but Rush never had much interest in education. He dropped out of Southeast Missouri State University after two semesters, and his father helped him get a job at his hometown radio station. For years Limbaugh roamed the country as a struggling radio DJ, news reader, and commentator. He thought he had left radio forever when he landed a job with the Kansas City Royals baseball club as a marketing manager, but in 1983 he went back to radio, working as a commentator on KMBZ in Kansas City.

After a few months of work, KMBZ fired Limbaugh for being too controversial. His next stop was Sacramento, where he filled in for his liberal-bashing predecessor, Morton Downey, Jr. In 1988 he was offered his own show in New York, where through word of mouth and his own self-promotion, Rush hit it big.

The *Rush Limbaugh Show* combines entertainment with current events that involve liberal issues. NOW conventions, Ted Kennedy, environmental activists, and Bill and Hillary Clinton are typical targets. Limbaugh asserts that he is the response to the liberal media, and therefore he is not required to give equal time to the other side because "I *am* equal time."

All callers are carefully screened, and only occasionally does Limbaugh accept a liberal caller. He has a policy of not having guests on the show, but "well . . . I'll make an exception for the president." Listeners can never be quite sure when Rush is serious or "Hey, we're just having fun here, lighten up."

Limbaugh and other radio and television talk-show hosts represent the new "call-in democracy." They are the first to sense the public mood, often receiving calls within an hour of a political event. Callers are not necessarily representative of the general public. Rather, they are usually the most intense and outraged of citizens. But their complaints are early warning signs for wary politicians.

---

newspaper reports of Ronald Reagan's commonplace speeches and time-worn slogans failed to capture his true audience appeal, the folksy, warm, comfortable, reassuring manner, the humor and humility, and the likable personality that made Reagan "the Great Communicator." Reagan prevailed over hostile reporters, editors, and commentators because he was able to effectively communicate directly to mass audiences.

The Media and Candidate Selection   The media strongly influence the early selection of candidates. Media coverage creates *name recognition,* an essential quality for any candidate. Early media "mentions" of senators, governors, and other political figures as possible presidential contenders help to sort out the field even before the election year begins. Conversely, media inattention can condemn aspiring politicians to obscurity.

The media sort out the serious candidates early in a race. They even assign front-runner status, which may be either a blessing or a curse, depending on subsequent media coverage. In presidential primaries, the media play the *expectations game*, setting vote margins that the front-runner must meet in order to maintain *momentum*. If the front-runner does not win by a large enough margin, the media may declare the runner-up the "real" winner. This sorting out of candidates by the media influences not only voters, but—more important—financial contributors. The media-designated favorite is more likely to receive campaign contributions; financial backers do not like to waste money on losers. And as contributions roll in, the favorite can buy more television advertising, adding momentum to the campaign.

In presidential elections, the media sorting process places great emphasis on the early primary states, particularly New Hampshire, whose primary in early February is customarily the first contest in a presidential election year. Less than 1 percent of convention delegates are chosen by this small state, but media coverage is intense, and the winner quickly becomes the media-designated front-runner.[9]

Perhaps the most striking example of media influence in presidential politics occurred in 1968 when anti–Vietnam War candidate Senator Eugene McCarthy challenged President Lyndon Johnson in the Democratic primary in New Hampshire. Johnson won with 60 percent of the vote, but the media reported McCarthy's 40 percent as a "stunning surprise," even a "moral victory." This deeply embarrassed President Johnson, who announced his decision not to seek reelection on March 31.

The Media and the Horse Race The media give election campaigns **horse-race coverage**: reporting on who is ahead or behind, what the candidates' strategies are, how much money they are spending, and, above all, what their current standing in the polls is. Such stories account for more than half of all television news coverage of an election. Additional stories are centered on *campaign* issues—

horse-race coverage Media coverage of electoral campaigns that concentrates on who is ahead and who is behind, and neglects the issues at stake.

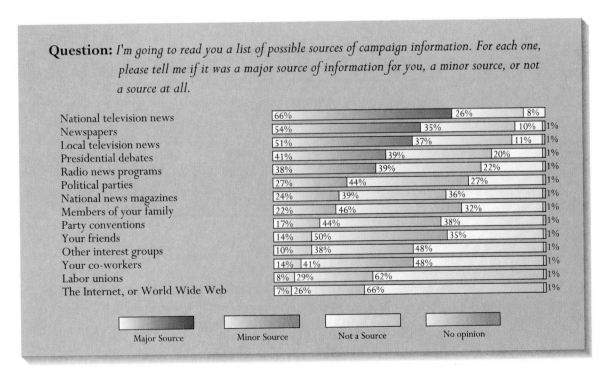

Question: *I'm going to read you a list of possible sources of campaign information. For each one, please tell me if it was a major source of information for you, a minor source, or not a source at all.*

	Major Source	Minor Source	Not a Source	No opinion
National television news	66%	26%	8%	
Newspapers	54%	35%	10%	1%
Local television news	51%	37%	11%	1%
Presidential debates	41%	39%	20%	1%
Radio news programs	38%	39%	22%	1%
Political parties	27%	44%	27%	1%
National news magazines	24%	39%	36%	1%
Members of your family	22%	46%	32%	1%
Party conventions	17%	44%	38%	1%
Your friends	14%	50%	35%	1%
Other interest groups	10%	38%	48%	1%
Your co-workers	14%	41%	48%	1%
Labor unions	8%	29%	62%	1%
The Internet, or World Wide Web	7%	26%	66%	1%

FIGURE 6-3 Sources of Political Campaign Information

Source: The survey was conducted jointly by *The Washington Post*, Harvard University, and the Kaiser Family Foundation; reported in *The Polling Report*, December 9, 1996.

What Do You Think?

Should the Media Report on the Private Lives of Public Officials?

Historically, reputable newspapers and magazines declined to carry stories about the sex lives of political figures. This unwritten ethic of journalism protected Presidents Franklin D. Roosevelt, Dwight D. Eisenhower, and John F. Kennedy during their political careers. But today, journalistic ethics (if there are any at all) do not limit reporting of sexual charges, rumors, or innuendos or public questioning of candidates and appointees about whether they ever "cheated on their spouse," "smoked marijuana," or "watched pornographic movies."

The media's rationale is that these stories reflect on the *character* of a candidate and hence deserve reporting to the general public as information relevant to their choice for national leadership. (See *What Do You Think?* "Should We Judge Presidents on Private Character or Performance in Office" in Chapter 11.) Yet it seems clear that scandalous stories are pursued by the media primarily for their commercial value. Sex sells; it attracts viewers and readers. But the media's focus on sexual scandal and other misconduct obscures other issues. Politicians defending themselves from personal attack cannot get their political themes and messages across to voters. Moreover, otherwise qualified people may stay out of politics to avoid the embarrassment to themselves and their families that results from invasion of personal privacy.

Popular reation to reports of President Clinton's sexual relationship with White House intern Monica Lewinsky suggests that most Americans separate private conduct from performance in office. Early in 1998, despite Clinton's denials, a majority of Americans believed that the allegations of sexual misconduct were "probably true":

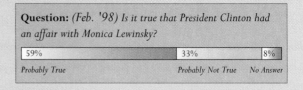

Question: *(Feb. '98) Is it true that President Clinton had an affair with Monica Lewinsky?*

| 59% | 33% | 8% |
| Probably True | Probably Not True | No Answer |

However, most believed that the affair was a "private matter":

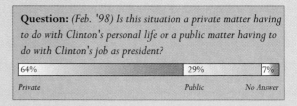

Question: *(Feb. '98) Is this situation a private matter having to do with Clinton's personal life or a public matter having to do with Clinton's job as president?*

| 64% | 29% | 7% |
| Private | Public | No Answer |

And, to the surprise of many media commentators, Clinton's job approval ratings *rose* markedly following the scandalous reports.

Even after Clinton's later public admission that he had had an "inappropriate relationship" with Lewinsky and had "misled" people about it, and even after the publication of the lurid Starr report with graphic sexual details of the relationship, the American public continued to approve of Clinton's performance in office:

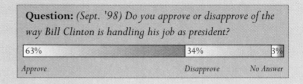

Question: *(Sept. '98) Do you approve or disapprove of the way Bill Clinton is handling his job as president?*

| 63% | 34% | 3% |
| Approve | Disapprove | No Answer |

controversies that arise on the campaign trail itself, including verbal blunders by the candidate—and *character* issues, such as the sex life of the candidate. In contrast, *policy* issues typically account for fewer than one-quarter of the television news stories on a presidential election campaign.

The Media as Campaign Watchdogs The media's bad-news bias is evident in election campaigns as well as in general news reporting. Negative stories about all presidential candidates usually outnumber positive stories.[10] The media generally see their function in political campaigns as reporting on the weaknesses, blun-

Moreover, most Americans did *not* believe that Clinton should be impeached and removed from office as a result of the affair:

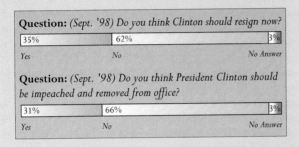

Question: *(Sept. '98) Do you think Clinton should resign now?*

35%	62%	3%
Yes	No	No Answer

Question: *(Sept. '98) Do you think President Clinton should be impeached and removed from office?*

31%	66%	3%
Yes	No	No Answer

Surveys of public opinion strongly suggest that Americans not only separate private conduct from performance in public office, but also oppose media reporting of private misconduct. The graph below illustrates how Americans distinguish between media reporting on public and private matters.

Sources: *New York Times*, February 24, 1998; CNN/*USA Today* poll, September 13, 1998.

Question: *For each of the following stories about public officials, please tell me whether you feel it should almost always be reported, whether it should sometimes be reported depending on the circumstances, or whether it should almost never be reported.*

When a public official…

…used military aircraft for personal trips without reimbursing the government?

| 76% | 16% | 7% | 1 |

…is found to have not paid federal income tax one time in the past?

| 69% | 21% | 9% | 1 |

…is found to have exaggerated his record of military service?

| 62% | 25% | 11% | 2 |

…is having an extramarital affair?

| 39% | 22% | 37% | 2 |

…is a homosexual?

| 33% | 21% | 43% | 3 |

…attended a party at which cocaine was used?

| 29% | 29% | 41% | 1 |

…is found to have been arrested for marijuana possession when he was a college student?

| 26% | 23% | 50% | 1 |

…had an extramarital affair six or seven years ago?

| 18% | 22% | 59% | 1 |

Almost always   Sometimes   Almost never   No opinion

Source: Gallup poll, May 8, 1991.

ders, and vulnerabilities of the candidates (see *What Do You Think?* "Should Media Report on the Private Lives of Public Officials?"). It might be argued that exposing the flaws of the candidates is an important function in a democracy. But the media's negative reporting about candidates and generally skeptical attitude toward their campaign speeches, promises, and advertisements may contribute to political alienation and cynicism among voters.

The media focus intense scrutiny on the personal lives of candidates—their marriages, sex lives, drug or alcohol use, personal finances, past friendships, military service, club memberships, and other potential sources of embarrassment.

FIGURE 6-4 Presidential Campaign Coverage by TV News in 1996

Source: Data from *Media Monitor*, December 1996, Center for Media and Public Affairs, Washington, D.C.

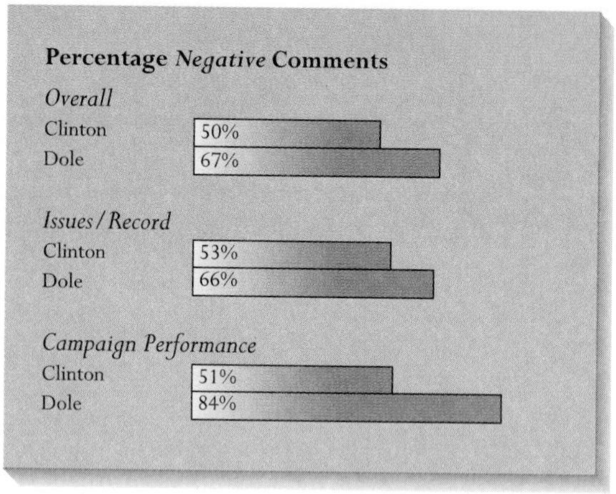

Percentage *Negative* Comments

Overall
Clinton 50%
Dole 67%

Issues/Record
Clinton 53%
Dole 66%

Campaign Performance
Clinton 51%
Dole 84%

Virtually any past error in judgment or behavior by a candidate is given heavy coverage. But the media defend their attention to personal scandal on the ground that they are reporting on the "character issue." Voters must have information on candidates' character as well as on their policy positions.

The Media and Political Bias   The media are very sensitive to charges of bias toward candidates or parties. Media people are overwhelmingly liberal and Democratic but generally try to deflect charges of political bias during an election campaign by giving almost equal coverage to both Democratic and Republican candidates. Moreover, the media report negatively on both Republicans and Democrats, although some scholars count more negative stories about Republican candidates (see Figure 6-4).

The media are generally more critical of front-runners than of underdogs during a campaign. A horse race loses audience interest if one horse gets too far ahead, so the media tend to favor the underdog. "Frontrunners and incumbents consistently experienced the least balanced, least favorable news coverage."[11] During the long presidential primary season, media attacks on an early favorite may result in gains for the underdog, who then becomes the new object of attack.

FREEDOM VERSUS FAIRNESS

Complaints about the fairness of media are as old as the printing press. Most early newspapers in the United States were allied with political parties; they were not expected to be fair in their coverage. It was only in the early 1900s that many large newspapers broke their ties with parties and proclaimed themselves independent. And it was not until the 1920s and 1930s that the norms of journalistic professionalism and accuracy gained widespread acceptance.

The Constitution protects the *freedom* of the press; it was not intended to guarantee *fairness.* The First Amendment's guarantee of freedom of the press was originally designed to protect the press from government attempts to silence criticism. Over the years, the U.S. Supreme Court has greatly expanded the meaning of the free-press guarantee.

No Prior Restraint   The Supreme Court has interpreted freedom of the press to mean that government may place no **prior restraint** on speech or

prior restraint   Power of government to prevent publication or to require approval before publication; generally prohibited by the First Amendment.

publication (that is, before it is said or published). Originally, this doctrine was designed to prevent the government from closing down or seizing newspapers. Today, the doctrine prevents the government from censoring any news items. In the famous case of the Pentagon Papers, the *New York Times* and *Washington Post* undertook to publish secret information stolen from the files of the State Department and Defense Department regarding U.S. policy in Vietnam while the war was still going on.[12] No one disputed the fact that stealing the secret material was illegal. What was at issue was the ability of the government to prevent the publication of stolen documents in order to protect national security. The Supreme Court rejected the national security argument and reaffirmed that the government may place no prior restraint on publication. If the government wishes to keep military secrets, it must not let them fall into the hands of the American press.

Press versus Electronic Media   In the early days of radio, broadcast channels were limited, and anyone with a radio transmitter could broadcast on any frequency. As a result, interference was a common frustration of early broadcasters. The industry petitioned the federal government to regulate and license the assignment and use of broadcast frequencies.

The Federal Communications Commission (FCC) was established in 1934 to allocate broadcast frequencies and to license stations for "the public interest, convenience and necessity." The act clearly instructed the FCC: "Nothing in this Act shall be understood or construed to give the Commission the power of censorship." However, the FCC views a broadcast license and exclusive right to use a particular frequency as a *public trust*. Thus broadcasters, unlike newspapers and magazines, are licensed by a government agency and must operate in the *public interest*.

The Equal-Time Requirement   The FCC requires radio and television stations that provide airtime to a political candidate to offer competing candidates the same amount of airtime at the same price. Stations are not required to give free time to candidates, but if stations choose to give free time to one candidate, they must do so for the candidate's opponents. But this **equal-time rule** does not apply to newscasts, news specials, or even long documentaries; nor does it apply to talk shows like *Larry King Live* (see *People in Politics:"Larry King Live"*). Nor does it apply to presidential press conferences or presidential addresses to the nation, although the networks now generally offer free time for a "Republican response" to a Democratic president, and vice versa. A biased news presentation does not require the network or station to grant equal time to opponents of its views. And it is important to note that newspapers, unlike radio and television, have never been required to provide equal time to opposing views (see *Compared to What? "America's TV Culture in Perspective"*).

LIBEL AND SLANDER

Communications that wrongly damage an individual are known in law as **libel** (when written) and **slander** (when spoken). The injured party must prove in court that the communication caused actual damage and was either false or defamatory. A damaging falsehood or words or phrases that are defamatory (such as "Joe Jones is a rotten son of a bitch") are libelous and are not protected by the First Amendment from lawsuits seeking compensation.

equal-time rule   Federal Communications Commission (FCC) requirement that broadcasters who sell time to any political candidate must make equal time available to opposing candidates at the same price.

libel   Writings that are false and malicious and are intended to damage an individual.

slander   Oral statements that are false and malicious and are intended to damage an individual.

Public Officials   Over the years, the media have sought to narrow the protection afforded public officials against libel and slander. In 1964 the U.S. Supreme Court ruled in the case of *New York Times v. Sullivan* that public officials did not have a right to recover damages for false statements unless they are made with "malicious intent."[13] The **Sullivan rule** requires public officials not only to show that the media published or broadcast false and damaging statements but also to prove they did so knowing that their statements were false and damaging or that they did so with "reckless disregard" for the truth or falsehood of their statements. The effect of the Sullivan rule is to free the media to say virtually anything about public officials. Indeed, the media have sought to expand the definition of "public officials" to "public figures"—that is, to include anyone they choose as the subject of a story.

Sullivan rule   Court guideline that false and malicious statements regarding public officials are protected by the First Amendment unless it can be proven they were known to be false at the time they were made or were made with "reckless disregard" for their truth or falsehood.

People in Politics

Larry King Live

Who turned presidential politics into talk-show entertainment? A strong argument can be made that Larry King was personally responsible for changing the nature of presidential campaigning. It was Larry King who nudged frequent talk-show guest Ross Perot into the presidential arena. And it was Larry King who demonstrated to the candidates that the talk-show format was a good way to reach out to the American people.

Larry King's supremacy in talk-show politics came late in life, after a half-century of hustling and hard knocks, no college education, bouts of gambling followed by bankruptcy, and multiple marriages. King has written five books about himself, describing his rise from Brooklyn neighborhoods; his friendships with Jackie Gleason, Frank Sinatra, and other celebrities; and his hardscrabble life. As he tells it, he hung around a New York radio station for five years before taking a bus to Miami to try his luck first as a disk jockey and later as a sports announcer. After a decade in Miami, he had his own TV interview show, a talk show on radio, and a newspaper column, and he was color commentator for the Miami Dolphins. He lived the fast life, running up huge debts and dealing in shady financial transactions. He was arrested in 1971 on grand larceny charges; they were dropped only because the statute of limi-

tations had expired. He lost his TV and radio shows and his newspaper column. He ended up in Shreveport, Louisiana, doing play by play for the World Football League's Shreveport Steamers. In 1975 he was bankrupt but back in Miami doing radio. In 1978 he moved to Washington to launch his Mutual Network radio talk show. As radio talk shows gained popularity, so did King. When CNN started twenty-four-hour broadcasting in 1982, the new TV network turned to King to do an evening interview show, *Larry King Live*. At first, the show merely filled the space between the evening and the late news. A decade later, the show was making news itself.

King's success is directly attributable to his accommodating style. He actually listens to his guests; he lets them speak for themselves; he unashamedly plugs their books, records, and movies. He does *not* attack his guests; he does not assume the adversarial, abrasive style preferred by reporters like Sam Donaldson, Dan Rather, and Mike Wallace. An old-fashioned liberal himself, King appears comfortable interviewing politicians of every stripe. He lets guests talk about themselves. He tosses "softball" questions: "If I were to interview the president about an alleged sexual affair, I wouldn't ask if he'd had one, I'd ask him, 'How does it feel to read these things about yourself?'"

With his emphasis on feelings, emotions, and motives rather than on facts, it is little wonder that King's style attracts politicians . . . or that *Larry King Live* is the highest rated show on CNN.

Source: Time, October 5, 1992, p. 76.

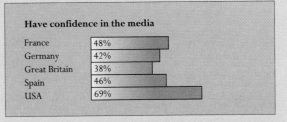

Compared to What?

America's TV Culture in Perspective

America is a TV culture. Americans rely more on television for news and entertainment than people in other advanced industrial nations do. Perhaps more important, Americans have greater confidence in the media than other peoples do. Consider, for example, the question "Would you say you have a great deal of confidence, only some confidence, hardly any confidence, or no confidence at all in the media—press, radio, and television?" When this question was asked of a national sample of Americans, 69 percent responded that they had a great deal or at least some confidence in the media. But majorities in four other countries—France, Great Britain, Germany, and Spain—said they had little or no confidence in the media (see "confidence in the media" figure).

How much do the media influence key decisions in society? A majority of people in both the United States and these same European nations believe the media exert a large influence on public opinion. Americans appear to be closer to unanimity on this point (88 percent) than are Europeans. When people are asked how much influence the media exerts on particular governing institutions—the executive, the legislature, and the judiciary—Americans are much more likely to perceive strong media influence than are Europeans (see "media influence" figure).

Source: Adapted from Lawrence Parisot, "Attitudes about the Media: A Five Country Study," *Public Opinion* 43 (January/February 1988): 18, 60.

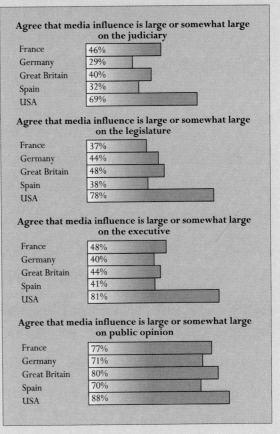

Have confidence in the media

France	48%
Germany	42%
Great Britain	38%
Spain	46%
USA	69%

Agree that media influence is large or somewhat large on the judiciary

France	46%
Germany	29%
Great Britain	40%
Spain	32%
USA	69%

Agree that media influence is large or somewhat large on the legislature

France	37%
Germany	44%
Great Britain	48%
Spain	38%
USA	78%

Agree that media influence is large or somewhat large on the executive

France	48%
Germany	40%
Great Britain	44%
Spain	41%
USA	81%

Agree that media influence is large or somewhat large on public opinion

France	77%
Germany	71%
Great Britain	80%
Spain	70%
USA	88%

"Absence of Malice"   The First Amendment protects the right of the media to be biased, unfair, negative, sensational, and even offensive. Indeed, even *damaging falsehoods* may be printed or broadcast as long as the media can show the story was not deliberately fabricated by them with malicious intent. In a CBS documentary, *The Uncounted Enemy: A Vietnam Deception,* broadcast in 1982, Mike Wallace charged General William C. Westmoreland, former commander of U.S. forces in Vietnam, with a "conspiracy" to deceive Congress, the president, and the American people about enemy troop strength. The documentary made no attempt to present different sides of the story or even to acknowledge that different intelligence analysts could arrive at different conclusions about enemy strength. CBS deleted from the broadcast all information and testimony it received supporting General Westmoreland's position

and spliced and doctored tapes and distorted quotes to make interviewees appear to attack the general when the full interview showed them to be defending him. By any journalistic standard the broadcast was unfair and biased.[14]

But the Constitution protects the right of a free press to be unfair. CBS did not have to prove that the general deceived his superiors; all CBS needed to show was that it had a reasonable basis for believing he did. At the libel trial, CBS produced a surprise witness, Westmoreland's own intelligence chief in Vietnam, who said that the general "withheld" intelligence estimates from Washington. The general withdrew his suit in exchange for a statement from CBS affirming the general's patriotism and "long and faithful service to his country." But CBS paid no monetary damages and declared it would "stand by the broadcast" despite "minor procedural violations of CBS news standards."

Shielding Sources   The media argue that the First Amendment allows them to refuse to reveal the names of their sources, even when this information is required in criminal investigations and trials. Thus far, the U.S. Supreme Court has not given blanket protection to reporters to withhold information from court proceedings. However, a number of states have passed *shield laws* protecting reporters from being forced to reveal their sources.

MEDIA EFFECTS: SHAPING POLITICAL LIFE

What effects do the media have on public opinion and political behavior? Let us consider media effects on (1) information and agenda setting, (2) values and opinions, and (3) behavior. These categories of effects are ranked by the degree of influence the media are likely to have over us. The strongest effects of the media are on our information levels and societal concerns. The media also influence values and opinions, but the strength of media effects in these areas is diluted by many other influences. Finally, it is most difficult to establish the independent effect of the media on behavior.

Information and Agenda-Setting Effects   The media strongly influence what we know about our world and how we think and talk about it. Years ago, foreign-policy expert Bernard Cohen, in the first book to assess the effects of the media on foreign policy, put it this way: "The mass media may not be successful in telling people what to think, but the media are stunningly successful in telling their audience what to think about"[15] (see *Up Close:* "The Media Age").

However, **information overload** diminishes the influence of the media in determining what we think about. So many communications are directed at us that we cannot possibly process them all. A person's ability to recall a media report depends on repeated exposure to it and reinforcement through personal experience. For example, an individual who has a brother in a trouble spot in the Middle East is more likely to be aware of reports from that area of the world. But too many voices with too many messages cause most viewers to block out a great deal of information.

Information overload may be especially heavy in political news. Television tells most viewers more about politics than they really want to know. Political scientist Austin Ranney writes, "The fact is that for most Americans politics is still far from being the most interesting and important thing in life. To them, politics is usually confusing, boring, repetitious, and above all irrelevant to the things that really matter in their lives."[16]

information overload   Situation in which individuals are subjected to so many communications that they cannot make sense of them.

Effects on Values and Opinions   The media often tell us how we *should* feel about news events or issues, especially those about which we have no prior feelings or experiences. The media can reinforce values and attitudes we already hold. However, the media seldom change our preexisting values or opinions. Media influence over values and opinions is reduced by **selective perception**, mentally screening out information or opinions we disagree with. People tend to see and hear only what they want to see and hear. For example, television news concentration on scandal, abuse, and corruption in government has not always produced the liberal, reformist values among viewers that media people expected. On the contrary, the focus of network executives on governmental scandals—Watergate, the Iran-contra scandal, the sexual antics of politicians, congressional check kiting, and so on—has produced feelings of general political distrust and cynicism toward government and the political system. These feelings have been labeled **television malaise**, a combination of social distrust, political cynicism, feelings of powerlessness, and disaffection from parties and politics that seems to stem from television's emphasis on the negative aspects of American life.

The media do not *intend* to create television malaise; they are performing their self-declared watchdog role. They expect their stories to encourage liberal reform of our political institutions. But the result is often alienation rather than reform.

Direct Effects on Public Opinion   Can the media change public opinion, and if so, how? For many years, political scientists claimed that the media had only minimal effects on public opinions and behavior. This early view was based largely on the fact that newspaper editorial endorsements seldom affected people's votes. But serious research on the effects of television tells a different story.

In an extensive study of eighty policy issues over fifteen years, political scientists examined public opinion polls on various policy issues at a first point in time, then media content over a following interval of time, and finally public opinion on these same issues at the end of the interval. The purpose was to learn if media content—messages scored by their relevance to the issue, their salience in the broadcast, their pro/con direction, the credibility of the news source, and quality of the reporting—changed public opinion. Although most people's opinions remained constant over time (opinion at the first time period is the best predictor of opinion at the second time period), opinion *changes* were heavily influenced by media messages. The authors concluded that "news variables alone account for nearly half the variance in opinion change." They also reported the following:

- Anchors, reporters, and commentators have the greatest impact on opinion change. Television newscasters have high credibility and trust with the general public. Their opinions are crucial in shaping mass opinion.

- Independent experts interviewed by the media have a substantial impact on opinion, but not as great as newscasters themselves.

- A popular president can also shift public opinion somewhat. Unpopular presidents do not have much success as opinion movers, however.

- Interest groups on the whole have a slightly negative effect on public opinion. "In many instances they seem to actually have antagonized the public and created a genuine adverse effect"; such cases include Vietnam War protesters, nuclear freeze advocates, and other demonstrators and protesters, even peaceful ones.[17]

selective perception
Mentally screening out information or opinions with which one disagrees.

television malaise   Generalized feelings of distrust, cynicism, and powerlessness stemming from television's emphasis on the negative aspects of American life.

Up Close

The Media Age

The print media—newspapers, magazines, and books—have played a major role in American politics since colonial times. But the electronic media—radio, television, and cable television—are relatively new forces.

Radio was widely introduced into American homes in the 1920s and 1930s, allowing President Franklin D. Roosevelt to become the first "media president," directly communicating with the American people through radio "fireside chats." After World War II, the popularity of television spread quickly; between 1950 and 1960, the percentage of homes with TV sets grew from 9 to 87.

Some notable political media innovations over the years:

- **1952:** The first paid commercial TV ad in a presidential campaign appeared, on behalf of Dwight D. Eisenhower. The black-and-white ad began with a voice-over—"Eisenhower answers the nation!"—followed by citizens asking favorable questions and Eisenhower responding, and ending with a musical jingle: "I like Ike." Although crude by current standards, it nevertheless set a precedent in media campaigning.

- **1952:** The "Checkers speech" by Eisenhower's running mate, Richard M. Nixon, represented the first direct television appeal to the people over the heads of party leaders. Nixon was about to be dumped from the Republican ticket for hiding secret slush-fund money from campaign contributors. He went on national television with an emotional appeal, claiming that the only personal item he ever took from a campaign contributor was his daughters' little dog, Checkers. Thousands of viewers called and wired in sympathy. Ike kept Nixon on the ticket.

- **1960:** The first televised debate between presidential candidates featured a youthful, handsome John F. Kennedy against a shifty-eyed Richard M. Nixon with a pronounced "five o'clock shadow." Nixon doggedly scored debater points, but JFK presented a cool and confident image and spoke directly to the viewers. The debate swung the popular tide toward Kennedy, who won in a very tight contest. Nixon attributed his defeat to his failure to shave before the broadcast.

- **1964:** The first "negative" TV ad was the "Daisy Girl" commercial sponsored by the Lyndon Johnson campaign against Republican conservative Barry Goldwater. It implied that Goldwater would start a nuclear war. It showed a little girl picking petals off a daisy while an ominous voice counted down "10-9-8-7 . . ." to a nuclear explosion, followed by a statement that Lyndon Johnson could be trusted to keep the peace.

- **1976:** President Gerald Ford was the first incumbent president to agree to a televised debate. (No televised presidential debates were held in the Nixon-Humphrey race in 1968 or in the Nixon-McGovern race in 1972. Apparently Nixon had learned his lesson.) Ford stumbled badly, and Jimmy Carter went on to victory. President Carter was unable to dodge debating Reagan in 1980, and televised debates became a political institution.

- **1982:** CNN (Cable News Network), introduced by the maverick media mogul Ted Turner, began twenty-four-hour broadcasting.

Effects on Behavior   Many studies have focused on the effects of the media on behavior: studies of the effects of TV violence, studies of the effects of television on children, and studies of the effects of obscenity and pornography.[18] Although it is difficult to generalize from these studies, television appears more likely to reinforce behavioral tendencies than to change them. For example, televised violence may trigger violent behavior in children who are already predisposed to such behavior, but televised violence has little behavioral effect on average children.[19] Nevertheless, we know that television advertising sells products. And we know that political candidates spend millions to persuade audiences to go out and vote for them on election day. Both manufacturers and politicians create name recognition,

The first televised presidential election debates were in 1960 between Senator John F. Kennedy and Vice President Richard Nixon. Nixon came armed with statistics, but his dour demeanor, "five o'clock shadow," and stiff presentation fared poorly in contrast to Kennedy's open, relaxed, confident air.

- **1991:** The Persian Gulf War was the first war to be fought live on television. (Although film and videotape reports of the Vietnam War had been important molders of public opinion in America, the technology of that era did not allow live reporting. In the Gulf War, the Iraqi government permitted CNN to continue live broadcasts from Baghdad, including spectacular coverage of the first night's air raids on the city.

- **1992:** In the presidential election, television talk shows became a major focus of the campaign. Wealthy independent candidate Ross Perot actually conducted an all-media campaign, rejecting in-person appearances in favor of such media techniques as half-hour "infomercials."

- **1994–95:** The arrest and trial of celebrity O. J. Simpson on murder charges so domi-

nated the national news that more television time was devoted to the O. J. story than to the actions of the president and Congress.

- **1996:** The presidential election was given less television time and newspaper space than previous elections. Clinton's large lead throughout the campaign, public boredom with Whitewater and other scandals, and Dole's lackluster performance frustrated reporters in search of drama. Network TV news gave Clinton twice as much positive coverage as Dole.

- **1997-98:** Sex scandals involving Bill Clinton dominated the news and talk shows, but public opinion polls gave the president the highest approval ratings of his two terms in office.

employ product differentiation, try to associate with audiences, and use repetition to communicate their messages. These tactics are designed to affect our behavior both in the marketplace and in the election booth.

Political ads are more successful in motivating a candidate's supporters to go to the polls than they are in changing opponents into supporters. It is unlikely that voters who dislike a candidate or are committed to another candidate will be persuaded by political advertising to change their votes. But many potential voters are undecided, and the support of many others is dubbed "soft." Going to the polls on election day requires effort—people have errands to do, it may be raining, they may be tired. Television advertising is more effective with the marginal voters.

Politics in Cyberspace

The Media

Major News Organizations

Most major national news organizations, both print and broadcast, now post up-to-date news online. Here are some to look for:

ABC	http://www.abc.com
CBS	http://www.cbs.com
NBC	http://www.msnbc.com
CNN	http://www.cnn.com
USA Today	http://www.usatoday.com
New York Times	http://www.nytimes.com
Washington Post	http://www.washingtonpost.com

The Center for Media and Public Affairs
http://www.cmpa.com

The Center for Media and Public Affairs is a nonprofit, Washington-based think tank that studies how the media treat social and political issues.

The Drudge Report
http://www.drudgereport.com

The upstart Matt Drudge uses his Web site to present unabashedly tabloid coverage of Washington politics without concern for the niceties of journalistic ethics that constrain reporters and commentators working for established news organizations. Drudge proudly boasts that 80 percent of what he reports is true. The site also provides links to all major news agencies.

SUMMARY NOTES

- The mass media in America not only report on the struggle for power; they are participants themselves in that struggle.

- It is only through the media that the general public comes to know about political events, personalities, and issues. Newsmaking—deciding what is or is not "news"—is a major source of media power. Media coverage not only influences popular discussion but also forces public officials to respond.

- Media power also derives from the media's ability to set the agenda for public decision making—to determine what citizens and public officials will regard as "crises," "problems," or "issues" to be resolved by government.

- The media also exercise power in their interpretation of the news. News is presented in story form; pictures, words, sources, and story selection all contribute to interpretation.

- The media play a major role in socializing people to the political culture. Socialization occurs in news, entertainment, and advertising.

- The politics of the media are shaped by their economic interest in attracting readers and viewers.

This interest largely accounts for the sensational and negative aspects of news reporting.

- The professional environment of newspeople encourages an activist, watchdog role in politics and government. The politics of most newspeople are liberal and Democratic.

- Political campaigning is largely a media activity. The media have replaced the parties as the principal linkage between candidates and voters. But the media tend to report the campaign as a horse race, at the expense of issue coverage, and to focus more on candidates' character than on their voting records or issue positions.

- The First Amendment guarantee of freedom of press protects the media from government efforts to silence or censor them and allows the media to be "unfair" when they choose to be. The Federal Communication Commission exercises some modest controls over the electronic media, since the rights to exclusive use of broadcast frequencies is a *public trust*.

- Public officials are afforded very little protection by libel and slander laws. The Supreme Court's Sullivan rule allows even damaging falsehoods to be written and broadcast as long as newspeople themselves do not deliberately fabricate lies with "malicious intent" or "reckless disregard."

- Media effects on political life can be observed in (1) information and agenda setting, (2) values and opinions, and (3) behavior—in that order of influence. The media strongly influence what we know about politics and what we talk about. The media are less effective in changing existing opinions, values, and beliefs than they are in creating new ones. Nevertheless, the media can change many people's opinions, based on the credibility of news anchors and reporters. Direct media effects on behavior are limited. Political ads are more important in motivating supporters to go to the polls, and in swinging undecided or "soft" voters, than in changing the minds of committed voters

SELECTED READINGS

ANSOLABEHERE, STEPHEN, ROY BEHR, and SHANTO IYENGAR. *The Media Game: American Politics in the Television Age.* New York: Macmillan, 1993. A comprehensive text assessing the changes in the political system brought about by the rise of television since the 1950s.

FALLOWS, JAMES. *Breaking the News: How the Media Undermine American Democracy.* New York: Pantheon Books, 1996. An argument that today's arrogant, cynical, and scandal-minded news reporting is turning readers and viewers away and undermining support for democracy.

GRABER, DORIS A. *Mass Media and American Politics.* 5th ed. Washington, D.C.: Congressional Quarterly Press, 1996. A wide-ranging description of media effects on campaigns, parties, and elections, as well as on social values and public policies.

LICHTER, ROBERT S., STANLEY ROTHMAN, and LINDA S. LICHTER. *The Media Elite.* Bethesda, Md.: Adler and Adler, 1986. A thorough study of the social and political values of top leaders in the mass media, based on extensive interviews of key people in the most influential media outlets.

LIMBAUGH, RUSH. *The Way Things Ought to Be.* New York: Simon & Schuster, 1992. Humor and bombast by the popular conservative radio and television personality.

MEDVED, MICHAEL. *Hollywood versus America.* New York: HarperCollins, 1992. An assault on the entertainment establishment, charging it with corrupting American culture with "sleaze and self-indulgence," a "preference for the perverse," and "a bias for the bizarre" that bashes religion, the family, business, the military, and American institutions generally.

PATTERSON, THOMAS E. *Out of Order.* New York: Random House, 1994. The antipolitical bias of the media poisons national election campaigns; policy questions are ignored in favor of the personal characteristics of candidates, their campaign strategies, and their standing in the horse race.

PRINDLE, DAVID F. *Risky Business.* Boulder, Colo.: Westview Press, 1993. An examination of the politics of Hollywood, its liberalism, activism, self-indulgence, and celebrity egotism.

SABATO, LARRY J. *Feeding Frenzy: How Attack Journalism Has Transformed American Politics.* New York: Free Press, 1992. A strong argument that the media prefer "to employ titillation rather than scrutiny" and as a result produce "trivialization rather than enlightenment."

WEST, DARRELL M. *Air Wars.* Washington, D.C.: Congressional Quarterly Press, 1993. An assessment of the effects of television advertisements in election campaigns from 1952 through 1992.

ASK YOURSELF ABOUT POLITICS

1 Generally speaking, how would you identify yourself: as a Republican, Democrat, independent, or something else?

Republican ☐   Democrat ☐
Independent ☐   Other ☐

2 Which major political party better represents the interests of people like yourself?

Republican ☐   Democrat ☐

3 Does the Republican Party favor the rich more than the middle class or poor?

Yes ☐   No ☐

4 Does the Democratic Party favor the poor more than the middle class or rich?

Yes ☐   No ☐

5 Which major party does a better job of protecting the Social Security system?

Republican ☐   Democrat ☐

6 Which major party does a better job of handling foreign affairs?

Republican ☐   Democrat ☐

7 Should elected officials be bound by their party's platform?

Yes ☐   No ☐

8 Do we need a third party to challenge the Republican and Democratic parties?

Yes ☐   No ☐

CHAPTER OUTLINE

FEATURES

How much power do politi-
cal parties really have to
determine who gets what
in America? We hear the terms
Republican and *Democratic* linked to
people and to policies, but do these
parties have real power beyond that
of organizing for elections?

THE POWER OF ORGANIZATION

In the struggle for power, organization grants advantage. Italian political scientist Gaetano Mosca once put it succinctly: "A hundred men acting uniformly in concert, with a common understanding, will triumph over a thousand men who are not in accord and can be dealt with one by one."[1] Thus politics centers on organization—on organizing people to win office and to influence public policy.

Political organizations—parties and interest groups—function as intermediaries between individuals and government. They organize individuals to give them power in selecting government officials—who governs—and in determining public policy—for what ends. Generally, **political parties** are more concerned with winning public office in elections than with influencing policy, whereas *interest groups* are more directly concerned with public policy and involve themselves with elections only to advance their policy interests (see Figure 7-1). In other words, parties and interest groups have an informal division of functions, with parties focusing on personnel and interest groups focusing on policy. Yet both organize individuals for more effective political action.

AMERICAN PARTIES: A HISTORICAL PERSPECTIVE

Parties are *not* mentioned in the Constitution. Indeed, the nation's Founders regarded both parties and interest groups as "factions," citizens united by "some common impulse of passion, or of interest, adverse to the rights of other citizens, or to the permanent and aggregate interests of the community." The Founders viewed factions as "mischievous" and "dangerous."[2] Yet the emergence of parties was inevitable as people sought to organize themselves to exercise power over who governs (see Figure 7-2).

The Emergence of Parties: Federalists and Democratic-Republicans In his Farewell Address, George Washington warned the nation about political parties: "Let me . . . warn you in the most solemn manner against the baneful effects of the spirit of party generally."[3] As president, Washington stood above the factions that were coalescing around his secretary of treasury, Alexander Hamilton, and around his former secretary of state, Thomas Jefferson. Jefferson had resigned from Washington's cabinet in 1793 to protest the fiscal policies of

political organizations Parties and interest groups that function as intermediaries between individuals and government.

political parties Organizations that seek to achieve power by winning public office.

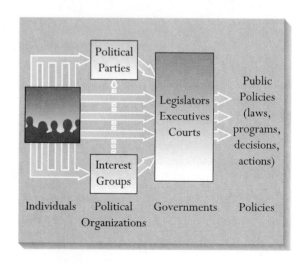

FIGURE 7-1 Political Organizations as Intermediaries

All political organizations function as intermediaries between individuals and government. Parties are concerned primarily with winning elected office; interest groups are concerned with influencing policy.

FIGURE 7-2 Change and Continuity in the American Party System

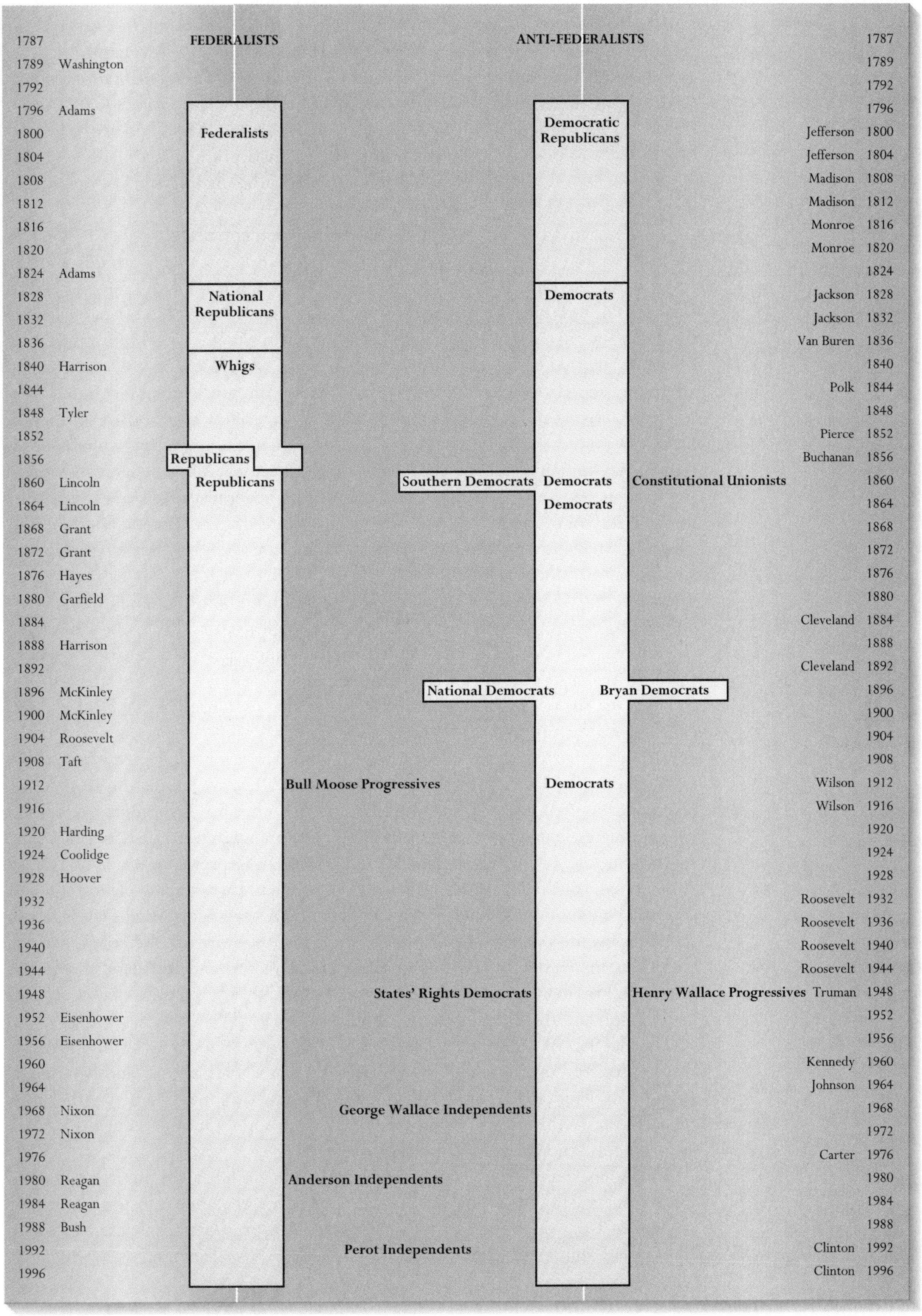

Year	(Left / Federalists)			(Right / Anti-Federalists)	Year
1787	**FEDERALISTS**		**ANTI-FEDERALISTS**		1787
1789	Washington				1789
1792					1792
1796	Adams				1796
1800	**Federalists**		**Democratic Republicans**	Jefferson	1800
1804				Jefferson	1804
1808				Madison	1808
1812				Madison	1812
1816				Monroe	1816
1820				Monroe	1820
1824	Adams				1824
1828	**National Republicans**		**Democrats**	Jackson	1828
1832				Jackson	1832
1836				Van Buren	1836
1840	Harrison	**Whigs**			1840
1844				Polk	1844
1848	Tyler				1848
1852				Pierce	1852
1856	**Republicans**			Buchanan	1856
1860	Lincoln	**Republicans**	**Southern Democrats** Democrats **Constitutional Unionists**		1860
1864	Lincoln		Democrats		1864
1868	Grant				1868
1872	Grant				1872
1876	Hayes				1876
1880	Garfield				1880
1884				Cleveland	1884
1888	Harrison				1888
1892				Cleveland	1892
1896	McKinley		**National Democrats** **Bryan Democrats**		1896
1900	McKinley				1900
1904	Roosevelt				1904
1908	Taft				1908
1912		**Bull Moose Progressives**	**Democrats**	Wilson	1912
1916				Wilson	1916
1920	Harding				1920
1924	Coolidge				1924
1928	Hoover				1928
1932				Roosevelt	1932
1936				Roosevelt	1936
1940				Roosevelt	1940
1944				Roosevelt	1944
1948		**States' Rights Democrats**	**Henry Wallace Progressives**	Truman	1948
1952	Eisenhower				1952
1956	Eisenhower				1956
1960				Kennedy	1960
1964				Johnson	1964
1968	Nixon	**George Wallace Independents**			1968
1972	Nixon				1972
1976				Carter	1976
1980	Reagan	**Anderson Independents**			1980
1984	Reagan				1984
1988	Bush				1988
1992		**Perot Independents**		Clinton	1992
1996				Clinton	1996

Hamilton, notably his creation of a national bank and repayment of the state's Revolutionary War debts with federal funds. Washington had endorsed Hamilton's policies, but so great was the first president's prestige that Jefferson and his followers directed their fire not against Washington but against Hamilton, John Adams, and their supporters, who called themselves **Federalists** after their leaders' outspoken defense of the Constitution during the ratification process. By the 1790s, Jefferson and Madison, as well as many **Anti-Federalists** who had initially opposed the ratification of the Constitution, began calling themselves *Republicans* or *Democratic-Republicans*, terms that had become popular after the French Revolution in 1789.

Adams narrowly defeated Jefferson in the presidential election of 1796. This election was an important milestone in the development of the parties and the presidential election system. For the first time, two candidates campaigned as members of opposing parties, and candidates for presidential elector in each state pledged themselves as "Adams's men" or "Jefferson's men." By committing themselves in advance of the actual presidential vote, these pledged electors enabled voters in each state to determine the outcome of the presidential election.

Party activity intensified in anticipation of the election of 1800. Jefferson's Democratic-Republican Party first saw the importance of organizing voters, circulating literature, and rallying the masses to their causes. Many Federalists viewed this early party activity with disdain. Indeed, the Federalists even tried to outlaw public criticism of the federal government by means of the Alien and Sedition Acts of 1798, which among other things made it a crime to publish false or malicious writings against the (Federalist) Congress or president or to "stir up hatred" against them. These acts directly challenged the newly adopted First Amendment guarantees of freedom of speech and press. But in the election of 1800, the Federalists went down to defeat. Democratic-Republican electors won a **majority** (more than half the votes cast) in the Electoral College.

However, the original Constitution provided that each presidential elector could cast two votes; the person getting the most votes won the presidency and the runner-up won the vice presidency. If no one won a majority, the president would be elected by the House of Representatives. In 1800 each Democratic-Republican elector cast one of his votes for Jefferson and the other for Aaron Burr, Jefferson's vice presidential running mate. But the result was an unintended tie between Jefferson and Burr, throwing the election into the House of Representatives. (The Twelfth Amendment, ratified in 1804, remedied the problem by requiring electors to cast separate votes for president and vice president.) A few disgruntled Federalists in the House considered giving Burr their votes just to embarrass Jefferson, and the ambitious Burr encouraged this chicanery. But in the end, the House selected Jefferson. President Adams and the Federalists turned over the reins of government to Jefferson and the Democratic-Republicans.

The election of 1800 was a landmark in American democracy—the first time that control of government passed peacefully from one party to another on the basis of an election outcome. As commonplace as that may seem to Americans today, the peaceful transfer of power from one group to another remains a rarity in many political systems around the world.

Jefferson's Democratic-Republican Party—later to be called the Democrats—was so successful that the Federalist Party never regained the presidency or control of Congress. The Federalists tended to represent merchants, manufacturers, and shippers, who were concentrated in New York and New England.

Federalists   Those who supported the U.S. Constitution during the ratification process and who later formed a political party in support of John Adams's presidential candidacy.

Anti-Federalists   Those who opposed the ratification of the U.S. Constitution and the creation of a strong national government.

majority   Election by more than 50 percent of all votes cast in the contest.

The Democratic-Republicans tended to represent agrarian interests, from large plantation owners to small farmers. In the mostly agrarian America of the early 1800s, the Democratic-Republican Party prevailed. Jefferson easily won reelection in 1804, and his allies James Madison and James Monroe overwhelmed their Federalist opponents in subsequent presidential elections. By 1820, the Federalist Party had ceased to exist. Indeed, for a few years, it seemed as if the new nation had ended party politics.

Jacksonian Democrats and Whigs Partisan politics soon reappeared, however. The Democratic-Republicans had already begun to fight among themselves by the 1824 presidential election. Andrew Jackson won a **plurality** (at least one more vote than anyone else in the race) but not a majority of the popular and Electoral College vote, but he then lost to John Quincy Adams in a close decision by the factionalized House of Representatives. Jackson led his supporters to found a new party, the **Democratic Party,** to organize popular support for his 1828 presidential bid, which succeeded in ousting Adams.

Jacksonian ideas both *democratized* and *nationalized* the party system. Under Jackson, the Democratic Party began to mobilize voters on behalf of the party and its candidates. It pressed the states to lower property qualifications for voting in order to recruit new Democratic Party voters. The electorate expanded from 365,000 voters in 1824 to well over a million in 1828 and over 2 million in 1840. The Democratic Party also pressed the states to choose presidential electors by popular vote rather than by state legislatures. Thus Jackson and his Democratic successor, Martin Van Buren, ran truly national campaigns directed at the voters in every state.

At the same time, Jackson's opponents formed the Whig Party, named after the British party of that name. Like the British Whigs, who opposed the power of the king, the American Whigs charged "King Andrew" with usurping the powers of Congress and the people. The Whigs quickly adopted the Democrats' tactics of national campaigning and popular organizing. By 1840, the Whigs were able to gain the White House, running William Henry Harrison—nicknamed "Old Tippecanoe" from his victory at Tippecanoe over Native Americans in 1811—and John Tyler and featuring the slogan "Tippecanoe and Tyler too."

Post–Civil War Republican Dominance Whigs and Democrats continued to share national power until the slavery conflict that ignited the Civil War destroyed the old party system. The Republican Party had formed in 1854 to oppose the spread of slavery to the western territories. By the election of 1860, the slavery issue so divided the nation that four parties offered presidential candidates: Lincoln the Republican, Stephen A. Douglas the northern Democrat, John C. Breckinridge the southern Democrat, and John Bell the Constitutional Union Party candidate. No party came close to winning a majority of the popular vote, but Lincoln won in the Electoral College.

The new party system that emerged from the Civil War featured a victorious **Republican Party** that generally represented the northern industrial economy and a struggling Democratic Party that generally represented a southern agricultural economy. The Republican Party won every presidential election from 1860 to 1912 except for two victories by Democratic reformer and New York governor Grover Cleveland (see *Up Close*: "The Donkey and the Elephant").

Yet the Democratic Party offered a serious challenge in the election of 1896 and realigned the party affiliations of the nation's voters. The Democratic Party nomi-

plurality Election by at least one vote more than any other candidate in the race.

Democratic Party One of the main parties in American politics; it traces its origins to Thomas Jefferson's Democratic-Republican Party, acquiring its current name under Andrew Jackson in 1828.

Republican Party One of the two main parties in American politics; it traces its origins to the antislavery and nationalist forces that united in the 1850s and nominated Abraham Lincoln for president in 1860.

The Donkey and the Elephant

The popular nineteenth-century cartoonist Thomas Nast is generally credited with giving the Democratic and Republican parties their current symbols: the donkey and the elephant. In *Harper's Weekly* cartoons in the 1870s, Nast critically portrayed the Democratic Party as a stubborn mule "without pride of ancestry nor hope of posterity." During this period of Republican Party dominance, Nast portrayed the Republican Party as an elephant, the biggest beast in the political jungle. Now both party symbols are used with pride.

In the 1870 cartoon on the left, published following the death of Lincoln's Secretary of War E.M. Stanton, Nast shows a donkey (labeled "Copperheads," a disparaging term for the mostly Democratic Northerners who were sympathetic to the South during the Civil War) kicking the dead Stanton, who is portrayed as a lion. The 1874 cartoon on the right features the elephant as the Republican Vote and the donkey masquerading as a lion.

nated William Jennings Bryan, a talented orator and a religious fundamentalist. Bryan sought to rally the nation's white "have-nots" to the Democratic Party banner, particularly the debt-ridden farmers of the South and West. His plan was to stimulate inflation (and thus enable debtors to pay their debts with "cheaper," less valuable dollars) through using plentiful, western-mined "free silver," rather than gold, as the monetary standard. He defeated Cleveland's faction and the "Gold Democrats" in the 1896 Democratic Party convention with his famous Cross of Gold speech: "You shall not crucify mankind upon a cross of gold."

But the Republican Party rallied its forces in perhaps the most bitter presidential battle in history. It sought to convince the nation that high tariffs, protection for manufacturers, and a solid monetary standard would lead to prosperity for industrial workers as well as the new tycoons. The campaign, directed by Marcus Alonzo Hanna, attorney for John D. Rockefeller's Standard Oil Company, spent an unprecedented $16 million (an amount in inflation-adjusted dollars that has never been equaled) to elect Republican William McKinley, advertised as the candidate who would bring a "full dinner pail" to all. The battle also produced one of the largest voter turnouts in history. McKinley won in a landslide. Bryan ran twice again but lost by even larger margins. The Republican Party solidified the loyalty of industrial workers, small-business owners, bankers, and large manufacturers, as well as black voters, who respected "the party of Lincoln" and despised the segregationist practices of the southern Democratic Party.

So great was the Republican Party's dominance in national elections that only a split among Republicans enabled the Democrat Woodrow Wilson to capture the presidency in 1912. Republican Theodore Roosevelt (who became president following McKinley's assassination and had won reelection in 1904) sought to recapture the presidency from his former protégé, Republican William Howard Taft. In the **GOP** convention ("Grand Old Party," as the Republicans began labeling themselves), party regulars rejected the unpredictable Roosevelt in favor of Taft, even though Roosevelt had won the few primary elections that had recently been initiated. An irate Teddy Roosevelt launched a third, progressive party, the "Bull Moose," which actually outpolled the Republican Party in the 1912 election—the only time a third party has surpassed one of the two major parties in U.S. history. But the result was a victory for the Democratic candidate, former Princeton political science professor Woodrow Wilson. Following Wilson's two terms, Republicans again reasserted their political dominance with victories by Warren G. Harding, Calvin Coolidge, and Herbert Hoover.

The New Deal Democratic Party   The promise of prosperity that empowered the Republican Party and held its membership together faded in the light of the Great Depression. The U.S. stock market crashed in 1929, and by the early 1930s, one-quarter of the labor force was unemployed. Having lost confidence in the nation's business and political leadership, in 1932 American voters turned out incumbent Republican President Herbert Hoover in favor of Democrat Franklin D. Roosevelt, who promised the country a **New Deal.**

GOP   "Grand Old Party"—a popular label for the Republican Party.

New Deal   Policies of President Franklin D. Roosevelt during the depression of the 1930s that helped form a Democratic Party coalition of urban working-class, ethnic, Catholic, Jewish, poor, and southern voters.

Franklin Roosevelt campaigning among coal miners in West Virginia during the presidential election campaign of 1932. Roosevelt's optimism and "can-do" attitude in the face of the Great Depression helped cement the New Deal Democratic coalition that won him the presidency.

More than just bringing the Democrats to the White House, the Great Depression marked another party realignment. This time, traditionally Republican voting groups changed their affiliation and enabled the Democratic Party to dominate national politics for a generation. This realignment actually began in 1928, when Democratic presidential candidate Al Smith, a Catholic, won many northern, urban, ethnic voters away from the Republican Party. By 1932, a majority New Deal Democratic coalition had been formed in American politics. It consisted of the following groups:

- Working classes and union members, especially in large cities.
- White ethnic groups who had previously aligned themselves with Republican machines.
- Catholics and Jews.
- African Americans, who ended their historic affiliation with the party of Lincoln to pursue new economic and social goals.
- Poor people, who associated the New Deal with expanded welfare and Social Security programs.
- Southern whites, who had provided the most loyal block of Democratic voters since the Civil War.

To be sure, this majority coalition had many internal factions: southern "Dixiecrats" walked out of the Democratic Party convention in 1948 to protest a party platform that called for an end to racial discrimination in employment. But the promise of a New Deal—with its vast array of government supports for workers, elderly and disabled people, widows and children, and farmers—held this coalition together reasonably well. President Harry Truman's **Fair Deal** proved that the coalition could survive its founder, Franklin Roosevelt. Republican Dwight D. Eisenhower made inroads into this coalition by virtue of his personal popularity and the Republican Party's acceptance of most New Deal programs. But John F. Kennedy's "New Frontier" demonstrated the continuing appeal of the Democratic Party tradition. Lyndon Johnson's **Great Society** went further than the programs of any of his predecessors in government intervention in the economic and social life of the nation. Indeed, it might be argued that the excesses of the Great Society laid the foundation for a political reaction that eventually destroyed the old Democratic coalition and led to yet another new party alignment (see Figure 7-3).

A New Republican Majority   The American political system underwent massive convulsions in the late 1960s as a result of both the civil rights revolution at home and an unpopular war in Vietnam. Strains were felt in all of the nation's political institutions, from the courts to the Congress to the presidency. And when Lyndon Johnson announced his decision not to run for reelection in 1968, the Democratic Party erupted in a battle that ultimately destroyed its majority support among presidential voters.

At the 1968 Democratic Party convention in Chicago, Vice President Hubert Humphrey controlled a majority of the delegates inside the convention hall, but antiwar protesters dominated media coverage outside the hall. When Chicago police attacked unruly demonstrators with batons, the media broadcast to the world an image of the nation's turmoil. In the presidential campaign that followed, both candidates—Democrat Hubert Humphrey and Republican Richard Nixon—

Fair Deal   Policies of President Harry Truman extending Roosevelt's New Deal and maintaining the Democratic Party's voter coalition.

Great Society   Policies of President Lyndon Johnson that promised to solve the nation's social and economic problems through government intervention.

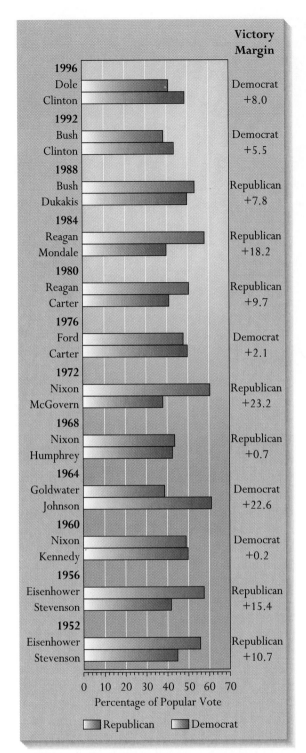

Victory Margin

Year	Candidates	Margin
1996	Dole / Clinton	Democrat +8.0
1992	Bush / Clinton	Democrat +5.5
1988	Bush / Dukakis	Republican +7.8
1984	Reagan / Mondale	Republican +18.2
1980	Reagan / Carter	Republican +9.7
1976	Ford / Carter	Democrat +2.1
1972	Nixon / McGovern	Republican +23.2
1968	Nixon / Humphrey	Republican +0.7
1964	Goldwater / Johnson	Democrat +22.6
1960	Nixon / Kennedy	Democrat +0.2
1956	Eisenhower / Stevenson	Republican +15.4
1952	Eisenhower / Stevenson	Republican +10.7

Percentage of Popular Vote
0 10 20 30 40 50 60 70

■ Republican   ■ Democrat

FIGURE 7-3 The Parties in Presidential Voting

Despite the dominance of the Democratic Party in terms of numbers of registered voters, Republicans have won seven of the eleven presidential elections since 1952, indicating that, at the presidential level, voters are not always loyal to their party.

presented nearly identical positions supporting the U.S. military commitment in Vietnam while endorsing a negotiated, "honorable" settlement of the war. But the image of the Democratic Party became associated with the street protesters. Inside the convention hall, pressure from women and minorities led party leaders to adopt changes in the party's delegate-selection process for future conventions to

Battles between so-called hippie demonstrators and police in Chicago during the Democratic National Convention in 1968 bolstered Republicans' arguments that government by the Democrats had led to a breakdown in fundamental values and that the nation had to shift gears in order to restore "law and order."

assure better representation of these groups—at the expense of Democratic office-holders (see "Making Party Rules" later in this chapter for more details).

In 1972 the Democratic Party convention strongly reflected the views of anti-war protesters, civil rights advocates, feminist organizations, and liberal activists generally. The visibility of these activists, who appeared to be well to the left of both Democratic Party voters and the electorate in general, allowed the Republican Party to portray the Democratic presidential nominee, George McGovern, as an unpatriotic liberal, willing to "crawl to Hanoi" and to sacrifice the nation's honor for peace. It also allowed the Republicans to characterize the new Democratic Party as soft on crime, tolerant of disorder, and committed to racial and sexual quotas in American life. Richard Nixon, never very popular personally, was able to win in a landslide in 1972. The Watergate scandal and Nixon's forced resignation only temporarily stemmed the tide of "the new Republican majority." Democrat Jimmy Carter's narrow victory over Republican Gerald R. Ford in 1976 owed much to the latter's pardon of Nixon.

The Reagan Coalition   Under the leadership of Ronald Reagan, the Republican Party was able to assemble a majority coalition that dominated presidential elections in the 1980s, giving Reagan landslide victories in 1980 and 1984 and George Bush a convincing win in 1988. The **Reagan Coalition** consisted of the following groups:

Reagan Coalition Combination of economic and social conservatives, religious fundamentalists, and defense-minded anticommunists who rallied behind Republican President Ronald Reagan.

- Economic conservatives concerned about high taxes and excessive government regulation, including business and professional voters who had traditionally supported the Republican Party.
- Social conservatives concerned about crime, drugs, and racial conflict, including many white ethnic voters and union members who had traditionally voted Democratic.

- Religious fundamentalists concerned about such issues as abortion and prayer in schools.

- Southern whites concerned about racial issues, including affirmative action programs.

- Internationalists and anticommunists who wanted the United States to maintain a strong military force and to confront Soviet-backed Marxist regimes around the world.

Reagan held this coalition together in large part through his personal popularity and his infectious optimism about the United States and its future. Although sometimes at odds with one another, economic conservatives, religious fundamentalists, and internationalists could unite behind the "Great Communicator." Reagan's presidential victory in 1980 helped to elect a Republican majority to the U.S. Senate and encouraged Democratic conservatives in the Democrat-controlled House of Representatives to frequently vote with Republicans. As a result, Reagan got most of what he asked of Congress in his first term: cuts in personal income taxes, increased spending for national defense, and slower growth of federal regulatory activity. With the assistance of the Federal Reserve Board, inflation was brought under control. But Reagan largely failed to cut government spending as he had promised, and the result was a series of huge federal deficits. Reagan appointed conservatives to the Supreme Court and the federal judiciary (see Chapter 13), but no major decisions were reversed (including the *Roe v. Wade* decision, protecting abortion); social conservatives had to be content with the president's symbolic support.

During these years, the national Democratic Party was saddled with an unpopular image as the party of special-interest groups. As more middle-class and working-class voters deserted to the GOP, the key remaining loyal Democratic constituencies were African Americans and other minorities, government employees, union leaders, liberal intellectuals in the media and universities, feminist organizations, and environmentalists. Democratic presidential candidates Walter Mondale in 1984 and Michael Dukakis in 1988 were obliged to take liberal positions to win the support of these groups in the primary elections. Later, both candidates sought to move toward the center of the ideological battleground in the general election. But Republican Party strategists were able to "define" Mondale and Dukakis through negative campaign advertising (see Chapter 8) as liberal defenders of special-interest groups. The general conservative tilt of public opinion in the 1980s added to the effectiveness of the GOP strategy of branding Democratic presidential candidates with the "*L* word" (*liberal*).

Clinton and the "New" Democrats   Yet even while Democratic candidates fared poorly in presidential elections, Democrats continued to maintain control of the House of Representatives, to win back control of the U.S. Senate in 1986, and to hold more state governorships and state legislative seats than the Republicans. Thus the Democratic Party retained a strong leadership base on which to rebuild itself.

During the 1980s, Democratic leaders among governors and senators came together in the **Democratic Leadership Council** to create a "new" Democratic Party closer to the center of the political spectrum. The chair of the Democratic Leadership Council was the young, energetic, and successful governor of Arkansas, Bill Clinton. The concern of the council was that the Democratic Party's traditional support for social justice and social welfare programs was

Democratic Leadership Council Organization of party leaders who sought to create a "new" Democratic Party to appeal to middle-class, moderate voters.

overshadowing its commitment to economic prosperity. Many council members argued that a healthy economy was a prerequisite to progress in social welfare. The council became closely identified with *neo-liberal* arguments (see Chapter 2) about the need for government to stimulate economic growth, productivity, and competitiveness in world markets. Not all Democrats agreed with the council agenda. African American leaders (including the Reverend Jesse Jackson), as well as liberal and environmental groups, feared that the priorities of the council would result in the sacrifice of traditional Democratic Party commitments to minorities, poor people, and the environment.

In the 1992 presidential election, Bill Clinton was in a strong position to take advantage of the faltering economy under George Bush, to stress the "new" Democratic Party's commitment to the middle class, and to avoid being labeled as a liberal defender of special interests. At the same time, he managed to rally the party's core activist groups—liberals, intellectuals, African Americans, feminists, and environmentalists. Many liberals in the party deliberately soft-pedaled their views during the 1992 election in order not to offend voters, hoping to win with Clinton and then fight for liberal programs later. Clinton won with 43 percent of the vote, to George Bush's 38 percent. Independent Ross Perot captured a surprising 19 percent of the popular vote, including many voters who were alienated from both the Democratic and the Republican parties. Once in office, Clinton appeared to revert to liberal policy directions rather than to pursue the more moderate line he had espoused as a "new" Democrat. Yet polls continued to suggest that voters favored *moderate* and *conservative* political labels, as well as many specific policy proposals that Clinton opposed, including the Balanced Budget Amendment, congressional term limits, and cutbacks in social welfare spending. As Clinton's ratings sagged, the opportunity arose for a Republican resurgence.

Republican Resurgence   A political earthquake shook Washington in the 1994 congressional elections, when the Republicans for the first time in forty years

Republican freshman representatives meet with the press during a showdown with President Clinton over the budget in the fall of 1995.

J.C. Watts, Jr., Can the Republican Party Attract African Americans?

African Americans are the most loyal group of Democratic Party voters. Rarely do Republican candidates win more than 10 percent of the black vote. But J.C. Watts of Oklahoma, one of only two African American Republican members of Congress, argues: "Democrats just don't pay attention to African Americans because they are already the most loyal voting block in the ranks. And the Republicans have said, 'We don't have to pay attention because they vote Democrat.' I want to change all that."

Julius Caesar Watts, Jr., graduated from Eufaula High School in Oklahoma and won a football scholarship to the University of Oklahoma, where he quarterbacked the Sooners to two consecutive Big Eight championships. He twice defeated the Florida State Seminoles in Orange Bowl games in 1981 and 1982, and was named MVP of both games. He graduated with a degree in journalism and went on to play quarterback in the Canadian Football League for six years. Returning to Norman, Oklahoma, to work in real estate, he was soon recruited by the Republican Party to run for the state's elected Corporation Commission. He became the first African American to be elected to statewide office in Oklahoma since Reconstruction.

"J.C.'s" name recognition and fame in Oklahoma football circles, and his strong commitment to Christian values, made him a favorite speaker at events across the state. He is a leader in the Fellowship of Christian Athletes and a frequent guest preacher in the Southern Baptist Church.

In 1994 Watts undertook a politically daunting challenge—running for Congress as an African American Republican in an overwhelmingly white Democratic district. He won the GOP primary in a five-candidate field and went on to face a liberal Democrat in the general election. Watts stood by his conservative beliefs, including opposition to homosexuals in the military, opposition to abortion except to save the life of the woman, support for a balanced budget, and support for a two-year limit on welfare benefits. He won a near-landslide 58 percent of the vote.

The national Republican Party has featured J.C. Watts in many of its key events in the hopes of attracting more conservative African Americans to the GOP. In 1997 Watts gave the Republican response to President Clinton's State of the Union Address on national television: "I didn't get my values from Washington. I got my values from a strong family, a strong church, and a strong neighborhood . . . I was taught, in the words of Dr. Martin Luther King Jr., to judge a man not by the color of his skin but by the content of his character. And I was taught that character is doing what's right, when nobody's looking."

captured the House of Representatives, regained control of the Senate, and captured a majority of the nation's governorships. Not a single Republican incumbent lost, but Democratic incumbents lost two Senate, thirty-five House, and five governor races (see *People in Politics:* J. C. Watts, Jr., Can the Republican Party Attract African Americans?"). Republicans won a large majority of open-seat races and for the first time in history won more seats in the South than the Democrats. This southern swing to the Republicans in congressional elections seemed to confirm the realignment of southern voters that had begun earlier in presidential elections. Just two years after a Democratic president had been elected, the GOP won its biggest nationwide victory since the Great Depression.

Clinton Holds On   Following the Republican victory, the Democratic Party appeared to be in temporary disarray. The new Republican House Speaker, Newt

Gingrich, tried to seize national policy leadership; Clinton was widely viewed as a failed president. But the Republicans quickly squandered their political opportunity. They had made many promises in a well-publicized "Contract with America"—a balanced federal budget, congressional term limits, a middle-class tax cut, welfare reform, and more—but they delivered little. Majority Leader Bob Dole failed by one vote to pass the Balanced Budget Amendment in the Senate. President Clinton took an unexpectedly hard line toward GOP spending cuts and vetoed several budget bills. When the federal government officially "closed down" for lack of appropriated funds, the public appeared to blame Republicans. Polls showed a dramatic recovery in the president's approval ratings. Clinton skillfully portrayed GOP leaders, especially Newt Gingrich, as "extremists" and himself as a responsible moderate prepared to trim the budget, reduce the deficit, and reform welfare, "while still protecting Medicare, Medicaid, education, and the environment." By early 1996, Clinton had set the stage for his reelection campaign.

Bill Clinton is the first Democratic president to be *re*elected since Franklin D. Roosevelt. Clinton rode to victory on a growing economy. In 1996 most Americans thought the nation's economy was excellent or good (57 percent), compared to very few (19 percent) who thought so when Bush had sought reelection in 1992. They were willing to put aside doubts about Clinton's character, and they ignored Republican Bob Dole's call for tax reductions. Clinton won with 49 percent of the popular vote to Dole's 41 percent and Perot's 8 percent. But Clinton's victory failed to rejuvenate the Democratic Party's fortunes across the country. The GOP retained its majorities in both houses of Congress.

POLITICAL PARTIES AND DEMOCRATIC GOVERNMENT

"Political parties created modern democracy and modern democracy is unthinkable save in terms of parties."[4] Traditionally, political scientists have praised parties as indispensable to democratic government. They have argued that parties are essential for organizing popular majorities to exercise control over government. The development of political parties in all the democracies of the world testifies to the underlying importance of parties to democratic government. But political parties in the United States have lost their preeminent position as instruments of democracy. Other structures and organizations in society—interest groups, the mass media, independent campaign organizations, primary elections, social welfare agencies—now perform many of the functions traditionally regarded as prerogatives of political parties. Nevertheless, the Democratic and Republican parties remain important organizing structures for politics in the United States.

"Responsible" Parties in Theory   In theory, political parties function in a democracy to organize majorities around broad principles of government in order to win public office and enact these principles into law. A "responsible" party should:

- Adopt a platform setting forth its principles and policy positions.
- Recruit candidates for public office who agree with the party's platform.

- Inform and educate the public about the platform.
- Organize and direct campaigns based on platform principles.
- Organize the legislature to ensure party control in policy making.
- Hold its elected officials responsible for enacting the party's platform.

If responsible, disciplined, policy-oriented parties competed for majority support, *if* they offered clear policy alternatives to the voters, and *if* the voters cast their ballots on the basis of these policy options, *then* the winning party would have a "policy mandate" from the people to guide the course of government. In that way, the democratic ideal of government by majority rule would be implemented.

Winning Wins over Principle   However, the **responsible party model** never accurately described the American party system. The major American parties have been loose coalitions of individuals and groups seeking to attract sufficient votes to gain control of government. *Winning has generally been more important than any principles or policies.* America's major parties must appeal to tens of millions of voters in every section of the nation and from all walks of life. If a major party is to acquire a majority capable of controlling the U.S. government, it cannot limit its appeal by relying on a single unifying principle. Instead, it must form coalitions of voters from as many sectors of the population as it can. Major American parties therefore usually do not emphasize particular principles or ideologies so much as try to find a common ground of agreement among many different people. This emphasis does not mean no policy differences exist between the American parties. On the contrary, each party tends to appeal to a distinctive coalition of interests, and therefore each party expresses somewhat distinctive policy views (see *What Do You Think?* "Popular Images of the Democratic and Republican Parties").

In their efforts to win, major American political parties strive to attract the support of the large numbers of people near the center of public opinion. Generally more votes are at the center of the ideological spectrum—the middle-of-the-road—than on the extreme liberal or conservative ends. Thus *no real incentive exists for vote-maximizing parties to take strong policy positions in opposition to each other.* As the Democratic and Republican policy positions approach the center, the parties seem to echo each other, and critics attack them as Tweedledee and Tweedledum (see Figure 7-4).

The Erosion of Traditional Party Functions   Parties play only a limited role in campaign organization and finance. Campaigns are generally directed by professional campaign management firms or by the candidates' personal organizations, not by parties. Party organizations have largely been displaced in campaign activity by advertising firms, media consultants, pollsters, and others hired by the candidates themselves (see Chapter 8).

American political parties also play only a limited role in recruiting candidates for elected office. *Most political candidates today are self-recruited.* People initiate their own candidacies, first contacting friends and financial supporters. Often in state and local races, candidates contact party officials only as a courtesy, if at all.

The major American political parties cannot really control who their **nominee**—the party's entry in a general election race—will be. Rather, party **nominations** for most elected offices are won in *primary elections.* In a **primary**

responsible party model
System in which competitive parties adopt a platform of principles, recruiting candidates and directing campaigns based on the platform, and holding their elected officials responsible for enacting it.

nominee   Political party's entry in a general election race.

nomination   Political party's selection of its candidate for a public office.

What Do You Think?

Popular Images of the Democratic and Republican Parties

What do Americans think of the Democratic and Republican parties? Generally speaking, the Democratic Party has been able to maintain an image of "the party of the common people," and the Republican Party has long been saddled with an image of "favoring the rich."

But when it comes to popular perceptions of each party's ability to deal with problems confronting the nation, the Democratic and Republican parties appear evenly matched. The Republican Party is trusted to "do a better job" in handling foreign affairs and maintaining a strong national defense. It also enjoys a reputation of being better at "holding down taxes."

The Democratic Party enjoys its greatest advantage on "compassion issues" like helping poor, elderly, and homeless people. And the Democrats have long enjoyed the support of the high-voter-turnout over-sixty-five age group because it is trusted to do a better job "protecting the Social Security system."

Source: Surveys by Gallup and CBS News/*New York Times,* reported in *American Enterprises* (March/April 1994): 78–80; and NBC News/*Wall Street Journal,* reported in *The Polling Report,* September 1997.

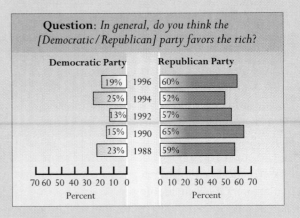

Question: *In general, do you think the [Democratic/Republican] party favors the rich?*

Democratic Party		Republican Party
19%	1996	60%
25%	1994	52%
13%	1992	57%
15%	1990	65%
23%	1988	59%

70 60 50 40 30 20 10 0 — Percent   0 10 20 30 40 50 60 70 — Percent

---

Question: *When it comes to…, which party do you think would do a better job: the Democratic Party, the Republican Party, both about the same, or neither? ("Both" and "Neither" responses not shown.)*

Democratic Party   **Republican Party**

Republican Advantages

Democratic		Republican
31%	…dealing with national defense…	56%
24%	…dealing with the economy…	34%
23%	…reducing the federal deficit…	31%
26%	…dealing with taxes…	31%

Fairly Evenly Matched

21%	…dealing with crime…	27%
17%	…reducing the drug problem…	19%
32%	…reforming the welfare system…	30%

Democratic Advantages

33%	…dealing with Social Security…	19%
40%	…dealing with education…	20%
42%	…dealing with problems of health care…	18%
51%	…protecting the enivornment…	12%

80 60 40 20 0 — Percentage   0 20 40 60 80 — Percentage

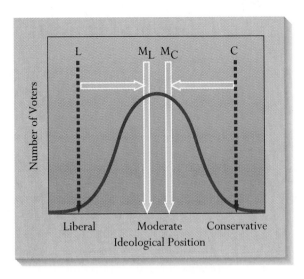

FIGURE 7-4 Winning versus Principle

Why don't we have a party system based on principles, with a liberal party and a conservative party, each offering the voters a real ideological choice? Let's assume that voters generally choose the party closest to their own ideological position. If the liberal party (L) took a strong ideological position to the left of most voters, the conservative party (C) would move toward the center, winning more moderate votes, even while retaining its conservative supporters, who would still prefer it to the more liberal opposition party. Likewise, if the conservative party took a strong ideological position to the right of most voters, the liberal party would move to the center and win. So both parties must abandon strong ideological positions and move to the center, becoming moderate in the fight for support of moderate voters.

election, registered voters select from among a party's members who meet minimum legal standards and choose to run. The primary winner then becomes the party's nominee. Party leaders may endorse a candidate in a primary election and may even work to try to ensure the victory of their favorite, but the voters in that party's primary select the nominee.

Once nominated, candidates have little need of their parties, because they usually communicate directly with voters through the mass media. Television has replaced the party organization as the principal medium of communication between candidates and voters. Candidates no longer rely much on party workers to carry their message from door to door. Instead, candidates can come directly into the voters' living room via television.

Even if the American parties wanted to take stronger policy positions and to enact them into law, they would not have the means to do so. *American political parties have no way to bind their elected officials to the party platform or even to their campaign promises.* Parties have no strong disciplinary sanctions to use against members of Congress who vote against the party's policy position. The parties cannot deny them renomination. At most, the party's leadership in Congress can threaten the status, privileges, and pet bills of disloyal members (see Chapter 10). Party cohesion, where it exists, is more a product of like-mindedness than of party discipline.

Finally, American political parties no longer perform social welfare functions—trading off social services, patronage jobs, or petty favors in exchange for votes. Traditional party organizations, or **machines,** especially in large cities, once helped immigrants get settled in, found **patronage** jobs in government for party

primary elections Elections to choose party nominees for public office; may be open or closed.

machine Tightly disciplined party organization, headed by a boss, that relies on material rewards—including patronage jobs—to control politics.

patronage Appointment to public office based on party loyalty.

workers, and occasionally provided aid to impoverished but loyal party voters. But *government bureaucracies have replaced the political parties as providers of social services.* Government employment agencies, welfare agencies, civil service systems, and other bureaucracies now provide the social services once undertaken by political machines in search of votes.

PARTIES AS ORGANIZERS OF ELECTIONS

Despite the erosion of many of their functions, America's political parties survive as the principal institutions for organizing elections. Party nominations organize electoral choice by narrowing the field of aspiring office seekers to the Democratic and Republican candidates in most cases. Very few independents are elected to high political office in the United States. Democratic or Republican Party nominations are sought by most serious aspirants for state and national office, often a year or two in advance of the actual election (see *People in Politics:* "George W. Bush, Republican Presidential Hopeful"). **Nonpartisan elections**—elections in which there are no party nominations and all candidates run without an official party label—are common only in local elections, for city council, county commission, school board, judgeships, and so on. Party conventions are still held in many states in every presidential year, but these conventions seldom have the power to determine the parties' nominees for public office.

Party Conventions   Historically, party nominations were made by caucus or convention. The **caucus** was the earliest nominating process; party leaders (party chairs, elected officials, and "bosses") would simply meet several months before the election and decide on the party's nominee themselves. The early presidents—Thomas Jefferson, James Madison, James Monroe, and John Quincy Adams—were nominated by caucuses of Congress members. Complaints about the exclusion of people from this process led to nominations by convention—large meetings of delegates sent by local party organizations—starting in 1832. Andrew Jackson was the first president to be nominated by convention. The convention was considered more democratic than the caucus.

For nearly a century, party conventions were held at all levels of government—local, state, and national. City or county conventions included delegates from local **wards** and **precincts,** who nominated candidates for city or county office, for the state legislature, or even for the House of Representatives when a congressional district fell within the city or country. Only Nebraska has nonpartisan elections for its unicameral (one-house) state legislature. State conventions included delegates from counties and nominated governors, U.S. senators, and other statewide officers. State parties chose delegates to the Republican and Democratic national conventions every four years to nominate a president.

Party Primaries   Today, primary elections have largely replaced conventions as the means of selecting the Democratic and Republican nominees for public office.[5] Primary elections, introduced as part of the progressive reform movement of the early twentieth century, allow the party's voters to choose the party's nominee directly. The primary election was designed to bypass the power of party organizations and party leaders and to further democratize the nomination process. It

nonpartisan elections
Elections in which candidates do not officially indicate their party affiliation; often used for city, county, school board, and judicial elections.

caucus   Nominating process in which party leaders select the party's nominee.

ward   Division of a city for electoral or administrative purposes or as a unit for organizing political parties.

precinct   Subdivision of a city, county, or ward for election purposes.

George W. Bush, Republican Presidential Hopeful

George W. Bush had never held public office before being elected governor of Texas. But the son of former president George Bush not only enjoyed widespread name recognition in the Lone Star State (perhaps even name confusion), but also served as the managing general partner of the homestate Texas Rangers American League baseball team. His victory over popular incumbent governor Ann Richards in 1994 and his landslide re-election in 1998 propelled him to the top of the Republican presidential opinion polls.

Born in 1946 into the Bush family's tradition of wealth, privilege, and public service (Bush's grandfather was a U.S. senator from Connecticut and chairman of Yale University's governing board), George W. followed his father to Yale University and later received an M.B.A. from Harvard. And like his father, he founded a Texas oil and gas exploration company. He remained in the energy business until 1986 when he went to Washington to run his father's presidential campaign.

George W. reflects his father's moderate Republicanism. Yet his political style fits comfortably with Texas "good old boys." Early in his administration he supported legislation that gave law-abiding adult Texans the right to carry concealed handguns. Yet at the same time he did little to restrict abortion in his state despite cries from his Christian conservative supporters to do so. A strong economy has allowed him to improve public services in the state while lowering school property taxes. Texas remains one of the few states that has no state income tax. Bush failed, however, to broaden the state's sales tax to include tax on services. He has supported educational reform by opposing the practice of "social promotion" in urging the public schools in Texas to require every third-, fifth-, and eighth-grade pupil to pass statewide tests before advancing to the next grade.

Bush has helped lead the gradual realignment of Texas away from its traditional Democratic roots and toward its current Republican coloration. (In 1998 Republicans not only occupied the governorship and both of the state's U. S. Senate seats but also all other statewide elected offices.) Yet George W. has proven that he can work with Democrats in the Texas legislature. His style is to meet privately and frequently with his Democratic opponents and to remain on friendly personal terms with them. He is willing to accept legislative compromises and he tries to avoid controversy wherever possible. But, perhaps as a result of this style, Bush is unable to point to any landmark achievement in his administration (comparable, for example, to Christine Whitman's slashing of income taxes in New Jersey).

George W. currently leads all other potential Republican 2000 presidential candidates in opinion polls. (Only Colin Powell, who has steadfastly refused to be a candidate, is more popular among Republicans than Bush.)

Only one other son (John Quincy Adams) ever followed his father (John Adams) to the White House. But George W. Bush is in a strong position to lead the Republican Party into the next century.

generally succeeded in doing so, but it also had the effect of seriously weakening political parties, since candidates seeking a party nomination need only appeal to party *voters*—not *leaders*—for support in the primary election.[6]

Primary elections to choose each party's nominee may be open or closed. **Closed primaries** allow only voters who are registered as Democrats or Republicans to vote in their party's primaries. Voters who wish to cast ballots in a particular party's primary must declare their party affiliation sometime before the

closed primaries Primary elections in which voters must declare (or have previously declared) their party affiliation and can cast a ballot only in their own party's primary election.

(a)

(b)

(c)

(d)

Political parties as organizers of elections. (a) The Executive Committee of the Republican National Convention in Chicago in 1880. Conventions emerged as the main way for parties to select candidates in the nineteenth century. (b) Bob Dole celebrates after winning a crucial set of primaries on Super Tuesday. Today party candidates are determined by primary elections rather than by convention. (c) Parties also seek to attract voters through registration drives. (d) President Clinton campaigning on his way to the Democratic National Convention in Chicago. Parties provide the organizational structure for political campaigns.

open primaries Primary elections in which a voter may cast a ballot in either party's primary election.

raiding Organized effort by one party to get its members to cross over in a primary and defeat an attractive candidate in the opposition party's primary.

primary. Persons registered as independents cannot vote in either party's primary. Thus closed primaries tend to discourage people from officially registering as independents, even if they think of themselves as independent. About half the states hold closed primaries.[7] **Open primaries** allow voters to choose on election day in which party primary they wish to participate. Anyone, regardless of prior party affiliation, may choose to vote in either party's primary. Voters simply request the ballot of *one* party or the other. (Only in Alaska and Washington can primary voters cast ballots in *both* party primaries.) About half the states hold open primaries. Open primaries provide opportunities for voters to *cross over* party lines and vote in the primary of the party they usually do not support. One concern about open primaries is their potential for **raiding**, an organized effort by one party to get its members to cross over in a primary and defeat an attractive candidate in the opposition party's primary, thus strengthening the raiding party's chances in the general election. However, little evidence shows that large numbers of voters connive in such a fashion.

Some states hold a **runoff primary** when no candidate receives a majority or a designated percentage of the vote in the party's first primary election. A runoff primary is limited to the two highest vote-getters in the first primary. Runoff elections are more common in the southern United States.[8] In most states, only a plurality of votes is needed to win a primary election.

General Elections Several months after the primaries and conventions, the **general election** (usually held in November, on the first Tuesday after the first Monday for presidential and most state elections) determines who will occupy elective office. Winners of the Democratic and Republican primary elections must face each other—and any independent or minor-party candidates—in the general election. Voters in the general election may chose any candidate, regardless of how they voted earlier in their party's primary or whether they voted in the primary at all.

Independent and minor-party candidates can get on the general election ballot, although the process is usually very difficult. Most states require independent candidates to file a petition with the signatures of several thousand registered voters. The number of signatures varies from state to state and office to office, but it may range up to 5 or 10 percent of *all* registered voters, a very large number that, in a big state especially, presents a difficult obstacle. The same petition requirements usually apply to minor parties, although some states automatically carry a minor party's nominee on the general election ballot if that party's candidate or candidates received a certain percentage (for example, 10 percent) of the vote in the previous general election.

WHERE'S THE PARTY?

The Democratic and Republican parties are found in different political arenas (see Figure 7-5). There is, first of all, the **party-in-the-electorate**—the voters who identify themselves as Democrats or Republicans and who tend to vote for the candidates of their party. The party-in-the-electorate appears to be in decline today. Party loyalties among voters are weakening. More people identify themselves as independents, and more **ticket splitters** divide their votes between candidates of different parties for different offices in the same general election, and more voters cast their ballots without regard to the party affiliation of the candidates than ever before.

The second locus of party activity is the **party-in-the-government**—officials who received their party's nomination and won the general election. The party-in-the-government includes members of Congress, state legislators and local government officials, and elected members of the executive branch, including the president and governors.

Party identification and loyalty among elected officeholders (the party-in-the-government) are generally stronger than party identification and loyalty among

runoff primary Additional primary held between the top two vote-getters in a primary where no candidate has received a majority of the vote.

general election Election to choose among candidates nominated by parties and/or independent candidates who gained access to the ballot by petition.

party-in-the-electorate Voters who identify themselves with a party.

ticket splitter Person who votes for candidates of different parties for different offices in a general election.

party-in-the-government Public officials who were nominated by their party and who identify themselves in office with their party.

the party-in-the-electorate. Nevertheless, party loyalties among elected officials have also weakened over time. (We examine the role of parties in Congress in Chapter 9 and the president's party role in Chapter 10.)

Finally, there is the **party organization**—national and state party officials and workers, committee members, convention delegates, and others active in the party. The Democratic and Republican party organizations formally resemble the American federal system, with national committees, officers and staffs, and national conventions, 50 state committees, and more than 3,000 county committees with city, ward, and precinct levels under their supervision. State committees are not very responsive to the direction of the national committee; and in most states, city and county party organizations operate quite independently of the state committees. In other words, no real hierarchy of authority exists in American parties.

National Party Structure　The Democratic and Republican national party conventions possess *formal* authority over the parties. They meet every four years not only to nominate candidates for president and vice president but also to adopt a party platform, choose party officers, and adopt rules for the party's operation. Because the convention is a large body that meets for only three or four days, however, its real function is to ratify decisions made by national party leaders, as well as to formally nominate presidential and vice presidential candidates.

The Democratic and Republican national committees, made up of delegates from each state and territory, are supposed to govern party affairs *between* conventions.

party organization　National and state party officials and workers, committee members, convention delegates, and others active in the party.

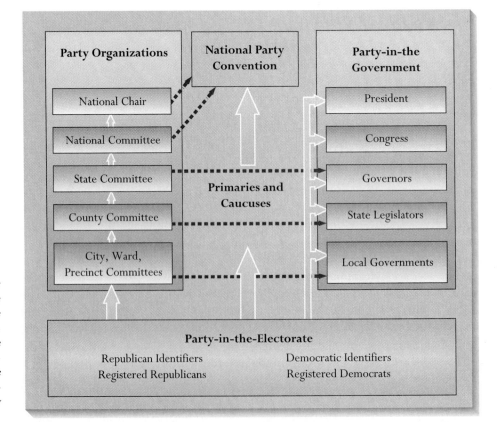

FIGURE 7-5　Where's the Party?

Even among Americans who strongly identify with a major party, there are differences among those who are strictly members of the party-in-the-electorate (voters), those who are members of the party-in-the-government (elected officials), and those who are members of the party organization (national and state party committee members).

But the *real* work of the national party organizations is undertaken by the national party chairs and staff. The national chair is officially chosen by the national committee but is actually chosen by the party's presidential candidate. If the party wins the presidency, the national chair usually serves as a liaison with the president for party affairs. If the party loses, the chair may be replaced before the next national convention. The national chair is supposed to be neutral in the party's primary battles, but when an incumbent president is seeking reelection, the national chair and staff lean very heavily in the president's favor.

The power of the national chair and staff lies in their ability to raise campaign funds and assist the party's candidates in presidential and congressional elections. The staff of the Republican National Committee (RNC) took the lead in fund raising in the 1980s, devising sophisticated computerized mailing lists and a huge file of potential contributors. The RNC used these funds to assist Republican candidates in House and Senate races, commission polls, develop campaign themes, analyze voter trends, and promote the party as a whole in national advertising. The success of the RNC inspired the Democratic National Committee (DNC) to emulate these activities. By 1992, the DNC was able to match the RNC in fund raising.

State Party Organizations   State party organizations consist of a state committee, a state chair who heads the committee, and a staff working at the state capital. Democratic and Republican state committees vary from state to state in composition, organization, and function. The state party chair is generally selected by the state committee, but this selection is often dictated by the party's candidate for governor. Membership on the state committee may range from about a dozen up to several hundred. The members may be chosen through party primaries or by state party conventions. Generally, representation on state committees is allocated by counties, but occasionally other units of government are recognized in state party organizations.

Most state party organizations maintain full-time staffs, including an executive director and public relations, fund-raising, and research people. These organizations help to raise campaign funds for their candidates, conduct registration drives, provide advice and services to their nominees, and even recruit candidates to run in election districts and for offices where the party would otherwise have no names on the ballot. Services to candidates may include advertising and media consulting, advice on election-law compliance, polling, research (including research on opponents), registration and voter identification, mailing lists, and even seminars on campaign techniques.

State committees are also supposed to direct the campaigns for important statewide elections—governors and U.S. senators. They are supposed to serve as central coordinating agencies for these election campaigns and as the party's principal fund-raising organization in the state. Today the role of the state committee is very often limited, however, because most candidates have their own campaign organizations.

Legislative Party Structures   The parties organize the U.S. Senate and House of Representatives, and they organize most state legislatures as well. The majority party in the House meets in caucus to select the speaker of the house as well as the House majority leader and whip (see "Organizing Congress: Party and Leadership" in Chapter 10). The minority party elects its own minority leader and whip. The majority party in the Senate elects the president pro tempore, who presides during the (frequent) absences of the vice president, as well as the Senate majority leader and whip. The minority party in the Senate elects its own minority leader and whip. Committee assignments in both the House and the Senate are allocated on a party basis; committee chairs are always majority-party members.

County Committees   The nation's 3,000 Republican and 3,000 Democratic county chairs probably constitute the most important building blocks in party organization in the nation. City and county party officers and committees are chosen in local primary elections; they cannot be removed by state or national party authorities.

NATIONAL PARTY CONVENTIONS

The Democratic and Republican parties are showcased every four years at the national party **convention.** The official purpose of these four-day fun-filled events is the nomination of the presidential candidates and their vice presidential running mates. Yet the presidential choices have usually already been made in the parties' **presidential primaries** and caucuses earlier in the year. By midsummer convention time, delegates pledged to cast their convention vote for one or another of the presidential candidates have already been selected. Not since 1952, when the Democrats took three convention ballots to select Adlai Stevenson as their presidential candidate, has convention voting gone beyond the first ballot. The possibility exists that in some future presidential race no candidate will win a majority of delegates in the primaries and caucuses, and the result will be a *brokered* convention in which delegates will exercise independent power to select the party nominee. But this event is unlikely.

The Democratic and Republican national conventions are really televised party rallies, designed to showcase the presidential nominee, confirm the nominee's choice for a running mate, and inspire television viewers to support the party and its candidates in the forthcoming general election. Indeed, the national party conventions are largely media events, carefully staged to present an attractive image of the party and its nominees. Party luminaries jockey for key time slots at the podium, and the party prepares slick videotaped commercials touting its nominee for prime-time presentation.

Convention Delegates   Over time, the spread of presidential primary elections has taken the suspense out of the national party conventions. As late as 1968, fewer than half of the delegates were selected in primary elections. But today, the selection of more than 80 percent of pledged delegates by the party's primary voters has greatly diminished the role of party officials in presidential selection.

Both parties award **delegates** to each state in rough proportion to the number of party voters in the state. Democratic Party rules currently require that all popularly elected delegates from each state be awarded to the presidential candidates according to their proportion of that state's primary or caucus vote, after the candidates reach a 15 percent vote threshold. Republican Party rules allow states either to apportion their delegates according to the primary or caucus vote or to adopt a winner-take-all system of awarding all state delegates to the state's primary election victor.

convention   Nominating process in which delegates from local party organizations select the party's nominees.

presidential primaries
Primary elections in the states in which voters in each party can choose a presidential candidate for its party's nomination. Outcomes help determine the distribution of pledged delegates to each party's national nominating convention.

delegate   Accredited voting member of a party's national presidential nominating convention.

Convention delegates are generally party activists, ideologically motivated and strongly committed to their presidential candidates.[9] Democratic delegates are much more *liberal* than Democratic voters, and Republican delegates are more *conservative* than Republican voters (see Figure 7-6). There is a slight tendency for Democratic and Republican delegates to differ in social backgrounds; usually more African Americans, women, and union members are found among Democratic delegates than among Republican delegates.

Making Party Rules   National party conventions make rules for the party, including rules governing the selection of delegates at the next party convention. Democrats are especially likely to focus on delegate selection rules. In 1972 the Democratic Party responded to charges that African Americans, women, and other minorities were underrepresented among the delegates by appointing a special commission chaired by Senator George McGovern to "reform" the party. The McGovern Commission took "affirmative steps" to ensure that the next convention would include "goals" for the representation of African Americans, women, and other minorities among the delegates in proportion to their presence in the Democratic electorate. The effect of these reforms was to reduce the influence of Democratic officeholders (members of Congress, governors, state legislators, and mayors) at the convention and to increase the influence of ideologically motivated activists. Later rule changes eliminated the *unit vote,* in which all delegates from a state were required to vote with the majority of the state's delegation and which required that all delegates who were pledged to a candidate vote for that candidate unless *released* by the candidate.

Then, in the 1980s, the Democratic Leadership Council pressed the party to reserve some convention delegate seats for **superdelegates**—elected officials and party leaders not bound to one candidate—with the expectation that these delegates would be more moderate than the liberal party activists. The notion was that the superdelegates would inject more balanced, less ideological political judgments into convention deliberations, thus improving the party's chances of victory in the general elections. As a result, many Democratic senators, governors, and members of Congress now attend the convention as superdelegates. If presidential candidates ever fail to win a

superdelegates   Delegates to the Democratic Party national convention selected because of their position in the government or the party and not pledged to any candidate.

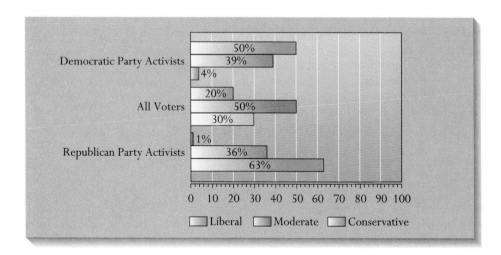

FIGURE 7-6 Ideologies of Voters Versus Party Activists

Democratic and Republican party activists (convention delegates in 1996) are far more likely to hold divergent liberal and conservative views than voters generally.

Source: NBC News/*Wall Street Journal* Poll as reported in *The Polling Report,* September 29, 1997.

Up Close

Democratic and Republican Platforms: Can You Tell the Difference?

These statements from the Democratic and Republican platforms in 1996 differ in both tone and substance.

Can you guess which statements are taken from the Democratic platform and which from the Republican?

Civil Rights

A. We continue to lead the fight to end discrimination on the basis of race, gender, religion, age, ethnicity, disability, and sexual orientation. . . . We support continued efforts . . . to end discrimination against gay men and lesbians and further their full inclusion in the life of the nation.

B. [W]e oppose discrimination based on sex, race, age, creed, or national origin and will vigorously enforce anti-discrimination statutes. We . . . endorse the Defense of Marriage Act to prevent states from being forced to recognize same-sex unions.

Abortion

A. [We] stand behind the right of every woman to choose, consistent with *Roe v. Wade*. . . . It is a fundamental constitutional liberty that individual Americans—not government—can best take responsibility for making the most difficult and intensely personal decisions regarding reproduction.

B. The unborn child has a fundamental individual right to life which cannot be infringed. We support a human life amendment to the Constitution. We oppose using public revenues for abortion and will not fund organizations which advocate it.

Taxes

A. We want to strengthen middle-class families by providing a $500 tax cut for children. We want to cut taxes to help families pay for education after high school and to guarantee the first two years of college.

B. In response to this unprecedented burden confronting America, we support an across-the-board, 15-percent tax cut to marginal tax rates. We believe such a cut should be the first step towards reducing overall tax burdens while promoting the economic growth . . .

Welfare

A. Thanks to [us], the new welfare bill includes the health care and child care people need so they can go to work confident their children will be cared for. Thanks to [us] the new welfare bill imposes time limits and real work requirements—so anyone who can work, does work, and so that no one who can work can stay on welfare forever.

B. The key to welfare reform is restoring personal responsibility and encouraging two-parent households. The path to that goal lies outside of official Washington. All able-bodied adults must be required to work, either in private sector jobs or in community work projects. Illegal aliens must be ineligible for all but emergency benefits. And a firm time limit for receipt of welfare must be enforced.

All **A** entries are Democrat. All **B** entries are Republican.

majority of delegates in the primaries, these superdelegates may some day control a nomination.

Party Platforms   National conventions also write party **platforms,** setting out the party's goals and policy positions. Because a party's platform is not binding on its nominees, platform *planks* are largely symbolic, although they often provide heated arguments and provide distinct differences between the parties to present to voters (see *Up Close:* "Democratic and Republican Platforms: Can You Tell the Difference?").

Selecting a Running Mate   Perhaps the only suspense remaining in national party conventions centers on the presidential nominee's choice of a vice presidential running mate. In 1956 Democratic presidential nominee Adlai Stevenson threw open the choice of a vice presidential nominee to the convention, which chose Tennessee Senator Estes Kefauver over young Massachusetts Senator John F. Kennedy. Normally, however, the choice is made by the presidential nominee. Even a presidential candidate who has decided on a running mate well in advance of the convention may choose to wait until the convention to announce the choice; otherwise there would be little real "news value" to the convention, and the television networks would give less coverage to it. By encouraging speculation about who the running mate will be, the candidate and the convention manager can sustain media interest. (For a discussion of various strategies in selecting a running mate, see "The Vice Presidential Waiting Game" in Chapter 11.)

The convention *always* accepts the presidential candidate's recommendation for a running mate. No formal rules require the convention to do so, but it would be politically unacceptable for the convention to override the first important decision of the party's presidential nominee. Convention delegates set aside any personal reservations they may have and unanimously endorse the presidential nominee's choice.

Campaign Kickoff   The final evening of the national conventions is really the kickoff for the general election campaign. The presidential nominee's acceptance speech tries to set the tone for the fall campaign. Party celebrities, including defeated presidential candidates, join hands at the podium as a symbol of party unity. Presidential and vice presidential candidates, spouses, and families assemble under balloons and streamers, amid the happy noise and hoopla, to signal the start of the general election campaign.[10]

THE PARTY VOTERS

Traditionally, the Democratic Party has been able to claim to be the majority party in the United States (see Figure 7-7). In opinion polls, those who "identified" with the Democratic Party generally outnumbered those who "identified" with the Republican Party. (**Party identification** is determined by response to the question, "Generally speaking, how would you identify yourself: as a Republican, Democrat, independent, or something else?") But the Democratic Party advantage among the voters has eroded over time, partly as a result of a gradual increase in the number of people who call themselves independents and partly as a result of recent Republican gains.[11]

platform   Statement of principles adopted by a political party at its national convention (specific portions of the platform are known as planks); a platform is not binding on the party's candidates.

party identification   Self-described identification with a political party, usually in response to the question, "Generally speaking, how would you identify yourself: as a Republican, Democrat, independent, or something else?"

**FIGURE 7-7 Party Identifi-
cation in the Electorate**

*For many years, the Democratic
Party enjoyed a substantial lead in
party identification among voters.
This Democratic lead eroded somewhat following the election of
Republican President Ronald
Reagan in 1980. Independent identification over the years has risen,
suggesting that many voters have
become disillusioned with both
parties. Relatively few people
consider themselves "strong" Democrats or Republicans.*

Source: Data from National Election
Studies, University of Michigan.

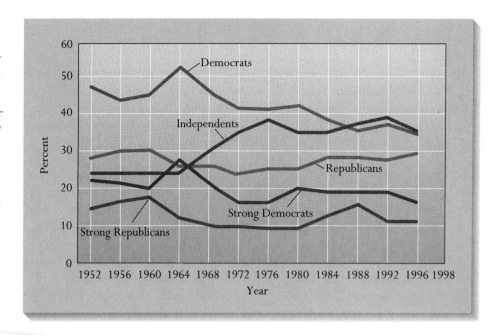

Growing Numbers of Independents Over time, Americans have grown
disenchanted with both parties. The Democratic and Republican parties have lost
identifiers, and the numbers of *independent identifiers* have increased substantially.
Indeed, in recent years more people have identified themselves as independents
than as either Democrats or Republicans.

Dealignment **Dealignment** describes the decline in attractiveness of the
political parties to the voters, the growing reluctance of people to identify themselves with either party, and a decrease in reliance on a candidate's party affiliation in voter choice. Dealignment is evident not only in the growing numbers of
self-described independents but also in the declining numbers of those who identify themselves as "strong" Democrats or Republicans. In short, the electorate is
less partisan than it once was.

Party Loyalty in Voting Despite the decline in partisan identification in the
electorate, it is important to note that *party identification is a strong influence in
voter choice in elections.* Most voters cast their ballot for the candidate of their
party. This is true in presidential elections (see Figure 7-8) and even more true
in congressional and state elections. Those who identify themselves as Democrats
are somewhat more likely to vote for a Republican presidential candidate than
those who identify themselves as Republicans are to vote for a Democratic presidential candidate. Republican Ronald Reagan was able to win more than one-quarter of self-identified Democrats in 1980 and 1984, earning these crossover voters
the label "Reagan Democrats."[12]

Realignment? Although Democratic Party loyalty has eroded over the last
twenty years, it is not clear whether or not this erosion is a classic party **realignment.**[13] Most scholars agree that party realignments occurred in the presidential

dealignment Declining
attractiveness of the parties to
the voters, a reluctance to identify strongly with a party, and a
decrease in reliance on party
affiliation in voter choice.

realignment Long-term shift
in social-group support for various political parties that creates
new coalitions in each party.

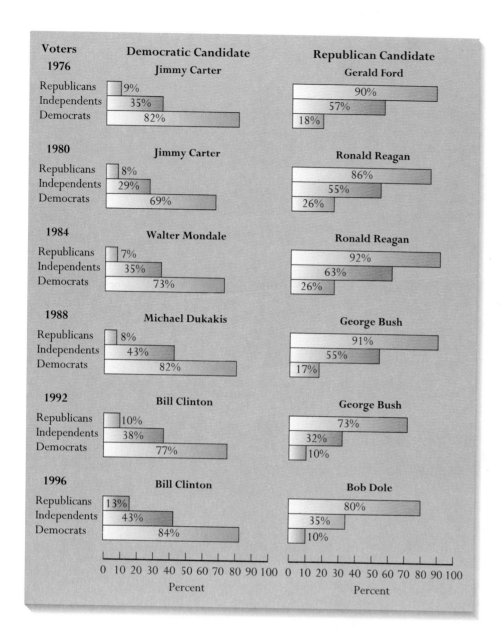

Voters 1976	Democratic Candidate Jimmy Carter	Republican Candidate Gerald Ford
Republicans	9%	90%
Independents	35%	57%
Democrats	82%	18%

1980	Jimmy Carter	Ronald Reagan
Republicans	8%	86%
Independents	29%	55%
Democrats	69%	26%

1984	Walter Mondale	Ronald Reagan
Republicans	7%	92%
Independents	35%	63%
Democrats	73%	26%

1988	Michael Dukakis	George Bush
Republicans	8%	91%
Independents	43%	55%
Democrats	82%	17%

1992	Bill Clinton	George Bush
Republicans	10%	73%
Independents	38%	32%
Democrats	77%	10%

1996	Bill Clinton	Bob Dole
Republicans	13%	80%
Independents	43%	35%
Democrats	84%	10%

Percent

Percent

FIGURE 7-8 Republican, Democratic, and Independent Voters in Presidential Elections

As the percentages here indicate, in recent years registered Democrats have been more likely to "cross over" and vote for a Republican candidate for president than registered Republicans have been to vote for the Democratic presidential candidate.

Source: New York Times.

elections of 1824 (Jackson, Democrats), 1860 (Lincoln, Republicans), 1896 (Bryan, Democrats), and 1932 (Roosevelt, Democrats). This historical sequence gave rise to a theory that realigning elections occur every thirty-six years. According to this theory, the election of 1968 should have been a realigning one. It is true that Richard Nixon's 1968 victory marked the beginning of a 24-year Republican era in presidential election victories that was broken only by Jimmy Carter in 1976. But there was relatively little shifting of the party loyalties of major social groups, and the Democratic Party remained the dominant party in the electorate and in Congress.

The Democratic Party still receives *disproportionate* support from Catholics, Jews, African Americans, less educated and lower income groups, blue-collar workers, union members, and big-city residents. The Republican Party still

The Anatomy of the Elephant

In the American two-party system, each party must endeavor to appeal to a broad coalition of voters in order to win a majority. But in so doing, each party incorporates an array of interests that often have different policy priorities. Differences among factions *within* both the Democratic and the Republican parties create internal tensions, which sometimes leads to open conflicts, especially in primary elections. Each party's presidential nominee must therefore expend considerable energy to patch over these internal party differences. (To understand how Bill Clinton managed to shore up the Democratic Party coalition, see *Up Close:* "Change with Moderation: Clinton's Winning Strategy" in Chapter 8, and *People*

Abortion rights is one of the issues dividing cultural conservatives from economic conservatives and economic supply-siders within the Republican Party.

receives *disproportionate* support from Protestants, whites, more educated and higher income groups, white-collar workers, nonunion workers, and suburban and small-town dwellers (see *Up Close:* "The Anatomy of the Elephant"). Disproportionate support does not mean these groups *always* give a majority of their votes to the indicated party, but only that they give that party a larger percentage of their votes than the party receives from the general electorate. This pattern of social-group voting and party identification has remained relatively stable over the years, even though the GOP has made some gains among many of the traditionally Democratic groups (see Figure 7-9 on page 226). The only major *shift* in social-group support has occurred among southern whites. This group has shifted from heavily Democratic in party identification to a substantial Republican preference. Thus it is questionable whether a true party realignment has occurred[14] (see *Across the USA:* "Democratic and Republican Party Strength in the States" on page 227).

in Politics: "Bill Clinton: The Ambivalent Presidency" in Chapter 11.)

Since Ronald Reagan's presidency, the Republican Party has been without a dominant, uniting figure. Neither George Bush nor Bob Dole as presidential candidates, nor congressional leaders Speaker of the House Newt Gingrich or Senate Majority Leader Trent Lott, has been able to appeal to all of the separate factions within the GOP. Although these factions are by no means clearly defined, we might categorize them as follows:

Economic Conservatives

- Priorities include balancing the budget, avoiding inflation, keeping interest rates low.
- Generally older, wealthier, mostly male, and stronger in the midwestern and northeastern states.
- Less concerned about moral issues such as drugs, crime, and homosexuality.
- Generally support abortion rights and affirmative action.
- Internationalists in world affairs; support world trade agreements and U.S. interventions in world crises.

Economic Supply-Siders

- Priorities include lower taxes and income tax reform (either flat tax or a national sales tax to replace the income tax).

- Less concerned about balanced budgets; believe that lower taxes will inspire economic growth.
- Generally younger, mostly male, and stronger in the West.
- Less concerned about crime; opposed to government actions restricting abortion or the medical use of marijuana; support equal opportunity but oppose racial preferences.
- Support free-trade agreements but often oppose U.S. interventions in foreign conflicts.

Cultural Conservatives

- Priorities include war on drugs, crime fighting, welfare reform.
- Less concerned with economic issues; prefer maintaining generous Social Security and Medicare benefits over balanced budget or lower taxes.
- Generally concerned with cultural decline, including pornography and incivility in daily life.
- Generally older, male and female, and stronger in Midwest and South.
- Strongly opposed to abortion, affirmative action, and laws protecting the rights of homosexuals.
- Nationalists in world affairs; oppose trade agreements they believe cost American jobs.

THIRD-PARTY PROSPECTS

There is widespread disillusionment in the United States with "politics as usual." This is reflected in the distrust expressed by Americans in their government (see *What Do You Think?* "Can You Trust the Government?" in Chapter 1), in their belief that the government is "run by a few big interests looking out for themselves" (see *What Do You Think?* "Is Government Run by a Few Big Interests Looking Out for Themselves?" in Chapter 1), and in their increasing dealignment from the Republican and Democratic parties. The public mood provides fertile ground for the emergence of **third parties** and independent candidates.

Third-Party Popularity In recent years, polls have reported that a majority of Americans favor the idea of a third party. The support for the *general idea* of a third party is usually favored by 55 to 65 percent of the American public.[15] But

third party Political party that challenges the two major parties in an election.

FIGURE 7-9 **Social-Group Support for the Democratic and Republican Parties**

FIGURE 7-9 Social-Group Support for the Democratic and Republican Parties

The Democratic Party draws disproportionate support from low-income, less educated, Catholic, Jewish, and African American voters. The Republican Party relies more heavily on support from high-income, college-educated, white Protestant voters.

Source: Data from National Election Studies, University of Michigan.

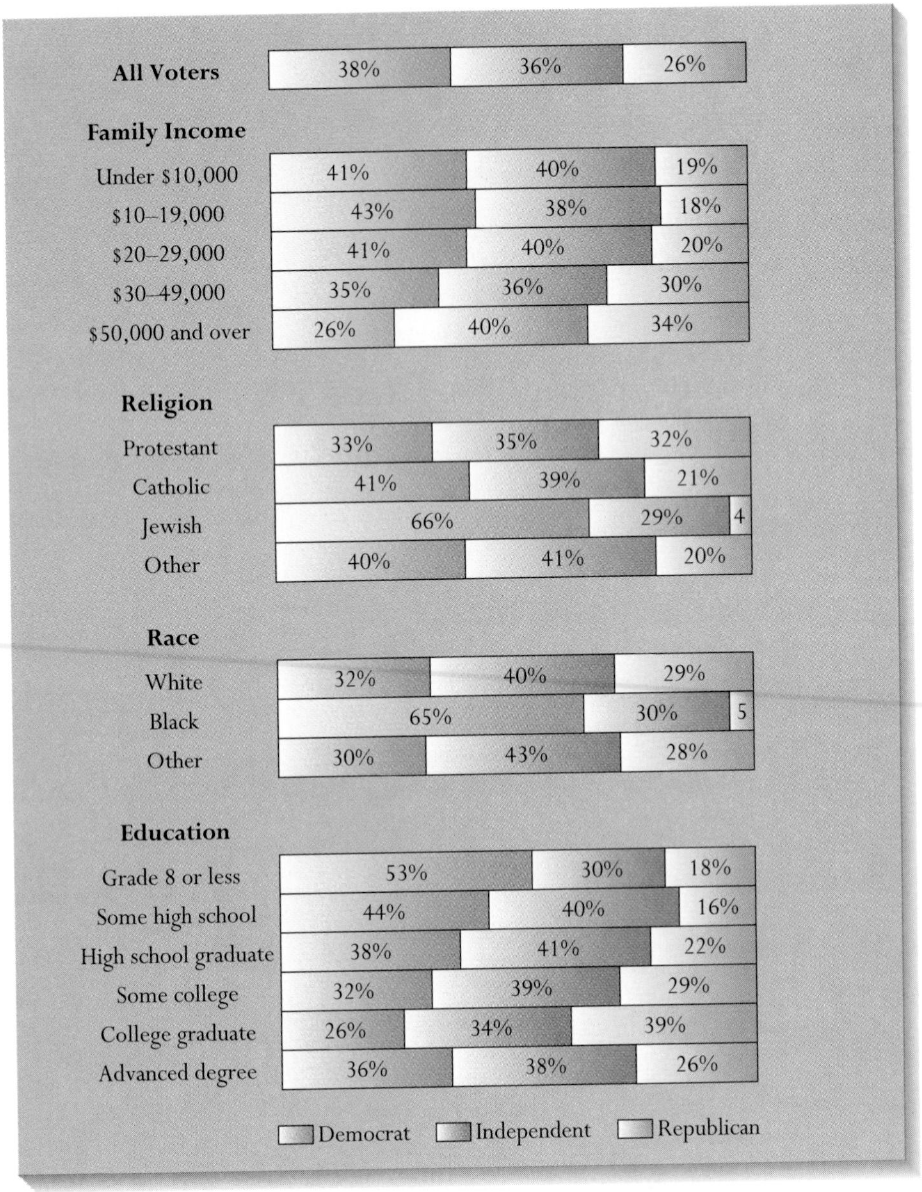

	Democrat	Independent	Republican
All Voters	38%	36%	26%
Family Income			
Under $10,000	41%	40%	19%
$10–19,000	43%	38%	18%
$20–29,000	41%	40%	20%
$30–49,000	35%	36%	30%
$50,000 and over	26%	40%	34%
Religion			
Protestant	33%	35%	32%
Catholic	41%	39%	21%
Jewish	66%	29%	4
Other	40%	41%	20%
Race			
White	32%	40%	29%
Black	65%	30%	5
Other	30%	43%	28%
Education			
Grade 8 or less	53%	30%	18%
Some high school	44%	40%	16%
High school graduate	38%	41%	22%
Some college	32%	39%	29%
College graduate	26%	34%	39%
Advanced degree	36%	38%	26%

this support for the general idea has never been matched by voter support for *specific* third-party or independent presidential candidates (see Table 7-1). And even the most popular of these candidates have failed to win the electoral votes of very many states (see *Up Close:* "Understanding the Electoral College" in Chapter 8). Third-party and independent movements in the twentieth century have been short-lived; by the next election, their supporters have been reabsorbed into the two-party system.

The Detached Center   In recent years legions of politically self-identified independents as well as ideologically self-identified moderates have grown dissatisfied with both the Democratic and Republican parties. Popular U.S. Senator Bill Bradley, in announcing his early retirement from the Senate, seemed to summarize the central problem confronting moderates: "The political debate has settled

Across the USA

Democratic and Republican Party Strength in the States

The Democratic and Republican parties compete in every state. Indeed, party competition within states has increased as the once heavily Democratic states of the "Solid South" have developed stronger Republican Party ties. But some voters have favored candidates of one party in gubernatorial and congressional elections and the other in presidential elections in recent years.

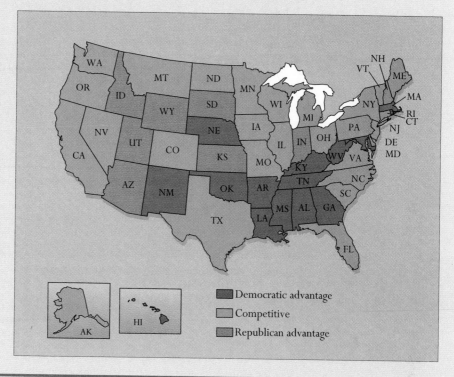

■ Democratic advantage
□ Competitive
■ Republican advantage

into two familiar ruts," he said. "The Republicans are infatuated with the 'magic' of the market and reflexively criticize government as the enemy of freedom, and the Democrats distrust the market, preach government as the answer to our problems and prefer the bureaucrats they know to the consumer they can't control."[16]

Ideological Separation of the Parties As ideologically driven political activists have gained influence in the Democratic and Republican parties, many moderate voters have been turned away. Often the fierce rhetoric of core Democratic activists (public employee unionists, feminists, environmentalists, and outspoken African American leaders) has alienated centrists and independents, just as the uncompromising stands of core Republican activists (religious fundamentalists, immigration opponents, anti-abortion activists) have done. Earlier, we observed that vote-maximizing parties would avoid extreme liberal or conservative positions and converge at the broad center of American opinion (see Figure 7-4). But often, activists in both parties—people who contribute money, work in campaigns, staff the party offices, vote regularly in party primaries, and frequently win seats as convention delegates—are more ideologically motivated than the general electorate. Many liberals among Democratic activists and many conservatives among

TABLE 7–1	Twentieth-Century Third-Party Presidential Votes		
Third-Party Presidential Candidates		Popular Vote (percentage)	Electoral Votes (number)
Theodore Roosevelt (1912), Progressive (Bull Moose) Party		27.4%	88
Ross Perot (1992), Independent		18.9	0
Robert M. La Follette (1924), Progressive Party		16.6	13
George C. Wallace (1968), American Independent party		13.5	46
Ross Perot (1996), Reform Party		8.5	0
John Anderson (1980), Independent		6.6	0

Republican activists are concerned primarily with their party's ideological stance, and they resist compromises designed to make their party more appealing to centrist voters. Moderates become disillusioned with both parties, and opportunities emerge for centrist, independent candidates.

Reform Party Prospects   In 1996 Ross Perot was successful in getting his Reform Party on the ballot in all fifty states. The party's convention spanned two weekends, between which members were asked to participate in a complicated electronic voting scheme. Perot himself emerged the predictable winner, and former Colorado governor Richard Lamm an embittered loser. But despite continued popular disillusionment with "politics as usual"—only 49 percent of the voting-age population cast ballots in 1996, the lowest turnout in seventy years—the Reform Party failed to challenge the major parties. Perot won only 9 percent of the popular vote for president. Perhaps independents were disenchanted with the autocratic style of Ross Perot and the Reform Party's too-close identification with the outspoken billionaire.

WHY THE TWO-PARTY SYSTEM PERSISTS

The two-party system is deeply ingrained in American politics. Although third parties have often made appearances in presidential elections, no third-party candidate has ever won the Oval Office. (Lincoln's new Republican Party in 1860 might be counted as an exception, but it quickly became a major party.) Very few third-party candidates have won seats in Congress. Many other democracies have multiple-party systems, so the question arises as to why the United States has had a two-party system throughout its history.

Cultural Consensus   One explanation of the nation's two-party system focuses on the broad consensus supporting the American political culture (see Chapter 2). The values of democracy, capitalism, free enterprise, individual liberty, religious freedom, and equality of opportunity are so widely shared that no party challenging these values has ever won much of a following. There is little support in the American political culture for avowedly fascist, authoritarian, or other antidemocratic parties. Moreover, the American political culture includes a strong belief in the separation of church and state. Political parties with religious affiliations, common in European democracies, are absent from American politics. Socialist parties have frequently appeared on the scene under various labels—the Socialist Party, the Socialist Labor Party, the Socialist Workers Party, and the Communist Party. But the largest popular vote ever garnered by a socialist candidate in a presidential election was the 6 percent won by Eugene V. Debs in 1912. In contrast, socialist parties have frequently won control of European governments.

On broad policy issues, most Americans cluster near the center. This general consensus tends to discourage multiple parties. There does not appear to be sufficient room for them to stake out a position on the ideological spectrum that would detach voters from the two major parties.

This cultural explanation blends with the influence of historical precedents. The American two-party system has gained acceptance through custom. The nation's first party system developed from two coalitions, Federalists and Anti-Federalists, and this dual pattern has been reinforced over two centuries.

Winner-Take-All Electoral System Yet another explanation of the American two-party system focuses on the electoral system itself. Winners in presidential and congressional elections, as well as in state gubernatorial and legislative elections, are usually determined by a plurality, winner-take-all vote. Even in elections that require a majority of more than 50 percent to win—which may involve a runoff election—only one party's candidate wins in the end. Because of the winner-take-all nature of U.S. elections, parties and candidates have an overriding incentive to broaden their appeal to a plurality or majority of voters. Losers come away empty-handed. There is not much incentive in such a system for a party to form to represent the views of 5 or 10 percent of the electorate.

Americans are so accustomed to winner-take-all elections that they seldom consider alternatives. In some countries, legislative bodies are elected by **proportional representation,** whereby all voters cast a single ballot for the party of their choice and legislative seats are then apportioned to the parties in proportion to their total vote in the electorate (see *Compared to What?* "Political Parties of the World"). Minority parties are assured of legislative seats, perhaps with as little as 10 or 15 percent of the vote. If no party wins 50 percent of the votes and seats, the parties try to form a coalition of parties to establish control of the government. In these nations, party coalition building to form a governing majority occurs *after* the election rather than *before* the election, as it does in winner-take-all elections systems.

Legal Access to the Ballot Another factor in the American two-party system may be electoral system barriers to third parties. The Democratic and Republican nominees are automatically included on all general election ballots, but third-party and independent candidates face difficult obstacles in getting their names listed. In presidential elections, a third-party candidate must meet the varied requirements of fifty separate states to appear on their ballots along with the Democratic and Republican nominees. These requirements often include filing petitions signed by up to 5 or 10 percent of registered voters. In addition, states require third parties

proportional representation Electoral system that allocates seats in a legislature based on the proportion of votes each party receives in a national election.

Political Parties of the World

Party politics vary throughout the world, but some general patterns are apparent. Multiparty systems occur in nations with proportional representation, whereas two-party systems occur in nations with winner-take-all elections. France has a unique two-step electoral system: all parties run candidates in a first election, and the top two candidates in each district face off in a second election. In Germany,

half of the Bundestag (national legislature) is chosen by proportional representation and half by winner-take-all district elections. Both the German and the French electoral systems support a multiparty system, although two-party coalitions dominate government. Small Communist parties are found in multiparty Western democracies, but wherever the Communist Party has taken power, it has established a one-party system. Most two-party systems have one party oriented more toward free markets and another party more toward a welfare state or democratic socialism.

Nation	System	Major Parties	Party Orientation
Australia	Two-party, winner take-all elections	Liberal Party Labor Party	Free enterprise Democratic socialism
Austria	Multiparty, proportional representation	Austrian Socialist Party Austrian Peoples Party Austrian Freedom Party	Democratic socialism Christian democratic Free enterprise, anti-immigration
Canada	Multiparty, winner-take-all elections	Liberal Party Progressive Conservative Party Le Parti Québecois New Democratic Party	Free enterprise, social reform Conservative, preservation of Canada Political sovereignty for Quebec Democratic socialism
China, People's Republic of	One-party system	Communist Party of China	Revolutionary class struggle, "market socialism"
Cuba	One-party system	Communist Party of Cuba	Revolutionary class struggle, socialism

to win 5 or 10 percent of the vote in the last election in order to retain their position on the ballot in subsequent elections. In 1980 independent John Anderson gained access to the ballot in all fifty states, as did independent Ross Perot in 1992. But just doing so required a considerable expenditure of effort and money that the major parties were able to avoid.

THIRD PARTIES IN THE U.S. SYSTEM

Despite the cultural and electoral barriers to victory, third parties, more accurately called minor parties, are a common feature of American politics. These parties can be roughly classified by the role they play in the political system.

Nation	System	Major Parties	Party Orientation
France	Multiparty, two elections, winner-take-all elections	Rally for the Republic Union for French Democracy Socialist Party Unified Socialist Party Communist Party National Front Greens	Nationalism, "Gaulist" Centrist, European outlook Democratic socialism Socialism Communist society Anti-immigration Environmentalism
Germany	Multiparty, half proportional representation, winner-take-all elections	Christian Democratic Union Social Democratic Party Free Democratic Party Greens	Christian conservative Democratic socialism Free Enterprise Environmentalism
Japan	Multiparty with a single dominant party, mixture of proportional representation and winner-take-all elections	Liberal Democratic Japan Socialist Party Komeito Party Japan Communist Party	Free enterprise Democratic socialism "Clean government" "Scientific socialism"
Israel	Multiparty with two major alignments, proportional representation	Likud Alignment Labour Alignment Liberal Party National Religious Party Communist Party	Nationalism Democratic socialism Free enterprise Religious orthodoxy Marxism-Leninism
United Kingdom	Modified two-party winner-take-all, elections	Conservative Party Labour Party Liberal Party	Free enterprise Social welfare state Free enterprise, centrist

Ideological Parties   **Ideological parties** exist to promote an ideology rather than to win elections. They use the electoral process to express their views and to rally activists to their cause, and they measure success not by victory at the polls but by their ability to bring their name and their views to the attention of the American public. The socialist parties, which have run candidates in virtually every presidential election in this century, are prime examples of ideological parties in the United States (see also *Up Close:* "The Libertarian Party: A Dissenting Voice").

ideological party   Third party that exists to promote an ideology rather than to win elections.

Protest Parties   **Protest parties** arise around popular issues or concerns that the major parties have failed to address. An important historical example of a protest party is the Populist Party of the late 1800s. It arose as a protest by midwestern farmers against eastern railroads, "trusts" and monopolies, and the

protest party   Third party that arises in response to issues of popular concern which have not been addressed by the major parties.

The Libertarian Party: A Dissenting Voice

Would you like to see the federal income tax repealed; the Internal Revenue Service abolished; foreign aid ended; all U.S. troops brought home from overseas; and individual choice "in all matters," from abortion to gun control to drug use? Would you like to eliminate government farm subsidies; end federal support for public broadcasting, science, and the arts; and "privatize" education and "charitize" welfare? These are the campaign promises of the Libertarian Party, whose presidential candidates' names appeared on the ballot in all fifty states in 1992 and 1996.

The Libertarian Party is unique in its uncompromising commitment to the classical liberal, eighteenth-century ideals of John Locke and Adam Smith. Libertarians oppose all interference by government in the private lives of citizens. They support unregulated free markets and the protection of private property rights. Thus they oppose environmental regulations, consumer protection laws, and laws that infringe on private property or "take" property for government use without just compensation to owners. They also oppose govern-

ment efforts to regulate private morals—including laws outlawing drug use, prostitution, gambling, and pornography—believing these activities should be the exclusive choice of consenting individuals. Libertarians are strict noninterventionists in international affairs; they are opposed to the North Atlantic Treaty Organization (NATO) alliance, to foreign aid, to military involvements outside of U.S. territory, and to virtually all spending for national defense.

Although the Libertarian Party candidate for president regularly receives less than 1 percent of the popular vote, Libertarian ideas have entered the nation's policy debates and influenced both major parties. Republican candidates have frequently adopted Libertarian arguments on behalf of deregulation of market activities; Democratic candidates frequently use Libertarian arguments about individual "choice" in the areas of abortion, school prayer, and homosexual activity. And both the Democratic and the Republican parties have vocal "isolationist" wings that borrow Libertarian, noninterventionist arguments against foreign aid, international alliances, and military expenditures. Thus the Libertarian Party, like other ideological parties, functions to promote ideas rather than win elections.

gold standard. The Populists threatened to capture the wave of popular support for railroad regulation, cheap money, and anti-monopoly legislation, and thus they endangered the established Democratic and Republican parties. But when the Democratic Party nominated William Jennings Bryan in 1896, the Populist Party officially endorsed Bryan and subsequently disappeared as a significant independent political organization. Later, Republican President Theodore Roosevelt would voice Populist "trust-busting" themes, stealing the rhetoric of the early Populist Party. Populist ideas were set forth again in a new Progressive Party, which nominated Robert M. La Follette for president in 1924; the Democratic and Republican parties both nominated conservative candidates that year, helping La Follette to win almost 17 percent of the popular vote.

Not all major protest movements have been accompanied by the formation of third parties. Indeed, protest leaders have often argued that a third-party effort distracts the movement from a more effective strategy of capturing control of one or both of the major parties. The labor-union-organizing movement of the 1930s and the civil rights and antiwar movements of the 1960s did not spark a separate third party but instead worked largely *within* the dominant Democratic Party to advance their goals.

After declining to run for another term in 1908 and encouraging the Republican Party to nominate William Howard Taft to fill his position, Teddy Roosevelt felt ready to return to the White House in 1912. When the Republican Party nominated President Taft again, Roosevelt formed his own independent party—the Progressive (Bull Moose) Party— and won more votes than any other third-party candidate in U.S. history, but still failed to win the presidency.

Single-Issue Parties   **Single-issue parties** have frequently formed around a particular cause. Single-issue parties are much like protest parties, although somewhat narrower in their policy focus. The Greenback Party of the late 1800s shared with the Populists a desire for cheap inflated currency in order to ease the burden of debt and mortgage payments by farmers. But the Greenback Party focused on a single remedy: an end to the gold standard and the issuance of cheap currency— "greenbacks."

Perhaps the most persistent of minor parties over the years has been the Prohibition Party. It achieved temporary success with the passage of the Eighteenth Amendment to the U.S. Constitution in 1919, which prohibited the manufacture, sale, or transportation of "intoxicating liquors," only to see its "noble experiment" fail and be repealed by the Twenty-first Amendment. Actually, the prohibitionists' successes were more directly attributable to their interest-group activity—lobbying in Congress and in state legislatures—than to the electoral threat of the Prohibition Party.

Splinter Parties   Finally, many third parties in American politics are really **splinter parties**, parties formed by a dissatisfied faction of a major party. Splinter parties may form around a particular individual, as did the Progressive (Bull Moose) Party of Theodore Roosevelt in 1912. As a popular former president, Teddy Roosevelt won more than 27 percent of the popular vote, outpolling Republican candidate William Howard Taft but allowing Democrat Woodrow Wilson to win the presidency.

Splinter parties also may emerge from an intense intraparty policy dispute. For example, in 1948 the States' Rights (Dixiecrat) Party formed in protest to the civil rights (fair employment practices) plan in the Democratic Party platform of that year and nominated Strom Thurmond for president. In 1968 George Wallace's American Independent Party won nearly 14 percent of the popular vote. Wallace attacked school desegregation and busing to achieve racial balance in schools, as well as crime in the streets, welfare "cheats," and meddling federal judges and bureaucrats. He abandoned his third-party organization in 1972 to run in the Democratic presidential primary elections. Following some Democratic primary victories, he was shot and disabled for life.

single-issue party   Third party formed around one particular cause.

splinter party   Third party formed by a dissatisfied faction of a major party.

Politics in Cyberspace

Political Parties

Keeping up with Republican and Democratic party affairs is relatively easy—just tap into the home pages of their Web site. And with a visit to the Web site of the Federal Elections Commission, you can check out for yourself the parties' major sources of funding.

Federal Elections Commission
http://www.fec.gov

The FEC site provides access to current financial reports filed by presidential, House and Senate campaigns.

Democratic National Committee
http://www.democrats.org

The Democratic National Committee Services Corporation's Web site posts the party platform, information about its current positions and past history, and membership information.

The Republican National Committee
http://www.rnc.com

The Republican National Committee Web site includes biographies on the party's leaders, membership information, and the party platform.

Communist Party, USA
http://ww.hartford-hwp.com/cp-usa

The Communist Party USA describes itself as "a Marxist-Leninist working-class party that unites Black, Brown and white, men and women, youth and seniors" and "speaks out from a working-class point of view on every vital issue."

Constitutional Action Party
http://www2.ari.net/home/CAP

The CAP, according to the party's Web page, "intends to become the new majority party in this county by uniting traditional values with a well-thought-out program of economic populism."

The Green Party USA
http://www.greens.org/usa

"The Greens/Green Party USA in the United States is part of the worldwide movement that promotes ecological wisdom, social justice, grassroots democracy and non-violence."

The Libertarian Party
http://www.lp.org

The Libertarian Party promotes "the American heritage of liberty, enterprise, and personal responsibility."

The Reform Party
http://www.reformparty.org

The Reform Party was created by Ross Perot, who ran as its presidential candidate in the 1996 election. The party won a spot on the ballot in all fifty states.

SUMMARY NOTES

- Organization grants advantage in the struggle for power. Political parties organize individuals and groups to exercise power in democracies by winning elected office.

- Political parties are not mentioned in the U.S. Constitution, yet they have played a central role in American political history. Major party realignments have occurred at critical points in American history, as major social groups shifted their political loyalties.

- In theory, political parties are "responsible" organizations that adopt a principled platform, recruit candidates who support the platform, educate the public about it, direct an issue-oriented campaign, and then organize the legislature and ensure that their candidates enact the party's platform.

- But in the American two-party system, winning office by appealing to the large numbers of people at the center of the political spectrum becomes more important than promoting strong policy positions. American parties cannot bind elected officials to campaign promises anyway.

- American parties have lost many of their traditional functions over time. Party nominations are won by individual candidates in primary elections rather than through selection by party leaders. Most political candidates are self-selected; they organize their own campaigns. Television has replaced the party as the principal means of educating the public. And government bureaucracies, not party machines, provide social services.

- Party nominations are won in primary elections as earlier caucus and convention methods of nomination have largely disappeared. Party primary elections in the various states may be open or closed and may or may not require runoff primaries. The nominees selected in each party's primary election then battle each other in the general election.

- The parties battle in three major arenas. The *party-in-the electorate* refers to party identification among voters. The *party-in-the-government* refers to party identification and organization among elected officials. The *party organization* refers to party offices at the local, state, and national levels.

- The Democratic and Republican parties are structured to include national party conventions, national committees with chairs and staff, congressional party organizations, state committees, and county and local committees.

- Since presidential nominations are now generally decided in primary elections—with pledged delegates selected before the opening of the national conventions and with party platforms largely symbolic and wholly unenforceable on the candidates—the conventions have become largely media events designed to kick off the general election campaign.

- *Dealignment* refers to a decline in the attractiveness of the parties to the voters, a growing reluctance of people to identify strongly with either party, and greater voter willingness to cross party lines. Despite dealignment, party identification remains a strong influence in voter choice.

- Opinion polls indicate that most Americans support the general idea of a third party, but throughout the twentieth century no third-party presidential candidate won very many votes.

- In the United States, many aspects of the political system—including cultural consensus, the winner-take-all electoral system, and legal restrictions to ballot access—place major obstacles in the way of success for third parties and independent candidates. Although never successful at gaining federal office in significant numbers, ideological, protest, single-issue, and splinter third parties have often been effective at getting popular issues on the federal agenda.

SELECTED READINGS

BECK, PAUL ALLEN. *Party Politics in America.* 8th ed. New York: Longman, 1997. An authoritative text on the American party system—party organizations, the parties-in-government, and the parties-in-the-electorate.

DOWNS, ANTHONY. *An Economic Theory of Democracy.* New York: Harper & Row, 1957. The classic work describing rational choice winning strategies for political parties and explaining why there is no incentive for vote-maximizing parties in a two-party system to adopt widely separate policy positions.

KEEFE, WILLIAM J. *Parties, Politics, and Public Policy in America.* 8th ed. Washington, D.C.: CQ Press, 1997. A comprehensive survey of American political parties, from the nominating process to campaign finance and the changing affiliations of voters.

LOWI, THEODORE E., and JOSEPH ROMANGE. *Debating the Two Party System.* Boulder, Colo.: Rowman & Littlefield, 1997. Lowi argues that the two-party system is no longer adequate to represent the people of a diverse nation; Romange counters that two parties help unify the country and instruct Americans about the value of compromise.

ROSENSTONE, STEVEN J., ROY L. BEHR, and EDWARD H. LAZARUS. *Third Parties in America.* 2nd ed. Princeton, N.J.: Princeton University Press, 1996. A review of the history of third parties in American politics with an analysis of the various causes of third-party movements.

WATTENBERG, MARTIN P. *The Decline of American Political Parties, 1952–1992.* Cambridge, Mass.: Harvard University Press, 1994. An authoritative discussion of increasing negative attitudes toward the parties and the growing dealignment in the electorate.

ZEIGLER, HARMON. *Political Parties in Industrial Democracies.* Itasca, Ill.: Peacock, 1992. An insightful comparative analysis of parties and interest groups in Western European nations, Japan, and the United States.

ASK YOURSELF ABOUT POLITICS

1. Should elected officials be bound by their campaign promises?
   Yes ☐ No ☐

2. Do you think that personal ambition, rather than civic duty, motivates most politicians?
   Yes ☐ No ☐

3. Do career politicians serve their constituents better than those who go into politics for just a short time?
   Yes ☐ No ☐

4. Should people vote on the basis of a candidate's personal character rather than his or her policy positions?
   Yes ☐ No ☐

5. Would you vote for a candidate who used negative ads to discredit an opponent?
   Yes ☐ No ☐

6. Do political campaign contributions have too much influence on elections and government policy?
   Yes ☐ No ☐

7. Are high campaign costs discouraging good people from becoming candidates?
   Yes ☐ No ☐

8. Should presdents be elected by direct popular vote?
   Yes ☐ No ☐

CHAPTER

8

CAMPAIGNS
AND
ELECTIONS
DECIDING WHO
GOVERNS

What real power do you
have in a democracy? By
casting ballots, citizens in
a democracy have the power to
determine who will represent them,
who will make up the government
under which they live. You, then, are
an integral part of the democratic
process every time you vote in an
election.

ELECTIONS IN A DEMOCRACY

Democratic government is government by "the consent of the governed." Elections give practical meaning to this notion of "consent." Elections allow people to choose among competing candidates and parties and to decide who will occupy public office. Elections give people the opportunity to pass judgment on current officeholders, either by reelecting them (granting continued consent) or by throwing them out of office (withdrawing consent).

In a representative democracy, elections function primarily to choose personnel to occupy public office—to decide "who governs." But elections also have an indirect influence on public policy, allowing voters to influence policy directions by choosing between candidates or parties with different policy priorities. Thus elections indirectly influence "who gets what"—that is, the outcomes of the political process.

Elections as Mandates?   However, it is difficult to argue that elections serve as "policy mandates"—that is, that elections allow voters to direct the course of public policy. Frequently, election winners claim a **mandate**—overwhelming support from the people—for their policies and programs. But for elections to serve as policy mandates, four conditions have to be met:

1. Competing candidates have to offer clear policy alternatives.
2. The voters have to cast their ballots on the basis of these policy alternatives alone.
3. The election results have to clearly indicate the voters' policy preferences.
4. Elected officials have to be bound by their campaign promises.[1]

As we shall see, none of these conditions is fully met in American elections. Often candidates do not differ much on policy questions, or they deliberately obscure their policy positions to avoid offending groups of voters. Voters themselves frequently pay little attention to policy issues in elections but rather vote along traditional party lines or group affiliations, or on the basis of the candidate's character, personality, or media image.

mandate Perception of popular support for a program or policy based on the margin of electoral victory won by a candidate who proposed it during a campaign.

President Clinton celebrates his reelection with his wife, Hillary Rodham Clinton, and their daughter, Chelsea. Clinton is the first Democrat to win a second term since Franklin Roosevelt. He fell just shy of 50 percent of the vote, however, and has had to face a Republican Congress.

Moreover, even in elections in which issues seem to dominate the campaign, the outcome may not clearly reflect policy preferences. Candidates take stands on a variety of issues. It is never certain on which issues the voters agreed with the winner and on which issues they disagreed yet voted for the candidate anyway.

Finally, candidates often fail to abide by their campaign promises once they are elected. Some simply ignore their promises, assuming voters have forgotten about the campaign. Others point to changes in circumstances or conditions as a justification for abandoning a campaign pledge.

Retrospective Judgment   Voters can influence future policy directions through retrospective judgments about the performance of incumbents, by either reelecting them or throwing them out of office.[2] Voters may not know what politicians will do in the future, but they can evaluate how well politicians performed in the past. When incumbent officeholders are defeated, it is reasonable to assume that voters did not like their performance and that newly elected officials should change policy course if they do not want to meet a similar fate in the next election. But it is not always clear what the defeated incumbents did in office that led to their ouster by the voters. Nor, indeed, can incumbents who won reelection assume that all of their policies are approved of by a majority of voters. Nevertheless, retrospective voting provides an overall judgment of how voters evaluate performance in office.

Retrospective voting is probably more important in presidential elections than in congressional elections. And most speculation about retrospective voting centers on the economy. Incumbent presidents seeking reelection in hard economic times have been regularly defeated by voters, and congressional candidates of the party in power during an economic downturn may suffer as well.

Protection of Rights   Elections also provide protection against official abuse. The long struggle for African American voting rights in the United States was premised on the belief that once black people acquired the right to vote, government would become more responsive to their concerns. In signing the Voting Rights Act of 1965, President Lyndon Johnson expressed this view: "The vote is the most powerful instrument ever devised by man for breaking down injustice and destroying the terrible walls which imprison men because they are different from other men."[3] The subsequent history of racial politics in America (see Chapter 15) suggests that the vote is more effective in eliminating discriminatory laws than it is in resolving social or economic inequities. Nevertheless, *without* the vote, we can be certain that government would have very little incentive to respond to popular needs.

POWER AND AMBITION

Personal ambition is a driving force in politics. Politics attracts people for whom *power*—the drive to shape the world according to one's own beliefs and values—and *celebrity*—the public attention, deference, name recognition, and social status that accompany public office—are more rewarding than money, leisure, or privacy. "Political office today flows to those who want it enough to spend the time and energy mastering its pursuit. It flows in the direction of ambition—and talent."[4]

Political ambition is the most distinguishing characteristic of elected officeholders. The people who run for and win public office are not necessarily the most intelligent, best informed, wealthiest, or most successful business or professional people. At all levels of the political system—from presidential candidates and

In 1996, most voters said that "compared to four years ago" they were "better off" or "about the same," rather than "worse off." This generally favorable retrospective judgment on Clinton's first term undermined Dole's chances of unseating the Democratic president.

members of Congress, to governors and state legislators, to city council and school board members—it is the most politically ambitious people who are willing to sacrifice time, family and private life, and energy and effort for the power and celebrity that come with public office.

Most politicians publicly deny that personal ambition is their real motivation for seeking public office. Rather, they describe their motives in highly idealistic terms: "civic duty," "service to community," "reforming the government," "protecting the environment," "bringing about change." These responses reflect the norms of our political culture. People are not supposed to enter politics to satisfy *personal* ambitions but rather to achieve *public* purposes. Many politicians do not really recognize their own drive for power or how much they crave celebrity. But if there were no personal rewards in politics, no one would run for office.

To achieve their ambitions, politicians must meet certain basic requirements and possess several key talents and skills.

Constitutional Requirements for Office The constitutional requirements for presidential and congressional candidates are very few:

- *President:* A natural-born citizen of the United States, a resident for at least fourteen years, and at least thirty-five years of age (Article II, Section 1). The Twenty-second Amendment to the U.S. Constitution, passed in 1951 after Franklin D. Roosevelt's unprecedented four elections to the presidency, imposes one more restriction: a person cannot be elected president more than twice, or more than once if having served more than two years of another president's term.
- *U.S. Senate:* A resident of the state from which elected, a citizen of the United States for at least nine years, and at least thirty years of age (Article I, Section 3).
- *U.S. House of Representatives:* A resident of the state from which elected, a citizen of the United States for at least seven years, and at least twenty-five years of age (Article I, Section 2).

Political Entrepreneurship One talent required of all politicians is **political entrepreneurship**—the ability to sell themselves to others as candidates, to raise money from contributors, to organize people to work on their behalf, and to communicate and publicize themselves through the media. Political parties no longer recruit candidates; candidates recruit themselves. Nor do interest groups recruit candidates; candidates seek out interest groups to win their support.

Political Temperament Perhaps the most important personal qualification is the willingness to work long and hard, to live, eat, and breathe politics every day. Occasionally people win high office who really do not like political campaigning; they view it as a torture they must endure in order to gain office and exercise power. But most successful politicians are people who really like politics—the meetings, appearances, speeches, interviews, handshaking—and really enjoy interacting with other people (see *People in Politics:* "Colin Powell, Saying No to Presidential Politics").

political entrepreneurship
Ability to sell oneself as a candidate for public office, including skills of organizing, fund raising, communicating, and publicizing.

Communication Skills Another important personal qualification is the ability to communicate with others. Politicians must know how to talk, and talk, and talk—to large audiences, in press conferences and interviews, on television, to reporters,

Colin Powell, Saying No to Presidential Politics

Colin Powell embodies the American dream: "a black kid of no early promise from an immigrant family of limited means who was raised in the South Bronx and somehow rose to become the National Security Adviser to the President of the United States and then Chairman of the Joint Chiefs of Staff." He also rose to be the American public's preferred choice for president of the United States, yet decided he did not have the "passion and commitment" for political life that he "felt every day of my thirty-five years as a soldier." Powell became the first person in modern political history to opt out of a presidential race while leading all other candidates, including the incumbent president, in the opinion polls.

Born in Harlem to Jamaican immigrant parents, Powell recounts his youth as proof that "it is possible to rise above conditions." After graduation from Morris High School in the South Bronx, Powell enrolled at The City College of New York on a ROTC scholarship. In 1958 he graduated with a degree in geology at the top of his ROTC class and was commissioned a second lieutenant in the U.S. Army. Powell went to South Vietnam as a military adviser in 1962 and returned for a second tour of service in 1968. In Vietnam, he was awarded two Purple Hearts, a Bronze Star for Valor, and the Legion of Merit.

In 1972 Powell returned to the classroom to pursue a master's degree in business administration from George Washington University and accept an appointment to the prestigious White House Fellows Program. As a White House Fellow, Powell was assigned to the Office of Management and Budget, where he worked under Caspar Weinberger, later secretary of defense in the Reagan Administration. Powell's career was on a fast track after his White House duty.

Powell was recalled to Washington in 1983 by Defense Secretary Weinberger to become senior military adviser to the secretary. Powell was active on behalf of Secretary Weinberger in opposing arms sales to Iran; he was overruled by President Ronald Reagan, but his memo urging that Congress be notified of the arms transfers would later give him good standing with the Congress after the Iran-contra scandal became public.

President George Bush chose General Powell in 1989 to head the Joint Chiefs of Staff, the nation's highest military position. It was Powell who helped convince the president that if military force were to be used to oust Saddam Hussein from Kuwait, it must be an overwhelming and decisive force, not gradual, limited escalation, as in Vietnam. Powell's televised press briefings during the war assured the American people of the competence and effectiveness of the U.S. military. The Gulf War victory restored the morale of U.S. military forces and the confidence of the American people in its military leadership. Powell retired from the army in 1993 when his term as chair of the Joint Chiefs of Staff ended and then wrote his inspiring autobiography, *My American Journey*.

To a great many Americans, Powell seemed to offer the nation what it most needed: a decisive leader with integrity and character, a political outsider untarnished by "politics as usual," and an African American whose "American journey" could serve as a model for all and ease the nation's racial divisions. He was frequently compared to Dwight D. Eisenhower, whose military leadership in World War II ushered him into the White House. Like Ike, Powell waited until after army retirement to declare himself a Republican and announce his support for a balanced federal budget, tax cuts, and a reduction in the size of government. He expressed moderate views on abortion rights and some forms of affirmative action and offered to help "the party of Lincoln move once again close to the spirit of Lincoln." Yet after "prayerful consideration," he announced that he would not be a candidate for president of the United States "or any elective office" in 1996.

Although polls continue to show him as America's top pick as a presidential candidate, Powell has devoted himself exclusively to volunteer activities, notably as chairman of a national campaign, "America's Promise—Alliance for Youth."

Source: Colin Powell, *My American Journey* (New York: Random House, 1995).

President Clinton prepares for an interview with reporters from the television news show 60 Minutes. *Successful politicians are skilled communicators; most truly enjoy the hard work and constant interaction with other people their careers entail.*

to small groups of financial contributors, on the phone, at airports and commencements, to their staffs, on the floor of Congress or the state legislature. It matters less what politicians say than how they look and sound saying it. They must communicate sincerity, compassion, confidence, and good humor, as well as ideas.

Professionalism   Politics is becoming increasingly professionalized. "Citizen officeholders"—people with business or professional careers who get into politics part time or for short periods of time—are being driven out of political life by career politicians—people who enter politics early in life as a full-time occupation and expect to make it their career. Politics increasingly demands all of a politician's time and energy. At all levels of government, from city council to state legislatures to the U.S. Congress, political work is becoming full-time and year-round. It is not only more demanding to *hold* office than it was a generation ago but also far more demanding to *run* for office. Campaigning has become more time consuming, more technically sophisticated, and much more costly.

Careerism   Professional political careers begin at a relatively early age. Politically ambitious young people seek out internships and staff positions with members of Congress, with congressional committees, in state legislators' or governors' offices, in mayors' offices, or in council chambers. Others volunteer to work in political campaigns. Many find political mentors from whom they learn how to organize campaigns, contact financial contributors, and deal with the media. Soon they are ready to run for local office or the state legislature. Rather than challenge a strong incumbent, they may wait for an open seat to be created by retirement, by reapportionment, or by its holder seeking another office. Or they may make an initial attempt against a strong incumbent of the opposition party in order to gain experience and win the appreciation of their own party's supporters for a good effort. Over time, running for and holding elective office become their career. They work harder at it than anyone else, in part because they have no real private-sector career to return to in case of defeat.

Lawyers in Politics   The prevalence of lawyers in politics is an American tradition. Among the fifty-five delegates to the Constitutional Convention in 1787, some twenty-five were lawyers. The political dominance of lawyers continues today, with lawyers filling more than half of U.S. Senate seats and nearly half of the seats in the U.S. House of Representatives.

It is sometimes argued that lawyers dominate in politics because of the parallel skills required in law and politics. Lawyers represent clients, so they can apply their professional experience to represent constituents in Congress. Lawyers are trained to deal with statutory law, so they are assumed to be reasonably familiar with the United States Code (the codified laws of the U.S. government) when they arrive in Congress to make or amend these statutes.

But it is more likely that people attracted to politics decide to go to law school fully aware of the tradition of lawyers in American politics. Moreover, political officeholding at the state and local level as well as in the national government can help a struggling lawyer's private practice through free public advertising and opportunities to make contacts with potential clients. Finally, there are many special opportunities for lawyers to acquire public office in "lawyers only" posts as judges and prosecuting attorneys in federal, state, and local governments. Law school graduates who accept modest salaries as U.S. attorneys in the Justice Department or in state or county prosecuting offices can gain invaluable experience for later use in either private law practice or politics.

Most of the lawyers in the Congress, however, have become professional politicians over time. They have left their legal practices behind.

THE ADVANTAGES OF INCUMBENCY

In theory, elections offer voters the opportunity to "throw the rascals out." But in practice, voters seldom do so. **Incumbents,** people already holding public office, have a strong advantage when they seek reelection. The reelection rates of incumbents for *all* elective offices—city council, mayor, state legislature, governor, and especially Congress—are very high. Since 1950, more than 90 percent of all members of the House of Representatives who have sought reelection have been successful. (Even in 1994, when Republicans wrested control of the House from the Democrats, the incumbent reelection rate was 92 percent. Only 35 of 382 incumbents seeking reelection lost, but all 35 were Democrats.) The success rate of U.S. Senate incumbents is not as great, but it is still impressive; since 1950, more than 70 percent of senators seeking reelection have been successful.

Why do incumbents win so often? This is a particularly vexing question, inasmuch as so many people are distrustful of government and hold politicians in low esteem. Congress itself is the focal point of public disapproval and even ridicule. Yet people seem to distinguish between Congress as an institution—which they distrust—and their own members of Congress—whom they reelect. The result is something of a contradiction: popular members of Congress serving in an unpopular Congress (see *What Do You Think:* "Why Do Voters Reelect Members of an Unpopular Congress?" in Chapter 10). Three major advantages tend to enhance incumbents' chances of winning: name recognition, campaign contributions, and the resources of office.

Name Recognition   One reason for incumbents' success is that they begin the campaign with greater *name recognition* than their challengers, simply because they are the incumbent and their name has become familiar to their constituents over the previous years. Much of the daily work of all elected officials, especially members

incumbent Candidate currently in office seeking reelection.

of Congress, is really public relations. Name recognition is a strategic advantage at the ballot box, especially if voters have little knowledge of policy positions or voting records. Voters tend to cast ballots for recognizable names over unknowns. Cynics have concluded that there is no such thing as bad publicity, only publicity. Even in cases of well-publicized scandals, incumbent members of Congress have won reelection; presumably voters preferred "the devil they knew" to the one they did not.

The somewhat lower rate of reelection of Senate versus House members may be a result of the fact that Senate challengers are more likely to have held high-visibility offices—for example, governor or member of Congress—before running for the Senate. Thus Senate challengers often enjoy some name recognition even before the campaign begins. Greater media attention to a statewide Senate race also helps to move the challenger closer to the incumbent in public recognition. In contrast, House challengers are likely to have held less visible local or state legislative offices or to be political novices, and House races attract considerably less media attention than Senate races do.

Campaign Contributions   Incumbents have a strong advantage in raising campaign funds, simply because individuals and groups seeking access to those already in office are inspired to make contributions. Challengers have no immediate favors to offer; they must convince a potential contributor that they will win office and also that they are devoted to the interests of their financial backers.[5]

Contributing individuals and interest groups show a strong preference for incumbents over challengers. They do not wish to offend incumbent officeholders by contributing to their challengers; doing so risks both immediate retribution and future "freezing out" in the likely event of the challengers' defeat. Thus only when an incumbent has been especially hostile to an organization's interest or in rare cases where an incumbent seems especially vulnerable will an interest group support a challenger. Yet challengers need even larger campaign war chests than incumbents to be successful. Challengers must overcome the greater name recognition of incumbents, their many office resources, and their records of constituency service. Thus even if incumbents and challengers had equal campaign treasuries, incumbents would enjoy the advantage.

Resources of Office   Successful politicians use their offices to keep their names and faces before the public in various ways—public appearances, interviews, speeches, and press releases. Congressional incumbents make full use of the **franking privilege** (free use of the U.S. mails) to send self-promotional newsletters to tens of thousands of households in their district at taxpayers' expense. They travel on weekends to their district virtually year-round, using tax-funded travel allowances, to make local appearances, speeches, and contacts.

Members of Congress have large staffs working every day over many years with the principal objective of ensuring the reelection of their members. Indeed, Congress is structured as an "incumbent-protection society" organized and staffed to help guarantee the reelection of its members (see "Home Style" in Chapter 10). Service to constituents occupies the energies of congressional office staffs both in Washington and in local district offices established for this purpose. Casework wins voters one at a time: tracing lost Social Security checks, ferreting out which federal loans voters qualify for and helping them with their applications, and performing countless other personal favors. These individual "retail-level" favors are supplemented by larger scale projects that experienced members of Congress can bring to their district or state

franking privilege   Free use of the U.S. mails granted to members of Congress to promote communication with constituents.

(roads, dams, post offices, buildings, schools, grants, contracts) or even undesirable projects (landfills, waste disposal sites, halfway houses) that they can keep out of their district. The longer incumbents have occupied the office, the more favors they have performed and the larger their networks of grateful voters.

CAMPAIGN STRATEGIES

Campaigning is largely a media activity, especially in presidential and congressional campaigns. Media campaigns are highly professionalized, relying on public relations and advertising specialists, professional fund raisers, media consultants, and pollsters. Campaign management involves techniques that strongly resemble those employed in marketing commercial products. Professional media campaign management includes developing a **campaign strategy**: compiling computerized mailing lists and invitations for fund-raising events; selecting a campaign theme and coming up with a desirable candidate image; monitoring the progress of the campaign with continual polling of the voters; producing television tapes for commercials, newspaper advertisements, signs, bumper stickers, and radio spots; selecting clothing and hairstyles for the candidate; writing speeches and scheduling appearances; and even planning the victory party.

Selecting a Theme Finding the right theme or slogan for a campaign is essential; this effort is not greatly different from that of launching an advertising campaign for a new detergent. A successful theme is one that characterizes the candidate or the electoral choice confronting the voters. A campaign theme need not be controversial; indeed, it need not even focus on a specific issue. It might be as simple as "a leader you can trust"—an attempt to "package" the candidate as competent and trustworthy.

Most media campaigns focus on candidates' personal qualities rather than on their stands on policy issues. Professional campaigns are based on the assumption that a candidate's "image" is the most important factor affecting voter choice. This image is largely devoid of issues, except in very general terms: for example, "tough on crime," "stands up to the special interests," "fights for the taxpayer," or "cares about you."

campaign strategy Plan for a political campaign, usually including a theme, an attempt to define the opponent or the issues, and an effort to coordinate images and messages in news broadcasts and paid advertising.

Lamar Alexander, seeking the Republican nomination in 1996, wears his trademark checked jacket to symbolize the outside-the-Washington, D.C.-beltway theme of his candidacy.

"Defining" the Opponent A media campaign also seeks to "define" the opponent in negative terms. The original negative TV ad is generally identified as the 1964 "Daisy Girl" commercial, aired by the Lyndon B. Johnson presidential campaign (see *Up Close:* "Dirty Politics"). Negative ads can serve a purpose in exposing the record of an opponent. But negative campaigns risk an opponent's counterattack charges of "mudslinging," "dirty tricks," and "sleaze."

Research into the opponent's public and personal background provides the data for negative campaigning. Previous speeches and writings can be mined for embarrassing or mean-spirited statements. The voting record of the opponent can be scrutinized for unpopular policy positions. Any evils that occurred during an opponent's term of office can be attributed to him or her, either directly ("She knew and conspired in it") or indirectly ("He should have known and done something about it"). Personal scandals or embarrassments can be developed as evidence of "character." If campaign managers fear that highly personal attacks on an opponent will backfire, they may choose to leak the information to reporters and try to avoid attribution of the story to themselves or their candidate.

Using Focus Groups and Polling Focus group techniques can help in selecting campaign themes and identifying negative characteristics in opponents. A **focus group** is a small group of people brought together to view videotapes, listen to specific campaign appeals, and respond to particular topics and issues. Media professionals then develop a campaign strategy around "hot-button" issues—issues that generate strong responses by focus groups—and avoid themes or issues that fail to elicit much interest.

The results of focus group work can then be tested in wider polling. Polling is a central feature of professional campaigning. Serious candidates for national and statewide offices almost always employ their own private polling firms, distinct from the national survey organizations that supply the media with survey data. Initial polling is generally designed to determine candidates' **name recognition**—the extent to which the voters recognize the candidates—and whatever positive and negative images are already associated with their names. "High negatives" of potential opponents may suggest an "attack" strategy, exploiting the weaknesses of the opponents.

High negatives for the candidate suggest the need for a strategy to overcome these images. For example, if the candidate is seen as too rich or too upper class or too "out of touch" with common people, then the campaign will show the candidate in blue jeans hanging out with factory workers in beer and pizza places. If the candidate's private life is under suspicion, then the campaign will feature appearances with a loving spouse and family attending church services. If the candidate is perceived as "too liberal," then centrist themes will be stressed; if seen as "too conservative," then moderation, warmth, and compassion will be emphasized. Astute campaign managers try not to completely reverse a candidate's previous political stances in order to deflect charges of "flip-flopping" and to avoid unintended images of insincerity.

Campaign polling is highly professionalized, with telephone banks, trained interviewers, and computer-assisted-telephone-interviewing (CATI) software that records and tabulates responses instantly and sends the results to campaign managers. In well-financed campaigns, polling is continual throughout the campaign, so that managers can assess progress on a daily basis. Polls chart the candidate's progress and, perhaps more important, help assess the effectiveness of specific campaign themes. If the candidate appears to be gaining support, the campaign stays on course. But if the candidate appears to be falling in the polls,

focus group In a political context, a small number of people brought together in a comfortable setting to discuss and respond to themes and issues, allowing campaign managers to develop and analyze strategies.

name recognition The extent to which voters know a candidate's name.

Up Close

Dirty Politics

Political campaigning frequently turns ugly with negative advertising that is vicious and personal. It is widely believed that television's focus on personal character and private lives—rather than on policy positions and governmental experience—encourages negative campaigning. But vicious personal attacks in political campaigns began long before television. They are nearly as old as the nation itself.

"If Jefferson is elected," proclaimed Yale's president in 1800, "the Bible will be burned and we will see our wives and daughters the victims of legal prostitution." In 1864 *Harper's Weekly* decried the "mudslinging" of the day, lamenting that President Abraham Lincoln was regularly referred to by his opponent as a "filthy storyteller, despot, liar, thief, braggart, buffoon, monster, Ignoramus Abe, robber, swindler, tyrant, fiend, butcher, and pirate."

Television's first memorable attack advertisement was the "Daisy Girl" commercial broadcast by Lyndon Johnson's presidential campaign in 1964 against his Republican opponent, Barry Goldwater. Although never mentioning Goldwater by name, the purpose of the ad was to "define" him as a warmonger who would plunge the world into a nuclear holocaust. The ad opens with a small, innocent girl standing in an open field plucking petals from a daisy and counting, "1, 2, 3 . . ." When she reaches 9, an ominous adult male voice begins a countdown: "10, 9, 8 . . ." as the camera closes in on the child's face. At "zero," a mushroom cloud appears, reflected in her eyes, and envelops the screen. Lyndon Johnson's voice is heard: "These are the stakes."

Frames from Lyndon Johnson's 1964 "Daisy Girl" commercial.

The infamous Willie Horton ad, broadcast by an independent organization supporting Republican George Bush in 1988, portrayed Democrat Michael Dukakis as weak on crime prevention. It featured a close-up mug shot of a very threatening convicted murderer, Willie Horton, with a voice proclaiming, "Dukakis not only opposes the death penalty, he allowed first-degree murderers to have weekend passes from prison. One was Willie Horton who murdered a boy in a robbery, stabbing him nineteen times. Despite a life sentence, Horton received ten weekend passes from prison." A final photo shows Dukakis, with a voice-over announcing, "Weekend prison passes, Dukakis weak on crime."

Clinton's 1996 negative TV ads described Dole as "wrong in the past, wrong for the future," and featured unflattering black-and-white photos of an aging Dole standing with Newt Gingrich. Dole's campaign found an old MTV show tape of Clinton joking about past drug use.

What are the effects of negative advertising? First of all, it works more often than not. Controlled experiments indicate that targets of attack ads are rated less positively by people who have watched these ads. Rarely do viewers penalize candidates for airing negative messages. Professional campaign managers are aware of the effectiveness of negative ads, and there is little likelihood that such ads will disappear over time. But another important effect of negative advertising is to make voters more cynical about politics and government in general. Indeed, some evidence indicates that negative campaigning by opposing candidates reduces voter turnout.

What, if anything, can be done? Government regulation of political speech directly contravenes the First Amendment. American democracy has survived negative campaigning for a long time. Some reform proposals have called for candidates to appear in person on camera when delivering an attack statement, or for media monitoring and criticism of attack messages as well as correction of erroneous positive claims. But it is unlikely that these reforms would have much of an impact on negative campaigning.

Source: Kathleen Hall Jamieson, *Dirty Politics: Deception, Distraction, and Democracy* (New York: Oxford University Press, 1992); also Stephen Ansolabehere et al., "Does Attack Advertising Demobilize the Electorate?" *American Political Science Review* 88 (December 1994): 829–38.

the campaign manager comes under intense pressure to change themes and strategies. As election day nears, the pressure increases on the trailing candidate to "go negative"—to launch even more scathing attacks on the opponent.

Incumbent versus Challenger Strategies   Campaign strategies vary by the offices being sought, the nature of the times, and the imagination and inventiveness of the candidates' managers. But incumbency is perhaps the most important factor affecting the choice of a strategy. The challenger must attack the record of the incumbent; deplore current conditions in the city, state, or nation; and stress the need for change. Challengers are usually freer to take the offensive; incumbents must defend their record in office and either boast of accomplishments during their term or blame the opposition for blocking them. Challengers frequently opt for the "outsider" strategy, capitalizing on distrust and cynicism toward government.

News Management   News management is the key to the media campaign. News coverage of the candidates is more credible in the eyes of viewers than paid advertisements. The campaign is planned to get the maximum favorable "free" exposure on the evening news as well as to saturate the media with paid commercial advertising. Each day a candidate must do something interesting and "newsworthy," that is, likely to be reported as news. Thus each day of the campaign is organized to win favorable coverage on the nightly television news and in the next day's newspapers. Pictures are as important as words. Candidates must provide good **photo ops** for the media—opportunities where they can be photographed in settings or backgrounds that emphasize their themes. For example, if the theme is patriotism, then the candidate appears with war veterans, at a military base, or at a flag factory. If the theme is education, the candidate appears at a school; if crime control, then with police officers; if environmentalism, then in a wilderness area; if the economy, then at a closed factory or unemployment line or soup kitchen for the homeless.

Words must also be carefully chosen for television reports. Themes must be stated in concise and catchy **sound bites** that will register in the viewers' minds. Candidates now understand that the news media will select only a few seconds of an entire day of speech making for broadcast. The average length of a network news sound bite has shrunk from forty-five to seven seconds over the last twenty years. Thus extended or serious discussion of issues during a campaign is sacrificed to the need for one-liners on the nightly news. Indeed, if a campaign theme cannot fit on a bumper sticker, it is too complex.

Consequently, each day's campaigning is a series of photo ops and sound bites, all prepared with the evening news in mind. Between events, candidates must scramble to various fund-raising events—dinners, parties, personal meetings with large contributors. Thus candidates balance their time between "getting out the message" and finding ways to pay for getting it out.

Paid Advertising   Television "spot" ads must be prepared prior to and during the campaign. They involve employing expensive television advertising and production firms well in advance of the campaign and keeping them busy revising and producing new ads throughout the campaign to respond to changing issues or opponents' attacks. Commercial advertising is the most expensive aspect of the campaign. Heavy costs are incurred in the production of the ads and in the purchase of broadcast time. The Federal Communications Commission (FCC) does not permit television networks or stations to charge more than standard commercial rates for political ads, but these rates are already high. Networks and stations are required to offer

photo ops   Staged opportunities for the media to photograph the candidate in a favorable setting.

sound bites   Concise and catchy phrases that attract media coverage.

the same rates and times to all candidates, but if one candidate's campaign treasury is weak or exhausted, an opponent can saturate broadcast airtime.

Free Airtime   All candidates seek free airtime on news and talk shows, but the need to gain free exposure is much greater for underfunded candidates. They must go to extremes in devising media events, and they must encourage and participate in free televised debates. The debate format is particularly well suited for candidates who cannot match their opponents in paid commercial advertising. Thus well-funded and poorly funded candidates may jockey over the number and times of public debates.

RAISING CAMPAIGN CASH

The professionalization of campaigning and the heavy costs of television advertising drive up the costs of running for office. Campaign costs are rising with each election cycle (see Figure 8-1). In the presidential election year 1996,

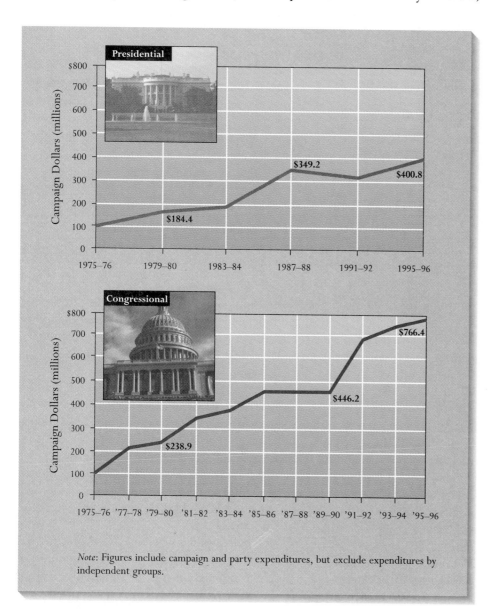

FIGURE 8-1   The Growing Costs of Campaigns

Source: Federal Elections Commission as reported in *Congressional Quarterly Weekly Reports*, April 5, 1997, p. 772.

Note: Figures include campaign and party expenditures, but exclude expenditures by independent groups.

What Do You Think?

How Big a Role Does Money Play in Politics?

Americans are clearly troubled by the role money plays in politics. About two-thirds believe excessive influence of political contributions on elections and government policy is a major problem with the system. A similar proportion feel this way about the conflicts of interest created when elected officials solicit or accept political contributions while they are making policy decisions. An even greater percentage believe the high cost of campaigns discourages good people from running for office.

Money is believed to obstruct good government in a variety of ways. At the very least, it is seen as distracting people's representatives from the jobs they were elected to do. A solid majority think elected officials in Washington spend too much time on political fund raising. But many see money's effects as much more pernicious than simply reducing the efficiency of the federal government. More than half of Americans believe political contributions often buy influence in Washington for one group by denying another group its fair say; as many as half think money often determines who gets

elected and appointed to federal office. Nearly half see the influence of money in politics seriously undermining democratic ideals by often leading elected officials to support policies they don't personally believe are best for the country.

Although most Americans express worry about the role of money in politics, relatively few know much about campaign finance. Despite their limited knowledge, Americans express clear preferences for what steps should be taken to reform campaign finance. Four proposals emerge as the public's top choices for reform. All four proposals are viewed favorably by more than two-thirds of adults:

- Banning all campaign contributions by people who are not American citizens.
- Requiring candidates for the U.S. House and Senate to raise a certain percentage of their campaign funds within their own states.
- Limiting how much of their own money wealthy candidates can spend on their campaigns.
- Limiting the amount of TV air time for political commercials.

But, to date, Congress has failed to pass any major campaign finance reform legislation.

campaign spending by *all* presidential and congressional candidates, the Democratic and Republican parties, and independent political organization topped *$2 billion* (see *What Do You Think?* "How Big a Role Does Money Play in Politics?"). Fund raising to meet these costs is the most important hurdle for any candidate for public office.

Paying for Campaigns   Campaign funds come from a wide range of sources—small donors, big donors, interest groups of every stripe, corporations, labor unions, even taxpayers. In some cases, candidates pay their own way (or most of it). More typically, however, candidates for high public office—particularly incumbents—have become adept at running their campaigns using other people's money, not their own. Sources of campaign cash for all congressional races in 1996 as well as the presidential race and spending by the national parties are shown in Table 8-1.

Public Money   All taxpayers have the option of helping fund presidential elections through public money by checking off a box on their income tax returns that allocates $3 of their tax money for the Presidential Election Campaign Fund. In reality, only about 13 percent of taxpayers have checked

Major Problems with Political System	Percentage Responding "Yes"
"Political contributions have too much influence on elections and government policy"	66%
"Elected officials seek or receive political contributions while making decisions about issues of concern to those giving money"	65
"Elected officials spend too much of their time raising money for selection campaigns"	63
"Good people are being discouraged from becoming candidates because of the high costs of campaigns"	71

How Frequently Does the Use of Money Buy Political Influence in Washington?	Percentage Responding "Often"
"Gives one group more influence by keeping another from having its fair say"	55%
"Determines election outcomes"	52
"Gets someone appointed to office who would not otherwise be considered"	50
"Keeps important legislation from being passed"	48
"Leads elected officials to support policies they don't think are best for the country"	45

Source: Princeton Survey Research Associates for the Center for Responsive Politics, Money and Politics Survey, 1997.

that box in the last couple of years, and recently the fund has been in jeopardy of not having enough money to make its promised payments to the candidates. In 1996 each of the major party presidential candidates got $61.8 million in public funds. (Ross Perot got $29 million, under a formula based on his vote total when he ran in 1992.) Public funds are also allocated to help the parties pay for their nominating conventions; the Democrats and Republicans each got about $12.4 million for that purpose in 1996.

Small Donations   Millions of Americans participate in campaign financing, either by giving directly to candidates or the parties, or by giving to political action committees, which then distribute their funds to candidates. For members of Congress, small donors typically make up about 20 percent of their campaign funds. The proportion is higher for presidential candidates and is highest of all in **hard money** contributions—money given directly to candidates' campaigns and subject to regulated limits. In 1995–96, both Clinton and Dole got about three-quarters of their hard-dollar contributions from donors giving less than $200. Beyond the total of dollars given, however, little is known about where all that money came from. Under federal law, donations under $200 need

hard money   Political contributions given directly to candidates' campaigns and subject to regulated limits.

TABLE 8-1	Sources of Campaign Cash in 1996 Elections	
Source	$ (millions)	Percentage of Total Campaign
Public (Taxpayer) Financing	$211	8.8%
Small Donations	$734	30.6
Large Individual Donors	$597	21.8
Political Action Committees (PACs)	$243	10.1
Soft money	$262	10.8
Candidates	$161	6.7
Other	$200	8.2
TOTAL	$2,400	

Source: Center for Responsive Politics, from Federal Elections Commission data.

not be itemized, so contributors' names and addresses are recorded only by the candidates and parties, not passed along to the Federal Election Commission as part of the public record.

Large Individual Donors   The single most important source of campaign dollars for Senate candidates, presidential candidates, and the political parties are individuals who can afford to write checks for $500, $1,000, or more. In all, some 630,000 donors did so in 1995–96, but despite their financial importance, these donors make up less than one-quarter of 1 percent of the nation's population. A $1,000 check is the preferred entry fee for "fat-cat" contributors; many give substantially more. They are the donors whose names are on the candidates' Rolodexes. They are the ones in attendance when the president, the Speaker of the House, or other top political dignitaries travel around the country doing fund raisers. They are also the ones who are wined, dined, prodded, and cajoled in a seemingly ceaseless effort by the parties and the candidates to raise funds for the next election.

Political Action Committees   **Political action committees (PACs)** are a mainstay of reelection campaigns in Congress, particularly in the House of Representatives, where they provide nearly 40 percent of the total contribution dollars for winning candidates. In the Senate, the proportion of money from PACs is lower—about 22 percent. Corporations and unions are not allowed to contribute directly to campaigns from corporate or union funds, but they may form PACs to seek contributions from managers and stockholders and their families, or union workers and their families. PACs are organized not only by corporations and unions but also by trade and professional associations, environmental groups, and liberal and conservative ideological groups. The wealthiest PACs are based in Washington, D.C. (see "PAC Power" in Chapter 9). PACs are very cautious; their job is to get a maximum return on their contributions, winning influence and goodwill with as many lawmakers as possible in Washington. There's no return on their investment if their recipients lose at the polls, therefore most PACs—particularly business PACs—give most of their dollars to incumbents seeking reelection. When the Democrats controlled Congress, business PACs split their dollars nearly evenly between Democrats and Repub-

Political Action Committee (PAC)   Organization created by a corporation, union, or other interest group to collect and distribute campaign funds to candidates.

licans. In 1996, with Republicans newly in control of both houses of Congress, they shifted their dollars heavily to the GOP, giving $2 in contributions to Republicans for every $1 they gave to Democrats. Labor PACs, however, did not back down from their traditional support of Democrats, even though they too raised their allocation to Republicans.

Soft Money   Under federal election law, hard money is used directly to benefit federal candidates such as the president and vice president. Soft money, in contrast, can be raised by the Democratic and Republican parties with no restrictions on amount or who can give. Technically, **soft money** is supposed to be used for party building, get-out-the-vote drives, issues education, and general party participation. In reality, both parties undertook an all-out blitz to raise as much soft money as possible in the 1996 election, an effort that had a lot more to do with electing the president than building the party.

Soft money is the fastest growing source of campaign funds (see Figure 8-2). Nearly all soft money is raised in large contributions—indeed, the reason soft money has been so popular with the parties is that it allows big donors to give without having to abide by the limits imposed on direct campaign contributions. Another advantage is that corporations, labor unions, and other groups can give directly from their organization's treasury, which they cannot legally do in contributions to candidates. For both the Democrats and the Republicans, corporate donations are the biggest single source of soft money.

Candidate Self-Financing   Candidates for federal office also pump millions into their own campaigns. Leading the field in 1996 was publishing magnate Steve Forbes, whose race for the Republican nomination for president was largely funded with $37 million from his personal fortune. In all, some 54 Senate candidates and 91 House candidates put $100,000 or more of their own money into their campaigns, through either outright gifts or personal loans. (Candidates who loan themselves the money to run are able to pay themselves back later from outside contributions.)

soft money   Political contributions, not subject to regulated limits, given to a party for activities such as party building or voter registration, but not directly for campaigns.

Confirming that politicians will willingly make fools of themselves, if necessary, to raise campaign cash, senators Trent Lott, Larry Craig, John Ashcroft, and James Jeffords appear as the "singing senators" during a Republican Party fundraising event.

FIGURE 8-2 **The Growth of Soft Money**

Source: Center for Responsive Politics, based on Federal Election Commission data.

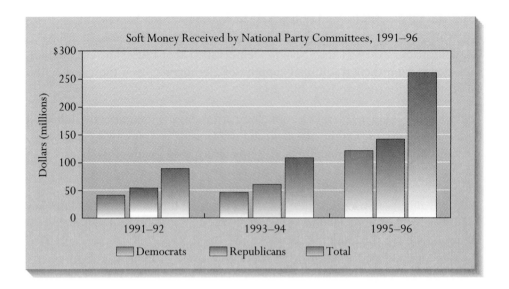

HOW MUCH DOES IT COST TO GET ELECTED?

Getting elected to public office has never been more expensive. The average winning campaign for the House of Representatives cost more than $673,000 in 1996 and over $700,000 in 1998. Ninety-four candidates for the House in 1996 spent more than a million dollars to get elected. The most expensive House campaign of all was the 1996 reelection effort of House Speaker Newt Gingrich, which cost nearly $6 million (see Table 8-2). In the Senate, the average seat cost about $5 million that year.

Republican Senator Phil Gramm of Texas once declared that "ready money" was a candidate's best friend and raising $20 million by January 1 of an election year would be the test that would separate potential presidential winners from the crowd of also-rans. (Gramm himself met his fund-raising goal but still went nowhere in the primaries and dropped out early.) Bill Clinton and Bob Dole, the eventual nominees, each spent more than $100 million in their campaigns, and their respective parties poured in millions more to help them indirectly. Under federal campaign rules, funding for the fall presidential campaigns is supposed to come entirely from the $3 taxpayers may put into the Presidential Election Campaign Fund. In reality, the general election campaign period is the most frenzied fund-raising season of all—with both parties raising as much money as they possibly can (see *Up Close:* "The President Shakes the Money Tree" on page 256).

WHAT DO CONTRIBUTORS "BUY"?

What does money buy in politics? A cynic might say that money can buy anything—for example, special appropriations for public works directly benefiting the contributor, special tax breaks, special federal regulations. Scandals involving the direct (quid pro quo) purchase of special favors, privileges, exemptions, and treatments have been common enough in the past, and they are likely to continue in the future. But campaign contributions are rarely made in the

TABLE 8-2

The Cost of Getting Elected to Congress

Senate	1996	1994
Average winner spent	$4,692,100	$4,569,940
Average loser spent	$2,773,756	$3,426,509
Most expensive campaign	$14,587,143	$29,969,695
	(Jesse Helms, R-N.C.)	(Michael Huffington, R-Calif.)

House of Representatives	1996	1994
Average winner spent	$673,739	$516,126
Average loser spent	$265,675	$236,715
Most expensive campaign	$5,577,715	$2,621,479
	(Newt Gingrich, R-Ga.)	(Richard E. Gephardt, D-Mo.)

form of a direct trade-off for a favorable vote. Such an arrangement risks exposure as bribery and may be prosecuted under the law. Campaign contributions are more likely to be made without any *explicit* quid pro quo but rather with a general understanding that the contributor has confidence in the candidate's good judgment on issues directly affecting the contributor. The contributor expects the candidate to be smart enough to figure out how to vote in order to keep the contributions coming in the future.

The Big-Money Contributors Big-money contributors—businesses, unions, professional associations—pump millions into presidential and congressional elections. Figure 8-3 on page 258 lists the top twenty-five contributors to candidates and parties in the 1996 election. Note that union contributions are heavily weighted toward Democrats, as are the contributions of the Association of Trial Lawyers. Businesses and business associations tend to split their contributions between the parties, but Republicans usually get the largest share.

Buying Access to Policy Makers Large contributors expect to be able to call or visit and present their views directly to "their" officeholders. At the presidential level, major contributors who cannot get a meeting with the president expect to meet at least with high-level White House staff or cabinet officials. At the congressional level, major contributors usually expect to meet or speak directly with their representative or senator. Members of Congress boast of responding to letters, calls, or visits by any constituent, but contributors can expect a more immediate and direct response than noncontributors can. Lobbyists for contributing organizations routinely expect and receive a hearing from members of Congress.

Buying Government Assistance Many individual large contributors do business with government agencies. They expect any representative or senator they have supported to intervene on their behalf with these agencies, sometimes acting to cut red tape, ensure fairness, and expedite their cases, and other times pressuring the

House Speaker Newt Gingrich with movie star Arnold Schwarzenegger. Politicians often seek the support of celebrities to boost their campaigns and help raise funds.

Up Close

The President Shakes the Money Tree

"Ready to start overnights right away," President Clinton wrote in his left-handed scrawl on a memo from the Democratic National Committee asking him to "energize" Democratic financial contributors in the 1996 presidential campaign. "Overnights" referred to invitations to wealthy donors to stay overnight in the White House Lincoln Bedroom as a reward for their soft-money contributions of $50,000 to $100,000 or more to the Democratic National Committee.

But sleepovers in the Lincoln Bedroom were only one of many access-for-cash schemes developed by the Clinton White House and Democratic National Committee during the presidential campaign. Indeed, the money drive included a unwritten memo of perks for donors, as shown in the table below.

President Clinton and the First Lady were reported to have invited more than a hundred guests for sleepovers in the White House and to have held hundreds of coffees, receptions, and tours for wealthy donors. The White House press secretary acknowledged, "It's clear that Mr. Clinton and the First Lady are social by nature. They enjoy entertaining in the White House."

The Democratic National Committee raised "somewhere between $100 and $125 million" in soft money in the 1996 presidential election. These funds were *in addition to* taxpayer-funded presidential campaign spending of $62 million for each of the Democratic and Republican nominees in the general election. The intensity of the money drive occupied much of Clinton's time during the election year. For the donors, "Mostly it's ego. It's to be able to sit around in a room with the President and later be able to say they had dinner with the President."

	Contribution Level	Perks
Saxophone Club	$250	Briefings by White House Staff; lapel pins
Women's Leadership Club	$1,000	Coffee with Hillary Clinton; reception with Tipper Gore
White House Coffee	$5,000	Coffee with President Clinton; tour of Oval Office
White House Dinner	$25,000–50,000	Dinner with President Clinton in small groups of 10–20
Lincoln Bedroom Sleepover	$50,000–100,000	Invitation to dinner, evening get-together, and White House overnight stay
President Golf Round	(Unknown)	Playing 9–18 holes of golf with President Clinton at Congressional Country Club, Potomac, Maryland

agencies for a favorable decision. Officials in the White House or the cabinet may also be expected to intervene on behalf of major contributors. There is little question raised when the intervention merely expedites consideration of a contributor's case, but pressure to bend rules or regulations to get favorable decisions raises ethical problems for officeholders (see "Congressional Ethics" in Chapter 10).

Individual Contributors Those who contribute to presidential and/or congressional campaign funds do so for a variety of reasons. Some contributors are ideologically motivated. They make their contributions based on their perception of the ideological position of the candidate (or perhaps their perception of the candidate's opponent). They may make contributions to congressional candidates across the country who share their policy views. Liberal and conservative

Many big-money contributors were invited by the Clintons to stay overnight in the Lincoln Bedroom in the White House.

But the intensity of the Democratic money drive in 1996 also led to some embarrassing disclosures and even the return of some contributions. Several major donors acknowledged before a Senate Judiciary Committee investigation that they made large contributions with the expectation of favorable review of their business ventures both at home and abroad. Evidence developed that foreign contributions (illegal under the federal campaign laws) were funneled through third persons (also an illegal practice) to the Clinton-Gore campaign and to the Democratic National Committee. Republicans in Congress objected to the use of federal property (the White House, including the Oval Office, the vice president's office, and so on) to solicit campaign funds. An especially controversial luncheon was held at a Buddhist temple near Los Angeles featuring Vice President Al Gore; Senate testimony from Buddhist nuns indicated they were reimbursed— illegally— for their political contributions. Among the more controversial entanglements:

- *John Huang*, a paid fund raiser for the Democratic National Committee and former Assistant Secretary of Commerce for International Trade, raised $3.4 million allegedly from foreign sources. He denied wrongdoing but fled to China.

- *Lippo Group*, a huge Indonesian conglomerate with ties to China, allegedly funneled contributions to the Democratic National Committee.

- *Charles Trie*, formerly the owner of a Chinese restaurant in Little Rock favored by Bill Clinton, raised more than $600,000 for the president's legal defense fund (defending Clinton from sexual harassment charges).

- *Buddhist Temple*, near Los Angeles, contributed $140,000 from improvised monks and nuns (reimbursed) following a personal appearance by Al Gore.

Equally embarrassing disclosures were made regarding Republican and Democratic congressional access—golf and dining with congress members, trips, receptions, and other exclusive events—in exchange for large campaign contributions. However, the use of the White House, the nation's revered symbol of government, for fund raising seemed more questionable than common Capitol Hill practices.

Source: All quotations from *New York Times*, December 27, 1996.

networks of contributors can be contacted through specialized mailing lists—for example, liberals through television producer Norman Lear's People for the American Way and conservatives through North Carolina Senator Jesse Helms's National Congressional Club. Feminists have been effective in soliciting individual contributions across the country and funneling them very early in a campaign to women candidates through EMILY's list. Ideological contributors may only get the satisfaction of knowing that they are financially backing their cause in the political process. Some contributors simply enjoy the opportunity to be near and to be seen with high-ranking politicians. Politicians pose for photos with contributors, who later frame the photos and hang them in their office to impress their friends, associates, and customers. About 7 to 10 percent of the population claims in national surveys to have contributed to candidates running for public

Rank	Contributor	Industry	Total Contributions	Percentage to Democrats	Percentage to Republicans
1.	Philip Morris*	Tobacco/Food	$4,208,505	21% / 79%	
2.	American Federation of State, County, and Muncipal Employees	Government Worker Unions	$4,017,553	99%	1%
3.	Assn. Trial Lawyers of America	Lawyers	$3,513,588	85%	14%
4.	National Education Assn.*	Teacher Unions	$3,283,143	96%	4%
5.	Teamsters Union*	Transport Unions	$3,164,297	96%	4%
6.	Laborers Union*	Building Trades Unions	$3,076,378	93%	7%
7.	United Auto Workers*	Manufacturing Unions	$3,023,288	99%	1%
8.	United Food & Commercial Workers Union	Miscellaneous Unions	$2,926,845	99%	1%
9.	International Brotherhood of Electrical Workers*	Electrical Workers Unions	$2,820,528	98%	2%
10.	American Medical Assn*	Doctors	$2,794,894	23% / 77%	
11.	Communications Workers of America*	Industrial Unions	$2,745,264	100%	0%
12.	AT&T*	Long Distance	$2,715,101	41% / 58%	
13.	Machinists/Aerospace Workers Union*	Industrial Unions	$2,565,493	100%	0%
14.	National Assn. of Realtors	Real Estate	$2,558,358	34% / 66%	
15.	Joseph E. Seagram & Sons*	Liquor/Movies/TV	$2,555,836	67% / 33%	
16.	American Federation of Teachers*	Teachers Unions	$2,423,088	99%	1%
17.	Natl. Auto Dealers Assn.	Auto Dealers	$2,421,575	19% / 81%	
18.	RJR Nabisco*	Tobacco/Food	$2,300,336	20% / 80%	
19.	United Parcel Service	Delivery Services	$2,176,700	35% / 65%	
20.	AFL-CIO*	Miscellaneous Unions	$2,165,224	98%	2%
21.	National Assn. of Letter Carriers*	Postal Unions	$2,151,219	89%	10%
22.	Federal Express Corp.	Delivery Services	$2,113,200	46% / 54%	
23.	Ernst & Young*	Accountants	$1,977,130	51% / 49%	
24.	Carpenters Union*	Bldg. Trades Unions	$1,888,472	96%	4%
25.	American Institute of CPAs	Accountants	$1,853,000	34% / 66%	

*Contributions came from more than one affiliate or subsidiary

To Democrats ☐   To Republicans ▨

FIGURE 8-3 The Big-Money Contributors

Figures include all contributions made to candidates or political parties in the 1995–96 election cycle by the listed organizations, their PACs, employees and immediate families. Included are direct contributions to candidates, as well as hard- and soft-money contributions to the political parties. Independent expenditures are not included, nor are expenditures on "issue ads" or other indirect or unreported election year expenses.

Source: *The Big Picture: Money Follows Power Shift on Capitol Hill* by Larry Makinson. Center for Responsive Politics, Washington, D.C. (Nov. 1997).

office. Contributors are disproportionately high-income, well-educated older people with strong partisan views (see Figure 8-4).

Fund-Raising Chores   Fund raising occupies more of a candidate's time than any other campaign activity. Candidates must personally contact as many individual contributors as possible. They work late into the evening on the telephone with potential contributors. Fund-raising dinners, cocktail parties, barbecues, fish frys, and so on, are scheduled nearly every day of a campaign. The candidate is expected to appear personally to "press the flesh" of big contribu-

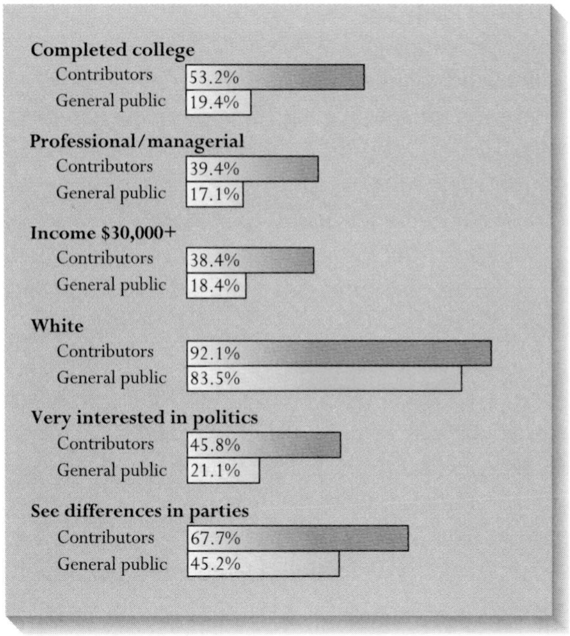

FIGURE 8-4 Characteristics of Individual Political Contributors

Completed college
Contributors 53.2%
General public 19.4%

Professional/managerial
Contributors 39.4%
General public 17.1%

Income $30,000+
Contributors 38.4%
General public 18.4%

White
Contributors 92.1%
General public 83.5%

Very interested in politics
Contributors 45.8%
General public 21.1%

See differences in parties
Contributors 67.7%
General public 45.2%

Contributors to political campaigns generally have better educations, higher incomes, and more professional positions than most Americans. They also are far more likely than average Americans to vote regularly and to hold strongly partisan views.

Source: Center for Political Studies, University of Michigan, *1990 National Election Study*. Data provided by the Interuniversity Consortium for Political and Social Research.

tors. Movie and rock stars and other assorted celebrities may also be asked to appear at fund-raising affairs to generate attendance. Dinners may run $250 to $1,000 a plate in presidential affairs, although often less in Senate or House campaigns. Tickets may be "bundled" to well-heeled individual contributors or sold in blocks to organizations. Fund-raising techniques are limited only by the imagination of the campaign manager.

REGULATING CAMPAIGN FINANCE

The **Federal Election Commission (FEC)** is responsible for enforcing limits on individual and organizational contributions to all federal elections, administering the public funding of presidential campaigns, and requiring full disclosure of all campaign financial activity in presidential and congressional elections. Enforcement of these federal election and campaign finance laws lies in the hands of the six-member FEC. Appointed by the president to serve staggered six-year terms, commission members are traditionally split 3 to 3 between Republicans and Democrats.

Limits on Contributions   The FEC limits direct individual contributions to a candidate's campaign to $1,000 per election and organizational contributions to $5,000 per election. But there are many ways in which individuals and organizations can legally surmount these limits. Contributors may give a candidate $1,000 for each member of their family in a primary election and then another $1,000 per member in the general election. Organizations may generate much more than the $5,000 limit by bundling (combining) $1,000 contributions from individual members. As noted earlier, both individuals and organizations can give unlimited amounts of soft money to the parties, as long as it is not spent directly on a particular candidate's campaign. Independent organizations can spend money beyond the FEC's limit for a presidential candidate or party in order to promote their political views, so long as these organizations do so "without cooperation or consultation with

Federal Election Commission (FEC) Agency charged with enforcing federal election laws and disbursing public presidential campaign funds.

the candidate of his or her campaign." Finally, as noted, individuals may spend as much of their own money on their own campaigns as they wish.[6]

By law, every candidate for federal office must file periodic reports with the FEC detailing both the income and the expenditures of their campaign. Individual contributors who give an aggregate of $200 or more must be identified by name, address, occupation, and employer. All PAC and party contributions, no matter how large or small, must also be itemized. In addition, PACs themselves must file reports with the FEC at least four times a year, detailing both the contributions received by the PAC and the names of candidates and other groups that received the PAC's donations.

Federal Funding of Presidential Elections   Federal funding, financed by the $3 checkoff box on individual income tax returns, is available to presidential candidates in primary and general elections, as well as to major-party nominating conventions. Candidates seeking the nomination in presidential primary elections can qualify for federal funds by raising $5,000 from private contributions no greater than $250 each in each of twenty states. In the general election, Democratic and Republican nominees are funded equally at levels determined by the FEC. In order to receive federal funding, presidential candidates must agree to FEC limits on their campaign spending in both primary and general elections. (Until 1992, all presidential candidates agreed to the FEC limits and accepted federal funding; but independent Texas billionaire H. Ross Perot funded his own campaign that year, rejecting federal funds, and publishing mogul Steve Forbes rejected federal funds in 1996 and paid for his own unsuccessful Republican presidential primary race.) Federal funding pays about one-third of the primary campaign costs of presidential candidates and all the *official* presidential campaign organization costs in the general election. The parties also receive federal funds for their nominating conventions. Should these regulations be changed? Reformers disagree sharply about how the limitations should be changed (see *A Conflicting View*: "Reforming Campaign Finance").

THE PRESIDENTIAL CAMPAIGN: THE PRIMARY RACE

The phrase *presidential fever* refers to the burning political ambition required to seek the presidency. The grueling presidential campaign is a test of strength, character, endurance, and determination. It is physically exhausting and mentally and emotionally draining. Every aspect of the candidates' lives—and the lives of their families—is subject to microscopic inspection by the news media. Most of this coverage is critical, and much of it is unfair. Yet candidates are expected to handle it all with grace and humor, from the earliest testing of the waters through a full-fledged campaign.

Media Mentions   Politicians with presidential ambitions may begin by promoting presidential *mentions* by media columnists and commentators. The media help to identify "presidential timber" years in advance of a presidential race simply by drawing up lists of potential candidates, commenting on their qualifications, and speculating about their intentions. Mentions are likely to come to prominent governors or senators who start making speeches outside of their state, who grab the media spotlight on a national issue, or who simply let it be known to the media "off the record" that they are considering a presidential race. Visiting New

A Conflicting View

Reforming Campaign Finance

Battles over campaign finance reform reflect conflict between the parties. Historically, Republicans enjoyed a greater ability to raise money from their more affluent loyalists. Democrats were usually more dependent on unions and political action committee (PAC) money. Political scientist Frank Sorauf writes, "Nothing colors the politics of regulating campaign finance as much as the central fact that the Congress is regulating its own electoral activity. . . . The members of Congress know campaign finance at first hand, and they know that even the slightest change in the structure of regulations may have considerable consequences for their own political careers."

Reform Goals Ideally, reform of campaign financing should minimize the opportunity for corruption, inspire voter confidence in the integrity of the political system, equalize influence between rich and poor, encourage competitive elections by giving challengers a fair chance against incumbents, and at the same time preserve free speech and the right of people to promote their views at election time. But it is not clear that any reform proposals could achieve all of these goals at once.

Eliminate PACs? Proposals to outlaw PACs and ban all contributions by corporations, unions, and interest groups raise constitutional questions about the right of groups to express their preferences and participate in the electoral process. The Supreme Court might strike down a congressional attempt to ban PACs as a violation of the First Amendment. Republicans might gain more from such a ban than Democrats; if PAC and union money were to be eliminated, individual contributions would become the only game in town, a situation that might favor Republicans.

Public Funding and Limits on Spending? It is frequently argued that congressional elections should be publicly funded and limits placed on congressional campaign spending, just as they are in presidential elections. Most members of Congress dislike the constant chore of asking people for money. Freeing

them from obligations to contributors would presumably reduce the influence of well-heeled special interests in congressional decision making. Members of Congress would no longer be obliged to give special consideration to the requests of wealthy individual contributors and big-spending PACs. Perhaps the general public would be less cynical about Congress and more confident of the fairness of the system.

But public funding would entail limits on campaign spending for the candidates. Equal limits for congressional incumbents and challengers would grant a strong advantage to incumbents, who already have name recognition and years of constituent contacts and services working on their behalf. Indeed, skeptics charge that public funding with campaign limits is really an "incumbent protection" plan.

Finally, many taxpayers are offended by the very idea of politicians using tax dollars to run for public office. Indeed, most taxpayers refuse even to check off $3 of their taxes for presidential campaigns.

Banning Soft Money? Current laws allow large contributions in soft money to political parties. Soft money allows big contributors to exercise disproportionate influence in party affairs. But this soft money also gives the parties what little direct influence they have over members of Congress. Cutting off party funding would further weaken the party system. A bill to ban soft money failed to pass Congress in 1997.

Curtailing Independent Spending? Independent spending on "issue ads" by organizations are currently allowed by law, so long as the independent persons or groups doing so do not coordinate with the candidate. But curtailing independent spending on political communication is likely to be an unconstitutional infringement on First Amendment–protected free speech. The Supreme Court ruled in *Buckley v. Valeo* (1976) that organizations and individuals may spend as much as they wish on political communications.

Source: Frank Sorauf, *Inside Campaign Finance* (New Haven, Conn.: Yale University Press, 1992), p. 191.

Up Close

Campaign 2000, Off and Running

The presidential election campaign of 2000 began on the morning following Bill Clinton's reelection in 1996. Potential presidential candidates in both parties began jockeying for position—appearing on news shows, "feeling out" potential supporters and contrib-utors, and "testing the waters" by traveling across the states for meetings and speeches. Favorite stops included Iowa, with the nation's first presidential party caucuses, and New Hampshire, with the nation's first presidential primary election. Campaign 2000 began especially early in both parties because for the first time since 1988, no incumbent president was in the race. And almost immediately, poll takers began reporting the "horse race."

Early Preferences for Republican Nominee (among Republicans)	Percentage Favoring
Texas Governor George W. Bush, son of the former president	19%
Elizabeth Dole, head of American Red Cross	14
Former congressional representative Jack Kemp	13
Former Vice President Dan Quayle	8
Business executive Steve Forbes	8
Tennessee Senator Fred Thompson	8
New Jersey Governor Christie Whitman	5
Political commentator Pat Buchanan	5
Former Tennessee Governor Lamar Alexander	4
House Speaker Newt Gingrich	4
New Hampshire Senator Bob Smith	2
Missouri Senator John Ashcroft	2
Other (vol.)	1
Undecided	7

Early Preferences for Democratic Nominee (among Democrats)	Percentage Favoring
Vice President Al Gore	33%
The Reverend Jesse Jackson	16
Former New Jersey Senator Bill Bradley	14
Missouri Congressman Dick Gephardt	7
Nebraska Senator Bob Kerrey	4
Massachusetts Senator John Kerry	4
Other (vol.)	3
Undecided	19

Hampshire and giving speeches there is viewed as "testing the waters" and a signal of presidential ambitions (see *Up Close:* "Campaign 2000, Off and Running").

Presidential Credentials   Political experience as vice president, governor, U.S. senator, or member of Congress not only inspires presidential ambition but also provides vital experience in political campaigning. However, virtually all presidential candidates testify that the presidential arena is far more challenging than politics at any other level. The experience of running for and holding high public office

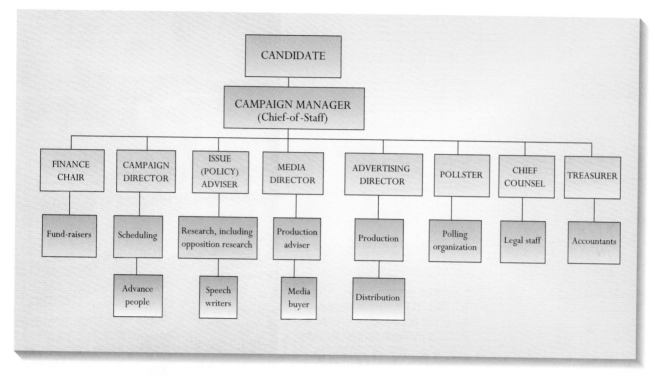

FIGURE 8-5 Typical Campaign Organization

Campaign organizations vary, but most assign someone to perform these tasks: funding, scheduling appearances, speech writing, media production and buying, polling, advertising, legal compliance, and check writing, even if, in local campaigns, all these tasks must be performed by the candidate or his or her family members.

appears to be a political requirement for the presidency. Some recent presidential aspirants (Independent Ross Perot, Republican Steve Forbes, and Republican Patrick Buchanan) have tried to make a virtue of their lack of previous political office holding, no doubt hoping to attract support from the many Americans who disdain "politics as usual." But in the twentieth century no major party nominee for president has not previously held office as vice president, governor, U.S. senator, or member of Congress except World War II hero General Dwight D. Eisenhower.

The Decision to Run   The decision to run for president involves complex personal and political calculations. Ambition to occupy the world's most powerful office must be weighed against the staggering costs—emotional as well as financial—of a presidential campaign.

Serious planning, organizing, and fund raising must begin at least two years before the general election. A staff must be assembled—campaign managers and strategists, fund raisers, media experts, pollsters, issues advisers and speech writers, lawyers and accountants—and supporters must be identified in key states throughout the nation. Paid and volunteer workers must be assembled (see Figure 8-5). Leaders among important interest groups must be contacted. A general campaign strategy must be developed, an organization put in place, and several millions of dollars in campaign contributions pledged in advance of the race. Often the decision to run hinges on whether initial pledges of campaign contributions appear adequate. The serious candidate must be able to anticipate contributions of $20 million or more for primary elections.

Presidential hopefuls multiply when the incumbent is forced to step down after serving two terms in office. Vice President Al Gore is the inside track for the Democratic nomination in 2000, but the Republican nomination has attracted a host of "wannabes."

A Strategy for the Primaries   The road to the White House consists of two separate races: the primary elections and caucuses leading to the Democratic and Republican party nominations, and the general election. Each of these races requires a separate strategy. The primary race requires an appeal to party activists and the more ideologically motivated primary voters in key states. The general election requires an appeal to the less partisan, less attentive, more ideologically moderate general election voters. Thus the campaign strategy developed to win the nomination must give way after the national conventions to a strategy to win the November general election (see *Up Close*: "Clinton's Winning Strategies: Change, with Moderation" on pages 266-267).

The New Hampshire Primary   The primary season begins in the winter snows of New Hampshire, traditionally the first state to hold a presidential primary election. New Hampshire is far more important *strategically* to a presidential campaign than it is in delegate strength. As a small state, New Hampshire supplies fewer than 1 percent of the delegates at the Democratic and Republican conventions. But the New Hampshire primary looms very large in media coverage and hence in overall campaign strategy. Although the popular Iowa party caucuses are held even earlier, New Hampshire is the nation's first primary, and the media begin speculating about its outcome and reporting early state-poll results months in advance.

The "expectations" game is played with a vengeance. Media polls and commentators set the candidates' expected vote percentages, and the candidates and their spokespersons try to deflate these expectations. On election night, the candidates' **spin doctors** sally forth among the crowds of television and newspaper reporters to give a favorable interpretation of the outcome. The candidates themselves appear at campaign headquarters (and, they hope, on national television) to give the same favorable spin to the election results. But the media itself—

spin doctor   Practitioner of the art of spin control, or manipulation of media reporting to favor one's own candidate.

particularly the television network anchors and reporters and commentators—interpret the results for the American people, determining the early favorites in the presidential "horse race."

New Hampshire provides the initial *momentum* for the presidential candidates. "Momentum" is more than just a media catchword. The Democratic and Republican winners in New Hampshire have demonstrated their voter appeal, their "electability." Favorable New Hampshire results inspire more financial contributions and thus the resources needed to carry the fight into the next group of primary elections. Unfavorable New Hampshire results tend to dry up contributions; weak candidates may be forced into an early withdrawal.

The "uncrowned" presidential nominee usually submits his choice for vice president in the run-up to the party's national convention. Here Jack Kemp, Bob Dole's 1996 running mate, accepts the nomination of the Republican Party at their national convention in San Diego.

The Front-End Strategy A **front-end strategy** places heavy emphasis on the results from New Hampshire and other early primary states. This strategy involves spending all or most of the candidate's available resources—time, energy, and money—on the early primary states, in the hopes that early victories will provide the momentum, in media attention and financial contributions, to continue the race. The front-end loading of the primary election schedule makes it especially important for candidates to raise "early money."

Super Tuesday Southern Strategy The primary road leads from New Hampshire to **Super Tuesday**, a cluster of primaries held in early March including Texas and Florida, the biggest prizes among the southern states. The decision of these states to hold early primaries on the same day was inspired by moderate Democrats in the 1980s who believed that their party's presidential losses in general elections were occurring because the nominees were too liberal. By holding presidential primaries in more moderate or conservative states early in the race, they hoped to give momentum to moderate candidates. However, in 1996 several states moved their primary elections ahead of the Super Tuesday states, including delegate-rich New York.

Big-State Strategy Presidential aspirants who begin the race with widespread support among party activists, heavy financial backing, and strong endorsements from the major interest groups can focus their attention on the big-state primaries. A **big-state strategy** generally requires more money, more workers, and better organization than a front-end strategy. But the big states—California, New York, Texas, Florida, Pennsylvania, Ohio, and Michigan—have the most delegates. The results of these primaries may determine the Democratic and Republican nominees, assuming that most or all of them are won by the same candidates. During the late March and April primaries, weaker candidates usually announce their withdrawals. It is rare that more than two candidates in each party survive as credible candidates into May and June. By this stage of the race, many uncommitted delegates begin to commit themselves and their convention vote to the leader.

Convention Showplace Once a presidential candidate has enough votes to assure nomination, this uncrowned winner must prepare for the party's convention. Organizing and orchestrating convention forces, dominating the platform and rules writing, enjoying the nominating speeches and the traditional roll call of the state delegations, mugging for the television camera when the nominating vote goes over the top, submitting the vice presidential nominee's name for convention approval, and preparing and delivering a rousing acceptance speech to begin the fall campaign are just a few of the many tasks awaiting the winner—and the winner's campaign team.

front-end strategy Presidential political campaign strategy in which a candidate focuses on winning early primaries to build momentum.

Super Tuesday Cluster of presidential primaries held in early March that includes important southern states.

big-state strategy Presidential political campaign strategy in which a candidate focuses on winning primaries in large states because of their high delegate counts.

Up Close

Clinton's Winning Strategies: Change, with Moderation

Prior to the 1992 presidential race, Democratic strategists were painfully aware that Republicans had won five of the previous six presidential elections. Northern liberal Democrats—Humphrey, McGovern, Mondale, Dukakis—had lost in campaigns in which Republicans had captured moderate as well as conservative voters. The strategic problem was diagnosed as follows: the party's liberal candidates enjoyed an advantage in primary elections, where low turnouts magnified the influence of the party's liberal constituencies; but in the general election, liberal candidates who won the party's nomination fared poorly among moderate swing voters.

Becoming a "Moderate" Bill Clinton had spent nearly twenty years shaping his image as a youthful "New Democrat" and positioning himself to run for president as a "moderate." He avoided the "liberal" tag with tough talk about workfare, the death penalty, and personal responsibility. He emphasized economic growth over income redistribution. He referred to government spending as "investment." His "putting people first" theme emphasized help for the middle class and avoided direct references to traditional Democratic groups: African Americans, feminists, environmentalists, labor unions, government employees.

Handling the Character Issue Bill Clinton almost lost the prize he had sought for a lifetime early in the 1992 Democratic primaries, when Gennifer Flowers held a nationally televised press conference to announce she had had a long-term affair with him. Rumors of marital infidelity had shadowed Clinton for many years. The same problem had driven Gary Hart out of the presidential race in 1988. But a tenacious Bill Clinton decided to confront the "bimbo issue" head-on. When Don Hewitt, producer of *60 Minutes*, offered Clinton a Sunday night prime-time interview just after the Super Bowl, the candidate accepted. With wife Hillary at his side, Bill Clinton told a huge nationwide audience that his marriage had survived shaky moments but it was rock solid now. He correctly calculated that the public was increasingly disgusted with the media's focus on sex scandals.

1992: Focusing on Change Clinton's 1992 campaign strategy was to hammer home, over and over again, a single theme: the economy is in bad shape, and the nation demands change. Yet in late spring, the most powerful voice for economic change in the nation was that of Ross Perot. Clinton was running third in the polls, trailing both President Bush and the independent billionaire. But Perot's focus on the economy and the need for change was detaching millions of middle-class voters from Bush and sending the president's popularity rating into a nosedive.

With the prospect of a three-person race looming, some Clinton strategists urged their candidate to jettison his moderate image in favor of cultivating the core liberal constituencies of the Democratic Party and thus eke out a plurality victory. But Clinton rejected this advice and insisted on sticking with the original game plan—moderation and change.

The Democratic convention was a celebration of Clinton's good fortune and sound political judgment. When the temperamental Perot unexpectedly withdrew from the race, millions of his disillusioned supporters were set adrift at precisely the moment Clinton was broadcasting his message of change to national audiences. Perot's middle-class, independent supporters flocked to Clinton's banner. By the end of the convention, Clinton had soared to a 20-point lead in the polls.

Taking Advantage of Opponent's Mistakes Clinton's single-minded focus on the economy and the need for change contrasted with the unfocused rambling of the Bush campaign. The Bush team at first implausibly tried to claim the "change" theme for itself, only to have voters ask why the president hadn't sought change in the previous four years. A subsequent attempt to focus on "family values" met with only limited success. Bush's attempts to remind voters of America's victories in the Cold War and the Gulf War seemed to backfire: they only proved that the president had focused his energies on foreign affairs rather than on problems at home. Bush's claim that the economy was not all that bad only seemed to show he was "out of touch" with the people.

Setting a Favorable Agenda Clinton went into the presidential debates in 1992 with one simple goal—to keep the focus of the campaign on the economy. Bush had a much more challenging task—

to refocus the campaign on Clinton's character and somehow overcome the Democrat's lead in the polls. Bush tried to tag Clinton as a Vietnam War protestor and draft dodger who lacked the personal stature to be commander-in-chief. But in the first debate Clinton nimbly deflected Bush's attack: "Your father was right to stand up to Joe McCarthy. You were wrong to attack my patriotism." Bush was awkward and uncomfortable in the attack mode.

In the final days of the campaign, Bush finally hit his stride with a fierce attack on Clinton's character. Could "Slick Willie"—a taxer, a spender, a liberal, a draft dodger, an antiwar demonstrator, and a liar—be trusted to run the country? But Bush's theme was negative and failed to give voters a reason to vote *for* the president. The Clinton team wanted the election to be a referendum on the economy, not on their candidate's character. In the end, that is what they got.

Although Clinton emerged only 5 percentage points ahead of Bush in the popular vote, the nation's desire for change was clearly evident in the combined votes for Clinton and Perot. Fully 62 percent of the voters chose to vote against incumbent president George Bush. Clinton prevailed in one of the toughest political campaigns in American history because he skillfully presented himself to the voters as an agent of change.

1996: Becoming Presidential   In his reelection campaign Bill Clinton reshaped his image into that of a responsible, centrist president: a president whose tireless efforts had improved the economy, reduced annual federal deficits, lowered the crime rate, and saved Medicare and Medicaid from mean-spirited Republicans in Congress. He shifted the public's attention away from his controversial early initiatives in office—his large tax increase, his confrontation with the military over homosexuals, and his unsuccessful national health care proposal. Instead, he focused on a series of modest but popular positions including the family leave act, portable health insurance, minimum two-day hospital stays following childbirth, the V-chip, school uniforms, a ban on assault weapons—positions that appealed especially to women voters. As incumbent president, he sailed through the presidential primaries in 1996 with no opposition.

"Defining" Bob Dole   General Colin Powell was the only potential opponent who led Clinton in presidential choice polls. When Powell removed himself

from contention, a loud sigh of relief was heard in the White House. Bob Dole—an aging, dour, occasionally grumpy, longtime congressional leader—was a welcome opponent. Indeed, as polls consistently reported Clinton's 20-plus percentage point lead over Dole, the only concern in the Clinton camp was overconfidence.

With the economy growing, the president had only to ask, "Are you better off now than when I took office?" But the Clinton campaign also sought to define Bob Dole as "wrong in the past, wrong for the future." Indeed, from the beginning Bob Dole seemed ill-suited as a presidential candidate: a Washington insider when the voters distrusted Washington; a congressional leader when Congress was the least-trusted branch of government; an aging World War II veteran out of touch with the baby-boomer electorate. Clinton television ads showed Dole acknowledging that "I voted against Medicare," raising fears among Dole's own senior generation voters. A modest Dole bounce in the polls after the GOP convention was quickly washed away.

Building the Bridge   The Clinton theme was an upbeat "bridge to the twenty-first century," suggesting his own forward-looking posture and subtly reminding voters of Dole's age. In the debates, Clinton remained cool, confident, and "presidential" in the face of Dole's barbs. "No insult," he said at one point, "ever cleaned up a toxic waste dump." Polls reported that although Americans thought Dole was more "honest and trustworthy" than Clinton, they still preferred Clinton as president.

Clinton was judged the clear winner of the debates, but viewership was down. The campaign was the dullest in recent times, as reflected in a half-century-record low voter turnout (48 percent). An embarrassing last-minute flap over Democratic campaign contributions from foreign sources seemed to raise Perot's vote just enough to prevent the president from winning 50 percent of the electorate. The final vote was Clinton 49 percent, Dole 41 percent, Perot 8 percent, with 2 percent going to minor party candidates.

Clinton won a second term—the first Democratic president since Franklin Roosevelt to do so—but he failed to win a policy mandate. Republicans maintained control of both houses of Congress, and scandals and investigations promised to follow the Clintons throughout their White House years. But Bill Clinton had again successfully shaped a winning image.

THE PRESIDENTIAL CAMPAIGN: THE GENERAL ELECTION BATTLE

Buoyed by the conventions—and often by postconvention bounces in the polls—the new nominees must now face the general electorate.

General Election Strategies   Strategies in the general election are as varied as the imaginations of campaign advisers, media consultants, pollsters, and the candidates themselves. As noted earlier, campaign strategies are affected by the nature of the times and the state of the economy; by the incumbent or challenger status of the candidate; by the issues, conditions, scandals, or events currently being spotlighted by the media; and by the dynamics of the campaign itself as the candidates attack and defend themselves.

Presidential election campaigns must focus on the **Electoral College**. The president is not elected by the national popular vote total but rather by a majority of the *electoral* votes of the states. Electoral votes are won by plurality, winner-take-all popular voting in each of the states (see *Up Close:* "Understanding the Electoral College" on pages 270-271). Thus a narrow plurality win in a state delivers *all* of that state's electoral votes. Big-state victories, even by very narrow margins, can deliver big electoral prizes. The biggest prizes are California with 54 electoral votes, New York with 33, and Texas with 32. With a total of 538 electoral votes at stake, *the winner must garner victories in states culminating in a minimum of 270 electoral votes.*

Targeting the Swing States   In focusing on the most populous states, with their large electoral votes, candidates must decide which of these states are "winnable," then direct their time, energy, and money to these *swing states.* Candidates cannot afford to spend too much effort in states that already seem to be solidly in their column, although they must avoid the perception that they are ignoring these strong bases of support. Neither can candidates waste much effort on states that already appear to be solidly in their opponent's column. So the swing states receive most of the candidates' time, attention, and television advertising money.

Regional Alignments   A glance at the Electoral College vote results in recent elections (see *Across the USA:* "How the States Voted") suggests that Republican candidates depend heavily on electoral votes from the South and the Mountain States. Florida and Texas are the keys to Republican presidential election strength. The Democratic presidential electoral base is found in the Northeast and upper Midwest. Even when Democratic candidates have lost in New York, Massachusetts, Pennsylvania, Illinois, Michigan, and Wisconsin, the vote margin in these states has been fairly close. California, with its prize of 54 electoral votes, is the most important swing state. California voters supported the Republican ticket in every election from 1968 to 1988; their swing to the Democratic ticket in 1992 and 1996 was a key component of Clinton's victories. Among the Republican "must-win" states in 1996, Dole held on to Texas but lost Florida.

The Presidential Debates   The nationally televised presidential debates are the central feature of the general election campaign. These debates attract more viewers than any other campaign event. Moreover, they enable a candidate to reach undecided voters and the opponent's supporters, as well as the candidate's own

Electoral College   The 538 presidential electors apportioned among the states according to their congressional representation (plus 3 for the District of Columbia) whose votes officially elect the president and vice president of the United States.

How the States Voted

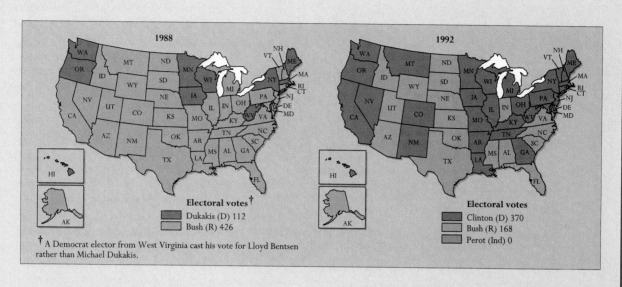

1988

Electoral votes †
- Dukakis (D) 112
- Bush (R) 426

† A Democrat elector from West Virginia cast his vote for Lloyd Bentsen rather than Michael Dukakis.

1992

Electoral votes
- Clinton (D) 370
- Bush (R) 168
- Perot (Ind) 0

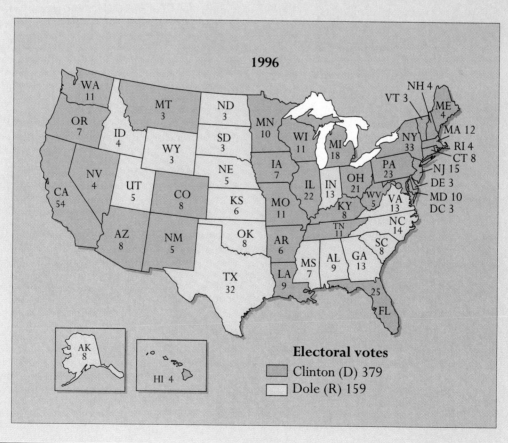

1996

WA 11
OR 7
ID 4
MT 3
ND 3
MN 10
WI 11
MI 18
NY 33
VT 3
NH 4
ME 4
MA 12
RI 4
CT 8
NJ 15
DE 3
MD 10
DC 3
PA 23
WV 5
VA 13
NV 4
UT 5
WY 3
SD 3
NE 5
IA 7
IL 22
IN 13
OH 21
KY 8
NC 14
CA 54
AZ 8
NM 5
CO 8
KS 6
MO 11
AR 6
TN 11
SC 8
GA 13
AL 9
MS 7
LA 9
OK 8
TX 32
FL 25
AK 8
HI 4

Electoral votes
- Clinton (D) 379
- Dole (R) 159

 **Up Close**

Understanding the Electoral College

The president of the United States is not elected by nationwide *popular* vote but rather by a majority of *electoral votes* of the states. The Constitution grants each state a number of electors equal to the number of its congressional representatives and senators combined (see map). Because representatives are apportioned to the states on the basis of population, the electoral vote of the states is subject to change after each ten-year census. No state has fewer than three electoral votes, because the Constitution guarantees every state two U.S. senators and at least one representative. The Twenty-third Amendment granted three electoral votes to the District of Columbia even though it has no voting members of Congress.

Voters in presidential elections are actually choosing a slate of presidential electors pledged to vote for their party's presidential and vice presidential candidates. The names of electors seldom appear on the ballot, only the names of the candidates and their parties. The slate that wins a *plurality* of the popular vote in a state (more than any other slate, not necessarily a majority) casts *all* of the state's vote in the Electoral College. This "winner-take-all" system in the states is not mandated by the Constitution; a state legislature could allocate a state's electoral votes in proportion to the split in the popular vote. The winner-take-all system in the states helps ensure that the Electoral College produces a majority for one candidate. Indeed, winning candidates usually garner a heavy majority in the Electoral College, even when they win the nationwide popular vote by only a modest margin.

The Electoral College never meets at a single location; rather, electors meet at their respective state capitols to cast their ballots around December 15, following the general election on the first Tuesday after the first Monday of November. The results are sent to the presiding officer of the Senate, the vice president, who in January presides over their count in the presence of both houses of Congress and formally announces the results. These procedures are usually considered a formality, but the U.S. Constitution does not *require* that electors cast their vote for the winning presidential candidate in their state, and occasionally "faithless electors" disrupt the process.

If no candidate wins a majority of electoral votes, the House of Representatives chooses the president from among the three candidates with the largest number of electoral votes, with each state casting *one* vote. The Constitution does not specify how House delegations should determine their vote, but by House rules, the state's vote goes to the candidate receiving a majority vote in the delegation.

Only two presidential elections have ever been decided formally by the House of Representatives. In 1800 Thomas Jefferson and Aaron Burr tied in the Electoral College because the Twelfth Amendment had not yet been adopted to separate presidential from vice presidential voting; all the Democratic-Republican electors voted for both Jefferson and Burr, creating a tie. In 1824 Andrew Jackson won the popular vote and more electoral votes than anyone else but failed to get a majority. The House chose John Quincy Adams over Jackson, causing a popular uproar and ensuring Jackson's election in 1828.

In addition, in 1876, the Congress was called on to decide which electoral results from the southern states to validate; a Republican Congress chose to validate enough electoral votes to allow Republican Rutherford B. Hayes to win, even though Democrat Samuel Tilden had won more popular votes. Hayes promised the Democratic southern states that in return for their acknowledgment of his presidential claim, he would end the military occupation of the South.

Finally, in 1888, the Electoral College vote failed to reflect the popular vote. Benjamin Harrison received 233 electoral votes to incumbent president Grover Cleveland's 168, even though Cleveland won about 90,000 more popular votes than Harrison. Harrison served a single lackluster term; Cleveland was elected for a second time in 1892, the only president to serve two nonconsecutive terms.

Constitutional proposals to reform the Electoral College have circulated for nearly two hundred years, but none has won widespread support. These reform proposals have included (1) election of the president by direct national popular vote; (2) allocation of each state's electoral vote in proportion to the popular vote each candidate received in the state; (3) allocation of electoral votes to winners of each congressional district and two to the statewide winners; (4) requirement that all electoral votes be cast for the state's winner, eliminating the possibility of faithless electors.

But most reform proposals create as many problems as they resolve. If the president is to be elected by direct nationwide popular vote, should a plurality vote be sufficient to win? Or should a national runoff be held in the event that no one receives a majority in the first election? Would proportional allocation of electoral votes encourage third-party candidates to enter the race in order to deny the leading candidate a majority?

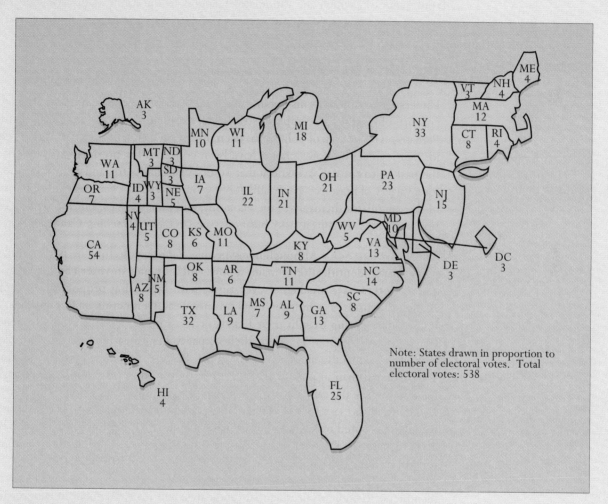

Note: States drawn in proportion to number of electoral votes. Total electoral votes: 538

In this map, each state is drawn in a size relative to the number of Electoral College votes it represented after the 1990 census.

Source: Holly Idelson, "Count Adds Seats in Eight States," *Congressional Quarterly Weekly Report* 48 (December 29, 1990), p. 4220.

partisans. Even people who usually pay little attention to politics may be drawn in by the drama of the confrontation (see *Up Close:* "The Presidential Debates").

The debates allow viewers an opportunity to see and hear candidates together and to compare their responses to questions as they stand side by side. The debates give audiences a better view of the candidates than they can get from thirty-second commercial ads or seven-second news sound bites. Viewers can at least judge how the candidates react under pressure.

However, the debates emphasize candidate image over substantive policy issues. Candidates must appear presidential. They must appear confident, compassionate, concerned, and good humored. They must not appear uncertain or unsure of themselves, or aloof or out of touch with viewers, or easily upset by hostile questions. They must avoid verbal slips or gaffes or even unpolished or awkward gestures. They must remember that the debates are not really debates so much as joint press conferences in which the candidates respond to questions with rehearsed mini-speeches and practiced sound bites.[7]

THE VOTER DECIDES

Understanding the reasons behind the voters' choice at the ballot box is a central concern of candidates, campaign strategists, commentators, and political scientists. Perhaps no other area of politics has been investigated so thoroughly as voting behavior. Survey data on voter choice have been collected for presidential elections for the past half century.[8] We know that voters cast ballots for and against candidates for a variety of reasons—party affiliation, group interests, characteristics and images of the candidates themselves, the economy, and policy issues. But forecasting election outcomes remains a risky business (see *Up Close*: "Tracking Campaigns").

Party Affiliation Although many people *claim* to vote for "the person, not the party," party identification remains a powerful influence in voter choice. Party ties among voters have weakened over time, with increasing proportions of voters labeling themselves as independents or only weak Democrats or Republicans, and more voters opting to split their tickets or cross party lines than did so a generation ago (see Chapter 7). Nevertheless, party identification remains one of the most important influences on voter choice. Party affiliation is more important in congressional than in presidential elections, but even in presidential elections the tendency to see the candidate of one's own party as "the best person" is very strong.

Consider the last four presidential elections (see Figure 8-6). Self-identified Republicans voted overwhelmingly for Reagan in 1984, for Bush in 1988, for Bush in 1992, and for Dole in 1996. Self-identified Democrats voted overwhelmingly for Mondale in 1984, Dukakis in 1988, and Clinton in 1992 and 1996.

Because Republican identifiers are outnumbered in the electorate by Democratic identifiers, Republican presidential candidates, and many Republican congressional candidates as well, *must* appeal to independent and Democratic crossover voters.

Group Voting We already know that various social and economic groups give disproportionate support to the Democratic and Republican parties (see Chapter 7). So it comes as no surprise that recent Democratic presidential candidates have received disproportionate support from African Americans, Catholics, Jews, less-educated and lower-income voters, and union workers; Republican presidential candidates have fared better among whites, Protestants, and better-educated and higher-income voters (see Figure 8-7). That

Up Close

Tracking Campaigns

Voter swings in loyalty during presidential campaigns suggest that the outcome of elections is by no means certain at the outset (see graphs). Tracking polls during the 1992 campaign showed large swings in opinion in midsummer, the time of the Democratic and Republican nominating conventions. In contrast, tracking polls in 1996 showed uncommon stability in Clinton's large lead over Dole throughout the campaign.

At the start of his 1992 reelection bid, George Bush enjoyed a comfortable lead in the polls. But in late spring, the independent candidacy of Ross Perot eroded Bush's support. Bill Clinton was mired in third place. The Bush campaign launched a strong attack on Perot, calling him temperamentally unfit to be president and encouraging the press to delve into his financial dealings and penchant for investigating his opponents. Perot's support began to drop in the polls, and he abruptly announced his withdrawal from the race on July 16, the start of the Democratic convention. Perot supporters were set adrift at precisely the moment that Bill Clinton was benefiting from favorable television coverage of the Democratic convention. Clinton soared ahead in the polls. The race narrowed somewhat in the fall, but Clinton never lost his lead.

In contrast to the volatile 1992 campaign, the presidential campaign of 1996 was so stable that voters appeared to lose interest. Clinton maintained a comfortable lead all year, dipping only slightly during the GOP convention in August and peaking during the September bombing of Iraq. Perot never mounted a serious threat. Clinton's margin of victory, however, was somewhat narrower than the tracking polls had forecast.

The "Horse Race": Tracking the Presidential Campaigns in the Polls

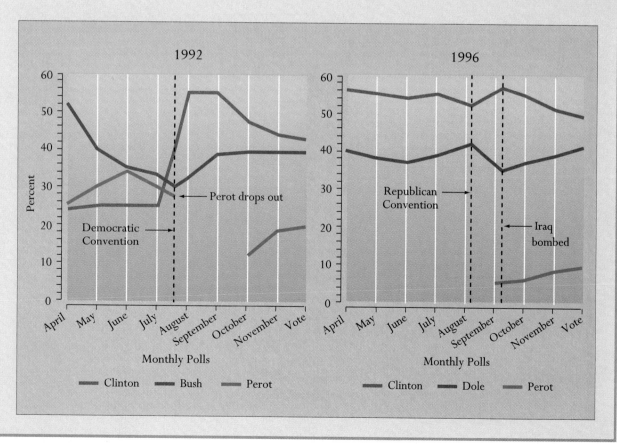

FIGURE 8-6 Party, Ideology, and Nature of the Times in Presidential Voting

Those who identify themselves as members of a major political party are highly likely to vote for the presidential candidates of their party. Likewise, those who identify themselves as liberals are more likely than average to vote for Democrats, and those who identify themselves as conservatives are more likely to vote for Republicans in presidential elections. In addition, voters who see the economic picture as better are more likely to vote for the incumbent; those who are concerned about the nation's economy are more likely to vote against the incumbent.

Source: Based on Gallup poll surveys; data for 1996 from *New York Times*, November 6, 1996.

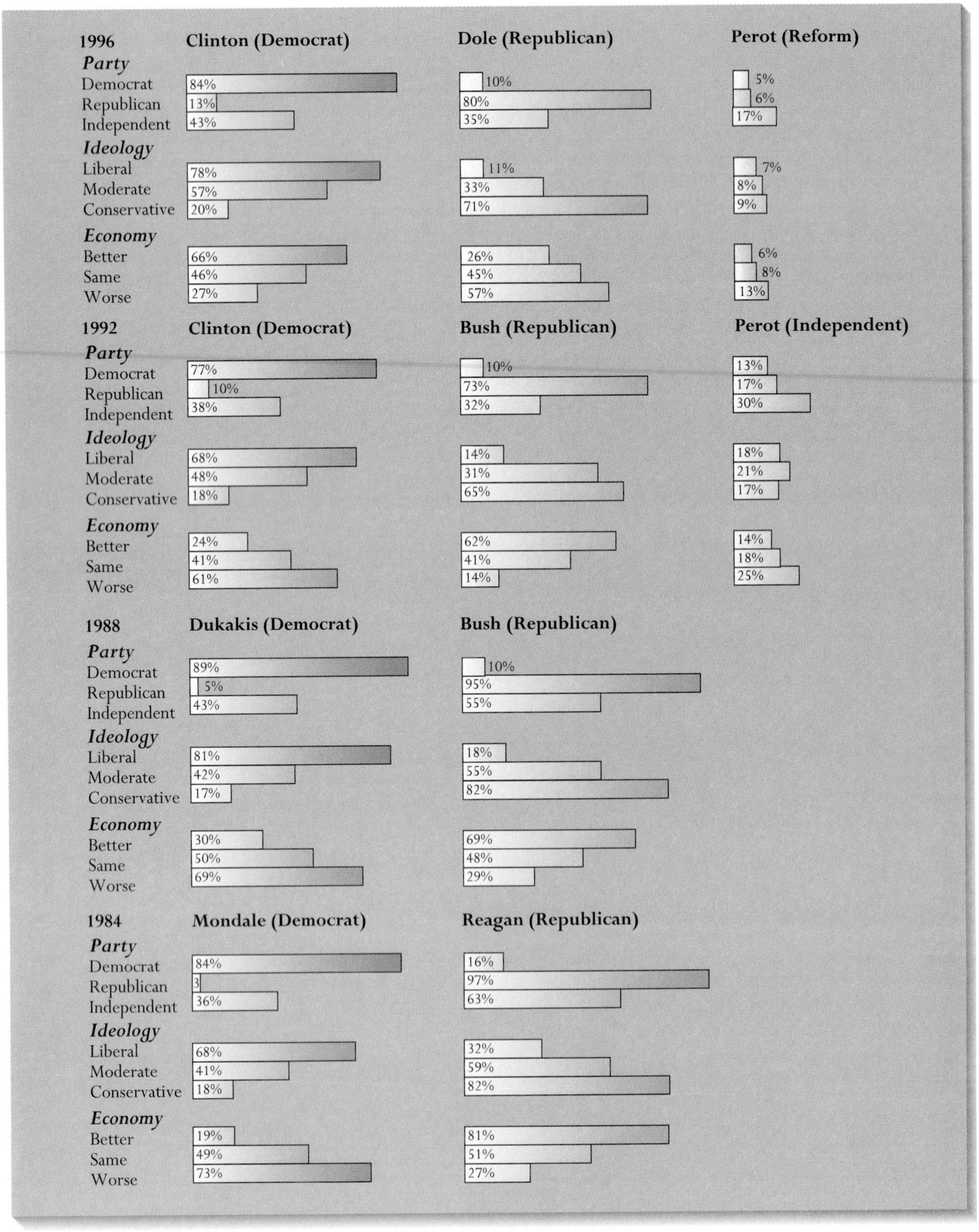

1996

	Clinton (Democrat)	Dole (Republican)	Perot (Reform)
Party			
Democrat	84%	10%	5%
Republican	13%	80%	6%
Independent	43%	35%	17%
Ideology			
Liberal	78%	11%	7%
Moderate	57%	33%	8%
Conservative	20%	71%	9%
Economy			
Better	66%	26%	6%
Same	46%	45%	8%
Worse	27%	57%	13%

1992

	Clinton (Democrat)	Bush (Republican)	Perot (Independent)
Party			
Democrat	77%	10%	13%
Republican	10%	73%	17%
Independent	38%	32%	30%
Ideology			
Liberal	68%	14%	18%
Moderate	48%	31%	21%
Conservative	18%	65%	17%
Economy			
Better	24%	62%	14%
Same	41%	41%	18%
Worse	61%	14%	25%

1988

	Dukakis (Democrat)	Bush (Republican)
Party		
Democrat	89%	10%
Republican	5%	95%
Independent	43%	55%
Ideology		
Liberal	81%	18%
Moderate	42%	55%
Conservative	17%	82%
Economy		
Better	30%	69%
Same	50%	48%
Worse	69%	29%

1984

	Mondale (Democrat)	Reagan (Republican)
Party		
Democrat	84%	16%
Republican	3	97%
Independent	36%	63%
Ideology		
Liberal	68%	32%
Moderate	41%	59%
Conservative	18%	82%
Economy		
Better	19%	81%
Same	49%	51%
Worse	73%	27%

FIGURE 8-7 Group Voting in Presidential Elections

Despite a great deal of attention in the popular press to a supposed gender gap in recent presidential elections, majorities of both women and men have given their support to the winning candidates. Likewise, voters in all age groups have basically followed the "majority-for-winner" formula. However, race, income, and education level do appear to influence voting patterns, with minorities, the poor, and those with little education voting heavily for Democratic candidates.

Source: Based on data from the Gallup poll surveys.

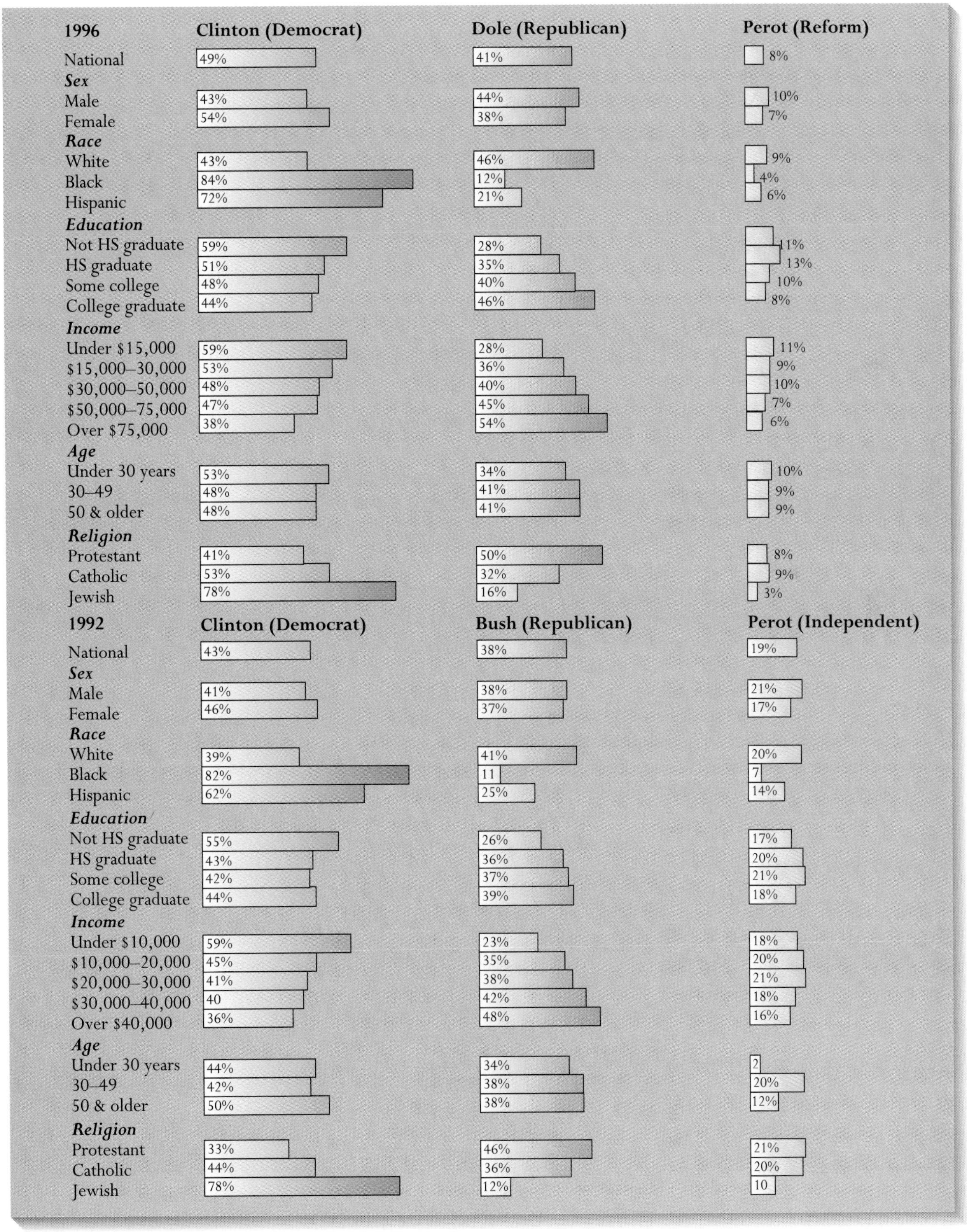

1996	Clinton (Democrat)	Dole (Republican)	Perot (Reform)
National	49%	41%	8%
Sex			
Male	43%	44%	10%
Female	54%	38%	7%
Race			
White	43%	46%	9%
Black	84%	12%	4%
Hispanic	72%	21%	6%
Education			
Not HS graduate	59%	28%	11%
HS graduate	51%	35%	13%
Some college	48%	40%	10%
College graduate	44%	46%	8%
Income			
Under $15,000	59%	28%	11%
$15,000–30,000	53%	36%	9%
$30,000–50,000	48%	40%	10%
$50,000–75,000	47%	45%	7%
Over $75,000	38%	54%	6%
Age			
Under 30 years	53%	34%	10%
30–49	48%	41%	9%
50 & older	48%	41%	9%
Religion			
Protestant	41%	50%	8%
Catholic	53%	32%	9%
Jewish	78%	16%	3%

1992	Clinton (Democrat)	Bush (Republican)	Perot (Independent)
National	43%	38%	19%
Sex			
Male	41%	38%	21%
Female	46%	37%	17%
Race			
White	39%	41%	20%
Black	82%	11	7
Hispanic	62%	25%	14%
Education			
Not HS graduate	55%	26%	17%
HS graduate	43%	36%	20%
Some college	42%	37%	21%
College graduate	44%	39%	18%
Income			
Under $10,000	59%	23%	18%
$10,000–20,000	45%	35%	20%
$20,000–30,000	41%	38%	21%
$30,000–40,000	40	42%	18%
Over $40,000	36%	48%	16%
Age			
Under 30 years	44%	34%	2
30–49	42%	38%	20%
50 & older	50%	38%	12%
Religion			
Protestant	33%	46%	21%
Catholic	44%	36%	20%
Jewish	78%	12%	10

Up Close

The Presidential Debates

Presidential debates attract more viewers than any other campaign activity. They produce vastly greater audiences than the candidates could garner by any other means. Most campaign activities—speeches, rallies, motorcades—reach only supporters. Such activities may inspire supporters to go to the polls, contribute money, and even work to get others to vote their way. But televised debates reach undecided voters as well as supporters, and they allow candidates to be seen by supporters of their opponent. Debates allow people to directly compare the responses of each candidate. Even if issues are not really discussed in depth, people see how presidential candidates react as human beings under pressure.

Kennedy-Nixon Televised presidential debates began in 1960 when John F. Kennedy and Richard M. Nixon confronted each other on a bare stage before an America watching on black-and-white TV sets. Nixon was the vice president in the popular presidential administration of Dwight Eisenhower; he was also an accomplished college debate-team member. He prepared for the debates as if they were college debates, memorizing facts and arguments. But he failed to realize that image triumphs over substance on television. Nixon was shifty-eyed and clearly in need of a shave or more makeup to hide his pronounced "five o'clock shadow." By contrast, Kennedy was handsome, cool, confident; whatever doubts the American people may have had regarding his youth and inexperience were dispelled by his polished manner. Radio listeners tended to think that Nixon won, and debate coaches scored him the winner. But television viewers preferred the glamorous young Kennedy. The polls shifted in Kennedy's direction after the debate, and he won in a very close general election. Nixon blamed his makeup man.

Carter-Ford President Lyndon Johnson avoided debating in 1964, and Nixon, having learned his lesson, declined to debate in 1968 and 1972. Thus televised presidential debates did not resume until 1976, when incumbent president Gerald Ford, perceiving he was behind in the polls, agreed to debate challenger Jimmy Carter. Ford made a series

of verbal slips—saying, for example, that the nations of Eastern Europe were free from Soviet domination. In that same year, the first vice presidential debate was held. In it, Republican Robert Dole's biting comments appeared mean-spirited in contrast to Democrat Walter Mondale's "Boy Scout" image. Both Carter and Mondale were widely perceived as having won their debates, and they went on to victory in the general election.

Reagan-Carter and Reagan-Mondale It was Ronald Reagan who demonstrated the true power of television. Reagan had lived his life in front of a camera. It was the principal tool of both of his trades—actor and politician. In 1980 incumbent president Jimmy Carter attempted to portray Reagan as a mean-spirited conservative ideologue who was a threat to peace. Carter talked rapidly and seriously about programs, figures, and budgets. But Reagan was master of the stage; he was relaxed, confident, joking. He appeared to treat the president of the United States as an overly aggressive, impulsive younger man, regrettably given to exaggeration ("There you go again."). When it was all over, it was clear to most viewers that Carter had been bested by a true professional in media skills.

However, in the first of two televised debates with Walter Mondale in 1984, Reagan's skills of a lifetime seemed to desert him. He stumbled over statistics and groped for words. Mondale was respectful of the presidency, somewhat stiff and ill at ease before the cameras but nevertheless clearheaded in his responses. Reagan's poor performance raised the only issue that might conceivably defeat him—his age. The president had looked and sounded *old*.

In preparation for the second debate, Reagan decided, without telling his aides, to lay the perfect trap for his questioners. When asked about his age and capacity to lead the nation, he responded with a serious deadpan expression to a hushed audience and waiting America: "I want you to know that I will not make age an issue in this campaign. I am not going to exploit for political purposes [pause] my opponent's youth and inexperience." The studio audience broke into uncontrolled laughter. Even Mondale had to laugh. With a classic one-liner, the president buried the age issue and won not only the debate but also the election.

Bush-Dukakis In 1988 Michael Dukakis ensured his defeat with a cold, detached performance in the presidential debates, beginning with the very first question. When CNN anchor Bernard Shaw asked, "Governor, if Kitty Dukakis were raped and murdered, would you favor an irrevocable death penalty for the killer?" The question demanded an emotional reply. Instead, Dukakis responded with an impersonal recitation of his stock positions on crime, drugs, and law enforcement. Bush seized the opportunity to establish an intimate, warm, and personal relationship with the viewers: "I do believe some crimes are so heinous, so brutal, so outrageous . . . I do believe in the death penalty." Voters responded to Bush, electing him.

Clinton-Bush-Perot The three-way presidential debates of 1992 drew the largest television audiences in the history of presidential debates. In the first debate, Ross Perot's Texas twang and down-home folksy style stole the show. Chided by his opponents for having no governmental experience, he shot back, "Well, they have a point. I don't have any experience in running up a $4 trillion dollar debt. I don't have any experience in gridlock government. I don't have any experience in creating the worst public school system in the industrialized world, the most violent crime-ridden society in the industrialized world. But I do have a lot of experience in getting things done." Perot's popularity in the polls, hardly visible at all

following his earlier abrupt withdrawal from the race, suddenly sprang to life again.

But it was Bill Clinton's smooth performance in the second debate, with its talk-show format, that seemed to wrap up the election. Ahead in the polls, Clinton appeared at ease walking about the stage and responding to audience questions with sympathy and sincerity. By contrast, George Bush appeared stiff and formal, and somewhat ill at ease with the "unpresidential" format. Bush made a modest comeback in the third and final debate with hard-hitting attacks on Clinton as a "waffler," but his modest recovery was too little and too late.

Clinton-Dole A desperate Bob Dole, running 20 points behind, faced a newly "presidential" Bill Clinton in their two 1996 debates. (Perot's poor standing in the polls led to his exclusion.) Dole tried to counter his image as a grumpy old man in the first encounter; his humor actually won more laughs from the audience than the president's more stately comments. Dole injected more barbs in the second debate, complaining of "ethical problems in the White House" and repeating the mantra "I keep my word," suggesting that Clinton did not. But Clinton remained cool and comfortable, ignoring the challenger and focusing on the nation's economic health. Viewers, most of whom were already in Clinton's court, judged him the winner of both debates.

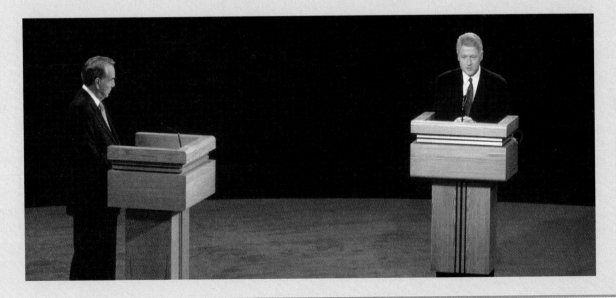

is, these groups have given a larger percentage of their vote to the Democratic or Republican candidates than the candidate received from the total electorate.

Among the more interesting group voting patterns is the serious *gender gap* affecting recent Republican candidates. Although Reagan won the women's vote in both 1980 and 1984, his vote percentages among men were considerably higher than among women. Bush lost the women's vote in both 1988 and 1992. In 1996 the gender gap widened, with a stunning 54 percent of women voting for Clinton as opposed to only 38 percent for Dole.[9] African Americans have long constituted the most loyal group of Democratic voters, regularly giving the Democratic presidential nominee 85 to 90 percent or more of their vote. The Hispanic vote is heavily Democratic, although a significant portion of Hispanics, notably Cuban Americans in Florida, are solidly Republican. Catholics are still more Democratic than Protestants, but Catholics favored Republican Ronald Reagan in 1980 and 1984. Catholics drifted back to the Democratic column in 1996.

Candidate Image   In an age of direct communication between candidates and voters via television, the image of candidates and their ability to relate to audiences have emerged as important determinants of voter choice. As party and group identifications have moderated and independent and middle-of-the-road identifications among voters have grown, the personal characteristics of candidates have become central to many voters. Indeed, the personal qualities of candidates are most important in the decision of less partisan, less ideological voters. Candidate image is most important in presidential contests, inasmuch as presidential candidates are personally more visible to the voter than candidates for lesser offices.[10]

It is difficult to identify exactly what personal qualities appeal most to voters. Warmth, compassion, strength, confidence, honesty, sincerity, good humor, appearance, and "character" all seem important. "Character" has become a central feature of media coverage of candidates (see Chapter 6). Reports of extramarital affairs, experimentation with drugs, draft dodging, cheating in college, shady financial dealings, conflicts of interest, or lying or misrepresenting facts receive heavy media coverage because they attract large audiences. But it is difficult to estimate how many voters are swayed by so-called character issues.

Attractive personal qualities can win support from opposition-party identifiers and people who disagree on the issues. John F. Kennedy's handsome and youthful appearance, charm, self-confidence, and disarming good humor defeated the heavy-jowled, shifty-eyed, defensive, and ill-humored Richard Nixon. Ronald Reagan's folksy mannerisms, warm humor, and comfortable rapport with television audiences justly earned him the title "The Great Communicator." Reagan disarmed his critics by laughing at his own personal flubs—falling asleep at meetings, forgetting names—and by telling his own age jokes. His personal appeal won more Democratic voters than any other Republican candidate has won in modern history, and he won the votes of many people who disagreed with him on the issues.

An important reservation regarding image voting: although many voters cite favorable or unfavorable personal characteristics of the candidates as the reason for their vote, it turns out that Democratic voters usually perceive favorable attributes in Democratic candidates and unfavorable attributes in Republican candidates, and Republican voters see just the opposite. In other words, the voters' perceptions of the candidates' personal qualities are influenced by the voters' party identifications and perhaps by their group affiliations as well. Thus evaluations of the candidates' personal characteristics may not be a significant independent determinant of voter choice, especially for people who identify themselves as strong Democrats or Republicans.

TABLE 8-3	Issues the Voters Cared about in 1996			
		Presidential Vote of Those Who Listed Issue as "Most Important"		
Rank	*Issue*	*Clinton*	*Dole*	*Perot*
1	Economy/jobs	60%	28%	10%
2	Medicare/Social Security	69	24	6
3	Taxes	18	75	6
4	Deficit	29	53	17
5	Education	79	16	3
6	Foreign policy	30	60	9

The Economy   Fairly accurate predictions of voting outcomes in presidential elections can be made from models of the American economy. Economic conditions at election time—recent growth or decline in personal income, the unemployment rate, consumer confidence, and so on—are related to the vote given the incumbent versus the challenger. Ever since the once-popular Republican incumbent Herbert Hoover was trounced by Franklin Roosevelt as the Great Depression of the 1930s deepened, politicians have understood that voters hold the incumbent party responsible for hard economic times.

Perhaps no other lesson has been as well learned by politicians: Hard economic times hurt incumbents and favor challengers. The economy may not be the only important factor in presidential voting, but it is certainly a factor of great importance. Some evidence indicates that it is not voters' *own* personal economic well-being that affects their vote but rather voter perception of *general* economic conditions. People who perceive the economy as getting worse are likely to vote against the incumbent party, whereas people who think the economy is getting better support the incumbent.[11] Thus voters who thought the economy was getting *worse* in 1992 supported challenger Bill Clinton over incumbent president George Bush. And more than twice as many people thought the economy was getting worse in that year than getting better. But the reverse was true in 1996; more people thought the economy was *better*, and the people who thought so voted heavily for incumbent Bill Clinton.

Issue Voting   Casting one's vote exclusively on the basis of the policy positions of the candidates is rare. Most voters are unaware of the specific positions taken by candidates on the issues. Indeed, voters often believe that their preferred candidate agrees with them on the issues, even when this is not the case. In other words, voters project their own policy views onto their favorite candidate more often than they decide to vote for a candidate because of his or her position on the issues.

However, when asked specifically about issues, voters are willing to name those they care most about. Voters do not always make their choices based on a candidate's stated policy positions, but voters *do* strongly favor candidates whose policy views they assume match their own. Only when a key issue takes center stage do voters really become aware of what the candidates actually propose to do. In the 1992 and 1996 elections, the economy was the issue that voters cared about most. In both elections, Clinton won the votes of the people most concerned about the economy (see Table 8-3). Clinton also won the strong support of people (especially senior citizens) concerned with Medicare and Social Security, as well as people concerned about education. Taxes, the deficit, and foreign policy were Bob Dole's best issues.

Politics in Cyberspace

Campaigns and Elections

Political campaigns can be followed on the Internet in several ways. For current political news, try CNN's allpolitics.com site. During a campaign, virtually all candidates for national office maintain a personal home page. These can usually be located through standard search engines using candidates names. To track campaign contributions to individual candidates for federal office, contact the Federal Elections Commission. A Washington think tank, the Center for Responsive Politics, specializes in providing information about the role that money plays in elections.

Federal Elections Commission
http://www.fec.gov

This site contains up-to-date information about candidates, parties and political action committees, databases for presidential and congressional elec-

tions, and a citizen's guide to campaign contributions and the law.

Emily's List
http://www.emilyslist.org

The Emily's list Web site identifies liberal pro-choice women candidates for federal and state offices and supports them by encouraging contributions to their campaigns and mobilizing women to vote for them.

Center for Responsive Politics
http://www.crp.org

The center's Web site is a gold mine of information regarding campaign finance. It provides specific, detailed, and researchable data bases on democratic and republican party contributions, PAC contributions, and corporate and individual contributors. It also provides the personal financial disclosure reports of each member of the U.S. House and Senate.

SUMMARY NOTES

- In a democracy, elections decide "who governs." But they also indirectly affect public policy, influencing "who gets what."

- Although winning candidates often claim a mandate for their policy proposals, in reality few campaigns present clear policy alternatives to the voters, few voters cast their ballots on the basis of policy considerations, and the policy preferences of the electorate can seldom be determined from election outcomes.

- Nevertheless, voters can influence future policy directions through retrospective judgments about the performance of incumbents, returning them to office or turning them out. Most retrospective voting appears to center on the economy.

- Personal ambition for power and celebrity drives the decision to seek public office. Political entrepreneurship, professionalism, and careerism have come to dominate political recruitment; lawyers have traditionally dominated American politics.

- Incumbents begin campaigns with many advantages: name recognition, financial support, goodwill from services they perform for constituents, large-scale public projects they bring to their districts, and the other resources of office.

- Campaigning for office is largely a media activity, dominated by professional advertising specialists, fund raisers, media consultants, and pollsters.

- The professionalization of campaigning and the heavy costs of a media campaign drive up the costs of running for office. These huge costs make candidates heavily dependent on financial support from individuals and organizations. Fund raising occupies more of a candidate's time than any other campaign activity.

- Campaign contributions are made by politically active individuals and organizations, including political action committees. Many contributions are made in order to gain access to policy makers and assistance with government business. Some contributors are ideologically motivated; others merely seek to rub shoulders with powerful people.

- Presidential primary election strategies emphasize appeals to party activists and core supporters, including the more ideologically motivated primary voters.
- In the general election campaign, presidential candidates usually seek to broaden their appeal to moder-

ate, centrist voters while holding on to their core supporters. Campaigns must focus on states where the candidate has the best chance of gaining the 270 electoral votes needed to win.

- Voter choice is influenced by party identification, group membership, perceived image of the candidates, economic conditions, and, to a lesser extent, ideology and issue preferences.

SELECTED READINGS

ABRAMSON, PAUL R., JOHN H. ALDRICH, and DAVID W. RHODE. *Change and Continuity in the 1996 Elections.* An in-depth analysis of the 1996 presidential and congressional elections assessing the impact of party loyalties, presidential performance, group memberships, and policy preferences on voter choice.

FIORINA, MORRIS P. *Retrospective Voting in American National Elections.* Princeton, N.J.: Princeton University Press, 1988. Argues that retrospective judgments guide voter choice in presidential elections.

FLANAGAN, WILLIAM H., and NANCY H. ZINGALE. *Political Behavior of the American Electorate.* 9th ed. Washington, D.C.: Congressional Quarterly Press, 1998. A brief but comprehensive summary of the extensive research literature on the effects of party identification, opinion, ideology, the media, and candidate image on voter choice and election outcomes.

GAIS, THOMAS L., and MICHAEL J. MALBIN. *The Day after Reform: Sobering Campaign Finance Lessons from the American States.* New York: Rockefeller Institute Press, 1997. A fifty-state survey of campaign finance laws with evaluations and recommendations for national reform.

IYENGAR, SHANTO, and STEPHEN ANSOLABEHERE. *Going Negative: How Political Advertisements Shrink and Polarize the Electorate.* New York: Free Press, 1996. The real problem with negative political ads is not that they sway voters to support one candidate over another, but that they reinforce the belief that all are dishonest and cynical.

MATALIN, MARY, and JAMES CARVILLE. *All's Fair: Love, War and Running for President.* New York: Random House and Simon & Schuster, 1994. Inside the presidential campaign of George Bush and Bill Clinton in 1992 by their respective campaign directors, who were romantically involved and were married after the campaign.

ROSENSTONE, STEVEN. *Forecasting Presidential Elections.* New Haven, Conn.: Yale University Press, 1985. A discussion of the models employed to forecast presidential election outcomes based on unemployment, inflation, and personal income statistics.

SABATO, LARRY J., and GLENN R. SIMPSON. *Dirty Little Secrets: The Persistence of Corruption in American Politics.* New York: Random House Times Books, 1996. A political scientist and a journalist combine to produce a lurid report on unethical and corrupt practices in campaigns and elections.

SORAUF, FRANK J. *Inside Campaign Finance.* New Haven, Conn.: Yale University Press, 1992. A comprehensive description of campaign financing in America, individual contributions, PACs, party funds, independent organizations, soft money, intermediaries and brokers, and so on, together with a balanced appraisal of the prospects and potential consequences of reform.

Chapter

9

INTEREST GROUPS GETTING THEIR SHARE AND MORE

What role do interest groups play in politics? Their organization, their money, and their influence in Washington raise the possibility that interest groups, rather than individuals, may in fact hold the real power in politics. They may be the "who" that determines the "what" that the rest of us get.

CHAPTER OUTLINE

FEATURES

INTEREST-GROUP POWER

Organization is a means to power—to determining who gets what in society. Interest groups are organizations that seek to influence government policy. Organization concentrates power, and concentrated power prevails over unorganized interests. The First Amendment to the Constitution recognizes "the right of the people peaceably to assemble, and to petition the government for a redress of grievances." Americans thus enjoy a fundamental right to organize themselves to influence government.

Electoral versus Interest-Group Systems   The *electoral system* is organized to represent geographically defined constituencies—states and congressional districts in Congress. The *interest-group system* is organized to represent economic, professional, ideological, religious, racial, gender, and issue constituencies.[1] In other words, the interest-group system supplements the electoral system by providing people with another avenue of participation. Individuals may participate in politics by supporting candidates and parties in elections, and also by joining **interest groups**, organizations that pressure government to advance their interests.

Interest-group activity provides more direct representation of policy preferences than electoral politics. At best, individual voters can influence government policy only indirectly through elections (see Chapter 8). Elected politicians try to represent many different—and even occasionally conflicting—interests. But interest groups provide concentrated and direct representation of policy views in government.

Checking Majoritarianism   The interest-group system gives voice to special interests, whereas parties and the electoral system cater to the majority interest. Indeed, interest groups are often defended as a check on **majoritarianism**, the tendency of democratic governments to allow the faint preferences of a majority to prevail over the intense feelings of minorities. However, the interest-group system is frequently attacked because it obstructs the majority from implementing its preferences in public policy. Interest-group power was once described and defended by a California state senator:

> About 90 percent of all legislation is conceived by special interests. It is merchandised by special interests. And probably less than 5 percent is inspired by governors, by individual legislators, by government itself. You say "Oh, isn't that evil!" The answer is, hell no, it isn't evil. That's what democracy is all about.[2]

Concentrating Benefits While Dispersing Costs   Interest groups seek special benefits, subsidies, privileges, and protections from the government. The costs of these *concentrated* benefits are usually *dispersed* to all taxpayers, none of whom individually bears enough added cost to merit spending time, energy, or money to organize a group to oppose the benefit. Thus the interest-group system concentrates benefits to the few and disperses costs to the many. The system favors small, well-organized, homogeneous interests that seek the expansion of government activity at the expense of larger but less well-organized citizen-taxpayers. Over long periods of time, the cumulative activities of many special-interest groups, each seeking concentrated benefits to themselves and dispersed costs to others, result in what has been termed

interest groups   Organizations that seek to influence government policy.

majoritarianism   Tendency of democratic governments to allow the faint preferences of the majority to prevail over the intense feelings of minorities.

From (a) the Whiskey Rebellion of 1794 to (b) violent early union protests like the Haymarket Riot of 1886 to (c) Carrie Nation's battle to ban liquor and (d) the women's suffrage movement of the late nineteenth and early twentieth centuries to (e) the civil rights marches of the 1960s and (f) the gay rights marches of the 1990s, protest has had a long and strong history for interest groups in the United States. Some protests have been violent and others peaceful, but by addressing key issues of the time, all have prompted public debate and many have resulted in changes in public policy.

Up Close

Superlobby: The Business Roundtable

The Business Roundtable was established in 1972 "in the belief that business executives should take an increased role in the continuing debates about public policy." The organization is composed of the chief executives of the 200 largest corporations in America and is financed through corporate membership fees. For many years, the U.S. Chamber of Commerce, the National Association of Manufacturers, the Business Council, and hundreds of industry associations such as the powerful American Petroleum Institute had represented business in traditional interest-group fashion. Why did business create this superorganization? The Business Roundtable itself says:

The answer is that business leaders believed there was a need that was not being filled, and they invented the Roundtable to fill it. They wanted an organization in which the chief executive officers of

leading enterprises take positions and advocate those positions. . . . The Roundtable therefore was formed with two major goals:

1. to enable chief executives from different corporations to work together to analyze specific issues affecting the economy and business; and
2. to present government and the public with knowledgeable, timely information, and with practical, positive suggestions for action.*

In brief, traditional interest-group representation was inadequate for the nation's top corporate leadership. It wished to come together *itself* to decide on public policy and press its views in Washington.

The power of the Business Roundtable stems in part from its "firm rule" that a corporate chief executive officer (CEO) cannot send a substitute to its meetings. Moreover, corporate CEOs lobby the Congress in person rather than sending paid lobbyists. Members of Congress are impressed when the chair of IBM appears at a congressional hearing on business regulation or when the chair of GTE speaks

---

organizational sclerosis, a society so encrusted with subsidies, benefits, regulations, protections, and special treatments for organized groups that work, productivity, and investment are discouraged and everyone's standard of living is lowered.

ORIGINS OF INTEREST GROUPS

James Madison viewed interest groups—which he called "factions"—as a necessary evil in politics. He defined a faction as "a number of citizens, whether amounting to a majority or a minority of the whole, who are united and actuated by some common impulse of passion, or of interest, adverse to the rights of other citizens, or to the permanent and aggregate interests of the community." He believed that interest groups not only conflict with each other but, more important, also conflict with the common good. Nevertheless, Madison believed that the origin of interest groups was to be found in human nature—"a zeal for different opinions concerning religion, concerning government, and many other points"—and therefore impossible to eliminate from politics.[3]

Protecting Economic Interests Madison believed that "the most common and durable source of factions, has been the various and unequal distribution of prop-

organizational sclerosis
Society encrusted with so many special benefits to interest groups that everyone's standard of living is lowered.

to a congressional committee about taxation, or when the chair of Prudential talks to Congress about Social Security, or when the head of B. F. Goodrich testifies before the Senate Judiciary Committee about antitrust policy. One congressional staff member explained, "If a corporation sends its Washington representative to our office, he's probably going to be shunted over to a legislative assistant. But the chairman of the board is going to get in to see the senator." Another aide echoed those sentiments: "Very few members of Congress would not meet with the president of a Business Roundtable corporation."[†]

The work of the Business Roundtable is organized by means of task forces on various issues of priority to its members. For example, there are task forces on education, the environment, government regulation, health, the federal budget, international trade, taxation, and welfare.

The Business Roundtable has experienced both victories and defeats in Congress. During the Ford and Carter administrations, the Roundtable successfully opposed the creation of a new federal consumer protec-

tion agency comparable to the Environmental Protection Agency. During the Reagan years, the Roundtable was at the forefront of "deregulation" and tax cutting. But the Roundtable lost a lengthy battle over mandated family leaves in 1993 when the Congress sent the Family Leave Act to President Bill Clinton to sign as his first major legislative victory. The Roundtable also was defeated in its opposition to the expansion of the Clean Air Act of 1990, which it believes imposes excessive compliance costs on industry and handicaps American corporations in global competition. And the Roundtable is regularly defeated in efforts to reform the nation's liability laws; its principal opponent in this struggle has been the Association of Trial Lawyers, some of whose members sit in the Congress itself. So even with all of its prestige and resources, the Business Roundtable does not win all of its battles.

---

[*]Quotations about the reasons for the establishment of the Business Roundtable from Business Roundtable public statement, "What the Roundtable Is," January 1988.

[†]*Time*, April 13, 1981, pp. 76–77.

erty." With genuine insight, he identified *economic interests* as the most prevalent in politics: "a landed interest, a manufacturing interest, a mercantile interest, a moneyed interest, with many lesser interests."[‡] From Madison's era to the present, businesspeople and professionals, bankers and insurers, farmers and factory workers, merchants and shippers have organized themselves to press their demands on government (see *Up Close:* "Superlobby: The Business Roundtable").

Advancing Social Movements   Major social movements in American history have spawned many interest groups. Abolitionist groups were formed before the Civil War to fight slavery. The National Association for the Advancement of Colored People (NAACP) emerged in 1910 to fight segregation laws and to rally public support against lynching and other violence against African Americans. Farm organizations emerged from the populist movement of the late nineteenth century to press demands for railroad rate regulation and easier credit terms. The small trade unions that workers formed in the nineteenth century to improve their pay and working conditions gave way to large national unions in the 1930s as workers sought protection for the rights to organize, bargain collectively, and strike. The success of the women's suffrage movement led to the formation of the League of Women Voters in the early twentieth century, and a generation later the feminist movement inspired the National Organization for Women (NOW).

Marian Wright Edelman, Lobbying for the Poor

As founder and president of the Children's Defense Fund, Marian Wright Edelman has become legendary in Washington as a persuasive and persistent lobbyist on behalf of civil rights and social welfare legislation. A close friend of the Kennedy family, Edelman regularly testifies at Senate committee hearings, providing rapid-fire statistics on the effects of poverty on African American children. Each year the Children's Defense Fund, with a staff of more than a hundred in its Washington headquarters and an $8 million annual budget, produces numerous reports on infant mortality, homelessness, prenatal care, child nutrition, drug use, child abuse, teenage pregnancy, and single-parent households.

Marian Wright grew up in segregated rural South Carolina, the academically gifted daughter of a Baptist minister with a strong commitment to social justice. At an early age, she worked at the Wright House for the Aged, which her father had established. She entered all-black Spelman College in Atlanta and studied abroad at the Sorbonne in Paris and the University of Geneva, intending to take up a career in the foreign service. But Wright changed her career plans when she became involved in the early civil rights struggles in Atlanta. After graduating from Spelman, she entered Yale Law School to prepare herself in civil rights law. Upon her graduation in 1963, she immediately went to work for the National Association for the Advancement of Colored People

Legal Defense Fund and traveled to Mississippi, where for four years she undertook the dangerous work of defending civil rights workers. In 1967 she met Peter Edelman, a Harvard Law School graduate and legislative aide to Senator Robert Kennedy; together they persuaded Kennedy to personally tour the most poverty-stricken areas of the Mississippi Delta, where the senator directly confronted hungry children living in miserable conditions.

The following year Wright and Edelman were married and settled in Washington, where she established the Washington Research Project, a public-interest research and lobbying organization on behalf of President Lyndon Johnson's War on Poverty. She maintained her Washington base even while directing the Harvard University Center for Law and Education during the several years that her husband served as vice president of the University of Massachusetts. In 1973 she organized the Children's Defense Fund in Washington with the support of private foundation grants and government grants and contracts. Part think tank and part lobbying organization, the Children's Defense Fund describes itself as an advocate for millions of "voiceless and voteless," neglected and abused, poor children. It was the principal lobbying group behind the Head Start program as well as federal child care and family leave legislation.

Marian Wright Edelman is especially effective as an advocate of social welfare programs with her lively style, sense of urgency, and wealth of information about children in poverty. "The real joy comes from achieving results, when you really see you've got a law that will protect children from being abused, that will provide them with proper health care and dental care. My greatest reward will be seeing thirteen million poor children lifted out of poverty."*

*New York Times, February 27, 1986, p. A10.

Seeking Government Benefits As government expands its activities, it creates more interest groups. Wars create veterans' organizations. The first large veterans' group—the Grand Army of the Republic—formed after the Civil War and successfully lobbied for bonus payments to veterans over the years. Today the American Legion, the Veterans of Foreign Wars, and the Vietnam Veterans of America engage in lobbying the Congress and monitor the activities of the Department of Veterans Affairs. As the welfare state grew, so did organizations seeking to obtain benefits for their members, including the nation's largest interest group, the American

Association of Retired Persons (AARP). Over time, organizations seeking to protect and expand welfare benefits for the poor also emerged (see *People in Politics:* "Marian Wright Edelman, Lobbying for the Poor"). Federal grant-in-aid programs to state and local governments inspired the development of governmental interest groups—the Council of State Governments, the National League of Cities, the National Governors Association, the U.S. Conference of Mayors, and so on—so that it is not uncommon today to see governments lobby other governments. Expanded government support for education led to political activity by the National Education Association, the American Federation of Teachers, the American Association of Land Grant Colleges and Universities, and other educational groups.

Responding to Government Regulation As more businesses and professions came under government regulation in the twentieth century, more organizations formed to protect their interests, including such large and powerful groups as the American Medical Association (doctors), the American Bar Association (lawyers), and the National Association of Broadcasters (broadcasters). Indeed, the issue of regulation—whether of public utilities, interstate transportation, mine safety, medicines, or children's pajamas—always causes the formation of interest groups. Some form to demand regulation; others form to protect their members from regulatory burdens.

THE ORGANIZED INTERESTS IN WASHINGTON

The Washington, D.C., telephone directory lists hundreds of organizations with their own offices in the capital and hundreds of additional firms of paid lawyers and lobbyists. Trade and professional associations and corporations have the most lobbies in Washington, but unions, public-interest groups, farm groups, and organized interests representing minorities, women, and the elderly also recognize that they need to be "where the action is." There are more than 22,000 national nonprofit organizations in the United States, several thousand of which are officially registered in Washington as lobbyists.[5] Among this huge assortment of organizations, many of which are very influential in their highly specialized fields, are a number of well-known interest groups. Even a partial list of organized interest groups provides some idea of both the depth and the breadth of such associations in U.S. political life and of the complexities facing modern legislators in trying to please such vastly different groups (see Table 9-1).

Business and Trade Organizations Traditionally, economic organizations have dominated interest-group politics in Washington. There is ample evidence that economic interests continue to play a major role in national policy making, despite the rapid growth over the last several decades of consumer and environmental organizations. Certainly in terms of the sheer number of organizations with offices and representatives in Washington, business and professional groups and occupational and trade associations predominate. More than half of the organizations with offices in Washington are business or trade associations, and another 15 percent are professional associations.

Business interests are represented, first of all, by large inclusive organizations, such as the U.S. Chamber of Commerce, representing thousands of local chambers

TABLE 9-1	Major Organized Interest Groups, by Type

Business

Business Roundtable
National Association of Manufacturers
National Federation of Independent
  Businesses
National Small Business Association
U.S. Chamber of Commerce

Trade

American Bankers Association
American Gas Association
American Iron and Steel Institute
American Petroleum Institute
American Truckers Association
Automobile Dealers Association
Home Builders Association
Motion Picture Association of America
National Association of Broadcasters
National Association of Real Estate
  Boards

Professional

American Bar Association
American Medical Association
Association of Trial Lawyers
National Education Association

Union

AFL-CIO
American Federation of State, County,
  and Municipal Employees
American Federation of Teachers
International Brotherhood of Teamsters
International Ladies' Garment Work-
  ers Union
National Association of Letter Carriers
United Auto Workers
United Steel Workers
United Postal Workers

Agricultural

American Farm Bureau Federation
National Cattlemen's Association

National Farmers Union
National Grange
National Milk Producers Federation
Tobacco Institute

Women

League of Women Voters
National Organization for Women

Public Interest

Common Cause
Consumer Federation of America
Public Citizen
Public Interest Research Groups

Ideological

American Conservative Union
Americans for Constitutional Action
  (conservative)
Americans for Democratic Action
  (liberal)
People for the American Way (liberal)
National Conservative Political Action
  Committee (conservative)

Single Issue

Mothers against Drunk Driving
National Abortion Rights Action
  League
National Rifle Association
National Right-to-Life Committee
Planned Parenthood Federation of
  America
National Taxpayers Union

Environmental

Environmental Defense Fund
Greenpeace
National Wildlife Federation
Natural Resources Defense Council
Nature Conservancy
Sierra Club
Wilderness Society

Religious

American-Israeli Public Affairs
  Committee
Anti-Defamation League of B'nai B'rith
Christian Coalition
National Council of Churches
U.S. Catholic Conference

Civil Rights

American Civil Liberties Union
American Indian Movement
Mexican-American Legal Defense and
  Education Fund
National Association for the Advance-
  ment of Colored People
National Urban League
Rainbow Coalition
Southern Christian Leadership Confer-
  ence

Age Related

American Association of Retired
  Persons
Children's Defense Fund

Veterans

American Legion
Veterans of Foreign Wars
Vietnam Veterans of America

Defense

Air Force Association
American Security Council
Army Association
Navy Association

Government

National Association of Counties
National Conference of State Legisla-
  tors
National Governors Association
National League of Cities
U.S. Conference of Mayors

of commerce across the nation; the National Association of Manufacturers; the Business Roundtable, representing the nation's largest corporations; and the National Federation of Independent Businesses, representing small business. Specific business interests are also represented by thousands of **trade associations**. These associations can closely monitor the interests of their specialized memberships.

trade associations Interest groups composed of businesses in specific industries.

Among the most powerful of these associations are the American Bankers Association, the American Gas Association, the American Iron and Steel Institute, the National Association of Real Estate Boards, the American Petroleum Institute, and the National Association of Broadcasters. In addition, many individual corporations and firms achieve representation in Washington by opening their own lobbying offices or by hiring experienced professional lobbying and law firms.

Professional Associations   Professional associations rival business and trade organizations in lobbying influence. The American Bar Association (ABA), the American Medical Association (AMA), and the National Education Association (NEA) are three of the most influential groups in Washington. For example, the American Bar Association, which includes virtually all of the nation's practicing attorneys, and its more specialized offspring, the American Association of Trial Lawyers, have successfully resisted efforts to reform the nation's tort laws (see "America Drowning in a Sea of Lawsuits," Chapter 13).

Many years ago, the AMA fought against national health insurance plans, arguing that socialized medicine would erode quality medical care. But when Medicare for the aged and Medicaid for the poor were pushed forward by President Lyndon Johnson in 1965, the AMA switched tactics, supporting the legislation as a means of bringing vast sums of tax money into the nation's health care system. The strategy proved immensely profitable: Medicare and Medicaid are the fastest growing programs in the federal budget, contributing heavily to medical cost inflation. Government payments also now account for nearly one-third of the average doctor's income. In recent years, the AMA and other powerful lobbies such as the Health Insurance Association of America have fought government efforts to regulate costs and practices. The AMA has been forced to accept government payment schedules for various procedures, but the cost of physicians' care continues to rise as more procedures are prescribed. The AMA remains vigorously opposed to any limits on physicians' decisions about care for their patients. Only about 45 percent of the nation's physicians are members of the AMA, down from nearly 75 percent thirty years ago. Many physicians believe they are better represented by more specialized medical groups (for example, the American College of Surgeons, the American Academy of Family Physicians, the American Society of Internal Medicine), especially in negotiations over government fee schedules for particular procedures.

Organized Labor   Labor organizations have declined in membership over the last several decades. The percentage of the nonagricultural work force belonging to unions has declined from about 35 percent in the 1950s to less than 15 percent today. This decline has occurred primarily as a result of changes in the economy: rapid growth of professional, managerial, finance, technical, sales, and service employment, where unions are weakest; and slower growth or stagnation of manufacture, mining, and construction employment, where unions are strongest. Yet even in manufacturing, union membership today is only about 20 percent of the work force.

Nevertheless, labor unions remain a major political influence in Congress and the Democratic Party. The AFL-CIO is a federation of more than one hundred separate unions with more than 14 million members. The AFL-CIO has long maintained a large and capable lobbying staff in Washington, and it provides both financial contributions and campaign services (registration, get-out-the-vote, information, endorsements) for members of Congress it favors. Many of the larger individual unions also maintain offices in Washington and offer campaign contributions and services.

Farm Organizations   Even though the farm population of the United States has declined from about 25 percent of the total population in the 1930s to less than 3 percent today, farmers—especially large agricultural producers—remain a very potent political force in Washington. Agricultural interests are organized both into large inclusive groups, such as the American Farm Bureau Federation and the National Grange, and into very effective specialized groups, such as the National Milk Producers and the National Cattlemen's Association. Small and low-income farmers are represented by the National Farmers Union.

Women's Organizations   Women's organizations date back to the antislavery societies in pre–Civil War America. The first generation of feminists—Lucretia Mott, Elizabeth Cady Stanton, Lucy Stone, and Susan B. Anthony—learned to organize, hold public meetings, and conduct petition campaigns as abolitionists. After the Civil War, women were successful in changing many state laws that abridged the property rights of married women and otherwise treated them as "chattel" (property) of their husbands. Women were also prominent in the Anti-Saloon League, which succeeded in outlawing prostitution and gambling in every state except Nevada and provided a major source of support for the Eighteenth Amendment (Prohibition). In the early twentieth century, the feminist movement concentrated on obtaining the vote (suffrage) for women. Today the League of Women Voters—a broad-based organization that provides information to voters—backs registration and get-out-the-vote drives and generally supports measures seeking to ensure honesty and integrity in government.

Interest in feminist politics revived in the wake of the civil rights movement of the 1960s. New organizations sprang up to compete with the conventional activities of the League of Women Voters by taking a more activist stance toward women's issues. The largest of these organizations is the National Organization for Women (NOW), founded in 1966.

Religious Groups   Churches and religious groups have a long history of involvement in American politics—from the pre–Civil War antislavery crusades, to the prohibition effort in the early twentieth century, to the civil rights movement of the 1960s. The leadership for the historic Civil Rights Act of 1964 came from the Reverend Martin Luther King, Jr., and his Southern Christian Leadership Conference. Today religious groups span the political spectrum, from liberal organizations such as the National Council of Churches and Anti-Defamation League of B'nai B'rith, to conservative and fundamentalist organizations, such as the Christian Coalition, often referred to as the "religious right" (see *Up Close:* "The Christian Coalition: Organizing the Faithful").

Public-Interest Groups   **Public-interest groups** claim to represent broad classes of people—consumers, voters, reformers, or the public as a whole. Groups with lofty-sounding names, such as Common Cause, Public Citizen, and the Consumer Federation of America, perceive themselves as balancing the narrow, "selfish" interests of business organizations, trade associations, unions, and other "special" interests. Public-interest groups generally lobby for greater government regulation of consumer products, public safety, campaign finance, and so on. Their reform agenda, as well as their call for a larger regulatory role for government, makes them frequent allies of liberal ideological groups, civil rights organizations, and environmental groups. Many public-interest groups were initially formed in

public-interest groups
Interest groups that claim to represent broad classes of people or the public as a whole.

Up Close

The Christian Coalition: Organizing the Faithful

Christian fundamentalists, whose religious beliefs are based on a literal reading of the Bible, have become a more significant political force in the United States through effective organization. Perhaps the most influential Christian fundamentalist organization today is the Christian Coalition with nearly 2 million active members throughout the country. Its former director, Ralph Reed, expresses the importance of organization: "You have to organize, organize, organize, and build and build, and train and train, so that there is a permanent vibrant structure of which people can be a part."*

Fundamentalist Christians are opposed to abortion, pornography, and homosexuality; they favor the recognition of religion in public life, including prayer in schools; and they despair at the decline of traditional family values in American culture, including motion pictures and television broadcasting. Historically fundamentalist Protestant churches avoided politics as profane and concentrated evangelical efforts on saving individual souls. Their few ventures into worldly politics—notably the prohibition movement in the early twentieth century—ended in defeat. Their strength tended to be in the southern, rural, and poorer regions of the country. They were widely ridiculed on the national media.

In the 1960s, television evangelism emerged as a religious force in the United States. The Reverend Pat Robertson founded the Christian Broadcasting Network (CBN) to air his popular *700 Club* and later purchased the Family Channel. But efforts by social conservatives to build a "moral majority" for political action largely failed, as did Robertson's presidential candidacy in 1988. Televangelists, including Jerry Falwell and Tammy Fay Baker, suffered popular disdain following some well-publicized scandals. As president, Ronald Reagan gave symbolic support to the political agenda of social and religious conservatives but concentrated instead on the concerns of economic conservatives (for deregulation and tax reduction) and anticommunist conservatives (for a military buildup and challenge to the Soviet Union).

Robertson eventually turned over his embattled political organization, the Christian Coalition, to a young, energetic, professional political organizer, Ralph Reed.

Under Reed's direction, the Christian Coalition rose in political influence across the country—in local politics, school board elections, state legislative and governors' races, and congressional politics. Building from the grass roots, in local communities and churches, Reed made the Christian Coalition perhaps the most powerful religious-based lobby in the nation. Although officially nonpartisan, the coalition represents an important force in Republican politics; religious fundamentalists may constitute as much as one-third of the party's voter support. The Christian Coalition does not officially endorse candidates, but its voter guides clearly indicate which candidates reflect the coalition's position on major issues. The distribution of more than 33 million of these guides, mostly in churches on the weekend before the Tuesday election, was credited with helping Republicans capture control of Congress in 1994. The political influence of the Christian Coalition in Republican politics, and the "religious right" generally, ensures that most GOP candidates for public office publicly express support for a "profamily" agenda. Indeed, the Christian Coalition issued its own "Contract with the American Family," following the lead of the Newt Gingrich–inspired "Contract with America," that summarizes the policy views of the coalition and many religious fundamentalists. These views included a constitutional amendment allowing prayer in public schools; vouchers for parents to send their children to private, religious schools; tax credits to families with children; banning late-term abortions as well as banning the use of taxpayer funds to pay for abortions; restrictions on pornography on cable television and the Internet; and a requirement that criminals make restitution to their victims after release. According to Reed, fundamentalist Christians "have finally gained a place at the table, a sense of legitimacy, and a voice in the conversation we call democracy."†

---

*Time, May 15, 1995, p. 35.

†Congressional Quarterly Weekly Report, May 20, 1995, p. 1449.

the 1970s by "entrepreneurs" who saw an untapped "market" for the representation of these interests.

Among the most influential public-interest groups are Common Cause, a self-styled "citizens' lobby," and the sprawling network of organizations created by consumer advocate Ralph Nader (see *People in Politics:* "Ralph Nader, People's Lobbyist" on pages 296–97). Common Cause tends to focus on election-law reform, public financing of elections, and limitations on political contributions. The Nader organization began as a consumer protection group focusing on auto safety but soon spread to encompass a wide variety of causes.

Single-Issue Groups   Like public-interest groups, **single-issue groups** appeal to principle and belief. But as their name implies, single-issue groups concentrate their attention on a single cause. They attract the support of individuals with a strong commitment to that cause. Single-issue groups have little incentive to compromise their position. They exist for a single cause; no other issues really matter to them. They are by nature passionate and often shrill. Their attraction to members is the intensity of their beliefs.

Among the most vocal single-issue groups in recent years have been the organizations on both sides of the abortion issue. The National Abortion Rights Action League (NARAL) describes itself as "pro-choice" and opposes any restrictions on a woman's right to obtain an abortion. The National Right-to-Life Committee describes itself as "pro-life" and opposes abortion for any reason other than to preserve the life of the mother. Other prominent single-issue groups include the National Rifle Association (opposed to gun control) and Mothers against Drunk Driving (MADD).

Ideological Groups   **Ideological organizations** pursue liberal or conservative agendas, often with great passion and considerable financial resources derived from true-believing contributors. The ideological groups rely heavily on computerized mailings to solicit funds from persons identified as holding liberal or conservative views. The oldest of the established ideological groups is the liberal Americans for Democratic Action (ADA), well known for its annual liberalism ratings of members of the Congress according to their support for or rejection of programs of concern. The American Conservative Union (ACU) also rates members of Congress each year. Overall, Democrats do better on the liberal list and Republicans on the conservative list, although both parties include some members whose policies frequently put them on the opposite side of the fence from the majority of their fellow party members (see Table 9-2). Other interest groups, such as the AFL-CIO, the National Taxpayers Union, and the National Abortion Rights Action League, also rate members of Congress, but these groups have a narrower focus than the ADA and ACU. Yet another prominent ideological group, People for the American Way, was formed by television producer Norman Lear to coordinate the efforts of liberals in the entertainment industry as well as the general public, but it issues no ratings.

Government Lobbies   The federal government's grant-in-aid programs to state and local governments (see Chapter 4) have spawned a host of lobbying efforts by these governments in Washington, D.C. Thus state- and local-government taxpay-

single-issue groups   Organizations formed to support or oppose government action on a specific issue.

ideological organizations
Interest groups that pursue ideologically based (liberal or conservative) agendas.

TABLE 9–2	Ideological Interest-Group Scores for U.S. Senators	
	Americans for Democratic Action (liberal)	*American Conservative Union (conservative)*
Most Liberal Senators		
Paul Wellstone (D-Minn.)	100	0
Tom Harkin (D-Iowa)	100	0
Daniel Patrick Moynihan (D-N.Y.)	100	0
Russell Feingold (D-Wisc.)	100	4
Edward Kennedy (D-Mass.)	95	0
John Kerry (D-Mass.)	95	5
Barbara Boxer (D-Calif.)	95	0
Most Liberal Republican Senators		
James Jeffords (R-Vt.)	85	12
John Chafee (R-R.I.)	65	30
Arlen Spector (R-Pa.)	55	46
Most Conservative Senators		
Jesse Helms (R-N.C.)	5	100
Larry Craig (R-Idaho)	0	100
Dirk Kempthorne (R-Idaho)	0	100
Don Nickles (R-Okla.)	5	100
Orrin Hatch (R-Utah)	5	100
Phil Gramm (R-Tex.)	5	100
Robert Smith (R-N.H.)	5	100
Paul Coverdell (R-Ga.)	5	100
Most Conservative Democratic Senators		
Ernest Hollings (D-S.C.)	55	22
John Breaux (D.-La.)	55	17

Source: Reported in *Congressional Quarterly.* Ratings for 104th Congress.

ers foot the bill to lobby Washington to transfer federal taxpayers' revenues to states and communities. The National Governors Association occupies a beautiful marble building, the Hall of the States, in Washington, along with representatives of the separate states and many major cities. The National League of Cities and the National Association of Counties also maintain large Washington offices, as does the U.S. Conference of Mayors. The National Conference of State Legislators sends its lobbyists to Washington from its Denver headquarters. These groups pursue a wide policy agenda and often confront internal disputes. But they are united in their support for increased federal transfers of tax revenues to states and cities.

LEADERS AND FOLLOWERS

Organizations require leadership. And over time leaders develop a perspective somewhat different from that of their organizations' membership. A key question in interest-group politics is how well organization leaders represent the views of their members.

Ralph Nader, People's Lobbyist

Much of the credit for the growth of public-interest groups in recent decades goes to Ralph Nader, the self-appointed "people's lobbyist" who achieved national celebrity as an advocate of consumer protection laws. From seat belts and nonsmoking sections to nuclear power regulation, insurance rates, food and drug legislation, and worker safety, Nader's influence has been widely felt in American society.

The child of Lebanese immigrants who operated a small bakery in Winsted, Connecticut, Nader graduated from the Woodrow Wilson School of Public and International Affairs at Princeton University magna cum laude, then went on to Harvard Law School, where he earned an LL.B. with distinction in 1958. After a short stint in the army, Nader opened a private law practice in Hartford, Connecticut, but soon left to travel throughout the world, working as a free-lance journalist for the *Christian Science Monitor*.

An article that Nader wrote for the *Harvard Law Review* on auto design and safety brought him to the attention of then-Acting Secretary of Labor (now U.S. Senator from New York) Daniel Patrick Moynihan. Moynihan hired the young attorney as a staff consultant on highway safety. While employed at the Department of Labor, Nader wrote and published his book *Unsafe at Any Speed* (1965), which charged that General Motors Corporation preferred styling to safety. Nader was thrust further into the national spotlight when he sued General Motors for invading his privacy by hiring private detectives to investigate him. With his $16 million in settlement money (plus substantial royalty and speaking income), Nader began to construct an organizational colossus (see figure). In 1969 Nader founded his Washington-based Center for Study of Responsive Law and staffed it with aggressive young lawyers. These "Nader's Raiders" launched attacks against a number of federal regulatory agencies, charging them with lax enforcement.

In 1971 Nader started Public Citizen, Inc., to enlist members of the general public in a broad array of causes. Nader has also formed a number of organizations that address more specific topics, such as the Citizens for Tax Justice, Aviation Consumer's Action, Center for Auto Safety, and Congress Watch. Nader was instrumental in the creation of the Occupational Safety and Health Administration and the Consumer Product Safety Commission, but Congress rejected his idea for a federal consumer protection agency.

Nader's independence and altruism, his contempt for bureaucratic lethargy and incompetence, and his posture as David fighting the corporate Goliaths of the world appealed to idealistic young people at colleges and universities across the nation. Capitalizing on his campus popularity, Nader formed hundreds of Public Interest Research Groups (PIRGs) and overcame the "free-rider" problem by pressuring university administrators on many campuses to add PIRG dues to student activities fees.

Nader has resigned from direct participation in most of the organizations he founded, leaving them to be managed by a new generation of consumer advocates. He continues to live in a low-rent boardinghouse in Washington, D.C., reportedly wearing one of the twelve pairs of shoes that he bought at an army PX in 1958. "I'm not an idealist. I think of myself as being very practical because I want to be effective. . . . Traditional reformers . . . didn't follow through by politically mobilizing a concerned constituency."

Nader ran for president in 1996 as a Green Party (environmental protection) candidate. He succeeded in getting his name on the ballot in California and several other states. But he campaigned very little and refused to solicit contributions. In public appearances he often seemed argumentative and self-righteous. He ended up with less than 1 percent of the popular vote nationwide.

Source: Adapted from "The Ralph Nader Trust," *Forbes*, September 17, 1990, pp. 120–21, by permission of Forbes Magazine; quotation from *Newsmakers* (Detroit: Gale Research, 1989), p. 360.

The Nader Network

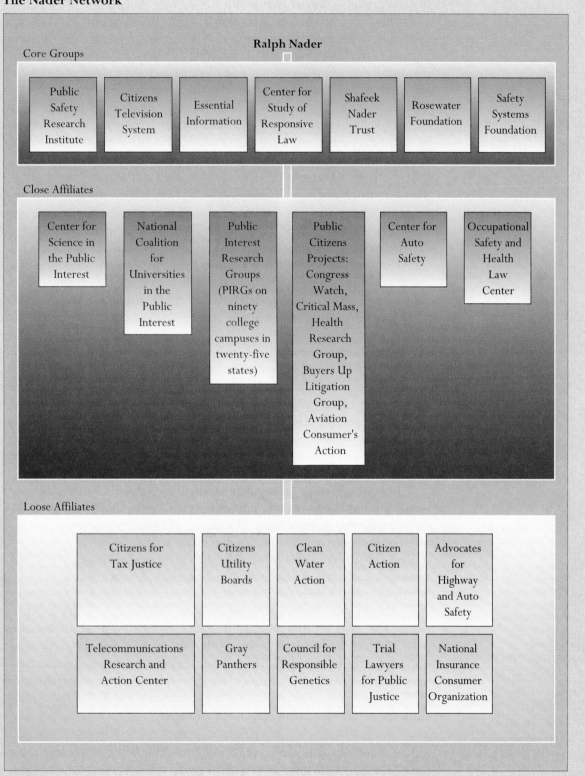

Core Groups

Ralph Nader

| Public Safety Research Institute | Citizens Television System | Essential Information | Center for Study of Responsive Law | Shafeek Nader Trust | Rosewater Foundation | Safety Systems Foundation |

Close Affiliates

Center for Science in the Public Interest

National Coalition for Universities in the Public Interest

Public Interest Research Groups (PIRGs on ninety college campuses in twenty-five states)

Public Citizens Projects: Congress Watch, Critical Mass, Health Research Group, Buyers Up Litigation Group, Aviation Consumer's Action

Center for Auto Safety

Occupational Safety and Health Law Center

Loose Affiliates

Citizens for Tax Justice

Citizens Utility Boards

Clean Water Action

Citizen Action

Advocates for Highway and Auto Safety

Telecommunications Research and Action Center

Gray Panthers

Council for Responsible Genetics

Trial Lawyers for Public Justice

National Insurance Consumer Organization

Interest-Group Entrepreneurs   People who create organizations and build membership in those organizations—**interest-group entrepreneurs**—have played a major role in strengthening the interest-group system in recent decades. These entrepreneurs help overcome a major obstacle to the formation of strong interest groups—the *free-rider* problem.

Free-riders are people who benefit from the efforts of others but do not contribute to the costs of those efforts. Not everyone feels an obligation to support organizations that represent their interests or views. Some people feel that their own small contribution will not make a difference in the success or failure of the organization's goals and, moreover, that they will benefit from any successes even if they are not members. Indeed, most organizations enroll only a tiny fraction of the people they claim to represent. The task of the interest-group entrepreneur is to convince people to join the organization, either by appealing to their sense of obligation or by attracting them through tangible benefits.

Marketing Membership   Interest-group entrepreneurs make different appeals for membership depending on the nature of the organization. Some appeal to passion or purpose, as, for example, those who seek to create ideological (liberal or conservative) organizations, public-interest organizations committed to environmental or consumer protection or governmental reform, and single-issue organizations devoted to the support or opposition of a single policy issue (gun control, abortion, and so on). Entrepreneurs of these organizations appeal to people's sense of duty and commitment to the cause rather than to material rewards of membership. By using sophisticated computerized mailing lists, they can solicit support from sympathetic people.[6]

Business, trade, and professional organizations usually offer their members many tangible benefits in addition to lobbying on behalf of their economic interests. These benefits may include magazines, journals, and newsletters that provide access to business, trade, and professional information as well as national conventions and meetings that serve as social settings for the development of contacts, friendships, and business and professional relationships. Some organizations also offer discount travel and insurance, credit cards, and the like, that go only to dues-paying members.

It is generally easier to organize smaller, specialized economic interests than larger, general, noneconomic interests. People more easily recognize that their own membership is important to the success of a small organization, and economic interests are more readily calculated in dollar terms.

Large organizations with broad goals—such as advancing the interests of all veterans or all retired people or all automobile drivers—must rely even more heavily on tangible benefits to solicit members. Indeed, some organizations have succeeded in recruiting millions of members (for example, the AARP with 33 million members, the American Automobile Association with 28 million members), most of whom have very little knowledge about the policy positions or lobbying activities of the organization. These members joined to receive specific benefits—magazines, insurance, travel tips, discounts. Leaders of these organizations may claim to speak for millions of members, but it is unlikely that these millions all share the policy views expressed by the leaders.

Organizational Democracy and Leader/Member Agreement   Most organized interest groups are run by a small group of leaders and activists. Few inter-

interest-group entrepreneurs   Leaders who create organizations and market memberships.

free-riders   People who do not belong to an organization or pay dues, yet nevertheless benefit from its activities.

est groups are governed democratically; members may drop out if they do not like the direction their organization is taking but rarely do they have the opportunity to directly challenge or replace the organization's leadership. Relatively few members attend national meetings, vote in organizational elections, or try to exercise influence within their organization. Thus the leadership may not always reflect the views of the membership, especially in large organizations that rely heavily on tangible benefits to recruit members. Leaders of these organizations enjoy considerable freedom in adopting policy positions and negotiating, bargaining, and compromising in the political arena.

The exception to this rule is the single-issue group. Because the strength of these groups is in the intensity of their members' beliefs, the leaders of such groups are closely tied to their members' views. They cannot bargain or compromise these views or adopt policy positions at variance with those of their members.

Class Bias in Membership   Americans are joiners. A majority of the population belong to at least one organization, most often a church. Yet membership in organized interest groups is clearly linked to socioeconomic status. Membership is greatest among professional and managerial, college-educated, and high-income persons.[7]

THE WASHINGTON LOBBYISTS

Washington is a labyrinth of interest representatives—lawyers and law firms; independent consultants; public and governmental relations firms; business, professional, and trade associations; and advocates of special causes. It is estimated that more than 14,000 people in Washington fit the definition of **lobbyist**, a person working to influence government policies and actions. These figures suggest at least twenty-five lobbyists for every member of Congress.

Who Are the Lobbyists?   Lobbyists in Washington, D.C., represent a broad array of concerns (see Table 9-3). They share a common goal—to influence the making and enforcing of laws—and common tactics to achieve this goal. Many lobbyists are the employees of interest-group organizations who devote all of their efforts to their sponsors.

lobbyist   Person working to influence government policies and actions.

TABLE 9-3	Types of Lobbyists	
Business, trade, and professional organization officers (approximately 2,200 organizations)		5,000
Representatives of individual corporations		1,500
Representatives of special causes		2,500
Lawyers registered as lobbyists		3,000
Public and governmental relations		2,500
Political action committee officers		200
Think tank officers		150

Source: Washington Representatives, 1995 (Washington, D.C.: Columbia Books, 1995).

Up Close

Washington's Most Powerful Lobbies

Fortune magazine sponsored a survey of more than 2,000 Washington "insiders," including members of Congress, their staffs, and White House officials, asking them to rank the most powerful lobbyists in the capital. The results were as follows:

The "Power 25"

1. American Association of Retired Persons
2. American Israel Public Affairs Committee
3. AFL-CIO
4. National Federation of Independent Business
5. Association of Trial Lawyers of America
6. National Rifle Association of America
7. Christian Coalition
8. American Medical Association
9. National Education Association
10. National Right to Life Committee
11. National Association of Realtors
12. American Bankers Association
13. National Association of Manufacturers
14. American Federation of State, County, and Municipal Employees
15. Chamber of Commerce of the U.S.A.
16. Veterans of Foreign Wars of the United States
17. American Farm Bureau Federation
18. Motion Picture Association of America
19. National Association of Home Builders of the U.S.
20. National Association of Broadcasters
21. American Hospital Association
22. National Governors' Association
23. American Legion
24. National Restaurant Association
25. International Brotherhood of Teamsters

Source: *Fortune*, December 8, 1997.

Some lobbying organizations rely heavily on their campaign contributions to achieve lobbying power; others rely on large memberships, and still others on politically active members who concentrate their attention on a narrow range of issues (see *Up Close:* "Washington's Most Powerful Lobbies").

Other lobbyists are located in independent law, consulting, or public relations firms that take on clients for fees. Independent lobbyists, especially law firms, are often secretive about whom they represent, especially when they represent foreign governments. Lobbyists frequently prefer to label their activities as "government relations," "public affairs," "regulatory liaison," "legislative counseling," or merely "representation."

In reality, many independent lawyers and lobbyists in Washington are "fixers" who offer to influence government policies for a price. Many are former government officials—former Congress members, cabinet secretaries, White House aides, and the like—who "know their way around." Their personal connections help to "open doors" to allow their paying clients to "just get a chance to talk" with top officials.

Regulation of Lobbies   The Constitution's First Amendment guarantee of the right "to petition the government for a redress of grievances" protects lobbying. But the government can and does regulate lobbying activities, primarily through disclosure laws. The Regulation of Lobbying Act requires lobbyists to register and to report how much they spend, but definitions of *lobbying* are unclear and enforcement is weak. Many large lobbying groups—for example, the National Association of Manufacturers, the American Bankers Association, and Americans for Constitutional Action—have never registered as lobbyists. These organizations claim that because lobbying is not their principal activity, they need not register under the law. In addition, financial reports of lobbyists grossly underestimate the extent of lobbying in Congress because the law requires reports of only money spent for direct lobbying before Congress, not money spent for public relations. Another weakness in the law is that it applies only to attempts to influence Congress; it does not regulate lobbying activities in administrative agencies or the executive branch.

Tax laws require nonprofit organizations to refrain from direct lobbying in order to retain their tax-free status. Under current tax law, individual contributions to nonprofit charitable and educational organizations are tax deductible, and the income of these organizations is tax free. But these organizations risk losing these tax preferences if a "substantial part" of their activities is "attempting to influence legislation."Thus, for example, Washington think tanks such as the Brookings Institution, the American Enterprise Institute, and the Heritage Foundation (see *Up Close:* "Think Tanks: The Battle of Ideas" in Chapter 2) refrain from direct lobbying even though they make policy recommendations. But the line between public affairs "education" and "lobbying" is very fuzzy.

THE FINE ART OF LOBBYING

Any activity directed at a government decision maker with the hope of influencing decisions is a form of **lobbying**. (The term arose from the practice of waiting in the lobbies of legislative chambers to meet and persuade legislators.) For organized interests, lobbying is continuous—in congressional committees, in congressional staff offices, at the White House, at executive agencies, at Washington cocktail parties. If a group loses a round in Congress, it continues the fight in the agency in charge of executing the policy, or it challenges the policy in the courts. The following year it resumes the struggle in Congress: It fights to repeal the offending legislation, to weaken amendments, or to reduce the agency's budget enough to cripple enforcement efforts.

Lobbying techniques are as varied as the imagination of interest-group leaders, but such activities generally fall into seven categories: (1) public relations; (2) access; (3) information; (4) grass-roots mobilization; (5) protests and demonstrations; (6) coalition building; and (7) campaign support. In the real world of Washington power struggles, all these techniques may be applied simultaneously, or innovative techniques may be discovered and applied at any time (see Figure 9-1).

Public Relations   Many interest groups actually spend more of their time, energy, and resources on **public relations**—developing and maintaining a favorable climate of opinion in the nation—than on direct lobbying of Congress. The mass media—television, magazines, newspapers—are saturated with expensive ads by oil companies, auto companies, chemical manufacturers, trade associations, teachers' unions, and many other groups, all seeking to create a favorable image for themselves with the general public. These ads are designed to go well beyond promoting the sale of particular products; they portray these organizations as patriotic citizens, protectors of the environment, providers of jobs, defenders of family values, and supporters of the American way of life. Generally, business interests have an advantage in the area of public relations because public relations and sales and marketing activities are synonymous. But paid advertising is less credible than

lobbying   Activities directed at government officials with the hope of influencing their decisions.

public relations   Building and maintaining goodwill with the general public.

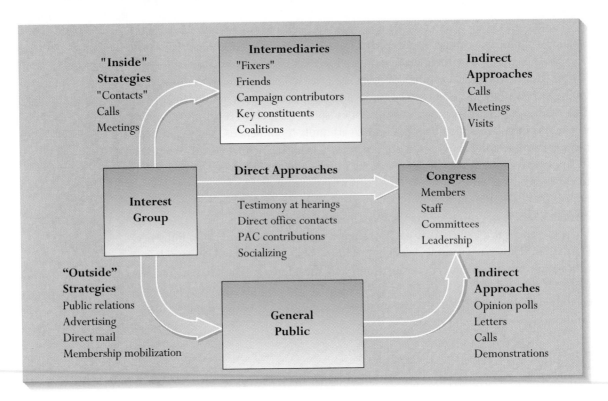

FIGURE 9-1   A Guide to the Fine Art of Lobbying

Interest groups seek to influence public policy both directly through lobbying and campaign contributions (inside strategy) and indirectly through public relations efforts to mold public opinion (outside strategy).

news stories and media commentary. Hence interest groups generate a daily flood of press releases, media events, interviews, reports, and studies for the media.

Access   "Opening doors" is a major business in Washington. To influence decision makers, organized interests must first acquire **access** to them. Individuals who have personal contacts in Congress, the White House, or the bureaucracy (or who say they do) sell their services at high prices. Washington law firms, public relations agencies, and consultants—often former insiders—all offer their connections, along with their advice, to their clients. The personal prestige of the lobbyist, together with the group's perceived political influence, helps open doors in Washington.

Washington socializing is often an exercise in access—rubbing elbows with powerful people. Well-heeled lobbyists regularly pay hundreds, even thousands, of dollars per plate at fund-raising dinners for members of Congress. Lobbyists regularly provide dinners, drinks, travel, vacations, and other amenities to members of Congress, their families, and congressional staff, as well as to White House and other executive officials. (Until recently, *honoraria*—direct payments to members of Congress for speaking to an organization—were common, but congressional ethics legislation now prohibits honoraria for House members and limits annual honoraria income for senators to 27 percent of their salaries.) These favors are rarely provided on a direct quid pro quo basis in exchange for votes. Rather, they are designed to gain access—"just a chance to talk."

access   Meeting and talking with decision makers, a prerequisite to direct persuasion.

Information   Once lobbyists gain access, their knowledge and information become valuable resources to those they lobby. Members of Congress and their staffs look to lobbyists for *technical expertise* on the issue under debate as well as *political information* about the group's position on the issue. Members of Congress must vote on hundreds of questions each year, and it is impossible for them to be fully informed about the wide variety of bills and issues they face. Consequently many of them (and administrators in the executive branch as well) come to depend on trusted lobbyists.

Lobbyists also spend considerable time and effort keeping informed about bills affecting their interests. They must be thoroughly familiar with the "ins and outs" of the legislative process—the relevant committees and subcommittees, their schedules of meetings and hearings, their key staff members, the best moments to act, the precise language for proposed bills and amendments, the witnesses for hearings, and the political strengths and weaknesses of the legislators themselves. In their campaign to win congressional and bureaucratic support for their programs, lobbyists engage in many different types of activities. Nearly all testify at congressional hearings and make direct contact with government officials on issues that affect them. In addition, lobbyists provide the technical reports and analyses used by congressional staffs in their legislative research. Engaging in protest demonstrations is a less common activity, in part because it involves a high risk of alienating some members of Congress (see Table 9-4).

Experienced lobbyists develop a reputation for accurate information. Most successful lobbyists do not supply faulty information; their success depends on maintaining the trust and confidence of decision makers. A reputation for honesty is as important as a reputation for influence.

Grass-Roots Mobilization　　Many organized interests lobby Congress from both the *outside* and the *inside*. From the outside, organizations seek to mobilize **grass-roots lobbying** of members of Congress by their constituents. Lobbyists frequently encourage letters and calls from "the folks back home." Larger organized interests often have local chapters throughout the nation and can

grass-roots lobbying
Attempts to influence government decision making by inspiring constituents to contact their representatives.

TABLE 9-4	**Activities of Professional Lobbyists**	
Activity	*Lobbyists Participating in Activity*
Testifying at hearings	99%
Contacting government officials directly	98
Making informal contacts over meals, and so on	95
Presenting research results	92
Helping write legislation	85
Mounting grass-roots lobbying campaigns	80
Telling legislators the impact of legislation in their districts	75
Pursuing litigation	72
Publicizing candidates' voting records	44
Making in-kind (work, skill) contributions to campaigns	24
Endorsing candidates publicly	22
Engaging in protests or demonstrations	20

Source: Kay Lehmann Schlozman and John T. Tierney, *Organized Interests and American Democracy* (New York: Harper & Row, 1986), p. 150.

AARP: The Nation's Most Powerful Interest Group

The American Association of Retired Persons (AARP) is the nation's largest and most powerful interest group, with nearly 33 million members. The AARP's principal interests are the Social Security and Medicare system programs, the nation's largest and most expensive entitlements. It led the fight in Congress against the Balanced Budget Amendment to the Constitution.

Like many other interest groups, the AARP has grown in membership not only by appealing to the political interests of retired people but also by offering a wide array of material benefits. For an $8 annual fee, members are offered a variety of services, including discounted rates on home, auto, and life insurance; discounted mail-order drugs; tax advisory services; discounted rates on hotels, rental cars, and so on; a newsletter, *The AARP Bulletin*; and a semi-monthly magazine, *Modern Maturity*.

Senior citizens are the most politically powerful age group in the population. They constitute 28 percent of the voting-age population, but because of their high voter-turnout rates, they constitute more than one-third of the voters on election day. Persons over sixty-five average a 68 percent turnout rate in presidential elections and a 61 percent rate

mobilize these local affiliates to apply pressure when necessary. Lobbyists encourage influential local people to visit the office of a member of Congress personally or to make a personal phone call on behalf of the group's position. And, naturally, members are urged to vote for or against certain candidates, based on their policy stances (see *Up Close:* "AARP: The Nation's Most Powerful Interest Group").

Experienced lawmakers recognize attempts by lobby groups to orchestrate "spontaneous" grass-roots outpourings of cards and letters. Pressure mail is often identical in wording and content. Nevertheless, members of Congress dare not

in congressional elections. In contrast, the turnout rate for those aged eighteen to twenty-one is 36 percent in presidential elections and 19 percent in congressional elections. In short, the voting power of senior citizens is twice that of young people. No elected official can afford to offend the seniors, and seniors strongly support generous Social Security and Medicare benefits.

The power of the "gray lobby" is clearly evident in the federal budget (see graph). The federal government invests relatively little in education, training, and social services for young people. Yet the federal government's most costly function is the support of the nation's senior citizens. Social Security, Medicare, and federal retirement programs now account for almost 40 percent of all federal spending.

At present there are no "means" (low-income) tests for Social Security and Medicare. These benefits go to the wealthy among the aged as well as the poor. And overall, the aged have higher average incomes and much more wealth than the rest of the population. Poverty among persons over sixty-five is 2 full percentage points below the national average. Seniors also are much more likely than other Americans to own their own homes with paid mortgages, to have larger bank accounts, and to own stocks and bonds.

The political power of senior citizens is so great that prospects for limiting current or even future increases in government benefits for the elderly are slim. Social Security is said to be the "third rail of American politics—touch it and you're dead."

Critics of the AARP argue that its lobbyists in Washington do not fairly represent the views of the nation's senior citizens, that few of its members know what its lobbying arm does at the nation's capital.

Young and Old in the Federal Budget

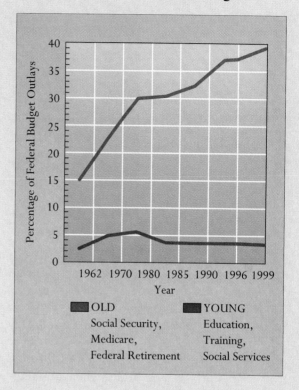

Source: Budget of the United States Government, 1999.

AARP keeps its dues low, and consequently its membership high, through its business ties with insurance companies, its magazine advertising revenue, and commercial royalties revenues for endorsing products and services. Only about one-third of its revenues come from members' dues. Its critics argue that its many business ties should bar it from claiming tax-free status as a nonprofit charitable and education organization.

ignore a flood of letters and telegrams from home, for the mail shows that constituents are aware of the issue and care enough to sign their names.

Another grass-roots tactic is to mobilize the press in the home district of a member of Congress. Lobbyists may provide news, analyses, and editorials to local newspapers and then clip favorable articles to send to lawmakers. Lobby groups may also buy advertisements in hometown newspapers.

Protests and Demonstrations   Interest groups occasionally employ protests and demonstrations to attract media attention to their concerns and thereby apply

Interest groups use campaign contributions to gain access to legislators and help elect people favorable to their goals. The National Rifle Association, for example, has contributed substantially over the years to Senator Phil Gramm of Texas, an opponent of gun control, shown here addressing workers at a gun factory.

pressure on officials to take action. For these actions to succeed in getting issues on the agenda of decision makers in Congress, in the White House, and in executive agencies, participation by the media, especially television, is essential. The media carry the message of the protest or demonstration both to the general public and directly to government officials (see "Protest as Political Participation" in Chapter 5).

Organized interest groups most often resort to protests and demonstrations when (1) they are frustrated in more traditional "inside" lobbying efforts; and/or (2) they wish to intensify pressure on officials at a specific point in time. Demonstrations typically attract media attention for a short time only. But media coverage of specific events can carry a clear message—for example, farmers driving tractors through Washington to protest farm conditions; motorcyclists conducting a giant "bike-in" to protest laws requiring helmets; cattle raisers driving steers down the Washington Mall to protest beef prices. The potential drawbacks to such activities are that the attention is short-lived and the group's reputation may be tarnished if the protest turns nasty or violent.

Coalition Building　Interest groups frequently seek to build **coalitions** with other groups in order to increase their power. Coalitions tend to form among groups with parallel interests: for example, the National Organization for Women, the League of Women Voters, and the National Abortion Rights Action League on women's issues. Coalitions usually form temporarily around a single piece of legislation in a major effort to secure or prevent its passage.

Campaign Support　Perhaps the real key to success in lobbying is the campaign contribution. Interest-group contributions not only help lobbyists gain access and a favorable hearing but also help elect people friendly to the group's goals. As the costs of campaigning increase, legislators must depend more heavily on the contributions of organized interests.

coalition A joining together of interest groups (or individuals) to achieve a common goal.

Most experienced lobbyists avoid making electoral threats. Amateur lobbyists sometimes threaten legislators by vowing to defeat them at the next election, but this tactic usually produces a hostile reaction among members of Congress. Legislators are likely to respond to crude pressures by demonstrating their independence and voting against the threatening lobbyist. Moreover, experienced members of Congress know that such threats are empty; lobbyists can seldom deliver enough votes to influence the outcome of an election.

Experienced lobbyists also avoid offering a campaign contribution in exchange for a specific vote.[8] Crude "vote buying" (bribery) is illegal and risks repulsing politicians who refuse bribes. **Bribery**, when it occurs, is probably limited to very narrow and specific actions—payments to intervene in a particular case before an administrative agency; payments to insert a very specific break in a tax bill or a specific exemption in a trade bill; payments to obtain a specific contract with the government. Bribery on major issues is very unlikely; there is too much publicity and too many participants for bribery to be effective (but see *Up Close*: "The Keating Five: Service to Constituents, for a Price?" in Chapter 10).

Instead of bribery, organized interests contribute to an incumbent member of Congress over a long period of time and leave it to the lawmaker to figure out how to retain their support. Only when a legislator consistently works against an organized interest will it consider contributing to that lawmaker's opponent in an election.

PAC POWER

Organized interest groups channel their campaign contributions through **political action committees (PACs)**. PACs are organized by corporations, labor unions, trade associations, ideological and issue-oriented groups, and cooperatives and nonprofit corporations to solicit campaign contributions and distribute them to political candidates.

Origins   The first PACs were created by organized labor to circumvent prohibitions against using union dues to finance elections. Corporations, like labor unions, had long been prohibited from making direct campaign contributions. Prior to passage of the Federal Election Campaign Act of 1974, which encouraged corporations to create their own PACs, PACs were relatively rare. But once begun, the PAC tide could not be stemmed (see Table 9-5). Today corporate PACs far

bribery   Giving or offering anything of value in an effort to influence government officials in the performance of their duties.

political action committees (PACs)   Organizations that solicit and receive campaign contributions from corporations, unions, trade associations, and ideological and issue-oriented groups, and their members, then distribute these funds to political candidates.

TABLE 9–5	The Growth of PACs			
	1974	*1980*	*1988*	*1998*
Corporate	89	1,206	1,816	1,836
Labor	201	297	354	358
Trade and professional	318	576	786	896
Ideological issue	—	374	1,115	1,259
All other	—	98	197	179
Total	608	2,551	4,268	4,528

Source: Federal Election Commission, 1998.

outnumber labor PACs. Trade and professional associations quickly organized their own PACs. Soon entrepreneurs for ideological, environmental, and single-issue groups created PACs. Increasingly political candidates turned to PACs as a major source of campaign financing.

Regulation   PACs are regulated by the Federal Election Commission (FEC), which requires them to register and report their finances and political contributions periodically. A registered PAC that has received contributions from more than fifty people and has contributed to at least five campaigns is eligible to contribute $5,000 to any candidate (per election), $15,000 to a party's national committee, and $5,000 to any other PAC. These limits mean that PACs can give five times as much to candidates in each election as can individuals, who are limited to $1,000. Individuals may, however, give $5,000 to any PAC. Thus the 1974 reform act, although intended to reform campaign financing, actually encouraged the growth of PACs and PAC power.

Distributing PAC Money   Because PAC contributions are in larger lumps than individual contributions, PAC contributions often attract more attention from members of Congress. PACs are also easier for politicians to deal with because there are far fewer PACs (about 4,000) than voters. The PACs listed in Table 9-6 give millions of dollars each year to finance the campaigns of their potential allies. The single largest distributor of PAC money to political candidates in 1996 was EMILY's List (see *Up Close:* "EMILY's List").

Most PACs use their campaign contributions to acquire access and influence with decision makers. Corporate, trade, and professional PAC contributions go

---

| TABLE 9-6 | The Big-Money PACs |

Corporate PACs

American Telephone and Telegraph Co. (AT&T PAC)
Federal Express Corporation PAC (FEPAC)
Team Ameritech (PAC)
Philip Morris (PHIL-PAC)
United Parcel Service (UPSPAC)
Lockheed Martin Employees PAC
Union Pacific Fund for Effective Government

Labor PACs

American Federation of State County & Municipal Employees (PEOPLE PAC)
United Automobile Workers (V-CAP)
Machinists Non-Partisan Political League

International Brotherhood of Electrical Workers
United Food & Commercial Workers (Active Ballot Fund)
Communications Workers of American (CWA-COPE)
United Steel Workers of America
AFL-CIO Committee on Political Education (AFL-CIO COPE)
Letter Carriers PAC

Trade and Professional PACs

Association of Trial Lawyers
National Education Association
American Medical Association
National Automobile Dealers
American Federation of Teachers
Realtors PAC
American Bankers Association

(BANKPAC)
National Association of Life Underwriters
National Association of Home Builders (BUILDPAC)

Ideological and Issue PACs

EMILY's List
National Rifle Association
Political Victory Fund
Women's Campaign Fund
National Committee for an Effective Congress
National Committee to Preserve Social Security and Welfare
National Right to Life PAC
Hollywood Women's PAC
GOPOC
Black America's PAC

Source: Federal Elections Commission, 1998.

EMILY's List

Fund raising is the greatest obstacle to mounting a successful campaign against an incumbent. And the most difficult problem facing challengers is raising money *early* in the campaign, when they have little name recognition and little or no standing in the polls.

EMILY's list is a politically adroit and effective effort to support liberal women candidates by infusing *early money* into their campaigns. EMILY stands for Early Money Is Like Yeast, because "it makes the dough rise." Early contributions provide the initial credibility that a candidate, especially a challenger, needs in order to solicit additional funds from individuals and organizations. EMILY is a fund-raising network of thousands of contributors, each of whom pays $100 to join and pledges to give at least $100 to two women from a list of candidates prepared by EMILY's leaders. Most of the contributors are professional women who appreciate EMILY's screening of pro-choice, liberal women candidates around the country. In 1996 EMILY helped distribute more than $9 million among liberal Democratic women candidates for Congress.

EMILY's list was begun by a wealthy heir to a founder of IBM, Ellen Malcolm. Malcolm graduated from Hollins College in Virginia in 1969 and joined the liberal public-interest group Common Cause as a volunteer. She later joined the staff of the National Women's Political Caucus. In 1980 she established her own private foundation, Windom Fund, to channel money to women and minority groups. (She reportedly invented the Windom name to preserve her own anonymity as the benefactor.) She created EMILY's list in 1985.

Women challengers for congressional races traditionally faced frustration in fund raising. Incumbent male officeholders enjoyed a huge fund-raising advantage because contributors expected them to win and therefore opened their wallets to gain access and goodwill. Contributing to women challengers, even by people who supported their views, was often considered a waste of money. EMILY's list has helped to overcome defeatism among both women candidates and contributors.

EMILY's list claims success in electing six current liberal Democratic women to the U.S. Senate (Barbara Boxer and Dianne Feinstein, both of California; Mary Landrieu, Louisiana; Carol Moseley-Braun, Illinois; Patty Murray, Washington; and Barbara Milkulski, Maryland) as well as forty-two liberal Democratic House members.

Senator Barbara Milkulski, Democrat of Maryland and a beneficiary of EMILY's list, at a news conference.

overwhelmingly to incumbents, regardless of party (see Table 9-7). Leaders of these PACs know that incumbents are rarely defeated, and they do not wish to antagonize even unsympathetic members of Congress by backing challengers. However, ideological and issue-oriented PACs are more likely to allocate funds according to the candidates' policy positions and voting records. Labor PACs give almost all of their contributions to Democrats. Ideological and issue-oriented PACs give money to challengers as well as incumbents; in recent years, these groups

TABLE 9-7	Distribution of PAC Contributions in Congressional Elections		

	Percentage of PAC Contributions		
	1995–96	*1993–94*	*1989–90*
All Candidates			
Incumbents	67%	72%	74%
Challengers	15	10	12
Open Seats	18	18	14
Senate			
Democrats	35	50	57
Republicans	65	50	43
House			
Democrats	50	67	67
Republicans	50	33	33

Source: Federal Elections Commission, 1998.

collectively favored Democrats as women's, environmental, abortion rights, and elderly groups proliferated.

The pattern of contributing to congressional incumbents resulted in a shift of contributions from Democrats to Republicans when the GOP took control of both houses of Congress after the 1994 election. PAC money is less important in the Senate than in the House. PAC contributions account for almost 40 percent of House campaign contributions; they only account for about 20 percent of Senate campaign contributions. Actually PACs contribute more *dollars* to the average senator than to the average House member. But because Senate campaigns cost so much more than House campaigns, PAC contributions are *proportionally* less. Senators must rely more on individual contributions than House members do.

LOBBYING THE BUREAUCRACY

Lobbying does not cease after a law is passed. Rather, interest groups try to influence the implementation of the law. Interest groups know that bureaucrats exercise considerable discretion in policy implementation (see "Bureaucratic Power" in Chapter 12). Thus many interests spend as much or more time and energy trying to influence executive agencies than Congress.

Lobbying the bureaucracy involves various types of activities, including monitoring regulatory agencies for notices of new rules and regulatory changes; providing reports, testimony, and evidence in administrative hearings; submitting contract and grant applications and lobbying for their acceptance; and monitoring the performance of executive agencies on behalf of group members. Groups may try to influence the creation of a new agency to carry out the law or influence the assignment of implementation to an existing "friendly" agency. They may try to influence the selection of personnel to head the implementing agency. They may lobby the agency to devote more money and personnel to enforcement of the law (or less, depending on a group's preference). They may argue for strict rules and regulations—or loose interpretations of the law—by the implementing agencies. Lobbyists frequently appear at administrative hearings to offer information. They often undertake to sponsor test cases of administrative regulations on behalf of affected members. In short, lobbying extends throughout the government.[9]

Iron Triangles   In general, interest groups strive to maintain close working relationships with the departments and agencies that serve their members or regulate their industries. Conversely, bureaucracies seek to nourish relationships with powerful "client" groups that are capable of pressuring Congress to expand their authority and increase their budgets. Both bureaucracies and interest groups seek close working relationships with the congressional committees that exercise jurisdictions over their policy function. Finally, members of Congress seek the political and financial support of powerful interest groups, and members also seek to influence bureaucrats to favor supportive interest groups.

The mutual interests of congressional committee members, organized groups, and bureaucratic agencies come together to form what has been labeled the "iron triangles" of American government. **Iron triangles** refer to stable relationships among interest groups, congressional committees, and administrative agencies functioning in the same policy area. Each of the three sides of these triangles depends on the support of the other two; their cooperation serves their own interests (see Figure 9-2).

In an iron triangle, bureaucracies, interest groups, and congressional committees "scratch each other's back." Bureaucrats get political support from interest groups in their requests for expanded power and authority and increased budgetary allocations. Interest groups get favorable treatment of their members by the bureaucracy. Congressional committee members get political and financial support from interest groups, as well as favorable treatment for their constituents and contributors who are served or regulated by the bureaucracy.

Iron triangles are more likely to develop in specialized policy areas over which there is relatively little internal conflict.[10] However, conflict, rather than cooperation, is more likely to characterize bureaucratic–congressional–interest-group relationships when powerful, diverse interests are at stake. For example, the Occupational Safety and Health Administration is caught between the demands of labor

iron triangles Mutually supportive relationships among interest groups, government agencies, and legislative committees with jurisdiction over a specific policy area.

FIGURE 9-2   Iron Triangles
The iron triangle approach provides a convenient way to look at the interrelationship among interest groups, executive agencies, and congressional committees. As this example shows, veterans' interest groups work closely with both the Department of Veterans Affairs (executive agency) and the House Veterans Affairs Committee.

unions and industry groups. The U.S. Forest Service is caught between the demands of environmental groups and the lumber industry. The Environmental Protection Agency is pressured by environmental groups as well as by industry and agriculture. These kinds of conflicts break open the iron triangles or prevent them from forming in the first place.

Policy Networks   Generally, we think of American government in terms of the separate branches—Congress, the president and the bureaucracy, and the courts—with interest groups portrayed as external to government itself. But it is also possible to envision government as a series of **policy networks**—interactions in a common policy area among interest-group leaders and lobbyists, members of Congress and their staff personnel, executive agency officials, lawyers and consultants, foundation and think tank people, and even reporters and journalists assigned to the field. Policy networks develop among people who share some knowledge and interest in a policy field—for example, weapons procurement, housing, environment, transportation, or energy—and who regularly interact with each other in the policy arena. Policy networks may include people who differ strongly with each other as well as people who share similar views. What they have in common is their policy expertise and regular interaction. They can participate in negotiations and reach compromises as well as try to outwit and outmaneuver each other.

Revolving Doors   It is not uncommon in Washington for people in a policy network to switch jobs, moving from a post in the government to a job in the private sector, or vice versa, or moving to different posts within the government. In one example, an individual might move from a job in a corporation (Pillsbury or General Mills) to the staff of an interest group (American Farm Bureau Federation), and then to the executive agency charged with implementing policy in the field (U.S. Department of Agriculture) or to the staff of a House or Senate committee with jurisdiction over the field (House Agricultural Committee or Senate Agriculture, Nutrition, and Forestry Committee). The common currency of moves within a network is both policy expertise and contacts within the field.

The term **revolving doors** is often used to criticize people who move from a government post (where they acquired experience, knowledge, and personal contacts) to a job in the private sector as a consultant, lobbyist, or salesperson. Defense contractors may recruit high-ranking military officers or Defense Department officials to help sell weapons to their former employers. Trade associations may recruit congressional staffers, White House staffers, or high-ranking agency heads as lobbyists, or these people may leave government service to start their own lobbying firms. Attorneys from the Justice Department, the Internal Revenue Service, and federal regulatory agencies may be recruited by Washington law firms to represent clients in dealings with their former employers. Following retirement, many members of Congress turn to lobbying their former colleagues.

Concern about revolving doors centers not only on individuals cashing in on their knowledge, experience, and contacts obtained through government employment, but also on the possibility that some government officials will be tempted to tilt their decisions in favor of corporations, law firms, or interest groups that promise these officials well-paid jobs after they leave government employment (see *What Do You Think?* "Is It What You Know or Who You Know?").

policy networks   Interaction in a common policy area among lobbyists, elected officials, staff personnel, bureaucrats, journalists, and private-sector experts.

revolving doors   The movement of individuals from government positions to jobs in the private sector, using the experience, knowledge, and contacts they acquired in government employment.

What Do You Think?

Is It What You Know or Who You Know?

A majority of paid lobbyists in Washington come to their jobs from government. The "revolving door" complaint is that these people exploit their government experience for private gain. A survey of Washington lobbyists revealed that 55 percent had held some government position before becoming a lobbyist. More had worked in the executive branch than in Congress, and a few had worked in both branches of government. Full-time staff lobbyists for interest groups had somewhat less government experience than independent lawyer lobbyists (78 percent of whom had government experience) and professional lobbying consultants (62 percent of whom had government experience).

How helpful is this experience, and, more important, is it "what you know" or "who you know" that counts most in lobbying? The "good old boy" theory of lobbying suggests that success depends mostly on contacts with officials, knowing them personally and maintaining warm relations with them, so that when they are asked to do something, they are most likely to respond favorably. But the knowledge theory of lobbying suggests that success is more a product of (1) knowledge about legislative and bureaucratic processes; and (2) substantive policy expertise.

When lobbyists themselves are asked questions on this topic, they acknowledge that government experience is important in lobbying (see table). Some 87 percent of lobbyists reported that their time in government was helpful in their present work; 80 percent said that it helped them to gain familiarity with the policy-making process; and 70 percent reported that it gave them familiarity with the issues. Government experience is also helpful in making contacts with decision makers. Contacts made through congressional experience appear to be more important than contacts made through executive branch experience. But, according to the lobbyists themselves, "what you know" is more important than "who you know."

Helpfulness of Government Experience

	Responses by Lobbyists with Congressional Experience	Responses by Lobbyists with Executive Experience
Government experience provides:		
Issue familiarity	72%	72%
Knowledge of decision-making process	92	81
Contacts in administration	48	53
Contacts in Congress	87	49

Source: Derived from Robert H. Salisbury et al., "Who You Know versus What You Know: The Uses of Government Experience for Washington Lobbyists," *American Journal of Political Science* 33 (February 1989): 175–195.

The Ethics in Government Act limits postgovernment employment in an effort to reduce the potential for corruption. Former members of Congress are not permitted to lobby Congress for one year after leaving that body. Former employees of executive agencies are not permitted to lobby their agency for one year after leaving government service, and they are not permitted to lobby their agency for two years on any matter over which they had any responsibility while employed by the government.

LOBBYING THE COURTS

Interest groups play an important role in influencing federal courts. Many of the key cases brought to the federal courts are initiated by interest groups. Indeed, **litigation** is becoming a favored instrument of interest-group politics. Groups that oppose a new law or an agency's action often challenge it in court as unconstitutional or as violating the law. Interest groups bring issues to the courts by (1) supplying the attorneys for individuals who are parties to a case; (2) bringing suits to the courts on behalf of classes of citizens; or (3) filing companion **amicus curiae** (literally "friend of the court") arguments in cases in which they are interested.

The nation's most powerful interest groups all have legal divisions specializing in these techniques. The American Civil Liberties Union is one of the most active federal court litigants on behalf of criminal defendants (see *Up Close:* "Politics and the ACLU" in Chapter 14). The early civil rights strategy of the National Association for the Advancement of Colored People (NAACP) was directed by its Legal Defense Fund under the leadership of Thurgood Marshall (see *People in Politics:* "Thurgood Marshall" in Chapter 15). The NAACP chose to sponsor a suit by Linda Brown against the Board of Education in her hometown—Topeka, Kansas—in order to win the historic 1957 desegregation decision.[11] The National Abortion Rights Action League (NARAL) is active in sponsoring legal challenges to abortion restrictions. The Environmental Defense Fund and the Natural Resources Defense Council specialize in environmental litigation.

The special rules of judicial decision making preclude direct lobbying of judges by interest groups (see "The Special Rules of Judicial Decision Making" in Chapter 13). Directly contacting federal judges about a case, letter writing, telephoning, and demonstrating outside of federal courtrooms are all considered inappropriate conduct. They inspire more resentment than support among federal judges. However, interest groups have been very active in direct lobbying of Congress over judicial appointments. Key interest groups supporting abortion rights—the National Abortion Rights Action League, People for the American Way, the National Organization for Women, and so on—have played a central role in confirmation battles (see *Up Close:* "The Confirmation of Clarence Thomas" in Chapter 13).

POLITICS AS INTEREST-GROUP CONFLICT

Politics can be viewed as a struggle among interest groups over government policy. Interest groups, rather than individual citizens, can be viewed as the principal participants in American politics.

Pluralism as Democratic Politics   Pluralism (see Chapter 2) is the idea that democracy can be preserved in a large, complex society through individual membership in interest groups that compete, bargain, and compromise over government policy. Individuals are influential in politics only when they act as part of, or on behalf of, groups. (Only leaders of organizations participate directly in policy making.) The group becomes the essential bridge between the individual and the government. Pluralists argue that interest-group politics is a natural exten-

litigation   Legal dispute brought before a court.

amicus curiae   Person or group other than the defendant or the plaintiff or the prosecution that submits an argument in a case for the court's consideration.

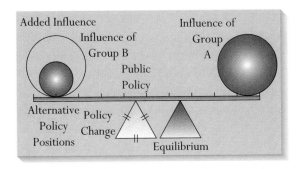

FIGURE 9-3 The Interest-Group Model

According to pluralist theorists, policy in a democracy is the result of various special-interest groups "reaching equilibrium"—arriving at a compromise position that requires all parties to give up something but gives all parties something they wanted.

sion of the democratic ideals of popular participation in government, freedom of association, and competition over public policy.

Pluralism portrays public policy at any given time as the equilibrium reached in the struggle among interest groups to influence policy (see Figure 9-3). This equilibrium is determined by the relative influence of interest groups. Changes in the relative influence of any interest group can be expected to result in changes in public policy; policy will move in the direction desired by the groups gaining in influence and away from the desires of groups losing influence.

According to this view of political life, government plays a passive role, merely "refereeing" group struggles. Public policy at any given moment represents the "equilibrium" point of the group pressures—the balance of competing interests. The job of politicians is to function as brokers of group interests, arranging compromises and balancing interests.

Balancing Group Power   Pluralism assumes that compromises *can* be arranged and that interests *can* be balanced in relatively stable fashion. It assumes that no single interest will ever become so dominant that it can reject compromise and proceed to impose its will on the nation without regard for the interests of other people. This assumption is based on several beliefs. The first is that interest groups act as a check on each other and that a system of *countervailing power* will protect the interests of all. For example, the power of big business will be checked by the countervailing power of big labor and big government.

A second belief is that *overlapping group membership* will tend to moderate the demands of particular groups and lead to compromise. Because no group can command the undivided loyalty of all its members, its demands will be less drastic and its leaders more amenable to compromise. If the leaders of any group go too far with their demands, those of its members who also belong to other groups endangered by these immoderate demands will balk.

A third belief is that radical programs and doctrinaire demands will be checked by the large, unorganized, but potentially significant *latent interest group* that is composed of all Americans who believe in toleration, compromise, and democratic processes.

Interest-Group Politics: How Democratic?   There are several problems with accepting pluralism as the legitimate heir to classic democratic theory. Democratic theory envisions public policy as the rational choice of individuals with equal influence who evaluate their needs and reach a majority decision with due regard for the rights of others. This traditional theory does not view public policy as a

Politics in Cyberspace

Interest Groups

Virtually all major organized interest groups sponsor Web sites to recruit members and get their messages into cyberspace. Among the more powerful Washington lobbying groups:

American Association of Retired Persons
http:www.aarp.org

National Rifle Association
http:www.nra.org

American Federation of Labor Congress of Industrial Organizations
http:www.aflcio.org

Organizations representing the full spectrum of ideological opinion can be found on the Web. Try, for example,

Americans for Democratic Action
http:www.ada.org

American Conservative Union
http:www.acu.org

For women's issues:

National Organization for Women
http:www.now.org

For an example of a public interest group:

Common Cause
http:www.commoncause.org

A conservative religious group:

Christian Coalition
http:www.cc.org

Civil rights and civil liberties:

American Civil Liberties Union
http:www.aclu.org

National Association for the Advancement of Colored People
http:www.naacp.org

And a single-interest group:

Mothers against Drunk Driving
http:www.madd.org

product of interest-group pressures. In fact, classic democratic theorists viewed interest groups and even political parties as intruders into an individualistic brand of citizenship and politics. Today critics of pluralism charge that interest groups dominate the political arena, monopolize access to governmental power, and thereby restrict individual participation rather than enhance it.

Pluralism contends that different groups of leaders make decisions about different issues, but critics charge that these leaders do not necessarily compete with each other. Rather, groups of leaders often allow other groups of leaders to govern their own spheres of influence without interference. Accommodation, rather than competition, may be the prevailing style of leadership interaction: "You scratch my back, and I'll scratch yours."

Another assumption of pluralism is that group membership enhances the individual's influence on policy. But only rarely are interest groups democratically governed. Individuals may provide the numerical strength for organizations, but interest groups are usually run by a small elite of officers and activists. Leaders of corporations, banks, labor unions, medical associations, and bar associations—whose views and agendas often differ from those of their membership—remain in control year after year. Very few people attend meetings, vote in organizational elections, or make their influence felt within their organization.

Finally, pluralists hope that the power of diverse institutions and organizations in society will roughly balance out and prevent the emergence of a power monopoly. Yet inequality of power among organizations is commonplace. Examples abound of narrow, organized interests achieving their goals at the expense of the broader, unorganized public. Furthermore, producer interests, bound together by economic ties, usually dominate less well-organized consumer groups and groups based on noneconomic interests. Special interests seeking governmental subsidies, payments, and "entitlements" regularly prevail over the broader yet unorganized interests of taxpayers.

Interest-Group Politics: Gridlock and Paralysis   Even if the pluralists are correct that the public interest is only the equilibrium of special-interest claims, some consensus among major interest groups is required if government is to function at all. Democracies require a sense of community and common purpose among the people. If the demands of special interests displace the public interest, government cannot function effectively. Uncompromising claims by conflicting special interests create policy *gridlock*. Yet if politicians try to placate every special interest, the result is confusing, contradictory, and muddled policy—or worse, no policy at all.

Interest-group paralysis and the resulting inability of government to act decisively to resolve national problems weaken popular confidence in government. "The function of government is to govern. A weak government, a government which lacks authority, fails to perform its function, is immoral in the same sense in which a corrupt judge, a cowardly soldier, or an ignorant teacher, is immoral."[12]

Over time, the continued buildup of special protections, privileges, and treatments in society results in "institutional sclerosis." Economist Mancur Olson argues that the accumulation of special interest subsidies, quotas, and protections leads to economic stagnation. Interest groups focus on gaining distributive advantages—a larger share of the pie for themselves—rather than on growth of the whole economy—a larger pie.[13] Major interest groups are more interested in winning income transfers to themselves through government action than in promoting the growth of national income. The more entrenched the interest-group system becomes, the slower the growth of the national economy.

SUMMARY NOTES

- Organizations concentrate power, and concentrated power prevails over diffused power. Interest groups are organizations that seek to influence government policy.

- The interest-group system supplements the electoral system as a form of representation. The electoral system is designed to respond to broad, majority preferences in geographically defined constituencies. The interest-group system represents narrower, minority interests in economic, professional, ideological, religious, racial, gender, and issue constituencies.

- Interest groups originated to protect economic interests, to advance social movements, to seek government benefits, and to respond to government activity. As government has expanded into more sectors of American life, more interest groups have formed to influence government policy.

- Washington lobbying groups represent a wide array of organized interests. But business, trade, and professional associations outnumber labor union, women's, public-interest, single-issue, and ideological groups.

- Interest-group formation has been aided in recent decades by entrepreneurs who create and build group memberships. They urge people to join organizations either by appealing to their sense of obligation or by providing an array of direct tangible benefits.

- Most organized groups are dominated by small groups of leaders and activists. Few groups are governed democratically; members who oppose the direction of the organization usually drop out rather than challenge the leadership. Group membership and especially group leadership over-represent educated, upper-middle-class segments of the population.

- Lobbying activities include advertising and public relations, obtaining access to government officials, providing them with technical and political information, mobilizing constituents, building coalitions, organizing demonstrations, and providing campaign support. Bribery is illegal, and most lobbyists avoid exacting specific vote promises in exchange for campaign contributions.

- Organized political action committees (PACs) proliferated following the 1974 "reform" of campaign finance laws. Most PAC money goes to incumbents; interest-group leaders know that incumbents are rarely defeated.

- The mutual interests of organized groups, congressional committees, and bureaucratic agencies sometimes come together to form "iron triangles" of mutual support and cooperation in specific policy areas. In many policy areas, loose "policy networks" emerge among people who share an interest and expertise—although not necessarily opinions—about a policy and are in regular contact with each other.

- The "revolving door" problem emerges when individuals use the knowledge, experience, and contacts obtained through government employment to secure high-paying jobs with corporations, law firms, lobbying and consulting firms, and interest groups doing business with their old agencies.

- Interest groups influence the nation's courts not only by providing financial and legal support for issues of concern to them but also by lobbying Congress over judicial appointments.

- Pluralism views interest-group activities as a form of democratic representation. According to the pluralists, public policy reflects the equilibrium of group influence and a reasonable approximation of society's preferences. Competition among groups, overlapping group memberships, and latent interest groups all combine to ensure that no single group dominates the system.

- Critics of pluralism warn that interest groups may monopolize power and restrict individual participation in politics rather than enhance it. They note that interest groups are not usually democratically governed, nor are their leaders or members representative of the general population. They warn that accommodation rather than competition may characterize group interaction and that narrow producer interests tend to achieve their goals at the expense of broader consumer (taxpayer) interests.

- The growing power of special interests, when combined with the declining power of parties and the fragmentation of government, may lead to gridlock and paralysis in policy making. The general public interest may be lost in the conflicting claims of special interests.

SELECTED READINGS

BERRY, JEFFREY M. *The Interest Group Society.* White Plains, N.Y.: Longman, 1997. An overview of lobbying in all three branches of government as well as grass-roots lobbying, within the context of democratic (Madisonian) theory.

CIGLER, ALLAN J., and BURDETT A. LOOMIS, EDS. *Interest Group Politics.* 4th ed. Washington, D.C.: Congressional Quarterly Press, 1994. A collection of essays examining interest-group politics.

HREBENAR, RONALD J. *Interest Group Politics in America.* 3rd ed. New York: M. E. Sharpe, 1996. A concise, readable, and timely introduction to the study of group power.

LOWI, THEODORE J. *The End of Liberalism.* New York: Norton, 1969. The classic critique of "interest-group liberalism," describing how special interests contribute to the growth of government and the development of "clientism."

MUCCIARONI, GARY. *Public Policy and Private Interests*. Washington, D.C.: Brookings, 1995. Identifying the factors that contribute to the victory or defeat of producer groups—firms, industries, professional and trade associations—in the policy process.

OLSON, MANCUR. *The Logic of Collective Action*. Cambridge, Mass.: Harvard University Press, 1965. A highly theoretical inquiry into the benefits and costs to individuals of joining groups and the obstacles (including the free-rider problem) to forming organized interest groups.

OLSON, MANCUR. *The Rise and Decline of Nations*. New Haven, Conn.: Yale University Press, 1982. Argues that, over time, the development of powerful special-interest lobbies has led to institutional sclerosis, inefficiency, and slowed economic growth.

SCHLOZMAN, KAY LEHMANN, and JOHN T. TIERNEY. *Organized Interests and American Democracy*. New York: Harper &

Row, 1986. Comprehensive examination of interest groups in American politics, with original survey data from Washington lobbyists.

TRUMAN, DAVID B. *The Governmental Process*. New York: Knopf, 1951. The classic description and defense of interest-group pluralism.

WALKER, JACK L. *Mobilizing Interest Groups in America: Patrons, Professions, and Social Movements*. Ann Arbor: University of Michigan Press, 1991. A study of mobilization and maintenance of interest groups, based on large-scale mail surveys of Washington-based membership associations. It includes chapters on how and why organizations are formed, what inducements members are offered, and what influences leaders' choices of strategy.

WOLPE, BRUCE E., and BERTRAM J. LEVINE. *Lobbying Congress*. 2nd ed. Washington, D.C.: CQ Press, 1996. A practical guide to lobbying on Capitol Hill written by experienced lobbyists.

ASK YOURSELF ABOUT POLITICS

1. Should members of Congress be limited in the number of terms they can serve?
   Yes ☐ No ☐

2. Should congressional districts be drawn to ensure that minorities win seats in Congress in rough proportion to their populations in the states?
   Yes ☐ No ☐

3. Should a party's candidates for Congress across the country join together and pledge to support specific policy positions?
   Yes ☐ No ☐

4. Would the nation be better served if the president and the majority Congress were from the same party?
   Yes ☐ No ☐

5. Is it ethical for Congress members to pay special attention to requests for assistance by people who make large campaign contributions?
   Yes ☐ No ☐

6. Are there too many lawyers in Congress?
   Yes ☐ No ☐

7. Are members of Congress obliged to vote the way their constituents wish, even if they personally disagree?
   Yes ☐ No ☐

CHAPTER

10

CONGRESS
POLITICS ON
CAPITOL HILL

Who are the members of Congress? How did they get there, and how do they manage to stay there? How did Congress—the official institution for deciding who gets what in America—get its powers, and how does it use them?

CHAPTER OUTLINE

The Powers of Congress

Congressional Apportionment and Redistricting

Getting to Capitol Hill

Life in Congress

Home Style

Organizing Congress: Party and Leadership

In Committee

On the Floor

Decision Making in Congress

Customs and Norms

Congressional Ethics

FEATURES

Across the USA: Apportionment of House Seats, 1990s

What Do You Think? Term Limits for Members of Congress?

What Do You Think? Why Do Voters Reelect Members of an Unpopular Congress?

People in Politics: Ben Nighthorse Campbell, Native American Voice in Congress

People in Politics: The Rise and Fall of Speaker Newt

People in Politics: Dick Gephardt, Minority Leader, Presidential Candidate, or Both?

Up Close: What Are They Talking About?

A Conflicting View: Congress Can Act Responsibly on Occasion

Up Close: The Keating Five: Service to Constituents, for a Price?

Politics in Cyberspace: Congress

321

THE POWERS OF CONGRESS

James Madison argued that the control of "faction" was "the principal task of modern legislation."[1] He meant that in enacting laws, legislators were really balancing interests, finding compromises, and resolving conflicts. Public policies—laws, regulations, and budgets—represent temporary balances of power among conflicting interests. As the relative power of these interests changes over time, new laws, amendments, and increases or decreases in funding will be enacted, reflecting new balances of power.

Constitutional Powers   The Constitution gives very broad powers to Congress. "All legislative Powers herein granted shall be vested in a Congress of the United States, which shall consist of a Senate and House of Representatives." The nation's Founders envisioned Congress as the first and most powerful branch of government. They equated national powers with the powers of Congress and gave Congress the most clearly specified role in national government (see Table 10-1).

Article I empowers Congress to levy taxes, borrow and spend money, regulate interstate commerce, establish a national money supply, establish a post office, declare war, raise and support an army and navy, establish a court system, and pass all laws "necessary and proper" to implement these powers. Congress may also propose amendments to the Constitution or call a convention to do so. Congress admits new states. In the event that no presidential candidate receives

---

TABLE 10-1   Constitutional Powers of Congress

Powers of Both House and Senate	Powers of House Only	Powers of Senate Only
• Appropriate money • Authorize borrowing • Levy taxes } "Power of the purse" • Regulate currency and punish counterfeiting • Establish post office and post roads • Make bankruptcy laws • Regulate interstate and foreign commerce • Establish rules of naturalization • Fix weights and measures • Make patent and copyright law • Provide for government of District of Columbia • Admit new states • Establish lower federal courts • Propose amendments to the Constitution • Declare war • Raise and support military forces } War-making powers • Provide for militia • "Make all laws which shall be necessary and proper for carrying into Execution the foregoing Powers, and all other powers vested by this Constitution in the Government of the United States" } Implied powers	• Originate tax bills • Bring impeachment charges	• Advise and consent to (ratify) treaties • Confirm appointments to Supreme Court and federal judiciary, ambassador, cabinet, and other high executive posts • Try impeachments

---

a majority of votes in the Electoral College, the House of Representatives selects the president. The Senate is called on for "advice and consent" to treaties and approves presidential nominations to executive and judicial posts. The House has the power to impeach, and the Senate to try, any officer of the U.S. government, including the president. Each **congressional session** convenes on January 3 following congressional elections in November of even-numbered years.

Institutional Conflict   Over two centuries, the separate branches of the national government—the Congress, the presidency and the executive branch, and the Supreme Court and federal judiciary—have struggled for power and preeminence in governing. This struggle for power among the separate institutions is precisely what the Founders envisioned. In writing the Constitution, they sought to create "opposite and rival interests" among the separate branches of the national government. "The constant aim," explained Madison, "is to divide and arrange the several offices in such a manner as that each may be a check on the other"[2] (see Appendix, *Federalist Papers*, No. 51). From time to time, first the Congress, then the presidency, and occasionally the Supreme Court have appeared to become the most powerful branch of government.

Throughout much of the twentieth century, Congress ceded leadership in national policy making to the president and the executive branch. Congress largely responded to the policy initiatives and spending requests originating from the president, executive agencies, and interest groups. Congress did not merely ratify or "rubber-stamp" these initiatives and requests; it played an independent role in the policy-making process. But this role was essentially a deliberative one, in which Congress accepted, modified, amended, or rejected the policies and budget requests initiated by others.

It is easier for the Congress to obstruct the policy initiatives of the president than it is to assume policy leadership itself. Congress can defeat presidential policy proposals, deny presidential budget requests, delay or reject presidential appointments, investigate executive agencies, hold committee hearings to spotlight improprieties, and generally immobilize the executive branch. It can investigate and question nominees for the Supreme Court and the federal judiciary; it can legislate changes in the jurisdiction of the federal courts; and it can try to reverse court decisions by amending laws or the Constitution itself. The Congress can even threaten to impeach the president or federal judges. But these are largely reactive, obstructionist actions, usually accompanied by a great deal of oratory.

From time to time, however, Congress has attempted to reassert national leadership. This effort was especially obvious in the 104th Congress, elected in 1994 and controlled by Republicans for the first time in forty years. The House of Representatives, under former Speaker Newt Gingrich, undertook to set the nation's policy agenda in a "Contract with America" that included term limits for Congress members, a balanced budget amendment to the Constitution, tax cuts, and welfare reform. Although most of the promises in this contract failed to pass and some were vetoed by the president, the important institutional lesson was that the Congress occasionally tries to seize the policy initiative. Nevertheless, over the long term, national leadership and policy initiative have tended to shift from Congress to the president.

Dividing Congressional Power: House and Senate   Congress must not only share national power with the executive and judicial branches of government;

congressional session Each Congress elected in November of even-numbered years meets the following January 3 and remains in session for two years. Since the first Congress to meet under the Constitution in 1789, Congresses have been numbered by session (for example, 104th Congress 1995–97, 105th Congress 1997–99, 106th Congress 1999–2001).

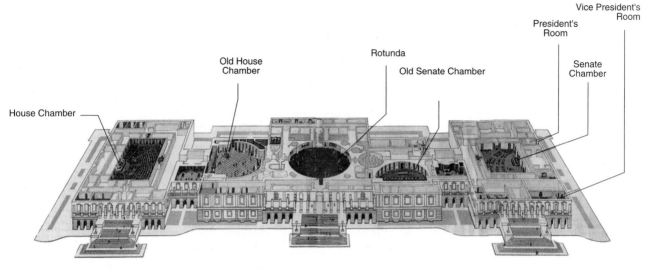

Vice President's Room

President's Room

Rotunda

Old House Chamber

Old Senate Chamber

Senate Chamber

House Chamber

FIGURE 10-1 Corridors of Power in Congress

The architecture and floor plan of the Capitol Building in Washington reflect the bicameral division of Congress, with one wing for the House of Representatives and one for the Senate.

it must share power within itself. The framers of the Constitution took the advice of the nation's eldest diplomat, Benjamin Franklin: "It is not enough that your legislature should be numerous; it should also be divided. . . . One division should watch over and control the other, supply its wants, correct its blunders, and cross its designs, should they be criminal or erroneous."[3] Accordingly, the U.S. Congress is **bicameral**—composed of two houses (see Figure 10-1).

No law can be passed and no money can be spent unless both the House of Representatives and the Senate pass identical laws. Yet the House and the Senate have very different constituencies and terms. The House consists of 435 voting members, elected from districts within each state apportioned on the basis of equal population. (The average congressional district since the 1990 census has a population of 571,700; the House also includes nonvoting delegates from Puerto Rico, the District of Columbia, Guam, the Virgin Islands, and American Samoa.) All House members face election every two years. The Senate consists of 100 members serving six-year terms, elected by statewide constituencies. Senate terms are staggered so that one-third of senators are elected every two years (see Table 10-2).

The House of Representatives, with its two-year terms, was designed to be more responsive to the popular mood. Representatives are fond of referring to their chamber as "the people's House," and the Constitution requires that all revenue-raising bills originate in the House. The Senate was designed to be a smaller, more deliberative body, with its members serving six-year terms. Indeed, the Senate is the more prestigious body. House members frequently give up their seats to run for the Senate; the reverse has seldom occurred. Moreover, the Senate exercises certain powers not given to the House: the power to ratify treaties and the power to confirm federal judges, ambassadors, cabinet members, and other high executive officials.

Domestic versus Foreign and Defense Policy   Congress is more powerful in domestic than in foreign and military affairs. It is freer to reject presidential initiatives in domestic policy areas such as welfare, health, education, the envi-

bicameral Any legislative body that consists of two separate chambers or houses; in the United States, the Senate represents 50 statewide voter constituencies, and the House of Representatives represents voters in 435 separate districts.

TABLE 10–2	**Comparing the House and Senate**	
	House of Representatives	*Senate*
Terms	Two years	Six years
Members	435	100
Elections	All every two years	One-third every two years
Constituencies	Congressional districts	States
Unique powers	Originate tax bills Bring impeachment charges	Advise and consent to (ratify) treaties by two-thirds vote Confirm appointments Try impeachment charges
Debate on bills	Limited by Rules Committee	Unlimited, except by unanimous consent or vote of cloture (three-fifths)
Member prestige	Modest; smaller personal staffs, fewer committee assignments	High; larger personal staffs, more committee assignments, always addressed as "Senator"
Leadership	Hierarchical, with speaker, majority and minority leaders and whips, and committees, especially Rules, concentrating power	Less hierarchical, with each senator exercising more influence on leadership, committees, and floor votes
Committees	Twenty standing committees Each member on two or three committees	Twenty standing committees Each member on four, five, or six committees

ronment, and taxation. But Congress usually follows presidential leadership in foreign and defense policy even though constitutionally the president and Congress share power in these arenas. The president is "Commander-in-Chief" of the armed forces, but only Congress can "declare war." The president appoints and receives ambassadors and "makes treaties," but the Senate must confirm appointments and provide "advice and consent" to treaties. Historically presidents have led the nation in matters of war and peace. Presidents have sent U.S. troops beyond the borders of the United States in military actions on more than two hundred occasions. In contrast, Congress has formally declared war only five times: the War of 1812, the Mexican War in 1846, the Spanish-American War in 1898, World War I in 1917, and World War II in 1941. Congress did not declare war in the Korean War (1950–53), the Vietnam War (1965–73), or the Persian Gulf War (1991).

The Vietnam experience inspired Congress to try to reassert its powers over war and peace. Military embarrassment, prolonged and indecisive fighting, and accumulating casualties—all vividly displayed on national television—encouraged Congress to challenge presidential war-making power. The War Powers Act of 1973, passed over the veto of President Richard Nixon, who was weakened by the Watergate scandal, sought to curtail the president's power to commit U.S. military forces to combat (see "Commander-in-Chief" in Chapter 11). But this act has not proven effective, and both Republican and Democratic presidents have continued to exercise war-making powers.

The Power of the Purse   Congress's real power in both domestic and foreign (defense) policy centers on its **power of the purse**—its power over federal

power of the purse
Congress's exclusive, constitutional power to authorize expenditures by all agencies of the federal government.

taxing and spending. Only Congress can "lay and collect Taxes, Duties, Imposts and Excises" (Article I, Section 8), and only Congress can authorize spending: "No Money shall be drawn from the Treasury, but in Consequence of Appropriations made by Law" (Article I, Section 9).

Congress jealously guards these powers. Presidents initiate taxing and spending policies by sending their budgets to the Congress each year (see "The Bureaucracy and the Budgetary Process" in Chapter 12 for details). But Congress has the last word on taxing and spending. The most important bills that Congress considers each year are usually the budget resolutions setting ceilings on various categories of expenditures and the later appropriations bills authorizing specific expenditures. It is often in these appropriations bills that Congress exercises its greatest influence over national policy. Thus, for example, the Congress's involvement in foreign affairs centers on its annual consideration of appropriations for foreign aid, its involvement in military affairs centers on its annual deliberations over the defense appropriations bill, and so on.

Oversight of the Bureaucracy Congressional **oversight** of the federal bureaucracy is a continuing process by which Congress reviews the activities of the executive branch. The *formal* rationale of oversight is to determine whether the purposes of laws passed by Congress are being achieved by executive agencies and whether appropriations established by Congress are being spent as intended. Often the *real* purpose is to influence executive branch decisions, secure favorable treatment for friends and constituents, embarrass presidential appointees, undercut political support for particular programs or agencies, lay the political groundwork for budgetary increases or decreases for an agency, or simply enhance the power of congressional committees and subcommittees and those who chair them.

Oversight is carried out primarily through congressional committees and subcommittees. Individual senators and representatives can engage in a form of oversight simply by writing or calling executive agencies, but committees and their staffs carry on the bulk of oversight activity. Because committees and subcommittees specialize in particular areas of policy making, each tends to focus its oversight activities on particular executive departments and agencies. Oversight is particularly intense during budget hearings. Subcommittees of both the House and the Senate Appropriations Committees are especially interested in how money is being spent by the agencies they oversee.

Oversight often begins when special-interest groups or constituents complain about bureaucratic performance. Minor complaints can be resolved by members of Congress or their staffs contacting the executive agency involved, but executive officials may also be called to a congressional committee or subcommittee hearing to explain and defend their actions. Sitting before a hostile congressional committee in the glare of television cameras and responding to unfriendly questions can be embarrassing and unpleasant. Thus executive officials have a powerful motivation to comply with the wishes of a member of Congress and escape such treatment.

Agenda Setting and Media Attention **Congressional hearings** and investigations often involve agenda setting—bringing issues to the public's attention and placing them on the national agenda. For agenda-setting purposes, congressional committees or subcommittees need the assistance of the media. Televised hearings and investigations are perhaps the most effective means by which Congress can attract attention to issues as well as to itself and its members.

oversight Congressional monitoring of the activities of executive branch agencies to determine if the laws are being faithfully executed.

congressional hearings Congressional committee sessions in which members listen to witnesses who provide information and opinions on matters of interest to the committee, including pending legislation.

Hearings and investigations are similar in some ways, but hearings are usually held on a specific bill in order to build a record of both technical information (what is the problem and how legislation might be crafted to resolve it) and political information (who favors and who opposes various legislative options). In contrast, investigations are held on alleged misdeeds or scandals. Although the U.S. Supreme Court has held that there must be some "legislative purpose" behind a **congressional investigation**, that phrase has been interpreted very broadly indeed.[4]

The *formal* rationale for congressional investigations is that Congress is seeking information to assist in its lawmaking function. But from the earliest Congress to the present, the investigating powers of Congress have often been used for political purposes: to rally popular support for policies or programs favored by Congress; to attack the president, high officials in the administration, or presidential policies or programs; to focus media attention and public debate on particular issues; or simply to win media coverage and popular recognition for members of Congress. Congressional investigators have the legal power to subpoena witnesses (force them to appear), administer oaths, compel testimony, and initiate criminal charges for contempt (refusing to cooperate) and perjury (lying). These powers can be exercised by Congress's regular committees and subcommittees and by committees appointed especially to conduct a particular investigation.

Congress cannot impose criminal punishments as a result of its investigations. (This would be a *bill of attainder* forbidden by Article I, Section 9 of the Constitution.) But the information uncovered in a congressional investigation can be turned over to the U.S. Department of Justice, which may proceed with its own criminal investigation and perhaps indictment and trial of alleged wrongdoers in federal courts.

Congressional investigations have long been used as an opportunity for Congress to expose wrongdoing on the part of executive branch officials. The first congressional investigation (1792) examined why General Arthur St. Clair had been defeated by the Indians in Ohio; the Crédit Mobilier investigations (1872–73) revealed scandals in the Grant Administration; the Select Committee on Campaign Practices, known universally as the "Watergate Committee," exposed the activities of President Richard Nixon's inner circle that led to impeachment charges and Nixon's forced resignation; a House and Senate Joint Select Committee conducted the Iran-contra investigation in the Reagan Administration; the Senate Special Whitewater Committee investigated matters related to Bill and Hillary Clinton's real estate investments in Arkansas; and a Senate investigating committee, chaired by Republican Fred Thompson, focused national attention in 1997 on presidential campaign fund-raising tactics (see Chapter 8, *Up Close:* "The President Shakes the Money Tree").

CONGRESSIONAL APPORTIONMENT AND REDISTRICTING

The Constitution states that "Representatives . . . shall be apportioned among the several states . . . according to their respective Numbers." It orders an "actual enumeration" (census) every ten years. And it provides that every state shall have at least one representative, in addition to two senators, regardless of population. But the Constitution is silent on the size of the House of Representatives. Congress itself determines its own size; for more than a century, it allowed itself to grow to accommodate new states and population growth. In 1910 it fixed the membership of the House at 435.

congressional investigation
Congressional committee hearings on alleged misdeeds or scandals.

Apportionment of House Seats, 1990s

When the number of seats in the House of Representatives stays constant, as it has at 435 seats since 1910, each census requires a reapportionment of seats among the states. States such as Arizona, which gained population between 1980 and 1990, gained seats. States such as Illinois, which lost population in that same period, lost seats. Changing population statistics do not affect Senate seats, however, since the Constitution stipulates that every state shall have two senators, elected by all voters in the state, regardless of the state's population.

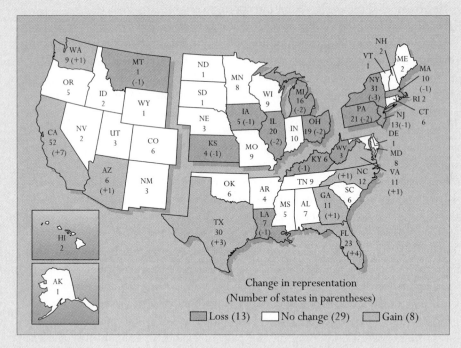

Change in representation
(Number of states in parentheses)

■ Loss (13)   □ No change (29)   ■ Gain (8)

apportionment The allocation of legislative seats to jurisdictions based on population. Seats in the U.S. House of Representatives are apportioned to the states on the basis of their population after every ten-year census.

malapportionment Unequal numbers of people in legislative districts resulting in inequality of voter representation.

Apportionment   **Apportionment** refers to the allocation of House seats to the states after each ten-year census. The Constitution does not specify a mathematical method of apportionment; Congress adopted a complex "method of equal proportion" in 1929, which so far has withstood court challenges (see *Across the USA:* "Apportionment of House Seats, 1990s," which shows the current apportionment, together with the states that gained and lost seats after the 1990 census).

Malapportionment   The Constitution does not determine how the states should apportion seats among their own citizens. State legislatures were long notorious for their **malapportionment**—congressional (and state legislative) districts with grossly unequal numbers of people. Some congressional districts had twice the average number of people per district, and others had only half as many. In 1962, for example, Georgia's congressional districts varied in size from a rural district of 272,154 to an Atlanta district of 823,860. In a district twice the size of the average district, the value of an individual's vote was heavily diluted. In a district half the size of the average, the value of an individual's vote was greatly magnified.

Enter the Supreme Court   Prior to 1962, the Supreme Court refused to intervene in apportionment, holding that this question belonged to the state legislatures and that the federal courts should avoid this "political thicket." So the Supreme Court's decision in the landmark case *Baker v. Carr* (1962) came as a surprise. The Court ruled that inequalities in voters' influence resulting from different-size districts violated the Equal Protection Clause of the Fourteenth Amendment. The case dealt with a complaint about Tennessee's state legislative districts, but the Court soon extended its holding to congressional districts as well.[5] "The conception of political equality from the Declaration of Independence to Lincoln's Gettysburg Address, to the Fourteenth, Fifteenth, Seventeenth, and Nineteenth Amendments, can mean only one thing—one person, one vote."[6]

The shift in the Supreme Court's policy raised a new question: How equal must districts be in order to guarantee voters "equal protection of the law"? The courts have ruled that only official U.S. Bureau of the Census figures may be used: estimated changes since the last census may *not* be used. In recent years, the courts have insisted on nearly exact mathematical equality in congressional districts.

"Enumeration"   Yet another constitutional issue arises over the use of the samples and estimates by the U.S. Bureau of the Census to correct what it perceives to be "undercounts." Undercounting is said to occur when certain populations are difficult to identify and count on an individual basis, for example, recent non–English-speaking immigrants to the United States, or residents of neighborhoods likely to mistake government census takers for law enforcement officers or other unwelcome government officials.

But the U.S. Constitution is very specific in its wording: It calls for an "actual Enumeration" (Article I, Section 2) of the population. Political leaders (usually Democrats) of states and cities with large immigrant and minority populations have urged the Census Bureau to substitute samples and estimates for actual head counts. Opponents of these substitutes (usually Republicans) will likely try to prevent the Census Bureau from using any methods other than actual counts. The issue may have to be settled by federal courts.

Redistricting   **Redistricting** refers to the drawing of boundary lines of congressional districts following the census. After each census, some states gain and others lose seats, depending on whether their populations have grown faster or slower than the nation's population. In addition, population shifts within a state may force districting changes. Congressional district boundaries are drawn by state legislatures in each state; a state's redistricting act must pass both houses of the state legislature and win the governor's signature (or be passed over a gubernatorial veto). The U.S. Justice Department and the federal judiciary are also deeply involved in redistricting issues, particularly questions of whether or not redistricting disadvantages African Americans or other minorities.

Gerrymandering   **Gerrymandering** is the drawing of district lines for political advantage (see Figure 10-2). The population of districts may be equal, yet the district boundaries are drawn in such a fashion as to grant advantage or disadvantage to specific groups of voters. Gerrymandering has long been used by parties in control of the state legislatures to maximize their seats in Congress and state legislatures.

Gerrymandering, with the aid of sophisticated computer-mapping programs and data on past voting records of precincts, is a highly technical task. But consider a simple example where a city is entitled to three representatives and the eastern

redistricting Drawing of legislative district boundary lines following each ten-year census.

gerrymandering Drawing district boundary lines for political advantage.

third of the city is Republican but the western two-thirds is Democratic (see Figure 10-3). If the Republicans could draw the district lines, they might draw them along a north-south direction to allow their party to win in one of the three districts. In contrast, if Democrats could draw the district lines, they might draw them along an east-west direction to allow their party to win all three districts by diluting the Republican vote. Such dividing up and diluting of a strong minority to deny it the power to elect a representative is called **splintering**. Often gerrymandering is not as neat as our example; district lines may twist and turn, creating grotesque patterns in order to achieve the desired effects. Another gerrymandering strategy—**packing**—is the heavy concentration of one party's voters in a single district in order to "waste" their votes and allow modest majorities of the party doing the redistricting to win in other districts.

Partisan Gerrymandering Generally, partisan gerrymandering does *not* violate federal court standards for "equal protection" under the Fourteenth Amendment. There is no constitutional obligation to allocate seats "to the contending parties in proportion to what their anticipated statewide vote will be."[7] However, the federal courts may intervene in political gerrymandering if it "consistently degrades a voter's or a group of voters' influence on the political process as a whole."[8] These vague standards set forth by the U.S. Supreme Court open the door to judicial intervention in particularly grievous cases of partisan gerrymandering.

The Politics of Redistricting Congressional district boundaries are drawn by state legislatures and governors, unless federal courts rule that these bodies have

splintering Redistricting in which a strong minority is divided up and diluted to prevent it from electing a representative.

packing Redistricting in which partisan voters are concentrated in a single district, "wasting" their majority vote and allowing the opposition to win by modest majorities in other districts.

acted illegally or unconstitutionally and step in to undertake the task themselves. Thus party control of state legislatures and governorships across the nation influences partisan gerrymandering and the protection of incumbents. During the reapportionment following the 1990 census, a majority of state legislative chambers across the nation were controlled by Democrats, and a majority of states had Democratic governors. As a result, the Democrats were well positioned to protect Democratic seats in the House of Representatives through careful, partisan redistricting plans. Republicans in many states were obliged to appeal to the courts and the Justice Department for relief. (In some cases, Republicans championed efforts to create African American and Hispanic districts, hoping to "pack" traditional Democratic-voting minorities into a few districts and thereby improve Republican chances in the remaining districts.) But political gerrymandering could not save the Democratic Congress in 1994. Republican House candidates nationwide won more than 54 percent of the total congressional votes cast and captured 230 seats (53 percent) in the House of Representatives.

Racial Gerrymandering   Racial gerrymandering to disadvantage African Americans and other minorities violates both the Equal Protection Clause of the Fourteenth Amendment and the Voting Rights Act of 1965. The Voting Rights Act specifies that redistricting in states with a history of voter discrimination or low voter participation must be "cleared" in advance with the U.S. Justice Department. The act extends special protection not only to African American voters but also to Hispanic, Native American, Alaska Native, and Asian voters.

In 1982 Congress strengthened the Voting Rights Act by outlawing any electoral arrangement that has the effect of weakening minority voting power. This *effects test* replaced the earlier *intent test,* under which redistricting was outlawed only if boundaries were intentionally drawn to dilute minority political influence. In *Thornburg v. Gingles* (1986), the Supreme Court interpreted the effects test to require state legislatures to redistrict their states in a way that maximizes minority representation in Congress and the state legislatures.[9] The effect of this ruling was to require **affirmative racial gerrymandering**—the creation of predominately African American and minority districts (labeled "majority-minority" districts) whenever possible. Following the 1990 census, redistricting in legislatures in states with large minority populations was closely scrutinized by the U.S. Justice Department and the federal courts. The result was a dramatic increase in African American and Hispanic representation in Congress.

affirmative racial gerrymandering   Drawing district boundary lines to maximize minority representation.

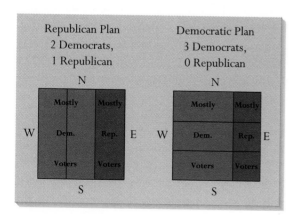

Republican Plan
2 Democrats,
1 Republican

N

Mostly | Mostly

W   Dem. | Rep.   E

Voters | Voters

S

Democratic Plan
3 Democrats,
0 Republican

N

Mostly | Mostly

W   Dem. | Rep.   E

Voters | Voters

S

FIGURE 10-3 Gerrymandering in Action

Depending on how an area is divided into districts, the result may benefit one party or the other. In this example, dividing the area so one district has virtually all the Republicans gives that party a victory in that district while ceding the other two districts to the Democrats. In contrast, Democrats benefit when Republican voters are divided among the three districts so that their votes are splintered.

FIGURE 10-4 **Affirmative Racial Gerrymandering**

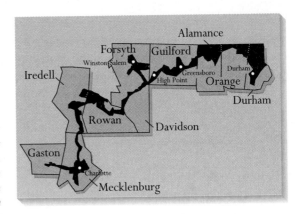

North Carolina's Twelfth Congressional District was drawn up to be a "majority-minority" district by combining African American communities over a wide region of the state. The U.S. Supreme Court in Shaw v. Reno (1993) ordered a court review of this district to determine whether it incorporated any common interest other than race. The North Carolina legislature redrew the district in 1997, lowering its black population from 57 to 46 percent, yet keeping its lengthy connection of black voters from Charlotte to Greensboro.

Nevertheless, the Supreme Court has expressed constitutional doubts about bizarre-shaped districts based *solely* on racial composition. In a controversial 5 to 4 decision in *Shaw v. Reno* (1993), Justice Sandra Day O'Connor wrote, "Racial gerrymandering, even for remedial purposes, may balkanize us into competing racial factions. . . . A reapportionment plan that includes in one district individuals who have little in common with one another but the color of their skin bears an uncomfortable resemblance to political apartheid"[10] (see Figure 10-4). Later the Court held that the use of race as the "predominant factor" in dividing district lines is unconstitutional: "When the state assigns voters on the basis of race, it engages in the offensive and demeaning assumption that voters of a particular race, because of their race, think alike, share the same political interests and will prefer the same candidates at the polls."[11] But the Court stopped short of saying that *all* race-conscious districting is unconstitutional. Several states redrew the boundaries of majority-minority districts trying to conform to the Court's opinions. Incumbent African American Congress members managed to hold on to their seats in these states. But the constitutional status of affirmative racial gerrymandering remains unclear.

GETTING TO CAPITOL HILL

Members of Congress are independent political entrepreneurs—selling themselves, their services, and their personal policy views to the voters in 435 districts and 50 states across the country. They initiate their own candidacies, raise most of their campaign funds from individual contributors, put together personal campaign organizations, and get themselves elected with relatively little help from their party. Their reelection campaigns depend on their ability to raise funds from individuals and interest groups and on the services and other benefits they provide to their constituents.

Who Runs for Congress? Members of Congress come from a wide variety of backgrounds, ranging from acting and professional sports to medicine and the ministry. However, exceptionally high percentages of senators and representatives have prior experience in at least one of three fields—law, business, or public

TABLE 10-3
Occupational Backgrounds of Members of Congress, 1997–1999

	House			Senate			Congress
	D	R	Total	D	R	Total	Total
Actor/Entertainer	0	1	1	0	1	1	2
Aeronautics	0	1	1	1	0	1	2
Agriculture	8	14	22	2	6	8	30
Artistic/Creative	1	1	2	0	0	0	2
Business or Banking	55	126	181	8	25	33	214
Clergy	1	0	1	0	1	1	2
Education	40	33	74	5	8	13	87
Engineering	1	7	8	0	0	0	8
Health Care	1	1	2	0	0	0	2
Journalism	4	7	12	2	7	9	21
Labor Officials	1	0	1	0	0	0	1
Law	87	85	172	26	27	53	225
Law Enforcement	8	2	10	0	0	0	10
Medicine	3	9	12	0	2	2	14
Military	0	1	1	0	1	1	2
Miscellaneous	0	5	5	0	0	0	5
Professional Sports	0	3	3	0	0	0	3
Public Service	54	46	100	9	17	26	126
Real Estate	3	20	23	2	3	5	28
Technical/Trade	0	1	1	0	0	0	1

Note: Because some members have more than one occupation, totals are higher than membership of Congress.

Source: Congressional Quarterly, February 12, 1997.

service (see Table 10-3). Members of Congress are increasingly career politicians, people who decided early in life to devote themselves to running for and occupying public office.[12] The many lawyers, by and large, are *not* practicing attorneys. Rather, the typical lawyer-legislator is a political activist with a law degree. These are people who graduated from law school and immediately sought public jobs—as federal or state prosecuting attorneys, as attorneys for federal or state agencies, or as staff assistants in congressional, state, or city offices. They used their early job experiences to make political contacts and learn how to organize a political campaign, find financial contributors, and deal with the media. Another group of Congress members are former businesspeople—not employees of large corporations, but people whose personal or family businesses brought them into close contact with government and their local community, in real estate, insurance, franchise dealerships, community banks, and so forth.

Competition for Seats   Careerism in Congress is aided by the electoral advantages enjoyed by incumbents over challengers. Greater name recognition, advantages in raising campaign funds, and the resources of congressional offices all combine to limit competition for seats in Congress and to reelect the vast majority of incumbents (see "The Advantages of Incumbency" in Chapter 8). A congressional district in which the incumbent regularly wins by a large margin

What Do You Think?

Term Limits for Members of Congress?

Declining confidence in government and increasing distrust of politicians have fueled a national grass-roots movement to limit the terms of public officials, notably members of Congress and state legislators. Although national polls regularly report that 70 percent or more of Americans favor congressional term limits, their enthusiasm is more than matched by the intense opposition on Capitol Hill. It is not likely Congress will ever vote to limit its own terms of office, especially since a constitutional amendment to do so requires a two-thirds vote of the members of both houses.

At the Constitutional Convention of 1787, Roger Sherman commented that Congress should be composed of "citizen-legislators" who would be expected to "return home and mix with the people." He feared that "by remaining at the seat of government, they would acquire the habits of the place, which might differ from those of their constituents." But after brief consideration, the Convention dropped the idea of limiting congressional terms.

Proponents of congressional term limits argue that citizen-legislators have largely been replaced by career politicians. Over time, professional office-holders become isolated from the lives and concerns of average citizens; they acquire an "inside the Beltway" (the circle of highways that surrounds Washington, D.C.) mentality. They respond to the media, to polls, and to interest groups but have no direct feeling for how their constituents live. Terms limits, proponents argue, would force politicians to return home and live under the laws that they make.

Proponents also argue that term limits would increase competition in the electoral system. Creating "open-seat" races on a regular basis would encourage more people to seek public office. Incumbents continually win reelection not because they are the most qualified people in their districts but rather because of the many electoral advantages granted by incumbency itself.

Opponents of term limits argue that they infringe on the voters' freedom of choice. If voters are upset with the performance of Congress or their state legislature, they can always limit "the rascals'" terms by not reelecting them. But if voters wish to keep popular, able, experienced, and hard-working legislators in office, they should be permitted to do so. Experience is a valuable asset in Washington. Voters reasonably want to be represented by members with knowledge and experience in public affairs.

Opponents also argue that inexperienced legislators would be forced to rely more on the policy information supplied them by bureaucrats, lobbyists, and staff people—term limits would thus weaken the institution of Congress, leaving it less capable of checking the power of the special interests. But proponents counter this argument by observing that the closest relationships have developed between lobbyists and senior members of Congress who have interacted professionally and socially over the years. And they note that the most powerful lobbying groups in Washington strongly oppose term limits.

The U.S. Supreme Court ruled in 1995 that the states cannot themselves limit the terms of their members of Congress: "Allowing individual states to adopt their own qualifications for Congressional service would be inconsistent with the framers' vision of a uniform national legislature representing the people of the United States. If the qualifications set forth in the text of the Constitution are to be changed, that text must be amended."

Justice John Paul Stevens, writing for the majority in the controversial 5 to 4 decision, argued that the Founders intended age, citizenship, and residency be the only qualifications for members of Congress. But Justice Clarence Thomas, in his dissenting opinion, set forth a compelling argument based on the Tenth Amendment: "I dissent. Nothing in the Constitution deprives the people of each state of the power to prescribe eligibility requirements for the candidates who seek to represent them in Congress. The Constitution is simply silent on this question. And where the Constitution is silent, it raises no bar to action by the states or the people."

(55 to 60 percent or more of the vote) is regarded as a **safe seat.** More than two-thirds of the members of the House of Representatives sit comfortably in safe seats. Even incumbents elected by close margins enjoy many advantages over challengers. The result is a reelection percentage for House members that usually exceeds 90 percent (see *What Do You Think?* "Term Limits for Members of Congress?"). The average reelection rate for U.S. senators is more than 80 percent (see Figure 10-5).

Aspirants for congressional careers are well advised to wait for open seats. **Open seats** in the House of Representatives are created when incumbents retire or vacate the seat to run for higher office. These opportunities occur on average in about 10 percent of House seats in each election. But every ten years reapportionment creates many new opportunities to win election to Congress. Reapportionment creates new seats in states gaining population, just as it forces out some incumbents in states losing population. Redistricting also threatens incumbents with new constituencies, where they have less name recognition, no history of casework, and perhaps no common racial or ethnic identification. Thus forced retirements and electoral defeats are more common in the first election following each ten-year reapportionment and redistricting of Congress.

Senate races are somewhat more competitive. Senate challengers are usually people who have political experience and name recognition as members of the House, governors, or other high state officials. Even so, most

safe seat Legislative district in which the incumbent regularly wins by a large margin of the vote.

open seat Seat in a legislature for which no incumbent is running for reelection.

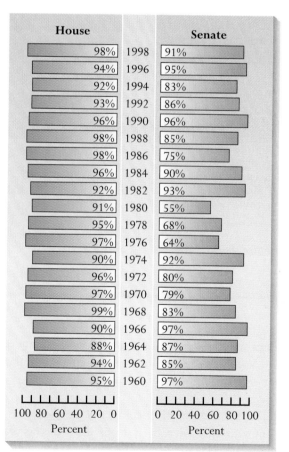

House		Senate
98%	1998	91%
94%	1996	95%
92%	1994	83%
93%	1992	86%
96%	1990	96%
98%	1988	85%
98%	1986	75%
96%	1984	90%
92%	1982	93%
91%	1980	55%
95%	1978	68%
97%	1976	64%
90%	1974	92%
96%	1972	80%
97%	1970	79%
99%	1968	83%
90%	1966	97%
88%	1964	87%
94%	1962	85%
95%	1960	97%

100 80 60 40 20 0   0 20 40 60 80 100
Percent   Percent

FIGURE 10-5 Incumbent Advantage

Despite periodic movements to "throw the bums out," voters in most districts and states routinely reelect their members of Congress. Although incumbents do not always retain their seats, the odds are strongly in their favor. In recent decades, more than 90 percent of representatives and 80 percent of senators who have sought reelection have been returned to Congress by voters in their districts or states.

Why Do Voters Reelect Members of an Unpopular Congress?

Congress is the least popular branch of government. Indeed, although the *most* popular institutions in the United States change from year to year, Congress in recent years has ranked at the *bottom* of the list (see figure on opposite page). What accounts for this lack of popularity? The belief that members of Congress "spend more time thinking about their own political futures than they do in passing legislation" may contribute to this sentiment. Well-publicized congressional scandals, pay raises, and lavish perks offend taxpayers. Congress also shares in the current general decline in popular trust in government.

But in an apparent paradox, most voters *approve of their own* representative (see figure below), even while Congress itself is the object of popular distrust and ridicule. A majority of voters believe that their own representatives "deserve reelection." This apparent contradiction is explained in part by differing expectations: Americans expect Congress to deal with national issues, but they expect their own representatives to deal with local concerns and even personal problems. Members of Congress understand this concern and consequently devote a great deal of their time to constituent service. Indeed, many members of Congress try to dissociate themselves from Congress, attacking Congress in their own campaigns and contributing to negative images of the institution. Finally, the national news media are highly critical of Congress, but local news media frequently portray local members of Congress in a more favorable light.

Percentage of Those Expressing Approval of Their Representatives and Congress

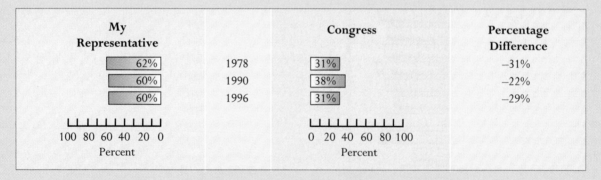

My Representative		Congress		Percentage Difference
62%	1978	31%		−31%
60%	1990	38%		−22%
60%	1996	31%		−29%

100 80 60 40 20 0   0 20 40 60 80 100
Percent   Percent

Source: 1973 and 1990 surveys by the Gallup Organization, as reported in *American Enterprise,* January–February 1991, p. 83; 1992 survey by Louis Harris, as reported in *American Enterprise,* May–June 1992, p. 103; 1996 by the Gallup Organization.

Senate incumbents seeking reelection are victorious over their challengers (see *What Do You Think?* "Why Do Voters Reelect Members of an Unpopular Congress?").

Turnover Despite a high rate of reelection of incumbents in Congress, **turnover** of membership in recent years has been fairly high. Turnover occurs more frequently as a result of retirement, resignation (sometimes to run for higher office), or reapportionment (and the loss of an incumbent's seat) than it does as a result of an incumbent's defeat in a bid for reelection.

turnover Replacement of members of Congress by retirement or resignation, by reapportionment, or (more rarely) by electoral defeat, usually expressed as a percentage of members newly elected.

Percentage of Those Expressing "Quite a Lot" or "a Great Deal" of Confidence in Various Institutions

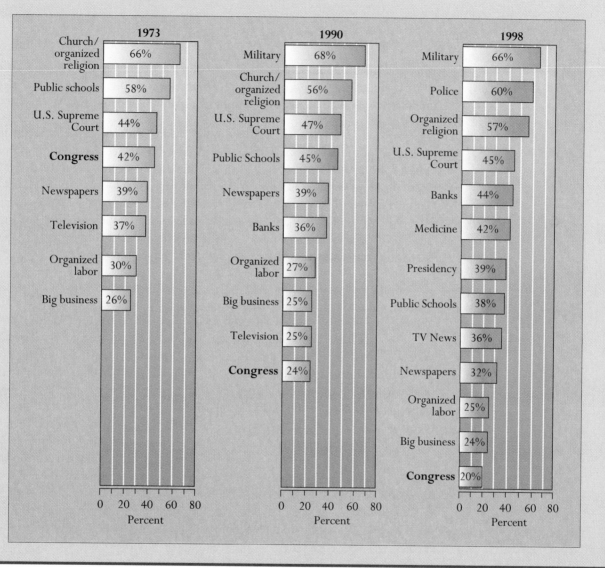

1973

Institution	Percent
Church/organized religion	66%
Public schools	58%
U.S. Supreme Court	44%
Congress	42%
Newspapers	39%
Television	37%
Organized labor	30%
Big business	26%

1990

Institution	Percent
Military	68%
Church/organized religion	56%
U.S. Supreme Court	47%
Public Schools	45%
Newspapers	39%
Banks	36%
Organized labor	27%
Big business	25%
Television	25%
Congress	24%

1998

Institution	Percent
Military	66%
Police	60%
Organized religion	57%
U.S. Supreme Court	45%
Banks	44%
Medicine	42%
Presidency	39%
Public Schools	38%
TV News	36%
Newspapers	32%
Organized labor	25%
Big business	24%
Congress	20%

The Congressional Electorate Congressional elections generally fail to arouse much interest among voters. Indeed, only about 60 percent of the general public can name one U.S. senator from their state, and only about 40 percent can name both of their U.S. senators. Members of the House of Representatives fare no better: less than half of the general public can name their representative.[13] But even constituents who know the names of their congressional delegation seldom know anything about the policy positions of these elected officials or about their votes on specific issues. Turnout in congressional *general elections* averages only about 35 percent in off-year (nonpresidential) elections. Turnout in congressional

TABLE 10-4	Congressional Campaign Spending	
	House	*Senate*
Average incumbent	$628,064	$5,015,685
Average challenger	$301,289	$2,418,075
Average open-seat candidate	$638,571	$2,970,018

Source: Federal Elections Commission, 1998.

primary elections seldom exceeds 15 to 20 percent of persons eligible to vote. This lack of public attentiveness to congressional elections gives a great advantage to candidates with high name recognition, generally the incumbents.

Independence of Congressional Voting   Congressional voting is largely independent of presidential voting. The same voters who elected Republican presidents in 1968, 1972, 1980, 1984, and 1988 simultaneously elected Democratic majorities to the House of Representatives. And while reelecting Democratic President Bill Clinton in 1996, voters simultaneously reelected Republican majorities in the House and Senate. It is unlikely that voters deliberately seek to impose *divided party government* on the nation. Rather, they cast their presidential and congressional votes on the basis of differing expectations of presidents versus members of Congress.[14]

Congressional Campaign Financing   Raising the $700,000 it can take to win a House seat or the $5 million for a successful Senate campaign is a major job in and of itself (see "How Much Does It Cost to Get Elected?" in Chapter 8). Even incumbents who face little or no competition still work hard at fund raising, "banking" contributions against some future challenger. Large campaign chests, assembled well in advance of an election, can also be used to frighten off would-be challengers. Campaign funds can be used to build a strong personal organization back home, finance picnics and other festivities for constituents, expand the margin of victory, and develop a reputation for invincibility that may someday protect against an unknown challenger.[15]

Incumbents in the House of Representatives raise and spend more than twice as much money as their challengers (see Table 10-4). Most individual contributors as well as business and corporate PACs are very pragmatic: they fund incumbents, regardless of party, in order to gain and maintain access to decision makers. Union PACs generally fund Democrats, based on the Democratic Party's perceived support for the goals of organized labor. Ideological PACs usually base their contributions on the perceived "correctness" of the voting records of members of Congress. Challengers thus must rely far more heavily on their own resources than do incumbents, although all candidates are free to spend as much of their own money as they wish.

Does money buy elections? In about 90 percent of all congressional races, the candidate who spends the most money wins. However, because most winning candidates are incumbents, the money probably reflects the expected political outcome rather than shapes it. But even in open-seat races, the candidate who spends the most money usually wins.

The Historic Democratic Party Dominance of Congress   For forty years (1954–94) Democrats enjoyed an advantage in congressional races; in fact, the Democratic Party was said to have a "permanent majority" in the House of Representatives (see Figure 10-6). Thus the Republican victory in the congressional elec-

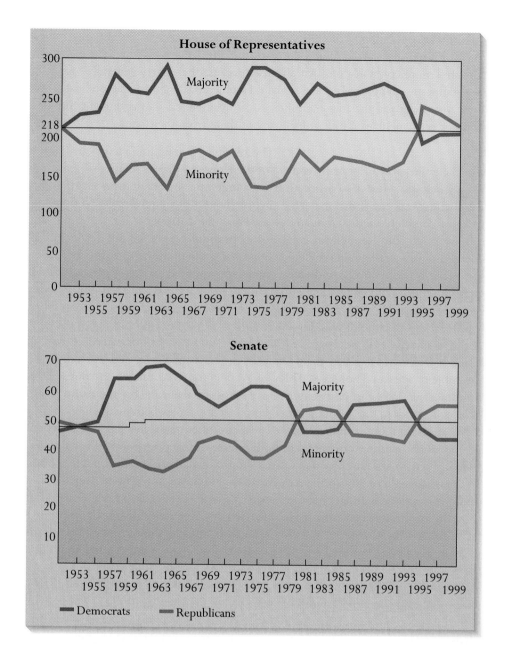

House of Representatives

Senate

■ Democrats ■ Republicans

FIGURE 10-6 Party Control of the House and Senate

Except for two very brief periods, Democrats continuously controlled both the House of Representatives and the Senate for more than forty years. The Democratic Party's "permanent" control of Congress was ended in 1994, when Republicans won majorities in both houses. Republicans retained control of Congress despite President Clinton's victory in 1996, and retained control by a slim margin in the House in 1998.

tion of 1994 was widely described as a political "earthquake." It gave the GOP control of the House for the first time in four decades, as well as control of the Senate.

The historic Democratic dominance of Congress was attributed to several factors. First, over those four decades more voters identified themselves with the Democratic Party than with the Republican Party (see Chapter 7). Party identification plays a significant role in congressional voting; it is estimated that 75 percent of those who identify themselves with a party cast their vote for the congressional candidate of their party.[16] Second, the Democratic advantage was buttressed by the fact that many voters considered local rather than national conditions when casting congressional votes. House campaigns were usually 435 separate local contests emphasizing personal qualities of the candidates and their ability to serve their district's constituents. Voters may have wanted to curtail overall federal spending in Washington (a traditional Republican promise), but they wanted a member of Congress who would "bring home the bacon." Although both Republican and Democratic congressional candidates usually promised to bring money and jobs to their districts, Democratic candidates appeared more creditable on such promises because their party generally supported large domestic-spending programs. Finally, Democratic congressional candidates over those years enjoyed the many advantages of incumbency. It was thought that only death or retirement would dislodge many of them from their seats.

The Republican "Revolution"?   The sweeping Republican victory in 1994—especially the party's capturing control of the House of Representatives—surprised many analysts.[17] Just two years after a Democratic president won election and Democrats won substantial majorities in both houses of Congress, the GOP gained its most complete victory in many years. How did it happen?

First of all, the Republican congressional candidates, under the leadership of Newt Gingrich, largely succeeded in *nationalizing* the midterm congressional election. That is, Republican candidates sought to exploit the voters' general skepticism about government and disenchantment with its performance. Voters were often unfamiliar with specific Republican promises, but they correctly sensed that the Republicans favored "less government."

The Democratic advantage in bringing "pork"—lucrative federal projects—to their districts was turned against them. Indeed, the most powerful House Democratic incumbent, Speaker Thomas S. Foley of Washington, was unable to convince his constituents in 1994 that his twenty years of service to them and his impressive record of bringing pork to the district justified his reelection. Foley became the first Speaker of the House in more than one hundred years to suffer defeat in a bid for reelection.

The GOP's capture of control of both houses of Congress in 1994 for the first time in forty years raised conservatives' hopes of a "revolution" in public policy. The new Republican House Speaker, Newt Gingrich, was the acknowledged leader of the revolution, with Republican Senate Majority Leader Bob Dole in tow. But soon the revolution began to fizzle out. Two key Republican campaign promises failed to pass the Congress: the House failed to muster the necessary two-thirds majority for a constitutional amendment to impose congressional term limits, and the Senate failed to do so on behalf of a balanced budget amendment.

But worse was yet to come for the Republicans. Congress passed several budget resolutions aimed at balancing the federal budget in seven years, only to see them vetoed. Clinton positioned himself as the defender of popular programs—Medicare, Medicaid, education, and the environment—consistently referring to congressional efforts to reduce the rate of growth in these programs as "cuts." The failure of Congress and the president to agree on appropriations temporarily shut down the federal government in 1995. To the surprise of the Republican leadership, opinion polls reported that Americans blamed the GOP Congress for the gridlock. Clinton's approval ratings rose, and Newt Gingrich was portrayed as a mean-spirited "extremist." Eventually Congress and the president agreed on a compromise budget, a welfare reform bill, and health insurance portability (see Chapter 17).

The Democratic Revival   Republicans succeeded in maintaining their control of Congress despite Clinton's reelection in 1996. Collectively, the voters seemed to say they preferred divided government, that they wanted a Republican Congress which would press for a balanced budget, but they also wanted a Democratic president who would defend popular middle-class entitlement programs. In short, voters seemed reluctant to allow either party to govern unchaperoned by the other.

Democrats gained house seats in both the 1996 and 1998 Congressional elections. Although the GOP retained a slim majority in the House of Representatives, the 1998 midterm election stunned Republicans. They had expected major gains in both the House (where they lost seats) and in the Senate (where they merely maintained their 55-45 margin). Democrats were encouraged because historically the party controlling the White House had *lost* seats in midterm elections.

Republican Congressional candidates throughout the nation had expected to benefit from Clinton's acknowledged sexual misconduct and the House impeachment investigation. But voters generally seemed to ignore the affair. Some Democratic voters may even have turned out especially to defend the still-popular president. Democratic leaders predicted that the weak GOP showing in 1998 would "take the steam out" of the House investigation.

In the U.S. Senate, Republican hopes to achieve a "filibuster proof" majority (60 seats) were dashed in the 1998 midterm election. Democrats held on to 45 seats. Illinois Republican Peter Fitzgerald defeated incumbent Democrat Carol Moseley-Brown, the only African American in the Senate; but powerful three-term New York Republican Senator Al D'Amato was defeated by Democrat Charles Schumer. The continued strength of the Democrats in Congress, together with President Clinton's veto power, ensured that Republicans acting alone could not enact a broad policy agenda.

LIFE IN CONGRESS

"All politics is local," declared former House Speaker Thomas P. "Tip" O'Neill, himself once the master of both Boston ward politics and the U.S. House of Representatives. Attention to the local constituency is the key to survival and success in congressional politics. If Congress often fails to deal responsibly with national problems, the explanation lies in part with the design of the institution. House members must devote primary attention to their districts and Senate members to their states. Only *after* their constituencies are served can they turn their attention to national policy making.

The "Representativeness" of Congress   The Constitution requires only that members of the House of Representatives be (1) residents of the state they represent (they need not live in their congressional district, although virtually all do so); (2) U.S. citizens for at least seven years; and (3) at least twenty-five years old. Senators must also be residents of the state they represent, but they must be at least thirty years old and U.S. citizens for at least nine years.

African Americans were first elected to Congress following the Civil War— seven black representatives and one black senator served in 1875. But with the end of Reconstruction, black membership in Congress fell to a single seat in the House from 1891 to 1955. Following the Civil Rights Act of 1964 and the Voting Rights Act of 1965, black membership in Congress rose steadily. Redistricting following the 1990 census resulted in many new "majority-minority" congressional districts. After the 1992 elections, black membership in the House rose dramatically (see Figure 10-7), with most elected from predominately African American districts. As a result, although African Americans today make up a little more than 12 percent of the U.S. population, they make up less than 9 percent of the House membership. Hispanics now account for 9 percent of the U.S. population but only about 4 percent of House membership. Only one Native American serves in Congress (see *People in Politics:* "Ben Nighthorse Campbell, Native American Voice in Congress").

FIGURE 10-7 Women and African Americans in Congress, 1951–1999

Although the House of Representatives is still far short of "looking like America," in recent years the number of African American and female members has risen noticeably. Both groups made particularly impressive advances in the 1992 elections, as did Hispanics. Nine women now serve in the Senate. The only African American woman to ever serve in that body, Democrat Carol Moseley-Braun of Illinois, lost her seat in 1998.

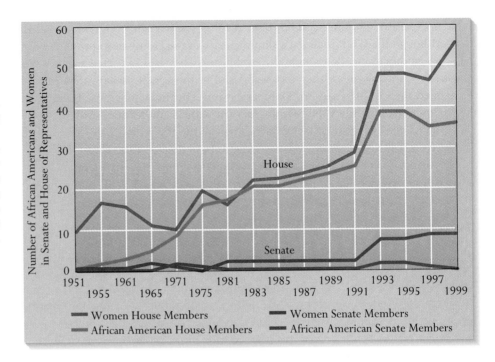

Number of African Americans and Women in Senate and House of Representatives

House

Senate

1951 1955 1961 1965 1971 1975 1981 1983 1985 1987 1989 1991 1993 1995 1997 1999

■ Women House Members   ■ Women Senate Members
■ African American House Members   ■ African American Senate Members

Congresswoman Marge Roukema of New Jersey meets with a staff member at her offices in Washington, D.C. Congressional staff play a key role in the legislative process.

Women have made impressive gains in both the House and the Senate in the last decade. The "year of the woman" election in 1992 brought a significant increase in the number of women in the House of Representatives. In 1998, women's representation in the House moved upward again; 56 women serve in the 106th Congress (1999–2001). In the Senate, California is represented by two Democratic women, Diane Feinstein and Barbara Boxer. They are joined by Democrats Patty Murry from Washington, Barbara Mikulski from Maryland, and Blanche Lincoln from Arkansas. Three Republican women serve in the Senate: Kay Hutchinson from Texas and Olympia Snowe and Susan Collins from Maine. Although this is the largest delegation of women ever to serve together in the U.S. Senate, it is still only 9 percent of that body.

Congressional Staff   Congress is composed of a great deal more than 535 elected senators and representatives. Congressional staff and other support personnel now total more than 25,000 people. Each representative has a staff of twenty or more people, usually headed by a chief of staff or administrative assistant and including legislative assistants, communications specialists, constituent-service personnel, office managers, secretaries, and aides of various sorts. Senators frequently have staffs of thirty to fifty or more people. All representatives and senators are provided with offices both in Washington and in their home districts and states. In addition, representatives receive more than $500,000 apiece for office expenses, travel, and staff; and senators receive $2 million or more, depending on the size of their state's population. Overall, Congress spends more than *$2 billion* on itself each year.

Congressional staff people exercise great influence over legislation.[18] Many experienced "Hill rats" have worked for the same member of Congress for many years. Many senior aides earn more than $100,000 per year. They become very familiar with "their" member's political strengths and vulnerabilities and handle much of the member's contacts with interest groups and constituents. Staff people, more than members themselves, move the legislative process—scheduling committee hearings,

Ben Nighthorse Campbell, Native American Voice in Congress

In an age of slick Ivy League career politicians, the colorful style of Ben Nighthorse Campbell is a welcome relief. Campbell is part Native American and official chief of the Northern Cheyenne nation. Growing up with an alchoholic father and a mother suffering from tuberculosis, he dropped out of high school and joined the Air Force, then later worked his way through the California State University at San Jose by driving a truck. Along the way, Campbell took up judo and won a spot on the U.S. Olympic team. His business skills in marketing Indian jewelry allowed him to go into cattle ranching and horse training in southwest Colorado and to win election to the House of Representatives in an upset in 1986. In 1988 and 1990, Colorado voters reelected him with more than 70 percent of the vote.

As a member of the House Agriculture Committee, Campbell was strongly supportive of ranching and mining interests, portraying himself as a social liberal and a fiscal conservative. When he announced his attention to run for the seat of retiring Democratic Senator Tim Wirth, environmental groups rushed to support his opponents, including former three-term governor Richard Lamm. But the witty and outspoken Campbell easily captured the Democratic nomination in a three-way race and entered the general election race with a wide lead over Republican state senator Terry Considine. The gap narrowed somewhat as Considine launched attack ads claiming Campbell was a pawn of the oil and mining companies, but Campbell, with his ponytail and trademark string tie, kept the confidence of Colorado voters and won a convincing 55 to 45 percent victory.

Campbell shocked his Democratic colleagues in the Senate in early 1995 when he announced his switch to the Republican Party. During his first two years in the Senate as a Democrat, he had given only lukewarm support to this party and President Bill Clinton, complaining that his moderate views were often out of sync with the Democratic leadership. Yet even while announcing his switch, he warned his new Republican colleagues that he would continue to support liberal positions on many social issues, including abortion.

Campbell's party change did not affect his popularity with Colorado voters. He won reelection as a Republican in 1998 with 62 percent of the vote. His Democratic opponent, Dottie Lamm, wife of former governor Richard Lamm, failed to exact family retribution for her husband's earlier loss to the charismatic Campbell. He can now boast that he has never lost an election in either party.

writing bills and amendments, and tracking the progress of such proposals through committees and floor proceedings. By working with the staff of other members of Congress or the staff of committees and negotiating with interest-group representatives, congressional staff are often able to work out policy compromises, determine the wording of legislation, or even outline "deals" for their member's vote (all subject to later approval by their member). With multiple demands on their time, members of Congress come to depend on their staff not only for information about the content of legislation but also for political recommendations about what position to take regarding it. Indeed, staff have become so important in the internal operations of Congress that members have less direct contact with each other than in the past, a situation that often makes modern congressional relations impersonal.

In addition to the personal staffs of members of Congress, congressional committees have their own staffs, ranging in size from 25 to more than 200 persons. Committee staffs are generally beholden to the committee chair and are often replaced when a new chair is named. Minority committee members do control some committee staff positions, however.

Support Agencies   In addition to the thousands of personal and committee staff who are supposed to assist members of Congress in research and analysis, four congressional support agencies provide Congress with information: the Library of Congress, the General Accounting Office, the Congressional Budget Office, and the Government Printing Office.

- The Library of Congress and its Congressional Research Service (CRS) are the oldest congressional support agencies. Members of Congress can turn to the Library of Congress for references and information. The CRS responds to direct requests of members for factual information on virtually any topic. It tracks major bills in Congress and produces summaries of each bill introduced. This information is available on computer terminals in members' offices.

- The General Accounting Office (GAO) has broad authority to oversee the operations and finances of executive agencies, to evaluate their programs, and to report its findings to Congress. Established as an arm of Congress in 1921, the GAO largely confined itself to financial auditing and management studies in its early years but expanded to more than five thousand employees in the 1970s and undertook a broad agenda of policy research and evaluation. Most GAO studies and reports are requested by members of Congress and congressional committees, but the GAO also undertakes some studies on its own initiative.

- The Congressional Budget Office (CBO) was created by the Congressional Budget and Impoundment Act of 1974 to strengthen Congress's role in the budgeting process. It was designed as a congressional counterweight to the president's Office of Management and Budget (see Chapter 14). The CBO supplies the House and Senate budget committees with its own budgetary analyses and economic forecasts, sometimes challenging those found in the president's annual budget.

- The Government Printing Office (GPO), created in 1860 as the publisher of the *Congressional Record*, now distributes over 20,000 different government publications in U.S. government bookstores throughout the nation.

Note that both the CBO and the OTA were created at a time when Congress was growing in power relative to a presidency weakened by Vietnam and Watergate. In these same years, Congress encouraged the GAO to undertake a more active and critical role relative to executive agencies. Thus the growth of congressional staff and supporting agencies is tied to the struggle for power between the legislative and executive branches.

Workload   Members of Congress claim to work twelve- to fifteen-hour days: two to three hours in committee and subcommittee meetings; two to three hours on the floor of the chamber; three to four hours meeting with constituents, interest groups, other members, and staff in their offices; and two to three hours attending conferences, events, and meetings in Washington.[19] Members of Congress may introduce anywhere from ten to fifty bills in a session of Congress. (A "session" convenes in January following a congressional election and extends for two years, until after the next election.) Most bills are introduced merely to exhibit the member's commitment to a particular group or issue. Cosigning a popular bill is a common practice; particularly popular bills may have 100 or 200 cosigners in the House of Representatives. Although thousands of bills are introduced, only 600 to 800 are passed in a session.

Members of Congress resent the notion that they are overpaid, underworked, pampered, self-seeking, corrupt, and ineffective. They respond to the bell calling them to the floor for a recorded vote 900 to 1,000 times a session. Each representative is a member of at least two standing committees and four subcommittees, and each senator may be a member of four committees and many more subcommittees. Thousands of committee and subcommittee meetings are scheduled each session.

Pay and Perks   Taxpayers can relate directly to what members of Congress spend on themselves, even while millions—and even billions—of dollars spent on government programs remain relatively incomprehensible. Taxpayers thus were enraged when Congress, in a late-night session in 1991, raised its own pay from $89,500 to $129,000. Congress claimed the pay raise was a "reform," since it was coupled with a stipulation that members of Congress would no longer be allowed to accept honoraria from interest groups for their speeches and appearances, thus supposedly reducing members' dependence on outside income. Many angry taxpayers saw only a 44 percent pay raise, in the midst of a national recession, for a Congress that was doing little to remedy the nation's problems. By 1998 automatic cost-of-living increases, also enacted by Congress, had raised members' pay to $138,600.

As the pay-raise debate raged in Washington, several states resurrected a constitutional amendment originally proposed by James Madison. Although passed by the Congress in 1789, it had never been ratified by the necessary three-quarters of the states. The 203-year-old amendment, requiring a House election to intervene before a congressional pay raise can take effect, was added as the Twenty-seventh Amendment when ratified by four states (for a total of thirty-nine) in 1992.

Even more damaging to public confidence in Congress have been revelations about the "perks" (privileges) accorded its members. For example, Congress had long maintained its own "bank"—actually more like an employee credit union—where members deposited their pay and wrote checks. Overdrafts were common, because members regularly wrote checks in anticipation of pay deposits. Some members clearly abused the privilege, writing hundreds of overdrafts totaling tens of thousands of dollars. Technically, no government (taxpayer) funds were involved. But when the "check-kiting" scandal was reported by the media in 1992, most people believed that members of Congress were abusing their power. Other perks also came under fire—travel and office expenses, the free congressional health club, free medical clinic, free parking, free video studios for making self-promotional tapes, free mailing privileges, and a subsidized dining room, gift shop, and barbershop.

HOME STYLE

Members of Congress spend as much time politically cultivating their districts and states as they do legislating. **Home style** refers to the activities of senators and representatives in promoting their images among constituents and personally attending to constituents' problems and interests.[20] These activities include members' allocations of their personnel and staff resources to constituent services; members' personal appearances in the home district or state to demonstrate personal attention; and members' efforts to explain their Washington activities to the voters back home.

Casework   **Casework** is really a form of "retail" politics. Members of Congress can win votes one at a time by helping constituents on a personal level. Casework can involve everything from tracing lost Social Security checks and Medicare claims to providing information about federal programs, solving problems with the Internal

home style   Activities of Congress members specifically directed at their home constituencies.

casework   Services performed by legislators or their staff on behalf of individual constituents.

Revenue Service, and assisting with federal job applications. Over time, grateful voters accumulate, giving incumbents an advantage at election time. Congressional staff do much of the actual casework, but letters go out over the signature of the member of Congress. One estimate of staff work suggests that House members' offices process more than 100 cases a week on average, and senators' offices process more than 300.[21] Senators and representatives blame the growth of government for increasing casework, but it is also clear that members solicit casework, frequently reminding constituents to bring their problems to their member of Congress.

Pork Barrel **Pork barreling** describes the efforts of senators and representatives to "bring home the bacon"—to bring federally funded projects, grants, and contracts that primarily benefit a single district or state to their home constituencies. Opportunities for pork barreling have never been greater: roads, dams, parks, and post offices are now overshadowed by redevelopment grants to city governments, research grants to universities, weapons contracts to local plants, "demonstration" projects of all kinds, and myriad other "goodies" tucked inside each year's annual appropriations bills. Members of Congress understand the importance of supporting each other's pork-barrel projects, cooperating in the "incumbent-protection society." Even though pork barreling adds to the public's negative image of Congress as an institution, individual members gain local popularity for the benefits they bring to home districts and states.

pork barreling Legislation designed to make government benefits, including jobs and projects used as political patronage, flow to a particular district or state.

Pressing the Flesh Senators and representatives spend a great deal of time in their home states and districts. Although congressional sessions last virtually all year, members of Congress find ways to spend more than a hundred days per year at home.[22] It is important to be seen at home—giving speeches and attending dinners, fund-raising events, civic occasions, and so on. To accommodate this aspect of home style, Congress usually follows a Tuesday-to-Thursday schedule of legislative business, allowing members to spend longer weekends in their home districts. Congress also enjoys long recesses during the late summer and over holidays.

Pork is in the eye of the beholder. These workers in Dallas are protesting the closing of the federally funded Superconducting Supercollider, a multibillion dollar project intended to advance research in particle physics. Some saw it as pork, others as essential to keeping the United States in the forefront of science research.

Puffing Images To promote their images back home, members make generous use of their **franking privilege** (free mailing) to send their constituents newsletters, questionnaires, biographical material, and information about federal programs. Newsletters "puff" the accomplishments of the member; questionnaires are designed more to flatter voters than to assess opinions; and informational brochures tout federal services members claim credit for providing and defending. Congress's penchant for self-promotion has also kept pace with the media and electronic ages. Congress now provides its members with television studios and support for making videotapes to send to local stations in home districts, and all members have addresses on the Internet.

ORGANIZING CONGRESS: PARTY AND LEADERSHIP

Congress is composed of people who think of themselves as leaders, not followers. They got elected without much help from their party. Yet they realize that their chances of attaining their personal goals—getting reelected and influencing policy—are enhanced if they cooperate with each other.[23]

Party Organizations in Congress The Democratic and Republican party organizations within the House of Representatives and the Senate are the principal bases for organizing Congress (see Figure 10-8). The leadership of each house of Congress, although nominally elected by the entire chamber, is actually chosen by secret ballot of the members of each party at a "conference" or caucus (see Table 10-5).

The parties and their leaders do not choose congressional candidates, nor can they deny them renomination; all members of Congress are responsible for their own primary and general election success. But party leadership in each chamber *can* help incumbents achieve their reelection goals. Each party in the House and Senate sponsors a campaign committee that channels some campaign funding to party members seeking reelection, although these Republican and Democratic congressional and senatorial campaign committees contribute less money than either PACs or individuals to the candidates.[24] Rather, good relations between members and their party's leadership are more important in the quest for power and influence in Washington.

Occasionally, congressional party leaders are urged to exercise more discipline over their members, to ensure that they support the party's position on key votes. Theoretically, party leaders in the House and Senate could do so by denying disloyal members appointment to preferred committees, by regularly burying their favorite bills, by cutting their pork-barrel projects from the budget, or by denying them party campaign funds. But except in very extreme cases, party leaders have been reluctant to employ these punishments. Members of Congress cherish their independence. They respect each other's need to get reelected. A member's vote lost today may be won next week if the member is not alienated by disciplinary action.

In the House: "Mr. Speaker" In the House of Representatives, the key leadership figure is the **Speaker of the House,** who serves as both presiding officer of the chamber and leader of the majority party. The Twenty-fifth Amendment to the Constitution stipulates that if the president and vice president simultaneously become unable to serve for any reason, the Speaker is to become president. In the House, the Speaker has many powers. The Speaker decides who shall be recognized

franking privilege Free mail service afforded members of Congress.

Speaker of the House Presiding officer of the House of Representatives.

FIGURE 10-8 The Organization of Congress

Aside from naming the Speaker of the House as head of that body's operations and the vice president as overseer of Senate deliberations, the Constitution is silent on the organization of Congress. Political parties have filled this gap: both majority and minority parties have their own leadership, which governs the appointment of members to the various committees, where the work of Congress actually takes place.

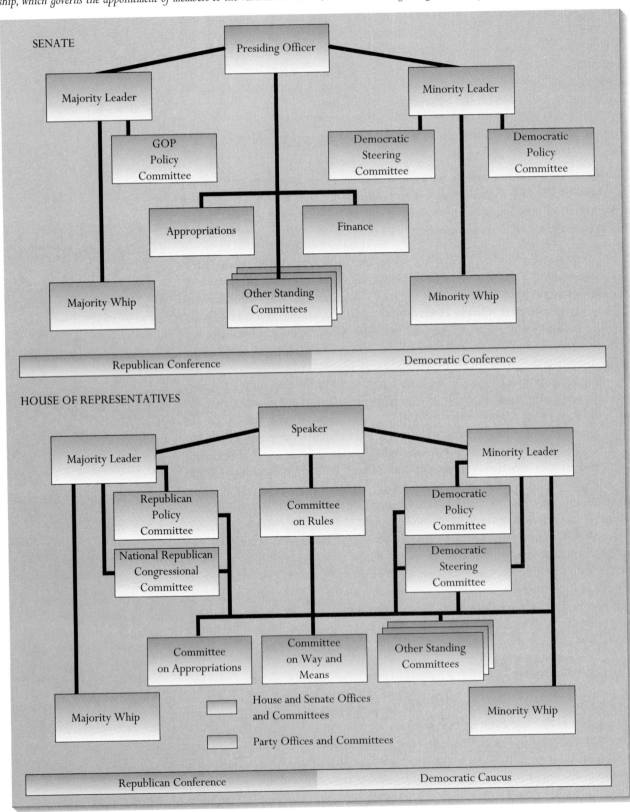

TABLE 10-5 **Leadership in Congress, 1999–2001**

Senate	
President Pro Tempore	Strom Thurmond (R-S.C.)
Majority Leader	Trent Lott (R-Miss.)
Majority Whip	Don Nickles (R-Okla.)
Minority Leader	Tom Daschle (D-S.D.)
Minority Whip	Harry Reid (D-Nev)
House	
Speaker	Dennis Hastert (D-Ill)
Majority Leader	Dick Armey (R-Tex.)
Majority Whip	Tom DeLay (R-Tex.)
Minority Leader	Richard Gephardt (D-Mo.)
Minority Whip	David Bonior (D-Mich.)

to speak on the floor and rules on points of order (with advice from the parliamentarian), including whether a motion or amendment is germane (relevant) to the business at hand. The Speaker decides to which committees new bills will be assigned and can schedule or delay votes on a bill. The Speaker appoints members of select, special, and conference committees and names majority-party members to the Rules Committee. And the Speaker controls both patronage jobs and office space in the Capitol. Although the norm of fairness requires the Speaker to apply the rules of the House consistently, the Speaker is elected by the majority party and is expected to favor that party. However, the effectiveness and success of the Speaker really rest "less on formal rules than on personal prestige, sensitivity to member needs, ability to persuade and skill at mediating disputes"[25] (see *People in Politics:* "The Rise and Fall of Speaker Newt").

House Leaders and Whips   The Speaker's principal assistant is the **majority leader.** The majority leader formulates the party's legislative program in consultation with other party leaders and steers the program through the House. The majority leader also must persuade committee leaders to support the aims of party leaders in acting on legislation before their committees. Finally, the majority leader arranges the legislative schedule with the cooperation of key party members.

The minority party in the House selects a **minority leader** whose duties correspond to those of the majority leader, except that the minority leader has no authority over the scheduling of legislation. The minority leader's principal duty has been to organize the forces of the minority party to counter the legislative program of the majority and to pass the minority party's bills. It is also the minority leader's duty to consult ranking minority members of House committees and to encourage them to adopt party positions and to follow the lead of the president if the minority party controls the White House (see *People in Politics:* "Dick Gephardt, Minority Leader, Presidential Candidate, or Both?").

In both parties, **whips** assist leaders in keeping track of the whereabouts of party members and in pressuring them to vote the party line. Whips are also responsible for ensuring the attendance of party members at important roll calls and for canvassing their colleagues on their likely support for or opposition to

majority leader   In the House, the majority party leader and second in command to the Speaker; in the Senate, the leader of the majority party.

minority leader   In both the House and Senate, the leader of the opposition party.

whips   In both the House and Senate, the principal assistants to the party leaders and next in command to those leaders.

The Rise and Fall of Speaker Newt

Newt Gingrich was the most powerful and controversial Speaker of the House in recent times. In the midterm congressional elections of 1994, the Republican Party not only captured control of the U.S. Senate but also for the first time in forty years won control of the House of Representatives. The GOP victory enabled the brash, brilliant, and pugnacious southern conservative Newt Gingrich to assume the office of Speaker. Indeed, Gingrich saw himself as the architect of his party's stunning victory through the Republican "Contract with America," which sought to nationalize the House election by setting forth clear party positions on key issues.

Newt Gingrich was born in a military hospital in 1943 while his father was fighting in World War II. Highly opinionated even as a youngster, Newt was voted "most intellectual" in his senior year in high school. He attended college on a federal war orphans scholarship, earning a Ph.D. in history from Tulane University in 1971.

Gingrich was a history professor at West Georgia College when he first ran for Congress, in 1974. Twice he ran and lost in a traditionally Democratic district, but on his third try, in 1978, he won election to the House by projecting a strong conservative image. Upon his arrival in Washington, Gingrich quickly acquired a reputation as a "bomb thrower" even within his own party by not only challenging the liberal Democratic majority leadership but also pushing moderate Republican minority leaders toward a more conservative stance. In 1986 he took control of a political action committee dedicated to helping Republicans and won the loyalty of many House Republicans to whom he directed money.

Gingrich mounted vicious attacks on Democrats in the Congress, even forcing the resignation of former House Speaker Jim Wright (Tex.) on ethics charges. In 1989 Gingrich won a narrow victory over a more senior and more moderate Republican for the post of minority whip, the second highest minority post in the House.

He opposed Republican President George Bush's agreement with congressional leaders to raise taxes in 1990, correctly perceiving the voters' wrath over Bush's broken "No new taxes!" promise. Although the media despised Gingrich's politics, his aggressive style soon made him the spokesperson for House Republicans. After soft-spoken minority leader Bob Michel (Ill.) retired, Gingrich assumed the GOP leadership post.

When national polls suggested he was not very popular with the American people (see table), Gingrich responded by saying that popularity is a price that a revolutionary leader must pay. As a player of "hardball politics," he often found himself on the receiving end of personal attacks; Democrats filed several ethics complaints over his political action committee and funding for his televised college course. When the House Ethics Committee fined Gingrich $300,000, GOP presidential candidate Bob Dole offered to loan Gingrich the money.

Newt Gingrich: Public Opinion

	1995	1996	1998
Favorable	34%	31%	24%
Unfavorable	37%	57%	62%
No opinion	29%	12%	14%

Although the GOP retained control of Congress in the 1996 and 1998 elections, Gingrich came under increasing attack from within his own party. Republican losses of House seats were blamed on his unpopular image among voters, his pursuit of the impeachment inquiry against a popular President Clinton, and on the failure of Congressional Republicans to project a clear and favorable policy agenda to the nation. Gingrich had managed to suppress the revolt against his leadership following the 1996 election, but militant opposition arose again when the GOP lost House seats in 1998.

In a surprise announcement three days after that election, Gingrich resigned from his Speaker's post and from Congress. Acknowledging criticism from fellow Republicans in the House, Gingrich said he would not "allow the party to cannibalize itself." House member Steve Largent expressed a popular feeling among Republicans, "We need likable, congenial messengers to carry our ideas."

After Bob Livingston of Louisiana reisgned as Speaker-designate, Republicans in the House chose Dennis Hastert of Illinois to replace Gingrich.

People in Politics

Dick Gephardt, Congressional Leader, Presidential Candidate, or Both?

House Minority Leader Richard A. Gephardt is frequently described as a "workaholic who combines a love of policy and a lust for politics." Recently he has also tried to combine his House Democratic leadership post with his personal ambition to be president of the United States. Indeed, this aspiration has led to clashes with his chief rival, Vice President Al Gore, as well as with President Clinton, whose support of Gore appears solid. The result is a House Democratic leader sometimes at odds with a Democratic White House.

Dick Gephardt has lived all of his life in St. Louis. He graduated from Northwestern University, where he was student body president, then attended the University of Michigan Law School. When he returned home, he served the powerful Democratic party in St. Louis as precinct captain and alderman. His party loyalty helped him win a seat in Congress in 1976. In 1984 he was elected chair of the House Democratic Caucus; in 1988, House Democratic leader (second only to the Democratic House Speaker); in 1994, minority leader, the top Democratic spot when Republicans gained control of the House.

But even as Gephardt was rising in the House Democratic Party hierarchy, he nurtured his ambition to occupy the White House. He briefly entered the 1988 race for the Democratic presidential nomination, easily won the Iowa caucus, but lost to Michael Dukakis in the New Hampshire primary and dropped out. President George Bush's popularity following victory in the Persian Gulf War led Gephardt and other prominent Democrats to sit out the 1992 presidential election, opening the way for Arkansas Governor Bill Clinton.

Early in his congressional career Gephardt compiled a moderate to conservative record, but as President Clinton moved to capture the Democratic Party's center, Gephardt assumed leadership of the party's liberal wing. He moved leftward in policy positions—supporting abortion rights, gun control, and health and welfare spending but opposing tax cuts, a balanced budget amendment, defense spending, and even Clinton's trade agreements, arguing that they undermined U.S. labor and environmental standards.

Gephardt contends that he is battling for "the heart and soul of the Democratic Party" and has gradually won over many its core constituencies, including labor, environmental groups, and abortion rights activists, who believe that President Clinton—and perhaps Al Gore, in his quest for the presidency—has moved too far toward the center. As party leader in the House, Gephardt is expected to be a "team player" supporting his president on key issues. But as a presidential contender he must set out his own political agenda, one that distinguishes him from his rival Al Gore. It is likely that Dick Gephardt will soon have to choose which role to pursue.

party-formulated legislation. Finally, whips are involved regularly in the formation of party policy and the scheduling of legislation.

In the Senate: "Mr. President" The Constitution declares the vice president of the United States to be the presiding officer of the Senate. But vice presidents seldom exercise this senatorial responsibility, largely because the presiding officer of the Senate has very little power. Having only 100 members, the Senate usually does not restrict debate and has fewer scheduling constraints than the House. The only significant power of the vice president is the right to cast a deciding vote in the event of a tie on a Senate roll call. In the usual absence of the vice president, the Senate is presided over by a *president pro tempore*. This honorific position is traditionally granted by the majority party to one of its senior stalwarts. The job of

While serving as a chairman of the powerful Appropriations Committee, Representative Bob Livingston raised millions of dollars to help finance the campaigns of House GOP candidates across the nation. He was the first choice of Republicans to succeed Gingrich, but he shocked his colleagues by resigning his seat after admitting to an extramarital affair. He called on President Clinton to follow his example.

standing committee
Permanent committee of the House or Senate that deals with matters within a specified subject area.

presiding over the Senate is so boring that neither the vice president nor the president pro tempore is found very often in the chamber. Junior senators are often asked to assume the chore. Nevertheless, speeches on the Senate floor begin with the salutation "Mr. President."

Senate Majority and Minority Leaders   Senate leadership is actually in the hands of the Senate majority leader, but the Senate majority leader is not as powerful in that body as the Speaker is in the House. With fewer members, all of whom perceive themselves as powerful leaders, the Senate is less hierarchically organized than the House. The Senate majority leader's principal power is scheduling the business of the Senate and recognizing the first speaker in floor debate. To be effective in policy making, the majority leader must be skilled in interpersonal persuasion and communication. Moreover, in the media age, the Senate majority leader must also be a national spokesperson for the party, along with the Speaker of the House. With a Democrat in the White House, Republican Senate Leader Trent Lott and Republican Speaker of the House Robert Livingston are their party's leading national officeholders. The minority party leader in the Senate represents the opposition in negotiations with the majority leader over Senate business. With the majority leader, the minority party leader tends to dominate floor debate in the Senate.

Career Paths within Congress   Movement up the party hierarchy in each house is the most common way of achieving a leadership position. The traditional succession pattern in the House is from whip to majority leader to Speaker. In the Senate, Republicans and Democrats frequently resort to election contests in choosing their party leaders, yet both parties have increasingly adopted a two-step succession route from whip to leader. Once in office, leaders in both parties are rarely removed.[26]

IN COMMITTEE

Much of the real work of Congress is done in committee. The floor of Congress is often deserted; C-SPAN focuses on the podium, not the empty chamber. Members dash to the floor when the bell rings throughout the Capitol signaling a roll-call vote. Otherwise they are found in their offices or in the committee rooms, where the real work of Congress is done.

Standing Committees   The committee system provides for a division of labor in the Congress, assigning responsibility for work and allowing members to develop some expertise. The committee system is as old as the Congress itself: the very first Congress regularly assigned the task of wording bills to selected members who were believed to have a particular expertise. Soon a system of **standing committees**—permanent committees that specialize in a particular area of legislation—emerged. House committees have thirty to forty members and Senate committees fifteen to twenty members each. The proportions of Democrats and Republicans on each committee reflect the proportions of Democrats and Republicans in the House and Senate as a whole. Thus the majority party has a majority of members on every committee; and every committee is chaired by a member of the majority party. The minority membership on each committee is led by the *ranking minority member,* the minority-party committee member with the most seniority.

The principal function of standing committees is the screening and drafting of legislation. With 6,000 to 8,000 or more bills introduced each session, the screening function is essential. The standing committees are the gatekeepers of Congress; less than 10 percent of the legislation introduced will pass the Congress. With rare exceptions, bills are not submitted to a vote by the full membership of the House or Senate without prior approval by the majority of a standing committee. Moreover, committees do not merely sort through bills assigned to them to find what they like. Rather, committees—or more often their subcommittees—draft (write) legislation themselves. Committees may amend, rewrite, or write their own bills. Committees are "little legislatures" within their own policy jurisdictions. Each committee guards its own policy jurisdiction jealously; jurisdictional squabbles between committees are common.

Decentralization and Subcommittees   Congressional subcommittees within each standing committee further decentralize the legislative process. At present, the House has about 90 subcommittees and the Senate about 70 subcommittees, each of which functions independently of its full committee (see Table 10-6). Subcommittees have fixed jurisdictions (for example, the House International Relations Committee has subcommittees on Africa, Asia and the Pacific, International Economic Policy, International Operations and Human Rights, and the Western Hemisphere); they meet and schedule their own hearings; and they have their own staffs and budgets. However, bills recommended by a subcommittee still

TABLE 10-6	Standing Committees in Congress
Senate	
Agriculture, Nutrition, and Forestry	Governmental Affairs
Appropriations	Indian Affairs
Armed Services	Judiciary
Banking, Housing, and Urban Affairs	Labor and Human Resources
Budget	Rules and Administration
Commerce, Science, and Transportation	Small Business
Energy and Natural Resources	Special Aging
Environment and Public Works	Veterans' Affairs
Finance	Select Ethics
Foreign Relations	Select Intelligence
House of Representatives	
Agriculture	National Security
Appropriations	Resources
Banking and Financial Services	Rules
Budget	Science
Commerce	Small Business
Education and the Workforce	Standards of Official Conduct
Government Reform and Oversight	Transportation and Infrastructure
House Oversight	Veterans' Affairs
International Relations	Ways and Means
Judiciary	Select Intelligence

require full standing-committee endorsement before being reported to the floor of the House or Senate. Full committees usually, but not always, ratify the decisions of their subcommittees.

Subcommittees decentralize power in Congress. Interest groups no longer concentrate their attention on a few senior standing-committee chairs and party leaders. Rather, they concentrate on those subcommittees dealing most directly with their concerns. Likewise, executive agencies must respond to subcommittees with policy oversight. Both lobbyists and bureaucrats must seek out "their" subcommittee and try to win the support of the chair and perhaps the ranking minority member. (For example, agents of the postal workers' union, the U.S. Postal Service, and private competitors such as FedEx and United Parcel Service all converge on the Post Office and Civil Service Subcommittee of the Senate Governmental Affairs Committee.) The result has been hundreds of policy networks, each featuring subcommittee members and staff, lobbyists with an interest in the subcommittee's field, and bureaucrats in the executive branch charged with implementing congressional policy in that field.

Chairing a committee or subcommittee gives members of Congress the opportunity to exercise power, attract media attention, and thus improve their chances of reelection. Often committees have become "fiefdoms" over which their chairs exercise complete control and jealously guard their power. This situation allows a very small number of House and Senate members to block legislation. Many decisions are not really made by the whole Congress. Rather, they are made by subcommittee members with a special interest in the policy under consideration. Although the committee system may satisfy the desire of members to gain power, prestige, and reelection opportunities, it weakens responsible government in the Congress as a whole.

Committee Membership   Given the power of the committee system, it is not surprising that members of Congress have a very keen interest in their committee assignments. Members strive for assignments that will give them influence in Congress, allow them to exercise power in Washington, and ultimately improve their chances for reelection. For example, a member from a big city may seek a seat on Banking, Finance, and Urban Affairs, a member from a farm district may

Senate Foreign Relations Committee chair Jesse Helms (right) enraged fellow Republicans by quashing the nomination of Republican William Weld, governor of Massachusetts, to be ambassador to Mexico. Helms, a conservative, was displeased with Weld's moderate politics. In contrast, Republican Senator Richard Lugar (left) strongly supported Weld. Helms's success reflects the power of committee chairs.

seek a seat on Agriculture, and a member from a district with a large military base may seek a seat on National Security or Veterans' Affairs. Everyone seeks a seat on Appropriations, because both the House and the Senate Appropriations committees have subcommittees in each area of federal spending.

Party leadership in both the House and the Senate largely determines committee assignments. These assignments are given to new Democratic House members by the Democratic Steering and Policy Committee; new Democratic senators receive their assignments from the Senate Democratic Steering Committee. New Republican members receive their committee assignments from the Republican Committee on Committees in both houses. The leadership generally tries to honor new members' requests and improve their chances for reelection, but because incumbent members of committees are seldom removed, openings on powerful committees are infrequent.

Seniority   Committee chairs are elected in the majority-party caucus. But the **seniority system** governs most movement into committee leadership positions. The seniority system ranks all committee members in each party according to the length of time they have served on the committee. If the majority-party chair exits the Congress or leaves the committee, that position is filled by the next *ranking majority-party member*. New members of a committee are initially added to the bottom of the ranking of their party; they climb the seniority ranking by remaining on the committee and accruing years of seniority. Members who stay in Congress but "hop" committees are usually placed at the bottom of their new committee's list.

The seniority system has a long tradition in the Congress. The advantage is that it tends to reduce conflict among members, who otherwise would be constantly engaged in running for committee posts. It also increases the stability of policy direction in committees over time. Critics of the system note, though, that the seniority system grants greater power to members from "safe" districts—districts that offer little electoral challenge to the incumbent. (Historically in the Democratic Party, these districts were in the conservative South, and opposition to the seniority system developed among liberal northern Democrats. But in recent years, many liberal big-city Democrats gained seniority and the seniority system again became entrenched.) The seniority rule for selecting committee chairs has been violated on only a few notable occasions.

Committee Hearings   The decision of a congressional committee to hold public hearings on a bill or topic is an important one. It signals congressional interest in a particular policy matter and sets the agenda for congressional policy making. Ignoring an issue by refusing to hold hearings on it usually condemns it to oblivion. Public hearings allow interest groups and government bureaucrats to present formal arguments to Congress. Testimony comes mostly from government officials, lobbyists, and occasional experts recommended by interest groups or committee staff members. Hearings are usually organized by the staff under the direction of the chair. Staff members contact favored lobbyists and bureaucrats and schedule their appearances. Committee hearings are regularly listed in the *Washington Post* and are open to the public. Indeed, the purpose of many hearings is not really to inform members of Congress but instead to rally public support behind an issue or a bill. The media are the real target audience

seniority system Custom whereby the member of Congress who has served the longest on the majority side of a committee becomes its chair and the member who has served the longest on the minority side becomes its ranking member.

of many public hearings, with committee members jockeying in front of the cameras for a "sound bite" on the evening news.

Markup   Once hearings are completed, the committee's staff is usually assigned the task of writing a report and **drafting a bill.** The staff's bill generally reflects the chair's policy views. But the staff draft is subject to committee **markup,** a line-by-line consideration of the wording of the bill. Markup sessions are frequently closed to the public in order to expedite work. Lobbyists are forced to stand in the hallways, buttonholing members as they go into and out of committee rooms.

It is in markup that the detailed work of lawmaking takes place. Markup sessions require patience and skill in negotiation. Committee or subcommittee chairs may try to develop consensus on various parts of the bill, either within the whole committee or within the committee's majority. In marking up a bill, members of a subcommittee must always remember that the bill must pass both in the full committee and on the floor of the chamber. Although they have considerable freedom in writing their own policy preferences into law, especially on the details of the legislation, they must give some consideration to the views of these larger bodies. Consultations with party leadership are not infrequent.

Most bills die in committee. Some are voted down, but most are simply ignored. Bills introduced simply to reassure constituents or interest groups that a representative is committed to "doing something" for them generally die quietly. But House members who really want action on a bill can be frustrated by committee inaction. The only way to force a floor vote on a bill opposed by a committee is to get a majority (218) of House members to sign a **discharge petition.** Out of hundreds of discharge petition efforts, only a few dozen have succeeded. The Senate also can forcibly "discharge" a bill from committee by simple majority vote; but because senators can attach any amendment to any bill they wish, there is generally no need to go this route.

ON THE FLOOR

A favorable "report" by a standing committee of the House or Senate places a bill on the "calendar." The word "calendar" is misleading, because bills on the calendar are not considered in chronological order, and many die on the calendar without ever reaching the floor.

House Rules Committee   Even after a bill has been approved by a standing committee, getting it to the floor of the House of Representatives for a vote by the full membership requires favorable action by the Rules Committee. The Rules Committee acts as a powerful "traffic cop" for the House. In order to reach the floor, a bill must receive a rule from the Rules Committee. The Rules Committee can kill a bill simply by refusing to give it a rule. A **rule** determines when the bill will be considered by the House and how long the debate on the bill will last. More important, a rule determines whether amendments from the floor will be permitted and, if so, how many. A **closed rule** forbids House members from offering any amendments and speeds up consideration of the bill in the form submitted by the standing committee. A **restricted rule** allows certain specified amendments to be considered. An **open rule** permits unlimited amendments. Most key bills are

drafting a bill   Actual writing of a bill in legal language.

markup   Line-by-line revision of a bill in committee by editing each phrase and word.

discharge petition   Petition signed by at least 218 House members to force a vote on a bill within a committee that opposes it.

rule   Stipulation attached to a bill in the House of Representatives that governs its consideration on the floor, including when and for how long it can be debated and how many (if any) amendments may be appended to it.

closed rule   Rule that forbids adding any amendments to a bill under consideration by the House.

restricted rule   Rule that allows specified amendments to be added to a bill under consideration by the House.

open rule   Rule that permits unlimited amendments to a bill under consideration by the House.

brought to the floor of the House with fairly restrictive rules. In recent sessions, about three-quarters of all bills reaching the floor were restricted, and an additional 10 to 15 percent were fully closed. Only a few bills were open.

In both houses, when a bill reaches the floor, the debate can be baffling to the uninitiated because of the terminology and conventions of speech used by the speakers (see *Up Close*: "What Are They Talking About?" for an explanation of selected terms used in congressional debates; see, also, the glossary items in the margins of this book).

Senate Floor Traditions   The Senate has no rules committee but relies instead on a **unanimous consent agreement** negotiated between the majority and minority leader to govern consideration of a bill. The unanimous consent agreement generally specifies when the bill will be debated, what amendments will be considered, and when the final vote will be taken. But as the name implies, a single senator can object to a unanimous consent agreement and thus hold up Senate consideration of a bill. Senators do not usually do so, because they know that a reputation for obstructionism will imperil their own favorite bills at a later date. Once accepted, a unanimous consent agreement is binding on the Senate and cannot be changed without another unanimous consent agreement. To get unanimous consent, Senate leaders must consult with all interested senators. Unanimous consent agreements have become more common in recent years as they have become more specific in their provisions.

The Senate cherishes its tradition of unrestricted floor debate. Senators may speak as long as they wish or even try to **filibuster** a bill to death by talking nonstop and tying up the Senate for so long that the leadership is forced to drop the bill in order to go on to other work. Senate rules also allow senators to place a "hold" on a bill, indicating their unwillingness to grant unanimous consent to its consideration. Debate may be ended only if sixty or more senators vote for **cloture,** a process of petition and voting that limits the debate. A cloture vote requires a petition signed by sixteen senators; two days must elapse between the petition's introduction and the cloture vote. If cloture passes, then each senator is limited to one hour of debate on the bill. Despite the obstacles to cloture, in recent years it has been used with increasing frequency.

Senate floor procedures also permit unlimited amendments to be offered, even those that are not "germane" to the bill. A **rider** is an amendment to a bill that is not germane to the bill's purposes.

These Senate traditions of unlimited debate and unrestricted floor amendments give individual senators considerably more power over legislation than individual representatives enjoy.

Floor Voting   The key floor votes are usually on *amendments* to bills rather than on their final passage. Indeed, "killer amendments" are deliberately designed to defeat the original purpose of the bill. Other amendments may water down the bill so much that it will have little policy impact. Thus the true policy preferences of senators or representatives may be reflected more in their votes on amendments than their vote on final passage. Members may later claim to have supported legislation on the basis of their vote on final passage, even though they earlier voted for amendments designed to defeat the bill's purposes.

Members may also obscure their voting records by calling for a voice vote—simply shouting "aye" or "nay"—and avoiding recording of their individual votes.

unanimous consent agreement   Negotiated by the majority and minority leaders of the Senate, it specifies when a bill will be taken up on the floor, what amendments will be considered, and when a vote will be taken.

filibuster   Delaying tactic by a senator or group of senators, using the Senate's unlimited debate rule to prevent a vote on a bill.

cloture   Vote to end debate—that is, to end a filibuster—which requires a three-fifths vote of the entire membership of the Senate.

rider   Amendment to a bill that is not germane to the bill's purposes.

Up Close

What Are They Talking About?

Visitors to Congress and TV viewers of C-SPAN are often confused by the language used during debates. Here some common phrases heard in the U.S. Congress, as well as state legislatures, are briefly defined.

Act Legislation that has passed both houses of Congress and been signed by or passed over the veto of the president, thus becoming law.

Bills Legislative proposals before Congress—designated "HR" in the House or "S" in the Senate plus the number assigned when they are introduced during the two-year congressional term.

Calendar A list of business awaiting possible action by each chamber. The Houses uses five legislative calendars (Corrections, Discharge, House, Private, and Union calendars). The Senate places all legislative matters reported from committee on one calendar.

Committee of the Whole All House members sitting as a committee, with its own chair, not the Speaker. A measure is debated and amendments may be proposed, with votes on amendments as needed. The committee, however, cannot pass a bill. When the committee completes its work, members may demand a roll-call vote on any amendment adopted in the Committee of the Whole. The final vote is on passage of the legislation.

Congressional Record The daily printed account of proceedings in both the House and Senate chambers, showing substantially verbatim debate, statements, and a record of floor action. Members are entitled to have their extraneous remarks printed in an appendix known as "Extension of Remarks."

Enacting Clause Key phrase in bills beginning, "Be it enacted by the Senate and House of Representatives . . ." A successful motion to strike it from legislation kills the measure.

Five-Minute Rule When the House sits as the Committee of the Whole, under the rule a member offering an amendment is allowed to speak five minutes in its favor and an opponent is allowed to speak five minutes in opposition.

Floor Manager Member who has the task of steering legislation through floor debate and the amendment process to a final vote in the House or the Senate.

Germane Pertaining to the subject matter of the measure at hand. All House amendments must be germane to the bill being considered. The Senate requires that amendments be germane when they are proposed to general appropriation bills, bills being considered once cloture has been adopted, or, frequently, when proceeding under a unanimous consent agreement placing a time limit on consideration of a bill.

Hopper Box on House clerk's desk where members deposit bills and resolutions to introduce them.

Motion In the House or Senate chamber, a request by a member to institute any one of a wide array of parliamentary actions.

Point of Order Objection raised by a member that the chamber is departing from rules governing its conduct of business.

Questions of Privilege Matters affecting members of Congress individually or collectively. Questions involving individual members are called questions of "personal privilege." A member rising to ask a question of personal privilege is given precedence over almost all other proceedings.

Quorum Number of members whose presence is necessary for the transaction of business. In the Senate and House, it is a majority of the membership.

Reading of Bills Traditional procedure required bills to be read three times before they were passed. This custom is of little modern significance. Normally a bill is considered to have its first reading when it is introduced and printed, by title, in the *Congressional Record*. The second reading comes when floor consideration begins. (This is the most likely point at which there is an actual reading of the bill, if there is any.) The third reading (again, usually by title) takes place when floor action has been completed on amendments.

Recommit to Committee A motion, made on the floor after a bill has been debated, to return it to the committee that reported it. If approved, recommittal usually is considered a death blow to the bill.

Reconsider a Vote A motion to reconsider the vote by which an action was taken can be made only by a member who voted on the prevailing side of the original question.

Report Document that explains the action of a committee when it returns a bill referred to it to the parent chamber.

Resolution A "simple" resolution, designated "H Res" or "S Res," deals with matters entirely within the prerogatives of one house or the other. It requires neither passage by the other chamber nor approval by the president, and it does not have the force of law. Resolutions are often used to express the sentiments of a house such as condolences to the family of a deceased member or to comment on foreign policy or executive business.

Standing Vote Nonrecorded vote used in both the House and Senate. (A standing vote also is called a division vote.) Members in favor of a proposal stand and are counted by the presiding officer.

Strike from the Record Remarks made on the House floor may offend some member, who moves that the offending words be expunged from the debate as published in the *Congressional Record*.

Substitute A motion, amendment, or entire bill introduced in place of the pending legislative business. Passage of a substitute measure kills the original measure by supplanting it.

Suspend the Rules Often a time-saving procedure for passing bills in the House. The wording of the motion, which may be made by any member recognized by the Speaker, is: "I move to suspend the rules and pass the bill . . ." A favorable vote by two-thirds of those present is required for passage.

Table a Bill Widely used parliamentary procedures used to block or kill amendments or other parliamentary questions. Motions to table are not debatable and require a simple majority vote. When approved, a tabling motion is considered the final disposition of that issue.

Unanimous Consent Proceedings of the House or Senate and action on legislation often take place upon the unanimous consent of the chamber, whether or not a rule of the chamber is being violated. Unanimous consent is used to expedite floor action.

U.S. Code A consolidation and codification of the general and permanent laws of the United States arranged by subject under 50 titles, the first 6 dealing with general or political subjects, and the other 44 alphabetically arranged from agriculture to war. The *U.S. Code* is updated annually, and a new set of bound volumes is published every six years.

Without Objection Used in lieu of a vote on noncontroversial motions, amendments, or bills that may be passed in either the House or Senate if no member voices an objection.

Yeas and Nays The Constitution requires that yea-and-nay votes be taken and recorded when requested by one-fifth of the members present.

Yielding When a member has been recognized to speak, no other member may speak unless he or she obtains permission from the member recognized. This permission is called yielding and usually is requested in the form, "Will the gentleman yield to me?"

FIGURE 10-9 How a Bill Becomes a Law

This diagram depicts the major hurdles a successful bill must overcome in order to be enacted into law. Few bills introduced travel this full path; less than 10 percent of bills introduced are passed by Congress and sent to the president for approval or veto. Bills fail at every step along the path, but most die in committees and subcommittees, usually from inaction rather than from being voted down.

Bill Introduction

Subcommittee Hearings

Committee Action

Floor Action

Conference Action

Presidential Decision

HOUSE

Bill is introduced and assigned to a committee, which refers it to the appropriate subcommittee.

Subcommittee
Subcommittee holds hearings and "marks up" the bill. If the bill is approved in some form, it goes to the full committee.

Committee
Full committee considers the bill. If the bill is approved in some form, it is "reported" to the full House and placed on the House calendar.

Rules Committee
Rules Committee issues a rule to govern debate on the floor. Sends it to the full House.

Full House
Full House debates the bill and may amend it. If the bill passes and it is in a form different from the Senate version, it must go to a conference committee.

SENATE

Bill is introduced and assigned to a committee, which refers it to the appropriate subcommittee.

Subcommittee
Subcommittee holds hearings, debates provisions and "marks up" the bill. If a bill is approved, it goes to the full committee.

Committee
Full committee considers the bill. If the bill is approved in some form, it is "reported" to the full Senate and placed on the Senate calendar.

Leadership
Majority and minority leaders negotiate "unanimous consent" agreements scheduling full Senate debate and vote on the bill.

Full Senate
Full Senate debates the bill. Senate may amend it. If the bill passes and is in a form different from the House version, it must go to a conference committee.

Conference Committee
Conference committee of senators and representatives meets to reconcile differences between bills. When agreement is reached, a compromise bill is sent back to both the House and the Senate.

President
President signs or vetoes the bill. Congress can override a veto by a two-thirds majority vote in both the House and Senate.

LAW

In contrast, a **roll-call vote** involves the casting of individual votes, which are reported in the *Congressional Record* and are available to the media and the general public. Electronic voting machines in the House allow members to insert their cards and record their votes automatically. The Senate, truer to tradition, uses no electronic counters.

Conference Committees   The Constitution requires that both houses of Congress pass a bill with identical wording. However, many major bills pass each house in different forms, not only with different wording but sometimes with wholly different provisions. Occasionally the House or the Senate will resolve these differences by reconsidering the matter and passing the other chamber's version of the bill. But about 15 percent of the time, serious differences arise and bills are assigned to **conference committees** to reach agreement on a single version for resubmission to both houses. Conference committees are temporary, with members appointed by the leadership in each house, usually from among the senior members of the committees that approved the bills.

Conference committees can be very powerful. Their final bill is usually (although not always) passed in both houses and sent to the president for approval. In resolving differences between the House and the Senate versions, the conference committee makes many final policy decisions. Although conference committees have considerable leeway in striking compromises, they focus on points of disagreement and usually do not change provisions already approved by both houses. Figure 10-9 summarizes the lawmaking process.

DECISION MAKING IN CONGRESS

How do senators and representatives decide about how they will vote on legislation? From an almost limitless number of considerations that go into congressional decision making, a few factors recur across a range of voting decisions: party loyalty, presidential support or opposition, constituency concerns, interest-group pressures, and the personal values and ideologies of members themselves.[27]

Party Voting   Party remains a significant influence on congressional voting. **Party votes** are roll-call votes on which a majority of voting Democrats oppose a majority of voting Republicans. Traditionally, party votes occurred on roughly *half* of all roll-call votes in Congress. But partisanship in Congress, as reflected in the percentage of party votes, has risen in recent years to over 60 percent of all roll-call votes (see Figure 10-10). Party votes decline slightly in election years (when representatives and senators are most concerned with how they look to voters).

Party unity is measured by the percentage of Democrats and Republicans who stick by their party on party votes. Republican Party unity has remained at fairly constant levels (75–85 percent) in both the House and the Senate over the past twenty years. Until recently, Democratic Party cohesion was weakened by the frequent defection of southern Democrats. But in the last several sessions, Democratic Party unity in the House has matched that of the Republican Party, with both parties holding the votes of over 80 percent of their members.

Why does party continue to be an important influence in congressional voting when party leaders cannot deny renomination to members or influence party primary elections in districts or states? First of all, Democratic and Republican

roll-call vote   Vote of the full House or Senate on which all members' individual votes are recorded and made public.

conference committee   Meeting between representatives of the House and Senate to reconcile differences over provisions of a bill passed by both houses.

party vote   Majority of Democrats voting in opposition to a majority of Republicans.

party unity   Percentage of Democrats and Republicans who stick with their party on party votes.

FIGURE 10-10 Party Voting in Congress

Partisanship varies over time in Congress. For many years, between 30 and 60 percent of votes in the House and Senate were party votes—votes on which a majority of Democrats were in opposition to a majority of Republicans—but in recent years the percentage has risen, indicating an increasingly partisan environment in Congress.

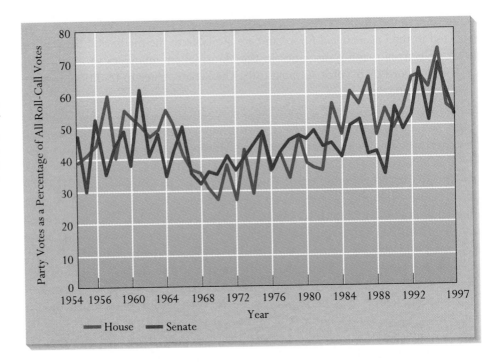

members of Congress tend to be ideologically distinct. Democratic members of both the House and the Senate are more liberal on social and economic issues than are Republican members. Thus ideological like-mindedness accounts for much of the party cohesion observed in congressional roll-call votes.

Conflict between the parties occurs frequently on domestic social and economic issues—welfare, housing and urban affairs, health, business regulation, taxing, and spending. On civil rights issues, voting often follows party lines on amendments and other preliminary matters but then swings to **bipartisan** voting on a final bill. This pattern suggests that the parties tend to agree on the general goals of civil rights legislation but not on the means. Traditionally, bipartisanship was the goal of both presidents and congressional leaders on foreign and defense policy issues. Since the Vietnam War, however, Democrats in the House have been more critical of U.S. military involvements (and defense spending in general) than have Republicans, although many Democrats in the Senate have continued to support presidential initiatives.

Party may also influence congressional voting even when ideology is not a concern. Members of Congress run under party labels. (Only one independent, Vermont's Bernard Sanders, serves in the House.) So there is some incentive for Democrats and Republicans in Congress to improve the image of their parties generally. The party leadership tries to appeal to party loyalty whenever it can. Members do have an interest in seeing their party win majority status in their chamber. Majority status means committee and subcommittee chairs, control over committee and subcommittee budgets and staff, and a better opportunity to get pork-barrel legislation passed. Finally, party leaders in the House and Senate do have modest favors to disperse. In short, party loyalty is not an insignificant factor in congressional voting.

Presidential Support or Opposition Presidential influence in congressional voting is closely tied to party. Presidents almost always receive their greatest support from members of their own party (see Figure 10-11). Indeed, the policy

bipartisan Agreement by members of both the Democratic and the Republican parties.

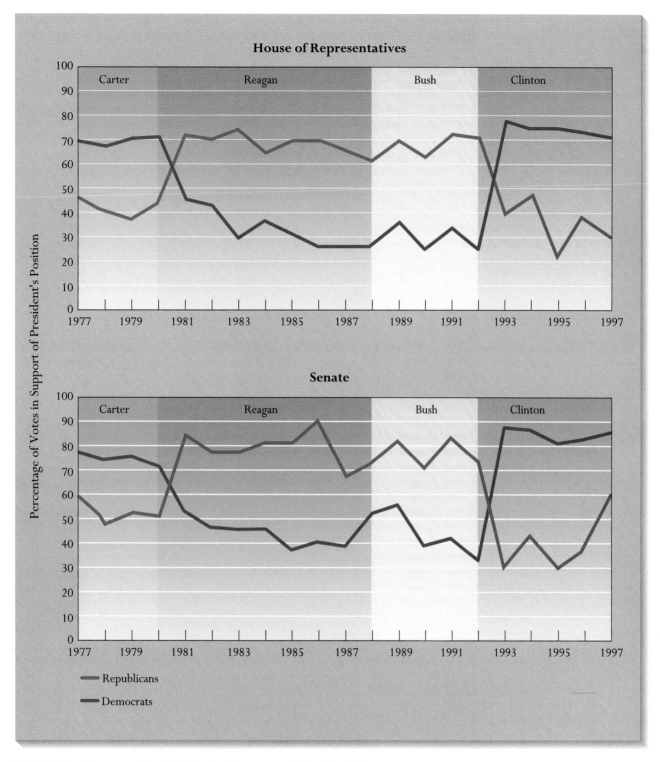

House of Representatives

Senate

Republicans

Democrats

FIGURE 10-11   Congressional Voting in Support of the President

Presidents always receive more support in Congress from members of their own party. Democratic presidents Jimmy Carter and Bill Clinton could count on winning large majorities of Democratic members' votes; Republican presidents Ronald Reagan and George Bush won large majorities of GOP members' votes. Percentages indicate congressional votes supporting the president on votes on which the president took a position.

Source: Norman J. Ornstein, Thomas E. Mann, and Michael J. Malbin, *Vital Statistics on Congress 1995–96* (Washington, D.C.: Congressional Quarterly Inc., 1996), pp. 206–7; updated by author.

gridlock associated with *divided government*—in past decades, a Republican president and a Democratic-controlled Congress, but beginning in 1995 a Democratic president and a Republican-controlled Congress—arises directly from the tendency of the opposition party to obstruct the president's policy proposals.

The decentralization of power in the congressional committee system also limits the president's ability to influence voting. The president cannot simply negotiate with the leadership of the House and Senate but instead must deal with scores of committee and subcommittee chairs and ranking members. To win the support of so many members of Congress, presidents often must agree to insert pork into presidential bills, promise patronage jobs, or offer presidential assistance in campaign fund raising.

If negotiations break down, presidents can "go over the heads" of Congress, using the media to appeal directly to the people to support presidential programs and force Congress to act. The president has better access to the media than Congress has. But such threats and appeals can only be effective when (1) the president himself is popular with the public; and (2) the issue is one about which constituents can be made to feel intensely.

Finally, presidents can threaten to veto legislation. This threat, expressed or implied, confronts congressional leaders, committee chairs, and sponsors of a bill with several options. They must decide whether to (1) modify the bill to overcome the president's objections; (2) try to get two-thirds of both houses to commit to overriding the threatened veto; or (3) pass the bill and dare the president to veto it, then make a political issue out of the president's opposition. Historically, less than 5 percent of vetoes have been overridden by the Congress. Unless the president is politically very weak (as Richard Nixon was during the Watergate scandal), Congress cannot count on overriding a veto. If members of Congress truly want to address an important problem and not just define a political issue, they must negotiate with the White House to write a bill the president will sign.

Constituency Influence   Constituency influence in congressional voting is most apparent on issues that attract media attention and discussion and generate intense feelings among the general public. If many voters in the home state or district know about an issue and have intense feelings about it, members of Congress are likely to defer to their constituents' feelings, regardless of the position of their party's leadership or even their own personal feelings.[28] Members of Congress from *safe seats* seem to be just as attuned to the interests of their constituents as members from competitive seats.

Constituency influence is particularly important on economic issues. Members from districts heavily dependent on a particular industry are routinely found protecting and advancing the interests of that industry. This kind of constituency representation is not unlike pork-barrel politics.

Constituencies may also exercise a subtle influence by conditioning the personal views of members. Many members were born, were raised, and continue to live in the towns they represent; over a lifetime they have absorbed and internalized the views of their communities. Moreover, some members of Congress feel an obligation to represent their constituents' opinions even when they personally disagree.

Members of Congress have considerable latitude in voting against their constituents' opinions if they choose to do so. Constituents, as noted earlier, lack information about most policy issues and the voting records of their senators and representatives. Even when constituents know about an issue and feel strongly about it, members can afford to cast a "wrong" vote from time to time. A long record of home-style politics—casework, pork barreling, visits, public appearances, and so on—can isolate members of Congress from the wrath generated by their voting records. Only a long string of "wrong" votes on issues important to constituents is likely to jeopardize an incumbent.

Interest-Group Influence   Inside the Washington Beltway, the influence of interest groups, lobbyists, and fund raisers on members of Congress is well understood. This influence is seldom talked about back home or on the campaign trail, except perhaps by challengers. Lobbyists have their greatest effects on the *details* of public policy. Congressional decisions made in committee rooms, at markup sessions, and around conference tables can mean billions of dollars to industries and tens of millions to individual companies. Pressures from competing interest groups can be intense as lobbyists buttonhole lawmakers and try to win legislative amendments that can make or break business fortunes. One of the most potent tools in the lobbyist's arsenal is money. The prohibitive cost of modern campaigning has dictated that dollars are crucial to electoral victory, and virtually all members of Congress spend more time than they would like courting it, raising it, and stockpiling it for the next election.

Voters may be wrong when they think that all members of Congress are crooks, but they are not far off the mark when they worry that their own representatives may be listening to two competing sets of constituents—the real constituents back home in the district and the cash constituents who come calling in Washington, D.C.[29]

Personal Values   It was the eighteenth-century English political philosopher Edmund Burke, himself a member of Parliament, who told his constituents: "You choose a member indeed; but when you have chosen him, he is not a member of Bristol, but he is a member of *Parliament*." Burke defended the classic notion of representatives as **trustees** who feel obligated to use their own best judgment about what is good for the nation as a whole. In this theory, representatives are not obligated to vote the views of their constituents. This notion contrasts with the idea of representatives as **delegates** who feel obligated to vote according to the views of "the folks back home" regardless of their own personal viewpoint. Most legislators *claim* to be trustees, perhaps because of the halo effect generated by the independence implied in the term.

Democratic political philosophers have pondered the merits of trustee versus delegate representation over the centuries, but the question only rarely arises in actual congressional deliberations. In many cases, members' own personal views and those of their constituents are virtually identical. (However, there is some evidence that members themselves may exaggerate the knowledge and issue-oriented tendencies of voters, since those most likely to communicate directly with their members of Congress are among the most knowledgeable and issue-oriented people in the district.[30]) Even when legislators perceive conflicts between their own views and those of their constituents, most attempt to find a compromise between these competing demands rather than choose one role or another exclusively. The political independence of members of Congress—their independence from party, combined with the ignorance of their constituents about most policy issues—allows members to give great weight to their own personal ideologies in voting.

trustees   Legislators who feel obligated to use their own best judgment in decision making.

delegates   Legislators who feel obligated to present the views of their home

CUSTOMS AND NORMS

Over time, institutions develop customs and norms of behavior to assist in their functioning. These are not merely quaint and curious folkways; they promote the purposes of the institution. Congressional customs and norms are designed to help members work together, to reduce interpersonal conflict, to facilitate bargaining and promote compromise, and in general to make life in Congress a little more pleasant.

Civility   Traditionally members of Congress understood that uncivil behavior— expressions of anger, personal attacks on character, ugly confrontations, flaming rhetoric—undermined the lawmaking function. Indeed, civility was encouraged by the longstanding custom of members of Congress referring to each other in elaborately courteous terms: "my distinguished colleague from Ohio," "the honorable representative from Pennsylvania," and the like. By custom, even bitter partisan enemies in Congress were expected to avoid harsh personal attacks on each other. The purpose of this custom was to try to maintain an atmosphere in which people who hold very different opinions can nevertheless function with some degree of decorum. Unfortunately, many of these customs and norms of behavior are breaking down. Individual ambition and the drive for power and celebrity have led to a decline in courtesy, cooperation, and respect for traditional norms. One result is that it has become increasingly difficult for Congress to reach agreement on policy issues. Another result is that life in Congress is increasingly tedious, conflict filled, and unpleasant (see *A Conflicting View:* "Congress Can Act Responsibly on Occassion").

In early 1997 concerned members of the House sponsored a weekend "Civility Retreat," inviting both members and their families in an effort to improve collegiality. Although more than two hundred members attended, just weeks later House members were heatedly arguing on the floor over calls for the impeachment of both President Clinton and Speaker Gingrich.

The Demise of the Apprenticeship Norm   Not too many years ago, "the first rule"[31] of congressional behavior was that new members were expected to be

New York's then representative Charles Schumer (he was elected senator in 1998) and other House Democrats display a blow-up of a newspaper headline mocking House speaker Newt Gingrich, to the objection of House Republicans. These kinds of displays are becoming increasingly common as traditional congressional norms of decorum and courtesy break down.

seen but not heard on the floor, to be studious in their committee work, and to be cooperative with party leaders. But the institutional norm of apprenticeship was swept aside in the 1970s as increasingly ambitious and independent senators and representatives arrived on Capitol Hill. Today new members of Congress feel free to grab the spotlight on the floor, in committee, and in front of television cameras. "The evidence is clear, unequivocal, and overwhelming: the [apprenticeship] norm is simply gone."[32] Nevertheless, experienced members are more active and influential in shaping legislation than are new members.[33]

Specialization and Deference The committee system encourages members of Congress to specialize in particular policy areas. Even the most independent and ambitious members can perceive the advantage of developing power and expertise in an area especially relevant to their constituents. Traditionally, members who developed a special expertise and accumulated years of service on a standing committee were deferred to in floor proceedings. These specialists were "cue givers" for party members when bills or amendments were being voted on. Members are still likely to defer to specialized committee members when the issues are technical or complicated, or when the issue is outside of their own area of policy specialization, but deference is increasingly rare on major public issues.

Bargaining Bargaining is central to the legislative process. Little could be achieved if individual members were unwilling to bargain with each other for votes both in committees and on the floor. A willingness to bargain is a longstanding functional norm of Congress.

Members of Congress are not expected to violate their consciences in the bargaining process. On the contrary, members respect one another's issues of conscience and receive respect in return. On most issues, however, members can and do bargain their support. "Horse trading" is very common in committee work.[34] Members may bargain in their own personal interest, in the interests of constituents or groups, or even in the interests of their committee with members of other committees. Because most bargaining occurs in a committee setting, it is seldom a matter of public record. The success and reputation of committee chairs largely depend on their ability to work out bargains and compromises.

Bargaining can assume different forms. Explicit trade-offs such as "If you vote for my bill, I'll vote for yours" are the simplest form of bargaining, but implicit understandings may be more common. Members may help other members in anticipation of receiving reciprocal help at some future unspecified time. Moreover, representatives who refuse to cooperate on a regular basis may find little support for their own bills. Mutual "back scratching" allows members to develop a reservoir of IOUs for the future. Building credit is good business for most members; one can never tell when one will need help in the future.

Bargaining requires a certain kind of integrity. Members of Congress must stick to their agreements. They must not consistently ask too high a price for their cooperation. They must recognize and return favors. They must not renege on promises. They must be trustworthy.

Conference-committee bargaining is essential if legislation acceptable to both houses is to be written. Indeed, it is expected that conferees from each house will bargain and compromise their differences. "Every House-Senate conference is expected to proceed via the methods of 'give and take,' 'trading

Congress Can Act Responsibly on Occasion

Congress is not always mired in partisanship, squabbling and gridlock. On occasion it acts responsibly in the national interest. Indeed, consider the following congressional landmarks in U.S. history:

Louisiana Purchase (1803)   President Thomas Jefferson offered to purchase from France nearly 830,000 square miles between the Mississippi and the Rockies for $15 million—about three cents an acre. There is no constitutional provision authorizing the federal government to buy foreign territory, but the Senate, accepting Jefferson's broad interpretation of the Constitution, approved the purchase. The House appropriated the money to consummate the deal. On December 29, 1803, the U.S. took possession of North America's heartland, doubling the nation's size with territory that would comprise 13 states.

Homestead Act (1862)   This Civil War-era legislation allowed any family head or adult male to claim 160 acres of prairie land for a $10 registration fee and a promise to live there continuously for five years. It opened up the midwestern United States for immediate settlement. The act drew thousands of English, Irish, Germans, Swedes, Danes, Norwegians, and Czechs to the U.S., pushing settlement farther west.

Social Security Act (1935)   The act was designed to secure "the men, women, and children of the nation against certain hazards and vicissitudes of life," explained President Franklin Roosevelt. The act's best-known measure is the social insurance system that provides monthly checks to the elderly.

National Labor Relations Act (1935)   By declaring workers had a right to join unions and bargain collectively with employers for pay raises and improved working conditions, the act spurred the growth of the nation's major industrial unions. Labor's Magna Carta also provided workers with the legal weapons to improve plant conditions and protect themselves from employer harassment.

G.I. Bill of Rights (1944)   The G.I. Bill of Rights, known officially as the Servicemen's Readjustment Act of 1944, offered to pay tuition for college or trade education to ex-World War II servicemen. It also mandated that they receive up to $500 a year for tuition, books, and supplies. Nearly 8 million veterans who took advantage of this first G.I. Bill and American higher education expanded rapidly as a result. Veterans also made use of the bill's guaranteed mortgages and low interest rates to buy new homes in the suburbs, inspiring a development boom.

Truman Doctrine (1947) and NATO (1949)   The Truman Doctrine initiated U.S. resistance to expansion of the Soviet Union into Western Europe following World War II, and the NATO Treaty has provided the framework for European Security for half a century. Truman declared to a joint session of Congress, "I believe that it must be the policy of the United States to support free people who are resisting attempted subjugation by armed minorities or by outside pressures."

Federal Highway Act (1956)   President Dwight D. Eisenhower was right when he said "More than any single action by the government since the end of the war, this one would change the face of America." The most expensive public-works project in U.S. history, the highway act built the 41,000 mile nationwide interstate-highway system.

Civil Rights Act of 1964   Only Congress could end racial segregation in privately-owned businesses and facilities. It did so by an overwhelming vote of both Houses in the Civil Rights Act of 1964. Injustices endure, but the end of segregated restaurants, theaters, and drinking fountains provided new opportunities for African-Americans and helped change white attitudes. In addition, Title VII of the act prohibits gender discrimination and serves as the legal bulwark for the women's rights.

Voting Rights Act of 1965   President Johnson signed this act in the same room in the Capitol where Abraham Lincoln had penned the Emancipation Proclamation. This legislation guaranteed all Americans the most fundamental of all rights—the right to vote. Between the 1964 and 1968 presidential elections, black voter registration increased 50 percent across the nation, even in the reluctant southern states, giving African Americans newfound political clout.

Medicare and Medicaid (1965)   Congress amended the Social Security Act of 1935 to provide for national health insurance for the aged (Medicare) and for the poor (Medicaid).

back and forth,' 'pulling and hauling,' 'horse-trading and compromise,' 'splitting the difference,' etc."[35]

Reciprocity   The norm of *reciprocity*—favors rendered should be repaid in kind—supports the bargaining process. Reciprocity may mean simply supporting a bill that is important to a colleague. But it may also extend to committees and subcommittees. In order to minimize intercommittee disputes over legislation, jurisdiction, or appropriations, "committees negotiate treaties of reciprocity ranging from 'I will stay out of your specialty if you will stay out of mine,' to 'I'll support your bill if you will support mine.' "[36]

The norm of reciprocity facilitates compromise and agreement and getting the work of Congress accomplished. Members who were willing to accept "half a loaf" traditionally accomplished more than those who insisted on a "whole loaf." But the norm of reciprocity may have weakened in recent years.

Logrolling   Perhaps the most celebrated and reviled form of reciprocity, **logrolling** is mutual agreement to support projects that primarily benefit individual members of Congress and their constituencies. Logrolling is closely associated with pork-barrel legislation. Yet it can occur in virtually any kind of legislation. Even interest-group lobbyists may logroll with each other, promising to support each other's legislative agendas.

Leader-Follower Relations   Because leaders have few means of disciplining members, they must rely heavily on their bargaining skills to solicit cooperation and get the work of Congress accomplished. Party leaders can appeal to members' concerns for their party image among the voters. Individual majority members want to keep their party in the majority—if for no other reason than to retain their committee and subcommittee chairs. Individual minority members would like their party to win control of their house in order to assume the power and privileges of committee and subcommittee chairs. Party leaders must appeal to more than partisanship to win cooperation, however.

To secure cooperation, leaders can grant—or withhold—some tangible benefits. A member of the House needs the Speaker's support to get recognition, to have a bill called up, to get a bill scheduled, to see to it that a bill gets assigned to a preferred committee, to get a good committee assignment, and to help a bill get out of the Rules Committee, for example.

Party leaders may also seek to gain support from their followers by doing favors that ease their lives in Washington, advance their legislative careers, and help them with their reelection. Favors from party leaders oblige members to respond to leaders' requests at a later time. Members themselves like to build up a reservoir of good feeling and friendship with the leadership, knowing that eventually they will need some favors from the leadership.

CONGRESSIONAL ETHICS

Although critics might consider the phrase *congressional ethics* to be an oxymoron, the moral climate of Congress today is probably better than in earlier eras of American history. Nevertheless, Congress as an institution has suffered from

logrolling   Bargaining for agreement among legislators to support each other's favorite bills, especially projects that primarily benefit individual members and their constituents.

well-publicized scandals that continue to prompt calls for reform (see *Up Close:* "The Keating Five: Service to Constituents, for a Price?").

Ethics Rules   Congress has an interest in maintaining the integrity of the institution itself and the trust of the people. Thus Congress has established its own rules of ethics. These rules include the following:

- *Financial disclosure:* All members must file personal financial statements each year.
- *Honoraria:* Members cannot accept fees for speeches or personal appearances.
- *Campaign funds:* Surplus campaign funds cannot be put to personal use. (A loophole allowed members elected before 1980 to keep such funds if they left office before January 1, 1993. A record number of House members resigned in 1992; many of them kept substantial amounts of campaign money.)
- *Gifts:* Members may not accept gifts worth more than $200 for representatives and $300 for senators (with annual increases in these amounts for inflation).
- *Free travel:* Members may not accept free travel from private corporations or individuals for more than four days of domestic travel and seven days of international travel per year. (Taxpayer-paid "junkets" to investigate problems at home or abroad or attend international meetings are not prohibited.)
- *Lobbying:* Former members may not lobby Congress for at least one year after retirement.

But these limited rules have not gone very far in restoring popular trust in Congress.

Expulsion   The Constitution gives Congress the power to discipline its own members. "Each House may . . . punish its Members for disorderly Behaviour, and, with the Concurrence of two thirds, expel a Member." But the Constitution fails to define *disorderly behavior.*

It seems reasonable to believe that criminal conduct falls within the constitutional definition of disorderly behavior. Bribery is a criminal act: it is illegal to solicit or receive anything of value in return for the performance of a government duty. During its notorious Abscam investigation in 1980, the Federal Bureau of Investigation set up a sting operation in which agents posing as wealthy Arabs offered bribe money to members of Congress while secretly videotaping the transactions. Six representatives and one senator were convicted. But criminal conviction does not automatically result in expulsion from Congress. In the Abscam case, only one defendant, Representative Michael Ozzie Myers (D-Pa.), was expelled, becoming the first member to be expelled since the Civil War. (Two other House members and the senator resigned rather than face expulsion, and the other three representatives were defeated for reelection. Perhaps the most interesting result of the Abscam investigation: only one member of Congress approached by the FBI, Democratic Senator Larry Presler of South Dakota, turned down the bribe.) The powerful chair of the House Appropriations Committee, Democrat Dan Rostenkowski (Ill.), was indicted by a federal grand jury in 1994 for misuse of congressional office funds; he refused to resign from Congress, but his Chicago constituents voted him out

Senator Bob Packwood of Oregon, facing expulsion by the Senate for sexual harassment charges, was forced to resign his Senate seat.

The Keating Five:
Service to Constituents,
for a Price?

The case of the Keating Five dates back to 1985, when Charles H. Keating, owner of the California-based Lincoln Savings and Loan, ran into difficulties with the Federal Home Loan Bank Board, which regulates the savings and loan industry. Keating invested Lincoln's government-insured funds in a wide variety of risky stocks, bonds, and commercial real estate ventures. When the Bank Board regulators charged that he had violated savings and loan regulations, Keating began to line up prominent politicians to pressure the board to drop its "vendetta" against him. Among those who agreed to intercede were U.S. senators Alan Cranston (D-Calif.), John Glenn (D-Ohio), Donald W. Riegle (D-Mich.), Dennis DeConcini (D-Ariz.), and John McCain (R-Ariz.).

Most of the senators' work on behalf of Keating consisted of contacting regulators and urging speedy and favorable consideration of his case. Regulators appeared ready to close down the shaky Lincoln S&L in early 1987 in order to save its remaining assets and limit the taxpayers' responsibility for additional losses. But Keating arranged to have his senators meet with top regulators and pressure them to postpone for two years the government's decision to close down the bankrupt S&L, a decision that eventually cost U.S. taxpayers *$2 billion.*

How did Keating win the active support of five U.S. senators in his fight against the Bank Board? Keating reciprocated by contributing a total of more than $1.5 million to their campaign chests and political causes. Nearly $1 million of these contributions went to Senator Alan Cranston; specific contributions of $250,000, $250,000, and $500,000 were made within days of Cranston's calls and meetings with Bank Board officials. Senator John Glenn received a total of $242,000 from

Keating, and John McCain received $110,000. Dennis DeConcini and Donald Riegle, who received $85,000 and $78,250, respectively, later returned those monies.

The key question in the subsequent Senate Ethics Committee investigation in 1991 was whether there was any direct connection between Keating's payments and the actions of the five senators on behalf of their benefactor. Bribery is an illegal exchange of official actions for payment. When Keating himself was asked whether his large campaign contributions brought him political influence, he replied, "I certainly hope so." Keating was later tried and convicted on fraud charges stemming from his S&L operations.

But Senator Cranston contended that he was just performing a service for a constituent. His "everyone does it" defense cited his own and other senators' efforts on behalf of defense contractors, automobile manufacturers, and others seeking specific government benefits and subsidies. "Nothing I did violated any law or specific Senate rule. . . . There is no evidence that I ever agreed to help Charles Keating in return for a contribution."*

But the Senate Ethics Committee found that Cranston's "impermissible pattern of conduct violated established norms of behavior in the Senate . . . [and] was improper and repugnant." The committee "strongly and severely reprimanded" Cranston but took no further action due to "extenuating circumstances. . . . Senator Cranston is in poor health . . . [and] has announced his intention not to seek reelection to the Senate." The Senate Ethics Committee also determined that the other four senators—DeConcini, Glenn, McCain, and Riegle—were guilty of "poor judgment" in conduct that gave "the appearance of impropriety." But the Ethics Committee offered little in the way of future guidance in handling constituent services and campaign contributions.

---

*U.S. Senator Alan Cranston, statement in the U.S. Senate, reported in *Congressional Quarterly Weekly Report,* November 23, 1991, p. 3437.

Politics in Cyberspace

Congress

Speaker of the House, Newt Gingrich, reportedly pushed Congress into cyberspace shortly after the 1994 Congressional elections when he asked the Library of Congress to create Thomas to provide citizens and legislators with access to Congressional records and documents.

Americans for Democratic Action

http://www.adaction.org

"The voice of liberal activists," ADA describes itself as an independent liberal political organization founded in 1947 and dedicated to promoting individual liberty and economic justice for all Americans.

Thomas

www.thomas.loc.gov

Sponsored by the Library of Congress, this is the best single source of legislative information on the net. The site includes current House and Senate legislative schedules, the status of all current bills, bill summaries, the results of role call votes, the text of the *Congressional Record,* and more. The site allows searches of recent legislation by topic, by short title, or by bill number. Summaries are available of bills from past Congresses back to 1973.

Senate and House

http://www.senate.gov

http://www.house.gov

These sites provide information about the two houses of Congress and provide links to the web pages of individual representatives and senators. Many of these individual Web sites are quite elaborate, featuring the legislator's picture, biography, policy positions, key votes, speeches, and so on.

House and Senate Committees

To connect to a House or Senate committee's Web page, add the committee name to the URL for the House or Senate home page. For example:

House Appropriations Committee

http://www.house.gov/appropriations

House Budget Committee

http://www.house.gov/budget

Senate Finance Committee

http://www.senate.gov/committee/finance

Senate Foreign Relations

http://www.senate.gov/committee/foreign_relations

Watchdog Groups

Several Congressional watchdog groups maintain interesting Web sites. Among them are the following:

Public Citizen Watch

http://www.citizen.org

Founded by Ralph Nader, this organization tracks legislation affecting drugs, medical devices, energy sources, and so on.

Pork Patrol

http://www.caguw.org/porkpatrol

Sponsored by Citizens Against Government Waste, this site includes a seven-part criteria for defining pork and publishes examples in a "Congressional Pig Book Summary." It also includes state rankings and "Oinkers Awards."

U.S. Term Limits

http://www.termlimits.org

This organization promotes term limits for both House and Senate members. In conjunction with state organizations, U.S. Term Limits asks candidates for public office to sign declarations stating that they intend to limit their own terms.

of office. Democratic Representative Mel Reynolds (Ill.) resigned in 1995, following his criminal conviction on charges of sexual misconduct. (A special election to fill his vacated seat was won by Jesse Jackson, Jr., son of the popular preacher, commentator, and former Democratic presidential contender.) Republican Senator Robert Packwood (Oreg.) resigned in 1995 in order to avoid official expulsion following a Senate Ethics Committee report charging him with numerous counts of sexual harassment of female staff.

Censure A lesser punishment in the Congress than expulsion is official **censure.** Censured members are obliged to "stand in the well" and listen to the charges read against them. It is supposed to be a humiliating experience and fatal to one's political career. In 1983 two members of Congress were censured for sexual misconduct with teenage congressional pages. Both were obliged to "stand in the well." Representative Daniel B. Crane (R-Ill.), who acknowledged a sexual relationship with a female page, was subsequently defeated for reelection. But Representative Gerry E. Studds (D-Mass.), who admitted to a homosexual relationship with a male teenage page, won reelection.

The threat of censure can be a potent one, though. In 1989, Speaker of the House Jim Wright (D-Tex.) was found to have circumvented ethics rules regarding outside financial payments to a member. He received heavy royalties on sales to interest groups of a book he authored. He also accepted large gifts from supporters, including the free use of an expensive condominium. He resigned the Speaker's post as well as his seat in Congress.

censure Public reprimand for wrongdoing, given to a member standing in the chamber before Congress.

SUMMARY NOTES

- The Constitution places all of the delegated powers of the national government in the Congress. The Founders expected Congress to be the principal institution for resolving national conflicts, balancing interests, and deciding who gets what. Today, Congress is a central battleground in the struggle over national policy. Congress generally does not initiate but responds to policy initiatives and budget requests originating from the president, the bureaucracy, and interest groups. Over time, the president and the executive branch, together with the Supreme Court and federal judiciary, have come to dominate national policy making.

- The Congress represents local and state interests in policy making. The Senate's constituencies are the 50 states, and the House's constituencies are 435 separate districts. Both houses of Congress, but especially the House of Representatives, wield power in domestic and foreign affairs primarily through the "power of the purse."

- Congressional powers include oversight and investigation. These powers are exercised primarily through committees. Although Congress claims these powers are a necessary part of lawmaking, their real purpose is usually to influence agency decision making, to build political support for increases or decreases in agency funding, to lay the political foundation for new programs and policies, and to capture media attention and enhance the power of members of Congress.

- Congress is gradually becoming more "representative" of the general population in terms of race and gender. Redistricting, under federal court interpretations of the Voting Rights Act, has increased African American and Hispanic representation in Congress. And women have significantly increased their presence in Congress in recent years. Nevertheless, women and minorities do not occupy seats in Congress proportional to their share of the general population.

- Members of Congress are independent political entrepreneurs. They initiate their own candidacies, raise their own campaign funds, and get themselves elected with very little help from their party. Members of Congress are largely career politicians who skillfully use the advantages of incumbency to stay in office. Incumbents outspend challengers by large margins. Interest-group political action committees and individual contributors strongly favor incumbents. Congressional elections are seldom focused on great national issues but rather on local issues and personalities and the ability of candidates to "bring home the bacon" from Washington and serve their constituents.

- Congress as an institution is not very popular with the American people. Scandals, pay raises, perks, and privileges reported in the media have hurt the image of the institution. Nevertheless, individual members of Congress remain popular with their districts' voters.

- Members of Congress spend as much time on "home-style" activities—promoting their images back home and attending to constituents' problems—as they do legislating. Casework wins votes one at a time, gradually accumulating political support back home, and members often support each other's "pork-barrel" projects.

- Despite the independence of members, the Democratic and Republican party structures in the House and Senate remain the principal bases for organizing Congress. Party leaders in the House and Senate generally control the flow of business in each house, assigning bills to committees, scheduling or delaying votes, and appointing members to committees. But leaders must bargain for votes; they have few formal disciplinary powers. They cannot deny renomination to recalcitrant members.

- The real legislative work of Congress is done in committees. Standing committees screen and draft legislation; with rare exceptions, bills do not reach the floor without approval by a majority of a standing committee. The committee and subcommittee system decentralizes power in Congress. The system satisfies the desires of members to gain power, prestige, and electoral advantage, but it weakens responsible government in the Congress as a whole. All congressional committees are chaired by members of the majority party. Seniority is still the major determinant of power in Congress.

- In order to become law, a bill must win committee approval and withstand debate in both houses of Congress. The rules attached to a bill's passage in the House can significantly help or hurt its chances. Bills passed with differences in the two houses must be reworked in a conference committee composed of members of both houses and then passed in identical form in both.

- In deciding how to vote on legislation, Congress members are influenced by party loyalty, presidential support or opposition, constituency concerns, interest-group pressures, and their own personal values and ideology. Party majorities oppose each other on roughly half of all roll-call votes in Congress. Presidents receive the greatest support in Congress from members of their own party.

- The customs and norms of Congress help reduce interpersonal conflict, facilitate bargaining and compromise, and make life more pleasant on Capitol Hill. They include the recognition of special competencies of members, a willingness to bargain and compromise, mutual "back scratching" and logrolling, reciprocity, and deference toward the leadership. But traditional customs and norms have weakened over time as more members have pursued independent political agendas.

- Congress establishes its own rules of ethics. The Constitution empowers each house to expel its own members for "disorderly conduct" by a two-thirds vote, but expulsion has seldom occurred. Some members have resigned to avoid expulsion; others have been officially censured yet remained in Congress.

SELECTED READINGS

DAVIDSON, ROBERT H., and WALTER J. OLESZEK. *Congress and Its Members.* 6th ed. Washington, D.C.: CQ Press, 1997. Authoritative text on Congress covering the recruitment of members, elections, house styles and hill styles, leadership, decision making, and relations with interest groups, presidency, and courts. Emphasizes tension between lawmaking responsibilities and desire to be reelected.

FENNO, RICHARD F. *Home Style*. Boston: Little, Brown, 1978. The classic description of how attention to constituency by members of Congress enhances their reelection prospects. Home-style activities, including casework, pork barreling, travel and appearances back home, newsletters, and surveys, are described in detail.

FIORINA, MORRIS P. *Congress: Keystone to the Washington Establishment*. 2nd ed. New Haven, Conn.: Yale University Press, 1989. A lively description of members of Congress as independent political entrepreneurs serving themselves by serving local constituencies and ensuring their own reelection, often at the expense of the national interest.

GINGRICH, NEWT. *To Renew America*. New York: Harper-Collins, 1995. The Republican Speaker of the House describes the "third wave information age" that will "empower and enhance" the lives of Americans and the "liberals, lawyers, and bureaucrats" who will try to block it to maintain their own power.

KAPTOR, MARCY. *Women of Congress*. Washington, D.C.: CQ Press, 1996. An account of the progress of women toward longer tenure, greater seniority, and more influential committee appointments and how women in Congress still differ from men on these factors.

OLESZEK, WALTER J. *Congressional Procedures and the Policy Process*. 4th ed. Washington, D.C.: CQ Press, 1995. An explanation of the interaction between congressional rules and policy making that includes a description of committee and floor procedures and an explanation of the role of the leadership.

ORNSTEIN, NORMAN J., THOMAS E. MANN, and MICHAEL J. MALBIN. *Vital Statistics on Congress*. Washington, D.C.: CQ Press, 1998. Published biennially. Excellent source of data on members of Congress, congressional elections, campaign finance, committees and staff, workload, and voting alignments.

SINCLAIR, BARBARA. *Legislators, Leaders, and Lawmaking: The U.S. House of Representatives in the Postreform Era*. Baltimore: Johns Hopkins University Press, 1995. A systematic examination of the role of majority party leadership in meshing the goals of individual members with the collective goals of the House.

SINCLAIR, BARBARA. *Unorthodox Lawmaking*. Washington, D.C.: CQ Press, 1997. A description of the various detours and shortcuts a major bill is likely to take in Congress, including five recent case studies.

 **ASK YOURSELF
ABOUT POLITICS**

① Do you approve of the way the president is handling his job?
Yes ⬤   No ⬤

② Should presidents have the power to take actions not specifically authorized by law or the Constitution that they believe necessary for the nation's well-being?
Yes ⬤   No ⬤

③ Should the American people consider private moral conduct in evaluating presidential performance?
Yes ⬤   No ⬤

④ Should Congress rally to support a president's decision to send U.S. troops into action even if it disagrees with the decision?
Yes ⬤   No ⬤

⑤ In addition to formal treaties, should all agreements with other countries require the approval of the Senate?
Yes ⬤   No ⬤

⑥ Should Congress have the authority to call home U.S. troops sent by the president to engage in military actions overseas?
Yes ⬤   No ⬤

⑦ Should Congress impeach and remove a president whose policy decisions damage the nation?
Yes ⬤   No ⬤

⑧ Is presidential performance more related to character and personality than to policy positions?
Yes ⬤   No ⬤

THE PRESIDENT
WHITE HOUSE POLITICS

CHAPTER OUTLINE

FEATURES

How much power does the president of the United States really have—over policies, over legislation, over the budget, over how this country is viewed by other nations, even over how it views itself?

PRESIDENTIAL POWER

Americans look to their president for "Greatness." The presidency embodies the popular "great man" view of history and public affairs—attributing progress in the world to the actions of particular individuals. Great presidents are those associated with great events: George Washington with the founding of the nation, Abraham Lincoln with the preservation of the Union, Franklin D. Roosevelt with the nation's

377

President Clinton attempts to introduce his new dog Buddy to his cat Socks. Because presidents are the most visible figures in government for most people, even their family pets receive media attention.

emergence from economic depression and victory in World War II (see *What Do You Think?* "How Would You Rate the Presidents?"). People tend to believe that the president is responsible for "peace and prosperity" as well as for "change." They expect their president to present a "vision" of America's future and to symbolize the nation.

The Symbolic President   The president personifies American government for most people. People expect the president to act decisively and effectively to deal with national problems. They expect the president to be "compassionate"—to show concern for problems confronting individual citizens.[1] The president, while playing these roles, is the focus of public attention and the nation's leading celebrity. Presidents receive more media coverage than any other person in the nation, for everything from their policy statements to their favorite foods to their dogs and cats.

Managing Crises   In times of crisis, the American people look to their president to take action, to provide reassurance, and to protect the nation and its people. It is the president, not the Congress or the courts, who is expected to speak on behalf of the American people in times of national triumph and tragedy.[2] The president gives expression to the nation's pride in victory. The nation's heroes are welcomed and its championship sports teams are feted in the White House Rose Garden.

The president also gives expression to the nation's sadness in tragedy and strives to help the nation go forward. When the *Challenger* spacecraft disintegrated before the eyes of millions of television viewers in 1986, President Ronald Reagan canceled his State of the Union Address and went on national television to give voice to the nation's feelings about the disaster and to explain it to children: "I want to say something to the schoolchildren of America who were watching the live coverage of the shuttle's takeoff. I know it is hard to understand, but sometimes painful things like this happen. It's part of the process of exploration and discovery. It's all part of taking a chance and expanding man's horizons. The future doesn't belong to the faint-hearted. It belongs to the brave."

Providing Policy Leadership   The president is expected to set policy priorities for the nation. Most policy initiatives originate in the White House and various departments and agencies of the executive branch, then are forwarded to Congress with the president's approval. Presidential programs are submitted to Congress in the form of messages, including the president's annual State of the Union Address, and in the Budget of the United States Government, which the president presents each year to Congress.

As a political leader, the president is expected to mobilize political support for policy proposals. It is not enough for the president to send policy proposals to Congress. The president must rally public opinion, lobby members of Congress, and win legislative battles. To avoid being perceived as weak or ineffective, presidents must get as much of their legislative programs through Congress as possible. Presidents use the threat of a veto to prevent Congress from passing bills they oppose; when forced to veto a bill, they fight to prevent an override of the veto. The president thus is responsible for "getting things done" in the policy arena.

Managing the Economy   The American people hold the president responsible for maintaining a healthy economy. Presidents are blamed for economic downturns, whether or not governmental policies had anything to do with market conditions. The president is expected to "Do Something!" in the face of high

What Do You Think?

How Would You Rate the Presidents?

From time to time, historians have been polled to rate U.S. presidents (see table). The survey ratings given the presidents have been remarkably consistent. Abraham Lincoln, George Washington, and Franklin Roosevelt are universally recognized as the greatest American presidents. It is more difficult for historians to rate recent presidents; the views of historians are influenced by their own (generally liberal and reformist) political views. Richard Nixon once commented, "History will treat me fairly. Historians probably won't."

Historians may tend to rank activist presidents who led the nation through war or economic crisis higher than passive presidents who guided the nation in peace and prosperity. Initially Dwight Eisenhower, who presided in the relatively calm 1950s, was ranked low by historians. But later, after comparing his performance with those who came after him, his steadiness and avoidance of war raised his ranking dramatically.

Arthur M. Schlesinger (1948)	Arthur M. Schlesinger, Jr. (1962)	Robert Murray (1982)	Arthur M. Schlesinger, Jr. (1996)	W. J. Ridings, S. B. McIver (1997)
Great	**Great**	**Presidential Rank**	**Great**	**Overall Ranking**
1. Lincoln	1. Lincoln	1. Lincoln	1. Lincoln	1. Lincoln
2. Washington	2. Washington	2. F. Roosevelt	2. Washington	2. F. Roosevelt
3. F. Roosevelt	3. F. Roosevelt	3. Washington	3. F. Roosevelt	3. Washington
4. Wilson	4. Wilson	4. Jefferson		4. Jefferson
5. Jefferson	5. Jefferson	5. T. Roosevelt	**Near Great**	5. T. Roosevelt
6. Jackson		6. Wilson	4. Jefferson	6. Wilson
	Near Great	7. Jackson	5. Jackson	7. Truman
Near Great	6. Jackson	8. Truman	6. T. Roosevelt	8. Jackson
7. T. Roosevelt	7. T. Roosevelt	9. J. Adams	7. Wilson	9. Eisenhower
8. Cleveland	8. Polk	10. L. Johnson	8. Truman	10. Madison
9. J. Adams	Truman (tie)	11. Eisenhower	9. Polk	11. Polk
10. Polk	10. J. Adams	12. Polk		12. L. Johnson
	11. Cleveland	13. Kennedy	**High Average**	13. Monroe
Average		14. Madison	10. Eisenhower	14. J. Adams
11. J. Q. Adams	**Average**	15. Monroe	11. J. Adams	15. Kennedy
12. Monroe	12. Madison	16. J. Q. Adams	12. Kennedy	16. Cleveland
13. Hayes	13. J. Q. Adams	17. Cleveland	13. Cleveland	17. McKinley
14. Madison	14. Hayes	18. McKinley	14. L. Johnson	18. J. Q. Adams
15. Van Buren	15. McKinley	19. Taft	15. Monroe	19. Carter
16. Taft	16. Taft	20. Van Buren	16. McKinley	20. Taft
17. Arthur	17. Van Buren	21. Hoover		21. Van Buren
18. McKinley	18. Monroe	22. Hayes	**Average**	22. Bush
19. A. Johnson	19. Hoover	23. Arthur	17. Madison	23. Clinton
20. Hoover	20. B. Harrison	24. Ford	18. J. Q. Adams	24. Hoover
21. B. Harrison	21. Arthur	25. Carter	19. B. Harrison	25. Hayes
	Eisenhower (tie)	26. B. Harrison	20. Clinton	26. Reagan
Below Average	23. A. Johnson	27. Taylor	21. Van Buren	27. Ford
22. Tyler		28. Tyler	22. Taft	28. Arthur
23. Coolidge	**Below Average**	29. Fillmore	23. Hayes	29. Taylor
24. Fillmore	24. Taylor	30. Coolidge	24. Bush	30. Garfield
25. Taylor	25. Tyler	31. Pierce	25. Reagan	31. B. Harrison
26. Buchanan	26. Fillmore	32. A. Johnson	26. Arthur	32. Nixon
27. Pierce	27. Coolidge	33. Buchanan	27. Carter	33. Coolidge
	28. Pierce	34. Nixon	28. Ford	34. Tyler
Failure	29. Buchanan	35. Grant		35. W. Harrison
28. Grant		36. Harding	**Below Average**	36. Fillmore
29. Harding	**Failure**		29. Taylor	37. Pierce
	30. Grant		30. Coolidge	38. Grant
	31. Harding		31. Fillmore	39. A. Johnson
			32. Tyler	40. Buchanan
				41. Harding
			Failure	
			33. Pierce	
			34. Grant	
			35. Hoover	
			36. Nixon	
			37. A. Johnson	
			38. Buchanan	
			39. Harding	

Note: These ratings result from surveys of scholars ranging in number from 55 to 950.

Sources: Arthur Murphy, "Evaluating the Presidents of the United States," *Presidential Studies Quarterly* 14 (1984): 117–26; Arthur M. Schlesinger, Jr., "Rating the Presidents: Washington to Clinton," *Political Science Quarterly* 112 (1997): 179–90; William J. Ridings and Stuart B. McIver *Rating the Presidents* (Secaucus, N.J.: Citadel Press, 1997).

Although far less glamorous than the job of Commander-in-Chief of the U.S. armed forces, commanding the nation's bureaucracy and overseeing the running of the civilian government usually occupies far more of a president's time. Here President Clinton meets with his cabinet.

unemployment, declining personal income, high mortgage rates, rising inflation, or even a stock market crash. Herbert Hoover in 1932, Gerald Ford in 1976, Jimmy Carter in 1980, and George Bush in 1992—all incumbent presidents defeated for reelection during recessions—learned the hard way that the general public holds the president responsible for hard economic times. Presidents must have an economic "game plan" to stimulate the economy—tax incentives to spur investments, spending proposals to create jobs, plans to lower interest rates (see Chapter 16).

Presidents themselves are partly responsible for these public expectations. Incumbent presidents have been quick to take credit for economic growth, low inflation, low interest rates, and low unemployment. And presidential candidates in recessionary times invariably promise "to get the economy moving again."

Managing the Government   As the chief executive of a mammoth federal bureaucracy with 2.8 million civilian employees, the president is responsible for implementing policy, that is, for achieving policy goals. Policy making does not end when a law is passed. Policy implementation involves issuing orders, creating organizations, recruiting and assigning personnel, disbursing funds, overseeing work, and evaluating results. It is true that the president cannot perform all of these tasks personally. But the ultimate responsibility for implementation—in the words of the Constitution, "to take Care that the Laws be faithfully executed"—rests with the president. Or as the sign on Harry Truman's desk put it: "THE BUCK STOPS HERE."

The Global President   Nations strive to speak with a single voice in international affairs; for the United States, the global voice is that of the president. As commander-in-chief of the armed forces of the United States, the president is a powerful voice in foreign affairs. Efforts by Congress to speak on behalf of the nation in foreign affairs and to limit the war-making power of the president have been generally unsuccessful. It is the president who orders American troops into combat. It is the president's finger that rests on the nuclear trigger.

CONSTITUTIONAL POWERS OF THE PRESIDENT

Popular expectations of presidential leadership far exceed the formal constitutional powers granted to the president. Compared with the Congress, the president has only modest constitutional powers (see Table 11-1). Nevertheless, presidents have pointed to a variety of clauses in Article II to support their rights to do everything from doubling the land area of the nation through purchase (Thomas Jefferson) to sending U.S. troops to keep the peace in Bosnia (Bill Clinton).

Who May Be President?   To become president, the Constitution specifies that a person must be a natural-born citizen at least thirty-five years of age and a resident of the United States for fourteen years.

Initially, the Constitution put no limit on how many terms a president could serve. George Washington set a precedent for a two-term maximum that endured until Franklin Roosevelt's decision to run for a third term in 1940 (and a fourth term in 1944). In reaction to Roosevelt's lengthy tenure, in 1947 Congress proposed the Twenty-second Amendment (ratified in 1951), which officially restricts the president to two terms (or one full term if a vice president must complete more than two years of the previous president's term).

Presidential Succession   Until the adoption of the Twenty-fifth Amendment in 1967, the Constitution had said little about presidential succession, other than designating the vice president as successor to the president "in Case of the Removal, . . . Death, Resignation, or Inability" and giving Congress the power to decide "what Officer shall then act as President" if both the president and vice

---

TABLE 11-1	The Constitutional Powers of the President

Chief Administrator
Implement policy: "take Care that the Laws be faithfully executed" (Article II, Section 3)
Supervise executive branch of government
Appoint and remove executive officials (Article II, Section 2)
Prepare executive budget for submission to Congress (by law of Congress)

Chief Legislator
Initiate policy: "give to the Congress Information of the State of the Union, and recommend to their Consideration such
  Measures as he shall judge necessary and expedient" (Article II, Section 3)
Veto legislation passed by Congress, subject to override by a two-thirds vote in both houses
Convene special session of Congress "on extraordinary Occasions" (Article II, Section 3)

Chief Diplomat
Make treaties "with the Advice and Consent of the Senate" (Article II, Section 2)
Exercise the power of diplomatic recognition: "receive Ambassadors" (Article II, Section 3)
Make executive agreements (by custom and international law)

Commander-in-Chief
Command U.S. armed forces: "The president shall be Commander-in-Chief of the Army and Navy" (Article II, Section 2)
Appoint military officers

Chief of State
"The executive Power shall be vested in a President" (Article II, Section 1)
Grant reprieves and pardons (Article II, Section 2)
Represent the nation as chief of state
Appoint federal court and Supreme Court judges (Article II, Section 2)

president are removed. The Constitution was silent on how to cope with serious presidential illnesses. It contained no provision for replacing a vice president. The incapacitation issue was more than theoretical: James A. Garfield lingered months after being shot in 1881; Woodrow Wilson was an invalid during his last years in office (1919–20); Dwight Eisenhower suffered major heart attacks in office; and Ronald Reagan was in serious condition following an assassination attempt in 1981.

The Twenty-fifth Amendment stipulates that when the vice president and a majority of the cabinet notify the Speaker of the House and the president pro tempore of the Senate in writing that the president "is unable to discharge the powers and duties of his office," then the vice president becomes *acting* president. To resume the powers of office, the president must then notify Congress in writing that "no inability exists." If the vice president and a majority of cabinet officers do not agree that the president is capable of resuming office, then the Congress "shall decide the issue" within twenty-one days. A two-thirds vote of both houses is required to replace the president with the vice president.

The disability provisions of the amendment have never been used, but the succession provisions have been. The Twenty-fifth Amendment provides for the selection of a new vice president by presidential nomination and confirmation by a majority vote of both houses of Congress. When Vice President Spiro Agnew resigned in the face of bribery charges in 1973, President Richard Nixon nominated the Republican leader of the House, Gerald Ford, as vice president; and when Nixon resigned in 1974, Ford assumed the presidency and made Nelson Rockefeller, governor of New York, his vice president. Thus Gerald Ford's two-year tenure in the White House marked the only time in history when the man serving as president had not been elected to either the presidency or the vice presidency. (If the offices of president and vice president are both vacated, then Congress by law has specified the next in line for the presidency as the Speaker of the House of Representatives, followed by the president pro tempore of the Senate, then the cabinet officers, beginning with the secretary of state.)

Impeachment　The Constitution grants Congress the power of **impeachment** over the president, vice president, and "all civil Officers of the United States" (Article II, Section 4). Technically, impeachment is a charge similar to a criminal indictment brought against an official. The power to bring charges of impeachment is given to the House of Representatives. The power to try all impeachments is given to the Senate, and "no Person shall be convicted without the Concurrence of two thirds of the Members present" (Article I, Section 3). Impeachment by the House and conviction by the Senate only remove an official from office; a subsequent criminal trial is required to inflict any other punishment.

The Constitution specifies that impeachment and conviction can only be for "Treason, Bribery, or other High Crimes and Misdemeanors." These words indicate that Congress is not to impeach presidents, federal judges, or any other officials simply because Congress disagrees with their decisions or policies. Indeed, the phrase implies that only serious criminal offenses, not political conflicts, can result in impeachment. Nevertheless, politics was at the root of the impeachment of President Andrew Johnson in 1867, and was a factor in the impeachment investigation opened by the House against President Clinton in 1998 (see *Up Close*: "Sex, Lies, Partisanship, and Impeachment"). Johnson was a southern Democrat who had remained loyal to the Union. Lincoln had chosen him as vice president in 1864 as a gesture of national unity. A Republican House impeached him on a party-line vote, but after a month-long trial in the Senate, the "guilty" vote fell one short of the two-thirds needed for removal.[3] In 1974, Richard Nixon resigned after

President Clinton greets well-wishers, including Monica Lewinsky, at a Democratic party event in January 1996. Clinton's acknowledged "inappropriate behavior" and his efforts to conceal his relationship with Lewinsky were the subjects of the impeachment investigation opened against him by the House in 1998.

impeachment　Equivalent of a criminal charge against an elected official; removal of the impeached official from office depends on the outcome of a trial.

Up Close

Sex, Lies, Partisanship, and Impeachment

Bill Clinton is the third president in the nation's history (following Andrew Johnson in 1867 and Richard Nixon in 1973) to be the subject of an impeachment investigation by the U.S. House of Representatives. The 1998 vote to begin an investigation against Clinton followed a report to the House by Independent Counsel Kenneth Starr that provided evidence of impeachable offenses, including perjury, obstruction of justice, witness tampering, and "abuse of power."

The Starr Report describes in graphic and lurid detail Clinton's sexual relationship with young White House intern Monica Lewinsky. It cites as impeachable offenses Clinton's lying about their relationship; his misleading testimony in a sworn statement in the Paula Jones case; his conversations with close friend Vernon Jordan about finding Lewinsky a job; his attempts to impede Starr's investigation; and his evasive testimony before Starr's grand jury.

Does engaging in extramarital sex and lying about it meet the Constitution's standard for impeachment—"Treason, Bribery, or other High Crimes and Misdemeanors"? Perjury—knowingly giving false testimony in a sworn legal proceeding—is a criminal offense. But does the Constitution envision more serious misconduct? According to Alexander Hamilton in *Federalist* 65, impeachment should deal with "the abuse or violation of some public trust." Is Clinton's acknowledged "inappropriate behavior" a private affair or a violation of the public trust?

How are such questions decided? Despite pious rhetoric in Congress about the "search for truth," "impartial investigation," and "unbiased constitutional judgment," the impeachment process, whatever the merits of the charges against a president, is political, not judicial. The House vote to impeach Clinton (228 to 106 on Article I perjury) was largely along partisan lines, with all but five Republicans voting "yes" and all but 5 Democrats voting "no." In 1863 the Republican House voted to impeach Democrat Andrew Johnson for defying the authority of Congress and deliberately violating the Tenure of Office Act, a newly enacted federal law, because he

opposed the Republicans' program for Reconstruction after the Civil War. Johnson avoided conviction and removal from office in the Senate by one vote. In 1974, the Democratically controlled House, with support from many Republicans, was about to vote articles of impeachment against Republican Richard Nixon—for obstruction of justice, abusing his constitutional authority, and failing to obey the committee's subpoenas—when Nixon resigned.

The Founders anticipated that impeachment would be a raucous, messy, and partisan process. Impeachable offenses, wrote Hamilton,

> are of a nature which may with peculiar propriety be denominated POLITICAL, as they relate chiefly to injuries done immediately to the society itself. The prosecution of them, for this reason, will seldom fail to agitate the passions of the whole community, and to divide it into parties more or less friendly or inimical to the accused. In many cases it will connect itself with the pre-existing factions, and will enlist all their animosities, partialities, influence, and interest on one side or on the other; and in such cases there will always be the greatest danger that the decision will be regulated more by the comparative strength of parties, than by the real demonstrations of innocence or guilt.

Why then, is the impeachment of a president so rare, even during periods of divided government? Because in a democracy, the ultimate jury is the people—through elections—and Congress knows that.

When Congress began its investigation of President Clinton, opinion polls found that more than 60 percent of the American people apparently did not believe his misconduct should result in his impeachment and removal from office. Republicans in Congress knew they had to move carefully in their proceedings or risk losing their seats. Backlash against the impeachment process may have contributed to the Republicans' loss of five seats in the 1998 elections. But a president's popularity can fade. President Nixon's public support had plummeted to a meager 24 percent before the 1974 vote of the House Judiciary Committee to recommend his impeachment. By placing the power of impeachment and removal in the hands of Congress, the Founders insured that ultimately this power would be held accountable to the people.

Watergate and the Limits of Presidential Power

Richard Nixon was the only president ever to resign the office. He did so to escape certain impeachment by the House of Representatives and a certain guilty verdict in trial by the Senate. Yet Nixon's first term as president included a number of historic successes. He negotiated the first ever strategic nuclear arms limitation treaty, SALT I, with the Soviet Union. He changed the global balance of power in favor of the Western democracies by opening relations with the People's Republic of China and dividing the communist world. In his second term, he withdrew U.S. troops from Vietnam, negotiated a peace agreement, and ended one of America's longest and bloodiest wars. But his remarkable record is forever tarnished by his failure to understand the limits of presidential power.

In early 1972, Nixon's attorney general, John Mitchell, became head of the Committee to Re-Elect the President (CREEP). Mitchell hired ex-CIA agent and author of spy novels E. Howard Hunt, Jr., and former FBI agent G. Gordon Liddy to gather intelligence about the Democratic opposition. On the night of June 17, 1972, five men with burglary tools and wiretapping devices were arrested in the offices of the Democratic National Committee in the Watergate Building in Washington. Also arrested were Hunt and Liddy, who had directed the break-in and bugging, and James W. McCord, Jr., security coordinator for CREEP. All pleaded guilty and were convicted, but

When the U.S. Supreme Court ruled that there is no "executive privilege" of a president to withhold possible evidence of illegal activities, Richard Nixon was forced to surrender tape recordings of conversations between himself and his closest aides. Arguing that the quality of the tape recordings made it difficult to distinguish what was being said, Nixon released "official" transcripts along with the tapes. Rather than placating his enemies, however, the transcripts provided evidence of Nixon's participation in the Watergate cover-up.

U.S. District Court Judge John J. Sirica believed that the defendants were shielding whoever had ordered and paid for the operation.

Although there is no evidence that Nixon himself ordered or had prior knowledge of the break-in, he discussed with his chief of staff, H. R. Halderman, and White House advisers John Ehrlichman and John Dean the advisability of payoffs to buy the defendants' silence. Hunt and the burglars subsequently received money and were told that executive clemency was possible if they remained silent about Mitchell's involvement. Nixon

the House Judiciary Committee recommended impeachment but before a vote by the full House (see *Up Close:* "Watergate and the Limits of Presidential Power").

Presidential Pardons The Constitution grants the president the power to "grant Reprieves and Pardons." This power derives from the ancient right to appeal to the king to reverse errors of law or justice committed by the court system. It is absolute: the president may grant pardons to anyone for any reason. The most celebrated use of the presidential pardon was President Ford's blanket pardon of former President Nixon "for all offenses against the United States which he, Richard Nixon, has committed or may have committed or taken part in." Ford defended the pardon as necessary to end "the bitter controversy and divisive national debate," but his actions may have helped cause his defeat in the 1976 election.

Executive Power The Constitution declares that the "executive Power" shall be vested in the president, but it is unclear whether this statement grants the

hoped his landslide electoral victory in November 1972 would put the matter to rest.

But a series of sensational revelations in the *Washington Post* kept the story alive. Using an inside source known only as Deep Throat, Bob Woodward and Carl Bernstein, investigative reporters for the *Post*, alleged that key members of Nixon's reelection committee and White House staff were actively involved in the break-in and, more important, in the subsequent attempts at a cover-up. Judge Sirica threatened Liddy and McCord with long prison sentences unless they told him who had ordered the break-in and made the cover-up payments. Liddy refused and subsequently served fifty-two months in Lewisburg federal penitentiary; McCord confessed and received a light sentence. Seven Nixon associates—including Mitchell, Ehrlichman, and Halderman—were indicted on charges of conspiracy to obstruct justice.

In February 1973 the U.S. Senate formed a Special Select Committee on Campaign Activities—the "Watergate Committee"—to delve into Watergate and related activities. The committee's nationally televised hearings enthralled millions of viewers with lurid stories of "the White House horrors." John Dean broke with the White House and testified before the committee that he had earlier warned Nixon the cover-up was "a cancer growing on the presidency." Then, in a dramatic revelation, the committee—and the nation—learned that President Nixon maintained a secret tape-recording system in the Oval Office. Hoping that the tapes would prove or disprove charges of Nixon's involvement in the cover-up, the committee issued a subpoena to the White House. Nixon refused to comply, arguing that the constitutional separation of powers gave the president an "executive privilege" to withhold his private conversations from Congress. However the U.S. Supreme Court, voting 8 to 0 in *United States v. Richard M. Nixon,* ordered Nixon to turn over the tapes.

On May 9, 1974, the Judiciary Committee of the House of Representatives, chaired by Peter Rodino (D-N.J.) convened to consider a series of articles of impeachment against President Nixon. Despite the rambling nature of the tapes, committee members interpreted them as confirming Nixon's involvement in the payoffs and cover-up. The committee passed two articles of impeachment: one accused Nixon of obstructing justice in the Watergate investigation; the other accused him of misusing his executive power and disregarding his constitutional duty to ensure that the laws be faithfully executed. Informed by congressional leaders of his own party that impeachment by a majority of the House and removal from office by two-thirds of the Senate were assured, on August 9, 1974, Richard Nixon resigned his office.

On September 8, 1974, new President Gerald R. Ford pardoned former President Nixon "for all offenses against the United States which he, Richard Nixon, has committed or may have committed or taken part in" during his presidency. In accepting the pardon, Nixon expressed remorse over Watergate and acknowledged grave errors of judgment, but he did not admit personal guilt. Upon his death in 1994, Nixon was eulogized for his foreign policy successes.

president any powers that are not specified later in the Constitution or given to the president by acts of Congress. In other words, does the grant of "executive Power" give presidents constitutional authority to act as they deem necessary *beyond* the actions specified elsewhere in the Constitution or specified in laws passed by Congress?

Contrasting views on this question have been offered over two centuries (see *A Conflicting View:* "Liberals, Conservatives, and Presidential Power"). President William Howard Taft provided the classic *narrow* interpretation of executive power:

> The true view of the executive function is, as I conceive it, that the president can exercise no power which cannot be fairly and reasonably traced to some specific grant of power or justly implied and included within such express grant as proper and necessary to its exercise. Such specific grants must be either in the federal constitution or in the pursuance thereof. There is no undefined residuum of power which can be exercised which seems to him to be in the public interest.[4]

A Conflicting View

Liberals, Conservatives, and Presidential Power

Liberals traditionally endorsed strong presidential leadership, viewing the president as a powerful initiator of social change. Franklin D. Roosevelt succeeded in ushering in the New Deal welfare state by presidential leadership, and Harry Truman was a feisty proponent of a liberal Fair Deal. Moderate Dwight Eisenhower was criticized by liberals for failing to use his great popularity to advance civil rights or social welfare programs. Liberals urged John F. Kennedy to be an activist president and strongly endorsed Lyndon Johnson's Great Society programs in education, welfare, and health. In his influential book *Presidential Power,* Harvard professor Richard E. Neustadt urged presidents to constantly strive to acquire as much power as possible because their constitutional authority is limited, noting that only by using their powers of persuasion can presidents achieve great change.[*] Liberal reform required forceful national leadership, and only the president could fulfill this role.

But liberals had a change of heart when presidents Lyndon Johnson and Richard Nixon pursued the Vietnam War. Liberals complained that both presidents were *too* powerful. What liberals had earlier praised as the *use* of presidential power was now described as the *abuse* of power. Liberal historian Arthur M. Schlesinger, Jr., attacked "the Imperial Presidency" and called for greater congressional power to restrain presidential actions, especially in war.[†] The Watergate scandal revealed further misuses of power and lawless actions.

Following the resignation of President Richard Nixon in 1974, Congress tried to reestablish its position as the first branch of government. It reasserted its authority in war making, in intelligence operations, and in the budgetary process. The War Powers Act of 1973 requires congressional approval within sixty days of the president's deployment of military forces; the Budget and Impoundment Control Act of 1974 establishes Congress's own budget office and prevents the president from impounding funds without congressional approval; and the Case Act requires the president to submit executive agreements to the Senate. Two weakened presidents—Republican Gerald Ford and Demo-

crat Jimmy Carter—suffered from the "post-Watergate" paralysis.

Conservatives were traditionally concerned about the concentration of power in the presidency. But by 1980, conservatives were calling for policy *changes:* lowering tax rates, slowing the growth of government, reducing the burdens of regulation, and restoring America's military power. Only strong presidential leadership could bring about these changes, and conservatives found that leadership in Ronald Reagan. Ronald Reagan liked to compare himself with Franklin D. Roosevelt: both presidents used the power, prestige, and media access of their office to redirect the nation. Like Roosevelt, Reagan had a clear vision and sense of the direction in which he wanted to move the nation; and, especially in his first term, he was extraordinarily successful in achieving his goals. Conservatives soon found themselves bashing the liberal Democratic Congress for failing to follow the president's lead in spending cuts and regulatory reform. Liberals, now well entrenched in Congress, were forced to defend that institution.

The sweeping Republican congressional victory in 1994, ending forty years of Democratic control of the House of Representatives and giving the GOP control of the Senate as well, again shifted the stances of liberals and conservatives regarding presidential power. Conservatives in the House under the speakership of Newt Gingrich reasserted the power of Congress, and liberals praised the checking powers of the president, Democrat Bill Clinton. But it soon became clear that a majority party in Congress cannot enact its own agenda over the opposition of the president.

Today, both liberals and conservatives have come to understand that the nation is poorly served by a weak presidency. Weakening the president does *not* mean turning back power to Congress or to the people. Weakening the president only means strengthening the special interests, deadlocking the legislative process, and crippling the ability of the government to deal with threats abroad and problems at home.

---

[*]Richard E. Neustadt, *Presidential Power* (New York: Wiley, 1960).

[†]Arthur M. Schlesinger, Jr., *The Imperial Presidency* (Boston: Houghton Mifflin, 1973).

Theodore Roosevelt, Taft's bitter opponent in a three-way race for the presidency in 1912, expressed the opposite view:

> I decline to adopt the view that what was imperatively necessary for the nation could not be done by the president unless he could find some specific authorization to do it. My belief was that it was not only his right but his duty to do anything that the needs of the nation demanded, unless such action was forbidden by the Constitution or by the laws.[5]

Although the constitutional question has never been fully resolved, history has generally sided with those presidents who have taken an expansive view of their powers. John F. Kennedy expressed the modern view of the constitutional presidency:

> The Constitution is a very wise document. It permits the president to assume just about as much power as he is capable of handling. . . . I believe that the president should use whatever power is necessary to do the job unless it is expressly forbidden by the Constitution.[6]

Some Historical Examples   U.S. history is filled with examples of presidents acting independently, beyond specific constitutional powers or laws of Congress. Among the most notable:

- George Washington issued a Proclamation of Neutrality during the war between France and Britain following the French Revolution, thereby establishing the president's power to make foreign policy.
- Thomas Jefferson, who prior to becoming president argued for a narrow interpretation of presidential powers, purchased the Louisiana Territory despite the fact that the Constitution contains no provision for the acquisition of territory, let alone authorizing presidential action to do so.
- Andrew Jackson ordered the removal of federal funds from the national bank and removed his secretary of the treasury from office, establishing the president's power to *remove* executive officials, a power not specifically mentioned in the Constitution.
- Abraham Lincoln, asking, "Was it possible to lose the nation yet preserve the Constitution?" established the precedent of vigorous presidential action in national emergencies: He blockaded southern ports, declared martial law in parts of the country, and issued the Emancipation Proclamation—all without constitutional or congressional authority.
- Franklin D. Roosevelt, battling the Great Depression during the 1930s, ordered the nation's banks to close temporarily. Following the Japanese attack on Pearl Harbor in 1941, he ordered the incarceration without trial of many thousands of Americans of Japanese ancestry living on the West Coast.

Checking Presidential Power   President Harry Truman believed that "the president has the right to keep the country from going to hell," and he was willing to use means beyond those specified in the Constitution or authorized by Congress. In 1952, while U.S. troops were fighting in Korea, steelworkers at home were threatening to strike. Rather than cross organized labor by forbidding the strike under the terms of the Taft-Hartley Act of 1947 (which he had opposed), Truman chose to seize the steel mills by executive order and continue their operations under U.S. government control. The U.S. Supreme Court ordered the steel mills returned to their owners, however, acknowledging that the president may have inherent powers to act in a national emergency but arguing that Congress had provided a legal remedy, however distasteful to the president. Thus the president can indeed act to keep the country from "going to hell," but if Congress has already acted to do so, the president must abide by the law.

Executive Privilege Over the years, presidents and scholars have argued that the Constitution's establishment of a separate executive branch of government entitles the president to **executive privilege**—the right to keep confidential communications from other branches of government. Public exposure of internal executive communications would inhibit the president's ability to obtain candid advice from subordinates and would obstruct the president's ability to conduct negotiations with foreign governments or to command military operations.

But Congress has never recognized executive privilege. It has frequently tried to compel the testimony of executive officials at congressional hearings. Presidents have regularly refused to appear themselves at congressional hearings and have frequently refused to allow other executive officials to appear or divulge specific information, citing executive privilege. The federal courts have generally refrained from intervening in this dispute between the executive and legislative branches. However, the Supreme Court has ruled that the president is not immune from court orders when illegal acts are under investigation. In *United States v. Nixon* (1974), the U.S. Supreme Court acknowledged that although the president might legitimately claim executive privilege where military or diplomatic matters are involved, such a privilege cannot be invoked in a criminal investigation. The Court ordered President Nixon to surrender tape recordings of White House conversations between the president and his advisers during the Watergate scandal. (See also *Up Close:* "William Jefferson Clinton versus Paula Corbin Jones.")

Presidential Impoundment The Constitution states that "no Money shall be drawn from the Treasury, but in Consequence of appropriations made by Law" (Article I, Section 9). Clearly the president cannot spend money *not* appropriated by Congress. But the Constitution is silent on whether the president must spend all of the money appropriated by Congress for various purposes. Presidents from Thomas Jefferson onward frequently refused to spend money appropriated by Congress, an action referred to as **impoundment**. But taking advantage of a presidency weakened by the Watergate scandal, the Congress in 1974 passed the Budget and Impoundment Control Act, which requires the president to spend all appropriated funds. The act does provide, however, that presidents may send Congress a list of specific **deferrals**—items on which they wish to postpone spending—and **rescissions**—items they wish to cancel altogether. Congress by *resolution* (which cannot be vetoed by the president) may restore the deferrals and force the president to spend the money. Both houses of Congress must approve a rescission; otherwise the government must spend the money.

The Constitution's Congressional Tilt The Constitution, reflecting the Founders' view of the preeminence of the legislative branch, gives the last word to the Congress in disputes with the president:

- The Congress can override the president's veto of legislation if it can muster a two-thirds vote in both houses.
- The Congress can impeach and remove the president from office.
- Only the Congress can appropriate money.
- Major presidential appointments require Senate confirmation.

executive privilege Right of a president to withhold from other branches of government confidential communications within the executive branch; although posited by presidents, it has been upheld by the Supreme Court only in limited situations.

impoundment Refusal by a president to spend monies appropriated by Congress; outlawed except with congressional consent by the Budget and Impoundment Control Act of 1974.

deferrals Items on which a president wishes to postpone spending.

rescissions Items on which a president wishes to cancel spending.

William Jefferson Clinton versus Paula Corbin Jones

The president is not "above the law"; that is, his conduct is not immune from judicial scrutiny. The president's official conduct must be lawful; federal courts may reverse presidential actions found to be unconstitutional or violative of laws of Congress. And presidents are not immune from criminal prosecution; they cannot ignore demands to provide information in criminal cases.[*] However, the Supreme Court has held that the president has "absolute immunity" from civil suits "arising out of the execution of official duties."[†] In other words, the president cannot be sued for damages caused by actions or decisions that are within his constitutional or legal authority.

But can the president be sued for *private* conduct beyond the scope of his official duties? In 1994 Paula Corbin Jones sued William Jefferson Clinton in federal district court in Arkansas, alleging that he made "abhorrent" sexual advances toward her in Little Rock in 1991 while he was governor and she was a state employee. She claimed that while working for the Arkansas Industrial Development Commission as a receptionist at a conference, she was approached by a state trooper who asked her to come to the governor's hotel suite. She claimed that the trooper escorted her to Clinton's room, but upon entering she found herself alone with the governor. She claimed he made sexual overtures, touched her inappropriately, and then exposed himself to her. She claims she fled the room but was subsequently treated in a rude and hostile manner by superiors at the commission for rejecting the governor's advances.

The president's lead attorney, Robert Bennett (brother of conservative commentator and former Reagan cabinet official William Bennett), stated that Clinton "has no recollection of ever meeting this woman" and "did not engage in any inappropriate or sexual conduct with this woman." But the president's defense team also argued that the president should be immune from civil actions, especially those arising from events alleged to occur before he assumed office. They argued that the president's constitutional responsibilities are so important and demanding that he must devote his undivided time and attention to them. He cannot be distracted by civil suits; otherwise a large volume of politically motivated frivolous litigation might undermine his ability to function effectively in office. At the very least, the president's attorney argued, the president should be given "temporary immunity" by postponing the case until after he leaves office.

However, in 1997 the U.S. Supreme Court rejected the notion of presidential immunity (as well as temporary immunity) from civil claims arising from actions outside of the president's official duties. Although advising lower courts to give "utmost deference to Presidential responsibilities" in handling the case, the Court held that "the doctrine of separation of powers does not require federal courts to stay all private actions against the president until he leaves office."[‡]

Subsequently, after reviewing the case, federal district judge Susan Wright dismissed Jones's charges as insufficient to prove sexual assault or harassment. "Although the Governor's alleged conduct, if true, may certainly be characterized as boorish and offensive, [it] . . . does not constitute sexual assault." And inasmuch as it was a single incident, "brief and isolated," and "did not involve any coercion or threats of reprisal," the alleged conduct by Clinton did not create a hostile work environment," evidence of which is required to sustain a claim of sexual harassment.[§]

Clinton later settled the case with a financial payment to Jones, but with no admission or apology. The settlement ended Jones's appeals and avoided possible reopening of the case.

---

[*]*United States v. Nixon* (1974).
[†]*Nixon v. Fitzgerald* (1982).
[‡]*Clinton v. Jones*, May 27, 1997.
[§]*Jones v. Clinton*, April 1, 1998

- The president is obliged by the Constitution to "take Care that the Laws be faithfully executed"—that is, the *laws of Congress*—regardless of any personal feelings about these laws.

Thus Congress is *constitutionally* positioned to dominate American government. But it is the president who *politically* dominates the nation's public affairs.

POLITICAL RESOURCES OF THE PRESIDENT

The real sources of presidential power are not found in the Constitution. The president's power is the *power to persuade*. As Harry Truman put it, "I sit here all day trying to persuade people to do things they ought to have sense enough to do without my persuading them. . . . That's all the powers of the president amount to."[7]

The president's political resources are potentially very great. The nation looks to the president for leadership, for direction, for reassurance. The president is the focus of public and media attention. The president has the capacity to mobilize public opinion, to communicate directly with the American people, and to employ the symbols of office to advance policy initiatives in both foreign and domestic affairs.

The Reputation for Power   A reputation for power is itself a source of power. Presidents must strive to maintain the image of power in order to be effective. A president perceived as powerful can exercise great influence abroad with foreign governments and at home with the Congress, interest groups, and the executive bureaucracy. A president perceived as weak, unsteady, bumbling, or error prone will soon become unpopular and ineffective.

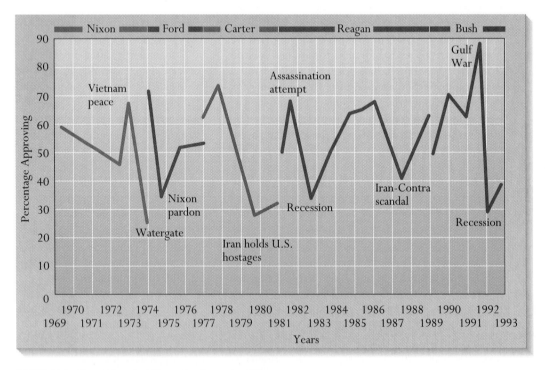

FIGURE 11-1   Presidential Popularity over Time

Americans expect a great deal from their presidents and are quick to give these leaders the credit—and the blame—for major events in the nation's life. In general, public approval (as measured by response to the question "Do you approve or disapprove of the way _____ is handling the job of president?") is highest at the beginning of a new president's term in office and declines from that point. Major military confrontations generally raise presidential ratings initially but can (as in the case of Lyndon Johnson) cause dramatic decline if the conflict drags on. In addition, public approval of the president is closely linked to the nation's economic health. When the economy is in recession, Americans tend to take a negative view of the president.

Presidential Popularity   Presidential popularity with the American people is a political resource. Popular presidents cannot always transfer their popularity into foreign policy successes or legislative victories, but popular presidents usually have more success than unpopular presidents.

Presidential popularity is regularly tracked in national opinion polls. For more than forty years, national surveys have asked the American public: "Do you approve or disapprove of the way _____ is handling his job as president?" (see Figures 11-1, 11-2). Analyses of variations over time in these poll results suggest some generalizations about presidential popularity.[8]

Presidential popularity is usually high at the beginning of a president's term of office, but this period can be very brief. The American public's high expectations for a new president can turn sour within a few months. A president's popularity will vary a great deal during a term in office, with sharp peaks and steep valleys in the ratings. But the general trend is downward.[9] Presidents usually recover some popularity at the end of their first term as they campaign for reelection.

Presidential popularity rises during crises. People "rally 'round the president" when the nation is confronted with an international threat or the president initiates a military action.[10] President George Bush, for example, registered the all-time high in presidential ratings during the Persian Gulf War. Likewise, the invasion of Grenada in 1983 and Panama in 1989 rallied support to the president. But prolonged warfare and stalemate erode popular support. In both the Korean and the Vietnam wars, initial public approval of the president and support for the war eroded over time as military operations stalemated and casualties mounted.[11]

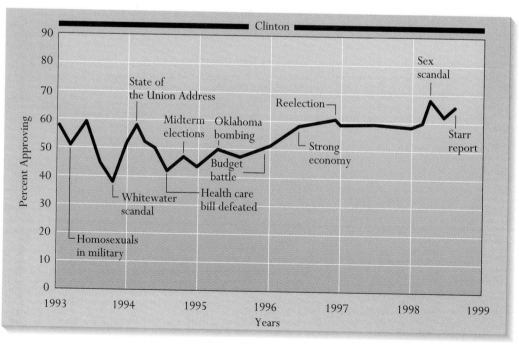

FIGURE 11-2   Bill Clinton's Popularity Ratings

During his first term, Bill Clinton experienced dips in popularity with his opening of military service to homosexuals, press coverage of the Whitewater scandal, and the defeat of his health care bill. But following the terrorist bombing of the Federal Building in Oklahoma City and his later battles with Congress over the budget, Clinton moved above the critical 50 percent approval level and maintained a positive rating throughout the 1996 presidential campaign. During his second term, the health of the nation's economy drove his approval over 60 percent, and, paradoxically, his ratings went up during a sex scandal.

What Do You Think?

Should We Judge Presidents on Private Character or Performance in Office?

In evaluating presidents, should we consider their private moral conduct or should we focus on how they perform their public duties? Can private morality be divorced from public trust? The sex scandals surrounding Bill Clinton, not only those alleged to have occurred before he was elected president, but also those alleged to have occurred in the Oval Office itself, brought these questions forcefully to the American people.

When allegations first emerged in January, 1998, that Clinton had had an affair with a twenty-one-year-old intern working at the White House, President Clinton himself emphatically denied the allegations, saying, "I did not have sexual relations with that woman, Ms. Lewinsky!" But a majority of the American people (62%) believed the allegations to be true.

Yet, while most Americans clearly believed the president had a sexual affair in the White House and subsequently lied about it, they also approved of the way Clinton was performing his job as president (see figure). Indeed, the public appeared to rally around the president following the allegations of sexual misconduct. Clinton's job rating, already a healthy 60 percent at the beginning of 1998, experienced a "Lewinsky bounce" following lurid news stories of the affair.

Later, even after Clinton's televised acknowledgment of behavior that was "wrong," the American people contintued to give him high approval ratings as president. Americans overwhelmingly opposed his impeachment and removal from office (68 percent) as well as his voluntary resignation (64 percent). When Clinton's grand jury testimony about the affair was aired on television, he again experienced a favorable "bounce" in job approval. Indeed, many people blamed the independent counsel Kenneth Starr for investigating the private life of the president (see *What Do You Think?* "Do We Need Special Prosecutors to Investigate Presidents?" in Chapter 13). And many people blamed the news media for focusing so much attention on the affair. At the same time, opinion polls indicate most Americans felt that the president did not "share their values" (56%), did not "show good judgment" (56%), and was not "honest and trustworthy" (62%).

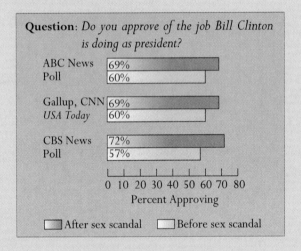

Question: *Do you approve of the job Bill Clinton is doing as president?*

Source: Copyright, *USA Today*. Reprinted with permission.

Major scandals may also hurt presidential popularity and effectiveness. The Watergate scandal produced a low of 22 percent approval for Nixon just prior to his resignation. Reagan's generally high approval ratings were blemished by the Iran-contra scandal hearings in 1987, although he ultimately left office with the highest approval rating of any outgoing president. But highly publicized allegations of sexual improprieties against President Clinton in early 1998 appeared to have the opposite effect; Clinton's approval ratings went *up*. Perhaps the public differentiates between private sexual conduct and performance in office (see *What Do You Think? Should We Judge Presidents on Private Character or Performance in Office?*).

Finally, economic recessions erode presidential popularity. Every president in office during a recession has suffered loss of popular approval, including President

In the 1998 midterm Congressional elections, Republicans were unable to capitalize politically on President Clinton's troubles. On the contrary, a last-minute backlash against the impeachment investigation appeared to help Democratic candidates. As the accompanying table shows, the "Lewinsky investigation" placed last in issues considered "very important" by the voters.

Issue Importance, 1998 Midterm Congressional Elections

Issue	"Very Important"
Education	88%
Budget surplus debate	76
Global and U.S. economy	76
HMO regulation	68
Middle class tax cuts	62
Party control of Congress	54
Campaign finance reform	49
Tobacco regulation	38
Impeachment debate	35
Lewinsky investigation	18

SOURCE: Pew Research Center for the People and the Press.

Various explanations have been offered for this apparent paradox—a public that believed the president had an affair in the White House and lied about it, that questioned his values and judgment, yet gave the president the highest approval ratings of his career and passed up the opportunity to punish his party in the elections. Many Americans believe that private sexual conduct is irrelevant to the performance of public duties. Private morality is viewed as a personal affair about which Americans should be nonjudgmental. Some people would emulate more "sophisticated" Europeans by ignoring the sex lives of political leaders. Others say, "If it's okay with Hillary, why should we worry?" Haven't we had adulterous presidents before, from Thomas Jefferson to John F. Kennedy, presidents who were ranked high in history? And many Americans believe that "they all do it." Indeed, in response to the question "Do you think most presidents have or have not had extramarital affairs while they were president?" some 59 percent say "most have," whereas only 33% percent say "most have not."

Others argue, nonetheless, that private character counts in presidential performance, indeed, that it is a prerequisite for public trust. The president, in this view, performs a symbolic role that requires dignity, honesty, and respect. A president publicly embarrassed by sexual scandal, diminished by jokes, and laughed at by late-night television audiences cannot perform this role. Clinton's problems raised questions about their possible effect on critical decisions he faced, for example as Commander-in-Chief during a time of tension with Iraq. The acceptance of a president's adulterous behavior, according to one commentator, lowers society's standards of behavior. "The president's legacy . . . will be a further vulgarization and demoralization of society."[*]

_____
[*]Gertrude Himmelfarb, "Private Lives, Public Morality," *New York Times,* February 9, 1998. Poll results reported in *The Polling Report,* February 9, 1998.

Reagan during the 1982 recession. But no president suffered a more precipitous decline in approval ratings than George Bush, whose popularity plummeted from its Gulf War high of 89 percent to a low of 37 percent in only a year, largely as a result of recession. Bill Clinton's approval ratings were only mediocre during his first term, but robust economic growth pushed his popularity to new highs in his second term (see Figure 11-3).

Access to the Media   The president dominates the news more than any other single person. All major television networks, newspapers, and newsmagazines have reporters (usually their most experienced and skilled people) covering the "White House beat."[12] The presidential press secretary briefs these reporters daily, but the

President Clinton answers questions during a press conference. These meetings with the press can be a double-edged sword. They give the president an opportunity to present his point of view to the public, but they also allow the press to raise issues a president might rather avoid.

president also may appear in person in the White House press room at any time. Presidents regularly use this media access to advance their programs and priorities.

Presidential press conferences can help mobilize popular support for presidential programs. Presidents often try to focus attention on particular legislative issues, and they generally open press conferences with a lengthy policy statement on these issues. But reporters' questions and subsequent reporting often refocus the press conference in other directions. The president cannot control the questions or limit the subject matter of press conferences. Indeed, the president cannot even ensure that the television networks—ABC, CBS, and NBC—will carry a presidential press conference live, although CNN, with its all-news format, always does so.

Presidents may also use direct television addresses from the White House. President Reagan, who held relatively few press conferences, made heavy use of national prime-time television appeals to mobilize support for his programs. Reagan's appeals frequently resulted in a deluge of telephone calls, wires, and letters to Congress in support of the president. George Bush and Bill Clinton were far less successful in this approach. Presidents must also weigh the drawbacks of television addresses. The networks now routinely give opposition leaders television time to respond following the president's address.

Finally, presidents can try to mobilize popular support for a program by public appearances, addresses, and speeches. The national meetings or conventions of influential groups such as the American Newspaper Association, the American Legion, the National Association of Manufacturers, the U.S. Chamber of Commerce, and the National Association for the Advancement of Colored People can provide a forum. So can college and university commencements.

Party Leadership   Presidents are leaders of their party, but this role is hardly a source of great strength. It is true that presidents select the national party chair, control the national committee and its Washington staff, and largely direct the national party convention. Incumbent presidents can use this power to help defeat challengers *within* their own parties. President Ford used this power to help defeat challenger Ronald Reagan in 1976; President Carter used it to help defeat challenger Ted Kennedy in 1980; and President Bush used it against challenger Pat Buchanan in 1992. But the role of party leader is of limited value to a president because the parties have few controls over their members (see Chapter 7).

Nevertheless, presidents enjoy much stronger support in Congress from members of their own party than from members of the opposition party. Some of the president's party support in Congress is a product of shared ideological values and policy positions. But Republican Congress members do have some stake in the success of a Republican president, as do Democratic members in the success of a Democratic president. Popular presidents may produce those few extra votes that make the difference for party candidates in close congressional districts.

CHIEF EXECUTIVE

The president is the chief executive of the nation's largest bureaucracy: 2.8 million civilian employees, 60 independent agencies, 14 departments, and the large Executive Office of the President. The formal organizational chart of the federal government places the president at the head of this giant structure (see Figure 12-1, "The Federal Bureaucracy," in Chapter 12). But the president cannot command this bureaucracy in the fashion of a military officer or a corporation president. When Harry Truman was preparing to turn over the White House to Dwight Eisenhower, he predicted that the general of the army would not understand the presidency: "He'll sit here and say 'Do this! Do that!' and nothing will happen. Poor Ike—it won't be a bit like the army. He'll find it very frustrating." Truman vastly underestimated the political skills of the former general, but the crusty Missourian clearly understood the frustrations confronting the nation's chief executive. The president does not command the executive branch of government but rather stands at its center—persuading, bargaining, negotiating, and compromising to achieve goals (see *People in Politics:* "Bill Clinton: The Ambivalent Presidency").

The Constitutional Executive The Constitution is vague about the president's authority over the executive branch. It vests executive power in the presidency and grants the president authority to appoint principal officers of the government "by and with the Advice and Consent of the Senate." Under the Constitution, the president may also "require the Opinion, in writing, of the principal Officer of each of the executive Departments, upon any Subject relating to the Duties of their respective Offices." This awkward phrase presumably gives the president the power to oversee operations of the executive departments. Finally, and perhaps most important, the president is instructed to "take Care that the Laws be faithfully executed."

At the same time, Congress has substantial authority over the executive branch. Through its lawmaking abilities, Congress can establish or abolish executive departments and regulate their operations. Congress's "power of the purse" allows it to determine the budget of each department each year and thus to limit or broaden or even "micromanage" the activities of these departments. Moreover, Congress can pressure executive agencies by conducting investigations, calling administrators to task in public hearings, and directly contacting agencies with members' own complaints or those of their constituents.

Bill Clinton,
The Ambivalent Presidency

No one doubts that William Jefferson Clinton is one of the most intelligent men ever to occupy the Oval Office and that his knowledge of the details of government and public policy exceeds that of any other recent president. But with no fixed ideological compass, the Clinton presidency has suffered "deep, near terminal ambivalence."[*]
Throughout his first term he weighed conflicting advice from moderates and liberals with reference to a single overriding goal—reelection. In his second term, he became free to pursue a consistent course and establish a recognized legacy. But he has continued to pursue multiple directions simultaneously.

Getting Started   Born Billy Blythe in rural Hope, Arkansas, three months after his father's death in an automobile accident (he assumed his stepfather's name of Clinton at age fifteen), young Bill learned that persistence and tenacity were the keys to success and acclaim. As a teenage delegate to Boys Nation, he won a handshake from President John F. Kennedy in 1963. He chose to attend Georgetown University in Washington to be near the nation's centers of power. As soon as he arrived in the capital he called on his state's senator, William J. Fulbright, chair of the Senate Foreign Relations Committee, and got a part-time job as a legislative aide. Clinton won a Rhodes Scholarship to Oxford University with the help of Senator Fulbright, himself a former Rhodes scholar. He never completed a degree at Oxford, but he cultivated friendships that would later enhance his public career. In London he helped organize anti–Vietnam War demonstrations, even while he worried that his antiwar activities might someday come back to haunt his political ambitions. When he received a draft notice, he promptly enrolled in the ROTC program at the University of Arkansas, making himself temporarily ineligible for the draft despite acknowledging that his real plans were to go to Yale Law School.

The Nation's Youngest Governor   Upon graduation from Yale, Clinton turned down offers to return to Washington as a congressional staff aide. He was anxious

to launch his own political career, and he knew that the road to elective office ran through his home state. Trying to capitalize on the Watergate scandal, he challenged a veteran Republican member of Congress in 1974. As a young antiwar activist with long 1960s-style hair, a Yale and Oxford background, and liberal friends such as Hillary Rodham coming from Washington to help in the campaign, he could have lost by a wide margin in conservative Arkansas. Instead, he came within a few votes of defeating a strong incumbent. In 1976 Clinton ran successfully for attorney general of Arkansas, and, in 1978, he jumped into the open gubernatorial contest and became the nation's youngest governor at age thirty-two.

Remolding His Image   As governor, Clinton first pushed a broad program of liberal reform for Arkansas, increasing taxes and expenditures. But he appeared to be an arrogant, crusading, liberal politician, out of touch with his conservative Arkansas constituency. He was defeated for reelection in 1980. His defeat "forever influenced the way he approached government and politics."[†] He proceeded to remold himself into a political moderate, calling for workfare to replace welfare, supporting the death penalty, and working to create a favorable business climate in Arkansas. He cut his hair, and his wife began using her married name so as not to offend social conservatives. The moderate strategy proved successful; he was elected governor once again in 1982. By most accounts, Bill Clinton was a successful governor.

Clinton's view that only a moderate Democrat could win the presidency was reinforced by Michael Dukakis's disastrous defeat in 1988. Just as he had shaped his image to fit his Arkansas constituents, Clinton molded his national image as a moderate, pro-business, Democrat, capable of winning back the support of the white middle class.

First Term Flip-Flops   Bill Clinton won the White House in 1992 with only 43 percent of the popular vote, hardly a mandate for comprehensive policy change. His first major battle—to retain homosexuals in the military—proved a disaster. Military chiefs, led by the popular General Colin Powell, resisted, and Clinton was forced to retreat. He succeeded in getting the Democratic-controlled Congress to pass a large tax increase, raising the top marginal income tax rate from 31 to nearly 40 percent. But in his second year, he stumbled badly in his massive national health care program, and his approval ratings sagged.

The sweeping Republican congressional victory in 1994 posed very important political choices for Clinton. Should he respond by moving back to the center, moderating his big spending plans and cooperating with Republicans in Congress on budget cutting and welfare reform? Or should he continue to fight for liberal policies, challenging the Republican Congress to reject his initiatives, and then campaign for reelection by castigating Congress? Typically, Clinton followed *both* paths simultaneously. He pressured Senate Democrats to defeat the balanced budget amendment and vetoed several Republican balanced budget plans. When the government temporarily "shut down," Clinton uncharacteristically stood firm and shifted blame to the Republican Congress. He cast himself as the defender of "Medicare, Medicaid, education, and the environment" against mean-spirited Republican budget cutters. Clinton's approval ratings began a long rise.

Shifting Toward Mini-Policies Election year brought still more policy shifts. He announced, "The era of big government is over." He signed the Republican welfare bill that he had vetoed twice. Rather than champion large-scale change in the fashion of Roosevelt's New Deal, Clinton shifted to what might be labeled the "Small Deal"—an assembly of small changes easily understood by the American people and not costing very much. This shift toward mini-policies—V-chips, school uniforms, gun control, time off for family emergencies, longer stays in maternity wards, for example—paid off among women voters at the polls. Although men appeared to divide their votes evenly between Clinton and Dole, the president won women voters by a stunning 54 to 38 margin.

A Mandate for What? At the start of his second term Clinton seemed to acknowledge that he had no mandate for new, large-scale government programs. He modestly observed in his election night victory speech: "Tonight we proclaim that the vital American center is alive and well." But even if he had sought to return to a liberal agenda, it is not likely that a Republican Congress would have allowed him to get very far. Indeed, Republicans and conservatives claimed that Clinton won reelection as a deficit-cutting, welfare-reforming, more-cops-on-the-beat president—that is, by "stealing" traditional Republican issues.

Second Term Drift? Critics of President Clinton describe his second term as "risk averse," adrift, and even aimless. Although he speaks on a multitude of policy proposals, he does not cite any single issue as his overriding priority.

Second-term presidents often become highly attentive to "their place in history," that is, to establishing a lasting legacy for which they will be forever remembered. But Clinton seems aware that presidential "greatness" is as much a product of the times as the man, perhaps acknowledging that he may not be ranked among the "great" presidents.

Yet Clinton's second-term popular approval ratings are high—over 60 percent—an impressive level for any president. These ratings appear to be immune to allegations of sexual misconduct. Most commentators attribute his high ratings to the nation's healthy economy—economic growth, low employment, low inflation.

The booming economy has also provided a temporary solution to what has been the most vexing of all government problems: continuing deficit spending. Robust economic growth has increased federal tax revenues enough to produce a projected balanced federal budget, a goal that eluded presidents and Congresses for over a quarter-century. Clinton and Congress have a far happier problem to debate—how to allocate any surplus revenues. Clinton's call to "save Social Security first" (before tax cutting or new spending programs) reflects majority public opinion.

The Rhetorical Presidency Bill Clinton enjoys talking about politics and public policy. Indeed, critics complain *talk*—"town hall" meetings, talk shows, dialogues, and discussions—has become the hallmark of his presidency. Clinton believes that people can come to understand each other better by talking. He is sincere in his desire to improve race relations in America; yet beyond creating a new advisory board (the Initiative on Race and Reconciliation) to discuss racial issues and giving frequent speeches on the topic, he has no specific policy agenda. On the affirmative action controversy (see Chapter 15) he provided only a trendy sound bite— "Mend it, don't end it"—but no specific recommendations regarding racial quotas or preferences.

Clinton is aware that there is no groundswell of public opinion in support of major new government programs. So he wisely limits his proposals to modest reforms. Yet the very modesty of his goals may forecast Clinton's place in history.

---

*Bob Woodward, *The Agenda,* New York: Simon & Schuster, 1994, p. 48.

†David Maranis, *First in His Class,* New York: Simon & Schuster, 1995, p. 400.

Executive Orders   Presidents frequently use **executive orders** to implement their policies. Executive orders may direct specific federal agencies to carry out the president's wishes, or they may direct all federal agencies to pursue the president's preferred course of action. In any case, they must be based on either a president's constitutional powers or on powers delegated to the president by laws of Congress. Presidents regularly issue 50 to 100 executive orders each year,[13] but some stand out. In 1948 President Harry Truman issued Executive Order 9981 to desegregate the U.S. armed forces. In 1967 President Lyndon Johnson issued Executive Order 11246 to require that private firms with federal contracts institute affirmative action programs.

Appointments   Presidential power over the executive branch derives in part from the president's authority to appoint and remove top officials. Presidents can shape policy by careful attention to top appointments—cabinet secretaries, assistant secretaries, agency heads, and White House staff. The key is to select people who share the president's policy views and who have the personal qualifications to do an effective job. However, in cabinet appointments political considerations weigh heavily: unifying various elements of the party; appealing for interest-group support; rewarding political loyalty; providing a temporary haven for unsuccessful party candidates; achieving a balance of racial, ethnic, and gender representation.[14] The appointment power gives the president only limited control over the executive branch of government. Of the executive branch's 2.8 million civilian employees, the president actually appoints only about 3,000. The vast majority of federal executive branch employees are civil servants—recruited, paid, and protected under civil service laws—and are not easily removed or punished by the president. Cabinet secretaries and heads of independent regulatory agencies require congressional confirmation, but presidents can choose their own White House staff without the approval of Congress.

Presidents have only limited power to remove the heads of independent regulatory agencies. By law, Congress sets the terms of these officials. Federal Communications Commission members are appointed for seven years; Securities and Exchange Commission members for five years; and Federal Reserve Board members, responsible for the nation's money supply, enjoy the longest term of any executive officials—fourteen years. Congress's responsibility for term length for regulatory agencies is supposed to insulate those agencies, in particular their quasi-judicial responsibilities, from "political" influence.

Even having a presidential appointee at the helm of a department does not always guarantee the president control over that department. Many political appointees are stymied by the career bureaucrats in departments and agencies who have the knowledge, skills, and experience to function with little or no supervision from their nominal political chiefs. Rather than carrying out the president's policies, some appointees "go native": they yield to the career bureaucrats, adopt the prevailing customs and values of their agencies, and seek the support of the bureaucrats, interest groups, and congressional committees that determine the agencies' future.

Republican presidents have an especially difficult task controlling the bureaucracy because a majority of career bureaucrats are Democrats.[15] When President Nixon tried to deal with this problem by shifting power from executive departments to his White House staff, the unhappy result was that the White House staff itself became a large and powerful bureaucracy, frequently locked in conflict with

executive order   Formal regulation governing executive branch operations issued by the president.

executive departments. President Reagan instead tried appointing committed conservatives to head key agencies, only to see them isolated and undermined by angry bureaucrats. Some lower-level bureaucrats supplied the media and Congress with damaging reports about Reagan appointees' activities (see "Bureaucratic Politics" in Chapter 12).

Budget Presidential authority also derives from the president's role in the budgetary process. The Constitution makes no mention of the president with regard to expenditures; rather, it grants the power of the purse to Congress. Indeed, for nearly 150 years, executive departments submitted their budget requests directly to the Congress without first submitting them to the president. But with the passage of the Budget and Accounting Act in 1921, Congress established the Office of Management and Budget (originally named the Bureau of the Budget) to assist the president in preparing an annual Budget of the United States Government for presentation to the Congress. The president's budget is simply a set of recommendations to the Congress. Congress must pass appropriations acts before the president or any executive department or agency may spend money. Congress can and frequently does alter the president's budget recommendations (see "The Politics of Budgeting" in Chapter 12).

With the Senate's consent, the president also appoints three professional economists of high standing to the Council of Economic Advisers (CEA). Created by the Employment Act of 1946, CEA analyzes trends in the economy and recommends to the president the fiscal and monetary policies necessary to avoid depression and inflation (see "Economic Decision Making" in Chapter 16).

The Cabinet   The **cabinet** is not mentioned in the U.S. Constitution; it has no formal powers. It consists of the secretaries of the executive departments and others the president may designate, including the vice president, the ambassador to the United Nations, the director of the Central Intelligence Agency, and the Special Trade Representative. According to custom, cabinet officials are ranked by the date their departments were created (see Table 11-2). Thus the Secretary of State is the senior cabinet officer, followed by the Secretary of the Treasury. They sit next to the president at Cabinet meetings; heads of the newest departments sit at the far ends of the table. The Defense Department was created by law in 1947, but the secretary of defense inherits the traditional posts—and rank—of the secretary of war and the secretary of the navy, which were created by the first Congress of the United States.

The cabinet rarely functions as a decision-making body. Cabinet officers in the United States are powerful because they head giant administrative organizations. The secretary of state, the secretary of defense, the secretary of the treasury, the attorney general, and, to a lesser extent, the other departmental secretaries are all people of power and prestige. But seldom does a strong president hold a cabinet meeting to decide important policy questions. More frequently, presidents know what they want and hold cabinet meetings only to help promote their views. Presidents who have tried to use the cabinet as a policy-making body have been disappointed. George Washington was frustrated by constant feuding between his secretary of the treasury, Alexander Hamilton, and his secretary of state, Thomas Jefferson. President Jimmy Carter promised "cabinet government" but soon found that meetings were little more than "adult show and tell." The cabinet is too large for serious discussion; its members are not necessarily familiar with issues beyond

cabinet   The heads (secretaries) of the executive departments together with other top officials accorded Cabinet rank by the president; only occasionally does it meet as a body to advise and support the president.

TABLE 11-2	The Cabinet Departments	
Department		Created
State		1789
Treasury		1789
Defense*		1947
Justice		1789
Interior		1849
Agriculture†		1889
Commerce		1913
Labor		1913
Health and Human Services‡		1953
Housing and Urban Development		1965
Transportation		1966
Energy		1977
Education		1979
Veterans' Affairs		1989

*Formerly the War and Navy Departments, created in 1789 and 1798, respectively.

†Agriculture Department created in 1862; made part of cabinet in 1889.

‡Originally Health, Education, and Welfare; reorganized in 1979, with the creation of a separate Department of Education.

their own department's sphere of activity; they are preoccupied with managing large bureaucracies. Finally, cabinet members are frequently appointed not for policy guidance but to cement the president's relationships with interest groups— agriculture, veterans, labor, and so forth—or to provide the administration with racial, ethnic, and gender balance.

The Constitution requires that "Officers of the United States" be confirmed by the Senate. In the past, the Senate rarely rejected a presidential cabinet nomination; the traditional view was that presidents were entitled to pick their own people and even make their own mistakes. In recent years, however, the confirmation process has become more partisan and divisive, with the Senate conducting lengthy investigations and holding public hearings on presidential cabinet nominees. In 1989 the Senate rejected President Bush's nomination of John Tower as secretary of defense in a partisan battle featuring charges that the former Texas senator was a heavy drinker. In 1993 President Clinton was obliged to withdraw the nomination of Zoe Baird as attorney general following Senate hearings featuring the charge that she had employed an illegal alien as a babysitter and had failed to pay the woman's Social Security taxes. The intense public scrutiny and potential for partisan attacks, together with financial disclosure and conflict-of-interest laws, may be discouraging some well-qualified people from accepting cabinet posts.

The National Security Council   The **National Security Council (NSC)** is really an "inner cabinet" created by law in 1947 to advise the president and coordinate foreign, defense, and intelligence activities. The president is chair, and the vice president, secretary of state, and secretary of defense are participating members. The chair of the Joint Chiefs of Staff and the director of the Central Intelligence Agency

National Security Council (NSC)   "Inner cabinet" that advises the president and coordinates foreign, defense, and intelligence activities.

serve as advisers to the NSC, which is headed by the special assistant to the president for national security affairs. The purposes of the council are to advise and coordinate policy, but in the Iran-Contra scandal, a staff member of the NSC, Lt. Col. Oliver North, undertook to implement security policy. Various investigative committees strongly recommended that the NSC staff confine itself to an advisory role.

White House Staff   Today, presidents exercise their powers chiefly through the White House staff.[16] This staff includes the president's closest aides and advisers. Over the years, the White House staff has grown from Roosevelt's small "brain trust" of a dozen advisers to several hundred people, many with impressive titles, such as assistant to the president, deputy assistant to the president, special assistant to the president, and counsel to the president.

Senior White House staff members are trusted political advisers, often personal friends and long-time associates of the president. Some enjoy office space in the White House itself and daily contact with the president (see Figure 11-3). Appointed without Senate confirmation, they are loyal to the president alone, not to departments, agencies, or interest groups. Their many tasks include the following:

- Providing the president with sound advice on everything from national security to congressional affairs, policy development, and electoral politics.
- Monitoring the operations of executive departments and agencies and evaluating the performance of key executive officials.
- Setting the president's schedule, determining whom the president will see and call, where and when the president will travel, and where and to whom the president will make personal appearances and speeches.
- Above all, the staff must protect their boss, steering the president away from scandal, political blunders, and errors of judgment.

The senior White House staff normally includes a chief of staff, the national security adviser, a press secretary, the counsel to the president (an attorney), a director of personnel (patronage appointments), and assistants for political affairs, legislative liaison, management, and domestic policy. Staff organization depends on each president's personal taste. Some presidents have organized their staffs hierarchically, concentrating power in the chief of staff. Others have maintained direct contact with several staff members.

CHIEF LEGISLATOR AND LOBBYIST

The president has the principal responsibility for the initiation of national policy. Indeed, about 80 percent of the bills considered by Congress originate in the executive branch. Presidents have a strong incentive to fulfill this responsibility: the American people hold them responsible for anything that happens in the nation during their term of office, whether or not they have the authority or capacity to do anything about it.

Policy Initiation   The Founders understood that the president would be involved in policy initiation. The Constitution requires the president to "give to the Congress Information of the State of the Union," to "recommend to their Consideration such Measures as he shall judge necessary and expedient" (Article II, Section 3). "On extraordinary Occasions" the president may call a recessed

FIGURE 11-3 The Clinton Administration's Corridors of Power

Presidents allocate office space in the White House according to their own desires. An office located close to the president's is considered an indication of the power of the occupant.

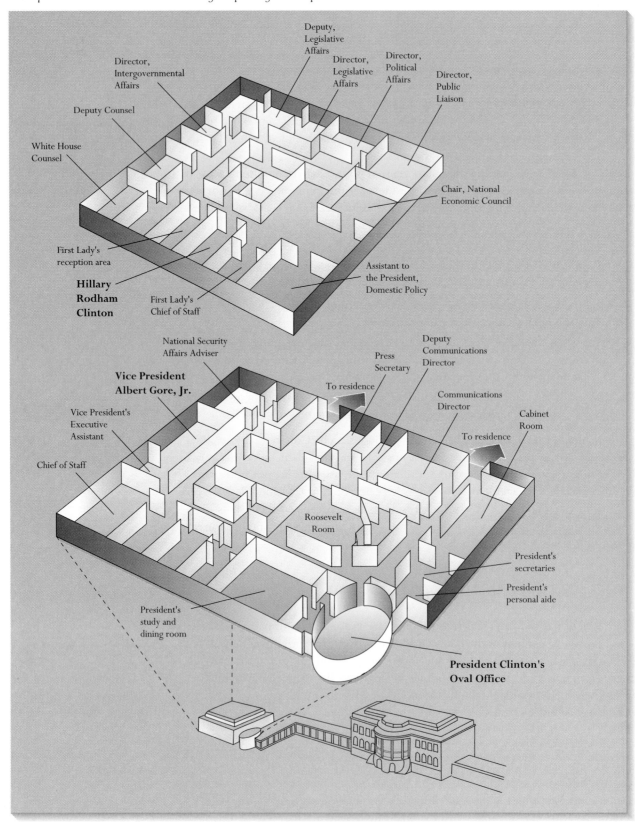

Congress into special session. Each year the principal policy statement of the president comes in the State of the Union message to Congress. It is followed by the president's Budget of the United States Government, which sets forth the president's programs with price tags attached. Many other policy proposals are developed by executive departments and agencies, transmitted to the White House for the president's approval or "clearance," and then sent to Congress.

Congress may not accept all or even most of the president's proposals. Indeed, from time to time it may even try to develop its own legislative agenda in competition with the president's. But the president's legislative initiatives usually set the agenda of congressional decision making. As one experienced Washington lobbyist put it, "Obviously when the president sends up a bill, it takes first place in the queue. All other bills take second place."[17]

White House Lobbying   Presidents do not simply send their bills to Congress and then await the outcome. The president is also expected to be the chief lobbyist on behalf of the administration's bills as they make their way through the legislative labyrinth. The White House staff includes "legislative liaison" people—lobbyists for the president's programs. They organize the president's legislative proposals, track them through committee and floor proceedings, arrange committee appearances by executive department and agency representatives, count votes, and advise the president on when and how to "cut deals" and "twist arms."

Presidents are not without resources in lobbying Congress. They may exchange many favors, large and small, for the support of individual members. They can help direct "pork" to a member's district, promise White House support for a member's pet project, and assist in resolving a member's problems with the bureaucracy. Presidents also may issue or withhold invitations to the White House for prestigious ceremonies, dinners with visiting heads of state, and other glittering social occasions—an effective resource because most members of Congress value the prestige associated with close White House "connections."

The president may choose to "twist arms" individually—by telephoning and meeting with wavering members of Congress. Arm twisting is generally reserved for the president's most important legislative battles. There is seldom time for a president to contact individual members of Congress personally about many bills in various stages of the legislative process—in subcommittee, full committee, floor consideration, conference committee, and final passage—in both the House and the Senate. Instead, the president must rely on White House staff for most legislative contacts and use personal appeals sparingly.

The Honeymoon   The **honeymoon period** at the very start of a president's term offers the best opportunity to get the new administration's legislative proposals enacted into law. Presidential influence in Congress is generally highest at this time both because the president's personal popularity is typically at its height and because the president can claim the recent election results as a popular mandate for key programs. Sophisticated members of Congress know that votes cast for a presidential candidate are not necessarily votes cast for that candidate's policy position (see "The Voter Decides" in Chapter 8). But election results signal members of Congress, in a language they understand well, that the president is politically popular and that they must give the administration's programs careful consideration. President Lyndon Johnson succeeded in getting the bulk of his Great Society program enacted in the year following his landslide victory in 1964. Ronald Reagan pushed through the

honeymoon period Early months of a president's term in which his popularity with the public and influence with the Congress are generally high.

largest tax cut in American history in the year following his convincing electoral victory over incumbent president Jimmy Carter in 1980. Bill Clinton was most successful with the Congress during his first year in office, in 1993, even winning approval for a major tax increase as part of a deficit-reduction package.

Presidential "Box Scores" How successful are presidents in getting their legislation through Congress? *Congressional Quarterly* regularly compiles "box scores" of presidential success in Congress—percentages of presidential victories on congressional votes on which the president took a clear-cut position. The measure does not distinguish between bills that were important to the president and bills that may have been less significant. But viewed over time (see Figure 11-4), the presidential box scores provide interesting insights into the factors affecting the president's legislative success.

The most important determinant of presidential success in Congress is party control. Presidents are far more successful when they face a Congress controlled by their own party. Democratic presidents John F. Kennedy and Lyndon Johnson enjoyed the support of Democratic-controlled Congresses and posted average success scores over 80 percent. Jimmy Carter was hardly a popular president, but he enjoyed the support of a Democratic Congress and an average of 76.8 percent presidential support. Republican presidents Richard Nixon and Gerald Ford fared

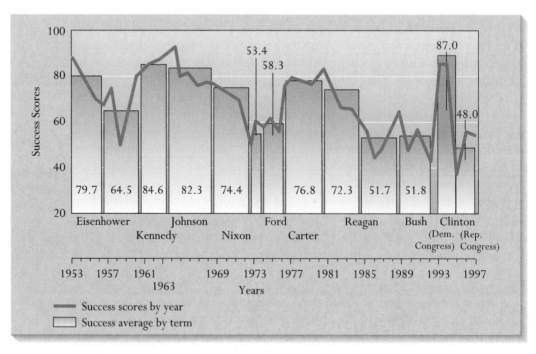

FIGURE 11-4 Presidential Success Scores in Congress

Presidential "box scores"—the percentage of times that a bill endorsed by the president is enacted by Congress—are closely linked to the strength of the president's party in Congress. For example, both Dwight D. Eisenhower and Ronald Reagan benefited from having a Republican majority in the Senate in their first terms and suffered when Democrats gained control of the Senate in their second terms. Democratic control of both houses of Congress resulted in significantly higher box scores for Democratic presidents John Kennedy, Lyndon Johnson, and Jimmy Carter than for Republicans Richard Nixon, Gerald Ford, and George Bush. Clinton was very successful in his first two years, when the Democrats controlled Congress, but when the Republicans won control following the 1994 midterm election, Clinton's box score plummeted.

poorly with Democrat-controlled Congresses. Republican president Ronald Reagan was very successful in his first term when he faced a Democratic House and a Republican Senate, but after Democrats took over both houses of Congress, Reagan's success rate plummeted. During the Reagan and Bush presidencies, divided party control of government (Republicans in the White House and Democrats controlling one or both houses of Congress) was said to produce **gridlock**, the political inability of the government to act decisively on the nation's problems. President Bill Clinton's notable achievements when Democrats controlled the Congress (1993–94), contrasted with his dismal record in dealing with Republican-controlled Congresses (1995–99), provide a vivid illustration of the importance of party in determining a president's legislative success.

The Veto Power   The **veto** is the president's most powerful weapon in dealing with Congress. The veto is especially important to a president facing a Congress controlled by the opposition party. Even the *threat* of a veto enhances the president's bargaining power with Congress.[18] Confronted with such a threat, congressional leaders must calculate whether they can muster a two-thirds vote of both houses to override the veto.

To veto a bill passed by the Congress, the president sends to Congress a veto message specifying reasons for not signing it. If the president takes no action for ten days (excluding Sundays) after a bill has been passed by Congress, the bill becomes law without the president's signature. However, if Congress has adjourned within ten days of passing a bill and the president has not signed it, then the bill does not become law; this outcome is called a **pocket veto**.

A bill returned to Congress with a presidential veto message can be passed into law over the president's opposition by a two-thirds vote of both houses. (A bill that has received a pocket veto cannot be overridden because the Congress is no longer in session.) In other words, the president needs only to hold the loyalty of more than one-third of *either* the House or the Senate to sustain a veto. If congressional leaders cannot count on the votes to **override**, they are forced to bargain with the president. "What will the president accept?" becomes a key legislative question.

The president's bargaining power with Congress has been enhanced over the years by a history of success in sustaining presidential vetoes.[19] From George Washington to Bill Clinton, more than 96 percent of all presidential vetoes have been sustained (see Table 11-3). For example, although Bush was unable to achieve much success in getting his own legislative proposals enacted by a Democratic Congress, he was extraordinarily successful in saying no. Of Bush's many vetoes, only one (regulation of cable TV) was overridden by Congress.[20] Clinton did not veto any bills when Democrats controlled Congress, but he began a series of vetoes in his struggle with the Republican Congress elected in 1994. He was able to sustain almost all of his vetoes because Republicans did not have two-thirds of the seats in both houses and most Democratic Congress members stuck with their president.

The Line-Item Veto   For many years, presidents, both Democratic and Republican, petitioned Congress to give them the **line-item veto**, the ability to veto some provisions of a bill while accepting other provisions. The lack of presidential line-item veto power was especially frustrating when dealing with appropriations bills because the president could not veto specific pork-barrel provisions from major spending bills for defense, education, housing, welfare, and so on. Finally, in 1996 Congress granted the president authority to "cancel" spending items in

gridlock   Political stalemate between the executive and legislative branches arising when one branch is controlled by one major political party and the other branch by the other party.

veto   Rejection of a legislative act by the executive branch; in the U.S. federal government, overriding of a veto requires a two-thirds majority in both houses of Congress.

pocket veto   Effective veto of a bill when Congress adjourns within ten days of passing it and the president fails to sign it.

override   Voting in Congress to enact legislation vetoed by the president; requires a two-thirds vote in both the House and Senate.

line-item veto   Power of the chief executive to reject some portions of a bill without rejecting all of it.

	TABLE 11-3	Presidential Vetoes		

President	Total Vetoes[*]	Vetoes Overridden	Percentage of Vetoes Sustained
F. Roosevelt	633	9	99%
Truman	250	12	95
Eisenhower	181	2	99
Kennedy	21	0	100
L. Johnson	30	0	100
Nixon	43	5	90
Ford	66	12	85
Carter	31	2	94
Reagan	78	8	91
Bush	46	1	98
Clinton (1st term)	17	1	94

[*]Regular vetoes plus pocket vetoes.

Source: Harold W. Stanley and Richard G. Niemi, *Vital Statistics on American Politics*, 5th ed. (Washington, D.C.: CQ Press, 1995), p. 258. Updated by author.

any appropriation act, any new entitlement, or any limited tax benefit. Such cancellation would take effect immediately unless blocked by a special "disapproval bill" passed by Congress. The president could veto the disapproval bill, and a two-thirds vote of both houses would be required to override the veto.

However, opponents of the line-item veto successfully challenged its constitutionality, arguing that it transfers legislative power—granted by the Constitution only to Congress—to the president. The U.S. Supreme Court agreed: "There is no provision in the Constitution that authorizes the president to enact or amend or repeal statutes." The line-item veto, the Court said, "authorizes the president himself to elect to repeal laws, for his own policy reasons" and therefore violates the law-making procedures set forth in Article I of the Constitution.

GLOBAL LEADER

The president of the United States is the leader of the world's largest and most powerful democracy. During the Cold War, the president of the United States was seen as the leader of the "free world." The threat of Soviet expansionism, the huge military forces of the Warsaw Pact, and Soviet-backed guerrilla wars around the world all added to the global role of the American president as the defender of democratic values. In today's post–Cold War world, Western Europe and Japan are formidable economic competitors and no longer routinely defer to American political leadership. But if a new stable world order based on democracy and self-determination is to emerge, the president of the United States must provide the necessary leadership.

Global leadership is based on a president's powers of persuasion. Presidents are more persuasive when the American economy is strong, when American military forces are perceived as ready and capable, and when the president is seen as having the support of the American people and Congress. America's allies as well as its enemies perceive the president as the controlling force over U.S. foreign and military policy. Only occasionally do they seek to bypass the president and appeal to the Congress or to American public opinion.

Presidents sometimes prefer their global role to the much more contentious infighting of domestic politics. Abroad, presidents are treated with great dignity as head of the world's most powerful state. In contrast, at home presidents must confront hostile and insulting reporters, backbiting bureaucrats, demanding interest groups, and contentious members of Congress.

Foreign Policy   As the nation's chief diplomat, the president has the principal responsibility for formulating U.S. foreign policy. The president's constitutional powers in foreign affairs are relatively modest. Presidents have the power to make treaties with foreign nations "with the Advice and Consent of the Senate." Presidents may negotiate with nations separately or through international organizations such as the North Atlantic Treaty Organization (NATO) or the United Nations, where the president determines the U.S. position in that body's deliberations. The Constitution also empowers the president to "appoint Ambassadors, other public Ministers, and Consuls" and to "receive Ambassadors." This power of **diplomatic recognition** permits a president to grant legitimacy to or withhold it from ruling groups around the world (to declare or refuse to declare them "rightful"). Despite controversy, President Franklin Roosevelt officially recognized the communist regime in Russia in 1933, Richard Nixon recognized the communist government of the People's Republic of China in 1972, and Carter recognized the communist Sandinistas' regime in Nicaragua in 1979. To date, all presidents have withheld diplomatic recognition of Fidel Castro's government in Cuba.

Presidents have expanded on these modest constitutional powers to dominate American foreign policy making. In part, they have done so as a product of their role as commander-in-chief. Military force is the ultimate diplomatic language. During wartime, or when war is threatened, military and foreign policy become inseparable. The president must decide on the use of force and, equally important, when and under what conditions to order a cease-fire or an end to hostilities.

Presidents have also come to dominate foreign policy as a product of the customary international recognition of the head of state as the legitimate voice of a government. Although nations may also watch the words and actions of the American Congress, the president's statements are generally taken to represent the official position of the U.S. government.

Treaties   Treaties the president makes "by and with the Advice and Consent of the Senate" are legally binding upon the United States. The Constitution specifies that "all Treaties made . . . under the Authority of the United States, shall be the supreme Law of the Land; and the Judges in every State shall be bound thereby" (Article VI). Thus treaty provisions are directly enforceable in federal courts.

Although presidents may or may not listen to "advice" from the Senate on foreign policy, no formal treaty is valid unless "two-thirds of the Senators present concur" to its ratification. Although the Senate has ratified the vast majority of treaties, presidents must be sensitive to Senate concerns. The Senate defeat of the Versailles Treaty in 1920, which formally ended World War I and established the League of Nations, prompted Presidents Roosevelt and Truman to include prominent Democratic and Republican members of the Senate Foreign Relations Committee in the delegation that drafted the United Nations Treaty in 1945 and the NATO Treaty in 1949.

Executive Agreements   Over the years, presidents have come to rely heavily on **executive agreements** with other governments rather than formal treaties.

President Clinton meeting with President Nelson Mandela of South Africa during Clinton's visit to Africa. Presidential visits emphasize the chief executive's foreign policy priorities and his international role as chief of state.

diplomatic recognition
Power of the president to grant "legitimacy" to or withhold it from a government of another nation (to declare or refuse to declare it "rightful").

executive agreement
Agreement with another nation signed by the president of the United States but less formal (and hence potentially less binding) than a treaty because it does not require Senate confirmation.

Although still part of the "Big Three" along with Prime Minister Winston Churchill of Great Britain (left) and Marshal Josef Stalin of the Soviet Union (right), it was a gravely ill President Franklin Roosevelt (middle) who traveled to Yalta, a port on Russia's Crimean peninsula, and negotiated secret executive agreements dividing Germany among the Allies in 1945. Germany remained divided until 1989, when protesters tore down the Berlin Wall and the Soviet Union under Mikhail Gorbachev acquiesced in the unification of Germany under a democratic government.

An executive agreement signed by the president of the United States has much the same effect in international relations as a treaty. However, an executive agreement does not require Senate ratification. Presidents have asserted that their constitutional power to execute the laws, command the armed services, and determine foreign policy gives them the authority to make agreements with other nations and heads of state without obtaining approval of the U.S. Senate. However, unlike treaties, executive agreements do not supersede laws of the United States or of the states with which they conflict, but they are otherwise binding on the United States.

The use of executive agreements in important foreign policy matters was developed by President Franklin Roosevelt. Prior to his administration, executive agreements had been limited to minor matters. But in 1940, Roosevelt agreed to trade fifty American destroyers to England in exchange for naval bases in Newfoundland and the Caribbean. Roosevelt was intent on helping the British in their struggle against Nazi Germany, but before the Japanese attack on Pearl Harbor in 1941, isolationist sentiment in the Senate was too strong to win a two-thirds ratifying vote for such an agreement. Toward the end of World War II, Roosevelt at the Yalta Conference and Truman at the Potsdam Conference negotiated secret executive agreements dividing the occupation of Germany between the Western Allies and the Soviet Union and granting the Soviet Union territory in the Japanese Kurile Islands in exchange for its entry into the war against Japan.

Congress has sometimes objected to executive agreements as usurping its own powers. In the Case Act of 1972, Congress required the president to inform Congress of all executive agreements within sixty days, but the act does not limit the president's power to make agreements. It is easier for Congress to renege on executive agreements than on treaties that the Senate has ratified. In 1973 President Nixon signed an executive agreement with South Vietnamese President Nguyen Van Thieu pledging that the United States would "respond with full force" if North Vietnam violated the Paris Peace Agreement that ended American participation in the Vietnam War. But when North Vietnam reinvaded the south in 1975, Congress rejected President Gerald Ford's pleas for renewed military aid to the South Vietnamese government, and Ford knew that it had become politically impossible for the United States to respond with force.

Intelligence   The president is responsible for the intelligence activities of the United States. Presidents have undertaken intelligence activities since the founding of the nation. During the Revolutionary War, General George Washington nurtured small groups of patriots living behind British lines who supplied him with information on Redcoat troop movements.[21] Today, the director of central intelligence (DCI) is appointed by the president (subject to Senate confirmation) and reports directly to the president. The DCI coordinates the activities of the Central Intelligence Agency, the National Security Agency (which monitors electronic broadcasts around the world), and the secret National Reconnaissance Office (which obtains information from satellites), as well as the intelligence activities of the Department of Defense.

The Central Intelligence Agency (CIA) is directly supervised by the DCI. It is responsible for the analysis, preparation, and distribution of intelligence to the president and the National Security Council. It is also responsible for the collection of human intelligence—reports obtained from foreign sources by CIA caseworkers around the world. And the CIA is responsible for all **covert action**—activities in support of the national interest of the United States that would be ineffective or counterproductive if their sponsorship were to be made public. For example, one of the largest covert actions undertaken by the United States was the support, for nearly ten years, of the Afghan rebels fighting Soviet occupation of their country during the Afghanistan War (1978–88). Public acknowledgment of such aid would have assisted the Soviet-backed regime in Afghanistan to claim that the rebels were not true patriots but rather "puppets" of the United States. The rebels themselves did not wish to acknowledge U.S. aid publicly, even though they knew it was essential to the success of their cause. Hence Presidents Carter and Reagan aided the Afghan rebels through covert action.

Covert action is, by definition, secret. And secrecy spawns elaborate conspiracy theories and flamboyant tales of intrigue and deception. In fact, most covert actions consist of routine transfers of economic aid and military equipment to pro-U.S. forces that do not wish to acknowledge such aid publicly. Although most covert actions would have widespread support among the American public if they were done openly, secrecy opens the possibility that a president will undertake to do by covert action what would be opposed by Congress and the American people if they knew about it.

In the atmosphere of suspicion and distrust engendered by the Watergate scandal, Congress passed intelligence oversight legislation in 1974 requiring a written "presidential finding" for any covert action and requiring that members of the House and Senate Intelligence Committees be informed of all covert actions. The president does not have to obtain congressional approval for covert actions; but

covert action   Secret intelligence activity outside U.S. borders undertaken with specific authorization by the president; acknowledgment of U.S. sponsorship would defeat or compromise its purpose.

Congress can halt such actions if it chooses to do so. For example, in 1982, Congress passed the controversial Boland Amendment, which ordered the president and executive branch not to spend federal funds to assist the Contra rebel forces in Nicaragua in their efforts to overthrow the communist Sandinistas' regime. The Reagan Administration's efforts to get around the Boland Amendment led directly to the Iran-Contra scandal (see *Up Close:* "Iran-Contra and the White House Staff").

COMMANDER-IN-CHIEF

Global power derives primarily from the president's role as commander-in-chief of the armed forces of the United States. Presidential command over the armed forces is not merely symbolic; presidents may issue direct military orders to troops in the field. As president, Washington personally led troops to end the Whiskey Rebellion in 1794; Abraham Lincoln issued direct orders to his generals in the Civil War; Lyndon Johnson personally chose bombing targets in Vietnam; and George Bush personally ordered the Gulf War cease-fire after 100 hours of ground fighting. All presidents, whether they are experienced in world affairs or not, soon learn after taking office that their influence throughout the world is heavily dependent upon the command of capable military forces.

War-making Power   Constitutionally, war-making power is divided between the Congress and the president. Article I, Section 8, says, "The Congress shall have Power . . . to . . . provide for the common Defence . . . to declare War . . . to raise and support Armies . . . to provide and maintain a Navy . . . to make Rules for the Government and Regulation of the land and naval forces." However, Article II, Section 2, says, "The President shall be Commander-in-Chief of the Army and Navy of the United States." In defending the newly written Constitution, the *Federalist Papers* construed the president's war powers narrowly, implying that the war-making power of the president was little more than the power to defend against imminent invasion when Congress was not in session.

In reality, however, presidents have exercised their powers as commander-in-chief to order U.S. forces into military action overseas on many occasions—from John Adams's ordering of U.S. naval forces to attack French ships (1789–99) to Harry Truman's decision to intervene in the Korean War (1951–53) to Lyndon Johnson's and Richard Nixon's conduct of the Vietnam War (1965–73), to George Bush's Operation Desert Storm (1991). The Supreme Court has consistently refused to hear cases involving the war powers of the president and Congress. Supreme Court Chief Justice William H. Rehnquist wrote before he was elevated to the Court,

> It has been recognized from the earliest days of the Republic, by the President, by Congress, and by the Supreme Court, that the United States may lawfully engage in armed hostilities with a foreign power without Congressional declaration of war. Our history is replete with instances of "undeclared wars" from the war with France in 1789–1800 to the Vietnamese War.[22]

Thus, although Congress retains the formal power to "declare war," in modern times wars are seldom "declared." Instead, they begin with direct military actions, and the president, as Commander-in-Chief of the armed forces, determines what those actions will be. Historically, Congress accepted the fact that only the president has the information-gathering facilities and the ability to act with the speed and

Iran-Contra and the White House Staff

Ronald Reagan entered the White House with a strong sense of mission: to restore American military strength and respect in world councils. But he seldom involved himself in the details of policy or its implementation. Instead, he relied heavily on the White House staff and key cabinet officers to guide his presidency.

President Reagan was strongly committed to the support of pro-Western resistance movements in communist-dominated nations. He believed that the Soviet "evil empire" should be rolled back, not merely contained, and that the United States should assist "freedom fighters" in Afghanistan, Angola, and Nicaragua. Although Congress supported these actions in Afghanistan and Angola, it voted in 1982 to cut off U.S. aid to the Contra rebel forces fighting the Soviet-backed Sandinista regime in Nicaragua. The Boland Amendment specifically prohibited all executive branch agencies from sending any more aid to the Contras. But Reagan clearly communicated to his White House staff (especially his national security advisers Robert McFarlane and later John Poindexter) his desire to find ways to keep the Contra movement supplied. A National Security Council staff officer, Marine Lt. Col. Oliver North, was especially active in soliciting assistance for the Contras from private sources and from friendly foreign governments in a deliberate effort to circumvent the congressional ban.

In November 1986 a Lebanese newspaper disclosed that the United States had been secretly shipping arms to Iran in an effort to secure the release of Americans held hostage in Lebanon by Iranian-backed terrorists. It was later revealed that national security adviser McFarlane and North had been directly involved in these arms-for-hostages dealings. President Reagan initially denied that the arms shipments were a ransom-for-hostages deal, but upon thorough investigation, the Tower Commission, an independent commission assigned to investigate the incident, reported: "Whatever the intent, almost from the beginning the initiative became a series of arms-for-hostages deals."[*]

But the worst news was yet to be revealed. At a nationally televised press conference, Attorney General Ed Meese revealed that money paid by the Iranians for the weapons shipments had been diverted to the Contras. The scheme to divert the "profits" from the arms deals to the contras had been concocted by North, with the knowledge of McFarlane and Poindexter, and perhaps CIA director William Casey (who became seriously ill and died before the investigation was complete). There is no direct evidence or testimony that Reagan himself knew of the scheme to direct profits from Iranian dealings to the Contras, but the president's strong support of the Contra cause led North to believe that the president approved of the diversion of arms-sales money.

Trading arms for hostages with the hated regime in Iran was enough to send President Reagan's approval ratings into a steep decline. His presidency was badly shaken; there were murmurs on Capitol Hill about beginning impeachment proceedings. It was the worst moment of the previously popular president's eight years in office. Congress held nationally televised hearings on what became known as the Iran-Contra scandal. His Marine Corps uniform covered with a chestful of medals, North acknowledged misleading the Congress, but his appearance captured the imagination and sympathy of many Americans. Thousands of telegrams poured into Congress attacking the investigators and praising the patriotism of the Marine. North was eventually convicted of having lied earlier to Congress about aid to the Contras, but his conviction was overturned on appeal.

Presidents have always dominated foreign policy and have traditionally withheld information from Congress. But the Reagan Administration was chastened even by the congressional committee's minority (Republican) report: "The Constitution gives important foreign policy powers to both Congress and the President. Neither can accomplish very much over the long term by trying to go it alone."[†]

---

[*]*The Tower Commission Report* (New York: Times Books, 1987), p. 80.

[†]Joel Brinkley, ed., *Report of the Congressional Committees Investigating the Iran-Contra Affair* (New York: Times Books, 1988).

secrecy required for military decisions during the periods of crisis. Not until the Vietnam War, and later during the Persian Gulf War, was there serious congressional debate over whether the president has the power to commit the nation to war.

War Powers Act   In the early days of the Vietnam War, the liberal leadership of the nation strongly supported the effort, and no one questioned Democratic President Lyndon Johnson's power to commit the nation to war. By 1969, however, many congressional leaders had withdrawn their support of the war. With a new Republican president, Richard Nixon, and a Democratic Congress, congressional attacks on presidential policy became much more partisan.

Antiwar members of Congress made several attempts to end the war by cutting off money for U.S. military activity in Southeast Asia. Such legislation only passed after President Nixon announced a peace agreement in 1973, however. It is important to note that Congress has *never* voted to cut off funds to support American armies while they were in the field.

Congress also passed the **War Powers Act**, designed to restrict presidential war-making powers, in 1973. (President Nixon vetoed the bill, but the Watergate affair undermined his support in Congress, which overrode his veto.) The act has four major provisions:

1. In the absence of a congressional declaration of war, the president can commit armed forces to hostilities or to "situations where imminent involvement in hostilities is clearly indicated by the circumstances" *only:*

   - To repel an armed attack on the United States or to forestall the "direct and imminent threat of such an attack."
   - To repel an armed attack against U.S. armed forces outside the United States or to forestall the threat of such attack.
   - To protect and evacuate U.S. citizens and nationals in another country if their lives are threatened.

2. The president must report promptly to Congress the commitment of forces for such purposes.

3. Involvement of U.S. forces must be no longer than sixty days unless Congress authorizes their continued use by specific legislation.

4. Congress can end a presidential commitment by resolution, an action that does not require the president's signature.

Presidential Noncompliance   The War Powers Act raises constitutional questions. A commander-in-chief clearly can order U.S. forces to go anywhere. Presumably, Congress cannot constitutionally command troops, yet that is what the act attempts to do by specifying that troops must come home if Congress orders them to do so or if Congress simply fails to endorse the president's decision to commit them. No president—Democrat or Republican—can allow Congress to usurp this presidential authority. Thus, since the passage of the War Powers Act, presidents have continued to undertake military actions, including the following:

- President Gerald Ford ordered U.S. forces to attack a Cambodian island in 1975 to free the U.S. merchant ship *Mayaguez;* forty-one marines died in the attack. Ford notified the Congress of his action only after the attack.
- President Jimmy Carter did not notify Congress before ordering U.S. military forces to attempt a rescue of American embassy personnel held hostage by Iran in 1980.

War Powers Act   Bill passed in 1973 to limit presidential war-making powers; it restricts when, why, and for how long a president can commit U.S. forces and requires notification of and, in many cases, approval by Congress.

- After President Reagan had committed troops to "peacekeeping" in Lebanon in 1982, Congress invoked the War Powers Act and attempted to limit U.S. marines to an eighteen-month stay. The president maintained that the act was unconstitutional and made it clear that the administration would keep the troops there as long as it desired. Only the deaths of 241 marines in a suicidal attack by an Islamic faction persuaded President Reagan to withdraw U.S. troops from Lebanon in 1983.

- In 1983 U.S. troops invaded the tiny Caribbean island of Grenada in the wake of a procommunist coup there. Informed after the fact, Congress chose not to invoke the War Powers Act in view of the invasion's rapid success.

- President Bush ignored the provisions of the War Powers Act in ordering the invasion of Panama in 1989 and in sending U.S. forces to Saudi Arabia in August 1990, following Saddam Hussein's invasion of Kuwait.

- Bush also claimed he had the constitutional power to order U.S. military forces to liberate Kuwait from Iraqi occupation, whether or not Congress authorized the action. Bush ordered military preparations to begin, and despite misgivings Congress voted to authorize the use of force a few days before U.S. air attacks began. Rapid military victory in the ensuing Gulf War silenced congressional critics.

- President Clinton ordered U.S. troops into Bosnia as part of a NATO "peacekeeping" operation in 1995.

The War Powers Act is not only constitutionally questionable but also politically weak. The president almost always enjoys great popular support in the initial stages of an international conflict. At this point, members of Congress are likely to be swept along and to endorse the president's action rather than invoking the War Powers Act and appearing unsupportive of U.S. troops. Only if the fighting goes badly, becomes protracted, or fails to produce decisive results is the War Powers Act likely to be invoked by Congress. Thus the War Powers Act remains largely a symbolic reminder to presidents that if things go badly, the Congress will desert them.

As Commander-in-Chief, President Clinton directed the United States Navy to enforce the ongoing UN sanctions against Iraq in the wake of the Gulf War.

Despite a Supreme Court ruling that segregation in education was illegal, many southern states continued to try to keep their schoolhouse doors closed to black students. Here Elizabeth Eckford, a fifteen-year-old resident of Little Rock, Arkansas, is denied entry to Central High School by a member of the National Guard under the orders of Governor Orval Faubus. Not until President Dwight Eisenhower sent the 101st Airborne Division to Little Rock were the high court's desegregation orders enforced.

Presidential Use of Military Force in Domestic Affairs   Democracies are generally reluctant to use military force in domestic affairs. Yet the president has the constitutional authority to "take Care that the Laws be faithfully executed" and, as Commander-in-Chief of the armed forces, can send them across the nation as well as across the globe. The Constitution appears to limit presidential use of military forces in domestic affairs to protecting states "against domestic Violence" and only "on Application of the [state] Legislature or the [state] Executive (when the Legislature cannot be convened)" (Article IV, Section 4). Although this provision would seem to require states themselves to request federal troops before they can be sent to quell domestic violence, historically presidents have not waited for state requests to send troops when federal laws, federal court orders, or federal constitutional guarantees are being violated.

Relying on their constitutional duty to "faithfully execute" federal laws and their command over the nation's armed forces, presidents have used military force in domestic disputes since the earliest days of the Republic. Perhaps the most significant example of a president's use of military force in domestic affairs was Dwight Eisenhower's 1957 dispatch of U.S. troops to Little Rock, Arkansas, to enforce a federal court's desegregation order. In this case, the president acted directly *against* the expressed wishes of the state's governor, Orval Faubus, who had posted state units of the National Guard at the entrance of Central High School to prevent the admission of black students that had been ordered by the federal court. Eisenhower officially called Arkansas's National Guard units into federal service, took personal command of them, and then ordered them to leave the high school. Ike then replaced the Guard units with U.S. federal troops under orders to enforce desegregation. Eisenhower's action marked a turning point in the struggle over school desegregation. The Supreme Court's historic desegregation decision in *Brown v. Board of Education of Topeka* might have been rendered meaningless had not the president chosen to use military force to secure compliance.

THE VICE PRESIDENTIAL WAITING GAME

The principal responsibility of the vice president is to be prepared to assume the responsibilities of the president. The phrase describing the job as "a heartbeat away from the presidency" is historically relevant: eight vice presidents have become president following the death of their predecessor. But vice presidents have not always been well prepared; Harry Truman, who succeeded Franklin Roosevelt while World War II still raged, had never even been informed about the secret atomic bomb project.

Political Selection Process   The political process surrounding the initial choice of vice presidential candidates does not necessarily produce the persons best qualified to occupy the White House. It is, indeed, a "crap shoot"[23]; if it produces a person well qualified to be president, it is only by luck. Candidates may *claim* that they select running mates who are highly qualified to take over as president, but this claim is seldom true.

Vice presidential candidates are chosen to give political "balance" to the ticket, to attract voters who might otherwise desert the party or stay home. Traditionally, Democratic presidential candidates sought to give ideological and geographical balance to the ticket. Northern liberal presidential candidates (Adlai Stevenson, John Kennedy) selected southern conservatives (John Sparkman, Estes Kefauver, Lyndon Johnson) as their running mates. Walter Mondale selected New York Congresswoman Geraldine Ferraro in a bold move to exploit the gender gap. Liberal Massachusetts Governor Michael Dukakis returned to the earlier Democratic tradition, choosing to run with conservative Texas Senator Lloyd Bentsen. Bill Clinton sought a different kind of balance: Al Gore's military service in Vietnam and his unimpeachable family life helped offset reservations about Clinton's avoidance of the draft and his past marital troubles.

While the vice president has no official duties under the Constitution except to act as presiding officer of the Senate, vice presidents have often been called upon to share at least some of the ceremonial duties of the presidency and are sometimes able to use their position to further causes they support. Here, Vice President Albert Gore, an environmentalist, addresses officials and environmental activists about efforts to clean up Santa Monica Bay in California.

Traditionally, Republican presidential candidates sought to accommodate either the conservative or moderate wing of their party in their vice presidential selections. Moderate Eisenhower chose conservative Nixon. Conservative Barry Goldwater's selection of William Miller, an unknown conservative member of the House, ensured his loss of moderate support in 1964. In 1980 conservative Reagan first asked his moderate predecessor, Gerald Ford, to join him on the ticket before turning to his moderate primary opponent George Bush, who in 1988 tapped conservative Senator Dan Quayle.

In 1996 Bob Dole gambled big in choosing the popular and charismatic—but opinionated and unpredictable—Jack Kemp as his running mate. Far behind in the polls, Dole could not afford a "safe" choice. He needed the former star quarterback of the Buffalo Bills to add excitement to the ticket, even at the risk of seeing Kemp call plays not approved by the coach.

Vice Presidential Roles Presidents determine what role their vice presidents will play in their administration. Constitutionally, the only role given the vice

People in Politics

Al Gore, Waiting for 2000

Vice President Al Gore stands silent and rigid behind the president so often that he could easily be mistaken for a Secret Service agent. Gore's stoic performance as loyal prop for Bill Clinton is the traditional vice president role. But Al Gore is no lightweight: he brings impressive presidential credentials to his office.

Young Al was born into a political dynasty. His father, Albert Gore, Sr., served four years in the House and eighteen years in the Senate as a strong supporter of FDR's New Deal and the Tennessee Valley Authority, which served his state and region. Young Al grew up in Washington, attended a prestigious private prep school, St. Alban's, and went on to Harvard. Apparently he set his sights on the presidency early in his career; his senior honors thesis was entitled "The Impact of Television on the Conduct of the Presidency." Like his father, Gore opposed the Vietnam War; yet when facing the draft in 1970, he volunteered and served as an army newspaper reporter in Saigon.

When he returned home, he took a job as a reporter for the Nashville newspaper, the *Tennessean.*

At the same time, he became a land developer with his Tanglewood Home Builders Company as well as a livestock and tobacco farmer. A devout Baptist, Gore briefly studied religion at Vanderbilt University before entering law school. Upon obtaining his law degree in 1976, he immediately jumped into the Democratic primary race for a Tennessee congressional seat. At age twenty-eight, he relied primarily on his father's name to defeat an experienced Democratic state legislator and go on to win the general election over token Republican opposition in the traditionally Democratic district.

As a member of Congress, Gore remained in close contact with his constituents, returning to Tennessee virtually every weekend and practicing "home-style" politics. Indeed, on some high-profile issues, including federal funding of abortions, Gore abandoned his liberalism to reflect his constituents' views. His wife, "Tipper," improved her husband's standing among social conservatives by leading a national effort to place warning labels on obscene recordings.

When Howard Baker, the Republican leader in the U.S. Senate, announced that he would not seek reelection in 1984, Gore quickly established himself as the leading Democratic contender to capture his Tennessee Senate seat. With his famous name, four congressional terms serving constituents, and growing personal stature in his state, Gore swept to victory. In the Senate, Gore began to focus on envi-

president is to preside over the Senate and to vote in case of a tie in that body. Presiding over the Senate is so tiresome that vice presidents perform it only on rare ceremonial occasions, but they have occasionally cast important tie-breaking votes. If the president chooses not to give the vice president much responsibility, the vice presidency becomes what its first occupant, John Adams, described as "the most insignificant office that ever the invention of man contrived or his imagination conceived." One of Franklin Roosevelt's three vice presidents, the salty Texan John Nance Garner, put it more pithily, saying that the job "ain't worth a bucket of warm spit" (reporters of that era may have substituted "spit" for Garner's actual wording).

The political functions of vice presidents are more significant than their governmental functions. Vice presidents are obliged to support their president and the administration's policies. But sometimes a president will use the vice president to launch strongly partisan political attacks on opponents while the president remains "above" the political squabbles and hence more "presidential." Richard Nixon served as a partisan "attack dog" for Eisenhower, then gave Spiro Agnew this task

ronmental issues. He fervently embraced a whole series of environmental causes and even published a controversial book on the topic, *Earth in the Balance*.

Gore made a brief run for the Democratic presidential nomination in 1988 but bowed out gracefully when Michael Dukakis beat him in the primaries. Early in the 1992 Democratic presidential preference polls, Gore was running behind only New York Governor Mario Cuomo. Bill Clinton was hardly recognized by voters outside of Arkansas. But like other Democratic heavyweights, Gore put his White House aspirations on hold: Bush's popularity following victory in the Gulf War appeared unassailable. Gore's decision helped created the vacuum that Bill Clinton leaped to fill.

Traditionally, Democratic presidential candidates sought to "balance" the national ticket by selecting vice presidential running mates from different regions of the country, from different generations, and from different ideological wings of the party. But in 1992 Bill Clinton wisely sought a new kind of balance. Beset by charges of marital infidelity and draft evasion, Clinton saw the advantage of selecting a devout family man and Vietnam veteran. And Gore's established presidential stature contrasted sharply with the popular image of Bush's running mate, the seemingly immature Dan Quayle. Clinton's selection of Al Gore put two southern baby boomers on the same ticket, but it convinced many voters that

Clinton was wise enough to select a vice president who was indeed qualified to become president.

Gore proved to be a loyal and self-effacing vice president. He carefully avoided any public disagreements with his president and consistently praised Clinton's performance in office. He chaired a "National Performance Review" designed to make cost-savings reforms in the federal bureaucracy (see Chapter 12). He coined the term *information superhighway* and initiated efforts to improve access to the Internet for both schoolchildren and the general public. He easily bested a bumbling Jack Kemp in a televised vice presidential candidate debate in 1996.

Gore leads all other Democrats in early presidential preference polling for 2000. But hidden potholes could cause him to stumble on his road to the White House. His strong support of international treaties requiring a cutback in U.S. environmental emissions places him in a tricky position between traditional Democratic interest groups—for example, labor unions that fear such cutbacks will create job losses—and environmental groups that fear global warming will produce various climatic disasters. His prominent role in soliciting campaign funds, including his ill-advised appearance at a Buddhist temple, appears to be the only smudge on his otherwise spotless character. Gore's presidential prospects depend on a continuing strong economy and his avoidance of entanglements in White House scandals.

The President

The White House

http://www.whitehouse.gov

The White House Web site (which is shown on page 169 of this text) is not only an excellent place to begin exploration of the national government, but also a good source of information on politics and public affairs from the President's viewpoint. It contains biographies of the president and vice president, White House history, a virtual library of White House documents, a daily briefing room with the latest press releases from the White House as well as presidential messages in presidential commission reports, and even a "White House for Kids" feature.

National Archives and Records Administration

http://www.nara.gov

This site is an important source for research on the history of the U.S. government and its various offices, including the presidency. It links to the official *U.S. Government Organizational Manual*, which provides organizational charts of each federal department and agency, the names of officials, government addresses and phone numbers, and a summary statement of each agency's purpose. It also provides addresses of presidential libraries and links to their Web sites.

Presidential Libraries

Ronald Reagan Library	*http://sunsite.unc.edu/lia/president/reagan.html*
Franklin D. Roosevelt Library	*http://www.academic.marist.edu/fdr/*
Jimmy Carter Library	*http://redbud.lbjlib.utexas.edu/carter/homepage/homepage.htm*
Eisenhower Center	*http://redbud.lbjlib.utexas.edu/eisenhower/ddehp.htm*
George Bush Presidential Library	*http://csdl.tamu.edu/bushlib/bushpage.html*
John F. Kennedy Presidential Library	*http://www.cs.umb.edu/jfklibrary/*
Richard M. Nixon Presidential Materials Staff	*http://sunsite.unc.edu/lia/president/nixon.html*
Gerald R. Ford Library	*http://www.lbjlib.utexas.edu/ford/index.html*
Lyndon Baines Johnson Library	*http://www.lbjlib.utexas.edu/*
Herbert Hoover	*http://hoover.nara.gov/*
Harry S. Truman	*http://www.lbjlib.utexas.edu/truman/*

in his own administration. George Bush was a much more reserved vice president, but Dan Quayle renewed the tradition of the vice president as political "hit man." The attack role allows the vice president also to help cement political support for the president among highly partisan ideologues. Vice presidents are also useful in campaign fund raising. Large contributors expect a personal touch; the president cannot be everywhere at once, so the vice president is frequently a guest at political fund-raising events. Presidents also have traditionally sent their vice presidents to attend funerals of world leaders and placed them at the head of governmental commissions.

Vice presidents themselves strive to play a more significant policy-making role, often as senior presidential adviser and confidant. Recent presidents have encouraged the development of the vice presidency along these lines. Walter Mondale, the first modern vice president to perform this function, had an office in the White House next to the president's, had access to all important meetings and policy decisions, and was invited to lunch privately each week with President Carter. As vice president, George Bush claimed to have participated in every major decision of the Reagan Administration. Vice President Al Gore was routinely stationed behind President Clinton during major policy pronouncements. Clinton reportedly gave great weight to Gore's views on the environment, on cost savings in government, and on information technology. Gore also spoke out aggressively in defense of Clinton's policies. Thus the senior advisory role is becoming institutionalized over time.

The Waiting Game   Politically, vice presidents are obliged to play a tortuous waiting game. They can use their time in office to build a network of contacts that can later be tapped for campaign contributions, workers, and support in their own race for the presidency, should they decide to run. But winning the presidency following retirement of their former boss requires a delicate balance (see *People in Politics:* "Al Gore, Waiting for 2000" on pages 416–17). They must show loyalty to the president in order to win the president's endorsement and also to help ensure that the administration in which they participated is judged a success by voters. At the same time, vice presidents must demonstrate that they have independent leadership qualities and a policy agenda of their own to offer voters. This dilemma becomes more acute as their boss's term nears its end.

Historically, only a few sitting vice presidents have won election to the White House: John Adams (1797), Thomas Jefferson (1801), Martin Van Buren (1837), and George Bush (1988). In addition, four vice presidents won election in their own right after entering the Oval Office as a result of their predecessors' death: Theodore Roosevelt (1901), Calvin Coolidge (1923), Harry Truman (1945), and Lyndon Johnson (1963). Only one nonsitting former vice president has been elected president: Richard Nixon (1968, after losing to Kennedy in 1960). Thus, out of the forty-six men who served the nation as vice president through 1992, only nine were ever elected to higher office.

SUMMARY NOTES

- The American presidency is potentially the most powerful office in the world. As head of state, the president symbolizes national unity and speaks on behalf of the American people to the world. And as commander-in-chief of the armed forces, the president has a powerful voice in national and international affairs. The president also symbolizes government for the American people, reassuring them in times of hardship and crises.

- As head of the government, the president is expected to set forth policy priorities for the nation, to manage the economy, to mobilize political support for the administration's programs in Congress, to manage the giant federal bureaucracy, and to recruit people for policy-making positions in both the executive and judicial branches of government.

- Popular expectations of presidential leadership far exceed the formal constitutional powers of the president: chief administrator, chief legislator, chief diplomat, commander-in-chief, and chief of state. The vague reference in the Constitution to "executive Power" has been used by presidents to justify actions beyond those specified elsewhere in the Constitution or in laws of Congress.

- It is the president's vast political resources that provide the true power base of the presidency. These include the president's reputation for power, personal popularity with the public, access to the media, and party leadership position.

- Presidential popularity and power are usually highest at the beginning of the term of office. Presidents are more likely to be successful in Congress during this honeymoon period. Presidents' popularity also rises during crises, especially during international threats and military actions. But prolonged indecision and stalemate erode popular support, as do scandals and economic recessions.

- As chief executive, the president oversees the huge federal bureaucracy. Presidential control of the executive branch is exercised through executive orders, appointments and removals, and budgetary recommendations to Congress. But the president's control of the executive branch is heavily circumscribed by Congress, which establishes executive departments and agencies, regulates their activities by law, and determines their budgets each year.

- Presidents are expected not only to initiate programs and policies but also to shepherd them through Congress. Presidential success scores in Congress indicate that presidents are more successful early in their term of office. Presidents who face a Congress controlled by the opposition party are far less successful in winning approval for their programs than presidents whose party holds a majority.

- The veto is the president's most powerful weapon in dealing with Congress. The president needs to hold the loyalty of only one more than one-third of either the House or the Senate to sustain a veto. Few vetoes are overridden. The threat of a veto enables the president to bargain in Congress for more acceptable legislation.

- During the long years of the Cold War, the president of the United States was the leader of the "free world." In the post–Cold War world, the president is still the leader of the world's most powerful democracy and is expected to exercise global leadership on behalf of a stable world order.

- Presidents have come to dominate foreign policy through treaty making, executive agreements, control of intelligence activities, and international recognition of their role as head of state. Above all, presidents have used their power as commander-in-chief of the armed forces to decide when to make war and when to seek peace.

- The global power of presidents derives primarily from this presidential role as Commander-in-Chief. Constitutionally, war-making power is divided between Congress and the president, but historically, it has been the president who has ordered U.S. military forces into action. In the War Powers Act, Congress tried to reassert its war-making power after the Vietnam War, but the act has failed to restrain presidents. Presidents have also used the armed forces in domestic affairs to "take Care that the Laws be faithfully executed."

- The principal responsibility of the vice president is to be prepared to assume the responsibilities of the president. However, the selection of the vice president is dominated more by political concerns than by consideration of presidential qualifications. Aside from officially presiding over the U.S. Senate, vice presidents perform whatever roles are assigned them by the president.

SELECTED READINGS

BARBER, JAMES DAVID. *The Presidential Character: Predicting Performance in the White House,* 4th ed. Englewood Cliffs, N.J.: Prentice Hall, 1992. An updated version of Barber's original thesis that a president's performance in office is largely a function of active/passive and positive/negative character; includes classifications of twentieth-century presidents through Reagan.

BRACE, PAUL, and BARBARA HINCKLEY. *Follow the Leader.* New York: Basic Books, 1992. The most marked increases in public approval of the president came on the heels of international crises, especially when the president responds with bold and decisive action.

BRODY, RICHARD A. *Assessing Presidents: The Media, Elite Opinion, and Public Support.* Stanford, Calif.: Stanford University Press, 1991. Develops the thesis that media and elite interpretations of presidential actions shape public evaluations of the president; includes analysis of the president's "honeymoon," "rally 'round the president" events, and the rise and fall of public approval ratings.

DiCLERICO, ROBERT E. *The American President*. 4th ed. Englewood Cliffs, N.J.: Prentice Hall, 1995. Comprehensive text on the presidency, focusing on selection, power, accountability, decision making, personality, and leadership.

DREW, ELIZABETH. *On the Edge: The Clinton Presidency*. New York: Simon & Schuster, 1994. A reporter's inside account of the Clinton presidency—"ambitious and uncertain, looking to the future and bounded by the past."

EDWARDS, GEORGE C., III. *At the Margins: Presidential Leadership of Congress*. New Haven, Conn.: Yale University Press, 1989. A systematic examination of the factors affecting presidential success in Congress, including presidential popularity, party support, and lobbying efforts.

KESSLER, RONALD. *Inside the White House*. New York: Pocket Books, 1995. Muckraking accounts of the "hidden lives" of presidents, from Lyndon Johnson to Bill Clinton.

LOWI, THEODORE. *The Personal President*. Ithaca, N.Y.: Cornell University Press, 1987. An examination of the presi-

dency from the perspective of the public and its reliance on the president for reassurance in crises.

MARANISS, DAVID. *First in His Class*. New York: Simon & Schuster, 1995. A biography of Bill Clinton, describing his overriding ambition, talent for politics, perseverance in the face of adversity, eagerness to please everyone, and tendency to shade the truth.

MILKUS, STANLEY, and MICHAEL NELSON. *The American Presidency: Origins and Development, 1776–1990*. Washington, D.C.: CQ Press, 1990. A comprehensive history of the presidency which argues that the institution is best understood by examining its development over time; describes the significant presidential actions in the early days of the Republic that shaped the office, as well as the modern era in which the president has replaced Congress and the political parties as the leading instrument of popular rule.

NEUSTADT, RICHARD E. *Presidential Power*. New York: Wiley, 1960. The classic argument that the president's power is the power to persuade, that the formal constitutional powers of the presidency provide only a framework for the president's use of persuasion, public prestige, reputation for power, and other personal attributes to exercise real power.

ASK YOURSELF ABOUT POLITICS

1. Do bureaucrats in Washington have too much power?
   Yes ◯ No ◯

2. Do you believe the bureaucrats in Washington really believe in the value of the programs they administer?
   Yes ◯ No ◯

3. Should the U.S. Postal Service and Amtrak be required to break even rather than receiving government subsidies to cover their deficits?
   Yes ◯ No ◯

4. Should the federal bureaucracy be managed by nonpartisan professionals rather than people politically loyal to the president?
   Yes ◯ No ◯

5. Should the federal bureaucracy at all levels reflect the gender and minority ratios of the total civilian work force?
   Yes ◯ No ◯

6. Do you believe the bureaucrats in Washington waste a lot of the money we pay in taxes?
   Yes ◯ No ◯

7. Do you believe the federal government is spending more money but delivering less service?
   Yes ◯ No ◯

8. Do you believe bureaucratic regulations of all kinds are hurting America?
   Yes ◯ No ◯

THE BUREAUCRACY BUREAUCRATIC POLITICS

CHAPTER OUTLINE

FEATURES

Power in Washington is not only exercised by the president, Congress, and courts, but also by 2.8 million federal bureaucrats—neither elected nor accountable to ordinary citizens—who determine in large measure who gets what in America.

BUREAUCRATIC POWER

Political conflict does not end after a law has been passed by Congress and signed by the president. The arena for conflict merely shifts from Capitol Hill and the White House to the **bureaucracy**—to the myriad departments, agencies, and bureaus of the federal executive branch that implement the law. Despite the popular impression that policy is decided by the president and Congress and merely implemented by the federal bureaucracy, in fact policy is also made by the bureaucracy. Indeed, it is often remarked that "implementation is the continuation of policy making by other means." The Washington bureaucracy is a major base of power in the American system of government—independent of Congress, the president, the courts, and the people. Indeed, controlling the bureaucracy has become a major challenge of democratic government (see *What Do You Think?* "Do Bureaucrats in Washington Have Too Much Power?").

The Nature of Bureaucracy "Bureaucracy" has become a negative term equated with red tape,[1] paper shuffling, duplication of effort, waste and inefficiency, impersonality, senseless regulations, and unresponsiveness to the needs of "real" people. But bureaucracy is really a form of social organization found not only in governments but also in corporations, armies, schools, and many other societal institutions. The German sociologist Max Weber described bureaucracy as a "rational" way for society to organize itself that has the following characteristics:

- **Chain of command**: Hierarchical structure of authority in which command flows downward.
- **Division of labor**: Work divided among many specialized workers in an effort to improve productivity.
- **Specification of authority**: Clear lines of responsibility with positions and units reporting to superiors.
- **Goal orientation**: Organizational goals determining structure, authority, and rules.
- **Impersonality**: All persons within the bureaucracy treated on "merit" principles, and all "clients" served by the bureaucracy treated equally according to rules; all activities undertaken according to rules; records maintained to assure rules are followed.[2]

Thus, according to Weber's definition, General Motors and IBM, the U.S. Marine Corps, the U.S. Department of Education, and all other institutions organized according to these principles are "bureaucracies."

The Growth of Bureaucratic Power Bureaucratic power has grown with advances in technology and increases in the size and complexity of society. The standard explanation for the growth of bureaucratic power in Washington is that Congress and the president do not have the time, energy, or expertise to handle the details of policy making. A related explanation is that the increasing complexity and sophistication of technology require technical experts ("technocrats") to actually carry out the intent of Congress and the president. Neither the president nor the 535 members of Congress can look after the myriad details involved in environmental protection, occupational safety, air traffic

bureaucracy Departments, agencies, bureaus, and offices that perform the functions of government.

chain of command Hierarchical structure of authority in which command flows downward; typical of a bureaucracy.

division of labor Division of work among many specialized workers in a bureaucracy.

specification of authority Clear lines of responsibility with positions and units reporting to superiors in a bureaucracy.

goal orientation Organizational goals that determine structure, authority, and rules in a bureaucracy.

impersonality Treatment of all persons within a bureaucracy on the basis of "merit" and of all "clients" served by the bureaucracy equally according to rule.

What Do You Think?

Do Bureaucrats in Washington Have Too Much Power?

Americans have always been suspicious of government power. Opinion polls regularly report that Americans believe "the federal government in Washington" has "too much power." A majority also believe that "major corporations" and "television news" have too much power.

But among federal government agencies, the tax-collecting Internal Revenue Service (IRS) is clearly the most feared. The power of the Central Intelligence Agency (CIA) and the Bureau of Alcohol, Tobacco and Firearms (ATF) also appears to raise concerns among Americans, no doubt in part because of adverse publicity in recent years. (The CIA was deeply embarrassed by the revelation that a high officer, Aldrich Ames, had been paid millions of dollars by Russian agents to work secretly on their behalf; the ATF was strongly criticized for attacking the Branch Davidian compound in Waco, Texas, in 1993.)

In contrast, the U.S. military enjoys a favorable reputation among most Americans, 80 percent of whom believe it has "about the right amount of power" or "not enough." Local government in America and local police are also perceived as having about the right amount or not enough power.

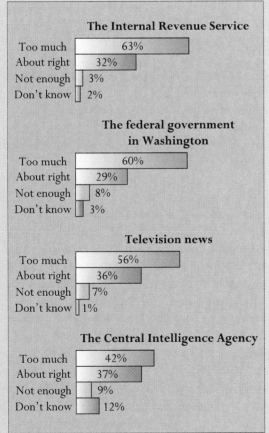

The Internal Revenue Service
- Too much — 63%
- About right — 32%
- Not enough — 3%
- Don't know — 2%

The federal government in Washington
- Too much — 60%
- About right — 29%
- Not enough — 8%
- Don't know — 3%

Television news
- Too much — 56%
- About right — 36%
- Not enough — 7%
- Don't know — 1%

The Central Intelligence Agency
- Too much — 42%
- About right — 37%
- Not enough — 9%
- Don't know — 12%

The Federal Bureau of Alcohol, Tobacco and Firearms
- Too much — 39%
- About right — 34%
- Not enough — 23%
- Don't know — 4%

The Federal Bureau of Investigation
- Too much — 32%
- About right — 48%
- Not enough — 16%
- Don't know — 4%

The military
- Too much — 17%
- About right — 57%
- Not enough — 23%
- Don't know — 3%

The local police in your community
- Too much — 13%
- About right — 55%
- Not enough — 31%
- Don't know — 1%

Source: Gallup Poll, 1995.

control, or thousands of other responsibilities of government. So the president and Congress create bureaucracies, appropriate money for them, and authorize them to draw up detailed rules, regulations, and "guidelines" that actually govern the nation. Bureaucratic agencies receive only vague and general directions from the president and Congress. Actual governance is in the hands of the Environmental Protection Agency, the Occupational Safety and Health Administration, the Federal Aviation Administration, and hundreds of similar agencies (see Figure 12-1).

But there are also political explanations for the growth of bureaucratic power. Congress and the president often deliberately pass vague and ambiguous laws. These laws allow elected officials to show symbolically their concerns for environmental protection, occupational safety, and so on, yet avoid the controversies surrounding actual application of those lofty principles. Bureaucracies must then give practical meaning to these symbolic measures by developing specific rules and regulations. If the rules and regulations prove unpopular, Congress and the president can blame the bureaucrats and pretend that these unpopular decisions are a product of an "ungovernable" Washington bureaucracy.

Finally, as the bureaucracy itself has grown in size and influence, it has become its own source of power. Bureaucrats have a personal stake in expanding the size of their own agencies and budgets and adding to their own regulatory authority. They can mobilize their "client" groups (interest groups that directly benefit from the agency's programs, such as environmental groups on behalf of the Environmental Protection Agency, farm groups for the Department of Agriculture, the National Education Association for the Department of Education) in support of larger budgets and expanded authority.

Bureaucratic Power: Implementation   Bureaucracies are not *constitutionally* empowered to decide policy questions. But they do so, nevertheless, as they perform their tasks of implementation, regulation, and adjudication.

Implementation is the development of procedures and activities to carry out policies legislated by Congress. It may involve creating new agencies or bureaus or assigning new responsibilities to old agencies. It often requires bureaucracies to translate laws into operational rules and regulations and usually to allocate resources—money, personnel, offices, supplies—to the new function. All of these tasks involve decisions by bureaucrats, decisions that drive how the law will actually affect society. In some cases, bureaucrats delay the development of regulations based on a new law, assign enforcement responsibility to existing offices with other higher priority tasks, and allocate few people with limited resources to the task. In other cases, bureaucrats act forcefully in making new regulations, insist on strict enforcement, assign responsibilities to newly created aggressive offices with no other assignments, and allocate a great deal of staff time and agency resources to the task. Interested groups have a strong stake in these decisions, and they actively seek to influence the bureaucracy.

Bureaucratic Power: Regulation   **Regulation** involves the development of formal rules for implementing legislation. The federal bureaucracy publishes about 60,000 pages of rules in the *Federal Register* each year. The Environmental Protection Agency (EPA) is especially active in developing regulations governing the handling of virtually every substance in the air, water, or ground. The rule-making process for federal agencies is prescribed by an Administrative

implementation   Development by the federal bureaucracy of procedures and activities to carry out policies legislated by Congress; it includes regulation as well as adjudication.

regulation   Development by the federal bureaucracy of formal rules for implementing legislation.

FIGURE 12-1 The Federal Bureaucracy

Although the president has constitutional authority over the operation of the executive branch, Congress creates departments and agencies and appropriates their funds, and Senate approval is needed for presidential appointees to head departments.

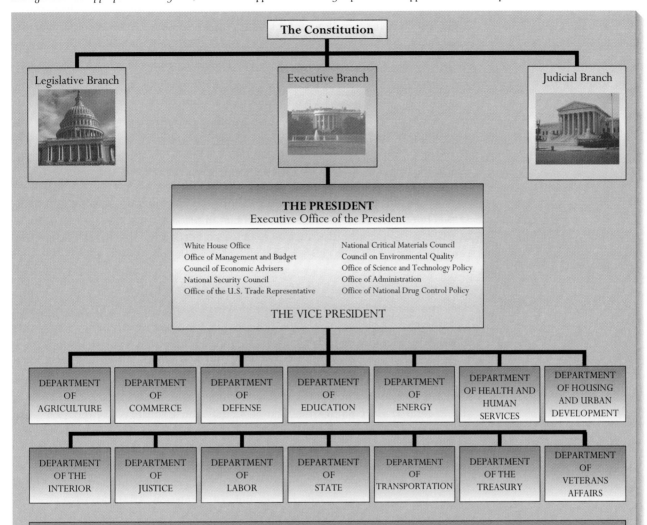

The Constitution

Legislative Branch

Executive Branch

Judicial Branch

THE PRESIDENT
Executive Office of the President

White House Office
Office of Management and Budget
Council of Economic Advisers
National Security Council
Office of the U.S. Trade Representative

National Critical Materials Council
Council on Environmental Quality
Office of Science and Technology Policy
Office of Administration
Office of National Drug Control Policy

THE VICE PRESIDENT

| DEPARTMENT OF AGRICULTURE | DEPARTMENT OF COMMERCE | DEPARTMENT OF DEFENSE | DEPARTMENT OF EDUCATION | DEPARTMENT OF ENERGY | DEPARTMENT OF HEALTH AND HUMAN SERVICES | DEPARTMENT OF HOUSING AND URBAN DEVELOPMENT |

| DEPARTMENT OF THE INTERIOR | DEPARTMENT OF JUSTICE | DEPARTMENT OF LABOR | DEPARTMENT OF STATE | DEPARTMENT OF TRANSPORTATION | DEPARTMENT OF THE TREASURY | DEPARTMENT OF VETERANS AFFAIRS |

INDEPENDENT ESTABLISHMENTS AND GOVERNMENT CORPORATIONS

ACTION
Administrative Conference of the U.S.
African Development Foundation
Central Intelligence Agency
Commission on Civil Rights
Commission on National and Community
  Service
Commodity Futures Trading Commission
Consumer Product Safety Commission
Defense Nuclear Facilities Safety Board
Environmental Protection Agency
Equal Employment Opportunity
  Commission
Export–Import Bank of the U.S.
Farm Credit Administration
Federal Communications Commission
Federal Deposit Insurance Corporation
Federal Election Commission

Federal Emergency Management Agency
Federal Housing Finance Board
Federal Labor Relations Authority
Federal Maritime Commission
Federal Mediation and Conciliation
  Service
Federal Mine Safety and Health Review
  Commission
Federal Reserve System
Federal Retirement Thrift Investment
  Board
Federal Trade Commission
General Services Administration
Inter–American Foundation
Interstate Commerce Commission
Merit Systems Protection Board
National Aeronautics and Space
  Administration
National Archives and Records
  Administration
National Capital Planning Commission

National Credit Union Administration
National Labor Relations Board
National Mediation Board
National Railroad Passenger Corporation
  (Amtrak)
National Science Foundation
National Transportation Safety Board
Nuclear Regulatory Commission
Occupational Safety and Health Review
  Commission
Office of Government Ethics
Office of Personnel Management
Office of Special Counsel
Panama Canal Commission
Peace Corps
Pennsylvania Avenue Development
  Corporation
Pension Benefit Guaranty Corporation

Postal Rate Commission
Railroad Retirement Board
Resolution Trust Corporation
Securities and Exchange Commission
Selective Service System
Small Business Administration
Tennessee Valley Authority
Thrift Depositor Protection Oversight
  Board
Trade and Development Agency
U.S. Arms Control and Disarmament
  Agency
U.S. Information Agency
U.S. International Development
  Cooperation Agency
U.S. International Trade Commission
U.S. Postal Service

Source: Chart prepared by U.S. Bureau of the Census.

Procedures Act, first passed in 1946 and amended many times. Generally, agencies must:

1. Announce in the *Federal Register* that a new regulation is being considered.
2. Hold hearings to allow interested groups to present evidence and arguments regarding the proposed regulation.
3. Conduct research on the proposed regulation's economic and environmental impacts.
4. Solicit "public comments" (usually the arguments of interest groups).
5. Consult with higher officials, including the Office of Management and Budget.
6. Publish the new regulation in the *Federal Register*.

Regulatory battles are important because formal regulations that appear in the *Federal Register* have the effect of law. Congress can amend or repeal a regulation only by passing new legislation and obtaining the president's signature. Controversial bureaucratic regulations often remain in place because Congress is slow to act, because key committee members block corrective legislation, or because the president refuses to sign bills overturning the regulation.

Bureaucratic Power: Adjudication   **Adjudication** involves bureaucratic decisions about individual cases. Rule making resembles the legislative process, and adjudication resembles the judicial process. In adjudication, bureaucrats decide whether a person or firm is failing to comply with laws or regulations and, if so, what penalties or corrective actions are to be applied. Regulatory agencies and commissions—for example, the National Labor Relations Board, the Federal Communications Commission, the Equal Employment Opportunity Commission, the Federal Trade Commission, the Securities and Exchange Commission—are heavily engaged in adjudication. Their elaborate procedures and body of previous decisions closely resemble the court system. Some agencies authorize specific hearing officers, administrative judges, or appellate divisions to accept evidence, hear arguments, and decide cases. Individuals and firms involved in these proceedings usually hire lawyers specializing in the field of regulation. Administrative hearings are somewhat less formal than a court trial, and the "judges" are employees of the agency itself. Losers may appeal to the federal courts, but the record of agency success in the federal courts discourages many appeals.

Bureaucratic Power: Administrative Discretion   Much of the work of bureaucrats is administrative routine—issuing Social Security checks, printing forms, delivering the mail. Routines are repetitive tasks performed according to established rules and procedures. Yet bureaucrats almost always have some discretion in performing even the most routine tasks. Discretion is greatest when cases do not exactly fit established rules, or when more than one rule might be applied to the same case, resulting in different outcomes. The Internal Revenue Service administers the hundreds of thousands of rules developed to implement the U.S. Tax Code, but each IRS auditing agent has wide discretion in deciding which rules to apply to a taxpayer's income, deductions, business expenses, and so on. Indeed, identical tax information submitted to different IRS offices almost always results in different estimates of tax liability. But even in more routine tasks, from processing Medicare applications to forwarding mail, individual bureaucrats can be friendly and helpful or hostile and obstructive.[3]

adjudication   Decision making by the federal bureaucracy as to whether or not an individual or organization has complied with or violated government laws and/or regulations.

Bureaucratic Power and Budget Maximization   Bureaucrats generally believe strongly in the value of their programs and the importance of their tasks. Senior military officers and civilian officials of the Department of Defense believe in the importance of a strong national defense, and top officials in the Social Security Administration are committed to maintaining the integrity of the retirement system and serving the nation's senior citizens. Beyond these public-spirited motives, bureaucrats, like everyone else, seek higher pay, greater job security, and added power and prestige for themselves.

These public and private motives converge to inspire bureaucrats to seek to expand the powers, functions, and budgets of their departments and agencies. Rarely do bureaucrats request a reduction in authority, the elimination of a program, or a decrease in their agency's budget. Rather, over time, **budget maximization**—expanding the agency's budget, staff, and authority as much as possible—becomes a driving force in government bureaucracies. This is especially true of discretionary funds. **Discretionary funds** are those that bureaucrats have flexibility in deciding how to spend, rather than money committed by law to specific purposes.[4] Thus bureaucracies continually strive to add new functions, acquire more authority and responsibility, and increase their budgets and personnel. Bureaucratic expansion is just one of the reasons that government grows over time (see *Up Close:* "Why Government Grows, and Grows, and Grows").

THE FEDERAL BUREAUCRACY

The federal bureaucracy—officially the executive branch of the U.S. government—consists of about 2.8 million civilian employees (plus 1.4 million persons in the armed forces) organized into 14 cabinet departments, 60 independent agencies, and a large Executive Office of the President (see Figures 12-1 and 12-2). The expenditures of *all* governments in the United States—the federal

budget maximization
Bureaucrats' tendencies to expand their agencies' budgets, staff, and authority.

discretionary funds
Budgeted funds not earmarked for specific purposes but available to be spent in accordance with the best judgment of a bureaucrat.

An Internal Revenue Service processing center. The IRS administers the nation's complex tax code, leaving wide discretion to its agents to determine how to apply the rules to individual taxpayers.

government, the 50 state governments, and some 86,000 local governments—now amount to more than $2.5 *trillion* (roughly 35 percent of the U.S. gross domestic product, or GDP). About two-thirds of this—more than $1.7 *trillion* a year (more than 23 percent of GDP)—is spent by the federal government. In contrast, at the start of the century, the federal government was very small relative to state and local governments, and federal spending was only about 2 percent

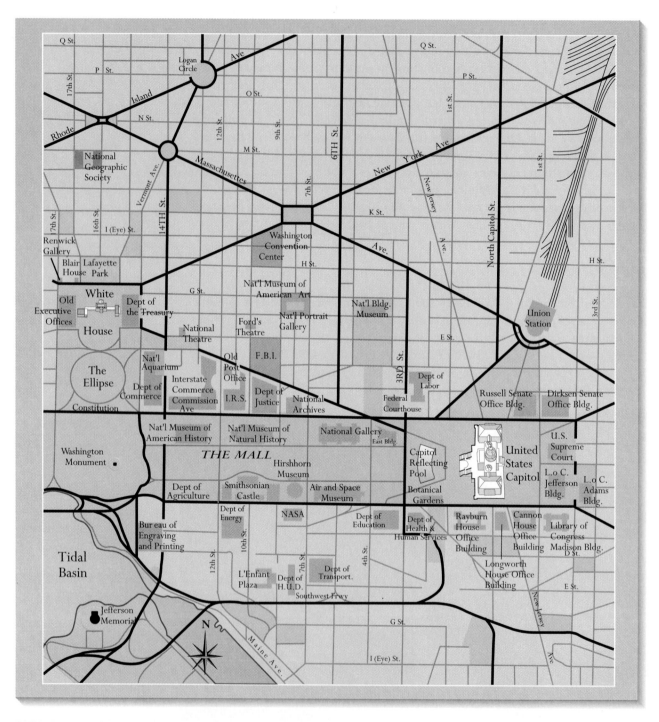

FIGURE 12-2 Corridors of Power in the Bureaucracy

This map shows the Capitol, the White House, and the major departments of the federal bureaucracy in Washington, D.C.

Why Government Grows, and Grows, and Grows

What accounts for the growth of government activity? Many theories offer explanations. The theories listed below are not mutually exclusive; indeed, probably all of the forces they identify contribute to government growth.

Societal Demands: Wagner's Law: In the nineteenth century, economist Adolf Wagner proposed a "law of increasing state activity"—the notion that government activity increased faster than economic output in all developing societies.[*] He attributed this growth to a variety of factors including increasing demands in a developed society for social services such as education, welfare, and public health.

Wars and Crises Another theory is based on the fact that during periods of social upheaval, especially war or economic turmoil, people willingly accept higher-than-normal levels of taxation. During these periods, then, government grows. But after the stressful period is over, government size does not return to its previous levels. Instead, governments substitute new expenditures for those accepted during the crisis. Thus expenditures increase during crisis periods but never return to the precrisis levels after the crisis passes.

Fiscal "Illusion" This explanation assumes that government officials can increase revenues, and then expenditures, by altering tax-collecting devices so that voters do not realize how much money government is actually taking from them. The federal income tax grew very rapidly *after* the introduction of federal tax "withholding" in 1943. Since that time, wage earners have not received all of the money they earn and have come to perceive the missing portion as "belonging" to the federal government. This illusion is also aided by government-mandated withholding of Social Security taxes.

Bureaucratic Expansionism Bureaucrats and legislators have a personal interest in expanding government budgets. Bureaucrats want to increase the amount of money they can spend and the number of employees under their supervision. Legislators want to increase the resources over which they have jurisdiction and to enhance the government benefits bestowed on their constituents.

Interest-Group Pressures This explanation assumes that interest groups want to increase the size of government programs that benefit their own members. Benefits are visible and concentrated. Costs are invisible in many cases or are of less significance to those who will clearly benefit. As each interest group is motivated to act on behalf of its own members, largely ignoring the associated costs, government grows.

Politicians Seeking Votes Politicians in competitive elections frequently promise their constituents visible and exaggerated benefits while hiding or minimizing the costs to other voters. When these promises become policies, government grows.

Cumulative Unintended Consequences The current size of the government is the result of previous efforts to solve earlier problems. Once established, bureaucracies and programs live on, even when their original tasks no longer need doing. Over the years, the effects of all these decisions accumulate beyond what anyone originally intended.

Incrementalism Governments expand because decision making is incremental. Presidents and members of Congress focus on a narrow range of new policy proposals and *increases* or *decreases* in the budget. Old programs are never reviewed as a whole every year. The value of existing programs is seldom reconsidered.

---

[*]Adolf Wagner's major work is *Grundlegung der Politischen Ökonomie* (Leipzig, 1883). This work is discussed at length in Alan T. Peacock and Jack Wiseman, *The Growth of Public Expenditures in the United Kingdom* (Princeton, N.J.: Princeton University Press, 1961).

of GDP. Nevertheless, government spending in the United States remains relatively modest compared to that of many nations (see *Compared to What?* "The Size of Government in Other Nations").

Cabinet Departments   Cabinet departments employ about 60 percent of all federal workers. Each of the fourteen departments is headed by a secretary (with the exception of the Justice Department, which is headed by the attorney general) who is appointed by the president and must be confirmed by the Senate. Each department is hierarchically organized; each has its own organization chart. Although organizational patterns differ among departments, the chart for the Department of Health and Human Services shown in Figure 12-3 is typical.

Government departments vary widely in the budgetary funds they control and in the number of personnel (see Table 12-1 on page 435). The largest budget belongs to the Department of Health and Human Services (HHS), primarily spent through its Social Security and Medicare and Medicaid outlays, which account for about 40 percent of all federal spending. The largest organization in the federal

 Compared to What?

The Size of Government in Other Nations

How does the size of the public sector in the United States compare with the size of the public sector in other countries? There is a great deal of variation in the size of government across countries. Government spending accounts for nearly three-fifths of the total output in Denmark, Sweden, and the Netherlands. Approximately one-half of the total income of Italy, Austria, Greece, France, Belgium, and Germany is channeled through the public sector. The high level of government spending in these countries primarily reflects greater public-sector involvement in the provision of housing, health care, retirement insurance, and aid to the poor and unemployed. The size of the public sectors in Australia, Japan, and Switzerland are approximately the same as in the United States; the size of government in South Korea and Hong Kong, two Asian nations where income has grown very rapidly in recent decades, is substantially smaller than that of the United States.

Governmental Percentage of Gross Domestic Product

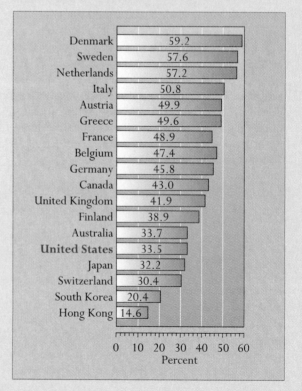

Source: OECD Economic Outlook, June 1990.

bureaucracy in terms of personnel is the Department of Defense (DOD), with nearly 1 million civilian employees in addition to 1.4 million military personnel. The Department of Defense is unique in that the civilian heads of the "Departments" of the Army, Navy, and Air Force are given the title "secretary" even though they really function as undersecretaries to the Secretary of Defense. This anomaly is a product of historical tradition: a secretary of war headed a separate War Department (created 1789) and the secretary of the navy headed a separate Department of the Navy (created 1798) until the creation of a unified Department of Defense in 1947.

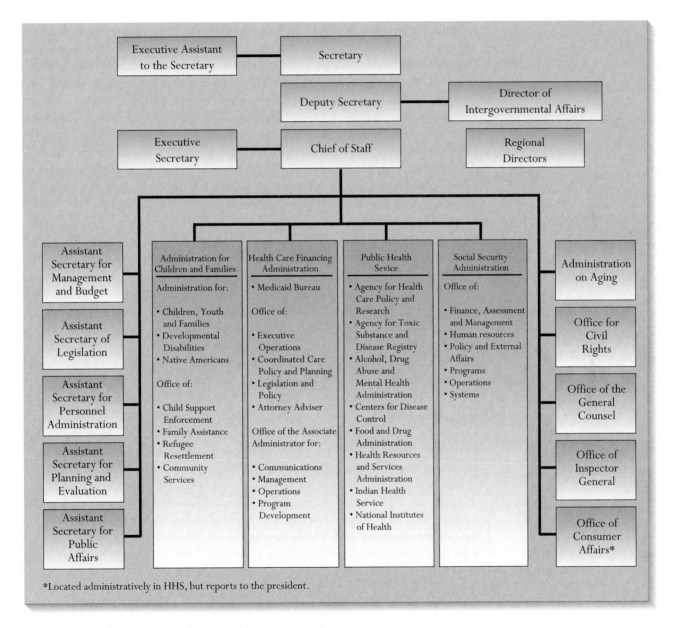

*Located administratively in HHS, but reports to the president.

FIGURE 12-3 Department of Health and Human Services

The internal structures of various cabinet-level departments differ somewhat in specifics, but this chart of the Department of Health and Human Services (HHS) is typical of most. It includes secretary, deputy secretary, assistant secretaries, and multiple "administrations" (subdepartments), agencies, offices, and services.

Cabinet status confers great legitimacy on a governmental function and prestige on the secretary, thus strengthening that individual's voice in the government. Therefore the elevation of an executive department to cabinet level often reflects political considerations as much as or more than national needs. Strong pressures from "client" interest groups (groups principally served by the department), as well as presidential and congressional desires to pose as defenders and promoters of particular interests, account for the establishment of all of the newer departments. President Woodrow Wilson appealed to the labor movement in 1913 when he separated out a Department of Labor from the earlier business-dominated Department of Commerce and Labor. In 1965 President Lyndon Johnson created the Department of Housing and Urban Development to demonstrate his concern for urban problems. Seeking support from teachers and educational administrators, President Jimmy Carter created a separate Department of Education in 1979 and changed the name of the former Department of Health, Education, and Welfare to the Department of Health and Human Services (perhaps finding the phrase "human services" more politically acceptable than "welfare"). President Ronald Reagan, never a favorite of educational groups, tried and failed to "streamline" government by abolishing the Department of Education. But Reagan himself added a cabinet post, elevating the Veterans' Administration to the Department of Veterans' Affairs in an attempt to ingratiate himself with veterans. President Clinton promised to elevate the Environmental Protection Agency (EPA) to a cabinet department.

Cabinet Department Functions   The relative power and prestige of each cabinet-level department is a product not only of its size and budget but also of the importance of its function. By custom, the "pecking order" of departments—and therefore the prestige ranking of their secretaries—is determined by their years of origin. Thus the Departments of State, Treasury, Defense (War), and Justice, created by the First Congress in 1789, head the protocol list of departments. Overall, the duties of the fourteen cabinet-level departments of the executive branch cover an enormous range—everything from providing mortgage insurance to overseeing the armed forces of the United States (see Table 12-1).

Cabinet Appointments   The Constitution requires that "Officers of the United States" be confirmed by the Senate. In the past, the Senate rarely rejected a presidential cabinet nomination; the traditional view was that presidents were entitled to pick their own people and even make their own mistakes. In recent years, however, the confirmation process has become more partisan and divisive, with the Senate conducting lengthy investigations and holding public hearings on presidential cabinet nominees. In 1989 the Senate rejected President Bush's nomination of John Tower as secretary of defense in a partisan battle featuring charges that the former Texas senator was a heavy drinker. In 1993 President Clinton was obliged to withdraw the nomination of Zoe Baird as attorney general following Senate hearings featuring the charge that she had employed an illegal alien as a babysitter and had failed to pay the woman's Social Security taxes. The intense public scrutiny and potential for partisan attacks, together with financial disclosure and conflict-of-interest laws, may be discouraging some well-qualified people from accepting cabinet posts (see *People in Politics:* "Who's Who in the Clinton Cabinet").

TABLE 12-1	Cabinet Departments and Functions

Department and Date Created	Function
State (1789)	Advises the president on the formation and execution of foreign policy; negotiates treaties and agreements with foreign nations; represents the United States in the United Nations and in the more than fifty major international organizations and maintains U.S. embassies abroad; issues U.S. passports and, in foreign countries, visas to the United States.
Treasury (1789)	Serves as financial agent for the U.S. government; issues all payments of the U.S. government according to law; manages the debt of the U.S. government by issuing and recovering bonds and paying their interest; collects taxes owed to the U.S. government; collects taxes and enforces laws on alcohol, tobacco, and firearms and on customs duties; manufactures coins and currency.
Defense (1947; formerly the War Department, created in 1789, and the Navy Department, created 1798)	Provides the military forces needed to deter war and protect the national security interest; includes the Departments of the Army, Navy, and Air Force.
Justice (1789)	Enforces all federal laws, including consumer protection, antitrust, civil rights, drug, and immigration and naturalization; maintains federal prisons.
Interior (1849)	Has responsibility for public lands and natural resources, for American Indian reservations, and for people who live in island territories under U.S. administration; preserves national parks and historical sites.
Agriculture (1889)	Works to improve and maintain farm income and to develop and expand markets abroad for agricultural products; safeguards standards of quality in the food supply through inspection and grading services; administers rural development, credit, and conservation programs; administers food stamp program.
Commerce (1913)	Encourages the nation's international trade, economic growth, and technological advancement; conducts the census; provides social and economic statistics and analyses for business and government; maintains the merchant marine; grants patents and registers trademarks.
Labor (1913)	Oversees working conditions; administers federal labor laws; protects workers' pension rights; sponsors job training programs; keeps track of changes in employment, price, and other national economic indicators.
Health and Human Services (1953 as Health, Education, and Welfare; reorganized with Education as a separate department in 1979)	Administers to social welfare programs for the elderly, children, and youths; protects the health of the nation against impure and unsafe foods, drugs, and cosmetics; operates the Centers for Disease Control; funds the Medicare and Medicaid programs; and operates the Social Security system.
Housing and Urban Development (1965)	Is responsible for programs concerned with housing needs, fair housing opportunities, and the improvement and development of the nation's communities; administers mortgage insurance programs, rental subsidy programs, and neighborhood rehabilitation and preservation programs.
Transportation (1966)	Is responsible for the nation's highway planning, development, and construction; also urban mass transit, railroads, aviation, and the safety of waterways, ports, highways, and oil and gas pipelines.
Energy (1977)	Is responsible for the research, development, and demonstration of energy technology; marketing of federal electric power; energy conservation; the nuclear weapons program; regulation of energy production and use; and collection and analysis of energy data.
Education (1979)	Administers and coordinates most federal assistance to education.
Veterans' Affairs (1989)	Operates programs to benefit veterans and members of their families.

Source: The United States Government Manual 1996/97 (Washington, D.C.: Government Printing Office, 1997).

People in Politics

Who's Who in the Clinton Cabinet

By custom, cabinet officials who served during a president's first term offer their resignations at the beginning of a second term. This allows the president to reshape his administration and allow cabinet members to exit more or less gracefully. Following his reelection, Clinton was given the opportunity to retain some of his top officials (for example, Treasury Secretary Robert Rubin, HHS Secretary Donna Shalala, Interior Secretary Bruce Babbitt, Education Secretary Richard Riley, Attorney General Janet Reno, and VA Secretary Jesse Brown), and replace others (for example, former Secretary of State Warren Christopher, former HUD Secretary Henry Cisneros, former Labor Secretary Robert Riech, former Agriculture Secretary Mike Espy, and former Energy Secretary Hazel O'Leary). This practice allows the president to rid the administration of people who are judged inadequate, as well as to bring in fresh new faces.

Clinton's Second Term Team

Madeleine K. Albright, Secretary of State Born in Czechoslovakia, her family escaped Nazi occupation and she earned a Ph.D. in international affairs at Columbia, taught at Georgetown University, served on the National Security Council staff in the Carter Administration, and served as U.S. Ambassador to the United Nations during Clinton's first term. A welcome relief following the sour-faced Warren Christopher as Secretary of State, Albright cultivates warm relationships with Congress, the media, and world diplomats.

Robert E. Rubin, Secretary of Treasury Former chairman of the giant Wall Street investment firm of Goldman, Sachs & Company. A graduate of Harvard University and Yale Law School. Multimillionaire investor. Most trusted of Clinton's advisers on economic affairs.

William S. Cohen, Secretary of Defense The lone Republican in the cabinet, former U.S. senator from Maine and member of the Senate Armed Forces and Intelligence committees. A graduate of Bowdoin College and Boston University Law School. Never served in the military.

Janet Reno, Attorney General The first woman attorney general and a holdover from Clinton's first term. A graduate of Cornell University and Harvard Law School. Politically unknown prior to her appointment, she had served as state attorney for Florida's Dade County (Miami). Her decisions to appoint independent counsel to investigate the White House and other cabinet members made her unwelcome in the Oval Office, but Clinton feared media backlash if he fired her.

William Daley, Secretary of Commerce Son of the legendary political "boss" and mayor of Chicago Richard J. Daley (and brother of the current mayor, Richard M. Daley). A banker and major Democratic Party fund raiser. A graduate of Loyola University and the John Marshall Law School in Chicago. He was confirmed by the Republican-controlled Senate only after promising not to make his department a partisan Democratic enclave.

Andrew M. Cuomo, Secretary of Housing and Urban Development Son of former New York Governor Mario Cuomo. Formerly outspoken manager of his father's political campaigns; married to Kerry Kennedy, daughter of former U.S. Senator Robert Kennedy and niece of President John F. Kennedy. A graduate of Fordham University and Albany Law School. Assistant HUD Secretary during Clinton's first term and earlier chairman of the New York City Commission on the Homeless.

Richard W. Riley, Secretary of Education Oldest cabinet member, former Democratic governor of South Carolina. A graduate of Furman University and University of South Carolina Law School and a long-term member of the South Carolina state legislature. As a former moderate southern reform governor himself, Clinton is reported to rely on Riley's advice on a broad range of topics.

Dan Glickman, Secretary of Agriculture A member of the U.S. House of Representatives for eighteen years, the Kansas Democrat had served on the House Agriculture Committee prior to his appointment in 1995. A graduate of the University of Michigan and George Washington University Law School. He replaced Clinton's first Secretary of Agriculture, Mike Espy, following the appointment of an independent counsel to investigate Espy.

President Clinton introduces members of his second-term team. Federico Pena is fourth from right; Alexis Herman is fifth from right; Andrew Cuomo is seventh from right (next to Vice President Gore); and Donna Shalala is just to the left of the lectern.

Bruce Babbitt, Secretary of the Interior Former governor of Arizona and an unsuccessful candidate for the Democratic presidential nomination in 1988. A graduate of Notre Dame University and Harvard Law School. A former lawyer and lobbyist for environmental organizations. Held over in his post by Clinton despite opposition to his federal land-use policies for western corporate interests.

Donna E. Shalala, Secretary of Health and Human Services Chancellor of the University of Wisconsin at the time of her appointment by Clinton in 1993. A Ph.D. in political science from Syracuse University, she taught at Columbia University and later served as president of Hunter College. A close friend of Hillary Clinton and an outspoken liberal (she defended P.C. speech at Wisconsin), Shalala reluctantly accepted Clinton welfare reform.

Alexis M. Herman, Secretary of Labor Formerly director of the Women's Bureau in the Department of Labor under President Carter and later a consultant to businesses and government on the employment of minorities and women. A graduate of Xavier University in New Orleans.

Rodney E. Slater, Secretary of Transportation Formerly administrator (head) of the Federal Highway Administration during Clinton's first term. Served Governor Clinton on the Arkansas State Highway Commission and later as special assistant for minority affairs. A native of Arkansas, but a graduate of Eastern Michigan University where he attended on a football scholarship; he earned a law degree from the University of Arkansas.

Federico F. Pena, Secretary of Energy Former mayor of Denver and driving force behind the city's expensive new airport. He served as Secretary of Transportation during Clinton's first term. A graduate of the University of Texas and the University of Texas Law School and a leading Hispanic Democratic legislator in Colorado.

Jesse Brown, Secretary of Veterans' Affairs A marine corps veterans wounded in Vietnam, Brown became a prominent Washington lobbyist for the Disabled American Veterans. A graduate of Chicago City College. Held over by Clinton from his first term, Brown is more popular with veterans than Clinton himself.

TABLE 12-2

Major Regulatory Bureaucracies

Commission	Date Created	Primary Functions
Federal Communications Commission (FCC)	1934	Regulates interstate and foreign communications by radio, television, wire, and cable.
Food and Drug Administration (FDA)	1930	Sets standards of safety and efficacy for foods, drugs, and medical devices.
Federal Home Loan Bank	1932	Regulates savings and loan associations that specialize in making home mortgage loans.
Federal Maritime Commission	1961	Regulates the waterborne foreign and domestic offshore commerce of the United States.
Federal Reserve Board (FRB)	1913	Regulates the nation's money supply by making monetary policy, which influences the lending and investing activities of commercial banks and the cost and availability of money and credit.
Federal Trade Commission (FTC)	1914	Regulates business to prohibit unfair methods of competition and unfair or deceptive acts or practices.
National Labor Relations Board (NLRB)	1935	Protects employees' rights to organize; prevents unfair labor practices.
Securities and Exchange Commission (SEC)	1934	Regulates the securities and financial markets (such as the stock market).
Occupational Safety and Health Administration (OSHA)	1970	Issues workplace regulations; investigates, cites, and penalizes for noncompliance.
Consumer Product Safety Commission (CPSC)	1972	Protects the public against product-related deaths, illnesses, and injuries.
Commodity Futures Trading Commission	1974	Regulates trading on the futures exchanges as well as the activities of commodity exchange members, public brokerage houses, commodity salespersons, trading advisers, and pool operators.
Nuclear Regulatory Commission (NRC)	1974	Regulates and licenses the users of nuclear energy.
Federal Energy Regulatory Commission (formerly Federal Power Commission)	1977	Regulates the transportation and sale of natural gas, the transmission and sale of electricity, the licensing of hydroelectric power projects, and the transportation of oil by pipeline.
Equal Employment Opportunity Commission (EEOC)	1964	Investigates and rules on charges of racial, gender, and age discrimination by employers and unions, in all aspects of employment.
Environmental Protection Agency (EPA)	1970	Issues and enforces pollution control standards regarding air, water, solid waste, pesticides, radiation, and toxic substances.

Source: The United States Government Manual 1996/97 (Washington, D.C.: Government Printing Office, 1997).

Independent Regulatory Commissions   Independent regulatory commissions differ from cabinet departments in their function, organization, and accountability to the president. Their function is to *regulate* a sector of society—transportation, communications, banking, labor relations, and so on (see Table 12-2). These commissions are empowered by Congress both to make and to enforce rules, and they thus function in a quasi-judicial fashion. To symbolize their impartiality, many of these organizations are headed by *commissions,* usually with five to ten members, rather than by a single secretary. Major policy decisions are made by majority vote of the commission. Finally, these agencies are more independent of the president than are cabinet departments. Their governing commissions are appointed by the president and confirmed by the Senate in the same fashion as cabinet secretaries, but their terms are fixed; they cannot be removed by the president.[5] These provisions are designed to insulate regulators from direct partisan or presidential pressures in their decision making.

A few powerful regulatory agencies remain inside cabinet departments. The most notable are the Food and Drug Administration (FDA), which remains in the Department of Health and Human Services and has broad authority to prevent the sale of drugs not deemed by the agency to be both "safe" and "effective"; the Occupational Health and Safety Administration (OSHA) in the Department of Labor, with authority to make rules governing any workplace in America; and the most powerful government agency of all, the Internal Revenue Service in the Treasury Department, with its broad authority to interpret the tax code, maintain records on every American, and investigate and punish alleged violations of the tax code.

Independent Agencies   Congress has created a number of independent agencies outside of any cabinet department. Like cabinet departments, these agencies are hierarchically organized with a single head—usually called an "administrator"—who is appointed by the president and confirmed by the Senate. Administrators have no fixed terms of office and can be dismissed by the president; thus they are independent only insofar as they report directly to the president rather than through a cabinet secretary. Politically, this independence ensures that their interests and budgets will not be compromised by other concerns, as may occur in agencies located within departments. (For more on their operations, see "Regulatory Battles" later in this chapter.)

Perhaps the most powerful independent agency is the Environmental Protection Agency (EPA), which is responsible for implementing federal legislation dealing with clean air, safe drinking water, solid waste disposal, pesticides, radiation, and toxic substances. EPA establishes and enforces comprehensive and complex standards for thousands of substances in the environment. It enjoys the political support of influential environmental interest groups, including the Environmental Defense Fund, Friends of the Earth, National Audubon Society, National Wildlife Federation, Natural Resources Defense Council, Sierra Club, and the Wilderness Society.

Government Corporations   Government corporations are created by Congress to undertake independent commercial enterprises. They resemble private corporations in that they typically charge for their services. Like private corporations, too, they are usually governed by a chief executive officer and a board of directors, and they can buy and sell property and incur debts.

Presumably, government corporations perform a service that the private enterprise system has been unable to carry out adequately. The first government corporation was the Tennessee Valley Authority, created by President Franklin Roosevelt during the Depression to build dams and sell electricity at inexpensive rates to impoverished citizens in the mid-South. In 1970 Congress created Amtrak to restore railroad passenger service to the United States. The U.S. Post Office had originally been created as a cabinet-level department, but in 1971 it became the U.S. Postal Service, a government corporation with a mandate from Congress to break even. Nevertheless, when the Postal Service and other government corporations have

Cleaning up an oil spill on a California beach. The Environmental Protection Agency is perhaps the most powerful independent agency in the bureaucracy.

During the administration of Andrew Jackson, the spoils system was perhaps more overt than at any other time in the history of the U.S. federal government. Jackson claimed he was trying to involve more of the "common folk" in the government, but his selection of advisers on the basis of personal friendship rather than qualifications sometimes caused him difficulties.

spoils system Selection of employees for government agencies on the basis of party loyalty, electoral support, and political influence.

merit system Selection of employees for government agencies on the basis of competence, with no consideration of an individual's political stance and/or power.

run recurring deficits in their operations, Congress has provided subsidies to make up the difference.

Contractors and Consultants   How has the federal government grown enormously in power and size, yet kept its number of employees at roughly the same level in recent years? The answer is found in the spectacular growth of private firms that live off federal contracting and consulting fees. Nearly one-fifth of all federal government spending flows through private contractors: for supplies, equipment, services, leases, and research and development. An army of scientists, economists, education specialists, management consultants, transportation experts, social scientists, and others are scattered across the country in universities, think tanks, consulting firms, and laboratories. Many are concentrated in the "beltway bandit" firms surrounding Washington, D.C.

The federal grant and contracting system is enormously complex; an estimated 150,000 federal contracting offices in nearly 500 agencies oversee thousands of outside contractors and consultants.[6] Although advertised bidding is sometimes required by law, most contracts and grants are awarded without competition through negotiation with favored firms or "sole source contracts" with organizations believed by bureaucrats to be uniquely qualified. Even when federal agencies issue public requests for proposals (RFPs), often a favored contractor has been alerted and advised by bureaucrats within the agency about how to win the award.

BUREAUCRACY AND DEMOCRACY

Traditionally, conflict over government employment centered on the question of partisanship versus competence. Should the federal bureaucracy be staffed by people politically loyal to the president, the president's party, or key members of Congress? Or should it be staffed by nonpartisan people selected on the basis of merit and protected from "political" influence?[7]

The Spoils System   Historically, government employment was allocated by the **spoils system**—selecting employees on the basis of party loyalty, electoral support, and political influence. Or as Senator William Marcy said in 1832, "They see nothing wrong in the rule that to the victors belong the spoils of the enemy."[8] The spoils system is most closely associated with President Andrew Jackson, who viewed it as a popular reform of the earlier tendency to appoint officials on the basis of kinship and class standing. Jackson sought to bring into government many of the common people who had supported him. Later in the nineteenth century, the bartering and sale of government jobs became so scandalous and time-consuming that presidents complained bitterly about the task. And when President James Garfield was shot and killed in 1881 by a disgruntled job seeker, the stage was set for reform.

The Merit System   The **merit system**—government employment based on competence, neutrality, and protection from partisanship—was introduced in the Pendleton Act of 1883. The act created the Civil Service Commission to establish a system for selecting government personnel based on merit, as determined by competitive examinations. In the beginning, "civil service" coverage included only about 10 percent of total federal employees. Over the years, however, more and more positions were placed under civil service, primarily at the behest of presidents who sought to "freeze in" their political appointees. By 1978 more than 90 percent of federal employees were covered by civil service or other merit systems.[9]

The civil service system established a uniform General Schedule (GS) of job grades from GS 1 (lowest) to GS 15 (highest), with an Executive Schedule added later for top managers and pay ranges based on an individual's time in the grade. Each grade has specific educational requirements and examinations. College graduates generally begin at GS 5 or above; GS 9 through GS 12 are technical and supervisory positions; and GS 13, 14, and 15 are midlevel management and highly specialized positions. The Executive Schedule (the "supergrades") are reserved for positions of greatest responsibility. (In 1995 annual pay ranged from roughly $20,000 to $35,000 for Grades 5–8, up to $50,000 to $90,000 for Grades 13–15, and over $100,000 for some Executive Schedule positions.) When a position in a federal agency opens up, the agency is supposed to receive the names of the three people earning the highest examination scores for that position grade. The agency is supposed to hire one of the three, with the other two remaining at the top of the register for the next opening. But agencies often set highly specialized job qualifications that relatively few applicants possess, and special preferences abound in federal employment regulations.

About two-thirds of all federal civilian jobs come under the General Schedule system, with its written examinations and/or training, experience, and educational requirements. Most of the other one-third of federal civilian employees are part of the "excepted services"; they are employed by various agencies that have their own separate merit systems, such as the Federal Bureau of Investigation, the Central Intelligence Agency, the U.S. Postal Service, and the State Department Foreign Service. The military also has its own system of recruitment, promotion, and pay.

The Problem of Responsiveness The civil service system, like most "reforms," eventually created problems at least as troubling as those in the system it replaced. First of all, there is the problem of a *lack of responsiveness* to presidential direction. Civil servants, secure in their protected jobs, can be less than cooperative toward their presidentially appointed department or agency heads. They can slow or obstruct policy changes with which they personally disagree. Each bureau and agency develops its own "culture," usually in strong support of the governmental function or client group served by the organization. Changing the culture of an agency is extremely difficult, especially when a presidential administration is committed to reducing its resources, functions, or services. Bureaucrats' powers of policy obstruction are formidable: they can help mobilize interest group support against the president's policy; they can "leak" damaging information to sympathizers in Congress or the media to undermine the president's policy; they can delay and/or "sabotage" policies with which they disagree.

The Problem of Productivity Perhaps the most troublesome problem in the federal bureaucracy has involved *productivity*—notably the inability to improve job performance because of the difficulties in rewarding or punishing civil servants. "Merit" salary rewards have generally proven ineffective in rewarding the performance of federal employees. More than 99 percent of federal workers regularly receive annual "merit" pay increases. Moreover, over time, federal employees have secured higher grade classifications and hence higher pay for most

TABLE 12-3	Firing a Bureaucrat: What Federal Employees Require before They Can Be Dismissed

- Written notice at least thirty days in advance of a hearing to determine incompetence or misconduct.
- A statement of cause, indicating specific dates, places, and actions cited as incompetent or improper.
- The right to a hearing and decision by an impartial official, with the burden of proof falling on the agency that wishes to fire the employee.
- The right to have an attorney and to present witnesses in the employee's favor at the hearing.
- The right to appeal any adverse action to the Merit Systems Protection Board.
- The right to appeal any adverse action by the board to the U.S. Court of Appeals.
- The right to remain on the job and be paid until all appeals are exhausted.

of the job positions in the General Schedule. This "inflation" in GS grades, combined with regular increases in salary and benefits, has resulted in many federal employees enjoying higher pay and benefits than employees in the private sector performing similar jobs.

At the same time, very poor performance often goes largely unpunished. Once hired and retained through a brief probationary period, a federal civil servant cannot be dismissed except for "cause." Severe obstacles to firing a civil servant result in a rate of dismissal of about one-tenth of 1 percent of all federal employees (see Table 12-3). It is doubtful that only such a tiny fraction are performing unsatisfactorily. A federal executive confronting a poorly performing or nonperforming employee must be prepared to spend more than a year in extended proceedings to secure a dismissal. Often costly substitute strategies are devised to work around or inspire the resignation of unsatisfactory federal employees—assigning them meaningless or boring tasks, denying them promotions, transferring them to distant or undesirable locations, removing secretaries or other supporting resources, and the like.

Civil Service Reform   Presidents routinely try to remedy some of the problems in the system (see *Up Close:* "Reinventing Government"). The Civil Service Reform Act of 1978 initiated by President Jimmy Carter,[10] replaced the Civil Service Commission with the Office of Personnel Management (OPM) and made OPM responsible for recruiting, examining, training, and promoting federal employees. Unlike the Civil Service Commission, OPM is headed by a single director responsible to the president. The act also sought to (1) streamline procedures through which individuals could be disciplined for poor performance; (2) establish merit pay for middle-level managers; and (3) create a Senior Executive Service (SES) composed of about 8,000 top people designated for higher Executive Schedule grades and salaries who also might be given salary bonuses, transferred among agencies, or demoted, based on performance.

But like many reforms, this act failed to resolve the major problems—the responsiveness and productivity of the bureaucracy. No senior executives were fired, demoted, or involuntarily transferred. The bonus program proved

"Reinventing" Government

How can we overcome "the bankruptcy of bureaucracy"—the waste, inefficiency, impersonality, and unresponsiveness of large government organizations? Solving the problem of bureaucracy is perceived as overcoming "the routine tendency to protect turf, to resist change, to build empires, to enlarge one's sphere of control, to protect projects and programs regardless of whether or not they are any longer needed."* The answer, according to current reformers, is to "reinvent government"—to focus on the needs of citizens, not bureaucrats, to inject competition into public service provision, to use market incentives whenever possible, to decentralize, and to encourage agencies to be mission-driven rather than rule-driven.

The notion of "reinventing government" gained popularity among centrist Democrats even before the Clinton Administration arrived in Washington. Some Democratic Party constituencies—notably government employees and their unions, teachers and their unions, and environmental groups—are concerned about the antibureaucratic thrust of many of the new reforms and fear the loss of government jobs to private contractors. But Clinton campaigned on the pledge to make government more efficient and responsive. Upon taking office, he assigned this task to Al Gore.

Vice presidents traditionally undertake symbolic roles in presidential administrations, but Al Gore responded to his assignment with considerable energy and enthusiasm, promptly producing a 168-page report of the National Performance Review, *Creating a Government That Works Better and Costs Less.*[†] The report includes 384 specific recommendations designed to put the "customer" (U.S. citizen) first, to "empower" government employees to get results, to cut red tape, to introduce competition and a market orientation wherever possible, and to decentralize government decision making. Many previous bureaucratic reform efforts had floundered, from Hoover Commission studies in the Truman and Eisenhower years to the Grace Commission in the Reagan Administration. But Bill Clinton boasted that the new effort would succeed because Vice President Gore was given the responsibility not just to devise

Making a point about red tape and bureaucratic inefficiency, President Clinton and Vice President Al Gore walk past two fork-lifts loaded with reams of federal rules and regulations before announcing their plans for "reinventing" government.

recommendations but to oversee their implementation as well.

How successful has Al Gore been at "reinventing" federal government? Periodically Gore has published "status reports" on the implementation of his National Performance Review recommendations. As expected, these reports present glowing accounts of "reinvention," bureaucratic "cultural change," "cutting red tape," and "putting customers first." But even after discounting for puffery, it seems clear that some progress has been achieved. The most impressive evidence is the overall decline in federal employment.

---

*David Osborne and Ted Gaebler, *Reinventing Government: How the Entrepreneurial Spirit Is Transforming the Public Sector* (New York: Addison-Wesley, 1992), pp. 23–24.

†Al Gore, *Creating a Government That Works Better and Costs Less* (Washington, D.C.: Government Printing Office, 1993).

TABLE 12-4	Women and Minorities in the Federal Bureaucracy			
	Percentage Female	Percentage Minority*	Percentage African American	Percentage Hispanic
Overall	48.7%	27.8%	16.5%	5.2%
By pay grade				
Lowest GS 1–4	74.8	43.2	29.4	7.0
GS 5–8	53.5	34.6	23.1	6.1
GS 9–12	32.9	22.1	11.8	5.0
GS 13–15	17.0	13.7	6.8	2.9
Executive	9.1	8.1	5.0	2.3
U.S. population	51.1	28.7	12.1	9.0

*African Americans and Hispanics, plus American Indians, Alaska Natives, Asians, and Pacific Islanders.

Source: Statistical Abstract of the United States, 1994, p. 346. Figures are for 1992.

difficult to implement: there are few recognized standards for judging meritorious work in the public service, and bonuses often reflect favoritism as much as merit.[11] Because the act creates a separate Merit Systems Protection Board to hear appeals by federal employees from dismissals, suspensions, and demotions, rates of dismissal for all grades have not changed substantially from earlier days.

Bureaucracy and Representation In addition to the questions of responsiveness and productivity, there is also the question of the representativeness of the federal bureaucracy. Today, the federal bureaucracy *as a whole* reflects fairly well the gender and minority ratios of the U.S. population. Nearly 49 percent of the total civilian work force is female, 16.5 percent is black, and 5.2 is Hispanic. However, a close look at *top* bureaucratic positions reveals a somewhat different picture. As Table 12-4 shows, only 9.1 percent of federal "executive" positions (levels GS 16–18) are filled by women, only 5.0 percent by blacks, and only 2.3 percent by Hispanics. Thus the federal bureaucracy, like other institutions in American society, is *un*representative of the general population in its top executive positions.

BUREAUCRATIC POLITICS

To whom is the federal bureaucracy really accountable? The president, Congress, or itself? Article II, Section 2, of the Constitution places the president at the head of the executive branch of government, with the power to "appoint Ambassadors, other public Ministers and Consuls, Judges of the Supreme Court, and all other Officers of the United States . . . which shall be established by Law." Appointment of these officials requires "the Advice and Consent of the Senate"—that is, a majority vote in the Senate. The Constitution also states that "the Congress may by Law vest the Appointment of such inferior Officers, as they think proper, in the President alone." If the bureaucracy is to be made accountable to the president, we would expect the president to directly appoint *policy-making* executive officers. But it is difficult to determine exactly how many positions are truly "policy making."

Presidential "Plums"   The president retains direct control over about 3,000 federal jobs. Some 700 of these jobs are considered policy-making positions. They include presidential appointments authorized by law—cabinet and subcabinet officers, judges, U.S. marshals, U.S. attorneys, ambassadors, and members of various boards and commissions. The president also appoints a large number of "Schedule C" jobs throughout the bureaucracy, which are described as "confidential or policy-determining" in character. Each new presidential administration goes through many months of high-powered lobbying and scrambling to fill these posts. Applicants with congressional sponsors, friends in the White House, or a record of loyal campaign work for the president compete for these "plums." Political loyalty must be weighed against administrative competence.

Whistle-Blowers   The question of bureaucratic responsiveness is complicated by the struggle between the president and Congress to control the bureaucracy. Congress expects federal agencies and employees to respond fully and promptly to its inquiries and to report candidly on policies, procedures, and expenditures. **Whistle-blowers** are federal employees (or employees of a firm supplying the government) who report government waste, mismanagement, or fraud to the media or to congressional committees or who "go public" with their policy disputes with their superiors. Congress generally encourages whistle-blowing as a means of getting information and controlling the bureaucracy, but the president and agency heads whose policies are under attack are often less kindly disposed toward whistle-blowers. In 1989 Congress passed the Whistleblower Protection Act, which established an independent agency to guarantee whistle-blowers protection against unjust dismissal, transfer, or demotion.

Agency Cultures   Over time, every bureaucracy tends to develop its own "culture"—beliefs about the values of the organization's programs and goals and close associations with the agency's client groups and political supporters. Many government agencies are dominated by people who have been in government service most of their lives, and most of these people have worked in the same functional field most of their lives. They believe their work is important, and they resist efforts by either the president or Congress to reduce the activities, size, or budget of their agency. Career bureaucrats tend to support enlargement of the public sector—to enhance education, welfare, housing, environmental and consumer protection, and so on.[12] Bureaucrats not only share a belief in the need for government expansion but also stand to benefit directly from increased authority, staffing, and funding as government takes on new and enlarged responsibilities.

Friends and Neighbors   Bureaucracies maintain their own cultures in part by staffing themselves. Informal practices in recruitment often circumvent civil service procedures. Very few people ever get hired by taking a federal civil service examination administered by OPM and then sitting and waiting to be called for an interview by an agency. Most bureaucratic hiring actually comes about through "networks" of personal friends and professional associates. People inside an agency contact their friends and associates when a position first becomes vacant; they then

whistle-blower Employee of the federal government or of a firm supplying the government who reports waste, mismanagement, and/or fraud by a government agency or contractor.

send their friends to OPM to formally qualify for the job. Thus inside candidates learn about an opening well before it appears on any list of vacant positions and can tailor their applications to the job description. Agencies may even send a "name request" to OPM, ensuring that the preselected person will appear on the list of qualified people. In this way, individuals sometimes move through many jobs within a specific policy network—for example, within environmental protection, within transportation, or within social welfare—shifting between the federal bureaucracy, state or local government, and private firms or interest groups in the same field. Network recruiting generally ensures that the people entering a bureaucracy will share the same values and attitudes of the people already there.

THE BUREAUCRACY AND THE BUDGETARY PROCESS

The federal government's annual budget battles are the heart of political process. Budget battles decide who gets what and who pays the cost of government. The budget is the single most important policy statement of any government.

The president is responsible for submitting the annual Budget of the United States Government—with estimates of revenues and recommendations for expenditures—for consideration, amendment, and approval by the Congress. But the president's budget reflects the outcome of earlier bureaucratic battles over who gets what. Despite highly publicized wrangling between the president and Congress each year—and occasional declarations that the president's budget is "DOA" (dead on arrival)—final congressional appropriations rarely deviate by more than 2 or 3 percent from the original presidential budget. Thus the president and the Office of Management and Budget in the Executive Office of the President have real budgetary power.

The Office of Management and Budget The Office of Management and Budget (OMB) has the key responsibility for budget preparation. In addition to this major task, OMB has related responsibilities for improving the organization and management of the executive agencies, for coordinating the extensive statistical services of the federal government, and for analyzing and reviewing proposed legislation (see *People in Politics:* "Franklin Raines, Balancing the Federal Budget").

Preparation of the budget begins when OMB, after preliminary consultations with the executive agencies and in accord with presidential policy, develops targets or ceilings within which the agencies are encouraged to build their requests (see Figure 12-4). Budget materials and instructions then go to the agencies, with the request that the forms be completed and returned to OMB. This request is followed by about three months of arduous work by agency budget officers, department heads, and the "grass-roots" bureaucracy in Washington, D.C., and out in the field. Budget officials at the bureau and departmental levels check requests from the smaller units, compare them with previous years' estimates, hold conferences, and make adjustments. The heads of agencies are expected to submit their completed requests to OMB by July or August. Although these requests usually remain within target levels, occasionally they include some "overceiling" items (requests above the suggested ceilings). With the requests of the spending agencies at hand, OMB begins its own budget review, including hearings at which top agency officials support their requests as convincingly as possible. Frequently OMB must say "no,"

People in Politics

Franklin Raines, Balancing the Federal Budget

As former director of the Office of Management and Budget (OMB), Franklin Delano Raines was principally responsible for the preparation of the federal government's 1999 $1.7 *trillion* budget. This was the nation's first balanced budget in thirty years! Raines himself was perhaps the Clinton White House's most respected official on Capitol Hill. Republican Congressional leaders described him as "a serious guy who understands what needs to be done."

The son of a maintenance man for the Seattle Parks Department, Raines won nearly every honor possible at his public high school—student body president, captain of the football team, statewide debate champion—while earning a near 4.0 grade-point average. He won a full scholarship to Harvard University in 1967 and impressed his political science professors there, including Daniel Patrick Moyhihan, now U.S. senator from New York. He went on to graduate from Harvard Law School and to win a Rhodes Scholarship to Oxford University in England (as had Bill Clinton a few years earlier).

Raines briefly worked at OMB in the Carter White House, but was soon recruited by the giant Wall Street investment firm of Lazard Freres. Later he became vice chairman of the Federal National Mortgage Association, known as Fannie Mae, the nation's largest investor in home mortgages. By the time President Clinton asked him to became OMB Director in 1996, Raines had accumulated millions in personal investments; he chose to serve at a considerable personal financial sacrifice. When the OMB staff first made note of his race in a press release, he ordered that it never happen again.

Saying "No" to outsized bureaucratic budget requests is the most difficult aspect of Raines job. But Raines must remain on "the cutting edge" if the president, Congress, and the nation are to reach the long-sought goal of a balanced federal budget. Following submission of the 1999 balanced federal budget to Congress, Raines returned to Fannie Mae to become its chairman.

that is, reduce agency requests. On rare occasions, dissatisfied agencies may ask the budget director to take their cases to the president.

The President's Budget   In December, the president and the OMB director devote much time to the key document, *The Budget of the United States Government*, which by now is approaching its final stages of assembly. Each budget is named for the **fiscal year** in which it *ends.* The federal fiscal year begins on October 1 and ends the following September 30. (Thus the *Budget of the United States Government Fiscal Year 2000* begins October 1, 1999, and ends September 30, 2000.) Although the completed document includes a revenue plan with general estimates for taxes and other income, it is primarily an expenditure budget. (Revenue and tax policy staff work center in the Treasury Department, not in the Office of Management and Budget.) In late January, the president presents Congress with the Budget of the United States Government for the fiscal year beginning October 1. After the budget is in legislative hands, the president may recommend further alterations as needs dictate.

House and Senate Budget Committees   The Constitution gives Congress the authority to decide how the government should spend its money: "No money shall be drawn from the Treasury, but in Consequence of Appropriations made by

fiscal year   Yearly government accounting period, not necessarily the same as the calendar year. The federal government's fiscal year begins October 1 and ends September 30.

FIGURE 12-4 The Budget Process

Development, presentation, and approval of the federal budget for any fiscal year takes almost two full years. The executive branch spends more than a year on the process before Congress even begins its review and revision of the president's proposals. The problems of implementing the budgeted programs then fall to the federal bureaucracy.

	WHO	WHAT	WHEN
 **Presidential budget making**	President and OMB	OMB presents long-range forecasts for revenues and expenditures to the president. President and OMB develop general guidelines for all federal agencies. Agencies are sent guidelines and forms for their budget requests.	January February March
	Executive agencies	Agencies prepare and submit budget requests to OMB.	April May June July
	OMB and agencies	OMB reviews agency requests and holds hearings with agency officials.	August September October
	OMB and president	OMB presents revised budget to president. President and OMB write budget message for Congress.	November December
	President	President presents budget for the next fiscal year to Congress.	January
 **Congressional budget process**	CBO and congressional committees	CBO reviews taxing and spending proposals and reports to House and Senate budget committees.	February– May
	Congress; House and Senate budget committees	Committees present first concurrent resolution, which sets overall total for budget outlays in major categories. Full House and Senate vote on resolution. Committees are instructed to stay within Budget Committee's resolution.	May June
	Congress; House and Senate appropriations committees and budget committees	Appropriations committees and subcommittees draw up detailed appropriations bills and submit them to budget committees for second concurrent resolution. The full House and Senate vote on "reconciliations" and second (firm) concurrent resolution.	July August September
	Congress and president	House and Senate pass various appropriations bills (nine to sixteen bills, by major functional category, such as "defense"). Each is sent to president for signature. (If sucessfully vetoed, a bill is revised and resubmitted to the president.)	September October
 **Executive budget implementation**	Congress and president	Fiscal year for all federal agencies begins October 1. If no appropriations bill for an agency has been passed by Congress and signed by the president, Congress must pass and the president sign a continuing resolution to allow the agency to spend at last years's level until a new appropriations bill is passed. If no continuing resolution is passed, the agency must officially cease spending government funds and must officially shut down.	After October 1

Law" (Article I, Section 9). The president's budget is sent initially to the House and Senate Budget Committees, which rely on their own bureaucracy, the Congressional Budget Office (CBO), to review the president's budget. Based on the CBO's assessment, these committees draft a first **budget resolution** (due May 15) setting forth target goals to guide congressional committees regarding specific appropriations and revenue measures. If proposed spending exceeds the targets in the budget resolution, the resolution comes back to the floor in a reconciliation measure. A second budget resolution (due September 15) sets binding budget figures for committees and subcommittees considering appropriations. In practice, however, these two budget resolutions are often folded into a single measure because Congress does not want to argue the same issues twice.

Congressional Appropriations Committees   Congressional approval of each year's spending is usually divided into thirteen separate appropriations bills (acts), each covering separate broad categories of spending (for example, defense, labor, human services and education, commerce, justice). These appropriations bills are drawn up by the House and Senate Appropriations Committees and their specialized subcommittees, which function as overseers of agencies included in their appropriations bills. Committee work in the House of Representatives is usually more thorough than it is in the Senate; the committee in the Senate tends to be a "court of appeal" for agencies opposed to House action. Each committee, moreover, has about ten largely independent subcommittees, each reviewing the requests of a particular agency or a group of related functions. Specific appropriations bills are taken up by the subcommittees in hearings. Departmental officers answer questions on the conduct of their programs and defend their requests for the next fiscal year; lobbyists and other witnesses testify. Although committees and subcommittees have broad discretion in allocating funds to the agencies they monitor, they must stay within overall totals set forth in the second budget resolution adopted by Congress.

Appropriations Acts   In examining the interactions between Congress and the federal bureaucracy over spending, it is important to distinguish between appropriations and authorization. An **authorization** is an act of Congress that establishes a government program and defines the amount of money it may spend. Authorizations may be for one or several years. However, an authorization does not actually provide the money that has been authorized; only an **appropriations act** can do that. In fact, appropriations acts, which are usually for a single fiscal year, are almost always *less* than authorizations; deciding how much less is the real function of the Appropriations Committees and subcommittees. (By its own rules, Congress cannot appropriate money for programs it has not already authorized.) Appropriations acts include both obligational authority and outlays.

Obligational authority permits a government agency to enter into contracts that will require the government to make payments beyond the fiscal years in question. **Outlays** must be spent in the fiscal year for which they are appropriated.

Continuing Resolutions and "Shutdowns"   All appropriations acts *should* be passed by both houses and signed by the president into law before October 1, the date of the start of the fiscal year. However, it is rare for Congress to meet this deadline, so the government usually finds itself beginning a new fiscal year without a budget. Constitutionally, any U.S. government agency for which Congress does not pass an appropriations act may not draw money from the Treasury and

budget resolution   Congressional bill setting forth target budget figures for appropriations to various government departments and agencies.

authorization   Act of Congress that establishes a government program and defines the amount of money it may spend.

appropriations act   Congressional bill that provides money for programs authorized by Congress.

obligational authority   Feature of some appropriations acts by which an agency is empowered to enter into contracts that will require the government to make payments beyond the fiscal year in question.

outlays   Actual dollar amounts to be spent by the federal government in a fiscal year.

Up Close

Bureaucratic Budget Strategies

How do bureaucrats go about "maximizing" their resources? Some of the most common budgetary strategies of bureaucrats are listed here. Remember that most bureaucrats believe strongly in the importance of their tasks; they pursue these strategies not only to increase their own power and prestige but also to better serve their client groups and the entire nation.

- *Spend it all:* Spend all of your current appropriation. Failure to use up an appropriation indicates the full amount was unnecessary in the first place, which in turn implies that your budget should be cut next year.

- *Ask for more:* Never request a sum less than your current appropriation. It is easier to find ways to spend up to current appropriation levels than it is to explain why you want a reduction. Besides, a reduction indicates your program is not growing, an embarrassing admission to most government administrators. Requesting an increase, at least enough to cover "inflation," demonstrates the continued importance of your program.

- *Put vital programs in the "base":* Put top priority programs into the basic budget—that is, that part of the budget within current appropriation levels. The Office of Management and Budget (OMB) and legislative committees seldom challenge programs that appear to be part of existing operations.

- *Make new programs appear "incremental":* Requested increases should appear to be small and should appear to grow out of existing operations. Any appearance of a fundamental change in a budget should be avoided.

- *Give them something to cut:* Give the OMB and legislative committees something to cut. Normally it is desirable to submit requests for substantial increases in existing programs and many requests for new programs, in order to give higher political authorities something to cut. This approach enables authorities to "save" the public untold millions of dollars and justify their claim of promoting "economy" in government. Giving them something to cut also diverts attention from the basic budget with its vital programs.

- *Make cuts hurt:* If your agency is faced with a real budget cut—that is, a reduction from last year's appropriation—announce pending cuts in vital and popular programs in order to stir up opposition to the cut. For example, the National Park Service might announce the impending closing of the Washington Monument. Never acknowledge that cuts might be accommodated by your agency without reducing basic services.

---

continuing resolution
Congressional bill that authorizes government agencies to keep spending money for a specified period at the same level as in the previous fiscal year; passed when Congress is unable to enact final appropriations measures by October 1.

thus is obliged to shut down. To get around this problem, Congress usually adopts a **continuing resolution** that authorizes government agencies to keep spending money for a specified period at the same level as in the previous fiscal year.

A continuing resolution is supposed to grant additional time for Congress to pass, and the president to sign, appropriations acts. But occasionally this process has broken down in the heat of political combat over the budget: the time period specified in a continuing resolution has expired without agreement on appropriations acts or even on a new continuing resolution. Shutdowns occurred during the bitter battle between President Bill Clinton and the Republican-controlled Congress over the Fiscal Year 1996 budget. In theory, the absence of either appropriations acts or a continuing resolution should cause the entire federal government to "shut down," that is, to cease all operations and expenditures for lack of funds. But in practice, such shutdowns have been only partial, affecting only "nonessential" government employees and causing relatively little disruption.

THE POLITICS OF BUDGETING

Budgeting is very political. Being a good "bureaucratic politician" involves (1) cultivating a good base of support for requests among the public at large and among people served by the agency; (2) developing interest, enthusiasm, and support for one's program among top political figures and congressional leaders; (3) winning favorable coverage of agency activities in the media; and (4) following strategies that exploit opportunities[13] (see *Up Close:* "Bureaucratic Budget Strategies").

Budgeting Is "Incremental"   The most important factor determining the size and content of the budget each year is last year's budget. Decision makers generally use last year's expenditures as a *base;* active consideration of budget proposals generally focuses on new items and requested increases over last year's base. The budget of an agency is almost never reviewed as a whole. Agencies are seldom required to defend or explain budget requests that do *not* exceed current appropriations; but requested increases *do* require explanation and are most subject to reduction by OMB or Congress.

The result of **incremental budgeting** is that many programs, services, and expenditures continue long after there is any real justification for them. When new needs, services, and functions arise, they do not displace older ones but rather are *added* to the budget. Budget decisions are made incrementally because policy makers do not have the time, energy, or information to review every dollar of every budget request every year. Nor do policy makers wish to refight every political battle over existing programs every year. So they generally accept last year's base spending level as legitimate and focus attention on proposed increases for each program.

Reformers have proposed "sunset" laws requiring bureaucrats to justify their programs every five to seven years or else the programs go out of existence, as well as **zero-based budgeting** that would force agencies to justify every penny requested—not just requested increases. In theory, sunset laws and zero-based budgeting would regularly prune unnecessary government programs, agencies, and expenditures and thus limit the growth of government and waste in government (see *What Do You Think?* "How Much Money Does the Government Waste?"). But in reality, sunset laws and zero-based budgeting require so much effort in justifying already accepted programs that executive agencies and legislative committees grow tired of the effort and return to incrementalism.

The "incremental" nature of budgetary politics helps reduce political conflicts and maintain stability in governmental programs. As bruising as budgetary battles are today, they would be much worse if the president or Congress undertook to review the value of *all* existing expenditures and programs each year. Comprehensive budgetary review would "overload the system" with political conflict by refighting every policy battle every year.[14]

Budgeting Is Nonprogrammatic   Budgeting is *nonprogrammatic* in that an agency budget typically lists expenditures under ambiguous phrases: "personnel services," "contractual services," "travel," "supplies," "equipment." It is difficult to tell from such a listing exactly what programs the agency is spending its money on. Such a budget obscures policy decisions by hiding programs behind meaningless phrases. Even if these categories are broken down into line items (for

incremental budgeting
Method of budgeting that focuses on requested increases in funding for existing programs, accepting as legitimate their previous year's expenditures.

zero-based budgeting
Method of budgeting that demands justification for the entire budget request of an agency, not just its requested increase in funding.

What Do You Think?

How Much Money Does the Government Waste?

Bureaucracy is often associated in the public's mind with waste and inefficiency. But it is very difficult to determine objectively how much money government really wastes. People disagree on the value of various government programs. What is "waste" to one person may be a vital governmental function to another. One very conservative south Georgia farmer once explained politics to his son: "There's only three things that government should ever do—defend our country in war, keep the highways paved, and provide the peanut allotment." But even those who believe a government program is necessary may still believe some of the money going to that program is wasted by the bureaucracy.

Indeed, over the last twenty years, nearly two-thirds of Americans have described the government as wasting "a lot" of money rather than "some" or "not very much" (see graph). Belief in the wastefulness of government rose during the Vietnam War and Watergate years, just as confidence and trust in government declined.

Is public opinion correct in estimating that "a lot" of money is wasted? The General Accounting Office is an arm of Congress with broad authority to audit the operations and finances of federal agencies. GAO audits have frequently found fraud and mismanagement amounting to 10 percent or more of the spending of many agencies it has reviewed, which suggests that $170 *billion* of the overall federal budget of $1.7 trillion may be wasted.[*] Citizens' commissions studying the federal bureaucracy place an even higher figure on waste. The Grace Commission estimated waste at more than 20 percent of federal spending, more than enough to eliminate annual deficits.[†]

[*]General Accounting Office, *Federal Evaluation Issues* (Washington, D.C.: General Accounting Office, 1989).

[†]*President's Private Sector Survey on Cost Control* (Grace Commission Report) (Washington, D.C.: Government Printing Office, 1984).

Question: *Do people in the government waste a lot of the money we pay in taxes, some of it, or not very much of it?*

1996
- A lot: 63%
- Some: 33%
- Not very much: 4%

1988
- A lot: 64%
- Some: 34%
- Not very much: 3%

1984
- A lot: 65%
- Some: 29%
- Not very much: 4%

1972
- A lot: 66%
- Some: 30%
- Not very much: 2%

1968
- A lot: 59%
- Some: 34%
- Not very much: 4%

1964
- A lot: 47%
- Some: 44%
- Not very much: 6%

Source: National Election Studies.

example, under "personnel services," the line-item budget might say, "John Doaks, Assistant Administrator, $65,000"), it is still next to impossible to identify the costs of various programs.

For many years, reformers have called for budgeting by programs. **Program budgeting** would require agencies to present budgetary requests in terms of the end products they will produce or at least to allocate each expense to a specific program. However, bureaucrats are often unenthusiastic about program budgeting;

program budgeting Identifying items in a budget according to the functions and programs they are to be spent on.

it certainly adds to the time and energy devoted to budgeting, and many agencies are reluctant to describe precisely what it is they do and how much it really costs to do it. Moreover, some political functions are best served by *non*program budgeting. Agreement comes more easily when the items in dispute can be treated in dollars instead of programmatic differences. Congressional Appropriations Committees can focus on increases or decreases in overall dollar amounts for agencies rather than battle over even more contentious questions of which individual programs are worthy of support.

REGULATORY BATTLES

Bureaucracies regulate virtually every aspect of American life. Interest rates on loans are heavily influenced by the Federal Reserve Board. The National Labor Relations Board protects unions and prohibits "unfair labor practices." Safety in automobiles and buses is the responsibility of the National Transportation Safety Board. The Federal Deposit Insurance Corporation insures bank accounts. The Federal Trade Commission orders cigarette manufacturers to place a health warning on each pack. The Equal Employment Opportunity Commission investigates complaints about racial and sexual discrimination in jobs. The Consumer Product Safety Commission requires that toys be large enough that they cannot be swallowed by children. The Federal Communications Commission bans tobacco advertisements on television. The Environmental Protection Agency requires automobile companies to limit exhaust emissions. The Occupational Safety and Health Administration requires construction firms to place portable toilets at work sites. The Food and Drug Administration decides what drugs your doctor can prescribe. The list goes on and on. Indeed, it is difficult to find an activity in public or private life that is not regulated by the federal government (see *A Conflicting View:* "Bureaucratic Regulations Are Hurting America").

Federal regulatory bureaucracies are legislators, investigators, prosecutors, judges, and juries—all wrapped into one. They issue thousands of pages of rules and regulations each year; they investigate thousands of complaints and conduct thousands of inspections; they require businesses to submit hundreds of thousands of forms each year; they hold hearings, determine "compliance" and "noncompliance," issue corrective orders, and levy fines and penalties. Most economists agree that regulation adds to the cost of living, is an obstacle to innovation and productivity, and hinders economic competition. Most regulatory commissions are independent; they are not under an executive department, and their members are appointed for long terms by a president who has little control over their activities.

Traditional Agencies: Capture Theory   The **capture theory of regulation** describes how some regulated industries come to benefit from government regulation and how some regulatory commissions come to represent the industries they are supposed to regulate rather than representing "the people." Historically, regulatory commissions have acted against only the most wayward members of an industry. By attacking those businesses that gave the industry bad publicity, the commissions actually helped improve the public's opinion of the industry as a whole. Regulatory commissions provided symbolic reassurance to the public that the behavior of the industry was proper. Among the traditional

capture theory of regulation
Theory describing how some regulated industries come to benefit from government regulation and how some regulatory commissions come to represent the industries they are supposed to regulate rather than representing "the people."

A Conflicting View

Bureaucratic Regulations Are Hurting America

Today, bureaucratic regulations of all kinds—environmental controls, workplace safety rules, municipal building codes, government contracting guidelines—have become so numerous, detailed, and complex that they are stifling initiative, curtailing economic growth, wasting billions of dollars, and breeding popular contempt for law and government.

Consider, for example, the Environmental Protection Agency's rules and regulations, now *seventeen volumes* of fine print. Under one set of rules, before any land on which "toxic" waste was once used can be reused by anyone for any purpose, it must be cleaned to near perfect purity. The dirt must be made cleaner than soil that has never been used for anything. The result is that most new businesses choose to locate on virgin land rather than incur the enormous expense of cleaning dirt, and a great deal of land previously used by industry sits vacant while new land is developed.

These and similar examples of "the death of common sense" in bureaucratic regulations are set forth by critic Philip K. Howard, who argues, "We have constructed a system of regulatory law that basically outlaws common sense."* The result is that we direct our energy and wealth into defensive measures, designed not to improve our lives but to avoid tripping over senseless rules. People come to see government as their adversary and government regulations as obstacles in their lives.

The explosive growth in federal regulations in the last two decades has added heavy costs to the American economy. The costs of regulations do not appear in the federal budget: rather, they are paid for by businesses, employees, and consumers. Indeed, politicians prefer a regulatory approach to the environment, health, and safety precisely because it forces costs on the private sector—costs that are largely invisible to voters and taxpayers. Yet as the costs of regulation multiply for American businesses, the prices of their products rise in world markets.

How large is the regulatory bill? Proponents of a regulatory activity usually object to estimating its cost. Politicians who wish to develop an image as protectors of the environment, of consumers, of the disabled, and so on, do not want to call attention to the costs of their legislation. Only recently has the Office of Management and Budget even attempted to estimate the costs of federal regulatory activity. Overall, regulatory activity costs Americans between $300 billion and $500 billion a year, an amount equal to about one-quarter of the total federal budget. This means that each of America's 100 million households pays about $4,000 per year in the hidden costs of regulation. Paperwork requirements consume more than 5 billion hours of people's time, mostly to comply with the administration by the Internal Revenue Service of the tax laws. However, the costs of environmental controls, including the Environmental Protection Agency's enforcement of clean air and water and hazardous waste disposal regulations, are the fastest growing regulatory costs.

The real question is whether the *benefits* of this regulatory activity—for example, cleaner air and water, safer disposal of toxic wastes, safer consumer products, fewer workplace injuries, fewer highway deaths, protections against discrimination, improved access for disabled, and so on—are greater or less than the costs. But assessing the value of benefits is extraordinarily difficult. Many people object on ethical grounds to economic estimates of the value of a human life saved.

Regulation also places a heavy burden on innovations and productivity. The costs and delays in winning permission for a new product tend to discourage invention and to drive up prices. For example, new drugs are difficult to introduce in the United States because the Food and Drug Administration (FDA) typically requires up to ten years of testing. Western European nations are many years ahead in their number of lifesaving drugs available; they speak of the "drug lag" in the United States. Critics charge that if aspirin were proposed for marketing today, it would not be approved by the FDA. Recently activists have succeeded in speeding up FDA approval of drugs to treat AIDS, but the agency has continued to delay the introduction of drugs to treat other diseases.

---

*Philip K. Howard, *The Death of Common Sense: How Law Is Suffocating America* (New York: Random House, 1995), pp. 10–11.

regulatory agencies that have been accused of becoming too close to their regulated industry are the Federal Communications Commission (FCC, the communications industry, including the television networks), the Securities and Exchange Commission (SEC, the securities industry and stock exchanges), the Federal Reserve Board (FRB, the banking industry), and National Labor Relations Board (NLRB, unions).

Commission members often come from the industry they are supposed to regulate, and after a few years in government, the "regulators" return to high-paying jobs in the industry, creating the *revolving door problem* described in Chapter 9. In addition, many regulatory commissions attract young attorneys fresh from law school to their staffs. Industry siphons off the "best and the brightest" of these, offering them much higher paying jobs as defenders against government regulation.[15] Over the years, then, some industries have come to support their regulatory bureaucracies. Industries have often strongly opposed proposals to reduce government controls. Proposals to deregulate railroads, interstate trucking, and airlines have met with substantial opposition from both the regulatory bureaucracies and the regulated industries, working together.

The Newer Regulators: The Activists In recent decades, Congress created several new "activist" regulatory agencies in response to the civil rights movement, the environmental movement, and the consumer protection movement. Unlike traditional regulatory agencies, the activist agencies do not regulate only a single industry; rather, they extend their jurisdiction to all industries. The Equal Employment Opportunity Commission (EEOC), the Environmental Protection Agency (EPA), and the Occupational Safety and Health Administration (OSHA) pose serious challenges to the business community. Many businesspeople argue that EEOC rules designed to prevent racial and sexual discrimination in employment and promotion (affirmative action guidelines) ignore the problems of their industry or their labor market and overlook the costs of training or the availability of qualified minorities. Likewise, many of OSHA's thousands of safety regulations appear costly and ridiculous to people in industry. The complaint about EPA is that it seldom considers the cost of its rulings to business or the consumer. Industry representatives contend that EPA should weigh the costs of its regulations against the benefits to the environment.

Deregulation The demand to deregulate American life was politically very popular during President Ronald Reagan's administration in the 1980s. But **deregulation** made only limited progress in curtailing the power of the regulatory bureaucracies. Arguments for deregulation centered on the heavy costs of compliance with regulations, the burdens these costs imposed on innovation and productivity, and the adverse impact of regulatory activity on the global competitiveness of American industry. In 1978 Jimmy Carter succeeded in getting Congress to deregulate the airline industry. Against objections by the industry itself, which *wanted* continued regulation, the Civil Aeronautics Board was stripped of its powers to allocate airline routes to various carriers and to set rates. At the end of 1984, the board went out of existence, the first major regulatory agency ever to be abolished. With the airlines free to choose where to fly and what to charge, competition on heavily traveled routes (such as from New York to Los Angeles) reduced fares dramatically while prices rose on less traveled routes served by a single airline. Competition caused airline profits to decline and financially weak airlines to declare

The deregulation of the airline industry contributed to the development of the hub-and-spoke system currently used by most airlines to reduce their costs. Here American Airlines aircraft congregate at the airline's hub in Dallas/Fort Worth. Although deregulation has caused fares to decrease on heavily competitive routes, critics charge that it has contributed to higher rates on noncompetitive routes.

deregulation Lifting of government rules and bureaucratic supervision from business and professional activity.

bankruptcy. Also, during the 1980s the Interstate Commerce Commission (ICC), the first regulatory commission ever established by the federal government, dating from 1887, was stripped of most of its power to set railroad and trucking rates. The ICC itself was finally abolished in 1995.

Reregulation   Deregulation threatens to diminish politicians' power and to eliminate bureaucrats' jobs. It forces industries to become competitive and diminishes the role of interest group lobbyists. So in the absence of strong popular support for deregulation, pressures to continue and expand regulatory activity will always be strong in Washington.

Airline deregulation brought about a huge increase in airline travel, from roughly 15 million passengers in 1980 to 42 million in 1990.[16] The airlines doubled their seating capacity and made more efficient use of their aircraft through the development of "hub-and-spoke" networks. Air safety continued to improve; fatalities per millions of miles flown declined; and by taking travelers away from far more dangerous highway travel, overall transportation safety was enhanced. But these favorable outcomes were overshadowed by complaints about congestion at major airports and increased flight delays, especially at peak hours. The major airports are publicly owned, and governments have been very slow in responding to increased air traffic. Congestion and delays are widely publicized, and politicians respond to complaints by calling for reregulation of airline travel.

Reregulation also gained impetus from the financial disaster in the savings and loan industry. During the 1970s, deregulation of the financial industry allowed savings and loan companies to expand well beyond their traditional function of providing home mortgage loans. Removing limits on the interest rates savings and loan firms could pay on deposits forced them to compete for depositors, which encouraged them to make riskier loans to recover their higher costs. But because the federal government guaranteed deposits (up to $100,000) through the Federal Deposit Insurance Corporation, the savings and loan companies were really risking money guaranteed by American taxpayers. Fraud and mismanagement played a role in the disaster, but the real problem was the "moral hazard" created by allowing these companies free rein with government-guaranteed funds. (If the U.S. government is going to guarantee deposits, then it must regulate their use. Or alternatively, if the financial industry is to be deregulated, then the government must also end its deposit insurance.) The federal government was obliged to spend about $200 billion to "bail out" the savings and loan industry and to reimburse insured depositors for their losses. The savings and loan disaster has resulted in tightened federal regulation of banking and savings institutions.

CONGRESSIONAL CONSTRAINTS ON THE BUREAUCRACY

Bureaucracies are unelected hierarchical organizations, yet they must function within democratic government. To wed bureaucracy to democracy, ways must be found to ensure that bureaucracy is responsible to the people. Controlling the bureaucracy is a central concern of democratic government. The federal bureaucracy is responsible to all three branches of government—the president, the

Attorney General Janet Reno and FBI director Louis Freeh testify before a Senate committee.

Congress, and the courts. Although the president is the nominal head of the executive agencies, Congress—through its power to create or eliminate and fund or fail to fund these agencies—exerts its full share of control. Most of the structure of the executive branch of government (see Figure 12-1) is determined by laws of Congress. Congress has the constitutional power to create or abolish executive departments and independent agencies, or to transfer their functions, as it wishes. Congress can by law expand or contract the discretionary authority of bureaucrats. It can grant broad authority to agencies in vaguely written language, thereby adding to the power of bureaucracies, which can then determine themselves how to define and implement their own authority. In contrast, narrow and detailed laws place constraints on the bureaucracy.

In addition to specific constraints on particular agencies, Congress has placed a number of general constraints on the entire federal bureaucracy. Among the more important laws governing bureaucratic behavior are these:

- *Administrative Procedures Act* (1946): Requires that agencies considering a new rule or policy give public notice in the *Federal Register*, solicit comments, and hold public hearings before adopting the new measures.

- *Freedom of Information Act* (1966): Requires agencies to allow citizens (and the media) to inspect all public records, with some exceptions for intelligence, current criminal investigations, and personnel actions.

- *Privacy Act* (1974): Requires agencies to keep confidential the personal records of individuals, notably their Social Security files and income tax records.

Senate Confirmation of Appointments   The U.S. Senate's power to confirm presidential appointments gives it some added influence over the bureaucracy.[17] It is true that once nominated and confirmed, cabinet secretaries and regulatory commission members can defy the Congress; only the president can remove them from office. Senators usually try to impress their own views on presidential appointees seeking confirmation, however. Senate committees holding confirmation hearings often subject appointees to lengthy lectures on how the members believe their departments or agencies should be run. In extreme cases, when presidential appointees do not sufficiently reflect the views of Senate leaders, their confirmation can be held up indefinitely or, in very rare cases, defeated in a floor vote on confirmation.

Congressional Oversight   Congressional oversight of the federal bureaucracy is a continuing activity.[18] Congress justifies its oversight activities on the ground that its lawmaking powers require it to determine whether the purposes of the laws it passed are being carried out. Congress has a legitimate interest in communicating legislative *intent* to bureaucrats charged with the responsibility of implementing laws of Congress. But often oversight activities are undertaken to influence bureaucratic decision making. Members of Congress may seek to secure favorable treatment for friends and constituents, try to lay the political groundwork for increases or decreases in agency appropriations, or simply strive to enhance their own power or the power of their committees or subcommittees over the bureaucracy.

Oversight is lodged primarily in congressional committees and subcommittees (see "In Committee" in Chapter 10) whose jurisdictions generally parallel those of executive departments and agencies. However, all too frequently, agencies are required to respond to multiple committee inquiries in both the House and the Senate. For example, the secretary of defense may be called to testify before both the House National Security and Senate Armed Forces committees, as well as the Defense Appropriations subcommittees of both the House and Senate Appropriations Committees, the Government Operations Committee of the House and the Senate Governmental Affairs Committee overseeing defense contracts, and the Senate Foreign Relations and House Foreign Affairs Committees. But the committee system in Congress often results in the development of close relationships between specific committees and subcommittees and their staffs and particular departments and agencies (see "Iron Triangles and Policy Networks" in Chapter 9).

Congressional Appropriations   The congressional power to grant or to withhold the budget requests of bureaucracies and the president is perhaps Congress's most potent weapon in controlling the bureaucracy. Spending authorizations for executive agencies are determined by standing committees with jurisdiction in various policy areas, such as armed services, judiciary, education, and labor (see Table 10-4), and appropriations are determined by the House and Senate Appropriations Committees, and more specifically their subcommittees with particular jurisdictions. These committees and subcommittees exercise great power over executive agencies. The Defense Department, for example, must seek *authorizations* for new weapons systems from the House and Senate Armed Services Committees and *appropriations* to actually purchase these weapons from the House and Senate Appropriations Committees, especially their Defense Appropriations subcommittees.

Congress frequently undertakes to control the specific policies and actions of executive agencies through strings it attaches to appropriations measures. Congressional committees and subcommittees may write detailed instructions into appropriations acts about how money is to be spent, thus denying either the president or the bureaucracy any real discretion in implementing programs. For example, in some cases, the Defense Department has been forced to buy weapons it does not need or want simply because an influential member of Congress wrote a pork-barrel provision into the defense appropriations act.

casework Services performed by legislators and their staffs on behalf of individual constituents

Congressional Investigation   Congressional investigations offer yet another tool for congressional oversight of the bureaucracy. Historically, congressional investigations have focused on scandal and wrongdoing in the executive branch (see "Oversight of the Bureaucracy" in Chapter 10). Occasionally, investigations even produce corrective legislation, although they more frequently produce changes in agency personnel, procedures, or policies. Investigations are more likely to follow media reports of waste, fraud, or scandal than to uncover previously unknown problems. In other words, investigations perform a political function for Congress—assuring voters that the Congress is taking action against bureaucratic abuses. Studies of routine bureaucratic performance are likely to be undertaken by the General Accounting Office (GAO), an arm of Congress and frequent critic of executive agencies. GAO may undertake studies of the operations of executive agencies on its own initiative but more often responds to requests for studies by specific members of Congress.

Casework   Perhaps the most frequent congressional oversight activities are calls, letters, and visits to the agencies by individual members of Congress seeking to influence particular actions on behalf of themselves or their constituents. A great deal of congressional **casework** involves intervening with executive agencies on behalf of constituents[19] (see Chapter 10). Executive departments and agencies generally try to deal with congressional requests and inquiries as favorably and rapidly as the law allows. Pressure from a congressional office will lead bureaucrats to speed up an application, correct an error, send information, review a case, or reinterpret a regulation to favor a client with congressional contacts. But bureaucrats become very uncomfortable when asked to violate established regulations on behalf of a favored person or firm (see *Up Close*: "The Keating Five: Service to Constituents, for a Price?" in Chapter 10). The line between serving constituents and unethical or illegal attempts to influence government agencies is sometimes very difficult to discern.

INTEREST GROUPS AND BUREAUCRATIC DECISION MAKING

Interest groups understand that great power is lodged in the bureaucracy. Indeed, interest groups exercise an even closer oversight of bureaucracy than do the president, Congress, and courts, largely because their interests are directly affected by day-to-day bureaucratic decisions. Interest groups focus their attention on the particular departments and agencies that serve or regulate their own members or that function in their chosen policy field. For example, the American Farm Bureau Federation monitors the actions of the Department of Agriculture; environmental lobbies—such as the National Wildlife Federation, the Sierra Club, and the Environmental Defense Fund—watch over the Environmental Protection Agency as well as the National Park Service; the American Legion, Veterans of Foreign Wars, and Vietnam Veterans "oversee" the Department of Veterans Affairs. Thus specific groups come to have a proprietary interest in "their" specific departments and agencies. Departments and agencies understand that their "client" groups have a continuing interest in their activities.

Many bureaucracies owe their very existence to strong interest groups that successfully lobbied Congress to create them. The Environmental Protection

Lobbying Washington can take many forms. Although most professional lobbyists operate quietly within the halls of the nation's capital, groups of private citizens often take to the streets to get their message across. Demonstrations may capture the attention of the media and thus may force bureaucrats and politicians at least to consider a group's cause, but the attention span of both media and Washington power brokers can be extremely short. Here people with disabilities demonstrate in front of the White House for continued support of attendant care.

Politics in Cyberspace

The Bureaucracy

Every cabinet department and virtually all independent regulatory commissions and agencies maintain their own Web sites. The White House Web site, www.whitehouse.gov, has links to all other executive branch sites as well. Or Web users can contact cabinet departments directly:

Agriculture	www.usda.gov
Commerce	www.doc.gov
Defense	www.dla.mil/defenselinks
Education	www.ed.gov
Energy	www.doe.gov
Health and Human Services	www.os.dhhs.gov
Housing and Urban Development	www.hud.gov
Interior	www.dol.gov
Justice	www.usdoj.gov
Labor	www.dol.gov
State	www.state.gov
Treasury	www.ustreas.gov
Transportation	www.dot.gov
Veterans' Affairs	www.va.gov

Many key agencies within departments have their own sites, for example:

Food and Drug Administration	www.fda.gov
National Institute of Health	www.hihf.gov
Federal Bureau of Investigation	www.fbi.gov

One of the most frequently visited sites on the Web is that of the National Aeronautics and Space Administration:

NASA	www.nic.nasa.gov

Other interesting federal Web sites include the following:

National Science Foundation	www.nsf.gov
National Endowment for the Humanities	www.nehfed.us
The Peace Corps	www.peacecorps.gov
The Smithsonian Institution	www.si.edu

Agency owes its existence to the environmental groups, just as the Equal Employment Opportunity Commission owes its existence to civil rights groups. Thus many bureaucracies nourish interest groups' support to aid in expanding their authority and increasing their budgets (see "Iron Triangles and Policy Networks" in Chapter 9).

Interest groups can lobby bureaucracies directly by responding to notices of proposed regulations, testifying at public hearings, and providing information and commentary. Or interest groups can lobby Congress either in support of bureaucratic activity or to reverse a bureaucratic decision. Interest groups may also seek to "build fires" under bureaucrats by holding press conferences, undertaking advertising campaigns, and soliciting media support for agency actions. Or interest groups may even seek to influence bureaucracies through appeals to the federal courts.

JUDICIAL CONSTRAINTS ON THE BUREAUCRACY

Judicial oversight is another source of restraint on the bureaucracy. Bureaucratic decisions are subject to review by the federal courts. Federal courts can even issue *injunctions* (orders) to an executive agency *before* it issues or enforces a regulation or undertakes a particular action. Thus the judiciary poses a check on bureaucratic power.

Judicial Standards for Bureaucratic Behavior   Historically, the courts have stepped in when agency actions have violated laws passed by Congress, when agencies have exceeded the authority granted them under the laws, when the agency actions have been adjudged "arbitrary and unreasonable," and when agencies have failed in their legal duties under the law. The courts have also restrained the bureaucracy on procedural grounds—ensuring proper notice, fair hearings, rights of appeal, and so on. In short, appeal to the courts must cite failures of agencies to abide by substantive or procedural laws.

Judicial oversight tends to focus on (1) whether or not agencies are acting beyond the authority granted them by Congress; and (2) whether or not they are abiding by rules of procedural fairness. It is important to realize that the courts do not usually involve themselves in the *policy* decisions of bureaucracies. If policy decisions are made in accordance with the legal authority granted agencies by Congress, and if they are made with procedural fairness, the courts generally do not intervene.

Bureaucrats' Success in Court   Bureaucracies have been very successful in defending their actions in federal courts. Individual citizens and interest groups seeking to restrain or reverse the actions or decisions of executive agencies have been largely *unsuccessful*. One study reported that the Federal Trade Commission won 91 percent of the cases they argued before the Supreme Court; the National Labor Relations Board won 75 percent; and the Internal Revenue Service won 73 percent. Only the Immigration and Naturalization Service had a mediocre record of 56 percent.[20] Independent agencies enjoy greater support from the courts than cabinet departments.[21]

What accounts for this success? Bureaucracies have established elaborate administrative processes to protect their decisions from challenge on procedural grounds. Regulatory agencies have armies of attorneys, paid for out of tax monies, who specialize in these narrow fields of law. It is very expensive for individual citizens to challenge agency actions. Corporations and interest groups must weigh the costs of litigation against the costs of compliance before undertaking a legal challenge of the bureaucracy. Excessive delays in court proceedings, sometimes extending to several years, add to the time and expense of challenging bureaucratic decisions.

SUMMARY NOTES

- The Washington bureaucracy—the departments, agencies, and bureaus of the executive branch of the federal government—is a major base of power in American government. Political conflict does not end when a law is passed by Congress and signed by the president. The arena merely shifts to the bureaucracy.

- Bureaucratic power has grown with increases in the size of government, advances in technology, and the greater complexity of modern society. Congress and the president do not have the time, resources, or

expertise to decide the details of policy across the wide range of social and economic activity in the nation. Bureaucracies must draw up the detailed rules and regulations that actually govern the nation. Often laws are passed for their symbolic value; bureaucrats must give practical meaning to these laws. And the bureaucracy itself is not sufficiently powerful to get laws passed adding to its authority, size, and budget.

- Policy implementation is the development of procedures and activities and the allocation of money, personnel, and other resources to carry out the tasks mandated by law. Implementation includes regulation—the making of detailed rules based on the law—as well as adjudication—the application of laws and regulations to specific cases. Bureaucratic power increases with increases in administrative discretion.

- Bureaucracies usually seek to expand their own powers, functions, and budgets. Most bureaucrats believe strongly in the value of their own programs and the importance of their tasks. And bureaucrats, like everyone else, seek added power, pay, and prestige. Bureaucratic expansion contributes to the growth of government.

- The federal bureaucracy consists of 2.8 million civilian employees in 14 cabinet departments and more than 60 independent agencies, as well as a large Executive Office of the President. Federal employment is not growing, but federal spending, especially for entitlement programs, is growing rapidly. Today federal spending amounts to more than 23 percent of GDP, and federal, state, and local government spending combined amounts to about 35 percent of GDP.

- Historically, political conflict over government employment centered on the question of partisanship versus competence. Over time, the "merit system" replaced the "spoils system" in federal employment, but the civil service system raised problems of responsiveness and productivity in the bureaucracy. Civil service reform efforts have not really resolved these problems.

- The president's control of the bureaucracy rests principally on the powers to appoint and remove policy-making officials, to recommend increases and decreases in agency budgets, and to recommend changes in agency structure and function.

- But the bureaucracy has developed various means to insulate itself from presidential influence. Bureaucrats have many ways to delay and obstruct policy decisions with which they disagree. Whistle-blowers may inform Congress or the media of waste, mismanagement, or fraud. A network of friends and professional associates among bureaucrats, congressional staffs, and client groups helps create a "culture" within each agency and department. The bureaucratic culture is highly resistant to change.

- Women and minorities are represented in overall federal employment in proportion to their percentages of the U.S. population. However, women and minorities are not proportionately represented in the higher levels of the bureaucracy.

- Budget battles over who gets what begin in the bureaucracy as departments and agencies send their budget requests forward to the president's Office of Management and Budget. OMB usually reduces agency requests in line with the president's priorities. The president submits spending recommendations to Congress early each year in the Budget of the United States Government. Congress is supposed to pass its appropriations acts prior to the beginning of the fiscal year, October 1, but frequently falls behind schedule.

- Budgeting is incremental, in that last year's agency expenditures are usually accepted as a base and attention is focused on proposed increases. Incrementalism saves time and effort and reduces political conflict by not requiring agencies to justify every dollar spent, only proposed increases each year. Nonprogrammatic budgeting also helps reduce conflict over the value of particular programs. The result, however, is that many established programs continue long after the need for them has disappeared.

- Bureaucracies regulate virtually every aspect of our lives. The costs of regulation are borne primarily by business and consumers; they do not appear in the federal budget. In part for this reason, a regulatory approach to national problems appeals to elected officials who seek to obscure the costs of government activity. It is difficult to calculate the true costs and benefits of much regulatory activity. After a brief period of deregulation in the 1980s, regulation has regained popular favor.

- Congress can exercise control over the bureaucracy in a variety of ways: by creating, abolishing, or reorganizing departments and agencies; by altering their authority and functions; by requiring bureaucrats to testify before congressional committees; by undertaking investigations and studies through the General Accounting Office; by intervening directly on behalf of constituents; by instructing presidential nominees in Senate confirmation hearings and occasionally delaying or defeating nominations; and especially by withholding or threatening to withhold agency appropriations or by writing very specific provisions into appropriations acts.

- Interest groups also influence bureaucratic decision making directly by testifying at public hearings and providing information and commentary, and indirectly by contacting the media, lobbying Congress, and initiating lawsuits.

- Judicial control of the bureaucracy is usually limited to determining whether agencies have exceeded the authority granted them by law or have abided by the rules of procedural fairness. Federal bureaucracies have a strong record of success in defending themselves in court.

SELECTED READINGS

GORE, AL. *Creating a Government That Works Better and Costs Less.* Washington, D.C.: Government Printing Office, 1993. Specific recommendations for "reinventing" government by making citizens "customers," introducing competition, cutting red tape, and privatizing government services.

GORE, AL. *The Best Kept Secrets in Government.* New York: Random House, 1996. Gore's own evaluation of progress in "reinventing the way Washington works."

HENRY, NICHOLAS. *Public Administration and Public Affairs.* 6th ed. Upper Saddle River, NJ: Prentice Hall, 1995. Authoritative introductory textbook on public organizations (bureaucracies), public management, and policy implementation.

HOWARD, PHILIP K. *The Death of Common Sense: How Law Is Suffocating America.* New York: Random House, 1995. Outrageous stories of bureaucratic senselessness coupled with a plea to allow bureaucrats flexibility in achieving the purposes of laws and holding them accountable for outcomes.

JOHNSON, RONALD N., and GARY D. LIBECAP. *The Federal Civil Service System and the Problem of Bureaucracy.* Chicago: University of Chicago Press, 1994. A convincing argument that civil service was not a product of a moral crusade by reformers against politicians but rather a result of presidents and Congresses competing to maximize their power.

KETTL, DONALD F. *Civil Service Reform.* Washington, D.C.: Brookings Institution, 1996. A brief introduction to the problems confronting government managers and some recommendations for reform.

OSBOURNE, DAVID, and TED GAEBLER. *Reinventing Government.* New York: Addison-Wesley, 1992. The respected manual of the "reinventing government" movement with recommendations to overcome the routine tendencies of bureaucracies and inject "the entrepreneurial spirit" in them.

SCHICK, ALLEN. *The Federal Budget: Politics, Policy, Process.* Washington, D.C.: Brookings Institution, 1995. A comprehensive explanation of the federal budgetary process.

WILDAVSKY, AARON. *The New Politics of the Budgetary Process.* Glenview, Ill.: Scott Foresman, 1988. The revised version of the classic work on politics and incrementalism in budgeting, including strategies by bureaucrats, the Office of Management and Budget, the president, and Congress, with emphasis on the collapse of political consensus, the entitlements problem, and the failure of budget-balancing efforts.

WILSON, JAMES Q. *Bureaucracy: What Government Agencies Do and Why They Do It.* New York: Basic Books, 1989. In the author's words, "an effort to depict the essential features of bureaucratic life in the government agencies of the United States." Examining what really motivates middle-level public servants, Wilson argues that congressional attempts to "micromanage" government activities hamper the ability of bureaucrats to do their jobs.

 ## ASK YOURSELF
ABOUT POLITICS

1 Have the federal courts grown too powerful?
Yes ☐   No ☐

2 Is it really democratic to allow federal court judges, who are appointed, not elected, and serve for life, to overturn laws of an elected Congress and president?
Yes ☐   No ☐

3 Should the Constitution be interpreted in terms of the original intentions of the Founders rather than the morality of society today?
Yes ☐   No ☐

4 Should presidents appoint only judges who agree with their judicial philosophy?
Yes ☐   No ☐

5 Should the Senate confirm Supreme Court appointees who oppose abortion?
Yes ☐   No ☐

6 Should the Supreme Court be able to decide whether or not there can be organized prayer in schools?
Yes ☐   No ☐

7 Is there a need to appoint special prosecutors to investigate presidents and other high officials?
Yes ☐   No ☐

CHAPTER 19

COURTS
JUDICIAL
POLITICS

CHAPTER OUTLINE

Judicial Power

Activism versus Self-Restraint

Structure and Jurisdiction of Federal Courts

The Special Rules of Judicial Decision Making

The Politics of Selecting Judges

Who Is Selected?

Supreme Court Decision Making

Checking Court Power

FEATURES

People in Politics: John Marshall and Early Supreme Court Politics

People in Politics: Sandra Day O'Connor, Holding the Middle Ground

Across the USA: Geographic Boundaries of Federal Courts

A Conflicting View: America Drowning Itself in a Sea of Lawsuits

What Do You Think? Do We Need Special Prosecutors to Investigate Presidents?

Up Close: The Confirmation of Clarence Thomas

People in Politics: William Rehnquist, Leading the Conservative Bloc

Up Close: Privacy, Abortion, and the Constitution

Politics in Cyberspace: The Judiciary

Do the Supreme Court and the federal judiciary in fact have the real power to shape public policies in the United States?

JUDICIAL POWER

"There is hardly a political question in the United States which does not sooner or later turn into a judicial one."[1] This observation by French diplomat and traveler Alexis de Tocqueville, although made in 1835, is even more accurate today. It is the Supreme Court and the federal judiciary, rather than the president or Congress, that has taken the lead in deciding many of the most heated issues of American politics. It has undertaken to:

465

- Eliminate racial segregation and decide about affirmative action.
- Ensure separation of church and state and decide about prayer in public schools.
- Determine the personal liberties of women and decide about abortion.
- Define the limits of free speech and free press and decide about obscenity, censorship, and pornography.
- Ensure equality of representation and require legislative districts to be equal in population.
- Define the rights of criminal defendants, prevent unlawful searches, limit the questioning of suspects, and prevent physical or mental intimidation of suspects.
- Decide the life-or-death issue of capital punishment.

Courts are "political" institutions. Like Congress, the president, and the bureaucracy, courts decide who gets what in American society. Judges do not merely "apply" the law to specific cases. Years ago, former Supreme Court Justice Felix Frankfurter explained why this mechanistic theory of judicial objectivity fails to describe court decision making:

> The meaning of "due process" and the content of terms like "liberty" are not revealed by the Constitution. It is the Justices who make the meaning. They read into the neutral language of the Constitution their own economic and social views. . . . Let us face the fact that five Justices of the Supreme Court are the molders of policy rather than the impersonal vehicles of revealed truth.[2]

Constitutional Power of the Courts   The Constitution grants "the judicial Power of the United States" to the Supreme Court and other "inferior Courts" that Congress may establish. The Constitution guarantees that the Supreme Court and federal judiciary will be politically independent: judges are appointed, not elected, and hold their appointments for life (barring commission of any impeachable offenses). It also guarantees that their salaries will not be reduced during their time in office. The Constitution goes on to list the kinds of cases and controversies that the federal courts may decide. The list is very broad; almost any issue can become a federal case. Federal judicial power extends to any case arising under the Constitution and federal laws and treaties, to cases in which officials of the federal government or of foreign governments are a party, and to cases between states or between citizens of different states.

Interpreting the Constitution: Judicial Review   The Constitution is the "supreme Law of the Land" (Article VI). Judicial power is the power to decide cases and controversies and, in doing so, to decide what the Constitution and laws of Congress really mean. This authority—together with the guaranteed independence of judges—places great power in the Supreme Court and the federal judiciary. Indeed, because the Constitution takes precedence over laws of Congress as well as state constitutions and laws, it is the Supreme Court that ultimately decides whether Congress, the president, the states, and their local governments have acted constitutionally.

The power of **judicial review** is the power to invalidate laws of Congress or of the states that conflict with the U.S. Constitution. Judicial review is not specifically mentioned in the Constitution but has long been inferred from it. Even before the states had approved the Constitution, Alexander Hamilton wrote in

judicial review   Power of the courts, especially the Supreme Court, to declare laws of Congress, laws of the states, and actions of the president unconstitutional and invalid.

1787 that "limited government . . . can be preserved in practice no other way than through the medium of courts of justice, whose duty it is to declare all acts contrary to the manifest tenor of the Constitution void."[3] But it was the historic decision of *Marbury v. Madison* (1803)[4] that officially established judicial review as the most important judicial check on congressional power (see *People in Politics:* "John Marshall and Early Supreme Court Politics"). Writing for the majority, Chief Justice Marshall constructed a classic statement in judicial reasoning as he proceeded step by step to infer judicial review from the Constitution's Supremacy (Article VI) and Judicial Power (Article III, Section 1) Clauses:

- The Constitution is the supreme law of the land, binding on all branches of government: legislative, executive, and judicial.
- The Constitution deliberately establishes a government with limited powers.
- Consequently, "an act of the legislature repugnant to the Constitution is void." If this were not true, the government would be unchecked and the Constitution would be an absurdity.
- Under the judicial power, "It is emphatically the province and duty of each of the judicial departments to say what the law is."
- "So if a law be in opposition to the Constitution . . . the court must determine which of these conflicting rules governs the case. This is the very essence of judicial duty."
- "If, then, the courts are to regard the Constitution, and the Constitution is superior to any ordinary act of the legislature, the Constitution, and not such ordinary act, must govern the case to which they both apply."
- Hence, if a law is repugnant to the Constitution, the judges are duty bound to declare that law void in order to uphold the supremacy of the Constitution.

Arguments over Judicial Review   The power of the federal courts to invalidate *state* laws and constitutions that conflict with federal laws or the federal Constitution is easily defended. Article VI states that the Constitution and federal laws and treaties are the supreme law of the land, "any Thing in the Constitution or Laws of any State to the Contrary notwithstanding." Indeed, the Constitution specifically obligates state judges to be "bound" by the Constitution and federal laws and to give these documents precedence over state constitutions and laws in rendering decisions. Federal court power over state decisions is probably essential to maintaining national unity: fifty different state interpretations of the meaning of the Constitution or of the laws and treaties of Congress would create unimaginable confusion. Thus the power of federal judicial review over state constitutions, laws, and court decisions is seldom questioned.

Today, the power of federal courts to invalidate laws of Congress and actions of the president is also widely accepted. No serious challenge to the power of judicial review has emerged in American politics. But we still might ask: Why should an appointed court's interpretation of the Constitution prevail over the views of an elected Congress and an elected president? Members of Congress and presidents swear to uphold the Constitution, and we can assume they do not pass laws they believe to be unconstitutional. Because both houses of Congress and the president must approve laws, why should federal courts be allowed to set aside these decisions? Is not judicial review, especially by unelected justices appointed for life, undemocratic?

John Marshall and Early Supreme Court Politics

John Marshall was a dedicated Federalist. A prominent Virginia lawyer, he was elected a delegate to Virginia's Constitution-ratifying convention, where he was instrumental in winning his state's approval of the document in 1788. Later Marshall served as secretary of state in the administration of John Adams, where he came into conflict with Adams's vice president, Thomas Jefferson.

In the election of 1800, Jefferson's Democratic-Republicans crushed Adams's Federalist Party. But Adams, taking advantage of the fact that his term of office would not expire until the following March,* sought to pack the federal judiciary with Federalists. The lame duck Federalist majority in the Senate confirmed the appointments, and John Marshall was sworn in as Chief Justice of the Supreme Court on February 4, 1801. Many of these "midnight appointments" came at the very last hours of Adams's term of office.

At that time, a specified task of the secretary of state was to deliver judicial commissions to new judges. When Marshall left his position as secretary of state to become Chief Justice, several of these commissions were still undelivered. Jefferson and the Democratic-Republicans were enraged over this last-minute Federalist chicanery, so when Jefferson assumed office in March, he ordered his new secretary of state, James Madison, not to deliver the remaining commissions. William Marbury, one of the disappointed Federalist appointees, brought a lawsuit to the Supreme Court, asking it to issue a writ of mandamus ("we command") to James Madison, ordering him to do his duty and deliver the valid commission.

The Judiciary Act of 1789, which established the federal court system, had included a provision granting original jurisdiction to the Supreme Court to issue writs of mandamus. The case, therefore, came directly to new Chief Justice John Marshall,

who had failed to deliver the commission in the first place. (Today, we expect justices who are personally involved in a case to "recuse" themselves—that is, not to participate in that case, allowing the other justices to make the decision—but Marshall's actions were typical of his time.)

John Marshall realized that if he issued a direct order to Madison to deliver the commission, Madison would probably ignore it. The Court had no way to enforce such an order, and Madison had the support of President Jefferson. Issuing the writ would create a constitutional crisis in which the Supreme Court would most likely lose power. But if the Court failed to pronounce Madison's actions unlawful, it would lose legitimacy.

Marshall resolved his political dilemma with a brilliant judicial ploy. Writing for the majority in *Marbury v. Madison,* he announced that Madison was wrong to withhold the commission but that the Supreme Court could not issue a writ of mandamus because Section 13 of the Judiciary Act of 1789, which gave the Court original jurisdiction in the case, was unconstitutional. Giving the Supreme Court *original* jurisdiction conflicted with Article III, Section 2, of the Constitution, which gives the Supreme Court original jurisdiction only in cases affecting "Ambassadors, other public Ministers and Consuls, and those in which a State shall be a Party." "In all other Cases," the Constitution states that the Court shall have appellate jurisdiction. Thus Section 13 of the Judiciary Act was unconstitutional.

By declaring part of an act of Congress unconstitutional, Marshall accomplished multiple political objectives. He avoided a showdown with the executive branch that would undoubtedly have weakened the Court. He left Jefferson and Madison with no Court order to disobey. At the same time, Marshall forced Jefferson and the Democratic-Republicans to acknowledge the Supreme Court's power of judicial review—the power to declare an act of Congress unconstitutional. (To do otherwise would have meant acknowledging Marbury's claim.) Thus Marshall sacrificed Marbury's commission to a greater political goal, enhancing the Supreme Court's power.

---

*Not until the adoption of the Twentieth Amendment in 1933 was the president's inauguration moved up to January.

The Use of Judicial Review   Judicial review is potentially the most powerful weapon in the hands of the Supreme Court. It enables the Court to assert
its power over the Congress, the president, and the states and to substitute its
own judgment for that of other branches of the federal government and the
states. However, the Supreme Court has been fairly restrained in its use of judicial review to void acts of Congress. Prior to the Civil War, the Supreme Court
invalidated very few laws of any kind. Since that time, however, the general
trend has been for the U.S. Supreme Court to strike down more *state* laws as
unconstitutional. In contrast, the Court has been relatively restrained in its
rejection of *federal* laws; over two centuries the Court has struck down fewer
than 150 of the more than 60,000 laws passed by Congress.

Nevertheless, some of the laws overturned by the Supreme Court have been
very important. In 1857 the Court ruled in the case of *Dred Scott v. Sandford*[5]
that the Missouri Compromise of 1820, which had restricted the expansion of
slavery into U.S. territories, was invalid; this decision helped to bring about
the Civil War. The Court overturned several important New Deal laws in the
early 1930s in a direct effort to restrict the federal government's role in regulating the economy. The Court's frontal attack on President Franklin Roosevelt
and the Democratic Congress created a constitutional crisis when Roosevelt
responded with a proposal to "pack" the Court, to increase its traditional nine-
member size to fifteen, so that his additional appointees—New Deal supporters—would dominate. (There is no constitutional provision specifying nine
members; Congress could, if it chose to do so, change the number of justices
on the Court.) The Court reversed its anti–New Deal stance in the late 1930s
(inspiring the jibe "A switch in time saved nine") and began to interpret the
federal government's powers much more broadly.[6] In *Buckley v. Valeo* (1976),[7] the
Court struck down provisions of the Federal Election Campaign Act that had
limited the amount individuals could spend to finance their own campaigns or
express their own independent political views. In *United States v. Lopez* (1995),
the Supreme Court struck down Congress's Gun-Free School Zones Act as an
unconstitutional expansion of the interstate commerce power and an invasion
of powers reserved to the states. Overall, however, the Supreme Court's use of
judicial review against the Congress has been restrained.

The Supreme Court has only rarely challenged presidential power. The Court
has overturned presidential policies both on the grounds that they conflicted
with laws of Congress and on the grounds that they conflicted with the Constitution. In *Ex parte Milligan* (1866),[8] for example, the Court held (somewhat
belatedly) that President Abraham Lincoln could not suspend the writ of habeas
corpus in rebellious states during the Civil War. In *Youngstown Sheet and Tube Co.
v. Sawyer* in 1952,[9] it declared President Harry Truman's seizure of the nation's
steel mills during the Korean War to be illegal. In 1974 it ordered President
Richard Nixon to turn over taped White House conversations to the special
Watergate prosecutor, leading to Nixon's forced resignation.[10] And in 1998 the
Court held that President Bill Clinton was obliged to respond to a civil suit
even while serving in office (see *Up Close:* "William Jefferson Clinton versus
Paul Corbin Jones" in Chapter 11).

The Supreme Court has used its power of judicial review far more frequently
to invalidate state laws. Some of these decisions had impact far beyond the individual states on trial. For example, the historic 1954 decision in *Brown v. Board of
Education of Topeka,* declaring segregation of the races in public schools to be

unconstitutional, struck down the laws of twenty-one states[11] (see Chapter 15). The 1973 *Roe v. Wade* decision, establishing the constitutional right to abortion, struck down anti-abortion laws in more than forty states.[12]

Interpreting Federal Laws   The power of the Supreme Court and the federal judiciary does not rest on judicial review alone. The courts also make policy in their interpretation of **statutory laws**—the laws of Congress. Frequently, Congress decides that an issue is too contentious to resolve. Members of Congress cannot themselves agree on specific language, so they write, sometimes deliberately, vague, symbolic language into the law—words and phrases like "fairness," "equitableness," "good faith," "good cause," and "reasonableness"—effectively shifting policy making to the courts by giving courts the power to read meaning into these terms.

The Supreme Court's Policy Agenda   The Supreme Court, and federal courts generally, deal with a very wide range of policy issues. However, the overwhelming majority of cases decided by the Court involve disputes that arise out of government activity—disputes in which a government or a government agency is one party and an individual or firm is the contending party. The Supreme Court dominates policy making in the areas of (1) civil rights and the treatment of women and minorities; (2) the procedural rights of criminal defendants; and (3) freedom of speech, press, and religion. It is estimated that more than half of all the cases decided by the Supreme Court involve these three issue areas.[13] Some of these cases involve interpretations of statutory law, especially the Civil Rights Act of 1964, the Voting Rights Act of 1965, and later amendments of these acts by Congress. But in most civil rights and civil liberties cases, the Court must determine the meaning of the Constitution itself—the meaning of the First Amendment's freedom of speech and press and religion, the meaning of the Equal Protection Clause of the Fourteenth Amendment, and the meaning of the Due Process Clause of the Fifth and Fourteenth Amendments.

The Court is active in determining the nature of American federalism (see Chapter 4), resolving disputes between states and the federal government. It has also played a key role in refereeing the struggle for power between Congress and the president. Finally, the Court devotes considerable attention to government regulatory activity—environmental protection, banking and securities regulation, labor-management relations. The Supreme Court is noticeably absent from the areas of national defense and international relations, leaving these issues to the president and Congress to resolve.

ACTIVISM VERSUS SELF-RESTRAINT

Supreme Court Justice Felix Frankfurter once wrote: "The only check upon our own exercise of power is our own sense of self-restraint. For the removal of unwise laws from the statute books, appeal lies not to the courts but to the ballot and to the processes of democratic government."[14]

Judicial Self-Restraint   The idea behind **judicial self-restraint** is that judges should not read their own philosophies into the Constitution and should

statutory laws   Laws made by act of Congress or the state legislatures, as opposed to constitutional law.

judicial self-restraint   Self-imposed limitation on judicial power by judges deferring to the policy judgments of elected branches of government.

Sandra Day O'Connor, Holding the Middle Ground

For nearly two hundred years, the U.S. Supreme Court was America's most exclusive all-male club. After 101 male justices, Sandra Day O'Connor was named to the Supreme Court by President Ronald Reagan in 1981. On the high court, O'Connor has succeeded in molding a moderate bloc of votes that holds the balance of power on the Supreme Court between liberal and conservative blocs. More important, perhaps, O'Connor has taken the lead in shaping Court policy on women's issues, including the most controversial issue of all—abortion.

Sandra Day grew up on her family's large Arizona ranch, graduated from Stanford with honors, and went on to Stanford Law School, where she finished near the top of her class (along with now Chief Justice of the Supreme Court William Rehnquist, who was first in the class). After graduation, she married John Jay O'Connor, a Phoenix attorney, and had three sons. She entered Arizona politics about the time her youngest son entered school. In 1969 she was appointed to fill a vacancy in the Arizona state senate and was later elected twice to that body, where she rose to become majority leader in 1973. She left the Arizona legislature in 1975 to become a Phoenix trial judge and in 1979 was appointed by a Democratic governor to the Arizona Court of Appeals, an intermediate court that does not hear major constitutional issues.

O'Connor had some business experience: she was formerly a director of the First National Bank of Arizona and Blue Cross/Blue Shield of Arizona. But until her appointment to the U.S. Supreme Court, she was an obscure state court judge. Her service as a Republican leader in the Arizona state senate qualified her as a moderately conservative party loyalist. However, it appears that her professional and political friendships had more to do with bringing her to President Ronald Reagan's attention than her record as a jurist. She had known both Justice Rehnquist and former Chief Justice Warren Burger for many years, and Barry Goldwater, Arizona's senior U.S. senator and Republican warhorse, had been her mentor in Arizona Republican politics. When Reagan's political advisers told him during the presidential campaign that he was not doing well among women voters (he opposed the Equal Rights Amendment), he responded by pledging to appoint a woman to the Supreme Court. Reagan's fulfillment of his campaign pledge was a politically popular decision. Feminist groups felt forced to support the appointment, even though O'Connor's record in Arizona was moderately conservative.

In her early Court deliberations, Justice O'Connor generally reflected the moderate conservatism of recent Republican appointees, but on gender questions she took an independent role from the beginning. Over time, her independent course has made her a swing vote on many key policy issues, from affirmative action to abortion. Indeed, her leadership of the Court on the abortion issue has preserved the constitutional right to abortion.

avoid direct confrontations with Congress, the president, and the states whenever possible. The argument for judicial self-restraint is that federal judges are not elected by the people and therefore should not substitute their own views for the views of elected representatives. Judicial activism encourages people to believe that federal courts—rather than Congress, the president, or state governments— should decide all important matters. As Justice Sandra Day O'Connor (see *People in Politics:* "Sandra Day O'Connor, Holding the Middle Ground") argued in her Senate confirmation hearings, "The courts should interpret the laws, not make them. . . . I do not believe it is a function of the Court to step in because times have changed or social mores have changed."[15]

Wisdom versus Constitutionality   A law may be unwise, unjust, or even stupid and yet still be constitutional. One should not equate the wisdom of a law with its constitutionality, and the Court should decide only the constitutionality and not the wisdom of a law. Justice Oliver Wendell Holmes once lectured a younger colleague, sixty-one-year-old Justice Harlan Stone, on this point:

> Young man, about 75 years ago I learned that I was not God. And so, when the people . . . want to do something I can't find anything in the Constitution expressly forbidding them to do, I say, whether I like it or not, "Goddamn it, let 'em do it."[16]

However, the actual role of the Supreme Court in the nation's power struggles suggests that the Court indeed often equates wisdom with constitutionality. People frequently cite broad phrases in the Fifth and Fourteenth Amendments establishing constitutional standards of "due process of law" and "equal protection of the laws" when attacking laws they believe are unfair or unjust. Most Americans have come to believe that unwise laws must be unconstitutional. If so, then the courts must be the final arbiters of fairness and justice.

Original Intent   Should the Constitution be interpreted in terms of the intentions of the Founders or according to the morality of society today? Most jurists agree the Constitution is a living document, that it must be interpreted by each generation in the light of current conditions, and to do otherwise would soon render the document obsolete. But in interpreting the document, whose values should prevail—the values of the judges or the values of the Founders? The doctrine of **original intent** takes the values of the Founders as expressed in the text of the Constitution and attempts to apply these values to current conditions. Defenders of original intent argue that the words in the document must be given their historical meaning and that meaning must restrain the courts as well as the legislative and executive branches of government. That is, the Supreme Court should not set aside laws made by elected representatives unless they conflict with the original intent of the Founders. Judges who set aside laws that do not accord with their personal views of today's moral standards are simply substituting their own morality for that of elected bodies. Such decisions lack democratic legitimacy because there is no reason why judges' moral views should prevail over those of elected representatives.

Judicial Activism   However, the doctrine of original intent carries little weight with proponents of judicial activism. The idea behind **judicial activism** is that the Constitution is a living document whose strength lies in its flexibility, and judges should shape constitutional meaning to fit the needs of contemporary society. The argument for judicial activism is that viewing the Constitution as a broad and flexible document saves the nation from having to pass dozens of new constitutional amendments to accommodate changes in society. Instead, the courts need to give contemporary interpretations to constitutional phrases, particularly general phrases such as "due process of law" (Fifth Amendment), "equal protection of the laws" (Fourteenth Amendment), "establishment of religion" (First Amendment), and "cruel and unusual punishment" (Eighth Amendment).

original intent   Judicial philosophy under which judges attempt to apply the values of the Founders to current issues.

judicial activism   Making of new law through judicial interpretations of the Constitution.

Stare Decisis Conflicts between judicial activism and judicial self-restraint are underscored by questions of whether to let past decisions stand or to find constitutional support for overturning them. The principle of **stare decisis,** which means the issue has already been decided in earlier cases, is a fundamental notion in law. Reliance on **precedent** gives stability to the law; if every decision were new law, then no one would know what the law is from day to day. Yet the Supreme Court has discarded precedent in many of its most important decisions: *Brown v. Board of Education* (1954), which struck down laws segregating the races; *Baker v. Carr* (1962), which guaranteed equal representation in legislatures; *Roe v. Wade* (1973), which made abortion a constitutional right; and many other classic cases. Former Justice William O. Douglas, a defender of judicial activism, justified disregard of precedent as follows:

> The decisions of yesterday or of the last century are only the starting points. . . . A judge looking at a constitutional decision may have compulsions to revere the past history and accept what was once written. But he remembers above all else that it is the Constitution which he swore to support and defend, not the gloss which his predecessors may have put on it. So he comes to formulate his own laws, rejecting some earlier ones as false and embracing others. He cannot do otherwise unless he lets men long dead and unaware of the problems of the age in which he lives do his thinking for him.[17]

Rules of Restraint Even an activist Supreme Court adheres to some general rules of judicial self-restraint, however, including the following:

- The Court will pass on the constitutionality of legislation only in an actual case; it will not advise the president or Congress on constitutional questions.
- The Court will not anticipate a question on constitutional law; it does not decide hypothetical cases.
- The Court will not formulate a rule of constitutional law broader than that required by the precise facts to which it must be applied.
- The Court will not pass on a constitutional question if some other ground exists on which it may dispose of the case.
- The Court will not pass on the validity of a law if the complainants fail to show that they have been injured by the law, or if the complainants have availed themselves of the benefits of the law.
- When doubt exists about the constitutionality of a law, the Court will try to interpret the law so as to give it a constitutional meaning and avoid the necessity of declaring it unconstitutional.
- Complainants must have exhausted all remedies available in lower federal courts or state courts before the Supreme Court will accept review.
- The Court will invalidate a law only when a constitutional issue is crucial to the case and is substantial, not trivial.
- Occasionally the Court defers to Congress and the president, classifies an issue as a political question, and refuses to decide it. The Court has generally stayed out of foreign and military policy areas.
- If the Court holds a law unconstitutional, it will confine its decision to the particular section of the law that is unconstitutional; the rest of the statute stays intact.

stare decisis Judicial precept that the issue has already been decided in earlier cases and the earlier decision need only be applied in the specific case before the bench; the rule in most cases, it comes from the Latin for "the decision stands."

precedent Legal principle that previous decisions should determine the outcome of current cases; the basis for stability in law.

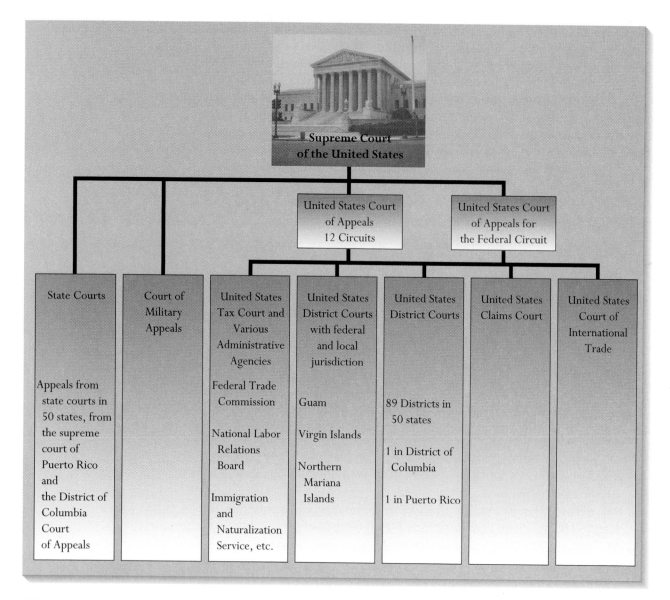

FIGURE 13-1 Structure of Federal Courts

The federal court system of the United States is divided into three levels: the courts of original jurisdiction (state courts, military courts, tax courts, district courts, claims courts, and international trade courts); U.S. Courts of Appeals (which hear appeals from all lower courts except state and military panels); and the U.S. Supreme Court, which can hear appeals from all sources.

STRUCTURE AND JURISDICTION OF FEDERAL COURTS

jurisdiction Power of a court to hear a case in question.

original jurisdiction Refers to a particular court's power to serve as the place where a given case is initially argued and decided.

The federal court system consists of three levels of courts—the Supreme Court, the Courts of Appeals, and the district courts—together with various special courts (see Figure 13-1). Only the Supreme Court is established by the Constitution, although the number of justices is determined by Congress. Article III authorizes Congress to establish such "inferior Courts" as it deems appropriate. Congress has designed a hierarchical system with a U.S. Court of Appeals

TABLE 13-1

Jurisdiction of Federal Courts

Supreme Court of the United States	United States Courts of Appeals	United States District Courts
Appellate jurisdiction (cases begin in a lower court); hears appeals, at its own discretion, from: 1. Lower federal courts 2. Highest state courts Original jurisdiction (cases begin in the Supreme Court) over cases involving: 1. Two or more states 2. The United States and a state 3. Foreign ambassadors and other diplomats 4. A state and a citizen of a different state (if begun by the state)	No original jurisdiction; hear only appeals from: 1. Federal district courts 2. U.S. regulatory commissions 3. Certain other federal courts	Original jurisdiction over cases involving: 1. Federal crimes 2. Civil suits under the federal law 3. Civil suits between citizens of states where the amount exceeds $50,000 4. Admiralty and maritime cases 5. Bankruptcy cases 6. Review of actions of certain federal administrative agencies 7. Other matters assigned to them by Congress

divided into 12 regional circuit courts, a federal circuit, and 89 district courts in the fifty states and one each in Puerto Rico and the District of Columbia. Table 13-1 describes their **jurisdiction** and distinguishes between **original jurisdiction**—where cases are begun, argued, and initially decided—and **appellate jurisdiction**—where cases begun in lower courts are argued and decided on **appeal.**

The Supreme Court is the "court of last resort" in the United States, but it hears only a very small number of cases each year. In a handful of cases, the Supreme Court has original jurisdiction; these concern primarily disputes between states (or states and residents of other states), disputes between a state and the federal government, and disputes involving foreign dignitaries. However, most Supreme Court cases are appellate decisions involving cases from state supreme courts or cases tried first in a U.S. District Court.

District Courts   **District courts** are the original jurisdiction trial courts of the federal system. Each state has at least one district court, and larger states have more (New York, for example, has four). There are more than six hundred federal district judges, each appointed for life by the president and confirmed by the Senate. The president also appoints a U.S. marshall for each district to carry out orders of the court and maintain order in the courtroom. District courts hear criminal cases prosecuted by the Department of Justice as well as civil cases. As trial courts, the district courts make use of both **grand juries** (called to hear evidence and, if warranted, to indict a defendant by bringing formal criminal charges) and **petit (regular) juries** (which determine guilt or innocence). District courts may hear as many as 300,000 cases in a year, including 50,000 criminal cases.

Courts of Appeals   Federal **circuit courts** (see *Across the USA:* "Geographic Boundaries of Federal Courts") are appellate courts. They do not hold trials or accept new evidence but consider only the records of the trial courts and oral or

appellate jurisdiction
Particular court's power to review a decision or action of a lower court.

appeal   In general, requests that a higher court review cases decided at a lower level. In the Supreme Court, certain cases are designated as appeals under federal law; formally, these must be heard by the Court.

district courts   Original jurisdiction trial courts of the federal system.

grand juries   Juries called to hear evidence and decide whether defendants should be indicted and tried.

petit (regular) juries
Juries called to determine guilt or innocence.

circuit courts   The twelve appellate courts that make up the middle level of the federal court system.

Geographic Boundaries of Federal Courts

For administrative convenience, the U.S. District Courts are organized into twelve circuits (regions), plus the Federal Circuit (Washington, D.C.). Within each region, circuit court judges form panels to hear appeals from district courts.

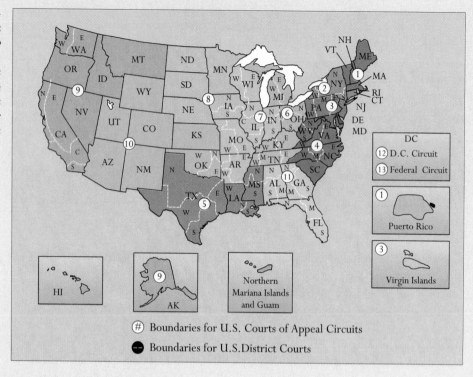

(#) Boundaries for U.S. Courts of Appeal Circuits

— Boundaries for U.S. District Courts

written arguments (**briefs**) submitted by attorneys. Federal law guarantees everyone the right to appeal, so the Court of Appeals has little discretion in this regard. Appellate judges themselves estimate that more than 80 percent of all appeals are frivolous—that is, without any real basis. There are more than a hundred circuit judges, each appointed for life by the president subject to confirmation by the Senate. Normally, these judges serve together on a panel to hear appeals. More than 90 percent of the cases decided by the Court of Appeals end at this level. Further appeal to the Supreme Court is not automatic; it must be approved by the Supreme Court itself. Because the Supreme Court hears very few cases, in most cases the decision of the circuit court becomes law.

Supreme Court   The Supreme Court of the United States is the final interpreter of all matters involving the Constitution and federal laws and treaties, whether the case began in a federal district court or in a state court. Appeals to the U.S. Supreme Court may come from a state court of last resort (usually a state's supreme court) or from lower federal courts. The Supreme Court determines whether to accept an appeal and consider a case. It may do so when there is a "substantial federal question" presented in a case or when there are "special and important reasons," or it may reject a case—with or without explaining why.

briefs   Documents submitted by an attorney to a court, setting out the facts of the case and the legal arguments in support of the party represented by the attorney.

In the early days of the Republic, the size of the Supreme Court fluctuated, but since 1869 the membership has remained at nine: the Chief Justice and eight associate justices. The Supreme Court is in session each year from October through June, hearing oral arguments, accepting written briefs, conferring, and rendering opinions.

Appeals from State Courts   Each of the fifty states maintains its own courts. The federal courts are not necessarily superior to those courts; state and federal courts operate independently. State courts have original jurisdiction in most criminal and civil cases. Because the U.S. Supreme Court has appellate jurisdiction over state supreme courts as well as over lower federal courts, the Supreme Court oversees the nation's entire judicial system, but the great bulk of cases begin and end in the state court systems. The federal courts do not interfere once a case has been started in a state court except in very rare circumstances. And Congress has stipulated that legal disputes between citizens of different states must involve $50,000 or more to be heard in federal courts. Moreover, parties to cases in state courts must "exhaust their remedies"—that is, appeal their case all the way through the state court system—before the federal courts will hear an appeal. Appeals from state supreme courts go directly to the U.S. Supreme Court and not to a federal district or circuit court. Such appeals are usually made on the grounds that a federal question is involved in the case—that is, a question has arisen regarding the application of the Constitution or a federal law.

Federal Cases   Some 10 million civil and criminal cases are begun in the nation's courts each year (see *A Conflicting View:* "America Drowning Itself in a

Justices of the Supreme Court. Front row, from the left: Antonin Scalia, John Paul Stevens, Chief Justice William Rehnquist, Sandra Day O'Connor, and Anthony Kennedy. Back row, from the left: Ruth Bader Ginsburg, David Souter, Clarence Thomas, and Stephen Breyer.

America Drowning Itself in a Sea of Lawsuits

America is threatening to drown itself in a sea of lawsuits. Civil suits in the nation's courts exceed 10 *million* per year. There are more than 805,000 lawyers in the United States (compared to about 650,000 physicians), more than three times as many as in 1960. These lawyers are in business, and their business is litigation. Generating business means generating lawsuits. And just as businesses search for new products, lawyers search for new legal principles on which to bring lawsuits. They seek to expand legal liability for civil actions—that is, to expand the definition of civil wrongdoings, or torts.

Unquestionably, the threat of lawsuits is an important safeguard for society, compelling individuals, corporations, and government agencies to behave responsibly toward others. Because victims require compensation for *actual* damages incurred by the wrongdoing of others, liability laws protect all of us.

But we need to consider the social costs of frivolous lawsuits, especially those brought without any merit but initiated in the hope that individuals or firms will offer a settlement just to avoid the expenses of defending themselves. Legal expenses and excessive jury awards leveled against corporations increase insurance premiums for businesses and service providers, including physicians and hospitals. The risk of lawsuits forces physicians to practice "defensive medicine," ordering expensive tests, multiple consultations with specialists, and expensive procedures not because they are adjudged medically necessary but rather to protect themselves from the possibility of a lawsuit.

Product Liability The threat of lawsuits discourages new products from entering the marketplace by raising their cost through extensive testing and perhaps modification to ensure near-perfect safety. Virtually any accident involving a commercial product can inspire a product liability suit. An individual who gets cut opening a can of peas can sue the canning company. A woman who spills hot coffee on herself while driving sues the fast-food restaurant for making the coffee too hot. Real estate brokers are sued by buyers unhappy in their new homes. Bar owners are sued by persons injured by intoxicated patrons driving home. Hotels pay damages to persons raped in their rooms. Coastal cities with beaches are successfully sued by relatives of persons who drowned in the ocean.

Third-Party Suits Defendants in civil cases are not necessarily the parties directly responsible for damages to the plaintiff. Instead, wealthier third parties, who may indirectly contribute to an accident, are favorite targets of lawsuits. For example, if a drunk driver injures a pedestrian but the driver has only limited insurance and small personal wealth, a shrewd attorney will sue the bar that sold the driver the drinks instead of the driver. Insurance premiums have risen sharply for physicians seeking malpractice insurance, as have premiums for recreation facilities, nurseries and day-care centers, motels, and restaurants. Trial lawyers have been successful in coaxing ever-larger damage awards out of juries, especially against corporations, insurance companies, and governments. Many of these awards are reduced on appeal, but the trend in awards is unmistakably upward.

Sea of Lawsuits"). Fewer than 300,000 (3 percent) of the cases are begun in the federal courts. About 5,000 are appealed to the Supreme Court each year, but the Court hears only about 200 of them. The Constitution "reserves" general police powers to the states. That is, civil disputes and most crimes—murder, robbery, assault, and rape—are normally state offenses rather than federal crimes and thus are tried in state and local courts.

Federal court caseloads have risen in recent years (see Figure 13-2), in part because more civil disputes are being brought to federal courts. In addition, the U.S. Justice Department is prosecuting more criminal cases as federal law enforce-

"Pain and Suffering" Awards High jury awards in liability cases, sometimes running into tens of millions of dollars, cover much more than the doctor bills, lost wages, and cost of future care for injured parties. Most large damage awards are for *pain and suffering*. Pain and suffering awards are *added* compensation for the victim, beyond actual costs for medical care and lost wages.

"Joint and Severable" Liability A legal rule known as *joint and severable liability* allows a plaintiff to collect the entire award from any party that contributed in any way to an accident if other defendants cannot pay. If, for example, a drunk driver crosses a median strip and crashes into another car, leaving its driver crippled, the victim may sue the city for not placing a guard railing in the median strip. The rule encourages trial lawyers to sue the party "with the deepest pockets," that is, the wealthiest party rather than the party most responsible for the accident. Unsophisticated juries can be emotionally manipulated into granting huge damage awards, especially against businesses, municipalities, and insurance companies.

Contingency Fees Many lawsuits are initiated by lawyers who charge fees on a contingency basis; the plaintiff pays nothing unless the attorney wins an award. Up to half of that award may go to the attorney in expenses and fees. Trial attorneys argue that many people could not afford to bring civil cases to court without a contingency fee contract.

Reform Proposals Legal reform centers on discouraging the worst abuses of the system. Some of the most common reform proposals are the following:

- *Loser pay rule:* requiring the losing party in a civil action to pay the attorney fees and court costs of the winning party. This rule would discourage baseless suits designed to force settlements by threatening defendants with high costs. It encourages strong cases because claimants know that they would be reimbursed for costs if they win.

- *Contingency fees limits:* requiring that the parties suffering damages, rather than attorneys, receive the bulk of court awards. A related reform would require attorneys to provide written notice of all expenses, charges, and fees to their clients.

- *"Pain and suffering" damage caps:* limiting awards for noneconomic damages as well as "punitive" awards to $250,000.

- *Ending "joint and severable" liability:* limiting the responsibility of any defendant to his or her actual contribution to the wrongdoing rather than holding the wealthiest defendant responsible for all damages.

Reform Politics Reforming the nation's liability laws presents major challenges to the political system. The reform movement can count on support from some normally powerful interest groups—insurance companies, manufacturers, drug companies, hospitals, and physicians. But legal reform is an anathema to the legal profession itself, notably the powerful Association of Trial Lawyers. And lawyers compose the single largest occupational background of Congress members—indeed, of politicians generally.

ment agencies—such as the Federal Bureau of Investigation (FBI), Drug Enforcement Administration (DEA), Internal Revenue Service (IRS), and Bureau of Alcohol, Tobacco and Firearms (ATF)—have stepped up their investigations. Most of this recent increase is attributable to enforcement of federal drug laws.

Traditionally, federal crimes were offenses directed against the U.S. government, its property, or its employees or were offenses involving the crossing of state lines. Over the years, however, Congress has greatly expanded the list of federal crimes so that federal and state criminal court jurisdictions often overlap, as they do, for example, in most drug violations.

FIGURE 13-2 Caseloads in Federal Courts

Increasing caseloads in the federal courts have placed a heavy burden on prosecutors and judges. Although the increase in civil suits in the federal courts is the result of more plaintiffs insisting on taking their cases to the federal level both originally and on appeal, the increase in criminal cases is the result of Congress's decision to make more crimes—especially drug-related crimes—federal offenses and to pursue such criminals more vigorously.

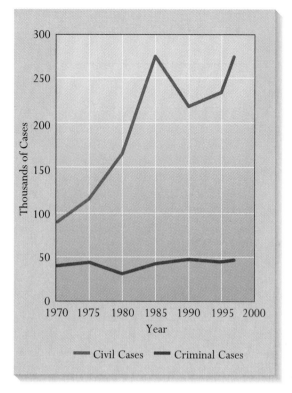

THE SPECIAL RULES OF JUDICIAL DECISION MAKING

Courts are political institutions that resolve conflict and decide about public policy. But unlike Congress, the presidency, and the bureaucracy, the courts employ highly specialized rules in going about their work.

Cases and Controversies   One overriding characteristic of the way courts work is that they do not initiate policy but rather wait until a case or controversy is brought to them for resolution. A case must involve two disputing parties, one of which must have incurred some real damage as a result of the action or inaction of the other. Federal courts do *not* render "advisory" opinions about pending legislation or executive actions. They do *not* issue policy declarations or decide hypothetical cases. Federal courts do *not* render opinions about whether or not proposed laws of Congress are constitutional. Rather, the courts wait until disputing parties bring a case to them that requires them to interpret the meaning of a law or determine its constitutionality in order to resolve the case. Only then do courts render opinions.

The vast majority of cases do *not* involve important policy issues. Courts determine the guilt or innocence of criminal defendants. Courts enforce contracts and award damages to victims of negligence in **civil cases**. And courts render these decisions on the basis of established law. Only occasionally do courts make significant policy decisions.

Adversarial Proceedings   Underlying judicial decision making is the assumption that the best way to decide an issue is to allow two disputing parties to present arguments on each side. Judges in the United States do not investigate cases, ques-

civil cases Noncriminal court proceedings in which a plaintiff sues a defendant for damages in payment for harm inflicted.

tion witnesses, or develop arguments themselves (as they do in some European countries). This **adversarial system** depends on quality of argument on each side, which means it often depends on the capabilities of attorneys. There is no guarantee that the adversarial process will produce the best policy outcomes.

Standing   To bring an issue into court as a case, individuals or firms or interest groups must have **standing**; that is, they must be directly harmed by a law or action. People cannot "go to court" simply because they do not like what the government is doing. Merely being taxpayers does not entitle people to claim that they are damaged by government actions.[18] Individuals or firms automatically have standing when they are prosecuted by the government for violation of laws or regulations. Thus one way to gain standing in order to challenge the legality of a regulation or the constitutionality of a law is to violate the regulation or law and invite the government to prosecute.

To sue the government, plaintiffs must show they have suffered financial damages, loss of property, or physical or emotional harm as a direct result of the government's action. (The party initiating a suit and claiming damages is the **plaintiff**; the party against whom a suit is brought is the **defendant**. The ancient legal doctrine of **sovereign immunity** means that one cannot sue the government without the government's consent. But by law, the U.S. government allows itself to be sued in a wide variety of contract and negligence cases. A citizen can also personally sue to force government officials to carry out acts that they are required by law to perform or for acting contrary to law. The government does not allow suits for damages as a result of military actions.

Class Action Suits   **Class action suits** are cases brought into court by individuals on behalf not only of themselves but also of all other persons "similarly situated." That is, the party bringing the case is acting on behalf of a "class" of people who have suffered the same damages from the same actions of the defendant. One of the most famous and far-reaching class action suits was *Brown v. Board of Education of Topeka* (1954). The plaintiff, Linda Brown of Topeka, Kansas, sued her local board of education on behalf of herself and all other black pupils who were forced to attend segregated schools, charging that such schools violated the Equal Protection Clause of the Fourteenth Amendment. When she won the case, the Court's ruling affected not only Linda Brown and the segregated public schools in Topeka but also all other black pupils similarly situated across the nation (see Chapter 15).

Since the *Brown* case, class action suits have grown in popularity. These suits have enabled attorneys and interest groups to bring multimillion-dollar suits against corporations and governments for damages to large numbers of people, even when none of them has individually suffered sufficient harm to merit bringing a case to court. For example, an individual overcharged by an electric utility would not want to incur the expense of suing for the return of a few dollars. But if attorneys sue the utility on behalf of a large number of customers similarly overcharged, the result may be a multimillion-dollar settlement from which the attorneys can deduct their hefty fees. In recent years, the courts have tightened the rules governing class action suits in order to stem the huge tide of suits generated by the legal profession. Today, federal courts generally require attorneys bringing class action suits to notify each member of the class on whose behalf the case is said to be brought.

adversarial system   Method of decision making in which an impartial judge or jury or decision maker hears arguments and reviews evidence presented by opposite sides.

standing   Requirement that the party who files a lawsuit have a legal stake in the outcome.

plaintiffs   Parties initiating suits and claiming damages. In criminal cases, the state acts as plaintiff on behalf of an injured society and requests fines and/or imprisonment as damages. In civil suits, the plaintiff is the injured party and seeks monetary damages.

defendants   Parties against whom a criminal or civil suit is brought.

sovereign immunity   Legal doctrine that individuals can sue the government only with the government's consent.

class action suits   Cases initiated by parties acting on behalf of themselves and all others similarly situated.

Legal Fees Going to court requires financial resources. Criminal defendants are guaranteed an attorney, without charge if they are poor, by the Sixth Amendment's guarantee of "Assistance of Counsel" (see Chapter 14).[19] However, persons who wish to bring a *civil* suit against governments or corporations must still arrange for the payment of legal fees. The most common arrangement is the **contingency fee**, in which plaintiffs agree to pay expenses and share one-third or more of the money damages with their lawyers if the case is won. If the case is lost, neither plaintiffs nor their lawyers receive anything for their labors. Lawyers do not usually participate in such arrangements unless the prospects for winning the case are good and the promised monetary reward is substantial. Civil suits against the government have increased since Congress enacted a law requiring governments to pay the attorneys' fees of citizens who successfully bring suit against public officials for violation of their constitutional rights.

Remedies and Relief Judicial power has vastly expanded through court determination of **remedies and relief**. These are the orders of a court following a decision that are designed to correct a wrong. In most cases, judges simply fine or sentence criminal defendants to jail or order losing defendants in civil suits to pay monetary damages to the winning plaintiffs. In recent years, however, federal district court judges have issued sweeping orders to governments to correct constitutional violations. For example, a federal district judge took over operation of the Boston public schools for more than ten years to remedy *de facto* (an existing, although not necessarily deliberate, pattern of) racial segregation. A federal district judge ordered the city of Yonkers, New York, to build public housing in white neighborhoods. A federal district judge took over the operation of the Alabama prison system to ensure proper prisoner treatment. A federal district judge ordered the Kansas City, Missouri, school board to increase taxes to pay for his desegregation plan. (This case reached the Supreme Court, which held that a federal court does have the power to

contingency fees Fees paid to attorneys to represent the plaintiff in a civil suit and receive in compensation an agreed-upon percentage of damages awarded (if any).

remedies and reliefs
Orders of a court to correct a wrong, including a violation of the Constitution.

Whitewater special prosecutor Kenneth Starr speaks to reporters soon after it was announced that he was investigating events connected with an alleged affair between President Clinton and Monica Lewinsky.

levy taxes—a power reserved to the legislature in English-speaking countries for centuries—when necessary to implement a constitutional guarantee.)[20]

Appointments of Independent Counsels   The Ethics in Government Act of 1978 grants federal courts the power, upon request of the attorney general, to appoint an independent counsel or "special prosecutor" to investigate and prosecute violations of federal law by the president and other high officials (see *What Do You Think?* "Do We Need Special Prosecutors to Investigate Presidents?").

THE POLITICS OF SELECTING JUDGES

The Constitution specifies that all federal judges, including justices of the Supreme Court, shall be appointed by the president and confirmed by a majority vote of the Senate. Judicial recruitment is a political process: presidents almost always appoint members of their own party to the federal courts. More than 80 percent of federal judges have held some political office prior to their appointment to the court. More important, political philosophy now plays a major role in the selection of judges. Thus the appointment of federal judges has increasingly become an arena for conflict between presidents and their political opponents in the Senate.

The Politics of Presidential Selection   Presidents have a strong motivation to select judges who share their political philosophy. Judicial appointments are made for life. The Constitution stipulates that federal judges "shall hold their Offices during good Behaviour." Although a rather vague phrase, it has come to mean a virtually guaranteed life term. A president cannot remove a judge for any reason, and Congress cannot impeach judges just because it dislikes their decisions.

This independence of the judiciary has often frustrated presidents and Congresses. Presidents who have appointed people they thought were liberals or conservatives to the Supreme Court have sometimes been surprised by the decisions of their appointees. An estimated one-quarter of the justices of the Supreme Court have deviated from the political expectations of the presidents who appointed them.[21] For example, Chief Justice Earl Warren, perhaps the most liberal and activist chief justice in the Court's history, was appointed by Republican President Dwight Eisenhower. Previously the governor of California, Warren lacked judicial experience and received his appointment as a reward for swinging his state's delegation to Eisenhower at the 1952 Republican national convention. Eisenhower later complained that the Warren appointment was "the biggest damn mistake I ever made."

It is important to recognize that presidents' use of political criteria in selecting judges has a democratic influence on the courts. Presidents can campaign on the pledge to make the courts more liberal or conservative through their appointive powers, and voters are free to cast their ballots on the basis of this pledge. For example, Bill Clinton's promise to appoint judges who support abortion rights appears to have influenced some voters in his presidential races.

Political Litmus Test   Traditionally, presidents and senators have tried to discern where a Supreme Court candidate fits on the continuum of liberal activism versus conservative self-restraint. Democratic presidents and senators usually prefer liberal judges who express an activist philosophy. Republican presidents usually

Do We Need Special Prosecutors to Investigate Presidents?

The Ethics in Government Act of 1978, passed in the wake of the Watergate scandal in the Nixon Administration, provides for the appointment of an independent counsel (special prosecutor) to investigate alleged crimes by the president and other high officials. The goal was to *take politics out of* the investigation of wrongdoing in high places. (Nixon had fired Attorney General Elliot Richardson and Justice Department prosecutor Archibald Cox in 1973 for investigating Watergate.) The act, generally referred to as the independent counsel law, obliges the attorney general "upon specific and credible evidence of federal crime" by a high government official to ask a three-judge federal panel to appoint an independent counsel from outside the Justice Department and to define the counsel's scope of investigation. The independent counsel is authorized to conduct the investigation, bring indictments, and prosecute cases in federal court. The attorney general can dismiss a special prosecutor only for "good cause."

The independent counsel law was challenged in the U.S. Supreme Court as transferral of executive power ("to take care that the laws be faithfully executed"—Article II) to the judicial branch of government in violation of the separation of powers in the U.S. Constitution.* But the Court upheld the law, noting that the attorney general, an executive branch official appointed by the president, had to request the judiciary to appoint the independent counsel.

Whatever the original intent of the act, special prosecutors have often been accused of *bringing politics into* the criminal justice system. Indeed, special prosecutor Kenneth Starr's dogged pursuit of Bill and Hillary Clinton was deemed a "witch-hunt" by friends of the president. The First Lady linked Starr to "a vast right-wing conspiracy" trying to reverse the outcome of two presidential elections.

Starr was appointed in 1994 with a mandate to investigate crimes stemming from the Clintons' relation with Whitewater Development Corporation, an Arkansas land development firm owned in part by the Clintons while Bill Clinton was governor. However, over the years, Starr successfully petitioned the three-judge federal oversight panel to expand his investiga-

tion to include the suicide of White House official Vince Foster, the firing of seven White House travel office employees, and the alleged misuse of FBI background files. And in early 1998, Starr's investigation was expanded again to include whether or not President Clinton committed perjury or asked others to do so in an effort to cover up sexual affairs.

Both Starr's political background and his investigatory methods have come under heavy fire. He first practiced law in Los Angeles under William French Smith, Republican Ronald Reagan's attorney general and was later appointed to the U.S. Court of Appeals by Reagan; Starr stepped down in 1989 to become Republican President George Bush's solicitor general. His investigatory methods have included keeping former Clinton business partner Susan McDougal in jail for over a year, and threatening to bring perjury and obstruction of justice charges against Monica Lewinsky and others to force them to testify against Clinton.

Is the special counsel law being abused? Media reports of wrongdoing and partisan attacks in Congress have sparked appointments of several special prosecutors. To deflect criticism from themselves, attorneys general often ask a federal court to make the appointment. (Janet Reno faced considerable political pressure to request yet another prosecutor to investigate Democratic Party fund raising in 1996, but she declined to do so.) Moreover, many allege that a special prosecutor comes under heavy political pressure to bring indictments. With no limits on time or money spend on investigations, prosecutors have frequently expanded their investigation beyond the original allegations in order to bring indictments against their targets. As one observer put it: "If I have three FBI agents, three IRS agents, an unlimited amount of time, and an unlimited amount of money, I can indict anybody."

Congress could reform the special counsel law by reducing the number of officials covered by the statute to the president, vice president, and attorney general; by limiting inquiries to events that took place only while the accused were in office (the Whitewater land deal, for example, took place over twenty years ago); by limiting the time and money that can be spent (the Iran-Contra investigation lasted seven years and cost $50 million); and by preventing prosecutors from broadening their investigation beyond the original allegations.

Morrison v. Olson, 487 U.S. 654 (1988).

Independent Counsel Investigations

	Target; Allegation*	Year	Outcome
Carter Administration	White House chief of staff Hamilton Jordan; cocaine use	1979–80	No charges
	Campaign manager Timothy Kraft; cocaine use	1980–81	No charges
Reagan Administration	Labor Secretary Raymond Donovan; larceny and fraud	1981–82	No charges
	White House counselor Edwin Meese; financial improprieties	1984	No charges
	Assistant Attorney General Theodore Olsen; lying to Congress	1986–89	No charges
	White House aide Michael Deaver; lying about lobbying activities	1986–90	Convicted of perjury
	Reagan officials illegally selling arms to Iran and diverting profits to the Nicaraguan contras—Iran-Contra scandal	1986–93	14 indictments; 7 guilty pleas, 4 convictions nullified by presidential pardons
	White House aide Lyn Nofziger and Attorney General Edwin Meese; Wedtech Corporation contracting scandal	1987–88	2 indictments; 1 acquittal by jury; 1 conviction overturned on appeal
	Assistant Attorney General W. Lawrence Wallace; finance-related allegation	1987	No charges
	Department of Housing and Urban Development; fraud, favoritism, and mismanagement	1990	14 indictments[†]; others pending; 10 guilty pleas; 3 convictions
Bush Administration	Search of Clinton's passport file	1992–96	No charges
Clinton Administration	Bill and Hillary Clinton and others; Whitewater land deal	1994–present	12 indictments[†]; others pending; 10 guilty pleas; 3 convictions
	Investigations resulting from the expanded scope of the Whitewater inquiry:		
	Suicide of White House counsel Vince Foster		No charges
	White House travel office firings		Pending
	Misuse of FBI background files		Pending
	President Clinton; perjury in sex scandal		Pending
	Secretary of Agriculture Mike Espy; illegal gratuities	1994–present	10 indictments[†]; 6 guilty pleas; 3 convictions; 4 acquittals
	HUD Secretary Henry Cisneros; lying to FBI about size of payments made to mistress	1995–present	3 indictments; trials pending
	Commerce Secretary Ronald Brown	1995–96	Case closed after Brown's death in plane crash

*Some investigations that did not result in indictments have remained sealed by court order.

[†]Some indictments cover more than one person.

prefer conservative judges who express a philosophy of judicial self-restraint. Until very recently, both the president and the Senate denied using any political "litmus test" in judicial recruitment. A **litmus test** generally refers to recruitment based on a nominee's stand on a single issue. Since the Supreme Court ruling on *Roe v. Wade* (1973), however, the single issue of abortion has come to dominate the politics of judicial recruitment. Although Presidents Ronald Reagan and George Bush denied applying a litmus test on this issue, many observers believe their nominees were selected with the expectation that they would help reverse *Roe v. Wade.* President Clinton was forthright in his pledge to nominate only justices who specifically support the *Roe v. Wade* decision.

Competence and Ethics   Although competence and ethics may be of lesser importance than party and political philosophy, they are serious considerations for the attorney general and Justice Department as they assist the president in screening nominees for federal judgeships. Given the close scrutiny to which the media and the Senate now subject nominees, even minor violations of laws or moral standards can lead to Senate rejection, especially when senators dislike a candidate's judicial philosophy. Questions of competence and ethics can seldom be separated from politics.

The Politics of Senate Confirmation   All presidential nominations for the federal judiciary, including the Supreme Court, are sent to the Senate for confirmation. The Senate refers them to its powerful Judiciary Committee, which holds hearings, votes on the nomination, and then reports to the full Senate, where floor debate may precede the final confirmation vote.

The Senate's involvement in federal district judgeships traditionally centered on the practice of **senatorial courtesy**. If senators from the president's party from the same state for which an appointment was being considered disapproved of a nominee, their Senate colleagues would defeat the nomination. But if the president and senators from that party agreed on the nomination, the full Senate, even if controlled by the opposition, customarily confirmed the nomination. During the Reagan-Bush years, however, partisan divisions between these Republican presidents and Senate Democrats eroded the tradition of senatorial courtesy.

Supreme Court nominations have always received close political scrutiny in the Senate. Over the last two centuries, the Senate has rejected or refused to confirm about 20 percent of presidential nominees to the high court, but only five nominees in this century (see Table 13-2). In the past, most senators believed that presidents deserved to appoint their own judges; the opposition party would get its own opportunity to appoint judges when it won the presidency. Only if the Senate found some personal disqualification in a nominee's background (for example, financial scandal, evidence of racial or religious bias, judicial incompetence) would a nominee likely be rejected. But publicity and partisanship over confirmation of Supreme Court nominees have increased markedly in recent years.

The Bork Battle   The U.S. Senate's rejection of President Ronald Reagan's nomination of Judge Robert H. Bork in 1987 set a new precedent in Senate confirmation of Supreme Court nominees. The Senate rejected Bork because of his views, not because he lacked judicial qualifications. Bork had a reputation for "conservative activism"—a desire better to reflect the "original intent" of the

litmus test   In political terms, a person's stand on a key issue that determines whether he or she will be appointed to public office or supported in electoral campaigns.

senatorial courtesy   Custom of the U.S. Senate with regard to presidential nominations to the judiciary to defer to the judgment of senators from the president's party from the same state as the nominee.

TABLE 13-2	Senate Confirmation Votes on Supreme Court Nominations since 1950		
Nominee	President	Year	Vote
Earl Warren	Eisenhower	1954	NRV*
John Marshall Harlan	Eisenhower	1955	71–11
William J. Brennan	Eisenhower	1957	NRV
Charles Whittaker	Eisenhower	1957	NRV
Potter Stewart	Eisenhower	1959	70–17
Byron White	Kennedy	1962	NRV
Arthur Goldberg	Kennedy	1962	NRV
Abe Fortas	Johnson	1965	NRV
Thurgood Marshall	Johnson	1967	69–11
Abe Fortas[†]	Johnson	1968	Withdrawn[‡]
Homer Thornberry	Johnson	1968	No action
Warren Burger	Nixon	1969	74–3
Clement Haynsworth	Nixon	1969	Defeated 45–55
G. Harrold Carswell	Nixon	1970	Defeated 45–51
Harry Blackmun	Nixon	1970	94–0
Lewis Powell	Nixon	1971	89–1
William Rehnquist	Nixon	1971	68–26
John Paul Stevens	Nixon	1975	98–0
Sandra Day O'Connor	Reagan	1981	99–0
William Rehnquist[†]	Reagan	1986	65–33
Antonin Scalia	Reagan	1986	98–0
Robert Bork	Reagan	1987	Defeated 42–58
Douglas Ginsburg	Reagan	1987	Withdrawn
Anthony Kennedy	Reagan	1988	97–0
David Souter	Bush	1990	90–9
Clarence Thomas	Bush	1991	52–48
Ruth Bader Ginsburg	Clinton	1993	96–3
Stephen G. Breyer	Clinton	1994	87–9

*No recorded vote.

[†]Elevation to Chief Justice.

[‡]Nomination withdrawn after Senate vote failed to end filibuster against nomination; vote was 45 to 43 to end filibuster, and two-thirds majority was required.

Source: Congressional Quarterly, *The Supreme Court: Justice and the Law* (Washington, D.C.: Congressional Quarterly, 1983), p. 179; updated by the author.

Constitution's framers by rolling back some of the Supreme Court's broad interpretations of privacy rights, free speech, and equal protection of the law. Perhaps most controversial were his views on *Roe v. Wade;* he had labeled the Court's striking down of state laws prohibiting abortion as "wholly unjustifiable judicial usurpation of state legislative authority."

Unlike previous nominees, Bork was subjected by the Senate Judiciary Committee to extensive case-by-case questioning in nationally televised confirmation hearings, during which the bearded, scholarly Bork presented a poor TV image. The Democrat-controlled U.S. Senate rejected his nomination. Victory in the Bork battle encouraged liberal interest groups to closely scrutinize the personal lives

The Confirmation of Clarence Thomas

Television coverage of Senate confirmation hearings on Clarence Thomas's appointment to the Supreme Court in 1991 captivated a national audience. The battle pitted blacks against whites (as well as against other blacks), men against women, and liberals against conservatives. The conflict raised just about every "hot-button" issue in American politics, from abortion rights and affirmative action to the most explosive new issue—sexual harassment.

Born to a teenage mother who earned $10 a week as a maid, Clarence Thomas and his brother lived in a dirt-floor shack in Pin Point, Georgia, where they were raised by strict, hardworking grandparents who taught young Clarence the value of education and sacrificed to send him to a Catholic school. He excelled academically and went on to mostly white Immaculate Conception Seminary College in Missouri to study for the Catholic priesthood. But when he overheard a fellow seminarian express satisfaction at the assassination of Dr. Martin Luther King, Jr., Thomas left the seminary in anger and enrolled at Holy Cross College, where he helped found the college's Black Student Union, and went on to graduate with honors and to win admission to Yale Law School.

Upon graduating from Yale, Thomas took a job as assistant attorney general in Missouri and later became a congressional aide to Republican Missouri Senator John Danforth. In 1981 he accepted the post

as head of the Office of Civil Rights in the Department of Education, using the position to speak out on self-reliance, self-discipline, and the value of education. In 1982 he was named chair of the Equal Employment Opportunity Commission (EEOC), where he successfully eliminated much of that agency's financial mismanagement and aggressively pursued individual cases of discrimination. At the same time, he spoke out against racial "quotas" and imposed minority hiring goals only on employers with proven records of discrimination. In 1989 President Bush nominated him to the U.S. Court of Appeals, and he was easily confirmed by the Senate.

In tapping Thomas for the Supreme Court, the White House reasoned that the liberal groups who had blocked the earlier nomination of conservative Robert Bork would be reluctant to launch personal attacks on an African American. With the opposition fractured, the White House saw an opportunity to push a strong conservative nominee through the Democrat-dominated Senate Judiciary Committee and win confirmation by the full Senate.

But behind the scenes, liberal interest groups, including the National Abortion Rights Action League, People for the American Way, and the National Organization for Women, were searching for evidence to discredit Thomas. On the third day of the hearings, a University of Oklahoma law professor, Anita Hill, a former legal assistant to Thomas both at the Department of Education and later at the Equal Employment Opportunity Commission, contacted the staff of the Judiciary Committee with charges that Thomas had

and political views of subsequent nominees. Indeed, the Bork battle set the stage for an even more controversial political struggle—the confirmation of Justice Clarence Thomas (see *Up Close:* "The Confirmation of Clarence Thomas").

WHO IS SELECTED?

What background and experiences are brought to the Supreme Court? Despite often holding very different views on the laws, the Constitution, and their interpretation, the justices of the U.S. Supreme Court tend to share a common background of education at the nation's most prestigious law schools and prior judicial experience.

sexually harassed her in both jobs. Later she went on to give a nationally televised press conference, elaborating on her charges against Thomas. Her bombshell became a media extravaganza.

Thomas himself flatly denied the charges. Appealing to the huge national television audience watching the Senate Judiciary Committee hearings live, he declared, "This is not American; this is Kafkaesque. It has got to stop. It must stop for the benefit of future nominees and our country. Enough is enough." A convincing witness on her own behalf, Anita Hill began by saying that only three months after coming to the civil rights office in the Department of Education, Thomas, who was then single, asked her to go out with him. Hill stated that although she declined, Thomas continued to ask her out and initiated sexual conversations with her that included references to pubic hair, penis size, and sex with animals.

Democrats on the committee treated Hill with great deference, asking her to talk about her feelings and provide even more explicit details of Thomas's alleged misconduct. But Senator Arlen Specter, a Republican moderate with a history of strong support for abortion rights, was not convinced that Hill was telling the truth. Why, he asked, with her legal education and knowledge of civil rights, had she failed to report this harassment? Why did she accept another job at the EEOC from Thomas if she had been harassed by him earlier at the Department of Education? Why had she made many calls to Thomas over the years leaving messages with his secretary such as "Please call."

Given a final opportunity to rebut Hill's charges, Thomas did so very emphatically: "This is a circus. It's a national disgrace. And from my standpoint as a black American, as far as I'm concerned, it is a high-tech lynching for uppity blacks who in any way deign to think for themselves."

In the end, there was no way to determine who was telling the truth, and "truth" in Washington is, at any rate, often determined by opinion polls. An astonishing 86 percent of the general public said they had watched the televised hearings. A majority of blacks as well as whites and a majority of women as well as men sided with the nominee.* In a fitting finale to the bitter and sleazy conflict, the final Senate confirmation vote was 52 to 48, the closest vote in the history of such confirmations. The best that can be said about the affair was that it placed the issue of sexual harassment on the national agenda.

*Gallup Opinion Reports, October 15, 1991, p. 209.

Law Degrees There is no constitutional requirement that Supreme Court justices be attorneys, but every person who has ever served on the High Court has been trained in law. Moreover, a majority of the justices have attended one or another of the nation's most prestigious law schools—Harvard, Yale, and Stanford (see Table 13-3).

Judicial Experience Historically, about half of all Supreme Court justices have been federal or state court judges. Many justices have served some time as U.S. attorneys in the Department of Justice early in their legal careers. Relatively few have held elected political office; among today's justices, only Sandra Day O'Connor ever won an election (to the Arizona state legislature), but one

TABLE 13-3

The Supreme Court

Justice	Age at Appointment	President Who Appointed	Law School	Position at Time of Appointment	Years as a Judge
William H. Rehnquist					
Original appointment	47	Nixon (1971)	Stanford	Asst. Attorney General	0
Chief Justice	61	Reagan (1986)			15
John Paul Stevens	50	Ford (1976)	Northwestern	U.S. Court of Appeals	5
Sandra Day O'Connor	51	Reagan (1981)	Stanford	State Court	6
Antonin Scalia	50	Reagan (1988)	Harvard	U.S. Court of Appeals	4
Anthony M. Kennedy	51	Reagan (1988)	Harvard	U.S. Court of Appeals	12
David H. Souter	50	Bush (1990)	Harvard	State Supreme Court	13
Clarence Thomas	43	Bush (1991)	Yale	U.S. Court of Appeals	2
Ruth Bader Ginsburg	60	Clinton (1993)	Columbia	U.S. Court of Appeals	13
Stephen G. Breyer	56	Clinton (1994)	Harvard	U.S. Court of Appeals	14

chief justice—William Howard Taft—previously held the nation's highest elected post, the presidency.

Age Most justices have been in their fifties when appointed to the Court. Presumably this is the age at which people acquire the necessary prominence and experience to bring themselves to the attention of the White House and Justice Department as potential candidates. At the same time, presidents seek to make a lasting imprint on the Court, and candidates in their fifties can be expected to serve on the Court for many more years than older candidates with the same credentials.

Race and Gender No African American had ever served on the Supreme Court until President Lyndon Johnson's appointment of Thurgood Marshall in 1967. A Howard University Law School graduate, Marshall had served as counsel for the National Association for the Advancement of Colored People Legal Defense Fund and had personally argued the historic *Brown v. Board of Education* case before the Supreme Court in 1954. He served as solicitor general of the United States under President Lyndon Johnson before his elevation to the high court. Upon Marshall's retirement in 1991, President George Bush sought to retain minority representation on the Supreme Court, yet at the same time to reinforce conservative judicial views. His choice of Clarence Thomas created a firestorm of controversy before his eventual confirmation by the U.S. Senate.

No woman had served on the Supreme Court prior to the appointment of Sandra Day O'Connor by President Ronald Reagan in 1981. O'Connor was Reagan's first Supreme Court appointment. Although a relatively unknown Arizona state court judge, she had the powerful support of Arizona Republican Senator Barry Goldwater and Stanford classmate Justice William Rehnquist. The second woman to serve on the high court, Ruth Bader Ginsburg, had served as an attorney for the American Civil Liberties Union while teaching at Columbia Law School and had argued and won several important gender discrimination cases. President Jimmy Carter appointed her in 1980 to the U.S. Court of

Appeals, where she acquired a reputation as a judicial moderate. President Bill Clinton elevated her to the Supreme Court in 1993.

SUPREME COURT DECISION MAKING

The Supreme Court sets its own agenda: it decides what it wants to decide. Of the more than 5,000 requests for hearing that come to its docket each year, the Court issues opinions on only about 200 cases. Another 150 or so cases are decided *summarily* (without opinion) by a Court order either affirming or reversing the lower court decision. The Supreme Court refuses to rule at all on the vast majority of cases that are submitted to it. Thus the rhetorical threat to "take this all the way to the Supreme Court" is usually an empty one. It is important, however, to realize that a refusal to rule also creates law by allowing the decision of the lower court to stand. That is why the U.S. Circuit Courts of Appeals are powerful bodies.

Setting the Agenda: Granting Certiorari   Most cases reach the Supreme Court when a party in a case appeals to the Court to issue a **writ of certiorari** (literally to "make more certain"), a decision by the Court to require a lower federal or state court to turn over its records on a case.[22] To "grant certiorari"— that is, to decide to hear arguments in a case and render a decision—the Supreme Court relies on its *rule of four:* four justices must agree to do so. Deciding which cases to hear takes up a great deal of the Court's time.

What criteria does the Supreme Court use in choosing its policy agenda—that is, in choosing the cases it wishes to decide? The Court rarely explains why it accepts or rejects cases, but there are some general patterns. First, the Court accepts cases involving issues that the justices are interested in. The justices are clearly interested in the area of First Amendment freedoms—speech, press, and religion. Members of the Court are also interested in civil rights issues under the Equal Protection Clause of the Fourteenth Amendment and the civil rights laws and in overseeing the criminal justice system and defining the Due Process Clauses of the Fifth and Fourteenth Amendments.

In addition, the Court seems to feel an obligation to accept cases involving questions that have been decided differently by different circuit courts of appeals. The Supreme Court generally tries to see to it that "the law" does not differ from one circuit to another. Likewise, the Supreme Court usually acts when lower courts have made decisions clearly at odds with Supreme Court interpretations in order to maintain control of the federal judiciary. Finally, the Supreme Court is more likely to accept a case in which the U.S. government is a party and requests a review, especially when an issue appears to be one of overriding importance to the government. In fact, the U.S. government is a party in almost half of the cases decided by the Supreme Court.

Hearing Arguments   Once the Supreme Court places a case on its decision calendar, attorneys for both sides submit written briefs on the issues. The Supreme Court may also allow interest groups to submit **amicus curiae** (literally, "friend of the court") briefs. This process allows interest groups direct access to the Supreme Court. In the affirmative action case of *University of California Regents v. Bakke* (1978),[23] the Court accepted 59 amicus curiae briefs representing more than 100 interest

writ of certiorari   Writ issued by the Supreme Court, at its discretion, to order a lower court to prepare the record of a case and send it to the Supreme Court for review. Most cases come to the Court as petitions for writs of certiorari.

amicus curiae   Literally, "friend of the court"; a person, private group or institution, or government agency that is not a party to a case but participates in the case (usually through submission of a brief) at the invitation of the court or on its own initiative.

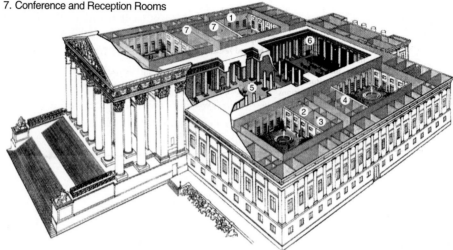

1. Courtyards
2. Solicitor General's Office
3. Lawyers' Lounge
4. Marshall's Office
5. Main Hall
6. Courtroom
7. Conference and Reception Rooms

FIGURE 13-3 Corridors of Power in the Supreme Court

This cutaway shows the location of the principal offices and chambers of the Supreme Court building.

groups. The U.S. government frequently submits amicus curiae arguments in cases in which it is not a party. The **solicitor general** of the United States is responsible for presenting the government's arguments both in cases in which the government is a party and in cases in which the government is merely an amicus curiae.

Oral arguments before the Supreme Court are a time-honored ritual of American government. They take place in the marble "temple"—the Supreme Court building across the street from the U.S. Capitol in Washington, D.C. (see Figure 13-3). The justices, clad in their black robes, sit behind a high "bench" and peer down at the attorneys presenting their arguments. Arguing a case before the Supreme Court is said to be an intimidating experience. Each side is usually limited to either a half-hour or an hour of argument, but justices frequently interrupt with their own pointed questioning. Court watchers sometimes try to predict the Court's decision from the tenor of the questioning. Oral argument is the most public phase of Supreme Court decision making, but no one really knows whether these arguments ever change the justices' minds.

In Conference   The actual decisions are made in private conferences among the justices. These conferences usually take place on Wednesdays and Fridays and cover the cases argued orally during the same week. The Chief Justice (currently William Rehnquist; see *People in Politics:* "William Rehnquist, Leading the Conservative Bloc") presides, and only justices (no law clerks) are present. It is customary for the Chief Justice to speak first on the issues, followed by each associate justice in order of seniority. A majority must decide which party wins or loses and whether a lower court's decision is to be affirmed or reversed.

Writing Opinions   The *written* opinion determines the actual outcome of the case (votes in conference are not binding). When the decision is unanimous, the

solicitor general Attorney in the Department of Justice who represents the U.S. government before the Supreme Court and any other courts.

William Rehnquist, Leading the Conservative Bloc

In the more than two hundred years of Supreme Court history, the Court has contained some of the finest legal minds of its time (as well as its share of less-than-brilliant legalists). Only three men, however, have been "promoted" from the post of associate justice to Chief Justice: Edward D. White (Chief Justice from 1910 to 1921), Harlan F. Stone (Chief Justice from 1941 to 1946), and the current Chief Justice, William H. Rehnquist.

Rehnquist grew up in the affluent Milwaukee suburb of Shorewood, where his mother was a civic activist and local Republican leader. After serving in the Army Air Corps during World War II as a weather observer in North Africa, he took advantage of the G.I. Bill to attend Stanford University, where he graduated Phi Beta Kappa with a degree in political science in 1948. He went on to graduate school at Harvard, earning a master's degree, then returned to Stanford to attend law school, finishing at the top of his class and winning the chance to serve as a clerk for the late Justice Robert H. Jackson, one of the Court's more conservative thinkers. When his internship at the Supreme Court ended, Rehnquist moved to Arizona to begin private practice. In Phoenix, he became active in the Arizona State Republican Party and worked on the presidential campaigns of Barry Goldwater in 1964 and Richard Nixon in 1968.

Following Nixon's election, Rehnquist went to Washington as assistant attorney general. On several occasions, Rehnquist publicly criticized the Supreme Court as having gone too far in protecting the rights of the accused.

When a seat on the Supreme Court became open in 1971, Nixon, who had pledged in his campaign to appoint "judicial conservatives" to the Court, nominated Rehnquist, anticipating that the rela-

tively young conservative (age forty-seven) would serve for a long time. The nomination sparked a debate in the Senate over what Rehnquist's opponents labeled his "ultraconservative" philosophy. Numerous civil rights groups and liberals spoke against him in the Senate Judiciary Committee's hearings, but Rehnquist successfully defended his positions, responding calmly and professionally to hostile questions by Senators Edward Kennedy and Birch Bayh. The Senate voted 68 to 26 in favor of confirming the nomination.

Rehnquist arrived at the Court just as it was beginning to reconcile years of judicial activism under recently retired Chief Justice Earl Warren with the more restrained approach of Chief Justice Warren Burger. But Burger never followed a true conservative or restraintist position; the Chief Justice frequently led the Court in upholding defendants' rights, court-ordered desegregation, and affirmative action plans. As a result, Rehnquist wrote so many "lone dissenting" opinions that his law clerks presented him with a Lone Ranger doll. In *Roe v. Wade* in 1973, Rehnquist wrote in his dissenting opinion (which only Justice Byron White joined) that "Abortion involves the purposeful termination of potential life" and is therefore "beyond the rubric of personal privacy."

Over time Rehnquist began to find additional support on the Court for his positions, not because he had changed but because the Court membership changed. In 1986, after fifteen years on the Court, Rehnquist was nominated by President Reagan to the position of Chief Justice upon Burger's retirement. At the same time, Reagan nominated another strong conservative, Antonin Scalia, to take Rehnquist's seat as associate justice. Again Rehnquist came under sharp attack in the Senate Judiciary Committee, but no one really doubted his brilliance in constitutional law. The Senate tradition of confirming presidential nominees (barring evidence of incompetence or lack of ethics) still held sway, and Rehnquist was confirmed.

With the appointment of this conservative leader to the most conservative Court in fifty years, many observers looked for major changes in the high court's decisions. Instead, Rehnquist has wound up the leader of only the most conservative members on the Court.

Chief Justice traditionally writes the opinion. In the case of a split decision, the Chief Justice may take on the task of writing the **majority opinion** or assign it to another justice in the majority. If the Chief Justice is in the minority, the senior justice in the majority makes the assignment. Writing the opinion of the Court is the central task in Supreme Court policy making. Broadly written opinions may effect sweeping policy changes; narrowly written opinions may decide a particular case but have very little policy impact. The reasons cited for the decision become binding law, to be applied by lower courts in future cases. Yet despite the crucial role of opinion writing in Court policy making, most opinions are actually written by law clerks who are only recent graduates of the nation's prestigious law schools. The justices themselves read, edit, correct, and sometimes rewrite drafts prepared by clerks, but clerks may have a strong influence over the position taken by justices on the issues.

In addition, the views of the legal profession itself—as reflected by the American Bar Association (ABA) as well as the numerous law reviews published by law schools—influence the Court in subtle yet important ways. Often new interpretations of laws or the Constitution first appear in prestigious law journals, then are borrowed by Supreme Court clerks preparing drafts of opinions by justices, and finally become law when incorporated into majority opinions.

A draft of the opinion is circulated among members of the majority. Any majority member who disagrees with the reasoning in the opinion, and thus disagrees with the policy that is proposed, may either negotiate changes in the opinion with others in the majority or write a concurring opinion. A **concurring opinion** agrees with the decision about which party wins the case but sets forth a different reason for the decision, proposing, in fact, a different policy position.

Justices in the minority often agree to present a **dissenting opinion**. The dissenting opinion sets forth the views of justices who disagree with both the decision and the majority reasoning. Dissenting opinions do not have the force of law. They are written both to express opposition to the majority view and to appeal to a future Court to someday modify or reverse the position of the majority. Occasionally, the Court is unable to agree on a clear policy position on particularly vexing questions. If the majority is strongly divided over the reasoning behind their decision and as many as four justices dissent altogether from the decision, lower courts will lack clear guidance and future cases will be decided on a case-by-case basis, depending on multiple factors occurring in each case (see, for example, "Affirmative Action in the Courts" in Chapter 15). The absence of a clear opinion of the Court, supported by a unified majority of the justices, invites additional cases, keeping the issue on the Court's agenda until such time (if any) as the Court establishes a clear policy on the issue.

Voting Blocs   Although liberal and conservative voting blocs on the Court are visible over time, on any given case particular justices may deviate from their perceived ideological position. Many cases do not present a liberal-conservative dimension. Each case presents a separate set of facts, and even justices who share a general philosophy may perceive the central facts of a case differently. Moreover, the liberal-versus-conservative dimension sometimes clashes with the activist-versus-self-restraint dimension. Although we generally think of liberals as favoring activism and conservatives self-restraint, occasionally those who

majority opinion   Opinion in a case that is subscribed to by a majority of the judges who participated in the decision.

concurring opinion   Opinion by a member of a court that agrees with the result reached by the court in the case but disagrees with or departs from the court's rationale for the decision.

dissenting opinion   Opinion by a member of a court that disagrees with the result reached by the court in the case.

	TABLE 13-4	Liberal and Conservative Voting Blocs on the Supreme Court	
	The Warren Court	*The Burger Court*	*The Rehnquist Court*
	1968	1975	1999
Liberal	Earl Warren Hugo Black William O. Douglas Thurgood Marshall William J. Brennan Abe Fortas	William O. Douglas Thurgood Marshall William J. Brennan	John Paul Stevens Ruth Bader Ginsburg Stephen G. Breyer
Moderate	Potter Stewart Byron White	Potter Stewart Byron White Lewis Powell Harry Blackmun	Anthony Kennedy Sandra Day O'Connor David Souter
Conservative	John Marshall Harlan	Warren Burger William Rehnquist	William Rehnquist Antonin Scalia Clarence Thomas

favor self-restraint are obliged to approve of legislation that violates their personal conservative beliefs because opposing it would substitute their judgment for that of elected officials. So ideological blocs are not always good predictors of voting outcomes on the Court.

Over time, the composition of the Supreme Court has changed, as has the power of its various liberal and conservative voting blocs (see Table 13-4). The liberal bloc, headed by Chief Justice Earl Warren, dominated Court decision making from the mid-1950s through the end of the 1960s. The liberal bloc gradually weakened following President Richard Nixon's appointment of Warren Burger as Chief Justice in 1969, but not all of Nixon's appointees joined the conservative bloc; Justice Harry Blackmun and Justice Lewis Powell frequently joined in voting with the liberal bloc. Among Nixon's appointees, only William Rehnquist has consistently adopted conservative positions. President Gerald Ford's only appointee to the Court, John Paul Stevens, began as a moderate and drifted to the liberal bloc. As a result, the Burger Court, although generally not as activist as the Warren Court, still did not reverse any earlier liberal holdings.

President Ronald Reagan, who had campaigned on a pledge to restrain the liberal activism of the Court, tried to appoint conservatives. His first appointee, Sandra Day O'Connor, turned out to be less conservative than expected, especially on women's issues and abortion rights. When Chief Justice Burger retired in 1986, Reagan seized on the opportunity to strengthen the conservative bloc by elevating Rehnquist to Chief Justice and appointing a strong conservative, Antonin Scalia, to the Court. Reagan added Anthony Kennedy to the Court in 1988, giving Rehnquist and the conservative bloc the opportunity to form a majority if they could win over Byron White, a moderately conservative justice and the Court's senior member, having been appointed by President John F. Kennedy in 1962. Had President Reagan succeeded in getting the powerful conservative voice of Robert Bork on the

Privacy, Abortion, and the Constitution

No other issue has generated more emotional, political, and legal controversy for the Supreme Court than abortion. Yet prior to the 1973 Court decision in *Roe v. Wade*, abortion was not a significant issue in American national politics. Since the 1800s, abortions for any purpose other than saving the life of the mother had been criminal offenses under most state laws. About a dozen states acted in the late 1960s to permit abortions in cases of rape or incest or to protect the physical (and, in some cases, mental) health of the mother. Relatively few abortions were performed under these laws, however, because of the red tape involved—review of each case by several concurring physicians, approval of a hospital board, and so forth. Then in 1970, New York, Alaska, Hawaii, and Washington enacted laws that in effect permitted abortion at the request of the woman involved and the concurrence of her physician. During this period, a growing pro-abortion coalition formed, including the American Civil Liberties Union, a new National Association for the Repeal of Abortion Laws, Planned Parenthood, and women's organizations, including the National Organization for Women.

The Right to Privacy Meanwhile, the Supreme Court was developing a new constitutional right—the right of privacy—partly in response to a case brought to it by Planned Parenthood in 1965. When Estelle Griswold opened a birth control clinic on behalf of the Planned Parenthood League of Connecticut, the state found her in violation of a Connecticut law prohibiting the use of contraceptives. She challenged the constitutionality of the statute, and in its ruling in *Griswold v. Connecticut* the Supreme Court struck down the law by a vote of 7 to 2.

Although the majority agreed that a right to privacy could be found in the Constitution, members of the majority could not agree on where it was to be found. Justice Douglas found it in "the penumbras formed by emanations from" the First, Third, Fourth, Ninth, and Fifteenth Amendments. Justices Goldberg, Warren, and Brennan found it in the Ninth Amendment: "The enumeration of the Constitution of certain rights, shall not be contrived to deny or disparage others retained by the people." Justice Harlan found the right in the word "liberty" in the Fourteenth Amendment. The fact that Griswold dealt with reproduction gave encouragement to groups advocating abortion rights.

Roe v. Wade In 1969 Norma McCorvey sought an abortion in Texas, but the doctor refused, citing a state law prohibiting abortion except to save a woman's life. McCorvey bore the child and gave it up for adoption but then enlisted the aid of two young attorneys, Linda Coffee and Sarah Weddington, who challenged the Texas law in federal courts on a variety of constitutional grounds, including the right to privacy. Amicus curiae briefs were filed by a wide assortment of groups on both sides of the issue. McCorvey became "Jane Roe," and the case became one of the most controversial in the Court's history.[1]

Again divided 7 to 2 (despite membership changes), the Supreme Court ruled that the constitutional right of privacy as well as the Fourteenth Amendment's guarantee of "liberty" included a woman's decision to bear or not to bear a child. The Court ruled that the word "person" in the Constitution did not include the unborn child; therefore, the Fifth and Fourteenth Amendments' guarantee of "life, liberty, or property" did not protect the "life" of the fetus. The Court also ruled that a state's power to protect the health and safety of the mother could not justify any restriction on abortion in the first three months of pregnancy. Between the third and sixth months of pregnancy, a state could set standards for abortion procedures in order to protect the health of women, but a state could not prohibit abortions. Only in the final three months could a state prohibit or regulate abortion to protect the unborn.

Rather than end the political controversy over abortion, *Roe v. Wade* set off a conflagration. A new movement was mobilized to restrict the scope of the decision and if possible to bring about its overturn. Congress defeated efforts to pass a constitutional amendment restricting abortion or declaring that life begins at conception. However, when Congress banned the use of federal funds under Medicaid (medical care for the poor) for abortions except to protect the life of a woman, the Supreme Court upheld the ban, holding that there was no constitutional obligation for governments to pay for abortions.[2]

The Battle over Restrictions Initial efforts by some states to restrict abortion ran into Supreme Court opposition. But opponents of abortion won a victory in *Webster v. Reproductive Health Services* in 1989.[3]

Pro-life and pro-choice activists confront each other outside the Supreme Court in 1992 after the justices issued their ruling in Planned Parenthood of Pennsylvania v. Casey.

In this case, the Supreme Court upheld a Missouri law denying the use of public facilities or employees in performing or assisting in abortions. More important, the justices recognized the state's "interest in the protection of human life when viability is possible" and upheld Missouri's requirement for a test of "viability" after twenty weeks and a prohibition on abortions of a viable fetus except to save a woman's life. The vote on *Webster* was a signal to pro-life groups that the Supreme Court's position might be changing.

Reaffirming Roe v. Wade   Abortion has become such a polarizing issue that "pro-choice" and "pro-life" groups are generally unwilling to search out a middle ground. Yet the current Supreme Court appears to have chosen a policy of affirming a woman's right to abortion while upholding modest restrictions, as evidenced by the Court's ruling in *Planned Parenthood of Pennsylvania v. Casey* (1992).[4]

In this case, the Supreme Court considered a series of restrictions on abortion enacted by Pennsylvania: that physicians must inform women of risks and alternatives; that women must wait twenty-four hours after requesting an abortion before having one; and that minors must have the consent of parents or a judge. It struck down the requirement that spouses be notified.

Justice Sandra Day O'Connor took the lead in forming a moderate, swing bloc on the Court, consisting of herself, Anthony Kennedy, and David Souter. (Harry A. Blackmun and John Paul Stevens voted to uphold *Roe v. Wade* with *no* restrictions, making the vote 5 to 4.) Her majority opinion strongly reaffirmed the fundamental right of abortion, both on the basis of the Fourteenth Amendment and on the principle of stare decisis. But the majority also upheld states' rights to protect any fetus that reached the point of "viability." The Court went on to establish a new standard for constitutionally evaluating restrictions: they must not impose an "undue burden" on women seeking abortion or place "substantial obstacles" in her path. All of Pennsylvania's restrictions met this standard and were upheld except spousal notification.

Despite outcries from both pro-choice and pro-life forces, the *Casey* decision puts the Supreme Court almost exactly where opinion polls suggest most Americans are: generally supporting a woman's right to choose an abortion early in pregnancy but also supporting many restrictions on the exercise of that right.

---

[1] *Roe v. Wade,* 410 U.S. 113 (1973).

[2] *Harris v. McRae,* 448 U.S. 297 (1980).

[3] *Webster v. Reproductive Health Services,* 492 U.S. 490 (1989).

[4] *Planned Parenthood v. Casey,* 510 U.S. 110 (1992).

Court, it is possible that many earlier liberal decisions, including *Roe v. Wade,* would have been reversed. But the Senate rejected Bork; David Souter, the man ultimately confirmed, compiled a moderate record.

Liberals worried that the appointment of conservative Clarence Thomas as a replacement for the liberal Thurgood Marshall would give the conservative bloc a commanding voice in Supreme Court policy making. But no solid conservative majority emerged. Justices Rehnquist, Scalia, and Thomas are considered the core of the conservative bloc, but they must win over at least two of the more moderate justices in order to form a majority in a case. President Bill Clinton's appointees, Ruth Bader Ginsburg and Stephen G. Breyer, came to the Court with reputations as moderate judges, but they have generally supported liberal views on the Supreme Court. On key questions, the moderate bloc has the deciding vote (see *Up Close:* "Privacy, Abortion, and the Constitution").

CHECKING COURT POWER

Many people are concerned about the extent to which we now rely on a nonelected judiciary to decide key policy issues rather than depending on a democratically elected president or Congress.

Legitimacy as a Restraint in the Judiciary   Court authority derives from legitimacy rather than force. By that we mean that the courts depend on their authority being seen as rightful, on people perceiving an obligation to abide by court decisions whether they agree with them or not. The courts have no significant force at their direct command. Federal marshals, who carry out the orders of federal courts, number only a few thousand. Courts must rely primarily on the executive branch for enforcement of their decisions.

Today most Americans believe that Supreme Court decisions are authoritative statements about the Constitution and that people have an obligation to obey these decisions whether they agree with them or not. Thus public opinion constrains other public officials—from the president, to governors, to school superintendents, to law enforcement officials—to obey Supreme Court decisions. Their constituents do not hold them personally responsible for unpopular actions ordered by the Supreme Court or federal judges. On the contrary, their constituents generally expect them to comply with court decisions.

The institutional legitimacy of the federal courts was tested in the civil rights battles of the 1950s and 1960s. In 1957 Governor Orval Faubus of Arkansas used state National Guard troops to halt federal marshals from escorting black students into a segregated Little Rock high school pursuant to a federal court order. President Dwight Eisenhower had his personal doubts about the wisdom of federal court-ordered desegregation, but the governor's open defiance of a federal court order could not be tolerated by a president sworn "to preserve, protect, and defend the Constitution of the United States." Eisenhower ordered U.S. Army troops to Little Rock to enforce the federal court's order, a decision that proved a historic turning point in the civil rights movement. But Eisenhower's decision also greatly strengthened federal courts, ensuring that the full force of the federal government would be used to gain compliance with their decisions.

Widespread opposition to Supreme Court policy can obstruct and delay its implementation. For example, the Supreme Court's 1963 ruling that prayer and

Bible-reading exercises in public schools violated the No Establishment Clause of the First Amendment was very unpopular (see Chapter 14). Many public school systems simply ignored the decision. Enforcement required individuals or groups in school districts throughout the country to bring separate suits in federal courts. In school districts where no one strongly objected to prayer or where objectors did not have the will or resources to bring suit against school officials, the practice continued. Congress did not feel disposed to cut off federal funds to schools that allowed prayer, and the president was not disposed to send federal troops into the schools to halt Bible reading. Only gradually were prayers and other religious observances deleted from public school exercises.

Compliance with Court Policy   Federal and state court judges must apply Supreme Court policies when ruling on cases in their own courts.[24] Occasionally lower courts express their disagreement with the Supreme Court in an opinion, even when they feel obliged to carry out the High Court's policy. At times, lower federal and state courts try to give a narrow interpretation to a Supreme Court decision with which they disagree. But judges who seek to defy the Supreme Court face the ultimate sanction of reversal on appeal by the losing party. Professional pride usually inspires judges to avoid reversals of their judgments by higher courts even though a long record of reversals is not grounds for impeachment or removal of a federal judge.

Public officials who defy Supreme Court rulings risk lawsuits and court orders mandating compliance. Persons injured by noncompliance are likely to file suit against noncomplying officials, as are interest groups that monitor official compliance with the policies they support. These suits are expensive, time consuming, and potentially embarrassing to government officials and agencies. Once a court order is issued, continued defiance can result in fines and penalties for contempt of court.

The president of the United States is subject to federal court orders. Historically, this notion has been challenged: early presidents believed they were separate and at least co-equal to the courts and that their own determination about the legality or constitutionality of their own acts could not be overturned by the courts. President Andrew Jackson could—and did—say: "John Marshall has made his decision. Now let him enforce it," expressing the view that the president was not obliged to enforce court decisions he disagreed with.[25] But in the course of 200 years, the courts—not the president—have gained in legitimacy as the final authority on the law and the Constitution. Today a president who openly defied the Supreme Court would lose any claims to legitimacy and would risk impeachment by Congress.

The case of Richard Nixon illustrates the weakness of a modern president who would even consider defying the Supreme Court. When Nixon sought to invoke executive privilege to withhold damaging tapes of White House conversations in the Watergate investigation (see *Up Close:* "Watergate and the Limits of Presidential Power" in Chapter 11), federal district judge John Sirica rejected his claim and ordered that the tapes be turned over to the special prosecutor in the case. In arguments before the Supreme Court, Nixon's lawyers contended that the president would not have to comply with a Supreme Court decision to turn over the tapes. Yet when the Court ruled unanimously against him, Nixon felt bound to comply and released tapes that were very damaging to his cause. But Nixon understood that refusal to abide by a Supreme Court decision would most

Politics in Cyberspace

The Judiciary

The Federal Judiciary
www.uscourts.gov

The judicial branch of the U.S. government maintains a site, which is a clearinghouse of information about all federal courts.

Cornell University Law School
www.law.cornell.edu

The decisions of the U.S. Supreme Court can be found at many sites. This site, one of the most frequently used, includes all opinions of the Supreme Court since 1990, plus a collection of the most important historical decisions of the Court. Decisions can be accessed by name, topic, or date.

Lexis/Nexis

Most law firms have direct access to commercial online services, notably Lexis/Nexis, to assist their attorneys in legal research. Lexis/Nexis provides paying subscribers access to full texts of federal and state cases, statutes, regulations, and public records. Most law schools now subscribe to Lexis/Nexis and provide their students with access to it.

assuredly have resulted in impeachment. Under the circumstances, compliance was the better of two unattractive choices.[26]

Presidential Influence on Court Policy   The president and Congress can exercise some restraint over court power through the checks and balances built into the Constitution. Using the office's powers of appointment, presidents have effectively modified the direction of Supreme Court policy and influenced lower federal courts as well. Certainly presidents must await the death or retirement of Supreme Court justices and federal judges, and presidents are constrained by the need to secure Senate confirmation of their appointees. However, over time presidential influence on the courts can be significant. During their combined twelve years in the White House, Ronald Reagan and George Bush were able to fill 70 percent of federal district and appellate court judgeships and six of nine Supreme Court positions with their own appointees. As noted earlier, however, their appointees did not always reflect these presidents' philosophy of judicial self-restraint in rendering decisions. Nevertheless, the federal courts tilted in a somewhat more conservative direction. President Bill Clinton's appointments generally strengthened liberal, activist impulses throughout the federal judiciary.

Congressional Checks on the Judiciary   The Constitution gives Congress control over the structure and jurisdiction of federal district and appellate courts, but congressional use of this control has been restrained. Only the Supreme Court is established by the Constitution; Article III gives Congress the power to "ordain and establish" "inferior" courts. In theory, Congress could try to limit court jurisdiction to hear cases that Congress did not wish it to decide. Congress has used this power to lighten the federal courts' workload; for example, Congress has limited the jurisdiction of federal courts in cases between citizens of different states by requiring that the dispute involve more than $50,000. But Congress has never used this power to change court policy—for example, by removing federal court jurisdiction over school prayer cases or desegregation cases. Indeed federal courts would probably declare unconstitutional any congressional attempt to limit their power to interpret the Constitution by limiting jurisdiction.

Likewise, although Congress could, in theory, expand membership on the Supreme Court, the custom of a nine-member Supreme Court is now so deeply ingrained in American government that "court packing" is politically unthinkable. Franklin Roosevelt's unsuccessful 1937 attempt to expand the Supreme Court was the last serious assault on its membership. However, President Jimmy Carter succeeded in getting Congress to add a large number of federal district judgeships, and he used these new posts to appoint more women and minorities to the federal judiciary.

A more common congressional constraint on the Supreme Court is amending statutory laws to reverse federal court interpretations of these laws that Congress believes are in error. Thus when the Supreme Court decided that civil rights laws did not mandate a cutoff of all federal funds to a college upon evidence of discrimination in a single program but only the funds for that program,[27] Congress amended its own laws to require the more sweeping remedy. Likewise, when the Supreme Court ruled that existing civil rights legislation put the burden of proof of discrimination on plaintiffs rather than employers, Congress passed the Civil Rights Act of 1991, which requires employers to show why tests and other recruitment practices are a "business necessity." Although members of Congress frequently berate the Court for what they see as misreading of the laws, all Congress needs to do to reverse a Court interpretation of those laws is to pass amendments to them.

Constitutional amendment is the only means by which the Congress and the states can reverse a Supreme Court interpretation of the Constitution itself. After the Civil War, the Thirteenth Amendment abolishing slavery reversed the Supreme Court's *Dred Scott* decision (1857) that slavery was constitutionally protected. The Sixteenth Amendment (1913) gave Congress the power to impose an income tax, thus reversing the Supreme Court's earlier decision in *Pollock v. Farmer's Loan*[28] holding income taxes illegal (1895). But recent attempts to reverse Supreme Court interpretations of the Constitution by passing constitutional amendments on the issues of prayer in public schools, busing, and abortion have all failed to win congressional approval. The barriers to a constitutional amendment are formidable: a two-thirds vote of both houses of Congress and ratification by three-quarters of the states. Thus for all practical purposes, the Constitution is what the Supreme Court says it is.

Congress can impeach federal court judges, but only for committing crimes, not for their decisions. Although impeachment is frequently cited as a constitutional check on the judiciary, it has no real influence over judicial policy making. Only five federal court judges have ever been impeached by the House, convicted by the Senate, and removed from office, although two others were impeached and another nine resigned to avoid impeachment. In 1989 Federal District Court Judge Alcee Hastings became the first sitting judge in more than fifty years to be impeached, tried, and found guilty by the Congress. He was convicted by the Senate of perjury and conspiracy to obtain a $150,000 bribe; but a federal district court judge ruled that he should have been tried by the full Senate, not a special committee of the Senate. Hastings declared the ruling a vindication; in 1992 he won a congressional seat in Florida, becoming the first person ever to become a member of the House after being impeached by that same body. Even criminal convictions do not ensure removal from office, although judges have resigned under fire.

- Great power is lodged in the Supreme Court of the United States and the federal judiciary. These courts have undertaken to resolve many of the most divisive conflicts in American society. The judicial power is the power to decide cases and controversies, and in so doing to decide the meaning of the Constitution and laws of Congress.

- The power of judicial review is the power to invalidate laws of Congress or of the states that the federal courts believe conflict with the U.S. Constitution. This power is not specifically mentioned in the Constitution but was derived by Chief Justice John Marshall from the Supremacy Clause and the meaning of judicial power in Article III.

- The Supreme Court has been fairly restrained in its use of judicial review with regard to laws of Congress and actions of presidents; it has more frequently overturned state laws. The federal courts also exercise great power in the interpretation of the laws of Congress, especially when statutory language is vague.

- Arguments over judicial power are reflected in the conflicting philosophies of judicial activism and judicial self-restraint. Advocates of judicial restraint argue that judges must not substitute their own views for those of elected representatives and the remedy for unwise laws lies in the legislature, not the courts. Advocates of judicial activism argue that the courts must view the Constitution as a living document and its meaning must fit the needs of a changing society.

- The federal judiciary consists of three levels of courts—the Supreme Court, the U.S. Courts of Appeals, and the U.S. District Courts. The district courts are trial courts that hear both civil and criminal cases. The courts of appeals are appellate courts and do not hold trials but consider only the record of trial courts and the arguments (briefs) of attorneys. More than 90 percent of federal cases end in appeals courts. The Supreme Court can hear appeals from state high courts as well as lower federal courts. The Supreme Court hears only about 200 cases a year.

- Courts function under general rules of restraint that do not bind the president or Congress. The Supreme Court does not decide hypothetical cases or render advisory opinions. The principle of stare decisis, or reliance on precedent, is not set aside lightly.

- In the wake of the Watergate scandal, Congress passed an Ethics in Government Act in 1978 authorizing federal courts, upon application by the attorney general, to appoint independent counsels (special prosecutors) to investigate allegations against the president or other high federal officials. The intent of the law was to take politics out of the investigation of the highest officials, but the record of special prosecutors suggests that politics nonetheless drives many investigations.

- The selection of Supreme Court justices and federal judges is based more on political considerations than legal qualifications. Presidents almost always appoint judges from their own party, and presidents increasingly have sought judges who share their ideological views. However, because of the independence of judges once they are appointed, presidents have sometimes been disappointed in the decisions of their appointees. In addition, Senate approval of nominees has become increasingly politicized, with problems most evident when different parties control the White House and the Senate.

- The Supreme Court sets its own agenda for policy making, usually by granting or withholding certiorari. Generally four justices must agree to grant certiorari for a case to be decided by the Supreme Court. The Supreme Court has been especially active in policy making in interpreting the meaning of the Fourteenth Amendment's guarantee of "equal protection of the laws," as well as of the civil rights and voting rights acts of Congress. It has also been active in defining the meaning of freedom of press, speech, and religion in the First Amendment and "due process of law" in the Fifth Amendment. The federal courts are active in overseeing government regulatory activity. But federal courts have generally left the areas of national security and international relations to the president and Congress. In addition, the Court tends to accept cases involving questions decided differently by different courts of appeal, cases in which lower courts have challenged Supreme Court interpretations, and cases in which the U.S. government is a party and it requests review.

- Liberal and conservative blocs on the Supreme Court can be discerned over time. Generally, liberals have been judicial activists and conservatives have been restraintists. Today a moderate bloc appears to hold the balance of power.

- Court power derives primarily from legitimacy rather than force. Most Americans believe that Supreme Court decisions are authoritative statements about the Constitution and people have an obligation to obey these decisions whether they agree with them or not. Although early presidents thought of themselves as constitutional co-equals with the Supreme Court and not necessarily bound by Court decisions, today it would be politically unthinkable for a president to ignore a court order.

- There are very few checks on Supreme Court power. Presidents may try to influence Court policy through judicial nominations, but once judges are confirmed by the Senate they can pursue their own impulses. Congress has never tried to use its power to limit the jurisdiction of federal courts in order to influence judicial decisions.

- Only by amending the Constitution can Congress and the states reverse a Supreme Court interpretation of its meaning. Congress can impeach federal judges only for committing crimes, not for their decisions.

SELECTED READINGS

ABRAHAM, HENRY J. *The Judicial Process*. 6th ed. New York: Oxford University Press, 1993. Comprehensive survey of judicial politics and processes in the United States, England, and France. Provides an introduction to the nature and sources of law, as well as the organization, functioning, and staffing of the courts.

BAUM, LAWRENCE. *The Supreme Court*. 6th ed. Washington, D.C.: CQ Press, 1997. Readable introduction to the Supreme Court as a political institution, covering the selection and confirmation of judges, the nature of the issues decided by courts, the process of judicial decision making, and the impact of Supreme Court decisions.

CARP, ROBERT A., and RONALD AIDHAM. *The Federal Courts*. 3rd ed. Washington, D.C.: CQ Press, 1998. Overview of the federal judicial system, arguing that federal judges and Supreme Court justices function as part of the political system and engage in policy making that influences all our lives.

EPSTEIN, LEE, and JACK KNIGHT. *The Choices Justices Make*. Washington, D.C.: CQ Press, 1998. Account of the U.S. Supreme Court's strategic political decision making based on both public records and the private papers of justices.

NAGEL, ROBERT F. *Judicial Power and American Character*. New York: Oxford University Press, 1994. Critique of judicial reasoning as a mask for the exercise of power.

SCHWARTZ, BERNARD. *A History of the Supreme Court*. New York: Oxford University Press, 1995. Comprehensive one-volume history of the nation's highest court and the influence the Court has had on American politics and society.

U.S. Supreme Court decisions are available at most public and university libraries as well as at law libraries in volumes of *United States Reports*. Court opinions are cited by the names of the parties, for example, *Brown v. Board of Education of Topeka*, followed by a reference number such as 347 U.S. 483 (1954). The first number in the citation (347) is the volume number; "U.S." refers to *United States Reports*; the subsequent number is the page on which the decision begins; the year the case was decided is in parentheses.

Congress OF THE United ...

begun and held at the City of New-York, on

Wednesday the fourth of March, one thousand seven hundred and ...

THE *Conventions of a number of the States, having at the time of their adopting the Con...*

or abuse of its powers, that further declaratory and restrictive clauses should be added: And as extending the ground of public confidence in the G...

RESOLVED *by the Senate and House of Representatives of the United States...*

concurring that the following Articles be proposed to the Legislatures of the several States, as amendments to the Constitution of the United States...

said Legislatures, to be valid to all intents and purposes, as part of the said Constitution; viz.

ARTICLES *in addition to, and amendment of the Constitution of the United States...*

of the several States, pursuant to the fifth Article of the original Constitution.

Article the first.... After the first enumeration required by the first Article of the Constitution, there shall be one Representative for every thirty thou...
which, the proportion shall be so regulated by Congress, that there shall be not less than one hundred Representatives...
until the number of Representatives shall amount to two hundred; after which the proportion shall be so regulated by Congr...
nor more than one Representative for every fifty thousand persons.

Article the second... No law, varying the compensation for the services of the Senators and Representatives, shall take effect, until an election of Re...

Article the third..... Congress shall make no law respecting an establishment of religion, or prohibiting the free exercise thereof; or abridging the freedo...
assemble, and to petition the Government for a redress of grievances

Article the fourth.... A well regulated militia, being necessary to the security of a free State, the right of the people to keep and bear Arms, sha...

Article the fifth...... No Soldier shall, in time of peace be quartered in any house, without the consent of the owner, nor in time of war, but in a...

Article the sixth..... The right of the people to be secure in their persons, houses, papers, and effects, against unreasonable searches and seizures...

ASK YOURSELF ABOUT POLITICS

1 Do you think the government has become so large and powerful that it poses a threat to the rights and freedoms of ordinary citizens?
Yes ☐   No ☐

2 Do you believe that using tax funds to pay tuition at church-affiliated schools violates the separation of church and state?
Yes ☐   No ☐

3 Do we have a constitutional right to physician-assisted suicide?
Yes ☐   No ☐

4 Should we have the right to burn the American flag?
Yes ☐   No ☐

5 Should federal or local governments be able to censor what motion pictures are shown in public theaters?
Yes ☐   No ☐

6 Should organizations like the Ku Klux Klan and the American Nazi Party be permitted to hold marches and rallies?
Yes ☐   No ☐

7 Do law-abiding citizens have a constitutional right to carry a handgun for self-protection?
Yes ☐   No ☐

8 Is the death penalty a "cruel and unusual" punishment?
Yes ☐   No ☐

Government power defends your most basic rights to life, liberty, and the pursuit of happiness while at the same time ensuring that all other Americans have the same rights. The Founders guaranteed individual liberty in the earliest days of our nation through the first ten amendments to the Constitution—our Bill of Rights.

POWER AND INDIVIDUAL LIBERTY

To the authors of the Declaration of Independence, individual liberty was inherent in the human condition. It was not derived from governments or even from constitutions. Rather, governments and constitutions existed to make individual liberty more secure:

We hold these truths to be self-evident, that all men are created equal, that they are endowed by their Creator with certain unalienable Rights, that among these are Life, Liberty and the pursuit of Happiness. That to secure these rights, Governments are instituted among Men, deriving their just powers from the consent of the governed.

Authority and Liberty   To avoid the brutal life of a lawless society, where the weak are at the mercy of the strong, people form governments and endow them with powers to secure peace and self-preservation (see *People and Politics:* "Thomas Hobbes and the Need for Leviathan" in Chapter 1). People voluntarily relinquish some of their individual freedom to establish a government that is capable of protecting them from their neighbors as well as from foreign aggressors. This government must be strong enough to maintain its own existence or it cannot defend the rights of its citizens.

But what happens when a government becomes too strong and infringes on the liberties of its citizens? How much liberty must individuals surrender to secure an orderly society? This is the classic dilemma of free government: people must create laws and governments to protect their freedom, but the laws and governments themselves restrict freedom.

Democracy and Personal Liberty   When democracy is defined only as a *decision-making process*—widespread popular participation and rule by majority—it offers little protection for individual liberty. Democracy must also be defined to include *substantive values*—a recognition of the dignity of all individuals and their equality under law. Otherwise, some people, particularly "the weaker party, or an obnoxious individual" would be vulnerable to deprivations of life, liberty, or property simply by decisions of majorities (see "The Paradox of Democracy" in Chapter 1). Indeed, the "great object" of the Constitution, according to James Madison, was to preserve popular government yet at the same time to protect individuals from "unjust" majorities.[1]

The purpose of the Constitution—and especially its Bill of Rights, the first ten amendments, passed by the First Congress in September 1789 and ratified by the states—is to limit governmental power over the individual, that is, to place personal liberty beyond the reach of government (see Table 14-1). Each individual's rights to life, liberty, and property, due process of law, and equal protection of the law are not subject to majority vote. Or, as Supreme Court Justice Robert Jackson once declared,

> The very purpose of a Bill of Rights was to withdraw certain subjects from the vicissitudes of political controversy, to place them beyond the reach of majorities and officials, and to establish them as legal principles to be applied by the courts. One's right to life, liberty, and property, to free speech, a free press, freedom of worship and assembly, and other fundamental rights may not be submitted to vote: they depend on the outcome of no elections.[2]

Nationalizing the Bill of Rights   The Bill of Rights begins with the words "*Congress* shall make no law . . . ," indicating that it was originally intended to limit only the powers of the federal government. The Bill of Rights was added to the Constitution because of fear that the *federal* government might become too powerful and encroach on individual liberty. But what about encroachments by state and local governments and their officials? For more than one hundred years, the U.S. Supreme Court, reflecting what it saw as the intentions of the framers, refused to

TABLE 14-1	Constitutionally Protected Rights

The Bill of Rights

The first ten amendments to the Constitution of the United States, passed by the First Congress of the United States in September 1789 and ratified by the states in December 1791.

Amendments	Protections
First Amendment: Religion, Speech, Press, Assembly, Petition Congress shall make no law respecting an establishment of religion, or prohibiting the free exercise thereof; or abridging the freedom of speech, or of the press; or the right of the people peaceably to assemble, and to petition the Government for a redress of grievances.	Prohibits government establishment of religion. Protects the free exercise of religion. Protects freedom of speech. Protects freedom of the press. Protects freedom of assembly. Protects the right to petition government "for a redress of grievances."
Second Amendment: Right to Bear Arms A well regulated Militia, being necessary to the security of a free State, the right of the people to keep and bear Arms, shall not be infringed.	Protects the right of people to bear arms and states to maintain militia (National Guard) units.
Third Amendment: Quartering of Soldiers No Soldier shall, in time of peace, be quartered in any house, without the consent of the Owner, nor in time of war, but in a manner to be prescribed by law.	Prohibits forcible quartering of soldiers in private homes in peacetime, or in war without congressional authorization.
Fourth Amendment: Searches and Seizures The right of the people to be secure in their persons, houses, papers, and effects, against unreasonable searches and seizures, shall not be violated, and no Warrants shall issue, but upon probable cause, supported by Oath or affirmation, and particularly describing the place to be searched, and the persons or things to be seized.	Protects against "unreasonable searches and seizures." Requires warrants for searches of homes and other places where there is a reasonable expectation of privacy. Judges may issue search warrants only with "probable cause"; and such warrants must be specific regarding the place to be searched and the things to be seized.
Fifth Amendment: Grand Juries, Double Jeopardy, Self-Incrimination, Due Process, Protection against Government Takings of Property No person shall be held to answer for a capital, or otherwise infamous crime, unless on a presentment or indictment of a Grand jury, except in cases arising in the land or naval forces, or in the Militia, when in actual service in time of war or public danger; nor shall any person be subject for the same offence to be twice put in jeopardy of life or limb; nor shall he be compelled in any criminal case to be a witness against himself, nor be deprived of life, liberty, or property, without due process of law; nor shall private property be taken for public use, without just compensation.	Requires that, before trial for a serious crime, a person (except military personnel) must be indicted by a grand jury. Prohibits double jeopardy (trial for the same offense a second time after being found innocent). Prohibits the government from forcing any person in a criminal case to be a witness against himself or herself. Prohibits the government from taking life, liberty, or property "without due process of law." Prohibits government from taking private property without paying "just compensation."
Sixth Amendment: Fair Trial In all criminal prosecutions, the accused shall enjoy the right to a speedy and public trial, by an impartial jury of the State and district wherein the crime shall have been committed, which district shall have been previously ascertained by law, and to be informed of the nature and cause of the accusation; to be confronted with the witnesses against him; to have compulsory process for obtaining witnesses in his favor, and to have the Assistance of Counsel for his defense.	Requires that the accused in a criminal case be given a speedy and public trial, and thus prohibits prolonged incarceration without trial or secret trials. Requires that trials be by jury and take place in the district where the crime was committed. Requires that the accused be informed of the charges, have the right to confront witnesses, have the right to force supporting witnesses to testify, and have the assistance of counsel.

TABLE 14-1   **Constitutionally Protected Rights** *(continued)*

Amendments	*Protections*
Seventh Amendment: Trial by Jury in Civil Cases In Suits at common law, where the value in controversy shall exceed twenty dollars, the right of trial by jury shall be preserved, and no fact tried by a jury, shall be otherwise reexamined in any Court of the United States, than according to the rules of the common law.	Requires a jury trial in civil cases involving more than $20. Limits the degree to which factual questions decided by a jury may be reviewed by another court.
Eighth Amendment: Bail, Fines and Punishment Excessive bail shall not be required, nor excessive fines imposed, nor cruel and unusual punishments inflicted.	Prohibits excessive bail. Prohibits excessive fines. Prohibits cruel and unusual punishment.
Ninth Amendment: Unspecified Rights Retained by People The enumeration in the Constitution, of certain rights, shall not be construed to deny or disparage others retained by the people.	Protection of unspecified rights (including privacy) that are not listed in the Constitution. The Constitution shall not be interpreted to be a complete list of rights retained by the people.
Tenth Amendment: Rights Reserved to the States The powers not delegated to the United States by the Constitution, nor prohibited by it to the States, are reserved to the States respectively, or to the people.	States retain powers that are not granted by the Constitution to the national government or prohibited by it to the states.

Rights in the Text of the Constitution

Several rights were written into the text of the Constitution in 1787 and thus precede in time the adoption of the Bill of Rights.

Article I Section 9: Habeas Corpus, Bills of Attainder, and Ex Post Facto Laws The privilege of the Writ of Habeas Corpus shall not be suspended, unless when in Cases of Rebellion or Invasion the public Safety may require it. No Bill of Attainder or ex post facto Law shall be passed.	Habeas corpus prevents imprisonment without a judge's determination that a person is being lawfully detained. Prohibition of bills of attainder prevents Congress (and states) from deciding people guilty of a crime and imposing punishment without trial. Prohibition of ex post facto laws prevents Congress (and states) from declaring acts to be criminal that were committed before the passage of a law making them so.

Thirteenth and Fourteenth Amendments

The Bill of Rights begins with the words "Congress shall make no law . . ." indicating that it initially applied only to the *federal* government. Although states had their own constitutions that guarantee many of the same rights, for more than a century the Bill of Rights did not apply to state and local governments. Following the Civil War, the Thirteenth, Fourteenth, and Fifteenth (voting rights) Amendments were passed, restricting *state* governments and their local subdivisions. But not until many years later did the U.S. Supreme Court, in a long series of decisions, apply the Bill of Rights against the states.

Thirteenth Amendment Neither slavery nor involuntary servitude, except as a punishment for crime whereof the party shall have been duly convicted, shall exist within the United States, or any place subject to their jurisdiction.	Prohibits slavery or involuntary servitude except for punishment by law; applies to both governments and private citizens.
Fourteenth Amendment All persons born or naturalized in the United States, and subject to the jurisdiction thereof, are citizens of the United States and of the State wherein they reside. No State shall make or enforce any law which shall abridge the privileges or immunities of citizens of the United States; nor shall any State deprive any person of life, liberty, or property, without due process of law; nor deny to any person within its jurisdiction the equal protection of the laws.	Protects "privileges and immunities of citizenship." Prevents deprivation of life, liberty, or property "without due process of law"; this phrase incorporates virtually all of the rights specified in the Bill of Rights. Prevents denial of "equal protection of the laws" for all persons.

make the protections of the Bill of Rights binding on state and local governments. States had their own constitutions with many of the same rights, but state constitutions were enforceable only in state courts.[3]

With the addition of the Fourteenth Amendment to the Constitution following the Civil War, the question of the applicability of the Bill of Rights to the states arose anew. The Fourteenth Amendment includes the words "No State shall . . ."; its provisions are directed specifically at states. This amendment was designed to secure equality for newly freed slaves, but its provisions guaranteed that no one could be denied "the privileges or immunities of citizens," "life, liberty, or property," "due process of law," or "equal protection of the laws." Do these general phrases incorporate the protections of the Bill of Rights—make them applicable against *state* actions?

Initially, the U.S. Supreme Court rejected the argument that the Privileges or Immunities Clause[4] and the Due Process Clause[5] incorporated the Bill of Rights. But beginning in the 1920s, the Court handed down a long series of decisions that gradually brought about the **incorporation** of almost all of the protections of the Bill of Rights into the "liberty" guaranteed against state actions by the Due Process Clause of the Fourteenth Amendment. In *Gitlow v. New York* (1925), the Court ruled that "freedom of speech and of the press—which are protected by the First Amendment from abridgment by Congress—are among the fundamental personal rights and liberties protected by the due process clause of the Fourteenth Amendment from impairment by the states."[6] Over time, the Court applied the same reasoning in incorporating almost all provisions of the Bill of Rights into the Fourteenth Amendment's Due Process Clause (see Table 14-2).

FREEDOM OF RELIGION

Americans are a very religious people. Belief in God and church attendance are more widespread in the United States than in any other advanced industrialized nation.

incorporation In constitutional law, the application of almost all of the Bill of Rights to the states through the Fourteenth Amendment.

TABLE 14-2	The Nationalization of the Bill of Rights		
Year	Amendment	Protection	Case
1925	First	Freedom of speech	*Gitlow v. New York*
1931	First	Freedom of press	*Near v. Minnesota*
1932	Sixth	Rights to counsel in capital cases	*Powell v. Alabama*
1937	First	Freedom of assembly	*DeJonge v. Oregon*
1940	First	Free exercise of religion	*Cantwell v. Connecticut*
1947	First	No establishment of religion	*Everson v. Board of Education*
1948	Sixth	Public trial	*In re Oliver*
1949	Fourth	No unreasonable searches and seizures	*Wolf v. Colorado*
1962	Eighth	No cruel and unusual punishments	*Robinson v. California*
1963	Sixth	Right to counsel in felony cases	*Gideon v. Wainwright*
1964	Fifth	Freedom from self-incrimination	*Malloy v. Hagan*
1967	Sixth	Speedy trial	*Klopfer v. North Carolina*
1968	Sixth	Jury trial in all criminal cases	*Duncan v. Louisiana*
1969	Fifth	No double jeopardy	*Benton v. Maryland*

In 1990 the Supreme Court ruled against two Native Americans who had been fired from their jobs as drug counselors for taking peyote during religious ceremonies of the Native American Church. The Court maintained that the Free Exercise Clause does not exempt individuals from complying with valid laws regulating conduct. In this picture, a Native American holy man performs a ceremony outside the Court as it hears arguments on the case.

Free Exercise Clause Clause in the First Amendment to the Constitution that prohibits the federal government from restricting religious beliefs and practices.

Although many early American colonists came to the new land to escape religious persecution, they frequently established their own government-supported churches and imposed their own religious beliefs on others. Puritanism was the official faith of colonial Massachusetts, and Virginia officially established the Church of England. Only two colonies (Maryland and Rhode Island) provided for full religious freedom. In part to lessen the potential for conflict among the states, the framers of the Bill of Rights sought to prevent the new national government from establishing an official religion or interfering with religious exercises.[7] The very first words of the First Amendment set forth two separate prohibitions on government: "Congress shall make no law respecting an *establishment of religion,* or prohibiting the *free exercise* thereof." These two restrictions on government power—the Free Exercise Clause and the No Establishment Clause—guarantee separate religious freedoms.

Free Exercise of Religion   The **Free Exercise Clause** prohibits government from restricting religious beliefs or practices. Although the wording of the First Amendment appears absolute ("Congress shall make no law . . ."), the U.S. Supreme Court has never interpreted the phrase to protect *any* conduct carried on in the name of religion. In the first major decision involving this clause, the Court ruled in 1879 that polygamy could be outlawed by Congress in Utah Territory even though some Mormons argued that it was part of their religious faith. The Court distinguished between belief and behavior, saying that "Congress was deprived of all legislative power over mere opinion [by the First Amendment], but was left free to reach actions which were in violation of social duties."[8] The Court also employed the Free Exercise Clause to strike down as unconstitutional an attempt by a state to prohibit private religious schools and force all children to attend public schools.[9] This decision protects the entire structure of private religious schools in the nation.

Later, the Supreme Court elaborated on its distinction between religious belief and religious practice. *Beliefs* are protected absolutely, but with regard to religious *practices,* the Court has generally upheld governmental restrictions when enacted for valid secular purposes.[10] Thus the government can outlaw religious practices that threaten health, safety, or welfare. The Free Exercise Clause does *not* confer the *right* to practice human sacrifice or even the ceremonial use of illegal drugs.[11] Individuals must comply with valid and neutral laws even if these laws restrict religious practices.

But the Supreme Court has continued to face many difficulties in applying its "valid secular test" to specific infringements of religious freedom. When some Amish parents refused to allow their children to attend any school beyond the eighth grade, the State of Wisconsin argued that its universal compulsory school attendance law had a valid purpose: the education of children. The Amish parents argued that high school exposed their children to worldly influences and values contrary to their religious beliefs. The Supreme Court sided with the Amish, deciding that their religious claims outweighed the legitimate interests of the state in education.[12] But the Supreme Court approved of an Internal Revenue Service action revoking the tax-exempt status of Bob Jones University because of its rules against interracial dating or marriage among its students. The school argued that its rule was based on religious belief, but the Court held that the government had "an overriding interest in eradicating racial discrimination in education."[13] And the Supreme Court struck down an attempt by a Florida city to outlaw the Santeria (a mix of Catholicism and voodoo) practice of slaughtering animals in religious ceremonies.[14]

No Establishment of Religion   Various meanings have been ascribed to the First Amendment prohibition against the "establishment" of religion. The first meaning—what the writers of the Bill of Rights had in mind—is that it merely prohibits the government from officially recognizing and supporting a national church, like the Church of England in that nation. A second meaning is somewhat broader: the government may not prefer one religion over another or demonstrate favoritism toward or discrimination against any particular religion, but it might recognize and encourage religious activities in general. The most expansive meaning is that the **No Establishment Clause** creates "a wall of separation between church and state" that prevents government from endorsing, aiding, sponsoring, or encouraging any or all religious activities. In 1947 Justice Hugo Black, writing for the Court majority, gave the following definition of this **wall-of-separation doctrine:**

> Neither a state nor the Federal Government can set up a church. Neither can pass laws which aid one religion, aid all religions, or prefer one religion over another. Neither can force nor influence a person to go to or to remain away from church . . . or force him to profess a belief or disbelief in any religion. . . . No tax in any amount, large or small, can be levied to support any religious activities or institutions, whatever they may be called, or whatever form they may adopt to teach or practice religion. Neither a state nor the Federal Government can, openly or secretly, participate in the affairs of any religious organizations or groups and vice versa. In the words of Jefferson, the clause against establishment of religion by law was intended to erect "a wall of separation between Church and State."[15]

Yet even while erecting this high rhetorical wall between church and state, the Court in this case upheld a state's provision of school bus service to parochial school pupils at public expense on the grounds that the buses did not directly aid religion but merely helped all children in the community proceed safely to and from school.[16] Although the Supreme Court has generally voiced its support for the wall-of-separation doctrine, on several occasions it has permitted cracks to develop in the wall. In allowing public schools to give pupils regular releases from school to attend religious instructions given outside of the school, Justice William O. Douglas wrote that the state and religion need not be "hostile, suspicious or even unfriendly."[17]

What Constitutes "Establishment"?   It has proven difficult for the Supreme Court to reconcile this wall-of-separation interpretation of the First Amendment with the fact that religion plays an important role in the life of most Americans. Public meetings, including sessions of the Congress, often begin with prayers;[18] coins are inscribed with the words "In God We Trust"; and the armed forces provide chaplains for U.S. soldiers.

The Supreme Court has set forth a three-part *Lemon test* for determining whether a particular state law constitutes "establishment" of religion and thus violates the First Amendment. To be constitutional, a law affecting religious activity:

1. Must have a secular purpose.
2. As its primary effect, must neither advance nor inhibit religion.
3. Must not foster "an excessive government entanglement with religion."[19]

Using this three-part test the Supreme Court held that it was unconstitutional for a state to pay the costs of teachers' salaries or instructional materials in parochial schools. The justices argued that this practice would require excessive government controls and surveillance to ensure that funds were used only for secular

No Establishment Clause   Clause in the First Amendment to the Constitution that is interpreted to require the separation of church and state.

wall-of-separation doctrine   The Supreme Court's interpretation of the No Establishment Clause that laws may not have as their purpose aid to one religion or aid to all religions.

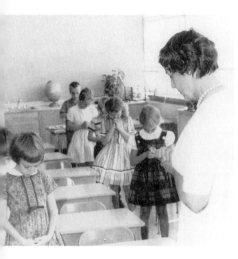

Although the Supreme Court ruled in 1962 (Engle v. Vitale) that even voluntary prayer in public schools was an unconstitutional violation of the separation of church and state under the First Amendment, the question of prayer in the schools remains a heated one. Indeed, recent court rulings regarding nondenominational prayers at graduation ceremonies and sporting events have, if anything, further confused the issue.

instruction and thus involved "excessive entanglement between government and religion." However, the Court has upheld the use of tax funds to provide students attending church-related schools with nonreligious textbooks, lunches, and transportation. And the Court has upheld a state's granting of tax credits to parents whose children attend private schools, including religious schools.[20] The Court has also upheld government grants of money to church-related colleges and universities for secular purposes.[21]

The High Court has upheld tax exemptions for churches on the grounds that "the role of religious organizations as charitable associations, in furthering the secular objectives of the state, has become a fundamental concept in our society."[22] It held that schools must allow after-school meetings on school property by religious groups if such a privilege is extended to nonreligious groups.[23] Deductions on federal income tax returns for church contributions are also constitutional. The Supreme Court allows states to close stores on Sundays and otherwise set aside that day, as long as there is a secular purpose—such as "rest, repose, recreation and tranquility"—in doing so.[24] However, the Supreme Court has held that a Christmas nativity scene on public property is an official "endorsement" of Christian belief and therefore violates the No Establishment Clause of the First Amendment.[25]

Prayer in the School   The Supreme Court's most controversial interpretation of the No Establishment Clause involved the question of prayer and Bible-reading ceremonies conducted by public schools. The practice of opening the school day with prayer and Bible-reading ceremonies was once widespread in American public schools. To avoid the denominational aspects of these ceremonies, New York State's Board of Regents substituted the following nondenominational prayer, which it required to be said aloud in each class in the presence of a teacher at the beginning of each school day: "Almighty God, we acknowledge our dependence upon Thee, and we beg Thy blessings upon us, our parents, our teachers, and our country." New York argued that this brief prayer did not violate the No Establishment Clause, because the prayer was denominationally neutral and because student participation in the prayer was voluntary. However, in *Engle v. Vitale* (1962), the Supreme Court stated that "the constitutional prohibition against laws respecting an establishment of a religion must at least mean in this country it is no part of the business of government to compose official prayers for any group of the American people to recite as part of a religious program carried on by government." The Court pointed out that making prayer voluntary did not free it from the prohibitions of the No Establishment Clause, and that clause prevented the *establishment* of a religious ceremony by a government agency regardless of whether the ceremony was voluntary.[26]

One year later, in the case of *Abington School District v. Schempp,* the Court considered the constitutionality of Bible-reading ceremonies in the public schools. Here again, even though the children were not required to participate, the Court found that Bible reading as an opening exercise in the schools was a religious ceremony. The justices went to some trouble in the majority opinion to point out that they were not "throwing the Bible out of the schools." They specifically stated that the *study* of the Bible or of religion, when presented objectively and as part of a secular program of education, did not violate the First Amendment; but religious *ceremonies* involving Bible reading or prayer established by a state or school did.[27]

State efforts to encourage "voluntary prayer" in public schools have also been struck down by the Supreme Court as unconstitutional. When the State of Alabama authorized a period of silence for "meditation or voluntary prayer" in public schools, the Court ruled that this action was an "establishment of religion." The Court said the law had no secular purpose, that it conveyed "a message of state endorsement and promotion of prayer," and that its real intent was to encourage prayer in public schools. In a stinging dissenting opinion, Chief Justice Warren Burger noted that the Supreme Court itself opened its session with a prayer and that both houses of Congress opened every session with prayers led by official chaplains paid by the government. "To suggest that a moment of silence statute that includes the word *prayer* unconstitutionally endorses religion manifests not neutrality but hostility toward religion."[28]

Religious Freedom Restoration? Congress sought to intervene in government-religion disputes with a Religious Freedom Restoration Act in 1993. Traditionally, the Supreme Court had employed a "compelling interest" test to decide whether government could ban a religious practice; that is, the government had to prove a compelling public interest to justify even a nondiscriminatory law or regulation that infringed on the free exercise of religion.[29] But when the Court appeared to relax that test and to hold that religious beliefs cannot excuse persons from compliance with *any* otherwise valid law, Congress saw an opportunity to align itself with religion. It acted to exempt people from government laws or regulations that burden their religious freedom unless the government can prove that the burden is "the least restrictive means of furthering a compelling interest."[30] But the Supreme Court responded by declaring the act unconstitutional, asserting in *City of Boerne v. Flores* (1997) that only the courts can interpret the meaning of the Constitution and that Congress had overstepped it powers trying to do so itself.

FREEDOM OF SPEECH

Although the First Amendment is absolute in its wording ("Congress shall pass *no* law . . . abridging the freedom of speech"), the Supreme Court has never been willing to interpret this statement as a protection of *all* speech. What kinds of speech does the First Amendment protect from government control, and what kinds of speech may be constitutionally prohibited?

Clear and Present Danger Doctrine The classic example of speech that can be prohibited was given by Justice Oliver Wendell Holmes in 1919: "The most stringent protection of free speech would not protect a man in falsely shouting 'fire' in a theater and causing a panic."[31] Although Holmes recognized that the government may prevent speech that creates a serious and immediate danger to society, he objected to government attempts to stifle critics of its policies, such as the Espionage Act of 1917 and the Sedition Act of 1918. The Sedition Act prohibited, among other things, speech that was meant to discourage the sale of war bonds; "disloyal" speech about the government, the Constitution, the military forces, or the flag of the United States; and speech that urged the curtailment of war production. In the case of *Gitlow v. New York,* the majority supported the right of the government to curtail any speech that "tended to subvert or imperil the government," but Holmes dissented, arguing that "Every idea is an incitement. It offers itself for belief and if believed it is acted on unless some other belief outweighs it."[32] Unless the expression of an idea created a *serious and immediate danger,* Holmes argued that it should be tolerated and combated or defeated only by the expression of better ideas. This standard for determining the limits of free expression became known as the **clear and present danger doctrine.** Government should not curtail speech merely because it *might tend* to cause a future danger: "The question in every case is whether the words used are used in such circumstances and are of such a nature as to create a clear and present danger that they will bring about the substantive evils that Congress has a right to prevent."[33] Holmes's dissent inspired a long struggle in the courts to strengthen constitutional protections for speech and press (see *Up Close:* "The American Civil Liberties Union").

Although Holmes was the first to use the phrase "clear and present danger," it was Justice Louis D. Brandeis who later developed the doctrine into a valuable constitutional principle that the Supreme Court gradually came to adopt. Brandeis explained that the doctrine involved two elements: (1) the clearness or seriousness of the expression; and (2) the immediacy of the danger flowing from the speech. With regard to immediacy he wrote,

> No danger flowing from speech can be deemed clear and present, unless the incidence of the evil apprehended is so imminent that it may befall before there is opportunity for full discussion. If there be time to expose through discussion the falsehood and fallacies, to avert the evil by the processes of education, the remedy to be applied is more speech, not enforced silence.

And with regard to seriousness he wrote,

> Moreover, even imminent danger cannot justify resort to prohibition [of speech] . . . unless the evil apprehended is relatively serious. Prohibition of free speech and assembly is a measure so stringent that it would be inappropriate as the means for averting a relatively trivial harm to society. . . . There must be the probability of serious injury to the State.[34]

Preferred Position Doctrine   Over the years, the Supreme Court has given the First Amendment freedom of speech, press, and assembly a special **preferred position** in constitutional law. These freedoms are especially important to the preservation of democracy. If speech, press, or assembly are prohibited by government, the people have no way to correct the government through democratic processes. Thus the burden of proof rests on the *government* to justify any restrictions on speech, writing, or assembly.[35] In other words, any speech or writing is presumed constitutional unless the government proves that a serious and immediate danger would ensue if the speech were allowed.

The Cold War Challenge   Despite the Supreme Court's endorsement of the clear and present danger and preferred position doctrines, in times of perceived national crisis the courts have been willing to permit some government restrictions of speech, press, and assembly. At the outbreak of World War II, just prior to U.S. entry into that world conflict, Congress passed the Smith Act, which stated,

> It shall be unlawful for any person to knowingly or willfully advocate, abet, advise, or teach the duty, necessity, desirability, or propriety of overthrowing or destroying any government in the United States by force or violence, or by the assassination of any officer of any such government.

clear and present danger doctrine   Standard used by the courts to determine whether speech may be restricted; only speech that creates a serious and immediate danger to society may be restricted.

preferred position   Refers to the tendency of the courts to give preference to the First Amendment rights to speech, press, and assembly when faced with conflicts.

The American Civil Liberties Union

The American Civil Liberties Union (ACLU) is one of the largest and most active interest groups devoted to litigation. Its Washington offices employ a staff of several hundred people; it counts on some five thousand volunteer lawyers across the country; and it has affiliates in every state and most large cities. The ACLU claims that its sole purpose is defense of civil liberty, that it has no other political agenda, that it defends the Communist Party and the Ku Klux Klan alike—not because it endorses their beliefs but because "the Bill of Rights is the ACLU's only client."* And indeed on occasion it has defended the liberties of Nazis, Klansmen, and other right-wing extremists to express their unpopular views. But most ACLU work has involved litigation on behalf of liberal causes, such as abortion rights, resistance to military service, support for affirmative action, and opposition to the death penalty.

The ACLU was founded in 1920 by Roger Baldwin, a wealthy radical activist who opposed both capitalism and war. Baldwin graduated from Harvard University and briefly taught sociology at Washington University in St. Louis. He refused to be drafted during World War I and served a year's imprisonment for draft violation. In prison, Baldwin joined the Industrial Workers of the World (IWW, or the "Wobblies"), a radical labor union that advocated violence to achieve its goals. In the early 1920s, the ACLU defended socialists, "Bolsheviks," labor organizers, and pacifists against government coercion, including those arrested in the "Red Scare" raids of Attorney General Alexander Mitchell Palmer.

Later the ACLU concentrated its efforts on the defense of First Amendment freedoms of speech, press, religion, and assembly. ACLU member Felix Frankfurter, later a Supreme Court justice, set the tone: "Civil liberty means liberty for those whom we do not like or even detest." In the famous "Monkey Trial" of 1925, the ACLU helped defend schoolteacher John Scopes for having taught the theory of evolution in violation of Tennessee state law. Later, it played a supporting role in the litigation efforts of the National Association for the Advancement of Colored People in the elimination of segregation; it defended Vietnam War protesters; it brought cases to court to

In 1978 the ACLU defended the right of American Nazis to march in the Chicago suburb of Skokie, Illinois, home to many survivors of the Nazi holocaust in Europe.

ban prayer and religious exercise in public schools; it has opposed the death penalty and fought for abortion rights; and it defended the rights of people to burn the American flag as a form of symbolic speech.

The ACLU's decision to defend the right of the American Nazi Party to march through Skokie, Illinois, a Chicago suburb with a large Jewish population, including some Holocaust survivors, created a crisis in the organization. The ACLU had defended Nazis and Klansmen before, but the Skokie case engendered more publicity than any earlier cases involving right-wing extremists. Many members quit the organization and financial contributions temporarily declined.

Today, the ACLU is racked by internal arguments over politically correct speech codes and over whether "hate crimes" (crimes committed with racist, sexist, antihomosexual, and similar motives) should invoke harsher sentences than the same crimes committed for other motives. "Pure" First Amendment defenders in the organization oppose speech codes and hate crime legislation, while many liberal members rationalize these penalties on speech and thought.

Former Supreme Court Chief Justice Earl Warren once said of the ACLU, "It is difficult to appreciate how far our freedoms might have eroded had it not been for the Union's valiant representation in the courts of the constitutional rights of people of all persuasions."†

---

*William A. Donohue, *The Politics of the American Civil Liberties Union* (New Brunswick: Transaction Books, 1985), p. 3.

†Quoted in *ACLU Annual Report*, 1977, cited in ibid., p. 2.

Do We Have a Constitutional Right to Burn the American Flag?

Flag waving is an American political tradition. The American flag symbolizes nationhood and national unity. Most states and the federal government have laws forbidding "desecration" of the flag.

Flag desecration is a physical act, but it also has symbolic meaning—for example, hatred of the United States or opposition to government policies. At the 1984 Republican national convention in Dallas, Gregory Lee Johnson joined a protest march against Reagan Administration policies, then doused an American flag with kerosene and set fire to it. As it burned, he and others chanted, "America, the red, white, and blue, we spit on you." Police arrested Johnson and charged him with violating a Texas law against flag desecration. The American Civil Liberties Union came to Johnson's defense, arguing that flag burning is "symbolic speech" protected by the First Amendment.

In the case of *Texas v. Johnson* (1989), a majority of Supreme Court justices argued that "Johnson's burning of the flag was conduct sufficiently imbued with elements of communication to implicate the First Amendment." They declared that when speech and conduct are combined in the same expressive act, the government must show that it has "a sufficiently important interest in regulating the non-speech element to justify incident limitations on First Amendment freedoms." In this case, "preserving the flag as a symbol of nationhood and national unity" was not deemed sufficiently important to justify limiting Johnson's freedom of expression.*

The Court's decision caused a political uproar. President George Bush immediately condemned it, and public opinion polls showed massive opposition to it. Congress quickly passed the Flag Protection Act of 1989, mandating a one-year jail sentence and $1,000 fine for anyone who "knowingly mutilates, defaces, physically defiles, burns, maintains on the floor or ground, or tramples upon, any flag of the United States." But just as promptly, the Supreme Court, by the same 5 to 4 vote, struck down the new federal law as unconstitutional, using the same reasoning as expressed in the *Johnson* case. Congress was not finished with the issue. Its next effort centered on the

passage of a constitutional amendment: "The Congress and the states shall have the power to prohibit physical desecration of the flag of the United States." Because Congress was controlled by the Democrats, Republicans were convinced that the failure to pass the amendment would hurt Democratic Party candidates in the next election. (A June 1990 Gallup Poll revealed that 68 percent of Americans supported a constitutional amendment protecting the flag.) But Democratic leaders argued that the proposed amendment would alter the Bill of Rights and that Republicans were trying to "politicize the flag." The Democratic leadership also called for a quick vote to forestall efforts to rally strong public support for the amendment. Republicans led the fight for the amendment, but the political appeal of supporting the flag pulled a large number of Democratic members of the House to their side. Supporters paid homage to the flag:

> Too many people have paid for it with their blood. Too many people have marched behind it. Too many kids and parents and widows have accepted this triangle as the last remembrance of their loved ones. Too many to have this ever demeaned.

Opponents frequently quoted the Supreme Court's majority opinion:

> The way to preserve the flag's special role is not to punish those who feel differently about these matters. It is to persuade them that they are wrong. . . . We can imagine no more appropriate response to burning a flag than waving one's own, no better way to counter a flag-burner's message than by saluting the flag that burns. . . . We do not consecrate the flag by punishing its desecration, for in doing so we dilute the freedom that this cherished emblem represents.†

In the end, the flag amendment was defeated when it garnered a majority of House votes but fewer than required to pass a constitutional amendment by the necessary two-thirds vote. Likewise, a majority of the Senate has voted several times in favor of the amendment, but it has always fallen short of the necessary two-thirds vote.

Texas v. Johnson, 491 U.S. 397 (1989).
†Quotations from *Congressional Quarterly,* June 23, 1990, p. 2004.

Congress justified its action in terms of national security, initially as a protection against fascism during World War II, then later as a protection against communist revolution in the early days of the Cold War.

In 1949 the Department of Justice prosecuted Eugene V. Dennis and ten other top leaders of the Communist Party of the United States for violation of the Smith Act. A jury found them guilty of violating the act, and the party leaders were sentenced to jail terms ranging from one to five years. In 1951 the case of *Dennis v. United States* came to the Supreme Court on appeal. In upholding the conviction of the Communist Party leaders, the Court seemed to abandon Brandeis's idea that "present" meant "before there is opportunity for full discussion."[36] It seemed to substitute clear and *probable* for clear and *present*.

Since that time, however, the Supreme Court has returned to a policy closer to the original clear and present danger doctrine. As the Cold War progressed, Americans grew to view communism as a serious threat to democracy, but not a *present* danger. The overthrow of the American government advocated by communists was not an incitement to *immediate* action. A democracy must not itself become authoritarian to protect itself from authoritarianism. In later cases, the Supreme Court held that the mere advocacy of revolution, apart from unlawful action, is protected by the First Amendment.[37] It struck down federal laws requiring communist organizations to register with the government,[38] laws requiring individuals to sign "loyalty oaths,"[39] laws prohibiting communists from working in defense plants,[40] and laws stripping passports from Communist Party leaders.[41] In short, once the perceived Cold War crisis began to fade, the Supreme Court reasserted the First Amendment rights of individuals and groups.

The Supreme Court has ruled that Ku Klux Klan cross burnings constitute symbolic speech protected by the First Amendment.

Symbolic Speech The First Amendment's guarantees of speech, press, and assembly are broadly interpreted to mean **freedom of expression.** Political expression encompasses more than just words. For example, when Mary Beth Tinker and her brothers were suspended for wearing black armbands to high school to protest the Vietnam War, they argued that the wearing of armbands constituted **symbolic speech** protected by the First Amendment. The Supreme Court agreed, noting that the school did not prohibit all wearing of symbols but instead singled out this particular expression for disciplinary action.[42] The Court also held that wearing Ku Klux Klan hoods and gathering together to burn a cross[43] and even burning the American flag (see *What Do You Think?:* "Do We Have a Constitutional Right to Burn the American Flag?")[44] are protected expression. However, burning one's draft card does not constitute protected speech and exempt the burner from legal penalties for failure to carry such a card. The Court "cannot accept the view that an apparently limitless variety of conduct can be labeled 'speech.' "[45]

The Supreme Court continues to wrestle with the question of what kinds of conduct are symbolic speech protected by the First Amendment and what kinds of conduct are outside of this protection (see *What Do You Think?:* "Do We Have the Right to Die?"). Symbolic speech, like speech itself, cannot be banned just because it offends people. "If there is only one bedrock principle underlying the First Amendment, it is that the Government may not prohibit the expression of an idea simply because society finds the idea itself offensive or disagreeable."[46]

Speech and Public Order The Supreme Court has wrestled with the question of whether speech can be prohibited when it stirs audiences to public disorder, not because the speaker urges lawless action but because the audience reacts to the speech

freedom of expression Collectively, the First Amendment rights to free speech, press, and assembly.

symbolic speech Actions other than speech itself but protected by the First Amendment because they constitute political expression.

What Do You Think?

Do We Have the Right to Die?

In most states, for most of the nation's history, it has been a crime to assist another person to commit suicide. Michigan's prosecution of Dr. Jack Kevorkian for publicly participating in physician-assisted suicides launched a nationwide debate on the topic. More important, a group of physicians in Washington, along with their gravely ill patients, filed suit in federal court seeking a declaration that their state's law banning physician-assisted suicide violated the "liberty" guaranteed by the Fourteenth Amendment. They argued that mentally competent, terminally ill patients had the "right to die"; that is, they had a privacy right to request and receive aid in ending their life. They relied on the Supreme Court's previous rulings on abortion (see *Up Close:* "Privacy, Abortion, and the Constitution" in Chapter 13), contending that Washington's law placed an undue burden on the exercise of a privacy right. But the U.S. Supreme Court held that a law prohibiting "causing or aiding" a suicide did *not* violate the Fourteenth Amendment, that there is no *constitutional right* to physician-assisted suicide.* The Court implied that if the laws governing the practice are to be changed, they must be changed by legislatures, not by reinterpreting the Constitution. The Court observed that a number of states had recently reaffirmed their bans on physician-assisted suicide and that Congress specifically prohibits the use of federal funds for that purpose.

Nonetheless, public opinion generally favors physician-assisted suicide often referred to by supporters

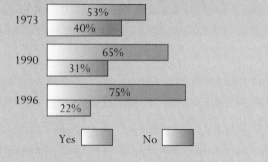

Question: *When a person has a disease that cannot be cured, do you think doctors should be allowed by law to end the patient's life by some painless means if the patient and his family request it?*

1973 53% / 40%
1990 65% / 31%
1996 75% / 22%
Yes / No

Source: Gallup Polls, reported in *The Polling Report,* July 28, 1997, p. 6.

as "the right to die." Indeed support appears to have grown over the years:

The Supreme Court exercised "judicial restraint" in its (6 to 3) decision *not* to declare physician-assisted suicide a constitutionally protected liberty. It left the question to Congress and state legislatures. It is likely that "the right to die" will be hotly debated by the people and their elected representatives in the years ahead.

---

*Washington v. Glucksberg (June 26, 1997).

---

with hostility. In short, can a speaker be arrested because of the *audience's* disorderly behavior? In an early case, the Supreme Court fashioned a *fighting words doctrine,* to the effect that words that "ordinary men know are likely to cause a fight" may be prohibited.[47] But later the Court seemed to realize that this doctrine, if broadly applied, could create a huge constitutional hole in the First Amendment guarantee of free speech. Authorities could curtail speech simply because it met with audience hostility. The Court recognized that "speech is often provocative and challenging. It may . . . have profound unsettling effects. . . . That is why freedom of speech, while not absolute, is nevertheless protected against censorship."[48] In recent years, the Court has consistently refused to allow government authorities to ban speech *before* it has occurred simply because they believe it *may* create a disturbance.

Many colleges and universities have undertaken to ban speech that is considered racist, sexist, homophobic, or otherwise "insensitive" to the feelings of women and minorities. Varieties of "speech codes," "hate codes," and sexual harassment regulations that prohibit verbal expressions raise serious constitutional questions, especially at state-supported colleges and universities. The First Amendment does not exclude insulting or offensive racist or sexist words or comments from its protection (see *Up Close:* "Political Correctness versus Free Speech on Campus").

Commercial Speech   Do First Amendment freedoms of expression apply to commercial advertising? The Supreme Court has frequently asserted that **commercial speech** is protected by the First Amendment. The Court held that states cannot outlaw price advertising by pharmacists[49] or advertising for services by attorneys[50] and that cities cannot outlaw posting "For Sale" signs on property, even in the interests of halting white flight and promoting racially integrated neighborhoods. Advertising is the "dissemination of information" and is constitutionally protected.[51]

However, the Court has also been willing to weigh the First Amendment rights of commercial advertisers against the public interest served by regulation.[52] In other words, the Court seems to suspend its preferred position doctrine with regard to commercial advertising and to call for a "balancing of interests." Thus the Supreme Court has allowed the Federal Communications Commission to regulate the contents of advertising on radio and television and even to ban advertising for cigarettes. The Federal Trade Commission enforces "truth" in advertising by requiring commercial packages and advertisers to prove all claims for their products.

Libel and Slander   Libel and slander have never been protected by the First Amendment against subsequent punishment (see "Libel and Slander" in Chapter 6). Once a communication is determined to be libelous or slanderous, it is outside of the protection of the First Amendment. The courts have traditionally defined "libel" as a "damaging falsehood." However, if plaintiffs are public officials they must prove that the statements made about them are not only false and damaging but also "made with actual malice"—that is, with knowledge that they are false or with "reckless disregard" of the truth—in order to prove libel.[53]

OBSCENITY AND THE LAW

Obscene materials of all kinds—words, publications, photos, videotapes, films— are also exempt from First Amendment protection. Most states ban the publication, sale, or possession of obscene material, and Congress bans its shipment in the mails. Because obscene material is not protected by the First Amendment, it can be banned without even an attempt to prove that it results in antisocial conduct. In other words, it is not necessary to show that obscene material would result in a clear and present danger to society, the test used to decide the legitimacy of *speech*. In order to ban obscene materials, the government need only prove that they are *obscene*.

Defining "obscenity" has confounded legislatures and the courts for years, however. State and federal laws often define pornography and obscenity in such terms as "lewd," "lascivious," "filthy," "indecent," "disgusting"—all equally as vague as "obscene." "Pornography" is simply a synonym for "obscenity." *Soft-core pornography* usually denotes nakedness and sexually suggestive poses; it is less likely to confront legal barriers. *Hard-core pornography* usually denotes explicit sexual activ-

commercial speech Advertising communications given only partial protection under the First Amendment to the Constitution.

Political Correctness versus Free Speech on Campus

Universities have a very special responsibility to protect freedom of expression. The free and unfettered exchange of views is essential to the advancement of knowledge—the very purpose of universities. For centuries universities have fought to protect academic freedom from pressures arising from the world *outside* of the campus—governments, interest groups, financial contributors—arguing that the university must be a protected enclave for free expression of ideas. But the latest threat to academic freedom arises from *within* universities—from efforts by administrations, faculty, and campus groups to suppress ideas, opinions, and language that are not "politically correct" (PC). PC activists seek to suppress opinions and expressions they consider to be racist, sexist, "homophobic," or otherwise "insensitive" to specified groups.*

Speech Codes The experience at the University of Michigan with its "Policy on Discrimination and Discriminatory Harassment" illustrates the battles occurring on many campuses over First Amendment rights. In 1988 a series of racial incidents on campus prompted the university to officially ban "any behavior verbal or physical" that "stigmatized" an individual "on the basis of race, ethnicity, religion, sex, sexual orientation, ancestry, age, marital status, handicap, or Vietnam-era veteran status" or that created "an intimidating, hostile, or demeaning environment for educational pursuits." A published guide provided examples of banned activity, which included the following:

- A male student makes remarks in class like "women just aren't as good in this field as men."
- Jokes about gay men and lesbians.
- Commenting in a derogatory way about a particular person or group's physical appearance or sexual orientation, or their cultural origins, or religious beliefs.

Free Speech In 1989 "John Doe," a psychology graduate student studying gender differences in personality traits and mental functions, filed suit in federal court requesting that the University of Michigan policy be declared a violation of the First Amendment. (He was permitted by the court to remain anonymous because of fear of retribution.) He was joined in his complaint against the university by the American Civil Liberties Union.

In its decision, the court acknowledged that the university had a legal responsibility to prevent racial or sexual discrimination or harassment. However, it did not have a right to

> establish an anti-discrimination policy which had the effect of prohibiting certain speech because it disagreed with ideas or messages sought to be conveyed. . . . Nor could the University proscribe speech simply because it was found to be offensive, even gravely so, by large numbers of people. . . . These principles acquire a special significance in the University setting, where the free and unfettered interplay of competing views is essential to the institution's educational mission. . . . While the Court is sympathetic to the University's obligation to ensure educational opportunities for all of its students, such efforts must not be at the expense of free speech.[†]

It seems ironic that students and faculty now must seek the protection of the federal courts from attempts by universities to limit speech. Traditionally, universities themselves fought to protect academic freedom. Academic freedom included the freedom of faculty and students to express themselves in the classroom, on the campus, and in writing, on controversial and sensitive topics, including race and gender. It was recognized that students often express ideas that are biased or ill informed, immature, or crudely expressed. But students were taught that the remedy for offensive language or off-color remarks or ill-chosen examples was more enlightened speech, not suppression.

---

*Dinesh D'Souza, *Illiberal Education: The Politics of Race and Sex on Campus* (New York: Vintage Books, 1992).

[†]*John Doe v. University of Michigan,* 721 F. Supp. 852 (1989).

ity. After many fruitless efforts by the Supreme Court to come up with a workable definition of "pornography" or "obscenity," a frustrated Justice Potter Stewart wrote in 1974, "I shall not today attempt further to define [hard-core pornography]. . . . But *I know it when I see it.*"[54]

Slackening Standards: **Roth v. United States**   The Court's first comprehensive effort to define "obscenity" came in *Roth v. United States* (1957). Although the Court upheld Roth's conviction for distributing pornographic magazines through the mails, it defined "obscenity" somewhat narrowly: "Whether to the average person applying contemporary community standards, the dominant theme of the material, taken as a whole, appeals to prurient interests."[55]

Note that the material must be obscene to the *average* person, not to children or particular groups of adults who might be especially offended by pornography. The standard is "contemporary," suggesting that what was once regarded as obscene might be acceptable today. Later, the *community standard* was clarified to mean the "society at large," not a particular state or local community.[56] The material must be "considered as a whole," meaning that even if a work includes some obscene material, it is still acceptable if its "dominant theme" is something other than "prurient."[57] The Court added that a work must be "utterly without redeeming social or literary merit" in order to be judged obscene.[58] The Court never really said what a "prurient" interest was but reassured everyone that "sex and obscenity are not synonymous."[59]

Tightening Standards: **Miller v. California**   The effect of the Roth decision, and the many and varied attempts by lower courts to apply its slippery standards, tended to limit law enforcement efforts to combat pornography during the 1960s and 1970s. The Supreme Court itself came under ridicule when it was learned that the justices had set up a movie room in the basement of the Supreme Court building to view films that had been brought before them in obscenity cases.[60]

So the Supreme Court tried again, in *Miller v. California* (1973), to give law enforcement officials some clearer standards in determining obscenity. Although the Court retained the "average person" and "contemporary" standards, it redefined "community" to mean the *local* community rather than the society at large. It also defined "prurient" as "patently offensive" representations or descriptions of "ultimate sex acts, normal or perverted, actual or simulated," as well as "masturbation, excretory functions, and lewd exhibition of the genitals." It rejected the earlier requirement that the work had to be "utterly without redeeming social value" in order to be judged obscene, and it substituted instead "lacks serious literary, artistic, political, or scientific value."[61]

The effect of the Supreme Court's *Miller* standards has been to increase the likelihood of conviction in obscenity-pornography cases.[62] It is easier to prove that a work lacks serious value than to prove that it is utterly without redeeming merit. Nevertheless, the *local community standard* allows sales of pornographic materials (by most people's standards) in adult bookstores and X-rated video stores in many cities throughout the nation.

Child Pornography   The Supreme Court has struck hard against child pornography—the "dissemination of material depicting children engaged in sexual conduct regardless of whether the material is obscene." Such conduct includes any visual depic-

Despite public concerns about the ability of children to gain access to obscene materials on the Internet, the Supreme Court, calling it the "most participatory form of mass speech yet developed," ruled that Congress cannot regulate the Internet's content.

tion of children performing sexual acts or lewdly exhibiting their genitals. The Court held that safeguarding children used in films or photographs from sexual exploitation and abuse was "a government objective of overriding importance."[63] In such cases, the existence of the material itself is evidence that a crime has been committed. Thus the test for *child* pornography is much stricter than the *Miller* standards.

The Information Highway   New technologies continue to challenge courts in the application of First Amendment principles. Currently the Internet, the global computer communication network, allows users to gain access to information worldwide. Thousands of electronic bulletin boards give computer users with communication modems access to everything from bomb-making instructions and sex conversations to obscene photos and even child pornography. Many commercial access services ban obscene messages and exclude bulletin boards with racially or sexually offensive commentary. But can *government* try to ban such material from the Internet without violating First Amendment freedoms?

Congress tried unsuccessfully to ban "indecent" and "patently offensive" communications from the Internet in its Communications Decency Act of 1996. Proponents of the law cited the need to protect children from pornography. But in *Janet Reno v. American Civil Liberties Union* (1997) the Supreme Court held the act unconstitutional: "Notwithstanding the legitimacy and importance of the Congressional goal of protecting children from harmful materials, we agree that the statute abridges freedom of speech protected by the First Amendment." The Supreme Court agreed with the assertion that "as the most participatory form of mass speech yet developed [the Internet] deserves the highest protection from government intrusion"

FREEDOM OF THE PRESS

Democracy depends on the free expression of ideas. Authoritarian regimes either monopolize press, radio, and television facilities themselves or subject them to strict licensing and censorship of their content. The idea of a free and independent press is deeply rooted in the evolution of democratic government.

No Prior Restraint Doctrine   Long before the Bill of Rights was written, English law protected newspapers from government restrictions or licensing prior to publication—a practice called **prior restraint.** This protection, however, does not mean that publishers are exempt from *subsequent punishment* for libelous, obscene, or other illegal publications. Prior restraint is more dangerous to free expression because it allows the government to censor the work prior to publication and forces the defendants to *prove* that their material should *not* be censored. In contrast, subsequent punishment requires a trial in which the government must prove that the defendant's published materials are unlawful.

In 1695 the great English jurist William Blackstone described the meaning of a free press as freedom from *prior* censorship:

> The liberty of the press . . . consists in laying no previous restraints upon publications, and not in freedom from censure for criminal matter when published. Every freeman has an undoubted right to lay what sentiments he pleases before the public. To forbid this is to destroy the freedom of the press; but if he published what is improper, mischievous or illegal, he must take the consequences of his own temerity.[64]

In *Near v. Minnesota* (1931), a muckraking publication accusing local officials of trafficking with gangsters had been barred from publishing under a Minnesota law that prohibited the publication of a "malicious, scandalous or defamatory newspaper." The Supreme Court, quoting Blackstone with approval, struck down the law as unconstitutional. Although *Near v. Minnesota* was a landmark decision affirming the *no-prior-restraint doctrine,* a close reading of the majority opinion reveals that the doctrine was not presented as absolute. Chief Justice Charles Evans Hughes noted that prior government censorship might be constitutional "if publication . . . threatened the country's safety in times of war."[65] Presumably, the government can prevent the publication of information on troop movements, invasion plans, or other military information when lives are at stake.

The question of whether or not the government can restrain publication of stories that present a serious threat to national security remains unanswered. For example, can the government restrain the press from reporting in advance on the time and place of an impending U.S. military action, thereby warning an enemy and perhaps adding to American casualties? In the most important case on this question, *New York Times v. United States* (1971), the Supreme Court upheld the right of the newspaper to publish secret documents that had been stolen from State Department and Defense Department files. The material covered U.S. policy decisions in Vietnam, and it was published while the war was still being waged. But five separate (concurring) opinions were written by justices in the majority as well as two dissenting opinions. Only two justices (Hugo Black and William O. Douglas) argued that government can *never* restrain any publication regardless of the seriousness or immediacy of the harm. Others in the majority cited the government's failure to show proof in this case that publication "would surely result in direct, immediate, and irreparable damage to our nation or its people."[66] Presumably, if the government had produced such proof, the case might have been decided differently. The media interprets the decision as a blanket protection to publish anything it wishes regardless of harm to government or society.

prior restraint   Government actions to restrict publication of a magazine, newspaper, or books on grounds of libel, obscenity, or other legal violations prior to actual publication of the work.

Although self-ratings by the movie industry have thus far kept it from government regulation, recent ratings have caused an uproar, both within the film industry and among the movie-going public. Just what separates an "R" film from an "NC-17" (formerly "X")? When Midnight Cowboy *first appeared in 1969, it was rated "X," but, with no changes, it was rerated as "R" after winning the Oscar for the best picture. More recently, critics have charged that the violence and steamy sex scenes of* Basic Instinct *went far beyond "R" standards, but it avoided an "NC-17" rating only because it was the product of a major film studio that was able to pressure the ratings board.*

shield laws Laws in some states that give reporters the right to refuse to name their sources or to release their notes in court cases; may be overturned by the courts when such refusals jeopardize a fair trial for a defendant.

Film Censorship The no-prior-restraint doctrine was developed to protect the print media—books, magazines, newspapers. When the motion picture industry was in its infancy, the Supreme Court held that films were "business, pure and simple" and were not entitled to the protection of the First Amendment.[67] But as films grew in importance, the Court gradually extended First Amendment freedoms to cover motion pictures.[68] However, the Supreme Court has not given the film industry the same strong no-prior-restraint protection it has given the press. The Court has approved government requirements for prior submission of films to official censors, so long as (1) the burden of proof that the film is obscene rests with the censor; (2) a procedure exists for judicial determination of the issue; and (3) censors are required to act speedily.[69] To avoid government-imposed censorship the motion picture industry adopted its own system of rating films:

G: suitable for all audiences

PG: parental guidance suggested

PG-13: parental guidance strongly suggested for children under thirteen

R: restricted to those seventeen or older unless accompanied by a parent or guardian

NC-17: no one under seventeen admitted

Some city governments have sought to restrict showing of NC-17 films, and their restrictions have been upheld by the Courts.[70]

Radio and Television Censorship The Federal Communications Commission was created in 1934 to allocate broadcast frequencies and to license stations. The exclusive right to use a particular frequency is a "public trust." Thus broadcasters, unlike newspapers and magazines, are licensed by the government and subject to government rules. Although the First Amendment protects broadcasters, the Supreme Court has recognized the special obligations that may be imposed on them in exchange for the exclusive right to use a broadcast frequency. "No one has a First Amendment right to a license or to monopolize a radio frequency; to deny a station license because 'the public interest' requires it, is not a denial of free speech."[71] Thus the Court has upheld FCC-imposed "equal time" and "fairness" rules against broadcasters, even while striking down state attempts to impose the same rules on newspapers.[72]

Media Claims for Special Rights The news media make various claims to special rights arising out of the First Amendment's guarantee of a free press. Reporters argue, for example, that they should be able to protect their news sources and are not obliged to give testimony in criminal cases when they have obtained evidence in confidence. However, the only witnesses the Constitution exempts from compulsory testimony are defendants themselves, who enjoy the Fifth Amendment's protection against "self-incrimination." The Supreme Court has flatly rejected reporters' claims to a privilege against compulsory testimony. "We cannot seriously entertain the notion that the First Amendment protects a newsman's agreement to conceal the criminal conduct of his source, or evidence thereof, on the theory that it is better to write about a crime than to do something about it."[73] The Court also has rejected the argument that media notes and records are confidential; instead, it sided with law enforcement officials who had used a valid warrant to search the *Stanford Daily's* offices for photos showing demonstrators who had attacked police.[74]

Despite these rulings, reporters regularly boast of their willingness to go to jail to protect sources, and many have done so. But the media have also pressured the nation's legislatures for protection. Congress has passed the Privacy Protection Act, which sharply limits the ability of law enforcement officials to search press offices, and many states have passed **shield laws** specifically protecting reporters from giving testimony in criminal cases.

Conflicting "Rights"   The conflict between reporters' "rights" to protect their sources under shield laws and the constitutional right of individuals to face their accusers when on trial is just one example of the many conflicts over "rights" in American life. In the case of shield laws, the courts have ruled that "rights" granted by law are not equal to rights granted by the Constitution and have imprisoned those who try to hide behind these laws. Sometimes, however, conflict pits two constitutional rights against one another, as when a judge places a **gag order** on individuals involved in a case. In such cases, the court has essentially decreed that the First Amendment rights of free speech and freedom of the press must be postponed so that the right of an individual to receive a fair and impartial trial is not destroyed.

FREEDOM OF ASSEMBLY AND PETITION

The First Amendment guarantees "the right of the people peaceably to assemble, and to petition the government for redress of grievances." The right to organize political parties and interest groups derives from the right of assembly. And freedom of petition protects most lobbying activities.

The Right of Association   Freedom of assembly includes the right to form and join organizations and associations. In an important case during the early civil rights movement, the State of Alabama attempted to harass the National Association for the Advancement of Colored People by requiring it to turn over its membership lists to authorities. The Supreme Court held the state's action to be an unconstitutional infringement of the freedom of association.[75]

The Supreme Court has also protected the right of students to form organizations. "First Amendment rights are available to teachers and students. It can hardly be argued that either teachers or students shed their constitutional rights at the school house gate."[76] Attempts by a college or university to deny official recognition to a student organization based on its views violates the right of association.

Protests, Parades, and Demonstrations   Freedom of assembly includes the right to peacefully protest, parade, and demonstrate. Authorities may, within reasonable limits, enact restrictions regarding the time, place, and manner of an assembly so as to preserve public order, smooth traffic flow, freedom of movement, and even peace and quiet. But these regulations cannot be unevenly applied to groups with different views. Thus authorities may require a permit to parade, but they cannot deny a permit to a group because of the nature of their cause. For example, the Supreme Court held that city authorities in Skokie, Illinois, acted unconstitutionally in prohibiting the American Nazi Party from holding a march in that city even though it was populated with large numbers of Jewish survivors of the Holocaust.[77] (As *What Do You Think?* "Freedom of Assembly for Whom?" illustrates, however, many Americans disagree with this interpretation.)

Picketing   Assemblies of people have a high potential for creating a public disturbance. Parades block traffic and litter the streets; loudspeakers assault the ears of

gag order   Order by a judge banning discussion or reporting of a case in order to ensure a fair and impartial trial.

What Do You Think?

Freedom of Assembly for Whom?

The general public lags far behind the Supreme Court, and well behind persons trained in the law, in adherence to the prevailing constitutional norms of freedom of assembly. Although most Americans express general support for the right to hold mass protests and demonstrations, they are unwilling to extend police protection to unpopular groups or to risk any protests that "might" result in violence. When the same questions are asked of a national sample of lawyers and judges, there is much greater understanding of the constitutional principles at stake and a much greater willingness to protect demonstrators.

The First Amendment right of assembly does not depend on the views of the group that is meeting. If a community regularly allows its civic auditorium to be used by organizations, it cannot deny use to a particular organization on the basis of its unpopular views. But the general public appears quite willing to deny the use of a community facility to advocates of unpopular causes. For example, although the right of association protects even Nazis, it is not likely that many university administrations would permit such an organization to meet on campus unless confronted with a court order to do so. Persons trained in the law are generally more cognizant of First Amendment rights, but even lawyers do not uniformly endorse the exercise of the right of assembly for all groups.

What Is Your Position on the Following Activities?	General Public	Lawyers and Judges
Mass student protest demonstrations . . .		
. . . should be allowed by college officials as long as they are nonviolent.	68%	88%
. . . have no place on the college campus and participating students should be punished.	21	9
. . . neither/undecided	12	3
When groups like the Nazis or other extreme groups require police protection at their rallies and marches, the community should . . .		
. . . supply and pay for whatever police protection is needed.	18	67
. . . prohibit such groups from holding rallies because of the costs and damages incurred.	57	14
. . . neither/undecided	25	20
Should a community allow its civic auditorium to be used . . .		
. . . by Protestant groups who want to hold a revival meeting?		
Yes	69	74
No	16	17
. . . right to life groups to preach against abortion?		
Yes	65	81
No	18	10
. . . gay liberation movements to organize for homosexual rights?		
Yes	26	65
No	59	26
. . . atheists who want to preach against God and religion?		
Yes	18	66
No	71	24
. . . foreign radicals who want to express their hatred of America?		
Yes	6	32
No	87	52
If some students at a college want to form a "Campus Nazi Club" . . .		
. . . they should be allowed to do so.	17	67
. . . college officials should ban such clubs from campus.	67	24
. . . neither/undecided	16	9

Source: Data from Herbert McClosky and Alida Brill, *Dimensions of Tolerance* (New York: Russell Sage Foundation, 1983).

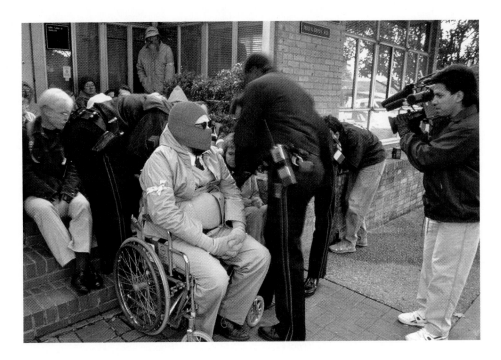

No rights are absolute. The freedom to assemble does not include the right to block public access to buildings. Congress reaffirmed this limitation in 1994 in a law guaranteeing access to abortion clinics.

local residents and bystanders; picket lines may block the free passage of others. Although the right of assembly is protected by the First Amendment, its exercise involves conduct as well as expression, and therefore it is usually subject to greater government regulation than expression alone. The Court has generally upheld reasonable use of public property for assembly, but it has not forced *private* property owners to accommodate speeches or assemblies. Airport terminals, shopping malls, and other open forums, which may or may not be publicly owned, have posed problems for the courts.

Freedom of assembly is currently being tested by opponents of abortion such as Operation Rescue that picket abortion clinics, hoping to embarrass and dissuade women from entering them. Generally the courts have placed strict limits on these demonstrations to ensure that people can move freely in and out of the clinics. Freedom of assembly does not include the right to block access to public or private buildings. And when abortion opponents demonstrated at the residence of a physician who performed abortions, the Supreme Court upheld a local ordinance barring assemblies in residential neighborhoods.[78] Physically obstructing access to buildings almost always violates state or local laws, as does the threat or use of force by picketers. In 1994 Congress passed a federal law guaranteeing access to abortion clinics, arguing that the federal government should act to guarantee a recognized constitutional right.

THE RIGHT TO BEAR ARMS

The Second Amendment to the U.S. Constitution states: "A well regulated Militia, being necessary to the security of a free State, the right of the people to keep and bear Arms, shall not be infringed."

Bearing Arms   What is meant by the right of the people "to keep and bear arms"? One view is that the Second Amendment confers on Americans an *individual*

The violent conclusion of the attempt by the Bureau of Alcohol, Tobacco and Firearms to enforce federal gun laws against the Branch Davidians in Waco, Texas. Members of citizen militia groups regard the ATF as a threat to their freedom to bear arms.

constitutional right, like the First Amendment freedom of speech or press (see *Across the USA:* "Gun Control and the Second Amendment"). The history surrounding the adoption of the Second Amendment reveals the concern of colonists with attempts by despotic governments to confiscate the arms of citizens and render them helpless to resist tyranny. James Madison wrote in the *Federalist Papers,* No. 46 that "the advantage of being armed which the Americans possess over the people of almost every other nation, forms a barrier against the enterprise of [tyrannical] ambition."[79] The Second Amendment was adopted with little controversy; most state constitutions at the time, like Pennsylvania's, declared that "the people have a right to bear arms for the defense of themselves and the state." Early American political rhetoric was filled with praise for an armed citizenry able to protect its freedoms by force if necessary.

State Militias   But many constitutional scholars argue that the Second Amendment protects only the *collective* right of the states to form militias—that is, their right to maintain National Guard units. They focus on the qualifying phrase "a well-regulated Militia, being necessary to the security of a free State." The Second Amendment merely prevents Congress from denying the states the right to organize their own military units. If the Founders had wished to create an individual right to bear arms, they would not have inserted the phrase about a "well-regulated militia." (Opponents of this view argue that the original definition of a militia included all free males over eighteen.) Interpreted in this fashion, the Second Amendment does *not* protect private groups who form themselves into militias, nor does it guarantee citizens the right to own guns.

Citizen "Militias"   In recent years, self-styled citizen "militias" have cropped up across the nation. They are armed groups who more or less regularly get together dressed in camouflage to engage in military tactics and training. They generally view federal government agencies, and often the United Nations, as potential threats to their freedom. They view themselves as modern-day descendants of the

Gun Control and the Second Amendment

One subject of contention in the debate over gun control is whether or not law abiding citizens should be permitted to carry concealed handguns. Laws on this issue vary from state to state.

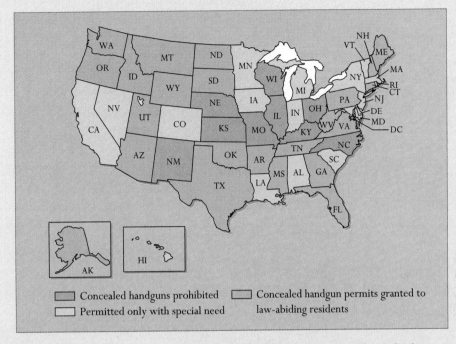

☐ Concealed handguns prohibited
☐ Permitted only with special need
☐ Concealed handgun permits granted to law-abiding residents

Attempts at gun control legislation frequently follow murders or assassination attempts on prominent figures. The Federal Gun Control Act of 1968 was a response to the assassinations of Senator Robert F. Kennedy and Martin Luther King, Jr., in that year. It banned mail-order sales of handguns and required that manufacturers place serial numbers on all firearms, that dealers record all sales, and that dealers be licensed by the Bureau of Alcohol, Tobacco and Firearms. In 1993 Congress passed the Brady Act, requiring a seven-day waiting period for the purchase of a handgun. The act is named for James S. Brady, former press secretary to President Ronald Reagan, who was severely wounded in the 1981 attempted assassination of the president. The Crime Control Act of 1994 banned the manufacture or sale of "assault weapons," generally defined to include both automatic and semiautomatic rifles and machine pistols. Opponents of these acts believe they are empty political gestures that erode the Second Amendment right to bear arms.

Proponents of gun control cite the U.S. Supreme Court decision in *United States v. Miller* (1939). In this case, the Court considered the constitutionality of the federal National Firearms Act of 1934, which, among other things, prohibited the transportation of sawed-off shotguns in interstate commerce. The defendant claimed that Congress could not infringe on his right to keep and bear arms. But the Court responded that a sawed-off shotgun had no "relationship to the preservation or efficiency of a well-regulated militia."* The clear implication of this decision is that the right to bear arms refers only to a state's right to maintain a militia. But even if an individual has a constitutional right to own a gun, the Supreme Court is likely to approve of reasonable restrictions on that right, including waiting periods for purchases, reporting, and registration. No constitutional right is viewed as absolute.

The Second Amendment does not necessarily include the right to carry a hidden gun. Currently about half of the states grant concealed weapons carrying permits to applicants who have never been convicted of a felony. (Generally a "concealed weapon" refers to a handgun carried on a person or within immediate reach in an automobile.) Nine states and the District of Columbia prohibit the carrying of concealed weapons altogether. Other states require applicants for permits to prove that they have a specific need to carry a weapon.

---

*United States v. Miller, 307 U.S. 174 (1939).

American patriot militias who fought in the Revolutionary War. Indeed, the Militia Act of 1792 *required* "every free white male citizen of the respective states, resident therein, who is or shall be of the age of 18 years and under the age of 45 years" to be enrolled in the militia and equipped with "a good musket," a bayonet, and "24 rounds of ammunition." This law was not changed until 1912, when National Guard units replaced state militia.

Citizen militia groups frequently come into conflict with federal firearms regulations. Enforcement of these regulations is the responsibility of the Bureau of Alcohol, Tobacco and Firearms. It was the ATF's violent efforts to enforce federal gun laws that led to the deaths of more than seventy people at the Branch Davidian compound in Waco, Texas, in 1993. Radical militia groups have pledged to enforce their right to bear arms with violence if necessary.

CRIME, VIOLENCE, AND THE CONSTITUTION

Crime, violence, and social disorder are common ills confronting all societies. But democratic societies must balance any remedies with respect for the dignity of individuals. For democratic societies, government repression, invasions of privacy, and police misconduct are evils at least as dangerous as crime and violence. It is not surprising that half of the amendments in the Bill of Rights are related to matters involving criminal justice.

Crime in America   How much crime is there in America? Official **crime rates** are based on the Federal Bureau of Investigation's *Uniform Crime Reports,* but these annual FBI reports themselves are based on crimes reported to state and local law enforcement agencies. The FBI has established a uniform classification of certain crimes: *violent crimes* (crimes against persons)—murder and non-negligent manslaughter, forcible rape, robbery, and aggravated assault; and *property crimes* (crimes against property only)—burglary, larceny, arson, and theft, including auto theft (see Table 14-3).

crime rates   Numbers of crimes reported to law enforcement authorities in relation to the population.

Crime Rates   National crime rates more than doubled between 1965 and 1975, and "law and order" became an important political issue. Since the early 1980s, however, crime rates have leveled off and even declined from their record years (see Figure 14-1). Many speculate that this pattern reflects age-group changes in the popu-

TABLE 14-3	Official Crime Rates (Offenses Reported to Police per 100,000 Population)			
	1980	*1985*	*1990*	*1997*
Crime against Persons	597	538	732	644
Murder	10	8	9	7
Forcible rape	37	34	41	36
Robbery	251	217	257	301
Aggravated assault	299	279	424	405
Crimes against Property	5,353	4,637	5,089	4,409
All Reported Crimes	5,950	5,175	5,821	5,067

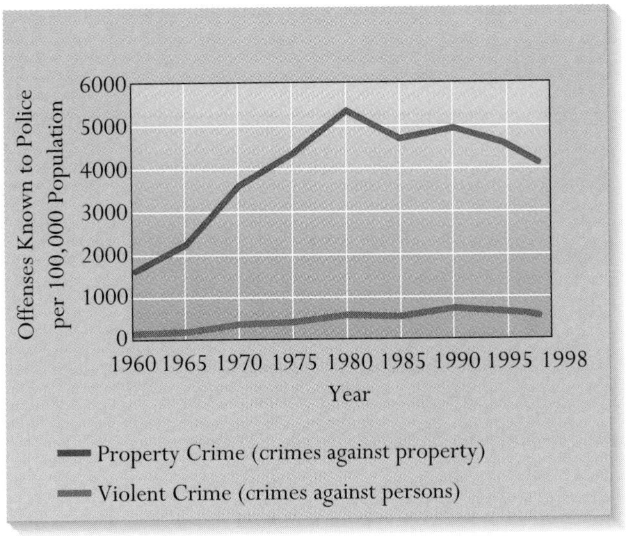

FIGURE 14-1 Crime Rates in the United States

lation: the early rise in crime reflected the large numbers of baby boomers reaching "crime-prone" age groups (fifteen to twenty-four) at that time. Crime rates leveled off when this age group was no longer increasing as a percentage of the population and were expected to keep falling. But instead, crime rates moved upward again. The new factor in the crime rate equation appeared to be the widespread popularity of "crack" cocaine and other illegal drugs. Perhaps as many as one-half of all crimes today are drug related (see *A Conflicting View:* "Legalize Drugs to Reduce Crime").

Crime on the Wane?   Law enforcement officials attribute the recent decline in the crime rate to successful crime-fighting strategies such as "crackdowns," more aggressive "community policing," and longer prison sentences for repeat offenders, including "three strikes you're out" laws. In support of this claim, they observe that the greatest reductions in crime have occurred in the nation's largest cities, especially those such as New York that have adopted tougher law enforcement practices. However, although overall crime rates are down, juvenile crime is on the rise. So it is by no means certain that crime rates will not rise again in future years.

Victimization   Many crimes are not reported to the police and therefore cannot be counted in the official crime rates shown in Table 14-3. In an effort to learn the real amount of crime in the nation, the U.S. Justice Department regularly surveys a national sample of people, asking whether they have been a victim of a crime during the past year.[80] These surveys reveal that the **victimization rate** is many times greater than the official crime rate. Between 30 and 40 million of the nation's 265 million inhabitants say they have been a victim of a crime in the preceding year; 6 million say they have been victims of violent crime. The number of forcible rapes is three to five times greater than the number reported to police, burglaries three times greater, and robbery more than twice the reported rate. Only auto theft and murder statistics are reasonably accurate, indicating that most people call the police when their car is stolen or someone is murdered.

Why do people fail to report crime to the police? The most common reason given by interviewees is the feeling that police cannot be effective in dealing with

victimization rate   Incidence of crime as reported in public opinion polls; exceeds the crime rate because it takes into account individuals who are victimized but decline to take the issue to the police.

Legalize Drugs to Reduce Crime

Drug offenses currently account for almost half of all prison sentences meted out by federal courts.* The average federal sentence for drug crimes—possession, trafficking, or manufacturing of illegal substances—is seven years; the federal minimum sentence for possession of illegal drugs is five years. Almost half of the federal prison population is serving time for drug offenses. Nearly 1 million persons are arrested each year for drug violations. The United States imprisons a larger proportion of its population than any other advanced nation. Is all this too high a price to pay for the "war on drugs"?

The U.S. government's National Institute on Drug Abuse regularly surveys Americans to ask whether they have ever used particular drugs and whether they have used them in the past year or month. These surveys suggest that about 13 million people, or less than 6 percent of the U.S. population, have used an illicit drug in the previous thirty days (see figure). Marijuana is the most commonly used illicit drug, followed by cocaine. An estimated 10 million are regular users of marijuana, or about 4 percent of the population, although many more have smoked it at least once. About 53 percent of the adult population have consumed alcoholic beverages in the previous month and 24 percent have smoked cigarettes.

According to the survey evidence, the numbers of people using illicit drugs has declined in recent years. However, the U.S. Drug Enforcement Administration (DEA) reports increased numbers of cocaine seizures and drug arrests each year. There appear to be no significant reductions in the volume of drugs entering the country or reaching the streets.

The failure of antidrug policies to produce any significant reductions in drug supply or demand, coupled with the high costs of enforcement and the loss of civil liberties, has caused some observers to propose the legalization of drugs and government control of their production and sales. "Prohibition" failed earlier in the century to end alcohol consumption, and the crime, official corruption, and enormous cost of futile efforts to stop drinking eventually forced the nation to end Prohibition. Similarly, it is argued that the legalization of drugs would end organized crime's profit monopoly over the drug trade, raise billions of dollars by legally taxing drugs, end the strain

Drug Use in the United States

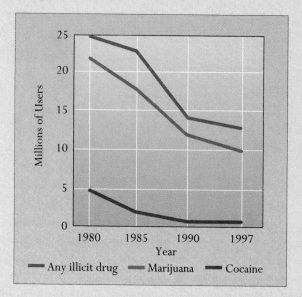

on relations with Latin American nations caused by efforts to eradicate drugs, and save additional billions in enforcement costs that could be used for education and treatment. If drugs were legally obtainable under government supervision, it is argued that many of society's current problems would be alleviated: the crime and violence associated with the drug trade, the corruption of public officials, the spread of diseases associated with drug use, and the many infringements of personal liberty associated with antidrug wars.

But even the suggestion of drug legalization offends Americans who believe that legalization would greatly expand drug use in the country. Cheap, available drugs would greatly increase the numbers of addicted persons, creating a "society of zombies" that would destroy the social fabric of the nation. Cocaine and heroin are far more habit forming than alcohol, and legalization would encourage the development of newer and even more potent and addictive synthetic drugs. Whatever the health costs of drug abuse today, it is argued that legalization would produce public health problems of enormous magnitude. Whatever the damages to society from drug-related crime and efforts to prohibit drugs, the damages to society from cheap, available drug usage would be far greater.

---

*Statistical Abstract of the United States, 1997, p. 217.

Source: U.S. Substance Abuse and Mental Health Services Administration, Natural Household Survey on Drug Abuse, annual.

the crime. Other reasons included the feeling that the crime was "a private matter" or that the victim did not want to harm the offender. Fear of reprisal was mentioned less frequently, usually in cases of assaults and family crimes.[81]

RIGHTS OF CRIMINAL DEFENDANTS

While society needs the protection of the police, it is equally important to protect society from the police. Arbitrary searches and arrests, imprisonment without trial, forced confessions, beatings and torture, secret trials, tainted witnesses, excessive punishments, and other human rights violations are all too common throughout the world. The U.S. Constitution limits the powers of the police and protects the rights of the accused (see Table 14-4).

The Guarantee of the Writ of Habeas Corpus   One of the oldest and most revered rights in English common law is the right to obtain a **writ of habeas corpus,** which is a court order directing public officials who are holding a person in custody to bring the prisoner into court and explain the reasons for confinement. If a judge finds that the prisoner is being unlawfully detained, or finds insufficient evidence that a crime has been committed or that the prisoner could have committed it, the judge must order the prisoner's release. Thus the writ of habeas corpus is a means to test the legality of any imprisonment.

The writ of habeas corpus was considered so fundamental to the framers of the Constitution that they included it in the original text of Article I: "The privilege of the Writ of Habeas Corpus shall not be suspended, unless when in Cases of Rebellion or Invasion the public Safety may require it." Despite the qualifying phrase, the Supreme Court has never sanctioned suspension of the writ of habeas corpus even during wartime. President Abraham Lincoln suspended the writ of habeas corpus in several areas during the Civil War, but in the case of *Ex parte Milligan* (1866), the Supreme Court ruled that the president had acted unconstitutionally.[82] (With the war over, however, the Court's decision had no practical effect.) Again, in 1946, the Supreme Court declared that the military had had no right to substitute military courts for ordinary courts in Hawaii during World War II, even though Hawaii was in an active theater of war.[83] State courts cannot issue writs of habeas corpus to federal officials, but federal judges may issue such writs to state officials whenever there is reason to believe that a person is being held in violation of the Constitution or laws of the United States.

The Prohibition of Bills of Attainder and Ex Post Facto Laws   Like the guarantee of habeas corpus, protection against bills of attainder and ex post facto laws was considered so fundamental to individual liberty that it was included in the original text of the Constitution. A **bill of attainder** is a legislative act inflicting punishment without judicial trial. An **ex post facto law** is a retroactive criminal law that works against the accused—for example, a law that makes an act criminal after the act is committed or a law that increases the punishment for a crime and applies it retroactively. Both the federal government and the states are prevented from passing such laws.

The fact that relatively few cases of bills of attainder or ex post facto laws have come to the federal courts does not diminish the importance of these protections. Rather, it testifies to the widespread appreciation of their importance in a free society.

writ of habeas corpus   Court order directing public officials who are holding a person in custody to bring the prisoner into court and explain the reasons for confinement; the right to habeas corpus is protected by Article I of the Constitution.

bill of attainder   Legislative act inflicting punishment without judicial trial; forbidden under Article I of the Constitution.

ex post facto law   Retroactive criminal law that works against the accused; forbidden under Article I of the Constitution.

TABLE 14-4	Individual Rights in the Criminal Justice Process	

Rights	*Process*
Fourth Amendment: Protection against unreasonable searches and seizures Warranted searches for sworn "probable cause." Exceptions: consent searches, safety searches, car searches, and searches incident to a valid arrest.	**Investigation by law enforcement officers** Expectation that police act lawfully.
Fifth Amendment: Protection against self-incrimination Miranda rules (see Figure 14-2) **Habeas corpus** Police holding a person in custody must bring that person before a judge with cause to believe that a crime was committed and the prisoner committed it.	**Arrest** Arrests based on warrants issued by judges and magistrates. Arrests based on crimes committed in the presence of law enforcement officials. Arrests for "probable cause."
Eighth Amendment: No excessive bail Defendant considered innocent until proven guilty; release on bail and amount of bail depends on seriousness of crime, trustworthiness of defendant, and safety of community.	**Hearing and bail** Preliminary hearing in which prosecutor presents testimony that a crime was committed and probable cause for charging the accused.
Fifth Amendment: Grand jury (federal) Federal prosecutors (but not necessarily state prosecutors) must convince a grand jury that a reasonable basis exists to believe the defendant committed a crime and he or she should be brought to trial.	**Indictment** Prosecutor, or a grand jury in federal cases, issues formal document naming the accused and specifying the charges.
Sixth Amendment: Right to Counsel Begins in investigation stage, when officials become "accusatory"; extends throughout criminal justice process. Free counsel for indigent defendants.	**Arraignment** Judge reads indictment to the accused and ensures that the accused understands charges and rights and has counsel. Judge asks defendant how to choose a plea: Guilty, *nolo contendere* (no contest), or not guilty. If defendant pleads guilty or no contest, a trial is not necessary and defendant proceeds to sentencing.
Sixth Amendment: Right to a speedy and public trial Impartial jury. Right to confront witnesses. Right to compel favorable witnesses to testify.	**Trial** Impartial judge presides as prosecuting and defense attorneys present witnesses and evidence relevant to guilt or innocence of defendant and make arguments to the jury. Jury deliberates in secret and issues a verdict.
Fourth Amendment: Exclusionary rule Illegally obtained evidence cannot be used against defendant.	
Eighth Amendment: Protection against cruel and unusual punishments	**Sentencing** If the defendant is found not guilty, the process ends. Defendants who plead guilty or no contest and defendants found guilty by jury are sentenced by fine, imprisonment, or both by the judge.
Fifth Amendment: Protection against double jeopardy Government cannot try a defendant again for the same offense.	**Appeal** Defendants found guilty may appeal to higher courts for reversal of verdict or a new trial based on errors made anywhere in the process.

Unreasonable Searches and Seizures   Individuals are protected by the Fourth Amendment from "unreasonable searches and seizures" of their private "persons, houses, papers, and effects." The Fourth Amendment lays out specific rules for searches and seizures of evidence: "No warrants shall issue, but upon probable cause, supported by Oath or affirmation, and particularly describing the place to be searched, and the persons or things to be seized." Judges cannot issue a **search warrant** just to let police see if an individual has committed a crime; there must be "probable cause" for such issuance. The indiscriminate searching of whole neighborhoods or groups of people is unconstitutional and is prevented by the Fourth Amendment's requirement that the place to be searched must be specifically described in the warrant. The requirement that the things to be seized must be described in the warrant is meant to prevent "fishing expeditions" into an individual's home and personal effects on the possibility that some evidence of unknown illegal activity might crop up. The only exception is if police, in the course of a valid search for a specified item, find other items whose very possession is a crime—for example, illicit drugs.

But the courts also permit police to undertake various other "reasonable" searches *without* a warrant: searches in connection with a valid arrest; searches to protect the safety of police officers; searches to obtain evidence in the immediate vicinity and in the suspect's control; searches to preserve evidence in danger of being immediately destroyed; and searches with the consent of a suspect. Indeed, most police searches today take place without warrant under one or another of these conditions. The Supreme Court has also allowed automobile searches and searches of open fields without warrants in many cases. The requirement of "probable cause" has been very loosely defined; even a "partially corroborated anonymous informant's tip" qualifies as "probable cause" to make a search, seizure, or arrest.[84] And if the police, while making a warranted search or otherwise lawfully on the premises, see evidence of a crime "in plain view," they may seize such evidence without further authorization.[85]

Arrests   The Supreme Court has not applied the warrant requirement of the Fourth Amendment to arrests. Rather, the Court permits arrests without warrants

search warrant Court order permitting law enforcement officials to search a location in order to seize evidence of a crime; issued only for a specified location, in connection with a specific investigation, and on submission of proof that "probable cause" exists to warrant such a search.

Unlike soldiers in a conventional war, U.S. police officers face restraints on how far they can go in their war on crime. Although some charge that these restrictions have made it easy for criminals to escape the consequences of their actions, others argue that forcing law enforcement officials to follow the law is not only reasonable but also results in stronger cases and increased chances of conviction.

(1) when a crime is committed in the presence of an officer; and (2) when an arrest is supported by "probable cause" to believe that a crime has been committed by the person apprehended.[86] However, the Court has held that police may not enter a home to arrest its occupant without either a warrant for the arrest or the consent of the owner.[87]

Indictment The Fifth Amendment requires that an **indictment** be issued by a **grand jury** before a person may be brought to trial on a felony offense. This provision was designed as a protection against unreasonable and harassing prosecutions by the government. In principle, the grand jury is supposed to determine whether the evidence submitted to it by government prosecutors is sufficient to place a person on trial. In practice, however, grand juries spend very little time deliberating on the vast majority of cases. Neither defendants nor their attorneys are permitted to testify before grand juries without the prosecution's permission, which is rarely given. Thus the prosecutor controls the information submitted to grand juries and instructs them in their duties. In almost all cases, grand juries accept the prosecution's recommendations with little or no discussion. Thus grand juries, whose hearings are secret, do not provide much of a check on federal prosecutors, and their refusal to indict is very rare.

Self-Incrimination and the Right to Counsel Freedom from self-incrimination had its origin in English common law; it was originally designed to prevent persons from being tortured into confessions of guilt. It is also a logical extension of the notion that individuals should not be forced to contribute to their own prosecution, that the burden of proof rests on the state. The Fifth Amendment protects people from both physical and psychological coercion.[88] It protects not only accused persons at their own trial but also witnesses testifying in trials of other persons, civil suits, congressional hearings, and so on. Thus "taking the Fifth" has become a standard phrase in our culture: "I refuse to answer that question on the grounds that it might tend to incriminate me." The protection also means that judges, prosecutors, and juries cannot use the refusal of people to take the stand at their own trial as evidence of guilt. Indeed, a judge or attorney is not even permitted to imply this to a jury, and a judge is obligated to instruct a jury *not* to infer guilt from a defendant's refusal to testify.

It is important to note that individuals may be forced to testify when they are not themselves the object of a criminal prosecution. Government officials may extend a grant of **immunity from prosecution** to a witness in order to compel testimony. Under a grant of immunity, the government agrees not to use any of the testimony against the witness; in return, the witness provides information that the government uses to prosecute others who are considered more dangerous or more important than the immune witness. Because such grants ensure that nothing the witnesses say can be used against them, immunized witnesses cannot refuse to answer under the Fifth Amendment.

The Supreme Court under Chief Justice Earl Warren greatly strengthened the Fifth Amendment protection against self-incrimination and the right to counsel in a series of rulings in the 1960s:

- *Gideon v. Wainwright* (1963): Equal protection under the Fourteenth Amendment requires that free legal counsel be appointed for all indigent defendants in all criminal cases.[89]

indictment Determination by a grand jury that sufficient evidence exists to warrant trial of an individual on a felony charge; necessary before an individual can be brought to trial.

grand jury Jury charged only with determining whether sufficient evidence exists to support indictment of an individual on a felony charge; the grand jury's decision to indict does not represent a conviction.

immunity from prosecution Grant by the government to an individual of freedom from prosecution on a particular charge in return for testimony by that individual that might otherwise be self-incriminating.

METROPOLITAN POLICE DEPARTMENT	WAIVER
Warning As To Your Rights	
You are under arrest. Before we ask you any questions you must understand what your rights are.	1. Have you read or had read to you the warning as to your rights?_____
You have the right to remain silent. You are not required to say anything to us at any time or to answer any questions. Anything you say can be used against you in court.	2. Do you understand these rights? _____
	3. Do you wish to answer any questions? _____
You have the right to talk to a lawyer for advice before we question you and to have him with you during questioning.	4. Are you willing to answer questions without having an attorney present? _____
If you cannot afford a lawyer and want one, a lawyer will be provided for you.	5. Signature of defendant on line below.
	_____
If you want to answer questions now without a lawyer present, you will still have the right to stop answering at any time. You also have the right to stop answering at any time until you talk to a lawyer.	6. Time _____ Date _____
	7. Signature of officer _____
	8. Signature of witness _____

FIGURE 14-2 The Miranda Warning

Since the U.S. Supreme Court's ruling in the case of Miranda v. Arizona *in 1966, law enforcement officials at all levels have routinely carried "Miranda rights" cards, which they read to accused individuals immediately after their arrest. This procedure has largely eliminated defendants' abilities to obtain dismissals and/or acquittals on the basis of ignorance of their rights or lack of proper counsel.*

- *Escobedo v. Illinois* (1964): Suspects are entitled to confer with counsel as soon as police investigation focuses on them or once "the process shifts from investigatory to accusatory."[90]

- *Miranda v. Arizona* (1966): Before questioning suspects, a police officer must inform them of all their constitutional rights, including the right to counsel (appointed at no cost to the suspect if necessary) and the right to remain silent. Although suspects may knowingly waive these rights, the police cannot question anyone who at any point asks for a lawyer or declines "in any manner" to be questioned. If the police commit an error in these procedures, the accused goes free, regardless of the evidence of guilt.[91] Figure 14-2 shows a typical "Miranda rights" card carried by police to ensure that they issue the proper warnings to those under arrest.

It is very difficult to determine the extent to which these decisions have really hampered efforts to halt the rise in crime in the United States. Studies of police behavior following these decisions show that at first police committed many procedural errors and guilty persons were freed, but after a year or so of adjustment to the new rules, successful prosecutions rose to the same level achieved before the decisions.[92]

The Exclusionary Rule   Illegally obtained evidence and confessions may *not* be used in criminal trials. If police find evidence of a crime in an illegal search or if they elicit statements from suspects without informing them of their rights to remain silent or to have counsel, the evidence or statements produced are not admissible in a trial. This **exclusionary rule** is one of the more controversial procedural rights that the Supreme Court has extended to criminal defendants. The rule is also unique to the United States: in Great Britain evidence obtained illegally may be used against the accused, although the accused may bring charges against the police for damages.

The rule provides *enforcement* for the Fourth Amendment guarantee against unreasonable searches and seizures, as well as the Fifth Amendment guarantee against compulsory self-incrimination and the guarantee of counsel. Initially applied only in federal cases, in *Mapp v. Ohio* (1961) the Supreme Court extended the exclusionary rule to all criminal cases in the United States.[93] A *good faith exception* is made "when law enforcement officers have acted in objective good faith or their transgressions have been minor."[94] But the exclusionary rule is frequently attacked for the high price it extracts from society—the release of guilty criminals. Why punish society because of the misconduct of police? Why not punish police directly, perhaps with disciplinary measures imposed by courts that discover errors, instead of letting guilty persons go free?

Bail Requirements   The Eighth Amendment says only that "*excessive* bail shall not be required." This clause does not say that pretrial release on bail will be available to all. The Supreme Court has held that "in our society liberty is the norm, and detention prior to trial or without trial is the carefully limited exception." Pretrial release on bail can be denied on the basis of the seriousness of the crime (bail is often denied in murder cases), the trustworthiness of the defendant (bail is often denied when the prosecution shows that the defendant is likely to flee before trial), or, in a more controversial exception, when release would threaten "the safety of any other person or the community."[95] If the court does not find any of these exceptions, it must set bail no higher than an amount reasonably calculated to ensure the defendant's later presence at trial.

Most criminal defendants cannot afford the bail money required for pretrial release. They must seek the services of a bail bondsman, who charges a heavy fee for filing the bail money with the court. The bail bondsman receives all of the bail money back when the defendant shows up for trial. But even if the defendant is found innocent, the bail bondsman retains the charge fee. (Thus the system is said to discriminate against poor defendants who cannot afford the bondsman's fee.) The failure of a criminal defendant to appear at his or her trial is itself a crime and subjects the defendant to immediate arrest as well as forfeiture of bail. Most states authorize bail bondsmen to find and arrest persons who have "jumped bail," return them to court, and thereby recover the bail money.

Fair Trial   The original text of the Constitution guaranteed jury trials in criminal cases, and the Sixth Amendment went on to correct weaknesses the framers saw in the English justice system at that time—closed proceedings, trials in absentia (where the defendant is not present), secret witnesses, long delays between arrest and trial, biased juries, and the absence of defense counsel. Specifically, the Sixth Amendment guarantees the following:

● The right to a speedy and public trial.

exclusionary rule   Rule of law that evidence found in an illegal search or resulting from an illegally obtained confession may not be admitted at trial.

- An impartial jury chosen from the state or district where the crime was committed.
- The right to confront (cross-examine) witnesses against the accused.
- The right of the accused to compel (subpoena) favorable witnesses to appear.
- The right of the accused to be represented by counsel.

Over the years the courts have elaborated on these elements of a fair trial so that today trial proceedings follow a rigidly structured format. First, attorneys make opening statements. The prosecution describes the crime and how it will prove beyond a reasonable doubt that the defendant committed it. The defense attorney argues either that the crime did not occur or that the defendant did not do it. Next, each side, again beginning with the prosecution, calls witnesses who first testify on "direct examination" for their side, then are cross-examined by the opposing attorney. Witnesses may be asked to verify evidence that is introduced as "exhibits." Defendants have a right to be present during their own trials (although an abusive and disruptive defendant may be considered to have waived his or her right to be present and be removed from the courtroom).[96] Prosecution witnesses must appear in the courtroom and submit to cross-examination (although special protection procedures, including videotaped testimony, may be used for children).[97] Prosecutors are obliged to disclose any information that might create a reasonable doubt about the defendant's guilt,[98] but the defendant may not be compelled to disclose incriminating information.

After all of the witnesses offered by both sides have been heard and cross-examined, prosecution and defense give their closing arguments. The burden of proof "beyond a reasonable doubt" rests with the prosecution; the defense does not need to prove that the accused is innocent, only that reasonable doubt exists regarding guilt.

Juries must be "impartial": they must not have prejudged the case or exhibit bias or prejudice or have a personal interest in the outcome. Judges can dismiss jurors for "cause." During jury selection, attorneys for the prosecution and defense are allowed a fixed number of "peremptory" challenges of jurors (although they cannot do so on the basis of race).[99] Jury selection is often regarded by attorneys as the key to the outcome of a case; both sides try to get presumed sympathetic people on the jury. In well-publicized cases, judges may "sequester" a jury (keep them in a hotel away from access to the mass media) in order to maintain impartiality. Judges may exclude press or television to prevent trials from becoming spectacles if they wish.[100] By tradition, English juries have had twelve members; however, the Supreme Court has allowed six-member juries in non-death-penalty cases.[101] Also by tradition, juries should arrive at a unanimous decision. If a jury cannot do so, judges declare a "hung" jury and the prosecutor may schedule a retrial. Only a "not guilty" prevents retrial of a defendant. Traditionally, it was believed that a lack of unanimity raised "reasonable doubt" about the defendant's guilt. But the Supreme Court has permitted nonunanimous verdicts in some cases.[102]

Plea Bargaining   Few criminal cases actually go to trial. More than 90 percent of criminal cases are plea bargained.[103] In **plea bargaining,** the defendant agrees to plead guilty and waives the right to a jury trial in exchange for concessions made by the prosecutor, perhaps the dropping of more serious charges against the defendant or a pledge to seek a reduced sentence or fine. Some critics of plea bargaining view it as another form of leniency in the criminal justice system that

Despite national attention on the Oklahoma City bombing, the trial of defendant Timothy McVeigh did not become a media spectacle like the O.J. Simpson trial because the trial judge barred television cameras from the courtroom.

plea bargaining   Practice of allowing defendants to plead guilty to lesser crimes than those with which they were originally charged in return for reduced sentences.

reduces its deterrent effects. Other critics view plea bargaining as a violation of the Constitution's protection against self-incrimination and guarantee of a fair jury trial. Prosecutors, they say, threaten defendants with serious charges and stiff penalties in order to force a guilty plea. Still other critics see plea bargaining as an "under-the-table" process that undermines respect for the criminal justice system.

Yet it is vital to the nation's court system that most defendants plead guilty. The court system would quickly break down from overload if any substantial proportion of defendants insisted on jury trials.

THE DEATH PENALTY

Perhaps the most heated debate in criminal justice policy today concerns capital punishment. Opponents of the death penalty argue that it violates the prohibition against "cruel and unusual punishments" in the Eighth Amendment to the Constitution. They also argue that the death penalty is applied unequally. A large proportion of those executed have been poor, uneducated, and nonwhite. In contrast, many Americans feel that justice demands strong retribution for heinous crimes— a life for a life. A mere jail sentence for a multiple murderer or rapist-murderer seems unjust compared with the damage inflicted on society and the victims. In many cases, a life sentence means less than ten years in prison under the current early-release and parole policies in many states. Convicted murderers have been set free, and some have killed again.

Prohibition against Unfair Application   Prior to 1971, the death penalty was officially sanctioned by about half of the states. Federal law also retained the death penalty. However, no one had actually suffered the death penalty since 1967 because of numerous legal tangles and direct challenges to the constitutionality of capital punishment.

In *Furman v. Georgia* (1972), the Supreme Court ruled that capital punishment, as then imposed, violated the Eighth and Fourteenth Amendment prohibitions against cruel and unusual punishment and due process of law. The justices' reasoning in the case was very complex. Only Justices William J. Brennan and Thurgood Marshall declared that capital punishment itself is cruel and unusual. The other justices in the majority felt that death sentences had been applied unfairly; some individuals received the death penalty for crimes for which many others received much lighter sentences. These justices left open the possibility that capital punishment would be constitutional if it was specified for certain kinds of crime and applied uniformly.[104]

After this decision, a majority of states rewrote their death penalty laws to try to ensure fairness and uniformity of application. Generally, these laws mandate the death penalty for murders committed during rape, robbery, hijacking, or kidnapping; murder of prison guards; murder with torture; and multiple murders. They call for two trials to be held—one to determine guilt or innocence and another to determine the penalty. At the second trial, evidence of "aggravating" and "mitigating" factors must be presented; if there are aggravating factors but no mitigating factors, the death penalty is mandatory.

Death Penalty Reinstated   The revised death penalty laws were upheld in a series of cases that came before the Supreme Court in 1976. The Court concluded

Politics in Cyberspace

Civil Liberties

The Cornell University Law School
http://www.law.cornell.edu

This site provides access to historic decisions of the U.S. Supreme Court, including its landmark decisions on civil liberties.

American Civil Liberties Union
http://www.aclu.org

The ACLU provides a generally liberal perspective on civil liberties. Its Web site includes information about many recent First Amendment–based challenges to state and federal laws, as well as information on student rights, voting rights, workers' rights, and other topics.

American Center for Law and Justice
http://www.aclj.org

The ACLJ is a conservatively oriented public-interest law firm founded by Pat Robertson. Its Web site provides information about such issues as challenges by religious groups to restrictions on prayer and other religious expression in schools and restrictions on anti-abortion protests.

---

that "the punishment of death does *not* invariably violate the Constitution." The majority decision noted that the framers of the Bill of Rights had accepted death as a common penalty for crime. Although acknowledging that the Constitution and its amendments must be interpreted in a dynamic fashion, reflecting changing moral values, the Court's majority noted that most state legislatures have been willing to reenact the death penalty and hundreds of juries have been willing to impose that penalty. Thus "a large proportion of American society continues to regard it as an appropriate and necessary criminal sanction." Moreover, the Court held that the social purposes of retribution and deterrence justify the use of the death penalty; this ultimate sanction is "an expression of society's moral outrage at particularly offensive conduct."[105]

The Court reaffirmed that *Furman v. Georgia* struck down the death penalty only where it was invoked in "an arbitrary and capricious manner." A majority of the justices upheld the death penalty in states where the trial was a two-part proceeding, provided that during the second part the judge or jury was given relevant information and standards for deciding whether to impose the death penalty. The Court approved the consideration of "aggravating and mitigating circumstances." The Court also called for automatic review of all death sentences by state supreme courts to ensure that none is imposed under the influence of passion or prejudice, that aggravating factors are supported by the evidence, and that the sentence is not disproportionate to the crime. However, the court disapproved of state laws making the death penalty mandatory in all first-degree murder cases, holding that such laws were "unduly harsh and unworkably rigid."

Racial Bias   The death penalty has been challenged as a violation of the Equal Protection Clause of the Fourteenth Amendment because of racial bias in the application of the punishment. White murderers are just as likely to receive the death penalty as black murderers. However, some statistics show that if the *victim* is white there is a greater chance that the killer will be sentenced to death than if the victim is black. Nevertheless, the U.S. Supreme Court has ruled that statistical disparities in the race of victims by itself does not bar the use of the death penalty in all cases. There must be evidence of racial bias against a particular defendant in order for the Court to reverse a death sentence.[106]

Delays   Once imposed, the death penalty is, of course, irreversible. It is the ultimate punishment, and it must not be imposed if there is any doubt whatsoever about the defendant's guilt. Yet how many opportunities should death row inmates have to challenge their convictions and sentences? The writ of habeas corpus is guaranteed in the Constitution, but how many habeas corpus petitions should federal courts allow a condemned prisoner to submit? Attorneys for prisoners often generate new claims for last-minute appeals, expecting that federal courts will delay executions for future hearings and adjudications. Sometimes these claims are repetitive and frivolous. Currently, multiple appeals and writs by prisoners mean more than a decade between death sentence and execution.

In recent years, the Supreme Court has limited habeas corpus petitions of prisoners who have already exhausted their appeals and filed one claim in federal court and lost, and prisoners who failed to follow state rules of appeal. But what if genuine new evidence is uncovered after all appeals have been exhausted? Prisoners must then rely on governors' pardons (or, in federal cases, a presidential pardon).

SUMMARY NOTES

- Laws and government are required to protect individual liberty. Yet laws and governments themselves restrict liberty. To resolve this dilemma, constitutions seek to limit governmental power over the individual. In the U.S. Constitution, the Bill of Rights is designed to place certain liberties beyond the reach of government.

- Initially the Bill of Rights applied against only the federal government, not state or local governments. But over time, the Bill of Rights was nationalized, as the Supreme Court applied the Due Process Clause of the Fourteenth Amendment to all governments in the United States.

- Freedom of religion encompasses two separate restrictions on government: government must not establish religion or prohibit its free exercise. Although the wording of the First Amendment is absolute ("Congress shall make no law . . .") the Supreme Court has allowed some restrictions on religious practices that threaten health, safety, or welfare.

- The Supreme Court's efforts to maintain "a wall of separation" between church and state have proven difficult and controversial. The Court's banning of prayer and religious ceremony in public schools more than thirty years ago remains politically unpopular today.

- The Supreme Court has never adopted the absolutist position that all speech is protected by the First Amendment. The Court's clear and present danger doctrine and its preferred position doctrine recognize the importance of free expression in a democracy, yet the Court has permitted some restrictions on expression, especially in times of perceived national crisis.

- The Supreme Court has placed obscenity outside of the protection of the First Amendment, but it has encountered considerable difficulty in defining "obscenity."

- Freedom of the press prevents government from imposing prior restraints (censorship) on the news media except periodically in wartime, when it has been argued that publication would result in serious harm or loss of life. The Supreme Court has allowed greater government authority over radio and television than over newspapers, on the grounds that radio and television are given exclusive rights to use specific broadcast frequencies.

- The First Amendment guarantee of the right of assembly and petition protects the organization of political parties and interest groups. It also protects the right of people to peacefully protest, parade, and demonstrate. Governments may, within reasonable limits, restrict these activities for valid reasons but may not apply different restrictions to different groups based on the nature of their views.

- The Second Amendment guarantees "the right of the people to keep and bear arms." However, it is frequently argued that this is not an individual right to possess a gun, but rather a collective right of the states to maintain National Guard units.

- Crime rates in the United States are currently declining. Yet a free society must balance any remedies to the crime problem against potential infringements of the rights of its citizens.

- The Constitution includes a number of important procedural guarantees in the criminal justice system: the writ of habeas corpus; prohibitions against bills of attainder and ex post facto laws; protection against unreasonable searches and seizures; protection against self-incrimination; guarantee of legal counsel; protection against excessive bail; guarantee of a fair public and speedy trial by an impartial jury; the right to confront witnesses and to compel favorable witnesses to testify; and protection against cruel or unusual punishment.

- The Supreme Court's exclusionary rule helps to enforce some of these procedural rights by excluding illegally obtained evidence and self-incriminating statements from criminal trials. In the 1960s, Court interpretations of the Fourth and Fifth Amendments strengthened the rights of criminal defendants. Police procedures adjusted quickly, and today there is little evidence that procedural rights greatly hamper law enforcement.

- Few criminal cases go to trial. Most are plea bargained, with the defendant pleading guilty in exchange for reduced charges and/or a lighter sentence. Although this practice is frequently criticized, without plea bargaining the nation's criminal court system would break down from case overload.

- The Supreme Court has ruled that the death penalty is not a "cruel and unusual punishment," but the Court has insisted on fairness and uniformity of application.

SELECTED READINGS

ELSHTAIN, JEAN BETHKE. *Democracy on Trial.* New York: Basic Books, 1995. "Communitarian" argument that America's emphasis on personal rights erodes the common good and subverts democracy.

EPSTEIN, LEE. *Constitutional Law for a Changing America: Rights, Liberties and Justice.* 3rd ed. Washington, D.C.: CQ Press, 1997. Updated edition of an authoritative text on civil liberties and the rights of the criminally accused. It describes the political context of Supreme Court decisions and provides key excerpts from the most important decisions.

GARROW, DAVID. *Liberty and Sexuality: The Right to Privacy and the Making of Roe v. Wade.* New York: Macmillan, 1994. Historical account of the background and development of the right to sexual privacy.

HENTOFF, NAT. *Free Speech for Me—But Not for Thee.* New York: HarperCollins, 1992. Account of how both the right and the left in America try to suppress the opinions of those who disagree with them.

HICKOK, EUGENE W., ed. *The Bill of Rights: Original Meaning and Current Understanding.* Charlottesville: University of Virginia Press, 1991. Essays on civil liberty and current controversies surrounding individual liberties guaranteed in the Bill of Rights.

KOBYLKA, JOSEPH F. *The Politics of Obscenity.* Westport, Conn.: Greenwood Press, 1991. Comprehensive review of Supreme Court obscenity decisions, arguing that the *Miller* case in 1973 was a turning point away from a more permissive to a more restrictive approach toward sexually oriented material. It examines the litigation strategies of the American Civil Liberties Union and other groups in obscenity cases.

LEWIS, ANTHONY. *Gideon's Trumpet.* New York: Random House, 1964. The extraordinary story of Clarence Gideon and how his handwritten habeas corpus plea made its way to the U.S. Supreme Court, resulting in the guarantee of free legal counsel for poor defendants in felony cases.

McCLOSKY, HERBERT, and ALIDA BRILL. *Dimensions of Tolerance.* New York: Russell Sage Foundation, 1983. Using public opinion surveys, the authors assess popular and elite support for constitutional liberties; they conclude that intolerance is widespread in the mass public but that community and legal elites give greater support to constitutional principles.

ASK YOURSELF ABOUT POLITICS

1 Does the U.S. Constitution require the government to be color blind with respect to different races in all its laws and actions?
Yes ☐ No ☐

2 If a city's schools are mostly black and the surrounding suburban schools are mostly white, should busing be used to achieve a better racial balance?
Yes ☐ No ☐

3 Are differences between blacks and whites in average income mainly a product of discrimination?
Yes ☐ No ☐

4 Do you generally favor affirmative action programs for women and minorities?
Yes ☐ No ☐

5 Do you believe racial and sexual preferences in employment and education discriminate against white males?
Yes ☐ No ☐

6 Should gender equality receive the same level of legal protection as racial equality?
Yes ☐ No ☐

7 Do dirty jokes and foul language at work constitute sexual harassment?
Yes ☐ No ☐

CHAPTER OUTLINE

FEATURES

Equality has long been the central issue of American politics. What do we mean by equality? And what, if anything, should government do to achieve it?

THE POLITICS OF EQUALITY

Equality has been the central issue of American politics throughout the history of the nation. It is the issue that sparked the nation's only civil war, and it continues today to be the nation's most vexing political concern.

Conflict begins over the very definition of "equality" (see "Dilemmas of Equality" in Chapter 2). Although Americans agree in the abstract that everyone is equal, they disagree over what they mean by "equality." Traditionally, equality meant "equality of *opportunity*": an equal opportunity to develop individual talents and abilities and to be rewarded for work, initiative, merit, and achievement. Over time, the issue of equality has shifted to "equality of *results*": an equal sharing of income and material rewards. With this shift in definition has come political conflict over the question of what, if anything, government should do to narrow the gaps between rich and poor, men and women, blacks and whites, and all other groups in society. Achieving greater equality of results requires government policies that modify the effects of equality of opportunity—that is, policies leading to **redistribution** of income, wealth, jobs, promotions, admissions, and other benefits.

A related issue arises over whether "equality" is to be defined in individual or group terms. Traditionally, Americans thought of equality as the fair treatment of all *individuals,* rather than the treatment afforded particular *groups* such as racial and ethnic minorities, women, or disabled people. Inequality among groups takes on even greater political significance than inequality among individuals. Disparities between men and women, blacks and whites, and various ethnic groups spur political activity, as people in disadvantaged groups come to see their common plight and organize themselves for remedial political action.[1]

The nation's long struggle over equality has produced a number of constitutional and legal milestones in civil rights. These are summarized in Table 15-1. Much of the politics of civil rights centers on the development and interpretation of these guarantees of equality.

SLAVERY, SEGREGATION, AND THE CONSTITUTION

In penning the Declaration of Independence in 1776, Thomas Jefferson affirmed that "All men are created equal." Yet from 1619, when the first slaves were brought to Jamestown, Virginia, until 1865, when the Thirteenth Amendment to the Constitution outlawed the practice, slavery was a way of life in the United States. Africans were captured, enslaved, transported to America, bought and sold, and used as personal property.

Slavery and the Constitution   The Constitution of 1787 recognized and protected slavery in the United States. Article I stipulated that slaves were to be counted as three-fifths of a person for purposes of representation and taxation; it also prohibited any federal restriction on the importation of slaves until 1808. Article IV even guaranteed the return of escaped slaves to their owners. The Founders were aware that the practice of slavery contradicted their professed belief in "equality," and this contradiction caused them some embarrassment. Thus they avoided the word "slave" in favor of the euphemism "person held to Service or Labour" in writing the Constitution.

redistribution   Government policies meant to shift assets from one group to another.

TABLE 15-1 Guarantees of Civil Rights

Thirteenth Amendment (1865)

Neither slavery nor involuntary servitude, except as a punishment for crime whereof the party shall have been duly convicted, shall exist within the United States, or any place subject to their jurisdiction.

Fourteenth Amendment (1868)

No State shall make or enforce any law which shall abridge the privileges or immunities of citizens of the United States; nor shall any State deprive any person of life, liberty, or property, without due process of law; nor deny to any person within its jurisdiction the equal protection of the laws.

Fifteenth Amendment (1870)

The rights of the citizens of the United States to vote shall not be denied or abridged by the United States or by any State on account of race, color, or previous condition of servitude.

Nineteenth Amendment (1920)

The right of the citizens of the United States to vote shall not be denied or abridged by the United States or by any State on account of sex.

Civil Rights Acts of 1866, 1871, and 1875

Acts passed by the Reconstruction Congress following the Civil War. The Civil Rights Act of 1866 guaranteed newly freed persons the right to purchase, lease, and use real property. The Civil Rights Act of 1875 outlawed segregation in privately owned businesses and facilities, but in the Civil Rights Cases (1883), the Supreme Court declared the act an unconstitutional expansion of federal power, ruling that the Fourteenth Amendment limits only "State" actions. Other provisions of these acts were generally ignored for many decades. But the Civil Rights Act of 1871 has been revived in recent decades; the act makes it a federal crime for any person acting under the authority of state law to deprive another of rights protected by the Constitution.

Civil Rights Act of 1957

The first civil rights law passed by Congress since Reconstruction. It empowers the U.S. Justice Department to enforce voting rights, established the Civil Rights Division in the Justice Department, and created the Civil Rights Commission to study and report on civil rights in the United States.

Civil Rights Act of 1964

A comprehensive enactment designed to erase racial discrimination in both public and private sectors of American life. Major titles of the act: I. outlaws arbitrary discrimination in voter registration and expedites voting rights suits; II. bars discrimination in public accommodations, such as hotels and restaurants, that have a substantial relation to interstate commerce; III. and IV. authorize the national government to bring suits to desegregate public facilities and schools; V. extends the life and expands the power of the Civil Rights Commission; VI. provides for withholding federal funds from programs administered in a discriminatory manner; VII. establishes the right to equality in employment opportunities.

Civil Rights Act of 1968

Prohibits discrimination in the advertising, financing, sale, or rental of housing, based on race, religion, or national origin and, as of 1974, sex. A major amendment to the act in 1988 extended coverage to the handicapped and to families with children.

Voting Rights Act

Enacted by Congress in 1965 and renewed and expanded in 1970, 1975, and 1982, this law has sought to eliminate restrictions on voting that have been used to discriminate against blacks and other minority groups. Amendments in 1975 (1) required bilingual ballots in all states; (2) required approval by the Justice Department or a federal court of any election law changes in states covered by the act; (3) extended legal protection of voting rights to Hispanic Americans, Asian Americans, and Native Americans. The 1982 act provides that *intent* to discriminate need not be proven if the *results* demonstrate otherwise. Although the 1982 extension does not require racial quotas for city councils, school boards, or state legislatures, a judge may under the law redraw voting districts to give minorities maximum representation.

Supreme Court Chief Justice Roger Taney, ruling in the notorious case of *Dred Scott v. Sandford* in 1857, reflected the racism that prevailed in early America:

> They had for more than a century before been regarded as beings of an inferior order, and altogether unfit to associate with the white race, either in social or political relations; and so far inferior, that they had no rights which the white man was bound to respect; and that the negro might justly and lawfully be reduced to slavery

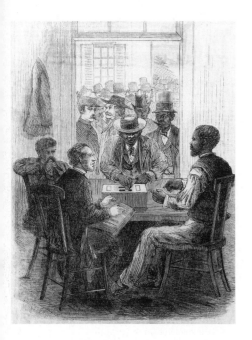

The Thirteenth, Fourteenth, and Fifteenth Amendments to the Constitution, as well as other legislation passed during Reconstruction, opened the ballot box and access to political office to the freedmen of the South. However, these gains were soon largely reversed by Jim Crow laws and segregation.

abolition movement Social movement before the Civil War whose goal was to abolish slavery throughout the United States.

for his benefit. He was bought and sold, and treated as an ordinary article of merchandise and traffic, whenever a profit could be made by it.

This opinion was at that time fixed and universal in the civilized portion of the white race.[2] Taney's decision in this case interpreted the Constitution in terms of the *original intent* of the Founders. The ruling upheld slavery and the constitutional guarantee given slave owners for the return of slaves escaping to nonslave states.

Emancipation and Reconstruction A growing number of Americans, especially members of the **abolition movement**, disagreed with Taney. In 1860 internal party divisions over the slavery issue led to a four-way race for the presidency and the election of Abraham Lincoln. Although personally opposed to slavery, Lincoln had promised during the campaign not to push for abolition of slavery where it existed. Many southerners were unconvinced, however, and on December 20, 1860 (three months before Lincoln's inauguration), South Carolina became the first state to secede from the Union, touching off the Civil War.

The Civil War was the nation's bloodiest war. (Combined deaths of Union and Confederate forces matched the nation's losses in World War II, even though the nation's population in 1860 was only 31 million compared to 140 million during World War II.) Very few families during the Civil War did not experience a direct loss from that conflict. As casualties mounted, northern Republicans joined abolitionists in calling for emancipating, or freeing, the slaves simply to punish the Rebels. They knew that much of the South's power depended on slave labor. Lincoln also knew that if he proclaimed the war was being fought to free the slaves, military intervention by the British on behalf of the South was less likely. Accordingly, on September 22, 1862, Lincoln issued his Emancipation Proclamation. Claiming his right as Commander-in-Chief of the army and navy, he declared that, as of January 1, 1863, "all persons held as slaves within any State, or designated part of a State, the people whereof shall then be in rebellion against the United States, shall be then, thenceforward, and forever free." The Emancipation Proclamation did not come about as a result of demands by the people. It was a political and military action by the president intended to help preserve the Union.

The Emancipation Proclamation freed slaves in the seceding states, and the Thirteenth Amendment in 1865 abolished slavery everywhere in the nation. But freedom did not mean civil rights. The Fourteenth Amendment, passed in 1867 by a Republican Congress that intended to reconstruct southern society after the Civil War and ratified the next year, made "equal protection of the laws" a command for every state to obey. The Fifteenth Amendment, passed in 1869 and ratified in 1870, prohibited federal and state governments from abridging the right to vote "on account of race, color, or previous condition of servitude." In addition, Congress passed a series of civil rights laws in the 1860s and 1870s guaranteeing the newly freed slaves protection in the exercise of their constitutional rights. Between 1865 and the early 1880s, the success of Reconstruction was evident in widespread black voting throughout the South, the presence of many blacks in federal and state offices, and the admission of blacks to theaters, restaurants, hotels, and public transportation.[3]

The Imposition of Segregation Political support for Reconstruction policies soon began to erode. In the Compromise of 1877, the national government agreed to end military occupation of the South, give up its efforts to rearrange southern society, and lend tacit approval to white supremacy in that region. In return, the southern states pledged their support to the Union, accepted national supremacy, and agreed to permit the Republican presidential candidate, Rutherford B. Hayes, to assume the presidency, although the Democratic candidate, Samuel Tilden, had received more popular votes in the disputed election of 1876.

As white southerners regained political power and blacks lost the protection of federal forces, the Supreme Court moved to strike down Reconstruction laws. In the Civil Rights Cases of 1883, the Supreme Court declared federal civil rights laws preventing discrimination by private individuals to be unconstitutional.[4] By denying Congress the power to protect blacks from discrimination by businesses and individuals, the Court paved the way for the imposition of segregation as the prevailing social system of the South. In the 1880s and 1890s, white southerners imposed segregation in public accommodations, housing, education, employment, and almost every other sector of private and public life. By 1895 most southern states had passed laws *requiring* racial segregation in education and in public accommodations. At the time, more than 90 percent of the African American population of the United States lived in these states.

Segregation became the social instrument by which African Americans were "kept in their place"—that is, denied social, economic, educational, and political equality. In many states, **Jim Crow** followed them throughout life: birth in segregated hospital wards, education in segregated schools, residence in segregated housing, employment in segregated jobs, eating in segregated restaurants, and burial in segregated graveyards. Segregation was enforced by a variety of public and private sanctions, from lynch mobs to country club admission committees. But government was the principal instrument of segregation in both the southern and the border states of the nation. (For a look at the political reactions of African Americans to segregation, see *Up Close:* "African American Politics in Historical Perspective.")

Early Court Approval of Segregation　Segregation was imposed despite the Fourteenth Amendment's guarantee of "equal protection of the laws." In the 1896 case of *Plessy v. Ferguson,* the Supreme Court upheld state laws requiring segregation. Although segregation laws involved state action, the Court held that segregation of the races did not violate the Equal Protection Clause of the Fourteenth Amendment so long as people in each race received equal treatment. Schools and other public facilities that were **separate but equal** were constitutional, the Court ruled.

> The object of the amendment was undoubtedly to enforce the absolute equality of the two races before the law, but in the nature of things it could not have been intended to abolish distinctions based upon color, or to enforce social, as distinguished from political, equality, or a commingling of the two races upon terms unsatisfactory to either. Laws permitting, and even requiring, their separation in places where they are liable to be brought into contact do not necessarily imply the inferiority of either race to the other, and have been generally, if not universally, recognized as within the competency of the state legislatures in the exercise of their police power.[5]

The effect of this decision was to give constitutional approval to segregation; the decision was not reversed until 1954.

Jim Crow　Second-class-citizen status conferred on blacks by southern segregation laws; derived from a nineteenth-century song-and-dance act (usually performed by a white man in blackface) that stereotyped blacks.

separate but equal　Ruling of the Supreme Court in the case of *Plessy v. Ferguson* (1896) to the effect that segregated facilities were legal as long as the facilities were equal.

Up Close

African American Politics in Historical Perspective

Many early histories of Reconstruction paid little attention to the political responses of African Americans to the imposition of segregation. But there were at least three distinct types of response: accommodation to segregation; the formation of a black protest movement and resort to legal action; and migration out of the South (to avoid some of the worst consequences of white supremacy) coupled with political mobilization of black voters in large northern cities.

Accommodation   The foremost African American advocate of accommodation to segregation was well-known educator Booker T. Washington (1856–1915). Washington enjoyed wide popularity among both white and black Americans. An adviser to two presidents (Theodore Roosevelt and William Howard Taft), he was highly respected by white philanthropists and government officials. In his famous Cotton States' Exposition speech in Atlanta in 1895, Washington assured whites that blacks were prepared to accept a separate position in society: "In all things that are purely social we can be as separate as the fingers, yet one as the hand in all things essential to mutual progress."*

Washington's hopes for black America lay in a program of self-help through education. He himself had attended Hampton Institute in Virginia, where the curriculum centered around practical trades for African Americans. Washington obtained some white philanthropic support in establishing his own Tuskegee Institute in Tuskegee, Alabama, in 1881. His first students helped build the school. Early curricula at Tuskegee emphasized immediately useful vocations, such as farming, teaching, and blacksmithing. One of Tuskegee's outstanding faculty members, George Washington Carver, researched and devel-

oped uses for southern crops. Washington urged his students to stay in the South, to acquire land, and to build homes, thereby helping to eliminate ignorance and poverty.

Protest   While Booker T. Washington was urging African Americans to make the best of segregation, a small group was organizing in support of a declaration of black resistance and protest that would later rewrite American public policy. The leader of this group was W.E.B. Du Bois (1868–1963), a historian and sociologist at Atlanta University. In 1905 Du Bois and a few other black intellectuals met in Niagara Falls, Canada, to draw up a platform intended to "assail the ears" and sear the consciences of white Americans. The Niagara Statement listed the major injustices perpetrated against African Americans since Reconstruction: the loss of voting rights, the imposition of Jim Crow laws and segregated public schools, the denial of equal

Booker T. Washington

W.E.B. Du Bois

job opportunities, the existence of inhumane conditions in southern prisons, the exclusion of blacks from West Point and Annapolis, and the federal government's failure to enforce the Fourteenth and Fifteenth Amendments. Out of the Niagara meeting came the idea of a nationwide organization dedicated to fighting for African Americans, and on February 12, 1909, the one hundredth anniversary of Abraham Lincoln's birth, the National Association for the Advancement of Colored People (NAACP) was founded.

Du Bois himself was on the original board of directors of the NAACP, although a majority of the early board members and financial contributors were white. Du Bois was also the NAACP's first director of research and the editor of its magazine, *Crisis*. The NAACP began a long and eventually successful campaign to establish black rights through legal action. Over the years, this organization brought hundreds of court cases at the local, state, and federal court levels on behalf of African Americans denied their constitutional rights.

Migration and Political Mobilization   World War I provided an opportunity for restive blacks in the South to escape the worst abuses of white supremacy by migrating en masse to northern cities. Between 1916 and 1918, an estimated half-million African Americans moved north to fill the labor shortage caused by the war effort. Most arrived in big northern cities only to find more poverty and segregation, but at least they could vote, and they did not encounter laws requiring segregation in public places.

The progressive "ghettoization" of African Americans—their migration from the rural South to the urban North and their increasing concentration in central cities—had profound political, as well as social, implications. The ghetto provided an environment conducive to political mobilization. As early as 1928, African Americans in Chicago were able to elect one of their own to the U.S. House of Representatives. The election of Oscar de Priest, the first black member of Congress from the North, signaled a new turn in American urban politics by announcing to white politicians that they would have to reckon with the black vote in northern cities. The black ghettos would soon provide an important element in a new political coalition that was about to take form: the Democratic Party of Franklin Delano Roosevelt.

The increasing concentration of African Americans in large, politically competitive, "swing" states provided black voters with new political power—not only to support the Democratic Party coalition in national politics but also to elect African Americans to local public office. Today African American mayors serve, or have served, in cities as diverse as New York, Chicago, Los Angeles, Detroit, Philadelphia, Atlanta, and New Orleans.

---

*Quoted in Henry Steele Commager, ed., *The Struggle for Racial Equality* (New York: Harper & Row, 1967), p. 19.

EQUAL PROTECTION OF THE LAWS

The initial goal of the civil rights movement was to eliminate segregation laws, especially segregation in public education. Only after this battle was well under way could the civil rights movement turn to the fight against segregation and discrimination in all sectors of American life, *private* as well as *public.*

The NAACP and the Legal Battle   The National Association for the Advancement of Colored People (NAACP) and its Legal Defense and Education Fund led the fight to abolish lawful segregation. As chief legal counsel to the fund, Thurgood Marshall (see *People in Politics:* "Thurgood Marshall, Advocate of Equal Protection") began a long legal campaign to ensure equal protection of the law for African Americans. Initially, the NAACP's strategy focused on achieving the "equal" portion of the separate-but-equal doctrine. Segregated facilities, including public schools, were seldom "equal," even with respect to physical conditions, teachers' salaries and qualifications, curricula, and other tangible factors. In other words, southern states failed to live up even to the segregationist doctrine of separate but equal. In a series of cases, Marshall and other NAACP lawyers convinced the Supreme Court to act when segregated facilities were clearly unequal. For example, the Court ordered the admission of individual blacks to white public universities where evidence indicated that separate black institutions were inferior or nonexistent.[6]

But Marshall's goal was to prove that segregation *itself* was inherently unequal whether or not facilities were equal in all tangible respects. In other words, Marshall sought a reversal of *Plessy v. Ferguson* and a ruling that separation of the races was unconstitutional. In 1952 Marshall led a team of NAACP lawyers in a suit to admit Linda Brown to the white public schools of Topeka, Kansas, one of the few segregated school systems where white and black schools were equal with respect to buildings, curricula, teachers' salaries, and other tangible factors. In choosing the *Brown* suit, the NAACP sought to prevent the Court from simply ordering the admission of black pupils because tangible facilities were not equal and to force the Court to review the doctrine of segregation itself.

Brown v. Board of Education of Topeka   On May 17, 1954, the Court rendered its historic decision in the case of *Brown v. Board of Education of Topeka:*

> Segregation of white and colored children in public schools has a detrimental effect upon the colored children. The impact is greater when it has the sanction of law, for the policy of separating the races is usually interpreted as denoting the inferiority of the Negro group. A sense of inferiority affects the motivation of a child to learn. Segregation with the sanction of law, therefore, has a tendency to retard the educational and mental development of Negro children and to deprive them of some of the benefits they would receive in a racially integrated school system. Whatever may have been the extent of psychological knowledge of the time of *Plessy v. Ferguson,* this finding is amply supported by modern authority. Any language in *Plessy v. Ferguson* contrary to this source is rejected. . . . We conclude that in the field of public education the doctrine of "separate but equal" has no place. Separate educational facilities are inherently unequal.[7]

The Supreme Court decision in *Brown* was symbolically very important. Although it would be many years before any significant number of black children would

Thurgood Marshall, Advocate of Equal Protection

The modern civil rights movement in the United States began with the historic Supreme Court decision in *Brown v. Board of Education of Topeka* in 1954. And the individual most responsible for bringing about that decision was Thurgood Marshall (1908–93), then chief counsel for the NAACP Legal Defense Fund. Marshall directed the NAACP's legal strategy against segregation, and he personally argued the *Brown* case before the Supreme Court. His later appointment to the Supreme Court as the first African American to serve on that body was a fitting recognition of his immense contribution to civil rights law in the United States.

Marshall grew up in Baltimore, the son of a railroad car steward. He attended all-black Lincoln University in Chester, Pennsylvania, and following his cum laude graduation in 1930 he entered Howard University Law School in Washington, D.C. Shortly after graduation in 1933, Marshall became counsel for the Baltimore chapter of the NAACP. In 1940 he became the director and chief counsel of the NAACP's newly formed and semiautonomous Legal Defense and Education Fund, a position he held for more than twenty years.

Marshall coordinated the NAACP's broad legal attack against discrimination in voting, housing, public accommodations, and education. He personally argued thirty-two cases for the NAACP before the Supreme Court, winning twenty-nine of them, including the landmark decision in the *Brown* case. President John F. Kennedy appointed Marshall as a judge on the U.S. Circuit Court of Appeals in 1961. Four years later, President Lyndon Johnson appointed him solicitor general of the United States in 1965, making Marshall the first African American to serve as the nation's chief counsel. In that capacity, Marshall personally argued nineteen more cases before the Supreme Court, including the important case of *South Carolina v. Katzenbach,* upholding the constitutionality of the Voting Rights Act.* Announcing Marshall's appointment to the Supreme Court, President Johnson noted that few other attorneys in the history of the nation had ever argued as many cases before the Supreme Court as Thurgood Marshall. Marshall was confirmed by a vote of 69 to 11 in the Senate in 1967.

In his more than two decades on the Supreme Court, Marshall was the most consistent member of the liberal voting bloc. He regularly voted against restrictions on abortions, against capital punishment, and for affirmative action and racial set-aside programs. Upon his retirement in 1991, his seat on the Court was taken by Clarence Thomas.

South Carolina v. Katzenbach, 383 U.S. 301 (1966).

---

attend previously all-white schools in the South, the decision by the nation's highest court stimulated black hopes and expectations. Indeed, *Brown* started the modern civil rights movement. As the African American psychologist Kenneth Clark wrote, "This [civil rights] movement would probably not have existed at all were it not for the 1954 Supreme Court school desegregation decision, which provided a tremendous boost to the morale of blacks by its clear affirmation that color is irrelevant to the rights of American citizens."[8]

Enforcing Desegregation   The *Brown* ruling struck down the laws of twenty-one states as well as congressional laws segregating the schools of the District of Columbia.[9] Such a far-reaching exercise of judicial power was bound to meet with difficulties in enforcement, and the Supreme Court was careful not to risk its own authority. It did not order immediate national desegregation but rather required state and local authorities, under the supervision of federal district courts, to proceed with "all deliberate speed" in desegregation.[10] For more than fifteen years, state and school districts in the South waged a campaign of resistance to desegregation. Delays in implementing school desegregation continued until 1969, when the Supreme Court rejected a request by Mississippi officials for further delay, declaring that all school districts were obligated to end their dual school systems "at once" and "now and hereafter" to operate only integrated schools.[11]

Busing and Racial Balancing   Federal district judges enjoy wide freedom in fashioning remedies for past or present discriminatory practices by governments. If a federal district court anywhere in the United States finds that any actions by governments or school officials have contributed to racial imbalances (for example, drawing school district attendance lines that separate black and white pupils), the judge may order the adoption of a desegregation plan to overcome racial imbalances produced by official action. A large number of cities have come under federal district court orders to improve racial balances in their schools through busing.

In the important case of *Swann v. Charlotte-Mecklenburg County Board of Education* (1971), the Supreme Court upheld the following:

- The use of racial balance requirements in schools and the assignment of pupils to schools based on race.
- "Close scrutiny" by judges of schools that are predominantly of one race.
- Gerrymandering of school attendance zones as well as "clustering" or "grouping" of schools to achieve racial balance.
- Court-ordered busing of pupils to achieve racial balance.[12]

The Court was careful to note, however, that racial imbalance in schools is not itself grounds for ordering these remedies unless it is also shown that some present or past governmental action contributed to the imbalance.

De Facto Segregation   However, in the absence of any past or present governmental actions contributing to racial imbalance, states and school districts are *not* required by the Fourteenth Amendment to integrate their schools. For example, where central-city schools are predominantly black and suburban schools are predominantly white owing to residential patterns, cross-district busing is not required unless some official action brought about these racial imbalances. Thus in 1974 the Supreme Court threw out a lower federal court order for massive busing of students between Detroit and fifty-two suburban school districts.[13] Although Detroit city schools are 70 percent black and the suburban schools almost all white, none of the area school districts segregated students within their own boundaries. This important decision means that largely black central cities surrounded by largely white suburbs will remain segregated in practice because there are not enough white students living within the city boundaries to achieve integration.

De facto segregation is more common in the northern metropolitan areas than in the South. The states with the largest percentages of African American students attending schools that have 90 to 100 percent minority enrollments are Illinois (62 percent), Michigan (60 percent), New York (57 percent), and New Jersey (54 percent). The persistence of de facto segregation, together with a renewed interest in the quality of education, has caused many civil rights organizations to focus their attention on improving the quality of schools in urban areas rather than trying to desegregate these schools.

de facto segregation   Racial imbalances not directly caused by official actions but rather by residential patterns.

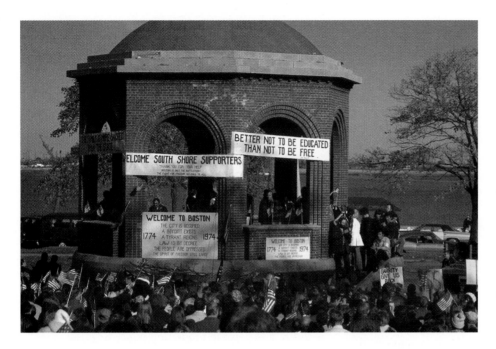

Many school districts in the South and elsewhere have operated under federal court supervision for many years. How long should court supervision continue, and what standards are to be used in determining when desegregation has been achieved once and for all? The Rehnquist-led Supreme Court in recent years has undertaken to free some school districts from direct federal court supervision. Where the last vestiges of state-sanctioned discrimination have been removed "as far as practicable," the Supreme Court has allowed lower federal courts to dissolve racial balancing plans even though imbalances due to residential patterns may continue to exist.[14]

THE CIVIL RIGHTS ACTS

The early goal of the civil rights movement was to eliminate discrimination and segregation practiced by *governments,* particularly states and school districts. When the civil rights movement turned to *private* discrimination—discrimination practiced by private owners of restaurants, hotels, motels, and stores; private employers, landlords, and real estate agents; and others who were not government officials—it had to take its fight to the Congress. The Constitution does not govern the activities of private individuals. Only Congress at the national level could outlaw discrimination in the private sector. Yet prior to 1964, Congress had been content to let the courts struggle with the question of civil rights. New political tactics and organizations were required to put the issue of equality on the agenda of Congress.

Martin Luther King, Jr., and Nonviolent Direct Action   Leadership in the struggle to eliminate discrimination and segregation from private life was provided by a young African American minister, Martin Luther King, Jr. (see *People in Politics:* "Martin Luther King, Jr., 'I Have a Dream' "). Under King, the civil rights movement developed and refined political techniques for use by American minorities, including **nonviolent direct action**. Nonviolent direct action is a

nonviolent direct action   Strategy used by civil rights leaders such as Martin Luther King, Jr., in which protesters break "unjust" laws openly but in a "loving" fashion in order to bring the injustices of such laws to public attention.

People in Politics

Martin Luther King, Jr., "I Have a Dream"

"If a man hasn't discovered something he will die for, he isn't fit to live."*

For Martin Luther King, Jr., (1929–1968), civil rights was something to die for, and before he died for the cause, he would shatter a century of southern segregation and set a new domestic agenda for the nation's leaders. King's contributions to the development of nonviolent direct action won him international acclaim and the Nobel Peace Prize.

King's father was the pastor of one of the South's largest and most influential African American congregations, the Ebenezer Baptist Church in Atlanta, Georgia. Young Martin was educated at Morehouse College in Atlanta and received a Ph.D. in religious studies at Boston University. Shortly after beginning his career as a Baptist minister in Montgomery, Alabama, in 1955, a black woman, Rosa Parks, refused to give up her seat to whites on a Montgomery bus, setting in motion a year-long bus boycott in that city. Only twenty-six years old, King was thrust into national prominence as the leader of that boycott, which ended in the elimination of segregation on the city's buses. In 1957 King founded the Southern Christian Leadership Conference (SCLC) to provide encouragement and leadership to the growing nonviolent protest movement against segregation.

Perhaps the most dramatic application of nonviolent direct action occurred in Birmingham, Alabama, in the spring of 1963. Under King's direction, the SCLC had chosen that city as a major site for demonstrations during the centennial year of the Emancipation Proclamation. By its own description the "Heart of Dixie," Birmingham was the most rigidly segregated large city in the United States at the time. King believed that if segregation could be successfully challenged in Birmingham, it might begin to crumble throughout the South. Thousands of African Americans, ranging from schoolchildren to senior citizens, staged protest marches in Birmingham from May 2 to May 7. Although the demonstrators conducted themselves in a nonviolent fashion, police and firefighters under the direction of Police Chief Eugene "Bull" Connor attacked the demonstrators with fire hoses, cattle prods, and police dogs, all in clear view of national television cameras. Thousands of demonstrators were dragged off to jail, including King. (It was at this time that King wrote his "Letter from Birmingham Jail," explaining and defending nonviolent direct action.) But Connor's "victory" was short-lived. Pictures of police brutality flashed throughout the nation and the world, touching the consciences of many white Americans.

King was also the driving force behind the most massive application of nonviolent direct action in U.S. history: the great "March on Washington" in August 1963, during which more than 200,000 black and white marchers converged on the nation's capital. The march ended at the Lincoln Memorial, where King delivered his most eloquent appeal, entitled "I Have a Dream."

> I still have a dream. It is a dream deeply rooted in the American dream. I have a dream that one day this nation will rise up and live out the true meaning of its creed: "We hold these truths to be self-evident, that all men are created equal."

form of protest that involves breaking "unjust" laws in an open, "loving," nonviolent fashion. The purpose of nonviolent direct action is to call attention—to "bear witness"—to the existence of injustice. In the words of Martin Luther King, Jr., such civil disobedience "seeks to dramatize the issue so that it can no longer be ignored"[15] (see also *A Conflicting View: "Sometimes It's Right to Disobey the Law"* in Chapter 1).

King formed the Southern Christian Leadership Conference (SCLC) in 1957 to develop and direct the growing nonviolent direct action movement. During the next few years, the SCLC overshadowed the older NAACP in leading the fight

I have a dream that one day on the red hills of Georgia, sons of former slaves and sons of former slave-owners will be able to sit down together at the table of brotherhood.

I have a dream that one day, even in the state of Mississippi, a state sweltering with the heat of injustice, sweltering with the heat of oppression, will be transformed into an oasis of freedom and justice.

I have a dream my four little children will one day live in a nation where they will not be judged by the color of their skin but by content of their character. . . .

And when this happens, and when we allow freedom to ring, when we let it ring from every village and hamlet, from every state and city, we will be able to speed up that day when all of God's children—black men and white men, Jews and Gentiles, Catholics and Prostestants—will be able to join hands and to sing in the words of the old Negro spiritual, "Free at last, free at last; thank God Almighty, we are free at last."[†]

It was in the wake of the March on Washington that President John F. Kennedy sent to the Congress a strong civil rights bill that would be passed after his death—the Civil Rights Act of 1964. That same year, King received the Nobel Peace Prize.

Yet even after passage of this act, voting registrars in many southern counties continued to keep African Americans off of the voting rolls through a variety of discriminatory tactics. In 1965 King again took action. Selma, the county seat of Dallas County, Alabama, was chosen as the site to dramatize the voting rights problem. King organized a fifty-mile march from Selma to the state capitol in Montgomery. He didn't get very far. Acting on orders of Governor George Wallace to disband the marchers, state troopers did so with a vengeance—using tear gas, nightsticks, and whips. This time, however, the national government intervened: in his capacity as Commander-in-Chief of the armed forces, President Lyndon Johnson ordered the National Guard to protect the demonstrators, and the march continued. During the march, Johnson went on television to address a special joint session of Congress, urging passage of new legislation to assure African Americans the right to vote, and Congress responded with the Voting Rights Act of 1965.

White racial violence in the early 1960s, including murders and bombings of black and white civil rights workers, shocked and disgusted many whites in both the North and the South. In 1963 Medgar Evers, the NAACP's state chair for Mississippi, was shot to death by a sniper as he entered his Jackson home. That same year, a bomb killed four young black girls attending Sunday school in Birmingham. On the evening of April 3, 1968, King spoke to a crowd in Memphis, Tennessee, in eerily prophetic terms. "I just want to do God's will. And He's allowed me to go to the mountain. And I've looked over, and I've seen the promised land. I may not get there with you. But I want you to know tonight, that we, as a people will get to the promised land. So I'm happy tonight. I'm not worried about anything. I'm not fearing any man."[††] On the night of April 4, 1968, the world's leading exponent of nonviolence was killed by an assassin's bullet.

---

[*]Martin Luther King, Jr., speech, June 23, 1963, Detroit, Michigan.

[†]Martin Luther King, Jr., "I Have a Dream" speech, August 28, 1963, at the Lincoln Memorial, Washington, D.C., printed in David J. Garrow, *Bearing the Cross: Martin Luther King, Jr., and the Southern Christian Leadership Conference* (New York: Vintage Books, 1988), pp. 283–84.

[††]Martin Luther King, Jr., speech, April 3, 1968, Memphis, Tennessee, in ibid., p. 621.

against segregation. Where the NAACP had developed its strategy of court litigation to combat discrimination by *governments,* now the SCLC developed nonviolent direct action tactics to build widespread popular support and to pressure Congress to outlaw discrimination by *private businesses.*

The year 1963 was perhaps the most important for nonviolent direct action. The SCLC focused its efforts in Birmingham, Alabama, where King led thousands of marchers in a series of orderly and peaceful demonstrations. When police attacked the marchers with fire hoses, dogs, and cattle prods—in full view of national television cameras—millions of viewers around the country came to understand the

In the civil rights march of 1963 more than 200,000 people marched peacefully on Washington, D.C., to end segregation. It was here that Martin Luther King, Jr., delivered his famous "I Have a Dream" speech.

injustices of segregation. The Birmingham action set off demonstrations in many parts of the country. The theme remained one of nonviolence, and it was usually whites rather than blacks who resorted to violence in these demonstrations. Responsible black leaders remained in control of the movement and won widespread support from the white community.

The culmination of King's nonviolent philosophy was a huge yet orderly march on Washington, D.C., held on August 28, 1963. More than 200,000 blacks and whites participated in the march, which was endorsed by many civic leaders, religious groups, and political figures. The march ended at the Lincoln Memorial, where Martin Luther King, Jr., delivered his most eloquent appeal, entitled "I Have a Dream." Congress passed the Civil Rights Act of 1964 by better than a two-thirds favorable vote in both houses; it won the overwhelming support of both Republican and Democratic members of Congress.

The Civil Rights Act of 1964   Signed into law on July 4, 1964, the Civil Rights Act of 1964 ranks with the Emancipation Proclamation, the Fourteenth Amendment, and the *Brown* case as one of the most important steps toward full equality for African Americans. Among its most important provisions are the following:

Title II: It is unlawful to discriminate or segregate persons on the grounds of race, color, religion, or national origin in any public accommodation, including hotels, motels, restaurants, movies, theaters, sports arenas, entertainment houses, and other places that offer to serve the public. This prohibition extends to all business establishments whose operations affect interstate commerce or whose discriminatory practices are supported by state action.

Title VI: Each federal department and agency is to take action to end discrimination in all programs or activities receiving federal financial assistance in any form. This action may include termination of financial assistance to persistently discriminatory agencies.

Title VII: It is unlawful for any employer or labor union to discriminate against any individual in any fashion in employment because of the individual's race, color, religion, sex, or national origin. The Equal Employment Opportunity Commission is established to enforce this provision by investigation, conference, conciliation, persuasion, and, if need be, civil action in federal court.

The Civil Rights Act of 1968   For many years "fair housing" had been considered the most sensitive area of civil rights legislation. Discrimination in the sale and rental of housing was the last major civil rights problem on which Congress took action. Discrimination in housing had not been mentioned in the comprehensive Civil Rights Act of 1964. Prohibiting discrimination in the sale or rental of housing affected the constituencies of northern members of Congress; earlier public accommodations provisions had their greatest effect in the South.

Prospects for a fair housing law were poor at the beginning of 1968. However, when Martin Luther King, Jr., was assassinated on April 4, the mood of Congress and the nation changed dramatically. Congress passed a fair housing law as tribute to the slain civil rights leader. The Civil Rights Act of 1968 prohibited discrimination in the sale or rental of a dwelling to any person on the basis of race, color, religion, or national origin.

EQUALITY: OPPORTUNITY VERSUS RESULTS

Although the gains of the civil rights movement were immensely important, these gains were primarily in *opportunity* rather than in *results*. The civil rights movement of the 1960s did not bring about major changes in the conditions under which most African Americans lived in the United States. Racial politics today center around the *actual* inequalities between blacks and whites in incomes, jobs, housing, health, education, and other conditions of life.

Continuing Inequalities   The issue of inequality today is often posed as differences in the "life chances" of blacks and whites. Figures can reveal only the bare outline of an African American's "life chances" in this society (see Table 15-2). The average income of a black family is 60 percent of the average white family's income. Over 30 percent of all black families live below the recognized poverty line, whereas less than 12 percent of white families do so. The black unemployment rate is more than twice as high as the white unemployment rate. Blacks are less likely to hold prestigious executive jobs in professional, managerial, clerical, or sales work. They do not hold many skilled craft jobs in industry but are concentrated in operative, service, and laboring positions. The civil rights movement opened up new opportunities for African Americans. But equality of *opportunity* is not the same as equality of *results*.

Policy Choices   What public policies should be pursued to achieve equality in America? Is it sufficient that government eliminate discrimination, guarantee equality of opportunity, and apply color-blind standards to both blacks and whites? Or should government take **affirmative action** to overcome the results of past unequal treatment of blacks—preferential or compensatory treatment to assist black applications for university admissions and scholarships, job hiring and promotion, and other opportunities for advancement in life?

affirmative action   Any program, whether enacted by a government or by a private organization, whose goal is to overcome the results of past unequal treatment of minorities and/or women by giving members of these groups preferential treatment in admissions, hiring, promotions, or other aspects of life.

TABLE 15-2	**Minority Life Chances**				

	Median Income of Families				
	1970	*1975*	*1980*	*1985*	*1995*
White	$10,236	$14,268	$21,904	$29,152	$42,646
Black	6,279	8,779	12,674	16,786	25,970
Hispanic	—	9,551	14,716	19,027	24,570

	Percentage of Persons below Poverty Level			
	1975	*1980*	*1985*	*1995*
White	9.7%	10.2%	11.4%	11.2%
Black	31.3	32.5	31.3	29.3
Hispanic	26.9	25.7	29.0	30.3

	Unemployment Rate		
	1980	*1985*	*1996*
White	6.3%	6.2%	4.7%
Black	14.3	15.1	10.5
Hispanic	10.1	10.5	8.9

	Education: Percentage of Persons over Twenty-Five Completing	
	High School	*College*
White	83%	24%
Black	74	14
Hispanic	53	9

Source: *Statistical Abstract of the United States, 1997,* pp. 159, 398, 469.

Shifting Goals in Civil Rights Policy   For decades, the emphasis of government policy was on equal *opportunity.* This early nondiscrimination approach began with President Harry Truman's decision to desegregate the armed forces in 1948 and carried through to Title VI and Title VII of the Civil Rights Act of 1964, which eliminated discrimination in federally aided projects and private employment. Gradually, however, the goal of the civil rights movement shifted from the traditional aim of equality of opportunity through nondiscrimination alone to affirmative action involving the establishment of "goals and timetables" to achieve greater equality of results between blacks and whites. While avoiding the term **quota**, the notion of affirmative action tests the success of equal opportunity by observing whether blacks achieve admissions, jobs, and promotions in proportion to their numbers in the population.

Affirmative Action   Affirmative action programs were initially developed in the federal bureaucracy. Federal executive agencies were authorized by the Civil Rights Act of 1964 to develop "rules and regulations" for desegregating any organization or business receiving federal funds. In 1965 President Lyndon B. Johnson signed Executive Order 11246, requiring all federal agencies and businesses contracting with the federal government to practice affirmative action. In 1972 the

quota Provision of some affirmative action programs in which specific numbers or percentages of positions are open only to minorities and/or women.

U.S. Office of Education issued guidelines that mandated "goals" for university admissions and faculty hiring of minorities and women. The Equal Employment Opportunity Commission (EEOC), established by the Civil Rights Act of 1964, is responsible for monitoring affirmative action programs in private employment.

Federal officials generally measure "progress" in affirmative action in terms of the number of disadvantaged group members admitted, employed, or promoted. The pressure to show "progress" can result in relaxation of traditional measures of qualifications, such as test scores and educational achievement. Advocates of affirmative action argue that these measures are not good predictors of performance on the job or in school and are biased in favor of white culture. State and local governments, schools, colleges and universities, and private employers are under pressure to drop these standards.

AFFIRMATIVE ACTION IN THE COURTS

The constitutional question posed by affirmative action programs is whether or not they discriminate against whites in violation of the Equal Protection Clause of the Fourteenth Amendment. A related question is whether or not affirmative action programs discriminate against whites in violation of the Civil Rights Act of 1964, which prohibits discrimination "on account of race," not just discrimination against blacks. Clearly, these are questions for the Supreme Court to resolve, but unfortunately the Court has failed to develop clear-cut answers.

The Bakke Case In the absence of a history of racial discrimination, the Supreme Court has been willing to scrutinize affirmative action programs to ensure that they do not directly discriminate against whites. In *University of California Regents v. Bakke* (1978), the Supreme Court struck down a special admissions program for minorities at a state medical school on the grounds that it excluded a white applicant because of his race and violated his rights under the Equal Protection Clause.[16] Allan Bakke applied to the University of California Davis Medical School two consecutive years and was rejected; in both years, black applicants with significantly lower grade point averages and medical aptitude test scores were accepted through a special admissions program that reserved sixteen minority places in a class of one hundred.[17] The University of California did not deny that its admissions decisions were based on race. Instead, it argued that its racial classification was "benign," that is, designed to assist minorities. The special admissions program was designed to (1) "reduce the historical deficit of traditionally disfavored minorities in medical schools and the medical profession"; (2) "counter the effects of societal discrimination"; (3) "increase the number of physicians who will practice in communities currently underserved"; and (4) "obtain the educational benefits that flow from an ethnically diverse student body."

The Supreme Court held that these objectives were legitimate and that race and ethnic origin *may* be considered in reviewing applications to a state school without violating the Fourteenth Amendment's Equal Protection Clause. However, the Court also held that a separate admissions program for minorities with a specific quota of openings which were unavailable to white applicants *did* violate the Equal Protection Clause. The Court ordered the university to admit Bakke to its medical school and to eliminate the special admissions program. It recommended that California consider an admissions program developed at Harvard, which considers disadvantaged racial or ethnic background as a "plus" in an overall evaluation of an application but does not set numerical quotas or exclude any person from competing for all positions.

Reaction to the decision was predictable: supporters of affirmative action, particularly government officials from affirmative action programs, emphasized the Supreme Court's willingness to allow minority status to be considered a positive factor; opponents emphasized the Supreme Court's unwillingness to allow quotas that exclude whites from competing for some positions. Because Bakke had "won" the case, many observers felt that the Supreme Court was not going to permit racial quota systems.

Affirmative Action as a Remedy for Past Discrimination   The Supreme Court has continued to approve of affirmative action programs where there is evidence of past discriminatory practices. In *United Steelworkers of America v. Weber* (1979), the Supreme Court approved a plan developed by a private employer and a union to reserve 50 percent of higher paying, skilled jobs for minorities. Kaiser Aluminum Corporation and the United Steelworkers Union, under federal government pressure, had established a program to get more blacks into skilled technical jobs; only 2 percent of the skilled jobs were held by blacks in the plant in question, and 39 percent of the local work force was black. When Weber, a white male, was excluded from the training program while blacks with less seniority and fewer qualifications were accepted, he filed suit in federal court claiming that the plan violated Title VII of the Civil Rights Act of 1964 by discriminating against him because of his race. But the Supreme Court held that "employers and unions in the private sector [are] free to take such race-conscious steps to eliminate manifest racial imbalances in traditionally segregated job categories. We hold that Title VII does not prohibit such . . . affirmative action plans." Weber's reliance on the clear language of Title VII was "misplaced." According to the Court, it would be "ironic indeed" if the Civil Rights Act were used to prohibit voluntary private race-conscious efforts to overcome the past effects of discrimination.[18] In *United States v. Paradise* (1987), the Court upheld a rigid 50 percent black quota system for promotions in the Alabama Department of Safety, which had excluded blacks from the ranks of state troopers prior to 1972 and had not promoted any blacks higher than corporal prior to 1984. In a 5 to 4 decision, the majority stressed the long history of discrimination in the agency as a reason for upholding the quota system. Whatever burdens imposed on innocent parties were outweighed by the need to correct the effects of past discrimination.[19]

Case Questioning Affirmative Action   The Supreme Court has continued to express concern about whites who are directly and adversely affected by government action solely because of their race. In *Firefighters Local Union 1784 v. Stotts* (1984), the Court ruled that a city could not lay off white firefighters in favor of black firefighters with less seniority.[20] In *City of Richmond v. Crosen Co.* (1989), the Supreme Court held that a minority **set-aside program** in Richmond, Virginia, which mandated that 30 percent of all city construction contracts must go to "blacks, Spanish-speaking, Orientals, Indians, Eskimos, or Aleuts," violated the Equal Protection Clause of the Fourteenth Amendment.[21]

It is important to note that the Supreme Court has never adopted the color-blind doctrine, first espoused by Justice Harlan in his dissent from *Plessy v. Ferguson,* that "Our Constitution is colorblind, and neither knows nor tolerates classes among citizens." If the Equal Protection Clause required the laws of the United States and the states to be truly color blind, then no racial guidelines, goals, or quotas would be tolerated. Occasionally this view has been expressed in recent minority dissents.[22]

set-aside program   Program in which a specified number or percentage of contracts must go to designated minorities.

However, the Court has held that racial classifications in law must be subject to "strict scrutiny." This means that race-based actions by government—any disparate treatment of the races by federal, state, or local public agencies—must be found necessary to remedy past proven discrimination, or to further clearly identified, compelling, and legitimate government objectives. Moreover, race-based actions must be "narrowly tailored" so as not to adversely affect the rights of individuals. In striking down a federal construction contract "set-aside" program for small businesses owed by racial minorities, the Court expressed skepticism about governmental racial classifications: "There is simply no way of determining what classifications are 'benign' and 'remedial' and what classifications are in fact motivated by illegitimate notions of racial inferiority or simple racial politics."[23]

Absence of a Clear Constitutional Principle   The Supreme Court's decisions on affirmative action have not provided the nation with a clear and coherent interpretation of the Constitution. No clear rule of law, or legal test, or constitutional principle tells us what is permissible and what is prohibited in the way of racially conscious laws and practices.

Indeed, at least one Circuit Court of Appeals has held that any use of race as a university admission factor violates the Equal Protection Clause of the Fourteenth Amendment. This decision in *Hopwood v. Texas* requires the University of Texas system to end racial preferences in admission. The U.S. Supreme Court affirmed this Court of Appeals decision, yet warned that it may not fully agree with the Circuit Court opinion.[24] Thus the constitutionality of affirmative action programs remains unclear. Nevertheless, over time some general tendencies in Supreme Court policy can be identified. Affirmative action programs are *more likely to be found constitutional* when:

- They are adopted in response to a past proven history of discrimination.
- They are "narrowly tailored" so as not to adversely affect the rights of individuals.
- They do not absolutely bar whites or men from competing or participating.
- They serve clearly identified, compelling, and legitimate government objectives.

The thorny issue of affirmative action continues to arouse passions among both supporters and opponents.

BATTLES OVER AFFIRMATIVE ACTION

Political battles over affirmative action have been waged in the Congress and the states, as well as in the federal courts. Politicians are very much aware of survey results showing that most Americans favor affirmative action when it is expressed in the abstract. But they are equally aware that the poll results are much different when "preferences" or "quotas" are mentioned. Congress, ever mindful of the polls, has tried to find a way to advance affirmative action while avoiding direct reference to preferences or quotas.

Affirmative Action in the Workplace   The Civil Rights Act of 1964, Title VII, bars racial or sexual discrimination in employment. But how can persons who feel they have been passed over for jobs or promotions go about the task of proving that discrimination was involved? Evidence of direct discrimination

Up Close

Black and White Opinion on Affirmative Action

Blacks and whites differ over the extent of discrimination in American society today and what, if anything, should be done about it. Blacks are far more likely than whites to believe that racial discrimination is the principal reason why blacks, on the average, have lower incomes and poorer housing than whites. Although 70 percent of blacks believe these differences are "mainly due to discrimination," only 47 percent of whites think so.

Affirmative Action Given these different views on the extent of discrimination, it is not surprising that blacks and whites also differ on "affirmative action." There is widespread debate over the meaning of the term *affirmative action*. Insofar as it is interpreted to mean greater effort to make sure *opportunities* are equally open to all—that is, making sure

schools and jobs are equally available to all races and both sexes—there is little controversy over its desirability. But affirmative action becomes controversial when it is interpreted to mean equality of *results* in admissions, jobs, and promotions. And the proposed use of "preferences" and "quotas" to ensure equality of results among races and sexes produces polarization of opinion among Americans.

Levels of support for affirmative action often depend on the wording of the question. If the question is posed simply in terms of support for or opposition to "affirmative action," without specifying preferences or quotas, then whites as well as blacks favor it. Moreover, if affirmative action is defined in terms of "encouraging" minorities or providing job training or special education "to make them better qualified," most Americans, both black and white, are supportive. However, black and white opinion differs sharply over whether "diversity" is an important goal for colleges in universities, and whether "quotas" ought to be established for racial minorities.

Question: *Do you feel that compared with whites, blacks...*

Blacks

- Get equal pay for equal work in unskilled jobs: 31%
- Get equal pay for equal work in executive jobs: 33%
- Are promoted as rapidly to higher ranks of employment: 13%
- Have as good a chance of getting into skilled craft unions: 41%

Whites

- Get equal pay for equal work in unskilled jobs: 72%
- Get equal pay for equal work in executive jobs: 78%
- Are promoted as rapidly to higher ranks of employment: 39%
- Have as good a chance of getting into skilled craft unions: 69%

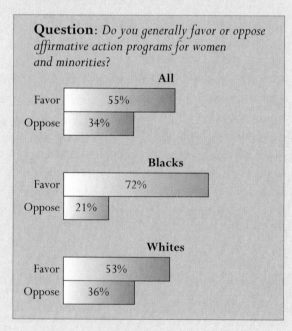

Question: *Do you generally favor or oppose affirmative action programs for women and minorities?*

All
- Favor: 55%
- Oppose: 34%

Blacks
- Favor: 72%
- Oppose: 21%

Whites
- Favor: 53%
- Oppose: 36%

is often difficult to obtain. Can underrepresentation of minorities or women in a work force be used as evidence of discrimination in the absence of any evidence of direct discriminatory practices? If an employer uses a requirement or test that has a disparate effect on minorities or women, who has the burden of proof of showing that the requirement or test is relevant to effective job performance?

Question: *Do you favor or oppose providing job training for minorities and women to make them qualified for better jobs?*

All

Favor 82%

Oppose 17%

Blacks

Favor 94%

Oppose 6%

Whites

Favor 80%

Oppose 18%

Question: *Do you favor or oppose providing special educational classes for minorities and women to make them better qualified for college?*

All

Favor 75%

Oppose 22%

Blacks

Favor 90%

Oppose 9%

Whites

Favor 73%

Oppose 24%

Question: *In order to make up for past discrimination, do you favor or oppose programs which impose quotas for racial minorities?*

All

Favor 19%

Oppose 72%

Blacks

Favor 48%

Oppose 37%

Whites

Favor 15%

Oppose 78%

Question: *How important do you think it is for a college to have a racially diverse student body— that is, a mix of blacks, whites, Asians, Hispanics, and other minorities? Is it very important? Somewhat important? Or not very important at all?*

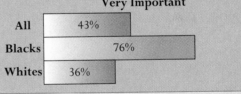

Very Important

All 43%

Blacks 76%

Whites 36%

Sources: Gallup poll, reported in *USA Today,* March 24, 1995; CBS News/*New York Times* poll, reported in *The Polling Report,* December 22, 1997.

The Supreme Court responded to both of these questions in its interpretation of the Civil Rights Act in *Wards Cove Packing Co., Inc. v. Antonio* in 1989.[25] In a controversial 5 to 4 decision, the Court held that statistical imbalances in race or gender in the workplace were not sufficient evidence by themselves to prove discrimination. And the Court ruled it was up to plaintiffs to prove that an employer had no business reason for requirements or tests which had an adverse impact on minorities or women. This decision clearly made it more difficult to prove job discrimination.

Civil Rights and Women's Equity Act of 1991 Civil rights groups were highly critical of what they regarded as the Supreme Court's "narrowing" of the Civil Rights Act protections in employment. They turned to Congress to rewrite portions of the Civil Rights Act to "restore" these protections. Business lobbies, however, believed that accepting statistical imbalances as evidence of discrimination or that shifting the burden of proof to employers would result in hiring by "quotas" simply to avoid lawsuits. After nearly two years of negotiations on Capitol Hill and a reversal of President George Bush's initial opposition, Congress produced the Civil Rights and Women's Equity Act of 1991.[26] Among the more important provisions of the act were these:

- *Statistical imbalances:* The mere existence of statistical imbalance in an employer's work force is not, by itself, sufficient evidence to prove discrimination. However, statistical imbalances may be evidence of employment practices (rules, requirements, academic qualifications, tests) that have a "disparate impact" on minorities or women.

- *Disparate employment practices:* Employers bear the burden of proof that any practice which has a "disparate impact" is necessary and has "a significant and manifest relationship to the requirements for effective job performance."

Public Opinion and Affirmative Action Most Americans agree that discrimination still exists in American society, even if they do not agree on what should be done about it. However, blacks and whites have come to hold very different opinions about the extent of discrimination today and about what, if anything, should be done about it (see *Up Close:* "Black and White Opinion on Affirmative Action" on pages 564–65). Few Americans object to actions taken to remedy proven discrimination by private employers, public officials, or university administrations. But resentment among whites toward preferential treatment of minorities appears to be growing.

The California Civil Rights Initiative National rethinking of affirmative action was inspired by a citizen's initiative placed on the ballot in California by popular petition. The California Civil Rights Initiative added the following phrase to that state's constitution:

> Neither the state of California nor any of its political subdivisions or agents shall use race, sex, color, ethnicity or national origin as a criterion for either discriminating against, or granting preferential treatment to, any individual or group in the operation of the State's system of public employment, public education or public contracting.

The key words are "or granting preferential treatment to . . ." Opponents argue that a constitutional ban on preferential treatment of minorities and women eliminates affirmative action programs in government, prevents governments from acting to correct historic racial or gender imbalances, and denies minorities and women the opportunity to seek legal protections in education and employment. (See *A Conflicting View:* "The Constitution Should Be Color Blind.")

A Conflicting View

The Constitution Should Be Color Blind

In 1896 a single voice spoke out against *all* racial classifications—Supreme Court Justice John Harlan opposing segregation: "Our Constitution is color-blind and neither knows nor tolerates classes among the citizens." He was *dissenting* from the Supreme Court's majority opinion in the infamous case of *Plessy v. Ferguson*, which approved the segregationist doctrine of "separate but equal." Unfortunately, the ideal of a color-blind society remains almost as elusive today as it was more than a hundred years ago.

Martin Luther King, Jr., had a dream that "our children will one day live in a nation where they will not be judged by the color of their skin but by the content of their character." Can that dream be made a reality?

Over time, the civil rights movement shifted its focus from *individual rights* to *group benefits*. Affirmative action programs classify people by group membership, thereby challenging a belief widely held in the United States—that people be judged on individual attributes like character and achievement, rather than on race or gender. Racial and gender preferences are currently encountered in hiring and promotion practices in private and public employment and in college in university admissions, scholarships, and faculty recruitment. "New" groups—homosexuals, for example—seek to be classified among the preferred groups. The result has been increased intergroup tension in many arenas—on the job, in schools, and on college campuses.

Affirmative action programs divide Americans into two classes—those who enjoy legally mandated preferential treatment, and those who do not. Majority support for civil rights laws is weakening under growing resentment among those who are denied preferential treatment.

Some early supporters of affirmative action have come to view race-conscious programs as no longer necessary. They argue that disadvantages in society today are based more on class than on race.

If preferences are to be granted at all, in their view, they should be based on economic disadvantage, not race.

Misgivings also have been expressed by a few African American scholars about the unfair stigmatizing of the supposed beneficiaries of affirmative action—a resulting negative stereotyping of blacks as unable to advance on merit alone. Race-conscious government policies, they argue, have done more harm than good. African American economist Glenn Loury claims that proponents of affirmative action have an inferiority complex: "When blacks say we have to have affirmative action, please don't take it away from us, it's almost like saying, you're right, we can't compete on merit. But I know that we can compete." Conservative columnist William Bennett says that "toxic" race relations, aggravated by affirmative action, have led to damaging forms of new segregation: "Affirmative action has not brought us what we want—a color-blind society. It has brought us an extremely color conscious society. In our universities we have separate dorms, separate social centers. What's next—water fountains? That's not good and everybody knows it."

Many argue that affirmative action has caused the civil rights movement to lose widespread public support and instead become contentious and divisive. In fact, civil rights has become such a hot topic that most elected officials now prefer to avoid it. As one anonymous member of Congress put it, "The problem is political correctness—you can't talk openly." President Bill Clinton's sound bite on affirmative action—"Mend it, don't end it"—straddles the issue without resolving the controversy that surrounds it.

Many supporters of affirmative action would ideally prefer a color-blind society—the dream evoked by Martin Luther King, Jr., in his speech at the civil rights march. However, they see race-conscious policies as necessary to remedy the effects of both past and current discrimination: "If we abandon affirmative action we return to the old white boy network."

Source: Quotations reported in *Newsweek*, February 13, 1996.

Opponents challenged the California Civil Rights Initiative in federal courts arguing that by preventing minorities and women from seeking preferential treatment under law, the initiative violated the Equal Protection Clause of the Fourteenth Amendment. But a Circuit Court of Appeals held, and the U.S. Supreme Court affirmed, that "[A] ban on race or gender preferences, as a matter of law or logic, does not violate the Equal Protection Clause in any conventional sense. . . . Impediments to preferential treatment do not deny equal protection."[27] The success of the California Initiative has inspired similar movements in other states.

GENDER EQUALITY AND THE FOURTEENTH AMENDMENT

The historical context of the Fourteenth Amendment implies its intent to guarantee equality for newly freed slaves, but the wording of its Equal Protection Clause applies to "any person." Thus the text of the Fourteenth Amendment could be interpreted to bar any gender differences in the law, in the fashion of the once proposed yet never ratified Equal Rights Amendment. But the Supreme Court has not interpreted the Equal Protection Clause to give the same level of protection to gender equality as to racial equality. Indeed, in 1873 the Supreme Court specifically rejected arguments that this clause applied to women. The Court once upheld a state law banning women from practicing law, arguing that "The natural and proper timidity and delicacy which belongs to the female sex evidently unfits it for many of the occupations of civil life. . . . The paramount destiny and mission of women are to fulfill the noble and benign offices of wife and mother. This is the law of the Creator."[28]

Early Feminist Politics   The earliest active feminist organizations grew out of the pre–Civil War antislavery movement. There the first generation of feminists—including Lucretia Mott, Elizabeth Cady Stanton, Lucy Stone, and Susan B. Anthony—learned to organize, hold public meetings, and conduct petition campaigns. After the Civil War, women were successful in changing many state laws that abridged the property rights of married women and otherwise treated them as "chattel" (property) of their husbands. By the early 1900s activists were also successful in winning some protections for women in the workplace, including state laws limiting women's hours of work, working conditions, and physical demands. At the time, these laws were regarded as "progressive."

The most successful feminist efforts of the 1800s centered on protection of women in families. The perceived threats to women's well-being were their husbands' drinking, gambling, and consorting with prostitutes. Women led the Anti-Saloon League, succeeded in outlawing gambling and prostitution in every state except Nevada, and provided the major source of moral support for the Eighteenth Amendment (Prohibition).

In the early twentieth century, the feminist movement concentrated on women's suffrage—the drive to guarantee women the right to vote. The early suffragists employed mass demonstrations, parades, picketing, and occasional disruption and civil disobedience—tactics similar to those of the civil rights movement of the 1960s. The culmination of their efforts was the 1920 passage of the Nineteenth Amendment to the Constitution: "The right of citizens of the United States to vote

Elizabeth Cady Stanton addresses a meeting. Stanton, with Lucretia Mott and others, organized one of the defining moments in feminist politics in the United States—the Seneca Falls convention of 1848. Participants at the convention approved a Declaration of Sentiments, modeled on the Declaration of Independence, that demanded legal and political rights for women, including the right to vote.

shall not be denied or abridged by the United States or by any State on account of sex." The suffrage movement spawned the League of Women Voters; in addition to women's right to vote, the League has sought protection of women in industry, child welfare laws, and honest election practices.

Judicial Scrutiny of Gender Classifications   In the 1970s, the Supreme Court became responsive to arguments that sex discrimination might violate the Equal Protection Clause of the Fourteenth Amendment. In *Reed v. Reed* (1971), it ruled that sexual classifications in the law "must be reasonable and not arbitrary, and must rest on some ground of difference having fair and substantial relation to . . . important governmental objectives."[29] This is a much more relaxed level of scrutiny than the Supreme Court gives to racial classification in the law. Since then, the Court has also made these rulings:

- A state can no longer set different ages for men and women to become legal adults[30] or purchase alcoholic beverages.[31]
- Women cannot be barred from police or firefighting jobs by arbitrary height and weight requirements.[32]
- Insurance and retirement plans for women must pay the same monthly benefits (even though women on the average live longer).[33]
- Schools must pay coaches in girls' sports the same as coaches in boys' sports.[34]

Continuing Gender Differences   The Supreme Court continues to wrestle with the question of whether some gender differences can be recognized in law. The question is most evident in laws dealing with sexual activity and reproduction. The Court has upheld statutory rape laws that make it a crime for an adult male to have sexual intercourse with a female under the age of eighteen, regardless of her consent. "We need not to be medical doctors to discern that young men and young women are not similarly situated with respect to the problems and the risks of sexual intercourse. Only women may become pregnant, and they suffer disproportionately the profound physical, emotional and psychological consequences of sexual activity."[35]

Women's participation in military service, particularly combat, raises even more controversial questions regarding permissible gender classifications. The Supreme Court appears to have bowed out of this particular controversy. In upholding Congress's draft registration law for men only, the Court ruled that "the constitutional power of Congress to raise and support armies and to make all laws necessary and proper to that end is broad and sweeping."[36] Congress and the Defense Department are responsible for determining assignments for women in the military. Women have recently won assignments to air and naval combat units but remain excluded from combat infantry, armor, artillery, and special forces.

Aims of the Equal Rights Amendment   The proposed Equal Rights Amendment to the U.S. Constitution, passed by Congress in 1972 but never ratified by the states, was worded very broadly: "Equality of rights under the law shall not be denied or abridged by the United States or any State on account of sex." Had it been ratified by the necessary thirty-eight states, it would have eliminated most, if not all, gender differences in the law. Without ERA, many important guarantees of equality for women rest on laws of Congress rather than on the Constitution.

GENDER EQUALITY IN THE ECONOMY

As cultural views of women's roles in society have changed and economic pressures on family budgets have increased, women's participation in the labor force has risen. The gap between women's and men's participation in the nation's work force is closing over time.[37] With the movement of women into the work force, feminist political activity has shifted toward economic concerns—gender equality in education, employment, pay, promotion, and credit.

Gender Equality in Civil Rights Laws   Title VII of the Civil Rights Act of 1964 prevents sexual (as well as racial) discrimination in hiring, pay, and promotions. The Equal Employment Opportunity Commission, the federal agency charged with eliminating discrimination in employment, has established guidelines barring stereotyped classifications of "men's jobs" and "women's jobs." The courts have repeatedly struck down state laws and employer practices that differentiate between men and women in hours, pay, retirement age, and so forth.

The Federal Equal Credit Opportunity Act of 1974 prohibits sex discrimination in credit transactions. Federal law prevents banks, credit unions, savings and loan associations, retail stores, and credit card companies from denying credit because of sex or marital status. However, these businesses may still deny credit for a poor or nonexistent credit rating, and some women who have always maintained accounts in their husband's name may still face credit problems if they apply in their own name.

Title IX of the Education Act Amendment of 1972 deals with sex discrimination in education. This federal law bars discrimination in admissions, housing, rules, financial aid, faculty and staff recruitment and pay, and—most troublesome of all—athletics. The latter problem has proven very difficult because men's football and basketball programs have traditionally brought in the money to finance all

Employees of the Mitsubishi automobile plant in Normal, Illinois, demonstrated outside the offices of the Equal Employment Opportunity Commission in Chicago in April, 1996, in support of the company after it became the target of a sexual harassment investigation. The company provided transportation to the demonstration and paid the workers for the day.

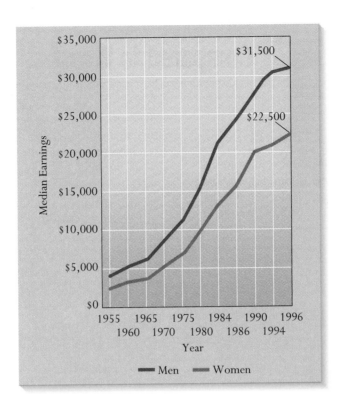

FIGURE 15-1 **Median Earnings by Gender**

The continuing "earnings gap" between men and women reflects a division in the labor market between traditionally male higher paying occupations and traditionally female lower paying positions.

Source: *Statistical Abstract of the United States, 1997.*

other sports, and men's football and basketball have received the largest share of school athletic budgets.

The Earnings Gap　Despite protections under federal laws, women continue to earn substantially less than men do. Today women, on average, earn only about 71 percent of what men do (see Figure 15-1). This earnings gap is not primarily a product of **direct discrimination**; women in the same job with the same skills, qualifications, experience, and work record are not generally paid less than men. Such direct discrimination has been illegal since the Civil Rights Act of 1964. Rather, the earnings gap is primarily a product of a division in the labor market between traditionally male and female jobs, with lower salaries paid in traditionally female occupations[38] (see *Compared to What?* "The Earnings Gap in Democratic Nations").

The Dual Labor Market and "Comparable Worth"　The existence of a "dual" labor market, with male-dominated "blue-collar" jobs distinguishable from female-dominated "pink-collar" jobs, continues to be a major obstacle to economic equality between men and women. These occupational differences result from cultural stereotyping, social conditioning, and training and education—all of which narrow the choices available to women. Although significant progress has been made in reducing occupational sex segregation (see Figure 15-2), many observers nevertheless doubt that sexually differentiated occupations will be eliminated in the foreseeable future.

As a result of a growing recognition that the wage gap is more a result of occupational differentiation than direct discrimination, some feminist organizations have turned to a new approach—the demand that pay levels in various occupations be determined by **comparable worth** rather than by the labor market.

direct discrimination　Now illegal practice of differential pay for men versus women even when those individuals have equal qualifications and perform the same job.

comparable worth　Argument that pay levels for traditionally male and traditionally female jobs should be equalized by paying equally all jobs that are "worth about the same" to an employer.

The Earnings Gap in Democratic Nations

The earnings gap between men and women in the United States persists. The International Labor Organization's comparisons indicate that for every dollar an American man earns in a week, an American woman earns an average of 74 cents.

In many advanced democracies, the earnings gap is significantly smaller (see graph). In France, for exam-

ple, women's wages are estimated to be 82 percent of men's wages. However, in Japan, women's earnings relative to men's are much worse than in the United States: the average weekly wage of women in Japan is only half that of men.

Source: International Labor Organization, *We're Number One* (New York: Vintage Books, 1992, p. iii.

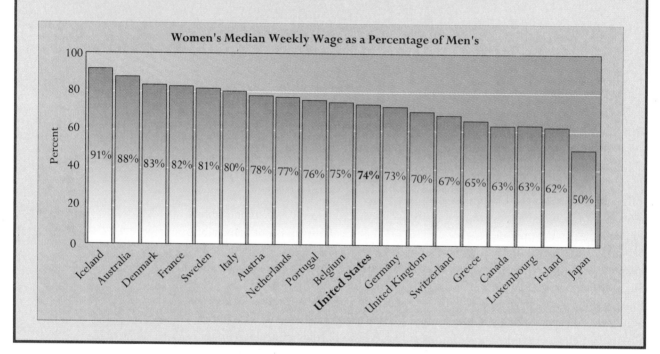

Comparable worth goes beyond paying men and women equally for the same work and calls for paying the same wages for jobs of comparable value to the employer. Advocates of comparable worth argue that governmental agencies or the courts should evaluate traditionally male and female jobs to determine their "worth" to the employer, perhaps by considering responsibilities, effort, knowledge, and skill requirements. Jobs adjudged to be "comparable" would be paid equal wages. Government agencies or the courts would replace the labor market in determining wage rates.

But comparable worth raises problems of implementation: Who would decide what wages should be for various jobs? What standards would be used to decide? EEOC has rejected the notion of comparable worth and declined to recommend wages for traditionally male and female jobs. And so far, the federal courts have refused to declare that differing wages in traditionally male and female occupations

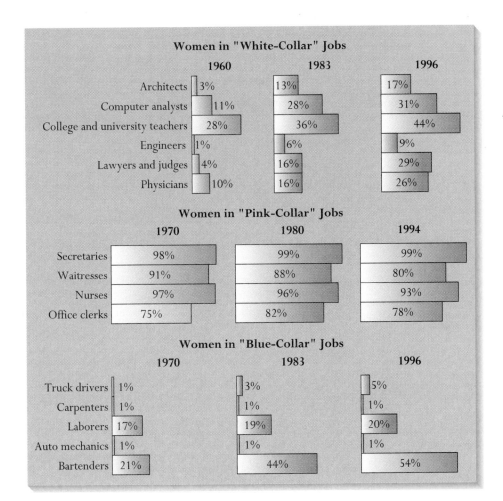

Women in "White-Collar" Jobs

	1960	1983	1996
Architects	3%	13%	17%
Computer analysts	11%	28%	31%
College and university teachers	28%	36%	44%
Engineers	1%	6%	9%
Lawyers and judges	4%	16%	29%
Physicians	10%	16%	26%

Women in "Pink-Collar" Jobs

	1970	1980	1994
Secretaries	98%	99%	99%
Waitresses	91%	88%	80%
Nurses	97%	96%	93%
Office clerks	75%	82%	78%

Women in "Blue-Collar" Jobs

	1970	1983	1996
Truck drivers	1%	3%	5%
Carpenters	1%	1%	1%
Laborers	17%	19%	20%
Auto mechanics	1%	1%	1%
Bartenders	21%	44%	54%

FIGURE 15-2 Gender Differentiation in the Labor Market

Most of the earnings gap between men and women in the U.S. labor force today is the result of the different job positions held by the two sexes. Although women are increasingly entering "white-collar" occupations long dominated by men, they continue to be disproportionately concentrated in "pink-collar" service positions. "Blue-collar" jobs have been the most resistant to change, remaining a male bastion, although women bartenders now outnumber men.

Sources: U.S. Department of Labor, *Employment in Perspective: Working Women* (Washington, D.C.: Government Printing Office, 1983); National Research Council, National Academy of Sciences, *Women's Work, Men's Work* (Washington, D.C.: National Academy Press, 1985); U.S. Bureau of Labor Statistics, *Employment Earnings,* 1997.

constitute evidence of sexual discrimination in violation of federal law. However, some state governments and private employers have undertaken to review their own pay scales to determine if traditionally female occupations are underpaid.

The "Glass Ceiling"   Few women have climbed the ladder to become president or chief executive officer or director of the nation's largest industrial corporations, banks, utilities, newspapers, or television networks.[39] Large numbers of women are entering the legal profession, but few are senior partners in the nation's largest and most prestigious law firms. Women are more likely to be found in the presidential cabinet than in the corporate boardroom.

The barriers to women's advancement to top positions are often very subtle, giving rise to the phrase **glass ceiling**. In explaining "why women aren't getting to the top," one observer argues that "At senior management levels competence is assumed. What you're looking for is someone who fits, someone who gets along, someone you trust. Now that's subtle stuff. How does a group of men feel that a woman is going to fit? I think it's very hard." Or, as a woman bank executive says, "The men just don't feel comfortable."[40]

There are many other explanations for the glass ceiling, all controversial: women choose staff assignments rather than fast-track, operating-head assignments. Women are cautious and unaggressive in corporate politics. Women have lower expectations about peak earnings and positions, and these expectations

glass ceiling   "Invisible" barriers to women rising to the highest positions in corporations and the professions.

What Do You Think?

What Constitutes Sexual Harassment?

The hearings on Clarence Thomas's nomination to the Supreme Court brought unprecedented levels of media scrutiny to the issue of sexual harassment. It inspired a wave of complaints to the U.S. Equal Employment Opportunity Commission, state and federal courts, corporate personnel offices, and colleges and universities. Various surveys report that up to one-third of female workers say they have experienced sexual harassment on the job.[*] But it is not always clear exactly what kind of behavior constitutes "sexual harassment."

The U.S. Supreme Court has provided some guidance in the development of sexual harassment definitions and prohibitions. Title VII of the Civil Rights Act of 1964 makes it "an unlawful employment practice to discriminate against any individual with respect to his [sic] compensation, terms, conditions or privileges of employment because of such individual's race, color, religion, sex, or national origin." In the employment context, the U.S. Supreme Court has approved the following definition of sexual harassment:

> Unwelcome sexual advances, requests for sexual favors, and other verbal or physical conduct of a sexual nature constitute sexual harassment when (1) submission to such conduct is made either explicitly or implicitly a term or condition of an individual's employment; (2) submission to or rejection of such conduct by an individual is used as the basis for employment decisions affecting such individual; or (3) such conduct has the purpose or effect of unrea-

sonably interfering with an individual's work performance or creating an intimidating, hostile, or offensive working environment.[†]

There are no great difficulties in defining sexual harassment when jobs or promotions are conditioned on the granting of sexual favors. But several problems arise in defining a "hostile working environment." This phrase may include offensive utterances, sexual innuendoes, dirty jokes, the display of pornographic material, and unwanted proposals for dates. First, it would appear to include speech and hence raise First Amendment questions regarding how far speech may be curtailed by law in the workplace. Second, the definition depends more on the subjective feelings of the individual employee about what is "offensive" and "unwanted" than on an objective standard of behavior easily understood by all. Justice Sandra Day O'Connor wrestled with the definition of a "hostile work environment" in *Harris v. Forklift* in 1993. She held that a plaintiff need not show that the utterances caused psychological injury but that a "reasonable person," not just the plaintiff, must perceive the work environment to be hostile or abusive. Presumably a single incident would not constitute harassment; rather, courts should consider "the frequency of the discriminatory conduct," "its severity," and whether it "unreasonably interferes with an employee's work performance."[††]

What behaviors does a "reasonable person" believe to be sexual harassment? Some polls indicate that women are somewhat more likely to perceive sexual harassment in various behaviors than men (see figure). But neither women nor men are likely to perceive it to include repeated requests for a date, the telling of dirty jokes, or comments on attractive-

become self-fulfilling. Women bear children, and even during relatively short maternity absences they fall behind their male counterparts. Women are less likely to want to change locations than men, and immobile executives are worth less to a corporation than mobile ones. Women executives in sensitive positions come under even more pressure than men in similar posts. Women executives believe they get much more scrutiny than men and must work harder to succeed. And at all levels, increasing attention has been paid to sexual harassment (see *What Do You Think?* "What Constitutes Sexual Harassment?"). Finally, it is important to note that affirmative action efforts by governments—notably the EEOC—are directed primarily at entry-level positions rather than senior management posts.

ness—even though these behaviors often inspire formal complaints.

Many university policies go well beyond both Supreme Court rulings and opinion polls in defining what constitutes sexual harassment, including the following:

- "remarks about a person's clothing"
- "suggestive or insulting sounds"
- "leering at or ogling of a person's body"
- "nonsexual slurs about one's gender"
- "remarks that degrade another person or group on the basis of gender."

The National Association of Scholars worries that overly broad and vague definitions of sexual harassment can undermine academic freedom and inhibit classroom discussions of important yet sensitive topics including human sexuality, gender differences, sexual roles, and gender politics. Teaching and research on such topics, in their view, must not be constrained by the threat that the views expressed will be labeled "insensitive," "uncomfortable," or "incorrect"; faculty must feel free to provide their best academic and professional advice to students, collectively and individually, without fear that their comments will be officially labeled as "offensive" or "unwelcome"; and students must feel free to express themselves on matters of gender, whether or not their ideas are biased, immature, or crudely expressed.

---

*Washington Post National Weekly Edition, March 7, 1993.

†Meritor Savings Bank v. Vinson, 477 U.S. 57 (1986).

††Harris v. Forklift Systems, 126 L. Ed. 2d 295 (1993).

Question: *Here is a list of some different situations. We're interested in knowing whether you think they are forms of sexual harassment—not just inappropriate or in bad taste, but sexual harassment.*

Definitely is sexual harassment...

Situation	Men	Women
If a male boss makes it clear to a female employee that she must go to bed with him for a promotion	91%	92%
If a male boss asks very direct questions of a female employee about her personal sexual practices and preferences	59%	68%
If a female boss asks very direct questions of a male employee about his personal sexual practices and preferences	47%	57%
If a man once in a while asks a female employee of his to go out on dates, even though she has said no in the past	15%	21%
If a man once in a while tells dirty jokes in the presence of female employees	15%	16%
If a male boss tells a female employee that she looks very attractive today	3%	5%

☐ Men   ☐ Women

Source: Roper Organization as reported in American Enterprise, September/October, 1993, p. 93.

HISPANIC POLITICS

Hispanics—a term the U.S. Census Bureau uses to refer to Mexican Americans, Puerto Ricans, Cubans, and others of Spanish-speaking ancestry and culture—now comprise over 11 percent of the U.S. population (see Table 15-3). The largest Hispanic subgroup is Mexican Americans. Some are descendants of citizens who lived in the Mexican territory annexed to the United States in 1848, but most have come to the United States in accelerating numbers in recent years. The largest Mexican American populations are found in Texas, Arizona, New Mexico, and California. Puerto Ricans constitute the second largest Hispanic subgroup. Many still retain ties to the commonwealth and move back and forth from Puerto Rico

TABLE 15-3	Minorities in America—2000	
	Number	*Percentage of Population*
African Americans	35,456,000	12.9%
Hispanic Americans	31,366,000	11.4
Asian or Pacific Islander Americans	11,246,000	4.1
Native Americans, Eskimos, Aleuts	2,402,000	0.9
Total Population	274,634,000	100.0

Source: Statistical Abstract of the United States, 1997, p. 35.

to New York. Cubans make up the third largest subgroup; most have fled from Fidel Castro's Cuba and live mainly in the Miami metropolitan area. Each of these Hispanic groups has encountered a different experience in American life. Indeed, some evidence indicates that these groups identify themselves separately, rather than as Hispanics.[41]

If all Hispanics are grouped together for statistical comparisons, their median family income level is well below that of whites (see Table 15-2). Hispanic poverty and unemployment rates are also higher than those of whites. The percentage of Hispanics completing high school and college education is well below that of both whites and blacks, suggesting language or other cultural obstacles in education. Yet within these overall racial comparisons, there are wide disparities among subgroups as well as among individuals.

Mexican Americans   The Mexican American population in the southwestern United States is growing very rapidly; it doubled in size between 1980 and 1990. For many years, agricultural business encouraged immigration of Mexican farm laborers willing to endure harsh conditions for low pay. Many others came to the United States as *indocumentados*—undocumented, or illegal, aliens. In the Immigration Reform Act of 1986 Congress offered amnesty to all undocumented workers who had entered the United States prior to 1982. But the act also required employers, under threat of penalties, to hire only people who can provide documentation of their legal status in the country. The result has been an increase in discrimination against Hispanics in hiring, as well as a booming business in counterfeit green (employment) and Social Security cards.

Economic conditions in Mexico and elsewhere in Central America continue to fuel immigration, legal and illegal, to the United States. But with lower educational levels, average incomes of Mexican American families in the United States are lower and the poverty rate is higher than the general population. Although Mexican Americans have served as governors of Arizona and New Mexico and have won election to the U.S. Congress, their political power does not yet match their population percentages. Mexican American voter turnout is lower than other ethnic groups, perhaps because many are resident aliens or illegal immigrants not eligible to vote, or perhaps because of cultural factors that discourage political participation.[42]

Puerto Ricans   Residents of Puerto Rico are American citizens because Puerto Rico is a commonwealth of the United States. Puerto Rico's commonwealth government resembles that of a state, with a constitution and elected governor and legislature, but the island has no voting members of the U.S. Congress and no electoral votes for president. As citizens, Puerto Ricans can move anywhere in the United States; many have immigrated to New York City.

Median family income in Puerto Rico is higher than anywhere else in the Caribbean but only half that of the poorest state in the United States. Puerto Ricans have not fared as well economically as other Hispanic groups within the United States: Puerto Ricans have lower median family incomes and higher poverty percentages, in part perhaps because of lower work force participation. One explanation centers on the history of access to federal welfare programs on the island and the resulting social dependency it fostered among some Puerto Rican families.[43]

Puerto Ricans have long debated whether to remain a commonwealth of the United States, apply for statehood, or seek complete independence from the United States. As citizens of a commonwealth, Puerto Ricans pay no U.S. income tax (although their local taxes are substantial) while receiving all the benefits that U.S. citizens are entitled to—Social Security, welfare assistance, food stamps, Medicaid, Medicare, and so forth. If Puerto Rico chose to become a state, its voters could participate in presidential and congressional elections, but its taxpayers would not enjoy the same favorable cost-benefit ratio they enjoy under commonwealth status. Some Puerto Ricans also fear that statehood would dilute the island's cultural identity and force English on them as the national language.

As a state, Puerto Rico would have two U.S. senators and perhaps six U.S. representatives. The island's majority party, the Popular Democratic Party, is closely identified with the Democratic Party, so most of these new members would likely be Democrats. But the island's New Progressive Party, identified with the Republican Party, supports statehood, and many GOP leaders believe their party should appeal to Hispanic voters. If Puerto Ricans were to choose independence, a new constitution for the Republic of Puerto Rico would be drawn up by the islanders themselves.

All of the participants in the debate agree that Puerto Ricans themselves should vote on the matter by referendum. (In a 1967 referendum, 60 percent of Puerto Ricans voted to remain a commonwealth, 39 percent voted for statehood, and less than 1 percent for independence.) Congress is currently planning another referendum, but arguments over the conditions associated with various options, as well as who should be allowed to vote (Puerto Ricans currently living on the mainland or only those currently residing on the island) have slowed action.

Cuban Americans Many Cuban Americans, especially those in the early waves of refugees from Castro's revolution in 1959, were skilled professionals and businesspeople, and they rapidly set about building Miami into a thriving economy. Although Cuban Americans are the smallest of the Hispanic subgroups, today they are better educated and enjoy higher incomes than the others. They are well organized politically, and they have succeeded in electing Cuban Americans to local office in Florida and to the U.S. Congress.

Hispanics in Congress Hispanic representation in the U.S. House of Representatives had risen to 18 by 1995. This figure—about 4 percent of the House membership—suggests continuing underrepresentation of the 11 percent of the U.S. population that is Hispanic. Cuban Americans tend to identify with the Republican Party, and the two Republican Hispanic House members are both Cuban Americans from the Miami area; all other Hispanic House members are Democrats.

NATIVE AMERICANS: TRAILS OF TEARS

Christopher Columbus, having erred in his estimate of the circumference of the globe, believed he had arrived in the Indian Ocean when he first came to the Caribbean. He mistook the Arawaks there for people of the East Indies, calling them *Indios,* and this Spanish word passed into English as "Indians"—a word that came to refer to all Native American peoples. But at the time of the first European contacts, these peoples had no common ethnic identity; hundreds of separate cultures and languages were thriving in the Americas. Although estimates vary, most historians believe 7 to 12 million people lived in the land that is now the United States and Canada; 25 million more lived in Mexico; and as many as 60 to 70 million in all lived in the Western Hemisphere, a number comparable to Europe's population at the time.

In the centuries that followed, the Native American population of the Western Hemisphere was devastated by warfare, by famine, and, most of all, by epidemic diseases brought from Europe. Overall, the Native population fell by 90 percent, the greatest known human disaster in world history. In the Europeans' conquest of the Americas, smallpox wreaked the greatest havoc, followed by measles, bubonic plague, influenza, typhus, diphtheria, and scarlet fever. Superior military technology, together with skill in exploiting hostilities between Native nations, gradually overcame the resistance of Native peoples. By 1910 only 210,000 Native Americans lived in the United States. Their population has slowly recovered to the current 2.2 million (less than 1 percent of the U.S. population). Many live on reservations and trust lands, the largest of which is the Navajo and Hopi enclave in the southwestern United States (see *Across the USA:* "Native American Peoples").

The Trail of Broken Treaties   In the Northwest Ordinance of 1787, Congress, in organizing the western territories of the new nation, declared, "The utmost good faith shall always be observed toward the Indians. Their lands and property shall never be taken from them without their consent." And later, in the Intercourse Act of 1790, Congress declared that public treaties between the United States government and the independent Native nations would be the only legal means of obtaining "Indian" land.

As president, George Washington forged a treaty with the Creeks: in exchange for land concessions, the United States pledged to protect the boundaries of the Creek nation and to allow the Creeks themselves to punish all violators of their laws within these boundaries. This semblance of legality was reflected in hundreds of treaties that followed. (Indeed, in recent years some Native American nations have successfully sued in federal court for reparations and return of lands obtained in violation of the Intercourse Act of 1790 and subsequent treaties.) Yet Native lands were constantly invaded by whites. The resulting Native resistance typically led to wars that ultimately resulted in great loss of life among warriors and their families and the further loss of Native land. The cycle of invasion, resistance, military defeat, and further land concessions continued for a hundred years.

"Indian Territories"   Following the purchase of the vast Louisiana Territory in 1803, President Thomas Jefferson sought to "civilize" the Natives by promoting farming in "reservations" that were located west of the Mississippi River. But soon, peoples who had been forced to move from Ohio to Missouri were forced to move again to

Native American Peoples

This map shows the locations of the principal Native American reservations in the United States. Tribal governments officially govern these reservations. (Alaska Natives, including Aleuts and Eskimos, live mostly in 200 villages widely scattered across rural Alaska; twelve regional Native American corporations administer property and mineral rights on behalf of Native peoples in that state.)

survive the relentless white expansion. President James Monroe designated as "Indian territory" most of the Great Plains west of the Missouri River. Native peoples increasingly faced three unattractive choices: assimilation, removal, or extinction.

In 1814 the Creeks, encouraged by the British during the War of 1812 to attack American settlements, faced an army of Tennessee volunteer militia led by Andrew Jackson. At the Battle of Horseshoe Bend, Jackson's cannon fire decimated the Creek warriors. In the uneven Treaty of Fort Jackson, the Creeks, Choctaws, and Cherokees were forced to concede millions of acres of land.

By 1830 the "Five Civilized Tribes" of the southeastern United States (Cherokees, Chickasaws, Choctaws, Creeks, and Seminoles) had ceded most but not all of their lands. When gold was discovered on Cherokee land in northern Georgia in 1829, whites invaded their territory. Congress, at the heeding of the old "Indian fighter" President Andrew Jackson, passed the Removal Act, ordering the forcible relocation of the Natives to Oklahoma Indian Territory. The Cherokees tried to use the whites' law to defend their land, bringing their case to the U.S. Supreme Court. When Chief Justice John Marshall held the Cherokees were a "domestic dependent nation" that could not be forced to give up its land, President Jackson replied scornfully, "John Marshall has made his decision. Now let him enforce it." He sent a 7,000-strong army to pursue Seminoles into the huge Florida Everglades swamp and forced 16,000 Cherokees and other peoples on the infamous "Trail of Tears" march to Oklahoma in 1838.

Encroachment on the Indian Territory of the Great Plains was not long in coming. First, the territory was crossed by the Santa Fe and Oregon Trails, and a series of military forts were built to protect travelers. In 1854, under pressure from railroad interests, the U.S. government abolished much of the Indian Territory to create the Kansas and Nebraska territories, which were immediately opened to white settlers. The Native peoples in these lands—including Potawatomis, Kickapoos, Delawares, Shawnees, Miamis, Omahas, and Missouris—were forced to sign treaties accepting vastly reduced land reservations. But large, warlike buffalo-hunting nations remained in the northern Dakotas and western Great Plains: the Sioux, Cheyennes, Arapahoes, Comanches, and Kiowas. (Other smaller peoples inhabited the Rockies to California and the Pacific Northwest; the sedentary Pueblos, Hopis, and Pimas and the migrating Apaches and Navajos occupied the Southwest.) The Plains peoples took pride in their warrior status, often fighting among themselves.

"Indian Wars"   The "Indian Wars" were fought between the Plains nations and the U.S. Army between 1864 and 1890. Following the Civil War, the federal government began to assign boundaries to each nation and created the Bureau of Indian Affairs (BIA) to "assist and protect" Native peoples on their "reservations." But the reservations were repeatedly reduced in size until subsistence by hunting became impossible. Malnutrition and demoralization of the Native peoples were accelerated by the mass slaughter of the buffalo; vast herds, numbering perhaps as many as 70 million, were exterminated over the years. The most storied engagement of the long war occurred at the Little Bighorn River in Montana on June 25, 1876, where Civil War hero General George Armstrong Custer led elements of the U.S. Seventh Calvary to destruction at the hands of Sioux and Cheyenne warriors led by Chief Crazy Horse, Sitting Bull, and Gall. But "Custer's last stand" inspired renewed army campaigns against the Plains peoples; the following year, Crazy Horse was forced to surrender. In 1881 destitute Sioux under Chief Sitting Bull returned from exile in Canada to surrender themselves to reservation life. Among the last peoples to hold out were the Apaches, whose famous warrior Geronimo finally surrendered in 1886. Sporatic fighting continued until 1890, when a small malnourished band of Lakota Sioux were wiped out at Wounded Knee Creek.

The Attempted Destruction of Traditional Life   The Dawes Act of 1887 governed federal Native American policy for decades. The thrust of the policy was to break up Native lands, allotting acreage for individual homesteads in order to assimilate Natives into the white agricultural society. Farming was to replace hunting, and traditional Native customs were to be shed for English language and schooling. But this effort to destroy culture never really succeeded. Although Native peoples lost more than half of their 1877 reservation land, few lost their communal ties or accumulated much private property. Life on the reservations was often desperate. Natives suffered the worst poverty of any group in the United States, with high rates of infant mortality, alcoholism, and other diseases. The BIA, notoriously corrupt and mismanaged, encouraged dependency and regularly interfered with religious affairs and customs.

The New Deal   The New Deal under President Franklin D. Roosevelt came to Native Americans in the form of the Indian Reorganization Act of 1934. This act sought to restore Native tribal structures by recognizing these nations as instruments of the federal government. Land ownership was restored, and elected Native tribal councils were recognized as legal governments. Efforts to force assimilation were largely abandoned. The BIA became more sensitive to Native culture and began employing Native Americans in larger numbers.

Yet the BIA remained "paternalistic," frequently interfering in tribal "sovereignty." Moreover, in the 1950s Congress initiated a policy of "termination" of sovereignty rights for specific nations that consented to relinquish their lands in exchange for cash payments. Although only a few nations chose this course, the results were often calamitous: after the one-time cash payments were spent, Native peoples became dependent on state social welfare services and often slipped further into poverty and alcoholism.

The American Indian Movement The civil rights movement of the 1960s inspired a new activism among Native American groups. The American Indian Movement (AIM) was founded in 1968 and attracted national headlines by occupying Alcatraz Island in San Francisco Bay. Violence flared in 1972 when AIM activists took over the site of the Wounded Knee battle and fought with FBI agents. Several Native nations succeeded in federal courts and Congress to win back lands and/or compensation for lands taken from them in treaty violations. Native culture was revitalized, and Vine Deloria's *Custer Died for Your Sins* (1969) and Dee Brown's *Bury My Heart at Wounded Knee* (1971) became national best-selling books.

Native Americans Today The U.S. Constitution (Article I, Section 8) grants Congress the full power "to regulate Commerce . . . with the Indian Tribes." States are prevented from regulating or taxing Native peoples or extending their courts' jurisdiction over them unless authorized by Congress. The Supreme Court recognizes Native Americans "as members of quasi-sovereign tribal entities"[44] with powers to regulate their own internal affairs, establish their own courts, and enforce their own laws, all subject to congressional supervision. Thus, for example, many Native peoples chose to legalize gambling, including casino gambling, on reservations in states that otherwise prohibited the activity. As citizens, Native Americans have the right to vote in state as well as national elections. Those living off of reservations have the same rights and responsibilities as other citizens. Ben Nighthorse Campbell, U.S. senator from Colorado, is the only tribal member

The Foxwoods Casino, on the Pequot Indian Reservation in Connecticut, has brought the tribe a new-found prosperity.

(Northern Cheyenne) currently serving in Congress (see *People in Politics:* "Minority Faces in Congress" in Chapter 10).

The Bureau of Indian Affairs in the Department of the Interior continues to supervise reservation life, and Native Americans enrolled as members of nations and living on reservations are entitled to certain benefits established by law and treaty. Nevertheless, these peoples remain the poorest and least healthy in the United States, with high incidences of infant mortality, suicide, and alcoholism. Approximately half of all Native Americans live below the poverty line.

THE RIGHTS OF DISABLED AMERICANS

Disabled Americans were not among the classes of people protected by the landmark Civil Rights Act of 1964. Yet they have long suffered both direct and indirect obstacles to participation in education, employment, and access to public accommodations. Throughout most of the nation's history, little thought was given to making public or private buildings or facilities accessible to blind, deaf, or mobility-impaired people.[45] Not until the Education of Handicapped Children Act of 1975 did the federal government mandate that the nation's public schools provide free education to handicapped children.

The Americans with Disabilities Act (ADA) of 1990 is a sweeping law that prohibits discrimination against disabled people in private employment, government programs, public accommodations, and telecommunications. The act is vaguely worded in many of its provisions, requiring "reasonable accommodations" for disabled people that do not involve "undue hardship." This means disabled Americans do not have exactly the same standard of protection as minorities or women, who are protected from discrimination *regardless* of hardship or costs. (It also means that attorneys, consultants, and bureaucrats will make handsome incomes over the years interpreting the meaning of these phrases.) Specifically the ADA includes the following protections:

The most recent Americans to pressure Congress and the courts for protection of rights long denied them are the nation's disabled citizens. In 1990 disability rights activists succeeded in getting Congress to pass the Americans with Disabilities Act, which mandates the removal of many barriers that have kept handicapped people from working, traveling, and enjoying leisure activities. Nevertheless, many obstacles remain. Here, activists demonstrate in favor of the act.

- *Employment:* Disabled people cannot be denied employment or promotion if, with "reasonable accommodation," they can perform the duties of the job. (Excluded from this protection are people currently using illegal drugs, gambling compulsively, or exhibiting certain other abnormal behavior.) Reasonable accommodation need not be made if doing so would cause "undue hardship" on the employer.

- *Government programs:* Disabled people cannot be denied access to government programs or benefits. New buses, taxis, and trains must be accessible to disabled persons, including those in wheelchairs.

- *Public accommodations:* Disabled people must enjoy "full and equal" access to hotels, restaurants, stores, schools, parks, museums, auditoriums, and the like. To achieve equal access, owners of existing facilities must alter them "to the maximum extent feasible"; builders of new facilities must ensure that they are readily accessible to disabled persons unless doing so is structurally impossible.

- *Communications:* The Federal Communications Commission is directed to issue regulations that will ensure telecommunications devices for hearing- and speech-impaired people are available "to the extent possible and in the most efficient manner."

INEQUALITY AND THE CONSTITUTION

Americans frequently claim "rights" that have no basis in the U.S. Constitution—for example, the "right" to an education, to medical care, to decent housing, to retirement benefits, to a job. The U.S. Constitution *limits* government; it protects individuals *from* government oppression. The U.S. Constitution does not mandate that governments act wisely or compassionately.

Constitutional versus Legal Rights There is no requirement in the U.S. Constitution that governments establish education, welfare, or social security programs or provide housing, job training, or unemployment compensation. Whatever benefits individuals derive from these government programs, they do so as a matter of law, not as a constitutional right.

> The importance of a service performed by the State does not determine whether it must be regarded as fundamental for purposes of examination under the equal protection clause. . . . Education, of course, is not among the rights afforded explicit protection under our federal Constitution. Nor do we find any basis for saying it is implicitly so protected.[46]

"Reasonable" Classifications Governments by law may classify people according to income, age, illness, disability, or any other "reasonable" standard in administering its programs. However, the Supreme Court has interpreted the Equal Protection Clause to mean only that governments may not practice "invidious" discrimination—that is, establish discriminatory classifications in the law which are "arbitrary and unreasonable" and have "no rational basis."[47] *Reasonable* classifications of individuals by law—those that serve a legitimate government purpose—are *not* unconstitutional. Yet the Equal Protection Clause obligates governments to treat equally all persons who are "similarly situated"—to treat every person who falls into a particular class in the same fashion as every other person in that class. Thus all persons who meet the eligibility requirements stated in the law must

Politics in Cyberspace

Civil Rights

A variety of information on civil rights is available on the Internet.

U.S. Commission on Civil Rights
http://www.usccr.gov

The U.S. government's official clearinghouse for information regarding discrimination or denial of equal protection of laws is the U.S. Commission on Civil Rights. The Commission was first established by Congress in 1957 to submit reports, findings, and recommendations to the president and Congress. It has produced over 150 public reports and studies on civil rights matters; all are available to the public free of charge.

U.S. Equal Employment Opportunity Commission
http://www.eeoc.gov

The U.S. Equal Employment Opportunity Commission also maintains a Web site with facts about employment discrimination as well as information on how to file a charge under Title VII of the Civil Rights Act of 1994, the Americans with Disabilities Act, the Age Discrimination in Employment Act, and the Equal Pay Act.

Many civil rights organizations also maintain their own Web sites.

National Association for the Advancement of Colored People
http://www.naacp.org

The NAACP is the nation's oldest civil rights organization. Its Web site includes information on the organization's history, structure, leadership, and current concerns.

National Organization for Women
http://www.now.org

The Web site of the National Organization for Women (NOW) includes studies on key issues, including violence against women, abortion and reproductive rights, and sexual harassment.

Center for Individual Rights
http://www.wdn.com

The Center for Individual Rights is a think tank that advocates and defends *individual* over *group* rights. It opposes affirmative action programs that include racial or gender quotas or preferences. It frequently engages in litigation and submits friends of the court briefs on behalf of individuals who have been denied employment or admission to universities based on their majority group status.

receive the same benefits. For example, if Congress establishes a public health care program for people sixty-five years of age and over (Medicare), then everyone in that age classification is entitled to the benefits of the program. Because the benefits of these programs are *legal* entitlements, not *constitutional* rights, however, Congress may choose to change the benefits or eligibility requirements at any time.

Protections for Poor Americans   The Constitution ensures that poor people are protected in their legal and political rights. Included among the specific protections given indigent persons are these:

- *Free legal counsel in criminal cases:* "From the very beginning, our state and national constitutions have laid great emphasis on procedures and substantial safeguards designed to assure fair trials before impartial tribunals in which every defendant stands equal before the law. This noble ideal cannot be realized if the poor man charged with a crime has to face his accusers without the lawyer to assist him."[48]

- *No tax or financial requirement for voting:* "A state violates the equal protection clause of the Fourteenth Amendment whenever it makes the affluence of the voter or payment of any fee an electoral standard."[49] This decision extended the Twenty-fourth Amendment's ban on poll taxes for national elections to state elections as well.

But the poor cannot demand government funding as a matter of constitutional right in order to exercise other recognized rights. For example, freedom of the press does not mean that the government must buy a printing press for anyone unable to afford one. Congress, in the controversial Hyde Amendment in 1977, denied the use of Medicaid funds for poor women seeking abortions, and the Supreme Court rejected arguments that federal funding of abortions was required by the Constitution. Even though the Court reaffirmed that abortion was a consti-tutional right, "it simply does not follow that a woman's freedom of choice carries with it a constitutional entitlement to the financial means to avail herself of the protected choices. . . . Although the government may not place obstacles in the path of a woman's exercise of her freedom of choice, it need not remove those not of its own creation."[50]

Income Inequality   Governments in the United States are not under any constitutional requirement to eliminate inequality of income or wealth. (The Founders believed that "dangerous leveling" was a violation of the right to prop-erty and to use and dispose of the fruits of one's own labors.) For example, repre-sentatives of poor, black, and Hispanic groups have charged that differences in public school spending per pupil among school districts in a state discriminate unconstitutionally against poor children. Although the state governments do not discriminate against the poor in their funding (on the contrary, most states have equalization programs written into state law giving more aid to schools serving poor students), it is argued that spending differences among local school districts violates the Equal Protection Clause of the Fourteenth Amendment. But the Supreme Court has ruled that disparities in school funding created by depen-dence on local property tax revenue and inequalities among districts in the value of property and amount of revenue raised does *not* violate the Equal Protection Clause. "We cannot say that such disparities are the product of a system that is so irrational as to be invidiously discriminatory."[51] Some *state* courts, however, have ruled that these same disparities violate *state* constitutional guarantees of equal protection.[52]

SUMMARY NOTES

- Equality has long been the central issue of Ameri-can politics. Today, most Americans agree that all individuals should have an equal opportunity to make of their lives whatever they can without arti-ficial barriers of race, class, gender, or ethnicity. Political conflict arises over what, if anything, government should do to achieve greater equality of results—the reduction of gaps between rich and poor, men and women, blacks and whites, and other groups in society.

- The original Constitution of 1787 recognized and protected slavery. Not until after the Civil War did the Thirteenth Amendment (1865) abolish slavery. But the Fourteenth Amendment's guarantee of "equal protection of the laws" and the Fifteenth Amend-ment's guarantee of voting rights were largely ignored in southern states after the federal government's Reconstruction efforts ended. Segregation was held constitutional by the U.S. Supreme Court in its "sepa-rate but equal" decision in *Plessy v. Ferguson* in 1896.

- The NAACP led the long legal battle in the federal courts to have segregation declared unconstitutional as a violation of the Equal Protection Clause of the Fourteenth Amendment. Under the leadership of Thurgood Marshall, a major victory was achieved in the case of *Brown v. Board of Education of Topeka* in 1954.

- The struggle over school desegregation continues even today. Federal courts are more likely to issue desegregation orders (including orders to bus pupils to achieve racial balance in schools) in school districts where present or past actions by government officials contributed to racial imbalances. Courts are less likely to order desegregation where racial imbalances are a product of residential patterns.

- The courts could eliminate *governmental* discrimination by enforcing the Fourteenth Amendment of the Constitution; but only Congress could end private discrimination through legislation. Martin Luther King, Jr.'s campaign of nonviolent direct action helped bring remaining racial injustices to the attention of Congress. Key legislation includes the Civil Rights Act of 1964, which bans discrimination in public accommodations, government-funded programs, and private employment; the Voting Rights Act of 1965, which authorizes strong federal action to protect voting rights; and the Civil Rights Act of 1968, which outlaws discrimination in housing.

- Today, racial politics center around continuing inequalities between blacks and whites in the areas of income, jobs, housing, health, education, and other conditions of life. Should the government concentrate on "equality of opportunity" and apply "color-blind" standards to both blacks and whites? Or should government take "affirmative action" to assist blacks and other minorities to overcome the results of past unequal treatment?

- Generally the Supreme Court is likely to approve of affirmative action programs when these programs have been adopted in response to a past proven history of discrimination, when they are narrowly tailored so as not to adversely affect the rights of individuals, when they do not absolutely bar whites from participating, and when they serve clearly identified, compelling, and legitimate government objectives.

- Congress is aware that public opinion generally supports affirmative action in the abstract but that white opinion rejects the specific notions of racial preferences and quotas. Recent battles in Congress have focused on whether statistical imbalances are evidence of discrimination and whether employers should bear the burden of proof that test requirements or practices with a disparate impact on minorities are related to job performance.

- The Equal Protection Clause of the Fourteenth Amendment applies to "any person," but traditionally the Supreme Court has recognized gender differences in laws. Nevertheless, in recent years the Court has struck down gender differences where they are unreasonable or arbitrary and unrelated to legitimate government objectives.

- Gender discrimination in employment has been illegal since the passage of the Civil Rights Act of 1964. Nevertheless, differences in average earnings of men and women persist, although these differences have narrowed somewhat over time. The earnings gap appears to be mainly a product of lower pay in occupations traditionally dominated by women and higher pay in traditionally male occupations. Although neither Congress nor the courts have mandated wages based on comparable worth of traditional men's and women's jobs in private employment, many governmental agencies and some private employers have undertaken to review wage rates to eliminate gender differences.

- Economic conditions in Mexico and other Spanish-speaking nations of the Western Hemisphere continue to fuel large-scale immigration, both legal and illegal, into the United States. But the political power of Mexican Americans, the nation's largest Hispanic group, does not yet match their population percentage. Their voter turnout remains lower than that of other ethnic groups in the United States.

- Since the arrival of the first Europeans on this continent, Native American peoples have experienced cycles of invasion, resistance, military defeat, and land concessions. Today Native American peoples collectively remain the poorest and least healthy of the nation's ethnic groups.

- The most recent major civil rights legislation is the Americans with Disabilities Act of 1990, which prohibits discrimination against disabled persons in private employment, government programs, public accommodations, and communications.

- The Equal Protection Clause does not bar government from treating persons in various income classes differently. However, governments must treat every individual in a class equally, and the classifications must not be "arbitrary" or "unreasonable." The poor cannot demand benefits or services as a matter of constitutional rights; but once government establishes a social welfare program by law, it must provide equal access to all persons "similarly situated."

SELECTED READINGS

BARKER, LUCIUS J., and MACK H. JONES. *African Americans and the American Political System*, 3rd ed. Upper Saddle River, N.J.: Prentice Hall, 1994. Comprehensive analysis of African American politics, examining access to the judicial arena, the interest-group process, political parties, Congress, and the White House.

CONWAY, M. MARGARET. *Women and Public Policy: A Revolution in Progress.* Washington, D.C.: CQ Press, 1994. Coverage of a broad range of policy areas that affect women, including education, employment, health, marriage and family law, and child care.

FOX-GENOVESE, ELIZABETH. *Feminism Is Not the Story of My Life.* New York: Doubleday, 1995. Critique of radical feminism for failing to understand the central importance of marriage and motherhood in women's lives, and a discussion of how public policy could ease the clashing demands of work and family on women.

GLAZER, NATHAN. *Affirmative Discrimination.* Cambridge, Mass.: Harvard University Press, 1987. Argues that the focus of current civil rights policy on group rights, rather than individual rights, is not only ineffective but also destructive of race relations in America.

HACKER, ANDREW. *Two Nations.* New York: Charles Scribner's Sons, 1992. Argues that race is the principal political division in American society and racial separation, hostilities, and inequalities are at dangerous levels today.

HERO, RODNEY E. *Latinos and the U.S. Political System.* Philadelphia: Temple University Press, 1992. General history of political participation of major Latino groups, arguing that different cultural behaviors limit their ability to participate in the interest-group system and policy-making process as currently structured.

KLUEGEL, JAMES R., and ELIOT R. SMITH. *Beliefs about Inequality.* New York: Aldine de Gruyter, 1986. Comprehensive description of Americans' beliefs and attitudes about inequality, based on extensive survey data, including evidence of changes in beliefs over time as well as inconsistencies and contradictions.

MCGLEN, NANCY E., and KAREN O'CONNER. *Women, Politics, and American Society.* Upper Saddle River, N.J.: Prentice Hall, 1996. Comprehensive text contrasting women's rights and realities in politics, employment, education, reproduction, and family.

SIGELMAN, LEE, and SUSAN WELCH. *Black Americans' Views of Racial Inequality.* Cambridge, Mass.: Cambridge University Press, 1991. Analysis of survey research showing that black perceptions of racial inequality in America are considerably different from white perceptions. Although remaining optimistic about the future, blacks see discrimination as commonplace and are much more likely than whites to attribute black-white differences in education, occupation, and income to racism.

THERNSTROM, STEPHEN, and ABIGAIL THERNSTROM. *America in Black and White.* New York: Simon & Schuster, 1997. Information-rich analysis tracing social and economic progress of African Americans and arguing that gains in education and employment were greater *before* the introduction of affirmative action programs.

ASK YOURSELF ABOUT POLITICS

1. Do you believe government efforts to manage the economy usually make things better or worse?
   Better ☐ Worse ☐

2. Do you believe the government should spend more during recessions to ease economic hardship even if it means larger government deficits?
   Yes ☐ No ☐

3. Do you think the federal government will ever balance the budget?
   Yes ☐ No ☐

4. If Congress could reduce government spending, should the money saved be used to balance the budget rather than cut taxes?
   Yes ☐ No ☐

5. Should the government spend more money for education even if doing so increases the deficit?
   Yes ☐ No ☐

6. Do you believe all wage earners should pay the same percentage of income in taxes (a flat tax)?
   Yes ☐ No ☐

7. Would you favor ending all deductions, including those for charitable contributions, if income taxes could be lowered to no more than 17 percent?
   Yes ☐ No ☐

POLITICS AND THE ECONOMY

CHAPTER OUTLINE

FEATURES

POLITICS AND ECONOMICS

What is the proper relationship between government and the economy? How much influence should the government exercise over the production and distribution of goods and services in this country?

Earlier, we observed that one of America's foremost political scientists, Harold Lasswell, defined "politics" as "who gets what, when, and how." One of America's foremost economists, Paul Samuelson, defined "economics" as "deciding what shall be produced, how, and for whom."[1] The similarity between these definitions is based on the fact that both the political system and the economic system provide society with means for deciding about the production and distribution of goods and services. The political system involves *collective* decisions—choices made by communities, states, or nations—and relies on government *coercion* through laws, regulations, taxes, and so on to implement them. A **free-**

The founder of classical economics, Scottish economist Adam Smith (1723–90), was a strong proponent of laissez-faire and free markets. He argued that government should keep out of economic matters as much as possible, relying instead on the "invisible hand" of the marketplace to rectify temporary economic problems such as recessions and inflation.

free-market economic system Economic system in which individual choices by consumers and firms determine what shall be produced, how much, and for whom; this economic system relies on voluntary exchanges of buying and selling

political economy Study of relationships among politics and economics and governments and markets.

inflation Rise in the general level of prices, not just the prices of some products.

recession Decline in the general level of economic activity.

economic growth Increase in the nation's total economic output.

market economic system involves *individual* decisions—choices made by millions of consumers and thousands of firms—and relies on *voluntary exchange* through buying, selling, borrowing, contracting, and trading to implement them. Both politics and markets function to transform popular demands into goods and services, to allocate costs, and to distribute goods and services.

One of the key questions in any society is how much to rely on government versus the marketplace to provide goods and services. This question of the proper relationship between governments and markets—that is, between politics and economics—is the subject of **political economy**. The United States is primarily a free-market economy, but the federal government strongly influences economic activity.

COMPETING ECONOMIC THEORIES

Various economic theories compete for preeminence as guides to government involvement in a free-market economy. These theories attempt to explain the forces that influence *demand*—the willingness and ability of individuals and firms to purchase goods and services (everything from cars and houses to dry cleaning and restaurant meals)—and *supply*—the willingness and ability of other individuals and firms to produce these products. Economic theories also attempt to explain the forces that influence the economy as a whole and can result in inflation, recession, or growth. **Inflation** is a rise in the *general level* of prices, not just the prices of some products. **Recession** is a decline in the general level of economic activity, usually coupled with an increase in unemployment. **Economic growth** is an increase in the nation's total economic output, usually measured by the real (inflation-adjusted) gross domestic product.

Classical Theory   **Classical economic theory** views a market economy as a self-adjusting mechanism that will achieve full employment, maximum productivity, and stable prices if left alone by the government. The rise or fall of prices will influence the decisions of millions of people and will bring into balance the demand for and supply of goods and labor, countering both recession and inflation.

Keynesian Theory   The Great Depression of the 1930s shattered popular confidence in classical economics. During the 1930s, the unemployment rate in the United States averaged 18 percent, reaching 25 percent in the worst year, 1933. Even in 1936, seven years after the great stock market crash of 1929, unemployment remained at 18 percent of the work force, raising questions about the ability of the market to stabilize itself and ensure high employment and output.

In analyzing this worldwide economic depression, the British economist John Maynard Keynes concluded that economic instability was a product of fluctuations in *demand*. **Keynesian economic theory** suggested that the economy could fall into a recession and *stay there* unless government added to demand by spending more money itself and lowering taxes. This combination of spending more and taxing less means that, during a recession, government would not be able to balance its budget. Rather, during recessions government would have to incur deficits to add to demand, spending more than it receives in revenue. To counter inflationary trends, governments should take just the opposite steps. During inflations, when strong consumer demand pushes up prices, government should cut its own spending, raise taxes, and run a surplus in the budget, thus reducing overall demand.

Employment Act of 1946   Keynesian ideas dominated U.S. economic policy making for nearly a half century. These ideas were written into the Employment Act of 1946, specifically pledging the federal government "to promote maximum employment production and purchasing power" through its taxing and spending policies. This act created the Council of Economic Advisers to "develop and recommend to the president national economic policies" and required the president to submit to Congress an annual economic report assessing the state of the economy.

Although most economists endorsed government deficits to counter recessions, it became increasingly clear over time that politicians were unable to end deficit spending after recessions were over. Politicians were more fearful of unemployment than of inflation, and because Keynesian theory portrayed these events as opposite ends of a seesaw, many politicians saw every reason to continue deficit spending. Even during inflation, politicians failed to enact the spending cuts and tax increases recommended by Keynes.

Other problems with Keynesian economic analysis surfaced in the 1970s, when unemployment and inflation occurred simultaneously, in defiance of Keynesian theory. Forty years of Keynesian efforts to manipulate aggregate demand had produced **stagflation**: inflation and high interest rates combined with unemployment and a stagnant economy. The nation experienced runaway "double-digit" (over 10 percent) annual inflation rates and a low rate of economic growth. President Ronald Reagan dubbed Keynesian economics "the failed policies of the past."

Supply-Side Economics   **Supply-side economic theory** (sometimes referred to as neo-classical economics) rejects Keynesianism's short-term manipulation of demand. Instead, supply-siders argue that the key is economic growth, which increases the overall supply of goods and services and thereby holds down prices, thus reducing or ending inflation altogether. More important, growth increases everyone's standard of living by increasing the availability of goods and services at stable prices.

Supply-side economists believe the free market is better equipped than government to bring about lower prices and more supplies of what people need and

classical economic theory   School of economic thought that focuses on economic efficiency and presumes the forces of demand and supply will automatically adjust to restore stable prices after a brief period of inflation.

Keynesian economic theory   School of economic thought that calls for government intervention to control recessions and inflation; government is to increase spending and incur deficits to prop up demand during a recession and curtail spending and take in a tax surplus to reduce demand during inflationary periods.

stagflation   Simultaneous occurrence of high rates of inflation and unemployment.

supply-side economic theory   School of economic thought that focuses on economic growth and argues that government taxing and spending are detrimental to such growth.

want. Government, they argue, is the problem, not the solution. High taxes penalize hard work, creativity, investment, and savings. Government should provide tax incentives to encourage investment and savings; tax rates should be lowered to encourage work and enterprise. Overall government spending should be held in check. Government regulations should be minimized in order to increase productivity and growth. Overall, government should act to stimulate production and supply rather than demand and consumption.

Monetarist Economics   Keynesian theory recommended not only changes in government spending and taxation to speed up or slow down demand but also changes in the money supply. During a recession, Keynes recommended expanding the supply of money available to individuals and businesses by easing bank reserve requirements (the amount banks are legally required to keep on hand and so cannot lend out) and lowering bank interest rates. Similarly, during inflationary periods, government was supposed to tighten the supply of money by increasing bank reserve requirements and increasing interest rates. Thus by increasing or decreasing the overall supply of money, government could "fine-tune" the economy.

However, **monetarist economic theory** contends that economic stability can only be achieved by holding the rate of monetary growth to the same rate as the economy's own growth. Led by Nobel Prize–winning economist Milton Friedman (see *People in Politics:* "Milton Friedman, In Defense of Free Markets"), monetarists challenge the view that manipulating the money supply can effectively influence economic activity. They argue that, over the long run, real income depends on actual economic output. Increasing the supply of money faster than output only creates inflation. The value of each dollar declines because there is more money to buy the same amount of goods. In short, monetarists believe that government tinkering with the money supply is the problem, not the solution.

Politics and Economic Theory   Keynesian economics calls for government to play a *greater* role in the economy, manipulating overall demand through its taxing, spending, and borrowing policies. Generally, political liberals are more comfortable with Keynesian economics because it is consistent with their belief in the use of government to correct societal problems. Political conservatives, who generally call for minimal government intervention in the economy, tend to espouse classical, supply-side economics. Liberals generally favor government intervention in economic affairs, whereas conservatives perceive government as the cause of rather than the solution to economic problems (see "Ideologies: Liberalism and Conservatism" in Chapter 2).

ECONOMIC DECISION MAKING

National **fiscal policy** focuses on the taxing, spending, and borrowing activities of the national government. Economic policy making takes place within the same system of separated powers and checks and balances that governs all federal policy making (see "Separation of Powers and Checks and Balances" in Chapter 3), with both the Congress and the president sharing responsibility for economic policy. Within the executive branch, responsibility for economic policy is divided among the White House, the Office of Management and Budget, the Treasury Department, the Council of Economic Advisers, and the powerful and independent Federal Reserve Board.

monetarist economic theory   School of economic thought that argues economic stability can be achieved only by holding the rate of monetary growth to the rate of the economy's own growth.

fiscal policy   Economic policies involving taxing, spending, and deficit levels.

Milton Friedman, In Defense of Free Markets

Economist Milton Friedman is perhaps the world's most influential spokesperson on behalf of free-market economics. He has spent a lifetime arguing that free markets are indispensable for human freedom and dignity. In 1976 Friedman was awarded a Nobel Prize in economics for his work in monetary policy.

Friedman was born in Brooklyn, New York, the son of working-class immigrants who stressed the importance of education. Young Friedman was an excellent high school student who went on to major in economics at Rutgers University, where he worked his way through college with a number of odd jobs. Upon graduation in 1932, Friedman was awarded a scholarship to attend graduate school at the University of Chicago. After earning his M.A. in economics, he worked in Washington, D.C., at various posts before returning to Columbia University for his Ph.D. in 1943. In 1946 he joined the faculty at the University of Chicago.

In his book *Studies in the Quantity Theory of Money* (1956) and in testimony before the Joint Congres-sional Economic Committee, Friedman argued against the prevailing economic philosophy of John Maynard Keynes and its prescription of increased government borrowing and spending to stimulate the economy. Friedman contended that a gradual, steady, continuous rate of increase in the money supply would be the best policy for achieving stable economic growth. Friedman and other economists who support this theory are known as *monetarists*.

In Friedman's view, the chief cause of recession and inflation is fluctuation in the nation's money supply. In an influential book, *A Monetary History of the United States* (1963), Friedman presented extensive historical evidence of the effect of money supply on the economic health of the nation. But Friedman's most widely read works are his cogent defenses of individual freedom and dignity. In *Capitalism and Freedom* (1962), he argued convincingly that free markets are essential to individual freedom and that government intervention in the marketplace inevitably curtails individual liberty and substitutes the judgment of a privileged few for the decisions of the people. In his television series *Free to Choose,* he brought his free-market ideas to a wide audience. According to Friedman, "The preservation of freedom requires limiting narrowly the role of government and placing primary reliance on private property, free markets and voluntary arrangements."

Congress and the President The Constitution of the United States places all taxing, borrowing, and spending powers in the hands of Congress. Article I grants Congress the "Power to lay and collect Taxes, Duties, Imposts and Excises, to pay the Debts and provide for the common Defence and general Welfare of the United States," and "to borrow Money on the Credit of the United States." It also declares that "No Money shall be drawn from the Treasury, but in Consequence of Appropriations made by Law." For nearly 150 years the power to spend was interpreted in a limited fashion: Congress could only spend money to perform powers specifically enumerated in Article I, Section 8, of the Constitution. But the Supreme Court has since ruled that the phrase "to pay the Debts and provide for the common Defence and general Welfare" may be broadly interpreted to authorize congressional spending for any purpose that serves the general welfare. Thus today there are no constitutional limits on Congress's spending power. Congress's borrowing power has always been unlimited constitutionally; and as yet there is no constitutional requirement for a balanced budget.

The Constitution gives the president no formal powers over taxing and spending or borrowing, stating only that the president "shall . . . recommend to [Congress's]

Consideration such Measures as he shall judge necessary and expedient" (Article II, Section 3). From this meager constitutional grant of power, however, presidents have gradually acquired leadership over national economic policy. The principal instrument of executive economic policy making is the Budget of the United States Government, which the president submits annually to Congress. The budget sets forth the president's recommendations for spending for the forthcoming fiscal year; revenue estimates, based on existing taxes or recommendations for new or increased tax levels; and estimates of projected deficits and the need for borrowing when, as has usually been the case of late, spending recommendations exceed revenue estimates (see Figure 12-4, "The Budgetary Process," for more detail).

The President's Economic Team   The president's recommendations to Congress regarding taxing, spending, and borrowing are influenced by advice received from three sources:

1. The Office of Management and Budget (OMB), responsible for preparing the Budget of the United States Government, exerts a powerful influence on the expenditure side of the budget. OMB supervises the year-long process of checking, reviewing, and modifying the budget requests of every federal department and agency.

2. The Department of the Treasury and the secretary of the treasury have the principal responsibility for estimating revenues and, if requested by the president, for drawing up new tax proposals and forecasting how much revenue they might produce. The Treasury Department also manages the nation's huge national debt—the result of its cumulative annual deficits. The Treasury must continually sell **government bonds** to banks and other investors, both foreign and domestic, in order to cover payments on previous deficits as well as to fund current deficits. In doing so, the Treasury Department determines interest rates on federal bonds, and it pays out interest charges on the national debt—charges that now amount to over 15 percent of all federal spending.

3. The Council of Economic Advisers (CEA), which forecasts economic conditions and recommends economic policies, is composed of three professional economists and a small staff. In theory, the CEA gives the president unbiased forecasts of economic trends and impartial analyses of economic issues. It does so principally in the annual Economic Report of the President, which the CEA prepares. But because the president chooses the members of the CEA, it often produces economic reports that reflect the president's thinking.

The Federal Reserve Board (the Fed)   Most economically advanced democracies have central banks whose principal responsibility is to regulate the supply of money, both currency in circulation and bank deposits. And most of these democracies have found it best to remove this responsibility from the direct control of elected politicians. Politicians everywhere are sorely tempted to inflate the supply of money in order to fund projects and programs with newly created money instead of new taxes. Nations pay for this approach with a general rise in prices and a reduction in goods and services available to private firms and individuals—inflation. Indeed, nations whose control of the money supply has fallen victim to irresponsible governments have experienced inflation rates of 500 to 1,000 percent per year, which is to say that their money became worthless.

government bonds   Certificates of indebtedness that pay interest and promise repayment on a future date.

People in Politics

Alan Greenspan, Inflation Fighter at the Fed

Economist Alan Greenspan was first appointed chair of the Federal Reserve Board in 1987 by President Ronald Reagan. Today, Greenspan must accommodate monetary policy to the Clinton Administration's taxing and spending policies to ensure a healthy economy.

Born in New York City, Alan Greenspan studied music at the prestigious Julliard School and enjoyed a brief but successful career as a professional saxophone player in a big swing band before returning to the classroom at New York University. He received an M.A. in economics in 1950 under the tutelage of Arthur F. Burns, who served as chair of the Federal Reserve from 1970 to 1978. After graduation, Greenspan formed his own economic consulting company, Townsend-Greenspan, which provided economic forecasts for some of America's largest corporations. In his spare time, Greenspan completed his Ph.D. at New York University and became a fan of the social philosopher and writer Ayn Rand. Greenspan embraced Rand's vision of a society in which every person could realize his or her own potential in any chosen field without government interference or regulation.

Greenspan began his public service in the Nixon Administration, serving on commissions and task forces, including the Commission on an All-Volunteer Armed Force. In 1974 President Nixon appointed Greenspan to chair the Council of Economic Advisers, a position Greenspan continued to hold under President Gerald Ford. When the Carter Administration came to Washington in 1977, Greenspan returned to running his private company.

In the early 1980s, Fed chair Paul Volker instituted a tight money policy that ultimately brought down the high rates of inflation which had plagued the nation for most of the 1970s. After initially claiming credit for what was really Volker's success in reducing inflation, the Reagan Administration, especially Secretary of the Treasury James Baker (later George Bush's secretary of state), eventually complained that Volker's anti-inflationary policies were too stringent. In August 1987 the Democrat Volker handed in his resignation and Reagan nominated Greenspan to follow him.

Like Reagan, Greenspan opposed higher taxes, but what the president had hoped would be a loyal Republican soldier often acted independently and disagreed with the administration over expanding the money supply. Greenspan's management of the Fed has been generally well received, and he has earned credibility with his fellow economists by avoiding the Washington political game. He is credited for his quick reaction to the stock market crash on October 19, 1987, when he ensured that Federal Reserve Banks would have enough cash on hand to prevent panic following the record drop in stock prices. During the 1991 recession, Greenspan pushed interest rates down to a twenty-year low and cut required Federal Reserve funds in half in order to ease credit. As independent as the Fed itself, he has frequently criticized presidents and the Congress regarding the huge federal deficits. In 1996 President Clinton nominated Greenspan for a third term as Fed chairman.

The Federal Reserve System of the United States is largely independent of either the president or Congress. Its independent status is a result not only of law but also of its structure. It is run by a seven-member board of governors who are appointed by the president, with the consent of the Senate, for fourteen-year terms. Members may not be removed from the board except for "cause"; no member has ever been removed since the creation of the board in 1913. The board's chair serves only a four-year term, but the chair's term overlaps that of the president, so that new presidents cannot immediately name their own chair (see *People in Politics:* "Alan Greenspan, Inflation Fighter at the Fed").

The task of the **Federal Reserve Board (the Fed)** is to regulate the money supply and by so doing to help avoid both inflation and recession. The Fed oversees the operation of the nation's twelve Federal Reserve Banks, which actually issue the nation's currency, called "Federal Reserve Notes." The Federal Reserve Banks are banker's banks; they do not directly serve private citizens or firms. They hold the deposits, or "reserves," of banks; lend money to banks at "discount rates" that the Fed determines; buy and sell U.S. Government Treasury bonds; and assure regulatory compliance by private banks and protection of depositors against fraud. The Fed determines the reserve requirements of banks and otherwise monitors the health of the banking industry. The Fed also plays an important role in clearing checks throughout the banking system.

The Fed's influence over the economy is mainly through **monetary policy**—increasing or decreasing the supply of money and hence largely determining interest rates. When inflation threatens, the Fed typically acts to limit ("tighten") the supply of money and raise interest rates by (1) raising the reserve requirement of banks and thereby reducing the amount of money they have to loan out; or (2) raising the discount rate and thereby the cost of borrowing by banks; or (3) selling off government bonds to banks and others in "open market operations," thereby reducing the funds banks can lend to individuals and businesses. When economic slowdowns threaten, the Fed typically acts to expand ("ease") the money supply and lower interest rates by taking the opposite of each action just described.

Politics and Monetary Policy   Although it is the Fed that makes monetary policy, voters typically hold the president responsible for recessions. Hence presidents frequently tries to persuade ("jawbone") the independent Fed into lowering interest rates, especially in an election year, believing a temporary stimulus to help win the election is worth whatever inflationary effects it might create after the election.[2] Congress, too, is usually aligned on the side of "easy" money. But Fed members are mainly bankers and economists who understand the threats posed by inflation; so are the members of the Federal Advisory Council, presidents of the twelve Federal Reserve Banks who advise the Fed. Thus tension frequently arises between the Fed, with its concern about inflation, and the president and Congress, with their concern about recession.

When the Fed deviates from the desires of the president and Congress for increases in the money supply and lower interest rates, the Fed's independence often comes under attack. Congress frequently threatens to curtail the independence of the Fed by shortening the terms of members or otherwise bringing them under the direction of the president or Congress. Despite these attempts to intimidate the Fed into abandoning its own judgment and following the lead of the president and Congress, over the years the Fed has established itself as a strong independent guardian of the nation's money supply.

THE PERFORMANCE OF THE AMERICAN ECONOMY

Underlying the power of nations and the well-being of their citizens is the strength of their economy—their total productive capacity. The United States produces more than $7 trillion worth of goods and services in a single year for its 265 million people—more than $25,000 worth of output for every person.

Federal Reserve Board (the Fed)   Independent agency of the executive branch of the federal government charged with overseeing the nation's monetary policy.

monetary policy   Economic policies involving the money supply and interest rates.

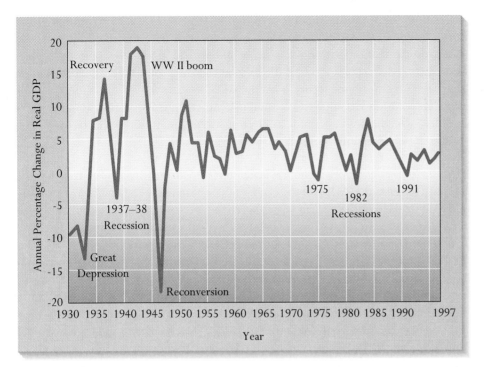

FIGURE 16-1 Economic Growth

The tendency for periods of economic growth to alternate with periods of contraction has led to the concept of the business cycle—the idea that at least some fluctuation is normal, even healthy, helping to keep the economy growing in the long run by keeping prices from getting too high. In recent decades, government intervention in the economy appears to have succeeded in reducing, although not in altogether eliminating, the depths of recessions to which the nation was formerly prone.

Source: Data from Council of Economic Advisors, *Economic Indicators,* February 1998.

Economic Growth **Gross domestic product (GDP)** is a widely used measure of the performance of the economy.[3] GDP is a nation's total production of goods and services for a single year valued in terms of market prices. It is the sum of all the goods and services that people have been willing to pay for, from wheat production to bake sales, from machine tools to maid service, from aircraft manufacturing to bus rides, from automobiles to chewing gum. GDP counts only final purchases of goods and services (that is, it ignores the purchase of steel by car makers until it is sold as a car) to avoid double counting in the production process. GDP also excludes financial transactions (such as the sale of bonds and stocks) and income transfers (such as Social Security, welfare, and pension payments) that do not add to the production of goods and services. Although GDP is expressed in current dollar prices, it is often recalculated in constant dollar terms to reflect real values over time, adjusting for the effect of inflation. GDP estimates are prepared each quarter by the U.S. Department of Commerce; these figures are widely reported and closely watched by the business and financial community.

Growth in real (constant dollar) GDP measures the performance of the overall economy. Economic recessions and recoveries are measured as fluctuations or swings in the growth of GDP. For example, a recession is usually defined as negative GDP growth in two or more consecutive quarters. Historical data reveal that periods of economic growth have traditionally been followed by periods of contraction, giving rise to the notion of *economic cycles.* Prior to 1950, economic cycles in the United States produced extreme ups and downs, with double-digit swings in real GDP. In recent decades, however, economic fluctuations have been more moderate. The United States still experiences economic cycles, but many economists believe that countercyclical government fiscal and monetary policy has succeeded in achieving greater stability (see Figure 16-1).

Voters today appear to hold the incumbent president more responsible than ever for *any* economic contraction, as George Bush learned to his sorrow in 1992.

gross domestic product (GDP) Measure of economic performance in terms of the nation's total production of goods and services for a single year, valued in terms of market prices.

The nation experienced a modest recession in 1991 and a weak recovery in 1992. Bush correctly claimed that the 1991 recession was not very deep by historical standards and that the nation was already on the road to recovery before the election. But media reporting of continual plant closings and voters' concerns that their own jobs were not secure outweighed GDP growth figures on election day. President Clinton has enjoyed continuing economic growth throughout his years in office, which helps explain his reelection victory in 1996 and his favorable job ratings in public opinion polls (see Chapter 11).

Unemployment   From a political standpoint, the **unemployment rate** may be the most important measure of the economy's performance. The unemployment rate is the percentage of the civilian labor force who are looking for work or waiting to return to or begin a job. Unemployment is different from not working; people who have retired or who attend school and people who do not work because of sickness, disability, or unwillingness are not considered part of the labor force and so are not counted as unemployed. People who are so discouraged about finding a job that they have quit looking for work are also not counted in the official unemployment rate. The unemployed do include people who have been terminated from their last job (34 percent) or temporarily laid off from work (15 percent), as well as people who voluntarily quit (15 percent), and those who have recently entered (10 percent) or reentered (27 percent) the labor force and are now seeking employment.

The unemployment rate is measured each month by the U.S. Department of Labor. It does so by contacting a random sample of more than 50,000 households in many locations throughout the country. Trained interviewers ask a variety of questions to determine how many (if any) members of the household are either working or have a job but did not work at it because of sickness, vacation, strike, or personal reasons (employed); or whether they have no job but are available for work and actively seeking a job (unemployed). The unemployment rate fluctuates with the business cycle, reflecting recessions and recoveries (see Figure 16-2). Generally, unemployment lags behind GDP growth, going down only after the

unemployment rate Percentage of the civilian labor force who are not working but who are looking for work or waiting to return to or to begin a job.

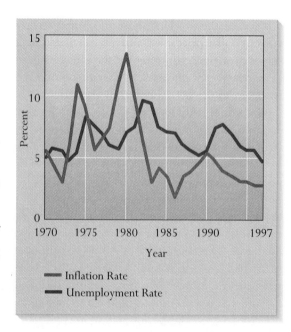

FIGURE 16-2 Unemployment and Inflation

Economic growth during the 1980s lowered both the inflation and unemployment rates, freeing the nation from the stagflation (combined inflation and high unemployment) that had characterized much of the 1970s. Unemployment rose during the recession of 1990–91 while inflation remained in check. Recent years have brought good economic news—low unemployment and low inflation.

Source: *Budget of the United States Government, 1997.*

Just how bad can inflation get? Between the two world wars, inflation in Germany reached such levels that the nation's currency was often weighed, rather than counted, in order to speed transactions.

recovery has begun. Following years of economic growth in the 1990s, the nation's unemployment rate fell to near record lows, below 5 percent.

Inflation   Inflation erodes the value of the dollar because higher prices mean that the same dollars can now purchase fewer goods and services. Thus inflation erodes the value of savings, reduces the incentive to save, and hurts people who are living on fixed incomes. When banks and investors anticipate inflation, they raise interest rates on loans in order to cover the anticipated lower value of repayment dollars. Higher interest rates, in turn, make it more difficult for new or expanding businesses to borrow money, for home buyers to acquire mortgages, and for consumers to make purchases on credit. Thus inflation and high interest rates slow economic growth.

In the 1990s the Fed has been very successful in keeping down the rate of inflation, and as a result, keeping down overall interest rates as well. Low interest rates have contributed to the nation's booming economy by encouraging businesses to borrow money for expansion and consumers to buy more on credit.

"UNCONTROLLABLE" GOVERNMENT SPENDING AND FEDERAL BUDGET PRIORITIES

The expenditures of all governments in the United States—federal, state, and local governments combined—amount to about 34 percent of GDP (see *Up Close:* "How Big Is Government and What Does It Do?" in Chapter 1). The federal government itself spends more than $1.7 trillion each year—about 23 percent of GDP.

"Uncontrollable" Spending   Much of the growth of federal government spending over the years is attributed to *uncontrollables* in the federal budget. Uncontrollables are budget items committed to by past policies of Congress that are not easily changed in annual budget making. Sources of uncontrollable spending include the following:

- *Entitlement programs:* Federal programs that provide classes of people with a legally enforceable right to benefits are called **entitlement programs**.

entitlement programs   Social welfare programs that provide classes of people with legally enforceable rights to benefits.

Transfers and Entitlements Drive Government Spending

Traditionally, governments in the United States have provided for national defense, police and fire protection, roads, education, and other public goods and services. These "public goods" cannot readily be provided by private markets because if one individual or firm purchased them, everyone else would get a "free ride"—that is, would use them without paying. Government involvement in these areas is not surprising. But these traditional public functions are not responsible for the growth of government in recent years.

Income Transfers   Recent expansions in the relative size of government are almost exclusively the result of increased governmental involvement in "income transfer" activities. The government has become a redistributor of income from one group to another—from the working population to retirees, from the employed to the unemployed,

from the taxpayers to the disadvantaged (such as low-income households with dependent children). In 1955 income transfers were about 5 percent of the GDP. Today, however, the government redistributes about 15 percent of total national output away from producers to persons "entitled" by law to receive government benefits.

Entitlements   Entitlement programs account for more than half of all federal spending. Virtually everyone who has examined the federal government's budget—economists, politicians, and private citizens—understands that "capping entitlements" is the only way to slow the growth of federal spending. The problem is the political gridlock that has arisen over what programs will be "capped."

Note that most entitlement payments do *not* go to the poor. The largest share of entitlements—Social Security, Medicare, veterans' and federal retirement—goes to retirees. These three programs alone account for two-thirds of all entitlement payments. Payments to the poor and unemployed—welfare, Medicaid, and unemployment insurance—account for less than one-third of federal entitlement spending.

Entitlements in the Federal Budget

	Billions of Dollars	Percentage
Entitlement, Total	$1,038	59.9%
Social Security	396	22.9
Medicare	207	11.9
Medicaid	143	8.1
Federal retirement	77	4.4
Welfare entitlement	148	8.6
Veterans' benefits	43	2.5
Unemployment insurance	• 26	1.5
Defense	265	15.3
Domestic	174	10.0
Interest	242	14.0
International	14	0.8
Total Federal Spending	1,733	100.0

Source: Budget of the United States Government, 1999.

Entitlement programs account for more than half of all federal spending, including Social Security, Medicare and Medicaid, food stamps, federal employees' retirement pensions, and veterans' benefits (see *Up Close:* "Transfers and Entitlements Drive Government Spending"). These entitlements are benefits that past Congresses have pledged the federal government to pay. Entitlements are not really uncontrollable. Congress can always amend the basic laws that established them, but doing so is politically difficult and might be regarded as abandonment of a public trust. As more people become "entitled" to government benefits—for example, as more people reach retirement ages and claim Social Security benefits—federal spending increases.

- *Indexing of benefits:* Another reason that spending increases each year is that Congress has authorized automatic increases in benefits to match inflation. Benefits under such programs as Social Security are tied to the Consumer Price Index. This **indexing** pushes up the cost of entitlement programs each year, even when the number of recipients stays the same, thus running counter to federal efforts to restrain inflation. Moreover, because the Consumer Price Index includes interest payments for new housing and the cost of new cars and appliances, it generally *over*estimates the needs of older recipients for cost-of-living increases.

- *Increasing costs of in-kind benefits:* Rises in the cost of major **in-kind (noncash) benefits**, particularly the medical costs of Medicaid and Medicare, also guarantee growth in federal spending. These in-kind benefit programs have risen faster in cost than cash benefit programs.

- *Interest on the national debt:* Interest payments have grown rapidly as a percentage of all federal spending. The federal government has a long history of deficits. In 1998 the president sent the first **balanced budget** to the Congress in thirty years. But the accumulated deficits still leave the government with a **national debt** of over $5.5 trillion. Interest payments on this debt now make up about 14 percent of total federal spending.

- *Backdoor spending and loan guarantees:* Some federal spending does not appear on the budget. For example, spending by the Postal Service is not included in the federal budget. No clear rule explains why some agencies

indexing Tying of benefit levels in social welfare programs to the general price level.

in-kind (noncash) benefits Benefits of a social welfare program that are not cash payments, including free medical care, subsidized housing, and food stamps.

balanced budget Government budget in which expenditures and revenues are equal, so that no deficit or surplus exists.

national debt Total current debt owed by the national government, produced by deficit spending over many years.

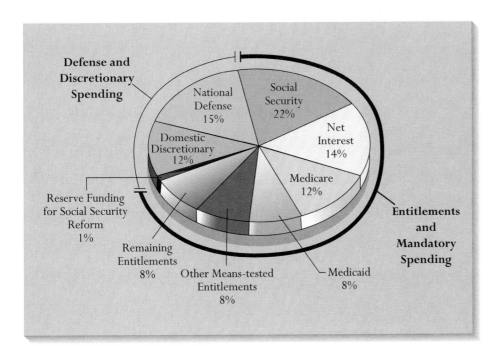

FIGURE 16-3 Federal Budget Shares

Mandatory spending—spending commitments in existing laws, notably Social Security, Medicare, Medicaid, and other entitlements, plus interest on the national debt—accounts for about two-thirds of the federal budget. Discretionary spending, including defense, accounts for only about one-third of the budget.

are in the budget and others are not, but "off-budget" agencies have the same economic effects as other government agencies. Another form of **backdoor spending** is found in government-guaranteed loans. Initially government guarantees for loans—Federal Housing Administration (FHA) housing loans, Guaranteed Student Loans, veterans' loans, and so forth— do not require federal money. The government merely promises to repay the loan if the borrower fails to do so. Yet these loans create an obligation against the government.

backdoor spending Spending by agencies of the federal government whose operations are not included in the federal budget.

mandatory spending Spending required by previous laws.

discretionary spending Spending for programs not previously mandated by law.

Federal Budget Priorities   Federal budget shares (the percentage of outlays devoted to various functions) reflect the spending priorities of the national government. Entitlements and other **mandatory spending** (principally interest on the national debt) heavily outweigh defense and **discretionary spending** combined (see Figure 16-3 on page 601). Spending on programs designed to assist senior citizens (Social Security and Medicare) heavily outweigh defense spending, welfare spending, and all discretionary spending. Today Social Security payments are the

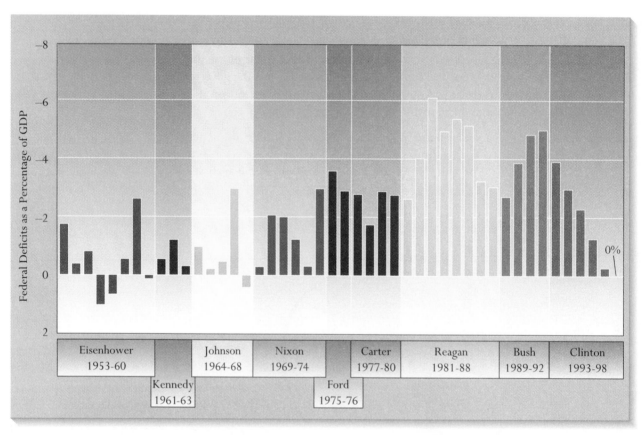

FIGURE 16-4   Deficits through the Years

This figure shows annual federal deficits as percentages of the GDP. Note that the federal government incurred deficits for thirty years, under both Republican and Democratic presidential administrations. A strong economy, and resulting increases in revenues flowing to the federal government, allowed President Bill Clinton to announce the first budget surplus in fiscal year 1999.

Source: Congressional Budget Office (September 1997) and Budget of the United States Government, 1999.

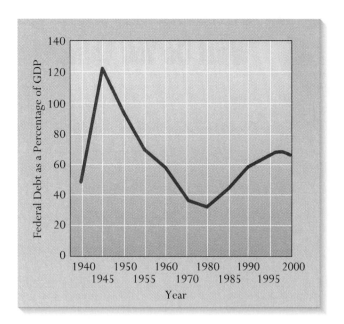

largest single item in the federal budget. Over time defense spending has declined from over 50 percent of the federal budget at the height of the Cold War in the early 1960s to 14 percent today. Medical costs—Medicare for elderly and Medicaid for the poor—are currently the fastest growing items in the federal budget.

THE DEBT BURDEN

The U.S. federal government incurred a **deficit** every year from 1969 to 1988—that is, its expenditure exceeded its revenues (see Figure 16-4). The accumulated national debt is over $5.5 trillion, or $20,000 for every man, woman, and child in the nation. This government debt is owed mostly to U.S. banks and financial institutions and private citizens who buy Treasury bonds. Only about 13 percent of the debt is owed to foreign banks and individuals. As old debt comes due, the U.S. Treasury Department sells new bonds to pay off the old; that is, it continues to "roll over" or "float" the debt. Despite its size in dollars, the debt today is smaller as a percentage of GDP than at some periods in U.S. history. For example, to pay the costs of fighting World War II, the U.S. government ran up a debt equivalent to over 100 percent of GDP. The current $5.5 trillion debt, although the highest in history in dollar terms, is equal to only about 68 percent of GDP (see Figure 16-5).

The ability to float such a huge debt depends on public confidence in the U.S. government—confidence that it will continue to pay interest on its debt, that it will pay off the principal of bonds when they come due, and that the value of the bonds will not decline over time because of inflation.

Default and Hyperinflation No one expects the United States ever to **default** on its debt—that is, to refuse to pay interest or principal when it comes due—although other debt-ridden nations have done so in the past and many threaten to do so today. But there is always the possibility that a future administration in Washington might **monetarize the debt**—that is, simply print

deficit Imbalance in the annual federal budget in which spending exceeds revenues.

default Refusal or inability to pay a debt.

monetarize a debt System of debt reduction in which a government simply prints more money and uses that money to pay its debts; because such money is more plentiful and thus worth less, inflation (and sometimes hyperinflation) results.

What Do You Think?

Will We Really Have a Budget Surplus and, If So, What Should We Do with It?

Thirty years of deficit spending have left Americans skeptical that the federal government can really balance its budget, let along produce a surplus. Despite President Clinton's 1998 presentation to Congress of a balanced *Budget of the United States Government FiscalYear 1999,* over two-thirds of Americans in national opinion polls doubt this goal will be realized.

Whether prematurely or not, Washington politicians are already arguing over what to do with a projected surplus of $20 to $40 billion a year over the next five years. Liberals have long chafed under the constraints that deficits have placed on the possibility of enacting new social welfare spending programs. They welcome projected surpluses as an opportunity to make new "investments" in children, health care, education, and the environment.

Conservatives argue that projected surpluses should be used to reduce taxes or to pay off part of the national debt, or some combination of both. They contend that surplus tax dollars should be returned to the American people so they can decide for themselves how to spend them. If any surplus is retained in Washington, they want it to be used to pay down the nation's $5.5 trillion debt, which would further reduce interest rates and spur additional economic growth.

Most Americans are aware that the Social Security and Medicare programs face enormous financial problems in the years ahead as more and more baby boomers retire. A majority of Americans appear to agree with President Clinton's announced priority for the use of budget surpluses: "Save Social Security first!"

Finally, it is interesting to note that more Americans credit "good economic conditions" (77 percent) for reducing deficits than they do either President Clinton (63 percent) or Republicans in Congress (54 percent).

Question: *President Clinton has just announced that his proposed budget for 1999 will be balanced. Do you think...*

The budget will be balanced in 1999	23%
Political or economic factors will prevent the budget from being balanced in 1999	69%

Question: *If the budget is balanced in 1999, do you think that it will stay balanced for the next several years?*

Yes	26%
No	63%

Question: *If the government has a budget surplus, what priority (top, high, low, or none) should these proposals be given?*

Percent responding "top priority"

Strengthen Social Security	32%
Reduce the national debt	31%
Strengthen Medicare	28%
Increase funding for schools	25%
Cut income taxes for most Americans	22%
Provide tax credit to parents for child care	20%
Provide tax credit to reduce pollution	15%
Increase spending on highway construction	11%

Source: Reported in *USA Today*, February 6, 1998; based on *USA Today*/CNN/Gallup.

---

hyperinflation Annual inflation rates of 100 to 1,000 percent or more.

currency and use it to pay off bondholders. Such currency would flood the nation and soon become worthless. **Hyperinflation**—annual inflation rates of 100 to 1,000 percent or more—would leave U.S. bondholders with worthless money. Both default and hyperinflation are unlikely, but the existence of a high federal deficit means that such disasters are not unthinkable.

Interest Burden for Future Generations   Interest payments on the national debt come from current taxes and so divert money away from *all* other government programs. Even if the federal government manages to balance its current budgets, these payments will remain obligations of the children and grandchildren of the current generation of policy makers and taxpayers.

The Politics of Deficits   Despite all the pious rhetoric about the need to "balance the budget," for decades neither presidents nor Congresses, Democrats nor Republicans, were willing to reduce expenditures or to raise taxes sufficiently to balance the budget. Deficit financing appeals to politicians. It allows them to provide high levels of government benefits while avoiding the unpopular step of raising taxes. To be sure, the burden of future interest payments is shifted to young people and future generations. But elected politicians know they will be long gone before these burdens are fully realized; their time frame is the next election. Many politicians are reluctant to cross swords with politically active older voters, who are more concerned with generous Social Security and Medicare benefits than with interest payments that will be paid by later generations.

Washington's Budget Battles   Occasionally, budget battles have temporarily "shut down" the federal government. The Constitution states that "no money shall be drawn from the Treasury, but in Consequence of Appropriations made by Law" (Article I, Section 9), suggesting that if Congress fails to pass, and the president to sign, appropriations acts, the government must close for lack of funds. But when this has actually occurred, only "nonessential" offices actually have closed. After bitter and prolonged negotiations in 1995 between Democratic President Bill Clinton and Republican congressional leaders Bob Dole and Newt Gingrich, agreement was reached on a pledge to balance the budget. But such pledges do not bind the president or Congress in future years.

The Long-Sought Balanced Budget   Economic growth began to shrink annual deficits after the 1991–92 recession. Increased economic activity in the nation increased federal tax revenues. A Republican-controlled Congress slowed the growth of federal spending. President Clinton did not introduce any major new spending programs after his comprehensive health care program failed to pass Congress in 1993 (see Chapter 17). But despite all of the chest thumping by both Democrats and Republicans in Washington, the decline in the size of deficits was produced by the nation's dynamic economy. Its performance in the 1990s was much stronger than either politicians or economists expected. The projected zero budget deficit, originally established by the president and Congress as a goal to be reached in 2002, was announced by the president in 1998 (see *What Do You Think?* Will We Really Have a Budget Surplus and, If So, What Should We Do with It?).

Trading on the floor of the New York Stock Exchange. The prolonged economic expansion of the 1990s increased the government's tax revenues beyond earlier estimates, creating the possibility of a sooner-than-expected balanced budget.

THE TAX BURDEN

The tax burden in the United States is modest compared to burdens in other advanced democracies (see *Compared to What?* "Tax Burdens in Advanced Democracies"). Federal revenues are derived mainly from (1) individual income taxes, (2) corporate income taxes, (3) Social Security payroll taxes, (4) estate and gift taxes, and (5) excise taxes and custom duties.

Compared to What?

Tax Burdens in Advanced Democracies

Americans complain a lot about taxes. But from a global perspective, overall tax burdens in the United States are relatively low (see figure). Federal, state, and local taxes in the United States amount to about 30 percent of the gross domestic product (GDP), slightly below the burden carried by the nation's leading competitors, Japan and Germany. U.S. taxes are well below the burdens imposed in Sweden, Denmark, and other nations with highly developed welfare systems.

Top marginal tax rates in many nations were reduced during the 1980s. For example, the top rate in Great Britain was lowered from 60 to 40 percent, in Japan from 70 to 50 percent, and in Sweden from 80 to 65 percent. Both in the United States and abroad, the notion that excessively high tax rates discourage work, savings, and investment, as well as slow economic growth, won acceptance (although how high is "excessive" is obviously open to different interpretations). Moreover, in a global economy, with increased mobility of individuals and firms, pressures push nations to keep their top tax rates within reasonable limits. Corporations can shift their assets to low-tax jurisdictions, and high personal income tax rates can even threaten a "brain drain" of talented individuals.

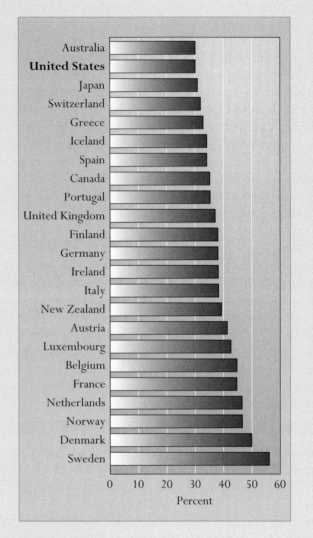

Tax Revenues as a Percentage of GDP

---

individual income tax Taxes on individuals' wages and other earned income, the primary source of revenue for the U.S. federal government.

Individual Income Taxes The **individual income tax** is the federal government's largest source of revenue (see Figure 16-6). Individual income is now taxed at five rates: 15, 28, 31, 36, and 39.6 percent, with these rising rates geared to increasing income "brackets." These are *marginal rates,* a term that economists use to mean additional. That is, income up to the top of the lowest bracket is taxed at 15 percent; additional income in the next bracket is taxed at 28 percent, up to a top marginal rate of 39.6 percent on income over $250,000. A personal exemption for each taxpayer and dependent together with a standard deduction for married couples and a refundable earned income tax credit ensure that the poorest families pay no income tax. (However, they still must pay Social Security taxes on wages.) Tax brackets, as well as the personal exemption and standard deduction, are indexed annually to protect against inflation.

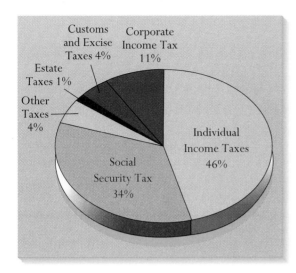

FIGURE 16-6 Sources of Federal Income

Individual income taxes make up the largest portion of the federal government's revenues (46 percent). The government also relies heavily on the second largest source of its revenues, Social Security taxes.

Source: Budget of the United States Government, 1999.

The income tax is automatically deducted from the paychecks of employees. This "withholding" system is the backbone of the individual income tax. There is no withholding of nonwage income such as dividends on investments, but taxpayers with such income must file a "Declaration of Estimated Taxes" and pay this estimate in quarterly installments. Before April 15 of each year, all income-earning Americans must report their taxable income for the previous year to the Internal Revenue Service on its 1040 Form.

Americans are usually surprised to learn that half of all personal income is *not* taxed. To understand why, we must know how the tax laws distinguish between *adjusted gross income* (an individual's total money income minus expenses incurred in earning that income) and *taxable income* (that part of adjusted gross income subject to taxation). Federal tax rates apply only to *taxable* income.

Tax expenditures are tax revenues lost to the federal government because of exemptions, exclusions, deductions, and special treatments in tax laws. Federal government revenues from individual and business income taxes would be substantially higher were it not for special provisions in tax laws that enable taxpayers to avoid paying taxes on often substantial sums of income. Although each of these "loopholes" supposedly has a larger social goal behind it (for example, the deductibility of mortgage interest is supposed to stimulate the purchase—and construction—of homes, keeping up the value of those assets for current homeowners and keeping the construction industry employed), critics charge that many cost far more than they are worth to society. These are the major tax expenditures in federal tax law:

- Personal exemptions
- Deductibility of mortgage interest on homes
- Deductibility of property taxes on first and second homes
- Deferral of capital gains on home sales
- Deductibility of charitable contributions
- Credit for child-care expenses
- Exclusion of employer contributions to pension plans and medical insurance
- Partial exclusion of Social Security benefits

tax expenditures Revenues lost to the federal government because of exemptions, exclusions, deductions, and special-treatment provisions in tax laws.

- Exclusion of interest on public-purpose state and local bonds
- Deductibility of state and local income taxes
- Exclusion of income earned abroad
- Accelerated depreciation of machinery, equipment, and structure
- Medical expenses over 7.5 percent of income

There is a continual struggle between proponents of special tax exemptions to achieve social goals and those who believe the tax laws should be simplified and social goals met by direct government expenditures. Much of the political infighting in Washington involves the efforts of interest groups to obtain exemptions, exclusions, deductions, and special treatments in tax laws.[4] Former Congressman Dan Rostenkowski of Chicago, once the chair of the House Ways and Means Committee, which writes the nation's tax laws, admitted,

> We gave oil companies breaks to fuel our oil industry. We gave real estate incentives to build more housing. We sharpened our technology with research and development credits. We gave tax breaks to encourage people to save. We pile one tax benefit on top of another—each one backed with good intention.

> Unfortunately it didn't take too long before those with the best accountants and lawyers figured out how to beat the system . . . and the cost of government was shifted to families like those in my neighborhood who don't have the guile to play the game of hide-and-seek with the IRS. . . .

> In the end tax reform comes down to a struggle between the narrow interests of the few—and the broad interests of working American families.[5]

Corporate Income Taxes   The corporate income tax provides only about 11 percent of the federal government's total revenue. The Tax Reform Act of 1986 reduced the top corporate income tax from 46 to 34 percent (raised to 35 percent in 1993). However, prior to this act, corporations found many ways of reducing their taxable income, often to zero. The result was that many very large and profitable corporations paid little or nothing in taxes. Some of the most notorious of these corporate tax breaks were modified or eliminated in the Tax Reform Act of 1986. Religious, charitable, and educational organizations, as well as labor unions, are exempt from corporate income taxes except for income they may derive from "unrelated business activity."

Who really bears the burden of the corporate income tax? Economists differ over whether the corporate income tax is "shifted" to consumers or whether corporations and their stockholders bear its burden. The evidence on the **incidence**—that is, who actually bears the burden—of this tax is inconclusive.[6]

Social Security Taxes   The second largest source of federal revenue is the Social Security tax. It is withheld from paychecks as the "FICA" deduction, an acronym that helps hide the true costs of Social Security and Medicare from wage earners. To keep up with the rising number of beneficiaries and the higher levels of benefits voted for by Congress, including generous automatic cost-of-living increases each year, the Social Security taxes rose to 15.3 percent. (The Social Security tax is 12.4 percent and the Medicare tax is 2.9 percent; all wage income is subject to the Medicare tax, but wage income above a certain level—$65,400 in 1998—is not subject to the Social Security tax.)

incidence   Actual bearer of a tax burden.

Taxes collected under FICA are earmarked (by Social Security number) for the account of each taxpayer. Workers thus feel they are receiving benefits as a right rather than as a gift of the government. However, less than 15 percent of the benefits being paid to current recipients of Social Security can be attributed to their prior contributions. Current taxpayers are paying more than 85 percent of the benefits received by current retirees.

Today a majority of taxpayers pay more in Social Security taxes than income taxes. Indeed, combined employer and employee Social Security taxes now amount to over $8,500 for each worker at the top of the wage base. If we assume that the employer's share of the tax actually comes out of wages that would otherwise be paid to the employee, then more than 75 percent of all taxpayers pay more in Social Security taxes than in income taxes.

Estate and Gift Taxes   Taxation of property left to heirs is one of the oldest forms of taxation in the world. Federal estate taxes begin on estates of $600,000 and levy a tax of 37 percent on accounts above this level. Because taxes at death otherwise could be avoided by simply giving estates to heirs while the giver is still alive, a federal gift tax is also levied on anyone who gives gifts in excess of $10,000 annually.

Excise Taxes and Custom Duties   Federal excise taxes on the consumption of liquor, tobacco, gasoline, telephones, air travel, and other so-called luxury items, together with custom taxes on imports, provide about 4 percent of total federal revenues.

TAX POLITICS

The politics of taxation centers around the question of who actually bears the heaviest burden of a tax—especially which income groups must devote the largest proportion of their income to taxes. **Progressive taxation** requires high-income groups to pay a larger percentage of their incomes in taxes than low-income groups. **Regressive**

progressive taxation
System of taxation in which higher income groups pay a larger percentage of their incomes in taxes than do lower income groups.

Appropriating symbolism from a famous Revolutionary War era event—the Boston Tea Party, in which Massachusetts Patriots tossed a cargo of tea into Boston Harbor to protest a British-imposed tax—Republican leaders in favor of scrapping the current tax code toss a copy of it into the same harbor. Tax policy has been a volatile issue for both Democrats and Republicans recently, as voters send conflicting messages about their preferences for tax cutting versus budget balancing.

What Do You Think?

Should We Enact a Flat Tax?

More than a hundred years ago, Supreme Court Justice Stephen J. Field, in striking down as unconstitutional a progressive income tax enacted by Congress, predicted that such a tax would lead to class wars: "Our political contests will become a war of the poor against the rich, a war constantly growing in intensity and bitterness."* But populist sentiment in the early twentieth century—the anger of midwestern farmers toward eastern rail tycoons and the beliefs of impoverished southerners that they would never have incomes high enough to pay an income tax—helped secure the passage of the Sixteenth Amendment to the U.S. Constitution. The federal income tax passed by Congress in 1914 had a top rate of 7 percent; less than 1 percent of the population had incomes high enough to be taxed. Today the top rate is 39.6 percent (actually over 42 percent when mandated phaseouts of deductions are calculated); about half of the population pays income taxes.

The current income tax progressively penalizes all the behaviors that produce higher incomes—work, savings, investment, and initiative. And whenever incomes are taxed at different rates, people will figure out ways to take advantage of the differential. They will hire lawyers, accountants, and lobbyists to find or create exemptions, exclusions, deductions, and preferential treatments for their own sources of income. The tax laws will become increasingly lengthy and complex. Today about half of all personal income is excluded from federal income taxation. The U.S. Tax Code, originally 14 pages long, is now 9,400 pages, and Internal Revenue Service regulations interpreting the tax code run more than 100,000 pages.

The Internal Revenue Service (IRS) is the most intrusive of all government agencies, overseeing the finances of every tax-paying citizen and corporation in America. It maintains personal records on more than 100 million Americans and requires them to submit more than a billion forms each year. It may levy fines and penalties and collect taxes on its own initiative; in disputes with the IRS, the burden of proof falls on the taxpayer, not the agency. Its 110,000 employees spend $8 billion per year reviewing tax returns, investigating taxpayers, and collecting revenue. Americans pay an additional $30 billion for the services of tax accountants and preparers, and they waste some $200 billion in hours of record keeping and computing their taxes.

Should we replace the current federal income tax system with a simple flat tax that could be calculated on a postcard? Reformers believe the elimination of all exemptions, exclusions, deductions, and special treatment, and the replacement of current progressive tax rates with a flat 19 percent tax on all forms of income, even excluding family incomes under $25,000, would produce just as much revenue as the current complicated system. It would sweep away the nation's army of tax accountants and lawyers and lobbyists, and increase national productivity by relieving taxpayers of millions of hours of record keeping and tax preparation. A flat tax could be filed on a postcard form (see facing page). Removing progressive rates would create incentives to work, save, and invest in America. It would lead to more rapid economic growth and improve efficiency by directing investments to their most productive uses rather than to tax avoidance. It would eliminate current incentives to underreport income, overstate exemptions, and avoid and evade taxation. Finally, by

---

regressive taxation System of taxation in which lower income groups pay a larger percentage of their incomes in taxes than do higher income groups.

taxation takes a larger share of the income of low-income groups. **Proportional (flat) taxation** requires all income groups to pay the same percentage of their income in taxes (see *What Do You Think?* "Should We Enact a Flat Tax?"). Note that the *percentage of income* paid in taxes is the determining factor. Most taxes take more money from the rich than the poor, but a progressive or regressive tax is distinguished by the percentages of income taken from various income groups.

The Argument for Progressivity   Progressive taxation is generally defended on the principle of ability to pay; the assumption is that high-income groups can

exempting a generous personal and family allowance, the flat tax would be made fair.

Opinion polls indicated that a flat tax rate is preferred over the current progressive rate system by a large majority of Americans. However, many Americans also support deductions for home mortgages and charitable contributions. This suggests a major political weakness in the flat tax idea: even if enacted, politicians will gradually erode the uniformity, fairness, and simplicity of a flat tax by introducing popular deductions. Lobbyists for special tax treatments will continue to pressure the Congress, and, over time, deductions, exemptions, and exclusions will creep back into the tax laws.

—————————————————
*Pollock v. Farmer's Loan, 158 U.S. 601 (1895).

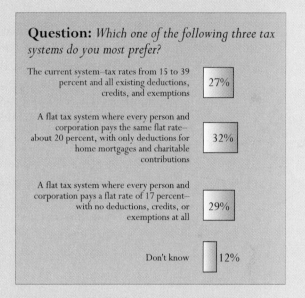

Form 1	Individual Wage Tax	1995
Your first name and initial (if joint return, also give spouse's name and initial)	Last name	Your social security number
Home address (number and street including apartment number or rural route)		Spouse's social security number
City, town, or post office, state, and ZIP code		Your occupation
		Spouse's occupation

1 Wages and salary	1
2 Pension and retirement benefits	2
3 Total compensation (*line 1 plus line 2*)	3
4 Personal allowance	
(a) 0 $16,500 for married filing jointly	4a
(b) 0 $9,500 for single	4b
(c) 0 $14,000 for single head of household	4c
5 Number of dependents, not including spouse	5
6 Personal allowances for dependents (*line 5 multiplied by $4,500*)	6
7 Total personal allowances (*line 4 plus line 6*)	7
8 Taxable compensation (*line 3 less line 7, if positive; otherwise zero*)	8
9 Tax (*19% of line 8*)	9
10 Tax witheld by employer	10
11 Tax due (*line 9 less line 10, if positive*)	11
12 Refund due (*line 10 less line 9, if positive*)	12

Question: *Which one of the following three tax systems do you most prefer?*

The current system–tax rates from 15 to 39 percent and all existing deductions, credits, and exemptions — 27%

A flat tax system where every person and corporation pays the same flat rate— about 20 percent, with only deductions for home mortgages and charitable contributions — 32%

A flat tax system where every person and corporation pays a flat rate of 17 percent— with no deductions, credits, or exemptions at all — 29%

Don't know — 12%

Source: Survey by Princeton Survey Research Associates for *Newsweek*, April 6–7, 1995, reported in American Enterprise, July/August 1995, p. 69.

afford to pay a larger percentage of their incomes into taxes at no more of a sacrifice than that required of lower income groups to devote a smaller proportion of their income to taxation. This assumption is based on what economists call *marginal utility theory* as it applies to money; each additional dollar of income is slightly less valuable to an individual than preceding dollars. For example, a $5,000 increase in the income of an individual already earning $100,000 is much less valuable than a $5,000 increase to an individual earning only $10,000 or to an individual with no income at all. Hence, it is argued that added dollars of income can be taxed at higher rates without violating equitable principles.

proportional (flat) taxation System of taxation in which all income groups pay the same percentage of their income in taxes.

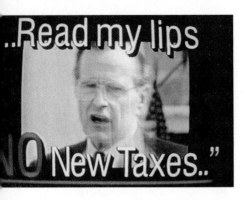

George Bush's pledge "Read my lips, no new taxes" helped him to victory in 1988. But breaking the pledge in 1990 contributed heavily to his defeat in 1992.

The Argument for Proportionality   Opponents of progressive taxation generally assert that equity can only be achieved by taxing everyone at the same percentage of their income, regardless of the size of their income. Progressivity penalizes initiative, enterprise, and the risk taking necessary to create new products and businesses. It also reduces incentives to expand and develop the nation's economy. Moreover, by taking more income from high-income groups, governments take the money that is most likely to otherwise go into business investments and stimulate economic growth. Highly progressive taxes curtail growth and make everyone poorer.

Reagan's Reductions in Progressivity   Certainly the most dramatic change in federal tax laws during the Reagan years was the reduction in the progressivity of individual income tax rates (see Figure 16-7). The top marginal tax rate fell from 70 percent when President Reagan took office to 28 percent following enactment of tax reform in 1986. The Tax Reform Act of 1986 reduced fourteen rate brackets to only two rate brackets, 15 and 28 percent.

"Read My Lips"   At the Republican National Convention in 1988, presidential nominee George Bush made a firm pledge to American voters that he would veto any tax increases passed by the Democratic-controlled Congress: "Read my lips! No new taxes." Yet in a 1990 budget summit with Democratic congressional leaders, President Bush agreed to add a top marginal rate of 31 percent to the personal income tax. Breaking his solemn pledge on taxes contributed heavily to Bush's defeat in the 1992 presidential election.

"Soak the Rich"   Proposals to "soak the rich" are always politically very popular. President Clinton pushed Congress to raise the top marginal tax rates to 36 percent for families earning $140,000, and to 39.6 percent for families earning $250,000. But these new top rates do not raise much revenue, partly because very few people have annual incomes in these categories. Moreover, high rates encourage people to seek tax-sheltered investments—to use their capital less efficiently to create tax breaks for themselves rather than to promote new business and new jobs. High taxes also encour-

FIGURE 16-7   Top Personal Income Tax Rates

The top marginal personal income tax rate fell dramatically during the Reagan administration, then began to creep upward again under Presidents Bush and Clinton.

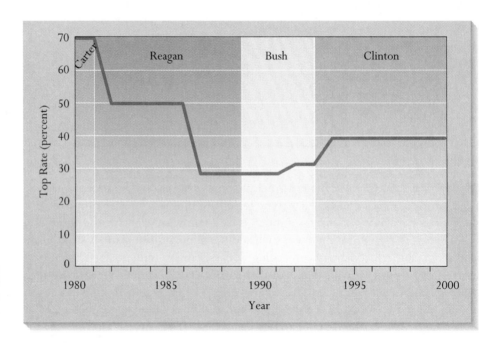

Politics in Cyberspace

The Economy

The Internet provides a wealth of information relating to the U.S. economy.

The Federal Reserve
http://www.bog.frb.fed.us

The Federal Reserve Web site details the purposes and functions of the Federal Reserve system and presents biographies of the board of governors and presidents of the Federal Reserve District banks. A search engine provides researchers with additional information on the board's working papers, surveys, enforcement actions, and legal interpretations.

Office of Management and Budget
http://www.whitehouse.gov/WH/EOP/OMB

OMB's official Web site provides direct access to the latest annual *Budget of the United States Government.*

National Bureau of Economic Research
http://www.nber.org

The NBER Web site provides access to the NBER Macro History Database with 3,500 monthly, quarterly, or annual sets of economic statistics.

Council of Economic Advisers
http://www.whitehouse.gov/WH/EOP/CEA/html

CEA's Web site includes the *Economic Report of the President* (annual) with past, current, and projected statistics on GDP, consumer price index, unemployment, personal income, wages, productivity, prices, interest rates, corporate profits, and government finance.

Concord Coalition
http://www.concordcoalition.org

The Concord Coalition is a nonprofit organization dedicated to federal budget deficit reduction and passage of a Balanced Budget Amendment to the U.S. Constitution. Its Web site includes charts and graphs and position papers on the budget and even a scorecard rating Congress members on their ability to make "tough choices" to eliminate deficits.

---

age high-bracket taxpayers to engage in *tax avoidance* (legal methods of reducing taxes) as well as *tax evasion* (illegal methods of reducing or eliminating taxes).

Capital Gains Taxation   All income is *not* taxed equally under federal income tax laws. (Indeed, interest income from municipal bonds is totally tax free, encouraging many wealthy investors to put their money into these "munies.") The tax code distinguishes between earned income and **capital gains**—profits from the buying and selling of property, including stocks, bonds, and real estate. Currently capital gains are taxed at a top marginal rate of 28 percent, compared to the top marginal rate of 39.6 percent for earned income.

Why should income earned from *working* be taxed at a higher rate than income earned from *investing?* The real estate industry, together with investment firms and stockbrokers, argue that high tax rates on capital gains discourage investment and economic growth. (But if it is true that high taxes discourage investment, high taxes must also discourage work, and both capital and labor are required for economic growth.) But the political power of investors, especially in the Republican Party, places heavy downward pressure on capital gains tax rates.

capital gains   Profits from buying and selling property including stocks, bonds, and real estate.

A major goal of tax reform has been to treat all income equally. The Tax Reform Act of 1986 eliminated preferential treatment for capital gains, but this preference was restored by President Bush and Congress in 1991: the top rate on earned income was pushed to 31 percent while the capital gains rate stayed at 28 percent. And again in 1993, when President Clinton raised the top rate on earned income to 39.6 percent, he quietly allowed the lower capital gains rate to remain the same. But the Republican Congress lowered capital gains taxation even further, granting additional preferential treatment for capital gains that brings the effective tax rate on such income to 20 percent.

SUMMARY NOTES

- A central policy issue is deciding how much to rely on government versus the marketplace to produce and distribute goods and services. The United States is primarily a free-market economy, but federal fiscal and monetary policies exercise a strong influence over economic activity.

- Classical economic theory views the marketplace as the most efficient means of producing and distributing goods and services. Market prices, determined by millions of individuals and thousands of firms, will adjust for recession, if government does not interfere.

- During the Great Depression of the 1930s, however, Keynesian economics came to dominate national policy making; Keynes argued that during a recession, government must apply countercyclical policies to increase demand, incurring deficits in order to add to total demand. During strong growth cycles, governments should amass surpluses to counter the threat of inflation.

- Supply-side economics focuses on stimulating growth rather than manipulating demand. Governments should lower taxes, reduce spending, and curtail regulations in order to stimulate production. The Reagan Administration lowered taxes but failed to curtail spending and thereby ran up the largest peacetime deficits in the nation's history.

- Monetarist economic theory contends that economic stability can only be achieved by holding the rate of monetary growth to the same rate as the economy's growth. It argues that government attempts to tinker with the money supply cause inflation.

- Both the president and the Congress have responsibilities for economic policy making. The independent Federal Reserve Board regulates the money supply and influences interest rates. When inflation threatens, the Fed is expected to "tighten" the money supply; when recession threatens, it is expected to "ease" the money supply.

- The performance of the economy can be measured by GDP growth and the unemployment and inflation rates.

Politically the unemployment rate may be the most important of these measures of economic performance.

- Annual federal budget deficits over the past thirty years led to a national debt of $5.5 trillion. Neither Democrats nor Republicans, presidents nor Congresses, were willing to reduce spending or raise taxes sufficiently to erase these annual deficits. The interest payments on this debt are now more than 15 percent of total federal expenditures, diverting money from all other government functions. Deficits slow economic growth by taking capital away from the private sector and keeping interest rates high.

- Economic growth produced a balanced budget in 1998, and continued growth promises modest surpluses in the next few years. Arguments in Washington now center on what to do with the surplus—pay down the debt, cut taxes, save it for future Social Security payments, or initiate new social welfare programs.

- Tax politics centers on the question of who actually bears the burden of a tax. The individual income tax, the largest source of federal government revenue, is progressive, with higher rates levied at higher income levels. Progressive taxation is defended on the ability-to-pay principle. But half of all personal income, and a great deal of corporate income, is untaxed, owing to a wide variety of exemptions, exclusions, deductions, and special treatments on tax laws. These provisions are defended in Washington by a powerful array of interest groups.

- The Reagan Administration reduced top income tax rates from 70 to 28 percent, believing high rates discouraged work, savings, and investment, and thereby curtailed economic growth. But George Bush agreed to an increase in the top rate to 31 percent. Bill Clinton pushed Congress to raise the top rates to 36 and 39.6 percent, arguing that rich people had benefited from Reagan's "trickle down" policies and must now be forced to bear their "fair share."

SELECTED READINGS

AARON, HENRY J., and CHARLES L. SCHULTZE, EDS. *Setting Domestic Priorities.* Washington, D.C.: Brookings Institution, 1992. A series of policy recommendations from the liberal Brookings Institution intended to guide the Clinton Administration in dealing with health care, welfare reform, education, crime, infrastructure development, and taxation.

CLINTON, BILL, and AL GORE. *Putting People First.* New York: Times Books, 1992. Comprehensive listing of the Democratic nominees' campaign promises to reduce deficits, stimulate the economy, lower taxes, and provide for children, the elderly, families, the environment, and so on. It is interesting to compare these promises with actual presidential programs.

LIEBERMAN, CARL. *Making Economic Policy.* Englewood Cliffs, N.J.: Prentice Hall, 1991. A brief introduction to taxing, spending, monetary, and regulatory policy.

MARSHALL, WILL, and MARTIN SCHRAM, EDS. *Mandate for Change.* New York: Berkeley Books, 1993. A series of studies and recommendations for policy changes from the neo-liberal Progressive Policy Institute, focusing on enterprise economics.

PHILLIPS, KEVIN. *The Politics of Rich and Poor.* New York: Random House, 1990. A controversial argument that Reagan Administration economic policies made the rich richer and the poor poorer. The book is often cited to justify new and heavier taxes on affluent Americans.

SAMUELSON, ROBERT. *The Good Life and Its Discontents: The American Dream in an Age of Entitlement.* New York: Times Books, 1996. Although the U.S. economy remains the world's richest and most productive, an "entitlement culture" is limiting the nation's potential and creating insecurity and dissatisfaction among Americans.

WOLFF, EDWARD N. *Top Heavy.* New York: Twentieth Century Fund Press, 1995. A study of the increasing inequality of wealth in the United States and an argument for taxing financial wealth (bank accounts, stocks, bonds, property, houses, cars, and so forth) as well as income.

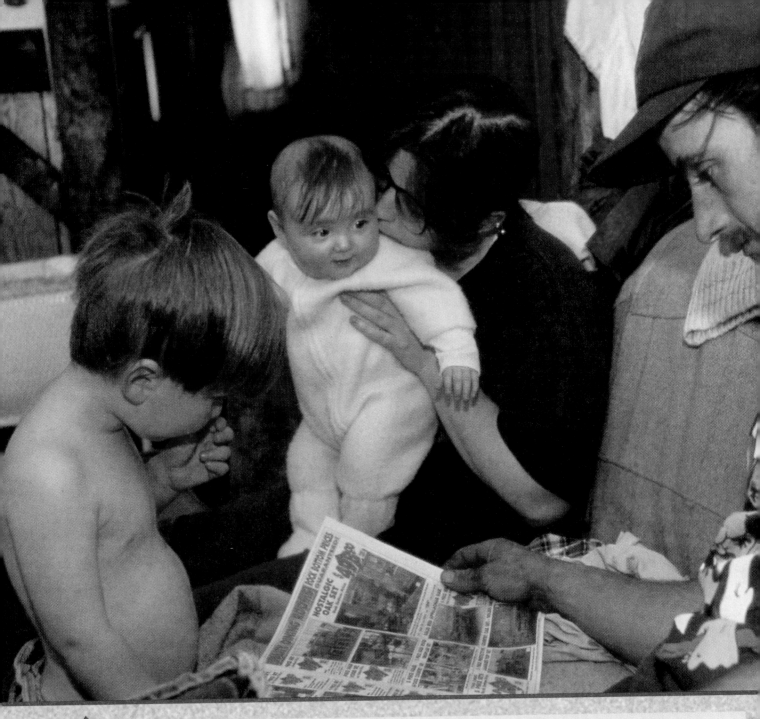

ASK YOURSELF ABOUT POLITICS

1 Do you believe the government should aid people who are unable to take care of themselves, such as the very young and the very old?
Yes [ ] No [ ]

2 Do you think government welfare programs perpetuate poverty?
Yes [ ] No [ ]

3 Should all retirees receive Social Security benefits regardless of their personal wealth or income?
Yes [ ] No [ ]

4 Should Medicaid pay for nursing home care without forcing beneficiaries to use up all their savings and income?
Yes [ ] No [ ]

5 Should Social Security pay you back only what you have put in during your working years?
Yes [ ] No [ ]

6 Should the states rather than the federal government decide about welfare policy?
Yes [ ] No [ ]

7 Should there be a time limit on how long a person can receive welfare payments?
Yes [ ] No [ ]

8 Should government provide health care insurance for all Americans?
Yes [ ] No [ ]

POLITICS AND SOCIAL WELFARE

CHAPTER OUTLINE

Power and Social Welfare

Poverty in the United States

Social Welfare Policy

Senior Power

Politics and Welfare Reform

Health Care in America

Politics and Health Care Reform

FEATURES

Up Close: Who Are the Poor?

Up Close: Homelessness in America

A Conflicting View: Government as the Cause of Poverty

Across the USA: Welfare Reform

Up Close: Is Welfare Reform Working?

Compared to What? Health and Health Care Costs in Advanced Democracies

People in Politics: Hillary Rodham Clinton and Health Care Policy Making

Politics in Cyberspace: Social Welfare

Through its social welfare policies, the federal government has the power to redistribute income among people. But most government payments to individuals do not go to poor people but rather to senior citizens whose voting power heavily influences elected officials.

POWER AND SOCIAL WELFARE

Social welfare policy largely determines who gets what from government—who benefits from government spending on its citizens and how much they get. This vast power has made the federal government a major *redistributor* of income from one group to another—from the working population to retirees, from the employed to the unemployed, from taxpayers to poor people. Direct payments to individuals—Social Security, welfare, pension, and other **transfer payments**—now account for more than half of all federal government outlays.

When most Americans think of social welfare programs, they think of poor people. An estimated 35 to 40 million people in the United

States (13 to 15 percent of the population) have incomes below the official **poverty line**—that is, their annual cash income falls below what is required to maintain a decent standard of living. If the approximately $1 trillion spent per year for social welfare were directly distributed to the nation's poor people, each poor person—man, woman, and child—would receive $25,000 per year.

Why does poverty persist in a nation where total social welfare spending is more than four times the amount needed to eliminate poverty? Because poor people are *not* the principal beneficiaries of social welfare spending. Most social welfare spending, including the largest programs—Social Security and Medicare—goes to the *nonpoor* (see Figure 17-1). Less than one-third of federal social welfare spending is **means tested**—that is, distributed on the basis of the recipient's income. The middle classes, not the poor, are the major beneficiaries of the nation's social welfare system.

POVERTY IN THE UNITED STATES

How much poverty really exists in the United States? It depends on how you define the term "poverty." The official definition used by the federal government focuses on the cash income needed to maintain a "decent standard of living." The official poverty line is only a little more than one-third of the median income of all American families.[1] It takes into account the effects of inflation, rising each year with the rate of inflation. (For example, in 1990, the official poverty line for an urban family of four was $13,359 per year; by 1998 the poverty line had risen to about $16,500.)

Liberal Criticism   The official definition of poverty has many critics. Some liberal critics believe poverty is underestimated for several reasons:

1. The official definition includes cash income from welfare and Social Security, and without this government assistance, the number of poor would be much higher, perhaps 25 percent of the total population.

transfer payments   Direct payments (either in cash or in goods and/or services) by governments to individuals as part of a social welfare program, not as a result of any service or contribution rendered by the individual.

poverty line   Official standard regarding what level of annual cash income is sufficient to maintain a "decent standard of living"; those with incomes below this level are eligible for most public assistance programs.

means-tested spending   Spending for benefits that is distributed on the basis of the recipient's income.

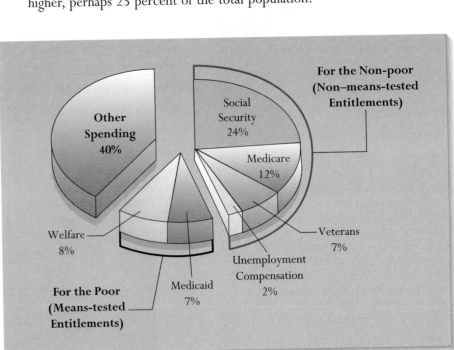

FIGURE 17-1 Entitlement Programs in the Federal Budget

Source: Budget of the United States Government, 1999.

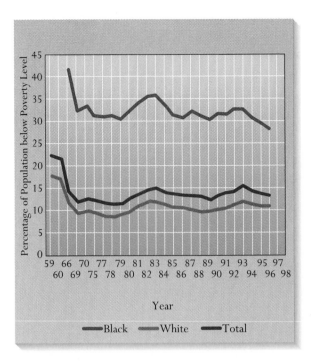

FIGURE 17-2 Poverty in the United States

Before 1970, poverty in the United States had been declining over time. But for the past thirty years, the poverty rate has held relatively steady at 13 to 15 percent of the total population. Black Americans have experienced poverty at roughly three times the rate of white Americans.

2. The official definition does not count the many "near poor," the 45 to 50 million Americans, or 19 percent of the population, living below 125 percent of the poverty level.

3. The official definition does not take into account regional differences in the cost of living, climate, or accepted styles of living.

4. The official definition does not consider what people *think* they need to live. (The poverty line is well below what most Americans think they need to survive.)

Conservative Criticism   Some conservative critics also challenge the official definition of poverty, arguing the following:

1. It does not consider the value of family assets. Elderly people who own their own mortgage-free homes, furniture, and automobiles may have incomes below the poverty line yet not suffer hardship.

2. Many families and individuals who are officially counted as poor do not *think* of themselves as "poor people"—for example, students who deliberately postpone income to secure an education.

3. Many persons (poor and nonpoor) underreport their real income, a practice that leads to overestimates of the number of poor.

4. Most important, the official definition of poverty excludes "in-kind" (noncash) benefits given to poor people by governments. If these benefits—including food stamps, free medical care, public housing, and school lunches—were "costed out" (calculated as cash income), there may be only half as many poor people as shown in official statistics.

Temporary Poverty   Poor people are often envisioned as a permanent "underclass" living most of their lives in poverty. But most poverty is not long term. Tracing poor families over time presents a different picture of the nature of poverty from the "snapshot" view taken in any one year (see Figure 17-2). For example,

Who Are the Poor?

Poverty occurs in many kinds of families and in all races and ethnic groups. However, some groups experience poverty (low income) in greater proportions than the national average (see figure).

Poverty is most common among families headed by women. The incidence of poverty among these families is four times greater than that for married couples. These women and their children constitute over two-thirds of all of the persons living in poverty in the United States. About one of every five children in the United States lives in poverty. These figures describe what has been labeled the "feminization of poverty" in the United States. Clearly, poverty is closely related to family structure. The disintegration of the traditional husband-wife family is the single most influential factor contributing to poverty today.

Blacks also experience poverty in much greater proportions than whites. Over the years, the poverty rate among blacks in the United States has been almost three times higher than the poverty rate among whites. Poverty among Hispanics is also significantly greater than among whites.

In contrast, elderly people in America experience *less* poverty than the nonaged. The aged are not poor, despite the popularity of the phrase "the poor and the aged." The percentage of persons over sixty-five years of age with low incomes is *below* the national average.

Percentage Living below the Poverty Level

Total population	13.8%
Husband-wife families	5.6%
Families w/female heads	32.4%
Whites	11.2%
Blacks	29.3%
Hispanics	30.3%
Over age 65	10.6%
Under age 18	20.8%

Source: Statistical Abstract of the United States, 1997.

Moreover, elderly people are much wealthier in terms of assets and have fewer expenses than the nonaged. They are more likely than younger people to own homes with paid-up mortgages. Medicare pays a large portion of their medical expenses. With fewer expenses, elderly people, even with relatively smaller cash incomes, experience poverty differently from the way a young mother with children experiences it. The declining poverty rate among elderly people is a relatively recent occurrence, however. Continuing increases in Social Security benefits over the years are largely responsible for this singular "victory" in the war against poverty.

over the last decade 13 to 15 percent of the nation's population has been officially classified as poor in any one year. However, only *some* poverty is persistent: about 6 to 8 percent of the population remains in poverty for more than five years. Thus about half of the people who are counted as poor are experiencing poverty for only a short period of time. For these temporary poor, welfare is a "safety net" that helps them through hard times.

Persistent Poverty About half of the people on welfare rolls at any one time are *persistently poor,* that is, likely to remain on welfare for five or more years. For these people, welfare is a more permanent part of their lives.

Because they place a disproportionate burden on welfare resources, persistently poor people pose serious questions for social scientists and policy makers. Prolonged poverty and welfare dependency create an **underclass** that suffers from many social ills—teen pregnancy, family instability, drugs, crime, alienation, apathy, and irresponsibility.[2] Government educational, training, and jobs programs, as well as many other social service efforts, fail to benefit many of these people.

underclass People who have remained poor and dependent on welfare over a prolonged period of time.

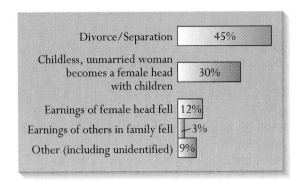

Divorce/Separation	45%
Childless, unmarried woman becomes a female head with children	30%
Earnings of female head fell	12%
Earnings of others in family fell	3%
Other (including unidentified)	9%

FIGURE 17-3 How to Become Poor: Personal Events Associated with Welfare Reliance

Many individuals fall below the poverty line because of their life situations. Women and children are especially likely to suffer poverty because divorced mothers (and their children) have the highest incidence of poverty nationwide. This has prompted some critics of modern society to argue that the cycle of poverty can only be addressed by a return to "traditional values," including the nuclear, two-parent family.

Source: Greg J. Duncan and Saul D. Hoffman, "Welfare Dynamics and the Nature of Need," paper presented at Policy Sciences Program Conference, Florida State University, Tallahassee, March 5–6, 1986, using data from University of Michigan Panel Study of Income Dynamics.

Family Structure Poverty and welfare dependency are much more frequent among female-headed households with no husband present than among husband-wife households (see *Up Close:* "Who Are the Poor?"). Unwed parenthood may be fashionable on television, but it is ill advised for young women hoping to avoid economic hardship for themselves and their children (see Figure 17-3).[3] Rising proportions of children living in poverty (from 15 percent in 1970 to more than 20 percent in 1995) are associated with rising proportions of births to unmarried women (see Figure 17-4). Traditionally, "illegitimacy" was held in check by powerful religious and social structures. But these structures have weakened over time, and the availability of welfare cash benefits, food stamps, medical care, and government housing has removed much of the economic hardship once associated with unwed motherhood. Indeed, it is sometimes argued that government welfare programs, however well meaning, end up perpetuating poverty and social dependency.

Teen Pregnancy Teenage motherhood is usually a path to poverty. "Babies having babies" is closely associated with social welfare dependency. But births to teenage mothers—the number of births per 1,000 women 15 to 19 years of age—has actually declined during the 1990s. Liberals claimed that this modest victory is a product of better sex education and condom distribution in schools.

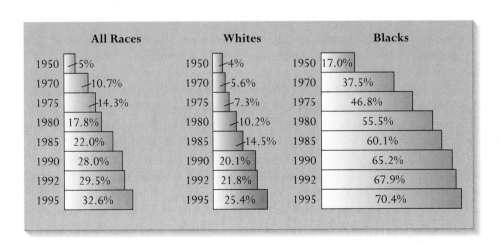

All Races		Whites		Blacks	
1950	5%	1950	4%	1950	17.0%
1970	10.7%	1970	5.6%	1970	37.5%
1975	14.3%	1975	7.3%	1975	46.8%
1980	17.8%	1980	10.2%	1980	55.5%
1985	22.0%	1985	14.5%	1985	60.1%
1990	28.0%	1990	20.1%	1990	65.2%
1992	29.5%	1992	21.8%	1992	67.9%
1995	32.6%	1995	25.4%	1995	70.4%

FIGURE 17-4 Births to Unmarried Women

The rate of children born to unmarried women rose through 1995. Recent reports indicate a leveling off of births to unmarried women, at approximately one-third of all births.
Source: Statistical Abstract of the United States, 1997, p. 78.

Up Close

Homelessness in America

The most visible social welfare problem in the United States is the nation's homeless people, who wander about in the larger cities suffering exposure, alcoholism, drug abuse, and chronic mental illness. No one knows their total number, but the best systematic estimate is 250,000 to 350,000.*

The issue of homelessness has become so politicized that an accurate assessment of the problem and a rational strategy for dealing with it have become virtually impossible. The term "homeless" is used to describe many different situations. Many are *street people* who sleep in subways, bus stations, parks, or the streets. Some of them are temporarily traveling in search of work; some have left home for a few days or are youthful runaways; others have roamed the streets for months or years. In contrast, *sheltered homeless people* have obtained housing in shelters operated by local governments or private charities. As the number of shelters has grown in recent years, the number of sheltered homeless people has also grown. But most of the sheltered homeless people come from other housing, not the streets. These are people who have recently been evicted from rental units or have previously lived with family or friends. They often include families with children; the street people are virtually all single persons.

About half of all street people are chronic alcoholic and drug abusers; an additional one-fourth to one-third are mentally ill.† Alcohol and drug abusers, especially "crack" cocaine users, are the fastest-growing groups among homeless people. Moreover, homeless people who are alcohol and drug abusers and/or mentally ill are by far the most likely to remain on the streets for long periods of time. Among the 15 to 25 percent of homeless people who are neither mentally ill nor dependent on alcohol or drugs, homelessness is likely to be temporary.

The current plight of homeless people is primarily a result of various "reforms" in public policy, notably the "deinstitutionalization" of care for the mentally ill and the newly recognized rights of individuals to refuse treatment; the "decriminalization" of vagrancy and public intoxication; and urban renewal, which has eliminated many low-rent apartments and cheap hotels.

Deinstitutionalization, a policy advanced by mental health care professionals and social welfare activists in the 1960s and 1970s after the introduction of new psychotropic drug therapies, has resulted in the release of all but the most dangerous mental patients from state-run mental hospitals. Advocates of deinstitutionalization argued that aside from drugs, no psychiatric therapies have much success among the long-term mentally ill. Drug therapies can be administered on an outpatient basis; they usually do not require hospitalization. So it was argued that patients could not rightfully be kept in

Conservatives claimed that it is a result of teaching abstinence, as well as welfare reforms requiring teenagers to reside with their parents and continue schooling as conditions for cash payments. According to federal survey data, teenage girls are having less sex *and* making more use of birth control.

The "Truly Disadvantaged"   The nation's largest cities have become the principal location of virtually all of the social problems confronting our society—poverty, homelessness (see *Up Close:* "Homelessness in America"), racial tension, drug abuse, delinquency, and crime. These problems are all made worse by their concentration in large cities. Yet the concentration of social ills in cities is a relatively recent occurrence; as late as 1970, there were higher rates of poverty in rural America than in the cities.

Why has the inner city become the locus of social problems? Some observers argue that changes in the labor market from industrial goods-producing jobs to

A family eating a Christmas Eve lunch for the needy and homeless, prepared by a Washington, D.C., mission.

ing an illegal substance or is found in court to be "a danger to himself or others," which means a person must commit a serious act of violence before the courts will intervene. For many homeless people—victimized by cold, exposure, and hunger, by the availability of alcohol and illegal drugs, and by the violent street crimes perpetrated against them—this means the "freedom to die with their rights on."

Community-based care has failed for many substance abusers and chronically mentally ill street people. Many are "uncooperative"; they are isolated from society; they have no family members or doctors or counselors to turn to for help. The nation's vast social welfare system provides them little help. They cannot handle forms, appointments, or interviews; the welfare bureaucracy is intimidating. Lacking a permanent address, many receive no Social Security, welfare, or disability checks. Shelters provided by private charities, such as the Salvation Army, or by city governments are more helpful to the temporarily homeless than to chronic alcohol or drug abusers or mentally ill people. Few shelters offer treatment for alcohol or drug abusers, and some refuse disruptive people.

mental institutions against their will; people who had committed no crimes and who posed no danger to others should be released. Much of the resulting problem arose because many of these patients were unable, on their own, to maintain the schedule for their outpatient treatment.

Decriminalization of public intoxication has also added to the numbers of street people. Involuntary confinement of substance abusers is now banned unless a person is arrested while possess-

---

*Peter H. Rossi, *Down and Out in America* (Chicago: University of Chicago Press, 1989).

†As reported in a twenty-seven-city survey by the U.S. Conference of Mayors. See *U.S. News and World Report,* January 15, 1990, pp. 27–29.

professional, financial, and technical service-producing jobs have increasingly divided the labor market into low-wage and high-wage sectors.[4] The decline in manufacturing jobs, together with a shift in remaining manufacturing jobs and commercial (sales) jobs to the suburbs, has left inner-city residents with fewer and lower paying job opportunities. The rise in joblessness in the inner cities has in turn increased the concentration of poor people, added to the number of poor single-parent families, and increased welfare dependency.

SOCIAL WELFARE POLICY

Public welfare has been a recognized responsibility of government in English-speaking countries for many centuries. As far back as the Poor Relief Act of 1601, the English Parliament provided workhouses for the "able-bodied poor" (the

TABLE 17-1 **Major Federal Social Welfare Programs**

Social Insurance Programs	Beneficiaries (millions)	Public Assistance Programs	Beneficiaries (millions)
Social Security		*Cash Aid*	
Retirement	30.1	Assistance to Families (formerly AFDC)	13.9
Survivors	7.4	Supplemental Security Income (SSI)	6.5
Disabled	5.8	General assistance	0.9
Total	43.4		
		Medical Care	
Unemployment Compensation		Medicaid	36.3
Total	8.0	Veterans	1.5
		Indians	1.3
Government Retirement and Veterans		Maternal and child health	4.6
Veterans	3.4		
Federal employees	2.8	*Food Benefits*	
State and local	4.9	Food stamps	28.9
		School lunches	14.0
Medicare		Women, Infants, Children (WIC)	6.5
Total	37.5	Child and adult care food	5.2
		Elderly nutrition	1.1
		Housing Benefit	
		Total	4.3
		Education Aid	
		Pell Grants	3.8
		Staffed Loans	4.5
		Head Start	0.5
		Job Training	
		Total	1.8
		Energy Assistance	
		Total	6.1

Source: U.S. Bureau of the Census, *Statistical Abstract of the United States, 1997,* pp. 115, 118, 375.

social insurance programs Social welfare programs to which beneficiaries have made contributions so that they are entitled to benefits regardless of their personal wealth.

public assistance programs Those social welfare programs for which no contributions are required and only those living in poverty (by official standards) are eligible; includes food stamps, Medicaid, and Family Assistance.

unemployed) and poorhouses for widows and orphans, elderly and handicapped people. Today, nearly one-third of the U.S. population receives some form of government benefits: Social Security, Medicare or Medicaid, disability insurance, unemployment compensation, government employee retirement, veterans' benefits, food stamps, school lunches, job training, public housing, and cash public assistance payments (see Table 17-1). More than half of all families in the United States include at least one person who receives a government check. Thus the "welfare state" now encompasses a very large part of our society.

The major social welfare programs can be classified as either **social insurance** or **public assistance**. This distinction is an important one that has on occasion become a major political issue. If the beneficiaries of a government program are required to have made contributions to it before claiming any of its benefits, and if they are entitled to the benefits regardless of their personal wealth—as in Social Security and Medicare—then the program is said to be financed on the social insurance principle. If the program is financed out of general tax revenues and if recipients are required to show that they are poor before claiming its benefits—as in Temporary Assistance to Needy Families, Supplemental Security Income, and Medicaid—then the program is said to be financed on the public assistance principle. Public assistance programs are generally labeled as "welfare."

Entitlements　**Entitlements** are government benefits for which Congress has set eligibility criteria—age, income, retirement, disability, unemployment, and so on. Everyone who meets the criteria is "entitled" to the benefit.

Most of the nation's major entitlement programs were launched either in the New Deal years of the 1930s under President Franklin D. Roosevelt (Social Security, Unemployment Compensation, Aid to Families with Dependent Children, now called Temporary Assistance to Needy Families, and Aid to Aged, Blind, and Disabled, now called Supplemental Security Income) or in the Great Society years of the 1960s under President Lyndon B. Johnson (food stamps, Medicare, Medicaid).

Social Security　Begun during the Depression, **Social Security** is now the largest of all entitlements; it comprises two distinct programs. The Old Age and Survivors Insurance program provides monthly cash benefits to retired workers and their dependents and to survivors of insured workers. The Disability Insurance program provides monthly cash benefits for disabled workers and their dependents. An automatic, annual cost-of-living adjustment (COLA) for both programs matches any increase in the annual inflation rate.

With more than 43 million beneficiaries, Social Security is the single largest spending program in the federal budget. About 96 percent of the nation's paid work force is covered by the program, which is funded by a payroll tax on employers and employees. Retirees can begin receiving benefits at age sixty-two (full benefits at age sixty-five), regardless of their personal wealth or income (see "Senior Power" later in this chapter).

Unemployment Compensation　**Unemployment compensation** temporarily replaces part of the wages of workers who lose their jobs involuntarily and helps stabilize the economy during recessions. The U.S. Department of Labor oversees the system, but states administer their own programs, with latitude within federal guidelines to define weekly benefits and other program features. Benefits are funded by a combination of federal and state unemployment taxes on employers.

Supplemental Security Income　**Supplemental Security Income (SSI)** is a means-tested, federally administered income assistance program that provides monthly cash payments to needy elderly (sixty-five or older), blind, and disabled people. A loose definition of "disability"—including alcoholism, drug abuse, and attention deficiency among children—has led to a rapid growth in the number of SSI beneficiaries.

Family Assistance　**Family Assistance**, officially Temporary Assistance to Needy Families, (formerly AFDC, or Aid to Families with Dependent Children), is a grant program to enable the *states* to assist needy families. States now operate the program and define "need"; they set their own benefit levels and establish (within federal guidelines) income and resource limits. Prior to welfare reform in 1996, AFDC was a *federal* entitlement program. The federal government now

entitlements Any social welfare program for which there are eligibility requirements, whether financial or contributory.

Social Security Social insurance program composed of the Old Age and Survivors Insurance program, which pays benefits to retired workers who have paid into the program and their dependents and survivors, and the Disability Insurance program, which pays benefits to disabled workers and their families.

unemployment compensation Social insurance program that temporarily replaces part of the wages of workers who have lost their jobs.

Supplemental Security Income (SSI) Public assistance program that provides monthly cash payments to the needy elderly (sixty-five or older), blind, and disabled.

Family Assistance Public assistance program that provides monies to the states for their use in helping needy families with children.

mandates a two-year limit on benefits, a five-year lifetime limit, and other requirements (see "Politics and Welfare Reform" later in this chapter).

Medicare   **Medicare** is a two-part program that helps elderly and disabled people pay acute-care (as opposed to long-term-care) health costs. Hospital Insurance (Part A) helps pay the cost of hospital inpatient and skilled nursing care. Anyone sixty-five or older who is eligible for Social Security is automatically eligible for Part A benefits. Also eligible are people under sixty-five who receive Social Security disability or railroad retirement disability and people who have end-stage kidney disease. Part A is financed primarily by the 1.45 percent payroll tax collected with Social Security (FICA) withholding.

Supplemental Medical Insurance (Part B) is an optional add-on taken by virtually all those covered by Part A. It pays 80 percent of covered doctor and outpatient charges. Monthly premiums deducted from Social Security benefit checks finance about 25 percent of the costs of Part B, and most of the rest comes from government revenues.

Medicaid   **Medicaid** is a joint federal-state program providing health services to low-income Americans. Most Medicaid spending goes to elderly and nonelderly disabled people. However, women and children receiving benefits under AFDC automatically qualify for Medicaid, as does anyone who gets cash assistance under SSI. States can also offer Medicaid to the "medically needy"—those who face crushing medical costs but whose income or assets are too high to qualify for SSI or Family Assistance, including pregnant women and young children not receiving Family Assistance. Medicaid also pays for long-term nursing home care, but only after beneficiaries have used up virtually all of their savings and income.

Food Stamps   The **food stamp program** provides low-income household members with coupons that they can redeem for enough food to provide a minimal nutritious diet. The program is overseen by the federal government but administered by the states.

Medicare   Social insurance program that provides health care insurance to elderly and disabled people.

Medicaid   Public assistance program that provides health care to the poor.

food stamp program   Public assistance program that provides low-income households with coupons redeemable for enough food to provide a minimal nutritious diet.

Most of America's social welfare programs began in either the Great Depression of the 1930s or the War on Poverty in the 1960s. At the outset of the Depression, millions of unemployed Americans, like the New Yorkers in a bread line in the photo at left, had only private charities to turn to for survival. The War on Poverty of the 1960s was a reaction to the persistence of extreme poverty, like that of the rural family in the photograph at right, in the midst of the prosperity that followed World War II.

SENIOR POWER

Senior citizens are the most politically powerful age group in the population. They constitute 28 percent of the voting-age population, but, more important, because of their high voter turnout rates, they constitute more than one-third of the voters on election day. Persons over age sixty-five average a 68 percent turnout rate in presidential elections and a 61 percent rate in congressional elections. By comparison, those aged eighteen to twenty-one have a turnout rate of 36 percent in presidential elections and 19 percent in congressional elections, so the voting power of senior citizens is twice that of young people. Moreover, seniors are well represented in Washington; the American Association of Retired Persons (AARP) is the nation's largest organized interest group (see *Up Close:* "AARP: The Nation's Most Powerful Interest Group" in Chapter 9). No elected officials can afford to offend seniors, and seniors strongly support generous Social Security benefits.

The Aged in the Future   The baby boom from 1945 to 1960 produced a large generation of people who crowded schools and colleges in the 1960s and 1970s and encountered stiff competition for jobs in the 1980s. During the baby boom, women averaged 3.5 births during their lifetime. Today, the birthrate is only 1.8 births per woman, less than the 2.1 figure required to keep the population from declining. (Current U.S. population growth is a product of immigration.) The baby boom generation will be retiring beginning in 2010, and by 2030 they will constitute more than 20 percent of the population. Changes in lifestyle—less smoking, more exercise, better weight control—may increase the aged population even more. Medical advances may also extend life expectancy.

The Generational Compact   The framers of the Social Security Act of 1935 created a "trust fund" with the expectation that a reserve would be built up from social insurance taxes paid by working persons. The reserve would earn interest, and the interest and principal would be used in later years to pay benefits. In theory, Social Security is an insurance program. (Payments are recorded by name and Social Security number.) Many people believe that they get back what they paid during their working years. Reality, however, has proven much different.

Social Security is now financed on a pay-as-you-go system, rather than a reserve system. Today, the income from all social insurance premiums (taxes) pays for current Social Security benefits. This generation of workers is paying for the benefits of the last generation, and this generation must hope that its future benefits will be financed by the next generation of workers. Taxing current workers to pay benefits to current retirees may be viewed as a compact between generations. Each generation of workers in effect agrees to pay benefits to an earlier generation of retirees and expects the next generation will pay for its retirement.

The Rising Dependency Ratio   Because current workers must pay for the benefits of current retirees and other beneficiaries, the **dependency ratio** becomes an important component of evaluating the future of Social Security. The dependency ratio for Social Security is the number of recipients as a percentage of the number of contributing workers. Americans are living longer and increasing the dependency ratio. A child born in 1935, when the Social Security system was created, could expect to live only to age sixty-one, four years *less* than the retirement age of sixty-five. The life expectancy of a child born in 1990 is

Well organized and known to take their outrage to the voting booth in substantial numbers, senior citizens enjoy enormous influence over the nation's politicians. They have successfully fought off efforts to reduce the benefits of social welfare programs for the elderly and also to increase the costs of many public services to seniors. In addition to massive letter-writing campaigns, senior citizens have shown themselves more than willing to adopt the techniques of young antiwar protesters in the 1960s, marching on government headquarters to make their complaints clear.

dependency ratio   In the Social Security system, the number of recipients as a percentage of the number of contributing workers.

seventy-four years, nine years *beyond* the retirement age. In the early years of Social Security, there were ten workers supporting each retiree—a dependency ratio of 10 to 1. But today, as the U.S. population grows older—due to lower birthrates and longer life spans—there are only three workers for each retiree, and by 2010 the dependency ratio will be two workers for each retiree.

Burdens on Generation X   With fewer workers to support each retiree, the burdens of Social Security on the current generation of young Americans will become unsupportable. Members of Generation X will pay many times more into Social Security than they will ever get out of it.

The Trust Fund Myth   Income from the Social Security tax currently exceeds payments to beneficiaries. The "surplus" is officially used to purchase U.S. government bonds. However, Social Security taxes are lumped together with general tax revenues in the federal budget as "current revenues," which offset *all* current expenditures of the federal government. Thus the Social Security surplus hides some deficits in overall federal spending, and the use of the "trust fund" to purchase government bonds aids the federal government in financing its debts. In short, the trust fund is merely an accounting gimmick; current Social Security taxes are being used to finance current spending, and future retirement benefits will have to be paid from future revenues.

Cost-of-Living Increases   Currently, the annual Social Security cost-of-living adjustments (**COLAs**) are based on the Consumer Price Index, which estimates the cost of all consumer items each year. These costs include home buying, mortgage interest, child rearing, and other costs that many retirees do not confront. Moreover, most *workers* do not have the same protection against inflation as retirees; average wage rates do not always match increases in the cost of living. Hence, over the years, COLAs have improved the economic well-being of Social Security recipients relative to all American workers.

Wealthy Retirees   Social Security benefits are paid to *all* eligible retirees, regardless of whatever other income they may receive. There is no means test for Social Security benefits. As a result, large numbers of affluent Americans receive government checks each month. They paid into Social Security during their working years, and they can claim these checks as an entitlement under the social insurance principle. But currently their benefits far exceed their previous payments.

Because elderly people experience less poverty than today's workers (see *Up Close:* "Who Are the Poor?" earlier in this chapter) and possess considerably more wealth, Social Security benefits constitute a "negative" redistribution of income— that is, a transfer of income from poorer to richer people. The elderly are generally better off than the people supporting them.

The "Third Rail" of American Politics   Social Security is the most expensive program in the federal budget, but also the most politically sacrosanct. Politicians regularly call it the "third rail of American politics"—touch it and die. Because Social Security and Medicare are entitlement programs, their spending grows automatically each year as numbers of beneficiaries increase and COLAs raise benefit levels. Because they are entitlement programs with strong political support, spending on them is sometimes called "uncontrollable."

COLAs   Annual cost-of-living adjustments mandated by law in Social Security and other welfare benefits.

But Congress can change or repeal any law it passes. Lawmakers can reduce entitlements, including Social Security and Medicare, in a variety of ways. They can legislate reductions in benefit levels; limit eligibility (for example, by increasing the age at which Social Security benefits begin); limit COLAs; or introduce means tests to deny benefits to high-income retirees.

POLITICS AND WELFARE REFORM

Americans confront a clash of values in welfare policy. Americans are a generous people; they believe government should aid those who are unable to take care of themselves, especially children, disabled people, and elderly people. But Americans are worried that welfare programs encourage dependency, undermine the work ethic, and contribute to illegitimate births and the breakup of families. As Harvard sociologist David Ellwood explains,

> Welfare brings some of our most precious values—involving autonomy, responsibility, work, family, community and compassion—into conflict. We want to help those who are not making it, but in so doing, we seem to cheapen the efforts of those who are struggling hard just to get by. We want to offer financial support to those with low incomes, but if we do, we reduce the pressure on them and their incentive to work. We want to help people who are not able to help themselves, but then we worry that people will not bother to help themselves. We recognize the insecurity of single-parent families, but, in helping them, we appear to be promoting or supporting their formation.[5]

Although social insurance programs (Social Security, Medicare, and Unemployment Compensation) are politically popular and enjoy the support of large numbers of active beneficiaries, public assistance programs (Family Assistance, SSI, Medicaid) are far less popular. A variety of controversies surround welfare policy in the United States.

"As far as I'm concerned, they can do what they want with the minimum wage, just as long as they keep their hands off the maximum wage."

Drawing by Mankoff. © 1989 The New Yorker Magazine.

Poverty and Public Policy   Can the government itself create poverty by fashioning social welfare programs and policies that destroy incentives to work, encourage families to break up, and condemn the poor to social dependency? Can the social welfare system sentence many people to a life of poverty who would otherwise form families, take low-paying jobs, and perhaps with hard work and perseverance gradually pull themselves and their children into the mainstream of American life?

The effect of generous welfare benefits and relaxed eligibility requirements on employment has been argued for centuries. Surveys show that the poor prefer work over welfare, but welfare payments may produce subtle effects on the behavior of the poor. People unwilling to take minimum wage jobs may never acquire the work habits required to move into better paying jobs later in their lives. Welfare may even help to create a dependent and defeatist subculture, lowering personal self-esteem and contributing to joblessness, illegitimacy, and broken families.

There is little doubt that social dependency and family structure are closely related. As noted earlier, poverty is much more frequent among female-headed households with no husband present than among husband-wife households. As births to unmarried women rise, poverty and social dependency increase. (In 1970, only 11 percent of births were to unmarried women; by 1995 this figure had risen to 31 percent of all births and 69 percent of minority births.) The troubling question is whether welfare policy ameliorates some of the hardships confronting unmarried mothers and their children, or whether it actually contributes to social dependency by mitigating the consequences of unmarried motherhood (see *A Conflicting View:* "Government as the Cause of Poverty").

Reform Politics   A political consensus grew over the years that long-term social dependency had to be addressed in welfare policy. The fact that most nonpoor mothers work convinced many *liberals* that welfare mothers had no special claim to stay at home with their children. And many *conservatives* acknowledged that some transitional assistance—education, job training, continued health care, and day care for children—might be necessary to move welfare mothers into the work force.

Although President Clinton had once promised "to end welfare as we know it," it was the Republican-controlled Congress elected in 1994 that proceeded to do so. The Republican-sponsored welfare reform bill ended the 60-year-old federal "entitlement" for low-income families with children—the venerable AFDC program. In its place the Republicans devised a "devolution" of responsibility to the states through federal block grants—Temporary Assistance to Needy Families—lump sum allocations to the states for cash welfare payments with benefits and eligibility requirements decided by the states. Conservatives in Congress imposed tough-minded "strings" to state aid, including a two-year limit on continuing cash benefits and a five-year lifetime limit; a "family cap" that would deny additional cash benefit to women already on welfare who bear more children; the denial of cash welfare to unwed parents under 18 years of age unless they live with an adult and attend school; and the denial of federally funded public assistance to illegal immigrants as well as legal immigrants who have not become citizens.

Democrats in Congress obtained some modifications to these requirements, as well as guarantees that states would not reduce their welfare funding below previous years' AFDC spending; exemptions from time limits and work requirements for some portion of welfare recipients; and community service alternatives to work requirements.

Government as the Cause of Poverty

Does the government itself create poverty by fashioning social welfare programs and policies that destroy incentives to work, encourage teenage pregnancies, and condemn the poor to social dependency? Does the current social welfare system unintentionally sentence many people to a life of poverty who would otherwise form families, take low-paying jobs, and perhaps, with hard work and perseverance, gradually pull themselves and their children into the mainstream of American life?

Poverty in the United States steadily *declined* from 1950, when about 30 percent of the population was officially poor, to 1970, when about 13 percent of the population was poor. During this period of progress toward the elimination of poverty, government welfare programs were minimal. Federal payments were available to elderly, blind, and disabled poor people. There were small Aid to Families with Dependent Children (AFDC) programs for women with children who lived alone; eligibility was restricted and welfare authorities checked to see if an employable male lived in the house. Welfare roles were modest; only about 1 to 2 percent of American families received AFDC payments.

Following the addition of many new Great Society welfare programs, the downward trend in poverty ended. Indeed, the number and proportion of the population living in poverty began to move upward (see Figure 17-2 in text). This was a period in which AFDC payments were significantly increased and eligibility rules were relaxed. The food stamp program, initiated in 1965, became a major welfare benefit. Medicaid, also initiated in 1965, became the costliest of all public assistance programs by the late 1970s. Federal aid to elderly, blind, and disabled people was merged into a new Supplemental Security Income program, and the number of recipients of this program quadrupled.

Why did the downward trend in poverty end in the 1970s? Discrimination did not become significantly worse during this period; on the contrary, the civil rights laws enacted in the 1960s were opening up many new opportunities for African Americans.

Poverty was reduced among elderly people due to generous increases in Social Security benefits. The greatest increases in poverty occurred in families headed by working-age persons. In short, it is difficult to find alternative explanations for the continuation of poverty. We are obliged to consider the possibility that *policy* changes—new welfare programs, expanded benefits, and relaxed eligibility requirements—contributed to maintaining poverty.

According to Charles Murray, the persons hurt most by current welfare policies are poor people themselves. In his controversial book *Losing Ground,* he argued that current social welfare policy provides many disincentives to family life. According to Murray, generous welfare programs encourage poor young women to start families before they have sufficient job skills to support themselves; poor young men are allowed to escape their family responsibilities. Surveys show that poor people prefer work over welfare, but welfare payments may subtly affect their behavior. Persons unwilling to take minimum wage jobs may never acquire the work habits required to move into better paying jobs later in life. Welfare may even help create a dependent and defeatist subculture, lowering personal self-esteem and contributing further to joblessness, illegitimacy, and broken families. Murray's policy prescription was a drastic one.

> [He recommended] scrapping the entire federal welfare and income-support structure for working-age persons. It would leave the working-age person with no recourse whatever except the job market, family members, friends, and public or private locally funded services—cut the knot, for there is no way to untie it.[*]

The result, he argued, would be less poverty and illegitimacy and more upward mobility, freedom, and hope for poor people. "The lives of large numbers of poor people would be radically changed for the better." The obstacle to this solution is not only the politicians and bureaucrats who want to keep their dependent clients but also, more important, the majority of well-meaning middle-class Americans who support welfare programs.

---

[*]Charles Murray, *Losing Ground* (New York: Basic Books, 1984), pp. 227–28.

Across the USA

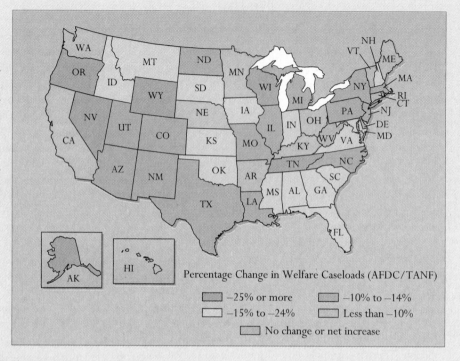

Welfare Reform

Even before welfare reform was enacted by Congress in 1996, many states had applied for and received "waivers" from the federal government to experiment with their own reforms. Wisconsin, under Republican Governor Tommy Thompson, led the way, reducing its welfare rolls by one-third. All states have reduced their welfare rolls.

Percentage Change in Welfare Caseloads (AFDC/TANF)

- −25% or more
- −15% to −24%
- −10% to −14%
- Less than −10%
- No change or net increase

President Clinton vetoed the first welfare reform bill passed by Congress in early 1996, but as the presidential election neared, he reversed himself and signed the welfare reform act, establishing the Temporary Assistance to Needy Families program (see *Across the USA:* "Welfare Reform"). The final program compromised many of the key issues: the family cap and school and adult supervision for teenage mothers was left to the states to decide; states were obliged to spend at least 75 percent of the funds previously spent on AFDC; states can exempt up to 20 percent of welfare recipients from time limits and work requirements. Food stamps, SSI, and Medicaid were continued as federal "entitlements." President Clinton promised to "improve" welfare reform, by eliminating restrictions on immigrant aid, making community service an alternative to work requirements, and so on. But continuing GOP control of Congress promises strong opposition to any efforts to "undo" welfare reform (see *Up Close:* "Is Welfare Reform Working?").

HEALTH CARE IN AMERICA

The United States spends more of its resources on health care than any other nation (see *Compared to What?* "Health and Health Care Costs in Advanced Democracies"). Nevertheless, the United States ranks well below other advanced democracies in key measures of the health of its people such as life expectancy and infant death rate. Moreover, unlike most other advanced democracies, which make provision

Is Welfare Reform Working?

Welfare reform, officially Temporary Assistance to Needy Families, was passed by Congress in 1996; its provisions took effect in 1997. By early 1998 the Clinton Administration, as well as Republican congressional sponsors of welfare reform, were declaring it a success. Their claim was based primarily on the rapid exodus of over 2 million people from the nation's welfare rolls.

The number of welfare recipients in the nation dropped below 10 million—the lowest number in more than twenty-five years. Fewer than 4 percent of Americans are now on welfare—the smallest proportion since 1970. No doubt some of this decline is attributable to strong growth of the economy: declines in welfare rolls began *before* Congress passed its welfare reform law, and some decline may have occurred without reform. Many states had initiated their own reforms under "waivers" from the federal government even before Congress acted.

Virtually all states have now developed work programs for welfare recipients. Applicants for welfare benefits are now generally required to enter job-search programs, to undertake job training, and to accept jobs or community service positions.

Yet, although nearly everyone agrees that getting people off welfare rolls and onto payrolls is the main goal of reform, there are major obstacles to the achievement of this goal. First of all, a substantial portion (perhaps 25 to 40 percent) of long-term welfare recipients have handicaps—physical disabilities, chronic illnesses, learning disabilities, alcohol or drug

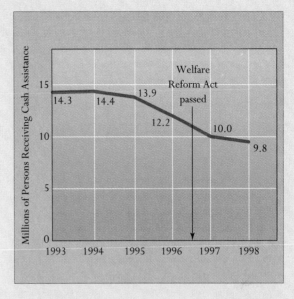

Source: As reported in *New York Times*, February 2, 1997, and January 21, 1998.

abuse problems—that prevent them from holding a full-time job. Many long-term recipients have no work experience (perhaps 40 percent), and two-thirds of them did not graduate from high school. Almost half have three or more children, making day-care arrangements a major obstacle. It is unlikely that any counseling, education, job training, or job placement programs could ever succeed in getting these people into productive employment. Policymakers argue whether or not there are 5 million jobs available to unskilled mothers, but even if there were, most would be low paying and might not lift the women out of poverty.

Programs such as this Riverside, California "Jobs Club" try to help welfare recipients find jobs in the wake of reforms intended to reduce welfare dependency.

Health and Health Care Costs in Advanced Democracies

Americans spend more than any other nation in the world for health care (see figure). They spend over 50 percent more than Canadians and nearly 100 percent more than Japanese. Few people object to heavy spending for health care if they get their money's worth. But cross-national comparisons of health statistics indicate that Americans on the average are less healthy than citizens in other advanced democracies. The United States ranks *below* many

other advanced nations in life expectancy and infant death rates—two commonly used measures of national health.

The United States offers some of the most advanced and sophisticated medical care in the world, attracting patients from the countries that rank well ahead of it in various health measures. The United States is the locus of some of the most advanced medical research, attracting medical researchers from throughout the world. But the high quality of medical care available in the United States, combined with the poor health statistics of the general public, suggest that the nation's health care problems center more on access to care and education and prevention of health problems than on the quality of care available.

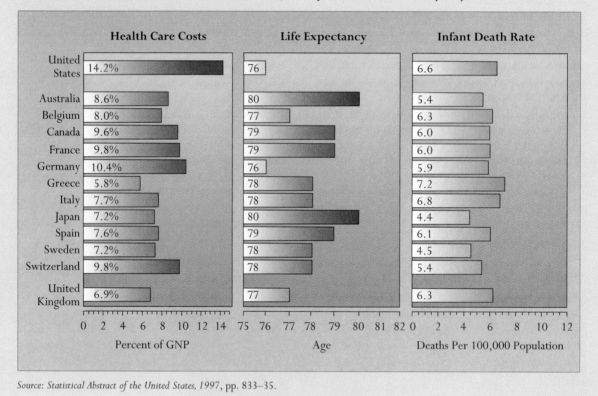

	Health Care Costs	Life Expectancy	Infant Death Rate
United States	14.2%	76	6.6
Australia	8.6%	80	5.4
Belgium	8.0%	77	6.3
Canada	9.6%	79	6.0
France	9.8%	79	6.0
Germany	10.4%	76	5.9
Greece	5.8%	78	7.2
Italy	7.7%	78	6.8
Japan	7.2%	80	4.4
Spain	7.6%	79	6.1
Sweden	7.2%	78	4.5
Switzerland	9.8%	78	5.4
United Kingdom	6.9%	77	6.3
	Percent of GNP	Age	Deaths Per 100,000 Population

Source: Statistical Abstract of the United States, 1997, pp. 833–35.

for health care for all citizens, Americans have no guarantee of access to medical care. In short, the American health care system is the most expensive and least universal in its coverage in the world.

The Health of Americans Historically, most reductions in death rates have resulted from public health and sanitation improvements, including immunizations, clean public water supplies, sanitary sewage disposal, improved diets, and increased standards of living. Many of the leading causes of death today (see Table 17-2),

TABLE 17-2	Leading Causes of Death			
	Deaths per 100,000 Population per Year			
	1960	1970	1980	1995
All causes	954.7	945.3	883.4	875.4
Heart disease	369.0	362.0	336.0	281.3
Stroke (cerebrovascular)	108.0	101.9	75.5	58.9
Cancer	149.2	162.8	183.9	204.2
Accidents	52.3	56.4	46.7	35.1
Pneumonia	37.3	30.9	24.1	31.3
Diabetes	16.7	18.9	15.5	21.8
AIDS	N.A.	N.A.	N.A.	16.2
Suicide	10.6	11.6	11.9	12.0
Homicide	4.7	8.3	10.7	9.6

Source: *Statistical Abstract of the United States, 1997*, p. 97.

including heart disease, stroke, AIDS, and suicide, are closely linked to heredity, personal habits and lifestyles (smoking, eating, drinking, exercise, stress, sexual practices), and the physical environment—factors over which doctors and hospitals have no direct control. Thus some argue that the greatest contribution to better health is likely to be found in altered personal habits and lifestyles rather than in more medical care.

Thanks to improved health care habits as well as breakthroughs in medical technology, Americans are living longer than ever before. Public awareness programs concerning the risks associated with many causes of death—including heart disease, strokes, accidents, pneumonia, diabetes, and emphysema—have probably contributed to declines in these causes of death. However, much of this decline has been offset by a rise in deaths from cancer, despite growth in spending for research and treatment.

Access to Care   A major challenge in health care is to extend coverage to all Americans. Today, about 85 percent of the nation's population is covered by either government or private health insurance. Government pays about 43 percent of all health care costs—through Medicare for the aged, Medicaid for the poor, and other government programs, including military and veterans' care. Private insurance pays for 39 percent of the nation's health costs. Direct payments by patients account for only 18 percent (see Figure 17-5).

But about 15 percent of the U.S. population—an estimated 35 to 40 million Americans—have *no* medical insurance. These include workers and their dependents whose employers do not offer a health insurance plan as well as unemployed people who are not eligible for Medicare or Medicaid. Another 30 million Americans suffer gaps in insurance coverage in any year owing to unemployment or shifts in jobs. People who lack health insurance may postpone or go without needed medical care or may be denied medical care by hospitals and physicians in all but emergency situations. Confronted with serious illness, they may be obliged to impoverish themselves in order to become eligible for Medicaid. Any unpaid medical bills must be absorbed by hospitals or shifted to paying patients and their insurance companies.

FIGURE 17-5 Who Pays the Medical Bills?

Critics of America's current health insurance system refer to it as a "patchwork" of different payment sources. About 43 percent of the nation's medical bills are paid by government, including 18 percent under Medicare for elderly people and 14 percent under Medicaid for poor people. Patient payments account for little more than 18 percent.

Source: *Statistical Abstract of the United States, 1995,* p. 109.

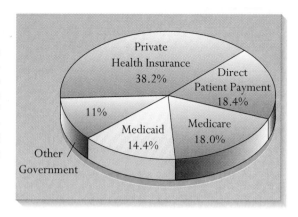

Coverage Gaps   Even people who *do* have health insurance often confront serious financial problems in obtaining medical care owing to inadequate coverage. Medicare, like most private insurance plans, requires patients to pay some *initial* charges called **deductibles**. The purpose of deductibles is to discourage unnecessary treatment. Patients must also make up any difference between doctors' actual charges and the rates allowed by their insurance plans. Indeed, only an estimated half of the doctors in the nation accept Medicare rates as payment in full. In addition, Medicare and many private insurance plans do not pay for prescription drugs, eyeglasses, hearing aids, or routine physical examinations.

More important, perhaps, Medicare does not pay for long-term care or catastrophic illness. Medicare covers only the first 60 days of hospitalization; it covers nursing home care for 100 days only if the patient is sent there from a hospital. In 1988 Congress attempted to remedy this problem by adding catastrophic health care coverage to Medicare. The program was jettisoned, however, in the face of a strong protest from seniors who opposed the tax surcharge on Medicare enrollees (elderly people) that was to have funded this coverage. Apparently senior citizens wanted their added benefits paid for by working people; if forced to pay themselves, they would rather not have the benefits.

As the number and proportion of the elderly population grows in the United States (eighty years and over is the fastest growing age group in the nation), the need for long-term nursing home care grows. Medicaid assistance to needy people is paid to nursing home patients, but middle-class people cannot qualify for Medicaid without first "spending down" their savings. Long-term nursing home care threatens their assets and their children's inheritance. Private insurance policies covering long-term care are said to be too expensive. So senior citizen groups have lobbied heavily for long-term nursing home care to be paid for by taxpayers under Medicare.

Health Care Cost Inflation   No system of health care can provide as much as people will use. Anyone whose health and life may be at stake will want the most thorough diagnostic testing, the most constant care, the most advanced treatment. Sworn to preserve life, doctors, too, want the most advanced diagnostic and treatment facilities available for their patients. Under conditions of uncertainty in a medical situation—and there is always some uncertainty—physicians are trained to seek more consultations, run more tests, and try new therapeutic approaches. Any tendency for doctors to limit testing and treatment is countered by the threat of malpractice suits; it is always easier to order one more test or procedure than to risk even the tiniest chance that failing to do so will some day be cause for a court suit. So both patients

deductibles   Initial charges in insurance plans, paid by beneficiaries.

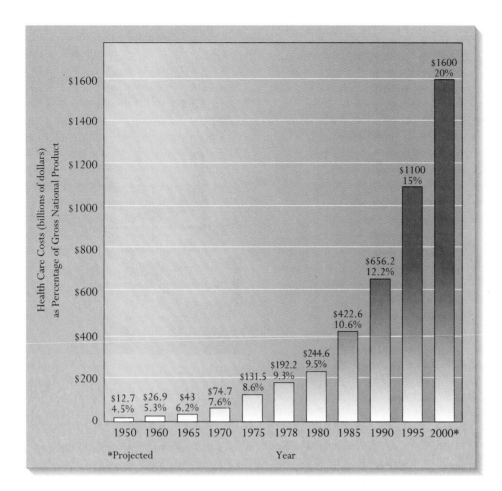

FIGURE 17-6 **The Growth of Health Care Costs in the United States**

Source: *Statistical Abstract of the United States, 1996.* Projection by Congressional Budget Office, in *Congressional Quarterly Weekly Report,* March 13, 1993, p. 596.

and doctors push up the costs of health care, particularly when the public or private insurers foot the bill. Advances in medical technology have produced elaborate and expensive equipment. Hospitals that have made heavy financial investment in this equipment must use it as often as possible. As a result, the costs of health care in the United States have risen to about 15 percent of the nation's total economic output (GDP) and these costs are likely to grow even more (see Figure 17-6).

Coping with Costs Both private and government insurers have made efforts to counter rising costs. Private insurers have negotiated discounts with groups of physicians and with hospitals—**preferred provider organizations (PPOs)**—and have implemented rules to guide physicians about when patients should and should not receive costly diagnostic and therapeutic procedures—**managed care**. Medicare no longer pays hospitals based on costs incurred; instead it pays fixed fees based on primary and secondary diagnoses at the time of admission. Both government and private insurers have encouraged the expansion of **health maintenance organizations (HMOs)**, groups that promise to provide a stipulated list of services to patients for a fixed fee and that are able to provide care at lower total costs than can other providers.

But many of the efforts by both private insurers and governments to control costs have created new problems. These include cost-control regulations and restrictions that add to administrative costs and create a mountain of paperwork for physicians and hospitals, and frustration and anger among both health care workers and

preferred provider organizations (PPOs) Groups of hospitals and physicians who have joined together to offer their services to private insurers at a discount.

managed care Programs designed to keep health care costs down by the establishment of strict guidelines regarding when and what diagnostic and therapeutic procedures should be administered to patients under various circumstances.

health maintenance organizations (HMOs) Health care provider groups that provide a stipulated list of services to patients for a fixed fee that is usually substantially lower than such care would otherwise cost.

Lack of health insurance forces many Americans to postpone regular visits to a doctor and to rely on crowded hospital emergency rooms when they become sick.

patients. Doctors and hospitals argue that the *administrative* costs imposed by these cost-control measures far exceed whatever savings are achieved. Patients and doctors complain that preapproval of treatment by insurance companies often removes medical decisions from the physician and patient and places them in the hands of insurance company employees.

POLITICS AND HEALTH CARE REFORM

Health care reform centers on two central problems: controlling costs and expanding access. These problems are related: expanding access to Americans who are currently uninsured and closing gaps in coverage requires increased costs, even while a central thrust of reform is to bring down overall health care costs.

National Health Insurance Plans   Liberals have long sought the creation of a Canadian-style health care system in which the federal government would provide health insurance for all Americans in a single national plan paid for by general tax increases. Under **national health insurance** all Americans would be entitled to a stipulated list of services from physicians, hospitals, and nursing homes, regardless of their employment, age, medical status, or income level. The federal government would be the "single payer" of health care costs through increased taxes. Hospitals would operate on budgets periodically negotiated with the government. Government fee schedules would dictate payments to physicians. Patients also might have to pay some share of the costs at the time of illness. This approach to health care would shift most costs from the private to the public sector. Although these plans are generally popular in Canada and Western Europe, proposals for federal nationwide insurance systems have consistently failed to win broad political support in the United States.

Employer-based Plans   Others have advanced the notion of universal coverage through mandated employer-based insurance for most workers combined with

national health insurance   Government-provided insurance to all citizens paid from tax revenues.

government subsidies to pay the insurance costs for people living below the poverty line and to assist others in purchasing insurance.

A majority of American employees are currently enrolled in employer-based plans, but these plans vary a great deal in coverage and cost to employees. And, of course, they do not cover the self-employed or unemployed. The federal government has never *mandated* employers to provide health insurance to their workers.

Clinton's Failed Comprehensive Health Care Plan   In 1992 a committee headed by First Lady Hillary Rodham Clinton proposed a comprehensive plan to restructure completely the nation's health care system (see *People in Politics:* "Hillary Rodham Clinton and Health Care Policy Making"). The Clinton health plan was incorporated into a very complex, 1,342-page bill that would have reorganized the entire health care industry in America—nearly one-sixth of the nation's economy. Its key elements included the following:

- Mandated employer-paid health insurance for workers and their dependents (80 percent of costs, with a cap of 7.9 percent of payroll).
- Mandated "comprehensive" benefits, including prescription drugs, mental health and substance abuse treatment, childhood immunization, dental coverage, eyeglasses for children, and all pregnancy-related services, including abortion.
- Health insurance for all citizens and legal residents. Government subsidies would be provided for small employers and persons not covered by employer-mandated insurance.
- Cost containment by a national health board that would set an overall health care budget and allocate totals to health alliances around the country.

The Clinton plan failed to pass Congress for a variety of reasons. The choice of a comprehensive plan that would have restructured one-sixth of the economy, as opposed to more modest incremental reforms, may have been the initial mistake. The complex plan caused a great deal of public confusion and enabled opponents— notably the health insurance industry with its effective "Harry and Louise" television ads—to raise fears about the effects of the plan on consumers. Liberals in Congress, who favored a Canadian-style government health care system paid for by tax increases, were only lukewarm supporters of the president's plan. Republicans were able to brand the president's bill as a "government takeover" of health care. The president was unwilling to consider more modest reforms. After months of debate, public opinion polls showed a majority of Americans were opposed to Clinton's plan.

Kennedy-Kassebaum Act   Some modest reforms were enacted in 1996 in the Kennedy-Kassebaum Act, named for its bipartisan sponsorship by liberal Democratic Senator Edward M. Kennedy and moderate Republican Senator Nancy Kassebaum. This act guarantees the "portability" of health insurance— allowing workers to maintain their insurance coverage if they lose or change jobs. Their new employer's health insurance company cannot deny them insurance for "preexisting conditions."

Health Insurance for Children and the "Near Elderly"   In his second term, President Clinton shifted his health care strategy from his earlier comprehensive plan to more modest incremental proposals to expand government health insurance. He advocated the expansion of Medicaid to cover children who would

Hillary Rodham Clinton and Health Care Policy Making

Hillary Rodham Clinton is not the first politically powerful First Lady. That distinction belongs to Eleanor Roosevelt; however, in Roosevelt's era the power of the First Lady was exercised in a more subtle fashion. As chair of the president's health care task force, Hillary Rodham Clinton possessed official responsibility for a key area of national policy making. But her influence extends well beyond the health care field to virtually all areas of presidential responsibility, earning her the label "co-president."

Hillary Rodham grew up in suburban Chicago, the daughter of wealthy parents who sent her to the private, prestigious Wellesley College. A 1969 honors graduate with a counterculture image—horn-rimmed glasses, long, straggling hair, no makeup—she was chosen by her classmates to give a commencement speech—a rambling statement about "more immediate, ecstatic, and penetrating modes of living."

At Yale Law School Hillary met a long-haired, bearded Rhodes scholar from Arkansas, Bill Clinton, who was just as politically ambitious as she was. Both Hillary and Bill received their law degrees in 1973. Bill returned to Arkansas to build a career in state politics, and Hillary went to Washington as an attorney—first for a liberal lobbying group, the Children's Defense Fund, and later on the staff of the House Judiciary Committee seeking to impeach President Richard Nixon. But Rodham and other Yale grads traveled to Arkansas to help Clinton run unsuccessfully for Congress in 1974. Hillary decided to stay with Bill in Little Rock; they married before his next campaign, a successful run for state attorney general in 1976. Hillary remained Hillary Rodham, even as her husband went on to the governorship in 1978. She taught briefly at the University of Arkansas Law School and eventually joined Little Rock's influential Rose law firm. She

kept her Washington ties with the Children's Defense Fund. She also became a director of Wal-Mart Stores, TCBY Enterprises, the LaFarge Corporation, and the federal government's Legal Services Corporation.

Her husband's 1980 defeat for reelection as governor was blamed on his liberal leanings; therefore, in his 1982 comeback Bill repackaged himself as a moderate and centrist. Hillary cooperated by becoming Mrs. Bill Clinton, shedding her horn-rims for contacts, blonding her hair, and echoing her husband's more moderate line. These tactics helped propel them back into the governor's mansion. Hillary soon became a full partner in the Rose firm, regularly earning more than $200,000 a year (while Bill earned only $35,000 as Arkansas governor). She won national recognition as one of the "100 most influential lawyers in the United States," according to the *American National Law Journal.* She chaired the American Bar Association's Commission on Women and the Profession.

In January 1993 newly elected president Bill Clinton named Hillary head of the President's Task Force on National Health Reform. Once installed as the "health czar," she moved expeditiously in the corridors of power. Her task force assembled a formidable array of staff, consultants, and committees and produced a 1,342-page bill that reorganized the nation's entire health care system. The *New York Times* dubbed her "St. Hillary" because of her unyielding commitment and determination[*]—qualities that did not stand her in good stead with powerful interest groups such as the American Medical Association and the American Association of Retired Persons, or with the members of Congress in whose hands the fate of the health care plan rested.

Indeed, Hillary's uncompromising liberalism may have contributed to the defeat of the Clinton comprehensive health care plan. She blamed "the special interests" for its defeat. Later, she avoided direct policy-making responsibilities, lowering her public profile and assuming a more traditional, supporting First Lady role.

---

[*]*New York Times Magazine,* May 23, 1993, p. 64.

not otherwise qualify as poor but who are not covered by private insurance. And he proposed to extend Medicare to the "near elderly," persons between the ages of 55 and 65, who have no health insurance.

Interest-Group Battles   Interest-group battles over the details of health care reform have been intense. Virtually everyone has a financial stake in any proposal to reorganize the nation's health care system.

- Employers, especially small businesses, are fearful of added costs.
- Physicians strongly oppose price controls and treatment guidelines, as well as programs that take away patient choice of physician or force all physicians into health maintenance organizations (HMOs). Overall, support is strongest among those physicians most likely to benefit from the low-cost plans—general family practitioners—and weakest among those most likely to lose—medical specialists.
- Psychiatrists, psychologists, mental health and drug abuse counselors, physical therapists, chiropractors, optometrists, and dentists all want their own services covered. Providing such "comprehensive" services greatly increases costs.
- Drug companies want to see prescription drugs paid for, but they vigorously oppose price controls on drugs.
- Hospitals want all patients to be insured but oppose government payment schedules.
- Medical specialists fear that proposals for managed care will result in fewer consultations, and medical manufacturers fear it will limit use of high-priced equipment.
- The powerful senior citizens' lobby wants added benefits—including coverage for drugs, eyeglasses, dental care, and nursing homes—but fears folding Medicare into a larger health care system.
- Veterans' groups want to retain separate VA hospitals and medical services.
- Opponents of abortion rights are prepared to do battle to keep national coverage from including such procedures, whereas many supporters of abortion rights will not back any plan that excludes abortion services.

Harry and Louise puzzle over the Clinton health care plan in one of a series of ads sponsored by the health insurance industry that helped kill the plan.

Although polls show that a majority of Americans are willing to pay higher taxes for comprehensive health care, many are willing to see increases only in "sin taxes" on alcohol, tobacco, and guns.

SUMMARY NOTES

- Social welfare policy largely determines who gets what from government; over half of the federal budget is devoted to "human resources." The government is a major redistributor of income from group to group.
- The poor are not the principal beneficiaries of social welfare spending. Only about one-fifth of all federal social welfare spending is means tested. Most social welfare spending, including the largest programs—Social Security and Medicare—goes to the middle class.
- About 13 to 15 percent of the U.S. population falls below the annual cash income level that the federal government sets as its official definition of poverty.

Politics in Cyberspace

Social Welfare

A number of government agencies and private organizations maintain Web sites devoted to social welfare and health-care issues.

Department of Health And Human Services
http://www.dhhs.gov

In addition to information on federal social welfare programs, the HHS Web site includes a "health finder" gateway to health and human service information.

Healthfinder
http://www.healthfinder.gov

The Healthfinder Web site can lead you to selected on-line publications, databases, Web sites, and support and self-help groups, as well as government agencies and not-for-profit organizations that provide information on health and human services needs.

Fedstats
http://www.fedstats.gov

This is the federal government's search engine for statistics maintained on the Internet by all federal departments and agencies. An alphabetical index includes many social welfare topics, including children, health care, causes of death, life expectancy, infant mortality, HIV/AIDS, poverty, and unemployment.

Children's Defense Fund
http://www.childrensdefense.org

The Children's Defense Fund lobbies vocally in Washington on behalf of "the needs of the poor, minorities, children, and those with disabilities."

American Medical Association
http://www.ama-assn.org

The American Medical Association is the leading organization representing the nation's physicians. Its Web site includes press releases, policy statements, legislative positions, information for medical consumers, and access to the prestigious *Journal of the American Medical Association*.

Urban Institute
http://www.urban.org

The Urban Institute is a nonprofit policy research organization established in Washington, D.C., in 1968. It investigates social and economic problems confronting the nation, and government policies and public and private programs designed to alleviate them.

But this definition includes cash income from welfare programs; without government aid, perhaps 25 percent of the population would fall below the poverty line. In contrast, the official poverty count includes many people receiving in-kind benefits and others for whom low current incomes do not create real hardship.

- Poverty is temporary for many families, but some poverty is persistent—lasting five years to a lifetime. Prolonged poverty and welfare dependency create an "underclass" beset by many social and economic problems. Poverty is more frequent among families headed by single mothers; about one of every five children in the United States is raised in poverty.

- Nearly one-third of the U.S. population receives some form of government payments or benefits. Entitlements are government benefits for which Congress has set eligibility criteria by law. Social Security and Medicare are the largest entitlement programs. The elderly are entitled to these benefits regardless of their income or wealth.

- Senior citizens are politically powerful; they vote more often than younger people and they have powerful lobbying organizations in Washington. Social Security is the largest single item in the federal budget. Yet proposals to modify Social Security or Medicare benefits are politically dangerous. Nevertheless, concerns over the future financing of these programs, which are now being funded out of current receipts, have led some politicians to call for reconsideration of COLAs and of payments to wealthy retirees.

- Public assistance programs, including Family Assistance, Supplemental Security Income, and food stamps, require recipients to show that they are poor in order to claim benefits.

- Social welfare policies seek to alleviate hardship; at the same time they seek to avoid creating disincentives to work. Cash welfare payments may, for example, encourage teenage pregnancies, undermine family foundations, and contribute to long-term social dependency. Welfare reforms center on moving former welfare recipients into the work force. But doing so may require increased spending on education, job training, health care, and child care.

- Welfare reform in 1996 offers block grants to the states to replace federal entitlements to cash payments and sets time limits on welfare enrollment.

- Americans spend more on health care than citizens of any other nation, yet we fail to insure almost 15 percent of the population. And the United States ranks below many other advanced nations in common health measures.

- Health care reform centers on two related problems—extending health insurance coverage to all Americans and containing the skyrocketing costs of health care. Proposals for extending coverage include national health insurance and mandatory employer-sponsored health insurance, as well as more modest proposals to extend government programs to children and all persons over fifty-five.

- President Clinton failed to win passage in Congress of a large-scale comprehensive restructuring of health care in the United States. But Congress acted to guarantee continuing employer insurance coverage for workers who lose or change jobs.

SELECTED READINGS

JENKS, CHRISTOPHER. *Rethinking Social Policy: Race, Poverty, and the Underclass.* Cambridge, Mass.: Harvard University Press, 1992. Series of essays by a leading commentator on social welfare policy, including the thesis that welfare dependency is primarily a product of the fact that low-wage jobs pay less than welfare.

JENKS, CHRISTOPHER, and PAUL E. PETERSON, EDS. *The Urban Underclass.* Washington, D.C.: Brookings Institution, 1991. Collection of essays arguing that "the most important problem—the rise in the percentage of children living in poverty—is due to the increasing number of female-headed households and the decline in the earnings of young men."

KELSO, WILLIAM A. *Poverty and the Underclass.* New York: New York University Press, 1994. Excellent introduction to the debate about poverty in America, summarizing the existing research on the causes of poverty and describing how contemporary views of the poor are changing.

MARMOR, THEODORE R., JERRY L. MASHAW, and PHILIP L. HARVEY. *America's Misunderstood Welfare State.* New York: Basic Books, 1990. An argument that ideological debate over welfare overstates major criticisms of the welfare state and obscures general agreement among Americans on the structure of the "opportunity-insurance state."

MEAD, LAWRENCE M. *The New Politics of Poverty.* New York: Basic Books, 1992. A persuasive argument that the underlying problem of poverty today is one of social values—resocializing the dependent poor—rather than the provision of jobs.

MURRAY, CHARLES. *Losing Ground.* New York: Basic Books, 1984. A well-argued, yet controversial, thesis that government social welfare programs, by encouraging social dependence, have had the unintended and perverse effect of slowing and even reversing earlier progress in reducing poverty, crime, ignorance, and discrimination.

WILSON, WILLIAM JULIUS. *The Truly Disadvantaged.* Chicago: University of Chicago Press, 1987. The thesis that the growth of the underclass is primarily a result of the decline of manufacturing jobs and their shift to the suburbs, and the resulting concentration of poor, jobless, isolated people in the inner city.

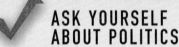

ASK YOURSELF ABOUT POLITICS

1 Has the United Nations been effective in maintaining world peace?
Yes ☐   No ☐

2 Should the United States and NATO intervene in regional conflicts in Eastern Europe?
Yes ☐   No ☐

3 Should the United States build a ballistic missile defense system even if it is very costly?
Yes ☐   No ☐

4 Is Russia likely to pose a military threat to Western Europe anytime in the future?
Yes ☐   No ☐

5 Is the president justified in placing U.S. troops in danger where U.S. vital interests are not at stake?
Yes ☐   No ☐

6 Are U.S. military force levels today sufficient to deal with potential regional aggressors such as Iran, Iraq, and North Korea?
Yes ☐   No ☐

7 Should the United States destroy all of its nuclear weapons now that the Cold War is over?
Yes ☐   No ☐

POLITICS AND NATIONAL SECURITY

18

CHAPTER OUTLINE

Power among Nations

The Legacy of the Cold War

The Nuclear Threat

Post–Cold War Threats

The Use of Military Force

Military Force Levels

FEATURES

A Conflicting View: We Should Defend Ourselves against a Ballistic Missile Attack

What Do You Think? What Should Be Our Foreign Policy Priorities?

Up Close: The Use of Force: Operation Desert Storm

Compared to What? Citizens' Knowledge of the World

Politics in Cyberspace: National Security

America must decide how to use its national power in world affairs. Should we intervene with military forces in pursuit of humanitarian goals and to keep the peace in war-torn lands? Or should we only use military force when vital national interests are at stake?

POWER AMONG NATIONS

International politics, like all politics, is a struggle for power. The struggle for power is global; it involves all the nations and peoples of the world, whatever their goals or ideals. As the distinguished political scientist Hans Morgenthau once observed,

> Whatever the ultimate aims of international politics, power is always the immediate aim. Statesmen and peoples may ultimately seek freedom, security, prosperity, or power itself. They may define their goals in terms of a religious, philosophic, economic, or social ideal. . . . But whenever they strive to realize their goal by means of international politics, they are striving for power.[1]

The struggle for power among nations has led to many attempts over the centuries to bring order to the international system.

The Balance-of-Power System One method of trying to bring order to international relations is the **balance-of-power** system. In the eighteenth and nineteenth centuries, nations deliberately attempted to stabilize international relations by creating systems of alliances designed to balance the power of one group of nations against the power of another, and thus to discourage war. For almost an entire century—from the end of the Napoleonic Wars (1815) until the outbreak of World War I (1914)—the balance-of-power system appeared to be at least partially effective in Europe. But an important defect in the balance-of-power system is that a small conflict between two nations which are members of separate alliances can draw all the member nations of both alliances into the conflict and thus can quickly turn a small conflict into a major war. This is essentially what happened in World War I, when a minor conflict in the Balkan nations resulted in a very destructive war between the Allied Powers (England, France, Russia, and eventually the United States) and the Central Powers (Germany, Austria-Hungary, and Turkey). Indeed, World War I proved so destructive (10 million men were killed on the battlefield between 1914 and 1918) it provoked a worldwide demand to replace the balance-of-power system with a new arrangement—collective security.

Collective Security Originally, **collective security** meant that *all* nations would join together to guarantee each other's "territorial integrity and existing political independence" against "external aggression" by any nation. This was the idea behind the League of Nations, established in 1919. However, opposition to international involvement was so great in the United States after World War I that, after a lengthy debate, the Senate refused to enroll the United States in the League of Nations. More important, the League of Nations failed to deal with acts of aggression by the Axis Powers—Germany, Japan, and Italy—in the 1930s. During that decade, Japan invaded Manchuria, Italy invaded Ethiopia, and Germany dismembered Czechoslovakia. The result was a war even more devastating than World War I: World War II cost more than 40 million lives, both civilian and military.

Formation of the United Nations Even after World War II, the notion of collective security remained an ideal of the victorious Allied Powers. The Charter of the United Nations, signed in 1945, provided for the following organization:

- The Security Council, with eleven member nations, five of them being permanent members—the United States, the **Soviet Union** (whose membership is now held by Russia), Britain, France, and China—and each having the power to veto any action by the Security Council.
- The General Assembly, composed of all the member nations, each with a single vote.
- The Secretariat, headed by a Secretary General with a staff at United Nations headquarters in New York.
- Organizations to handle specialized affairs—for example, the Economic and Social Council, the Trusteeship Council, and the International Court of Justice at The Hague in the Netherlands.

The Security Council has the "primary responsibility" for maintaining "international peace and security." The General Assembly has authority over "any matter affecting the peace of the world," although it is supposed to defer to the Security Council when the council has already taken up a particular security matter. No

balance of power Attempt to bring order to international relations in the eighteenth and nineteenth centuries by creating a system of alliances among nations so the relative strength of each alliance balanced that of the others.

collective security Attempt to bring order to international relations by all nations joining together to guarantee each other's "territorial integrity" and "independence" against "external aggression."

Soviet Union The Union of Soviet Socialist Republics (USSR) consisting of Russia and its bordering lands and ruled by the communist regime in Moscow, officially dissolved in 1991.

nation has a veto in the General Assembly; every nation has one vote, regardless of its size or power. Most resolutions can be passed by a majority vote.

The United Nations in the Cold War   The United Nations (UN) proved largely ineffective during the long Cold War confrontation between the communist nations, led by the Soviet Union, and the Western democracies, led by the United States. The UN grew from its original 51 member nations to 185, but most of those nations were headed by authoritarian regimes of one kind or another. The Western democracies were outnumbered in the General Assembly, and the Soviet Union frequently used its veto to prevent action by the Security Council. Anti-Western and antidemocratic speeches became common in the General Assembly.

During the Cold War, the UN was overshadowed by the confrontation of the world's two **superpowers**: the United States and the Soviet Union. Indeed, international conflicts throughout the world—in the Middle East, Africa, Latin America, Southeast Asia, and elsewhere—were usually influenced by some aspect of the superpower struggle.

Regional Security   The general disappointment with the United Nations as a form of collective security gave rise as early as 1949 to a different approach: **regional security**. In response to aggressive Soviet moves in Europe, the United States and the democracies of Western Europe created the **North Atlantic Treaty Organization (NATO)**. In the NATO treaty, fifteen Western nations agreed to collective regional security: they agreed that "an armed attack against one or more [NATO nations] . . . shall be considered an attack against them all." The United States made a specific commitment to defend Western Europe in the event of a Soviet attack. A joint NATO military command was established (with Dwight D. Eisenhower as its first commander) to coordinate the defense of Western Europe.

After the formation of NATO, the Soviets made no further advances into Western Europe. The Soviets themselves, in response to NATO, drew up the Warsaw Pact, a comparable treaty with their own Eastern European satellite nations. But for many years the real deterrent to Warsaw Pact expansion was not the weak NATO armies but rather the pledge of the United States to use its strategic nuclear bomber force to inflict "massive retaliation" on the Soviet Union itself in the event of an attack on Western Europe.

The Warsaw Pact disintegrated following the dramatic collapse of the communist governments of Eastern Europe in 1989. Former Warsaw Pact nations—Poland, Hungary, Romania, Bulgaria, and East Germany—threw out their ruling communist regimes and demanded the withdrawal of Soviet troops from their territory. The Berlin Wall was dismantled in 1989, and Germany was formally reunified in 1990, bringing together the 61 million prosperous people of West Germany and the 17 million less affluent people of East Germany. (Unified Germany continues as a member of NATO.) The Communist Party was ousted from power in Moscow, and the Soviet Union collapsed in 1991. Its former member nations, including Russia, Ukraine, and Belarus, continue to struggle toward democratic reforms.

The UN Today   The end of the Cold War has injected new vitality into the United Nations. Russia inherited the UN Security Council seat of the former Soviet Union, and the government of President Boris Yeltsin has generally cooperated in UN efforts to bring stability to various regional conflicts. No longer are these

superpowers   Refers to the United States and the Soviet Union after World War II, when these two nations dominated international politics.

regional security   Attempt to bring order to international relations during the Cold War by creating regional alliances between a superpower and nations of a particular region.

North Atlantic Treaty Organization (NATO)   Mutual-security agreement and joint military command uniting the nations of Western Europe, initially formed to resist Soviet expansionism.

Senate Foreign Relations Committee Chairman Jesse Helms (right) shows U.N. Secretary General Kofi Annan to his office. Helms, insisting on financial cutbacks at the U.N., has helped block the payment of delinquent dues the United States owes the international organization.

conflicts "proxy" wars between the superpowers. Greater cooperation among the permanent members of the Security Council (the United States, Great Britain, France, China, and Russia) has brought "a new world order" to international politics. The UN has sent blue-helmeted "peacekeeping" forces to monitor cease-fires in many troubled areas of the world. But the United Nations and its Security Council must rely on "the last remaining superpower," the United States, to take the lead in enforcing its resolutions.

The United Nations has created a huge bloated bureaucracy at its headquarters in New York City. Its costs, and the costs of UN peacekeeping missions, have been high. The United States is assessed the largest single-nation share of the UN budget (25 percent). But the United States is regularly delinquent in its payments; the Congress has insisted on reductions and efficiencies in the UN budget as a prerequisite to U.S. payment. Secretary of State Madeleine Albright has urged Congress to support the United Nations, arguing that when the United States undertakes a peacekeeping mission alone it pays all of the costs and its troops run all of the risks; whereas, if the UN does so, the United States pays only one-quarter of the costs and its troops share the risks with those of other nations.

THE LEGACY OF THE COLD WAR

For more than forty years following the end of World War II, the United States and the Soviet Union confronted each other in the protracted political, military, and ideological struggle known as the **Cold War**.

Origins   During World War II, the United States and the Soviet Union joined forces to eliminate the Nazi threat to the world. The United States dismantled its military forces at the end of the war in 1945, but the Soviet Union, under the brutal dictatorship of Josef Stalin, used the powerful Red Army to install communist governments in the nations of Eastern Europe in violation of wartime agreements to allow free elections. Stalin also ignored pledges to cooperate in a unified allied occupation of Germany; Germany was divided, and in 1948 Stalin unsuccessfully tried to oust the United States, Britain, and France from Berlin in a year-long "Berlin Blockade." Former British Prime Minister Winston Churchill warned the United States as early as 1946 that the Soviets were dividing Europe with an "Iron Curtain." When Soviet-backed communist forces threatened Greece and Turkey in 1947, President Harry S. Truman responded with a pledge to "support free people who are resisting attempted subjugation by armed minorities or by outside pressures," a policy that became known as the **Truman Doctrine**.

Containment   The United States had fought two world wars to maintain democracy in Western Europe. The new threat of Soviet expansionism and communist world revolution caused America to assume world leadership on behalf of the preservation of democracy. In an influential article in the Council on Foreign Relation's journal, *Foreign Affairs,* the State Department's Russian expert, George F. Kennan, called for a policy of **containment**:

> It is clear that the main element of any United States policy toward the Soviet Union must be that of a long-term, vigilant containment of Russian expansive tendencies. . . . Soviet pressure against the free institutions of the western world is something that can be contained by the adroit and vigilant application of counterforce.[2]

Cold War   Political, military, and ideological struggle between the United States and the Soviet Union following the end of World War II and ending with the collapse of the Soviet Union's communist government in 1991.

Truman Doctrine   U.S. foreign policy, first articulated by President Harry S. Truman, that pledged the United States to "support free peoples who are resisting attempted subjugation by armed minorities or by outside pressures."

containment   Policy of preventing an enemy from expanding its boundaries and/or influence, specifically the U.S. foreign policy vis-à-vis the Soviet Union during the Cold War.

To implement the containment policy, the United States first initiated the **Marshall Plan**, named for Secretary of State George C. Marshall, to rebuild the economies of the Western European nations. Marshall reasoned that *economically* weak nations were more susceptible to communist subversion and Soviet intimidation. The subsequent formation of NATO provided the necessary *military* support to contain the Soviet Union.

The Korean War   The first military test of the containment policy came in June 1950, when communist North Korean armies invaded South Korea. President Truman assumed that the North Koreans were acting on behalf of their sponsor, the Soviet Union. The Soviets had already aided Chinese communists under the leadership of Mao Zedong in capturing control of mainland China in 1949. The United States quickly brought the Korean invasion issue to the Security Council. With the Soviets boycotting this meeting because the Council had refused to seat the new communist delegation from China, the Council passed a resolution calling on member nations to send troops to repel the invasion.

America's conventional (non-nuclear) military forces had been largely dismantled after World War II. Moreover, President Truman insisted on keeping most of the nation's forces in Europe, fearing that the Korean invasion was a diversion to be followed by a Soviet invasion of Western Europe. But General Douglas MacArthur, in a brilliant amphibious landing at Inchon behind North Korean lines, destroyed a much larger enemy army, captured the North Korean capital, and moved northward toward the Chinese border. Then in December 1950, disaster struck American forces as a million-strong Chinese army entered the conflict. Chinese troops surprised the Americans, inflicting heavy casualties, trapping entire units, and forcing U.S. troops to beat a hasty retreat. General MacArthur urged retaliation against China, but Truman sought to keep the war "limited." When MacArthur publicly protested political limits to military operations, Truman dismissed the popular general. The Korean War became a bloody stalemate.

Dwight Eisenhower was elected president in 1952 in large measure because of public frustration over "Korea, communism, and corruption." Eisenhower had promised to "go to Korea" to end the increasingly unpopular war. He also threatened to use nuclear weapons in the conflict but eventually agreed to a settlement along the original border between North and South Korea. Communist expansion in Korea was "contained," but at a high price: the United States lost more than 38,000 men in the war.

The Cuban Missile Crisis   Throughout the Cold War, the Soviet Union sought to expand its political and military presence among **Third World** nations. Many nations of Africa and Asia had recently replaced British, French, and Dutch colonial regimes, and resentment toward colonialism fueled anti-Western and anti-American politics around the world. The United States initially welcomed Fidel Castro's overthrow of the repressive Batista regime in Cuba in 1959, but when Castro allied his government with Moscow and invited Soviet military intervention into the Western Hemisphere, Washington sought his ouster. Under President Eisenhower, the Central Intelligence Agency (CIA) had planned a large "covert" operation—an invasion of Cuba by a brigade of Cuban exiles. Newly installed President John F. Kennedy approved the Bay of Pigs operation in early 1961, but when Castro's air force destroyed the makeshift invasion fleet offshore, Kennedy refused to provide U.S. air support. The surviving Cubans were forced to surrender.

Marshall Plan   U.S. program to rebuild the nations of Western Europe in the aftermath of World War II in order to render them less susceptible to communist influence and takeover.

Third World   Those nations of the world that remain economically underdeveloped.

The young president was tested again in 1961, when the Russians erected the Berlin Wall, physically dividing that city. Despite heated rhetoric, Kennedy did nothing. Eventually the wall would become a symbol of Soviet repression.

The most serious threat of nuclear holocaust during the entire Cold War was the Cuban missile crisis. In 1962 Soviet Premier Nikita Khrushchev sought to secretly install medium-range nuclear missiles in Cuba in an effort to give the Soviet Union nuclear capability against U.S. cities. In October 1962 intelligence photos showing Soviet missiles at Cuban bases touched off a thirteen-day crisis. President Kennedy rejected advice to launch an air strike to destroy the missiles before they could be activated. Instead, he publicly announced a naval blockade of Cuba, threatening to halt Soviet missile-carrying vessels at sea by force if necessary. The prospect of war appeared imminent; U.S. nuclear forces went on alert. Secretly, Kennedy proposed to withdraw U.S. nuclear missiles from Turkey in exchange for Soviet withdrawal of nuclear missiles from Cuba. Khrushchev's agreement to the deal appeared to the world as a backing down; Secretary of State Dean Rusk would boast, "We were eyeball to eyeball, and they blinked." Kennedy would be hailed for his statesmanship in the crisis; Khrushchev would soon lose his job.

The Vietnam War   U.S. involvement in Vietnam grew out of the policy of containment. President Eisenhower had declined to intervene in the former French colony in 1956 when communist forces led by Ho Chi Minh defeated French forces at the battle of Dien Bien Phu. The resulting Geneva Accords divided that country into North Vietnam, with a communist government, and South Vietnam, with a U.S.-backed government. When South Vietnamese communist (Vietcong) guerrilla forces threatened the South Vietnamese government in the early 1960s, President Kennedy sent a force of more than 12,000 advisers and counterinsurgency forces to assist in every aspect of training and support for the Army of the Republic of Vietnam (ARVN). By 1964 units of the North Vietnamese Army (NVA) had begun to supplement the Vietcong guerrilla forces in the south. Unconfirmed reports of an attack on U.S. Navy vessels by North Vietnamese torpedo boats led the U.S. Congress to pass the Gulf of Tonkin Resolution, which authorized the

President Kennedy meeting with his Cabinet during the Cuban missile crisis, which brought the United States and the Soviet Union to the brink of nuclear war in 1962.

president to take "all necessary measures" to repel any armed attack against any U.S. forces in Southeast Asia.

In February 1965 President Lyndon B. Johnson ordered U.S. combat troops into South Vietnam and authorized a gradual increase in air strikes against North Vietnam. The fateful decision to commit U.S. ground combat forces to Vietnam was made without any significant effort to mobilize American public opinion, the government, or the economy for war. On the contrary, the president minimized the U.S. military effort, placed numerical limits on U.S. troop strength in Vietnam, limited bombing targets, and underestimated North Vietnam's military capabilities as well as expected U.S. casualties. U.S. ground troops were forbidden to cross into North Vietnam, and only once (in Cambodia in 1970) were they instructed to attack NVA forces elsewhere in Indochina.

Washington committed more than 500,000 troops to a war of attrition, a war in which U.S. firepower was expected to inflict sufficient casualties on the enemy to force a peace settlement. But over time, the failure to achieve any decisive military victories eroded popular support for the war.

On January 31, 1968, the Vietnam holiday of Tet, Vietcong forces blasted their way into the U.S. embassy compound in Saigon and held the courtyard for six hours. The attack was part of a massive, coordinated Tet offensive against all major cities of South Vietnam. U.S. forces responded and inflicted very heavy casualties on the Vietcong. By any military measure, the Tet offensive was a "defeat" for the enemy and a "victory" for U.S. forces. Yet the Tet offensive was Hanoi's greatest *political* victory. Television pictures of bloody fighting in Saigon and Hue seemed to mock President Johnson's promises of an early end to the war. The media launched a long and bitter campaign against the war effort.

On March 31, 1968, President Johnson went on national television to make a dramatic announcement: he halted the bombing of North Vietnam and asked Hanoi for peace talks, concluding, "I shall not seek, and I will not accept, the nomination of my party for another term as your president." Formal peace talks opened in Paris on May 13.

American objectives in Vietnam shifted again with the arrival in Washington of the new president, Richard Nixon, and his national security adviser, Henry Kissinger. Nixon and Kissinger knew the war must be ended, but they sought to end it "honorably." The South Vietnamese could not be abruptly abandoned without threatening the credibility of American commitments everywhere in the world. They also sought a peace settlement that would give South Vietnam a reasonable chance to survive. Toward these ends, they worked to create **détente**—relaxation of tension—with the Soviet Union and a new relationship with communist China. But even in the absence of a settlement with the communists in Vietnam, Nixon began the withdrawal of U.S. troops under the guise of "Vietnamization" of the war effort. ARVN forces were required to take up the burden of fighting as U.S. forces withdrew.

Unable to persuade Hanoi to make even the slightest concession at Paris, President Nixon sought to demonstrate American strength and resolve. In December 1972 the United States unleashed a devastating air attack directly on Hanoi for the first time. Critics at home labeled Nixon's action "the Christmas bombing," but when negotiations resumed in Paris in January, the North Vietnamese quickly agreed to peace on the terms that Kissinger and Le Duc Tho had worked out earlier.

The South Vietnamese government lasted two years after the agreement. The United States fulfilled none of its pledges, to either South or North Vietnam. Congress refused to provide significant military aid to the South Vietnamese. The

détente Relaxation of strained relations between nations, specifically used to refer to the relaxation of tensions between the United States and the Soviet Union during the Cold War.

Watergate scandal forced Nixon's resignation in August 1974. In early 1975 Hanoi decided that the Americans would not "jump back in" and therefore "the opportune moment" was at hand for a new invasion. President Gerald Ford's requests to Congress for emergency military aid to the South Vietnamese fell on deaf ears. U.S. Ambassador Graham Martin, embarrassed by his government's abandonment of Vietnam, delayed implementation of escape plans until the last moment. As Saigon (now Ho Chi Minh City) fell to the North Vietnamese in April 1975, the United States abandoned hundreds of thousands of loyal Vietnamese who had fought alongside the Americans for years.[3] The spectacle of U.S. Marines using their rifle butts to keep desperate Vietnamese from boarding helicopters on the roof of the U.S. embassy "provided a tragic epitaph for twenty-five years of American involvement in Vietnam."[4]

The Vietnam Syndrome   America's humiliation in Vietnam had lasting national consequences. The United States suffered 47,378 battle deaths and missing-in-action among the 2.8 million U.S. personnel who served in Vietnam. A new isolationism permeated American foreign policy following defeat in Vietnam. The slogan "No more Vietnams" was used to oppose any U.S. military intervention, whether or not U.S. vital interests were at stake. Disillusionment replaced idealism. American leaders had exaggerated the importance of Vietnam; now Americans were unwilling to believe their leaders when they warned of other dangers.

In the late 1970s the Soviet Union rapidly expanded its political and military presence in Asia, Africa, the Middle East, Central America, and the Caribbean. The United States did little to respond to this new wave of Soviet expansionism until the Soviet invasion of Afghanistan in 1979, when President Jimmy Carter authorized the largest covert action in CIA history—the military support of the Afghan guerrilla forces fighting Soviet occupation. The Soviets suffered a heavy drain of human and economic resources in their nine-year war in Afghanistan, which some dubbed "Russia's Vietnam."

Rebuilding America's Defenses   The decision to rebuild Western military forces and reassert international leadership on behalf of democratic values gained

The Vietnam War Memorial in Washington, D.C., is inscribed with the names of the nearly 50,000 Americans who died in Vietnam. America's defeat fostered a lasting skepticism about the wisdom of foreign military intervention, leading to a new isolationism in foreign policy.

widespread support in the Western world. In 1979 President Jimmy Carter presented Congress with the first request for an increase in defense spending in more than a decade. British Prime Minister Margaret Thatcher, French President François Mitterrand, and German Chancellor Helmut Kohl all pledged to increase their defense efforts and all held fast against a "nuclear freeze" movement that would have locked in Soviet superiority in European-based nuclear weapons. When the Reagan Administration arrived in Washington in 1981, the defense buildup had already begun.

The Reagan defense buildup extended through 1985—with increases in defense spending, improvements in strategic nuclear weapons, and, perhaps more important, the rebuilding and reequipping of U.S. conventional forces. The American and NATO defense buildup, together with the promise of a new, expensive, and technologically sophisticated race for ballistic missile defenses, forecast heavy additional strains on the weak economy of the Soviet Union. Thus, in 1985, when new Soviet President Mikhail Gorbachev came to power, the stage was set for an end to the Cold War.

Gorbachev, Perestroika, and Glasnost   Mikhail Gorbachev was committed to **perestroika** (restructuring)—the reform and strengthening of communism in the nation. Differing with many earlier interpretations of Marxism-Leninism, he increasingly turned to the principle of "material interest"—large rewards for better labor and management performance. He also encouraged greater decentralization in industry and less reliance on centralized state direction. At the same time, he called for **glasnost** (openness) in Soviet life and politics, removing many restrictions on speech, press, and religion and permitting free elections, with noncommunist candidates running for and winning elective office.

Gorbachev also announced reductions in the size of the Soviet military and reached agreements with the United States on the reduction of nuclear forces. More important, in 1988 he announced that the Soviet Union would no longer use its military forces to keep communist governments in power in Eastern European nations. This stunning announcement, for which he received the Nobel Peace Prize in 1990, encouraged opposition democratic forces in Poland (the Solidarity movement), Czechoslovakia, Hungary, Bulgaria, Romania, and East Germany. Gorbachev refused to intervene to halt the destruction of the Berlin Wall, despite pleas by the East German hard-line communist leader Erich Honecker.

The Collapse of Communism   Gorbachev's economic and political reforms threatened powerful interests in the Soviet Union—the Communist Party *apparatchniks* (bureaucrats), who were losing control over economic enterprises; the military leaders, who opposed the withdrawal of Soviet troops from Germany and Eastern Europe; the KGB police, whose terror tactics were increasingly restricted; and central government officials, who were afraid of losing power to the republics. These interests slowed perestroika and forced Gorbachev into many compromises that led to a rapid deterioration of the Soviet economy and the emergence of disorders and disturbances in various republics seeking independence. Democratic forces, led by Boris Yeltsin, the first elected president of the Russian Republic, were strongly critical of Gorbachev's reluctance to speed reforms. But when hard-liners in the Communist Party, the military, and the KGB attempted the forcible removal of Gorbachev in August 1991, democratic forces rallied to his support. Led by Yeltsin, thousands of demonstrators took to the streets, Soviet military

perestroika   Russian term meaning "restructuring," referring to Mikhail Gorbachev's policy of restructuring the Soviet system.

glasnost   Russian term meaning "openness," referring to Mikhail Gorbachev's removal of many restrictions on individual freedom in the Soviet Union.

The destruction of the Berlin Wall in 1989 dramatically symbolized the end of the Cold War and the collapse of Soviet authority over Eastern Europe.

forces stood aside, and the coup crumbled. Gorbachev was temporarily restored as president, but Yeltsin emerged as the most influential leader in the nation. The failed coup hastened the demise of the Communist Party. The party's offices and activities were suspended, and investigations of party complicity in the coup attempt were initiated. The party lost legitimacy with the peoples of Russia and the other republics.

The Disintegration of the Soviet Union   Strong independence movements in the republics of the Soviet Union emerged as the authority of the centralized Communist Party in Moscow waned. Lithuania, Estonia, and Latvia—nations that had been forcibly incorporated into the Soviet Union in 1939—led the way to independence in 1991. Soon all of the fifteen republics of the Soviet Union declared their independence, and the Union of Soviet Socialist Republics officially ceased to exist after December 31, 1991. Its president, Mikhail Gorbachev, no longer had a government to preside over. The red flag with its hammer and sickle atop the Kremlin was replaced with the flag of the Russian Republic.

THE NUCLEAR THREAT

Nuclear weaponry has made the world infinitely more dangerous. During the Cold War, the nuclear arsenals of the United States and the Soviet Union threatened a human holocaust. Yet, paradoxically, the very destructiveness of nuclear weapons caused leaders on both sides to exercise extreme caution in their relations with each other. Scores of wars, large and small, were fought by different nations during the Cold War years, yet American and Soviet troops never engaged in direct combat against each other.

Deterrence   To maintain nuclear peace during the Cold War, the United States relied primarily on the policy of **deterrence**. Deterrence is based on the notion that a nation can dissuade a rational enemy from attacking by maintaining the capacity to destroy the enemy's homeland even *after* the nation has suffered a well-executed surprise attack by the enemy. Deterrence assumes that the worst may happen—a surprise first strike against a nation's nuclear forces. It emphasizes **second-strike capability**—the ability of a nation's forces to survive a surprise attack by the enemy and then to inflict an unacceptable level of destruction on the enemy's homeland. Deterrence is really a *psychological* defense against attack; no effective physical defense against a ballistic missile attack exists even today.

MAD Balance of Terror   By the early 1970s, a nuclear balance existed between the superpowers. Neither side could consider launching a nuclear attack because of the terrible consequences that the other side could inflict in retaliation. If neither side could be assured of destroying the other side's retaliatory missiles in a first strike, then a mutual "balance of terror" maintained the nuclear peace. In effect, the populations of each nation were being held hostage against a nuclear attack. Commentators labeled this balance of terror as **mutual assured destruction** deterrence, or MAD.

Limiting Nuclear Arms: SALT   The United States and the Soviet Union engaged in negotiations over nuclear arms control for many years. The development of reconnaissance satellites in the 1960s made it possible for each nation to monitor the strategic weapons possessed by the other. Space photography made cheating on agreements more difficult and thus opened the way for both nations to seek stability through arms control.

Following the election of Richard Nixon as president in 1968, the United States, largely guided by former Harvard professor Henry Kissinger (national security adviser to the president and later secretary of state), began negotiations with the Soviet Union over strategic nuclear arms. In 1972 the two nations concluded two and a half years of Strategic Arms Limitation Talks (SALT) about limiting the nuclear arms race. The agreement, **SALT I**, consisted of a treaty limiting antiballistic missiles (ABMs) and an agreement placing a numerical ceiling on offensive missiles. The ABM treaty reflected the MAD theory that the populations of each nation should be *un*defended in order to hold them hostage against a first strike. Under the offensive-missiles agreement, each side was frozen at the total number of offensive missiles, completed or under construction. Both sides could construct new and more destructive missiles as long as they dismantled an equal number of older missiles. Each nation agreed not to interfere in the satellite intelligence-gathering activities of the other nation. SALT I was the first step forward on the control of nuclear arms; both sides agreed to continue negotiations.

After seven years of difficult negotiations, the United States and the Soviet Union produced the lengthy and complicated **SALT II** treaty in 1979. It set an overall limit on "strategic nuclear launch vehicles"—ICBMs, SLBMs, bombers, and long-range Cruise missiles—at 2,250 for each side. It also limited the number of missiles that could have multiple warheads (MIRVs) and banned new types of

deterrence   U.S. approach to deterring any nuclear attack from the Soviet Union by maintaining a second-strike capability.

Second-strike capability   Ability of a nation's forces to survive a surprise nuclear attack by the enemy and then to retaliate effectively.

Mutual assured destruction (MAD)   Nuclear peace maintained by the capability of each side's missile forces to survive a first strike and inflict heavy damages in retaliation against the aggressor's population.

SALT I   First arms limitation treaty between the United States and the Soviet Union, signed in 1972, limiting the total number of offensive nuclear missiles; the treaty reflected the theory that the population centers of both nations should be left undefended.

SALT II   Lengthy and complicated treaty between the United States and Soviet Union, agreed to in 1979 but never ratified by the U.S. Senate, that set limits on all types of strategic nuclear launch vehicles.

ICBMs, with the exception of one new type of ICBM for each side. When the Soviet Union invaded Afghanistan in 1974, President Carter withdrew the SALT II treaty from Senate consideration. However, President Carter, and later President Reagan, announced that the United States would abide by the provisions of the unratified SALT II treaty as long as the Soviet Union did so.

Reducing Nuclear Arms: START   In negotiations with the Soviets, the Reagan Administration established three central principles of arms control—reductions, equality, and verification. The new goal was to be *reductions* in missiles and warheads, not merely limitations on future numbers and types of weapons, as in previous SALT talks. To symbolize this new direction, President Reagan renamed the negotiations the Strategic Arms *Reductions* Talks, or START.

The **START I** Treaty signed in Moscow in 1991 by presidents George Bush and Mikhail Gorbachev was the first agreement between the nuclear powers that actually resulted in the reduction of strategic nuclear weapons. (Earlier, the Intermediate-Range Nuclear Forces INF Treaty of 1987 eliminated missiles with an intermediate range, between 300 and 3,800 miles; although the portion of each side's nuclear weapons covered by the INF Treaty was small, it set the pattern for future arms control agreements in its provisions for reductions, equality, and verification.) The START I Treaty reduced the total number of deployed strategic nuclear delivery systems (ICBMs, SLBMs, and piloted bombers) to no more than 1,600, a 30 percent reduction from the SALT II level.

The capstone of strategic nuclear arms control is the far-reaching **START II** agreement, signed in 1993 by U.S. President Bush and Russian President Yeltsin. This agreement promises to eliminate the threat of a first-strike nuclear attack by either side. Its most important provision is the agreement to eliminate all multiwarhead (MIRVed) land-based missiles by the year 2003. The Russians will dismantle their powerful SS-18 missiles, the most dangerous threat to the nuclear balance of power. The United States will dismantle the MX missile and convert the three-warheaded Minuteman IIIs into single-warhead missiles. START II also calls for the reduction of overall strategic warheads to 3,500, slashing the nuclear arsenals of both nations by more than two-thirds from Cold War levels (see Figure 18-1).

START I   First treaty between the United States and the Soviet Union that actually reduced the strategic nuclear arms of the superpowers, signed in 1991.

START II   Capstone of strategic nuclear arms control requiring the United States and Russia to reduce total nuclear warheads by more than two-thirds from Cold War levels and to eliminate all multiwarhead land-based missiles by 2003.

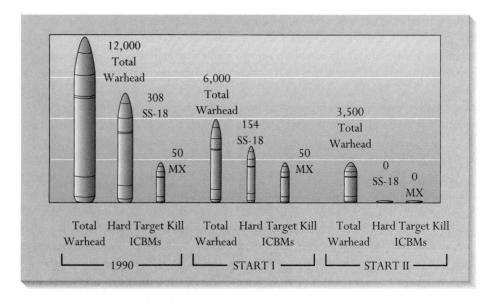

FIGURE 18-1 Strategic Nuclear Arms under START Treaties

Implementation of the Start II Treaty will reduce the total number of warheads in both the United States and Russia by over two-thirds and will completely eliminate hard target kill ICBMs.

The USS Kentucky, *a Trident-class nuclear-powered ballistic missile submarine. The Trident program has survived post–Cold War cuts in the U.S. strategic weapons arsenal.*

Continued Minimal Deterrence   Democratic developments in Russia have radically changed the U.S. assessment of the intentions of Russia's leaders, but its nuclear capabilities remain awesome. The United States has been assured that rational and responsible leaders remain in command and control of this enormous destructive force and that strategic nuclear weapons will be dismantled on schedule in accord with the START treaties. However, defense policy makers in both the Bush and the Clinton administrations have urged the continued maintenance of sufficient strategic nuclear forces to deter nuclear attack or intimidation by any leadership groups that might someday come into control of the awesome arsenal of the former Soviet Union.

To implement minimal deterrence, the United States currently plans to maintain 500 single-warhead Minuteman missiles and to reconfigure most remaining long-range bombers to carry conventional (non-nuclear) weapons. Only the Trident submarine program is relatively unaffected by the cuts in strategic weaponry; the United States maintains a total of eighteen of these ballistic-missile-carrying submarines.

Nuclear Terrorism   Even as the threat of a large-scale nuclear attack recedes, the threats arising from "nondeterrable" sources are increasing. Today, the principal nondeterrable threats are estimated to be (1) missiles launched by a terrorist nation; (2) unauthorized missile launches by elements within the former Soviet Union during periods of internal crisis and turmoil; and (3) accidental missile launches. Global nuclear and ballistic missile proliferation steadily increases over time the likelihood of these types of threats. Terrorist, unauthorized, and accidental launches are considered "nondeterrable" because the threat of nuclear retaliation is largely meaningless.

The threat of mass terror weapons—nuclear, chemical, or biological weapons, especially those carried by medium- or long-range missiles—is likely to increase

A Conflicting View

We Should Defend Ourselves against a Ballistic Missile Attack

For over a half-century, since the terrible nuclear blasts of Hiroshima and Nagasaki in Japan in 1945, the world has avoided nuclear war. Peace has been maintained by deterrence—by the threat of devastating nuclear attacks that would be launched in retaliation to an enemy's first strike. But in 1983 President Ronald Reagan urged that instead of deterring war through fear of retaliation, the United States should seek a technological defense against nuclear missiles, one that would eventually render them "impotent and obsolete."

> Our nuclear retaliating forces have deterred war for forty years. The fact is, however, that we have no defense against ballistic missile attack. . . . In the event that deterrence failed, a president's only recourse would be to surrender or to retaliate. Nuclear retaliation, whether massive or limited, would result in the loss of millions of lives. . . .

If we apply our great scientific and engineering talent to the problem of defending against ballistic missiles, there is a very real possibility that future presidents will be able to deter war by means other than threatening devastation to any aggressor—and by a means which threatens no one.[*]

"Star Wars"   Reagan's Strategic Defense Initiative (SDI) was a research program designed to explore means of destroying enemy nuclear missiles in space before they could reach their targets. Following President Reagan's initial announcement of SDI in March 1983, the press quickly labeled the effort "Star Wars." In theory, a ballistic missile defense (BMD) system could be based in space, orbiting over enemy missile-launching sites. Should an enemy missile get through the space-based defense, a ground-based BMD system would attempt to intercept warheads as they reentered the atmosphere and approached their targets. SDI included research on laser beams, satellite surveillance, computerized battle-management systems, and "smart" and "brilliant" weapons systems.

Global Protection   SDI under President Reagan was a very ambitious program with the goal of creating an "impenetrable shield" that would protect not

---

dramatically in the next century. Iraq, Iran, and Libya, for example, are all likely to acquire mass terror weapons and long-range delivery systems in the absence of any action by the United States to prevent them from doing so. North Korea is already reported to possess nuclear weapons and to be developing long-range missiles to carry them. Defending against terrorist, unauthorized, or accidental missile attacks requires the development and deployment of **ballistic missile defense (BMD)** systems, weapons capable of detecting, intercepting, and destroying ballistic missiles while they are in flight. At present there is no defense against a ballistic missile attack on American cities. Currently, some research is under way on ballistic missile defenses, but plans to actually deploy this defense to protect the U.S. population have been postponed indefinitely (see *A Conflicting View:* "We Should Defend Ourselves against a Ballistic Missile Attack").

POST–COLD WAR THREATS

The end of the Cold War did not eliminate all threats to America's national security. But it did force the United States to reexamine its defense policies, force levels, strategies and tactics, and budget requirements in the light of current and potential threats.

ballistic missile defense (BMD)   Weapons systems capable of detecting, intercepting, and destroying missiles in flight.

only the population of the United States but the population of our allies as well. Reagan argued that such a shield would allow the United States to dismantle its retaliatory nuclear forces, since they would no longer be necessary. Thus during the early Reagan years, SDI focused on developing space-based BMD systems. Later, more realistic goals envisioned combining deterrence with defense; BMDs would be employed to degrade a Soviet first strike and thereby protect U.S. retaliatory forces from complete destruction.

Protection against Nuclear Terrorism   The end of the Cold War refocused SDI away from defense against a massive Russian missile attack to more limited yet more likely threats. Today the principal nuclear threats are missiles launched by a terrorist nation, unauthorized missiles launched by elements within the former Soviet Union, and accidental missile launches. President Bush redirected SDI toward a program called GPALS—Global Protection against a Limited Strike.

The Gulf War experience demonstrated that deterrence may not protect the United States against a ballistic missile attack by a terrorist regime. The success of the Patriot antiballistic missile in destroying short-range Iraqi Scud missiles during the Gulf War demonstrated that enemy missiles could be intercepted in flight. The Patriot is a ground-based "tactical" weapon designed to protect specific military targets. Although developed by the army rather than by SDI, the Patriot silenced critics who had claimed that a successful intercept of an incoming missile was impossible.

The Future of BMDs   Despite the Gulf War experience, opposition to SDI continued in Congress. As a Reagan-era initiative, partisanship tended to cloud the debate over SDI. Although the Democrat-controlled Congress funded most of the money requested by presidents Reagan and Bush for SDI, Congress increasingly diverted money away from research on space-based interceptors toward ground-based systems.

In 1993 President Clinton's secretary of defense, Les Aspin, announced the termination of the separate SDI organization, but he reassured the nation that research would continue on ground-based ballistic missile defenses. However, plans to actually deploy these defenses to protect the U.S. population were postponed indefinitely.

---

[*]President Ronald Reagan, *The President's Strategic Defense Initiative,* The White House, January 3, 1985.

For the first time in almost fifty years, the United States had to design its foreign and defense policies in the absence of the dominant focus provided by the Soviet threat (see *What Do You Think?* "What Should Be Our Foreign Policy Priorities?").

Guarding against a Reversal of Democratic Trends   If Russia, Ukraine, and the other new republics make a full transition to democracy and capitalism, the next century promises much more peace and prosperity for the peoples of the world than the last century. But if they fail, the United States and Western nations will be confronted with many dangers, including the following:

- Continuing economic deterioration in Russia may undermine the weak traditions of democracy. The specter of a "Weimar Russia," in which initial advances toward democracy fail and an authoritarian leader emerges, haunts Europeans who remember the failure of the brief Weimar democracy in Germany before the rise of Adolf Hitler.

- The collapse of the democratic movement may usher in a neo-communist, nationalistic, militarist Russian regime. Such a regime may seek to reassert its control of the new independent republics, or even reassert dominance in Poland and other Eastern European nations.

What Do You Think?

What Should Be Our Foreign Policy Priorities?

During the Cold War, U.S. foreign policy centered on containing Soviet expansionism. But the end of the Cold War required a reassessment of our foreign policy priorities: What should be America's goals in world affairs? What are the vital interests of the United States? What, if anything, should we do to promote democratic values—human rights, self-determination, free markets—around the world? What, if anything, should we do to bring about peace in the Middle East, Africa, the former Yugoslavia, including Bosnia, and in other trouble spots in the world? What, if anything, should we do to prevent hostile regimes from acquiring chemical, biological, or nuclear weapons of mass destruction?

American public opinion is usually less focused on foreign affairs than on domestic issues. Unless war is directly threatened, relatively few Americans spend much time thinking about the Middle East, Korea, Bosnia, or even Cuba, only 90 miles from our shore. Polls asking Americans to rank specific foreign policy priorities (see figure) suggest that they evaluate foreign policy from a domestic viewpoint, giving top priority to international issues that affect life in the United States. Although most Americans would like to see democracy, human rights, and living standards advanced throughout the world, they are more likely to give greater priority to protecting American jobs, preventing the spread of weapons of mass destruction, combating the drug trade, and ensuring low oil prices.

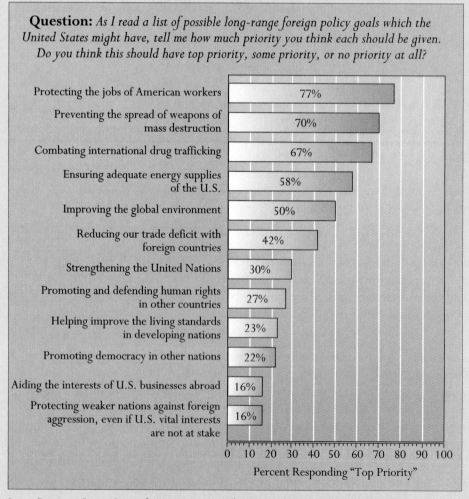

Question: *As I read a list of possible long-range foreign policy goals which the United States might have, tell me how much priority you think each should be given. Do you think this should have top priority, some priority, or no priority at all?*

Protecting the jobs of American workers — 77%
Preventing the spread of weapons of mass destruction — 70%
Combating international drug trafficking — 67%
Ensuring adequate energy supplies of the U.S. — 58%
Improving the global environment — 50%
Reducing our trade deficit with foreign countries — 42%
Strengthening the United Nations — 30%
Promoting and defending human rights in other countries — 27%
Helping improve the living standards in developing nations — 23%
Promoting democracy in other nations — 22%
Aiding the interests of U.S. businesses abroad — 16%
Protecting weaker nations against foreign aggression, even if U.S. vital interests are not at stake — 16%

Percent Responding "Top Priority"

Source: Princeton Survey Research Associates, September 4–11, 1997, as reported in *The Polling Report*, October 27, 1997.

- Continuing differences between the republics of the former Soviet Union, and the rekindling of ancient hatreds among ethnic groups, may result in armed conflict. With nuclear weapons, the potential for disaster is far greater than in other regions of the world that have experienced ethnic conflicts.
- A breakdown of nuclear command and control may result in the sale of nuclear weapons to terrorists or terrorist regimes.

The Russian government is already confronted with the problem of consolidating its authority throughout the Russian Republic itself. Many non-Russian ethnic minorities remain within its borders, including the Muslims of Chechnya, who have already resorted to arms to assert their independence.

Western Europe and the Future of NATO   The residual threat to Western Europe posed by Russian forces, even under a hostile regime, is currently very weak. The Russian military, more than 4 million strong as late as 1990, is now down to fewer than 2 million, a number smaller than the forces of the European NATO countries, exclusive of U.S. forces. Moreover, Russian military morale is reported to be low and equipment in disrepair. Even if an anti-Western regime were to emerge in Moscow, considerable time would be required to reconstitute a Russian force capable of threatening Western Europe.

The United States currently agrees with its Western European allies that NATO should remain as the anchor of American commitment to European security. But a question confronting policy makers is the level of U.S. troop deployments in Europe. The total withdrawal of U.S. military forces from Europe would probably mean an end to the NATO alliance. The United States has already reduced its "forward presence" in Europe by more than half. Proponents of a continued U.S. military presence in Europe argue that it provides reassurance and stability as democracy emerges in Eastern Europe; they note that both its old allies and its new friends in Europe have urged the United States to remain involved in European security. Opponents counter that the Western European nations are now quite capable of shouldering the burden of their own security.

NATO Expansion   Yet another post–Cold War question that confronted NATO was whether or not to expand its security protections to the newly democratic nations of Eastern Europe. Three nations—Poland, Hungary, and the Czech Republic—made an especially credible appeal for membership. All three peoples had previously attempted to resist Soviet (Russian) military intervention during the Cold War, and all exhibited a strong commitment to democracy. It was argued that opening NATO to these new members would encourage democratic developments throughout Eastern Europe. But Russia strongly objected to NATO expansion, viewing it as an incursion of Western powers in the East and a threat to Russia's security. Some American advisers warned that expanding NATO would undermine democratic forces in Russia and encourage the return of nationalist, anti-Western politics there. The United States and NATO proceeded to admit Poland, Hungary, and the Czech Republic to full membership in 1998, after reassuring Russia of the alliance's peaceful intentions.

European Ethnic Conflicts   Religious and ethnic conflicts in Europe are as old as the recorded history of the continent. A question confronting the United States and NATO is whether such conflicts threaten the security of Western

U.S. troops taking part in a joint U.S.–South Korean military exercise. North Korea remains a serious threat to South Korea.

Europe, and, if so, what to do about them. Media coverage of the hardship, death, and destruction resulting from these conflicts puts added pressure on democratic governments to undertake humanitarian and "peacekeeping" roles. A combination of security and humanitarian concerns drew NATO into Bosnia in 1995 to assist in resolving war among Serbs, Croats, and Muslims. The United States provides about one-third of the NATO military forces deployed in Bosnia as peacekeepers.

Regional Threats   The most likely threats today are those posed by regional aggressors. Saddam Hussein's Iraq is the model of a new regional threat. Potential regional aggressors include the following:

- *Iraq:* Saddam Hussein's million-strong army, with its 5,000 tanks, was reduced to one-third its size in the Gulf War. The UN-sponsored economic blockade of Iraq has hampered that nation's efforts to rebuild these conventional forces to their former size. However, Iraq continues to harbor Scud missiles and continues in its efforts to acquire weapons of mass destruction— nuclear, chemical, and biological.

- *Iran:* Iran has been rebuilding its million-strong army since the end of its war with Iraq, shopping for both conventional weapons and nuclear components in world arms markets. China and the former Soviet Union have supplied it with surface-to-surface missiles. Iran has also acquired a submarine force for operations in the Persian Gulf and a sizable air force. Iran supports terrorist groups throughout the Middle East and provides a beacon for violent Islamic fundamentalism. The Israelis consider Iran to be the principal threat to peace and stability in the region.

- *Syria:* Syria's military forces are impressive, with more than 700,000 men and 4,000 tanks. But with the collapse of the Soviet Union, its key supplier, Syria will now need to pay for weapons in hard currency—a commodity in short supply in Syria. Syria remains officially at war with Israel, and its troops occupy most of Lebanon.

- *Libya:* Muammar al-Qaddafi's military forces are not a major threat, yet Libya remains a major base for worldwide terrorist activity.

- *North Korea:* North Korea remains the most authoritarian and militarist regime in the world. It devotes a very large proportion of its economy to its military, even impoverishing its people to do so. It supports a million-strong army with 4,000 tanks, a large air force, and a large submarine force. North Korea's nuclear weapons program is very advanced. Its former "Great Leader," Kim Il-Sung, never renounced his intention to reunify Korea by force, nor has his son who replaced him, "Dear Leader" Kim Jong Il. In recognition of South Korea's burgeoning economy and progressive strengthening of its armed forces, the United States has undertaken a gradual reduction of American ground forces in South Korea. However, some U.S. ground forces are likely to remain in place near the border to deter invasion by North Korea. South Korea's army remains only about half as large as that of North Korea; in the event of war, the United States would need to provide immediate air combat support.

- *China:* The People's Republic of China now possesses the world's largest armed forces—more than 3 million soldiers, nearly 10,000 tanks, and more than 4,000 combat aircraft. China has ICBMs with multihead nuclear warheads capable of reaching the United States. China has always asserted that Taiwan is a province of China (as has the government of the Republic of China in Taiwan); Beijing continues to declare unification a goal. It has stated a preference for peaceful reunification, but the threat of force has always been present. The Beijing government's policies toward Hong Kong, the former British colony incorporated into the People's Republic of China in 1997, will signal China's future course. Beijing continues to voice support for market reforms of its economy, but it acted with brutal force to suppress the democracy movement in Tiananmen Square in 1989.

- *Terrorism:* The threat of terrorism creates two military requirements. The first is the ability to punish nations that sponsor terrorism and to dissuade other nations from continuing their support of terrorism. In 1986 the United States struck at Libya in a limited air attack in response to various Libyan-supported acts of terrorism around the world. In 1993 the United States struck Iraq's intelligence center in Baghdad in response to a foiled plot to assassinate former president George Bush. These types of operations are carried out by conventional military forces. The second requirement is the ability to take direct action against terrorists to capture or kill them or to free their hostages. These operations are carried out by highly trained, specially equipped Special Operations Forces.

Unanticipated Threats   The United States anticipated very few of the dozens of crises that required the use of military force over the past decade. Few would have forecast that U.S. troops would be engaged in combat in Grenada in 1983, or Panama in 1989, or even the Persian Gulf in 1991. General Colin Powell has tried to convince the Congress that "The real threat is the unknown, the uncertain. In a very real sense, the primary threat to our security is instability and unpreparedness to handle a crisis or war that no one expected or predicted. But it is difficult to convince taxpayers or their elected representatives to prepare for the unknown."[5]

THE USE OF MILITARY FORCE

American troops advancing against the background of burning oil fields in Kuwait during the Gulf War in 1991. President Bush argued that forcing Iraq's Saddam Hussein out of Kuwait was a clearly defined military objective and a vital interest of the United States.

All modern presidents have acknowledged that the most agonizing decisions they have made were to send U.S. military forces into combat. These decisions cost lives. The American people are willing to send their sons and daughters into danger—and even to see some of them wounded and killed—but *only* if a president convinces them that the outcome "is worth dying for." A president must be able to explain why they lost their lives and to justify their sacrifice.

To Protect Vital Interests   The U.S. military learned many bitter lessons in its long bloody experience in Vietnam. Among those lessons are these:

- The United States should commit its military forces only in support of vital national interests.

- If military forces are committed, they must have clearly defined military objectives—the destruction of enemy forces and/or the capture of enemy-held territory.

- Any commitment of U.S. forces must be of sufficient strength to ensure overwhelming and decisive victory with the fewest possible casualties.

- Before committing U.S. military forces, there must be some reasonable assurances that the effort has the support of the American people and their representatives in Congress.

- The commitment of U.S. military forces should be a last resort, after political, economic, and diplomatic efforts have proven ineffective.

President George Bush argued that his decision to use military force in the Gulf War in 1990–91 met these guidelines: that preventing Iraq's Saddam Hussein from gaining control of the world's oil supply and developing nuclear and chemical weapons were vital national interests; that political and economic sanctions were not effective; and that he had defined clear military objectives—the removal of Iraqi troops from Kuwait and the destruction of Iraq's nuclear and chemical weapon capabilities (see *Up Close:* "The Use of Force: Operation Desert Storm" on pages 666-67). And he authorized a large military commitment that led to a speedy and decisive victory.

These guidelines for the use of military force are widely supported within the U.S. military itself.[6] Contrary to Hollywood stereotypes, military leaders are extremely reluctant to go to war when no vital interest of the United States is at stake, where there are no clear-cut military objectives, without the support of Congress or the American people, or without sufficient force to achieve speedy and decisive victory with minimal casualties. They are wary of seeing their troops placed in danger merely to advance diplomatic goals, or to engage in "peacekeeping," or to "stabilize governments," or to "show the flag." They are reluctant to undertake humanitarian missions while being shot at. They do not like to risk their soldiers' lives under "rules of engagement" that limit their ability to defend themselves.

In Support of Important Political Objectives   In contrast to military leaders, political leaders and diplomats often reflect the view that "war is a continuation of politics by other means"—a view commonly attributed to nineteenth-century German theorist of war Karl von Clausewitz. Military force may be used to protect interests that are important but not necessarily vital. Otherwise, the

United States would be rendered largely impotent in world affairs. A diplomat's ability to achieve a satisfactory result often depends on the expressed or implied threat of military force. The distinguished international political theorist Hans Morgenthau wrote, "Since military strength is the obvious measure of a nation's power, its demonstration serves to impress others with that nation's power."[7]

Currently American military forces must be prepared to carry out a variety of missions in addition to the conduct of conventional war:

- Demonstrating U.S. resolve in crisis situations.
- Demonstrating U.S. support for democratic governments.
- Protecting U.S. citizens living abroad.
- Striking at terrorist targets to deter or retaliate.
- Peacemaking among warring factions or nations.
- Peacekeeping where hostile factions or nations have accepted a peace agreement.
- Providing humanitarian aid often under warlike conditions.

In pursuit of such objectives, recent U.S. presidents have sent troops to Lebanon in 1982 to stabilize the government (Reagan), to Grenada in 1983 to rescue American medical students and restore democratic government (Reagan), to Panama in 1989 to oust drug-trafficking General Manuel Antonio Noriega from power and to protect U.S. citizens (Bush), to Somalia in 1992–93 to provide emergency humanitarian aid (Bush and Clinton), to Haiti in 1994 to restore constitutional government (Clinton), and to Bosnia for peacekeeping among warring ethnic factions (see Table 18-1). In addition, U.S. military forces have been used in various counterterrorist

TABLE 18-1	Major Deployments of U.S. Military Forces since World War II	
Year	Area	President
1950–53	Korea	Truman
1958	Lebanon	Eisenhower
1961–64	Vietnam	Kennedy
1962	Cuban waters	Kennedy
1965–73	Vietnam	Johnson, Nixon
1965	Dominican Republic	Johnson
1970	Laos	Nixon
1970	Cambodia	Nixon
1975	Cambodia	Ford
1980	Iran	Carter
1982–83	Lebanon	Reagan
1983	Grenada	Reagan
1989	Panama	Bush
1990–91	Persian Gulf	Bush
1992–93	Somalia	Bush, Clinton
1994–95	Haiti	Clinton
1995–	Bosnia	Clinton

Source: Statistical Abstract of the United States, 1997, p. 97.

The Use of Force: Operation Desert Storm

The nation's military leadership learned hard lessons from Vietnam: define clear military objectives, use overwhelming and decisive military force, move swiftly and avoid protracted stalemate, minimize casualties, and be sensitive to the image of the war projected back home. Saddam Hussein's invasion of Kuwait on August 2, 1990, was apparently designed to restore his military prestige after an indecisive war against Iran, to secure additional oil revenues to finance the continued buildup of Iraqi military power, and to intimidate (and perhaps invade) Saudi Arabia and the Gulf states, thereby securing control over a major share of the world's oil reserves. On paper, Iraq possessed the fourth largest military force in the world, with 1 million troops, battle hardened from eight years of war with Iran. Iraqi weapons included over 5,000 tanks, 10,000 other armored vehicles, 4,000 artillery pieces, 700 combat aircraft, and surface-to-air missiles. In addition Iraq had deadly chemical weapons, which it had previously used against Iran and its own Kurdish population.*

The Iraqi invasion met with a surprisingly swift response by the United Nations, with Security Council resolutions condemning the invasion, demanding an immediate withdrawal, and imposing a trade embargo and economic sanctions. President George Bush immediately set to work to stitch together a coalition military force that would eventually include thirty nations. Early on, the president described the U.S. military deployment as "defensive," but he soon became convinced that neither diplomacy nor an economic blockade would dislodge Saddam from Kuwait and so ordered the military to prepare an "offensive" option.

The top U.S. military commanders—including the chair of the Joint Chiefs of Staff, General Colin Powell, and the commander in the field, General Norman Schwartzkopf—had been field officers in Vietnam, and they were resolved not to repeat the mistakes of that war. They were reluctant to go into battle without the full support of the American people. If ordered to fight, they wanted to employ overwhelming and decisive military force; they wanted to avoid the gradual escalation, protracted conflict, target limitations, and political inference in the conduct of the war that had characterized the U.S. military's efforts in Vietnam. Accordingly, they presented the president with a plan that called for a very large military buildup; elements of six army divisions and two marine divisions, with 1,900 tanks, 930 artillery pieces, 500 attack helicopters, and more than 1,000 combat aircraft. Coalition forces also included British and French heavy armored units, and Egyptian, Syrian, Saudi, and other Arab forces.

When President Bush announced this massive buildup of forces on November 8, however, he immediately faced a barrage of criticism at home for abandoning his earlier defensive posture. U.S. Senator Sam Nunn, respected chair of the Senate Armed Services Committee, opened hearings that urged the president to continue economic sanctions and avoid the heavy casualties a land war was expected to produce. But Bush was convinced that sanctions would not work, that Saddam would hold out for years, that eventually the political coalition backing the embargo would break up. He believed Saddam would become an increasingly powerful opponent who would soon dominate the Arab world and Middle East oil reserves. Unless stopped quickly, Saddam would soon acquire nuclear weapons. On November 29, 1990, Secretary of State James Baker won the support of UN Security Council members, including the Soviet Union (with China abstaining), for a resolution authorizing coalition forces to "use all necessary means" against Iraq unless it withdrew from Kuwait by January 15, 1991. Following a lengthy debate in the Congress, on January 12 President Bush won a similar resolution in the House (250–183) and the Senate (52–47).

From Baghdad, CNN reporters Bernard Shaw and Peter Arnett were startled on the night of January 16 when Operation Desert Storm began with an air attack on key installations in the city. Iraqi forces were also surprised, despite the prompt timing of the attack; Saddam had assured them that the United States lacked the resolve to fight, and that even if war broke out, U.S. public opinion would force a settlement as casualties rose.

The success of the coalition air force was spectacular. More than 110,000 combat missions were flown with only 39 aircraft losses, none in air combat. Most Iraqi aircraft were compelled to stay on the ground because runway and control facilities were destroyed; 38 Iraqi planes were shot down in combat, and 140 escaped to Iran. Strategic targets—including nuclear facilities, chemical warfare plants, command centers, and military communications—were repeatedly attacked. "Smart" weapons performed superbly. American TV audiences saw videotapes of laser-guided "smart bombs" entering the doors and air shafts of enemy bunkers. Civilian damage was lower than in any previous air war. The Patriot antiballistic missile system proved effective against Scuds; in more than eighty firings at Israel and Saudi Arabia, only one strike occurred, killing twenty-seven in a marine barracks. After five weeks of air war, intelligence estimated that nearly half the Iraqi tanks and artillery in the field had been destroyed, demoralized troops were hiding in deep shelters, and the battlefield had been isolated and "prepared" for ground operations.

General Schwartzkopf's plan for the ground war emphasized deception and maneuver. He wanted the Iraqis to believe the main attack would come directly against Kuwait's southern border and would be supported by a marine landing on the coast. While Iraqi forces prepared for attacks from the south and the east coast, he sent heavily armed columns in a "Hail Mary" play—a wide sweep to the west, outflanking and cutting off Iraqi forces in the battle area. The Iraqi forces, blinded by air attacks and obliged to stay in their bunkers, would not be able to know about or respond to the flanking attack. On the night of February 24, the ground attack began. Marines breached ditches and minefields and raced directly to the Kuwait airport; army helicopter air assaults lunged deep* into Iraq; armored columns raced northward across the desert to outflank Iraqi forces and then attack them from the west, while a surge in air attacks kept Iraqi forces holed up in their bunkers. Iraqi troops surrendered in droves, highways from Kuwait city became a massive junkyard of Iraqi vehicles, and Iraqi forces that tried to fight were quickly destroyed. After 100 hours of ground fighting, President George Bush ordered a cease-fire.

The United States had achieved a decisive military victory quickly and with remarkably few casualties. The president resisted calls to expand the original objectives of the war and go on to capture Baghdad, to destroy the Iraqi economy, to encourage Iraq's disintegration as a nation, or to kill Saddam, although it was expected that his defeat would lead to his ouster. Although the war left many political issues unresolved, it was the most decisive military outcome the United States had achieved since the end of World War II. President Bush chose to declare victory and celebrate the return of American troops.

The Gulf War taught the nation a number of lessons about the effective use of military power:

- The rapid employment of overwhelming forces is both politically and militarily superior to gradual escalation and employment of minimum force. The use of overwhelming force reduces total casualties and achieves an earlier and more decisive victory.

- The nation's political leadership is vastly more effective when it concentrates on developing and maintaining foreign and domestic political support for a war while leaving the planning and execution of military operations to the military leadership.

- A rapid conclusion of hostilities ensures that public support will not erode over time and that protracted combat and a steady stream of casualties will not fuel antiwar sentiments.

- Military force can capture territory and destroy enemy forces, but it cannot guarantee peace. Even a military-weakened Saddam Hussein remains a threat to stability in the Middle East.

- Perhaps the most important lesson, however, is that the end of the Cold War does *not* mean that the United States no longer requires military power.[†]

*International Institute for Strategic Studies, *The Military Balance 1991–92* (London: IISS, 1991).

[†]See Harry G. Summers, Jr., *On Strategy II: A Critical Analysis of the Gulf War* (New York: Dell, 1992).

actions, for example, by President Carter in Iran in 1980 in an unsuccessful attempt to rescue U.S. hostages, by President Reagan against Libya in 1986 to discourage terrorism, and by President Clinton in 1993 against Iraq in response to a plot to assassinate former President Bush.

Proponents of these more flexible uses of U.S. military forces usually deny any intent to be the "world's policeman." Rather, they argue that each situation must be judged independently on its own merits—weighing the importance of U.S. goals against expected costs. No military operation is without risk, but some risks may be worth taking to advance important political interests even though these interests may not be deemed "vital" to the United States. The media, particularly television, play an influential role in pressuring the president to use military force. Pictures of torture and killing, starvation and death, and devastation and destruction from around the world provide a powerful emotional stimulus to U.S. military intervention. Generally a president can count on an initial "rally 'round the flag" surge in popular support for a military action, despite overall poor public knowledge of international politics (see *Compared to What?* "Citizens' Knowledge of the World" on page 670). But if casualties mount during an operation, if no victory or end appears in sight, then press coverage of body bags coming home, military funeral services, and bereaved families create pressure on a president to end U.S. involvement. Unless the U.S. military can produce speedy and decisive results with few casualties, public support for military intervention wavers and critical voices in Congress arise.

MILITARY FORCE LEVELS

Overall military force levels in the United States are threat driven—that is, determined by the size and nature of the perceived threats to national security. It is true that particular weapons systems or base openings or closings may be driven by political forces such as the influence of defense contractors in Congress or the power of a member of Congress from a district heavily affected by defense spending. And not everyone in the White House and Congress, or even in the Defense Department, agrees on the precise nature of the threats confronting the United States now or in the future. Yet defense policy planning and the "sizing" of U.S. military forces are based on an assessment of the threats confronting the nation.

For nearly a half-century the Soviet threat drove defense policy, force planning, training, strategy and tactics, weapons research and procurement, troop deployments, and defense budgeting. The fundamental change in the world balance of power inspired a complete reexamination of defense policy and force sizing.

Reductions in Forces   Post–Cold War military force reductions began in 1990 under Secretary of Defense Richard Cheney in the Bush Administration. The initial plan called for a reduction of total U.S. military personnel from 2.1 to 1.6 million in 1995 (see Table 18-2). This plan envisioned a continuing "forward presence" in NATO but reduced U.S. forces in Europe by more than half. Consistent with the view that regional aggressors would be the most likely threats to U.S. interests in the future, forces designed principally to meet these threats suffered fewer cuts.

Later as President Bill Clinton's first secretary of defense, Les Aspin argued that the end of the Cold War required a complete "bottom-up" review of the threats

TABLE 18-2	Military Force Levels		
	End of Cold War, 1990	*Bush Administration, 1992*	*Clinton Administration, 1999*
Active duty personnel	2.1 million	1.6 million	1.4 million
Army divisions	18	12	10
Marine expeditionary forces	3	3	3
Navy carrier battle groups	15	12	11
Air force fighter wings	24	15	13

Source: Budget of the United States Government 1999 and previous annual budgets.

confronting the nation. Currently Clinton defense policy argues that Russia is no longer a major security threat to the United States or to NATO Europe. The U.S. military contribution to NATO can be reduced to symbolic levels. Whatever military threats might arise in Europe can be treated as regional conflicts.

Iraqi-Equivalent Regional Threats   Military force levels are currently designed to confront major Iraqi-equivalent regional threats. U.S. military force levels are based on the experience of defeating Iraq speedily and decisively in the Gulf War. But current planning also envisions the possibility that a second aggressor might decide to challenge the United States somewhere else in the world while its forces were involved in an Iraqi-equivalent war. For example, if U.S. forces were involved in the Persian Gulf against Iraq or Iran, North Korea might decide to take advantage of the situation and launch an invasion of South Korea. Therefore the United States currently plans to maintain sufficient additional U.S. forces to "fight and win two nearly simultaneous major regional conflicts." The ambiguous wording—"nearly simultaneous"—recognizes that the United States may not be able to airlift and sealift sufficient forces to fight and win two regional wars at the same time. American forces would be obliged to hold one aggressor (principally with air power) while defeating the other; once one aggressor was defeated, the United States could then redeploy sufficient forces to defeat a second aggressor.

Future Force Levels   The revised threat assessment rationalizes deep cuts in military forces and defense budgets in the Clinton Administration. The army will field ten active combat divisions and the air force thirteen fighter wings. (A U.S. Army division includes 15,000 to 18,000 troops; an air force fighter wing includes approximately seventy-two combat aircraft.) The navy will deploy eleven active (one training) carrier battle groups. (A carrier battle group typically includes one aircraft carrier with 75 to 85 aircraft, plus defending cruisers, destroyers, frigates, attack submarines, and support ships.) The marine corps is scheduled to retain all three of its marine expeditionary forces (each includes one marine division, one marine air wing, and supporting services).

Criticism   Although most defense experts agree on the assessment of the threat—the need to prepare to fight and win two major regional conflicts

Compared to What?

Citizens' Knowledge of the World

As the sole superpower left on earth, the United States is expected to assume leadership in support of democracy around the world. But how well prepared are the American people for global leadership?

If a basic knowledge of world geography is required to understand international politics, then the American people are ill prepared for their global responsibility. Young Americans ranked dead last in geographic knowledge among nine nations surveyed in 1988. On average, young Americans were able to correctly locate only seven of sixteen places on a world map. Older Americans did somewhat better. But the ignorance of

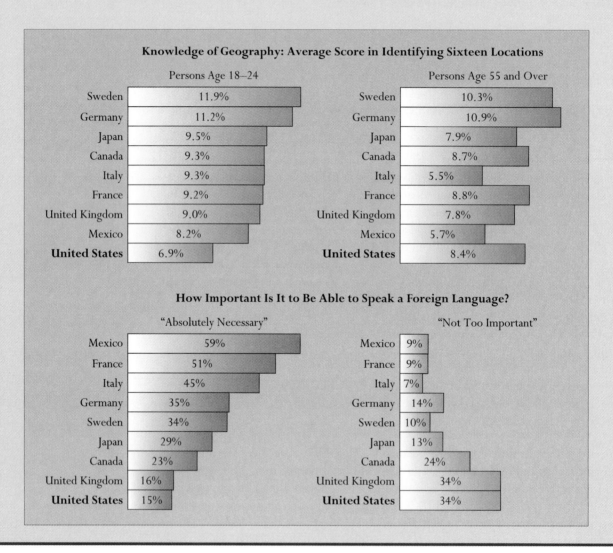

Knowledge of Geography: Average Score in Identifying Sixteen Locations

Persons Age 18–24

Sweden	11.9%
Germany	11.2%
Japan	9.5%
Canada	9.3%
Italy	9.3%
France	9.2%
United Kingdom	9.0%
Mexico	8.2%
United States	6.9%

Persons Age 55 and Over

Sweden	10.3%
Germany	10.9%
Japan	7.9%
Canada	8.7%
Italy	5.5%
France	8.8%
United Kingdom	7.8%
Mexico	5.7%
United States	8.4%

How Important Is It to Be Able to Speak a Foreign Language?

"Absolutely Necessary"

Country	Percent
Mexico	59%
France	51%
Italy	45%
Germany	35%
Sweden	34%
Japan	29%
Canada	23%
United Kingdom	16%
United States	15%

"Not Too Important"

Country	Percent
Mexico	9%
France	9%
Italy	7%
Germany	14%
Sweden	10%
Japan	13%
Canada	24%
United Kingdom	34%
United States	34%

simultaneously—many believe the projected force levels are inadequate for these tasks. Opponents contend that the reduced numbers of army and air force combat units and the limited transport and support services available to the military are inadequate for two major regional conflicts. Casualties can be kept low only when overwhelming military force is employed quickly and decisively,

American youth is particularly worrisome; over time the map of the earth is becoming increasingly unrecognizable to the American people.

Americans have less interest in foreign language capability than other peoples. It is true that today English is widely spoken in the world and most American tourists can get by with no foreign language skills. But language skills will become essential as we move toward a global economy. To see how well you would do, take the test here. Match the numbers on the map with the places listed.

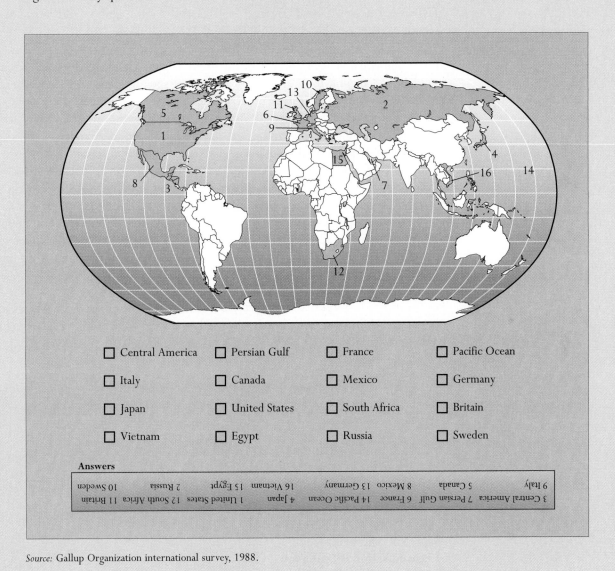

☐ Central America	☐ Persian Gulf	☐ France	☐ Pacific Ocean
☐ Italy	☐ Canada	☐ Mexico	☐ Germany
☐ Japan	☐ United States	☐ South Africa	☐ Britain
☐ Vietnam	☐ Egypt	☐ Russia	☐ Sweden

Answers

9 Italy   5 Canada   8 Mexico   13 Germany   16 Vietnam   15 Egypt   2 Russia   10 Sweden
3 Central America   7 Persian Gulf   6 France   14 Pacific Ocean   4 Japan   1 United States   12 South Africa   11 Britain

Source: Gallup Organization international survey, 1988.

as it was in Operation Desert Storm. Lives are lost when minimal forces are sent into combat, when they have inadequate air combat support, or when they are extended over too broad a front. Potential regional foes—for example, Iran and North Korea—deploy modern heavy armor and artillery forces. The United States benefited from a six-month buildup of its heavy forces in the

Gulf region before Operation Desert Storm began; such a period of preparation is unlikely in a future conflict. The deployment of U.S. troops for humanitarian and "peacekeeping" missions detracts from their readiness to respond to a major regional threat. More important, perhaps, the minimal force levels projected would severely tax the nation's ability to respond to two conflicts simultaneously in opposite ends of the globe. Critics charge current defense policy and military force levels were determined more by a desire to cut the defense budget than by a careful consideration of the forces required for national security.

Historical Trends in Defense Spending   In the early Cold War years, defense spending claimed a major share of U.S. resources (see Figure 18-2). In 1955 defense spending in the United States was 58 percent of all federal expenditures and equaled 10.5 percent of the gross national product. By 1965 defense spending had shrunk to 40.1 percent of federal spending and to 7.5 percent of the GNP. The Vietnam War caused defense spending to temporarily surge upward, but following President Nixon's decision to gradually withdraw U.S. forces from that conflict, defense spending began a long decline. By 1978 defense spending was down to 23 percent of federal spending and 4.5 percent of the GNP. This was the lowest defense "effort" the United States had made since before World War II. By the end of the Carter Administration, defense spending as a percentage of the GNP began to creep upward. Reagan's defense buildup brought defense spending to 6.5 percent of the GNP and 29 percent of the total federal budget by 1986. But during his second term, President Reagan and Secretary of Defense Caspar Weinberger fought a losing battle against a Congress determined to limit military spending.

Post–Cold War Defense Spending   The achievement of the Cold War objectives of the U.S. national defense policy led to a welcome result—a lessening of

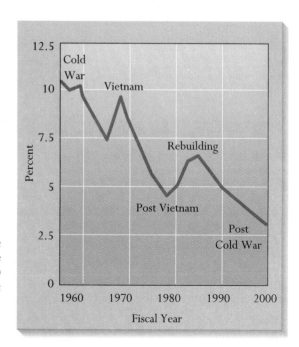

FIGURE 18-2 The Price of Peace: National Defense Outlays as a Percentage of GDP

Current spending on defense occupies a smaller percentage of the U.S. budget (as a percentage of gross national product) than it has at any time since the start of the Cold War.

Source: *Budget of the United States Government, 1993.*

Politics in Cyberspace

National Security

The Internet offers an almost limitless wealth of information on world affairs. National security information is also easily available on the Net from official U.S. government sources.

Defenselink
http://www.defenselink.mil

The defenselink site is a locus for information on national security affairs. It contains the latest Pentagon news releases, biographies of and recent public statements by key defense officials, the secretary of defense's *Annual Report to the President and Congress,* facts on U.S. military forces, weapons, and deployments, as well as direct links to Web sites maintained by the Army, Navy, Air Force, and Marine Corps.

Central Intelligence Agency
http://www.odci.gov

The Central Intelligence Agency's official Web site includes a history of the agency, a description of its organization, a statement of its mission, a "virtual tour" of its headquarters, and a link to the Center for the Study of Intelligence that provides previously classified documents to historians, political scientists, and interested citizens. (All users must consent to possible monitoring and auditing of usage.) It also provides an overview of the entire U.S. intelligence community, including the National Security Agency, National Reconnaissance Office, Defense Intelligence Agency, and the intelligence branches of the Army, Navy, Air Force, and Marine Corps.

National Security Council
http://www.whitehouse.gov/WH/EOP/NSC/html

The National Security Council is the president's principal forum for considering national security

and foreign policy issues with senior national security advisers and cabinet officials. The Web site provides details about the members and functions of the council and the text of the annual *National Security Strategy.*

NATO
http://www.nato.int

Originally formed after the Second World War to discourage Soviet expansion and protect Western Europe, today NATO peacekeeping forces undertake peacekeeping and crisis management missions throughout the world. NATO Online provides researchers with information about the alliance's current activities and membership, the text of speeches by NATO officials, and the text of the original treaty signed in 1949.

Arms Control and Disarmament Agency
http://www.acdi.gov

This Web site provides complete texts of all arms control treaties including the first and second SALT and START treaties.

Council on Foreign Relations
http://www.cfr.org

The CFR is the most influential private policy organization in the United States. Its journal *Foreign Affairs* regularly includes semiofficial policy proposals, commentaries, and statements.

United Nations
http://www.un.org

The official Web site of the United Nations includes a complete description of its organization, membership, and offices, as well as publications, statistics, documents, and treaties.

---

the threat to national security and a reduction in national defense spending. U.S. defense spending has steadily declined in real dollars since 1986; U.S. military strength has been cut by nearly half. Defense spending is projected to decline to less than 15 percent of federal spending and less than 3 percent of the nation's GNP. These are levels roughly comparable to those that prevailed before Pearl Harbor was attacked in 1941.

- The struggle for power is global. Leaders and peoples of the world protect and advance their goals and ideals through the exercise of power.

- There is no world government capable of legislating and enforcing rules of international politics. But various efforts to stabilize relations among nations have been attempted, including the balance-of-power system of alliances in the eighteenth and nineteenth centuries, the collective security arrangements of the League of Nations and the United Nations in the twentieth century, and the regional security approach of the North Atlantic Treaty Organization.

- The United Nations was largely ineffective during the Cold War, the confrontation between the Western democracies led by the United States and communist bloc nations led by the Soviet Union. During these years, the Western nations relied principally on the strength of the North Atlantic Treaty Organization (NATO) to deter war in Europe.

- For nearly fifty years, the Cold War largely directed U.S. foreign and defense policy. The United States sought to contain Soviet military expansionism and world communist revolutionary forces in all parts of the globe. U.S. involvement in the Korean and Vietnam wars grew out of this containment policy.

- During the Cold War years, U.S. and Soviet military forces never engaged in direct combat against each other, although many "proxy" conflicts took place throughout the world. The most serious threat of nuclear war occurred during the Cuban missile crisis in 1962.

- To maintain nuclear peace, the United States relied primarily on the policy of deterrence—dissuading the Soviets from launching a nuclear attack by maintaining survivable second-strike forces capable of inflicting unacceptable levels of destruction in a retaliating attack.

- In 1970 President Richard Nixon and National Security Adviser Henry Kissinger began negotiations with the Soviet Union with a view to limiting the nuclear arms race. These Strategic Arms Limitation Talks produced the SALT I agreement in 1972, and later, under President Jimmy Carter, the SALT II agreement in 1979. Both agreements set limits on future strategic weapons development but failed to reduce existing weapons stockpiles.

- President Ronald Reagan renamed the negotiations START, emphasizing the goal of reductions in weapons rather than limitations, and stressing equality and verification. The INF Treaty in 1987 was the first agreement that actually reduced nuclear arms, although it covered only intermediate-range weapons in Europe. Later the START I (1991) and START II (1993) treaties called for reducing nuclear arsenals by two-thirds from Cold War levels.

- The end of the Cold War followed the ouster of communist governments in Eastern Europe in 1989, the unification of Germany in 1990, the collapse of the Warsaw Pact communist military alliance in 1991, and the dissolution of the Soviet Union in 1991. Russia has inherited most of the nuclear weapons and military forces of the former Soviet Union as well as its seat in the UN Security Council.

- Current threats to peace and security are likely to be posed by regional aggressors. U.S. involvement in the Gulf War in 1990–91 is representative of the type of military action most likely to be undertaken in the future. Current defense policy calls for the United States to be prepared to fight two "Iraqi-equivalent wars" "nearly simultaneously."

- Current political threats to national security include a reverse of democratic trends in Russia and the emergence of a militarist and expansionist regime; European ethnic conflicts and wars; regional threats including Iraq, Iran, and North Korea; terrorism; and as-yet-unanticipated threats.

- Following the Vietnam War, many military leaders argued that U.S. forces should be used only to protect vital American interests, only in support of clearly defined military objectives, only with sufficient strength to ensure decisive victory with fewest possible casualties, only with the support of the American people and Congress, and only as a last resort.

- Recent presidents have used military forces to carry out a variety of missions in addition to conventional war, including peacekeeping, antiterrorist, and humanitarian activities. They have argued that the

risks were worth taking in light of the importance of the goals.

- U.S. military force levels and defense budgets are driven by perceived threats to national security. Thus the end of the Cold War has resulted in dramatic reductions in forces and budgets.

SELECTED READINGS

CLAUSEWITZ, KARL VON. *On War.* Edited and translated by Michael Howard and Peter Paret. Princeton, N.J.: Princeton University Press, 1984. The classic theory of war and military operations emphasizing their political character; first published in 1832.

INTERNATIONAL INSTITUTE FOR STRATEGIC STUDIES. *The Military Balance.* London: International Institute for Strategic Studies, published annually. Careful description of the military forces of more than 160 countries; this book is considered the most authoritative public information available.

KAGAN, DONALD. *On the Origins of War and the Preservation of Peace.* New York: Doubleday, 1995. Insights derived from comparative historical studies of the origins of great wars.

MAYERS, TEENA KARSA. *Understanding Nuclear Weapons and Arms Control.* 4th ed. New York: Brassey's, 1991. Well-illustrated primer on nuclear strategies and weapons, and a history of arms control negotiations and agreements.

NORTH, ROBERT C. *War, Peace, and Survival.* Boulder, Colo.: Westview Press, 1990. Overview of international relations, linking four levels of analysis—individual actors, nation-states, international relations, and global relations.

SNOW, DONALD M. *National Security: Enduring Problems in a Changing Defense Environment.* 2nd ed. New York: St. Martin's Press, 1991. Comprehensive overview of U.S. national security issues, reflecting the changing environment at the end of the Cold War.

SUMMERS, HARRY G., JR. *On Strategy II: A Critical Analysis of the Gulf War.* New York: Dell, 1992. Analysis of the Gulf War based on Clausewitz's classic principles of war. The strategic decisions leading to victory in the Gulf contrast markedly with the decisions in Vietnam that led to defeat, a topic covered in Summers's groundbreaking first book, *On Strategy: A Critical Analysis of the Vietnam War* (New York: Dell, 1984).

ASK YOURSELF ABOUT POLITICS

1. Are politics in Texas different from those of other states?
   Yes ☐   No ☐

2. Are Texans more conservative than the citizens of other states?
   Yes ☐   No ☐

3. Do race and ethnicity play a major role in Texas politics?
   Yes ☐   No ☐

4. Do some groups or interests in Texas have more influence or power than others in public policy decisions?
   Yes ☐   No ☐

5. Is Texas in a position to adapt to the global economy?
   Yes ☐   No ☐

6. Should Texas give more attention to assisting Mexico to develop a stable political and economic system?
   Yes ☐   No ☐

Chapter
19
THE SOCIAL AND ECONOMIC MILIEU OF TEXAS POLITICS

CHAPTER OUTLINE
Decades of Change and Challenge

Texas Myths

The Political Culture of Texas

The Peoples of Texas

Politics, Race, and Ethnicity

The Political Implications of Demographics

The Economy of Texas

Economic Regions of Texas

Transnational Regionalism

FEATURES
Up Close: Perpetuating an Image

What Do You Think? What's in a Name?

What Do You Think? Do Size and Geography Shape Texas Politics?

Compared to What? Texas in Comparison to Other States

Up Close: Will Welfare Reform Deter Illegal Immigration?

Politics in Cyberspace: The Social and Economic Milieu of Texas Politics

★ Social and economic factors are directly related to the distribution of political power and help determine who gets what in Texas politics.

DECADES OF CHANGE AND CHALLENGE

The frontier rural society of the cowboy is long gone. The Oil Patch, where wildcatters and roughnecks prevailed, has been replaced by the Silicon Prairie, "where venture capitalists and software engineers roam."[1] But Texas still has a rugged, bigger-than-life mystique that

677

annoys or amuses many non-Texans (see *Up Close:* "Perpetuating an Image"). In many subtle and not-so-subtle ways, Texans manifest this historical legacy in their speech, their can-do attitude, their celebrations of "Texan-ness," and their actions. But it hardly offers Texas and Texans immunity from the host of nagging, down-to-earth problems that confront most states at the start of the twenty-first century. Although most of these problems are not new, they have become increasingly important for Texas as it adjusts to a changing economy, a changing society, and a changing political landscape.

The 1980s were a tumultuous period of economic boom and bust for Texas. High oil and natural gas prices had put the state's economy in overdrive during the 1970s and early 1980s, but world energy prices plummeted in the mid-1980s, precipitating a major recession. Texas was battered by numerous bank and savings and loan failures, and many of the state's major financial institutions were reorganized. The real estate industry also went bust during the last part of the decade, and foreclosures on buildings and property escalated. Little new commercial or residential housing was built in the final years of the decade, and many support industries were forced into bankruptcy. During this same period, the state's economy was undergoing significant diversification, which contributed to economic recovery in the early 1990s.

Throughout the remainder of the 1990s, the Texas economy continued to expand and outperform the national economy. Technology has replaced energy as the state's largest employer, and Texas leads the nation in exports to Mexico. Three of the nation's ten largest cities are now located in Texas, and the state is the second largest in terms of total population. But with all of these changes, major problems still persist.

Challenges of the 1990s Sustained population growth, the continued transformation of the state's economy, environmental and water problems, and increased demands for governmental services pose tremendous challenges to the resources, capabilities, and structure of Texas government. The demographic characteristics of the state's population also are changing as racial and ethnic minority groups increase in size and as the population ages. Wealthy school districts have been forced to share revenue with their poor neighbors, but inequities in public education persist and pose a significant challenge for developing a work force that can compete in the global economy. Despite an unprecedented prison construction program and a decline in crime rates, many Texans still live in fear of crime. The lingering effects of the 1980s recession and high rates of unemployment or underemployment in various areas of the state, the influx of immigrants from Mexico, an aging population that requires long-term nursing care, and changes in the federal welfare laws have forced governments across the state to develop more effective and efficient means for assisting low-income populations. Finally, the state's growth has exacerbated environmental problems that affect the health and well-being of everyone.

These issues are the ingredients of contemporary Texas politics. They reflect the fundamental conflicts between competing interests and the way Texans decide who gets "what, when, and how."[2] Unfortunately, only a small part of the population is involved in developing solutions. Many people know little about their state and local governments, and the only time they show concern about government is when it fails to meet their demands or expectations. Such indifference and ignorance can be harmful to the public interest, particularly when Texas is undergoing critical changes.

The dime novel helped create the myth of Texas individualism by popularizing and exaggerating the image of the cowboy.

Up Close

As we begin our analysis of Texas government and politics, we ask why Texans and their public officials make the political choices they do. Why, for example, do expenditures for public education rank low in comparison to those in other states? How do we account for Texas's highly regressive tax system? Why are Texans so willing to fund the construction of highways and roads when their state ranks among the last in expenditures for public welfare?[3]

These policy issues relate directly to a variety of other questions about governmental institutions and the political system. Texas functions under a state constitution that most scholars agree is obsolete, yet when Texans had an opportunity to adopt a modern constitution, they refused to do so. Why are Texans content to continue to amend the present charter on a piecemeal basis? Why, until recently, was Texas a one-party Democratic state, and how can one explain the emergence of two-party politics? How can one confront a long legacy of racial discrimination? And what factors have forced changes in the relationships among the state's ethnic and racial groups? Do a few powerful individuals make the primary policy decisions for the state, or are there various competing centers of power? Many argue that special interests dominate state and local government, subordinating the public interest. Is this true? Have bitter, mudslinging political campaigns contributed to the public's loss of confidence in government and elected officials? Do Texans feel they are paying more but getting less for their tax dollars?

Most of these issues affect individual Texans personally. They pay the costs, even though they may not receive the direct benefits of every policy decision. The actions and decisions of governmental leaders can have an immediate and direct effect on people's lives, and, from time to time, those holding positions of power have made decisions that have cost Texans dearly. For example, the disastrous performance of the savings and loans and banks in Texas in the 1980s resulted, in large part, from the failure of state and federal governments to regulate the financial industry adequately.

The fundamental changes in the social, economic, and political structure of the state have required new solutions. Funding public education in the days of the one-room schoolhouse was relatively simple, but funding today's educational system in a way that provides equity among the state's 1,000-plus school districts is of an entirely different level of complexity.

The demographics, or population characteristics, of the state have changed dramatically since the 1940s, when Texas was still predominantly rural. Texas is now an urban state with urban problems. With an estimated population of 19.3 million in 1997, Texas now is the nation's second most populous state. Its ethnic and racial composition has changed, and it is now also home to a large number of individuals who were born and raised in other parts of the United States or abroad and have a limited sense of Texas history and politics. Although oil and natural gas are still important to the state's economy, economic diversification is the dominant theme promoted by business leaders, government officials, and economists.

Change places heavy demands on the state's basic governmental institutions, and there is increasing evidence that many of these institutions are incapable of responding adequately. As Texans face the accelerating change of the twenty-first century, they will need to give increased attention to modernizing and adapting government to these new realities.

This chapter introduces you to the people of Texas, the views they have of themselves, the state's political subcultures and economy, and the increased interdependence of Texas and Mexico. We refer to these factors generally as the *political environment*, a concept developed by political scientist David Easton to describe the context in which political institutions function.[4]

TEXAS MYTHS

Although most Texans have only a cursory knowledge of the state's governmental institutions, political history, and contemporary public policy, they do have views—often ill defined—of the state, its people, and its culture. Key elements of these views, shared by millions of Texans, are described by some scholars as *political myths*.

In recent years, serious scholarship has focused on myths as ways to assess people's views of their common historical and cultural experiences. A myth can be regarded as a "mode of truth . . . that codifies and preserves moral and spiritual values" for a particular culture or society.[5] Myths are stories, narratives, or phrases that are used to describe past events, explain their significance to successive generations, and provide an interpretive overview and understanding of a society. Myths provide a world picture or, in this case, a picture of the state of Texas. The relevance of a myth depends, in part, on the degree to which it approximates the events it is describing.

Texas has produced its own *myth of origin*, which continues to make a powerful statement about the political system and the social order on which it is based.[6] For many Texans, the battle of the Alamo clearly serves to identify the common experiences of independence and the creation of a separate, unique political order. No other state was a **republic** prior to joining the Union, and several scholars argue that independence and "going at it alone" from 1836 to 1845 resulted in a cultural experience that distinguishes the Texas political system from that of other states. A whole set of heroes came out of the formative period of Texas history, including many who fought and died at the Alamo or secured Texas independence on the San Jacinto battlefield. Texas schoolchildren are introduced to these heroes at a

republic Form of government in which representatives of the people, rather than the people themselves, govern.

very early age with field trips or "pilgrimages" to the Alamo in San Antonio and visits to the San Jacinto monument in Houston.

The Texas mythology also includes the Texas ranger and the cowboy. There are countless tales of the invincible, enduring ranger defeating overwhelming odds. Newspapers and dime novels in the nineteenth century introduced readers throughout the United States to the cowboy, who often was portrayed as an honest, hardworking individual wrestling with the harsh Texas environment. The cowboy's rugged **individualism**, with strong connotations of self-help, reflects a political culture in Texas that doesn't like to look to government as a solution to many problems.[7] It is the kind of individualism that continues to be exploited by political candidates in campaign ads and by the legislature in limited appropriations for welfare, health care, and other public assistance programs.

The frontier to which the Texas ranger and the cowboy belong is part of a cultural myth of limited government and unlimited personal opportunity. The frontier in the Texas experience also perpetuates the myths of "land as wilderness and land as garden."[8] These myths emphasize a need to dominate, control, and subdue the land, and they shape many contemporary attitudes toward land use in Texas.

The Texas myths, however, have been primarily the myths of the white (Anglo) population and have limited relevance to the cultural and historical experiences of many African American and Hispanic Texans. From the 1840s to the mid-1960s, such groups were excluded from full participation in Texas politics and the state's economic and social life. To many Hispanics, then, the Texas ranger is not a hero but a symbol of ruthless suppression.

Over the past thirty years, African Americans and Hispanics have made significant political and economic gains. Their share of the population, as well, has been increasing at a rate faster than that of Anglos, and they are expected to constitute a majority of the state's population after the first quarter of the twenty-first century.

As this shift occurs, Hispanic and African American historical experiences are likely to be incorporated into the mythology of the state, and some components of the mythology will be redefined. These revisions may already be under way, as demonstrated by the recent heated debates over what actually took place during the battle of the Alamo. According to newly published accounts, some of the Alamo's heroes surrendered to Mexican soldiers and were executed, rather than fighting to the death. African Americans in Texas have been successful, after several

individualism Attitude, rooted in classical liberal theory and reinforced by the frontier tradition, that citizens are capable of taking care of themselves with minimal governmental assistance.

Texans rally in Austin in celebration of Martin Luther King, Jr.'s birthday, which is now a national and a Texas holiday.

1998

In 1998 the U.S. Post Office issued a stamp commemorating Cinco de Mayo, *demonstrating the increased influence of Hispanic Americans in Texas as well as the rest of the United States.*

years of trying, in getting the legislature to make Martin Luther King, Jr.'s birthday a state holiday. And, for Hispanics, the *Cinco de Mayo* holiday celebrates common cultural and historical experiences.

THE POLITICAL CULTURE OF TEXAS

Texas shares the common institutional and legal arrangements that have developed in all fifty states, including a commitment to personal liberties, equality, justice, the rule of law, and popular sovereignty with its corresponding limitations on government. But there are differences among the states and even among regions within individual states. Texas is a highly diverse state, with racial and ethnic differences from one region to another and divergences in political attitudes and behavior that are reflected in the state's politics and public policies.

The concept of political culture (see Chapter 2) helps us evaluate some of these differences. **Political culture** has been defined as "the set of attitudes, beliefs, and sentiments which give order and meaning to a political process and which provide the underlying assumptions and rules that govern behavior in the political system."[9] The political culture of the state includes fundamental beliefs about the proper role of government, the relationship of the government to its citizens, and who should govern.[10] These complex attitudes and behaviors are rooted in the historical experience of the nation, shaped by the groups that immigrated to the United States and traveled across the continent to Texas.

One authority on American political culture, Daniel Elazar, believes that three political subcultures have emerged over time in the United States: the individualistic, the moralistic, and the traditionalistic. All three draw from the common historical legacy of the nation, but they have produced regional political differences. Sometimes they complement each other; at other times they produce conflict.[11]

The Individualistic Subculture The **individualistic** political view holds that politics and government function as a marketplace. Government does not have to be concerned with creating a good or moral society but exists for strictly "utilitarian reasons, to handle those functions demanded by the people it is created to serve."[12] Government should be limited, and its intervention in the private activities of its citizens kept to a minimum. The primary function of government is to assure the stability of a society so that individuals can pursue their own interests. In this view, politics is not a high calling but is like any other business venture in which skill and talent prevail and the individual can anticipate economic and social benefits. Politics can be perceived as a dirty business best left to those willing to soil their hands. This tradition may well contribute to political corruption, and members of the electorate who share this view may not be concerned when governmental misdeeds are revealed. New policies are more likely to be initiated by interest groups or private individuals than by public officials.

The Moralistic Subculture The **moralistic** subculture regards politics as one of the "great activities of man in his search for the good society."[13] Politics, it maintains, is the pursuit of the common good. Unlike the attitude expressed in the individualistic subculture that governments are to be limited, the moralistic subculture considers government a positive instrument with a responsibility to promote the general welfare. Politics, therefore, is not to be left to the few but is a responsibility of every individual. Politics is a duty and possibly a high calling.

political culture Widely shared set of views, attitudes, beliefs, and customs of a people as to how their government should be organized and run.

individualistic subculture View that government should interfere as little as possible in the private activities of its citizens while assuring that adequate public facilities and a favorable business climate are available to permit individuals to pursue their self-interests.

moralistic subculture View that government's primary responsibility is to promote the public welfare and it should actively use its authority and power to improve the social and economic well-being of its citizens.

This cultural tradition has a strong sense of service. It requires a high standard for those holding public office and believes public office is not to be used for personal gain. Politics may be organized around political parties, but this tradition has produced nonpartisanship, in which party labels and organizations are eliminated or play a reduced role. This tradition produces a large number of "amateur" or "nonprofessional" political activists and officeholders and has little toleration for political corruption. From the moralistic perspective, governments should actively intervene to enhance the social and economic lives of their citizens. Public policy initiatives can come from officeholders as well as from those outside the formal governmental structure.

The Traditionalistic Subculture   The **traditionalistic** political subculture holds that there is a hierarchical arrangement to the political order. This hierarchy serves to limit the power and influence of the general public while allocating authority to a few individuals who constitute a self-perpetuating **elite**. The elite may enact policies that benefit the general public, but doing so is secondary to its interests and objectives. Public policy reflects the interests of those who exercise influence and control, and the benefits of public policy go disproportionately to the elite.

Family and social relationships rather than mass political participation form the basis for maintaining this elite structure. In fact, in many regions of the country where traditionalistic patterns existed, there were systematic efforts to reduce or eliminate the participation of the general public. Although political parties may exist in such a subculture, they have only minimal importance. Many of the states characterized by the traditionalistic subculture were southern states in which two-party politics was replaced by factionalism within the Democratic Party.[14]

Historical Origins of Political Subcultures   The historical origins of these three subcultures can be explained, in part, by the early settlement patterns of the United States and by the cultural differences among the groups of people who initially settled the eastern seaboard. In very general terms, the New England colonists, influenced by Puritan and congregational religious groups, spawned the moralistic subculture. Settlers with entrepreneurial concerns and individualistic attitudes tended to locate in the mid-Atlantic states, and the initial settlement of the South was dominated by elites who aspired, in part, to recreate a semifeudal society.

As expansion toward the frontiers progressed, there were identifiable migration patterns from the initial three settlement regions. Texas was settled primarily by people holding the individualistic and traditionalistic views of a political system. The blending of these two views, along with the historical experience of the Republic and the frontier, contributed to the distinct characteristics of Texas's political culture.[15]

These two political subcultures have merged to shape Texans' general views of what governments should do, who should govern, and what constitutes good public policy. Given the characteristics of these two traditions, one might well conclude, as have many scholars, that the Texas political culture is conservative. Politics in Texas is designed to minimize the role of government, is hostile toward taxes—especially those allocated for social services—and is potentially manipulated by the few for their narrow advantages.

Some scholars have reservations about the concept of political subcultures because it is a complex theory that is difficult to test. Their reservations are

traditionalistic subculture   View that political power should be concentrated in the hands of a few elite citizens who belong to established families or influential social groups. Public policy basically serves the interests of this small group.

elite   Small group of people who exercise disproportionate power and influence in the policy-making processes.

Although they comprise only a small percentage of the state's current population, one enduring legacy of the Native Americans is the name Texas, which is derived from the earlier term Tejas, which means "friends" or "allies" and was used by the Spanish to describe the Native American population.

legitimate, but we know of no other single theory that presents such a rich historical perspective on the relationship of settlement patterns in the state and the evolution of political attitudes and behavior.

THE PEOPLES OF TEXAS

The politics and government of Texas can be understood, in part, from the perspective of the people living in the state. What follows is a descriptive analysis of a select number of demographic characteristics of Texans. In subsequent chapters, we examine the relationship of race, ethnicity, and other demographic characteristics to partisan behavior, public opinion, institutional power, and public policy.

Native Americans   Only three small Native American groups (Alabama-Coushatta, Tigua, and Kickapoo) live on reservations in Texas, and the Native American population is less than one-half of 1 percent of the state's total population.

In the early nineteenth century, at least twenty-three different Native American groups resided in Texas (see *What Do You Think?* "What's in a Name?"). During the period of the Republic, President Sam Houston attempted to follow a policy of "peace and friendship" with the Native Americans, but he was followed by President Mirabeau B. Lamar, who set out to "expel, defeat, or exterminate" them. As the European populations expanded to lands belonging to various Native American groups, conflict ensued, and most of the Native American population was eventually eliminated or displaced to other states.[16]

Hispanics   In the eighteenth and nineteenth centuries, neither Spain nor Mexico was very successful in convincing Hispanics to settle in the Tejas territory of Mexico. The Spanish regarded it as a border province with relatively little value except as a strategic buffer between Spanish colonies and those held by the British and the French. By the time Mexico declared its independence from Spain in 1821, the total Texas population under Spanish control was estimated to be approximately 5,000. With the rapid expansion of Anglo American immigration to Texas in the 1820s and 1830s, Hispanics became a small minority of the population.[17]

Some Hispanics were part of the Texas independence movement from Mexico, and after independence in 1836, such individuals as José Antonio Navarro and Juan Seguin became part of the Republic's political establishment. But the Anglo migration rapidly overwhelmed the Hispanic population and greatly reduced its political and economic power. There was even an effort at the Constitutional Convention of 1845 to strip Hispanics of the right to vote. The attempt failed, but it was an early indication of Anglo hostility toward the Hispanic population.[18]

By 1887 the Hispanic population had declined to approximately 4 percent of the state's total. In 1930 it was 12 percent, concentrated in the border counties from Brownsville to El Paso (see Figure 19-1). There were modest increases in the Hispanic population until it reached 18 percent of the state's population in 1970, after which it grew at a more rapid rate. By 1990 it had reached 25 percent, spurred by immigration from Mexico and other Latin American countries as well as by higher birthrates among Hispanic women. In addition to their traditional concentrations in the Rio Grande Valley and South-Central Texas, large Hispanic populations are found in most metropolitan areas. Except for the Asian population, which is still considerably smaller, the Hispanic population is growing at a significantly higher rate than any other population.

The Hispanic population will probably continue to increase at a higher rate than others, and by 2000, the Hispanic population is projected to represent 31 percent of the state's total; by 2020, this figure may grow to 41 percent. This growth has already produced significant political power and influence: two Hispanics have been elected to statewide office and, following redistricting and legal challenges to city, county, school board, and state legislative districts, Hispanics in 1994 held approximately 2,200 elected positions in Texas, the highest number of any state.

The regions of the state where Hispanics were concentrated (South Texas and along the Mexican border) before their more widespread migration to cities were areas heavily influenced by the traditionalistic subculture. Extreme poverty, low levels of education, and local economies based on agriculture contributed to the development of political systems dominated by a few Anglos, who often considered Hispanics second-class citizens. Hispanics' increasing political clout, however, has produced major political and governmental changes in those regions.

African Americans   Some African Americans lived in Texas during the colonization period, but the modern story of African American settlement did not begin until after independence in 1836. When Texas was part of Mexico, Mexican law restricted slavery within the territory. During the period of the Republic and early statehood prior to the U.S. Civil War, there was a significant increase in the African American population as Americans settling in Texas brought cotton cultivation and the slavery system with them. At the time of the Civil War, 30 percent of the state's residents were African American, but that percentage declined after the war. By 1960 it had leveled off to 12 percent, about the same level counted in the 1990 census (see Figure 19-1). African Americans are

Year	Total Population	Percent Anglo †	Percent African American	Percent Hispanic	Percent Other
1860	604,215	63.2%	30.3%	6.5%	
1930	5,824,715	73.3%	14.7%	12.0%	
1950	7,711,194	74.3%	12.7%	13.0%	
1960	9,579,677	72.6%	12.4%	15.0%	
1970	11,196,730	69.1%	12.5%	18.4%	
1980	14,229,191	65.6%	12.0%	21.0%	1.4%
1990	16,986,510	60.3%	11.9%	25.5%	2.3%
2000	20,318,262*	54.7%	11.4%	30.8%	3.1%

* Population projected to the year 2000
† White, not of Hispanic origin

FIGURE 19-1   Ethnic and Racial Composition of Texas, 1860–2000

Note: The Hispanic total for 1970 based on "Persons of Spanish language or surname." Data for Asian and other populations were not tabulated by the Bureau of the Census prior to 1980.

Source: Terry G. Jordan with John L. Bean, Jr., and William M. Holmes, *Texas: A Geography* (Boulder, Colo.: Westview Press, 1984), pp. 81, 83; U.S. Censuses, 1860–1990; Population Estimates and Projections Program, Texas State Data Center, Department of Rural Sociology, Texas A&M University System, *Projections of the Population of Texas and Counties in Texas by Age, Sex, Race/Ethnicity for 1990 to 2030,* February 1994.

expected to represent between 11 and 12 percent of the state's population during the next twenty-five years.

There is a large concentration of African Americans in East Texas, where white southerners and their slaves originally settled. African Americans are also concentrated in the urban areas of Dallas, Fort Worth, Austin, and Houston. Relatively few African Americans live in the western counties or in the counties along the border with Mexico. The increased number of African American state legislators, city council members, county commissioners, and school board trustees representing urban communities is an indication of the political power of the African American population in selected areas. In 1993, the most recent year for which data were available, there were 472 African American elected officials in Texas, but only one African American had been elected to statewide office.

The slaveholding whites who migrated to Texas from the lower southern states brought with them the dominant values of the traditionalistic political subculture. Although slaves were freed after the Civil War, continued political and economic discrimination against African Americans was commonplace in the eastern part of Texas into the 1960s. As in South Texas, the politics of East Texas served the interests of the white elites.

Attorney General Dan Morales, who retired in 1998, is the first Hispanic to have won election to a statewide administrative position. His victory reflected the increasing influence of Hispanics in Texas.

Anglos   In the vernacular of Texas politics, the white population is referred to as "Anglos," although there is no census designation by that name. The term includes Jews, Irish, Poles, and just about any other individual who is designated by the U.S. Bureau of the Census as "non-Hispanic white."

Scholars have identified two distinct early patterns of Anglo migration into Texas from other states. These patterns, as well as population movements through much of the late nineteenth and early twentieth centuries, largely explain the regional locations of the state's two dominant political subcultures.

In the early nineteenth century, the first Anglos moving to Texas were from the upper South—Tennessee, Kentucky, Arkansas, and North Carolina—a region significantly influenced by the individualistic subculture of limited government. The earliest settlements were primarily in what is now Northeast Texas in the Red River Valley. After Mexican independence from Spain, there was a second wave of immigration from the upper South. Few of the early colonists were plantation slaveholders from the lower South.

After Texas became independent, slavery was legalized, and settlers from the lower South began arriving. By the outbreak of the Civil War, Anglos who had moved to Texas from the lower South were roughly equal in number to those from the upper South. Arrivals from the slaveholding lower South initially settled in southeastern Texas near Louisiana, but soon they began to move northward and westward.

A line between Texarkana and San Antonio in effect divides Texas subcultures. Most of those Anglos who settled north and west of this line were from the upper South and heavily influenced by the individualistic subculture, which favors limited government. Anglos who settled south and east of the line were by and large from the lower South and shaped by its traditionalistic subculture.

This pattern of immigration and settlement continued after the Civil War. It was primarily those populations from the upper South who pushed westward to the Panhandle and West Texas. This expansion introduced to the western part of the state the cultural experience of those who resisted the notion that government

What Do You Think?

What's in a Name?

The Native American legacy of Texas lives on in the state's name. The word "Texas" comes from *Tejas*, which means "friends" or "allies." As Spanish explorers and missionaries moved across Texas, they encountered a Native American confederacy, the Hasinai. It was to this particular group that they applied the term, and eventually the Anglo form of the name became the permanent name of the region and then the state.

In 1989 the Texas Department of Transportation proposed changing the state's vehicle license plates to include the phrase, "The Friendship State." The proposal was dropped, however, because of a generally hostile public reaction. Some Texans apparently found the phrase incompatible with the state's rugged frontier image. The irony is that the state's very name, which means "friendship," is used almost every day by these same people.

Source: Rupert N. Richardson, Ernest Wallace, and Adrian N. Anderson, *Texas: The Lone Star State*, 6th ed. (Englewood Cliffs, N.J.: Prentice Hall, 1993), p. 1.

---

existed to solve society's ills. To this day, West Texas is still one of the most politically conservative areas of the state.[19]

In 1860 Anglos constituted approximately 63 percent of Texas' population (see Figure 19-1). The Anglo population increased until it reached 74 percent in 1950. But by 1990 the stabilization of the African American population and the increase in the Hispanic population had reduced the Anglo proportion to 60 percent. It is projected that Anglos will account for only 55 percent of Texas's population by the year 2000 and will continue to decline as a percentage of the total population through the first three decades of the twenty-first century.

The Anglo population is diverse, as exhibits in the Institute of Texan Cultures in San Antonio remind us. Towns throughout Texas are identified with immigrants of national origin other than Anglo-Saxon, and these national groups brought with them a rich heritage. Castroville, for example, is identified with the Alsatians; New Braunfels and Fredericksburg, the Germans; Panna Maria, the Poles; West and Hallettsville, the Czechs.

The Asian American Population   In 1980 Asian Americans accounted for 0.8 percent of Texas's population, but by 1990 the figure had grown to 1.9 percent. By 2000 the Asian American population will constitute 2.6 percent of the state total, which is projected to increase to 4.2 percent by 2020. This rapid increase parallels national trends. Changes in immigration policy and the dislocation of Asians due to war and political persecution have resulted in larger numbers of Asian immigrants entering the United States since the 1970s.

The largest concentration of Asian Americans in Texas is in Houston, where two Asian Americans have been elected to major public offices: Hannah Chow was elected judge of Harris County Criminal Court-at-Law No. 5 in 1986, and community activist Martha Wong was elected to the Houston City Council in 1993. Another Houstonian, Robert Gee, became one of the first Asian Americans to hold a state office when Governor Ann Richards appointed him to the Texas Public Utility Commission in 1991.

POLITICS, RACE, AND ETHNICITY

Today few Texans don the robes of the Ku Klux Klan and march in support of white supremacy. A state law barring African Americans from voting in party primaries was declared unconstitutional in the 1940s, and many other laws intended to reduce the political participation of African Americans and Hispanics have been eliminated. The federal Voting Rights Act, which was enacted in 1965 and extended to Texas in 1975, has also helped open up state and local electoral systems to minorities. There is still evidence of employment and housing discrimination, and opposition to the desegregation of a public housing project in Vidor received national publicity in 1993. But restrictive codes prohibiting a specific group of people from buying residential property have been declared unconstitutional, and federal and state laws have given minorities greater access to jobs.

Nonetheless, race and ethnicity are implicit issues in many contemporary political and policy discussions. Throughout the debate on restructuring the school finance system, the protagonists were identified as the "rich" and "poor" school districts of the state. But, in large part, these were alternative terms for "nonminority" and "minority" school systems. There have been bitter debates about redistricting to increase Hispanic and African American representation in the state legislature and the U.S. Congress. And although many poor Anglos live in Texas, the disproportionately high poverty rates among minority groups often influence discussions about social services. Many state and local elections show evidence of polarized voting along ethnic lines. Race and ethnicity also emerge in jury selection, employment patterns, contracts with state and local governments, and expenditures for public health and social service programs.

More than forty years ago, V.O. Key, a Texan scholar of American politics, concluded that Texas politics was moving from issues of race to issues of class and economics. He argued that voters in Texas "divide along class lines in accord with their class interests as related to liberal and conservative candidates."[20] In part, he was correct, in that unabashed racial bigotry and public demagoguery are, by and large, no longer part of the political mainstream. In part, though, he was incorrect and much too optimistic. If the state divides on economic issues, this division puts the majority of Anglos on one side and the majority of Hispanics and African Americans on the other.[21]

THE POLITICAL IMPLICATIONS OF DEMOGRAPHICS

Population Increase   Over the past fifty years, the population of Texas has increased at rates much higher than the national average (see Figure 19-1). According to the 1990 census, the population of Texas was 16,986,510, an increase of 2.7 million people in ten years. The 1997 estimate of 19.3 million made Texas the second most populous state in the nation. The population is expected to exceed 20 million by the 2000 census, a projected rate of growth for the decade of 19.6 percent.[22]

Birthrates explain part of the population increase, but migration from other states has also been a significant factor. In recent decades, demographers (those who study populations) have described a nationwide shift in population from the Northeast and Midwest to the South and West. For each of the censuses from 1940 to 1970, in-migration accounted for less than 10 percent of Texas's growth. But

Members of white supremacist groups demonstrate against the desegregation of a public housing project in Vidor, Texas.

in-migration jumped to 58.5 percent of the total growth between 1970 and 1980.[23] Between 1980 and 1990, it contributed 34.4 percent.[24]

Although it is expected to become less significant in the future, in-migration has already contributed to the restructuring of Texas's traditional one-party, Democratic political system into a two-party system. Many new residents came from states with strong Republican Party traditions and brought their affiliation with them. In the long run, in-migration may affect additional elements of the state's political culture.

The increase in population places demands on all levels of government, and many local governments throughout Texas are hard pressed to provide adequate services. Many Texas cities, for example, are already running out of landfill space. Environmental laws make it difficult to obtain new licenses for garbage and waste disposal, and without these additional facilities, new population growth cannot be serviced. The increased population has also raised questions about the adequacy of water supplies and has clogged streets and highways in urban and suburban areas.

The Aging Population Texans, along with other Americans, are aging. In 1990, 10.1 percent of the state's population was older than sixty-five, and the percentage was expected to increase to 17 percent by 2030.[25] This aging population will place unprecedented demands on the public and private sectors for goods and services, including expanded health care and long-term care.

Urbanization Although Texas was a rural state during the first 100 years of its history, approximately 80 percent of the state's population now resides in areas classified by the Bureau of the Census as urban (see Figure 19-2). **Urbanization** and suburban sprawl now characterize Texas's settlement patterns, and many urban corridors and suburban areas cross county boundaries. Residents of these areas often encounter problems that cut across political jurisdictions, and local governments sometimes find it difficult to resolve them.

The dramatic growth of Texas's largest cities is shown in Table 19-1. From 1960 to 1990, the population of Houston and El Paso nearly doubled. Dallas increased by 48 percent and San Antonio, 60 percent. Arlington had a population of only 44,775 in 1960, but in 1990 its population was 261,721, an increase of 548

urbanization Process by which a predominantly rural society or area becomes urban.

TABLE 19-1	Ten Largest Texas Cities						
City	*1900*	*1920*	*1940*	*1960*	*1980*	*1990*	*1997*
Houston	44,633	138,276	384,514	838,219	1,595,138	1,630,553	1,818,613
San Antonio	53,321	161,379	253,854	587,718	785,880	935,933	1,114,579
Dallas	42,638	158,976	294,734	679,684	904,078	1,006,877	1,062,218
El Paso	15,906	77,560	96,810	276,687	425,259	515,342	592,442
Austin	22,258	34,876	87,960	186,545	345,496	465,622	572,288
Fort Worth	26,688	106,482	177,662	356,268	385,164	447,619	481,480
Arlington	1,079	3,031	4,240	44,775	160,113	261,721	300,160
Corpus Christi	4,703	10,522	57,301	167,690	231,999	257,453	275,100
Lubbock	0	4,051	31,853	128,691	173,979	186,206	194,202
Garland	819	1,421	2,233	38,501	138,857	180,650	191,904

Sources: U.S. Censuses, 1900–1990; Texas State Data Center, 1997.

FIGURE 19-2 Urban and Rural Population of Texas, 1850–1990

Source: U.S. Censuses, 1850–1990.

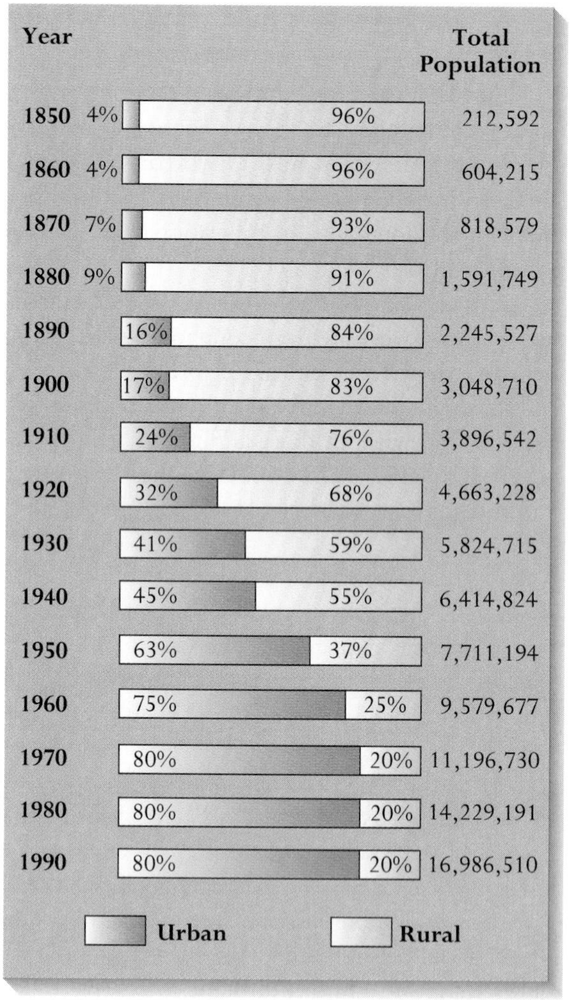

Year	Urban %	Rural %	Total Population
1850	4%	96%	212,592
1860	4%	96%	604,215
1870	7%	93%	818,579
1880	9%	91%	1,591,749
1890	16%	84%	2,245,527
1900	17%	83%	3,048,710
1910	24%	76%	3,896,542
1920	32%	68%	4,663,228
1930	41%	59%	5,824,715
1940	45%	55%	6,414,824
1950	63%	37%	7,711,194
1960	75%	25%	9,579,677
1970	80%	20%	11,196,730
1980	80%	20%	14,229,191
1990	80%	20%	16,986,510

Urban □   Rural □

percent. During this thirty-year period, Austin's population increased by 250 percent. All of these cities continued to show growth from 1990 to 1997.

Three of the ten largest cities in the United States are in Texas, and, like urban areas throughout the country, Texas's largest cities are increasingly populated by minorities. This trend results from higher birthrates among minority populations, urban migration patterns, and what is often referred to as "white flight" from the cities to suburban areas. Minority groups now account for the majority of the population in five of Texas's ten largest cities (Houston, San Antonio, Dallas, El Paso, and Corpus Christi). These minority residents include Hispanics, African Americans, and Asian Americans—groups that do not always constitute a cohesive bloc of interests. As minority growth continues, there will be areas of potential conflict among these groups.

population density Number of residents living within the boundaries of a city, county, or state in relationship to the land area. Population density is a significant factor in determining the level of local public services.

Population Density **Population density** refers to the number of people per square mile in a specific political jurisdiction. The greater the number of people living in close proximity, the greater the number of problems that emerge as people disagree over the use of land and resources. Complex social and economic relationships produce increased demands for government regulation, controls, and intervention (see *What Do You Think?* "Do Size and Geography Shape Texas Politics?").

What Do You Think?

Do Size and Geography Shape Texas Politics?

Texas is a big state. Covering 267,339 square miles, it is second only to Alaska in land mass. Although Texans appear to have adjusted to long distances—blithely driving 50 miles for a night out—visitors from out of state are often overwhelmed by Texas's size and diversity. The distance from Texarkana in Northeast Texas to El Paso in far West Texas is about 800 miles, and a person living in Texarkana is closer to Chicago than to El Paso. Brownsville in far South Texas is closer to Mexico City than it is to Texline in the Texas Panhandle.

Many would argue that perceptions of the state's size have helped shape political attitudes and concepts, and size has obviously affected state policy. Roads and highways, for example, have historically received a significant—and some would argue a disproportionate—share of the state's budget. Economic development in such a large, diverse state required a commitment to highway construction, and roads were regarded as essential to the development of an integrated economy.

One scholar argued that the great distances in Texas were politically important because they made it difficult for a politician to develop a personal following, such as could be cultivated in many smaller states. Size and distance deterred the development of a statewide political machine similar to those that developed in Virginia and Louisiana in the 1920s and

1930s. Although there have been regional or local political machines, such as the now-defunct Parr machine in South Texas, none extended statewide.

Size also contributes to the high cost of political campaigns. Candidates in the 1990 gubernatorial race spent more than $50 million to communicate with and mobilize Texas voters. There are twenty separate media markets in the state, and the cost of communicating with the voters is likely to increase.

A traveler driving across Texas is struck by the diversity in topography, climate, and vegetation. The state's "landforms range from offshore bars and barrier beaches to formidable mountains, from rugged canyons, gorges, and badlands to totally flat plains."* The western part of the state is dry and semiarid; the east is humid and subtropical, producing extremes in precipitation. South Texas often enjoys a tropical winter, whereas North Texas experiences cold winters with snowfall. The growing seasons in the south are virtually year-round; those in the north are approximately 180 days. East Texas is characterized by its piney woods, semiarid South Texas by its brush country.

Geography shaped historical migration and land use in Texas, and, although modern technology can partially compensate for climate and geography, geography continues to shape the economies and population patterns of the state.

---

*Terry G. Jordan with John L. Bean, Jr., and William M. Holmes, *Texas: A Geography* (Boulder, Colo.: Westview Press, 1984), p. 7.

There are marked differences in the population and density of Texas's 254 counties. Loving County in West Texas has a population of about 100 persons living in an area of 671 square miles. The most populous county is Harris County (Houston), with more than 3.1 million people living in 1,734 square miles. The problems and issues that Loving County faces are significantly different from those in Harris County, yet both counties function with the same form of government created by the Texas Constitution of 1876.

Conflict in Texas politics has often divided along urban-rural lines. Redistricting battles and a host of other public policy issues are evidence of that. Until recently, the Texas legislature was dominated by rural lawmakers, many of whom were insensitive to urban needs. Moreover, many of urban Texas's problems are exacerbated by constitutional restrictions written when Texas was still a rural state.

Wealth and Income Distribution   There is a wide disparity in the distribution of income and wealth across the state. To make the *Forbes* 400 list in 1997, an individual had to have a net worth of $475 million. Twenty-nine Texans were on this list with an estimated combined net worth of $40 billion. The "poorest" of this group had a net worth of $490 million, and the "richest," computer magnate Michael Dell, had a net worth of $5.5 billion.[26]

The vast majority of Texans have incomes or assets that come nowhere near those of the superwealthy. The average family income in Texas in 1989 was $31,553, and the average household income was $27,016, both below the national averages (see Table 19-2). By 1995 the average household income in the United States was $34,076, whereas the average household income in Texas was $32,039.[27]

By all measures of income, Hispanics and African Americans fall significantly below the Anglo population. According to the 1990 census, 39 percent of Hispanic households and 43 percent of African American households in Texas reported incomes below $15,000, but only 22 percent of Anglo households and a similar portion of the Asian American population reported incomes below that level. By contrast, 27 percent of Anglo households but only 9 percent of Hispanic households and 10 percent of African American households reported incomes above $50,000.

Many Texans live in severe poverty. Seven of the twenty poorest counties in the nation are in Texas. These are border counties (Dimmit, Hidalgo, Maverick, Starr, Willacy, Zapata, and Zavala) with large Hispanic populations and unemployment rates that are twice the state average. The per capita income (total income divided by the population) for Texas was $12,904 in 1989. For the Anglo population, it was significantly higher, but for African Americans, the figure was $8,102, and for Hispanics, $6,663.

In 1995 the poverty-level guidelines used in Texas to establish eligibility for many federal and state programs were $15,569 for a family of four and $7,763 for one person. According to the U.S. Bureau of the Census, 17.4 percent of the state's population, or 3.27 million people, fell below the poverty level. The impact of poverty was felt disproportionately by children, persons older than sixty-five, Hispanics, African Americans, and those living in one-parent households.[28]

Poverty is likely to worsen in Texas. Without significant changes in educational levels and expanded economic opportunities, approximately 20 percent of the state's households may fall below the poverty level by 2030, and income disparity will be especially problematic for minorities.[29]

| TABLE 19-2 | U.S. and Texas Income Figures, 1990 Census |

| | United States | Texas | | | | | |
	All Persons	All Persons	Anglos	Hispanics	African Americans	Native Americans	Asian Americans
Median income*							
Household	$30,056	$27,016	$31,475	$19,233	$17,853	$23,340	$30,792
Families	35,225	31,553	38,051	20,121	20,613	27,218	35,729
Per capita income	14,420	12,904	16,469	6,663	8,102	11,086	12,029
Percent of persons							
below poverty level	13.1%	18.1%	9.7%	33.0%	31.0%	20.8%	15.7%

*1989 dollars.

Source: Bureau of the Census, *1990 Census of Population: Social and Economic Characteristics.*

Financial resources can be translated into political power and influence, and some Texans clearly have greater clout than others.

Education and Literacy Public education has been a dominant issue in state politics for many years now. Litigation has forced the legislature to consider changes in the funding of public schools, and education will be a primary factor in determining whether Texas can successfully compete in a new global economy.

Over the next decade, 80 percent of the new jobs created in Texas will be in service industries. Most of these jobs will require increased reading, writing, and math skills, and high school dropouts will find fewer and fewer employment opportunities. Some experts predict that 50 percent of the jobs that will be created in the United States in the next decade will require a college education, compared to only 22 percent in the mid-1990s.[30] Texas faces a crisis in public education, and the state's ability to resolve it will directly affect the financial well-being of many Texans (see *Compared to What?* "Texas in Comparison to Other States").

According to the 1990 census, 72 percent of Texans twenty-five and older had completed high school, and 20 percent had completed college (see Figure 19-3). But there are wide disparities in the educational levels of the three major ethnic-racial groups. Sixty-six percent of the adult African Americans in Texas had completed high school, and 12 percent had completed college. Among Hispanics, 45 percent had completed high school, and approximately 7 percent had college degrees. Some 82 percent of the Anglo population age twenty-five and older had graduated from high school, and 25 percent had completed college.

Education not only helps determine a person's employment and income potential but also affects his or her participation in politics. Individuals with high educational levels are much more likely to be informed about politics and to participate in the political process than those who are less educated.

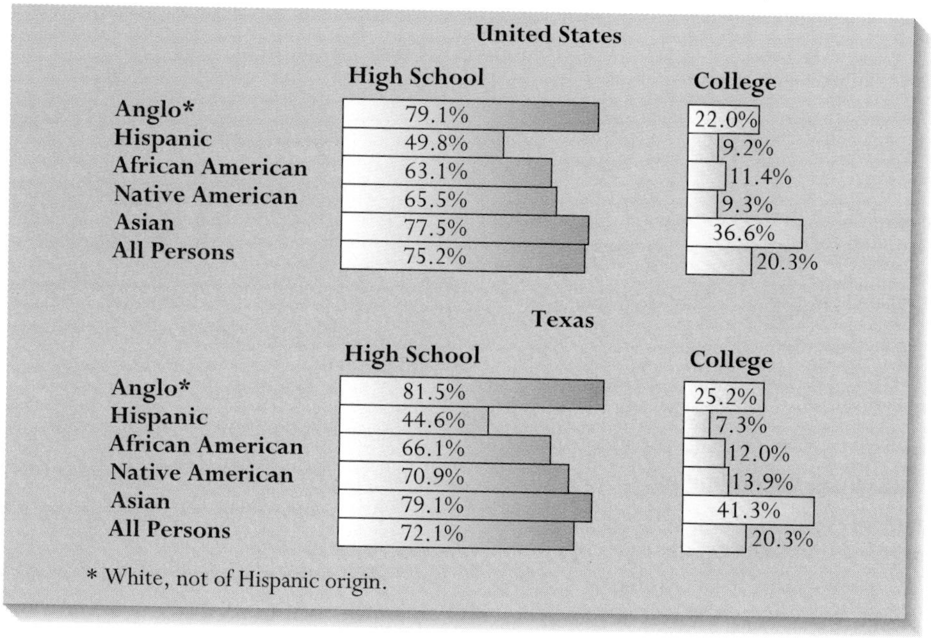

United States

	High School		College	
Anglo*	79.1%		22.0%	
Hispanic	49.8%		9.2%	
African American	63.1%		11.4%	
Native American	65.5%		9.3%	
Asian	77.5%		36.6%	
All Persons	75.2%		20.3%	

Texas

	High School		College	
Anglo*	81.5%		25.2%	
Hispanic	44.6%		7.3%	
African American	66.1%		12.0%	
Native American	70.9%		13.9%	
Asian	79.1%		41.3%	
All Persons	72.1%		20.3%	

* White, not of Hispanic origin.

FIGURE 19-3 Texas and U.S. Educational Attainment by Race and Ethnicity, 1990, for Population Age 25 and Older

Source: U.S. Bureau of the Census, *1990 Census of Population: Social and Economic Characteristics.*

Compared to What?

Texas in Comparison to Other States

Among the fifty states, Texas ranks:

#1 in total exports to Mexico ($27.4 billion in 1996)

in number of public school teachers (234,216 in 1994–1995)

in state prisoner incarceration rate (659 prisoners per 100,000 population in 1995)

in population change from 1990 to 1996 (2,141,926)

#2 in population (18.7 million in 1995)

in percentage of population that is Hispanic (28.3 percent in 1995)

#3 in gross state product ($476 billion in 1996)

in U.S. Department of Defense expenditures ($16.93 billion in 1995)

#4 in number of *Fortune* 500 companies (37 in 1996)

in institutions of higher learning (179 in 1996)

in deaths from AIDS-related causes (2,745 in 1994)

#5 in state sales tax rate (6.25 percent as of 1995)

#6 in average household size (2.75 persons per household in 1994)

in business failure rate (90 failures per 10,000 businesses in 1995)

#7 in enrollment in private institutions of higher education (111,493 in 1994)

in percentage of households receiving food stamps (14.2 percent in 1995)

#8 in teen unemployment (21.5 percent unemployment for teens age 16–19 in 1993)

in safety belt usage rate (72 percent in 1995)

#9 in robbery rate (253 robberies per 100,000 people in 1992)

#10 in percentage of school-age children living in poverty (23.1 percent in 1995)

#11 in education spending as a percentage of total state and local government spending (33.7 percent in 1993)

#12 in burglary rate (1,168 burglaries per 100,000 people in 1994)

#13 in per capita state lottery net proceeds to the state ($50.46 million in 1994)

#14 in hazardous waste sites on the National Priorities List (28 in 1996)

#15 in divorce rate (5.4 divorces per 1,000 population in 1994)

#16 in percentage of state legislators who are African American (8.8 percent in 1993)

#17 in percentage of the population that is African American (12.1 percent in 1995)

in percentage of murders involving firearms (69.2 percent in 1995)

#18 in average annual pay ($25,959 in 1994)

#19 in death rate by suicide (12.8 suicides per 100,000 population in 1992)

#20 in percentage of adults who smoke (23.66 percent in 1995)

in state tax rate on gasoline (20 cents per gallon in 1995)

Source: Texas Comptroller of Public Accounts, July 1994, July 1996; Kathleen O'Leary Morgan, Scott Morgan and Neal Quitno, *State Rankings 1997: A Statistical View of the 50 States* (Lawrence, Kans.: Morgan Quitno Press, 1997); *Texas Economic Quarterly*, September 1997.

THE ECONOMY OF TEXAS

Politics, government, and economics are inextricably linked. An economy that is robust and expanding provides far more options to government policy makers than an economy in recession. A healthy tax base requires an expanding economy, and when the economy goes through periods of recession, state and local governments are confronted with the harsh realities of having to increase taxes or cut back on public services, usually at a time when more people need governmental assistance.

At the beginning of the 1980s, Texas had experienced a sustained period of growth, and state government was able to adopt new policies and expand existing services with only minimal tax increases. But by 1991, the state had experienced a decade of economic boom and bust with two severe recessions, and the legislature had been forced to restrict public services and impose a series of significant tax increases.

Historically, the health of the Texas economy had been linked to oil and natural gas. In 1981, for example, 27 percent of the state's economy was tied to energy-related industries. The decade started with rapid increases in the world price of oil, and there was an economic boom throughout the financial, construction, and manufacturing sectors of the state's economy.[31]

But a series of national and international events soon produced major problems. World oil prices began to drop in 1981, resulting in serious unemployment problems in the Gulf Coast and Plains regions of the state. There was a disastrous decline in the value of the Mexican peso, which had a negative impact on the economies of border cities and counties; and in 1983 a harsh freeze in South Texas and a severe drought in West Texas had serious adverse effects on the agricultural sector. Some regions of the state were insulated from these conditions, but other areas experienced a significant economic downturn.[32]

Economic disaster struck again in 1986, with a 60 percent drop in the price of oil and corresponding reductions in the price of natural gas. Drilling activity in the state plummeted and was followed by a loss of 84,000 energy-related jobs. The problem was compounded by a worldwide slump in the electronics industry. These events hurt the construction and real estate sectors of the economy and, in turn, manufacturing and retail trade. For sixteen straight months in 1986 and 1987, the state's employment rate dropped, with a loss of an estimated 233,000 jobs.[33]

These economic reversals had a disastrous effect on Texas's banks and savings and loan institutions. "In 1987 and 1988, more Texas financial institutions failed than at any other time since the Great Depression," the state comptroller's office reported.

For much of the twentieth century, oil played a dominant role in the Texas economy, as the derricks in this photo of the town of Kilgore in the 1930s reflect. But with increased U.S. reliance on imported oil and the subsequent decline in Texas oil exploration and production, the Texas economy has become more diversified, reducing its reliance on oil and natural gas.

And the pattern of bank failures continued through 1990. The federal government developed a plan to bail out institutions that were covered by federal deposit insurance. But as the magnitude of the problem became clearer, there was a bitter debate over its causes, including the deregulation of the savings and loan and banking industries, inadequate government scrutiny of banking practices, a frenzy of speculation with questionable or unsecured loans, and outright fraud and malfeasance.[34]

State and local governments consequently suffered declines in revenues. With falling property values, local governments that depended on the property tax were particularly vulnerable. The legislature convened in special session in 1986 to pass an $875 million tax bill and cut the state budget by about $580 million in an attempt to "patch up" the widening holes in projected state revenues. In 1987 the legislature, mandated by the state constitution to a "pay as you go" system of government and denied the option of deficit financing, enacted a $5.6 billion tax bill, including an increase in the sales tax, a **regressive tax** that most adversely affects low-income people.[35]

By 1988 the economy was recovering, with slow, modest growth in most of the state. Oil and natural gas, although still important to the economy, were being replaced as the driving force in economic expansion. Increased manufacturing and the expansion of service industries, in particular, were responsible for the incremental recovery the state experienced through 1990. The state's growth rate declined again in 1991, reflecting broad recessionary patterns of the national economy. But beginning in 1992 and continuing through 1998, the Texas economy improved at a moderate pace. For much of the period from 1989 through 1997, the growth of the Texas economy outpaced national trends, and the pattern was expected to extend through 2000 (see Figure 19-4).

regressive tax   Tax that imposes a disproportionately heavier burden on low-income people than on the more affluent.

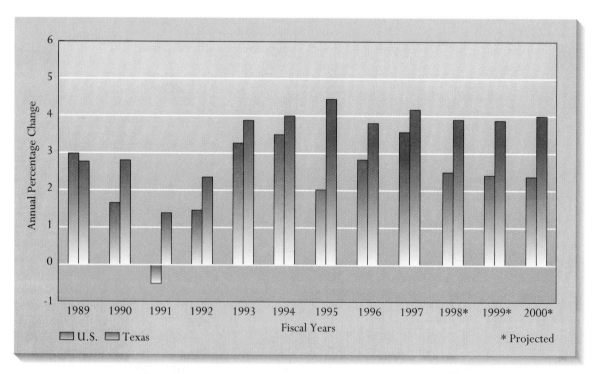

FIGURE 19-4   Texas and U.S. Economic Growth, 1989–2000
Source: Texas Comptroller of Public Accounts.

Because of the significant changes in the Texas economy, a number of experts argue that the state is now less vulnerable to the volatility of the energy industry. Based on 1996 figures, only 10 percent of the state's economy was tied to oil- and gas-related industries.[36] Texas ranked first in the number of new jobs created for five consecutive years (1990–94) and continued to rank second or third through 1998. More than half of these new jobs were linked to services and trade. Construction rebounded by 1994, and government employment expanded, in part because of a large prison construction program.[37] In addition, a restructured financial industry experienced a noticeable recovery by 1993.[38]

Clouding the picture, however, were a peso devaluation in 1994, recession in Mexico in 1995, and post–Cold War reductions in U.S. defense spending, which had accounted for 5.7 percent of the gross state product in 1987. By 2005 defense spending should account for only about 3 percent of the state's economy.[39]

In 1997 Texas had a gross state product of $521 billion (in 1992 dollars). By comparison, the gross domestic product of the United States that year was $6.9 trillion. The Texas economy was the third largest among the states, following California and New York. If Texas were a nation, its economy would rank eleventh in the world.[40]

Texas has experienced **economic diversification**. It has shifted from overreliance on energy to manufacturing, services, and trade with foreign countries. The largest growth sector has been in service industries, which range from low-paid restaurant workers to high-salaried medical and legal professionals.

A second notable change is the emerging shift to high-tech industries. Many economic and political leaders believe the state's future must be directly tied to these developing industries, and the state and many cities have developed aggressive recruitment programs that include economic development bonds and tax abatements for high-tech companies.

The term *high-tech* is generally used to describe business activities that produce new technology based on highly sophisticated computer applications. Companies that make semiconductors, microprocessors, and computer hardware and software clearly fall into this category, as do companies that produce telecommunications devices, fiber optics, aerospace guidance systems, and some medical instruments.[41] These industries have been joined by new biotechnology industries involved in producing new medicines, vaccines, and genetic engineering of plants and animals. Houston and Dallas have emerged as centers for biotechnology, with some development also occurring in San Antonio, Austin, and Fort Worth.[42]

There also is a trend, in both Texas and in the United States as a whole, toward what is often referred to as the **globalization of the economy**. Throughout the 1980s, as world oil prices directly affected the state, Texans were made keenly aware of their increased dependence on the world economy. But this development is much more complex. Foreign investment in Texas business has become increasingly common. Moreover, Texas exported $84.3 billion in goods and services in 1997 with approximately 37 percent going to Mexico.[43] The North American Free Trade Agreement among the United States, Mexico, and Canada, discussed later in this chapter, has already produced changes in the economic relationships among these countries, and more economic interdependence for North America is anticipated.

economic diversification
Development of new and varied business activities. New businesses were encouraged to relocate or expand in Texas after the oil and gas industry, which had been the base of the state's economy, suffered a major recession in the 1980s.

globalization of the economy Increased interdependence in trade, manufacturing, and commerce as well as most other business activities between the United States and other countries.

ECONOMIC REGIONS OF TEXAS

The economic diversity of Texas can be described in terms of ten distinct economic regions (see Figure 19-5). There are marked differences among these areas.[44] One may be undergoing rapid growth while another may be experiencing a recession.

The High Plains Region is made up of forty-one counties and includes Amarillo and Lubbock. Home of the XIT Ranch and Palo Duro Canyon, the region experienced a 1.2 percent decline in population from 1980 to 1990, but modest population growth was projected over the next decade. Agricultural production, whose major source of water is the Ogallala Aquifer, is a dominant industry. Related businesses include agricultural services, food processing, and the manufacturing of feed, fertilizers, and farm machinery and equipment. Oil and gas production is still an important component of the region's economy, but employment in the energy industry has declined from earlier periods.

The Northwest Texas Region includes thirty counties and the cities of Wichita Falls and Abilene. It had virtually no population growth between 1980 and 1990 and was expected to lose population during this decade. Agriculture and related businesses are important to the region's economy. The area is also home to several major oil and gas fields, but many jobs were lost in the crash of the energy industry in the 1980s. There is some employment in manufacturing, including construction-related

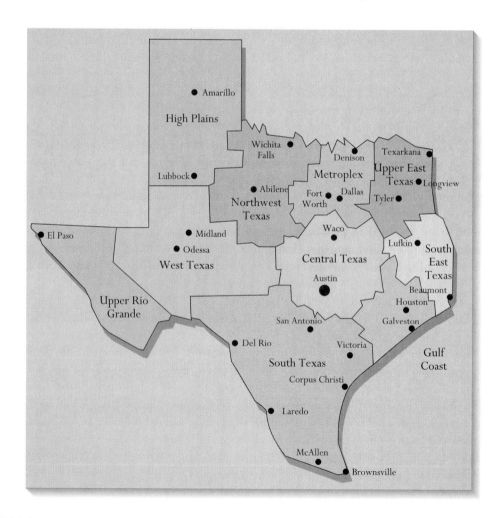

FIGURE 19-5 Economic Regions of Texas

Source: Texas Comptroller of Public Accounts.

products and apparel. Government employment is higher than the state average, primarily because of prisons in Abilene and Wichita Falls. The service sector also is a major source of employment.

The Metroplex Region includes nineteen counties and, with the cities of Dallas, Fort Worth, Sherman, and Denison, has the greatest concentration of large and middle-sized cities in the state. Population growth was 30.8 percent from 1980 to 1990, significantly higher than the state's overall 19.4 percent growth. The area is a major financial center, with regional offices of the Federal Reserve Bank and the Federal Home Loan Bank. It also has the Dallas Market Center (the world's largest trade complex) and the Dallas-Fort Worth International Airport. This region's manufacturing base is the most diversified in the state. The area is also home to growing and highly specialized electronics and communications industries. Health and business services industries also provide many jobs.

The Upper East Texas Region encompasses twenty-three counties and the cities of Texarkana, Marshall, Longview, and Tyler. Between 1980 and 1990, its population growth was significantly lower than the state's and was expected to continue to lag behind. Historically, the region's economy has been based on oil and gas, lumber, cotton, and cattle, but it has diversified over the past few decades. The area is now more manufacturing intensive than the state as a whole. Military-related manufacturing will decline with cutbacks in government defense spending, but the manufacture of lumber products will continue to show healthy growth, buoyed by home construction. Despite earlier losses, the oil and gas industry will continue to play a key role in the region's economy.

The Southeast Texas Region encompasses fifteen counties that extend from the upper Gulf Coast into the Piney Woods of East Texas and include Beaumont, Port Arthur, and Orange. From 1980 to 1990, its population increased by only 1.8 percent, and growth was expected to remain slow. Since the discovery of the famous Spindletop oil field in 1901, this area has been especially dependent on oil and gas production and refining and related industries, such as petrochemicals. Timber also plays a significant role in the region's economy. Future economic growth is projected in construction, health services, and poultry processing.

The Gulf Coast Region includes fourteen counties and the cities of Houston (the state's largest), Galveston, Texas City, and Angleton. The area has the Johnson Space Center and the Port of Houston, the second largest in the nation. Its population increased at about the same rate as the state's during the 1980s, but its growth was expected to exceed the state's during the 1990s. It has a diverse economy and is a center for petroleum and chemical production, water transportation, and trade. The Texas Medical Center, the world's largest medical complex, is in Houston, an important city in the development of the biotechnology industry. This region has long had a more cosmopolitan outlook than other parts of the state, and it is in an optimum position to capitalize on the globalization of the state's economy.

The Central Texas Region includes thirty counties of Central Texas and the cities of Austin, Waco, Killeen, Temple, Bryan, and College Station. Its economy is a well-balanced blend of agriculture, natural resources, trade, government, education, and industry. From 1980 to 1990, its population grew by 28 percent, and it was expected to remain one of the state's fastest growing areas. With three state universities, a military base in Killeen, and state government operations in Austin, government employment plays a larger economic role here than anywhere else in Texas, although government-related economic growth was expected to slow down. The region has become a center for high-tech industries, anchored by Microelectronics and Computer Technology Corporation (MCC) and Sematech (two research consortiums) and large university research programs. Manufacturing jobs were expected to show strong growth in the 1990s. Gains were also projected in the service sector, particularly in health care and business services.

The South Texas Region is geographically diverse and takes in forty-seven counties from the Texas Hill Country to the Lower Rio Grande Valley. It includes San Antonio, Victoria, Corpus Christi, Brownsville, McAllen, and Laredo. The population grew by 19 percent during the 1980s, and more growth was projected. Corpus Christi is the sixth largest port in the country, and the region has the state's largest number of foreign trade zones, where products from other countries can be imported with no tariffs until they are transported into domestic markets. The area along the Mexican border, however, includes some of the poorest counties in the United States and has high unemployment rates. Their economies received a boost from the construction of new product-assembly plants in Mexico, and more economic stimulus was anticipated from the North American Free Trade Agreement. Government employment, services, and trade were the largest sources of employment in this region, but cuts in defense spending were expected to take a toll in the government sector. There is considerable oil and gas production. Chemical and petrochemical production, which was expected to grow significantly during the 1990s, is centered in Corpus Christi, Victoria, and Calhoun County. Agriculture, livestock, and food processing are also important to the region. San Antonio is known internationally for its major tourist attractions—the Alamo, Sea World, and Fiesta Texas—and tourism will continue to be a growth industry.

The West Texas Region includes thirty counties and the cities of San Angelo, Odessa, and Midland. Its population increased by 8 percent during the 1980s, but more than one-third of its counties lost population, and only modest growth was expected during the 1990s. Economic diversification may be more difficult for this region than for any other area of the state because of its strong historic dependence on the energy industry. Long associated with oil and gas production and related manufacturing industries, this region was particularly hard hit with job losses during the energy bust of the 1980s. Agriculture also is important to the area, with the production of livestock, cotton, and a variety of other crops. Government jobs provide approximately 21 percent of the region's employment and were projected to increase during the 1990s.

The Upper Rio Grande Region consists of six counties located in the Chihuahuan Desert and includes El Paso (the oldest city in Texas) and Big Bend National Park. The population in this region grew by 23 percent between 1980 and 1990 and was expected to grow at a higher rate than the state's overall growth during the 1990s. With its close economic ties to Mexico, this area was hurt in the early 1980s by the sharp decline of the Mexican economy. But rapid industrialization along both sides of the border in the latter part of the decade produced impressive job gains, and the North American Free Trade Agreement was expected to benefit the region further. The manufacturing sector accounts for more than 19 percent of the region's employment. Economic and population growth in this area have prompted increased concerns in both Mexico and the United States about environmental impacts on the Rio Grande.

TRANSNATIONAL REGIONALISM

Texas shares a 900-mile border with Mexico, and common problems and interests that bond the two neighbors in **transnational regionalism** have taken on increased importance since the mid-1980s.

Historically, relations between the United States and Mexico have often been strained. The United States fought a war against Mexico in 1846–48, and on numerous later occasions, American troops entered Mexican territory, ostensibly to protect U.S. economic and national security interests. Apprehension about U.S. objectives resulted in Mexican policies on trade, commerce, and foreign ownership of property that were designed to insulate the country from excessive foreign influence and domination. Nevertheless, the interests of the two countries have long been bound by geopolitical factors, economics, and demographics. One Mexican author has compared the interdependence of the two countries to so-called Siamese twins, warning that "if one becomes gangrenous, the other twin will also be afflicted."[45]

Maquiladoras   Changes in the economic relationships between Mexico and the United States began with the **maquiladora program**, an initiative under Mexico's Border Industrialization Program in 1964 to boost employment, foreign exchange, and industrial development. It was also designed to transfer technology to Mexico, help train workers, and develop managerial skills among Mexican nationals.[46]

The concept was to develop twin plants, one in the United States and one in Mexico, under a single management. The plant in the United States would manufacture parts, and its Mexican counterpart would assemble them into a product, which, in turn, would be sent back to the United States for further processing or for shipping to customers.[47] Parts shipped into Mexico would not be subject to the normal tariffs, and the tax imposed on the assembled product would be minimal. In 1984 Mexico changed its laws to permit the United States and other foreign

transnational regionalism
The expanding economic and social interdependence of South Texas and Mexico.

maquiladora program
Policies initiated by Mexico in 1964 to stimulate economic growth along the U.S.-Mexico border.

The ever-expanding trade between Mexico and the United States is evident in this line of trucks waiting to cross the border in El Paso.

countries to establish these relationships throughout Mexico, rather than just on the border, and to permit 100 percent foreign ownership of the assembly plants in Mexico. The latter step was a radical departure from previous Mexican law, which prohibited such foreign ownership.[48]

The maquiladora program has not resulted in the construction of a significant number of manufacturing plants on the Texas side of the border because American companies have used existing plants throughout the United States to produce parts to be assembled in Mexico. Nevertheless, Texas's border counties have benefited through the creation of thousands of support jobs in transportation, warehousing, and services.[49]

With Mexico's membership (since 1986) in the international General Agreement on Tariffs and Trade (GATT) and the implementation of the North American Free Trade Agreement, the maquiladora program will continue to play a major role in transnational economic development. American organized labor opposes the program, arguing that the maquiladoras drain jobs from the United States. But the program provides a source of inexpensive labor for American businesses, which have complained for years that they cannot compete against lower foreign labor costs.

The North American Free Trade Agreement (NAFTA) Negotiations on a free trade agreement in 1991 marked a significant change in the relationship between Mexico and the United States. The negotiations were precipitated, in part, by world economics and the emergence of regional trading zones. But the administration of Mexican President Carlos Salinas de Gortari was also reacting to the failure of Mexico's economic policies of the 1980s and a fear of economic isolation. The end of the Cold War, a reduction in Central American conflicts, and internal population pressures were additional factors.[50]

The convergence of interests of the United States, Mexico, and Canada produced the **North American Free Trade Agreement (NAFTA)** to reduce tariffs and increase trade among the three countries. It created the world's largest trading bloc, with a combined population of approximately 400 million and a combined gross national product of more than $8 trillion in 1997.[51] Approved by the U.S. Congress in late 1993, the agreement had the strong support of the Texas business community, Governor Ann Richards, both U.S. senators from Texas, and twenty-four of the state's thirty members of the U.S. House of Representatives.

The treaty has increased trade among the three countries, strengthening previous economic ties and creating new ones. Texas has experienced significant economic changes from these new relationships, but the benefits have not been uniformly distributed throughout the state. The regions expected to benefit most in terms of new manufacturing jobs are the Dallas-Fort Worth area and Houston because of their concentrations of chemical and electronics industries.[52]

Some people on both sides of the U.S.-Mexico border fear that NAFTA will adversely affect their country. Labor unions in the United States are particularly concerned that lower labor costs in Mexico will drain jobs from the United States. Some manufacturers argue that labor and capital costs in Mexico will threaten their American markets. Some Texas officials fear that opening up the state's highways to Mexican trucks will create safety problems, and American trucking interests, including owners and drivers, oppose the competition from Mexican trucks on U.S. highways. In Mexico, there is concern that American corporations will dominate and reduce Mexico's control over its own economy. And, finally, envi-

North American Free Trade Agreement (NAFTA) Treaty among the United States, Canada, and Mexico that created the world's largest trading bloc. Approved by the U.S. Congress in 1993, the treaty is designed to reduce tariffs and increase trade among the three countries.

ronmentalists have argued that increased commerce will compound air and water pollution problems.

A number of American critics of NAFTA have also raised questions about Mexican political corruption and human rights violations, the continued domination of Mexican politics by the Revolutionary Institutional Party (PRI), and increased drug smuggling into the United States. Drug-related violence and alleged collusion between high-ranking Mexican officials and drug smugglers have sparked a heated debate over Mexican efforts to fight the drug problem.

Texas Attorney General Dan Morales, speaking to a group of law enforcement officers in November 1997, blamed NAFTA for opening the border to increased drug smuggling into Texas. Some 11,000 to 12,000 trucks were crossing the border each day at Laredo, he said. "Without thorough inspection of Mexican trucks, these Mexican [drug] cartels will feel like NAFTA means the North American Free Trafficking Agreement," he said.[53] But a spokesman for the National Office of Drug Control Policy said crackdowns on drug trafficking in Florida—not NAFTA—were responsible for increased smuggling along the U.S.-Mexican border. Mexican and South American drug traffickers had sought new routes, he said.[54]

The potential for political instability in Mexico surfaced dramatically with the uprising on January 1, 1994, of the Zapatistas, a peasant-based guerrilla movement centered in Chiapas. Although some efforts were made to address the Zapatistas' grievances, the massacre of 45 people in late 1997 by gunmen with alleged links to the ruling party cast more shadows on Mexico's political system. Presidential candidate Luis Donaldo Colosio was assassinated in March 1994, and José Francisco Ruiz Massieu, secretary general of the ruling party, was killed in September of that year. There is still widespread suspicion in the United States and Mexico that officials of the ruling party were involved in these murders.

With the devaluation of the peso in late 1994 and the beginning of a serious Mexican recession in 1995, further concern was expressed about the instability of the Mexican economy and its potential for destabilizing the Mexican political system. The Clinton Administration responded with an economic rescue plan for Mexico. President Clinton maintained that the collapse of the Mexican economy threatened to weaken the U.S. dollar, hurt exports, and generate disruption in other Latin American countries. It was also feared that social unrest could spill over into the United States, with an increase in illegal immigration.[55] The Mexican government responded with austere economic measures and repaid its guaranteed loans before they were due. By early 1997, there were signs that the Mexican economy was slowly improving, but concerns about corruption and social unrest continued.

The Free Trade Commission, based in Mexico City, is the central agency responsible for implementing NAFTA. Assisted by twenty-one committees, subcommittees, and advisory groups, it is charged with resolving disputes and developing and administering procedures, measures, and standards authorized by the agreement.[56]

Three agencies were created under side agreements to NAFTA, and they will coordinate efforts to address common problems arising under the treaty. The Border Environmental Cooperation Commission is responsible for environmental issues and differences that may arise among the three nations. The Commission for Labor Cooperation seeks to improve working conditions and living standards and strengthen the enforcement of domestic labor laws through the use of trade sanctions and other penalties. The Working Group on Emergency Action will address import surges that may have an adverse effect on individual industries in the three countries. In addition, the North American Development Bank, which is located in San Antonio, was created by the United States and Mexico to fund infrastructure and environmental projects along the U.S.-Mexico border.[57]

Trade Patterns between Texas and Mexico   The United States and Texas clearly profit from Mexico's prosperity. U.S. exports to Mexico were $12.4 billion in 1986 and $71.4 billion in 1997 (Table 19-3). Imports from Mexico, now the United States's third largest trading partner, were $73 billion in 1996. Exports to Mexico directly contribute to hundreds of thousands of jobs in the United States. More than 5 percent of the employment in Texas is directly or indirectly related to trade with Mexico. It has been estimated that for each $1 billion of exports, an additional 22,000 jobs are created north of the border.[58] Texas's exports to Mexico increased from $8.8 billion in 1987 to $31 billion in 1997 and constituted approximately 44 percent of all U.S. exports to Mexico. And trade between Texas and Mexico was expected to continue to increase.

The sheer volume of the movement of goods, services, and people is obvious on the highways leading into Mexico and in the long lines of autos and trucks at border crossings in Brownsville, Laredo, and El Paso. An estimated 100 million legal border crossings are made into Texas from Mexico each year. Truck crossings at Laredo, the nation's largest inland port, were projected to be 16,000 per day by the year 2000. This growth in commerce has also highlighted some severe infrastructure problems. An estimated $6 billion to $8 billion will be needed to build and improve roads, streets, bridges, water and sanitation systems, and other needs on both sides of the border. The North American Development Bank was established, in part, to address these needs.

Common Borders, Common Problems   To anyone living on the border, the economic interdependence of the United States and Mexico is evident every day. Thousands of pedestrians, cars, and trucks move across the international bridges, to and from the commercial centers on both sides of the Rio Grande. When the Mexican economy suffered a precipitous decline in 1982, the peso devaluation

---

TABLE 19-3   **Texas and U.S. Exports to Mexico, 1992–1997**

Year	Texas Exports to Mexico	U.S. Exports to Mexico	Texas as a Percentage of United States Exports
1992	$18,839,147,837	$40,597,450,983	46.40%
1993	$20,379,583,586	$41,635,494,403	48.95%
1994	$23,849,512,126	$50,840,265,077	46.91%
1995	$21,863,456,716	$46,311,454,997	47.21%
1996	$27,376,088,512	$56,760,822,874	48.23%
1997	$31,172,597,636	$71,378,310,454	43.67%
Percent change, 1992–1997	65.47%	75.82%	

Source: Massachusetts Institute for Social and Economic Research and the U.S. Census Bureau (based on "origin of movement to port" state-level data series).

severely disrupted the Texas border economy, causing unemployment to skyrocket and a considerable number of U.S. businesses to fail.

Although much of the effort toward improving relations between the United States and Mexico has focused on potential economic benefits, other complex problems confronting both countries also merit attention. One is health care. On both sides of the border, many children have not been immunized against basic childhood diseases. On the Texas side are more than 1,200 *colonias*—rural, unincorporated slums that have substandard housing, roads, and drainage and, in many cases, lack water and sewage systems. These conditions have contributed to severe health problems, including hepatitis, dysentery, and tuberculosis. Higher than normal numbers of both Texan and Mexican children along the border have been born with serious birth defects. Public health facilities in Texas report that Mexican women come across the border to give birth to their children in American facilities. This practice, which has the effect of creating "binational families," increases the burden on public hospitals—and taxpayers—in Texas. Children born in the United States are U.S. citizens, entitled to various public services.[59]

Industrial development and population growth along the border also increase environmental problems. U.S. antipollution laws have been more stringent than those of Mexico, but air and water pollution generated in Mexico do not stop at the border. The side agreements to NAFTA provide a basic framework for addressing these problems, but some have argued that a country such as Mexico, under enormous pressure to industrialize rapidly, is less likely to be concerned with environmental issues. In addition, U.S. efforts to impose its environmental standards on Mexico could be interpreted as another American effort to dominate the country.[60] In June 1994 several maquiladora plants in Matamoros, across the border from Brownsville, settled lawsuits alleging that pollution caused rare birth defects in children born in Texas. A report published by Public Citizen, a public interest group organized by Ralph Nader, concluded in late 1995 that public health and the environment on the U.S.-Mexico border had worsened since NAFTA was approved in 1993.[61]

Regional interdependence, although perhaps not recognized by most people on both sides of the border, has taken on greater importance in the press and in academic, business, and labor communities in the United States. Transnational public policies are emerging, creating legal issues in product liability, insurance, copyrights, and patents that must still be resolved. The governors of Mexican and U.S. border states have their own association, the Border Governors Conference, which meets regularly to discuss such issues as free trade, the environment, education, and tourism. Recent Texas governors have supported efforts to improve relations with Mexico, and Texas state agencies have been given increased authority to work in cooperative efforts with Mexican officials.[62] Private groups have also organized to address transnational issues and pressure governments on both sides of the border to develop policies and allocate resources to resolve common problems.

Illegal Immigration　　Population growth in Texas has always been affected by migration from other states and foreign countries. But the proximity of Texas to Mexico has put the state in the center of a long-running dispute over the illegal immigration of large numbers of Mexicans and other Latin Americans. In 1994 an estimated 3.5 million to 4 million people, mostly from Mexico and Central America, were living in the United States illegally.[63] Many enter through Texas and proceed to other areas of the country, but others remain in the state.

The failure of the Mexican economy and the attraction of employment opportunities north of the border have been major reasons for this migration, although political instability and persecutions in Central America have also been significant factors. Large portions of the Texas and American economies were built on the availability of low-cost, low-skilled Mexican labor.[64] If arrested, illegal workers were returned to Mexico, but, until recently, it was not illegal for American employers to hire them.[65]

In 1986 the U.S. Congress enacted the Immigration Reform and Control Act, which imposed fines on employers who hired illegal aliens and mandated jail sentences for flagrant violators. Potential employees had to provide documentation, and employers had to verify their employees' citizenship. The new law also provided a means for giving legal status, or amnesty, to hundreds of thousands of illegal immigrants who had moved to the United States before January 1, 1982. It also granted temporary status to agricultural workers who could satisfy specific residency requirements.[66]

By 1996 it was clear that this law had not stemmed the tide of illegal immigration because Mexicans were still drawn to the economic opportunities available in the United States. Throughout the Southwest, hundreds of thousands of illegal workers were being arrested and detained before being returned home, and the movement of Mexican workers into Texas and the rest of the United States remained a controversial political issue (see *Up Close:* "Will Welfare Reform Deter Illegal Immigration?").

Children of illegal immigrants can represent a heavy financial burden for many school districts along the border. Undocumented workers also increase demands on public health care programs. Some citizens, particularly unskilled workers, view the illegal arrivals as a threat to their jobs and standard of living.[67]

Up Close

Will Welfare Reform Deter Illegal Immigration?

In addition to changes in the immigration laws, the U.S. Congress passed major welfare reforms in 1996, cutting off most public assistance to both legal and illegal immigrants into the United States.

Critics of the previous welfare system had argued that the accessibility of public funds and services was a strong attraction to immigrants. They argued that American taxpayers had no obligation to support anyone who entered the country illegally or even legal immigrants who could not support themselves.

With some exceptions for medical emergencies, the 1996 welfare reform law barred illegal immigrants from receiving benefits provided by a federal agency or by federal funds, including welfare, retirement, health, disability, food assistance, or unemployment benefits. States are also prohibited from providing state or local benefits to illegal immigrants unless state officials pass specific laws making immigrants eligible for aid from state or local funds.

Although there are some exceptions for emergency medical care and education, most legal immigrants, even those already in the country when the law was changed, are now ineligible for federal supplemental security income and food stamps until they become citizens. Those who come to the United States legally since the law was passed will be denied most federal welfare benefits for five years. States, however, can assist legal immigrants with benefits funded entirely by state or local funds. The law also places additional financial responsibilities on people who sponsor immigrants.

These welfare changes were designed to discourage persons who are unable to support themselves and perceive the possibility of easy access to public assistance from immigrating to the United States. But will they create insurmountable obstacles for immigrants who come to the United States to escape desperate economic, political, or social conditions in their own countries? Only time will tell if these restrictions have the intended results.

Source: Jeffrey L. Katz, "Welfare Overhaul Law," *Congressional Quarterly Weekly Report* 54 (September 21, 1996), pp. 2696–2705.

Politics in Cyberspace

The Social and Economic Milieu of Texas Politics

A number of state and national organizations maintain web sites with information about the economy, demography, and political culture of Texas.

State of Texas
http://www.state.tx.us

The state's Web page provides links to state agencies, local and county governments, and councils of states along with references to sources providing economic and travel information.

The University of Texas at Austin
http://www.utexas.edu/texas

The University of Texas maintains "Web Texas," which serves as the official www registration site for Texas Web servers and provides links to all currently registered Texas Web pages. It includes commercial, organizational, governmental, and educational Web sites.

U.S. Bureau of the Census
http://www.census.gov

Population and economic data for the state are provided by the Bureau of the Census, which conducts the decennial census and a wide range of demographic

studies between censuses. For state and county data, use the "Other Official Stats/FedStats" icon.

Office of the Comptroller
http://www.window.texas.gov

The comptroller's office maintains a database for the Texas economy. This site offers easy access to Texas state agencies, economic data, tax rules, government performance reviews, the Texas Constitution, and the latest Lotto Texas results.

Texas State Data Center
http://www-txsdc.tamu.edu

The Texas State Data Center is part of the Department of Rural Sociology at Texas A & M University. The center provides "ready access to Texas census information and other information on the population of Texas." In addition to the census data, the center also provides population estimates and projections.

Texas State Electronic Library (TSEL)
http://link.tsl.texas.gov

The TSEL provides a link to state and local agencies as well as to Texas libraries and newspapers.

Piper Resources
http://www.piperinfo.com/state/states.html

Piper Resources provides convenient access to a wide variety of links to state agencies and government information.

There is a widespread belief in Texas that the state's citizens carry the burden for the failure of the federal government to develop policies to stem the illegal flow. In 1994 Texas joined several other states in filing lawsuits seeking reimbursement from the federal government for billions of dollars in state and local expenditures attributed to illegal immigration.

Some members of the U.S. Congress in 1995 and 1996 attempted to enact comprehensive immigration reforms to restrict both legal and illegal immigration. A coalition of immigrant advocacy groups and business interests was able to block key provisions of the original proposal, and by the time the final measure was enacted in late 1996, its provisions were directed primarily against illegal immigrants. The new law authorized funds for improvements to a border fence in California and additional Immigration and Naturalization Service border guards and inspectors. The measure also increased the penalties for smuggling illegal immigrants and using fraudulent documents and made it easier to detain illegal immigrants or deport them after their arrival in the United States.[68]

- Texas has experienced significant demographic, social, and economic changes over the past four decades that have transformed state politics, governmental institutions, and public policy.

- Texans, in part, explain and understand themselves in terms of political myths that provide generalized views of the state, its common historical experience, its people, and its institutions.

- Individualistic and traditionalistic political subcultures provided the basis for the beliefs Texans hold about what government should do, who should govern, and what constitutes good public policy. The traditionally conservative politics and public policies of the state, along with the dominant role of an elite structure, are rooted in these cultural patterns.

- Demographically, Texas is diverse. There has been a dramatic increase in the overall population, with significant increases among Hispanics and Asian Americans. The state will have a "majority minority" population in the first quarter of the twenty-first century.

- Politics in the state is largely shaped by the ethnic and racial composition of the population, and, although the interests of minorities were historically neglected, they are now receiving increased attention. This attention can be attributed, in part, to the increased number of minorities elected to state and local offices.

- Despite its size and sense of "wide open spaces," Texas is an urban state, with eight out of ten Texans living in urban areas.

- Wide disparities in wealth and income levels in Texas point to the political influence of class as well as of race and ethnicity.

- There are also wide disparities in educational levels in Texas. African Americans and Hispanics have a larger proportion of high school dropouts, fewer college graduates, and overall lower levels of education than Anglo Texans. Improved literacy and the development of a technologically competent work force are essential to the state's ability to compete in the global economy.

- The 1980s began with an economic boom, but, during most of the decade, the state was plagued by significant economic problems. Economic diversification aided recovery, and during much of the last decade of the twentieth century, economic growth in Texas outpaced national growth.

- There are ten distinct economic regions in Texas. Population growth and economic development in these regions vary considerably, and periods of economic downturn and recovery are not felt uniformly across the state.

- The economy of Texas has become bound to the economies of the Mexican border states with the development of the maquiladora program, Mexico's membership in the General Agreement on Tariffs and Trade, and the North American Free Trade Agreement.

- Texas attracts many illegal immigrants from Mexico and other Latin American countries, who place additional pressures on the state's economy and ability to provide adequate education, health care, and other services.

- Environmental, economic, and health care issues are problems of transnational regionalism that demonstrate the necessity for governments and businesses on both sides of the Rio Grande to work together in developing solutions.

SELECTED READINGS

BOUVIER, LEON F., and DUDLEY L. POSTON, JR. *Thirty Million Texans?* (Washington, D.C.: Center for Immigration Studies, 1993).

BUENGER, WALTER L., and ROBERT A. CALVERT, eds. *Texas through Time: Evolving Interpretations* (College Station: Texas A&M University Press, 1991).

CALVERT, ROBERT A., and ARNOLDO DELEON. *The History of Texas* (Arlington Heights, Ill.: Harlan Davidson, 1990).

CHAMPAGNE, ANTHONY, and EDWARD J. HARPHAM. "The Changing Political Economy of Texas," in *Texas Politics: A Reader*, eds. Anthony Champagne and Edward J. Harpham (New York: W.W. Norton, 1997), pp. 3–15.

ELAZAR, DANIEL. *American Federalism: A View from the States* (New York: Thomas Y. Crowell, 1966).

FEHRENBACH, T. R. *Lone Star: A History of Texas and the Texans* (New York: Macmillan, 1968).

HILL, KIM QUAILE. *Democracy in the Fifty States* (Lincoln: University of Nebraska Press, 1994).

JORDAN, TERRY G., with JOHN L. BEAN, JR., and WILLIAM M. HOLMES. *Texas: A Geography* (Boulder, Colo.: Westview Press, 1984).

LANGLEY, LESTER D. *MexAmerica: Two Countries, One Future* (New York: Crown, 1988).

MARTINEZ, OSCAR J. *Troublesome Border* (Tucson: University of Arizona Press, 1988).

McCOMB, DAVID G. *Texas: A Modern History* (Austin: University of Texas Press, 1989).

METZ, LEON C. *Border: The U.S.-Mexico Line* (El Paso: Mangan Books, 1989).

MONTEJANO, DAVID. *Anglos and Mexicans in the Making of Texas, 1836–1986* (Austin: University of Texas Press, 1987).

MURDOCK, STEVE H., MD. NAZRUL HOQUE, MARTHA MICHAEL, STEVE WHITE, and BEVERLY PECOTTE. *The Texas Challenge: Population Change and the Future of Texas* (College Station: Texas A&M University Press, 1997).

O'CONNOR, ROBERT F., ed. *Texas Myths* (College Station: Texas A&M University Press, 1986).

RICHARDSON, RUPERT N., ERNEST WALLACE, and ADRIAN N. ANDERSON. *Texas: The Lone Star State.* 7th ed. (Upper Saddle River, N.J.: Prentice Hall, 1997).

WEINTRAUB, SIDNEY. *A Marriage of Convenience: Relations between Mexico and the United States* (New York: Oxford University Press, 1990).

WRIGHT, BILL. *The Tigua: Pueblo Indians of Texas* (El Paso: Texas Western Press, 1993).

ZAMORA, EMILIO. *The World of the Mexican Worker in Texas* (College Station: Texas A&M University Press, 1993).

Constitution of the State of Texas

Preamble.

Humbly invoking the blessings of Almighty God, the people of the State of Texas, do ordain and esta[blish]

Article I.
Bill of Rights.

That the general, great and essential principles of liberty and free government may be recognized and

Sec. 1. Texas is a free and indepedent State, subject only to the Constitution of the United States, and of the Union depend upon the preservation of the right of local self-government, unimpaired to all the States.

Sec. 2. All political power is inherent in the people, and all free governments are founded on their author[ity] of Texas stands pledged to the preservation of a republican form of government, and, subject to this limitation only, they have their government in such manner as they may think expedient.

Sec. 3. All freemen, when they form a social compact, have equal rights, and no man, or set of men, [are entitled to exclusive] brivileges, but in consideration of public services.

Sec. 4. No religious test shall ever be required as a qualification to any office, or public trust, in this [State,] [nor shall any one be excluded from holding office] on account of his religious sentiments, provided he acknowledge the existence of a Supreme Being.

Sec. 5. No person shall be disqualified to give evidence in any of the Courts of this State on account of his re[ligious opinions,] but all oaths or affirmations shall be administered in the mode most binding upon the conscience, and shall be taken su[bject]

Sec. 6. All men have a natural and indefeasible right to worship Almighty God according to the di[ctates of their own consciences. No man shall be com]belled to attend, erect or support any place of worship, or to maintain any ministry against his consent. No human aut[hority ought, in any case whatever, to control or interfere] with the rights of conscience in matters of religion, and no preference shall ever be given by law to any religious soc[iety. But it shall be the duty of] the Legislature to pass such laws as may be necessary to protect equally every religious denomination in the pea[ceable enjoyment of its own mode of worship.]

Sec. 7. No money shall be appropriated, or drawn from the Treasury for the benefit of any sect, o[r religious society,] nor shall property belonging to the State be appropriated for any such purposes.

Sec. 8. Every person shall be at liberty to speak, write or publish his opinions on any subject, bein[g responsible for the abuse of that privilege; and no] law shall ever be passed curtailing the liberty of speech or of the press. In prosecutions for the publication of papers, investigat[ing the conduct of officers, or men in public capacity,] when the matter published is proper for public information, the truth thereof may be given in evidence. And in all indi[ctments for libels, the jury shall have the right to deter]mine the law and the facts, under the direction of the Court, as in other cases.

✓ **ASK YOURSELF ABOUT POLITICS**

1. Should every voter in Texas have to vote on a strictly local issue, such as whether a particular county should have a constable?
   Yes ___ No ___

2. Should Texas prepare its budgets each year rather than for two-year periods?
   Yes ___ No ___

3. Should Texas make it more difficult to amend its constitution?
   Yes ___ No ___

4. Should voters in Texas be able to sign petitions to put specific issues on the ballot?
   Yes ___ No ___

5. Should judges be appointed rather than elected?
   Yes ___ No ___

6. Does Texas need a new constitution?
   Yes ___ No ___

CHAPTER 20

THE TEXAS CONSTITUTION

CHAPTER OUTLINE

The Constitutional Legacy

General Principles of the Texas Constitution

Weaknesses and Criticisms of the Constitution of 1876

Constitutional Change and Adaptation

Constitutional Restraints and the Ability to Govern

FEATURES

Up Close: Budget Restrictions

Across the USA: States Frequently Amend Their Constitutions

What Do You Think? It Depends on How You Say It

Up Close: A Lot of Trouble for a Minor Office

What Do You Think? Do the Voters Really Care?

People in Politics: Martha Whitehead Campaigned to End Her Job

Politics in Cyberspace: The Texas Constitution

THE CONSTITUTIONAL LEGACY

The year was 1874, and unusual events marked the end of the darkest chapter in Texas history—the Reconstruction era and the military occupation that followed the Civil War. Texans, still smarting from some of the most oppressive laws ever imposed on American citizens, had overwhelmingly voted their governor out of office, but he refused to leave the Capitol and hand over his duties to his elected successor. For several tense days, the city of Austin was divided into two armed camps of people—those supporting the deposed governor, Edmund J. Davis, and those supporting the man who defeated him at the polls, Richard Coke. Davis finally gave up only after the Texas militia turned against him and marched on the Capitol.

That long-ago period bears little resemblance to modern Texas, but the experience still casts a long shadow over state government. The state constitution written by Texans at the close of Reconstruction was designed to put strong restraints on government to guard against future

> The Texas Constitution does more than define the institutions of government. It structures the power and influence that groups and individuals can wield in deciding who gets what, when, and how.

Budget Restrictions

Like most other states and unlike the federal government, Texas—thanks to a constitutional requirement—operates on a pay-as-you-go basis that prohibits deficit financing. The comptroller must certify that each budget can be paid for with anticipated revenue from taxes, fees, and other sources. Although that provision is designed to protect taxpayers and keep state government solvent, other sections of the constitution make it more difficult for the legislature to meet the state's budgetary needs adequately and fairly.

One handicap is the two-year budget period necessitated by the fact that the legislature meets in regular session only every other year. Critics, including many legislators and state agency directors, say two-year budgets require too much guesswork and cause inadequate funding of some programs and wasteful spending in other areas. Voters in 1985 approved a constitutional amendment to allow the governor and legislative leaders to transfer funds between programs or agencies to meet emergencies when the legislature is not in session. But that provision only partially addressed the problem.

The legislature's control over the budget-setting process is further restricted by constitutional requirements that dedicate significant portions of state revenue to specific purposes. Three-fourths of the revenue from the motor fuels tax is automatically set aside for highways and the remaining one-fourth for public education. The Permanent School Fund and the Permanent University Fund are land- and mineral-rich endowments that help support the public schools and boost funding for the University of Texas and Texas A&M University systems.

The legislature can bend the pay-as-you-go requirement by issuing general obligation bonds, serviced by future tax revenues, to build prisons and other public facilities. Such bonds require voter approval in the form of constitutional amendments, several of which, totaling more than $3 billion, have been approved in recent years to build new prisons. That debt will have to be paid off with tax dollars over the next generation.

abuses, and most of those restraints remain in place today. The Texas Constitution, adopted in 1876 and amended many times since, is so restrictive that many scholars and politicians believe it is counterproductive to effective modern governance. They believe the document, which is bogged down with statutory detail, is a textbook example of what a constitution should *not* be. State government functions despite its constitutional shackles: a weak chief executive, an outdated and part-time legislature, a poorly organized judiciary, and dedicated funds that limit the state's budgetary options (see *Up Close:* "Budget Restrictions"). But a total rewrite of the constitution has been elusive, thanks to numerous special interests who find security in the present document—from holders of obsolete offices to beneficiaries of dedicated funds and bureaucrats who fear change.

Texas has had seven constitutions (Table 20-1), and understanding this constitutional legacy is critical to understanding contemporary Texas politics and public policy. The first constitution was adopted in 1827, when the state was still part of Mexico. The second was drafted when Texas declared its independence from Mexico in 1836 and became a republic, and the third was adopted in 1845, when the state joined the Union. The fourth constitution was written when Texas joined the Confederacy in 1861, and the fifth was adopted when the state rejoined the Union in 1866. The sixth constitution was adopted in 1869 to satisfy the Radical Reconstructionists' opposition to the 1866 constitution, and the seventh constitution was adopted in 1876 after the termination of Reconstruction policies. Each of Texas's seven constitutions was written in a distinct historical setting. And although there are significant differences among these documents, each contributed to the state and local governments that exist in Texas today.

The Texas Constitution in a Comparative Perspective **Constitutions** do not lend themselves to easy reading. The formal legal language often obscures the general objectives of the document and its relevance to contemporary issues of political power and public policy. Scholars believe, first, that constitutions should be brief and should include general principles rather than specific legislative provisions. In other words, constitutions should provide a basic framework for government and leave the details to be imposed in **statutory law**. Second, these experts say, constitutions should make direct grants of authority to specific institutions, so as to increase the responsiveness and the accountability of individuals elected or appointed to public office. Scholars also believe that constitutions should provide for orderly change but should not be written in such a restrictive fashion that they require continual modifications to meet contemporary needs.[1]

Amended only twenty-seven times since its ratification in 1788, the U.S. Constitution is a concise 7,000-word document that outlines broad basic principles of authority and governance. No one would argue that the government of the 1990s is comparable to that of the 1790s, yet the flexibility of the U.S. Constitution makes it as relevant now as it was in the eighteenth century. It is often spoken of as "a living charter or document" that does not have to be continually amended to meet society's ever-changing needs and conditions. As discussed in Chapter 3, its reinterpretations by the courts, the Congress, and the president have produced an expansion of powers and responsibilities within the framework of the original language of the document.

By contrast, the Texas Constitution—like those of many other states—is an unwieldy, restrictive document. With 80,000-plus words, it has been on a life-

constitution Legal structure of a political system, establishing government bodies and defining their powers.

statutory law Law enacted by a legislative body.

TABLE 20-1	**The Seven Texas Constitutions**

1827: Constitution of Coahuila y Tejas
The first Texas constitution, adopted in 1827. It recognized Texas as a Mexican state with Coahuila.

1836: Constitution of the Republic
The constitution, adopted March 16, 1836, by Texas colonists declaring independence from Mexico. Under this constitution, Texas functioned as an independent republic for nine years.

1845: Constitution of 1845
The constitution under which Texas was admitted to the United States.

1861: Civil War Constitution
The constitution adopted by Texans after the state seceded from the Union and joined the Confederacy in 1861.

1866: Constitution of 1866
The short-lived constitution under which Texas sought to be readmitted to the Union after the Civil War and before the Radical Reconstuctionists took control of the U.S. Congress.

1869: Reconstruction Constitution
The constitution centralizing power in state government and weakening local governments. It reflected the sentiments of Radical Reconstructionists, not of most Texans.

1876: Texas Constitution
The constitution adopted at the end of Reconstruction, amended many times since, and still in effect. Highly restrictive and antigovernment, this constitution places strict limitations on the powers of the governor, the legislature, and other state officials.

support system—the piecemeal amendment process—for most of its existence. It is less a set of basic governmental principles than a compilation of detailed statutory language reflecting the distrust of government that was widespread in Texas when it was written. In effect, it attempts to diffuse political power among many different institutions.

The historical constitutional experiences of Texas parallel those of many southern states that have had multiple constitutions in the post–Civil War era. The southern states, Texas included, are the only states whose constitutions formally acknowledge the supremacy of the U.S. Constitution, a provision required by the Radical Reconstructionists for readmission of the former Confederate states to the Union.

The Constitution of Coahuila y Tejas, 1827   Sparsely populated Texas was part of Mexico when that country secured its independence from Spain in 1821, about the same time that Stephen F. Austin and others initiated Anglo colonization of Texas. Initially, Anglo Texans appeared to be willing to be incorporated into the Mexican political system as long as there was limited intrusion by the Mexican government into their daily affairs. In 1824 the new Republic of Mexico adopted a constitution for a federal system of government that recognized as a single state Texas and Coahuila, its neighbor south of the Rio Grande. Saltillo, Mexico, was the state capital.

The Constitution of Coahuila y Tejas, completed in 1827, provided for a **unicameral** legislature of twelve deputies, including two from Texas, elected by the people. Most of the legislators were from the more populous, Spanish-speaking Coahuila, and the laws were published in Spanish, which few Texas colonists understood. The executive department included a governor and a vice governor. The governor enforced the law, led the state militia, and granted pardons. The constitution made Catholicism the state religion, although that requirement was not enforced among Texas's Anglo settlers. Additionally, Anglo Texans were not subject to military service, taxes, or custom duties. In effect, Texas served as a buffer between Mexico and various Native American peoples and the United States.

But with increased Anglo immigration and the perceived threat of U.S. imperial or expansionary policies, Mexico soon attempted to extend its control over Texas. This effort reinforced cultural differences between the Anglo and Spanish populations and would eventually lead to revolution by Anglo Texans.[2]

This formative period produced some enduring contributions to the Texas constitutional tradition. Elements of the Mexican legal system are still to be found in property and land laws, water laws and water rights, and community property laws. One justification for the Revolution of 1836 was the failure of the Mexican government to provide sufficient funding for public education. But although there were expectations of funding by the central government, a "concept of local control over school development was firmly established."[3] This paradox has raised a continuing constitutional question and is central to the current issue of funding of public education.

The Constitution of the Republic of Texas, 1836   During the late 1820s and the early 1830s, increased immigration from the United States into the territory of Texas heightened tension between the Anglo settlers and the Mexican government. Mexico's efforts to enforce its laws within Texas produced conflicts between cultures, legal traditions, and economic interests that resulted in open rebellion by the colonists.

At the same time, Mexico was embroiled in its own internal dissension. It struggled to stabilize its political system but did not have the legacy and social and polit-

unicameral   Having a single legislative body.

ical institutions to ensure a successful democratic system. In many respects, the events in Texas were a footnote to the power politics in Mexico. Had the autonomy of Texas that was provided for under the Mexican constitution of 1824 been maintained, the history of this region might well have been different.

Increased internal conflict among competing Mexican interests resulted in the seizure of power by the popular general Antonio López de Santa Anna Perez de Lebron. Santa Anna began to systematically suspend the powers of the Mexican Congress and local governments, and in October 1835, the national constitution of 1824 was voided. Mexico adopted a new constitution providing for a **unitary system** with power centralized in the national Congress and the presidency. The principle of **federalism**, which divided power and authority between the national government and the states, was repudiated. This major change intensified conflict between the national government and the Mexican states. Texas was not the only area of Mexico where the principles of federalism were highly regarded, and although Texas was eventually successful in establishing its autonomy, several other Mexican states were subjected to harsh military retaliation.

As the Mexican government under Santa Anna attempted to regain control over Texas, colonists who initially supported the national government and those who expressed ambivalence were slowly converted to the cause of independence. Stephen F. Austin had consistently supported the position that Texas was a Mexican state, and he represented the views of a large part of the Anglo population living in Texas. But when Mexican troops moved across the Rio Grande into Texas in the autumn of 1835, Austin sent out a call for resistance.

The numerous special interests that later were to obstruct the course of constitutional development in Texas were missing at the small settlement of Washington-on-the-Brazos in 1836. The fifty-nine male colonists who convened to declare Texas's independence from Mexico on March 2 and to adopt a constitution for the new republic two weeks later had two overriding interests: the preservation of their fledgling

unitary system Constitutional arrangement whereby authority rests with the national government; subnational governments have only those powers given them by the national government.

federalism Constitutional arrangement in which power is formally divided between national and subnational governments.

Faced with the advancing Mexican armies, Texans hastily met in the small settlement of Washington-on-the-Brazos, declared their independence on March 2, 1836, and wrote the Constitution of the Republic, which was adopted on March 16, 1836.

nation and the preservation of their own lives. By the time they had completed their work, the Alamo—only 150 miles away—had fallen to a large Mexican army under Santa Anna, and a second Mexican force had arrived north of the Rio Grande. Accordingly, the constitution writers wasted little time on speech making.

Consequently, the Constitution of the Republic, adopted on March 16, 1836, was not cluttered with the details that weaken the present Texas Constitution. It drew heavily on the U.S. Constitution, and since forty-four of the fifty-nine delegates were from the South, from the constitutions of several southern states. The document created an elected **bicameral** congress and provided for an elected president. Members of the clergy were prohibited from serving as president or in congress, and there was no official, state-preferred religion. Slavery was legal, but importation of slaves from any country other than the United States was illegal. Free African Americans had to have congress's permission to leave Texas.

Approximately six weeks after the disastrous defeat at the Alamo, the Texas army, under Sam Houston, defeated Santa Anna's army at the battle of San Jacinto on April 21, 1836. The war of independence had been relatively short and involved limited casualties, but the problems of creating a stable political system under the new constitution were formidable. There was no viable government in place, no money for paying the costs of government, and no party system. And, although defeated, Mexico did not relinquish its claims to Texas and was to demonstrate in subsequent actions that it wanted to regain this lost territory. Nevertheless, the "transition from colony to constitutional republic was accomplished quickly and with a minimum of disorganization."[4]

Independence and national autonomy from 1836 to 1845 contributed significantly to the development of a sense of historical uniqueness among Texans. Although the effects on the state's political psyche may be difficult to measure, the "Lone Star" experience has been kept alive through school history texts, the celebration of key events, and the development of a mythology of the independence period.

The Constitution of 1845   During the independence movement and immediately thereafter, some Texans made overtures to the United States to annex Texas, but they were initially blocked by the issue of slavery and its relationship to economic and regional influence in U.S. politics. Increased immigration to Texas in the late 1830s and early 1840s, more interest among Texans in joining the Union, and expansionist policies of the U.S. government stepped up pressures for annexation. It was a major issue in the U.S. presidential campaign of 1844, and the election of James K. Polk accelerated the move toward Texas's admission to the United States in 1845.

The annexation bill approved by the U.S. Congress included a compromise that allowed slavery to continue in Texas.[5] Racial issues that emerged from this period continue to shape contemporary politics and public policy in the state. Texas still struggles with voting rights issues, inequities in funding of education, and the maldistribution of economic resources that directly affect the quality of life of many minorities.

The terms of Texas's admission into the Union also provided that Texas could divide itself into as many as five states, a provision largely forgotten until state representative David Swinford, a Republican from Dumas, made such a proposal in 1991. The idea attracted some newspaper headlines and some interest in the Panhandle, which is geographically isolated from most of Texas, but was not given serious consideration by Swinford's colleagues.

bicameral   Having two legislative bodies.

The state constitution drafted to allow Texas's annexation was about twice as long as the constitution of 1836. It borrowed not only from its predecessor but also from the constitutions of other southern states, particularly Louisiana.

The constitution of 1845 created an elected legislature that met biennially and included a house of representatives and a senate. It provided for an elected governor and an elected lieutenant governor, and it empowered the governor to appoint a secretary of state, attorney general, and state judges, subject to senate confirmation. The legislature chose a comptroller, treasurer, and land commissioner. But in 1850, Texas voters amended the constitution to make most state offices elective. In this respect, Texas was following a national pattern of fragmenting the powers of the executive branch of state government. Today Texas still has a plural executive system under which practically all statewide officeholders are elected independently of the governor, a system that contrasts sharply with the appointive cabinet system of executive government enjoyed by the president of the United States (see Chapter 11).

The constitution of 1845 protected private homesteads from foreclosure, guaranteed separate property rights for married women, and established a permanent fund for the support of public schools—provisions also found in the present constitution. The 1845 charter also recognized slavery, prohibited anyone who had ever participated in a duel from holding public office, and prohibited state-chartered banks. This constitution "worked so well that after several intervening constitutions, the people of Texas recopied it almost in toto as the Constitution of 1876."[6]

The Civil War Constitution, 1861   When Texas seceded from the Union in 1861, just before the outbreak of the Civil War, the state constitution was again revised. Although most of the provisions of the 1845 document were retained, significant changes were made in line with Texas's new membership in the Confederacy. Public officials were required to pledge their support of the Confederate constitution, greater protection was given to slavery, and the freeing of slaves was prohibited.

Any semblance of a two-party system had been destroyed by the issues of slavery and secession during the 1850s, and state politics was dominated by personalities and factions. Factionalism within the Democratic Party persisted for more than a hundred years, until the emergence of a two-party system in the 1980s.

The Civil War era also contributed to a legacy of states' rights, which was to persist well into the next century and spark an extended struggle for desegregation. Theoretically, the constitutional issue of the Civil War was whether a state, once having joined the Union, could leave it. The southern states subscribed to a view of the national government as a **confederacy**, and it was their position that a state could withdraw, or secede. Although the northern victory dispelled this interpretation, Texas, along with other southern states, found ways to thwart national policy through the 1960s. Their efforts were based, in part, on their continued arguments for states' rights.

The Constitution of 1866   After the Civil War, Texas was subject to national control through, first, a military government, then a provisional government headed by A. J. Hamilton, a former member of the U.S. Congress who had remained loyal to the Union. These were dark days for Texans. Although the state had experienced relatively few battles and had not suffered from the scorched-earth tactics used by Union generals elsewhere, the economy was in disarray. Many Texas families had also

confederacy National government created by states that relies on the states for its authority.

A Union general and later governor of Texas (1870–74), Edmund J. Davis conducted one of the most oppressive administrations in U.S. history. Texans reacted to such practices with restrictions built into the constitution of 1876.

Radical Reconstructionists The group of Republicans who took control of the U.S. Congress in 1866 and imposed hated military governments on the former Confederate states after the Civil War.

lost loved ones, and many surviving Confederate veterans had been wounded physically or psychologically. Although the national government developed policies to assist the newly freed slaves, these policies were never fully funded and were halfheartedly—and often dishonestly—carried out. And the presence of an occupation army heightened tension and shaped subsequent political attitudes.

The reconstruction plan initiated by President Abraham Lincoln but never fully implemented envisioned a rapid return to civilian government for the southern states and their quick reintegration as equals into the national political system. Requirements were modest: the abolition of slavery, the repudiation of the Secession Ordinance of 1861, and the repudiation of all debts and obligations incurred under the Confederacy.[7]

Texas voters revived the constitution of 1845 and amended it to include the stipulations required by the national government. But although slavery was eliminated and the freed slaves were given the right to hold property and were accorded legal rights before a jury, no black people could testify in any court case involving whites. And African Americans were denied the right to vote. The new constitution was adopted in June 1866, a new government was elected, and on August 20, 1866, President Andrew Johnson "declared the rebellion in Texas at an end."[8]

In short order, however, the mild reconstruction policies of Johnson were replaced by the severe policies of the **Radical Reconstructionists,** who captured control of Congress in 1866. The new Texas Constitution was invalidated by Congress, which passed, over the president's veto, the Reconstruction Acts that established military governments throughout the South. The civilian government initiated by the state constitution of 1866 was short-lived, and Texas functioned for two years under a reinstituted military government.

This period had an enduring impact on Texas constitutional law and politics. In a broad sense, it prolonged the full reintegration of Texas into the national political system, and, in specific terms, it transformed the constitutional tradition of Texas into one of hostility and suspicion toward government.

The Reconstruction Constitution, 1869   The Reconstruction Acts required a Texas constitution that would grant African Americans the right to vote and include other provisions acceptable to the U.S. Congress. A Republican slate of delegates to a new state constitutional convention produced a new charter that was published in 1869. It did not reflect the majority Texas sentiment of the time, but it conformed to Republican wishes. Centralizing more powers in state government while weakening local government, it gave the governor a four-year term and the power to appoint other top state officials, including members of the judiciary. It provided for annual legislative sessions, gave African Americans the right to vote, and, for the first time, provided for a centralized, statewide system of public schools. Texans were unhappy enough with their new constitution, but the widespread abuses of the document that followed under the oppressive and corrupt administration of Radical Republican Governor Edmund J. Davis paved the way for the shackles on state government that are still in place today.

In the 1869 election, the first under the new constitution, the military governor certified that Davis, a former Union Army officer, beat conservative Republican A. J. Hamilton by 39,901 to 39,092 votes. This outcome was allowed despite widespread, flagrant incidents of voter fraud, which were also ignored by President

Ulysses S. Grant and the U.S. Congress. A radical majority in the new Texas legislature then approved a series of authoritarian—and, in some respects, unconstitutional—laws proposed by Davis. They gave the governor the power to declare martial law and suspend the laws in any county and created a state police force under the governor's control that could deprive citizens of constitutional protections. The governor also was empowered to appoint mayors, district attorneys, and hundreds of other local officials. Another law that designated newspapers as official printers of state documents in effect put much of the press under government control.

Davis exercised some of the most repressive powers ever imposed on U.S. citizens. And Texans responded. First, in 1872, they elected a Democratic majority to the legislature that abolished the state police and repealed other oppressive laws. Then, in 1873, they elected a Confederate veteran, Democrat Richard Coke, governor by more than a 2-to-1 margin over Davis. Like the Radical Republicans in the previous gubernatorial election, the Democrats were not above abusing the democratic process, and, once again, voting fraud was rampant.

As described earlier in the chapter, Davis initially refused to leave office and appealed to President Grant for federal troops to help him retain power. Grant refused, and Davis finally gave up after the Texas militia turned against him and marched on the Capitol in January 1874. Bloodshed was avoided, Reconstruction was ending, and the constitution of 1869 was doomed.

The Constitution of 1876: Retrenchment and Reform   The restored Democratic majority promptly took steps to write a new constitution. A new constitutional convention convened in Austin on September 6, 1875. The delegates were all men. Most were products of a rural and frontier South, and, still smarting from Reconstruction abuses, they considered government a necessary evil that had to be heavily restricted. Many, however, had previous governmental experience. Initially, seventy-five Democrats and fifteen Republicans were elected delegates, but one Republican resigned after only limited service and was replaced by a Democrat.[9]

The vast majority of the delegates were white, and some disagreement remains over how many African Americans served in the convention. Some historians say there were six. According to one account, however, six African Americans were elected but one resigned after only one day of service and was replaced in a special election by a white delegate. All of the African American delegates were Republicans.[10]

Only four of the delegates were native Texans. Most had immigrated to Texas from other southern states, including nineteen—the largest single group—from Tennessee, which one author called the "breeding ground" of Texas delegates. Their average age was forty-five. The oldest was sixty-eight; the youngest was twenty-three.[11] Eleven of the delegates had been members of previous constitutional conventions in Texas, but there is disagreement over whether any had participated in drafting the Reconstruction constitution of 1869. In any event, the influences of the 1869 constitution were negative, not positive.

At least thirty of the delegates had served in the Texas legislature, two others had served in the Tennessee and Mississippi legislatures, two had represented Texas in the U.S. Congress, and two had represented Texas in the Confederate Congress. Delegates also included a former attorney general, a former lieutenant governor, and a former secretary of state of Texas; at least eight delegates had judicial experience. Many delegates had been high-ranking Confederate military officers. One, John H. Reagan, had been postmaster general of the Confederacy.[12] Reagan later would become a U.S. senator from Texas and would serve as the first chair of the Texas Railroad Commission.

Another delegate who epitomized the independent frontier spirit of the time was John S. "Rip" Ford, a native of South Carolina who had come to Texas in 1836 as a physician. He later became a lawyer, journalist, state senator, mayor of Austin, and Texas Ranger captain. In 1874 he was a leader of the militia that marched on the Capitol and forced Edmund J. Davis to relinquish the governor's office to his elected successor. Ford had been a secessionist delegate to the 1861 convention, which voted for secession and drafted a constitution. During the Civil War he had commanded a makeshift cavalry regiment that fought Union soldiers along the Texas-Mexico border.[13]

According to one account, delegates to the 1875 convention included thirty-three lawyers, twenty-eight farmers, three physicians, three merchants, two teachers, two editors, and one minister. At least eleven other delegates were part-time farmers who also pursued other occupations.[14] Other historians have come up with slightly different breakdowns, but all agree that the influence of agricultural interests was substantial in the writing of the new Texas charter.

About half the delegates were members of the Society of the Patrons of Husbandry, or the **Grange**. An organization formed to improve the lot of farmers, the Grange became politically active in the wake of national scandals involving abuses by big business and government. The Grange started organizing in Texas in 1873, and its influence was felt directly in constitutional provisions limiting taxes and governmental expenditures and restricting banks, railroads, and other corporations.

The delegates did not try to produce a document that would be lauded as a model of constitutional perfection or mistaken for a literary classic. They faced the reality of addressing serious, pressing problems—an immediate crisis that did not encourage debate over the finer points of academic or political theory or produce any prophetic visions of the next century.

The Civil War and Reconstruction had plunged the state into economic ruin and state government into deep debt, despite the heavy taxation of Texas citizens, particularly property owners. The bottom had fallen out of land prices, a disaster for what was still an agricultural state. Governmental corruption had been pervasive under the Davis administration, and the dictatorial powers that Davis had exercised, particularly the abuses of his hated state police, had left deep scars. Moreover, the national political scene under President Grant's two administrations (1869–77) had also been plagued by corruption and scandal.

The framers of the Texas constitution of 1876 reacted accordingly. In seeking to restore control of their state government to the people and reestablish economic stability, they fashioned what was essentially an antigovernment charter. Centralization was replaced with more local control, strict limits were placed on taxation, and short leashes were put on the legislature, the courts, and, especially, the governor.[15]

Texas's traditional agricultural interests, which had been called on to finance industrial development and new social services during the Reconstruction era, were once again protected from onerous governmental intrusion and taxation. The retrenchment and reform embodied in the new charter would soon hamper the state's commercial and economic development. But post-Reconstruction Texans applauded the multitude of restrictive details that the new constitution carried. They ratified the document in February 1876 by a resounding vote of 136,606 to 56,052.

Grange Organization formed in the late nineteenth century to improve the lot of farmers. The Grange influenced provisions in the Texas Constitution of 1876 limiting taxes and government spending and restricting big business, including banks and railroads.

GENERAL PRINCIPLES OF THE TEXAS CONSTITUTION

The Texas Constitution draws from the national constitutional tradition discussed earlier and embodies three dominant principles: popular sovereignty, limited government, and separation of powers.

The relatively short Preamble and the first three sections of the Bill of Rights express the underlying principle of **popular sovereignty**. As Article I, sections 2 and 3, make clear, it is a social compact, formed by free people, in which "all political power is inherent in the people, . . . founded on their authority, and instituted for their preservation." Although the language articulates the noble aspirations of a free and just society, it was limited in scope and application. Women and minorities were initially denied full citizenship rights. And although women gained the right to vote by amendment to the U.S. Constitution in 1920, African Americans and Hispanics have only recently received the full protections implicit in these statements.

The second major principle is **limited government**. The Texas Bill of Rights and other provisions throughout the constitution place limits on governmental authority and power. The constitution spells out the traditional rights of religious freedom, procedural due process of law, and other rights of the citizen in relation to the government.

The third major principle is that of **separation of powers**. Unlike the U.S. Constitution, in which this principle emerges through powers defined in the three articles that relate to the Congress, the president, and the judiciary, Article II of the Texas Constitution specifically provides for separation of powers. The Constitution of 1876 created three branches of government and established a system of checks and balances that assured that no single branch would dominate the others.

Lawmaking authority is vested in an elected legislature comprising a 150-member House of Representatives and a 31-member Senate. The Texas legislature meets in regular sessions in odd-numbered years and in special sessions of limited scope and duration when called by the governor. The sixty-five sections of Article III outline in excessive detail the powers granted and the restrictions imposed on the legislature.

An elected governor shares authority over the executive branch with several other independently elected statewide officeholders. The governor, who has limited constitutional powers, can veto bills approved by the legislature and can call and set the agendas for special legislative sessions.

Also elected are members of the judiciary—from justices of the peace, who have limited jurisdiction at the county level, to judges on the highest statewide appellate courts. The fact that the judiciary is elected rather than appointed reflects the strong preference of post-Reconstruction Texans for an independent judiciary and is a major difference from the federal government, in which judges are appointed by the president. Also unlike the federal system, in which the U.S. Supreme Court serves as the court of last resort in both civil and criminal appeals, Texas has two courts of last resort. The Texas Supreme Court has final jurisdiction over civil matters while the Texas Court of Criminal Appeals has final review of criminal cases.

popular sovereignty
Constitutional principle of self-government; belief that the people control their government and governments are subject to limitations and constraints.

limited government
Constitutional principle restricting governmental authority and spelling out personal rights.

separation of powers Division of powers among three distinct branches of government—the legislative, the executive, and the judicial—which serve as checks and balances on each other's actions.

WEAKNESSES AND CRITICISMS OF THE CONSTITUTION OF 1876

Executive Branch   Many experts believe that the Texas Constitution excessively fragments governmental authority and responsibility, particularly in the executive branch. Although there is a natural disposition for the public to look to the governor to establish policy priorities, the governor does not have control over other elected state executives but rather shares both authority and responsibility for policy with them. This situation can be problematic, as when former Republican Governor Bill Clements, for example, shared executive responsibilities with Democrats who sharply disagreed with his priorities. Even when the governor and other elected officials are of the same party, differences in personality, political philosophy, and policy objectives can produce tension and sometimes deadlock.

The governor's power has been further diffused by the creation over the years of numerous boards and commissions that set policy for executive agencies not headed by elected officials. Although the governor appoints most of those board members, they serve staggered six-year terms, which are longer than a governor's term. A newly elected governor—who cannot fire a predecessor's appointees—usually has to wait through most of his or her first term to gain a majority of appointees to most boards.

Fragmented authority and responsibility are also found in county governments, which are administrative agents of the state (see Chapter 25). Various elected county officials often clash over public policy, producing inefficiencies or failing to meet public needs. And just as voters are faced with a long ballot for statewide offices, they must also choose among a long, often confusing list of county officers. Because a long ballot discourages many people from voting, this obstacle reduces public accountability, an end result that the framers of the constitution of 1876 certainly never intended.

Legislative Branch   The constitution created a low-paid, part-time legislature to ensure the election of citizen-lawmakers who would be sensitive to the needs of their constituents, not of professional politicians who would live off the taxpayers. Unwittingly, however, the constitution writers also produced a lawmaking body easily influenced by special-interest groups. And the strict limitations placed on the legislature's operations and powers slow its ability to meet the increasingly complex needs of a growing, modern Texas.

In 1972 voters approved a constitutional change to lengthen the terms of the governor and other executive officeholders from two to four years. This change gives the governor more time to develop public policies with the prospect of seeing those policies implemented. But voters have repeatedly rejected proposals to provide for regular, annual legislative sessions, and legislative pay remains among the lowest in the country.

Judicial Branch   The Texas Constitution also created numerous locally elected judicial offices, including justice of the peace and county and district courts. Although there are appeal procedures, these judges have a great deal of autonomy, power, and influence through their local constituencies.

Education   Another example of decentralization is the public school system. The centralized school system authorized under the Reconstruction Constitution

African American participation in Texas politics has increased significantly since the 1960s as a result of the Voting Rights Act and of federal court decisions that overturned restrictive state laws that kept blacks from registering and voting.

of 1869 was abolished, and local authorities were given primary responsibility for supervising public education. The concept of "local control" over their schools is important to many Texans, but decentralization and wide disparities in local tax bases have produced an inequitable public education system.

Individual Rights   Although articulating a general commitment to democracy and individual rights, the constitution initially retarded democratic development in Texas. Like many other southern states, Texas had restrictive laws on voter participation. It levied a poll tax, which reduced the voting of minorities and poor whites until 1966, when an amendment to the U.S. Constitution and a decision by the U.S. Supreme Court outlawed it. Federal courts also struck down a Texas election system that excluded African Americans from voting in the Democratic primary, which was where elections were decided when Texas was a one-party state. The elimination of significant numbers of people from participating in elections helped perpetuate the one-party political system for approximately a hundred years.[16]

Consequence of Details   The Texas Constitution is burdened with excessive detail. Although few individuals are disposed to read the more than 80,000-word document, a person casually perusing it can find language, for example, governing the operation of hospital districts in Ochiltree, Castro, Hansford, and Hopkins counties. There also is a provision dealing with expenditures for relocation or replacement of sanitary sewer laterals on private property. Whereas the 7,000-word U.S. Constitution leaves the details of implementation to congressional legislation, the Texas Constitution often spells out the authority and power of a governmental agency in specific detail. Most experts agree that many constitutional articles are of a legislative nature and have no business in a constitution.[17] The excessive detail provides definitions and restrictions—continued legacies of the framers of the 1876 document.

Across the USA

States Frequently Amend Their Constitutions

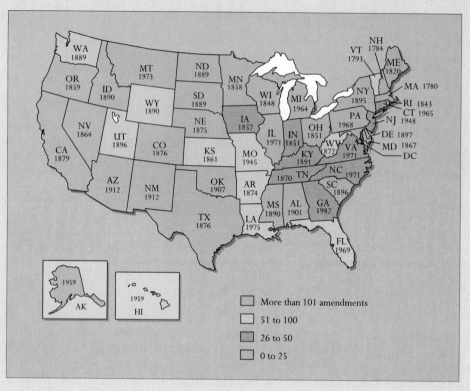

- ☐ More than 101 amendments
- ☐ 51 to 100
- ☐ 26 to 50
- ☐ 0 to 25

Source: Based on data from "State Constitutions," *The Book of the States: 1996–1997* (Council of State Governments, 1996), Table 1.1.

Consequently, there are obsolete provisions in the constitution. Article VI, which defines **suffrage**, prohibits anyone younger than twenty-one from voting. But that age limitation has been superseded by the Twenty-sixth Amendment to the U.S. Constitution, which lowered the voting age to eighteen. Some efforts have been made to "clean up" the constitution by eliminating such deadwood—fifty-six obsolete provisions were removed in 1969—but the problem persists.[18]

Another important criticism of the Texas Constitution focuses on the amendments and the amendment process. Alabama has passed more constitutional amendments than any other state, but Texas ranked fourth with 379 amendments from 1876 through 1997 (see *Across the USA:* "States Frequently Amend Their Constitutions"). In contrast, the U.S. Constitution has been amended only twenty-seven times since 1789, and ten of those amendments were adopted as the Bill of Rights immediately after the government organized. The numerous restrictions and prohibitions in the Texas Constitution require excessive amendments to enable state government to adapt to changing social, economic, and political conditions.

suffrage The right to vote.

It Depends on How You Say It

The legislature not only decides which constitutional amendments go to the voters but also determines the caption that appears on the ballot to describe a proposal. Because the entire text of an amendment is not printed on the ballot, the caption takes on increased importance and, in some cases, controversy. Opponents of some major amendments have accused lawmakers of trying to sneak proposals past the voters with misleading or inadequate ballot captions.

In 1989 the legislature proposed an amendment that would have more than tripled the $7,200 annual salary paid to lawmakers. It would also have removed the voters' control over future raises by tying legislative pay to a percentage of the governor's salary, which is set by the legislature. But the wording on the ballot simply said,

> The constitutional amendment to limit the salary of the lieutenant governor and the speaker of the House of Representatives to not more than one-half of the governor's salary and to limit the salary of a

member of the legislature to not more than one-fourth of the governor's salary.

Opponents of the proposal argued that the use of the word *limit* was an attempt to mislead voters into thinking the amendment could mean a pay reduction. In reality, the governor's salary, which had been freed from constitutional restraints in 1955, was then about $90,000 and was usually increased by the legislature each biennium. However, the voters were not confused. They rejected the amendment by a wide margin.

In 1987 voters rejected a constitutional amendment promoted by business interests and state leaders to allow a so-called freeport tax exemption for goods used in manufacturing that were only temporarily stored in Texas. The ballot caption identified the proposal as an amendment "relating to the exemption from ad valorem taxation of certain tangible personal property temporarily located within the state." A similar amendment was resubmitted by the legislature in 1989 and won voter approval. The 1989 ballot caption began, "The constitutional amendment promoting economic growth, job creation and fair tax treatment for Texans who export goods . . ." That obviously sounded much better to most voters.

CONSTITUTIONAL CHANGE AND ADAPTATION

Amendment   Although the drafters filled the Texas Constitution with a multitude of restrictive provisions, they also provided a relatively easy method of amending it. Although this piecemeal amendment process has enabled state government to meet some changing needs, it also has added thousands of words to the document.

Proposed constitutional amendments can be submitted only by the legislature. Approval by two-thirds of the House and the Senate puts them on the ballot, where adoption requires a majority vote (see *What Do You Think?* "It Depends on How You Say It"). Although voters had approved 379 amendments through 1997, they had rejected 168 others. Since the present charter was ratified in 1876, there have been only thirty-one years in which voters have not been asked to change it. The first amendment was adopted on September 2, 1879. A record twenty-five amendments were on the November 3, 1987, ballot. Seventeen were adopted, and eight were defeated.

Some amendments are of major statewide importance, but many have affected only a single county or a handful of counties or have been offered simply to rid the constitution of obsolete language (see *Up Close:* "A Lot of Trouble for a Minor Office"). One amendment approved by voters in 1993 affected only about 140

initiative   Procedure by which voters propose constitutional amendments or other laws through petitions subject to adoption by a popular vote.

referendum   Vote by the general electorate on a public policy issue, such as a constitutional amendment.

Up Close

families, two church congregations, and one school district in Fort Bend and Austin counties. It cleared up a title defect to their land.

Unlike voters in many other states, Texas citizens cannot force the placement of constitutional amendments on the ballot because Texas does not have the **initiative** and **referendum** on a statewide level. On taking office in January 1979 as Texas's first Republican governor since Reconstruction, Bill Clements made adoption of the initiative and referendum a priority. But these innovations could not take effect without a constitutional amendment, and the Democrat-controlled legislature—which did not want to give up such a significant policy prerogative to the electorate—ignored Clements.

In recent years, however, the legislature has demonstrated a tendency to seek political cover by selectively letting the voters decide some particularly controversial issues, such as a binding referendum in 1987 on the legalization of parimutuel betting on horse and dog racing. In 1993 the legislature proposed a constitutional amendment, which voters overwhelmingly endorsed, to prohibit a personal income tax in Texas without voter approval.

Constitutional Convention   The Constitution also provides for revision by constitutional convention, which the legislature can call with the approval of the voters. Convention delegates have to be elected, and their terms also are subject to voter approval. In 1919 voters overwhelmingly rejected a proposal for a constitutional convention. Subsequent efforts, including an attempt by Governor John Connally in 1967, to initiate reforms using a constitutional convention were also defeated.[19] Connally's efforts did, however, result in adoption of a "cleanup" amendment in 1969 that removed many obsolete provisions from the constitution, and it laid the groundwork for a constitutional convention in 1974.

Constitutional Reform Efforts of 1971–1975   The 1974 convention, the only one ever held under the present 1876 charter, ended in failure. Its delegates were the 181 members of the legislature. The constitutional convention of 1974 had its beginning in 1971, when state Representative Nelson Wolff of San Antonio and several other first-term legislators won the leadership's backing for a full-scale revision effort. In 1972 voters approved the necessary constitutional amendment that specified the convention would comprise house members and senators elected the same year.

In 1973 the legislature created a thirty-seven-member Constitutional Revision Commission to hold public hearings around the state and make recommendations to the convention. Members of the commission, chaired by former Texas Supreme Court Chief Justice Robert W. Calvert, were appointed by Governor Dolph Briscoe and other top state officials.

The constitutional convention, or "con-con," as it came to be called by legislators and members of the media, convened on January 8, 1974. House Speaker Price Daniel, Jr., was elected president, and Lieutenant Governor Bill Hobby, in an address to delegates, offered a prophetic warning: "The special interests of today will be replaced by new and different special interests tomorrow, and any attempt to draft a constitution to serve such interests would be futile and also dishonorable."[20]

Hobby's plea was ignored. Special interests dominated the convention, which finally adjourned in bitter failure on July 30, failing by three votes to get the two-thirds vote necessary to send a new constitution to Texas voters for ratification. The crucial fight was over a business-backed attempt to lock the state's right-to-work law into the constitution. The **right-to-work law** prohibits union membership as a condition of employment, so the effort was bitterly fought by organized labor.

right-to-work law   Law prohibiting the requirement of union membership in order to hold or get a job.

After three years of preparation and deliberations, the proposed constitution of 1974 failed by three votes in the final hectic session of the constitutional convention, when the gallery was filled with interested onlookers, including many representatives of labor.

What Do You Think?

Do the Voters Really Care?

Nelson Wolff, one of the legislators who began the constitutional revision effort in the 1970s and years later became mayor of San Antonio, noted a general lack of citizen interest in the work of the constitutional convention of 1974. In his book *Challenge of Change*, he wrote,

> The constitutional revision effort in Texas had attempted to use every means known to get citizen participation in the process. A toll-free telephone had been set up for the convention. Committees of the convention met at night and on weekends to provide working people an opportunity to testify. We provided to the best of our ability optimum conditions for testimony. Yet many people avoided participation in the revision process.*

Most people were not attentive to the details and nuances of constitutional revisions, and translating these complexities into arguments that made sense to the average voter was a difficult task.[†] Evidence also suggests that the advocates of constitutional reform were ineffective in their public relations campaign. The voter distrust and apathy played right into the hands of numerous special interests that did not want to give up the protections the old constitution afforded them.

---

* Nelson Wolff, *Challenge of Change* (San Antonio: Naylor, 1975), pp. 45–46.
[†] John E. Bebout, "The Problem of the Texas Constitution," in *The Texas Constitution: Problems and Prospects for Revision* (Arlington: Texas Urban Development Commission, 1971), p. 9.

Reflecting the sentiment of many other business groups, the Greater San Antonio Chamber of Commerce told convention delegates that such a guarantee against forced union membership should be in the constitution, even though it had been a state law since 1947 and was in no danger of being repealed. The right to work, the chamber wrote, "is considered by many to be so fundamental in nature as to require Constitutional protection."[21] The Texas AFL-CIO disagreed. Business was politically stronger than organized labor in Texas, but the two-thirds vote necessary to put a new constitution on the ballot was too high an obstacle.

The gallery in the house of representatives chamber, which served as the convention hall, was packed with labor representatives and other spectators when the final vote was taken, about a half-hour before the convention's midnight adjournment deadline. Daniel held the electronic voting board open for twenty-eight minutes, hoping three delegates could be persuaded to switch their votes, but time ran out. Tension and emotions were running so high that, at one point, state representative Jim Mattox of Dallas, who would later become attorney general, challenged Daniel's delay in announcing the vote and publicly called the convention president a liar.[22]

Although the right-to-work dispute took the brunt of the blame, other factors also worked against the revision effort (see *What Do You Think?* "Do the Voters Really Care?"). One was Governor Briscoe's refusal to exercise any significant leadership on behalf of a new state charter. Except for opposing proposals that he thought would further weaken the authority of the governor, he provided little input to the convention and did not attempt to twist delegates' arms to get enough votes to send the document to the electorate. Louisiana voters had approved a new state constitution in 1974, and Governor Edwin Edwards's strong support had been considered instrumental. Gubernatorial leadership in other states also appears to have been critical to successful constitutional conventions.

Another major obstacle was the convention's makeup. Texas, unlike most other states, chose to use the 181 members of the legislature as its constitutional convention. Soon after the convention began its work, many of them were facing reelection campaigns in the party primaries.

Additionally, a minority of legislators—dubbed "cockroaches" by President Daniel—did not want a new constitution and attempted to delay or obstruct the convention's work at every opportunity. Most legislators, even those who wanted a new constitution, reacted to their own political fears and ambitions. They were very susceptible to the influence of special interests, far more susceptible than most private-citizen delegates would likely have been. And special interests were legion at the convention. In addition to various business and professional groups and organized labor, many county officeholders whose jobs—protected by the constitution of 1876—were suddenly in jeopardy put pressure on the delegates.

Some county judges lobbied against a proposal to streamline the judiciary because they feared it would relieve them of judicial duties. Under the present constitution, county judges are primarily administrative officers and do not have to be lawyers, but they do have limited judicial responsibilities. So persistent was their lobbying that Daniel referred to some of them as a "wrecking crew." Representative DeWitt Hale of Corpus Christi, chair of the Committee on the Judiciary, was "disgusted because a handful of judges could be so disruptive to the convention."[23]

Influential regents, lobbyists, and alumni of the University of Texas and Texas A&M University systems guarded the Permanent University Fund, their rich constitutional endowment. Further, highway lobbyists, backed by thousands of contractors and businesspeople from throughout the state, fought any attempt to raid the highway trust fund, the constitutional provision that dedicates three-fourths of the revenue from the state motor fuels tax to highway projects.

Delegates tried to walk a tightrope over the emotionally charged issue of gambling. They yielded to the wishes of charitable and fraternal organizations and tentatively approved a provision to allow bingo and raffles to be conducted for charity, receiving some public ridicule for giving constitutional status to a game of chance. But delegates voted to retain the general constitutional prohibition against lotteries. In a letter to Robert W. Calvert, the chair of the Constitutional Revision Commission, Baylor University President Abner McCall had warned of considerable public opposition to any new constitution that legalized gambling: "The commission may adopt proposals to make the machinery of Texas government more efficient, but many of us will not trade a little more efficiency for a greater danger of corruption of government by state sponsored gambling."[24] The ban on lotteries was to remain in the constitution for another seventeen years, until Governor Ann Richards successfully promoted the creation of a state lottery as a new revenue source for state government in 1991.

During its next regular session, in 1975, the legislature, with the strong support of House Speaker Bill Clayton and Lieutenant Governor Bill Hobby, resurrected the constitutional revision effort. Lawmakers voted to present to Texans the basic document that the convention had barely rejected the previous summer in the form of eight separate constitutional amendments. The first three articles dealing with the separation of powers and the legislative and executive branches were combined into one ballot proposition. Each of the remaining seven propositions was a separate article, each to be independently approved or rejected by the voters. The most controversial issues that the 1974 convention had debated, such as right-to-work, were excluded. The streamlined amendments would have considerably shortened the

Martha Whitehead Campaigned to End Her Job

State Treasurer Martha Whitehead was a rarity in politics—an officeholder who campaigned to abolish her own job. The treasurer's post was created by the constitution of 1876 to manage the state's money, but by the 1990s it had become a relatively minor office overshadowed by the much larger fiscal operations of the state comptroller. It nevertheless still offered some political benefits for its occupants. Democrat Ann Richards, who was state treasurer for eight years,

used the office to launch a successful race for governor. Republican Kay Bailey Hutchison, the next treasurer, made it a springboard to the U.S. Senate. But Whitehead, a Democrat appointed by Richards in 1993 to complete Hutchison's term when Hutchison was elected to the U.S. Senate, held the office only a few months before deciding it was wasting taxpayers' money and needed to be abolished.

Pledging to lead a campaign to wipe the office off the books, Whitehead was elected to a new term in 1994 over a Republican opponent, Austin banker David Hartman, who argued that the treasurer's office should remain an independent agency to assure adequate checks and balances on state finances. The legislature placed a constitutional amendment on the November 1995 ballot to abolish the office and transfer its duties to the comptroller. The amendment was opposed by the State Republican Executive Committee but was overwhelmingly approved by voters. The comptroller's office estimated that taxpayers would save about $20 million during the first five years after the change. The elimination of the elected treasurer's post was effective on September 1, 1996. Some of the agency's 200 employees were transferred to the comptroller's office, but officials estimated that about 160 jobs would soon be phased out.

constitution and provided some major changes, including annual legislative sessions, a unified judicial system, and more flexibility in county government. It would have been a much more flexible, modern constitution than the 1876 document and had cost several million tax dollars and countless hours to produce. But voters rejected all eight propositions on November 4, 1975, some by margins of more than 2 to 1.

The legislature's stock fraud scandal of 1971 and the Watergate scandal that had forced the resignation of President Richard Nixon in 1974 had raised Texans' distrust of government, and the proposed new constitution had been drafted by state officials, not by private citizens.

Efforts to enact these proposals were further thwarted by Governor Briscoe. Although he had never taken an active role in the revision effort, three weeks before the 1975 election, he openly opposed the eight propositions and suggested that the existing constitution had served the state well and would continue to be adequate for the future.[25]

Further Piecemeal Reforms   So it was back to piecemeal constitutional changes. Between 1975 and 1997, 158 amendments were approved by Texas voters and 33 were rejected. Besides the lottery, amendments winning approval included the 1993 amendment to ban a personal income tax without voter approval and a series of propositions authorizing $3 billion in tax-backed bonds for a huge prison expansion program. In 1985 voters approved an amendment to give the governor and legislative leaders authority to deal with budgetary emergencies between legislative sessions. In 1995 they approved an amendment to abolish the state treasurer's office and transfer its duties to the comptroller (see *People in Politics:* "Martha Whitehead Campaigned to End Her Job"). And, in 1997, Texas voters by a wide margin approved a constitutional amendment to increase homeowners' $5,000 exemptions from school property taxes to $15,000. The measure, part of a property tax relief effort promoted by Governor George W. Bush, saved the average homeowner about $140 a year in local school taxes. Also in 1997, voters approved a constitutional amendment to allow Texas homeowners to use their homes as collateral for borrowing money for college educations and other consumer purposes. Texas was the last state to allow such home equity borrowing. Before the amendment was adopted, Texans' homesteads could be used as collateral only for loans to purchase a house or make improvements to it or for certain tax debts.

Constitutional Provisions, Interest Groups, and Elites   Only a small percentage of registered voters—often less than 20 percent—participate in elections when constitutional amendments are the only issues on the ballot (see Figure 20-1). When amendments are submitted to the voters during gubernatorial or presidential elections, the turnout is much higher. But in many instances, a relative handful of Texans ultimately decide on fundamental changes in government, which enhances their influence over the constitutional revision process.

Interest groups, which historically have been strong in Texas, work diligently to protect their concerns and objectives. They develop strategies to get provisions into the constitution that would benefit them and to keep provisions out of the constitution that they fear would hurt them. Because most amendments represent nonpartisan issues, a well-financed public relations campaign is likely to produce public support for an amendment.[26]

Interest groups are able to kill many proposed constitutional changes in the legislature, where the two-thirds vote requirement works to their advantage. Only a small fraction of constitutional amendments proposed by legislators get put on the ballot. Those that do usually have the support of one or more special-interest groups,

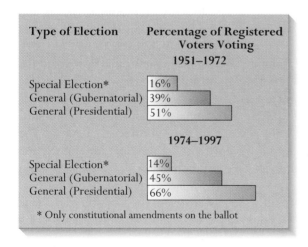

Type of Election	Percentage of Registered Voters Voting
1951–1972	
Special Election*	16%
General (Gubernatorial)	39%
General (Presidential)	51%
1974–1997	
Special Election*	14%
General (Gubernatorial)	45%
General (Presidential)	66%
* Only constitutional amendments on the ballot	

FIGURE 20-1 Turnout for Constitutional Amendments

Constitutional amendments can be presented to the voters in either a general election or a special election. Turnout rates are much higher during the gubernatorial and presidential elections, but it is not uncommon for less than 20 percent of the registered voters to turn out in a special election.

Source: Janice May, Amending the Texas Constitution, 1951–1972 (Austin: Texas Advisory Commission on Intergovernmental Relations, 1972); Secretary of State, Elections Division.

Politics in Cyberspace

The Texas Constitution

Most Texans have never seen or read the Texas Constitution, and although there are many provisions of the constitution that have little interest for most citizens, there are important sections of the constitution that merit a careful reading. For example, the provisions pertaining to the powers and responsibilities of the three branches of government are important to understanding how these institutions function, and for those interested in due process of law, the Bill of Rights should be consulted.

Texas Legislative Council
http:www.capitol.state.tx.us/txconst/toc.html

The entire text of the Texas Constitution can be downloaded from this site. In addition to an index to the constitution, the text of the constitution can be searched using key words.

Texas Legislature On-Line
http://www.capitol.state.tx.us

Access to legislative resolutions providing for constitutional amendments can be found here. Legislative intent and legislative histories of proposed constitutional amendments are also available.

Secretary of State
http://www.sos.state.tx.us

The office of the Secretary of State is responsible for compiling state election returns, including constitutional amendments. County level returns for constitutional amendments since 1993 can be accessed from this site.

League of Women Voters
http://main.org/leaguewv/home.html

The Texas League of Women Voters is a nonpartisan organization committed to increasing political participation, improving state and local government, and increasing public understanding of major policy issues. When constitutional amendments are submitted to voters, the league usually publishes information about the purpose and effects of the amendments.

---

which often finance publicity campaigns to promote the propositions to the voters. Few amendments attract organized opposition, but there have been exceptions.

In May 1993 strong opposition from wealthy school districts and Republicans defeated a constitutional amendment backed by Governor Ann Richards and Democratic legislative leaders that would have let the legislature redistribute education funds from wealthy to poor school districts in order to comply with a court order to equalize school funding. Opponents fanned voter distrust of the proposal by calling it a "Robin Hood" plan. Months later, it was revealed that the Republican National Committee, apparently hoping to damage Richards politically, had contributed $400,000 to the campaign against the amendment. That amount represented nearly 60 percent of the opposition's finances. The amendment's defeat came only a month before a court deadline for state action and forced the legislature to draft an eleventh-hour alternative plan to avoid shutting down public schools. The new plan didn't require a constitutional amendment, but it too forced wealthy school districts to share their revenue with poor districts. And it later was upheld by the Texas Supreme Court, which had a Republican majority.

Many of the recent successful attempts at constitutional change have reflected a pro-industry and economic development push that contrasts sharply

elites Small groups of people who exercise disproportionate power and influence in the policy-making processes.

with the antibusiness sentiment of the original constitutional framers. Recent amendments also have helped build up a public bonded indebtedness that the nineteenth-century constitution writers would have been unable to comprehend. Texas was rural then. It is now largely urban and is working to diversify and rebuild its economy in the wake of the disastrous oil and real estate busts of the 1980s. Business has repeatedly turned to state government for tax breaks and other economic incentives and has found receptive ears in the legislature and the governor's office.

Nine of the record twenty-five amendments on the November 1987 ballot were actively promoted as an economic development package by the Build Texas Committee, a bipartisan group of business and civic leaders. Voters approved most of the amendments, including bonds for new water projects and prisons.

Industry, with the unusual support of organized labor and environmentalists, won a major tax break through a constitutional amendment approved by Texas voters in 1993. It requires local governments to grant property tax exemptions for expensive pollution control equipment that businesses are required by state or federal law to install in their plants and other facilities. The business community supported the amendment because it represented untold millions of dollars in potential tax savings. Labor supported it because money not spent on taxes could mean more money spent on jobs. And environmentalists viewed it as an antipollution measure. Some local officials were fearful of the potential loss of large amounts of revenue to counties, school districts, and other local governments, but they were clearly overpowered.

It has been argued that the Texas Constitution serves the interests of a small number of **elites**—those individuals who control businesses and other dominant institutions in the state. This argument suggests that the severe constraints built into the constitution limit the policy options of state government and have historically thwarted the efforts of larger public-interest groups to restructure or improve the tax system, education policy, social services, health care, and other policies and programs that would benefit low- and middle-income Texans. Power is so fragmented that these groups have had to turn to the courts to force change. This same argument, incidentally, has often been made about the U.S. Constitution.

If this interpretation is accurate, it is ironic that those who framed the Texas Constitution of 1876 directed much of their wrath against railroads, banks, and other institutions that are today considered elitist. The tumultuous last quarter of the nineteenth century witnessed high levels of class and economic conflict, with the emergence of the Greenback and Populist political parties, which articulated the interests of the lower income groups. But monied business interests eventually were able to use the state constitution and subsequent legislation to reestablish their dominance over Texas government. Although the elite structure of the state has changed since 1876, some scholars argue that there has been a gradual transfer of power and control to new elites, who continue to exercise enormous influence over public policy.

Change through Court Interpretation   Some evidence indicates that Texas courts are now prepared to play a more expansive role in the interpretation of the constitution and, in turn, effect major changes in state policy. The best known example is the Edgewood school finance case, in which the courts invalidated the system of funding public education and ordered the legislature to provide more equity in tax resources among the state's more than 1,000 school districts. Wide disparities in spending on students between rich and poor districts—the result of wide disparities in local property values—violated the state constitution's requirement for an "efficient" system of public schools, the Texas Supreme Court ruled.

CONSTITUTIONAL RESTRAINTS AND THE ABILITY TO GOVERN

The nonpartisan League of Women Voters of Texas has been a long-suffering advocate of a total rewrite of the state constitution. Nevertheless, before each constitutional amendments election, it normally announces which propositions it endorses for the sake of good government and which it opposes. But League leaders lost their patience in 1987 with the placement of the record twenty-five amendments on the same ballot. They announced they would neither support nor oppose any amendment that year. Instead, they urged voters to examine the propositions carefully and complain to their legislators about the length of the ballot. "Enough is enough. Let us work together to halt this ridiculous system of running the government by means of the constitution," the League said. But without a new constitution, the only way state government can prepare for the challenges of the twenty-first century under a highly restrictive constitution written in the nineteenth is to continue this pattern of "amendomania."[27]

Prospects for Future Change   Experts can point out the many flaws of the Texas Constitution, but attempts at wholesale revision have not been successful. Numerous piecemeal changes have been made, but they have not addressed the fundamental criticisms of the charter. What is to be made of all this?

First, Texas has a long history of suspicion of government, and this tradition continues. Most people fear governmental abuses and excesses more than they worry about government's inability to respond quickly and efficiently to the needs of its citizens. In the vernacular of the layperson, "If it ain't broke, don't fix it." And it is not clear that the layperson regards the constitution as "broke."

Second, many groups and interests benefit from the existing constitution, and they have demonstrated a collective resolve to minimize change.

Finally, most Texans give little thought to changing the constitution because they are ill prepared to deal with the complexities of the document. Enormous problems must be overcome if citizens are to be educated and motivated to press for constitutional revision.

SUMMARY NOTES

- Texas, like most other states, has functioned under a series of constitutions, each of which has contributed to the state's constitutional legacy. Each is appropriately understood from the perspective of the period in which it was adopted.

- Texas currently operates under a constitution that was adopted following the Civil War and the Radical Reconstruction era, and the events of that period left an enduring legacy of suspicion of government, limited government, and fragmented governmental institutions. The 1876 constitution was predicated on the theory that governmental excesses could be minimized by carefully defining what governments could and could not do.

- The framers failed to anticipate that the limitations they imposed on governmental institutions would ultimately allow major economic interests within the state to dominate the policy-making process, often to the detriment of the lower socioeconomic groups.

- What the delegates to the Constitutional Convention of 1875 regarded as the strengths of the constitution—fragmented authority, detailed limitations on the power of governmental institutions, and decentralization—have served to limit the ability of state and local governments to adapt effectively to economic and demographic changes. The perceived solutions to many of the problems of 1875 have compounded the problems of state and local governments in the 1990s.

- Efforts to overhaul the Texas Constitution have failed. Consequently, the state has been forced to amend the document continually on a piecemeal basis. This process has produced some success in modernizing the charter, but many structural problems of state government require major institutional changes that cannot be resolved through this amendment process.

- In many ways, the Texas Constitution reflects the values of the state's conservative political culture, which continues to be suspicious of far-reaching constitutional changes. Moreover, constitutions and the debates that surround them are complex, and most people give little attention to these issues. Consequently, it is much easier to mobilize public opinion against rather than for wholesale change.

- Over the years, numerous groups have attempted to protect their interests through constitutional amendments. But the same groups usually oppose any proposed changes that threaten their influence, power, or benefits. Consequently, the interests of small segments of the state's population often prevail over the interests of the majority.

SELECTED READINGS

BRADEN, GEORGE D., ET AL. *The Constitution of the State of Texas: An Annotated and Comparative Analysis.* 2 vols. Austin: Texas Advisory Commission on Intergovernmental Relations, 1977.

BRUFF, HAROLD H. "Separation of Powers under the Texas Constitution." *Texas Law Review* 68 (June 1990): 1337–67.

CNUDDE, CHARLES F., and ROBERT E. CREW, JR. *Constitutional Democracy in Texas.* St. Paul: West, 1989.

HARRINGTON, JAMES C. "Framing a Texas Bill of Rights Argument." *St. Mary's Law Journal* 24 (1993): 399–442.

HIRCZY, WOLFGAN. "Texas Equal Rights Amendment: Twenty Years and a Few Surprises Later." *Texas Journal of Political Studies* 16 (Fall 1993): 22–46.

LUTZ, DONALD S. "The Texas Constitution." In *Perspectives on American and Texas Politics: A Collection of Essays*, eds. Donald S. Lutz and Kent L. Tedin, pp. 193–211. Dubuque, Iowa: Kendall/Hunt, 1987.

MAUER, JOHN WALKER. "State Constitutions in a Time of Crisis: The Case of the Texas Constitution of 1876." *Texas Law Review* 68 (June 1990): 1615–47.

MAY, JANICE C. *The Texas Constitution Revision Experience in the 70s.* Austin: Sterling Swift, 1975.

MCKAY, SETH SHEPARD. *Seven Decades of the Texas Constitution of 1876.* Lubbock: Texas Technical College, 1943.

MILLER, LAWRENCE. "The Texas Constitution," in *Texas Politics: A Reader*, eds. Anthony Champagne and Edward J. Harpham. New York: Norton, 1997, pp. 16–31.

PARKER, ALLAN E. "Public Free Schools: A Constitutional Right to Educational Choice in Texas." *Southwestern Law Journal* 45 (Fall 1991): 825–976.

WATTS, MIKAL, and BRAD ROCKWELL. "The Original Intent of the Educational Article of the Texas Constitution." *St. Mary's Law Journal* 21 (1990): 771–820.

WOLFF, NELSON. *Challenge of Change.* San Antonio: Naylor, 1975.

ASK YOURSELF ABOUT POLITICS

1. Do your elected officials care what you think about public policy and their decisions?
   Yes ☐ No ☐

2. Do working people have the same access to their state legislators as bank presidents do?
   Yes ☐ No ☐

3. Should a political party have the right to determine who can vote in its primary elections?
   Yes ☐ No ☐

4. Is there really any difference between the two major political parties in Texas?
   Yes ☐ No ☐

5. Should a candidate be allowed to accept unlimited amounts of money from special-interest groups?
   Yes ☐ No ☐

6. Should people be able to register to vote the day of an election?
   Yes ☐ No ☐

7. Should minority groups be represented in the Texas legislature in proportion to their share of the population?
   Yes ☐ No ☐

CHAPTER

21

INTEREST GROUPS, POLITICAL PARTIES, AND ELECTIONS IN TEXAS

Democracy is as much a struggle among competing interests at the state and local level as it is in Washington. How are the power and influence that affect the quality of life for millions of people distributed in Texas?

What Do You Think?

Is It Summer School or Recess for Lawmakers?

Lobbyists for numerous special-interest groups spent thousands of dollars entertaining and influencing Texas lawmakers during the 1997 legislative session, but they didn't stop there. Only a few weeks after their work in Austin had ended, many lobbyists and legislators headed to summer conferences, where the lawmakers were wined and dined some more.

Such conferences offer lawmakers from Texas the opportunity to discuss problems and exchange ideas with legislators from other states and to hear experts speak about a variety of important issues. They also offer special interests additional opportunities to purchase access to policymakers. The meeting schedules are usually crammed with opportunities for play as well as work. And most of the social events—dinners, golf games, tourist excursions, and other attractions—are sponsored by corporations and special-interest groups. Texas taxpayers, meanwhile,

pick up the tab for the legislators' airfare and hotel rooms. According to research by the *Austin American-Statesman*, taxpayers spent more than $265,000 on travel expenses for lawmakers attending three major out-of-state conferences in 1995 and 1996.

As many as half of Texas's lawmakers may attend one or more of these conferences in any given year. Some legislators conscientiously attend as many work sessions as they can. State Representative Bob Hunter of Abilene told the *Austin American-Statesman* he brings an empty suitcase to carry home the stacks of reports distributed to share with colleagues. "You glean some tremendous ideas," he said. Many other lawmakers, however, view the conferences more as social opportunities. "What did I do today? I played golf," Representative Pat Haggerty of El Paso told a reporter after skipping an afternoon's work session. "This [the golf course] is where you make the connections that are good for business, that are good for government, that are good for whatever," Haggerty said.

Source: Austin American-Statesman, November 2, 1997.

THE POWER OF INTEREST GROUPS

For a hundred years following the end of Reconstruction in the 1870s, the Democratic Party dominated Texas politics. In the past thirty years, however, the growing strength of the Republican Party has brought the era of Democratic Party dominance to an end. When it comes to shaping public policy, Republicans and Democrats alike take a back seat to the interests groups that have long dominated Texas's policy-making process and most likely will continue to do so.

Interest groups, whose priorities usually cross partisan lines, have long been strong in Texas politics. Their organizational strengths and initiatives are reflected in public policy, and those segments of Texas society that are unorganized are likely to have little, if any, impact on governmental decisions. The discussion of national interest groups in Chapter 9 is applicable to Texas, and many interest groups that function on the state and local level are linked to some extent to the national system.

Just as they do at the national level, interest groups in Texas spend millions of dollars a year trying to elect favored candidates or to influence the outcome of governmental decisions through a number of direct and indirect lobbying activities. Campaign contributions have always raised ethical questions of undue influence on policy makers and are a continuing source of controversy. Moreover, aggressive and often heavy-handed lobbying efforts contribute to the view that state and local governments are dominated by a few big interests looking out for themselves (see *What Do You Think?* "Is it Summer School or Recess for Lawmakers?").

interest group Organization seeking to influence government policy.

Lobbyists crowd into the senate chamber for a committee meeting during a regular legislative session.

Two studies, conducted more than twenty years apart, placed Texas among those states with strong interest-group systems.[1] Powerful pressure groups usually evolve in states with weak political parties, a condition that characterized Texas during most of this century.[2] During the many years that Texas was a one-party state, the Republican Party posed no serious challenge to the Democratic monopoly, and the Democratic Party was marked by intense factionalism. Although the conservative Democratic wing dominated state politics through the 1970s, interest groups often played a greater role in the policy-making process. Subsequent Republican growth has changed Texas's party system, but interest groups remain strong and, more often than not, still have a greater impact on the policy-making process than the political parties.

PLURALISM OR ELITISM?

There are thousands of interest groups at the state and local level in Texas. Some have long histories and a durable presence in the policy process; others are formed to address a specific need and disappear after a relatively short period. Although most groups have the potential to participate in policy making, many will not.

One can find evidence in Texas to support the pluralist view of power discussed in Chapter 1. **Pluralism** holds that significant numbers of diverse and competing interest groups serve to limit the power of any single group. Although most people do not actively participate in the policy-making process, they have access to the process through their group leaders. Pluralists believe there are numerous leadership opportunities within groups for people who want active roles.

The number of **lobbyists** has grown significantly over the past three decades, and the hundreds now registered in Austin represent a wide assortment of economic, social, civic, and cultural organizations. Supporters of the pluralist view say this growth proves the political system is open and accessible to new organizations. They argue that public officeholders are responsive to the needs and interests of a greater diversity of Texans than ever before.

Others insist that pluralist theories simply do not describe the realities of power and policy making in Texas. Convinced of the persuasiveness of **elitism**, they contend

pluralism Political system in which power is distributed among multiple groups.

lobbyists Individuals who attempt directly or indirectly to shape and influence the decisions of policy makers.

elitism Political system in which power is concentrated in the hands of a relatively small group of individuals or institutions.

that the ability to influence the most important policy decisions is monopolized by a few individuals who derive power from their leadership positions in organizations or institutions with great financial resources. In one view, from 1938 to 1957 Texas was "governed by conservatives, collectively dubbed **the Establishment**." This was a "loosely knit plutocracy comprised mostly of Anglo businessmen, oilmen, bankers and lawyers" that emerged in the late 1930s, in part, as a response to the liberal policies of the New Deal. They were extremely conservative, producing a "virulent" strain of conservatism marked by "Texanism" and "super-Americanism."[3]

The "traditionalistic-individualistic" political culture described in Chapter 19 was especially conducive to the dominance of the conservative establishment, which had little interest in the needs of the lower socioeconomic groups within the state. The exclusion of minorities from participation in elections and the low rates of voter turnout resulted in the election of public officials who were sympathetic to the views of the conservative elites. In addition, public opinion was manipulated by "unprincipled public relations men" and "the rise of reactionary newspapers."[4]

A more recent study of Texas politics argues that there is a group of Texans—extraordinarily wealthy or linked to large corporations—who constitute "an upper class in the precise meaning of the term: a social group whose common background and effective control of wealth bring them together politically." Although warning against the hasty conclusion that this upper class is a ruling class, the study describes their shared values, group cohesiveness, and interlocking relationships. The upper class has enormous political power. When united on specific policy objectives, its members have usually prevailed against "their liberal enemies concentrated in the working class." Moreover, the institutional arrangements of the state's economic and political structure work to produce upper-class unity that contributes to their successes in public policy.[5]

The sharply contrasting views of political power in Texas have produced an ongoing debate. To a large extent, the issue of who really controls Texas politics has not been resolved because of insufficient data to support one position over the other. There also is evidence that power relationships have changed over time. Historically, Texas government and public policy were dominated by an "upper class" or a "conservative establishment." But with the enormous social and economic changes that have taken place over the past twenty years, Texans may well be moving from an elitist system to some variation of pluralism.

DOMINANT INTEREST GROUPS IN TEXAS

Throughout much of this century, state government was dominated by large corporations, banks, oil companies, and agricultural interests that backed the conservative Democratic officeholders who had a stranglehold on the legislature, the courts, and the executive branch. Big business still carries a lot of weight in Austin and can purchase a lot of influence through major political contributions. State officials who want to build public support for new policy proposals usually solicit the support of the business community first.

But beginning in the 1970s, influence began to be more diffused. **Single-member districts** increased the numbers of minorities, Republicans, and liberal Democrats elected to the legislature (see Chapter 22). Consumer, environmental, and other public advocacy groups emerged. Organized labor, which had been shut out by the corporate establishment, found some common interests with the trial

"The Establishment" In the days of one-party Democratic politics in Texas, the Establishment was a loosely knit coalition of Anglo business and oil company executives, bankers, and lawyers who controlled state policy making through the dominant conservative wing of the Democratic Party.

single-member district Election system in which one person is elected to represent the people living within one geographic district.

lawyers, who earn fees suing businesses on behalf of consumers and other plaintiffs claiming damages or injuries caused by various companies or products. The decline of oil and gas production and the emergence of high-tech manufacturing and service industries also helped diffuse the business lobby into more competing factions.

Business Groups   The diverse business interests in Texas organize in three basic ways to influence the policy-making process. There are a few broad-based associations that represent business and industry in general, including the Texas Association of Business and Chambers of Commerce and the Texas Taxpayers and Research Association. Their overall goal is to maintain and improve on a favorable business climate.

The business community also organizes through trade associations, such as the Texas Bankers Association, the Texas Automobile Dealers Association, the Texas Independent Producers & Royalty Owners Association, the Wholesale Beer Distributors of Texas, and the Texas Chemical Council. These groups represent and seek to advance the interests of specific industries.

Finally, many individual companies retain their own lobbyists to represent them before the legislature and administrative agencies. Some wealthy individuals, such as computer magnate Ross Perot of Dallas, even hire their own lobbyists.

Although most business groups band together against organized labor, consumer advocates, and trial lawyers on major political and philosophical issues, the business lobby is far from monolithic (see *What Do You Think?* "Do Texas Lobbyists Look Out for Your Interests?"). There are numerous issues, including tax policy and utility regulation, on which companies or trade associations differ.

Professional Groups   A number of professional groups have played dominant roles in Texas politics and the policy-making process. One of the best known is the Texas Medical Association (TMA), which in recent years has joined forces with business against the trial lawyers in support of laws putting limits on malpractice suits and other damage claims against physicians and the business community. The TMA's political action committee is a major contributor of campaign dollars to candidates for the legislature and other state offices.

Litigation over medical malpractice, product liability, and workers' compensation has also expanded the influence of trial lawyers, who make their living representing injured persons. Individually and through their **political action committee**, Lawyers Involved for Texas (LIFT), trial lawyers have contributed millions of dollars to judicial, legislative, and other selected candidates since the 1970s. In the early 1980s, they succeeded in electing several Texas Supreme Court justices who shared their viewpoint, and the court issued major precedent-setting opinions making it easier for plaintiffs to win large damage awards from businesses, doctors, and insurance companies. The business and medical communities retaliated by boosting their own political contributions and lobbying efforts and, by 1990, had succeeded in tipping the Supreme Court's philosophical scale back to its traditional business-oriented viewpoint.

But the war over **tort law**, as these types of damage suits are called, continued to rage—before the judiciary and in the legislature. In 1995 the legislature enacted several laws backed by Governor George W. Bush to put significant restrictions on damage lawsuits.

Education Groups   In the past several years, educational interests have been very visible in the policy-making process in Austin, and higher education lobbying

political action committee   Committee organized by a corporation, labor union, trade association, ideological or issue-oriented group, cooperative, or nonprofit corporation for the purpose of collecting campaign contributions and distributing the money to political candidates.

tort law   Wrongful acts over which a damage lawsuit can be brought.

What Do You Think?

Do Texas Lobbyists Look Out for Your Interests?

During the 1997 session of the Texas legislature, 1,624 individuals representing hundreds of businesses, trade associations, and other interests registered as lobbyists. They ran the gamut from well-dressed corporate lobbyists with generous expense accounts to volunteer consumer and environmental advocates. Most were male, although the number of women lobbyists has increased in recent years, and many women now hold major lobbying positions. Most lobbyists came to their career by way of other occupations and jobs, but they have, on the whole, an acute understanding of the policy-making process and the points of access and influence in that process. The most successful lobbyists have developed the ability to pursue a wide range of tactics based on a comprehensive strategy.

Many lobbyists are former legislators. They bring to the process their legislative skills, personal relationships with former legislative colleagues, and expertise in substantive policy areas. A number of other lobbyists are former legislative staffers.

Many of the trade and professional associations, labor unions, and public interest groups have full-time staffers in Austin who function as their lobbyists. Many corporations also use their own employees to lobby in Austin. Some companies have governmental affairs departments or offices staffed by employees with experience in government or public affairs. In large corporations that do business across the country, the governmental affairs staffs may be rather large because such companies will attempt to follow the actions of numerous state legislatures, city councils, and the U.S. Congress.

A number of lawyers have developed successful lobby practices. Some of these professional freelancers, or "hired guns," specialize in specific policy areas; others represent a wide array of clients. Many work for the state's largest law firms, which have established permanent offices in Austin. Some of the top-notch freelancers are not attorneys, but they have a strong knowledge of the governmental process.

There are also some public relations firms that offer their services to interest groups. These companies specialize in "image creation" or "image modification." Although they may not handle the groups' direct lobbying efforts, they are often retained to assist in indirect lobbying. They are particularly adroit in developing relationships with the press, planning media campaigns, and assisting in political campaigns.

has been particularly effective. The changing global economy has enhanced the role of higher education in developing the state's future, and there is widespread public support for expanded access to higher education.

Most university regents, chancellors, and presidents are well connected politically. Although it is technically illegal for officials on the state payroll to try to influence legislation, universities are capable—through the use of donations and other nontax funds—of hiring a well-paid cadre of lobbyists. In 1991 the *Fort Worth Star-Telegram* counted at least twenty-two lobbyists on university payrolls, with salaries and expenses from September 1990 through July 1991 exceeding $1.6 million.[6]

Another effective lobbying source for universities, particularly the larger ones, are the armies of alumni—many of them politically influential—who are ready to make phone calls or write letters on behalf of their alma maters when the need arises. The business community is also a strong supporter of higher education.

The struggle for equity and quality in public elementary and secondary education in Texas, a major issue in the 1990s, has been complicated by more than two dozen groups representing various—and often conflicting—interests within the educational community. There are at least four different teachers' groups, one for school boards, one for school administrators, and still others for elementary school principals and secondary school principals. Separate groups have also been formed for urban school districts, suburban districts, rural districts, and districts with large numbers of special needs students. Virtually all these groups employ paid lobbyists, and although all claim to support educational quality, their primary goals are to protect the specific interests of their members. Together they produce much diversity of opinion on education and thereby reduce their own effectiveness.

Public Interest Groups   Most of the public interest groups represented in Austin are concerned with protecting consumers and the environment from big business, promoting stronger ethical standards for public officials, and increasing funding for health and human services programs for the poor, the elderly, the young, and the disabled. Many have full-time lobbyists, but grass-roots volunteer efforts and the adroit use of the mass media are crucial to their success. Among the most active are Common Cause, the Sierra Club, Consumers Union, Texas Consumers Association, Gray Panthers, Americans Disabled for Attendant Programs Today (ADAPT), and Public Citizen, a Texas affiliate of the national public interest group founded by consumer advocate Ralph Nader.

Minority Interest Groups   The advent of single-member urban legislative districts in the 1970s significantly increased the number of African American and Hispanic lawmakers and strengthened the influence of minority interest groups. These groups have often found that the courthouse is a shorter route to success than the statehouse, but the legislature has become increasingly attentive to their voices.

The League of United Latin American Citizens (LULAC) and the Mexican American Legal Defense and Educational Fund (MALDEF) are two of the better known Hispanic organizations. LULAC, founded in 1929, is the oldest and largest Hispanic organization in the United States and continues to be particularly influential in causes such as education and election reform in Texas. MALDEF, formed in San Antonio in 1968, fights in the courtroom for the civil rights of Hispanics. It has been successful in numerous battles over the drawing of political boundaries for governmental bodies in Texas and in lengthy litigation over public school finance. MALDEF represented the property-poor school districts that won a unanimous landmark Texas Supreme Court order in 1989 (*Edgewood* v. *Kirby*) for a more equitable distribution of education aid between rich and poor school districts. In 1997 MALDEF filed another major lawsuit over the public education system. In this suit, MALDEF contended that the Texas Assessment of Academic Skills (TAAS) test administered to Texas students discriminated against minorities. It asked a federal court to overturn a state requirement making passage of the exit-level TAAS test a condition for high school graduation.

The National Association for the Advancement of Colored People (NAACP) is a leader in promoting and protecting the interests of African Americans. The NAACP initiated many of the early court attacks on educational inequality and the disfranchisement of minorities. More recently, this group has worked hard to increase employment opportunities for African Americans in state agencies, particularly in higher paying administrative jobs.

In recent years, the Industrial Areas Foundation, a collection of well-organized church-supported community groups, has become a strong and effective voice for low-income minorities. Member groups include Valley Interfaith in South Texas, Communities Organized for Public Service (COPS) in San Antonio, The Metropolitan Organization (TMO) in Houston, and the El Paso Interreligious Sponsoring Organization (EPISO).

Organized Labor Groups   Organized labor has traditionally taken a back seat to business in Texas, a strong right-to-work state in which union membership cannot be required as a condition of employment. Antilabor sentiment ran particularly high in the 1940s and 1950s, at the height of the conservative Democratic establishment's control of Texas politics. Labor-baiting campaigns in which unions were portrayed as evil communist sympathizers were not uncommon then.[7]

Today there are pockets of strong labor influence in Texas, particularly in the southeastern part of the state, where thousands of petrochemical workers are unionized. Altogether Texas has about 200,000 union members and two dozen internationally affiliated unions. Among the largest unions are the Communications Workers of America, the International Brotherhood of Electrical Workers, the International Association of Machinists and Aerospace Workers, and the United Food and Commercial Workers International Union.

Unions can provide strong grass-roots support for political candidates through the distribution of campaign literature endorsing specific candidates, the use of union phone banks, and other get-out-the-vote efforts. Such union support has historically gone to Democratic candidates. In recent years, many labor-backed political candidates have not fared well in Texas, especially in statewide elections. Labor generally sides with the trial lawyers on such issues as workers' compensation, worker safety, and business liability for faulty products.

Government Lobbyists   Local governments are significantly affected by state laws and budgetary decisions. The stakes are particularly high now because most governments are finding revenue harder to raise—especially with the federal government passing the cost of numerous programs on to the state, and the state issuing similar mandates to local governments. As a result, counties, cities, prosecutors, metropolitan transit authorities, and various special districts are represented by lobbyists in Austin.

Many local governments belong to umbrella organizations, such as the Texas Municipal League, the Texas Association of Counties, and the Texas District and County Attorneys Association, which have full-time lobbyists. Several of the larger cities and counties also retain their own lobbyists. Mayors, city council members, and county judges also frequently travel to Austin to visit with legislators and testify for or against bills.

Agriculture Groups   Although Texas is now predominantly urban, agriculture is still an important part of the state's economy, and a number of agriculture groups are represented in Austin. Their influence is obviously strongest among rural legislators. But the Texas Farm Bureau—the largest such group and probably the most conservative—was instrumental in the 1990 defeat of liberal Democratic Agriculture Commissioner Jim Hightower, who had angered many agricultural producers and the chemical industry with tough stands on farm worker rights and pesticide regulation.

Other producer groups include the Texas and Southwestern Cattle Raisers Association, the Texas Nurseryman's Association, and the Texas Corn Producers Board.

Religious Groups   Many people, influenced in part by their views on separation of church and state, think religious groups have little or no legitimate role in the political process. Nevertheless, religious groups have helped influence policy in Texas, and the abortion issue and other social and economic issues have increased the presence of religious groups in Austin.

A number of religious groups have emerged since the 1940s with an identifiable right-wing orientation. These groups, predecessors to what is now known as the **Religious Right**, combined Christian rhetoric and symbols with anticommunist, antilabor, anti–civil rights, antiliberal, or anti–New Deal themes. Although these groups were often very small, they were linked to the extreme right wing of the Texas establishment, and they were the precursors of many of the conservative ideological groups that have emerged in American politics in the past twenty years.[8] Many of these organizations have gravitated toward the Republican Party[9] (see *Up Close*: "The Religious Right and Republican Growth"). With a strong organizational effort, religious conservatives were influential in a right-wing takeover of leadership positions in the Texas Republican Party in 1994.

Many religious denominations have boards or commissions responsible for monitoring governmental action. Although staff members or volunteers serving in this capacity may not register as lobbyists, they function much like lobbyists.

Churches across the state have formed community-based organizations to address the social and economic needs of the poor. In many regards, this is a redefinition of the Social Gospel, a church-based social movement of the late nineteenth and early twentieth centuries.

U.S. Senator Phil Gramm (R-Tex.) addressing a Christian Coalition conference in Washington.

THE DEVELOPMENT OF A TWO-PARTY SYSTEM IN TEXAS

The Texas party system has been restructured by the social and economic changes that the state has experienced over the past thirty years. Texas now has a strong Republican Party and a competitive **two-party system**, but for more than a century, Texas was a **one-party** Democratic state. There was no organized opposition party to mobilize those who felt excluded from the Democratic Party. Electoral politics was based on factions and personalities; the interests of the lower socioeconomic classes—especially minorities—were blatantly neglected.

The political transformation of Texas accelerated in the late 1990s. With one-party Democratic politics relegated to the history books, Texas Republicans enjoyed banner years. They captured a majority of the Texas senate for the first time since Reconstruction ended in the 1870s, narrowed the Democratic lead in the Texas house and, in 1998, swept all offices on the statewide general election ballot. That historic landslide under Governor George W. Bush gave Republicans all twenty-nine of Texas's statewide elected offices, a feat that was unheard of only a few years ago.

One-Party Politics   Texas's long domination by the Democratic Party can be traced to the period immediately after the Civil War, when the Republican Party was able to capture control of Texas government for a short period. Strong anti-Republican feelings were generated by the Reconstruction administration of Radical Republican Governor Edmund J. Davis, and the Republican Party was perceived by most Texans of that era to be the party of conquest and occupation. By the time the constitution of 1876 was implemented, the Republican Party's influence in state politics was negligible. From 1874 to 1961, no Republican won a statewide office in Texas, and in only a few scattered areas were Republicans elected to local offices.

The anti-Republicanism that evolved from the Civil War and Reconstruction, however, is only a partial explanation for the Democratic Party's longtime control

Religious Right   Political movement, based primarily in evangelical Protestant churches, that has played an increasingly prominent role in Texas and national politics.

two-party system   Political system that has two dominant parties, such as that of the United States.

one-party system   Domination of elections and governmental processes by a single party, which may be split into different ideological, economic, or regional factions. In Texas, the phrase is used to describe the period from the late 1870s to the late 1970s, when the Democratic Party claimed virtually all elected partisan offices.

The Religious Right and Republican Growth

As the Republican Party has expanded its support in Texas, it has experienced sharp, often bitter, philosophical and ideological differences among its members. Overwhelmingly conservative, Republicans are split along the lines of economic conservatism and "lifestyle" conservatism, such as that advocated by the Religious Right.

The Religious Right has long been part of the Texas political landscape.* Although its influence was occasionally manifested in conservative Democratic politics, it found far greater potential in the Republican Party for shaping electoral politics. Although there are secular components to the social conservative movement, it has strong religious overtones and draws considerable support from evangelical groups across the state. Some scholars attribute much of its success to its ability to mobilize voters who have traditionally been inactive and to bring them into the Republican Party. The Republicans' difficulty in attracting minority groups also leaves the social conservative wing with greater influence in the party. Conflict among Republicans over the abortion issue is a manifestation of the party's internal tension.

In 1990 one scholar concluded that the Religious Right had not taken over the Republican Party, "but its influence is significant and gives the Texas Republicans their particular stridency and, at times, their appearance of a Know-Nothing movement."[†] In 1994, however, the Religious Right was instrumental in a takeover by social conservatives of the Republican state convention and the party leadership.

Low voter turnout in the 1994 Republican primary enabled well-organized social conservatives to gain control of the party's precinct conventions and elect a majority of delegates to the June state convention. Sensing defeat, Fred Meyer, a traditional Republican who had guided the state party for six years during a period of growth and electoral success, stepped down and was replaced by Tom Pauken, a Dallas lawyer and former Reagan Administration official who courted Christian activists. Delegates also elected a new party vice chair, Christian activist Susan Weddington of San Antonio, and put other members of the Religious Right on the State Republican Executive Committee.

The Religious Right also was instrumental in the election of Republican George W. Bush over Democrat Ann Richards in the 1994 gubernatorial race. According to a survey of voters as they left the polls, 20 percent of the 4.4 million Texans who voted in that election identified themselves as white Christian fundamentalists. Of those, 84 percent said they voted for Bush. They also voted heavily for other Republican candidates.[‡]

Social and religious conservatives also took control of the 1996 Republican state convention and dominated the Texas delegation to the Republican National Convention. Some social conservatives, insisting the party retain its strong anti-abortion policy, tried to deny U.S. Senator Kay Bailey Hutchison a delegate's slot to the national convention because she favored abortion rights with some restrictions. Such a move would have been an unheard-of snub for a high-ranking officeholder from the party. Hutchison finally got on the delegate list with the help of Governor George W. Bush, U.S. Senator Phil Gramm, and Republican presidential nominee Bob Dole.

The State Republican Executive Committee elected Susan Weddington state party chair after Pauken resigned in 1997 to seek the Republican nomination for state attorney general.

---

*George Norris Green, *The Establishment in Texas Politics, 1938–1957* (Westport, Conn.: Greenwood Press, 1979), Chapter 5.

[†]Chandler Davidson, *Race and Class in Texas Politics* (Princeton, N.J.: Princeton University Press, 1990), p. 206.

[‡]*Dallas Morning News,* November 11, 1994.

of Texas politics. One classic study presents the provocative thesis that Texas politics might be better understood in terms of "modified class politics."[10]

As Texas's conservative agricultural leaders attempted to regain control over the state's political system after Reconstruction, the postwar economic devastation was dividing Texas along class lines. Small farmers, African Americans, and an emerging urban labor class suffered disproportionately from the economic depression of this period. They turned their discontent into support for agrarian third parties, particularly the Populist Party, which began to threaten the monopoly of the traditional Texas power structure.

To protect their political power, the established agricultural leaders moved to divide the lower social groups by directing the discontent of lower income whites against blacks. The rural elites, who manifested traditionalistic political values and wanted to consolidate power in the hands of the privileged few, also created alliances with the mercantile, banking, and emerging industrial leaders, who reflected the individualistic view of a limited government that served to protect their interests. Over the years, these two dominant forces consolidated political power and merged the politics of race with the politics of economics.

The elites were able to institutionalize their control through the adoption of constitutional restrictions and segregation legislation, called **Jim Crow laws**, designed to reduce the size of the electorate and the potential of a popular challenge to the establishment's political monopoly.[11]

The Texas Democratic Party, however, was not homogeneous. There were factions, regional differences, and personal political rivalries. Initially, there were no sustained, identifiable factions, as voting coalitions changed from election to election through much of the first third of the twentieth century. But the onset of the Great Depression in 1929, the election of President Franklin D. Roosevelt in 1932, and the policies of the New Deal reshaped Texas politics in the 1930s.

Factionalism in the Democratic Party   Franklin Roosevelt's administrations (1933–1945) articulated and developed a policy agenda radically different from that of the Republican Party, which had dominated national politics from 1860 to 1932. Government was to become a buffer against economic downturns as well as a positive force for change. Under Roosevelt, the regulatory function of the federal government was expanded to exercise control and authority over much of the nation's economy. The federal government also enacted programs such as Social Security, public housing, and labor legislation to benefit lower socioeconomic groups.

These national policies produced an active philosophical split within the Texas Democratic Party that was to characterize Texas politics for the next two generations. A majority of Texas voters supported Roosevelt in his four elections, and the Democratic Party maintained its monopoly over Texas politics. But competing economic interests clearly—and often bitterly—divided Texas Democrats along liberal and conservative lines.

A strong Republican Party did not emerge at this time in Texas or any other southern state because "southern conservative Democratic politicians, who would have been expected to lead such a realignment, or any politicians for that matter, did not relish jumping from a majority-status party to one in the minority."[12]

Despite some liberal successes under Governor James Allred, who was elected in 1934 and again in 1936, the conservative wing of the Democratic Party prevailed in state elections from the 1940s to the late 1970s. Democratic presidential candidates carried Texas in 1944, 1948, 1960, 1964, 1968, and

Jim Crow laws Legislation enacted by many states after the Civil War to limit the rights and power of African Americans.

1976, even though some of them were too liberal to suit the tastes of the state's conservative Democratic establishment.

At first glance, it might appear that the **bifactionalism** in the Democratic Party partially compensated for the lack of a competitive two-party system, but one scholar argued against that perception, concluding that factionalism resulted in "no-party politics." Factionalism results in discontinuity in leadership and group support, and the voter has no permanent reference point from which to judge the performance of the party or selected candidates. Because there are no clear distinctions between who holds power and who does not, the influence of pressure groups increases.[13] In one-party Democratic Texas, as noted, state government and public policy were susceptible to control by wealthy and corporate interests.

This bifactional pattern of state Democratic politics was tested by a number of factors, including the national party's increased commitment after 1948 to civil rights legislation. That development alienated segments of the white population and prompted many voters eventually to leave the Democratic Party and align with the Republicans.

Efforts by Texas oil interests to reestablish state control over the oil-rich tidelands also played a key role in the demise of one-party politics and the development of a two-party system. President Harry Truman, concerned about national security and federal access to these offshore oil resources, refused to accede to state demands and vetoed legislation favorable to Texas oil interests in 1952. That veto prompted a series of maneuvers orchestrated by Democratic Governor Allan Shivers to take the support of conservative Democrats to the Republican Party.

The "Shivercrats," as they were called, were successful in carrying Texas for the 1952 Republican presidential nominee, Dwight D. Eisenhower. This election helped establish a pattern of Texas's retaining its Democratic leanings in state and local elections but voting Republican in many presidential elections. Moreover, this election marked a shift in the state leadership of the Republican Party and led to efforts to create a party capable of winning local and statewide elections.[14]

In 1960 Democrat Lyndon B. Johnson ran both for election as vice president and for reelection as U.S. senator from Texas—a dual candidacy permitted under state law—and won both offices. His Republican opponent in the Senate race was John Tower, a relatively unknown college professor from Wichita Falls, who received 41 percent of the vote. After Johnson won the vice presidency and resigned from the Senate, a special election to fill the Senate seat was called in 1961. It attracted seventy-one candidates, including Tower, who defeated conservative Democrat William Blakely with 50.6 percent of the vote in a runoff.[15] Some evidence indicates that liberal Democrats, in retaliation for having been locked out of the power centers of their party and in anticipation of an ideological realignment of the party system, supported Tower in this election. The *Texas Observer*, an influential liberal publication, endorsed Tower with an argument for a two-party system. "How many liberals voted for Tower will never be known, nor will it be known how many 'went fishing,' " wrote a Republican campaign consultant.[16] Tower was reelected in 1966, 1972, and 1978, but no other Texas Republican won a statewide office until 1978, when Bill Clements was elected governor. Nevertheless, many students of Texas politics regard Tower's election in 1961 as a key factor in the development of the state's two-party system.[17]

Although Republicans made some gains in suburban congressional districts and local elections in the 1960s—including the election to Congress of a Houston Republican named George Herbert Walker Bush—the numbers were inconsequential. Most significant election battles continued to take place for a while longer within the Democratic Party, where the conservative wing generally prevailed until 1978.

bifactionalism Presence of two dominant factions organized around regional, economic, or ideological differences within a single political party. For much of the twentieth century, Texas functioned as a one-party system with two dominant factions.

Two-Party Politics in Texas   On the national level, **realignment** of political parties (see Chapter 7) is often associated with a critical election in which economic or social issues cut across existing party allegiances and produce a permanent shift in party support and identification.[18] What apparently has happened in Texas is that the state party system has been integrated into the national party system and now more closely approximates the political divisions which exist in states outside the South. Rather than occurring in one single election, this process has occurred over many years.

A major contributor to change was the civil rights movement. African Americans and Hispanics went to federal court to attack state laws requiring segregation and restricting minority voting rights. Successful lawsuits were brought against the white primary, the preprimary endorsement, the poll tax (all explained later in this chapter), and racial **gerrymandering** of political districts. Then minorities turned to the U.S. Congress for civil rights legislation, a process that produced the 1965 **Voting Rights Act**, which Congress extended to cover Texas after 1975.

Economic factors have also shaped minority political support and, in turn, have contributed to two-party development. African Americans and Hispanics are disproportionately low-income populations and generally support such governmental services as public housing, public health care, day care, and income support. These policies are associated with the liberal wing of the Democratic Party.

Minority organizations have made concerted efforts to register, educate, and mobilize the people in their communities. As the numerical strength of minorities increased, conservative Anglo Democrats found their position within the party threatened and began to look to the Republican Party as an alternative.

The large number of people who migrated to Texas from other states, particularly when the Sun Belt economy of the 1970s and early 1980s was booming and many northern industrial states were struggling, also contributed to two-party development in Texas. Many of these new arrivals were Republicans from states with strong Republican parties, and many of them settled in high-income, suburban, Anglo areas in Texas. Other significant factors were President Ronald Reagan's popularity in the 1980s and the 1978 election of Republican Governor Bill Clements, who encouraged many conservative Democratic officeholders to switch parties.

Other events of the 1970s and the 1980s demonstrated that the transformation of the Texas party system was well on its way. After a major stock fraud scandal, the Texas house elected a liberal Democrat, Price Daniel, Jr., as speaker in 1973. Three other moderate-to-liberal Democrats were also elected to statewide office in the early 1970s: Bob Armstrong as land commissioner in 1970, John Hill as attorney general in 1972, and Bob Bullock as comptroller in 1974.

In 1978 John Hill defeated Governor Dolph Briscoe, a conservative, in the Democratic primary and was subsequently defeated by Republican Bill Clements, then a political unknown, in the general election by a narrow margin of 17,000 votes. Four years later, Clements lost to Democratic Attorney General Mark White, but in 1986 he returned to defeat White in an expensive, bitter campaign. In the 1982 election, Democratic candidates who were considered liberal won additional statewide offices: Ann Richards was elected state treasurer; Jim Mattox, attorney general; Jim Hightower, agriculture commissioner; and Garry Mauro, land commissioner.

Party realignment was also reflected in the Texas legislature. In 1971 Republicans held only 12 of the 181 legislative seats. But by 1999 Republicans held 71 of the 150 house seats and 16 of the 31 senate seats.

realignment   Major shift in political party support or identification that usually occurs around a critical election. In Texas, realignment took place as a gradual transformation from a one-party system dominated by Democrats to a two-party system in which Republicans became competitive in elections.

gerrymandering   Drawing the boundaries of legislative districts in such a way as to increase the power of one group over another.

Voting Rights Act   Federal law designed to protect the voting rights of minorities by requiring the Justice Department's approval of changes in political districts and certain other electoral procedures. The 1965 act, as amended, has eliminated most of the restrictive practices that limited minority political participation.

The 1990 election further demonstrated how far the realignment process had gone. Democratic gubernatorial nominee Ann Richards defeated conservative business executive Clayton Williams, who had spent $6 million of his own money to win the Republican primary. But Republican Kay Bailey Hutchison was elected state treasurer, and Republican Rick Perry unseated liberal Democrat Jim Hightower to become agriculture commissioner. Republicans also retained one of the U.S. Senate seats from Texas when Phil Gramm easily won reelection to the seat once held by John Tower, and the GOP claimed 8 of the 27 congressional seats from Texas. The 1990 census has since increased the number of congressional seats from Texas to 30, and Republicans had won 13 of them by 1996.

In a special election in 1993 to fill the U.S. Senate seat vacated by Democrat Lloyd Bentsen when he was appointed secretary of the treasury by President Bill Clinton, Republican Kay Bailey Hutchison defeated Democrat Bob Krueger, thus giving the Republicans both U.S. Senate seats from Texas. Hutchison easily won reelection in 1994, despite a political and legal controversy over her administration of the state treasurer's office.

Also in 1994, Democratic Governor Ann Richards was unseated by Republican nominee George W. Bush, the son of former President George Bush. Republicans that year also captured four other statewide offices that had been held by Democrats, marking the most statewide gains by Republicans in any single election since Reconstruction. They won two additional seats on the Texas Railroad Commission, to give the party all three positions on that regulatory panel. They also won an additional seat on the Texas Supreme Court, giving Republicans a majority, and gained a seat on the Texas Court of Criminal Appeals. In district elections, Republicans won three additional seats on the State Board of Education, two additional congressional seats, one additional seat in the state senate, and one more in the Texas house.

In their historic sweep of statewide offices in 1996, Republicans gained a majority not only of the Texas senate for the first time since Reconstruction but also a majority of the Texas Court of Criminal Appeals. They also increased their majority on the Texas Supreme Court to 7 to 2. Democrats still held most seats in the Texas house, but their margin had been trimmed to 82 to 68. When the electoral dust had cleared that year, Republicans held 20 of Texas's 29 statewide elected offices, including the top three. That number increased to 21 in 1997, when Presiding Judge Michael McCormick of the Texas Court of Criminal Appeals switched from the Democratic to the Republican Party.

The Republicans' top priorities in 1998 were top reelect Bush governor, win the lieutenant governor's and attorney general's offices, and gain a majority of the Texas house. Lieutenant Governor Bob Bullock and Attorney General Dan Morales, two popular Democrats, chose not to seek reelection or any other office in 1998, and Republicans cashed in on the opportunity. With Bush winning reelection in a landslide, the GOP won every statewide race to give the Republicans control of all twenty-nine statewide elected offices. Republicans did not capture control of the Texas house but picked up three seats to narrow the Democratic margin to eight seats. In the governor's race, Bush carried 69 percent of the total vote against Democratic challenger Garry Mauro, the longtime land commissioner. Bush's support included a significant percentage of the Hispanic vote, more than 40 percent by some estimates.

U.S. Senator Kay Bailey Hutchison at a news conference after being found not guilty of charges she abused her previous office as Texas state treasurer.

Up Close

La Raza Unida

La Raza Unida, led by Jose Angel Gutierrez and Mario Compean, began in 1969 to organize in Crystal City in Zavala County and then extended its influence to Dimmit, La Salle, and Hildago counties.* Overwhelmingly Hispanic and poor, these counties were characteristic of many South Texas counties where the Anglo minority controlled both the political and economical institutions and there was little sensitivity to the needs of low-income residents. In 1972 Ramsey Muniz ran as the party's gubernatorial candidate. During the general election campaign, there was considerable speculation in the press and apprehension among conservative Democrats that La Raza would drain a sufficient number of votes away from Dolph Briscoe, the Democratic nominee, to give Henry "Hank" Grover, a right-wing Republican, the governorship. Briscoe won the election, but without a majority of the votes. The subsequent growth of liberal and minority influence within the Democratic Party, internal dissension within La Raza Unida, and legal problems encountered by Muniz contributed to the demise of this third party after 1978.

*Juan Gomez Quinones, *Chicano Politics* (Albuquerque: University of New Mexico Press, 1990), pp. 128–31.

Third Parties   There has been a tradition of third parties in Texas, including Grangers, Populists, Progressives, Socialists, Dixiecrats, the American Independent Party, Libertarians, and La Raza Unida (see *Up Close*: "La Raza Unida"). None has had statewide electoral success, a situation that can be explained in part by the cultural consensus supporting the two-party and winner-take-all election systems (see "Why the Two-Party System Persists" in Chapter 7). Most Americans do not tend to have highly cohesive political views, which are part of the appeal of many third parties.

The most successful third party in Texas in recent years has been the Libertarian Party. Libertarians have qualified for a place on the ballot in every Texas general election since 1986 because the party has succeeded in winning at least 5 percent of the vote in at least one statewide race during each election year. But the party has never won an elected office in Texas.

In addition to statewide third parties, local political organizations connected to neither the Democratic nor the Republican Party have been influential in some cities. Elections for city offices are nonpartisan, and most are held during odd-numbered years, when there are no state offices on the ballot. Cities such as San Antonio and Dallas developed citizens' associations, which controlled city governments for decades and maintained a virtual monopoly over city elections. But these local political parties have disappeared in recent years.

CHANGING PATTERNS OF PARTY SUPPORT AND IDENTIFICATION

The changes in party affiliations over the past forty years reinforce the argument that Texas is now a two-party state. In 1952, 66 percent of Texans called themselves Democrats, and only 6 percent claimed to be Republicans,[19] a pattern that changed little from 1952 to 1964. During the next decade, however, Republican Party

FIGURE 21-1 **Changing Party Affiliation in Texas, 1964–1996**

Source: The Texas Poll, 1989, copyrighted by Harte-Hanks Communications, Inc.; *The Texas Poll*, Summer 1993, Fall 1993, Winter 1996, Spring 1996, Fall 1996, copyrighted by Harte-Hanks Communications, Inc.

1996
Democrats 29%
Republicans 30%
1989
Democrats 32%
Republicans 31%
1984
Democrats 33%
Republicans 28%
1974
Democrats 59%
Republicans 16%
1964
Democrats 65%
Republicans 8%

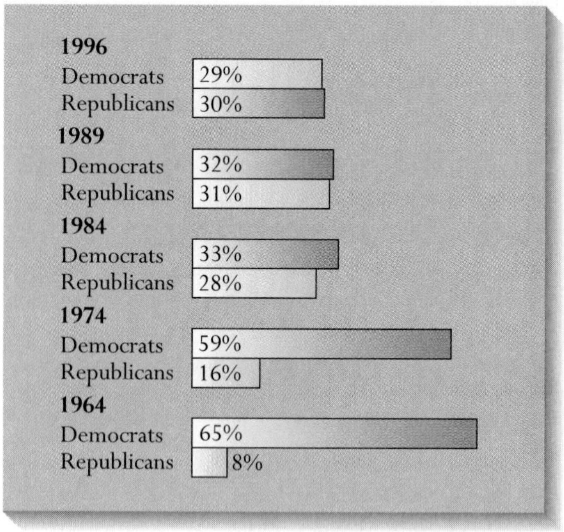

identification increased to 16 percent, and Democratic Party identification declined to 59 percent (see Figure 21-1).

Between 1975 and 1984, there was a dramatic decline in the number of voters who identified with the Democratic Party and a significant increase in those who identified with the Republican Party. By 1996 approximately 30 percent of Texas voters called themselves Republicans, and 29 percent identified as Democrats. This shift in party identification is reflected in increased competitiveness of local and state Republican candidates and Republican electoral victories. Data from *The Texas Poll* conducted in 1995 and 1996 provide a detailed demographic profile of voters identifying themselves as either Democrats, Republicans, or independents (see Figure 21-2).

The *Texas Poll* and other studies indicate marked differences in the social and economic characteristics of party identifiers. From these data, analysts have made the following generalizations:

The Republican Party is composed disproportionately of voters who fall into one or more of the following categories:

- College educated
- Newcomers
- Anglos
- Large metropolitan area residents
- Of higher income
- Younger than forty-five.

Democrats are strongly represented among:

- Minorities
- Older residents
- Native Texans
- Those with lower income levels
- Those with less education.[20]

FIGURE 21-2   Demographic Characteristics of Texas Voters, 1996

Source: *The Texas Poll*, Winter 1996, Spring 1996, Summer 1996, Fall 1996. Copyrighted by Harte-Hanks Communications, Inc. Used by permission. A total of 4,003 Texans were surveyed in these polls.

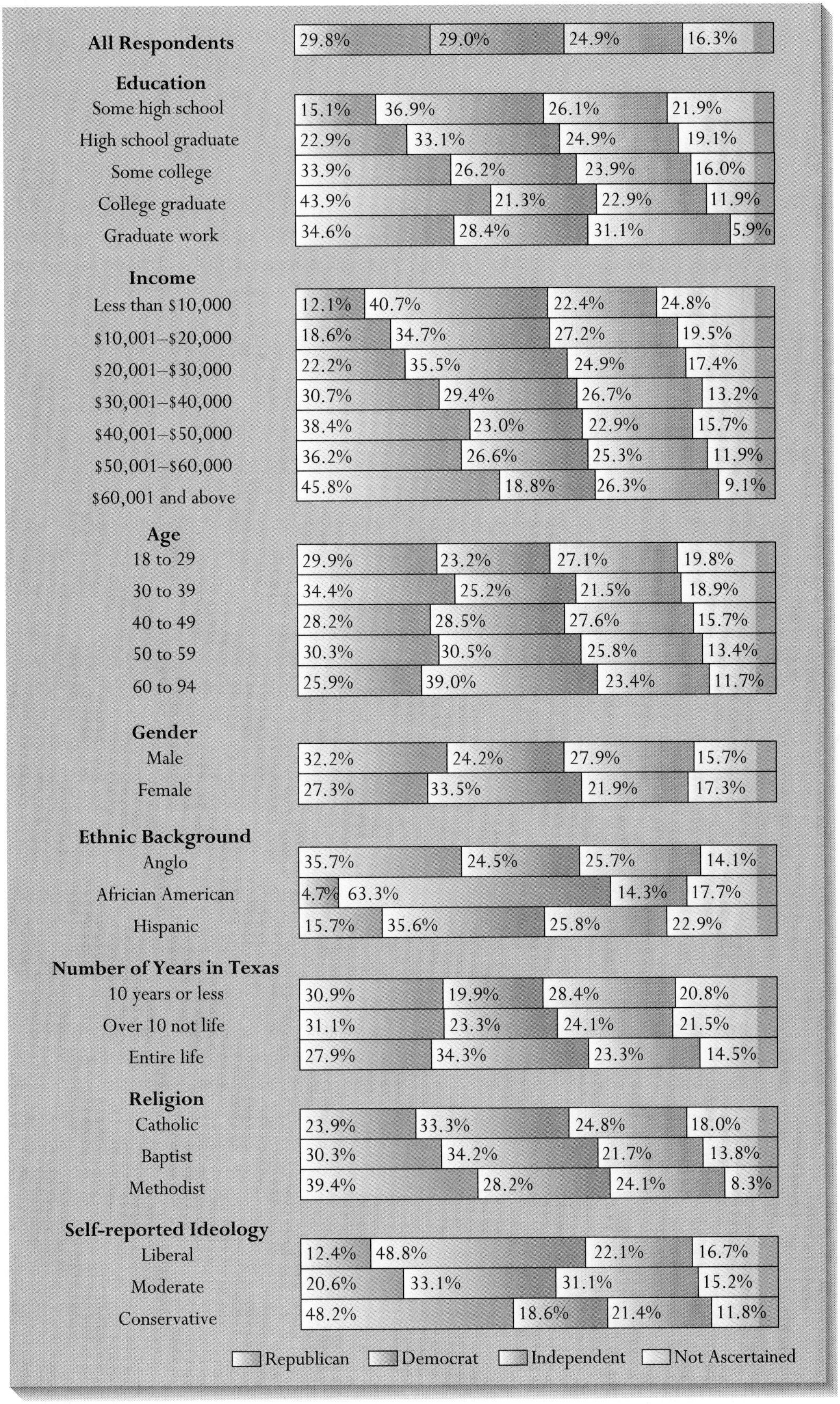

	Republican	Democrat	Independent	Not Ascertained
All Respondents	29.8%	29.0%	24.9%	16.3%
Education				
Some high school	15.1%	36.9%	26.1%	21.9%
High school graduate	22.9%	33.1%	24.9%	19.1%
Some college	33.9%	26.2%	23.9%	16.0%
College graduate	43.9%	21.3%	22.9%	11.9%
Graduate work	34.6%	28.4%	31.1%	5.9%
Income				
Less than $10,000	12.1%	40.7%	22.4%	24.8%
$10,001–$20,000	18.6%	34.7%	27.2%	19.5%
$20,001–$30,000	22.2%	35.5%	24.9%	17.4%
$30,001–$40,000	30.7%	29.4%	26.7%	13.2%
$40,001–$50,000	38.4%	23.0%	22.9%	15.7%
$50,001–$60,000	36.2%	26.6%	25.3%	11.9%
$60,001 and above	45.8%	18.8%	26.3%	9.1%
Age				
18 to 29	29.9%	23.2%	27.1%	19.8%
30 to 39	34.4%	25.2%	21.5%	18.9%
40 to 49	28.2%	28.5%	27.6%	15.7%
50 to 59	30.3%	30.5%	25.8%	13.4%
60 to 94	25.9%	39.0%	23.4%	11.7%
Gender				
Male	32.2%	24.2%	27.9%	15.7%
Female	27.3%	33.5%	21.9%	17.3%
Ethnic Background				
Anglo	35.7%	24.5%	25.7%	14.1%
African American	4.7%	63.3%	14.3%	17.7%
Hispanic	15.7%	35.6%	25.8%	22.9%
Number of Years in Texas				
10 years or less	30.9%	19.9%	28.4%	20.8%
Over 10 not life	31.1%	23.3%	24.1%	21.5%
Entire life	27.9%	34.3%	23.3%	14.5%
Religion				
Catholic	23.9%	33.3%	24.8%	18.0%
Baptist	30.3%	34.2%	21.7%	13.8%
Methodist	39.4%	28.2%	24.1%	8.3%
Self-reported Ideology				
Liberal	12.4%	48.8%	22.1%	16.7%
Moderate	20.6%	33.1%	31.1%	15.2%
Conservative	48.2%	18.6%	21.4%	11.8%

Republican   Democrat   Independent   Not Ascertained

THE PARTY ORGANIZATION

To carry out their functions, the two major parties in Texas have developed permanent and temporary organizations (see "Where's the Party?" in Chapter 7) built around geographic election districts, starting with the precinct. There is, however, no hierarchical arrangement to party organization. The party structure has been described as a "system of layers of organization," with each level—county, state, and federal—concentrating on the elections within its jurisdiction.[21]

There are no membership requirements for either the Democratic or the Republican Party. Party members do not have to pay dues, attend meetings, campaign for candidates, or make contributions. When people register to vote in Texas, they are not required to state their party preference. The right to participate in a party's electoral and nominating activities is based simply on voting in that party's primary election. When a person votes in one of the major party primaries, his or her voter registration card is stamped "Democrat" or "Republican."

The Permanent Organization   Election **precincts**—there were an estimated 8,700 in Texas in 1996—are created by the county commissioners of each of the 254 counties. Voters in each precinct elect a **precinct chair** in the party primary (see Figure 21-3). Any eligible voter within the precinct can file for this position, or the names of write-in candidates can be added to the ballot. The chair calls to order the precinct convention (discussed later) and serves as a member of the county executive committee. Many people do nothing with the position, but others contribute a great deal of time and energy to deliver the precinct's votes for their party's candidates in the general election.

The second level of the party organization is the **county executive committee**, which includes each precinct chair, and the **county chair**, who is elected to a two-year term by primary voters countywide. A major responsibility of the county chair and the executive committee is the organization and management of the primary election in their county. The county executive committee accepts filings by candidates and is also responsible for planning the county or district conventions. Funds for the management of primary elections are provided to the county party by the state through the secretary of state's office.

County committees may be well organized and may actively work to carry out a wide range of organizational and electoral activities, or they may meet irregularly and have difficulty getting a quorum of members to attend. The county chair is an unpaid position. But party organizations in some counties have successful ongoing fund-raising operations, and they support a party headquarters, retain professional staff, and are engaged in various party activities between elections.

At the state level, a party's permanent organization is the **state executive committee**, which is composed of sixty-four members, including the party's state chair and vice chair. When the parties meet in their biennial state conventions, two committee members—a man and a woman—are selected by delegation caucuses from each of the thirty-one state senatorial districts. The **state chair** and the **vice chair**, one of whom must be a woman, also are selected by the convention. The two top state party leaders and other executive committee members serve two-year terms and are unpaid.

Statewide candidates file for office with the executive committee, which is also responsible for planning and organizing the party's state convention and helps raise

---

precincts   Specific local voting areas created by county commissioners courts. The state election code provides detailed requirements for drawing up these election units.

precinct chair   Local officer in a political party who presides over the precinct convention and serves on the party's county executive committee. Voters in each precinct elect a chair in the party's primary election.

county executive committee   Panel responsible on the local level for the organization and management of a political party's primary election. It includes the party's county chair and each precinct chair.

county chair   Presiding officer of a political party's county executive committee. He or she is elected countywide by voters in the party primary.

state executive committee   Statewide governing board of a political party. It includes a man and a woman from each of the thirty-one state senatorial districts and the state chair and vice chair, who are selected by delegates to the party's biennial state convention.

state chair and vice chair   Two top state leaders of a political party, one of whom must be a woman. They are selected every two years by delegates to the party's state convention.

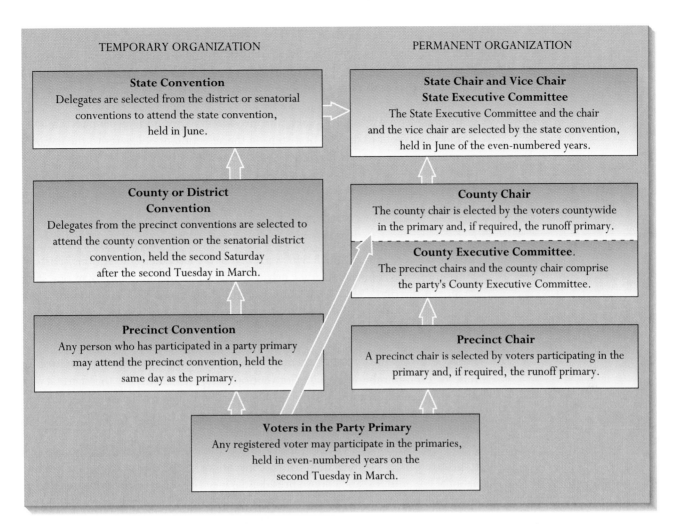

State Convention
Delegates are selected from the district or senatorial conventions to attend the state convention, held in June.

State Chair and Vice Chair
State Executive Committee
The State Executive Committee and the chair and the vice chair are selected by the state convention, held in June of the even-numbered years.

County or District Convention
Delegates from the precinct conventions are selected to attend the county convention or the senatorial district convention, held the second Saturday after the second Tuesday in March.

County Chair
The county chair is elected by the voters countywide in the primary and, if required, the runoff primary.

County Executive Committee.
The precinct chairs and the county chair comprise the party's County Executive Committee.

Precinct Convention
Any person who has participated in a party primary may attend the precinct convention, held the same day as the primary.

Precinct Chair
A precinct chair is selected by voters participating in the primary and, if required, the runoff primary.

Voters in the Party Primary
Any registered voter may participate in the primaries, held in even-numbered years on the second Tuesday in March.

FIGURE 21-3   Organization of Texas Political Parties

funds for the ongoing operations of the party. The committee serves to establish party policy, but day-to-day party operations are entrusted to the party's executive director and professional staff. The Texas Democratic Party and the Texas Republican Party have permanent staffs and headquarters in Austin.

Temporary Organizations   The temporary organizations of the political parties are the series of conventions held every two years, beginning on the day of the party primaries. They are particularly significant in presidential election years because they help select the state's delegates to the national party conventions. The convention system also helps organize the permanent party structure and brings party activists together to share common political concerns and shape party policies. Most Texans, however, have little knowledge of the convention system, and few participate in it.

Precinct Conventions   Anyone who votes in a party primary, held on the second Tuesday in March of even-numbered years, is eligible to participate in that party's **precinct convention**, normally held in the same place as the primary after voting stops at 7 P.M. The main business of the convention is the selection of

precinct convention   Meeting held by a political party in each precinct on the same day as the party primary. In presidential election years, the precinct conventions and the primaries are the first steps in the selection of delegates to the major parties' national nominating conventions.

delegates and alternate delegates to the county or senatorial district convention. Since 1972 the Democrats have used complex procedures designed to assure broad-based delegate representation by ethnicity, gender, and age. A precinct convention can also adopt resolutions to be submitted at the county or district conventions for possible inclusion in the party's platform.

In presidential election years, the presidential preference primary and the precinct conventions are the first steps in the selection of delegates to the national nominating conventions. Precinct conventions held in nonpresidential election years, however, are often poorly attended, and in many precincts no one shows up. Such low participation rates are cited by those who conclude that the political parties are in decline.

County or Senatorial District Conventions   County or state senatorial district conventions are held two weeks after the precinct conventions. District conventions are held in the larger urban counties that include more than one state senatorial district. Delegates elected at the precinct conventions constitute the membership of this second level of the convention process, which, in turn, elects delegates to the state convention.

State Conventions   The two major parties hold their **state conventions** in June of even-numbered years. Convention delegates certify to the secretary of state the names of those individuals who were nominated to statewide offices in the March primaries, adopt a party platform, and elect the state party chair, the vice chair, and the state executive committee.

In presidential election years, the state conventions also select delegates to their respective parties' national nominating conventions, elect members to their parties' national committees, and choose presidential electors. Electors from the party that carries Texas in the presidential race formally cast the state's electoral votes for that party's candidate in December after the general election.

The allocation of Texas delegates to the Republican national convention is determined by the presidential primary. Delegate selection committees named by the candidates nominate lists of delegates, who are selected at the state convention.

Texas delegates to the Democratic national convention are determined through a more complicated process based both on the primary vote and on candidate support from attendees at the series of party conventions, beginning at the precinct level.

PARTIES AND GOVERNMENT

state convention   Meeting held in June of even-numbered years by each of the two major political parties. Delegates to this convention elect the party's state leadership and adopt a party platform. In presidential election years, the state convention selects the delegates to the party's national nominating convention.

Political parties in Texas do not produce cohesive, policy-oriented coalitions in government and have been unable to hold their elected officials accountable or responsive to those supporting the party. Under ideal circumstances, some students of government believe, the two major parties would articulate clearly defined political philosophies and policies they would pursue if their candidates were elected. Once elected, persons supported by the party would be committed to these programs, giving the voters a clear standard by which to evaluate their performances in office. This perspective is often referred to as the *responsible party model* (see Chapter 7).

There are several reasons why Texas parties are incapable of functioning in this manner, none of which lessens the disenchantment and disgust that many voters feel toward political parties and politicians. First, the political parties in Texas are highly decentralized and unable to discipline members who pursue goals that conflict with the party's stated objectives. The large number of elected officials at both the state and the local level serves to diffuse party leadership.

Moreover, the coalitions that parties form with groups harboring different objectives, interests, and agendas make it next to impossible to develop clearly stated positions which would always differentiate one party from another. Philosophical, ideological, and programmatic differences among members and supporters of the same party result, for example, in ideological voting patterns in the legislature that cross party lines.

Another explanation for the lack of partisan accountability is the longstanding antiparty tradition of American politics. Many voters are ambivalent—even outright hostile—toward political parties, and the parties make only limited efforts to include a large number of individuals in their organizational activities.

MINORITIES AND POLITICAL PARTICIPATION

At a time when millions of people around the world have eliminated authoritarian political systems and made great sacrifices to win free and open elections, Texans congratulate themselves if one-third of the eligible population votes. Such a poor turnout cannot be blamed on a lack of opportunity. After decades of denying voting rights to large parts of the population, Texas now has one of the most progressive voter registration laws in the United States. Contemporary political campaigns, especially those for national and statewide offices, have high media visibility. People are bombarded by sophisticated television advertising campaigns, direct mail, phone bank solicitations for candidates, and daily news coverage. Yet something fundamental is disturbing Texas voters as well as voters across the nation. Statewide turnout rates in Texas are consistently low, and turnout rates in many local elections are downright appalling.

Texas has had a dark history of voter disfranchisement. The systematic exclusion of African Americans, Hispanics, and low-income whites was clearly undemocratic and created a political system in which the interests of a few could prevail over the interests of the majority.

Texas enacted a **poll tax** in 1902. Although not a large sum of money by today's standards, the $1.50 to $1.75 people had to pay in order to vote eliminated large numbers of people, especially those who were likely to support liberal social and economic policies and undermine the political establishment.[22] The poll tax was in effect for more than sixty years in Texas. It was outlawed for federal elections by the Twenty-fourth Amendment to the U.S. Constitution, adopted in 1964, but Texas retained it for state and local elections until November 1966.

In 1923 the Texas legislature enacted a law that denied African Americans the right to vote in the Democratic primary. After a series of challenges in the U.S. Supreme Court, the so-called **white primary** was finally eliminated in 1944 as a result of the court's decision in *Smith v. Allwright*.[23] But those who were intent on keeping African Americans from voting began to use a restrictive preprimary selection process to pick candidates, who then would be formally nominated in the Democratic primary and subsequently elected in the general election. Finally, in 1953, the Supreme Court also declared this arrangement unconstitutional.[24]

Until 1971 Texas had one of the most restrictive voter registration systems in the nation. Voters had to register annually between October 1 and January 31.

poll tax Tax that Texas and some other states required before people were allowed to vote. Its purpose was to discourage minorities and poor whites from participating in the political process. The tax was declared unconstitutional in the 1960s.

white primary Series of state laws and party rules that denied African Americans the right to vote in the Democratic primary in Texas in the first half of the twentieth century.

President Johnson, in a White House ceremony in 1964, signs the 24th Amendment to the Constitution barring the levying of a poll tax in federal elections. Texas soon followed with the elimination of the poll tax in state elections.

Voters who did not register in person at the county courthouse could be registered by deputy registrars. But deputy registrars could not mail a large number of registrations together; they were required to deliver or mail in only one registration form at a time. This requirement thwarted coordinated voter registration drives that targeted minorities and low-income populations.[25]

Court action eliminated this system, and the legislature—pressured by Common Cause, the League of Women Voters, and minority groups—enacted one of the most progressive voter registration systems in the country.[26] Permanent registration was implemented, and citizens could register by mail or in person up to thirty days before an election. The law also made it easier to organize large voter registration drives. In 1993 the U.S. Congress enacted "motor-voter registration," which requires states to provide facilities for voter registration where a person obtains a driver's license.

Women were not given the right to vote until the adoption of the Nineteenth Amendment to the U.S. Constitution in 1920. The adoption of the Twenty-sixth Amendment lowered the voting age from twenty-one to eighteen in 1971. Until the 1970s, property qualifications were used to exclude many voters from voting in local bond elections.

Even after the most obvious discriminatory practices against minorities were eliminated, there were more subtle, but just as pervasive, techniques for reducing the political power and influence of these same groups. One technique is racial gerrymandering of political boundaries. State legislators and many city council members are elected from single-member districts, each of which represents a specific number of people in a designated area. To minimize the possibilities of minority candidates being elected, policymakers could divide minority communities and attach them to predominantly nonminority communities. This tactic is called cracking. Or the minority communities could be consolidated into one district, a tactic called packing, with an 80 to 90 percent minority population, which would reduce the number of other districts in which minorities might have a chance of winning office.

At-large elections also have been used to reduce minority representation. At one time, members of the Texas house from urban counties were elected in multimember districts, which required candidates to win election in countywide races, a very difficult prospect for most minority candidates. The practice was eliminated in legislative races in the 1970s as a result of federal lawsuits. But many cities, school districts, and special districts across Texas continue to use at-large elections requiring candidates to run for office citywide or districtwide. The system dilutes minority representation in most communities in which it is used because of the higher costs of campaigning and the prevalence of polarized voting, in which minorities vote for minority candidates and Anglo voters, the majority, vote for white candidates.

POLITICAL GAINS BY MINORITIES AND WOMEN

Over the past thirty years, nevertheless, minorities have made substantial gains in the electoral process. Elimination of restrictive voting laws and adoption of a liberal voter registration system have contributed to an increase in minority voters across the state. So have voter registration and mobilization drives coordinated by groups such as the National Association for the Advancement of

Colored People and the Southwest Voter Registration Education Project. The federal Voting Rights Act, which was passed by the U.S. Congress in 1965 and extended to Texas ten years later, also has played a key role. Minority groups have used the Voting Rights Act to challenge discriminatory state and local election systems in the federal courts. An election system that dilutes minority voting strength is illegal, and the Voting Rights Act requires changes in the election systems of state or local governments, including redistricting plans, to be reviewed and precleared by the U.S. Justice Department or approved by the U.S. District Court in Washington, D.C. This law has been used with considerable success to eliminate at-large elections and attack racial gerrymandering of political districts. These changes enhanced election opportunities for African Americans and Hispanics, but the fight continued.

By the mid-1990s, the Voting Rights Act was under attack by conservatives. And the U.S. Supreme Court, in "reverse-discrimination" cases from Texas and Georgia, ruled that some congressional districts had been illegally gerrymandered to elect minority candidates.[27] In the Texas case, three federal judges held that the Texas legislature had violated the U.S. Constitution by designing two districts in Houston and one in the Dallas area to favor the election of African American or Hispanic candidates. The court redrew 13 congressional districts in Texas—the 3 minority districts and 10 districts adjoining them—and ordered special elections to fill the seats. Despite the redrawn boundaries, two incumbent African American congresswomen in the affected districts were reelected.

Hispanics   According to the 1995 population estimates, Hispanics made up 28 percent of Texas's population. But the Hispanic population is younger than the Anglo and African American populations, and Hispanics accounted for only 25 percent of Texans of voting age (Figure 21-4).

Hispanics also include a significant number of immigrants (an estimated 1 out of 7) who are not eligible to vote, thus reducing eligible Hispanic voters to approximately 20 percent of adult citizens. Approximately 15.5 percent, or 1,439,155, of the 9,268,679 Texas voters registered in October 1995 had Hispanic surnames. But in recent general elections, Hispanics were only 12 to 15 percent of Texas voters participating.[28] Voter turnout rates among Hispanics are lower, in part, because of the lower education and income levels of many Hispanics.

Approximately 42 percent of Hispanic adults interviewed in the *Texas Poll* said they identified with the Democratic Party (see Figure 21-2), but this percentage tells only part of the story. Based on voter interviews conducted on election day

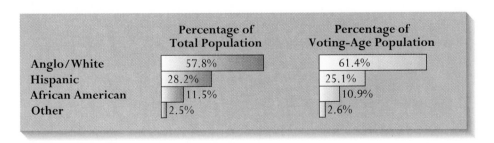

	Percentage of Total Population	Percentage of Voting-Age Population
Anglo/White	57.8%	61.4%
Hispanic	28.2%	25.1%
African American	11.5%	10.9%
Other	2.5%	2.6%

FIGURE 21-4   Breakdown of Texas Total Population and Voting-Age Population, 1995

Source: Populations Estimates and Projections Program, Texas State Data Center, Department of Rural Sociology, Texas A&M University System, *Projections of the Populations of Texas and Counties in Texas by Age, Sex, Race/Ethnicity for 1990 to 2030,* February 1994. Of the total population of 18,617,441, the number of Texas residents who were voting age in 1995 was 13,320,323.

Victor Morales campaigns from the back of a white pickup truck in his shoestring campaign for the U.S. Senate in 1996. Although he won an upset victory in the Democratic primary, he was unable to unseat Republican Phil Gramm in the general election.

by the Southwest Voter Research Project, Democratic candidates for president consistently receive more than 70 percent of the Hispanic vote.[29]

The increased electoral strength of the Hispanic population is borne out in Table 21-1, which compares the number of Hispanic elected officials in 1974 to those elected in 1994. The marked increase can be attributed to a more equitable apportionment of city, county, and school district political boundaries (see Chapter 22) and to the growth of the Hispanic population.

Only two Hispanics, Texas Supreme Court Justice Raul A. Gonzalez and Attorney General Dan Morales, have been elected to statewide office in Texas. Victor Morales, an Hispanic schoolteacher from Crandall, a small town in north Texas, generated some excitement and received national publicity when he ran for the U.S. Senate in 1996. Operating on a shoestring budget in the primary, Morales campaigned across Texas in a white pickup truck that became a symbol of his long-shot effort. To the surprise of most political observers, he defeated two incumbent congressmen and a politically experienced lawyer to win the Democratic nomination, a victory that demonstrated the influence of Hispanic voters in the Democratic primary. But this David versus Goliath challenge of Republican Senator Phil Gramm fell short in the general election campaign. Gramm outspent his Democratic challenger 6 to 1 and easily won reelection.

African Americans   African Americans constitute approximately 12 percent of the state's population, 11 percent of the voting-age population, and 9 to 10 percent of those who vote. Approximately 61 percent of Texas African Americans call themselves Democrats, but 80 to 90 percent of the African American vote is normally cast for Democratic candidates. Voting cohesively as a group, African Americans, like Hispanics, have considerable potential to influence the outcome of both primaries and general elections.

The increased political clout of the African American population is also manifested in the number of African American elected officials (Table 21-2). In 1970 only 29 African Americans were elected to public office in Texas. The number increased to 196 in 1980 and to 472 in 1993. Only one African American, Texas Court of Criminal Appeals Judge Morris Overstreet, has been elected to statewide office in Texas.

TABLE 21-1	Hispanic Elected Officials in Texas, 1974–1994		
	1974	*1984*	*1994*
Federal	2	3	5
State	13	25	36
County	102	152	222
Municipal	251	401	731
Judicial/Law Enforcement	172	291	389
School Board	—	555	763
Special District	—	—	69
Total	540	1,427	2,215

Sources: Juan A. Sepulveda, Jr., *The Question of Representative Responsiveness for Hispanics* (Cambridge, Mass.: Harvard College, Honors Thesis, March 1985); National Association of Latino Elected and Appointed Officials, *National Roster of Hispanic Elected Officials*, 1984 and 1994.

TABLE 21-2	African American Elected Officials in Texas, 1970–1993		
	1970	*1980*	*1993*
Federal	—	1	2
State	3	14	16
County	—	5	18
Municipal	16	75	305
Judicial/Law Enforcement	—	21	40
School Board	10	78	91
Special District	—	2	—
Total	29	196	472

Sources: Metropolitan Applied Research Center, Inc. and Voter Regional Council, Inc., *National Roster of Black Elected Officials.* Joint Center for Political Studies, *National Roster of Black Elected Officials, 1980, 1993.*

Women Historically, the world of Texas politics has been dominated by men. Prior to Ann Richards's election as state treasurer in 1982, only two women had been elected to statewide office. In addition to Richards, who was elected governor in 1990, four other women served in statewide offices in 1994. As governor, Richards also appointed more women to key positions on state boards and commissions than her predecessors.

More women were on the ballot for statewide offices in 1994 than in any previous election: 11 of the 32 Democratic and Republican nominees for 16 statewide offices were women. Although Richards lost her reelection bid, five other women won statewide offices that year.

By 1997 seven women were holding statewide offices in Texas, including one U.S. senator, one member of the Texas Railroad Commission, three members of the Texas Supreme Court, and two members of the Texas Court of Criminal Appeals. That same year, there were three women in the state senate and 30 in the Texas house, a significant increase over 1981, when the legislature included only one woman in the senate and 11 in the house.

Women are playing an increased role in local government as well, and this pattern can be expected to continue. Over the past two decades, the state's three largest cities—Houston, Dallas, and San Antonio—had women mayors. A 1995 survey by the Texas Municipal League counted 169 women mayors (14 percent) in the state's 1,173 cities. The 5,796 council members in the cities included 1,279 women, or 22 percent of the total. Women held 37, or 3.6 percent, of 1,016 county commissioners posts.[30]

ELECTIONS IN TEXAS

Texans have numerous opportunities to vote, often as many as three or four times a year. Although there are various rationales for this election scheduling by the legislature, evidence indicates that it contributes to "voter fatigue," reduced voter turnout, and the disproportionate influence of a few individuals in many local and special elections where voter turnout is usually the lowest. Turnout and interest are highest in the general election in presidential election years but can be

People in Politics

Does Anyone Know Me?

Statewide political candidates and officeholders often spend millions of dollars getting elected and reelected, but it seems that most of their constituents just aren't paying any attention. According to a 1997 Texas Poll, most Texans—82 percent of those surveyed—knew George W. Bush was the governor. But after that there was a huge dropoff in the public's ability to match the names of high-ranking state and federal officials with the offices they held.

The state attorney general could be identified by name by only 30 percent; the comptroller and the

land commissioner by 17 percent; the lieutenant governor by 16 percent, and the agriculture commissioner by 9 percent. Only 22 percent of the respondents could correctly name both Phil Gramm and Kay Bailey Hutchison as the two U.S. senators from Texas. "It's probably another indication that more and more people don't consider government very important to them, doesn't have much effect on their lives," said political consultant George Christian.

Source: The Texas Poll, Fall 1997, conducted for Scripps Howard by the Office of Survey Research of the University of Texas; Christian quoted in *Houston Chronicle*, November 23, 1997.

---

abysmally low in elections for school boards and the governing bodies of other single-purpose districts (see *People in Politics:* "Does Anyone Know Me?").

Primary Elections   Texas uses the **direct primary election**, adopted in 1903, to nominate major party candidates for public office. Administered by the political parties, primaries are held on the second Tuesday in March in even-numbered years. If no candidate receives a majority, the two top vote-getters must face each other in a runoff election. For practical purposes, Texas utilizes an **open primary** where voters do not register by party. People who vote in one party's primary, however, cannot vote in the other party's runoff election.

Voter turnout in the primary is traditionally lower than in the general election, but the emergence of a two-party system in Texas is producing appreciable changes in participation patterns in the Democratic and Republican primaries. During the period of one-party politics, the candidate who won the Democratic primary was the individual who was finally elected. From the 1920s through 1970, the rate of turnout for the Democratic primary never exceeded 35 percent of the voting-age population, and after the 1978 primary, the turnout rate dropped below 20 percent.[31] Approximately 12 percent of the voting-age population voted in the 1992 Democratic presidential primary, but only 7 percent in the 1996 Democratic presidential primary.

Through 1982, participation in the Republican primaries never exceeded 2.4 percent of the voting-age population.[32] One million voters, or 8 percent of the voting-age population, voted in the 1988 Republican presidential primary, but participation declined to 6.5 percent in the 1992 Republican presidential primary. Approximately 7.5 percent of voting-age Texans cast ballots in the 1996 Republican presidential primary.[33] With increased competition among Republican candidates, however, turnout in Republican primaries is likely to increase.

direct primary   Selection of candidates for government office through direct election by the voters of a political party.

General Elections   General elections for state and federal offices are held on the first Tuesday after the first Monday in November in even-numbered years. The names of the candidates nominated in the primaries by the two major parties are placed on a ballot, along with the names of third-party candidates who have submitted petitions bearing the names of eligible registered voters equal to 1 percent of the vote in the last gubernatorial election.

In the 1896 presidential election, the turnout rate was more than 80 percent of the eligible voting-age population, but in 1908, four years after the effective date of the poll tax, turnout had fallen to approximately 35 percent. During much of the period from 1910 to 1958, turnout rates in nonpresidential elections were less than 20 percent. Presidential elections generated a somewhat higher turnout, but in very few instances did the turnout rate exceed 40 percent of eligible voters.

Forty-seven percent of Texas's voting-age population cast ballots in the 1984 presidential race, 44 percent in the 1988 general election, approximately 50 percent in the spirited three-way presidential election of 1992, and 41 percent in 1996. But only 29 percent of the voting-age population cast general election ballots in the 1986 gubernatorial race, 32 percent in the 1990 race, and 34 percent in the 1994 gubernatorial election.

City, School Board, and Single-Purpose District Elections   Most local elections, which are nonpartisan, are held in May in odd-numbered years to minimize the convergence of issues in state and local races. Across the state, there are wide variations in the competitiveness of these elections, campaign costs, and turnout. But turnout rates rarely match those in the general election and are often abysmally low.

Special Elections   The legislature can submit constitutional amendments to the voters in a general election or schedule them in a special statewide election. Local governments also conduct special elections for bond issues, local initiatives and referenda, and the recall of public officials. Although these elections occasionally arouse high interest, turnout rates tend to be extremely low.

The governor also can call special elections to fill vacancies in certain offices, as was done in 1997 to fill the congressional seat vacated by the death of U.S. Representative Frank Tejeda of San Antonio.

Extended Absentee Balloting   In 1988 Texas made a major change in the requirements for **absentee** (or **early**) **voting** to permit any voter to cast a ballot from the twentieth day to the fourth day prior to an election. Special early voting areas are established—including many at shopping malls and other convenient locations—and voters don't have to provide an excuse for casting their ballots early. Consequently, there has been a notable increase in the number of early votes—20 percent to 30 percent of all votes in some areas. Extended early voting has forced candidates to identify two different sets of voters and develop strategies that require campaigns to "peak" twice. By 1994 seven other states had followed Texas's lead in eliminating another barrier to political participation.

CAMPAIGN FINANCES

Campaign Costs   No one knows precisely how much is spent every year on political campaigns in Texas because there is no single place where all this information is collected. Candidates for state office file campaign finance reports with the state Ethics Commission, but candidates for city councils, county offices, and school boards file reports with the jurisdictions in which they are running. Costs vary across the more than 2,000 governmental units, but

open primary   Primary election in which a voter may cast a ballot in either party's primary election.

absentee (or **early**) **voting**   Period before the regularly scheduled election date, during which voters are allowed to cast ballots. With recent changes in election law, a person does not have to offer a reason for voting absentee.

Politics in Cyberspace

Interest Groups, Political Parties, and Elections in Texas

Interest groups and political parties link individuals to the institutions of government and the policy making process. Although political parties function to mobilize voters and recruit candidates for public office, interest groups also play a significant role in electoral politics, and they are the dominant players in the policy making process.

Texas Ethics Commission
http://www.ethics.state.tx.us

Under Texas law, organizations that lobby the legislature are required to file with the Ethics Commission. This site provides names of registered lobbyists and their clients. It also organizes lobbyists by legislative subject matter. Candidates and political action committees are also required to file their financial statements with this agency.

Texas Democratic Party
http://www.txdemocrats.org

This site provides a range of information on the state party organization, county chairs, affiliate organizations, candidates, and policy issues.

Republican Party of Texas
http://www.texasgop.org

In addition to information about the Republican Party and links to other state party organizations, this site provides information about Republican candidates, the party platform, and a calendar of events.

Project Vote Smart
http://www.vote-smart.org

Project Vote Smart is a national nonpartisan organization that tracks the performance of approximately 13,000 national and state elected officials. The site provides information on the policy positions, campaign finances and expenditures, and job performance of the governor and state legislators.

Secretary of State
http://www.sos.state.tx.us

In addition to county election data for state offices, this office provides information on election law, election procedures, county officials, and maintains a program for voter education (Project V.O.T.E.).

modern campaign technology and paid media are extremely expensive, even on the local level. A few recent examples of campaign costs in selected races are illuminating.

City council races in major cities such as San Antonio, Houston, Fort Worth, and Dallas can easily cost $50,000 to $100,000. Bob Lanier spent $3 million getting elected mayor of Houston in 1991, and eight candidates spent more than $6.6 million in the 1997 race to succeed him. The 1997 winner, Lee Brown, spent more than $2.1 million alone, and the second-place finisher, businessman Rob Mosbacher, spent more than $3.5 million.[34] There have been reports of candidates for county commissioner spending $100,000 and of district judges in metropolitan counties spending more than $150,000. Historically, school board elections have been low budget, but it is not uncommon for slates of candidates in large urban school districts to spend $10,000 to $15,000 in low-turnout elections.

Many people believe that campaign expenditures in statewide races in Texas, particularly gubernatorial races, are excessive. But fueled by the rising costs of television advertising and other modern campaign techniques—and two-party competition—expenditures continue to increase. Total expenditures in the 1990 governor's race exceeded $50 million, making it the most expensive governor's race ever waged in the United States up to that point. The winner, Democrat Ann Richards, spent more than $12 million; the losing Republican nominee, Clayton Williams, spent more than $21 million. Richards spent more than $18 million on her unsuccessful reelection campaign in 1994, and Republican George W. Bush, the winner, spent more than $12 million.

Fund Raising   Soaring campaign costs have raised considerable concern about campaign fund raising and contributions in Texas, as they have nationally (see "Raising Campaign Cash," in Chapter 8). There is concern that elections are being bought and that major campaign contributors are purchasing influence in the policy-making process. Some critics of contemporary campaigns have argued that current practices are a form of legalized bribery, implying that public officials are available to the highest bidder.

Unlike the federal government, Texas places no limits on the amount of money a single individual or political action committee can contribute to most political candidates. The only exceptions in Texas are campaign contribution limits in judicial races, which were imposed by the legislature in 1995. There are no limits on how much a candidate in any race can contribute to his or her own campaign. Large contributions have long played a role in Texas politics, and, over the years, most large contributions have gone to the conservative candidates, both Democratic and Republican.

TABLE 21-3	Top PAC Contributors to Texas Candidates in Statewide Campaigns, 1990–1994	
PAC	*Base, operation*	*Amount*
Provost & Umphrey	Beaumont law firm*	$861,915
Bass Brothers PACs	Fort Worth	$664,945
Vinson & Elkins	Houston law firm	$532,052
Teamsters Union PAC	Dallas and Washington	$300,500
American Federation of State, County, and Municipal Employees Union	Austin labor group	$281,427
Winstead Seachrest & Minick	Dallas law firm	$275,529
Fulbright & Jaworski	Houston law firm	$268,841
Texas Real Estate PAC	Austin	$263,154
Nations Bank PAC	Dallas	$253,103
Baker & Botts	Houston law firm	$229,950
Texas United for Fundamental Fairness	Austin lawyers	$229,350
Texas Progress Fund	Fort Worth oil and agriculture	$224,000
Johnson & Gibbs	Dallas law firm	$219,000

*Previously Umphrey, Swearingen & Eddins.

Note: Totals include cash, loans, or in-kind contributions of $500 or more to political candidates in statewide races reported between January 1990 and February 28, 1994. Not included are federal or legislative races or candidate donations to their own campaigns.

Sources: Texas Ethics Commission, *Dallas Morning News* research.

Political Action Committees   Just as they have on the national level, political action committees (PACs) have increased their importance at the state and local level by bringing sophisticated fund-raising skills to political campaigns. Representing special interest groups or individual companies, PACs collect money from their members and are a ready source of campaign dollars. They are in the business of influencing elections. From 1990 to 1994, thirteen PACs, including several representing law firms, each made contributions in excess of $200,000 to candidates in statewide races in Texas (Table 21-3).[35]

Attempts at Reform   On the heels of the Sharpstown scandal, in which high-ranking state officials were given preferential treatment in the purchase of stock in an insurance company (see Chapter 22), the legislature enacted a major campaign finance disclosure law in 1973 that, with some changes, is now administered by the state Ethics Commission. Although it did not limit the size of political contributions, for the first time it required candidates to list the addresses as well as the names of donors and the amounts and dates of contributions. It also required political action committees contributing to candidates or officeholders to report the sources of their donations, which in the past had usually been hidden. Also for the first time, officeholders were required to file annual reports of their political contributions and expenditures—even during years when they were not seeking reelection—and candidates were required to report contributions and other financial activity that occurred after an election. A candidate also had to formally designate a campaign treasurer before he or she could legally accept political contributions. Campaign finance reform, however, remains a difficult and seemingly endless struggle.

SUMMARY NOTES

- Political power in Texas is related to the resources available to groups and organizations actively engaged in the political process. The great disparity in the distribution of resources raises fundamental questions about equity in access to policy makers and the decision-making process.

- Pluralist theorists argue that political power in Texas is distributed among a wide range of groups and interests, none of which has a monopoly on the institutions of government. Although there are marked differences in the resources of groups, there is sufficient competition and interaction among groups to achieve the goals of a democratic society. Public policy, in this view, reflects the compromise of competing interests.

- Advocates of elitist theory argue that political power in Texas is concentrated in the hands of a relatively small number of individuals who derive their resources from powerful institutional bases. These institutions are tied together with complex interlocking relationships, and access to their leadership posi-

tions is limited. Called the "Texas Establishment," those who monopolized power in the past were predominantly white males from the higher socioeconomic groups. Although there is some competition among these elites, there also is a great deal of consensus. Historically, the establishment has expressed indifference, if not hostility, toward the interests of labor, minorities, and the lower socioeconomic groups.

- The interest-group system in Texas was historically dominated by oil and gas, agriculture, and financial institutions. But dramatic changes in the state's economy, the political mobilization of minorities, and the development of public interest groups have produced considerable change. Not only are more groups now participating in the policy arenas, but some of the traditionally dominant groups apparently have experienced a dilution of their power. Policies directed to the interests of the lower socioeconomic groups are modest indications of these changes.

- For much of its political history, Texas had a one-party system, characterized by two dominant factions. This weak party system, based in part on the systematic exclusion of many citizens through discriminatory election laws, contributed to a powerful interest-group system. In Austin, as well as at the local level, the raw power of interest groups is seen in most aspects of the decision-making process, often to the detriment of the general public.

- Over the past thirty years, there have been significant changes in the state's party structure. One-party Democratic control has been transformed by complex economic, social, and political changes, and Texas is now a two-party state. The Texas electorate is divided somewhat equally among Democrats, Republicans, and independents.

- Historically, politics in Texas was configured around class and race, and these two factors are still primary dimensions of partisan alliances.

- Parties have rarely functioned as highly cohesive, disciplined organizations either in the electorate or government. With candidate-centered campaigns, many elected officials act as free agents, aligning with other groups and having little fear of recrimination from the political party.

- One of the most disturbing aspects of the contemporary Texas political system is the low voter turnout in most elections, despite the elimination of discriminatory election laws, the creation of an extended voting period, and easy voter registration.

- Although most discriminatory election barriers have been eliminated, racial gerrymandering and at-large election systems continue to generate controversy.

- Over the past thirty years, Hispanics and African Americans have realized substantial gains in the electoral process and increased success in winning election to public office. There has also been a dramatic increase in the number of women elected to public office.

- With varied election cycles for multiple levels of government, Texans are subjected to a continuous election process, contributing to "voter fatigue" and indifference.

- The costs of statewide campaigns, as well as many regional and local campaigns, have escalated over the past three decades. Although money may not buy public officials, it certainly buys access to them, and it creates the impression that well-organized interests, corporations, and wealthy individuals have a disproportionate influence on policy makers.

- Despite changes in the partisan lineup, Texans have not expressed a significant shift in their philosophical orientations over the past twenty years. Most Texans still classify themselves as moderate to conservative.

SELECTED READINGS

ANDERS, EVAN. *Boss Rule in South Texas: The Progressive Era*. Austin: University of Texas Press, 1982.

ANDERSON, JAMES E., RICHARD W. MURRAY, and EDWARD L. FARLEY. *Texas Politics*. 6th ed. New York: Harper-Collins, 1992.

BAUER, JOHN R. "Partisan Realignment and the Changing Political Geography of Texas." *Journal of Political Studies* 12 (Spring Summer 1990): 41–66.

DAVIDSON, CHANDLER. *Race and Class in Texas Politics*. Princeton, N.J.: Princeton University Press, 1990.

DYER, JAMES A., JAN E. LEIGHLEY, and ARNOLD VEDLITZ. "Party Identification and Public Opinion in Texas, 1984–1994: Establishing a Competitive Two-Party System," in *Texas Politics*, eds. Anthony Champagne and Edward J. Harpham (New York: W.W. Norton, 1997).

ELLIOTT, CHARLES P. "The Texas Trial Lawyers Association: Interest Group under Seige," in *Texas Politics*, eds. Anthony Champagne and Edward J. Harpham (New York: W.W. Norton, 1997).

GARCIA, IGNACIO. *United We Win: The Rise and Fall of La Raza Unida Party*. Tucson: Mexican American Studies and Research Center at the University of Arizona, 1989.

GREEN, GEORGE NORRIS. *The Establishment in Texas Politics: 1938–1957*. Westport, Conn.: Greenwood Press, 1979.

HREBENAR, ROBERT J., and CLIVE S. THOMAS, eds. *Interest Group Politics in Southern States*. Tuscaloosa: University of Alabama Press, 1992.

KEY, V. O. *Southern Politics*. New York: Vintage Books, 1949.

KNAGGS, JOHN R. *Two-Party Texas: The John Tower Era, 1961–1984*. Austin: Eakin Press, 1986.

LENCHNER, PAUL. "The Party System in Texas," in *Texas Politics*, eds. Anthony Champagne and Edward J. Harpham (New York: W.W. Norton, 1997).

SAN MIGUEL, GUADALUPE, JR. *Let Them Take Heed: Mexican Americans and the Campaign for Educational Equality in Texas, 1910–1981*. Austin: University of Texas Press, 1987.

ASK YOURSELF ABOUT POLITICS

1 With a full-time Congress passing laws in Washington, do we really need a state legislature?
Yes ⬜ No ⬜

2 Might our state representatives and senators do a better job if we paid them more?
Yes ⬜ No ⬜

3 Because the legislature is responsible for making laws, should all legislators be lawyers?
Yes ⬜ No ⬜

4 Do most state legislators in Texas stay in office too long?
Yes ⬜ No ⬜

5 Should the legislature be allowed to pass laws that cost money without getting voter approval first?
Yes ⬜ No ⬜

6 Do the men and women making laws in Texas really care about you?
Yes ⬜ No ⬜

7 Should the legislature pass all the governor's major priorities?
Yes ⬜ No ⬜

CHAPTER
22
THE TEXAS LEGISLATURE

CHAPTER OUTLINE

FEATURES

Even a part-time legislature still has considerable power over the laws that affect your life. And your interests often compete with those of other people and groups.

THE INSTITUTIONALIZATION OF THE TEXAS LEGISLATURE

Enormous social, political, and economic changes have occurred in Texas during the past generation, and the Texas legislature has had to scramble to keep pace—while undergoing many changes of its own.

Forty years ago, a rural-dominated legislature showed little concern for the problems of urban areas and minority groups. Operating within the context of one-party Democratic control and an interest-group system dominated by oil, finance, and agriculture, legislative leaders tied to conservative factions in the Democratic Party pursued selected policies that benefited those sectors of the Texas economy.

Today, Texas is the country's second most populous state and is more than 80 percent urban. The ethnic and racial characteristics of its population have changed, and still more changes are projected in its social composition. Texas has become a two-party state, its economy is diversifying, and, consequently, there are more demands today on lawmakers than in the past. The issues and policy questions that confront the Texas legislature are more complex, and the special interests demanding attention are more numerous and diverse.

Demographically and politically, the legislature also has undergone major changes. But lawmakers still have to operate under many nineteenth-century constitutional restrictions—including strict limits on when they can meet—that were written for a rural state in a bygone era.

The legislature, whose members are elected from districts throughout Texas, is the chief policy-making branch of state government. Its basic role is similar to that of Congress at the federal level, although there are major differences between the two institutions. The Texas legislature performs a variety of functions, but its primary task is to decide how conflicts between competing groups and interests are to be resolved—that is, who gets what, when, and how. Although often taken for granted, this orderly, institutionalized process of conflict management and resolution is critical to a stable political system.[1]

The Texas legislature has undergone significant institutional changes over the past 120 years. Some of these changes were due to external factors, such as the development of a two-party system within the electorate, changes in the interest-group system in Texas, and complex social and economic problems. Other changes were internal. They included the increased tenure of the membership, changing career and leadership patterns, expanded workload and length of sessions, the development and enforcement of complex rules and procedures, and the emergence of partisan divisions (see *Up Close:* "The 'Memorial Day Massacre'"). Political scientists describe these developments as **institutionalization**.[2]

Institutionalization varies throughout the fifty states. Some state legislatures are highly professional; others are not. In some states, salaries are high, turnover is limited, and legislators think in terms of legislative careers. Similarly, some legislatures have developed sophisticated staff and support services. By contrast, in other legislatures, members are poorly paid, turnover is high, legislative service is regarded as a part-time activity, and support services are limited. The Texas legislature falls somewhere between those legislatures that can be classified as highly professional and those that can be classified as amateur or citizen lawmaking bodies.[3] The institutionalization process has produced a more professional legislature in Texas, and this development is likely to continue in the future.

THE ORGANIZATION AND COMPOSITION OF THE TEXAS LEGISLATURE

Following the oppressive efforts of Governor Edmund J. Davis and the Reconstruction Republicans to centralize power (see Chapter 20), the delegates to the

institutionalization In the context of political science, the development of a legislative body into a formally structured system with stable membership, complex rules, expanded internal operations, and the delineation of staff functions.

bicameral legislature Lawmaking body, such as the Texas legislature, that includes two chambers.

Up Close

The "Memorial Day Massacre"

Despite strong Republican challenges of many Democratic incumbents in the 1996 legislative elections, partisanship was kept in check during most of the 1997 session. But partisan differences erupted on the evening of Memorial Day, one week before the session ended. They were ignited by fights over a bill to require parents to be notified before their minor daughters could receive abortions and a measure that would have prohibited the recognition of gay marriages in Texas. The two bills, both of which died, were major priorities of social conservatives, who formed a significant bloc among the 68 Republicans in the house.

After abortion rights supporters and other Democratic house members defeated efforts to debate both bills, Representative Arlene Wohlgemuth, a Republican from Burleson, used a technical procedural point to block consideration of 52 other bills remaining on the house's Memorial Day calendar. Wohlgemuth's move effectively killed most of the bills because that day was the deadline for the house to consider them on second reading. Sponsors managed to save only a few of the measures, including an education bill strongly supported by Governor George W. Bush, by tagging them on as amendments to related bills that had already won house approval.

Wohlgemuth said she was simply retaliating against house members who killed the bills on abortion restrictions and same-sex marriages, which social conservatives believed would have passed had they come to a vote. "I think that a statement needs to be made about why measures that are important to families, important to the people of this state, have not been heard, have not been voted on," she said.

Wohlgemuth's action wasn't entirely partisan because some of the bills that she killed or jeopardized, including Bush's education priority, were sponsored by other Republican legislators. But the action had strong partisan overtones and may have been a preview of future legislative sessions.

Representative Kent Grusendorf of Arlington, an outspoken Republican critic of Democratic Speaker Pete Laney, supported Wohlgemuth. He said committees controlled by Democrats had stalled bills that were important to Republicans and had majority support in the house.

But longtime Democratic Representative Dan Kubiak of Rockdale, in a speech on the house floor, strongly criticized Wohlgemuth's tactic. Kubiak said the incident—which he dubbed the "Memorial Day Massacre"—"was only the latest outbreak of the cancer that threatens not only this body, but the democratic process itself."

Source: Dallas Morning News, May 28, 1997.

---

constitutional convention in 1875 were distrustful, even fearful, of the excesses and abuses of big government. They created a part-time **bicameral legislature** comprising a 31-member senate and a 150-member house of representatives, and they placed strong restrictions on it. All other states also have bicameral legislatures except Nebraska, which has only one lawmaking body with 49 members. The sizes of other state senates range from 20 in Alaska to 67 in Minnesota; houses of representatives vary in size from 40 in Alaska to 400 in New Hampshire.[4]

Legislative Sessions   To curb lawmakers' power, the Texas constitutional framers limited **regular sessions** of the legislature to a maximum of 140 days every two years but gave the governor the authority to call **special sessions** when necessary. Lawmakers convene in regular session on the second Tuesday of January in odd-numbered years. Special sessions are limited to 30 days each and to subjects submitted by the governor, but there is no limit on the number of special sessions a governor can call.

regular session   The 140-day period in the odd-numbered years in which the legislature meets and can consider and pass laws on any issue or subject.

special session   Legislative session that can be called at any time by the governor. This session is limited to thirty days and to issues or subjects designated by the governor.

How Much Is a Legislator Worth?

Supporters of higher legislative pay in Texas say a raise is only fair because legislative service has become much more than a part-time job for many lawmakers, particularly during periods of frequent special sessions. They argue that the present low compensation level effectively restricts legislative service to wealthy individuals or those who have law practices or businesses in which partners or employees can take up the slack while they are in Austin. They believe higher pay would broaden the potential pool from which legislators are drawn—and perhaps improve the prospects for quality—by encouraging more salaried working people to run for legislative office.

The outside personal income of many legislators obviously does suffer while they are in office, but legislative service can enhance business and professional connections. Critics of higher legislative pay also note that candidates, many of whom spend thousands of dollars to get elected to the legislature, know the pay level before they run for the office. And Texas lawmakers have provided themselves with one of the best legislative retirement plans in the country. Retirement is computed on the basis of state district judges' salaries, which legislators raise during virtually every regular session, thereby increasing their own retirement benefits as well. Many former legislators receive pensions that are much larger than their paychecks were while they were in office.

There have been periods of frequent special sessions. From midsummer of 1986 through midsummer of 1987, for example, during a lingering budgetary crisis spawned by a depressed oil industry, the legislature convened for its regular 140-day session plus four special sessions, two of which lasted the maximum 30 days. The seventy-first legislature in 1989–90 held six special sessions to deal with equalization of school funding and the provision of medical expenses and other compensation for workers injured on the job. The seventy-second legislature had two special sessions in the summer of 1991 to write a new budget, pass a tax bill, make major changes in the criminal justice system, and redraw congressional district lines.

Some state officials and government experts believe the Texas legislature should have annual regular sessions, at least for budgetary purposes. Only six other state legislatures do not. But the change would require a constitutional amendment.

Terms of Office and Qualifications   Article III of the Texas Constitution contains the constitutional provisions pertaining to the structure, membership, and selection of the Texas legislature. Representatives serve two-year terms, and senators are elected to four-year, staggered terms. A senator has to be a qualified voter, at least twenty-six years old, a resident of Texas for five years preceding his or her election, and a resident of the district from which elected for at least one year. A representative must be a qualified voter, at least twenty-one years old, a Texas resident for two years, and a resident of the district represented for one year. There is no limit on the number of terms an individual can serve in the legislature.

Pay and Compensation   Members of both the house and the senate and their presiding officers have a base pay of $7,200 per year. This figure is set by the state constitution and can be raised only with voter approval. This is one of the lowest legislative pay levels in the country and was last increased in 1975 by a constitutional amendment that also set lawmakers' per diem, or personal expense allowance, at $30 a day while they were in session. The house and the senate authorize additional expense allowances for members to cover staff salaries and other costs of operating legislative offices.

In 1991 Texas voters approved a constitutional amendment creating a state Ethics Commission that could recommend legislative pay raises to the voters and change legislative per diem on its own. The commission set per diem at $95 per day for the 1997 legislative session.

By 1996 only Texas and four other states still retained constitutional limits on legislative pay. Compensation commissions now recommend legislative pay levels in some states; legislatures in twenty-three other states set their own salaries. In 1996 legislative pay ranged from a high of $72,000 a year in California, where lawmakers set their own salaries and are considered a full-time legislature, to a low of $100 a year in New Hampshire, which has annual sessions but a constitutional limit on salaries[5] (see *What Do You Think?* "How Much Is a Legislator Worth?").

Physical Facilities   The house chamber and representatives' offices have traditionally been located in the west wing of the state capitol, and the senate chamber and senators' offices in the east wing (see Figure 22-1). The pink granite building was completed in 1888, but the growth of state government and periodic renovations created a hodgepodge of cramped legislative offices. After one visitor died in a fire behind the senate chamber in 1983, it also became obvious that the building had become a firetrap. So in 1990 the state launched a $187 million capitol restoration and expansion project that included a four-story underground addition to the building. Legislative committee hearing rooms and many lawmakers' offices were relocated from the main building to the underground extension, which is connected to the original capitol and nearby office buildings by tunnels.

Completed in 1888 and recently renovated, the Texas capitol in downtown Austin houses the governor's office and meeting chambers for the house of representatives and the senate.

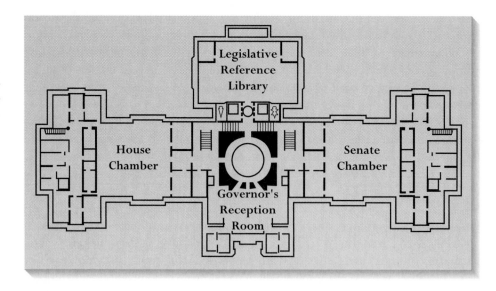

FIGURE 22-1 Corridors of Power in the Texas Capitol

The second floor of the Texas capitol, shown here, houses the senate and house chambers, the Legislative Reference Library, and the Governor's Reception Room.

When the legislature is in session, access to the floor of each chamber on the second floor of the capitol is restricted to lawmakers, certain state officials, some staff members, and accredited media representatives. The galleries, to which the public is admitted, overlook the chambers from the third floor of the capitol. In both the house and senate chambers, members have desks facing the presiding officer's podium, which, in turn, is flanked by desks of the clerical staff. Unlike the U.S. Congress, where seating is arranged by party affiliation, seats are assigned to state legislators by seniority.

Membership and Careers In 1971 the Texas legislature was overwhelmingly white, male, and Democratic. There were two African Americans in the 150-member house and one in the 31-member senate. The one African American senator was also the only woman in the senate. She was Barbara Jordan of Houston, who two years later would begin a distinguished career in the U.S. Congress. Frances Farenthold of Corpus Christi was the only woman in the house. She was a reform-minded lawmaker who was often referred to as "the Den Mother of the Dirty Thirty," a coalition of liberal Democrats and conservative Republicans who challenged the power of Speaker Gus Mutscher while a major political scandal in which he was involved was unfolding. In 1972 Farenthold ran a strong race for governor in the Democratic primary but lost a runoff election to Uvalde rancher Dolph Briscoe. There were eleven Hispanic members of the house and only one Hispanic senator in 1971. Only twelve legislators were Republicans—ten in the house and two in the senate.

By 1997 changing political patterns and attitudes, redrawn political boundaries, and court-ordered single-member districts for urban house members had significantly altered the composition of the legislature (see Table 22-1). During the regular session that year, there were 17 Republicans in the Senate, the first GOP majority in either chamber of the legislature since Reconstruction. The Senate also had two African American members, seven Hispanics, and three women.

The house in 1997 included 68 Republicans, 14 African Americans, 28 Hispanics, and 30 women. Representation from the urban and suburban areas of the state had grown, reflecting the population shifts accommodated by redistricting. In a special election to fill a house vacancy early in the 1991 session, Austin voters elected Texas's first openly gay legislator, Representative Glen Maxey.

TABLE 22-1	Comparative Profile of Texas Legislators, 1971–1997					
	House			*Senate*		
	1971	*1981*	*1997*	*1971*	*1981*	*1997*
Democrats	140	112	82	29	24	14
Republicans	10	38	68	2	7	17
Males	149	139	120	30	30	28
Females	1	11	30	1	1	3
Hispanics	11	17	28	1	4	7
African Americans	2	13	14	1	0	2
Anglos	137	120	108	29	27	22

Source: Texas house and senate rosters, 1971, 1981, 1997.

Law and business were the dominant occupations of legislators serving in 1997. Eleven of the 31 senators and 47 of the 150 house members were attorneys, although not all of them made their living practicing law. And some form of business involvement was reported by about the same number of legislators. The house included one retired airline pilot, one flight instructor, one physician, one retired physician, one orthodontist, and two chiropractors. One senator was trained both as an oral surgeon and an attorney, and another senator was a retired firefighter.

Senators' ages ranged from 31 to 64, with an average age of 50. The age range for members of the house was 24 to 72, with an average age of 47.

Various career patterns lead to election to the legislature.[6] Lawmakers include former members of city councils and school boards, former prosecutors, former legislative aides, and longtime Democratic and Republican party activists. Sixteen of the thirty-one senators in 1997 had previously served in the house. Many first-term legislators, however, arrive in Austin with relatively little political experience.

Legislative Turnover   Compared to other states, turnover in the Texas legislature is moderate, but relatively few individuals who serve can be considered career legislators. Only five senators and 12 house members entered the 1997 regular session with 20 or more years of legislative service. The average legislative experience in the senate was 9.8 years; house members had served an average of 6.6 years. In addition to the effects of redistricting of legislative seats every ten years, turnover is due to the low pay and the personal costs involved in running for public office. While in session, many legislators lose income from their regular sources of employment. Political ambition is also a factor. Many lawmakers who want to move up the political ladder serve only a few terms in the Texas house before running for the Texas senate, the U.S. Congress, or other state or local offices. Other legislators quit after a few sessions to become lobbyists.

REPRESENTATION AND REDISTRICTING

Many European legislatures use a system called *proportional representation*, in which legislative seats are allocated on the basis of each party's percentage of the total vote in an election. By contrast, the Texas legislature and most other American legislatures allocate seats geographically on the basis of **single-member districts**. The long legal and political battles over apportionment and redistricting address some of the fundamental questions of who should be represented and how they should be represented (see Chapter 10).

The Texas Constitution of 1876 provided that the legislature redraw state representative and senatorial districts every ten years, "at its first session after the publication of each United States decennial census," to reflect changing population patterns. But members of earlier rural-dominated legislatures were reluctant to apportion the legislative seats equitably to reflect the increased urbanization of the state, and inequities grew. In 1948 Texas voters approved a constitutional amendment creating the Legislative Redistricting Board to carry out redistricting responsibilities if the legislature failed to do so during the required session. The board includes the lieutenant governor, the speaker of the house, the attorney general, the comptroller, and the land commissioner.

But for many more years, the urban areas of the state were still denied equality in representation. After the 1960 census, it was possible for approximately 33 percent of the state's population to elect a majority of both the Texas house and the senate. And rural legislators tended to neglect urban problems.

Equality in redistricting finally came to Texas as a result of federal court intervention. In 1962 the U.S. Supreme Court, in the case of *Baker v. Carr*, applied the principle of equality to congressional districts. Then, in the case of *Reynolds v. Sims* (1964), the court held that state legislative districts had to be apportioned on the "one person, one vote" principle. Litigation in 1965 (*Kilgarlin v. Martin*) extended this ruling to Texas, and the "reapportionment revolution" was to produce dramatic changes in the composition and structure of the Texas legislature.[7] To a large degree, the increased representation of minorities and Republicans in Texas's lawmaking body is a result of the legal and political redistricting battles.

The Texas senate has always been elected by single-member districts, and after the 1970 census, the application of the "equality principle" to the senate resulted in districts that were comparable in size. The issues of racial and partisan gerrymandering—the practice of drawing lines to favor a particular individual or group (see Chapters 10 and 21)—were still to be resolved through subsequent litigation and federal legislation.

Rural members of the Texas house were also elected from single-member districts, but in the urban counties that had been allocated more than one representative, the elections were held in multimember districts. Each candidate for a house seat in an urban area had to run for election countywide, a practice that put ethnic and political minorities at a disadvantage because their votes were diluted by the dominant Anglo and Democratic populations.

In 1972 a three-judge federal court ruled that multimember districts in Dallas and Bexar counties were unconstitutional because they diluted the voting strength of African Americans in Dallas and Hispanics in Bexar. Coincidentally, the **at-large districts** diluted the voting strength of Republicans in both counties.

Despite the fact that 50 percent of Bexar County's population was Hispanic, under the at-large election system only one Hispanic from Bexar had served in the Texas house in 1971. Dallas County, which had a large African American population, had only one African American house member. Single-member districts in Harris County had been drawn by the Legislative Redistricting Board in 1971, and after the U.S. Supreme Court upheld the lower court's decision regarding Dallas

single-member district System in which a legislator, city council member, or other public official is elected from a specific geographic area.

at-large district Legislative or other political district, sometimes called a multimember district because two or more officials are elected from it, that includes an entire county, city, or other political subdivision.

Redistricting: Not Just a Matter of Numbers

The Mexican American Legal Defense and Educational Fund, Texas Rural Legal Aid, and the Texas Civil Rights Project sued the state over the 1991 redistricting plans drawn by the legislature, alleging that Texas house and senate districts had been gerrymandered to protect incumbents at the expense of minorities. After a state district judge in Edinburg ruled that the plans were unconstitutional, state Democratic leaders worked out a compromise with the minority plaintiffs, and the legislature in a January 1992 special session enacted new redistricting plans. But in a separate lawsuit brought by Republicans, a three-judge federal court in Austin took over the redistricting process.

The Republicans challenged the new districts as discriminatory against the GOP. The federal court upheld a redistricting plan for U.S. congressional districts. But the court, all of whose members were Republican appointees, voted 2 to 1 to order its own plans for Texas house and senate districts.

The court-ordered plan did not significantly change the proportion of Democratic and Republican seats in the Texas house after the 1992 elections, but it increased Republican strength in the senate by four seats at the expense of incumbent Democrats. Minority groups complained it reduced the poten-

tial number of minority senators. As a result, the senate that served during the 1993 regular session was much more conservative than that body had been in several years.

The 1992 elections were held under the court's plan only after a bitter political fight over the senate districts. Texas Attorney General Dan Morales, a Democrat, accused one of the federal judges, Jim Nowlin, of having possible improper contact with one or more Republican legislators in the drawing of the plan. State Representative George Pierce, a Republican senate candidate from San Antonio, acknowledged he had made some changes in San Antonio districts at Nowlin's request the day before the order was issued, but Pierce denied any wrongdoing. A federal judicial council investigated the allegations and reprimanded Nowlin but concluded that the judge had no ulterior motive in seeking Pierce's help.

Although Democrats were unable to block the 1992 elections under the court-ordered plan, they eventually prevailed in 1993 on an appeal to the U.S. Supreme Court, which upheld the senate plan that was drawn by the legislature to favor Democrats. That ruling required all thirty-one Texas senate seats to be up for election again in 1994—this time under the Democratic plan—but Republicans nevertheless gained another senate seat, bringing the GOP's total to fourteen. By 1997 Republicans had picked up three more senate seats and their first majority of the Texas senate since Reconstruction.

and Bexar counties, multimember legislative districts were soon eliminated in all other urban counties. After 1975 the U.S. Congress put Texas under the provisions of the federal Voting Rights Act, which prohibits the dilution of minority voting strength, requires clearance in advance of redistricting plans by the Department of Justice, and gives African Americans and Hispanics a strong weapon to use in challenging a redistricting plan in court.

By the mid-1990s, however, minorities believed their fight for equal representation was still far from over. The Voting Rights Act was under attack by conservatives. And the U.S. Supreme Court, in "reverse discrimination" cases from Texas and Georgia, ruled that some congressional districts had been illegally gerrymandered to elect minority candidates. The potential effect of those rulings on the redistricting of state legislative seats in Texas wouldn't be known until the next redistricting session in 2001 (see *A Conflicting View:* "Redistricting: Not Just a Matter of Numbers").

LEGISLATIVE LEADERSHIP

The highly institutionalized leadership structure found in the U.S. Congress (see Chapter 10) is only now beginning to emerge in the Texas legislature—and to only a limited extent. The Texas legislature has historically been dominated by a small group of Democratic lawmakers. With no significant party opposition or minority representation until recent years, legislative leadership was highly personal and dependent on the political relationships between the presiding officers and key legislators.

House Leadership   The presiding officer of the house of representatives is the **speaker**, who is elected by the house from among its membership. With the long tenures of Gib Lewis and his immediate predecessor in the speaker's office, Bill Clayton, there was not a contested speaker's race between 1975 and 1991. Lewis's decision not to seek reelection in 1992 prompted several house members to announce their candidacy for the post. But veteran Democratic Representative James E. "Pete" Laney, a farmer-businessman from Hale Center, secured the support of the necessary majority of house members several weeks before the 1993 legislature convened, and his election on the opening day of the session was unopposed.

It is illegal for a speaker candidate to make outright promises in return for members' pledges of support, but Laney's key supporters won choice leadership positions when the new speaker exercised one of his most significant formal powers and made committee assignments. Legislators know that the earlier they hop onto a winning bandwagon in a speaker's race, the better chance they will have of getting their preferred committee assignments or a chance to advance their legislative programs. Sometimes, however, choosing the winning candidate is difficult because

speaker   Presiding officer of the house of representatives.

Speaker Pete Laney presiding over the house of representatives.

TABLE 22-2	Recent Presiding Officers	
Lieutenant Governors	*When Served*	*Home*
Ben Ramsey	1951–1963	San Augustine
Preston Smith	1963–1969	Lubbock
Ben Barnes	1969–1973	DeLeon
Bill Hobby	1973–1991	Houston
Bob Bullock	1991–1999	Hillsboro
Rick Perry	1999–	Haskell
Speakers	*When Served*	*Home*
Reuben Senterfitt	1951–1955	San Saba
Jim T. Lindsey	1955–1957	Texarkana
Waggoner Carr	1957–1961	Lubbock
James A. Turman	1961–1963	Gober
Byron M. Tunnell	1963–1965	Tyler
Ben Barnes	1965–1969	DeLeon
Gus Mutscher	1969–1972	Brenham
Rayford Price	1972–1973	Palestine
Price Daniel Jr.	1973–1975	Liberty
Bill Clayton	1975–1983	Springlake
Gib Lewis	1983–1993	Fort Worth
James E. "Pete" Laney	1993–	Hale Center

Source: Texas Legislative Council, *Presiding Officers of the Texas Legislature, 1846–1982* (Austin: Texas Legislative Council, 1982); secretary of state.

the campaigning is conducted largely behind the scenes, with candidates making personal pleas to individual house members. Laney's main competitor had been Representative Jim Rudd of Brownfield, who, like Laney, had been a key committee chair under Lewis.

Until the 1950s, it was unusual for a speaker to serve more than one two-year term (see Table 22-2). The position was circulated among a small group of legislators who dominated the house. Clayton, a lawmaker from Springlake in West Texas, set a record by serving four consecutive terms before retiring in 1983. His successor, Lewis of Fort Worth, broke Clayton's record when he was elected to his fifth term in January 1991.

Unlike most of their predecessors, Clayton and Lewis devoted long hours to the job and kept large full-time staffs. With the complexities of a growing state putting more demands on the legislative leadership, recent senate leaders (lieutenant governors) have also made their jobs virtually full time and, like the speaker, have hired large staffs of specialists to research issues and help develop legislation. The presiding officers also depend on key committee chairs to take the lead in pushing their legislative priorities.

Laney has had a looser rein on the house than his predecessor. In 1993 he was active in efforts to meet a court deadline to restructure the school finance system. Then, in 1995, he joined Governor George W. Bush and Lieutenant Governor Bob Bullock in seeking changes in the civil justice system that curbed damage judgments against businesses and doctors. And, in 1997, he actively supported Bush's unsuccessful effort to replace a large chunk of local school property taxes with higher state taxes. Laney also encouraged opposing sides to find common ground on other major issues, but one of his own priorities was to improve the way the house conducted its business.

As he had promised during his campaign for speaker, Laney proposed and won significant changes in the house rules to alleviate the end-of-session logjams that in previous sessions had forced legislators to vote on many bills they had never seen. The rules changes also reduced the power of the Calendars Committee, which is discussed in more detail later in this chapter, and produced, in the view of many house members, a more democratic lawmaking process than existed under previous speakers.

The speaker appoints a speaker pro tempore, or assistant presiding officer, who is usually a close ally. In 1981 Speaker Clayton named the first African American, Representative Craig Washington of Houston, to the post. Although Clayton was a rural conservative and Washington was an urban liberal, Washington proved to be a critical member of the speaker's team. He also exercised considerable influence in the house on a wide range of issues of importance to minorities. Ten years later, Gib Lewis named another African American legislator, Representative Wilhelmina Delco of Austin, as the first woman speaker pro tempore.

The membership of most house committees is determined partly by seniority. The speaker has total discretion, however, in naming committee chairs and vice chairs and in appointing all the members of procedural committees, including the influential Calendars Committee.

Senate Leadership   The **lieutenant governor** is chosen by the voters in a statewide election to serve a four-year term as presiding officer of the senate. Unlike the vice president of the United States—the counterpart in the federal government, who has only limited legislative functions—the lieutenant governor is the senate's legislative leader. This office, which is elected independently of the governor, is often called the most powerful office in Texas state government because the lieutenant governor has the opportunity to merge a statewide electoral base into a dominant legislative role.[8] Lieutenant governors, however, get most of their power from the senate, not from the constitution, and to be successful they must learn to accommodate the individual senators—thirty-one of the strongest egos in Texas—who set the rules.

The lieutenant governor's power is based in part on the same coalitional strategies that are used by the speaker through committee assignments and relationships with interest groups. But the lieutenant governor has traditionally had more direct control over the senate's agenda than the speaker has over the house's agenda. Under longstanding senate rules, the lieutenant governor has determined when—and if—a committee-approved bill will be brought up for a vote by the full senate. In the house, the order of floor debate is determined by the Calendars Committee. Although that key panel is appointed by the speaker and is sensitive to the speaker's wishes, it represents an intermediate step that the lieutenant governor does not have to encounter.

The lieutenant governor also has had more formal control over the membership of senate committees than the speaker has over house panels. Under its rules, the senate traditionally has allowed the lieutenant governor to appoint members of all standing committees without regard to seniority or any other restrictions.

The senate has a president pro tempore, who is chosen by senators from among their membership. This position is rotated among the senators on a

lieutenant governor Presiding officer of the senate. This officeholder would become governor if the governor were to die, be incapacitated, or removed from office.

seniority basis. It is held for a limited period, and the holder of the position is third in line of succession to the governorship. Tradition dictates that the governor and the lieutenant governor both allegedly "leave" the state on the same day so the president pro tempore can serve as "governor for a day" at one point during his or her term.

Bill Hobby, a quiet-spoken media executive who served a record eighteen years as lieutenant governor before voluntarily leaving the office in January 1991, patiently sought consensus among senators on most major issues and rarely took the lead in promoting specific legislative proposals. One notable exception occurred in 1979, when Hobby tried to force senate approval of a presidential primary bill opposed by most Democratic senators. After Hobby served notice that he would alter the senate's traditional operating procedure to give the bill special consideration, twelve Democratic senators, dubbed the "Killer Bees," hid out for several days to break a **quorum** and keep the senate from conducting business. They succeeded in killing the primary bill and reminding Hobby that the senators set the rules. Another exception occurred in 1989 when Hobby, in an effort to break an impasse over workers' compensation reform, proposed a plan generally supported by business but vigorously opposed by trial lawyers and some of Hobby's own key senate leaders. This time, much of Hobby's proposal was eventually adopted.

Hobby's successor, Bob Bullock, had demonstrated strong leadership and a mercurial personality during sixteen years as state comptroller. Upon taking office as lieutenant governor, he had major policy and structural changes in mind for state government and was impatient to see them carried out by the legislature. Unlike Hobby, Bullock took the lead in making proposals and then actively lobbying for them. During his first session in 1991, he reportedly had shouting matches with some lawmakers behind closed doors and one day abruptly and angrily adjourned the senate when not enough members were present for a quorum at the scheduled starting time. But his experience and knowledge of state government and his tireless work habits won the respect of most senators and their support for most of his proposals.

Bullock, a Democrat, strengthened his leadership role during the 1993 and 1995 sessions and was actively involved in every major issue that the senate addressed. Recognizing that increases in Republican strength after the 1992 and 1994 elections made the senate more conservative than it had been in several years, and eager to strengthen his support in the business community, Bullock saw to it that compromises on major issues—including some long sought by business—were reached behind closed doors before they were made public. This approach kept controversy to a minimum and defused partisanship, but it distressed consumer advocates and environmentalists, who felt largely excluded from the process. It also prompted remarks that the senate had abandoned democracy. There were so many unanimous or near unanimous votes in the senate in 1993 that some house members joked that senators who wanted to show dissent voted aye with their eyes closed.[9]

Bullock's most controversial proposal during his first session in 1991 was a state income tax to improve state government's revenue base and reduce the high property taxes that Texans had to pay for the support of public schools. Texas was one of only a handful of states without an income tax, and there was strong opposition to one. Governor Ann Richards and Speaker Gib Lewis remained opposed to an income tax, as did a majority of the house, which, under the state constitution, has

Former Lieutenant Governor Bob Bullock, who retired in 1998.

quorum Required number of the members of a governing body who must be present so that official business, such as voting, can be conducted. In Texas, a quorum of the house and the senate is two-thirds of the membership. For committees, it is a majority of the members.

Republican Rick Perry was elected Texas lieutenant governor in 1998.

to initiate action on tax bills. So only a hybrid corporate income tax was passed, not a personal income tax.

Then, in 1993, Bullock surprised friends and foes alike by proposing a constitutional amendment to ban a personal income tax unless the voters approved one. Bullock was obviously seeking political cover on the issue for his 1994 reelection race, but he apparently also viewed his proposal as a way eventually to win Texans' approval of a personal income tax. The constitutional amendment, which voters overwhelmingly approved, provided that any such tax would have to be used to help fund public education and be accompanied by a reduction in unpopular school property taxes.

Bullock played a less active role during the 1997 session, after Republicans, for the first time this century, had won a majority of senate seats. He was strongly supportive of some key legislation, including a statewide water conservation and management plan, but did little to promote a property tax relief effort that Governor Bush had made his highest priority for the session. One key element of Bush's proposal, an increase in state taxes as a partial trade-off for lower school district taxes, died primarily because of strong senate opposition, which Bullock did not try to defuse.

A few days after the 1997 session ended, Bullock surprised the Texas political community by announcing that he would not seek reelection in 1998. Comptroller John Sharp, a Democrat, and Agriculture Commissioner Rick Perry, a Republican, quickly launched campaigns for the lieutenant governor's office. Without waiting for the election, some senators—both Democrats and Republicans—said they were interested in changing the senate rules to lessen the lieutenant governor's power over the senate agenda and over committee assignments, and to give more authority to the senators. They said changes should be considered regardless of whether the next lieutenant governor was a Democrat or a Republican and regardless of which party won a majority of senate seats in the 1998 elections. After Perry defeated Sharp, the rules remained unchanged.

Influence and Control over the Legislative Process   The power of each presiding officer to determine which committee will have jurisdiction over a specific bill gives the speaker and the lieutenant governor tremendous influence over the lawmaking process.

The speaker and the lieutenant governor control the legislative process through the application of the rules, including those set in the state constitution and those adopted by the house and the senate. Each presiding officer is advised on procedures by a parliamentarian. The speaker and the lieutenant governor do not participate in house or senate debate on bills and usually attempt to present an image of neutral presiding officers. Their formal powers, however, are further strengthened by their informal relationships with their committee leaders and interest groups, and they rarely lose control of the process.

In the senate, the lieutenant governor can vote only to break a tie. The speaker can vote on any issue in the house but normally abstains from voting except to break a tie or to send a signal to encourage reluctant or wavering house members to vote a particular way on an issue.

Leadership Teams   There is no formal division along party lines or a formal system of floor leaders in either the Texas house or the senate. The longtime one-party legislative system with the speaker's and lieutenant governor's control of committee appointments did not produce a leadership structure comparable to that of the U.S. Congress. The committee chairs constitute the speaker's and lieutenant governor's teams and usually act as their unofficial floor leaders in developing and building support for the leadership's legislative priorities. Most chairs are philosophically, if not always politically, aligned with the presiding officers.

THE COMMITTEE SYSTEM

The committee system is the backbone of the legislative process, and it is molded by the lieutenant governor and the speaker.[10] It is a screening process that decides the fate of most legislation.

The **committee** is where technical drafting errors and oversights in bills can be corrected and where compromise can begin to work for those bills that do eventually become law. Only 1,502 of the 5,727 bills and constitutional amendments introduced in the 1997 regular session won final legislative approval. Most of those that did not make it died in a senate or a house committee, many without ever being heard. Rarely does a committee kill a bill on an outright vote because there are much easier, less obvious ways to scuttle legislation. A bill can be gutted, or so drastically amended or weakened, that even its sponsor can hardly recognize it. Or it can be simply ignored.

Committee chairs have considerable power over legislation that comes to their committees. They may kill bills simply by refusing to schedule them for a hearing. Or, after a hearing, a chair may send a bill to a subcommittee that he or she stacks with members opposed to the legislation, thus allowing the bill to die slowly and quietly in the legislative deep freeze. Even if a majority of committee members want to approve a bill, the chair can simply refuse to recognize such a motion. Most chairs, however, are sensitive to the wishes of the presiding officers. If the speaker or the lieutenant governor wants a bill to win committee approval or another measure to die in committee, a chair will usually comply.

Referral to a **subcommittee**—which usually has three to five members—does not always mean the death of a bill. Subcommittees also help committees distribute the workload. They work out compromises, correct technical problems in bills, or draft substitute legislation to accommodate competing interest groups.

Standing Committees   The number and names of committees are periodically revised under house and senate rules, but there have been relatively few major changes in recent years. During the 1997 regular session, the senate had 15 **standing committees**, varying in membership from 5 to 13. Additionally, the entire senate was designated as a Committee of the Whole on Redistricting.

There are 37 standing committees in the house, with memberships ranging from 5 to 27 (Table 22-3). Most of these committees are substantive: that is, they hold public hearings and evaluate bills related to their areas, such as higher education, natural resources, or public health. A few committees are *procedural*, such as the Rules and Resolutions Committee, which handles many routine congratulatory resolutions, and the **Calendars Committee**, which schedules bills for debate by the full house.

committee   In the legislature, a group of lawmakers who review and hold public hearings on issues or bills they are assigned by the presiding officer. Committees that specialize in bills by subject matter are designated as standing committees. A bill has to win committee approval before it can be considered by the full house or senate. Most bills die in committees, which serve as a legislative screening process.

subcommittee   A few members of a larger committee appointed to review a particular bill and make recommendations on its disposition to the full committee.

standing committee Committee created by house or senate rules to consider legislation or perform a procedural role in the lawmaking process.

Calendars Committee Special procedural committee that schedules bills that already have been approved by other committees for floor debate in the house.

TABLE 22-3 Senate and House Standing Committees: 75th Legislature, 1997

	Number of Members		Number of Members
Senate		Criminal Jurisprudence	9
Administration	7	Economic Development	9
Criminal Justice	7	Elections	9
Economic Development	11	Energy Resources	9
Education	11	Environmental Regulation	9
Finance	13	Financial Institutions	11
General Investigating	5	General Investigating	5
Health and Human Services	11	Higher Education	9
Intergovernmental Relations	11	Human Services	9
International Relations,		Insurance	9
Trade and Technology	9	Judicial Affairs	9
Jurisprudence	7	Juvenile Justice and Family Issues	9
Natural Resources	11	Land and Resource Management	9
Nominations	7	Licensing and	
Revenue and Public		Administrative Procedures	9
Education Funding	11	Local and Consent Calendars	11
State Affairs	13	Natural Resources	9
Veterans' Affairs		Pensions and Investments	9
and Military Installations	5	Public Education	9
Committee of the Whole		Public Health	9
on Legislative and		Public Safety	9
Congressional Redistricting	31	Redistricting	11
		Revenue and Public	
House		Education Funding	11
Administration	11	Rules and Resolutions	11
Agriculture and Livestock	9	State Affairs	15
Appropriations	27	State, Federal and	
Business and Industry	11	International Relations	9
Calendars	11	State Recreational Resources	9
Civil Practices	9	Transportation	9
Corrections	9	Urban Affairs	9
County Affairs	9	Ways and Means	11

Source: Texas house and senate.

Some committees play more dominant roles in the lawmaking process than others, particularly in the house. The house State Affairs Committee, for example, handles many more major statewide bills than the committee on State, Federal and International Relations or the committee on Agriculture and Livestock. The house Urban Affairs and County Affairs committees handle several hundred bills of importance to local governments each session. The importance of a committee is determined by the area of public policy over which it has jurisdiction or by its role in the house's operating procedure.

The house Calendars Committee historically had more life and death power over legislation than any other committee because it set the order of debate on the house floor. During each regular session, it killed hundreds of bills that had been approved by various substantive committees by refusing to schedule them for debate by the full house or scheduling them so late in the session they did not have time to win senate approval. This committee traditionally worked closely with the speaker and was one means by which the speaker and the speaker's team controlled the house. Although many legislators bitterly complained that the committee kept their priority bills bottled up, some lawmakers defended the panel as a means of keeping controversial legislation—on which many members would rather not have to cast votes—from reaching the house floor.

Rules reforms backed by Speaker Laney in 1993 curtailed the Calendars Committee's powers. The panel still sets the schedule for floor debate, and it still kills bills. But it has to take recorded votes on the legislation it kills, and it has to act on a bill within a designated number of days after the measure has been approved by a substantive committee.

The state budget is the single most important bill enacted by the legislature because, through it, lawmakers determine how much money is spent on the state's public programs and services. In the house, the Appropriations Committee takes the lead in drafting state budgets, and the house Ways and Means Committee normally is responsible for producing any tax or revenue measures necessary to balance the budget. During the 1997 regular session, however, Speaker Laney appointed the Select Committee on Revenue and Public Education Funding to consider a tax redistribution plan proposed by Governor George W. Bush to lower school property taxes.

The two most important committees in the senate are the Finance Committee, which handles the budget and, usually, tax bills, and the State Affairs Committee, which, like its house counterpart, handles a variety of legislation of major statewide importance. But in 1997, Lieutenant Governor Bullock also appointed a separate committee to consider the governor's tax proposal.

Although committees have general areas of responsibility, legislative rules allow the lieutenant governor and the speaker some latitude in assigning bills. The presiding officer can ensure the death of a bill by sending it to a committee known to oppose it or can guarantee quick action on a measure by referring it to a friendly panel.

Standing Subcommittees   The formal standing subcommittee structure of the U.S. Congress has only begun to develop in the Texas legislature, where committee chairs traditionally appointed subcommittees as needed to handle specific bills.

Conference Committees   Legislation must be passed in exactly the same form by the house and the senate. If one chamber refuses to accept the other's version of a bill, a **conference committee** can try to resolve the differences. Conference committees of five senators and five representatives are appointed by the presiding officers. A compromise bill has to be approved by at least three senators and three house members who serve on the conference committee before it is sent back to the full house and the full senate for subsequent approval or rejection. Over the years, conference committees have drafted legislation in forms dramatically different from earlier versions approved by the house or senate. But because a conference committee is supposed to do no more than adjust the differences between the house bill and the senate bill, both chambers have to pass a concurrent resolution to allow the addition of significant new language.

Special Committees   **Special committees** are occasionally appointed by the governor, the lieutenant governor, and the speaker to study major policy issues,

conference committee
Panel of house members and senators appointed to work out a compromise on a bill if different versions of the legislation were passed by the house and the senate.

special committees Special panels appointed to study major policy issues.

such as tax equity or school finance. These panels usually include private citizens as well as legislators, and they usually recommend legislation. Standing legislative committees also study issues in their assigned areas during the **interims** between sessions, and the presiding officers can ask committees to conduct special investigations or inquiries pertaining to governmental matters.

RULES AND PROCEDURES

Laws are made in Texas according to the same basic process followed by the U.S. Congress and other state legislatures.[11] But as the discussion of the committee system already has indicated, legislative rules are complex and are loaded with traps where legislation can be killed. One often hears the remark around the capitol that "there are a lot more ways to kill a bill than to pass one." Legislators and lobbyists who master the rules can wield a tremendous amount of influence over the lawmaking process. Both the house and the senate have detailed rules governing the disposition of legislation, and each has a parliamentarian to help interpret them.

How a Bill Becomes a Law   The simplified outline of the process by which a bill becomes a law (Figure 22-2) starts with the introduction of a bill in the house or senate and its referral to a committee by the presiding officer, which constitutes **first reading**. That is the only reading most bills ever get.

A bill that wins committee approval can be considered on **second reading** by the full house or senate, where it is debated and often amended. Some amendments are designed to improve a bill, but others are designed to kill it by loading it down with controversial or objectionable provisions. Amendments that may be punitive toward particular individuals or groups are also sometimes offered. Such an amendment, which may be temporarily added to a bill only to be removed before the measure becomes law, is designed to give a group or perhaps a local official a message, or warning, that the sponsoring legislator expects his or her wishes to be heeded on a particular issue. Lawmakers also may offer amendments that they know have little chance of being approved merely to make favorable political points with constituents or special-interest groups.

If a bill is approved on second reading, it has to win one more vote on **third reading** before it goes to the other chamber for the same process. If the second chamber approves the bill without any changes, or amendments, it then goes to the governor for signature into law or for **veto**. The governor also can allow a bill to become law without his or her signature. This procedure is just the opposite of the pocket veto power afforded the president of the United States. If the president does not sign a bill approved by Congress by a certain deadline, it is automatically vetoed. If the governor of Texas does not sign or veto a bill by a certain deadline, it becomes law. A veto can be overridden and the bill allowed to become law by a two-thirds vote of both houses, although this approach is rarely attempted.

The governor must accept or reject a bill in its entirety except for the general **appropriations bill**, or state budget, from which he or she can delete specific spending proposals while approving others. This power is called a **line-item veto**. The budget and any other bill approved by the legislature that appropriates money has to be certified by the comptroller before it is sent to the governor. Texas has a **pay-as-you-go** government, and the comptroller must certify there will be enough revenue available to fund the bill.

interims   Periods between legislative sessions.

first reading   Introduction of a bill in the house or the senate and its referral to a committee by the presiding officer.

second reading   Initial debate by the full house or senate on a bill that has been approved by a committee.

third reading   Final presentation of a bill before the full house or senate.

veto   Power of the governor to reject, or kill, a bill passed by the legislature.

appropriations bill   Bill that authorizes the expenditure of money for a public program or purpose. In Texas, the general appropriations bill approved by the legislature every two years is the state budget.

line-item veto   Power of the Texas governor to reject certain parts of the general appropriations, or spending, bill without killing the entire measure.

pay-as-you-go   Constitutional requirement that prohibits the legislature from borrowing money for the state's operating expenses.

FIGURE 22-2 Basic Steps in the Texas Legislative Process

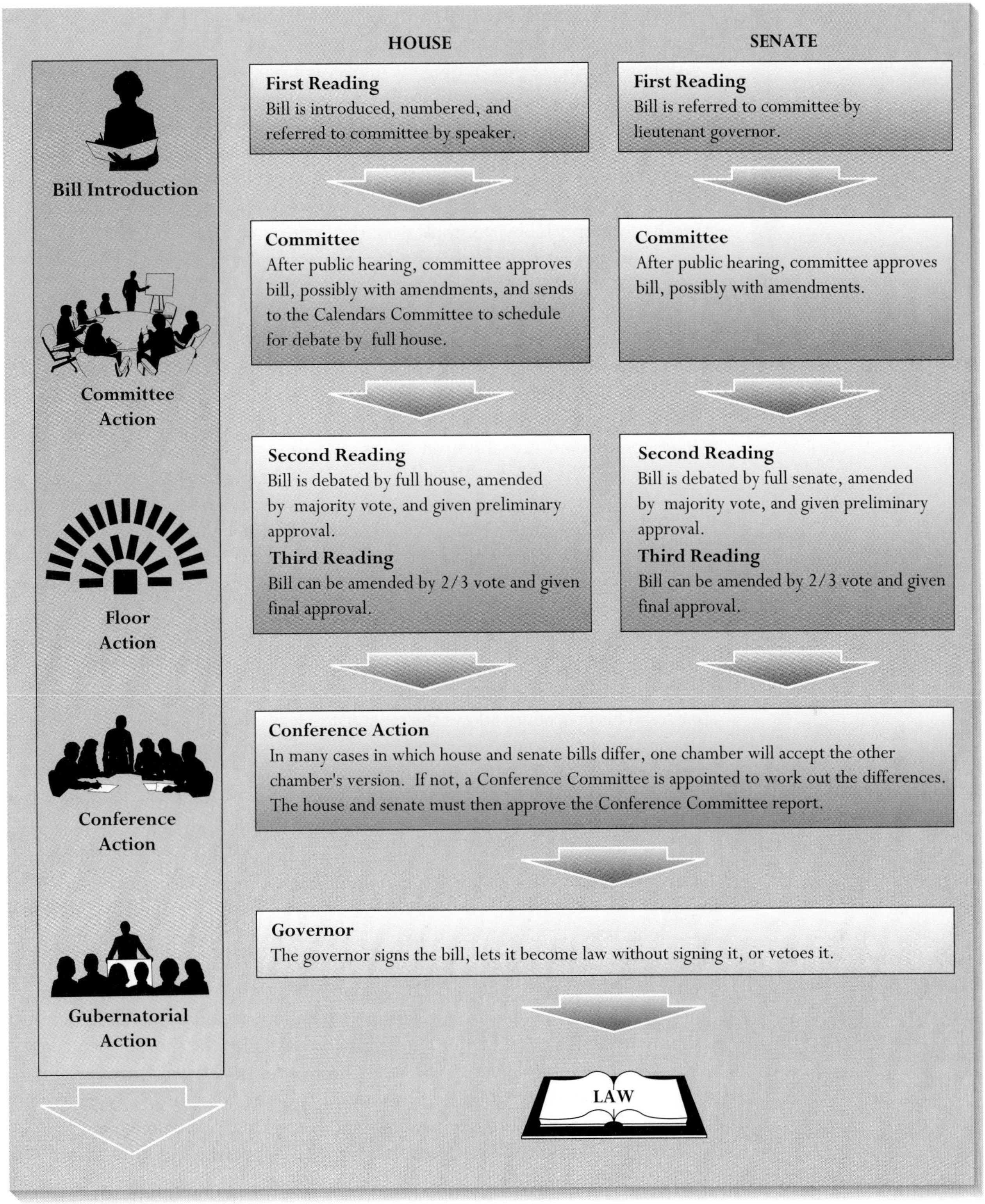

Bill Introduction

Committee Action

Floor Action

Conference Action

Gubernatorial Action

HOUSE

First Reading
Bill is introduced, numbered, and referred to committee by speaker.

Committee
After public hearing, committee approves bill, possibly with amendments, and sends to the Calendars Committee to schedule for debate by full house.

Second Reading
Bill is debated by full house, amended by majority vote, and given preliminary approval.
Third Reading
Bill can be amended by 2/3 vote and given final approval.

SENATE

First Reading
Bill is referred to committee by lieutenant governor.

Committee
After public hearing, committee approves bill, possibly with amendments.

Second Reading
Bill is debated by full senate, amended by majority vote, and given preliminary approval.
Third Reading
Bill can be amended by 2/3 vote and given final approval.

Conference Action
In many cases in which house and senate bills differ, one chamber will accept the other chamber's version. If not, a Conference Committee is appointed to work out the differences. The house and senate must then approve the Conference Committee report.

Governor
The governor signs the bill, lets it become law without signing it, or vetoes it.

LAW

State Senator Gonzalo Barrientos of Austin puts on comfortable shoes in anticipation of a lengthy filibuster.

two-thirds rule Rule under which the Texas senate has traditionally operated that requires approval of at least two-thirds of senators before a bill can be debated on the senate floor. It allows a minority of senators to block controversial legislation.

intent calendar Daily list of bills eligible for debate on the floor of the Texas senate, if the sponsor is recognized by the lieutenant governor.

tag Rule that allows an individual senator to postpone a committee hearing on any bill for at least forty-eight hours, a delay which can be fatal to a bill during the closing days of a legislative session.

filibuster Procedure that allows a senator to speak against a bill for as long as he or she can stand and talk. A filibuster can become a formidable obstacle or threat against controversial bills near the end of a legislative session.

If the second chamber amends the bill, the originating chamber must approve the change or request a conference committee. Any compromise worked out by a conference committee must be approved by both houses, without further changes, before it is sent to the governor.

All bills except revenue-raising measures can originate in either the house or the senate. Tax bills must originate in the house, although the legislative leadership severely bent that rule to win approval of a tax bill necessary to balance a new state budget in a 1991 special session. After the house had dismantled a $3.3 billion revenue bill recommended by its Ways and Means Committee and sent the senate nothing but a $30 million shell, Lieutenant Governor Bullock and the senate, in consultation with lobbyists, took over the writing of a new tax bill, which the house later approved.

Procedural Obstacles to Legislation   Pieces of legislation can encounter other significant procedural obstacles. In the house, there is the Calendars Committee, discussed earlier in this chapter. In the senate, there is the **two-thirds rule**.

The two-thirds rule for debating bills on the senate floor is a strong obstacle to controversial bills because it means that only eleven senators, if they are determined enough and not absent at the wrong time, can keep any measure from becoming law. This rule has also been a source of the lieutenant governor's power. After a bill is approved by a committee, its sponsor can have it placed on the daily **intent calendar**. If the sponsor is recognized by the lieutenant governor, he or she will seek senate permission to consider the bill. A sponsor can have majority senate support for a measure but watch it die if he or she cannot convince two-thirds of the senators to allow formal debate.

The two-thirds rule also gives a senator the opportunity to vote on both sides of an issue. Sometimes a senator will vote to bring up a bill and then vote against the measure when it is actually passed, as only a majority vote is required for approval. This procedure allows the senator to please the bill's supporters, give the sponsor a favor that can be repaid later, and, at the same time, tell the bill's opponents that he or she voted against the measure.

The senate rules also provide for tags and filibusters, both of which can be effective in killing bills near the end of a legislative session. A **tag** allows an individual senator to postpone a committee hearing on any bill for at least forty-eight hours, a delay that is often fatal in the crush of unfinished business during a session's closing days. The **filibuster**, a procedure that allows a senator to speak against a bill for as long as he or she can stand and talk, is usually little more than a nuisance to a bill's supporters early in a session, but it, too, can become a potent and ever-present threat against controversial legislation near the end of a session. Sometimes the mere likelihood of a filibuster is sufficient to kill a measure. Late in a session, the lieutenant governor may refuse to recognize the sponsor of a controversial bill for fear a filibuster will fatally delay other major legislative proposals. State Senator Bill Meier of Euless spoke for forty-three hours in 1977 against a bill dealing with the public reporting of on-the-job accidents. In so doing, he captured the world's record for the longest filibuster, which record he held for years.

Shortcuts, Obfuscation, and Confusion   Sponsors of legislation languishing in an unfriendly committee or subcommittee often try to resurrect their proposals by attaching them as amendments to related bills being debated on the house or senate floor. Such maneuvers are often successful, particularly if opponents are absent or if the sponsor succeeds in "mumbling" the amendment through without challenge. But the speaker or the lieutenant governor must find that such amendments are germane to the pending bill if an alert opponent raises a point of order against them.

To facilitate the passage of noncontroversial and local pieces of legislation, the house and the senate have periodic local and consent or local and uncontested **calendars**, which are conducted under special rules that allow scores of bills to be approved routinely and quickly by the full house or senate without debate. Bills of major statewide significance, even controversial measures, are sometimes placed on these calendars, but it takes only one senator or three representatives to have any bill struck. Legislators will sometimes knowingly let a controversial bill slip by on a local calendar without moving to strike it so as not to offend the sponsor or the presiding officer. But to protect themselves politically, should the bill become an issue later, they will quietly register a vote against the measure in the house or senate journal.

As noted earlier in this chapter, compromises on controversial legislation are often worked out behind closed doors long before a bill is debated on the house or senate floor or even afforded a public hearing. This approach to consensus building is arguably an efficient, businesslike way to enact legislation, but it also serves to discourage the free and open debate so important to the democratic process.

Recent speakers have also discouraged the taking of **record votes** during house floor debate on most bills. Many important issues are decided with **division votes**, which are taken on the computerized voting boards but leave no formal record once the boards are cleared. This approach saves the taxpayers some printing costs and can give lawmakers some respite from lobby pressure. But it also serves to keep the public in the dark about significant decisions made by their elected representatives.

Often legislators have made up their minds on an issue before the matter is debated on the floor. But when they are not familiar with a bill and have no political interest in it, they may simply vote the way the sponsor votes or the way the house or senate leadership wants them to vote. Despite what tourists in the gallery may think, legislators who raise their fingers above their heads when a vote is taken are not asking the presiding officer for a rest break. They are signaling the way they are voting and encouraging other lawmakers to vote the same way. One finger means yes; two fingers mean no.

When record votes are taken, house rules prohibit members from punching the voting buttons on other members' desks, but the practice occurs regularly. Sometimes members instruct a deskmate or another legislator to cast a specific vote for them if they expect to be off the floor when the vote is called for. Other legislators make a habit of punching the voting buttons at all the empty desks within reach. This practice is normally challenged only in cases of close votes, when members of the losing side request a roll-call verification of the computerized vote and the votes of members who do not answer the roll call are struck. The house was embarrassed in 1991 when a dead lawmaker was recorded as answering the daily roll call and voting on several record votes. The legislator had died in his Austin apartment, but his body was not discovered until several hours later. Meanwhile, colleagues had been pushing his voting button. This practice is not a problem in the senate, where the secretary of the senate calls the roll on record votes.

Partly because of the rules under which the legislature operates, partly because of the heavy volume of legislation, and partly because of political maneuvering, the closing weeks of a regular session are hectic. Legislators in both houses are asked

calendar Agenda or the list of bills to be considered by the house or the senate on a given day.

record vote Vote taken in the house or the senate of which a permanent record is kept, listing how individual legislators voted.

division votes Votes taken on the computerized voting boards in the Texas house but erased without being permanently recorded.

to vote on dozens of conference committee reports they do not have time to read. With hundreds of bills being rushed through the legislature to the governor's desk, mistakes occur. And deliberate attempts are made—often successfully—to slip major changes in law amid the confusion.

Three days before the 1991 regular session ended, the house without debate unanimously approved senate amendments to a routine liquor regulation bill that the house had approved earlier in the session. Only after the bill was already on its way to Governor Ann Richards did most house members learn that the senate changes provided numerous favors for the alcoholic beverage industry and included a particularly controversial provision to allow the sale of alcohol at Texas Stadium in Irving, home of the Dallas Cowboys football team. The latter provision would have superseded an Irving city ordinance. The house bill had been expanded from its original two pages to seventeen pages by liquor and beer lobbyists, and the Texas Stadium provision had been prepared by an attorney for the Cowboys and sponsored by Senator Bob Glasgow of Stephenville. Glasgow said he had been unaware of the dispute over the sale of alcohol at Texas Stadium, and he criticized Irving officials and their legislators and lobbyists for sleeping on the job.[12] But Senator John Leedom of Dallas complained that the maneuver reflected poorly on the senate, and he criticized beer and liquor lobbyists for their role. "It made us appear that we might not know what we're doing and that we were doing things in a sly way," Leedom said in a speech on the senate floor.[13] Governor Richards later vetoed the bill. But for every surprise bill or special-interest amendment that is caught, dozens slip through and become law. The rules reforms adopted by the house in 1993 only partially addressed the problem.

THE EMERGING PARTY SYSTEM

Unlike the U.S. Congress, the Texas legislature is not organized along party lines, with rules that automatically give leadership positions to members of the majority party. The arrangement in Texas is due primarily to the absence of Republican legislators for many years, and the more recent practice of rural Democrats aligning themselves with Republicans to produce a conservative coalition. As recently as 1971, the year before a federal court declared urban, countywide house districts unconstitutional, there were only ten Republicans in the house and two in the senate. As Republicans increased their numbers, they aligned themselves with conservative Democrats to control the policy-setting process, particularly in the house. This ideological coalition became increasingly important as single-member districts boosted not only the number of Republican lawmakers but also the number of moderate and liberal Democratic legislators elected from urban areas. It became a means of maintaining some legislative control for conservative Democrats as the base of power shifted in their own party.

Republicans and conservative Democrats formally organized the Texas Conservative Coalition in the house in the 1980s. The coalition remained a strong force in the 1990s, chaired for several years by Representative Warren Chisum of Pampa, who switched from the Democratic to the Republican Party in 1995. Chisum's mastery of the rules blocked many pieces of legislation on technicalities. One of the coalition's most publicized victories occurred in 1993, when it forced sponsors of a bill overhauling the state's Penal Code to retain a controversial, never-enforced ban on sodomy that had become a strong political statement for house conservatives.

On occasion, liberal Democrats and conservative Republicans have formed "unholy alliances," but these coalitions were usually short-lived. During the controversy over the Sharpstown stock fraud scandal in 1971, liberal Democrats and Republicans formed a loose coalition called "the Dirty Thirty" that continually harassed Speaker Gus Mutscher, who not only was a key figure in the scandal but also epitomized the rural conservative Democratic tradition of the statehouse.

The Growth of Partisanship With the growth of the Republican Party in Texas, it was inevitable that partisan differences would have increasing impact on the legislature. Bill Clayton, a conservative rural Democrat who was speaker during the 1981 redistricting session, was accused by many Democrats of having been excessively helpful to the Republicans in the creation of house districts where Republicans could be elected. As speaker, Clayton's base of power included Republicans, and after he retired from the legislature, he became a Republican.

Speaker Gib Lewis, a conservative urban Democrat, continued the tradition of appointing Republicans to major committee chairs. But partisan divisions increased in 1987 when Lewis, Democratic Lieutenant Governor Bill Hobby, and Republican Governor Bill Clements fought over a new state budget in the face of a huge revenue shortfall. On one side of the debate were moderate and liberal Democratic legislators, including inner-city and South Texas minorities whose constituents had the most to gain from a tax increase and the most to lose from deep cuts in spending on human services and educational programs. On the other side were a handful of conservative, primarily rural Democrats and Republicans with middle- and upper-middle-class suburban constituents who insisted on fiscal restraint. Clements eventually gave in and supported a tax increase, but most of the house Republicans continued to fight the measure until it was approved in a summer special session.

During the 1995 legislative session, when Democrats still held a majority of legislative seats, Lieutenant Governor Bob Bullock and Speaker Pete Laney, both Democrats, were strongly supportive of Republican Governor George W. Bush's legislative priorities. All three leaders cooperated in making major changes in public education and juvenile justice and setting limits on civil liability lawsuits.

After many bitterly contested legislative races, Republicans won their first majority of the senate in modern times during the 1996 elections and gained four seats in the house to narrow the Democratic majority in that body to 82 to 68. Nonpartisanship, however, still prevailed for the most part in the 1997 session. The senate, which had a 17 to 14 Republican majority, slammed the door on an attempt by Republican Governor George W. Bush to trade higher state taxes for major cuts in local school taxes, but opposition came from Democratic as well as Republican senators. Special interests who didn't want to pay the higher state taxes were a more significant factor than partisanship in the death of the tax bill. The house had approved the tax tradeoff, with Bush persuading many Republicans in the house to vote for the measure.

But there were some bitter fights with strong partisan overtones during the 1997 session over emotionally charged proposals strongly backed by social conservatives, a growing faction among Republican legislators. Those lawmakers fought hard, but unsuccessfully, for a bill that would have required parents to be notified before their minor daughters could receive abortions, a measure that would have prohibited recognition of gay marriages in Texas, and a proposal to allow some students to pay for tuition at private schools with state-backed vouchers.

State Senator Bill Ratliff (left) of Mount Pleasant, a key Republican member of the legislature, confers with state Representative Paul Sadler, a Democrat from Henderson, on education reform.

Now that Texas is a two-party state, partisanship will remain part of the legislative process. Before long, the legislature may even organize itself along the same partisan lines as the U.S. Congress—with distinct party positions, such as floor leaders, caucus leaders, and whips. If this were to happen, the legislative rules and powers of the presiding officers discussed earlier in this chapter would be significantly changed. But this development will depend on how fast Republican strength in the statehouse continues to grow and on the future leadership personalities that emerge in both parties. Another factor will be how well the two factions in the Republican Party—the traditional fiscal conservatives and the social conservatives—are able to accommodate each other's interests.

Republican Contenders   In 1989 Republicans formed their first **caucus** in the house, prompting speculation that they were preparing for an eventual partisan organization when they gained a majority of seats. Representative Tom Craddick of Midland, the Republican Caucus chair, dismissed such suggestions. But Democratic caucuses in the house and the senate are also taking on more importance and playing key roles in marshaling legislative support on selected issues.

Responding to stepped-up, well-financed Republican challenges of Democratic incumbents in the 1980s, both house and senate Democratic caucuses formed political action committees to raise campaign funds for Democratic legislators and legislative candidates. The Associated Republicans of Texas, which operates independently of the Texas Republican Party, has raised large sums of money for Republican legislative candidates, as have a number of national Republican organizations.

After dramatic gains in the 1992 and 1994 elections, Republicans held 14 of the 31 senate seats in 1995. The GOP gained another senate seat in the 1996 general election and—following the resignations of two Democratic senators—won two more seats in special elections to gain its first senate majority since Reconstruction. (Democratic Senator John Montford of Lubbock had resigned to become chancellor of the Texas Tech University System, and Democratic Senator Jim Turner of Crockett had quit after winning election to the U.S. Congress.)

The new Republican majority made no major changes in the senate rules for the 1997 session, leaving Democratic Lieutenant Governor Bob Bullock's strong powers over the legislative process intact. Bullock gave Republicans one new committee chairmanship and two additional seats on the budget-writing senate Finance Committee. But Democrats continued to chair most senate committees and had a 7 to 6 edge on the finance panel. Bullock appointed a Republican, Senator Bill Ratliff of Mount Pleasant, to chair the Finance Committee.

No candidate had the two-thirds support of the Republican Caucus necessary for a formal endorsement in the 1993 house speaker's race, but Democrat Pete Laney, the victor, was backed by a number of Republican house members and continued the practice of rewarding Republicans with leadership positions. That relationship was strained during the 1996 election, when some Republican groups recruited a Republican opponent against Laney in his West Texas district. Many Republican house members, however, supported the speaker against his long-shot challenger, and Laney easily won reelection. He appointed Republicans to chair 13 of the house's 37 committees in 1997.

When they gain a majority of house seats, Republicans are expected to try to elect one of their own as speaker. How a Republican speaker chooses committee chairs or views the house rules would be another key test in the development of a two-party system in the Texas legislature. Republicans made another strong push

caucus Group of legislators who band together for common political or partisan goals or along ethnic or geographic lines.

to gain a majority of house seats in the 1998 elections, but they fell short of winning their first house majority since Reconstruction.

OTHER LEGISLATIVE CAUCUSES

Hispanic and African American house members formed their own caucuses as their numbers began to increase in the 1970s in the wake of redistricting and the creation of urban single-member districts. Their cohesive **blocs** of votes have proved influential in speaker elections and the resolution of major statewide issues, such as health care for the poor, public school finance, and taxation. Their ability to broker votes has won them assignments as committee chairs and other concessions they may not otherwise have received. The Mexican American Legislative Caucus in the Texas house was chaired by Representative Hugo Berlanga, a Democrat from Corpus Christi, in 1997. The senate Hispanic Caucus was chaired by Senator Gregory Luna, a Democrat from San Antonio. Representative Al Edwards, a Democrat from Houston, chaired the Black Caucus in the house.

Some urban delegations, such as the group of legislators representing Harris County, the state's most populous county, have formed their own caucuses to discuss and seek consensus on issues of local importance. In Harris County's case, consensus is often difficult to achieve on local controversies because of the political, ethnic, and urban/suburban diversity within the delegation. Twenty-five house members—one-sixth of the body's membership—represented various parts of Houston and Harris County in 1997, and seven senators had districts that were within or included part of the county.

LEGISLATORS AND THEIR CONSTITUENTS

Although representative government is an essential component of American society, there are continued debates as to how people elected to public office should identify the interests and preferences of the people they represent.[14] Political theorists as well as legislators struggle with the problem of translating the will of the people into public policy. Most legislators represent diverse groups and interests in their districts. During a normal legislative session, there are thousands of proposed laws to consider, and legislators must constantly make decisions that may benefit or harm specific constituents.

Except for an occasional emotional issue—such as whether seat belts should be mandatory or private citizens should be allowed to carry pistols—many Texans pay little attention to what the legislature is doing. That is why they are often surprised to discover they have to pay a few extra dollars to register their cars or to learn that the fee for camping in a state park has suddenly increased. Very few Texans can identify their state representatives or senators by name, and far fewer can say what their legislators have voted for or against. This public inattention gives legislators great latitude when voting on public policies. It is also a major reason why most incumbent lawmakers who seek reelection are successful. Most legislative turnover is the result of voluntary retirements, not voter retribution.

Media coverage of the legislature is uneven. The large daily newspapers with reporters in Austin make commendable efforts to cover the major legislative issues

bloc Group of legislators who act together for a common goal regardless of party affiliation.

What Do You Think?

Isn't Something Missing?

The Texas legislature went on line in 1997 with its own official Web site at www.capitol.state.tx.us/ Voters could use their computers to learn about their state representatives and senators, read full texts and analyses of bills, check committee schedules, and even peruse the daily menus in the capitol dining room. In short, the Web site provided a wealth of information about the legislature and the state capitol.

One key ingredient, however, was missing. Records of how individual legislators voted on bills in committee or on the house and senate floor weren't available on the Internet, an omission that annoyed some Internet users. "There's no way the people can have a voice if they don't know how their representatives vote," one complained.

Record votes are listed in house and senate journals, which are distributed to public libraries, and are monitored by numerous special-interest and public-interest groups. But, with the growing use of computers, some people suspected that legislative leaders didn't want to make it any easier for political opponents to check up on lawmakers.

House Speaker Pete Laney said the legislative journals—with their recorded votes—would probably be put on the Internet eventually. "I think that all of these things will evolve," he said.

Source: Houston Chronicle, February 5, 1997.

and players and provide both spot news accounts and in-depth interpretation of the legislature's actions. All too frequently, however, such reports are limited by insufficient space and rarely include individual voting records or attempt to evaluate the performances of legislators from their readership areas. Most television and radio news shows provide only cursory legislative coverage.

Although legislators are aware of latent public opinion, they tend to be more responsive to the interest groups, or attentive publics, that operate in their individual districts or statewide.[15] People who are well informed and attentive to public policy issues are a relatively small portion of the total population, but they can be mobilized for or against an individual legislator. In some instances, they are community opinion leaders who, directly or indirectly, can communicate to other individuals information about a legislator's performance. Or they may belong to public-interest and special-interest groups that compile legislative voting records on selected issues of importance to their memberships. Although these records are only sporadically disseminated by the news media to the general public, they are mailed to the sponsoring groups' members. (See *What Do You Think?* "Isn't Something Missing?")

Many special-interest groups contribute thousands of dollars to a legislator's reelection campaign or to the campaign of an opponent. But politically astute legislators duly take note of all the letters, phone calls, e-mail messages, petitions, and visits by their constituents—plus media coverage—lest they lose touch with a significant number of voters with different views on the issues and become politically vulnerable.

A favorite voter-contact tool of many legislators is an occasional newsletter, which they mail to households in their districts at state expense. These mailings usually include photos of the lawmaker plus articles summarizing, in the best possible light, his or her accomplishments in Austin. Sometimes legislators also include a public opinion survey seeking constituent responses on a number of issues.

LEGISLATIVE DECISION MAKING

In addition to the formal rules of each legislative body, unwritten rules, or norms, shape the behavior of legislators and other actors in the lawmaking process. The legislature is like most other social institutions in that its members have perceptions of the institution and the process as well as the way they are expected to behave or carry out their responsibilities. Other participants also impose their views and expectations on lawmakers.[16]

The legislative process is designed to institutionalize conflict, and the rules and norms of the legislature are designed to give this conflict an element of civility. Debate is often intense and vigorous, and it may be difficult for some lawmakers to separate attacks on their positions from attacks on their personalities. But most legislators have learned the necessity of decorum and courtesy. Even if lawmakers believe some of their opponents in the house and senate are deceitful, personal attacks on other legislators are generally considered unacceptable. Personal attacks, even to the point of fistfights, occasionally occur, but they are rare.

With about 5,700 pieces of legislation introduced during a regular session—the level reached in 1997—no legislator could possibly read and understand each bill, much less the hundreds of amendments offered during floor debate. And although there are moments of high drama when issues of major statewide importance are being debated, most of the legislative workload is tedious and dull and produces little direct political benefit for most senators and representatives. But many of those bills contain hidden traps and potential controversies that can haunt a legislator later, often during a reelection campaign. So legislators use numerous information sources and rely on the norms of the process to assist them in decision making.

To make the process work, legislators must accommodate the competing interests they represent and achieve considerable reciprocity among themselves. An individual legislator usually has no direct political or personal interest in most bills because much legislation is local in nature and affects only a limited number of lawmakers and constituents. A legislator accumulates obligations as he or she supports another lawmaker's bill, with the full expectation that the action will be returned in kind.

A number of factors, however, help shape lawmakers' decisions on major legislation.[17] The wishes of constituents will be considered, particularly if there is a groundswell of opinion coming from a legislator's district. Legislators also exchange information with other lawmakers, particularly with members of the same caucus, those who share the same political philosophy, and colleagues from the same counties or regions of the state. Lawmakers often take their cues from bill sponsors or the speaker's and lieutenant governor's leadership teams. As the political parties develop more formal legislative structures, identifiable patterns of giving and taking cues are likely to emerge along party lines. That process is to some extent already under way, particularly on budgetary, taxation, and redistricting issues.

A legislator's staff also assists in the decision-making process, not only by evaluating the substantive merits of legislation but also by assessing the political implications of a lawmaker's decisions. The Legislative Budget Board and the Legislative Council provide technical information and expertise that can also be weighed by legislators.

Former Governor Ann Richards testifying before a legislative committee.

Interest groups are major sources of information and influence. Although an individual legislator will occasionally rail against a specific group, most lawmakers consider interest groups absolutely essential to the legislative process. Through their lobbyists, interest groups provide a vast amount of technical information and can signal the level of constituency interest, support, or opposition to proposed laws. A senator or representative can use interest groups to establish coalitions of support for a bill, and some legislators become closely identified with powerful interest groups because they almost always support a particular lobby's position.

The governor can also influence the legislature in several ways. He or she can raise the public's consciousness of an issue and can promote solutions through speeches and media appearances. The governor can communicate indirectly to individual lawmakers through the governor's staff, party leaders, and influential persons in a lawmaker's district. The governor can also personally appeal to lawmakers, in meetings one on one or with groups of legislators. At the beginning of each regular session, the governor outlines his or her legislative priorities in a State of the State Address to a joint session of the house and the senate, and the governor usually has frequent meetings with the lieutenant governor and the speaker throughout a session.

The governor may also visit the house or senate chamber in a personal show of support when legislation that he or she strongly advocates is being debated. Unlike most recent governors, Governor Ann Richards personally testified before legislative committees on several of her priorities, including ethics reform and government reorganization, during her first year in office. The intensity of a governor's arm twisting is often in the eye of the beholder, but it can include appeals to a lawmaker's reason or conscience, threats of retaliation, appeals for party support, and promises of a quid pro quo. The greatest threat that a governor can make is the possible veto of legislation or budget items of importance to a lawmaker. In special sessions, the governor can also negotiate with a lawmaker over whether to add a bill that is important to the legislator to the special session's agenda, which is controlled by the governor.

Legislators obtain information and support from other elected statewide officeholders, including the attorney general, the comptroller, and the land commissioner. These officials and lawmakers can assist each other in achieving political agendas.

The news media provide information and perspective on issues in broader political terms. In part, the policy agenda is established by those issues the media perceive to be important.

The relative importance of any groups or individuals on decision making is difficult to measure and varies from lawmaker to lawmaker and from issue to issue. Outside influences can also be tempered by a legislator's own attitude and opinion. On many issues, legislators are subject to competing advice and pressure. As much as a lawmaker might like to be all things to all people, that cannot be. She cannot please a chemical lobbyist, who is seeking a tax break for a new plant on the Gulf coast and also happens to be a large campaign contributor, and environmentalists, who fear the facility would spoil a nearby wildlife habitat. He cannot please the governor, who is promoting a lottery as a new state revenue source, and most of the voters in his district, who have consistently voted against gambling. The ultimate decision and its eventual political consequences are the legislator's.

Up Close

Legislative Reputations: Not All the Same

Some legislators become known for their commitment to producing good legislation. They spend endless hours developing programs and are repeatedly turned to by presiding officers to handle tough policy issues. Other lawmakers tend to look to their leadership for direction and cues, giving them considerable influence and power. And they are also essential to a productive legislative session.

Still other legislators earn reputations as grandstanders. Almost every legislator has shown off for the media or the spectators in the gallery at one time or another, but a number have developed a distinct reputation for this style of behavior. They appear to be more interested in scoring political points with their constituents or interest groups—with the objective of being reelected or seeking higher office—than with mastering the substance of legislation. Many of these lawmakers are lightweights who contribute little to the legislature's product. And although they may introduce many bills during a session, they may not be interested in the details of the lawmaking process and may find themselves unable to influence other legislators to support their legislation.

The legislature also has a number of opportunists, including members who pursue issues to produce personal or political benefits for themselves. They may sponsor legislation or take a position on an issue to curry favor with a special-interest group or benefit their personal businesses or professions. Legislative rules prohibit legislators from voting on issues in which they have a personal monetary interest, but individual lawmakers can interpret that prohibition as they see fit. Many lawmakers try to cash in on their legislative experience by becoming lobbyists after they leave office at considerably higher pay than they received as legislators.

Still other legislators appear to be little more than spectators. They enjoy the receptions and other perks of the office much more than the drudgery of the committee hearings, research, and floor debates. Some quickly become weary of the legislative process and, after a few sessions, decide against seeking reelection.*

---

*These legislative styles are similar to those developed by James David Barber, *The Lawmakers* (New Haven, Conn.: Yale University Press, 1965), Chapters 2 through 5.

Should lawmakers cast particular votes on the basis of the specific concerns of their districts, their personal convictions, the position of their political party, or the wishes of the special-interest groups that helped fund their campaigns? These issues reflect complex relationships between the legislator and the people represented. And because the overriding consideration for many lawmakers is reelection, the legislator must balance such factors carefully (see *Up Close:* "Legislative Reputations: Not All the Same").

THE DEVELOPMENT OF LEGISLATIVE STAFF

The quality of a legislator's staff can help determine his or her success, and both the quality and quantity of legislative staffs have been significantly enhanced since the early 1970s.[18] This growth reflects an emerging professional approach to lawmaking in an increasingly complex urban state. During recent regular sessions, the house has had about 900 employees, including part-time workers, and the Senate about 800. These figures include capitol and district office staff for individual senators and representatives, committee staffs, assistants to the lieutenant governor and the speaker, and other support staff hired directly by the house and the senate.

State Senator Ken Armbrister of Victoria talking with staff.

Additionally, there are permanent staff members assigned to the Legislative Budget Board, the legislature's financial research arm; the Legislative Council, which researches issues and drafts bills and resolutions for introduction by legislators; and the Legislative Reference Library, which provides resource materials for lawmakers, their staffs, and the general public. Other support staff are assigned to the Sunset Advisory Commission, which assists the legislature in periodic reviews of state agencies, and the state auditor, who is chosen by and reports to the legislative leadership.

Legislative staff range from part-time secretaries and clerks to lawyers and professionals who draft bills and direct research that results in major state laws. There are limits on the number of staff members and funds allocated for legislators' personal staffs. As a general rule, senators have more personal staff than house members. Staffing levels are usually reduced between sessions, and some members shut down their capitol offices entirely. Most lawmakers, however, maintain offices both in Austin and in their districts, even if such staffs sometimes only answer the phone.

A key support group in the house is the House Research Organization, which was organized as the House Study Group in the 1970s by a handful of primarily liberal lawmakers. The group's name was later changed, and its structure was reorganized to represent the entire house, but it still fills a strong research role. It is supported by funds from the house budget and is governed by a steering committee that represents a cross section of Democratic and Republican house members. During legislative sessions, its staff provides detailed analyses, including pro and con arguments, of many bills on the daily house calendar. During interim periods, it provides periodic analyses of proposed constitutional amendments and other issues. The senate formed a similar organization, the Senate Research Center, in 1991.

The quality of other resources available to lawmakers has also improved in recent years. Legislators and staff can routinely check the status of bills on computer terminals in their offices or at their desks in the house and senate chambers. Students, interest groups, and the public can also access this data through the Legislative Reference Library. In 1997 the Legislative Council established a Web site that includes committee schedules, bill texts and analyses, and other legislative information. Its address is www.capitol.state.tx.us/

LEGISLATIVE ETHICS AND REFORMS

The vast majority of legislators are honest, hard-working individuals. But the weaknesses of a few and the millions of dollars spent by special interests to influence the lawmaking process undermine Texans' confidence in their legislature and their entire state government. Although legislators cannot pass laws guaranteeing ethical behavior, they can set strong standards for themselves, other public officials, and lobbyists; and they can institute stiff penalties for those who fail to comply. Such reform efforts are periodically attempted, but, unfortunately, they usually issue from scandals and fall short of creating an ideal ethical climate.

Fallout from the Sharpstown stock scandal helped an outsider, Uvalde rancher Dolph Briscoe, win the 1972 gubernatorial race and also helped produce a large turnover in legislative elections (see *Up Close:* "The Sharpstown Stock Fraud Scandal"). In 1973 the legislature responded with a series of ethics reform laws, includ-

Up Close

The Sharpstown Stock Fraud Scandal

The Sharpstown stock fraud scandal rocked the state capitol in 1971 and 1972 and helped produce some far-reaching legislative and political changes. The scandal involved banking legislation sought by Houston banker-developer Frank Sharp and approved by the legislature in a special session in 1969, only to be vetoed by Governor Preston Smith. A lawsuit filed by the federal Securities and Exchange Commission broke the news that Smith, Speaker Gus Mutscher, Representative Tommy Shannon of Fort Worth (who had sponsored the bills), and other individuals had profited from stock deals involving Sharp's National Bankers Life Insurance Company. Much of their stock was purchased with unsecured loans from Sharp's Sharpstown State Bank. Mutscher, Shannon, and an aide to the speaker were later convicted of conspiracy to accept bribes. Mutscher, who had consolidated power in the house and was often regarded as iron-handed and arbitrary, was forced to resign. Later the house moved to limit the speaker's power through a modified seniority system for committee appointments. Subsequent speakers still exercised a great deal of power, but it was checked by expectations that the speaker would be more responsive to the membership. The media also started giving greater scrutiny and coverage to the activities of the speaker.

Source: Richard Morehead, *50 Years in Texas Politics* (Burnet, Tex.: Eakin Press, 1982), pp. 236–37.

---

ing requirements that lobbyists register with the secretary of state and report their expenditures. State officials were required to file public reports identifying their sources of income, although not specific amounts.

Weaknesses in those laws, however, were vividly demonstrated in 1989, when East Texas poultry producer Lonnie "Bo" Pilgrim distributed $10,000 checks to several senators in the capitol while lobbying them on workers' compensation reform, and the Travis County district attorney could find no law under which to prosecute him. There also were published reports that lobbyists had spent nearly $2 million entertaining lawmakers during the 1989 regular session without having to specify which legislators received the "freebies," thanks to a large loophole in the lobby registration law. The revelations—including frequent news stories about lobbyists treating lawmakers to golf tournaments, ski trips, a junket to Las Vegas for a boxing match, and limousine service to a Cher concert—created an uproar.

Some senators had angrily rejected Pilgrim's checks on the spot, and others returned them after the media pounced on the story. But the very next year, Pilgrim—a longtime political contributor—again contributed thousands of dollars to several statewide officeholders and candidates. This time the checks were not offered under the capitol dome but were sent through the mail, and they were gratefully accepted. Only one officeholder, who was passed over by Pilgrim in favor of his opponent, tried to make a campaign issue of the new contributions.

Despite all the headlines over ethical problems, legislative turnover was minimal in 1990. But in early December, about a month after the general election, a Travis County grand jury began investigating Speaker Gib Lewis's ties to a San Antonio law firm, Heard Goggan Blair and Williams. The firm had made large profits collecting delinquent taxes for local governments throughout Texas

Politics in Cyberspace

The Texas Legislature

The Texas Legislature enacts more than 1,000 bills in each legislative session, and many of these laws will have a direct impact on individuals and communities. Surveys of Texans indicate that very few know who their legislators are or what positions they have taken on public policy. In the past, information about the Texas Legislature was difficult to obtain, but now several sources make it possible to follow the actions of the legislature.

Texas Senate
http://www.senate.state.tx.us

This site provides biographical information, committee assignments, district data, and addresses for each member of the senate.

Texas House of Representatives
http://www.house.state.tx.us

This site provides direct access to live broadcasts of legislative proceedings, information pertaining to the legislative process in the house, information from the speaker's office, and general information about the capitol complex. It also provides biographical information, committee assignments, district data, and addresses for each member of the house.

Texas Legislative Council
http://www.tlc.state.tx.us

The Texas Legislative Council (TLC) is a state agency within the legislative branch. The TLC drafts bills and other legislative documents, conducts legal and public policy research, and produces informational publications for the senate and house of representatives.

Texas Legislature On-Line (TLOL)
http://www.capitol.state.tx.us

In addition to providing links to other legislative Web sites, such as the house, senate, Legislative Budget Board, state auditor, and the Sunset Commission, TLOL provides legislative histories, and access to bills, amendments, and statutes affected by proposed legislation.

under a law that allowed it to collect an extra 15 percent from the taxpayers as its fee. For several years, it had successfully defeated legislation that would have hurt its business. The *Fort Worth Star-Telegram* reported that Heard Goggan had paid about half of a $10,000 tax bill owed to Tarrant County by a business that Lewis partly owned.[19] And the *Houston Chronicle* reported that the grand jury was also looking into a trip Lewis had taken to a Mexican resort during the 1987 legislative session with four Heard Goggan partners and a lobbyist (all males) and six women (including a waitress from a topless nightclub in Houston).[20] The trip had been taken while a bill opposed by Heard Goggan was dying in a house committee.

On December 28, only twelve days before the 1991 regular legislative session was to convene and Lewis was to be reelected to a record fifth term as the house's presiding officer, grand jurors indicted him on two misdemeanor ethics charges. He was accused of soliciting, accepting, and failing to report an illegal gift from Heard Goggan—the partial payment of the tax bill. Lewis insisted he was innocent and vowed to fight the charges. He said the tax payment was the settlement of a legal dispute, and he angrily accused Travis County District Attorney Ronnie Earle, who headed the prosecution and had been publicly advocating stronger ethics laws, of using the grand jury to "influence the speaker's election." Lewis said that Earle was guilty of "unethical and reprehensible behavior."[21]

Lewis won a postponement of his trial under a law that automatically grants continuances to legislators when they are in session. The grand jury investigation, which prosecutors said would include other legislators or former legislators, continued for several more weeks, but no further indictments were issued.

Meanwhile, attention was focused on an ethics reform bill. Governor Ann Richards, who had campaigned for reform, testified before house and senate committees for tougher ethical requirements for state officials and lobbyists. The senate approved an ethics bill fairly early in the session, but the house did not act on its version of the bill until late in the session. The final bill was produced by a conference committee on the last night of the regular session in a private meeting and was approved by the house and the senate only a few minutes before the legislature adjourned at midnight. There was no time to print and distribute copies, and very few legislators knew for sure what was in the bill.

These events and the bill itself left a bad taste all around. Despite complaints that the measure was not strong enough and the controversy over the secretive way in which the final compromise had been written, Richards signed the bill. But she did so in the privacy of her office, not in the public ceremony that governors usually hold for their priority pieces of legislation. Ronnie Earle, the Travis County district attorney, was among those displeased with the legislation, but Richards called the new law a "very strong step in the direction of openness and ethics reform in this state."[22]

The new law required additional reporting of lobby expenditures and conflicts of interest between lobbyists and state officials, prohibited special interests from treating legislators to pleasure trips, prohibited lawmakers from accepting fees for speaking before special-interest groups, and created a new state Ethics Commission to review complaints about public officials.

But the measure did not put any limits on financial contributions to political campaigns, nor did it prohibit legislator-attorneys from representing clients before state agencies for pay. Moreover, it authorized the Ethics Commission to slap a bigger fine ($10,000) on someone who filed a frivolous complaint against a public official than the maximum fine ($5,000) that could be levied on an officeholder for violating the ethics law. That latter provision was viewed by many critics as an unreasonable effort to discourage citizen complaints. The new law also mandated that complaints filed with the Ethics Commission remain confidential unless the commission took action, a provision that would allow the commission to dismiss or sit on legitimate complaints without any public accounting.

In January 1992 Lewis announced that he would not seek reelection to another term in the house. In a plea bargain later the same month, prosecutors dropped the two ethics indictments against him in return for the speaker's "no contest" plea to two minor, unrelated charges. Lewis paid a $2,000 fine for failing to disclose publicly a business holding in 1988 and 1989, for which he had already paid a minor civil penalty to the secretary of state.

Lewis's decision to retire set off the first speaker's race in the house since 1975, and many house members, including most of the first-term legislators, used the campaign to bargain for reforms in the way the house conducted its business. As noted earlier, some of those reforms were adopted in 1993 with the support of the new speaker, Pete Laney, who, ironically, had been a longtime member of Lewis's team. The first-term legislators, in particular, had complained in 1991 that the house rules had been used to create an undemocratic process which catered to special interests and favored an inner circle of legislators close to the speaker.

SUMMARY NOTES

- Texas, the nation's second most populous state, has a part-time legislature that operates under detailed antigovernment restrictions drafted by nineteenth-century Texans in the wake of the repressive Reconstruction era. It is a lawmaking body that is not structured to respond readily to pressing late-twentieth-century needs and crises. Emergencies often require special legislative sessions and increase financial and personal pressures on lawmakers, who are among the lowest paid state legislators in the country. Legislative turnover in Texas is moderate.

- As recently as 1971, there was only a handful of African Americans, Hispanics, Republicans, and women in the 150-member house of representatives and the 31-member senate. But political realignment and federal court intervention in redistricting—particularly the ordering of single-member house districts for urban counties in 1972—have significantly increased the number of women, ethnic minorities, and Republicans in the legislature.

- Unlike the U.S. Congress, the Texas legislature is not organized along party lines and has only the tentative beginnings of an institutionalized leadership structure. The presiding officer of the house is the speaker, elected by the other house members. The presiding officer of the senate is the lieutenant governor, elected by the voters statewide.

- The most significant powers of the speaker and the lieutenant governor are the appointment of house and senate committees, which screen and draft legislation, and the assignment of bills to committees. The fate of most legislation is decided at the committee level. Although most house committees are partially appointed on the basis of seniority, the lieutenant governor has absolute control over the composition of senate committees. The presiding officers also play key roles in the development of major legislative proposals and, to a great extent, depend on their handpicked committee chairs to sell their legislative programs to house and senate colleagues.

- Traditionally, the powers of the presiding officers have been enhanced by the Calendars Committee in the house and the two-thirds rule in the senate. The Calendars Committee, composed entirely of speaker appointees, sets the schedule for floor debate in the house. The two-thirds rule provides that two-thirds of the senate must approve before any bill can be debated on the floor of that body. That means eleven senators can block, or kill, any piece of legislation which has majority support. The lieutenant governor decides which senate sponsors are recognized for consideration of specific bills.

- To be sent to the governor for signature into law, a bill must be approved after three readings in both the house and the senate. Referral to committee is first reading, which is as far as most bills progress. Many are never scheduled for a public hearing by the chairs of the committees to which they are assigned. Many others die in subcommittees to which they are sent after being heard by the full committee. And others do not survive the Calendars Committee in the house or the two-thirds rule in the senate. Those that do win committee approval are often amended, or changed.

- For those bills that survive the committee process, second reading is a crucial step. That is where most floor debate on legislation occurs and where many bills are further amended. If a bill is approved on second reading, it advances to third reading and then to the other legislative chamber, where it is referred to a committee and has to repeat the process.

- A bill must be approved in exactly the same form by both chambers. If the senate, for example, approves a house bill after making some changes in it, the house will have to concur in—or accept—the senate version, or a conference committee of house and senate members will have to be appointed to try to work out a compromise.

- The governor can sign a bill, veto it, or let it become law without his or her signature. The governor can use the line-item veto to delete specific spending provisions from the general appropriations bill, or state budget. All other bills must be accepted or rejected in their entirety.

- Tax bills must originate in the house. All other bills can originate in either chamber.

- The legislative rules and heavy volume of bills considered frequently allow lawmakers to sneak major controversial proposals into law by adding little noticed amendments to other bills.

- The growth of Republican strength has increased partisan activity in the legislature and fueled speculation that, sooner or later, attempts may be made to organize the legislature along the partisan lines of the U.S. Congress. Both major parties already have active legislative caucuses.

- Legislators' decisions are influenced by a number of factors, including constituents, interest groups, colleagues, staff, the governor, and the media.

- Legislators have increasingly come to rely on their staffs to develop legislation, perform constituent services, and act as liaisons to interest groups.

- Although most legislators are honest, hardworking individuals, the weaknesses of a few and the millions of dollars spent by special interests to influence the lawmaking process have undermined Texans' confidence in state government. Lawmakers make periodic efforts to strengthen their ethical standards, but usually only after well-publicized scandals.

SELECTED READINGS

ANDERSON, ARTHUR J. "Texas Legislative Redistricting: Proposed Constitutional and Statutory Amendments for an Improved Process." *Southwestern Law Journal* 43 (October 1989): 719–57.

BICKERSTAFF, STEVE. "State Legislative and Congressional Reapportionment in Texas: A Historical Perspective." *Public Affairs Comment* 37 (Winter 1991): 1–13.

BOULARD, GARRY. "Lobbyists as Outlaws." *State Legislatures* 22 (January 1996): 20–25.

BURKA, PAUL. "Bob Bullock: The Man Who Runs Texas Politics." *Texas Monthly* (September 1994): 100, 162–63.

DEATON, CHARLES. *The Year They Threw the Rascals Out.* Austin, Tex.: Shoal Creek Press, 1973.

DUBOSE, LOUIS, and GLEN UTTER. "Formal and Informal Rules Regulating Public Officials' Behavior." *Texas Journal of Political Studies* 10 (Fall/Winter 1988): 3–16.

EDWARDS, JULIE. "The Right to Vote and Reapportionment in the Texas Legislature." *Baylor Law Review* 41 (December 1989): 689–730.

FREEMAN, PATRICIA K. "A Comparative Analysis of Speakers' Career Patterns in U.S. State Legislatures." *Legislative Studies Quarterly* 20 (August 1995): 365–76.

HAMM, ROBERT, and ROBERT HARMEL. "Legislative Party Development and the Speaker System: The Case of the Texas House." *Journal of Politics* 55 (November 1993): 1140–51.

HERSKOWITZ, MICKEY. *Sharpstown Revisited: Frank Sharp and a Tale of Dirty Politics in Texas.* Austin: Eakin Press, 1994.

HICKOK, EUGENE W. *The Reform of State Legislatures and the Changing Character of Representation.* Boston: University Press of America, 1992.

MONCRIEF, GARY F., JOEL A. THOMPSON, and KARL T. KURTZ. "The Old Statehouse, It Ain't What It Used to Be." *Legislative Studies Quarterly* 21 (February 1996): 57–72.

MOONEY, CHRISTOPHER Z. "Citizens, Structures and Sister States: Influences on State Legislative Professionalism." *Legislative Studies Quarterly* 20 (February 1995): 47–67.

ROSENTHAL, ALAN. *Governors and Legislatures: Contending Powers.* Washington, D.C.: Congressional Quarterly Books, 1990.

TEXAS LEGISLATIVE COUNCIL. *Presiding Officers of the Texas Legislatures, 1946–1982.* Austin: Texas Legislative Council, 1982.

THORBURN, WAYNE. "The Growth of Republican Representation in the Texas Legislature: Coattails, Incumbency, Special Elections, and Urbanization." *Texas Journal of Political Studies* 11 (Spring/Summer 1989): 16–28.

ASK YOURSELF ABOUT POLITICS

1. Should the governor be Texas's most powerful officeholder?
   Yes ☐   No ☐

2. Should governors be able to appoint an attorney general and other executive officeholders of their choosing?
   Yes ☐   No ☐

3. Should governors be limited to a certain number of terms in office?
   Yes ☐   No ☐

4. Should new governors be able to fire policy makers appointed by predecessors and replace them with their own appointees?
   Yes ☐   No ☐

5. Should a nursing home owner be allowed to serve on a state board that regulates nursing homes?
   Yes ☐   No ☐

6. Are mismanagement and waste common in state agencies?
   Yes ☐   No ☐

7. Should elected officials be able to hire anyone they want regardless of the individual's job qualifications?
   Yes ☐   No ☐

CHAPTER

23

THE TEXAS EXECUTIVE AND BUREAUCRACY

CHAPTER OUTLINE

A Fragmented Government

The Structure of the Plural Executive

The Governor

Other Offices of the Executive Branch

Elected Boards and Commissions

The Texas Bureaucracy

The Growth of Government in Texas

Bureaucrats and Public Policy

Strategies for Controlling the Bureaucracy

FEATURES

People in Politics: Governor Bill Clements, On-the-Job Training

People in Politics: Governor Ann Richards, Saleswoman

Across the USA: Party Control of the Governor's Office, 1999

People in Politics: Governor George W. Bush, Consensus Builder

Up Close: What Can Happen to a Whistle-Blower?

What Do You Think? The Politics of Privatization

Politics in Cyberspace: The Texas Executive and Bureaucracy

To have the power to act on their priorities, Texas governors must sell their programs. A governor's effectiveness is largely determined by his or her ability to use informal resources to strengthen a weak office.

A FRAGMENTED GOVERNMENT

"One thing Texans have today is a state government that doesn't work very well," the state comptroller concluded after an exhaustive study of state agencies and programs. "It is time to rethink Texas government and how it provides basic services to the state's citizens."[1]

When that study was conducted in 1991, Texas had been operating under an inefficient, fragmented government for more than a century. Yet no changes in what could be considered the root of the problem—the basic governmental structure—have been made since.

805

For starters, in Texas no single elected official is ultimately responsible for the executive branch of state government—and for the quality of public services performed by thousands of state workers. Despite a public perception to the contrary, Texas has one of the weaker governors in the country (see Table 23-1). Unlike the president of the United States, the governor of Texas has no formal appointive cabinet through which to impose policy on the governmental bureaucracy. Several major state agencies are headed by independently elected officeholders who do not answer to the governor and sometimes do not even belong to the same political party. Approximately 250 other state agencies and universities are headed by boards and commissions appointed by the governor, but the governor has only indirect influence over them.

The office of governor is not without prestige and leadership opportunities. Candidates spend millions of dollars and countless hours campaigning for the job. It is the most visible state office. But it is institutionally weak, thanks to constitutional restrictions ensuring that no governor repeat the oppressive abuses of Governor Edmund J. Davis and his Reconstruction administration.[2]

Over the years, the governor's lot has improved somewhat. By constitutional amendment, voters empowered the legislature to raise the governor's salary, and the terms of office for the governor and most other statewide executive officeholders were lengthened from two to four years. In 1980 the governor was given the power, with the approval of the Texas senate, to remove board members he or she had personally appointed.[3] Nevertheless, these changes have not significantly enhanced the governor's authority. When Governor Ann Richards in 1991 tried to revive interest in giving the governor cabinet-style appointment powers over major state agencies, she had only limited success.

The governor can veto legislation and has the exclusive authority to schedule special sessions of the legislature and set their agendas. And, despite its limitations, the appointment power offers the governor an opportunity to make a strong mark on state government. The high visibility of the office also offers a ready-made public

TABLE 23-1	Institutional Powers of the Governors by State, 1994				
Strong	*Moderately Strong*		*Moderate*		*Weak*
Hawaii	Alaska	Missouri	Alabama	Mississippi	North Carolina
Iowa	Arizona	Montana	California	Nevada	South Carolina
Maryland	Arkansas	Nebraska	Colorado	New Hampshire	Vermont
New Jersey	Connecticut	New Mexico	Florida	Oklahoma	
New York	Delaware	North Dakota	Georgia	Texas	
Ohio	Illinois	Oregon	Idaho	Virginia	
Pennsylvania	Kansas	Rhode Island	Indiana	Washington	
Tennessee	Kentucky	South Dakota	Maine	Wyoming	
West Virginia	Louisiana	Utah	Massachusetts		
	Michigan	Wisconsin			
	Minnesota				

This scale was derived from scores for the governors' tenure potential, appointive powers, budgetary powers, veto powers, party control of state legislature, and the number of other statewide elected officials.

Source: Thad Beyle, "Governors: The Middlemen and Women in Our Political System," in *Politics in the American States*, 6th ed., eds. Virginia Gray and Herbert Jacob (Washington, D.C.: CQ Press, 1996), p. 237.

forum. Although the Texas Constitution limits the formal powers of the office, a governor's influence is shaped by his or her personality, political adroitness, staff appointments, and ability to define and sell an agenda that addresses broad needs and interests.

THE STRUCTURE OF
THE PLURAL EXECUTIVE

Article IV, Section 1, of the 1876 Constitution created a **plural executive branch**, which "shall consist of a Governor, who shall be the Chief Executive Officer of the State, a Lieutenant Governor, Secretary of State, Comptroller of Public Accounts, Treasurer, Commissioner of the General Land Office, and Attorney General." Elected officials added later to the executive branch were the agriculture commissioner, the three-member Railroad Commission, and the fifteen-member State Board of Education. Only the secretary of state is appointed by the governor. Members of the education board are elected from districts, and the other officeholders are elected statewide (see Figure 23-1). Article IV, Section 4, of the Texas Constitution requires most of these officials to be at least thirty years old and a resident of Texas for at least five years.

plural executive Fragmented system of authority under which most statewide executive officeholders are elected independently of the governor.

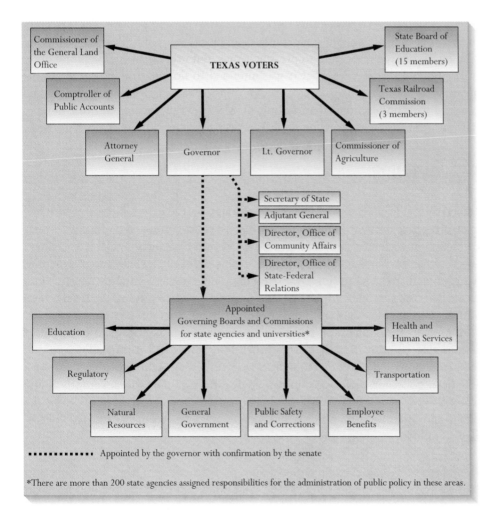

FIGURE 23-1 The Executive Branch in Texas

The executive branch in Texas is a combination of elected and appointed officials who administer more than two hundred state agencies.

Source: Comptroller of Public Accounts, *Breaking the Mold: A Report of the Texas Performance Review*, Vol. 1, p. 13.

The agencies headed by these elected officials are autonomous and, except for limited budgetary review, independent of the governor. In a confrontation with the governor over policy, agency heads can claim their own electoral mandates. For many years, there were only "scattered incidents of hostility within the executive branch," and elected officials generally "cooperated remarkably well with their chief executives"[4]—at least while Texas was a one-party Democratic state. During that period, party politics was dominated by conservatives, whose interests were generally served by state officials who believed it was in their own best political interests to cooperate with one another.

But the potential for conflict between the governor and other executive officials increased as Texas became a two-party state, and conflict is likely to become more common in the future, even among officials from the same party. During Republican Governor Bill Clements's first term (1979–83), the other elected officers in the executive branch were Democrats, including Attorney General Mark White, who frequently feuded with the governor. White jockeyed for the political advantage that allowed him to unseat Clements in 1982.

Democrat Jim Mattox also used the attorney general's office, which he held from 1983 to 1991, to prepare for a gubernatorial race. There was frequent speculation that some of his official actions were designed to increase his name identification and position himself on popular issues at the expense of both Governor White, a fellow Democrat, and Governor Clements, who returned to office in 1987.

When those holding office in a plural executive system have sharply different or competing agendas, it is difficult to develop coordinated policies. The governor, in an effort to avoid conflict, may pursue policies that are not likely to be disruptive, innovative, or responsive to pressing issues. But proponents of the plural executive contend that it does what it was intended to do: control and constrain the governor. Although collegial or collective decision making is often inefficient and can lead to deadlock, the advocates of the plural executive contend that democracy, in most instances, is to be preferred over efficiency.

THE GOVERNOR

Gubernatorial leadership styles have been as varied as the personalities that the chief executives have brought to their jobs. Some governors come to the office with well-defined policy agendas and attempt to exploit every resource available to achieve them. Other governors take a more limited view of the office. They adopt an administrative or managerial posture while leaving policy initiatives to other institutions or elected officials. Such governors tend to pursue new programs, especially those with far-reaching tax or social implications, with considerable caution.

Some governors thrive on the constant attention and political and social interactions that go with the office. They work long hours and continually engage in public relations and coalition building. Strange as it may seem, however, there have also been governors who were introverted, even shy, and who apparently found many aspects of the office distasteful. They often insulated themselves from the public and other political officials and seemed detached from the activities necessary to influence public policy.[5]

Backgrounds and Requirements for Governorship   The Texas Constitution has few requirements for a person who desires to run for governor. A gover-

Governor James E. "Pa" Ferguson was the only Texas governor to be removed from office through the impeachment process. Ferguson was impeached and convicted in 1917 during a controversy over his efforts to remove five University of Texas faculty members.

nor must be at least thirty years old, a U.S. citizen, and a resident of Texas for at least five years. There is also a vague requirement that no individual can be excluded from office for religious beliefs, "provided he acknowledges the existence of a Supreme Being" (Article I, Section 4). The constitution, however, does not spell out all the roadblocks to winning the office.

Until the election of Republican Bill Clements in 1978, every governor since 1874 had been a Democrat. Clements served two terms (1979–83 and 1987–91), and Republican George W. Bush was elected to the office in 1994, giving further evidence of the developing two-party system in Texas.

Most governors have been well-educated, middle-aged, and affluent white Protestant males. In many cases, their families were also active in public life and helped shape their careers. No minorities and only two women have been elected to the office. Miriam A. "Ma" Ferguson, whose husband, James E. "Pa" Ferguson, had earlier been governor, served two terms (1925–27 and 1933–35), and Ann Richards served one term (1991–95). By the time Richards became governor, only three women had ever been elected to any other statewide executive office in Texas. Richards, a Democrat, served two terms as state treasurer before being elected governor, and she was succeeded by Republican Kay Bailey Hutchison. From 1919 to 1923, Annie Webb Blanton was state superintendent of schools, an elective office that no longer exists.

With the rising costs of statewide political campaigns, a candidate's personal wealth or ability to raise large sums of money has taken on increased importance. Otherwise qualified individuals are dissuaded from running for governor and other offices because of the difficult burden of fund raising. Former Governor Bill Clements and fellow Republican Clayton Williams, a Midland business executive who lost the 1990 gubernatorial race to Richards, spent millions of dollars out of their own pockets on gubernatorial races that were their first bids for elective office (see *People in Politics*: "Governor Bill Clements, On-the-Job Training"). Their experience raises the possibility that personal wealth and the willingness to spend it on election campaigns will take on increased importance in future races.

Previous public service has provided gubernatorial aspirants with public recognition and ties to party leaders, interest groups, and public officials around the state. Texas governors have previously served in local and statewide offices, the legislature, and Congress. Preston Smith (1969–73) was a legislator and lieutenant governor before being elected governor. Dolph Briscoe (1973–79) also served in the legislature. Mark White (1983–87) served as secretary of state and then as attorney general. Ann Richards was a county commissioner and then state treasurer. Although he had never previously held elective office, Clements was a deputy U.S. secretary of defense prior to winning his first gubernatorial race. George W. Bush was elected governor in 1994 without any previous formal government experience. He had been an unofficial adviser to his father, former President George Bush. Table 23-2 lists the governors of Texas from 1870 to the present.

Impeachment and Incapacitation   A governor can be removed from office through **impeachment** proceedings initiated in the house of representatives and conviction by the senate in a trial on the impeachment charges. Texas is one of only a few states that have removed a governor with this procedure. In 1917 a controversy erupted over Governor James E. "Pa" Ferguson's efforts to remove five

First Lady Laura Bush applauds as her husband, Governor George W. Bush, delivers a speech. Bush was the second Republican to serve as governor of Texas in modern times.

impeachment   Procedure by which the legislature can remove a governor or certain other public officials from office for misconduct.

TABLE 23-2	Governors of Texas since 1870
Edmund J. Davis	1870–1874
Richard Coke	1874–1876
Richard B. Hubbard	1876–1879
Oran M. Roberts	1879–1883
John Ireland	1883–1887
Lawrence Sullivan Ross	1887–1891
James Stephen Hogg	1891–1895
Charles A. Culberson	1895–1899
Joseph D. Sayers	1899–1903
Samuel W.T. Lanham	1903–1907
Thomas Mitchell Campbell	1907–1911
Oscar Branch Colquitt	1911–1915
James E. Ferguson[*]	1915–1917
William Pettus Hobby	1917–1921
Pat Morris Neff	1921–1925
Miriam A. Ferguson	1925–1927
Dan Moody	1927–1931
Ross S. Sterling	1931–1933
Miriam A. Ferguson	1933–1935
James V. Allred	1935–1939
W. Lee O'Daniel	1939–1941
Coke R. Stevenson	1941–1947
Beauford H. Jester	1947–1949
Allan Shivers	1949–1957
Price Daniel	1957–1963
John Connally	1963–1969
Preston Smith	1969–1973
Dolph Briscoe, Jr.[†]	1973–1979
William P. Clements, Jr.	1979–1983
Mark White	1983–1987
William P. Clements, Jr.	1987–1991
Ann Richards	1991–1995
George W. Bush	1995–

[*]Only governor of Texas to be impeached and convicted.

[†]Prior to 1974, governors were elected for two-year terms of office.

Source: Texas Almanac, 1996–1997 (Dallas: The Dallas Morning News, Inc., 1995).

University of Texas faculty members. The governor vetoed the UT appropriations, and when he called a special legislative session to consider other funding, he was immediately faced with articles of impeachment based primarily on the misuse of public funds. He was ultimately convicted and removed from office, a landmark in the two decades of controversy that surrounded the husband-and-wife team of Pa and Ma Ferguson.[6]

If the governor dies, is incapacitated, or is impeached and convicted, the lieutenant governor replaces the governor until the next general election. When the governor leaves the state, the lieutenant governor serves as acting governor.

Salary and Perks of the Office In 1997 the governor of Texas was paid $99,122. The state also provides the governor with a mansion and a staff to maintain it, a security detail, travel expenses, and access to state-owned planes and cars.

Legislative Powers of the Governor   Governors have the opportunity to outline their legislative priorities at the beginning of each regular biennial session through the traditional State of the State Address to the legislature. The governor can also communicate with lawmakers—collectively or individually—throughout the session. In this fashion, the governor can establish a policy agenda, recommend specific legislation, and set the stage for negotiations with legislative leaders, other state officials, and interest groups. The governor's addresses and other formal messages to the legislature are well covered by the media. They give governors the opportunity to mobilize the public support that may be essential to the success of their initiatives.

The governor's effectiveness can be enhanced by the office's two major constitutional powers over the legislature: the veto and the authority to call and set the agenda for special legislative sessions.

The governor can call any number of **special sessions**, which can last as long as thirty days each, and designate the issues to be considered during each one. Sometimes the mere threat of a special session can be enough to convince reluctant lawmakers to approve a priority program of the governor or reach an acceptable compromise during a regular session. Most legislators, who are paid only part-time salaries by the state, dread special sessions because they interfere with their regular occupations and disrupt their personal lives. Governor Bill Clements, who called two special sessions on workers' compensation reform in 1989, used the threat of a third to convince a handful of senators to break a year-long impasse and approve legislation backed by the governor, a majority of the house, and the business community.

There also are risks in calling special sessions. The governor's influence and reputation are on the line, and further inaction by the legislature can become a political liability embarrassment. In some instances, the legislative leadership has liberally interpreted the subject matter of a governor's special session proclamation and considered bills not sought by the governor. Because the speaker and the lieutenant governor make the parliamentary rulings that determine whether a specific piece of legislation falls within the governor's call, the governor has to draft proclamations setting special session agendas very carefully. Once a special session is called, the governor can increase his or her bargaining power by adding legislators' pet bills to the agenda in exchange for the lawmakers' support of the governor's program.

The governor of Texas has one of the strongest **veto** powers of any governor. While the legislature is in session, the governor has ten days to veto a bill or let it become law without his or her signature. A veto can be overridden by a two-thirds vote of both the house and the senate. During the past fifty years, Governor Clements was the only governor to have a veto overridden. It was a local bill related to game management that the Democrat-dominated legislature voted to override during the Republican governor's first term. The governor has twenty days after the legislature adjourns to veto bills passed in the closing days of a session. Such vetoes are absolute because the only way the legislature can respond is to have the bill reintroduced in the next session.

The governor also has **line-item veto** authority over the state budget: that is, the governor can strike specific spending items without vetoing the

special session   Legislative session that can be called at any time by the governor. This session is limited to thirty days and to issues or subjects designated by the governor.

veto   Power of the governor to reject, or kill, a bill passed by the legislature.

line-item veto   Power of the governor to reject certain parts of an appropriations, or spending, bill without killing the entire measure.

Governor Bill Clements, On-the-Job Training

Bill Clements, a self-made multimillionaire who had founded an international oil drilling firm, personally funded much of his first campaign for governor in 1978. The man who shocked the Democratic establishment by defeating John Hill by 17,000 votes had held no previous elected office. His only governmental experience had been as deputy secretary of defense under Presidents Richard Nixon and Gerald Ford. Clements was an outsider, a Republican, a highly opinionated and blunt person, but he had a reputation for solid management skills. All the other elected statewide officials were Democrats, as were most legislators, although many lawmakers shared Clements's conservative views.

Upon arriving in Austin, Clements did not understand the limitations of the powers of the governor. In his election campaign, he had tapped a rather widely held view that state government was wasteful by proposing that 25,000 state jobs be eliminated. He also appealed to the popular notions of limited government and proposed that the Texas Constitution

be amended to allow private citizens to propose laws through a statewide initiative and referendum process. But he gradually learned that he could not run the statehouse and the bureaucracy single-handedly the way he had run the corporate boardroom, and he did not accomplish either of these goals.

In an interview years later, Clements admitted that he had not fully understood how state government worked when he first took office:

> Until I came to Austin and until I actually was in office and everything, I really didn't understand the detailed nuances of how the state government really functioned. I'd say it took me at least through that first legislative session. And by the time that was over, well, I began to understand exactly how the state government works.*

Clements eagerly exercised his veto power. During his first legislative session in 1979, he vetoed a near-record fifty-one bills. He also struck $252 million from the $20.7 billion state budget for 1980–81.

Clements generally received high marks for the quality of his staff and board appointments during his first term. He naturally appointed many fellow Republicans, who for years had been shut out of boards and commissions, and he also appointed many conservative Democrats. In part, his appointment strategies were designed to convert conservative Democrats to the Republican Party, thus

entire bill. All other bills have to be accepted or rejected in their entirety. In recent years, the legislature has restricted the governor's use of the line-item veto over the budget by making more lump-sum appropriations to agencies and giving agency heads more discretion in allocating the money among specific programs.

A governor may veto a bill for a number of reasons, including doubts about its constitutionality, objections to its wording, concerns that it duplicates existing law, or substantive differences with its policy. A governor's threat of a veto is often as effective as an actual veto because such threats can prompt legislators to make changes in their bills to meet the governor's objections.

Historic records on gubernatorial vetoes are not complete, but Governor Dan Moody was apparently one of the more frequent invokers of veto privileges. He vetoed 117 bills and resolutions between 1927 and 1931. Governor Richards vetoed 36 bills and resolutions in one regular and two special sessions in 1991 and allowed 228 bills to become law without her signature. Richards vetoed 26 bills and let another 19 become law without her signature in 1993. Governor Bush

extending and consolidating Republican gains across the state.

But Clements never developed effective ways of communicating with the legislature, the news media, and the general public, and he often found himself at odds with other elected officials and interest groups, primarily because of his outspokenness. He was often portrayed as insensitive, as someone inclined to "shoot from the lip" and worry about the consequences later.

At the end of his first term in 1982, Clements's job performance rating had dropped, his image had suffered, and the Texas economy had begun to show signs of weakness. A revitalized Democratic statewide political effort helped Mark White unseat Clements in a bitterly fought campaign.

In 1986 Clements became only the second person in Texas history to regain the governor's office after losing it. He spent his first six months back in Austin battling Lieutenant Governor Bill Hobby and Democratic legislators over the state budget. The problem was critical because revenue from existing taxes had fallen in the midst of a recession. Clements insisted on deep service cuts that would have allowed him to keep a 1986 campaign promise not to raise taxes, but he finally gave in during a summer special session in 1987 and signed a record $5.6 billion tax increase. The public's opinion of Clements, meanwhile, was plummeting. Two-thirds of the respondents to the Texas Poll that summer said they disapproved of the governor's

job performance. And Clements's negative ratings remained high throughout the remainder of his term. By the time he left the governor's office the second time, in 1991, he was widely viewed more as an obstructionist who would rather fight the Democratic majority in the legislature than as a leader who was ready to seek solutions to significant state problems.

Clements's two terms coincided with the emergence of a two-party system in Texas, and his candidacy and elections contributed significantly to this historic development. By proving that a Republican could win the governorship, Clements made the Republican Party attractive to many conservative Democrats, and many switched to the GOP.

In an interview shortly before leaving office for the last time, Clements assessed his contribution to the development of a two-party system:

> The electorate out there breaks down into about one-third Democrats, one-third Republicans, and one-third independents. Well, that is a significant change in the political profile of Texas. That's a historic change, and I guess I'd like to say that I put a brick in place to bring that about.[†]

Sources: *Houston Chronicle, December 2, 1990.
[†]Ibid.

vetoed 24 bills and let 6 become law without his signature in 1995, his first year in office. Bush vetoed 37 bills in 1997.

Budgetary Powers of the Governor   The governor of Texas has weaker budgetary authority than the governors of most states and the president of the United States. These budgetary constraints limit the governor's ability to develop a comprehensive legislative program. The legislature has the lead in budget setting, with a major role played by the **Legislative Budget Board** (LBB), a ten-member panel that includes the lieutenant governor, the speaker, and eight key lawmakers.

To meet emergencies between legislative sessions, the governor can propose the transfer of funds between programs or agencies, with the approval of the LBB. Or the LBB can recommend a funds transfer, subject to the governor's approval.

Appointive and Removal Powers of the Governor   Much of the state bureaucracy falls under the purview of more than two hundred boards and commissions that oversee various agencies created by state law. Most of these are

Legislative Budget Board   Panel that makes budgetary recommendations to the full legislature. It is chaired by the lieutenant governor and includes the speaker of the house and eight other key lawmakers.

part-time, unpaid positions whose occupants are heavily dependent on agency staffs and constituents for guidance. Although members of these boards are appointed by the governor and confirmed by the senate, the structure creates the potential for boards and commissions to become captives of the narrow constituencies they are serving or regulating and reduces their accountability to both the governor and the legislature.

Most board members serve six-year **staggered terms**. That means it takes new governors at least two years to get majorities favoring their policies on most boards. Resignations or deaths of board members may speed up the process, but governors cannot remove a predecessor's appointees. Governors, with the approval of two-thirds of the senate, can fire only their own appointees.

During her first year in office in 1991, Governor Ann Richards asked the legislature to give her the power to appoint the executive directors of state agencies directly; in the past, these officials had been hired by the various boards and commissions. In reorganizing a handful of agencies, the legislature gave the governor a small taste of the cabinet-style authority she had sought, but it hardly changed the system. The governor was given the authority to appoint a new commissioner to oversee several health and human service agencies, the executive director of the Department of Commerce, and the executive director of a new Department of Housing and Community Affairs. The governor retained her previous authority to appoint the secretary of state, the adjutant general, and the director of the Office of State-Federal Relations (see *People in Politics:* "Governor Ann Richards, Saleswoman").

The governor appoints individuals to boards and commissions with the approval of two-thirds of the senate. **Senatorial courtesy**, an unwritten norm of the senate, permits a senator to block the governor's nomination of a person who lives in that senator's district. The governor and staff members involved in appointments spend considerable time clearing potential nominees with senators because political considerations are as important in the confirmation process as a nominee's qualifications.

Individuals seek gubernatorial appointments for a variety of reasons, and the appointments process can be hectic, particularly at the beginning of a new governor's administration. Potential nominees are screened by the governor's staff to determine their availability and competence, political acceptability, and support by key interest groups. And although most governors would deny it, campaign contributions are a significant factor. A number of Governor Clements's appointees had made substantial contributions to his campaign.[7] Governors Richards and Bush also appointed several major contributors to important posts. One of Richards's most controversial appointments was that of Beaumont attorney Walter Umphrey to the Texas Parks and Wildlife Commission. Umphrey had ties to a company with a poor environmental record, but he had been the single biggest contributor to Richards's 1990 gubernatorial campaign, and he actively sought the parks and wildlife post. He and his law firm's political action committee had either donated or loaned Richards $350,000 in 1990.

The governor appoints individuals to fill vacancies on all courts at the district level or above. If a U.S. senator dies or resigns, the governor appoints a replacement. When a vacancy occurs in another statewide office, except for the lieutenant governor, the governor also appoints a replacement. All of these appointees must later win election to keep their seats.

staggered terms Terms that begin on different dates, a requirement for members of state boards and commissions appointed by the governor.

senatorial courtesy Unwritten practice that permits a senator to block the confirmation of a gubernatorial appointee who lives in the senator's district.

Governor Richards was particularly sensitive to constituencies that had historically been excluded from full participation in the governmental process and appointed a record number of women and minorities to state posts. About 45 percent of Richards's appointees during her four-year term were women, and about 35 percent were minorities. Her successor, Governor Bush, appointed women to 34 percent and minorities to 20 percent of the posts he filled during his first two years in office. Some minority legislators praised Bush for appointing minorities to several key positions, including a Hispanic, Tony Garza, as secretary of state.[8]

Judicial Powers of the Governor   Texas has an eighteen-member Board of Pardons and Paroles appointed by the governor. This panel decides when prisoners can be released early, and its decisions do not require action by the governor. The governor, however, does have the authority to grant executive clemency—acts of leniency or mercy—toward convicted criminals. One is a thirty-day stay of execution for a condemned murderer, which a governor can grant without a recommendation of the parole board. The governor, on recommendation of the board, can grant a full pardon to a criminal, a conditional pardon, or the commutation of a death sentence to life imprisonment.

If a person flees a state to avoid prosecution or a prison term, the U.S. Constitution, under the **Extradition** Clause, requires that person, upon arrest in another state, to be returned to the state from which he or she fled. The governor is legally responsible for ordering state officials to carry out such extradition requests.[9]

Military Powers of the Governor   The Texas Constitution authorizes the governor to function as the "commander-in-chief of the military force of the state, except when they are called into actual service of the United States" (Article IV, Section 7). The governor appoints the adjutant general to carry out this duty. Texas cannot declare war on another country, and the president of the United States has the primary responsibility for national defense. But when riots or natural disasters occur within the state, the governor can mobilize the Texas National Guard to protect lives and property and keep the peace. Should the United States go to war, the National Guard can be mobilized by the president as part of the national military forces. Although the Desert Shield and Desert Storm military operations against Iraq in the Persian Gulf in 1990–91 were not part of an officially declared war, a number of Texas National Guard units were called into active duty by the president and sent overseas.

Informal Resources of the Governor   Governors can compensate for the constitutional limitations on their office with their articulation of problems and issues, leadership capabilities, personalities, work habits, and administrative styles. Some governors relish being involved in the minutiae of building policy coalitions and devote much of their personal time to bringing about compromises and agreements. Other governors find such hands-on involvement distasteful, inefficient, and time consuming, and leave such "fine points" to subordinates.

As the most visible state official, governors sometimes get credit that belongs to others, but they can just as readily be blamed for problems beyond their control. For example, falling oil prices that had devastated the state's economy were a major factor in Mark White's loss of his 1986 reelection bid. White had no choice but to

extradition   Process by which a person in one state is returned to another state to face criminal charges.

People in Politics

Governor Ann Richards, Saleswoman

Taking her oath in January 1991, Ann Richards attempted to convince the public that her election marked the emergence of a "New Texas." She invited supporters to join her in a march up Congress Avenue to retake the capitol for "the people." And, hitting on the progressive Democratic themes of her campaign, she promised in her inaugural address a user friendly, compassionate state government that would expand opportunities for everyone, particularly minorities and women. But the euphoria of the day was tempered by the reality of a $4 billion-plus potential deficit, a court order for school finance reform that could make the shortfall even greater, and a grand jury investigation into legislative behavior that had eroded public confidence in state government.

Richards moved quickly to establish herself as an activist governor. The day after her inauguration, she continued a campaign assault on high insurance rates by marching over to a meeting of the State Board of Insurance to speak publicly against a proposed increase in auto insurance premiums. Unlike her recent predecessors, she also testified for her priorities before house and senate committees and used the media to attack the state bureaucracy.

Richards also quickly fulfilled a campaign promise to appoint more women and minorities to key positions in state government. She appointed the first African American to the University of Texas System Board of Regents, the first African American woman

to the Texas A&M University governing board, and the first Hispanic to the Texas Court of Criminal Appeals. Some 25 percent of her appointees during her first three months in office were Hispanic, 21 percent were African American, and 49 percent were women. Richards also named a disabled person to the Board of Human Services and a crime victim to the Board of Criminal Justice.*

With the state facing a revenue crunch, Richards took the lead in lobbying legislators for a constitutional amendment to create a state lottery. The lottery was a relatively safe issue on which to stake a leadership claim because polls indicated it had the strong support of most Texans as a new source of revenue for state government.

Most other major issues before the legislature during Richards's first year in office, however, were not so simple, and the new governor was less willing to strike specific policy positions on them. She preferred to support the initiatives of Democratic legislative leaders—or take the best bill they were willing to give her—rather than demand that legislators enact a specific plan. Detractors would say Richards's leadership wilted in the heat of legislative battle. Supporters would say she was a pragmatist who knew the limits of her office and recognized the necessity of political compromise.

The progressive goals that Richards had outlined in her campaign were also tempered by the reality that Texas was a predominantly conservative state. Despite promoting a vision of a "New Texas" that offered more compassion for the poor, improved health care for the sick, and greater educational opportunity for all, Richards took pains to establish credentials for fiscal restraint. She opposed a proposal for a personal income tax, even though it could have provided funds for a big boost in spending on health

call a special legislative session only a few months before the November election and, under the circumstances, probably exercised the best leadership that he could in convincing lawmakers to cut the budget and raise taxes. But it was not the type of leadership appreciated by most voters.

The Governor's Staff   Nineteenth-century governors had only three or four individuals to assist them, but staffs have grown with the increased complexity

and human services programs and education. And she eagerly embraced a thorough review of state spending practices that helped reduce the size of the revenue and tax bill she eventually signed during her first year in office.

Although Richards entered the 1993 legislative session with one of the highest public approval ratings of any governor in Texas history, she remained cautious during the entire session, apparently to save political capital for a 1994 reelection race. She joined Lieutenant Governor Bob Bullock and Pete Laney, the new house speaker, in insisting that a new state budget be written without an increase in state taxes. There was no tax bill, but the new budget did not allow the legislature to give teachers a pay raise, which had been another Richards priority, and it did not keep up with growing caseloads in health and human services programs.

In one of the most emotional issues of the session, Richards sided with police chiefs, mayors, physicians, and members of the clergy—and against a majority of the legislature—in killing a proposal to allow private citizens to carry handguns. (It was revived and approved under Governor George W. Bush two years later.) She successfully advocated an immunization program for children and actively promoted the legislature's efforts to comply with a Texas Supreme Court order for a constitutional school finance system but did not propose a plan of her own.

Richards staked out a strong anticrime position early in her term. In 1991 she ordered her appointees to the Board of Pardons and Paroles to curtail sharply a high rate of releases from state prisons, and she supported a huge prison expansion program. Richards also made economic development a major goal. She actively recruited companies to locate or expand in Texas and was instrumental in lobbying the U.S. Congress for approval of the North American Free Trade Agreement (NAFTA), even though NAFTA was bitterly opposed by organized labor, one of her key longtime supporters.

Richards was a national figure who was readily welcomed on Wall Street, at Hollywood parties, and in corporate boardrooms throughout the country. Many analysts believed her role as Texas's chief salesperson, or ambassador, was her greatest contribution to the state, along with the appointments that opened up the state policy-making process to a record number of women, Hispanics, and African Americans.

Richards, who had no legislative experience, did not seem to relish the often bloody give-and-take of the legislative process, but she obviously enjoyed her celebrity role as governor. During the 1993 session, Richards told reporters that she was not the kind of leader who could force results. Instead, she said, she tried to contribute to "an atmosphere in which good things can happen."[†]

Although Richards was unseated by Republican George W. Bush in 1994, polls indicated she remained personally popular with her constituents. But most conservative independent voters had never been comfortable with Richards politically. Voter discontent with the Democratic Party which swept the country that year contributed to her defeat. A number of other Democratic governors were also defeated, and Republicans captured control of both houses of the U.S. Congress. Richards's opposition to the handgun bill during the 1993 legislative session was another factor, particularly in key conservative areas of the state.

Sources: *Texas Government Newsletter*, February 25, 1991.
[†]Quoted in *Houston Chronicle*, June 2, 1993.

of state government and greater demands on the governor's time. By 1963, under John Connally, the governor's staff had grown to 68 full-time and 12 part-time employees.[10] Under the administration of Dolph Briscoe in the 1970s, the staff had further expanded to more than 300, but staff sizes were smaller in most subsequent administrations. At one point in her term, Ann Richards had almost 300 people on her staff. The number decreased to about 200 under George W. Bush, but Bush approved higher salaries for some of his key staffers.

Bush's top aide, executive assistant Joe Allbaugh, was paid $125,000 in 1995, or almost $26,000 more than the governor.[11]

The critical question involving staff is whether the governor has access to sufficient information on which to make decisions that produce good public policy and minimize the potential for controversy, conflict, and embarrassment. Under ideal circumstances, the staff enhances the governor's political, administrative, and policy-making capabilities. There have been instances, however, when governors have permitted staff to insulate them by denying access to persons with significant information or recommendations.

Governors generally choose staffers who are loyal and share their basic political attitudes. Because communication with the governor's various constituencies is fundamental to success, some staffers are chosen for their skills in mass communications and public relations. Others are hired for their expertise in specific policy areas. In many respects, staff members function as the governor's surrogates. Thus if one makes a mistake—particularly a serious mistake—the public perceives it as the governor's error.

The staff collects, organizes, and screens information, helps decide who sees the governor, and otherwise schedules the governor's time. Staffers also work on strategies to garner support for the governor's proposals from legislators, agencies, and interest groups. Because the governor often lacks the time to conduct discussions and negotiations, key staff members represent the governor in such meetings and in personal lobbying of lawmakers. Sometimes governors get involved personally, particularly if their participation is needed to break an impasse and bring about a solution.[12]

The Governor and the Mass Media Modern campaigns are increasingly shaped by the mass media, particularly television, and media-driven campaigns are often concerned more with image than with substance. Several candidates have had difficulty utilizing or exploiting the mass media to their advantage, and candidates—no matter how qualified—who do not understand the electronic media are likely to be rebuffed in their efforts to win major statewide office.

Once governors are elected, the mass media help shape their political and policy options. Governors who have failed to understand the impact of the media have often courted disaster. A governor who is readily accessible to reporters and understands the constraints under which the media operate is likely to develop a good working relationship with the press. But success with the media involves more than being accessible and friendly.

Governors call press conferences to announce new policies or to explain their positions on pending issues. They stage "news events," such as visits to classrooms to emphasize concern for educational quality or appearances at high-tech facilities to demonstrate a commitment to economic development. They or their staffers sometimes leak information to selected reporters to embarrass the opposition, put an action of the administration in the best possible light, or float a trial balloon to gauge legislative or public reaction to a proposal. Some governors have spent political funds to purchase radio or television time in an attempt to mobilize public opinion in support of pet proposals before the legislature. Overall, the timely use of the media can contribute significantly to the power and influence of a governor.

The Governor and the Political Party Historically, the political factions within one-party Democratic Texas were somewhat ill defined. Factionalism

Across the USA

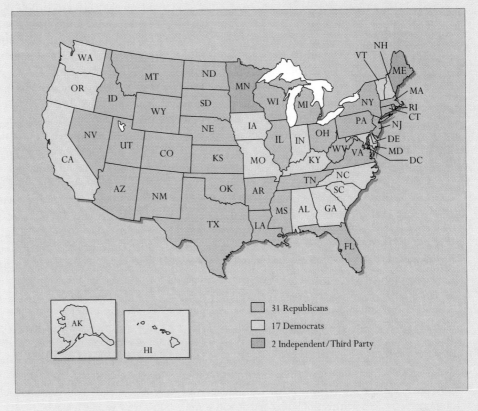

Party Control of the Governor's Office, 1999

In 1978 Texas elected Bill Clements to be its first Republican governor since Reconstruction. The defeat of Democrat Ann Richards by George W. Bush put the Texas executive back in the Republican camp in 1995.

31 Republicans
17 Democrats
2 Independent/Third Party

was often described in terms of liberal or conservative, but there also were complex urban-rural, regional, and economic differences. Democratic governors built policy coalitions around these factions, but there was little stability or continuity, and most governors derived only limited power from their position as party leader.

Under the two-party system, however, the political party is taking on more importance and may provide greater resources to the governor (see *Across the USA:* "Party Control of the Governor's Office, 1999"). During his second term, Bill Clements often had enough Republican votes in the house to thwart the will of the Democratic majority. A pattern of greater party cohesion and less bipartisan voting may develop with further growth of Republican legislative strength. If so, a governor of either party will attempt to use the party to garner support for his or her legislative program.

Upon taking office in 1995, Republican Governor George W. Bush enjoyed the support of party leaders for his own priorities—efforts to improve education, restrict civil lawsuits, reform juvenile justice, and change the welfare system. But he kept his distance from much of the agenda advocated by the social conservatives

Governor George W. Bush, Consensus Builder

George W. Bush, son of former President George Bush, had never held public office before being elected governor, but he had gained valuable political experience campaigning for and serving as an unofficial adviser to his father. The younger Bush became Texas's second Republican governor in modern times by conducting an effective campaign for improvements in the public schools, tougher penalties for juvenile offenders, and reform of the welfare and civil justice systems. He succeeded in winning approval for legislation addressing all four priorities during the 1995 legislative session, the first of his term.

Bush's public style was low key. He seemed to go out of his way to avoid controversy during his first year in office. But he remained focused on his four primary goals, and he was assisted by conservative Democratic legislative leaders who shared his views and sensed that public sentiment was on Bush's side. Although Democrats had majorities in both the house and the senate in 1995, the Texas legislature was dominated by conservatives of both parties, and some of the reforms the new governor wanted had already been initiated by Democratic officials.

Bush actively worked with legislators behind the scenes, making minor compromises, when necessary, on his policy priorities. The governor held frequent private meetings with house and senate members,

sometimes even dropping by their capitol offices unannounced. He had weekly breakfast meetings with Lieutenant Governor Bob Bullock and Speaker Pete Laney, two Democrats whose work was crucial to the governor's program. "We disagree, but you'll never read about it," Bush said of his meetings with the two legislative leaders. "The way to forge good public policy amongst the leadership of the legislative branch and executive branch is to air our differences in private meetings that happen all the time. The way to ruin a relationship is to leak things [to the media] and to be disrespectful of meeting in private."*

Bush also believed his decisive victory in the 1994 election had helped his cause in the legislature. "I won by 352,000 votes," he told reporters the day after the legislature adjourned. "And when you stand up in front of the legislature and outline a legislative agenda that was endorsed by the will of the people, that helps remind people that this is what Texans want."[†]

Unlike Governors Mark White, Bill Clements, and Ann Richards before him, Bush did not face budgetary problems in state government that could have distracted lawmakers' attention from his priorities. And unlike Richards, Bush supported legislation that gave adult Texans the right to carry concealed handguns. The gun bill was not one of Bush's major priorities, but it had been an issue in his victory over Richards. Bush signed the gun measure approved by lawmakers in 1995.

Bush faced a tougher challenge during the 1997 legislative session, when he made school property tax relief a major goal. He proposed that state government assume a larger share of the cost of funding the public schools by lowering local school

who had taken control of leadership positions in the Texas Republican Party in 1994 (see *People in Politics:* "Governor George W. Bush, Consensus Builder").

The Governor and Interest Groups   Successful governors seem to be consummate political animals who continually nurture relationships throughout the political system. A gubernatorial candidate aggressively solicits the endorsements and contributions of various groups. These groups, in turn, develop stakes in gubernatorial elections and usually assume that the candidates they support will be responsive to their interests. A governor's policy initiatives often include legislation of benefit to key support groups, which maintain active roles throughout the policy process.

taxes by about $3 billion a year. To replace the lost revenue, he proposed an increase in the state sales tax, the enactment of a new business tax, and the transfer of $1 billion in state budgetary savings to the public schools. The house rejected most of Bush's proposal and approved a controversial tax trade-off that would have increased numerous state taxes in exchange for major cuts in local school taxes. Bush lobbied Republican legislators for the house plan and helped convinced about half of the 68 Republicans in the house to vote for it. Assured that Bush was actively backing the plan, Speaker Laney helped persuade a large number of Democratic house members to vote for it. The bipartisan balancing act was necessary because many Republican legislators had campaigned against higher taxes of any kind and many Democratic lawmakers had previously been targeted by Republicans over the tax issue.

Despite the success in the house, the senate, which had a Republican majority in 1997, refused to approve a large increase in state taxes. Bush remained mostly in the background while the senate debated the issue. After it became obvious the house and the senate were in a stalemate, legislative negotiators requested the governor's active participation once again. But Bush was unable to forge any compromise to raise state taxes. The governor managed to salvage only a modest amount of property tax relief—about $140 a year for the average homeowner—by convincing the legislature to increase homestead exemptions, a form of tax break that homeowners get on their school taxes. The legislature used $1 billion in state budgetary savings to repay school districts for the revenue they lost from the higher exemptions.

In failing to win more substantial property tax relief, Bush was stymied by two major obstacles. One was strong opposition from business lobbyists to the proposed state tax increases. The other was the absence of a state budgetary crisis that would have forced the legislature to increase taxes. "We have a budget surplus. How do you start with a surplus and turn that into a tax bill? It's pretty hard to explain," stated Senator John Whitmire, a Democrat from Houston.[††]

Bush said he wanted to lower property taxes because they had become so high they were making home ownership difficult for many Texans. But there also was persistent speculation that Bush wanted to add a tax cut to his political résumé because it would make an attractive national issue should he follow in his father's footsteps and run for president. Some Democrats said Bush had failed as a leader because he had been unable to convince the legislature to enact a more substantial property tax cut package, but the governor dismissed the criticism. "I think people are going to say this is a man who set a very bold agenda and acted boldly," he said.[§] He said the higher homestead exemption that the legislature did pass was important.

With public opinion surveys showing Bush still highly popular with Texas voters and apparently unhurt by the tax controversy, he launched a reelection campaign later that year. He easily defeated Democratic challenger Garry Mauro.

Sources: *Quoted in *Houston Chronicle*, April 15, 1995.

[†]Quoted in *Houston Chronicle*, May 31, 1995.

[††]Quoted in *Houston Chronicle*, May 27, 1997.

[§]Quoted in *Dallas Morning News*, June 4, 1997.

OTHER OFFICES OF THE EXECUTIVE BRANCH

Lieutenant Governor   The **lieutenant governor** is the second highest ranking official in the state, but the executive powers of this office are limited. Were the governor to die, be incapacitated, or be removed from office, the lieutenant governor would become governor, but that eventuality has occurred only three times since 1900. In 1917 William P. Hobby replaced James E. Ferguson, who was impeached. Governor W. Lee O'Daniel resigned in 1941 to enter the U.S. Senate and was succeeded by Coke Stevenson. Governor Beauford Jester died in office in 1949 and was replaced by Allan Shivers.

lieutenant governor   Presiding officer of the senate. This officeholder would become governor if the governor were to die, be incapacitated, or be removed from office.

John Cornyn was elected Texas's first Republican attorney general in modern times.

The office of lieutenant governor is primarily a legislative office. The lieutenant governor, who need not belong to the same party as the governor and is elected independently of the governor, presides over the senate and has traditionally been given enormous power over the legislative process by the senate rules. The legislative powers and prerogatives far exceed those of the vice president on the federal level. Because of the lieutenant governor's key legislative role and statewide constituency, many experts consider this position one of the most powerful offices in state government. The lieutenant governor also chairs the Legislative Budget Board, which plays a key role in the state budgetary process.

Democrat Bill Hobby, son of the former governor, served a record eighteen years as lieutenant governor before retiring in 1991. He was succeeded by Democrat Bob Bullock, a former state comptroller and one of the most influential state officials in recent history (see Chapter 22). Bullock chose not to seek reelection in 1998, setting off a high-stakes campaign for the post. Agriculture Commissioner Rick Perry defeated Comptroller John Sharp to become Texas's first Republican lieutenant governor in modern times.

Attorney General   As the state's chief legal officer, the **attorney general** is called on to defend state laws enacted by the legislature and orders adopted by regulatory agencies. The office also enforces the state's antitrust and consumer protection laws and helps collect child support payments from delinquent noncustodial parents. Recent attorneys general have been kept busy defending the state or negotiating settlements in lawsuits challenging the constitutionality of state prisons, the public school finance system, the method of selecting state judges, and other major policies.

Unlike counterparts in the federal government and some other states, the Texas attorney general is primarily a civil lawyer. Except for representing the state in appeals of death penalty cases and assisting local prosecutors, the attorney general has relatively little responsibility for criminal law enforcement. Many candidates for the office campaign on tough law and order platforms, but responsibilities for criminal prosecution are vested in locally elected county and district attorneys. The attorney general also gives advisory opinions on the legality of actions of other state and local officials and is at the center of the policy-making process.[13]

In a major policy decision made independently of the governor, the legislature, and other state officials, Attorney General Dan Morales in 1996 filed a multibillion-dollar damage suit against tobacco companies, seeking reimbursement for public health care costs associated with smoking. Some other state officials supported Morales's decision, although others may have had reservations about the state's jumping into the tobacco controversy. But Morales acted within his authority as the state's chief legal officer. The decision was his alone to make.

Morales, a former Democratic state representative from San Antonio, was elected attorney general in 1990, becoming the second Hispanic elected to statewide office in Texas. He won reelection in 1994 over Republican Don Wittig, a state district judge from Houston. He chose not to run for a third term in 1998, leaving the contest for the office wide open. Republican John Cornyn, a former Texas supreme court justice, won the office.

Comptroller of Public Accounts   The **comptroller** is the state's primary tax administrator, accounting officer, and revenue estimator. Texas functions under a

attorney general   State's chief legal officer, who represents Texas in lawsuits and is responsible for enforcing the state's antitrust, consumer protection, and other civil laws.

comptroller of public accounts   State's primary tax administrator, accounting officer, and revenue estimator.

pay-as-you-go principle, which means the state cannot adopt an operating budget that exceeds anticipated revenue. The comptroller is responsible for providing the revenue estimates on which biennial state budgets are drafted by the legislature. A budget cannot become law without the comptroller's certification that it falls within the official revenue projection. The comptroller's office produces a revenue estimate of all projected state income for the two-year budget period by using sophisticated models of the state's economy.[14]

The comptroller's powerful role in budgetary affairs was enhanced by the legislature in 1990 with the additional authority to conduct management audits of local school districts, and again in 1991 with similar oversight authority over other state agencies. Through this process, Comptroller John Sharp identified billions of dollars' worth of potential savings for legislative budget writers and local school boards. Some of his proposals resulted in limited financial and organizational reforms.

Sharp, a Democrat, served two terms as comptroller. His decision to run for lieutenant governor in 1998 set off an aggressive campaign for the office. Republican Carole Keeton Rylander, a member of the Texas Railroad Commission, defeated Democrat Paul Hobby, a Houston businessman.

Carole Keeton Rylander won a close race to become Texas's first Republican state comptroller.

Commissioner of the General Land Office Texas retains ownership, including mineral rights, to approximately 22 million acres of public lands, which are managed by the state **land commissioner**. Revenues generated by mineral leases and other land uses are earmarked for education through the Permanent University Fund and the Permanent School Fund. This agency is also responsible for the Veterans' Land Program, which provides low-interest loans to veterans for the purchase of land and houses.

During sixteen years in office, Land Commissioner Garry Mauro, a Democrat, developed several environmental initiatives, including beach cleanup efforts and a program for cleaning up oil spills off the Texas coast. Mauro also took the lead in developing a coastal zone management plan to coordinate environmental protection efforts along the coast. Mauro's decision to run for governor in 1998 set off a scramble among would-be successors. Republican businessman David Dewhurst won the office.

pay-as-you-go principle Principle written into the Texas Constitution prohibiting state government from borrowing money to meet its operating budget.

land commissioner Elected official who manages the state's public lands and administers the Veterans' Land Program, which provides low-interest loans to veterans for the purchase of land and houses.

Houston businessman David Dewhurst was elected land commissioner in his first race for elective office.

Republican Susan Combs, a former state representative from Austin, was elected state agriculture commissioner in 1998.

agriculture commissioner
Elected official responsible for administering laws and programs that benefit agriculture.

secretary of state   Official who administers state election laws, grants charters to corporations, and processes the extradition of prisoners to other states. This officeholder is appointed by the governor.

state treasurer   Elective office created by the Constitution of 1876 to manage state funds. It was abolished by the voters in 1995, and its duties were transferred to the comptroller's office.

Railroad Commission
Three-member elected body that has some oversight over rail safety but now primarily regulates oil and natural gas production in Texas.

Commissioner of Agriculture   The **agriculture commissioner** is responsible for carrying out laws regulating and benefiting the agricultural sector of the state's economy. In addition to providing support for agricultural research and education, the agency is responsible for the administration of consumer protection laws in the areas of weights and measures, packaging and labeling, and marketing. Republican Rick Perry aggressively promoted Texas agricultural products during two terms as commissioner. Republican Susan Combs, a former legislator from Austin, defeated Democratic state representative Pete Patterson of Brookston for the agriculture post when Perry ran for lieutenant governor in 1998.

Secretary of State   The **secretary of state**, the only constitutional official appointed by the governor, has a variety of duties, including granting charters to corporations and processing the extradition of prisoners to other states. The primary function of this office, however, is to administer state election laws. That responsibility includes reviewing county and local election procedures, developing statewide policy for voter registration, and receiving and tabulating election returns.

State Treasurer   The Constitution of 1876 created a **state treasurer** to be the custodian of state funds. Shortly after taking office in 1993, however, Treasurer Martha Whitehead came to believe the office was no longer needed. She convinced the legislature and the voters to abolish it with a constitutional amendment, which was adopted in 1995 (see "Martha Whitehead Campaigned to End Her Job" in Chapter 20). The agency's duties were transferred to the comptroller's office.

ELECTED BOARDS AND COMMISSIONS

Only two of the more than two hundred boards and commissions that head most state agencies are elected. They are the Texas Railroad Commission and the State Board of Education.

Texas Railroad Commission   The **Railroad Commission** was originally designed to regulate intrastate (within Texas) operations of railroads. It also regulated intrastate trucking for many years. But it lost its trucking responsibilities and most of its railroad regulation to the federal government. It still retains some oversight over rail safety and regulates oil and natural gas production and lignite mining in Texas.

The commission includes three elected members who serve six-year staggered terms and rotate the position of chair among themselves. The oil and gas industry has historically focused much attention on this agency and made large campaign contributions to commission members. Many critics claim the commission is a prime example of a regulatory body that has been coopted by those interests it was created to regulate.

In 1991 Governor Ann Richards appointed Representative Lena Guerrero of Austin to the commission to succeed John Sharp, who had resigned after being elected comptroller. Guerrero was the first woman and first non-Anglo to serve on the regulatory body. But she lost the seat to Republican Barry Williamson in the 1992 election after the disclosure that she had falsely claimed to be a college graduate throughout her political career. Mary Scott Nabers became the second woman to serve on the commission when she was appointed by Richards in 1993 to succeed Democrat Bob Krueger, who had resigned to accept a short-lived interim appointment to the U.S. Senate. But Nabers was unseated in the 1994 election by Republican Carole Keeton Rylander. Republican Charles Matthews also unseated Democrat Jim Nugent, a longtime commissioner, in 1994 to give the GOP all three seats on the panel. Tony Garza succeeded Williamson and became the first Republican Hispanic elected to statewide office in Texas after Williamson ran an unsuccessful race for attorney general in 1998.

State Board of Education   Prior to educational reforms enacted in 1984, the **State Board of Education** was made up of twenty-seven members elected from congressional districts across the state. At the urging of reformers dissatisfied with student performance, the legislature provided for a new education board of fifteen members to be appointed by the governor and confirmed by the senate. The idea was to reduce the board's independence while new education reforms ordered by the legislature were being carried out. But the law also mandated that the board once again become an elected body within a few years. Some state leaders later proposed that the board remain appointive and put the question to the voters, who opted for an elected board in 1986. The present board has fifteen members elected from districts established by the legislature.

The day-to-day administration of the Texas Education Agency, the agency responsible for public education, is under the direction of the commissioner of education, who is appointed by the governor.

THE TEXAS BUREAUCRACY

A loosely connected, highly fragmented, and often confusing network of approximately 250 state agencies and universities with more than 300,000 employees is responsible for carrying out programs and policies approved and funded by the legislature and the governor. In addition, more than 950,000 other people are employed by school districts, cities, counties, and special districts in Texas.

This **bureaucracy** is often on the receiving end when someone complains about government. But without it, government would come to a grinding halt. The bureaucracy issues drivers' licenses, builds highways, distributes welfare checks, and performs myriad other public services. On an individual basis, the bureaucracy is the clerk, the inspector, the highway patrol officer, the computer programmer, the engineer, or occupational specialist delivering state services on a daily basis. On a larger scale, it is an assortment of agencies, some employing thousands of individuals, with designated responsibilities for specific public programs and services.

Although it is overstating the case to say that the bureaucracy runs state government, its role is enhanced in Texas because the legislature meets in regular session only five months every other year and the governor has only limited powers over the executive branch. The part-time boards and commissions that oversee most state agencies can exercise considerable independence in interpreting policies and determining the character and the quality of public services. Many boards heavily depend on the guidance of veteran administrators and career bureaucrats within their agencies.

THE GROWTH OF GOVERNMENT IN TEXAS

In 1967 there were 388,000 full-time state and local government employees in Texas. Thirty years later, there were more than three times that many (Table

State Board of Education   Elected panel that governs the administration of public education in Texas.

bureaucracy   Agencies of government and their employees responsible for carrying out policies and providing public services approved by elected officials.

TABLE 23-3	**Employment by Type of Government 1967–1992**			
	Full-Time Equivalent Employees			
Unit of Government	*1967*	*1977*	*1987*	*1992*
State	88,734	163,870	198,769	238,974
Counties	32,978	60,287	77,851	94,145
Municipalities	75,168	115,481	139,340	147,812
School Districts	177,734	282,492	400,035	460,212
Special Districts	13,698	18,917	29,687	42,156
Total Local	299,578	477,177	646,913	744,325
Total Texas	388,312	641,047	845,682	983,299

Sources: U.S. Department of Commerce, Bureau of the Census, *Census of Governments, 1967*, vol. 3, no. 2, table 15; *Census of Governments, 1977*, vol. 3, no. 2, table 13; *Census of Governments, 1987*, vol. 3, no. 2, table 14; *Census of Governments, 1992*, vol. 3, no. 2, table 14.

23-3). By 1995 Texas had 599 state and local government employees per 10,000 residents, making it eleventh highest in that category among the 50 states. Texas had only 143 state employees per 10,000 population, 39th among the states. But its 456 local government workers per 10,000 population ranked sixth highest among the states.[15] Many services performed by local governments—including education, fire and police protection, and sanitation services—require large numbers of professionals and other workers.

In recent years, there has been a substantial expansion of programs at all levels of government. State spending during the 1982–83 biennium was $25.6 billion, and only sixteen years later, the legislature appropriated $86 billion for the 1998–99 biennium. State spending grew at an annual rate of 9 percent, and population in Texas was increasing at an annual rate of 1.6 percent during most of this period. Nevertheless, Texas still ranks low in per capita expenditures: 49th among the states—$2,384 per person—in 1995. When combined state and local spending was compared, Texas rose to 41st, thanks partly to the large share of public school costs borne by local taxpayers. Still, in such key areas as per capita state spending on public health, education, welfare, and parks and recreation, Texas ranked behind most other states.[16]

Efforts to curtail government growth and spending have met with only marginal success. Texas citizens have come to expect a wide range of public services, and as the population grows, these expectations increase. The federal government, too, has imposed federal mandates on state and local governments that require additional expenditures and personnel. Moreover, the success of interest groups in winning approval of new programs adds to the growth of public employment. The state's financial problems in the late 1980s and early 1990s slowed the growth of public employment, but affected groups and interests continue their efforts to minimize reductions in programs and services.

Some 80 percent of state government employees work in three areas: higher education, public safety and corrections, and social services (which include public welfare and health care). Most employees of county governments work in social services, public safety and corrections, and general governmental administration (Table 23-4). Approximately one-third of city employees are engaged in fire and police protection, and another 30 percent work for city utilities and in housing, sewerage, sanitation, parks and recreation, and natural resources departments. Elementary and secondary school teachers are employees of local school districts.

BUREAUCRATS AND PUBLIC POLICY

The bureaucracy does more than carry out the policies set by the legislature: it is involved in virtually every stage of the policy-making process. The legislature usually broadly defines a program and gives the appropriate agency the responsibility for filling in the details.[17] Administrative agencies can sometimes interpret a vaguely worded law differently from its original legislative purpose. Although the legislature can use oversight committees and the budgetary process to control the bureaucracy, agencies often have resources and political influence that protect their prerogatives. Many appointed agency heads have political ties to interest groups affected by the work of their agencies, and these officials help develop policy alternatives and laws because legislators depend on their technical expertise.

Policy Implementation   Although one state agency may be primarily responsible for translating legislative intent into a specific program, other governmental bodies are also involved. The courts, for example, shape the actions of bureaucrats through their interpretation of statutes and administrative rules. And there may be jurisdictional and political battles between different agencies over program objectives.

In some cases, a new agency may have to be organized and staffed to carry out the goals of a new law. More often, however, the new responsibilities are assigned by the legislature to an existing agency, which develops the necessary rules, procedures, and guidelines for operating the new program. Additional employees are hired if the legislature provides the necessary funding. If not, responsibilities are reassigned among existing personnel. Sometimes tasks are coordinated with other agencies. Ultimately, all this activity translates into hundreds of thousands of daily transactions between governmental employees and the public.

TABLE 23-4	State and Local Employment by General Functions, 1992				
	State	*Counties*	*Cities/Towns*	*School Districts*	*Special Districts*
Education	36.0%	.8%	2.5%	100%	—
Social Services*	30.7%	27.9%	8.2%	—	52.7%
Public Safety & Corrections	13.6%	29.3%	33.1%	—	.3%
Transportation	6.0%	8.4%	8.3%	—	2.2%
Government Administration	5.7%	21.6%	8.8%	—	—
Environment/Housing	5.2%	2.8%	18.0%	—	13.3%
Utilities	—	—	12.0%	—	29.6%
All other	2.8%	9.2%	9.2%	—	1.9%
Total Employees	238,974	94,145	147,812	460,212	42,156

*Includes income maintenance.

Source: U.S. Department of Commerce, Bureau of the Census, *Census of Governments, 1992, Public Employment*, vol. 3, no. 2, table 14.

Almost everyone has heard horror stories about persons who have suffered abuse or neglect at the hands of public employees and agencies. Whether they involve an indigent family that fell through the cracks of the welfare system or a county jail prisoner who was lost in the administrative process of the judicial system, these stories tend to reinforce the suspicion and hostility that many people have toward bureaucracies and public employees. Unquestionably such abuses deserve attention and demand correction, yet thousands of governmental programs are successfully carried out with little or no fanfare and are fully consistent with the purpose of the authorizing legislation.

Most public employees take pride in what they do and attempt to be conscientious in translating policy objectives into workable public services. They are citizens and taxpayers who also receive services from other state and local agencies. A complex, interdependent state with more than 18 million people depends on the effectiveness and efficiency of governmental agencies. That activity appears, on the whole, to be mutually satisfactory or beneficial to most parties.

Obstacles to Policy Implementation As noted earlier, when things go wrong in state government and problems go unresolved, there is a tendency to blame the bureaucrats for excessive red tape, inefficiency, mismanagement, or incompetence. "Bureaucrat bashing" plays well politically, and many candidates for public office run on such campaigns. But in many cases they are unfairly blaming government employees for complex problems that policy makers have been unable, or unwilling, to resolve. One high-profile issue is the perennial struggle to improve the quality of the public education system. Some of the criticism directed at educational bureaucrats has been justified, but the legislature and the governor are ultimately responsible for the enactment of sound educational policies—and the development of a sufficient and equitable system of paying for them.

Some legislative policies may be misdirected, with little potential for producing the intended results. Or economic and social conditions may change, making programs inappropriate. In hindsight, administrators may also find that approaches different from those outlined by the legislature would have worked better; the legislature also frequently fails to fund programs adequately. In some cases, those charged with implementing a new policy may not have the know-how or the resources to make it work. And, finally, programs often produce unanticipated results.

The accountability and responsiveness of state and local agencies are also affected by other factors, including the influence of special interests. Thanks to the clout of special-interest lobbyists with the legislature, regulatory agencies are often headed by boards with a majority of members from the professions or industries they are supposed to regulate. Many taxpayers may feel this system is merely a legalized way of letting the foxes guard the henhouse. It is an extension of the **iron triangles** concept, whereby special interests seek to influence not only the legislators responsible for enacting laws but also the agencies responsible for enforcing them.

Business and professional groups argue that their professions can be effectively regulated only by individuals knowledgeable in their field. Although that argument has some validity, it also increases the potential for incestuous relationships that mock the regulatory process. There is always the possibility—and often the likelihood—that industry representatives serving on boards, commissions, or in agencies will be inclined to protect their industries against the best interests of consumers. This pattern of influence and control is often referred to as cooptation,

iron triangle Mutually supportive interrelationships among the interest groups, administrative agencies, and legislative committees involved in drafting the laws and regulations affecting a particular area of the economy or a specific segment of the population.

underscoring the possibility that agencies may be captured by the industries they are supposed to regulate. Licensing agencies may also seek to adopt unfair regulations designed to restrict new competitors from entering an industry.

Historically, many nine-member state regulatory boards included only industry representatives. But under the sunset review process, discussed in more detail later in this chapter, laws have gradually been changed to turn over some positions on most of those boards to members of the public. The Sunset Advisory Commission has concluded,

> Boards consisting only of members from a regulated profession or group affected by the activities of an agency may not respond adequately to broad public interests. This potential problem can be addressed by giving the general public a direct voice in the activities of the agency through representation on the board.[18]

Nevertheless, many industries are still able to flex their muscles with lawmakers. In 1991 Comptroller John Sharp, in his review of state agencies, recommended that most regulatory agencies be consolidated into an umbrella department that could not only save the state millions of dollars but also reduce the influence of some special interests over the bureaucracy. Lawmakers rejected the proposal and retained a hodgepodge of separate, small, industry-dominated agencies.

The "fox and the henhouse" approach to state regulation was highlighted again when Governor Ann Richards demanded that the Texas Department of Health crack down on deplorable conditions in some nursing homes. It was revealed that state inspectors had repeatedly found unsanitary conditions in three nursing homes partly owned by a member of the Texas Board of Health. The board member, an appointee of former Governor Bill Clements, denied any allegations of improper care but resigned after moving to another state.[19] Texas law in effect then required that one member of the eighteen-member health board be involved in the nursing home industry and the other members represent other health care professions.

STRATEGIES FOR CONTROLLING THE BUREAUCRACY

Elected policy makers can use several strategies to control bureaucracies and help ensure that policies are implemented as intended:

- Change the law or make legislation detailed enough to reduce or eliminate the discretionary authority of an agency.
- Overrule the bureaucracy and reverse or rescind an action or decision of an agency. With the independence of many agencies, boards, and commissions at the state level, the governor can reverse few agency decisions. Consequently, this step often requires legislative action.
- Transfer the responsibility for a program to another agency through administrative reorganization.
- Replace an agency head who is reluctant to or incapable of carrying out program objectives. But there are only a few agencies over which the governor can directly exercise such authority in Texas.
- Cut or threaten to reduce the budget of an agency to force compliance with policy objectives.

- Abolish an agency or program through sunset legislation.
- Pressure the bureaucracy to change with legislative hearings and public disclosures of agency neglect or inadequacies.
- Protect public employees who reveal incompetence, mismanagement, and corruption through **whistle-blower** legislation (see *Up Close:* "What Can Happen to a Whistle-Blower?").
- Enact **revolving door** restrictions to reduce or eliminate the movement of former state employees to industries over which they had regulatory authority.[20]

The Revolving Door   Over the years—at least until 1991—many regulatory agencies had become training grounds for young attorneys and other professionals taking their first jobs out of college or law school. They would work for state agencies for a few years for relatively low pay while gaining valuable experience in a particular regulatory area and making influential contacts in the state bureaucracy. Then they would leave state employment for higher paying jobs in the industries they used to regulate and would represent their new employers before the state boards and commissions for which they had once worked—or they would become consultants or join law firms representing regulatory clients. Former gubernatorial appointees to boards and commissions—not just hired staffers—also participated in this revolving door phenomenon, which raised ethical questions about possible insider advantages (see Chapter 12 and earlier discussion of iron triangles in this chapter).

An early step in restricting the revolving door was part of the 1975 law that created the Public Utility Commission (PUC); this law prohibited PUC members and key staffers from going to work for regulated utilities immediately after leaving the agency. The ethics reform law of 1991 expanded the restrictions to other agencies, but legislators refused to place similar restrictions on themselves. State senators and state representatives who were lawyers could continue to represent clients for pay before the state boards and commissions that operated under the laws and the budgets the legislators had enacted. For the first time, however, the 1991 ethics law did require legislators to report publicly who they represented for pay before state agencies.

Legislative Budgetary Control   Every two years, the legislature has traditionally set the budgets for state agencies, but subsequently provided little oversight as to how effectively the money was spent, unless there was a financial crisis that required a special legislative session or an emergency transfer of funds by the governor and the Legislative Budget Board. The most control that lawmakers exercised over agency spending, besides setting the bottom line, involved approving a number of line items in agency budgets that restricted portions of the funds to specific programs. That pattern also made those budgetary items vulnerable to the governor's line-item veto power, but it did not necessarily guarantee that money was eventually spent for designated purposes.

In recent years, the legislature has given agencies more discretion by including fewer specific spending items in favor of a greater consolidation of funds in agency budgets. Although that policy has reduced the governor's opportunities to exercise the line-item veto, proponents of the change in the budget pattern predicted it would lead to a more cost-efficient bureaucracy and give agency administrators greater flexibility in managing funds and meeting public needs.

whistle-blower   Public employee who reports illegal activities or "blows the whistle" on agency wrongdoing.

revolving door   Term describing the practice of former members of state boards and commissions or key employees of agencies leaving state government for more lucrative jobs with the industries they used to regulate.

Up Close

What Can Happen to a Whistle-Blower?

Governmental agencies make mistakes that can be very costly to the public in terms of financial waste or neglect. Texas has a whistle-blower protection law, which is designed to protect public employees who report wrongdoing within their agencies to their supervisors. If an employee is subjected to retaliation after having come forward, the law permits the worker to file a lawsuit against the offending agency.

A major test of the effectiveness of the law was brought by George Green, an architect for the Texas Department of Human Services (DHS). Green complained of shoddy construction on agency facilities, kickbacks, and noncompliance with contracts. He said his supervisors refused to take action against the offending contractors. After he went public with his charges, Green was fired by the agency for allegedly abusing sick leave time and making one unauthorized call on his state telephone—a 13-cent call to his father. Criminal charges were brought against him, and, although they were eventually dropped, he had spent $130,000 in legal fees, lost his job, and depleted many of his personal assets.

Green sued the state and won a $13.6 million judgment from a Travis County jury in 1991. The amount included $3.6 million in actual damages that Green had suffered and $10 million in punitive damages to punish the state for the way he had been treated. The state appealed, dragging out a resolution of the case, until the judgment was eventually upheld by the Texas Supreme Court in 1994. But the legislature was not in session that year, and state leaders said there was no money in the state budget to pay Green. So the whistle-blower had to wait for the legislature to convene in 1995. Green, meanwhile, was still unemployed and living off the generosity of friends and family and a personal loan he had made against a portion of his judgment.

By the time the legislature convened in January 1995, Green's judgment, with interest, had grown to almost $20 million, and interest continued to grow at the rate of more than $4,500 a day. The whistle-blower's case also was receiving considerable media attention, nationally as well as in Texas. But many legislators, particularly in the house, did not want to pay him the full amount, which they considered excessive. They particularly objected to the $10 million the jury had awarded as punitive damages and pointed out that taxpayers would ultimately have to pick up the tab.

Green refused to accept an amount smaller than the judgment and interest, and the 1995 session ended in late May without Green receiving any payment. Legislators, however, took steps to ensure that such a large whistle-blower judgment would never be awarded again. They changed the law to limit whistle-blower suit damages against the state to $250,000. Critics of the change warned it would seriously curtail whistle-blower suits—and damage an important taxpayer protection—because the best lawyers, whose fees are based on the size of a judgment, would no longer accept whistle-blower cases.

Finally, in November 1995, Green reached a compromise with legislative leaders. The Legislative Budget Board (LBB), which can transfer funds when the full legislature is not in session, approved a $13.8 million settlement, which Green accepted. Part of the money went to lawyers and a lobbyist who had helped Green collect payment, and $1 million went to an investor who had loaned Green money during his battle. Lieutenant Governor Bob Bullock, who chaired the LBB, apologized to Green and called his ordeal a "black mark on the history of Texas."[*]

Even then, Green's story continued. A former consultant sued Green for allegedly failing to pay him for helping Green collect the judgment from the state. In December 1996 another Travis County jury awarded the former consultant more than $600,000 in actual and punitive damages against Green.

Green's experience points to a major problem. Few public employees can afford to be subjected to this type of retaliation, and few have the resources to fight state government. Although the original intent of the law was to protect whistle-blowers and to encourage their coming forward with inside information, most state and local employees may have received a different message from the Green case and the legislature's decision to weaken the law.

Source: [*]Quoted in *Houston Chronicle*, November 16, 1995.

Sunset Legislation   Although Texas has been slow to modernize its budgetary process and other key functions of state government, it was one of the first states to require formal, exhaustive reviews of how effectively agencies are doing their jobs. The **sunset** law enacted in 1977 was so named because most agencies have to be periodically recreated by the legislature or automatically go out of business. Relatively few agencies—except for a number of inactive ones like the Pink Bollworm Commission and the Stonewall Jackson Memorial Board—have been abolished. But the obligatory review has produced some significant structural and policy changes in the state bureaucracy that the legislature may not have otherwise ordered. It has also expanded employment opportunities for lobbyists, because special-interest groups have much to win or lose in the sunset process. In many cases, special interests have succeeded in protecting the status quo.

Each agency is usually up for review every twelve years, under a rotating order set out in the sunset law. The review begins with the Sunset Advisory Commission, which includes four state representatives appointed by the speaker of the house, four senators appointed by the lieutenant governor, and two public members, one named by the speaker and the other by the lieutenant governor. The commission employs a staff that studies each agency up for review during the next regular biennial legislative session and reports its findings to the panel, which makes recommendations to the legislature.

In a few cases, the commission proposes that an agency—usually a minor one—be terminated or consolidated with another agency. In most cases, however, the commission recommends the continuation of an agency but outlines suggested changes in its organizational structure and/or operations. The future of the agency is then debated by the full legislature. If lawmakers fail to approve a sunset bill for any agency by September 1 of the year the agency is scheduled for review, the agency will be phased out of existence over the next year or terminated abruptly on September 1 if the legislature also refuses to approve a new budget for the agency. In recent years, however, the legislature has postponed controversial sunset decisions by passing special laws to allow some agencies to stay open past their review dates.

The Texas Higher Education Coordinating Board is subject to sunset review, but individual universities are not. Also exempted from sunset review are the courts and state agencies created by the constitution, such as the governor's office, the attorney general, the comptroller, and the General Land Office.

The sunset process has not reduced the size of the bureaucracy. By 1997 there were more than 300,000 full-time state employees, compared to about 164,000 in 1977, the year the sunset law was approved. Although more than forty agencies had been terminated or merged, others had been created in the interim (see Table 23-5). But Bill Wells, the Sunset Advisory Commission's former executive director, said the statistics did not tell the full story. He believed the sunset process had served to slow down the creation of new agencies. "You can't say how many [new agencies] would have been created if sunset hadn't heightened the awareness of the fact that we've got maybe too many agencies now," he said. "There is a heightened awareness of the fact that you need to go a little slower and you need to really have a problem before you create an agency."[21]

The sunset review process has helped rid state government of some deadwood, modernized some state laws and bureaucratic procedures, and made some agen-

sunset   Process under which most state agencies have to be periodically reviewed and re-created by the legislature or go out of business.

TABLE 23–5

Overview of Sunset Action, 1979–1997

Legislative Session	1979 66th	1981 67th	1983 68th	1985 69th	1987 70th	1989 71st	1991 72nd	1993 73rd	1995 74th	1997 75th	Totals
Agencies reviewed	26	28	32	31	20	30	30	31	18	21	267
Agencies continued	12	22	29	24	18	25	23	27	16	19	215
Agencies abolished outright	8	2	3	6	1	3	3	1	0	0	27
Agencies abolished and functions transferred	1	3	0	0	1	2	3	1	2	2	15
Agencies merged	4	1	0	0	0	0	1	2	0	0	8
Agencies separated	1	0	0	1	0	0	0	0	0	0	2

Source: Texas Sunset Advisory Commission, *Sunset Review in Texas: Summary of Process and Procedure*, October 1997.

cies more responsive and accountable to the public. The largest agencies and those with influential constituencies are usually the most difficult to change because special interests are working overtime and making large political contributions to protect their turf. In 1993, for example, the insurance lobby succeeded in weakening some regulatory reforms in the Department of Insurance sunset bill. In another case, there was such a high-stakes battle involving telephone companies, newspaper publishers, electric utilities, and consumers over the Public Utility Commission sunset bill that the legislature postponed action for two years. The lobby's influence over the 1993 sunset bills prompted Governor Ann Richards and some legislative leaders to suggest that the sunset process should be changed or repealed because it was being abused by special interests. But consumer advocates, who value the sunset process, blamed the problem on legislators who had difficulty saying no to lobbyists.

Performance Reviews   Facing a large revenue shortfall in 1991, the legislature directed Comptroller John Sharp to conduct unprecedented performance reviews of all state agencies to determine ways to eliminate mismanagement and inefficiency and to save tax dollars. Sharp recommended $4 billion in spending cuts, agency and funds consolidations, accounting changes, some minor tax increases, and increases in various state fees to reflect more accurately the costs of providing services. Pressure from special interests killed many of the recommendations, but the legislature adopted about $2.4 billion of the cuts. Sharp produced follow-up reports in 1993, 1995, and 1997. The comptroller also reviewed the operations of a number of local school districts and conducted special in-depth reviews of two of the largest state agencies, the Texas Department of Criminal Justice and the Texas Department of Mental Health and Mental Retardation.

One of Sharp's proposals adopted by the legislature in 1993 created the Council on Competitive Government, which was designed to give Texas businesses more opportunities to bid on state contracts and provide some state services more efficiently. It also allowed state agencies to bid on services performed by other state agencies if the bidding agencies thought they could do the work more efficiently. The council, which evaluates the proposals, includes the governor, lieutenant governor, comptroller, chair of the General Services Commission, and employee representative on the Texas Workforce Commission.[22]

What Do You Think?

The Politics of Privatization

Privatization, the process of the government contracting with private companies to provide public services, has become increasingly popular in recent years. Advocates say privatization promotes efficiency and saves taxpayers' money because private businesses know how to reduce waste to remain competitive. But as a major controversy over the Texas Lottery demonstrated, privatization does not always remove politics from the delivery of public services.

From its beginning, the Texas Lottery was operated by a private Rhode Island–based company, Gtech Corporation. State officials said Gtech, which also operated lotteries in a number of other states and foreign countries, had the necessary expertise to ensure the successful administration of the game. The company beat out another competitor for its first Texas contract in 1992. In 1996 the Texas Lottery Commission negotiated a new five-year contract with Gtech without taking bids. The contract was worth

$130 million a year to the company, which received a portion of the revenue from lottery ticket sales. Only a few months later, however, Gtech and the lottery were engulfed in controversy, and questions were being raised about Gtech's political connections.

The controversy erupted with a report that a close friend of Lottery Director Nora Linares had an undisclosed $30,000 contract with Gtech in 1992 and 1993. By the time news of the contract broke in late 1996, Linares's friend, Mike Moeller, was in federal prison on an unrelated bribery conviction stemming from his previous employment with the Texas Department of Agriculture. Linares said she hadn't known about the contract, but the controversy led to her firing by the Lottery Commission. It also sparked hundreds of news stories about Gtech and its insider connections. The company had hired several influential Texas lobbyists, including former Lieutenant Governor Ben Barnes, to help acquire and retain its lucrative contract. Other people and companies with political connections, it was revealed, also had contracts of one kind or another with the lottery—from advertising the games to providing supplies.

Some state government functions had been privatized before the council was created. One of the best known was the state lottery, which was administered from the beginning by a private company under a state contract (see *What Do You Think?* "The Politics of Privatization").

Merit Systems and Professional Management   At the turn of the century, public employees in Texas were hired on the basis of **political patronage**, or the personal relationships they had with elected or appointed officials. Little consideration was given to their skills, competence, or expertise. Few rules dictated terms of employment, advancement, or the rights or conduct of public employees, and wages and salaries varied widely from agency to agency. There also were high rates of employee turnover.

To serve the public and state workers more effectively, some reform advocates pushed for a **merit system** based, in part, on the Civil Service Commission created by the federal government for its workers in 1883 (see Chapter 12). Although some other states have developed comprehensive statewide employment or personnel systems administered by a single agency, the reform movement in Texas has not been as successful. Improvements have been made, but state government here continues to function under a decentralized personnel system, in part because the various elected executive officeholders have jealously guarded their prerogatives to hire and fire the people who work for them.

political patronage   Hiring of government employees on the basis of personal friendships or favors rather than ability or merit.

merit system   Personnel system in which public employees are selected for government jobs through competitive examinations and are systematically evaluated after being hired.

Politics in Cyberspace

The Texas Executive and Bureaucracy

Once legislation is enacted, the administrative agencies of the executive branch are responsible for implementing it. With the complex structure of the executive branch in Texas, it is often difficult for the citizen to determine who state officials are and which agencies are responsible for specific programs or public policies. It is even more difficult to determine the success or effectiveness of state policy.

Governor of Texas
http://www.governor.state.tx.us

The governor's web site offers up-to-date and archived news releases and speeches, information about ongoing initiatives, and a detailed description of the structure and functions of the governor's office. Links are provided to the important divisions or sections of the governor's office as well as to other state agencies.

State of Texas
http://www.state.tx.us

The state's web page provides links to more than 200 state agencies. Most of the state agencies have their own sites with detailed information about their organizational structure, programs, budgets, reports, and recent activities.

Office of the Comptroller
http://www.window.texas.gov

In addition to providing links to other state agencies, the comptroller's office provides a wide array of information about state taxes, management and accounting systems, and performance reviews of state operations and agencies.

National Governors Association (NGA)
http://www.nga.org

This bipartisan organization provides information on "Key State Issues" and monitors and analyzes the progress of important state policy issues. Information on the governors of all 50 states is also available.

Texas's personnel "system" is not a merit system but a highly fragmented arrangement with different agencies assigned various personnel responsibilities. Ultimately, the legislature has the legal authority to define personnel practices, and the biennial budget is the major tool used by legislators to establish some 1,300 job classifications and corresponding salary schedules. The legislature also establishes policies on vacations, holidays, and retirement. But the primary responsibility for carrying out personnel policies is still delegated to the various state agencies. An administrator can develop specific policies for an agency as long as the agency works within the general framework defined by the legislature.

All state job openings are required to be listed with the Texas Workforce Commission. Agencies also advertise for workers through the mass media and college placement centers. But many jobs still are filled as a result of friendships, other personal contacts, and the influence of key political players.

Higher and public education employees are subject to different employment policies, which are determined by individual university governing boards and local school districts. Unlike state government, many cities across Texas have adopted centrally administered merit systems organized around the accepted principles of modern personnel management.

- Although it is the most visible office in Texas government and the public believes it has considerable power, the office of governor is weak in formal powers.

- Unlike the president of the United States, Texas governors have no formal cabinet that serves at their pleasure. Texas has a "plural executive," which includes several other statewide officeholders elected independently of the governor. This diffusion of power was a reaction to the abuses of the Davis Administration during the Reconstruction era, but reform advocates argue that this structure diminishes the capacity of the executive branch to respond to the modern state's problems.

- Other elected officeholders in the executive branch are the lieutenant governor, the attorney general, the comptroller, the land commissioner, the agriculture commissioner, and members of the Texas Railroad Commission and the Texas State Board of Education. The top appointed official in the executive branch is the secretary of state. Although the lieutenant governor is part of the executive branch, the duties of that office are primarily legislative.

- Administrative responsibilities are further fragmented through approximately 250 boards and commissions authorized by statutory law. Although the governor appoints individuals to these boards, the governor's control is diluted by board members' staggered terms, the need for senatorial approval of the governor's appointments, and legal requirements relating to the composition of these boards.

- Besides appointments, the governor's main formal powers are the veto of legislation, line-item veto authority over the budget, and the authority to call and set the agenda for special sessions of the legislature.

- As part of the judicial powers, a governor can stay executions and, with the recommendation of the Board of Pardons and Paroles, grant full or conditional pardons or commute a death sentence to life imprisonment. The governor as commander-in-chief of the state's military force is responsible for maintaining order within the state and responding to various disasters by mobilizing the National Guard.

- Potentially, the governor also has a number of informal resources that can be used to shape public policy and the administrative process. Governors have used their staffs, their access to the mass media, their party roles, and their relationships to key interest groups to bring pressure to bear on legislators and other elected officials.

- More than one million Texans are employed by state and local governments. Collectively, they and the agencies for which they work are known as the bureaucracy. The bureaucracy has the primary responsibility of carrying out public policies adopted by the legislature and local governing bodies. But administrative agencies also are involved in virtually every stage of the policy-making process. Legislators depend on administrative agencies for advice when they draft public policies, and they rely on them to help assess the success or failure of policies.

- When things go wrong and problems go unresolved, there is a tendency to blame bureaucrats. But often government employees are unfairly blamed for complex problems that elected policy makers have been unwilling or unable to resolve. The fragmented structure of the executive branch of state government is, in itself, a major obstacle to the efficient, responsive delivery of public services. There also is the potential for agencies headed by appointed part-time boards to become unaccountable to the electorate and susceptible to the influence of special-interest groups.

- Through sunset legislation, Texas became one of the first states to require formal reviews of how effectively state agencies are doing their jobs. Most state agencies are subject to periodic review and reauthorization by the legislature. The process has not reduced the size of the bureaucracy, but it has helped rid state government of obsolete agencies and produced greater accountability. The legislature has also empowered the comptroller to conduct performance reviews of state programs to promote efficiency and reduce waste. In addition, Texas has adopted revolving door restrictions that prohibit former board members and key employees of regulatory agencies from going to work for regulated companies within a certain period after leaving their state posts.

- Although many local governments have adopted merit employment systems, state government functions under a decentralized personnel system. It is highly fragmented, with each agency largely free to set its own personnel policies.

SELECTED READINGS

BURKA, PAUL. "Four for Four." *Texas Monthly* 23 (June 1995): 107, 129–31.

___. "John Hall: A Man in His Environment." *Texas Monthly* 22 (September 1994): 116–17.

CONNALLY, JOHN B. *In History's Shadow: An American Odyssey.* New York: Hyperion, 1993.

CURRY, LANDON. "Politics of Sunset Review in Texas." *Public Administration Review* 50 (January/February 1990): 58–63.

DAVIS, J. WILLIAM. *There Shall Also Be a Lieutenant Governor.* Austin: Institute of Public Affairs, University of Texas, 1967.

DEBOER, MARVIN E., ed. *Destiny by Choice: The Inaugural Addresses of the Governors of Texas.* Fayetteville: University of Arkansas Press, 1992.

DICKSON, JAMES D. *Law and Politics: The Office of Attorney General in Texas.* Austin: Sterling Swift, 1976.

FREDERICK, DOUGLAS W. "Reexamining the Texas Railroad Commission," in *Texas Politics: A Reader*, eds. Anthony Champagne and Edward J. Harpham (New York: W.W. Norton, 1997).

GANTT, FRED, JR. *The Chief Executive in Texas: A Study in Gubernatorial Leadership.* Austin: University of Texas Press, 1964.

HAURWITZ, RALPH, and DAVE MCNEELY. "The Texas Emissions War." *State Legislatures* 21 (October/November 1995): 26–27, 29–31.

HENDRICKSON, KENNETH E. *Chief Executives of Texas: From Stephen F. Austin to John B. Connally, Jr.* College Station: Texas A&M University Press, 1995.

MCNEELY, DAVE. "Is the Sun Setting on the Texas Sunset Law?" *State Legislatures* 20 (May 1994): 17–20.

MORRIS, CELIA. *Storming the Statehouse: Running for Governor with Ann Richards and Dianne Feinstein.* New York: Scribner's Sons, 1992.

PRINDLE, DAVID. *Petroleum Politics and the Texas Railroad Commission.* Austin: University of Texas Press, 1981.

RESTON, JAMES, JR. *The Lone Star State: The Life of John Connally.* New York: Harper & Row, 1989.

SLACK, JAMES D. "Bureaucracy and Bureaucrats in Texas." In *Texas Public Policy*, ed. Gerry Riposa, pp. 187–91. Dubuque, Iowa: Kendall/Hunt, 1987.

TEXAS COMPTROLLER OF PUBLIC ACCOUNTS. "Public Payrolls." *Fiscal Notes* (July 1994): 12–13.

TEXAS GENERAL LAND OFFICE. *The Land Commissioners of Texas.* Austin: Texas General Land Office, 1986.

THOMPSON, PAT, and STEVEN R. BOYD. "Use of the Line Item Veto in Texas." *State and Local Government Review* 26 (Winter 1994): 38–45.

TOLLESON-RINEHART, SUE. *Claytie and the Lady: Ann Richards, Gender, and Politics in Texas.* Austin: University of Texas Press, 1994.

WELCH, JUNE R. *The Texas Governors.* Dallas: Yellow Rose Press, 1988.

ASK YOURSELF ABOUT POLITICS

1 Should an accused serial murderer be considered innocent until proven guilty?
Yes ⬭ No ⬭

2 Do you believe that the death penalty is "cruel and unusual punishment" in all circumstances?
Yes ⬭ No ⬭

3 Should a judge be required to try a lawsuit within one month after the suit is filed?
Yes ⬭ No ⬭

4 Do you think that a nonlawyer could be a good judge?
Yes ⬭ No ⬭

5 Should Texas establish its own courtroom rules, free of control by the federal courts?
Yes ⬭ No ⬭

6 Should the close relatives of a murder victim be allowed to witness the execution of their loved one's murderer?
Yes ⬭ No ⬭

7 Does the Ku Klux Klan have the same constitutional rights as the National Association for the Advancement of Colored People?
Yes ⬭ No ⬭

Chapter 24

THE TEXAS JUDICIARY

The courts often have the final say in how power is distributed, so understanding how they work can be crucial in gaining a share of that power.

CHAPTER OUTLINE

The Power of the Courts in Texas

The Structure of the Texas Court System

The Jury System

Judicial Procedures and Decision Making

Judicial Concerns and Controversies

Crime and Punishment

The Politics of Criminal Justice

Increased Policy Role of the State Courts

FEATURES

What Do You Think? Justice Delayed, Justice Denied?

People in Politics: Steve Mansfield, an Election Day Surprise

Up Close: An Attack on Affirmative Action

Up Close: A Public Case over Privacy

Up Close: Limited Reform

Up Close: Witnessing Executions

Up Close: Criminal Justice, an Expensive Headache

Up Close: More Is Involved Than Technicalities

Up Close: The Constitution Is for Everybody

Politics in Cyberspace: The Texas Judiciary

THE POWER OF THE COURTS IN TEXAS

In recent years, Texas courts have been beset by a series of controversies that have severely strained the principle of blind, impartial justice. Large campaign contributions to elected state judges from lawyers who practice before them have fueled a high-stakes war for philosophical and political control of the judiciary. The practice has drawn frequent

839

criticism and even raised questions in the national media about whether Texas courtrooms are "for sale."

Women and minorities, meanwhile, remain grossly underrepresented among the ranks of Texas judges. Even the basic structure of the judicial system—an assortment of about 2,600 courts of various, often overlapping jurisdictions—is so outdated that many experts believe it should be overhauled. But change does not come easily.

State courts resolve civil disputes over property rights and personal injuries. They also determine guilt or innocence and set punishment in criminal cases involving offenses against people, their property, and public institutions. And, to a more limited extent than the federal judiciary, they help set public policy by reviewing the actions of the executive and legislative branches of government. A civil dispute may stem from something as simple as a tenant's breaking an apartment lease to something as complex and potentially expensive as an auto manufacturer's liability for a defective brake system that contributes to the deaths or injuries of dozens of motorists. Criminal cases range from traffic offenses, punishable by fines, to capital murder, for which the death penalty can be imposed.

Some streamlining of Texas's judicial processes, especially at the appellate level, was accomplished in 1981. But the Texas judiciary, particularly in urban areas, has become overloaded by criminal cases and an increasingly litigious approach to civil disputes. It can take months to get a civil or a criminal case—one that is not settled out of court or in a plea bargain with prosecutors—to trial.

The State Courts in the Federal System   Like people in every state, Texans are subject to the jurisdiction of both state and federal courts. The federal judiciary has jurisdiction over violations of federal laws, including criminal offenses that occur across state lines, and over banking, securities, and other activities regulated by the federal government (see Chapter 13). Federal courts have also had major effects on state government policies and Texas's criminal justice system through interpretations and applications of the U.S. Constitution and federal laws.

Although Texas has a bill of rights in its constitution, the federal courts have taken the lead in protecting many civil and political rights, as when the U.S. Supreme Court declared the white primary election unconstitutional in *Smith v. Allwright* in 1944 (see Chapter 21).[1] Federal court intervention continues in the redistricting of legislative and congressional district lines. The federal judiciary also has ordered far-reaching improvements in the state prison system and restrictions on minority recruitment at state colleges and universities. And when police officers read criminal suspects their rights, the officers are complying with constitutional requirements determined by the U.S. Supreme Court in the *Miranda* case.[2]

Nevertheless, it is estimated that more than 95 percent of all litigation is based on state laws or local ordinances. Thus anyone involved in litigation is likely to be found in a state rather than a federal court.

The Legal Framework of the Judicial System   The U.S. and Texas constitutions form the basic legal framework of the Texas court system. Building on that framework, the Texas legislature has enacted codes of criminal and civil procedure to govern conduct in the courtroom and statutory laws for the courts to apply. Most criminal activities are defined and their punishments established in the Texas **Penal Code**. In criminal cases, the state—often based on charges made by another individual—initiates action against a person accused of a crime. The most serious criminal offenses, for which prison sentences can be imposed, are called **felonies**. More minor offenses, punishable by fines or short sentences in county jails, are called **misdemeanors**.

Civil lawsuits, which can be brought under numerous **statutes**, involve conflicts between two or more parties—individuals, corporations, governments, or other entities. Civil law governs contracts and property rights between private citizens, affords individuals an avenue for relief against corporate abuses, and determines liability for personal injuries. Administrative law includes enforcement powers over many aspects of the state's economy.

An individual with a grievance to be addressed has to take the initiative of going to court. A person can experience problems with a landlord who refuses to return a deposit, a dry cleaner who lost a suit, or a friend who borrowed and wrecked a car. But in a civil dispute, there is no legal issue to be resolved unless a lawsuit is filed. An injured person filing a lawsuit is a **plaintiff**. Because even the most minor disputes in the lowest courts can require professional assistance from a lawyer, a person will soon discover that the pursuit of justice can be very costly and time consuming.

Statutes and constitutional laws are subject to change through legislative action and popular consent of the electorate, and over the years there have been significant changes in what is legal and illegal, permissible and impermissible. At one time, for example, state law provided for a potential life prison sentence for the possession of a few ounces of marijuana. Small amounts are now considered a misdemeanor punishable by a fine. The legal drinking age was lowered to eighteen for a few years but was reestablished at twenty-one after parents and school officials convinced the legislature that the younger age had helped increase alcohol abuse among teenagers.

THE STRUCTURE OF THE TEXAS COURT SYSTEM

There are five levels of Texas courts, but some courts at different levels have overlapping authority and jurisdiction (see Figure 24-1). Some courts have only **original jurisdiction**; that is, they try or resolve only those cases being heard for the first time. They weigh the facts presented as evidence and apply the law in reaching a decision or verdict. Other courts have only **appellate jurisdiction**. They review the decisions of lower courts to determine if constitutional and statutory principles and procedures were correctly interpreted and followed. Appellate courts are empowered to reverse the judgments of the lower courts and to order cases to be retried if constitutional or procedural mistakes were made. Still other courts have both original and appellate jurisdiction.

At the highest appellate level, Texas has a **bifurcated court system**, with the nine-member Texas Supreme Court serving as the court of last resort in civil cases

Penal Code Body of law that defines most criminal offenses and sets a range of punishments that can be assessed.

felony Serious criminal offense that can be punished by imprisonment and/or a fine.

misdemeanor Minor criminal offense punishable by a fine and/or a short sentence in the county jail.

civil lawsuit Noncriminal legal dispute between two or more individuals, businesses, governments, or other entities.

statutes Laws enacted by a legislative body.

plaintiff Individual or party who initiates a lawsuit.

original jurisdiction Authority of a court to try or resolve a civil lawsuit or a criminal prosecution being heard for the first time.

appellate jurisdiction Authority of a court to review the decisions of lower courts to determine if the law was correctly interpreted and legal procedures were correctly followed.

bifurcated court system Existence of two courts at the highest level of the state judiciary. The Texas Supreme Court is the court of last resort in civil cases, and the Texas Court of Criminal Appeals has the final authority to review criminal cases.

FIGURE 24-1 Court Structure of Texas

Source: Office of Court Administration, 1998.

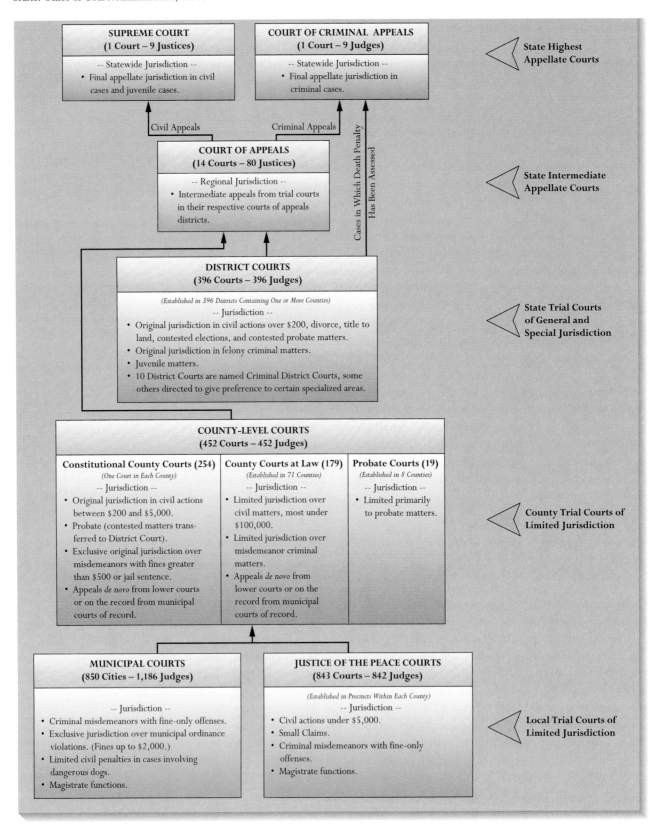

and the nine-member Texas Court of Criminal Appeals functioning as the court of last resort in criminal cases. Only one other state, Oklahoma, has a similar structure.[3]

Unlike federal judges, who are appointed by the president to lifetime terms, state judges, except for those on municipal courts, are elected to limited terms in partisan elections. Midterm vacancies, however, are filled by appointment. Vacancies on the justice of the peace and county courts are filled by county commissioners courts; vacancies on the district and appellate benches are filled by the governor.

Courts of Limited Jurisdiction   The lowest-ranking courts in Texas are municipal courts and justice of the peace courts. You or someone you know has probably appeared before a judge in one of these courts because both handle a large volume of traffic tickets. Some of these courts are big revenue raisers for local governments, and they are often accused of subordinating justice and fairness to financial considerations.

Some 850 **municipal courts** are established under state law, including some with multiple judges. The qualifications, terms of office, and methods of selecting municipal judges are determined by the individual cities, but they are generally appointed by the city council. Municipal courts have original and exclusive jurisdiction over city **ordinances**, but most of these courts are not courts of record, where a word-for-word transcript is made of trial proceedings. Only very rudimentary information is officially recorded in most of these courts, and any appeal from them is heard **de novo** by the higher court; that is, the second court has to conduct a new trial and hear the same witnesses and evidence all over again because no official record of the original proceedings was kept. The informality of these proceedings and the absence of a record add to the confusion and cost of using the system.[4] In response to these problems, the legislature in recent years has created municipal courts of record for some cities.

Each county in Texas is required to provide for one **justice of the peace court**, and each county government in the larger metropolitan areas may create sixteen (see Chapter 25). There are 843 of these courts in Texas. Justices of the peace are elected to four-year terms from precincts, or subdivisions of the county drawn by the commissioners court, which also sets their salaries. Justices of the peace are not required to be licensed attorneys, a situation that has generated much criticism of these courts.

Although their duties vary from county to county, justice of the peace courts, with certain restrictions, have original jurisdiction in civil cases when the amount in dispute is $5,000 or less and have original jurisdiction over criminal offenses that are punishable by fines only. In some areas of criminal law, they have overlapping jurisdiction with municipal courts. Justices of the peace also sit as judges of small-claims courts, and in many rural counties they serve as coroners. They also function as state magistrates with the authority to hold preliminary hearings to determine if there is probable cause to hold a criminal defendant.

These are not courts of record, and cases appealed from these courts are tried de novo in county courts, county courts-at-law, or district courts. Each justice court has an elected constable to serve warrants and perform other duties for the court.

County Courts   If there is confusion about the authority and jurisdiction of municipal and justice of the peace courts, it is compounded by the county courts. They were created by the Texas Constitution to serve the needs of the sparsely

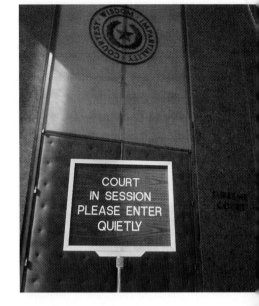

The Texas Supreme Court has jurisdiction over civil cases and disciplinary authority over state judges.

municipal court   Court of limited jurisdiction that hears cases involving city ordinances and primarily handles traffic tickets.

ordinances   Local laws enacted by a city council.

de novo   In a civil lawsuit or criminal trial, evidence is presented again before an appellate court because no record was kept of the evidence presented to the trial court.

justice of the peace court   Low-ranking court with jurisdiction over minor civil disputes and criminal cases.

Presiding Judge Michael J. McCormick of the Texas Court of Criminal Appeals recently switched from the Democratic to the Republican party.

populated, rural society that existed when the charter was written in 1875. But population growth and urbanization have placed enormous demands on the judicial system, and rather than modernize the system, the state has added courts while making only minor changes in the structure and jurisdiction of the older courts.

Each county has a **constitutional county court**. The holder of this office, the county judge, is elected countywide to a four-year term. This individual is the chief executive officer of the county and presides over the county commissioners court, the policy-making body of county government (see Chapter 25). Most urban county judges do not perform judicial duties, but county judges in many rural counties perform both executive and judicial functions, a dual responsibility that some experts believe is inconsistent with the Texas Constitution's separation-of-powers doctrine. Although a large number of county judges are lawyers, they are not required to be. They are required only to be "well informed in the law" and to take appropriate courses in evidence and legal procedures.

The constitutional county court shares some original civil jurisdiction with both the justice of the peace and the district court. It has original criminal jurisdiction over misdemeanors punishable by fines of more than $500 and jail sentences of one year or less. These courts also probate wills and have appellate jurisdiction over cases tried originally in justice of the peace and municipal courts.

Over the years, the legislature also has created 198 **statutory county courts**, or county courts-at-law, in more than 70 counties. Some specialize in probate cases and are called probate courts. These courts were designed to deal with specific local problems and, consequently, have inconsistent jurisdictions. Judges on these courts are elected countywide and have to be lawyers, but the authority of a particular court is defined by the legislation creating it. Some cannot hear civil disputes involving more than $2,500; others can hear disputes involving as much as $100,000. Drunken driving cases are the primary criminal cases tried before these courts.

Courts of General Jurisdiction   The primary trial court in Texas is the **district court**. Although there is some overlapping jurisdiction with county courts, the district courts have original jurisdiction over civil cases involving $200 or more in damages, divorce cases, contested elections, suits over land titles and liens, suits for slander or defamation, all criminal felony cases, and misdemeanors involving official misconduct. In recent years, the legislature has created district courts with specialized jurisdictions over criminal or civil law or over such specialties as family law—divorces and child custody cases. In some large metropolitan counties that have numerous district courts, the jurisdictions of the respective courts are determined by informal agreements among the judges. District court judges are elected to four-year terms, must be at least twenty-five years old, and must have practiced law or served as a judge of another court for four years prior to taking office.

The Texas Constitution gives the legislature the responsibility to define judicial districts, and, as expanding population produced greater caseloads, new districts were created. In 1981 there were 328 district courts. In 1998 there were 396 judicial districts, with one judge per district. A single county may be allocated more than one district court with overlapping geographical jurisdiction. Harris County, the state's most populous county, has fifty-nine district courts, each covering the entire county. By contrast, one rural district court may include several counties. As these courts evolved, little systematic consideration was given to the respective workloads of individual courts, and there are now great disparities in the number of people that district courts serve.

constitutional county court   County court created by the Texas Constitution, presided over by the county judge.

statutory county court   Court that exercises limited jurisdiction over criminal and/or civil cases. The jurisdiction of these courts varies from county to county.

district court   Primary trial court in Texas. It has jurisdiction over criminal felony cases and civil disputes.

Many urban counties suffer from a heavy backlog of cases that can delay a trial date in civil lawsuits and even some criminal cases for months or years (see *What Do You Think?* "Justice Delayed, Justice Denied?"). Delays in criminal cases have prompted a widespread use of plea bargains. In **plea bargaining**, a criminal defendant, through his or her lawyer, negotiates with prosecutors a guilty plea that will get a lesser sentence than the defendant could expect to receive if convicted in a trial. The process saves the state the time-consuming expense of a full-blown trial and has become an essential tool in clearing urban court dockets.

District Attorney John B. Holmes, Jr., has estimated that 90 percent of the more than thirty thousand felony cases filed in Harris County (Houston) each year are disposed of through plea bargains. Without plea bargains, the caseload would simply overwhelm the twenty-two Harris County district courts that handle criminal cases.

Harris County's civil district courts disposed of more than 88,000 lawsuits—divorces, personal injuries, tax disputes, and others—in fiscal year 1996 but left more than 70,000 other cases pending. Many civil lawsuits are resolved through negotiations between the opposing parties, but those that are tried and appealed can take several years to be resolved.

The wide disparities in populations and caseloads served by the various district courts prompted the adoption of a constitutional amendment in 1985 that created the Judicial Districts Board. That panel was responsible for redrawing judicial districts with an eye toward a more equitable distribution of the workload. But in 1994, yielding to pressure from incumbent judges who did not want to lose their offices, it issued recommendations that primarily preserved the status quo. Extensive changes by the legislature were considered unlikely.

Although the district court is the state's primary trial court and the state pays the district judges' base salaries, the counties pick up virtually all other district court expenses. The counties provide courtrooms, pay the courts' operating expenses, and supplement the judges' state pay.

Intermediate Courts of Appeals Fourteen intermediate **courts of appeals** that cover thirteen multicounty regions hear appeals of both civil and criminal cases from the district courts. Two courts, the First Court of Appeals and the Fourteenth Court of Appeals, are based in Houston and cover the same area. The Texas

plea bargaining Procedure that allows a person charged with a crime to negotiate a guilty plea with prosecutors in exchange for a lighter sentence than he or she would expect to receive if convicted in a trial.

court of appeals Intermediate-level court that reviews civil and criminal cases from the district courts.

What Do You Think?

Justice Delayed, Justice Denied?

Trial delays are bad enough for prosecutors and taxpayers. But they can be a nightmare for criminal defendants innocent of the charges against them, especially if they have to spend months in jail awaiting trial. In one case, a twenty-three-year-old construction worker from Mexico spent 575 days—more than

a year and a half—in the Tarrant County jail awaiting trial on charges of fondling a five-year-old girl.[*] When his case finally reached the courtroom, it took a jury forty-two minutes to find him innocent and free him. His room and board in jail had cost Tarrant County taxpayers $23,000. But his ordeal had cost him much more, and his case should make all of us ask how long justice can be delayed before it is justice denied.

[*]*Fort Worth Star-Telegram*, April 25, 1993.

Constitution provides that each court shall have a chief justice and at least two other justices, but the legislature can add to that number and has done so for most courts. Each Houston court has nine judges, and the Fifth Court of Appeals, in Dallas, has thirteen judges. Five of these intermediate courts, however, have only three members. Appellate judges are elected to six-year terms. They must be at least thirty-five years old and have at least ten years of experience as an attorney or a judge on a court of record.

All appellate courts combined had more than ten thousand cases pending on their dockets at the end of fiscal year 1996, with criminal cases accounting for about 70 percent of the total. But there are wide disparities in the caseloads between individual courts, with those in Houston and Dallas handling the lion's share. The Texas Supreme Court partially balances the load by transferring cases among courts. The courts of appeals normally decide cases in panels of three judges, but an entire court can hear some appeals.

Highest Appellate Courts   The creation of separate courts of last resort for civil and criminal cases was part of the effort by the constitutional framers of 1875 to fragment political power and decentralize the structure of state and local government. It was also based on the rationale that criminal cases should be tried more expeditiously, and the way to accomplish this was through a separate appellate court.

Although it decides only civil appeals, the **Texas Supreme Court** is probably viewed by most Texans as the titular head of the state judiciary, and it has been given some authority to coordinate the state judicial system.[5] The Supreme Court is charged with developing administrative procedures for the state courts and rules of civil procedure. It appoints the Board of Law Examiners, which is responsible for licensing attorneys, and has oversight of the State Bar, the professional organization to which all lawyers in Texas must belong. The Supreme Court also has disciplinary authority over state judges through recommendations of the State Commission on Judicial Conduct.

The Texas Supreme Court includes a chief justice and eight justices who serve staggered six-year terms. Table 24-1 lists the chief justices of the Texas Supreme Court. Three members are up for election every two years on a statewide ballot. Members must be at least thirty-five years old and must have been a practicing attorney, a judge of a court of record, or a combination of both for at least ten years.

The **Texas Court of Criminal Appeals**, which hears only criminal cases on appeal, includes a presiding judge and eight other judges elected statewide to staggered six-year terms. Table 24-2 lists the presiding judges of the Court of Criminal Appeals. The qualifications for members of this court are the same as those for the Texas Supreme Court.

Under the federal system, some decisions of the Texas Supreme Court and the Texas Court of Criminal Appeals can be appealed to the U.S. Supreme Court. Those cases have to involve a federal question or a right assured under the U.S. Constitution.

Texas Judges   In 1995, the last year for which extensive data were available, about two-thirds of the members of the intermediate and highest appellate courts had come to the bench from private law practice. One-third had previously served on lower courts. Most district judges had come to their offices from private law practice or from a prosecutor's office. There was greater diversity in career patterns for judges on the county courts, justice of the peace courts, and municipal courts, given the limited constitutional requirements for many of those positions.

Texas Supreme Court
Nine-member court with final appellate jurisdiction over civil lawsuits.

Texas Court of Criminal Appeals   Nine-member court with final appellate jurisdiction over criminal cases.

TABLE 24-1	Chief Justices of the Texas Supreme Court, 1876–Present	
Oran M. Roberts		1876–78
George F. Moore		1878–81
Robert S. Gould		1881–82
Asa H. Willie		1882–88
John W. Stayton		1888–94
Reuben R. Gaines		1894–1911
Thomas J. Brown		1911–15
Nelson Phillips		1915–21
C. M. Cureton		1921–40
W. F. Moore		1940–41
James P. Alexander		1941–48
J. E. Hickman		1948–61
Robert W. Calvert		1961–72
Joe R. Greenhill		1972–82
Jack Pope		1982–85
John L. Hill, Jr.		1985–88
Thomas R. Phillips		1988–Present

Source: Office of Chief Justice Thomas R. Phillips, Supreme Court of Texas.

TABLE 24-2	Presiding Judges, Court of Criminal Appeals, 1891*–Present	
John P. White		1891–92
James M. Hurt		1892–98
W. L. Davidson		1899–1913
A. C. Prendergast		1913–16
W. L. Davidson		1917–21
Wright C. Morrow		1921–39
Frank Lee Hawkins		1939–51
Harry N. Graves		1951–54
W. A. Morrison		1955–61
Kenneth K. Woodley		1961–65
W. T. McDonald		1965–66
W. A. Morrison		1966–67
Kenneth K. Woodley		1967–71
John F. Onion, Jr.		1971–89
Michael J. McCormick		1989–Present

*Court was restructured in 1891 through a constitutional amendment.

Source: Texas Almanac, 1996–1997 (Dallas: The Dallas Morning News, Inc., 1995).

The development of a two-party system in Texas has affected the partisan affiliation of state judges. Republicans have seen election gains and more appointments to judicial vacancies. A number of judges also have switched from the Democratic Party. Dallas County, in particular, has experienced considerable party switching by incumbent judges.[6] By 1995 more than 40 percent of the judges at the district court level and higher were Republicans.

Most Texas judges are white males. With increasing frequency, however, women as well as Hispanics and African Americans are entering the legal profession and running for judicial offices. As we discuss later in this chapter, minorities are pressing for changes in the judicial selection process to enhance their chances to serve on the bench.

The judicial election process has been diluted by a large number of appointments to judicial vacancies. The governor appoints judges to fill midterm vacancies that occur in the district and appellate courts. County commissioners courts fill midterm vacancies in county court-at-law and justice of the peace courts. In reality, therefore, Texas has a mixed judicial selection system.

All nine members of the Texas Court of Criminal Appeals in 1998 had initially been elected to their positions, but five of the nine members of the Texas Supreme Court had initially been appointed by a governor. More than one-third of the courts of appeals judges and almost one-half of the district court judges had initially been appointed.[7] Appointees are required to run for office in the next general election to keep their seats, but their incumbency can enhance their election chances.

The legislature has been under increasing political and legal pressure in recent years to change the way state judges are selected, an issue discussed in more detail later in this chapter.

Other Participants in the State Judiciary   County and district clerks, both elected offices, are custodians of court records. Bailiffs are peace officers assigned to the courts to help maintain order and protect judges and other parties from physical attacks. Other law enforcement officers play critical roles in the arrest, detention, and investigation of persons accused of crimes.

County attorneys and district attorneys are responsible for prosecuting criminal cases. Both positions are elected. Some counties do not have a county attorney. In those that do, the county attorney is the chief legal adviser to county commissioners, represents the county in civil lawsuits, and may prosecute misdemeanors. The district attorney prosecutes felonies and, in some counties, also handles misdemeanors. The district attorney represents one county in metropolitan areas and several counties in less populated areas of the state (see Chapter 25).

Other important players in the judicial process are the private citizens who serve on juries. Although there is some debate about the competency of a jury of ordinary citizens to make reasonable decisions on complex and technical civil and criminal matters, no acceptable alternatives have been found.

Efforts to Reform the Judicial System   Judicial reform has been a recurring issue in Texas politics. Small, incremental changes have been made since the 1970s, but many jurists and scholars continue to push for an overhaul of the state courts. In September 1989, Texas Supreme Court Chief Justice Thomas R. Phillips requested an in-depth study of the Texas judiciary by the Texas Research League, a privately financed, nonprofit group specializing in studies of state government.

The League concluded that the court system was fundamentally flawed and sorely in need of an overhaul. It made twenty-seven recommendations, including one that the legislature rewrite the judiciary article of the Texas Constitution to provide a fundamental framework for a unified court system.[8]

Despite a series of similar studies and reports, however, reform of Texas courts has been difficult. The public may have a lot to gain from judicial restructuring, but the primary stakeholders—the judges, the attorneys, the court administrative personnel, and litigants who benefit from delays, confusion, and inefficiency— have resisted change. Unless there is a popular demand for reform, there will be few structural changes in the judiciary until some or all of these participants perceive some advantages from reform.

THE JURY SYSTEM

The Grand Jury   Citizens serve on two kinds of juries—grand juries and trial, or petit, juries. The **grand jury** functions, in theory, to ensure that the government has sufficient reason to proceed with a criminal **prosecution** against an individual. It includes twelve persons selected by a district judge from a list proposed by a jury commission appointed by the local district judge or judges. Although the grand jury evolved to protect the individual against arbitrary and capricious behavior by governmental officials, a district attorney can exercise great control over a grand jury through deciding what evidence and which witnesses jurors will hear. There also have been allegations over the years that grand juries overrepresent the interests of upper social and economic groups and underrepresent minorities. Grand jury meetings and deliberations are conducted in private, and the accused is not allowed to have an attorney present during grand jury questioning.

grand jury   Panel that reviews evidence submitted by prosecutors to determine whether to indict, or charge, an individual with a criminal offense.

prosecution   Conduct of legal proceedings against an individual charged with a crime.

A grand jury usually meets on specified days of the week and serves for the duration of the district court's term, usually from three to six months. If at least nine grand jurors believe there is enough evidence to warrant a trial in a case under investigation, they will issue an **indictment**, or a "true bill"—a written statement charging a person or persons with a crime. A grand jury investigation also may result in no indictment, or a "no bill."

In some cases—especially when an investigation fails to produce a strong enough case for a felony indictment—grand juries issue indictments alleging misdemeanors. Most misdemeanors, however, are not handled by grand juries. They are handled by the district or county attorney, who prepares an **information**—a document formally charging an individual with a misdemeanor—on the basis of a complaint filed by a private citizen.

The Petit Jury   The jury on which most people are likely to be called to serve is the trial jury, or **petit jury**. Citizens who are at least eighteen years old and meet other minimal requirements are eligible for jury duty, and anyone refusing to comply with a jury summons can be fined for contempt of court. Persons older than sixty-five, individuals with legal custody of young children, and full-time students are exempted from jury duty. The legislature in 1991 increased the likelihood of an individual's being called to jury duty by providing that county and district clerks prepare jury summonses from lists of those Texans who have drivers' licenses or hold Department of Public Safety identification cards. Previously, prospective jurors had been chosen from voter registration lists, and it was believed that some Texans had not been registering to vote in order to avoid jury duty.

Six persons make up a jury in a justice of the peace or county court, and twelve in a district court. Attorneys for both sides in a criminal or civil case screen the prospective jurors, known as **veniremen**, before a jury is seated. In major felony cases, such as capital murder, prosecutors and defense attorneys may take several days to select a jury from among hundreds of prospects.

Attorneys for each side in a criminal case are permitted a certain number of peremptory challenges, which allow them to dismiss a prospective juror without

indictment   Written statement issued by a grand jury charging a person with a punishable offense.

information   Document formally charging a person with a misdemeanor.

petit jury   Panel of citizens that hears evidence in a civil lawsuit or a criminal prosecution and decides the outcome by issuing a verdict.

veniremen   Members of a panel from which a petit, or trial, jury is chosen.

An attorney addressing a jury in a state court in Dallas.

having to explain the reason, and an unlimited number of challenges for cause. In the latter case, the lawyer has to state why he or she believes a particular venireman would not be able to evaluate the evidence in the case impartially. The judge decides whether to grant each challenge for cause but can rule against a peremptory challenge only if he or she believes a prosecutor is trying to exclude prospective jurors because of their race, such as keeping African Americans off a jury that is to try an African American defendant. If that happens, the defendant is entitled to a new group, or panel, of prospective jurors.

In civil cases, attorneys for both sides determine whether any persons on the jury panel should be disqualified because they are related to one of the parties, have some other personal or business connection, or could otherwise be prejudiced. For example, a lawyer defending a doctor in a malpractice suit probably would not want to seat a prospective juror who had been dissatisfied with his own medical treatment. Such potential conflicts are discovered by attorneys' careful screening and questioning of veniremen.

Unanimous jury verdicts are required to convict a defendant in a criminal case. Jurors have to be convinced "beyond a reasonable doubt" that a defendant is guilty before returning a guilty verdict. In contrast, agreement of only ten of the twelve members of a district court jury and five of the six on a county court jury are sufficient to reach a verdict in a civil suit.

JUDICIAL PROCEDURES AND DECISION MAKING

Civil litigants and criminal defendants (except those charged with capital murder) can waive their right to a jury trial if they believe it would be to their advantage to have their cases decided by a judge. Following established procedures, which differ between civil and criminal cases and are enforced by the judge, the trial moves through the presentation of opening arguments by the opposing attorneys, examination and cross-examination of witnesses, presentation of evidence, rebuttal, and summation. Some trials can be completed in a few hours, but the trial of a complex civil lawsuit or a sensational criminal case can take weeks or months. Convicted criminal defendants or parties dissatisfied with a judge or jury's verdict in a civil lawsuit can then appeal their case to higher courts.

The procedure in appellate courts is markedly different from that in trial courts. There is no jury at the appellate level to rehear evidence. Instead, judges review the decisions and the procedures of the lower court for conformance to constitutional and statutory requirements. The record of the trial court proceedings and legal briefs filed by the attorneys are available for appellate judges to review.

Most civil and criminal appeals are initially made to one of the fourteen intermediate courts of appeals. Parties dissatisfied with decisions of the courts of appeals can appeal to the Texas Supreme Court or the Texas Court of Criminal Appeals.

Cases reach the Texas Supreme Court primarily on **writs of error** alleging that a lower court has ruled erroneously on points of law. Applications for writ of error seeking reversals of lower court decisions are distributed among the nine Supreme Court justices. The justices and their briefing attorneys then prepare memoranda on their assigned cases for circulation among the other court members. Meeting in private conference, the court decides which applications to reject outright—thus upholding the lower court decisions—and which to sched-

writ of error Formal allegation that constitutional or procedural mistakes were made by a lower court. Primary means by which cases reach the Texas Supreme Court.

ule for attorneys' oral arguments. A case will not be heard without the approval of at least four of the nine justices.

Oral arguments, in which the lawyers present their perspectives on the legal points at issue in their case and answer questions from the justices, are presented in open court. As many as twelve cases are usually scheduled for oral arguments during one week each month, and the responsibility for writing the majority opinions that state the court's decisions is determined by lot among the justices. It often takes several months after oral arguments before a decision is issued. Legal points and judicial philosophies are debated among the justices behind the closed doors of their conference room. But differences sometimes spill out for public view through split decisions and strongly worded dissenting opinions.

Most cases taken to the Texas Supreme Court on appeal are from one of the courts of appeals, but occasionally the Supreme Court receives a direct appeal from a district court. In 1980 the high court agreed to hear about 1 in every 8 applications for writ of error that it received. That ratio had been reduced to about 1 in 14 by 1990, partly because the court had changed its rules to increase from three to four the number of justices required to approve a hearing.

The Texas Supreme Court also acts on petitions for **writs of mandamus**, or orders directing a lower court or another public official to take a certain action. Many involve disputes over procedure or evidence in cases still pending in trial courts.

The Texas Court of Criminal Appeals has appellate jurisdiction in criminal cases that originate in the district and county courts. Death penalty cases are appealed directly to the Court of Criminal Appeals. Other criminal cases are appealed first to the intermediate courts of appeals. Either the defendant or the prosecution can appeal the courts of appeals' decisions to the Court of Criminal Appeals by filing petitions for discretionary review, which the high court may grant if at least four judges agree. The court sets one day a week aside for lawyers' oral arguments in the cases it agrees to review. The task of writing majority opinions is rotated among the nine judges.

JUDICIAL CONCERNS AND CONTROVERSIES

Throughout much of the 1980s and into the 1990s, Texas courts were at the center of conflict and controversy. Reports of large campaign contributions from lawyers to judges and judicial candidates raised allegations that Texas had the best justice money could buy. The Texas Supreme Court became a philosophical and political battleground, with billions of dollars at stake in crucial legal decisions. Meanwhile, minorities—who held a disproportionately small number of judicial offices—pressed for greater influence in electing judges. Lengthy ballots, particularly in urban areas, made it increasingly difficult for most voters to choose intelligently among judicial candidates (see *People in Politics*: "Steve Mansfield, an Election Day Surprise"). Although these issues and concerns may seem unrelated, they all shared one important characteristic: they cast a cloud over the Texas judiciary. Each, in its own way, undermined public confidence in the state courts and made many Texans question how just their system of justice is.

Judicial Activism In earlier chapters, we noted the historical domination of Texas politics and policies by the conservative, business-oriented establishment. For decades, that domination also applied to the judiciary, as insurance companies,

writ of mandamus Court order directing a lower court or another public official to take a certain action.

Steve Mansfield, an Election Day Surprise

Like most other candidates for the Texas Court of Criminal Appeals, Houston attorney Steve Mansfield received little publicity when he began a campaign in 1994 to unseat Democratic Judge Charles Campbell, a twelve-year incumbent. Running as a crime victims' advocate, he defeated an equally unknown attorney for the Republican nomination and then got more publicity than he wanted—all of it negative. In the middle of his campaign, it was revealed that Mansfield had lied about his personal and political background and had exaggerated his legal experience. He was primarily an insurance lawyer with little experience in criminal law. But he unseated Campbell, thanks to heavy straight-ticket Republican voting in a GOP landslide.

Bad publicity continued to dog Mansfield even after he took office. Texas Republican Party officials shunned him at a party fund raiser, and the Board of Law Examiners investigated the circumstances under which he had obtained a Texas law license, which he had to have to serve on the court. But at his swearing-in ceremony in January 1995, Mansfield promised to be a hardworking judge, and he spent his first year in office living up to his promise by authoring thirty-three opinions, slightly more than the court average. It was unknown how much of the actual research and writing could be credited to Mansfield and how much to the experienced staff he inherited from Campbell and was wise enough to retain. But, as he had promised during his campaign, Mansfield usually sided with the prosecution.

Several months after Mansfield took office, the State Bar publicly reprimanded him for his campaign lies. But the Board of Law Examiners did not challenge his law license, which cleared the way for him to remain on the court. Many judges, prosecutors, and other state officials considered Mansfield's election an embarrassment and a good argument for appointing, rather than electing, judges. But despite the controversy, Mansfield said he enjoyed his new job. "It's certainly been the greatest challenge I've ever faced. I've worked very hard to live up to the trust the people of Texas put in me," he said. [*]

Mansfield was not the first candidate of questionable qualifications to win election to a statewide court in Texas. The most infamous example was Donald B. Yarbrough. Yarbrough, also an unknown attorney from Houston, claimed that God had told him to run for the Texas Supreme Court. Thanks to his familiar name, he upset a much more qualified candidate, Appellate Judge Charles Barrow, for a seat on the high court in 1976. Yarbrough's name was similar to that of Don Yarborough, who had run unsuccessfully for governor two times in the 1960s, and that of former U.S. Senator Ralph Yarborough. Yarbrough spent approximately $350 campaigning; Barrow had the endorsement of the legal establishment.

Yarbrough, a Democrat, served about six months on the Supreme Court, then became the target of a criminal investigation and resigned as the legislature was preparing to remove him. After he left the court, he was convicted of lying to a grand jury investigating allegations that he plotted to have a banker killed and was sentenced to five years in prison. While free on bond during an appeal, he left the country to attend medical school in Grenada and refused to return when his appeal was denied. He finally was apprehended in the Caribbean, sentenced to two additional years for bond jumping, and imprisoned.

[*] Quoted in *Houston Chronicle*, June 28, 1995.

banks, utilities, and other large corporate entities became accustomed to favorable rulings from a Democratic, but conservative, Texas Supreme Court.

Establishment-oriented justices, usually elected with the support of the state's largest law firms, tended to view their role as strict constructionists. The legislature had the authority to enact public policy; the responsibility of the courts, they believed, was to narrowly interpret and apply the law. Judges were not to engage in setting policy but were to honor legal precedent and prior case law, which had generally favored the interests of corporations over those of consumers, laborers, and the lower social classes.

The establishment began to feel the first tremors of a philosophical earthquake in the 1970s. The Texas Trial Lawyers Association, whose members represent consumers in lawsuits against businesses, doctors, and insurance companies, increased its political activity. And in 1973, the legislature, with increased minority and female membership from single-member House districts ordered by the federal courts (see Chapter 22), enacted the Deceptive Trade Practices-Consumer Protection Act, which encouraged plaintiffs, or injured parties, to take their grievances to court. Among other things, the new law allowed plaintiffs to sue for attorneys' fees as well as compensatory and punitive damages.

Trial attorneys, who usually receive a healthy percentage of monetary damages awarded their clients, began contributing millions of dollars to successful Texas Supreme Court candidates, and judicial precedents started falling. A revamped court issued significant decisions that made it easier for consumers to win large judgments for medical malpractice, faulty products, and other complaints against businesses and their insurers. The new activist, liberal interpretation of the law contrasted sharply with the traditional record of the court. "All of a sudden, we have a magnificent Supreme Court, which is not controlled by a sinister, rich, opulent elite," trial attorney Pat Maloney of San Antonio, a major contributor to Supreme Court candidates, said in a 1983 interview with the *Fort Worth Star-Telegram*.[9]

The business community and defense lawyers accused the new court majority of exceeding its constitutional authority by trying to write its own laws. Some business leaders contended that the court's activism endangered the state's economy by discouraging new businesses from moving to Texas, a fear that was soon to be put to partisan advantage by Republican leaders.

At various times in the early and mid-1980s, the lineup on the Texas Supreme Court was viewed as 5 to 4 or 6 to 3 in favor of positions advocated by plaintiffs' attorneys. But the court also issued unanimous major opinions, sometimes coming down on the side of the plaintiffs, sometimes on the side of the defense.

Campaign Contributions and Judicial Politics   Controversy over the Texas Supreme Court escalated into a full-blown storm in 1986 when the Judicial Affairs Committee of the Texas House investigated two justices, Democrats C. L. Ray and William Kilgarlin, for alleged improper contact with attorneys practicing before the court. The two justices denied the allegations, made largely by former briefing attorneys, but never testified before the legislative panel. Both justices had consistently sided with plaintiffs' lawyers and had received considerable campaign support from them, and they contended the investigation was politically motivated and orchestrated by defense lawyers and corporate interests opposed to their judicial activism.

Chief Justice John L. Hill voluntarily testified before the committee and said he suspected but could not prove that information about the Supreme Court's deliberations on some cases had been improperly leaked to outsiders. Hill urged the committee to let the State Commission on Judicial Conduct, a state agency charged with investigating complaints of ethical violations by state judges, look into the allegations and "let the chips fall where they may."[10] The committee eventually concluded its investigation without recommending any action against the justices.

Hill, a former attorney general who had narrowly lost a gubernatorial race to Republican Bill Clements in 1978, had been a strong supporter of electing state judges and had spent more than $1 million winning the chief justice's seat in 1984. As did his colleagues on the court, he accepted many campaign contributions from lawyers. But in 1986, Hill announced that the "recent trend toward excessive political contributions in judicial races" had prompted him to change his mind.[11] He now advocated a so-called **merit selection** plan of gubernatorial appointments and periodic retention elections. But the other eight Supreme Court justices—like Hill, all Democrats—still favored the elective system, and the legislature ignored pleas for change.

Hill and two other Democratic justices resigned from the court before the 1988 elections, which were to focus even more attention on how expensive judicial races had become. The competing legal and financial interests in the state understood that the six Texas Supreme Court races on the ballot that year would help set the philosophy of the court for years to come. Consequently these were the most expensive court races in Texas history, with the twelve nominees raising $10 million in direct campaign contributions. Contributions to the winners averaged $836,347. Chief Justice Thomas R. Phillips, a Republican appointed by Governor Bill Clements to succeed Hill, limited contributions to $5,000 apiece and was able to raise approximately 90 percent of his funds from contributions of $500 or less. But he still managed to spend $2 million, the largest amount spent by a winning candidate. Other candidates depended heavily on large contributions ranging from $10,000 to $65,000. The smallest amount spent by a winning candidate was $449,290.[12] Reformers argued that such large contributions were creating an appearance of impropriety and eroding public confidence in the judiciary's independence.

But the successes of Republicans and conservative Democrats in the 1988 races probably hindered, more than helped, the cause of reforming the judicial selection process. The business and medical communities, which had considerable success fighting the plaintiffs' lawyers under the existing rules—with large campaign contributions of their own—viewed the new Texas Supreme Court as more conservative. "I'm a happy camper today," said one lobbyist for the Texas Medical Association, whose political action committee had supported two conservative Democratic winners and the three Republican victors.[13]

Legislative Reaction to Judicial Activism   The business community had also moved its war against the trial lawyers to the legislature, which in 1987 enacted a so-called **tort reform** package that attempted to put some limits on personal injury lawsuits and damage judgments entered by the courts. (A tort is a wrongful act over which a lawsuit can be brought.) Insurance companies, which had been lobbying nationwide for states to set limits on jury awards in personal injury cases, were major proponents of the legislation. They were joined by the Texas Civil Justice League, an organization of trade and professional associations, cities, and businesses formed in 1986 to seek similar changes in Texas tort law. The high-stakes campaign for change was enthusiastically supported by Governor Bill Clements but was opposed by consumer groups and plaintiffs' lawyers, who had been making millions of dollars from the judiciary's new liberalism.

Cities, businesses, doctors, and even charitable organizations had been hit with tremendous increases in insurance premiums, which they blamed on greedy trial lawyers and large court awards in malpractice and personal injury lawsuits. Trial lawyers blamed the insurance industry, which, they said, had started raising premiums to recoup losses in investment income after interest rates had fallen.

merit selection   Proposal under which the governor would appoint state judges from lists of potential nominees recommended by committees of experts. Appointed judges would have to run later in retention elections to keep their seats but would not have opponents on the ballot. Voters would simply decide whether a judge should remain in office or be replaced by another gubernatorial appointee.

tort reform   Changes in state law to put limits on personal injury lawsuits and damage judgments entered by the courts.

An article in the March 1, 1987, *Houston Chronicle* noted the high financial stakes in the fight. Members of the Senate Economic Development Committee alone reportedly had received $158,850 in political contributions from tort reform advocates in 1986 and $101,100 from those opposed to change. This Senate committee played a key role in developing the reform legislation.[14] Among other things, the new tort reform laws limited governmental liability, attempted to discourage frivolous lawsuits, and limited the ability of claimants to collect damages for injuries that were largely their own fault. They also set limits on punitive damages, which are designed to punish whoever caused an accident or an injury and are often awarded in addition to an injured party's compensation for actual losses.

Other limits on lawsuits were enacted in later legislative sessions. Some of the most significant were approved in 1995. Major priorities of Governor George W. Bush, these laws included even stricter limits on punitive damages and limited the liability of a party who is only partially responsible for an injury.

Judicial Impropriety   For the Texas Supreme Court, 1987 was even stormier than 1986 had been. In June, the State Commission on Judicial Conduct, which had investigated Justices Ray and Kilgarlin, issued public sanctions against each. Ray was reprimanded for seven violations of the Code of Judicial Conduct, including the acceptance of free airplane rides from attorneys practicing before the court and improper communication with lawyers about pending cases. Kilgarlin received a milder admonishment because two of his law clerks had accepted a weekend trip to Las Vegas from a law firm with cases pending before the court. Both justices were cited for soliciting funds from attorneys to help pay for litigation the justices had brought against the House Judicial Affairs Committee and a former briefing attorney who testified against them.

Later in 1987, the Texas judiciary, particularly the Texas Supreme Court, received negative publicity on a national scale when the high court upheld a record $11 billion judgment awarded Pennzoil Company in a dispute with Texaco, Inc. Several members of the Supreme Court were even featured on a network television program that questioned whether justice was "for sale" in Texas. The record judgment was awarded to Pennzoil after a state district court jury in Houston had determined that Texaco had wrongfully interfered in Pennzoil's attempt to acquire Getty Oil Company in 1984. Texaco, which sought protection under federal bankruptcy laws, later reached a settlement with Pennzoil, but it also waged a massive public relations campaign against the Texas judiciary.

In a segment on CBS-TV's *60 Minutes*, correspondent Mike Wallace pointed out that plaintiffs' attorney Joe Jamail of Houston, who represented Pennzoil, had contributed $10,000 to the original trial judge in the case and thousands of dollars more to Texas Supreme Court justices. The program also generally criticized the elective system that allowed Texas judges legally to accept large campaign contributions from lawyers who practiced before them. The program presented what had already been reported in the Texas media, but after the national exposure, Governor Clements and other Republicans renewed their attacks on the activist, Democratic justices. And some newspapers published editorials calling for a merit selection system of appointing judges.

In August 1987, a few months before the CBS program aired, Chief Justice Hill unexpectedly announced that he would leave the court in the middle of his six-year term on January 1, 1988, to return to private law practice and lobby as a private citizen for changing the judicial selection method. The legislature had refused to change the elective system earlier that year, and Hill's relationship with the other eight justices was strained. Part of the problem stemmed from the fact that all the other justices favored the continued election of judges. But personality differences were another source of friction.

Increased Partisanship and Republican Gains   Hill's resignation and the subsequent resignations in 1988 of two other Democratic justices—Robert M. Campbell and James Wallace—gave the Republicans a golden opportunity to make historic inroads on the high court. Party realignment, including midterm judicial appointments by Clements, had already increased the number of Republican judges across the state, particularly on district court benches in urban areas. But only one Republican had ever served on the Supreme Court in modern times. Will Garwood was appointed by Clements in 1979 to fill a vacancy on the court but was defeated by Democrat C. L. Ray in the 1980 election. GOP leaders already had been planning to recruit a Republican slate of candidates for the three Supreme Court seats that normally would have been on the ballot in 1988. Now, six seats were contested, including those held by three new Republican justices appointed by Clements to fill the unexpected vacancies. Even though a full Texas Supreme Court term is six years, the governor's judicial appointees have to run in the next election to keep their seats.

Clements appointed Thomas R. Phillips, a state district judge from Houston, to succeed Hill and become the first Republican chief justice since Reconstruction. Republicans won three of the six races in 1988, including Phillips's defeat of Democratic Justice Ted Z. Robertson, who had challenged the chief justice rather than run for reelection to his own seat.

The Texas Supreme Court's philosophical orientation did not change overnight, but change was on the way. One of the first major departures from a previous plaintiff-oriented ruling occurred in September 1990 when the court, in a 5 to 4 decision, upheld the constitutionality of limits on medical malpractice awards in wrongful death cases. Three years earlier, a more liberal court, in a 7 to 2 ruling, had struck down malpractice caps in personal injury cases. The new ruling was a major victory for the Texas Medical Association (TMA), which had contributed about $180,000 through its political arm to Supreme Court candidates in 1988 and helped unseat the author of the previous opinion, former Democratic Justice William Kilgarlin. The new majority opinion was written by Republican Justice Eugene Cook, one of the five successful candidates supported by the TMA.[15]

Conservatives made additional gains on the Supreme Court in 1990, with Republicans picking up a fourth seat. The partisan lineup remained 5 to 4 after the 1992 elections. In several key liability cases, the court continued to demonstrate a rediscovered philosophy favoring business defendants over plaintiffs.[16] Republicans gained a fifth Texas Supreme Court seat in 1994, to give the GOP a majority for the first time since Reconstruction. Republican challengers also unseated nineteen incumbent Democratic district judges in Harris County in strong straight-party voting. Republicans picked up a sixth and seventh seat on the Supreme Court after two Democratic justices resigned in midterm in 1995 and were replaced with Republican appointees of Governor George W. Bush.

Republicans maintained those gains by winning all four Supreme Court seats on the 1996 ballot. Three Republican justices were reelected in 1998, while Justice

Rose Spector, the only Democrat on the court's 1998 ballot, was unseated by Harriet O'Neill, an appellate judge from Houston. The Democrats lost their last seat on the court later in 1998, when Justice Raul A. Gonzalez retired in midterm.

In a 1997 study, Texas Citizen Action, a consumer advocacy group, concluded that the Texas Supreme Court strongly favored businesses and government agencies over consumers. In fifty-five "traditional injury" cases decided by the high court between August 30, 1996, and July 9, 1997, people who sued businesses or government agencies lost 71 percent of the time, according to the study. "The big winners . . . are the insurance companies, the medical community, and the government," said Walt Borges, director of Citizen Action's Court Watch program. "The court has tilted the playing field in favor of defendants. There is an appearance that the high court's justice is reserved for the moneyed, not the many."[17]

The Texas Supreme Court in a series of decisions throughout the 1990s weakened the discretion of juries in damage lawsuits, usually to the benefit of defendants, the *Texas Lawyer* concluded. Among other changes, the Supreme Court required new trial procedures so a jury would not know how wealthy a defendant was until it had determined liability for an injury. The idea apparently was to remove any possibility that a jury would render a judgment against a defendant simply because jurors knew the defendant could afford to pay. The high court also attempted to spell out when expert scientific evidence was reliable enough to be considered by juries, which previously had decided the credibility of such evidence themselves. And, in 1997, the Texas Supreme Court adopted a new rule that, according to plaintiffs' lawyers and some consumer advocates, would make it easier for defendants to get lawsuits against them dismissed without a full-blown trial.[18]

Minorities and the Judicial System   As the high-stakes battles were being waged over the Texas Supreme Court's philosophical and political makeup, minorities were actively seeking more representation in the Texas judiciary. But instead of pouring millions of dollars into judicial races, Hispanics and African Americans filed lawsuits to force change through the federal courts.

Throughout Texas history, Hispanics and African Americans have had difficulty winning election to state courts. The high cost of judicial campaigns, polarized voting along ethnic lines in the statewide or countywide races that are required of most judges, and low rates of minority participation in elections have minimized their electoral successes. The first Hispanic was seated on the Texas Supreme Court in 1984. The first African American was seated on the Texas Court of Criminal Appeals in 1990, and the first Hispanic in 1991.

Another factor limiting the number of minority judges is a proportional shortage of minority attorneys, from whose ranks judges are drawn. Fewer than 3 percent of the 11,000 attorneys in Dallas County in 1994, for example, were African American, and fewer than 2 percent were Hispanic.[19] State leaders' efforts to increase the number of minority lawyers were thwarted by an anti–affirmative action federal court ruling in 1996 and a related state attorney general's opinion, which prohibited Texas law schools and universities from giving preferential treatment to minorities in admissions, student aid, and other programs (see *Up Close:* "An Attack on Affirmative Action").

As of February 1989, a few months before a major lawsuit went to trial over the issue, only 35 of 375 state district judges were Hispanic, and only 7 were African American. Only 3 Hispanics and no African Americans were among the

Morris Overstreet of Amarillo became the first African American to win a statewide election in Texas when he won a seat on the Court of Criminal Appeals in 1990.

An Attack on Affirmative Action

The power of the federal courts over state policy was clearly demonstrated by a reverse-discrimination lawsuit filed by four white students who had been denied admission to the University of Texas School of Law. It had a far-reaching impact on efforts to promote racial and ethnic diversity in Texas's colleges and universities. Ruling in the so-called *Hopwood* case, a federal district judge in Austin said a law school admissions policy that had given preferences to minority applicants was unconstitutional. His decision was upheld by the Fifth U.S. Circuit Court of Appeals in 1996 and ultimately by the U.S. Supreme Court.* The nation's high court, however, did not reverse its earlier, landmark opinion in the *Bakke* case from California, which had held that race could be a factor in university admissions policies.† Thus Texas was the only state in which the new anti–affirmative action restrictions applied. The Fifth Circuit's decisions cover only Texas, Louisiana, and Mississippi, and Louisiana's and Mississippi's affirmative action policies were already under separate court orders.

In a related legal opinion in 1997, Texas Attorney General Dan Morales held that the *Hopwood* restrictions applied to admissions, student aid, and all other student policies at all colleges and universities in Texas. Morales's opinion was attacked as overly broad by many civil rights leaders and minority legislators, but it had the force of law. The Texas legislature, which met in 1997, attempted to soften the blow to affirmative action by enacting a new law that guaranteed automatic admissions to state universities for high school graduates who finished in the top 10 percent of their classes, regardless of their scores on college entrance examinations. The law was designed to give the best students from poor and predominantly minority school districts an equal footing in university admissions with better prepared graduates of wealthier school districts. The new law also allowed university officials to consider other admissions criteria, including a student's family income and parents' education level.

It would take several years for the effectiveness of the new law to be fully evaluated. There was little immediate change in minority enrollments at many Texas colleges after the *Hopwood* decision. But the more

flexible admissions standards applied only to entering undergraduate students, not to those seeking admission to law school and other professional schools. The dropoff in minority enrollment was particularly troubling at the UT law school the first year after the *Hopwood* restrictions went into effect. The first-year law class of almost 500 students in the fall of 1997 included only 4 African Americans and 25 Hispanics. There had been 31 African Americans and 42 Hispanics in the previous year's entering class. "The situation is desperate," said UT law school Dean Michael Sharlot.‡

By contrast, minority enrollment at the University of Houston law school did not immediately drop after the *Hopwood* ruling. Thirty Hispanics and eleven African Americans enrolled in the University of Houston's first-year law class in 1997, about the same number who enrolled in the first-year class in 1996. The University of Houston in 1997 deemphasized grades and test scores and gave more consideration to leadership, family hardship, and work experience of law school applicants.

Many higher education administrators and civil rights leaders were distressed by the *Hopwood* ruling. They said it was wrong to dismantle affirmative action programs that had been designed to improve the educational and professional opportunities of minorities, who had historically suffered from segregation and were still overrepresented among the nation's poor. They said it was particularly shortsighted to deemphasize minority recruitment efforts at a time when Hispanics and African Americans were only a few years away from making up a majority of the Texas population.

But Morales urged university officials to redouble their efforts to recruit disadvantaged students of all races. "We must express to young Texans the reality that in this country one is capable of rising as high as his or her individual talents, ability and hard work will allow," he said.§

Although the *Hopwood* decision applied only to Texas, race-neutral recruitment policies for student admissions also were imposed in California after voters in that state approved a 1996 initiative banning affirmative action.

---

*Hopwood v. Texas, 135 L Ed 1095 (1996).

†University of California Regents v. Bakke, 438 U.S. 265 (1978).

‡Quoted in Houston Chronicle, August 25, 1997.

§Quoted in Houston Chronicle, February 7, 1997.

80 judges on the 14 intermediate courts of appeals. Although they constituted at least one-third of the Texas population, African Americans and Hispanics held only 11.2 percent of the district judgeships and less than 4 percent of the intermediate appellate seats.[20] African Americans sat on only 3 of the 59 district court benches in Harris County (Houston), although they accounted for 20 percent of that county's population. African Americans held only 2 of 36 district judgeships in Dallas County, where they made up 18 percent of the population. Hispanics held 3 district court seats in Houston and 1 in Dallas.

Three African American judges in Dallas, who had been appointed by Governor Mark White to fill judicial vacancies, had been unseated in countywide elections. One was Jesse Oliver, a former legislator who had won election to the Texas House from a subdistrict within Dallas County but could not win a 1988 judicial race countywide. Oliver, a Democrat, had overwhelming African American support but lost about 90 percent of Dallas's white precincts.[21]

In a lawsuit tried in September 1989 in federal district court in Midland, attorneys for the League of United Latin American Citizens (LULAC) and other minority plaintiffs argued that the countywide system of electing state district judges violated the Voting Rights Act by diluting the voting strength of minorities. That federal law allows a federal court to strike down an electoral system which denies a protected class of voters an equal opportunity to elect officeholders of their choice. This case, *League of United Latin American Citizens et al. v. Mattox et al.*, took almost five years and two appeals to the U.S. Supreme Court to resolve. It did not change Texas's judicial selection system, but a summary of the case and its bumpy journey through the judicial process highlights the political stakes involved in the issue.

In November 1989, U.S. District Judge Lucius Bunton ruled that the countywide system was illegal in nine of the state's largest counties—Harris, Dallas, Tarrant, Bexar, Travis, Jefferson, Lubbock, Ector, and Midland. Those counties elected 172 district judges, almost half of the state's total, but had only a handful of minorities serving on the district courts. Bunton did not order an immediate remedy but strongly urged the legislature to address the issue in an upcoming special session that Governor Bill Clements had scheduled on workers' compensation. But most legislators opposed making any changes in the judicial selection process. And Clements, who opposed electing judges from subdistricts within a county, refused to add the issue to the special session's agenda.

Some Democratic leaders, including state party chair Bob Slagle and Attorney General Jim Mattox, favored the partisan election of trial judges from districts. Mattox angered Governor Clements and many Republican judges by agreeing to a district plan with the LULAC plaintiffs. That proposal would have required judges in the largest counties to run on partisan ballots from state representative districts in the 1990 elections and would have elected many minority candidates at the expense of incumbent judges. Bunton, however, rejected the Mattox-LULAC proposal. He ordered judges in the nine counties to run for election from districts, but in nonpartisan elections. Mattox then joined Secretary of State George Bayoud, the state's chief elections officer, and two district judges in asking the Fifth U.S. Circuit Court of Appeals to block Bunton's order. The federal appellate court granted the stay, and partisan countywide judicial elections were held as scheduled in 1990.

Ironically, one minority judge was outspoken in his opposition to district elections. State District Judge Felix Salazar of Houston did not seek reelection in

1990, at least in part because he disliked the prospect of having to run from a district rather than countywide. A Democrat, Salazar lived in a predominantly non-Hispanic white Houston neighborhood and in previous elections had been endorsed by a diversity of groups. He claimed that small districts could work against the interests of minorities because a judge from a conservative Anglo district could feel political pressure to sentence minority criminal defendants more harshly than whites. "The judge will have to espouse the feeling of the community. His district may think that's all right, and it will be hell unseating him," he told the *Houston Chronicle.*[22]

Other opponents of district elections argued that districts could also put undue pressure from minority communities on judges. But Jesse Oliver, the former African American legislator and judge who had been unseated in a countywide race in Dallas, did not agree that judicial districts would distort the administration of justice any more than countywide elections. "For one thing, if the community does exert pressure, then the white community is exerting all the pressure now because they are electing the judges in Dallas County," he said.[23]

Ruling in the Texas case and one from Louisiana in June 1991, the U.S. Supreme Court held that the Voting Rights Act applied to elections for the judiciary. But the high court did not strike down the at-large election system. "We believe that the state's interest in maintaining an electoral system—in this case, Texas's interest in maintaining the link between a district judge's [countywide] jurisdiction and the area of residency of his or her voters—is a legitimate factor to be considered" in determining whether the Voting Rights Act has been violated, the court wrote. But it also emphasized that the state's interest was only one factor to be considered and did not automatically outweigh proof of diluting minority votes.[24]

The U.S. Supreme Court returned the Texas lawsuit to the Fifth U.S. Circuit Court of Appeals for more deliberations, and, in January 1993, a three-judge panel of the Fifth Circuit ruled 2 to 1 that countywide elections illegally diluted the voting strength of minorities in eight counties—Harris, Dallas, Bexar, Tarrant, Jefferson, Lubbock, Ector, and Midland. Under pressure from minority legislators, Attorney General Dan Morales agreed to a settlement with the plaintiffs that would have required district elections for most of the judges in those counties and a ninth, Travis County. The settlement was endorsed by Governor Ann Richards, Democratic legislative leaders, and Democratic majorities in the Texas House and Senate. But it was opposed by Texas Supreme Court Chief Justice Thomas R. Phillips and state District Judges Sharolyn Wood of Houston and Harold Entz of Dallas, Republican defendants in the lawsuit.

The full Fifth Circuit rejected the settlement on a 9 to 4 vote in August 1993, holding that the "evidence of any dilution of minority voting power [in countywide judicial elections] is marginal at best."[25] The Fifth Circuit said partisan affiliation was a more significant factor than ethnicity in judicial elections. Then in January 1994, the U.S. Supreme Court brought the lawsuit to an end by upholding the Fifth Circuit's opinion. That left the issue of judicial selection in the hands of the Texas legislature, which for years had refused to change the elective system. State Senator Rodney Ellis, a Houston Democrat and a leading proponent of district elections, called the decision "devastating" and said it amounted to a "wholesale assault on civil rights." State District Judge Sharolyn Wood, a Houston Republican who had fought district elections, had a different reaction. "Hooray for Texas!" she said.[26]

By 1997, only 49 of the 494 state judges at the district court level and higher were Hispanic, and only 12 were African American.

Minority Judicial Appointments   Democratic Governor Mark White appointed the first Hispanic, Raul A. Gonzalez, the son of migrant workers, to the Texas Supreme Court in 1984 to fill a vacancy created by a resignation. Gonzalez made history a second time in 1986 by winning election to the seat and becoming the first Hispanic to win a statewide election in Texas. A native of Weslaco in the Rio Grande Valley, Gonzalez had been a state district judge in Brownsville and had been appointed to the Thirteenth Court of Appeals in Corpus Christi by Republican Governor Bill Clements in 1981.

Despite his background, Gonzalez, a Democrat, is one of the most conservative members of the Supreme Court. Consequently, he has come under frequent attack from plaintiffs' lawyers and, ironically, from many of the constituent groups within his own party who advocate increasing the number of minority judges. Gonzalez's reelection race in 1994, one of the most bitterly contested Supreme Court races in recent memory, proved that ethnicity can quickly take a backseat to judicial philosophy and partisanship.

Gonzalez defeated a strong challenge in the Democratic primary from Corpus Christi attorney Rene Haas, who was supported by trial lawyers, women's groups, consumer advocates, several key Democratic legislators, and a number of African American and Hispanic leaders in the Democratic Party. Gonzalez drew heavy financial support from business interests, insurance companies, and defense attorneys. He had angered many Democrats by siding with the Republican justices in a 5 to 4 decision upholding a state senate redistricting plan that favored Republicans in the 1992 legislative elections. And he angered many women, as well as trial lawyers, by voting with the court majority in two cases overturning damages awarded women who had complained of being emotionally and physically abused by men (see *Up Close*: "A Public Case over Privacy").

The Gonzalez-Haas race was often reduced to name calling in campaign mailings and TV commercials, with Haas accusing Gonzalez of defending men who abuse women and Gonzalez calling his challenger an "ambulance chaser." And, as such campaigns usually do, it made a lot of people wonder if this was the best way to choose members of one of the state's highest two courts.

Governor Ann Richards appointed the first Hispanic, Fortunato P. Benavides, to the Texas Court of Criminal Appeals in 1991 to fill a vacancy created by the death of Justice Marvin O. Teague. Benavides had been a justice on the Thirteenth Court of Appeals and a district judge and a county court-at-law judge in Hidalgo County. But his tenure on the statewide court was short-lived. He was narrowly unseated in 1992 by Republican Lawrence Meyers of Fort Worth, an Anglo, who became the first Republican elected to the criminal court. Benavides later was appointed by President Bill Clinton to the Fifth U.S. Circuit Court of Appeals.

Governor Bill Clements appointed the first African American, Louis Sturns, a Republican state district judge from Fort Worth, to the Texas Court of Criminal Appeals on March 16, 1990, to succeed Democratic Judge M. P. "Rusty" Duncan, who had died in an automobile crash. Because the vacancy had occurred after the 1990 party primaries, the State Republican Executive Committee put Sturns on the general election ballot as the GOP nominee for the seat. The State Democratic Executive Committee nominated another African American, Morris Overstreet, a county court-at-law judge from Amarillo. Overstreet narrowly defeated Sturns in the November general election to become the first African American elected to a statewide office in Texas.

Raul A. Gonzalez was the first Hispanic to serve on the Texas Supreme Court and the first Hispanic to win election to a statewide office in Texas.

Up Close

A Public Case over Privacy

A major courtroom dispute began as a youthful bedroom prank when Dan Boyles and a few of his teenage friends in Houston set up a video camera to secretly tape Boyles and his girlfriend having sex. The young woman, Susan Leigh Kerr, learned of the taping months later, after Boyles allegedly had showed the tape to other people. She sued her former boyfriend, claiming emotional distress. A Harris County jury agreed with Kerr and awarded her $1 million in damages. But Boyles appealed and, several years after the incident occurred, won a 6 to 3 ruling from the Texas Supreme Court, denying Kerr the damages. The court majority, although expressing sympathy toward Kerr, held that she could not collect damages for negligently inflicted emotional distress, the legal claim on which her suit had been based.

The ruling created an uproar. In a dissenting opinion, the court minority declared, "The rights of Texas women continue to slip away like sand through this majority's fingers." The Women and the Law Section of the State Bar accused the court of sexism. And, although Kerr later reached an out-of-court settlement with Boyles, women's groups and plaintiffs' attorneys also used the decision to campaign in 1994 against Supreme Court Justice Raul A. Gonzalez, who had sided with the majority against the young woman.

Gonzalez, who was reelected, acknowledged that Kerr had been victimized, but he said her lawyers had made a tactical mistake. He said they had sued for negligently inflicted emotional distress in order to collect damages under a homeowners' insurance policy covering Boyles. They had to claim negligence because such insurance policies cover only accidents or careless conduct, not intentional acts. Gonzalez and his colleagues in the court majority suggested that the result may have been different if Kerr's lawyers had sued under another legal theory.

Women in the Judiciary The first woman to serve as a state district judge in Texas was Sarah T. Hughes of Dallas, who was appointed to the bench in 1935 by Governor James V. Allred and served until 1961, when she resigned to accept an appointment by President John F. Kennedy to the federal district bench. Ironically, Hughes is best known for swearing a grim-faced Lyndon B. Johnson into office aboard Air Force One on November 22, 1963, following Kennedy's assassination in Dallas.

Ruby Sondock of Houston was the first woman to serve on the Texas Supreme Court. She had been a state district judge before Governor Bill Clements named her to the high court on June 25, 1982, to fill a vacancy temporarily. Sondock chose not to seek election to the seat and served only a few months. She later returned to the district bench.

Barbara Culver, a state district judge from Midland, became the second female Texas Supreme Court justice when Clements appointed her in February 1988 to fill another vacancy. Culver also served less than a year. She was unseated by Democrat Jack Hightower in the 1988 general election.

Democrat Rose Spector, a state district judge from San Antonio, became the first woman elected to the Supreme Court when she defeated Republican Justice Eugene Cook in 1992. A second woman, Republican Priscilla Owen, an attorney from Houston, was elected to the Supreme Court in 1994. Another woman, Deborah Hankinson, an appellate judge from Dallas, was appointed to the Supreme Court in 1997 by Gov. George W. Bush to fill a vacancy.

In 1994 Republican Sharon Keller, a former Dallas County prosecutor, became the first woman elected to the Texas Court of Criminal Appeals. Republican Sue Holland, a former state district judge from Plano, became the second woman elected to the criminal court in 1996. By 1997, 107 women held district or appellate judgeships in Texas.

The Search for Solutions   The debates and lawsuits over judicial elections and representation in Texas emphasize the significant role of the courts in policy making as well as day-to-day litigation. The composition of the courts makes a difference. Although some may argue that the role of a judge is simply to apply the law to the facts and issues of a specific case, judges bring to the courts their own values, philosophical views, and life experiences, and these factors serve to filter their interpretations of the law and determine the shape of justice for millions of people.

There is no one simple solution to all the problems and inequities outlined here. Strict limits on the amount of campaign funds that judges and judicial candidates could raise from lawyers and other special interests, for example, could reduce the appearance of influence peddling in the judiciary and temper the high-stakes war between the trial lawyers and the business community for philosophical control of the courts. Campaign finance reform could also help build or restore public confidence in the impartiality of the judiciary. Such reform, however, may not improve opportunities for minorities to win election to the bench. Nor would it shorten the long election ballots that discourage Texans from casting informed votes in judicial races.

The same shortcomings could be anticipated with nonpartisan judicial elections or a merit selection system, two frequently mentioned alternatives to Texas's system of partisan judicial elections. In nonpartisan elections, judges and judicial candidates would not run under Democratic, Republican, or other party labels. This arrangement would guard against partisan bickering on the multimember appellate courts and eliminate the possibility that a poorly qualified candidate could be swept into office by one-party, straight-ticket voting.

Under the merit selection plan (sometimes referred to as the Missouri Plan), the governor would appoint judges from lists of nominees recommended by committees of experts. The appointed judges would have to run later in retention elections to keep their seats, but they would not have opponents on the ballot. Voters would simply decide whether a judge should remain in office or be removed, to be replaced by another gubernatorial appointee.

Texas was one of only seven states in 1994 with a partisan election system for judges. Thirteen states had nonpartisan judicial elections, and approximately thirty used some sort of appointment or merit selection plan. Each alternative has its advantages, but none would necessarily eliminate undue political influence on the judiciary.

Under a merit selection system, interest groups could still apply pressure on the governor and the members of the committees making recommendations for appointments. Although a merit selection plan could be written to require the nominating panels to make ethnically diverse recommendations to the governor, that would not answer the question of how to structure the retention elections. Minority appointees could still be at a disadvantage in **retention elections** if they have to run countywide, rather than in smaller geographic districts. Despite their popularity among minority leaders, district elections for judges are still viewed by many decision makers as a form of **ward politics** that may be appropriate or desirable for legislative seats but not for judges. Judges, they argue, do not represent a particular constituency.

Attempts were made to overhaul the judicial selection process during the 1995 and 1997 legislative sessions, but they failed. In 1995, however, lawmakers set

Sarah T. Hughes (center), the first woman to serve as a district court judge in Texas, in 1961 was appointed a federal district court judge and in 1963 swore in Lyndon Johnson as president after John F. Kennedy was assassinated in Dallas.

Rose Spector, being sworn in, was the first woman elected to the Texas Supreme Court.

modest limits on campaign contributions to judges and judicial candidates and restricted the periods during which judges and judicial candidates could accept political donations (see *Up Close*: "Limited Reform").

CRIME AND PUNISHMENT

Under both the U.S. Constitution and the Texas Constitution, a person charged with a crime is presumed innocent until the state can prove guilt beyond a reasonable doubt to a judge or a jury. The state also has the burden to prosecute fairly— to follow principles of procedural due process outlined in constitutional and statutory law and interpreted by the courts. Even persons charged with the most heinous crimes retain these fundamental rights, and although there is often a public outcry about "coddling criminals," the process is designed to protect an individual from governmental abuses, to lessen the chance that an innocent person will be wrongly convicted of a crime.

In Texas, as well as in other states, these rights have sometimes been violated. But over the years, the federal courts, in particular, have strengthened their enforcement. Through a case-by-case process, the U.S. Supreme Court has applied the Bill of Rights to the states by way of the Due Process and the Equal Protection Clauses of the Fourteenth Amendment to the U.S. Constitution. The failure of police or prosecutors to comply with specific procedures for handling a person accused of a crime may result in charges against an individual being dropped or a conviction reversed on appeal.

Arrested suspects must be taken before a magistrate—usually a justice of the peace or a municipal court judge—to be formally informed of the offense or offenses with which they are charged and to be told their legal rights. Depending on the charges, a bond may be set to allow them to get out of jail and remain free pending their trials. They have the right to remain silent, to consult with an attorney and have an attorney present during questioning by law enforcement officers or prosecutors, and to be warned that any statement they make can be used against them in a trial. Defendants who cannot afford to hire a lawyer must be provided with court-appointed attorneys at taxpayer expense. Many of these protections were extended to the states by the U.S. Supreme Court in the landmark *Miranda* **ruling** in 1966.[27]

All criminal defendants have the right to a trial by jury but, except in capital murder cases, they may waive a jury trial and have their cases decided by a judge. Defendants may plead guilty, not guilty, or **nolo contendere** (no contest). Prosecutors and defense attorneys settle many cases through plea bargaining, a process described earlier in this chapter. The trial judge does not have to accept a plea bargain but usually does. When defendants choose to have their guilt or innocence determined by the judge, the judge also determines the punishment if they are convicted. A jury can return a guilty verdict only if all jurors agree that the defendant is guilty beyond a reasonable doubt. If a jury cannot reach a unanimous verdict, even after lengthy negotiations and prodding from the judge, the judge must declare a mistrial. In that case, the prosecution has to seek a new trial with another jury or drop the charges. In a jury trial, a defendant may choose to have the punishment also set by the jury. If not, it is determined by the judge.

In 1991 the Texas Court of Criminal Appeals took the major step of ordering, for the first time, an official definition of "reasonable doubt" that was to be submitted to every jury deciding a criminal case. According to the definition, evidence

retention elections Elections in which judges run on their own records rather than against other candidates. Voters cast their ballots on the question of whether the incumbent judge should stay in office.

ward politics Refers (often with negative connotations) to partisan politics linked to political favoritism.

Miranda **ruling** Far-reaching decision of the U.S. Supreme Court that requires law enforcement officers to warn a criminal suspect of his or her right to remain silent and have an attorney present before questioning.

nolo contendere A plea of "no contest" to a criminal charge.

Up Close

Limited Reform

After years of prodding by reform advocates, the Texas legislature in 1995 imposed the first limits on campaign contributions in state political races. The modest limits applied only to judges and judicial candidates. They restricted the periods during which judges and their challengers could raise political funds and limited individual contributions to $5,000 per election. But a judge could still receive as much as $30,000 from members of the same law firm and as much as $300,000 in total contributions from special interests through political action committees.

The 1996 races for the Texas Supreme Court—the first conducted under the new law—demonstrated how weak the new reforms were. Four Republican incumbents, including Chief Justice Thomas R. Phillips, still raised a combined $4 million, easily swamping fund-raising efforts by their unsuccessful challengers. One Republican justice, Greg Abbott, who had only a Libertarian opponent, offered to return contributions to donors after no Democrat filed against him. But few contributors asked for their money back.

Much of the Republicans' money came from defense lawyers, doctors, insurance companies, and other business interests who only a few years earlier had accused plaintiffs' lawyers of trying to use large campaign contributions to unduly influence the high court when it had a Democratic majority. Patrice Barron, a Houston attorney and Democrat who unsuccessfully ran against one of the incumbent justices, noted the irony. "It appears the court has become what [its new Republican majority] once condemned, but the buyers are different," she said.*

---

*Quoted in *Houston Chronicle*, September 22, 1996.

---

against a criminal defendant must be so convincing that jurors would be willing to rely on it "without hesitation" in the most important events in their own lives.[28]

Jury trials are required in **capital murder** cases, which are punishable by death or life in prison. Use of the death penalty is much more restricted in Texas and other states now than it was little more than a generation ago. Executions in Texas used to be carried out by electrocution at the state prison unit in downtown Huntsville. Some 361 individuals were executed in Texas from 1924 to 1964, when executions were suspended because of legal challenges.

In 1972 the U.S. Supreme Court halted executions in all the states by striking down all the death penalty laws then on the books as unconstitutional. The high court held that capital punishment, as then practiced, violated the constitutional prohibition against "cruel and unusual punishment" because it could be applied in a discriminatory fashion.[29] Not only could virtually any act of murder be punished by death under the old Texas law, but so could rape and certain other crimes.

In 1973 the Texas legislature rewrote the death penalty statute to try to meet the Supreme Court's standards by defining capital crimes as murder committed under specific circumstances. The list was expanded later and now includes the murder of a law enforcement officer or firefighter who is on duty, murder committed during the course of committing certain other major crimes, murder for hire, murdering more than one person, murder of a prison guard or employee, murder committed while escaping or attempting to escape from a penal institution, or murder of a child younger than six.

A jury that has found a person guilty of capital murder must answer certain questions about the defendant before choosing between death or life imprisonment, the only punishments available. Jurors are required to consider whether a

capital murder Murder committed under certain circumstances for which the death penalty or life in prison must be imposed.

THE TEXAS JUDICIARY • CHAPTER 24 **865**

probation Procedure under which a convicted criminal is not sent to prison if he or she meets certain conditions, such as restrictions on travel and associates.

parole Early release of an inmate from prison, subject to certain conditions.

convicted murderer will be a continuing danger to society as well as mitigating circumstances, including evidence of retardation, before deciding punishment.[30]

The first execution under the 1973 Texas law was carried out in 1982. By then the legislature, acting in 1977, had changed the method of execution from the electric chair to the intravenous injection of a lethal substance. By 1996 more than one hundred men were executed in Texas by lethal injection, and in 1998 Karla Faye Tucker was the first woman since the Civil War to be put to death, for killing two people with a pickax almost fifteen years earlier (see *Up Close:* "Witnessing Executions").

After capital murder, the most serious criminal offense is a first-degree felony— for example, aggravated sexual assault and noncapital murder—punishable by a prison sentence of five to ninety-nine years or life. Second-degree felonies, such as burglary of someone's home and bribery, are punishable by two to twenty years in prison. Third-degree felonies—including intentional bodily injury to a child and theft of trade secrets—are punishable by two to ten years in prison. State jail felonies, which include many property crimes, such as burglary of an office building, and minor drug offenses, are punishable by up to two years in a state-run jail or time in a community corrections program, each of which is supposed to emphasize rehabilitation as well as punishment.

The most minor crimes are classified as Class A, B, or C misdemeanors. Crimes such as public lewdness and harboring a runaway child are examples of Class A misdemeanors and are punishable by a maximum $4,000 fine and/or one year in a county jail. The unauthorized use of television cable decoding or falsely claiming to be a police officer are examples of Class B misdemeanors and carry a maximum sentence of 180 days in a county jail and a $2,000 fine. Class C misdemeanors include illegal gambling and the issuance of a bad check. They are punishable by a maximum $500 fine.

People convicted of crimes can be sentenced to **probation** (also called community supervision): they are not sent to prison but must meet certain conditions, such as restrictions on where they travel and with whom they associate. Except for those under the death penalty, convicted felons sentenced to prison can become eligible for **parole**—or early release under supervisory restrictions—after serving a portion of their sentence. Capital murderers sentenced to life in prison can be considered for parole after serving forty years.

A landmark federal court order in 1980 forced the state to spend billions of dollars expanding and improving its prison system and forced the legislature to reevaluate the punishment of some criminals (see *Up Close:* "Criminal Justice, an Expensive Headache").

THE POLITICS OF CRIMINAL JUSTICE

The Texas Court of Criminal Appeals must try to balance the constitutional rights of convicts against the public welfare, a role that puts the court at the center of major philosophical and political battles. Reversals of convictions, lengthy delays in the executions of those convicted of capital murder, concerns about procedural technicalities, and the release of individuals who are perceived by the public to be guilty have prompted accusations that the judiciary in general and the Court of Criminal Appeals in particular are soft on crime. Whether or not these perceptions are correct, they must be confronted in the political arena.

Death penalty protesters outside the Huntsville prison on the occasion of the execution of Karla Faye Tucker, the first woman to be put to death in Texas since the Civil War.

Witnessing Executions

After executions were resumed in Texas in 1982, they were witnessed only by a limited number of public officials plus as many as five people designated by the condemned, if he wished to have family members or friends present. Strong lobbying by crime victims' advocates convinced the Board of Criminal Justice in 1995 to expand the witness list to include as many as five relatives or friends of the condemned's murder victim or victims. Survivors said watching their loved ones' killers be put to death could help bring "closure" to their ordeal. The witness viewing area in the small death chamber in Huntsville was partitioned to separate the condemned's witnesses from those of the victim.

The first execution to be witnessed by the victims' loved ones was that of Leo Ernest Jenkins on February 9, 1996. Jenkins had been sentenced to die by lethal injection for the August 1988 murders of Mark Brandon Kelley, twenty-six, and his sister, Kara Denise Kelley Voss, twenty, during a robbery of their family's pawnshop in Houston. The execution was witnessed by the victims' parents, Linda and Jim Kelley; their sister, Robin Amanda Kelley; their grandmother, Angie Kelley; and Mark Kelley's widow, Lisa.

"This is justice in a big way. Believe me, justice was served tonight," Linda Kelley, the victims' mother, said. "I was angry. I was angry at him [Jenkins] when he died."*

_____

*Quoted in *Dallas Morning News*, February 10, 1996.

The combatants on one side of the debate include the prosecutors—the elected district and county attorneys—who do not like to see the convictions they have won reversed, partly because too many reversals could cost them reelection. Judges of the trial courts, who also periodically face the voters, are sensitive to reversals, too. So are the police and sheriffs' departments that arrest the defendants and provide the evidence on which criminal convictions are based.

On the other side of the debate are defense attorneys, who have an obligation to protect the rights and interests of their clients and who in their appeals often attack procedures used by police, prosecutors, and trial judges. Also on this side are civil libertarians, who insist that a criminal defendant's every right—even the most technical—be protected, and minority groups, who have challenged the conduct of trials when minorities have been excluded from juries weighing the fate of minority defendants (see *Up Close*: "More Is Involved Than Technicalities").

Throughout much of its history, the Texas Court of Criminal Appeals has been accused of excessive concern with legal technicalities that benefit convicted criminals.[31] The court reversed 42 percent of the cases appealed to it during the first quarter of the century, when Texas and many other states had a harsh system of criminal justice that often reflected class and racial bias at the trial level. By 1966 the reversal rate had dropped to 3 percent. But the defeat of incumbent judges, retirements, and the expansion of the court from three to five members in 1967 and to nine members in 1977 again changed its composition.

In the late 1980s, the Court of Criminal Appeals began to give mixed signals to the lower courts and other participants in the judicial system. Exercising a philosophy that was tagged "new federalism" by some critics, the court, using

Up Close

Criminal Justice, an Expensive Headache

An overcrowded and inadequately staffed prison system prompted U.S. District Judge William Wayne Justice of Tyler to declare Texas's prisons unconstitutional in 1980 in a landmark lawsuit brought by inmates (*Ruiz v. Estelle*). Among other things, the court ordered the population of prison units limited to 95 percent of capacity. That limit and an increase in the violent crime rate in the 1980s helped produce a criminal justice crisis that saw hundreds of dangerous convicts released from prison early and thousands of other criminals backlogged in overcrowded county jails.

The Ruiz lawsuit was settled in 1992, with the state promising to maintain constitutional prisons. In 1993 the legislature enacted a major package of criminal justice reforms. The minimum time that violent criminals would have to serve in prison before being eligible for parole was doubled—from one-fourth to one-half of their sentences. To make sure there was enough room to keep the most dangerous felons in prison longer, thousands of property and drug offend-ers were to be diverted into community corrections programs or a new system of state jails, where educa-tion, drug abuse treatment, and other rehabilitation programs were to be emphasized.

Financed by bond issues totaling $3 billion, a huge prison expansion program was completed in the mid-1990s. With more than 140,000 spaces, Texas finally had enough room for all its prisoners in its correc-tions system. Some counties had sufficient jail space to permit them to lease space to house convicts from other states. But criminal justice experts warned that the relief was only temporary, and by 1997, prison officials were making plans to expand the state's prison capacity again—by several thousand spaces. Lower parole rates and long prison sentences were once again taking their toll on the state's resources.

Also in 1997, the need for the state to more closely monitor several county jails that had been turned over to private operators became obvious. In a videotape shown on a national television program, private guards at the Brazoria County Jail near Houston were shown roughing up prisoners from Missouri. The inci-dent prompted Missouri officials to withdraw their convicts from privately operated jails in Texas.

---

the Texas Constitution, appeared to be moving in the direction of placing limi-tations on permissible evidence greater than those required by the U.S. Consti-tution and federal law. A 1987 ruling prohibited the use of videotaped testi-mony by a child who was sexually abused, and a 1988 ruling expanded a defendant's right to legal counsel. But the court subsequently issued contradic-tory decisions in 1989 and 1990 that suggested it was backing down from its new federalism approach.[32]

Then, after the 1990 elections produced significant changes in the court's membership, the new federalism issue resurfaced in the case of *William Randolph Heitman v. State*.[33] In this 1991 decision, the court ruled 7 to 2 that the Texas Consti-tution granted criminal defendants more protection against illegal searches and seizures by police than the U.S. Constitution did. Neil McCabe, a professor at South Texas College of Law, called the decision a "declaration of independence for the Texas judiciary in criminal cases" and said it followed a national trend. Prose-cutors were concerned that the decision could have a broader effect on criminal appeals.[34] But, once again, the court signaled a shift toward a more conservative philosophy after the 1994 elections of Judges Sharon Keller and Steve Mansfield had increased the number of Republicans on the court to three. During the first thirteen months the new judges were in office, for example, the court ordered the reinstatement of two death sentences it had reversed before Keller's and Mansfield's arrival. But *Texas Lawyer*, in an analysis, concluded that the court as a whole was "badly fractured, as evidenced by its inability to decide key issues with more than a plurality of judges."[35]

A Republican sweep of all three court seats on the 1996 ballot promised a more conservative court. Democratic Judge Frank Maloney, a former defense lawyer, was unseated by state District Judge Tom Price of Dallas. State District Judge Sue Holland of Plano and Williamson County prosecutor Paul Womack won races for open seats vacated by the retirement of two Democratic judges. A 6-to-3 Democratic majority had become a 6-to-3 Republican majority, the first GOP majority on the court since Reconstruction. Republicans increased their majority to 7 to 2 in 1997, when longtime Presiding Judge Mike McCormick, one of the court's most conservative members, switched from the Democratic to the Republican party. The Republican takeover of the court was completed in 1998, when Democrats lost their last two seats on the panel.

INCREASED POLICY ROLE OF THE STATE COURTS

The federal judiciary has traditionally had more influence than the state courts in molding public policy. Over the years, it has been at the center of political debate over the proper role of the judiciary in the policy-making process (see Chapter 13).

Much of the Texas Supreme Court's time is spent refereeing disputes between trial lawyers and insurance companies. But in recent years this court has increasingly played an active role in shaping broader public policies and addressing significant constitutional issues (see *Up Close*: "The Constitution Is for Everybody").

The Courts and Education   In one of its most significant and best known rulings, the Texas Supreme Court in the Edgewood school finance case in 1989

 Up Close

More Is Involved Than Technicalities

Randall Dale Adams and Clarence Lee Brandley owe their lives to the appellate process. Both men came perilously close to being executed for murders they apparently did not commit. Adams spent more than a decade behind bars before he was released in 1989, after a documentary film indicated he had been wrongfully convicted of the murder of a Dallas police officer. The Texas Court of Criminal Appeals ordered

a new trial, but the Dallas County district attorney chose not to retry him.

Brandley, an African American janitor at Conroe High School, was convicted by an all-white jury of the rape and murder of a sixteen-year-old girl, but the Court of Criminal Appeals reversed the conviction after being presented with evidence that Brandley had not received a fair trial and had been a victim of racial prejudice. Neither man would have lived long enough to win freedom had not the appellate process, which many prosecutors attack as too time consuming and too "technical," worked to delay their scheduled executions.

unanimously ordered major basic changes in the financing of public education to provide more equity between rich and poor school districts.[36] The lawsuit was brought against the state by poor districts after years of legislative inaction against a property tax-based finance system that had produced huge disparities in local education resources and in the quality of local schools.

The unanimity of the opinion, written by Justice Oscar Mauzy, a Democrat, surprised many legislators and school officials because two of the three Republican justices on the court at that time had initially been appointed by Governor Bill Clements, who had insisted that the courts had no business trying to tell the legislature what to do about school finance. The decision, which held that the school finance law violated a constitutional requirement for an efficient education system, was obviously the product of considerable compromise among the nine justices. Their deliberations were secret, but Justice Franklin Spears, a Democrat, told the *Fort Worth Star-Telegram*: "We wanted to speak with one voice. The opinion is a composite of many ideas, much brainstorming, much compromising." Mark Yudof, then dean of the University of Texas School of Law, said the court may have been determined to offer a united front because it attached as much importance to the school finance case as a united U.S. Supreme Court had to the landmark *Brown v. Board of Education of Topeka* desegregation case in the 1950s.[37]

Compliance with the school finance order did not come easily, however. A 1990 school finance law failed to meet the court's standards, so the court issued another order in 1991 and a third order in 1992 after the legislature again came up short. The court lost its unanimity on the third order, which struck down a 1991 law that had established special county education districts with a minimum property tax. In a challenge brought this time by wealthy school districts, a 7 to 2 court majority ruled that the tax was a statewide property tax prohibited by the Texas Constitution. Mauzy and fellow Democratic Justice Lloyd Doggett sharply dissented.

The legislature responded with still another school finance law in 1993. This law gave wealthy school districts several options for sharing revenue with poor districts, and it was challenged by both rich and poor districts. The rich districts objected to sharing their property wealth, and the poor districts argued that the new law was inadequately funded and did not sufficiently reduce the funding gap between rich and poor districts. The Texas Supreme Court upheld the law in a 5 to 4 decision in January 1995. By that time, a majority of the court's members were Republicans. In the majority opinion, Justice John Cornyn, a Republican, wrote:

> Children who live in property-poor districts and children who live in property-rich districts now have substantially equal access to the funds necessary for a general diffusion of knowledge. . . . It is apparent from the court's opinions that we have recognized that an efficient system does not require equality of access to revenue at all levels.

But Republican Justice Craig Enoch, who dissented, wrote that the state had failed to adequately provide for the public schools. He said the new law contributed to further "constitutional tensions" by promoting continued use of local property taxes.[38]

In 1992 a state district judge in Brownsville ruled that the state's system of funding higher education also was unconstitutional because it short-changed Hispanics in South Texas. But the Texas Supreme Court reversed that decision and upheld the higher education system.[39]

Up Close

The Constitution Is for Everybody

The Texas Supreme Court ruled in 1994 that a Ku Klux Klan leader had a constitutional right to keep Klan membership lists secret. The high court held that a state district judge had illegally jailed Michael Lowe for refusing to turn over the membership lists to state officials investigating the harassment and intimidation of African Americans attempting to desegregate a public housing project in Vidor. "The rights to form, discuss and express unpopular views are protected fundamental rights," the court said. "Where the organization advocates views which might subject members to ridicule . . . from the mere fact of membership, First Amendment associational rights are the basis for a qualified privilege against disclosure of membership lists."[*]

In an unusual twist, the white supremacist was represented by an African American civil liberties lawyer, Anthony Griffin of Galveston. The case, which Griffin took at the request of the American Civil Liberties Union, cost him another job—as chief Texas attorney for the National Association for the Advancement of Colored People. Griffin said he was "ecstatic" about the court's ruling. "I think it's a wonderful opinion for the state Supreme Court to reaffirm the virtue of the First Amendment," he said.[†]

---

[*]*Ex Parte Lowe*, 887 S.W.2d 1 (1994).

[†]Quoted in the *Houston Chronicle*, June 9, 1994.

In another education case with major implications, the Texas Supreme Court in 1994 upheld the right of Texas parents to educate their own children. Ending a ten-year legal battle, the court overturned a Texas Education Agency ruling that home schools were illegal. The court held that a home school was legitimate if parents used books, workbooks, or other written materials and met "basic education goals" by teaching basic subjects.[40]

The Courts and Abortion Rights   In 1998, the Texas Supreme Court upheld $1.2 million in damages against anti-abortion protesters who had staged massive demonstrations at Houston abortion clinics during the 1992 Republican National Convention. Some clinics had been vandalized and patients harassed. The high court also upheld most of the restrictions a lower court had set on protests near the clinics and the homes of several doctors who performed abortions. The court said it was trying to balance free speech rights with the rights of the.clinics to conduct business, the rights of women to have access to pregnancy counseling and abortion services, and the privacy rights of physicians. The court prohibited demonstrators from blocking access to clinics, intimidating patients, and engaging in other forms of aggressive behavior.[41] In a case from Florida, the U.S. Supreme Court had ruled in 1994 that judges could limit protests near abortion clinics but that restrictions had to be strictly limited.[42]

The Courts and Gay Rights   Deciding still another controversial issue, the Texas Supreme Court in 1996 ruled against the Log Cabin Republicans, a gay GOP group that had been denied a booth at the Republican State Convention in San Antonio. The court said the group had no grounds to sue the Republican Party for deprivation of rights under the Texas Constitution because the party was not a governmental agency.[43]

Politics in Cyberspace

The Texas Judiciary

Texas courts have a direct impact on the lives of Texans. There is a good chance that the average citizen of Texas will come into contact with a state or local court in his or her lifetime, whether as the victim of a crime, a party to a civil case, or as a citizen called for jury duty. Knowledge and information about the structure and procedures of the courts and the criminal justice system enhance one's ability to negotiate the legal processes.

Office of Court Administration
http://www.courts.state.tx.us

This agency provides administrative support and technical assistance to all courts in Texas. Links to all state appellate courts are found here along with information about the state court system.

Texas Department of Criminal Justice
http://www.tdcj.state.tx.us

This agency is responsible for the administration of the state's prison system. Organizational data can be found at this site along with statistics and reports on the prison population, prison sites, paroles, and programs designed to prevent recidivism.

Texas Juvenile Probation Commission
http://www.tjpc.state.tx.us

This agency works with local juvenile probation departments to rehabilitate juvenile offenders. This site provides information about state funding, training, certification, and monitoring of caseworkers and statistics on juvenile offenders.

Texas Youth Commission
http://www.tyc.state.tx.us

This site provides information on juvenile crime and correction in Texas.

Office of the Attorney General
http://www.oag.state.tx.us

Although the attorney general has limited responsibilities in criminal matters, this office has responsibilities for consumer law, elder protection, crime victim compensation, and child support services. Information on these issues can be found at this site.

Bureau of Justice Statistics
http://www.ojp.usdoj.gov/bjs

The Bureau of Justice Statistics is the primary source for criminal justice statistics in the United States. It "collects, analyzes, and disseminates information on crime, criminal offenders, victims of crime, and the operation of justice systems at all levels of government."

SUMMARY NOTES

- Texas has a confusing array of courts, many with overlapping jurisdictions. It is one of only two states with a bifurcated court system at the highest appellate level. The Texas Supreme Court is the court of last resort in civil cases and the Texas Court of Criminal Appeals in criminal cases.
- The judicial system is particularly inadequate in urban counties, where thousands of criminal cases each year are disposed of through plea bargains negotiated by prosecutors and defendants and where it can take years to resolve civil disputes.
- State judges, except those on municipal court benches, are elected in partisan elections. But there has been increasing political and legal pressure to change the selection process. Possible alternatives are nonpartisan elections, elections from geographic districts, or a merit selection plan under which the governor would appoint judges from lists of nominees recommended by experts. The latter plan would require the appointed judges to run later in retention elections to keep their seats, but they would not have opponents on the ballot.
- Grand juries are supposed to ensure that the government has sufficient evidence to proceed with a criminal prosecution against an individual. Petit, or trial, juries hear evidence and render verdicts in cases involving both civil and criminal matters.

- Litigants in civil cases and most criminal cases can waive a jury trial and have their cases decided by a judge. Trials move through opening statements, examination and cross-examination of witnesses, presentation of evidence, rebuttal, summation, and verdict.

- Cases can be appealed to appellate courts, where there are no juries. Appellate courts review the decisions and procedures of lower courts for conformity to constitutional and statutory requirements.

- Judges who espouse strict construction see their role as narrowly interpreting and applying the law while leaving public policy initiatives to the legislature. Judicial activists believe they should take a more expansive view of the law by reading broad policy implications into their decisions.

- The Texas Supreme Court became a battleground in the 1980s between trial attorneys who represent injured parties in damage lawsuits and the businesses, doctors, and insurance companies they sue. After trial lawyers began contributing millions of dollars to successful Supreme Court candidates, longtime judicial precedents that had favored the corporate establishment began to fall, and it became easier for plaintiffs to win huge damage awards.

- The business and medical communities retaliated by winning some legislative changes in the procedures under which lawsuits are tried and by increasing their political contributions in judicial races.

- Party realignment, including appointments by Governor Bill Clements to fill midterm vacancies, increased the number of Republican judges on trial courts in the 1980s. Soon Republicans won their first majority on the Texas Supreme Court in modern times.

- Women and minorities historically have been underrepresented on the state's court benches at all levels. In a lawsuit by minority plaintiffs, U.S. District Judge Lucius Bunton of Midland ruled in 1989 that the countywide system of electing district, or trial, judges in nine of the state's largest counties violated the federal Voting Rights Act by diluting the voting strength of minorities. But that ruling was reversed by the U.S. Supreme Court in 1994.

- The Texas Court of Criminal Appeals is at the center of philosophical and political disputes regarding the constitutional rights of convicted criminals. In a few key cases, the court has ruled that the Texas Constitution provides criminal defendants more protection than the U.S. Constitution does.

- The federal judiciary has traditionally had more influence than the state courts in molding public policy. But in recent years the Texas Supreme Court has increasingly played an active role in addressing significant constitutional issues.

SELECTED READINGS

BAUM, LAWRENCE. "Supreme Courts in the Policy Process," in *The State of the States*, ed. Carl E. Van Horn (Washington, D.C.: CQ Press, 1996), pp. 143–60.

CHAMPAGNE, ANTHONY. "Judicial Selection in Texas: Democracy's Deadlock," in *Texas Politics: A Reader*, eds. Anthony Champagne and Edward J. Harpham (New York: Norton, 1997), pp. 97–110.

CHAMPAGNE, ANTHONY, and GREG THIELEMANN. "Awareness of Trial Court Judges." *Judicature* 74 (February/March 1991): 271–76.

CHAPMAN, RONALD W. "Judicial Roulette: Alternatives to Single-Member Districts as a Legal and Political Solution to Voting-Rights Challenges to At-Large Elections." *SMU Law Review* 48 (January/February 1995) pp. 457–84.

HILL, JOHN. "Taking Texas Judges out of Politics: An Argument for Merit Election." *Baylor Law Review* 40 (Summer 1988): 340–66.

PARRISH, JAMES R. *A Two-Headed Monster: Crimes and Texas Prisons*. Austin: Eakin, 1989.

REAMY, GERALD S. *Criminal Offenses and Defenses in Texas*. Norcross, Ga.: Harrison, 1987.

SHARP, JOHN. *Texas Crime, Texas Justice*. Austin: Comptroller of Public Accounts, 1992.

TEXAS JUDICIAL COUNCIL, Office of Court Administration. *Texas Judicial System, 69th Annual Report*. Austin: Texas Judicial Council, 1997.

TEXAS RESEARCH LEAGUE. *The Texas Judiciary: A Structural-Functional Overview*. Report 1. Austin: Texas Research League, 1990.

TEXAS RESEARCH LEAGUE. *Texas Courts: A Proposal for Structural-Functional Reform*. Report 2. Austin: Texas Research League, 1991.

ASK YOURSELF ABOUT POLITICS

1 Are local governments more responsive to their citizens than the national government?
Yes ⬜ No ⬜

2 Should cities be able to choose any form of government they want?
Yes ⬜ No ⬜

3 Should Texas cities have the power to enact a local income tax to replace the sales and property tax?
Yes ⬜ No ⬜

4 Should every county in Texas be required to use the same form of government?
Yes ⬜ No ⬜

5 Should Texas enact laws giving school districts greater authority over local education?
Yes ⬜ No ⬜

6 With so many special districts in Texas, should the state attempt to consolidate local governments into larger, more comprehensive governmental units?
Yes ⬜ No ⬜

CHAPTER
25
LOCAL GOVERNMENT IN TEXAS
CITIES, TOWNS, COUNTIES, AND SPECIAL DISTRICTS

CHAPTER OUTLINE

The Power of Local Government

Local Governments in the Texas Political System

Municipal Government in Texas

Forms of City Government in Texas

Municipal Election Systems

City Revenues and Expenditures

Urban Problems in Texas

County Government in Texas

Criticisms of County Government

Special Districts in Texas

Independent School Districts

Councils of Government

Solutions to the Problems of Local Government

FEATURES

What Do You Think? Why Different Forms of City Government?

People in Politics: Ron Kirk and Lee Brown, History-Making Mayors

Up Close: The Job of the City Council Member

A Conflicting View: The Debate over Electoral Systems

What Do You Think? Circle C Ranch: A Subdivision's Fight against Austin

Up Close: Expensive Tax Breaks

Politics in Cyberspace: Local Government in Texas

What power do governments have over citizens? What power do citizens have over government? Because the 5,000 local governments in Texas are closest to the citizens and citizens can potentially have direct impact on their decisions, where does the power in Texas government really lie?

THE POWER OF LOCAL GOVERNMENT

Ever since the founding of the nation, Americans have expressed a strong belief in the right to local self-government.[1] In many areas of the young country, local governments existed long before there was a functioning state or federal government. Those early communities thus had limited expectations of what services the state or federal government might provide.

This history has led to the popular notion that local governments have fundamental rights based on the concept of local sovereignty, or ultimate power. Thomas Jefferson, for example, developed a theory of local government, designed in part to strengthen the powers of the states, in which local sovereignty was rooted in the sovereignty of the individual.[2] Some people suggest that this cultural legacy persists in grass-roots politics, the flight to suburbia, and the creation of neighborhood organizations. Today it is common to hear the opinion that local government is closest to the people and best represents their interests and desires.[3]

Although this traditional view is deeply held, the prevailing constitutional theory on the relationship of local governments to the state is the **unitary system**. Simply stated, this theory holds that local governments are the creations of the state. The powers, functions, and responsibilities that they exercise have been delegated or granted them by the state government, and no local government has sovereign powers. Numerous court cases have enunciated this principle, which is referred to as the **Dillon rule**, but the best summary is derived from an Iowa case in which a court held the following:

> The true view is this: Municipal corporations owe their origin to, and derive their powers and rights wholly from, the legislature. It breathes into them the breath of life, without which they cannot exist. As it creates, so it may destroy. If it may destroy, it may abridge and control. Unless there is some constitutional limitation on the right, the legislature might by a single act . . . sweep from its existence all of the municipal corporations in the State, and the corporations could not prevent it. We know of no limitation on this right so far as the corporations are concerned.[4]

The Dillon rule is now the prevailing theory defining the relationships of states and local governments, and it is applicable to local governments in Texas.

LOCAL GOVERNMENTS IN THE TEXAS POLITICAL SYSTEM

unitary system A constitutional arrangement whereby authority rests with the central government; regional governments have only those powers given them by the central government.

Dillon rule A principle holding that local governments are creations of state government and that their powers and responsibilities are defined by the state.

Local governments—counties, cities, school districts, and special districts—are created by the state and operate under limits set by the Texas Constitution and the legislature. They have found their capabilities and resources increasingly burdened by the pressing needs of a growing urban state. Some of this pressure has come from the state and federal governments ordering significant improvements in environmental, educational, health, and other programs but leaving cities, counties, and school districts to pick up much of the tab. Prior to the state's commitment to an extensive prison construction program in the 1990s, for example, the Texas government forced counties to spend millions of local taxpayer dollars to house state prisoners in county jails because it had failed adequately to address a criminal justice crisis. Local school districts and their payers of property tax are also at the mercy of the legislature, which has ordered expensive educational programs and

TABLE 25-1	Governments in the U.S. and Texas, 1992	
	United States	*Texas*
U.S. government	1	1
State government	50	1
Counties	3,043	254
Municipalities	19,279	1,171
Townships and towns	16,656	—
School districts	14,422	1,100
Special districts	31,555	*2,266
Total	85,006	4,793

*Of these special districts, 850 have property-based taxing authority.

Sources: U.S. Department of Commerce, Bureau of the Census, *1992 Census of Governments*, vol. 1, no. 1.

improved classroom standards without fully paying for them. Cities, too, find their budgetary problems exacerbated by state mandates. Local governments are the governments closest to the people, but they have to shoulder much of the responsibility—and often take much of the public outrage—for policy decisions made in Austin and Washington.

Although the legal position expressed by the Dillon rule subordinates local governments to the state, there are practical and political limitations on what the state can accomplish by means of local governments. More important, the state relies on local governments to carry out many of its responsibilities.[5]

Texas granted cities home rule authority in 1912. Home rule cities, discussed in more detail later, have considerable authority and discretion over their own local policies, but within limits set by state law. Texas voters approved a constitutional amendment in 1933 that also gave counties home rule authority, but no county established home rule government before the amendment was repealed in 1969.[6]

In a 1980 study, the Advisory Commission on Intergovernmental Relations ranked the states according to the discretionary authority they granted to their local governments. Texas ranked eleventh in a composite ranking that included all local subdivisions—cities, counties, school districts, and other special districts. But Texas ranked forty-third, or near the bottom, in the discretionary authority given to its counties alone, while ranking first in the discretionary authority given to its cities.[7]

The states vary considerably in the major responsibilities assigned to different levels of government. Texas, like most other states, assigns the primary responsibility for public education to local school districts while retaining the primary responsibility for highways, public welfare, and public health at the state level. Police protection, sanitation services, parks, recreation, and libraries are the primary responsibility of city governments. Public hospitals are a shared function of the state, county, and special districts.[8] Texas counties share with the state a primary responsibility for the court and criminal justice system. Altogether, there are close to 5,000 local governments in Texas (see Table 25-1).

MUNICIPAL GOVERNMENT IN TEXAS

Despite popular images of wide open spaces dotted with cattle and oil wells, Texas is an urban state. Some areas, particularly in West Texas, still offer a good deal of breathing room, but most Texans live in cities. First-time visitors to the state often express surprise at the size and diversity of Houston and Dallas and the more relaxed charm of San Antonio, whose Riverwalk reminds many tourists of some European cities. Austin, the seat of state government and location of a world-class university, is highly attractive to young professionals and high-technology businesses.

When the Texas Constitution was adopted in 1876, the state was rural and agrarian; less than 10 percent of the population lived in cities. According to the 1880 census, Galveston was the largest city, with a population of 22,248, followed by San Antonio with 20,550. Dallas, a relatively new settlement, had 10,358 residents, and Houston had 16,513. For most of the period from 1880 to 1920, San Antonio was Texas's largest city, but since the 1930 census, Houston has held that distinction.[9] In 1940 only 45 percent of Texans lived in urban areas, but by 1950, 60 percent of the population resided in cities. Since the 1970 census, eight of ten Texans have been living in cities.

Houston, Dallas, and San Antonio are among the ten largest cities in the United States. According to the 1990 census, Houston had a population of 1.6 million; Dallas, 1 million; and San Antonio, 936,000. By 1997 San Antonio, with a population of 1.1 million, had replaced Dallas as the state's second largest city. Five additional Texas cities—El Paso, Austin, Fort Worth, Corpus Christi, and Arlington—each had more than 250,000. Five of Texas's ten largest cities—Houston, Dallas, San Antonio, El Paso, and Corpus Christi—have minority populations exceeding 50 percent (see Table 25-2).

The more than 1,100 incorporated municipalities in Texas are diverse, and urban life, politics, and government have developed different styles across the state. The basic forms of city government are defined by statutory and constitutional law, but cities vary in their demographic makeup, their economies, the historical experiences that shaped their development, and their quality of life. There are local differences in economic stability, public safety, public education, health and environmental quality, housing, transportation, culture, recreation, and politics.[10]

TABLE 25-2 Select Characteristics of the Ten Largest Cities in Texas, 1990 and 1997

City	Total Population, 1990	1990 Population Characteristics						Total Population, 1997
		Percentage of Population Ages 65+	Percentage of Population under 18	Median Age	Percentage African American	Percentage Hispanic	Persons per Square Mile	
Houston	1,630,533	8.3%	26.7%	30.4	28.1%	27.6%	3020	1,818,613
Dallas	1,006,877	9.7	25.0	30.6	29.5	20.9	2941	1,069,338
San Antonio	935,933	10.5	29.0	29.8	7.0	55.6	2810	1,114,579
El Paso	515,342	8.7	31.9	28.7	3.4	69.0	2100	592,145
Austin	465,622	7.4	23.1	28.9	12.4	23.0	2138	572,288
Fort Worth	447,619	11.2	26.6	30.3	22.0	19.5	1592	481,277
Arlington	261,721	5.0	27.1	29.1	8.4	8.9	2814	300,160
Corpus Christi	257,453	10.1	30.2	30.6	4.8	50.4	1907	275,762
Lubbock	186,206	9.8	25.6	28.4	8.6	22.5	1789	194,202
Garland	180,650	5.5	30.0	30.1	8.9	11.6	3150	191,904
State Total	16,986,510	10.1	28.5	30.8	11.9	25.5	64	19,334,173

Sources: U.S. Department of Commerce, Bureau of the Census, *Selected Population and Housing Characteristics, 1990*, from the 1990 Census, Summary Tape File 1A (STFIA), Texas and Texas Counties; U.S. Department of Commerce, Bureau of Census, *Statistical Abstract of the U.S. 1991*, Table 40; Texas State Data Center, January 1, 1997, *Estimates of the Total Population of Counties and Places in Texas for July 1, 1996 and January 1, 1997*, table 1-2.

What Do You Think?

Why Different Forms of City Government?

Most major Texas cities have functioned under more than one form of government. Both Houston and San Antonio have functioned under all three primary forms described in this chapter. Changes in city charters often follow periods of intense political conflict, inertia, or inability to respond to long-term problems. Proposed changes in governmental structures and election systems often threaten groups and interests that have a stake in the way business is currently being conducted, and charter revisions have a tendency to polarize a community.

Does the form of government under which a city operates make any significant difference? Political scientists have spent a lot of time trying to answer that question, and although there is some consensus on the general weaknesses of the city commission, opinions are divided on the other forms of local government. The general public appears to pay little attention to city charters or governmental structures,

but elected officials and other city leaders, public employees, special-interest groups, minority leaders, and some reform-minded citizens consider the structure of city government a crucial issue.

A city charter spells out how a city will run its affairs and helps determine which citizens will influence policy making. In part, a charter is an expression of a city's social, economic, and political structure. Some scholars have concluded that the urban reform movements advocating nonpartisan at-large elections, often tied to council-manager government, were advancing middle- and upper-middle-class views and interests. The original intent of these changes may have been to encourage managerial efficiencies, but many urban governments became less responsive to the needs and interests of lower income groups and minority populations.

Sources: William Lyons, "Reform and Response in American Cities: Structure and Policy Reconsidered," *Social Science Quarterly* 59 (June 1978): 130; Robert Lineberry and Edmund Fowler, "Reformism and Public Policies in American Cities," *American Political Science Review* 61 (September 1967): 701–17; Willis D. Hawley, *Nonpartisan Elections and the Case for Party Politics* (New York: Wiley, 1973).

General Law and Home Rule Cities   The Texas Constitution provides for two general categories of cities: general law and home rule. **General law cities** have fewer than 5,000 residents and have more restrictions in organizing their governments, setting taxes, and annexing territory than do home rule cities. They are allowed only those powers specifically granted to them by the legislature. Most Texas cities—more than 800—are general law cities.

A city with more than 5,000 inhabitants can adopt any form of government its residents choose, provided it does not conflict with the state constitution (Article XI, Sections 4, 5) or statutes. This option is called **home rule** and is formalized through the voters' adoption of a **charter**, which is the fundamental document—something like a constitution—under which a city operates. A charter establishes a city's governing body, the organization of its administrative agencies and municipal courts, its taxing authority, and procedures for conducting elections, annexing additional territory, and revising the charter. There are about 350 home rule cities in Texas.

general law city City allowed to exercise only those powers specifically granted to it by the legislature. General law cities have fewer than 5,000 residents.

home rule city City with a population of more than 5,000, which can adopt any form of government residents choose, provided it does not conflict with the state constitution or statutes.

FORMS OF CITY GOVERNMENT IN TEXAS

Texas cities have experimented with three forms of government: the mayor-council, the council-manager, and the commission (see *What Do You Think?* "Why Different Forms of City Government?"). According to the *1992 Census of Governments,* there

charter Document, based on state authorization, which defines the structure, powers, and responsibilities of a city government.

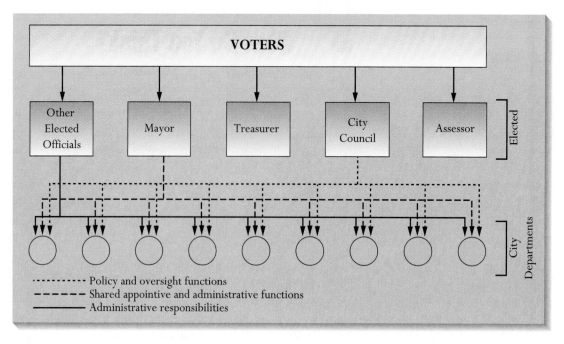

VOTERS

| Other Elected Officials | Mayor | Treasurer | City Council | Assessor | ⎤ Elected |

- - - - - - - - Policy and oversight functions
- - - - - - Shared appointive and administrative functions
———— Administrative responsibilities

City Departments

FIGURE 25-1   **Example of Weak Mayor Form of Government**

were 1,171 municipal governments in Texas, 874 of which were some variation of the mayor-council form and 287 of which had council-manager governments.[11]

Mayor-Council   The **mayor-council**, the most common form of municipal government in Texas, was derived from the English model of city government. The legislative function of the city is vested in the city council, and the executive function is assigned to the mayor. This type of government is based on the separation-of-powers principle, which also characterizes the state and federal governments.

In theory, the mayor, who is elected citywide, is the chief executive officer. In terms of power, however, there are two distinguishable forms of mayor—the **weak mayor** and the **strong mayor**—and in most Texas cities, the mayor is weak.

The city charter determines a mayor's strength. The weak mayor has little control over policy initiation or implementation. The mayor's powers may be constrained by one or more of the following: limited or no appointment or removal power over city offices, limited budgetary authority, and the election of other city administrators independently of the mayor (Figure 25-1). Under these circumstances, the mayor shares power with the city council over city administration and policy implementation and "is the chief executive in name only."[12] These restrictions limit both the political and the administrative leadership of the mayor. Although it is possible for a mayor to use noninstitutional resources to influence the city council and other administrators and to provide energetic leadership, there are formidable obstacles to overcome.[13]

A strong mayor has real power and authority, including appointive and removal powers over city agency heads (see Figure 25-2). Such appointments often require city council approval, but the appointees are responsible to the mayor and serve at mayoral discretion. The mayor has control over budget preparation and exercises some veto authority over city council actions. This form of city government clearly distinguishes between executive and legislative functions.

mayor-council   Form of city government in which the legislative function is invested in the city council and the executive function in the mayor.

weak mayor   Form of city government in which the mayor shares authority with the city council and other elected officials but has little independent control over city policy or administration.

strong mayor   Form of city government that gives the mayor considerable power, including budgetary control and appointment and removal authority over city department heads.

FIGURE 25-2 Example of Strong Mayor Form of Government

Source: Office of the Mayor, El Paso, Texas.

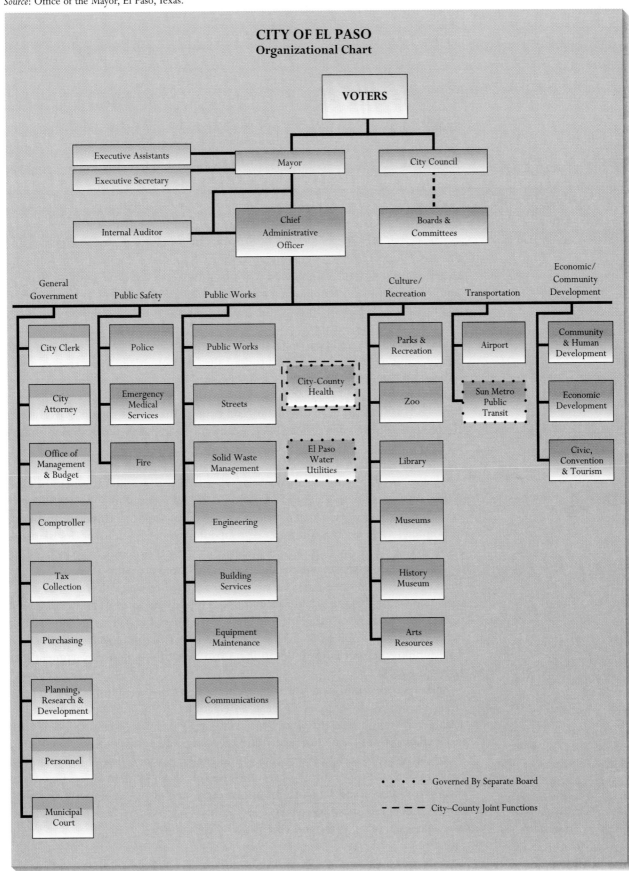

FIGURE 25-3 Example of a City Commission Form of Government

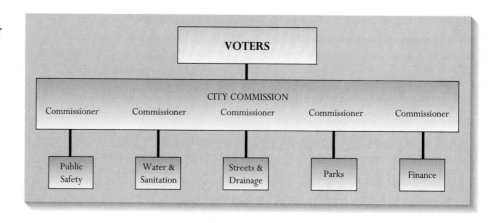

The strong mayor form of government is found in many of the larger American cities, but it has been adopted by only two major cities in Texas—Houston and El Paso. The form may be unpopular in the state because the strong mayor often was associated with urban political machines, ward politics, and political corruption. Moreover, the fragmentation of authority and responsibility in local government parallels that found in state government and is another reminder of the deep distrust of government that Reconstruction produced in Texas. Finally, the state's individualistic and traditionalistic subcultures (see Chapter 19) reinforce hostile attitudes toward governmental institutions that are potentially more responsive to lower socioeconomic groups.

City Commission   The commission and council-manager forms of government are products of the twentieth century. Both reflect, in part, efforts to reform city governments through administrative efficiency, the reduction of partisan conflict, and the adaptation of a businesslike approach to running city government.

The origin of the **city commission** is usually traced to the Texas island city of Galveston. After a hurricane and subsequent flooding devastated most of the city in 1900, the government then in office proved incompetent and incapable of responding. That crisis prompted a group of citizens to win the legislature's approval of a new form of government designed to be more responsive by combining the city's legislative and administrative functions in the offices of five city commissioners. City commissions were soon adopted by other major Texas cities, including Dallas, Houston, and San Antonio. But with the subsequent development of council-manager government as an alternative, there has been a marked decline in the city commission's popularity. It has been replaced in Houston, Dallas, and San Antonio, and only a few cities in Texas still have this form of government (see Figure 25-3).

Initially, the commission was supported as a businesslike approach to running city government. By eliminating partisan elections and combining the executive, administrative, and legislative functions, it was argued, cities could provide services more efficiently. But critics have identified several problems. The commission minimizes the potential for effective political leadership because no single individual can be identified as the person in charge. Moreover, there is minimal oversight and review of policies and budgets. Commissioners are elected primarily as policy makers, not administrators, and there are downsides to electing amateurs to administer increasingly technical and complex city programs.

city commission   Form of city government in which elected commissioners collectively serve as a city's policy-making body and individually serve as administrative heads of different city departments.

The few cities in Texas that use the pure form of commission government generally have three members—a mayor and two commissioners—who are assigned responsibilities for specific city functions such as water, sanitation, and public safety. Several of the commission cities now turn to a city administrator or manager, hired by the commission, to run the daily affairs of the city.

Council-Manager   After enthusiasm for the city commission waned, urban reformers, both in Texas and nationally, looked to the **council-manager** form of government. Its specific origins are disputed, but it was influenced by the commission. The first cities in Texas to use council-manager government were Amarillo and Terrell in 1913, and it soon became popular among home rule cities. Dallas and San Antonio have been the largest cities in the state to adopt it (see Figure 25-4). Its principal characteristics are professional city management, nonpartisan city elections, and a clear distinction between policy making and administration.

In some council-manager cities, the mayor is chosen by the city council from among its membership to preside over council meetings and fulfill a primarily symbolic role. But in other cities, the mayor is elected citywide, an arrangement that enhances the political position of the office without necessarily vesting it with formal legal authority. The mayor is usually a voting member of the city council but has few other institutional powers in a council-manager government. The mayor does, however, have the opportunity to become a visible spokesperson for the city and has a forum from which to promote ideas and programs (see *People in Politics:* "Ron Kirk and Lee Brown, History-Making Mayors" on page 886).

The city council is primarily responsible for developing public policy (see *Up Close:* "The Job of the City Council Member" on page 887). It creates, organizes, and restructures city departments, approves the city budget, establishes the tax rate, authorizes the issuance of bonds (subject to voter approval), enacts local laws (ordinances), and conducts inquiries and investigations into the operations and functions of city agencies.[14]

The council hires a full-time city manager, who is responsible for administering city government on a day-to-day basis. The manager hires and fires assistants and department heads, supervises their activities, and translates the policy directives of the city council into concrete action by city employees. The city manager is also responsible for developing a city budget for council approval and then supervising its implementation. Professionalism is one of the key attributes of the council-manager form of government. Initially, many city managers were engineers, but in recent years managers have tended to be generalists with solid skills in public finance. City managers are fairly well paid: in 1998 the salary of the city manager of San Antonio was $132,581, and the city manager of even a small city such as Seguin received $86,600.

There is a delicate line between policy making and administration, and a city manager is, in principle, supposed to be politically neutral. The overall effectiveness of city managers depends on three main factors: their relationship with their city council; their ability to develop support for their recommendations within the council and the community at large without appearing to have gone beyond the scope of their authority; and the overall perception of their financial and managerial skills. In the real world of municipal government, city managers play a central role in setting policy as well as carrying it out. Managers' adroit use of their resources and sensitivity to political factions and the personal agendas of elected officials are key to determining their success.

Alex Briseño was the first Hispanic to serve as city manager of San Antonio

council-manager   Form of city government in which policy is set by an elected city council, which hires a professional city manager to head the daily administration of city government.

FIGURE 25-4 Example of a Council-Manager Form of Government

Source: City of San Antonio, 1997.

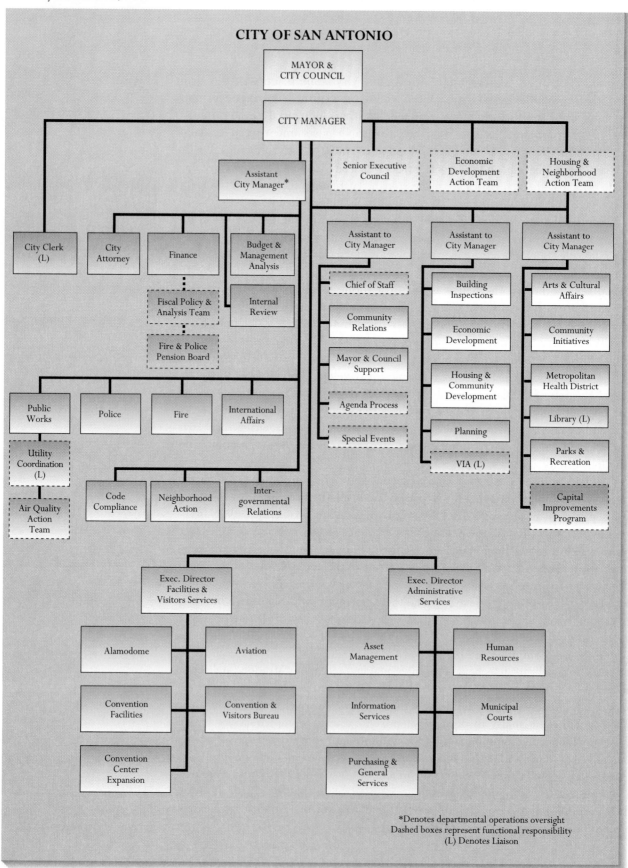

MUNICIPAL ELECTION SYSTEMS

Nonpartisan City Elections   Virtually every city in Texas elects its council members in **nonpartisan elections**. Claiming that there was no Democratic or Republican way to pave a street, city reformers who were part of the nonpartisan movement (1920s to 1950s) expressed a strong aversion to political parties and particularly to the urban political machines (see *A Conflicting View:* "The Debate over Electoral Systems" on page 888). To enforce separation of city elections from party politics, most municipal elections are held at times other than the party primaries or the general election.

The nonpartisan ballot—combined with at-large, citywide elections—has historically benefited higher social and economic groups. Parties and party labels normally serve as cues for voters. When they are eliminated in city elections, voters are forced to find different sources of information about candidates. Many local newspapers, which endorse candidates and decide how much coverage to give them, have ties to the dominant urban elites. Candidates from lower socioeconomic groups historically have had few contacts with the influential organizations that recruit, support, and endorse politicians. Although no longer in existence, San Antonio's Good Government League and Dallas's Citizens Charter Association controlled the recruitment and election of candidates in those two cities for several decades. Both organizations drew members from the Democratic and the Republican parties, but they reflected and pursued the interests of higher socioeconomic groups, often to the detriment of lower income and minority populations.

At-Large Elections   Another notable feature of city politics in Texas is the general use of citywide, or **at-large elections**. In 1992 there were 6,409 individuals elected to the governing bodies of 1,171 cities and towns in Texas. Some 5,649, or 88 percent, were elected at-large. Only 12 percent were elected from single-member districts, discussed in the following section.[15]

In an at-large election, all of a city's voters participate in the selection of all members of the city council. In a pure at-large system, every candidate runs against every other candidate. If there are eight candidates running for five positions on the city council, the candidates with the five highest vote totals are the winners. Many of these election systems have been struck down by the federal courts or by the U.S. Justice Department under the Voting Rights Act as discriminatory against minorities.

A variation of the at-large system is the **place system**. Candidates file for a specific council seat and run citywide for places, or positions. Cities using the place system may require that the winning candidate receive a simple plurality of votes (more votes than any other candidate running for the same position) or an absolute majority of votes (more than half the votes cast). If a city requires the latter and there are more than two persons in a race, **runoff elections** between the two highest vote-getters are often required.

Single-Member Districts   An alternative to at-large elections is the **single-member district**, or ward. Under this system, a city is divided into separate geographic districts, each represented by a different council member. A candidate must live in and run for election from a specific district, and voters can cast ballots only in the race for the council seat that represents their district. A person elected

nonpartisan elections
Elections in which candidates do not represent a political party.

at-large elections   Election systems under which officeholders are elected by voters in the entire city, school district, or single-purpose district.

place system   Form of at-large election in which candidates run for specific positions, or places, on a city council or other governing body.

runoff elections   Elections that are required if no candidate receives an absolute majority of the votes cast in a city council, school district, or party primary race. The runoff is between the two top vote-getters.

single-member district   System in which city council members, legislators, or other public officials are elected from specific geographical areas.

People in Politics

Ron Kirk and Lee Brown, History-Making Mayors

In one key respect, Ron Kirk's election as mayor of Dallas in 1995 was not all that unusual. He had the strong support of the city's business leaders, who liked his campaign pledge for more aggressive economic development. Kirk's election, however, made history. He was Dallas's first African American mayor. In a city well known for its conservatism and recent racial divisions, Kirk attracted a broad base of support that included both African Americans who had long been unhappy with the city's power structure and establishment whites.

A former Texas secretary of state under Governor Ann Richards, Kirk was elected to head a city council that included four other African Americans, two Hispanics, and eight whites. Dallas has a council-manager form of government, and its mayor's office is weak in terms of formal powers. But the high-profile post offered Kirk the opportunity to use the skills of salesmanship and persuasion that had served him so well during his campaign. Successful economic development, which he viewed as essential to the city's future, would improve racial harmony in Dallas,

he predicted. "It doesn't matter whether your ancestors come over on the *Mayflower*, or on a slave ship," he said. "We're all in the same boat now."*

Two years later, Lee Brown scored a similar historic victory in Houston, when he was elected that city's

first African American mayor. Brown, who earlier had been Houston's first African American police chief and drug policy director under President Bill Clinton, campaigned as a "mayor for all of Houston." Unlike Dallas, Houston has a strong mayoral office, giving Brown appointment powers over most city department heads and significant influence over city policies.

After taking 53 percent of the vote in a runoff against white businessman Rob Mosbacher, Brown told supporters at a victory celebration, "Another great barrier has fallen in the city of Houston—the doors of opportunity have opened wider for all of Houston's children."†

Brown received virtually all the African American vote and almost 30 percent of the white vote in the runoff. He and Mosbacher split the Hispanic vote. Brown said race was not an issue in the campaign.

---

*Quoted in *Governing*, July 1995, p. 108.
†Quoted in *Houston Chronicle*, December 8, 1997.

---

from a single-member district can, depending on the city's charter, be elected by a plurality or an absolute majority of votes.

Legal Attacks on At-Large Elections Hispanics and African Americans, through various advocacy groups such as the National Association for the Advancement of Colored People, the Mexican American Legal Defense and Educational Fund, Texas Rural Legal Aid, and the Southwest Voter Registration and Education Project, have challenged in federal courts the election systems used by numerous Texas cities. From the small East Texas town of Jefferson to El Paso, Houston, and Dallas, minority groups have challenged, with considerable success, the inequities of at-large elections and forced city governments to adopt electoral plans that give minorities a better chance of electing candidates to city councils. The ethnic and racial composition of city councils has changed dramatically over the past twenty years, with a marked increase in the number of Hispanics and African Americans elected to these governing bodies (see Chapter 21).

The Job of the City Council Member

Regardless of the form of government, most city councils in Texas are small, with five to fifteen members elected for two-year terms. Most council seats are elected at-large, or citywide, and council elections are nonpartisan. Council members in most cities can serve for an unlimited number of terms. Recent referenda on term limitations, however, have been held in several Texas cities, including San Antonio and Houston, which imposed a two-term limitation on council members in 1991.

In most cities, council members serve part time with little or no compensation. In most of the large cities, the pay is nowhere near commensurate with the time spent on the job. Council members in San Antonio are paid $20 per meeting; those in Dallas, $50 per meeting. Low salaries were part of the early urban reform tradition: the idea was that people would run for office out of a sense of civic duty rather than to advance themselves financially. Houston, whose strong mayor gives it a form of government different from that of most other Texas cities, pays its council members about $40,000 a year, but most council members do not consider that a full-time salary. The mayor of Houston is paid about $150,000 a year.

The frequency of council meetings varies. In many small towns, councils may meet for only a few hours each month, but councils in large cities meet much more frequently, usually weekly, with meetings lasting several hours. Cities are dealing with a wider range of complex issues than ever before, and demands on a council member's time are great. In addition to their policy-making roles, council members in large cities are faced with increased demands for constituent services. Many council members are finding that public service is extremely costly in terms of time lost from their families and the jobs or professions that provide their livelihoods.

Council members often complain that they had no idea how much time the public would demand of them and their families. The following commandments for surviving have been offered by Hal Conklin, a former mayor:

1. Make an honest inventory of the hours that your political commitment will take.
2. Establish a contract with your employer for the hours that you are going to spend in your political commitment.
3. Set office hours and stick to them.
4. Delegate and hold accountable staff members and volunteers.
5. Put unmonitored phone lines on answering machines, especially at home.
6. Distinguish between home hours and work hours.
7. Make a date with your spouse (or significant other) for the same time each week.
8. Exercise regularly each day; eat a stress controlled diet.
9. Start and end your day with activities that soothe the soul.
10. Keep your sense of humor.*

---

*Hal Conklin, "Ten Commandments for Surviving as a City Council Member," *Texas Town and City* 83 (June 1995): 12, 19.

CITY REVENUES AND EXPENDITURES

Despite a growing number of expensive needs that they are expected to address, Texas cities have limited financial resources. City governments depend disproportionately on **regressive taxes**, such as property taxes and fees for services. Moreover, the state limits the property tax rate that a city can impose and permits citizens to petition their city council for a **rollback election** to nullify any tax increase of more than 8 percent in a given year. Although there have been few rollback elections in the 1990s, the potential for such citizen initiatives serves to constrain policy makers.

regressive taxes Taxes that impose a disproportionately heavier burden on low-income people than on the more affluent.

rollback election Election in which local voters can nullify a property tax increase that exceeds 8 percent in a given year.

The Debate over Electoral Systems

There has been much debate over the most desirable form of city election system. Advocates of at-large, nonpartisan elections often warn of ward politics and the potential relationship of single-member districts to political machines, bosses, partisan conflict, corruption, and mismanagement. Even without corruption, they argue, council members elected from districts are concerned primarily with the interests of their own neighborhoods and may be more susceptible to trade-offs, swapping votes for programs and services that would benefit small segments of the community rather than the entire city. It has also been argued that district elections divide communities along racial, ethnic, or economic lines, thus resulting in high levels of political conflict. Moreover, proponents of at-large elections argue that their system produces higher caliber candidates, results in more media exposure for political campaigns, and permits a voter to participate in the selection of the entire city council rather than just one member.[*]

But critics of the at-large system believe that single-member districts make elected officials more responsive to the needs and interests of specific constituencies. They also argue that at-large elections discriminate against African Americans and Hispanics because of racially polarized voting and the dilution of the impact of minority voting strength. Furthermore, citywide election campaigns, especially in the larger cities, are much more expensive than district campaigns, thus adversely affecting the electoral chances of candidates from low-income, often minority, areas. It also has been argued that single-member districts produce a more diverse group of elected officials and ensure that a city council will consider a broader range of views and interests. At-large elections, critics say, permit a small group of individuals—the city's elites—to control the electoral process and the council by recruiting and financially supporting candidates to protect their interests.

[*]Tom Albin et al., *Local Government Election Systems* (Austin: Local Government Election Systems Policy Research Project, University of Texas, 1984), p. 2.

general obligation bonds Method of borrowing money to pay for new construction projects, such as prisons, mental hospitals, or school facilities. The bonds, which require voter approval, are repaid with tax revenue.

revenue bonds Bonds that are used to finance construction of a public facility and are repaid with income produced by the facility.

infrastructure Streets, waste disposal systems, libraries, and other public facilities built and operated by governments.

When the Texas economy went sour in 1985 and 1986, cities experienced revenue shortfalls from a decline in sales tax revenues, reductions in the assessed value of property, and the elimination of many federal assistance programs. By 1993, however, there were indications that the financial positions of most cities were improving as a result of a rebound in the real estate market and the overall improvement of the state's economy. By 1995 municipal financial conditions had improved dramatically, with revenues growing. Many cities, particularly larger ones, were able to enact modest tax reductions or maintain existing tax rates. Smaller cities across the state reported a less optimistic financial outlook.[16]

Although cities are required by law to balance their operating budgets, many municipal construction projects are financed by loans through the issuance of **general obligation bonds**, which are subject to voter approval. These bonds are secured by the city's taxing power. The city pledges its full faith and credit to the lender and, over a number of years, repays the bonds with tax revenue. Cities also fund various projects through **revenue bonds** that are payable solely from the revenues derived from an income-producing facility.[17] The poor economy of the late 1980s made it more difficult for cities to borrow money. And with a pent-up demand for improving **infrastructure** (streets, waste disposal systems, libraries, and other facilities), cities have entered an era of bond financing that has been radically altered by the performance of Wall Street and changes in state and federal tax laws.[18] Although city finances are improving, cities across the state continue to postpone capital spending for streets, roads, water systems, and other improvements.[19]

URBAN PROBLEMS IN TEXAS

During the 1970s and through the early 1980s, Texas cities were key participants in the dramatic economic growth of the state. Many older cities across the country—particularly in the East and the Midwest—"looked at their Texas counterparts and envied their capacity to attract population and business."[20] Texas cities had low taxes, a pro-business tradition, few labor unions with significant economic clout, an abundant work force, proximity to natural resources, and governing bodies that favored economic growth and development. By the late 1980s, however, economic conditions had changed dramatically, and many problems associated with older urban areas outside of Texas had arrived in the state.

The Graying of Texas Cities   The Texas population is aging, or graying. Americans are living longer, and older age groups are among the fastest growing segments of the population. As the population ages, additional pressures are placed on city government budgets. The local property tax, a major source of revenue for city governments, is stretched almost to its limits. Moreover, many Texas cities have granted, in addition to the standard **homestead exemption**, additional property tax exemptions for individuals older than sixty-five. As more and more people become old enough to claim these exemptions, younger taxpayers will be called on to shoulder the burden through higher tax rates.

"White Flight"   The population characteristics of Texas cities change over time, and major metropolitan areas are experiencing a "white flight" to the suburbs, a dramatic increase in the growth rate of minority populations, and small growth rates among Anglos in the central cities. Income levels for most minority Texans have always been lower than those of Anglos, and a larger proportion of the minority population falls below the poverty level. The increased concentration of lower income people in the central cities increases pressure for more public services, and a declining proportion of affluent property owners weakens the local tax bases that pay for the services.

Declining Infrastructures   Much concern has been expressed across Texas and the United States about the declining infrastructures of local governments. Streets, bridges, water and sewer systems, libraries, and other facilities must be continually maintained or expanded to support a growing population. Moreover, many Texas cities are out of compliance with federal standards for treating water and sewage and disposing of solid waste and must spend millions of dollars on physical improvements to avoid or reduce fines. Some capital improvements are paid for out of current operating budgets, but a more common practice is for cities to borrow money to improve roads, streets, water systems, and the like. These bonds are repaid from taxes on property. When property values decline—as they did in the late 1980s—cities are restrained by the constitution and statutes as to the indebtedness they can incur to support improvements.

   By the mid-1990s, property values had increased across most areas of the state, and cities had more opportunities to borrow money for capital improvements.

homestead exemption   Reduction in property taxes that some local governments grant on a taxpayer's residence.

Poor neighborhoods stand in sharp contrast to the nearby high-rise office buildings of downtown Houston.

Nevertheless, most cities have a large backlog of proposed projects and are often forced to put off or defer needed construction.

Crime and Urban Violence   Crime is one of the most pressing problems facing Texas cities and counties, just as it is in many other parts of the country. Although crime rates in most offense categories declined in the mid-1990s, numerous surveys indicated that many Texans believed crime was on the rise. Much of the problem is related to drug abuse, gang violence, and an increase in crime among juveniles. Expanded law enforcement patrols are proposed by political candidates and elected officials, but many city and county budgets cannot absorb the costs.

State- and Federal-Mandated Programs   Both federal and state governments have increasingly used mandates to implement public policy in recent years. A **mandate** is a law or regulation enacted by a higher level of government that compels a lower level of government to carry out a specific action. In simpler terms, it is a form of "passing the buck." Federal mandates cover a wide range of governmental functions including transportation, education for the disabled, water and air quality, and voter registration. States, meanwhile, have shifted much of the cost of public education to local governments.

Despite a decrease in federal funding for many urban problems during the 1980s, there has been an increase in federal mandates on the states, counties, and cities and an increase in state mandates on local governments, often with no corresponding financial support. In some cases, the state simply passes on the responsibility for—and the costs of—carrying out federal mandates to local governments. Congress enacted a law in 1995 to restrict unfunded mandates, but the law applied only to future, not existing, mandates. And such restrictions can still be circumvented if Congress chooses.

Although this practice may seem unfair and illogical, it is politically attractive to policy makers because they can "appease a large and vocal interest group which demands an extensive program without incurring the wrath of their constituents."

mandate   Law or regulation enacted by a higher level of government that compels a lower level of government to carry out a specific function.

Although they get the credit for such programs, they do not get the blame for their costs.[21] Cities across Texas claim that these unfunded requirements have them between a rock and a hard place. Unless there are changes in such practices, these cities will be out of compliance and subject to litigation. They are then likely to reduce other services or seek alternative sources of funding now denied them.

COUNTY GOVERNMENT IN TEXAS

Texas has 254 counties, more than any other state. Counties are administrative subunits of the state that were developed initially to serve a predominantly rural population. Created primarily to administer state law, they possess powers delegated to them by the state and have relatively few implied powers. Unlike home rule cities, counties lack the basic legislative power of enacting ordinances. They can carry out only those administrative functions granted them by the state. Counties administer and collect some state taxes and enforce a variety of state laws and regulations. They also build roads and bridges, administer local welfare programs, aid in fire protection, and perform other functions primarily local in nature.[22] All counties function under the same constitutional restrictions and basic organizational structure despite wide variations in population, local characteristics, and public needs.

According to 1997 population estimates, Loving County, the state's least populous, had only 97 residents, compared to 3,142,293 in Harris County, the most populous (see Table 25-3). Rockwall County includes only 147 square miles,

TABLE 25-3	Ten Largest and Ten Smallest Texas Counties, 1980–1997		
	1980 Population	*1990 Population*	*1997 Population**
Harris County	2,409,547	2,818,199	3,142,293
Dallas County	1,556,390	1,852,810	2,010,655
Tarrant County	860,880	1,170,103	1,322,221
Bexar County	988,800	1,185,394	1,328,219
El Paso County	479,899	591,610	679,842
Travis County	419,573	576,407	688,039
Hidalgo County	283,229	383,545	506,919
Denton County	143,126	273,525	358,957
Collin County	144,576	264,036	386,875
Nueces County	268,215	291,145	311,543
Glasscock County	1,304	1,447	1,477
Sterling County	1,206	1,438	1,402
Terrell County	1,595	1,410	1,232
Roberts County	1,187	1,025	873
Kent County	1,145	1,010	935
McMullen County	789	817	757
Borden County	859	799	753
Kenedy County	543	460	458
King County	425	354	358
Loving County	91	107	97

*Estimated population.

Source: U.S. Census, 1980 and 1990; Texas State Data Center, *Estimates of the Total Population of Counties and Places in Texas for July 1, 1996 and January 1, 1997*, table 2.

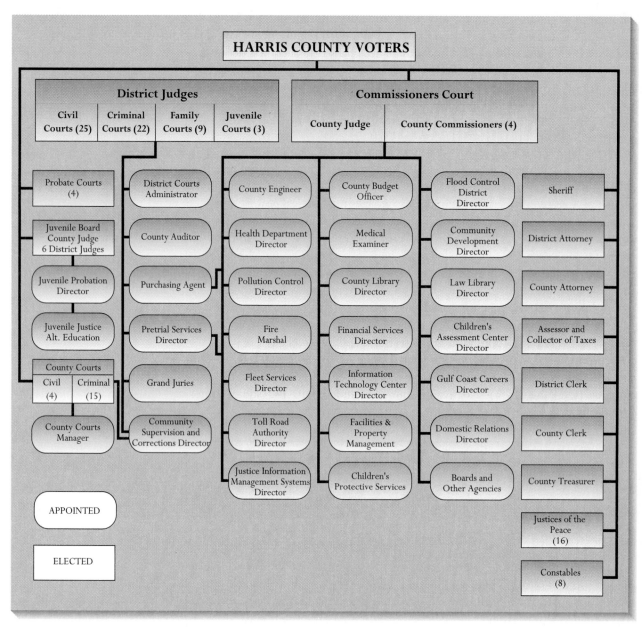

FIGURE 25-5 Example of a County Government Organization

Source: Harris County Budget Office, 1997.

whereas Brewster County covers 6,204 square miles. Jeff Davis County reported a 1998 budget of $945,683, paid its county judge $22,176 a year, and paid its county commissioners $120 per year. Harris County's 1994 budget was $1.34 billion. Its county judge was paid $108,000, and each of its commissioners received $93,408. Some 55 percent of Texas's residents live in the ten most populous counties.[23]

Structure of County Government The organizational structure of county government is highly fragmented, reflecting the principles of Jacksonian democracy (see Chapter 7) and the reaction of late-nineteenth-century Texans to Radical Reconstruction. The governing body of a county is the **commissioners court**, but it shares administrative functions with other independently elected officials (see Figure 25-5).

commissioners court Principal policy-making body for county government. It sets the county tax rate and supervises expenditures.

Moreover, the name "commissioners court" is somewhat misleading because that body has no judicial functions.

The Commissioners Court and County Judge   The commissioners court comprises a county judge, who is elected countywide, and four county commissioners, who are elected from a county's four commissioners precincts. Like other elected county officials, the judge and the commissioners serve four-year terms and are elected in partisan elections.

Until recent years, there were gross inequities in the population distributions among commissioners precincts in most counties. This issue of malapportionment came to a head in the 1968 case of *Avery v. Midland County*, in which the U.S. Supreme Court applied the "one person, one vote" principle to the counties and required districts to be equally apportioned.[24] Subsequently, Congress forced Texas to comply with the Voting Rights Act in 1975, and counties were required to consider the interests of minority populations in drawing up the boundaries for commissioners precincts. African Americans and Hispanics across the state have challenged county electoral systems and have increased minority representation on county commissioners courts.

The **county judge** presides over commissioners court, participates in the court's deliberations, and votes on issues before it. If there is a vacancy among the commissioners, the county judge appoints a replacement. If the county judge vacates the office, the commissioners choose a replacement.

The Texas Constitution also gives the county judge some judicial responsibilities but does not require the officeholder to be a lawyer. Most urban counties have county courts-at-law that relieve the county judge of judicial duties. However, county judges in some rural counties perform a judicial as well as an executive role, combining two sets of duties in one office.

The commissioners court fills midterm vacancies in other county offices. It also has authority over the county budget, which permits the court to exercise some influence, if not control, over other officeholders.[25] The court sets the annual tax rate, which is limited by the Texas Constitution, approves the tax roll, and supervises all expenditures of county money. Other county officials must obtain the court's authorization for personnel positions, salaries, and office expenses. Consequently, the budgetary process often sparks political disputes and other conflicts.

Historically, county road construction and maintenance were primary functions of commissioners court. The Optional Road Law of 1947 gave counties the authority to create a consolidated road system under the supervision of a county engineer, who relieved commissioners of road maintenance and other construction headaches. But the importance of roads to the commissioners and their constituents still generates political disputes.

County Clerk   The Texas Constitution provides for an elected **county clerk** to serve as the clerk of the commissioners court, the clerk of the county courts, and (in the smaller counties) the clerk of the district court. Over the years, the legislature has enacted hundreds of statutory provisions defining specific responsibilities of the office, prompting one writer to describe the office as the "dumping ground for miscellaneous functions of the county."[26] The office is the depository of a county's vital statistics, such as birth and death records, and documents related to real estate transactions. It issues marriage licenses and various other licenses required by state law.[27] The county clerk also serves as a county's chief elections administrator if the commissioners court has not created a separate elections administrator's office.[28]

county judge   Presiding officer of a county commissioners court. This office also has some judicial authority, which is assumed by separate county courts-at-law in most urban counties.

county clerk   Chief record-keeping officer of a county.

District Clerk   The **district clerk**, also elected countywide, assists the district court by maintaining custody of court documents and records.[29] In small counties, the county clerk is authorized to double as the district clerk, and seventy-one counties combined these two offices in 1994.[30]

County and District Attorneys   The state's legal interests in both civil and criminal matters are represented at the local level by one of three officers—the **county attorney**, the **district attorney**, or the criminal district attorney. The legislature has enacted numerous provisions for legal departments that vary from county to county. Some counties have no county attorney but have a criminal district attorney. Under state law, others are granted both a county attorney and a district attorney. District attorneys prosecute more serious cases, usually felonies, in the district courts, and the county attorneys prosecute lesser offenses, primarily misdemeanors, in the county courts.[31]

These officers can also provide legal advice and opinions to other county officials and give legal counsel to public officials or employees who have been sued for acts committed in carrying out their official duties. Upon request of the commissioners court, the district attorney or county attorney may initiate lawsuits on behalf of the county. Various other laws charge these attorneys with protecting the public health, assisting the state attorney general in cases involving deceptive trade practices, enforcing the state's election laws, collecting delinquent taxes, and even enforcing the Texas Communist Control Act of 1951.[32]

Tax Assessor-Collector   The property tax is the primary source of revenue for counties. Although the commissioners court sets property tax rates, the **tax assessor-collector**, another elected county officer, has the task of determining who owns a given piece of property, determining how much tax is owed on that property, then collecting the tax. In counties with fewer than 10,000 people, these responsibilities are assigned to the sheriff, unless voters decide to create a separate tax assessor-collector's office. A number of counties, especially those with fewer than 5,000 people, continue to let the sheriff handle the job.

Prior to reforms enacted in the 1970s, the tax assessor-collector also was responsible for appraising property or determining its value. This process was often steeped in politics because the higher the value of a piece of property, the more taxes its owner has to pay. Lowering property values for select friends or supporters gave those holding this office considerable power, which often was abused. In an effort to move toward greater consistency across the state and to enhance the professionalism of tax appraisals, the legislature now requires each county to create an appraisal district separate from the tax office.[33] Property tax appraisals are now conducted countywide by an **appraisal district** whose members represent other governmental units in the county. The district also certifies the tax rolls, and other governmental units are required by law to use its appraisals.[34]

County Law Enforcement   **Sheriffs** and **constables**, a county's law enforcement officers, are part of an old tradition under the Anglo-Saxon legal system. Each county has one sheriff with countywide jurisdiction, but the number of constables can vary. In counties with fewer than 18,000 residents, the commissioners court can designate the entire county as a single justice of the peace precinct or can create as many as four precincts, with each precinct assigned one constable. In the

---

district clerk   Elected county official who maintains custody of state district court records.

county attorney   Elected official who is the chief legal officer of some counties. He or she also prosecutes lesser criminal offenses, primarily misdemeanors, in county courts.

district attorney   Elected official who prosecutes more serious criminal offenses, usually felonies, before state district courts.

tax assessor-collector   Elected official who determines how much property tax is owed on the different pieces of property within a county and then collects the tax.

appraisal district   Local agency that determines the value of pieces of property in a county. All local governments are required to use its evaluations, or appraisals, for tax purposes.

sheriff   Elected official who is the chief law enforcement officer of a county.

constable   Elected law enforcement officer who is primarily responsible for executing court judgments, serving subpoenas, and delivering other legal documents.

large counties, as many as eight justice of the peace precincts can be created, with a constable assigned to each. Most counties have four constables.[35]

In a small rural county, the sheriff is the primary law enforcement officer for the entire county. But in urban counties, city police departments generally assume exclusive jurisdiction in the incorporated municipal areas, leaving the sheriff jurisdiction over the unincorporated areas. Most sheriffs have considerable discretion in the hiring, promotion, and firing of deputies and other employees, although some counties have adopted a merit employment system for the sheriff's office. The sheriff also serves as the administrative officer for the district and county courts.

Constables are authorized to patrol their precincts, make arrests, and conduct criminal investigations, but their primary function is to serve as administrative officers of the justice of the peace courts. They are responsible for serving **subpoenas**, executing judgments of the court, and delivering other legal documents.[36]

County governments are responsible for constructing and staffing county jails, which are managed in most counties by the sheriff and in some counties by a jail administrator. During the late 1980s and early 1990s, counties across the state pursued an aggressive policy of jail construction in response to court decisions, increased crime rates, and a shortage of state prison space. Jail construction was a "growth" industry during this period, but by the mid-1990s, some counties found that they had overextended their finances to construct these jails. They also were left with excess jail capacity after the state built new prisons. To compensate for these problems, several counties contracted with other states to house their prisoners in Texas jails.

All counties are authorized to create an office of **medical examiner**, who is appointed by the commissioners court and determines the cause of death of murder victims or others who die under suspicious or unusual circumstances. In counties that do not have a medical examiner, the justice of the peace is charged with conducting an **inquest** to determine if conditions warrant an autopsy.

Counties, either individually or as part of multicounty judicial districts, are required to provide facilities for a criminal probation office. Funded by the state, the chief adult probation officer of a county is chosen by the district judges, who supervise the office.

County Auditor

All counties with 10,000 or more people are required to have a **county auditor**, and smaller counties may have one if the commissioners court chooses. Two counties with fewer than 25,000 residents may jointly agree to hire an auditor to serve both counties. The county auditor is appointed by the district judges of the county for a two-year term. He or she is primarily responsible for reviewing every bill and expenditure of a county to assure its correctness and legality. Such oversight can, in effect, impose budgetary restrictions on the commissioners court and produce political conflict with other county officers.

The role of the auditor varies from county to county. In counties with more than 225,000 people, the auditor is the budget officer and prepares the county budget for submission to commissioners court unless an alternative has been authorized by the legislature.[37] In smaller counties, the commissioners court prepares the budget, based on estimates provided by the auditor.

County Treasurer

The **county treasurer** is responsible for receiving and disbursing county funds. Although this office has existed since 1846, its primary functions are now carried out by the county auditor, and constitutional amendments have eliminated the office in a number of counties.

The Crockett County Courthouse is located in Ozona in sparsely populated West Texas.

subpoenas Court orders requiring people to testify in court or before grand juries or to produce certain documents.

medical examiner Appointed official responsible for determining the cause of death of murder victims or others who die under suspicious or unusual circumstances.

inquest Examination by a justice of the peace or a medical examiner of unusual circumstances under which someone has died.

county auditor Appointed officer who is primarily responsible for reviewing every bill and expenditure of a county to assure it is correct and legal.

county treasurer Elected officer responsible for receiving and disbursing county funds.

CRITICISMS OF COUNTY GOVERNMENT

The structure of county government in Texas, designed for a rural state, has inhibited efforts of urban counties to respond to growing needs for public services. The state experimented with county home rule, but the provisions were so poorly written, confusing, and contradictory that local self-rule at the county level was never given a real chance.

Even though the county functions primarily as an extension, or administrative subdivision, of state government, there is limited supervision of the counties by the state and a wide disparity in the way counties interpret and administer their functions. The fragmentation represented by several independently elected officers always poses a danger of jurisdictional conflict, administrative inefficiency, and even government deadlock.

Like other local governments in Texas, counties rely heavily on the property tax for revenue but cannot exceed tax rate limits set by the state constitution. Those limits reflected a general apprehension about government when they were initially set in 1875; they now further restrict the counties' ability to provide services.

Historically, county courthouses have been associated with political patronage and the **spoils system**. Victorious candidates have claimed the right to appoint personal and political friends to work for them, and state courts have held that elected county officials have wide discretion in the selection of their employees. Reformers have advocated a **civil service system** for county employees based on merit and competitive examinations and offering job security from one election to the next. A 1971 law allows counties with more than 200,000 residents to create a civil service system, but it excludes several county offices, including the district attorney. An elected public official retains considerable control over the initial hiring of employees through a probationary period of six months.[38]

SPECIAL DISTRICTS IN TEXAS

Every day, Texans utilize the services of municipal utility districts (MUDs), water conservation and improvement districts (WCIDs), hospital districts, and a host of other administrative units, which some have deemed the "invisible governments" of the state.[39] Approximately 2,300 such governmental units across Texas have been classified as **special districts**, and every year additional ones are created. These include drainage districts, navigation districts, fresh water supply districts, river authorities, underground water districts, sanitation districts, housing authorities, soil conservation districts, MUDs, and WCIDs. School districts are also considered a form of special district.

Functions and Structures Special districts are units of local government created by the state to perform specific functions. Wide variations in their functions, taxing and borrowing authority, governance, and performance limit generalizations about them. Most special districts are authorized to perform a single function and are designated single-purpose districts. But some are multipurpose districts because the laws creating them permit them to provide more than one service to constituents. For example, in addition to providing water to people in their service areas, MUDs may assume responsibility for drainage, solid waste collection, firefighting, and parks and other recreational facilities.[40] Some districts, such as hospi-

spoils system System of filling public jobs by hiring friends and other politically connected applicants, regardless of their abilities.

civil service system System under which public employees are hired and promoted on their abilities. It features competitive examinations and offers job security from one election to another.

special districts Units of local government created by the state to perform specific functions not met by cities or counties, including the provision of public services to unincorporated areas.

tal districts, normally cover an entire county. Others, such as MUDs, cover part of one county; still others, such as river authorities, cover a number of counties.

A special district is governed by a board either appointed by other governmental units or elected in nonpartisan elections. The board members of hospital districts are appointed by county commissioners courts; city housing authority boards are appointed by mayors or city councils. Many of these districts have taxing and borrowing authority, but others have no taxing powers and are supported by user fees or funds dedicated to them by other governmental agencies. Many special districts are eligible for federal grants-in-aid.

Special districts exist for a variety of reasons. Independent school districts were created, in part, to depoliticize education and remove the responsibility for it from county and city governments. In some cases, existing governments are unwilling or unable—because of state restrictions on their tax, debt, or jurisdictional authority—to provide essential services to developing communities. So special districts are created to fill the gap.

The cost of providing a particular governmental service is another reason for the growth of special districts. By creating a special district that includes a number of governmental units and a larger population and tax base, the costs can be spread over a wider area. Special districts often are promoted by individuals, groups, or corporations for selfish gains. Builders, for example, sometimes develop plans for large tracts of land in the unincorporated areas of a county and then convince local governments or the legislature to create municipal utility or water districts to provide water and sewer services.

Some special districts have been designed to serve specific geographical areas. River basins that extend for thousands of square miles and cover ten or twenty counties have presented a particular problem. Because no existing governments had jurisdiction over the use of water resources in these basins, river authorities with multicounty jurisdictions were created.[41]

Consequences of Single-Purpose Districts   From one perspective, special districts compensate for the fragmentation of local government that exists throughout Texas. But, ironically, these districts contribute to further fragmentation and delay the development of comprehensive, multipurpose governmental units that could provide public services more efficiently. A special district has been called a "halfway house between cityhood and non-cityhood, between incorporation and non-incorporation."[42] Residents of a developing community or subdivision may not want to create a new city or become part of a nearby existing city, but they need certain fundamental services, such as water, electricity, and fire protection, some of which can be provided through the creation of special districts.

Many special districts are small operations with limited financial resources and few employees. Salaries often are low, and some districts have difficulty retaining the licensed technical people required to perform daily operations. In some cases, record-keeping and management operations are shoddy and amateurish, and the costs of providing services by many of these operations may actually be higher than what similar services cost in larger governmental systems. Special districts may also use outside legal and professional assistance, which can be very costly, and many districts lack the expertise to maximize their investments or borrowing potential.[43]

Some special districts expand their functions beyond the purpose for which they were created. The metropolitan transit authority in San Antonio, for example, authorized under state law to impose a 1 percent sales tax for public transportation, became involved in building the Alamodome, a multipurpose convention and sports facility. As governments expand their functions, there is a greater potential for intergovernmental rivalry, conflict, deadlock, and duplication of costs.

Except for the 1,000-plus independent school districts and a small number of other highly visible districts, such as river authorities, most special districts operate in anonymity. The public has only limited knowledge of their jurisdiction, management, operations, or performance. Many taxpayers may not even be aware they are paying taxes to some of these entities. There is little media coverage of their work, few individuals attend their board meetings, and turnout for their elections is extremely low. In the case of the governing boards appointed by other governmental agencies, the selection process is often dominated by a small number of individuals or groups who greatly influence the activities of the special district as well. This domination is probably the most pernicious aspect of special districts.

INDEPENDENT SCHOOL DISTRICTS

The **independent school district**, currently the basic organizational structure for public education in Texas, has its origins in the constitution of 1876. Cities and towns were allowed to create independent school districts and to impose a tax to support them. Initially, the city government served as the school board, but in 1879, school districts were permitted to organize independently of the city or town, elect their own boards of trustees, and impose their own school tax. But residents of rural areas, where most nineteenth-century Texans lived, were denied these powers and had the sole option of forming community schools. In effect, Texas operated under a dual school system, with the majority of students subject to the discretionary and often arbitrary powers of county governments.

Inequities in the Public Education System   From the very beginning, the inequities in the school system were clear to many parents, elected officials, and educators, and there were early efforts to reform and modernize public schools. Most were linked to national education reform movements: for example, the Peabody Education Board, a national organization, provided financial aid and technical support to the leaders of the state reform movement during the early part of the twentieth century. More recently, national attention has been directed to the problems of public education through widely publicized studies such as *A Nation at Risk: The Imperative for Educational Reform* (1983), which was conducted by the National Commission on Excellence in Education. Many national, state, and local organizations have attempted to identify the most serious problems in public education, develop alternatives for resolving these problems, and initiate related litigation or legislative and administrative reforms.

Reformers have focused much of their attention on compulsory education laws, adequacy and equity in school funding, quality curricula, and teacher preparation. Other reform efforts have been directed at the structure and governance of local school districts. The diverse and fragmented structure of Texas schools has been modified over the years through consolidation, greater uniformity in the organization of school districts, and the extension of the independent school district to virtually every community in the state.

independent school district   Specific form of special district that administers the public schools in a designated area.

Local School Governance   Although regulation and coordination are provided on a statewide level through the State Board of Education and the Texas Education

Agency (TEA), public education is now administered through approximately 1,050 local school districts. In 1998 the smallest district, the Doss Consolidated School District, had 16 students. The largest, the Houston Independent School District, had 209,375 students. The nine largest districts enrolled more than 800,000 of the 3.9 million students attending pre-kindergarten through grade 12 in Texas public schools during the 1997–98 school year. By contrast, 366 districts had fewer than 500 students each, serving a total of only 93,000 students. By 1998 students from minority ethnic or racial groups constituted 55 percent of the public school population in Texas, and their numbers were expected to increase.[44]

School districts are governed by **school boards**, ranging in size from three to nine members; most have seven. Trustees are elected in nonpartisan elections for terms that vary from two to six years, with most serving three-year terms. In 1997 approximately 140 of the 1,050 school districts elected their boards from single-member districts.[45] School districts with significant minority populations have shifted from at-large elections to single-member districting primarily as a consequence of lawsuits or threatened lawsuits by minority plaintiffs under the Voting Rights Act.

Most school board elections are held on the first Saturday in May, the same day most cities hold their elections. School board election turnouts are low, usually less than 10 percent of registered voters. But turnout increases when there are highly visible issues, such as the firing of a superintendent or a dramatic increase in taxes.

Recruiting qualified candidates for school boards is often difficult, and many times elections are uncontested. Individuals are encouraged to run by the superintendent, other members of the board, or key community leaders, many of whom point out that it is difficult to find people who are willing to give the required time and energy. Individuals often have little knowledge of what school board members do, and because many trustees serve for only one term, some boards have high turnover rates. Moreover, there is no way for a potential trustee to anticipate the amount of time it will take for briefings by the superintendent and staff, preparing for and participating in board meetings, and taking phone calls from parents and taxpayers. A board member must also deal with the political aspect of the job, including attendance at community functions and major school programs and meeting with teachers and taxpayer groups. Board members receive no salaries but are reimbursed for travel related to board business.

The most important decision that a school board makes is the hiring of a **school superintendent**. In organization and management structure, the school district is similar to the council-manager form of government. The board hires a superintendent, who is in charge of the district's day-to-day operations. Although the board has the primary policy-making responsibility for a district, part-time board members are often dominated by the superintendent and the superintendent's staff. School trustees and superintendents tend to talk about "keeping politics out of education," and superintendents often attempt to convey the impression that they serve simply to carry out the will of their boards. In most instances, however, a school board's agenda is established by the superintendent, and the board members depend on the superintendent and other professional staff members for information and policy recommendations. Very few board members have much time to devote to the district, and most have only limited knowledge of the laws affecting education. State law, in fact, restricts the intrusion of board members into the daily management and administration of a district. An excessively politicized school board that becomes involved in day-to-day administration can be called

school board Governing body of a school district. Its responsibilities include the development or approval of educational policies, approval of the budget, hiring of the superintendent, and other personnel matters.

school superintendent Top administrator of a school district hired by the elected school board to direct the district's daily operations.

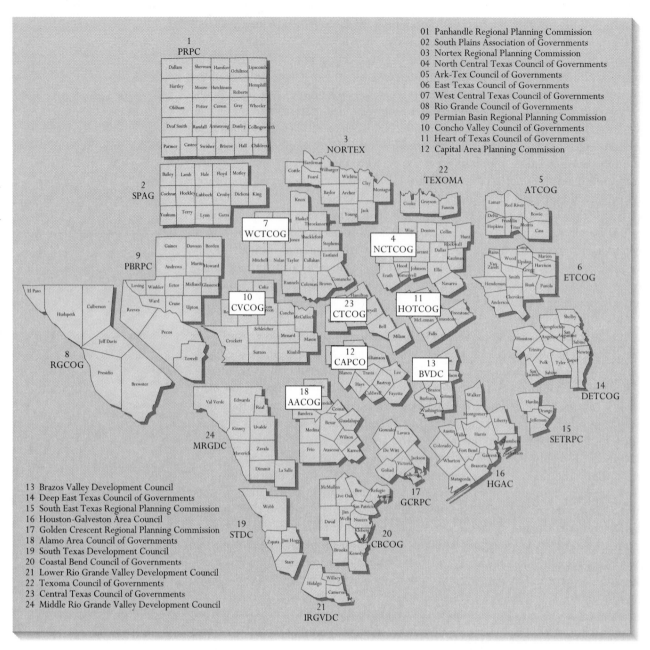

FIGURE 25-6 State Planning Regions
Source: Office of the Governor.

01 Panhandle Regional Planning Commission
02 South Plains Association of Governments
03 Nortex Regional Planning Commission
04 North Central Texas Council of Governments
05 Ark-Tex Council of Governments
06 East Texas Council of Governments
07 West Central Texas Council of Governments
08 Rio Grande Council of Governments
09 Permian Basin Regional Planning Commission
10 Concho Valley Council of Governments
11 Heart of Texas Council of Governments
12 Capital Area Planning Commission

13 Brazos Valley Development Council
14 Deep East Texas Council of Governments
15 South East Texas Regional Planning Commission
16 Houston-Galveston Area Council
17 Golden Crescent Regional Planning Commission
18 Alamo Area Council of Governments
19 South Texas Development Council
20 Coastal Bend Council of Governments
21 Lower Rio Grande Valley Development Council
22 Texoma Council of Governments
23 Central Texas Council of Governments
24 Middle Rio Grande Valley Development Council

to task by the Texas Education Agency. In an extreme case, the TEA can even take over the management of a school district.

COUNCILS OF GOVERNMENT

council of government (COG) Council comprised of representatives of other governments in a defined region of the state.

Councils of government (COGs), or regional planning commissions, were created under the Texas Regional Planning Act of 1965 (see Figure 25-6). That law was enacted, in part, to comply with federal regulations requiring local planning and review procedures.[46] These organizations evolved over the years to take on additional duties, including comprehensive planning and service responsibilities for employment and job training, criminal justice, economic development, health, aging, early childhood development, alcoholism, drug abuse, transportation, land resource management, environmental quality, and rural development.[47]

Twenty-four regional councils of government in Texas each serve a specific geographic area. Membership is voluntary; in 1996 more than 1,900 counties, cities, school districts, and other special districts were members of COGs. Each COG decides the composition and structure of its governing body, so long as two-thirds of its members are elected officials from counties or cities. Regional councils have no regulatory authority or powers comparable to those of other local governments, and decisions of COGs are not binding on their members.[48]

Member governments pay dues, but the primary sources of funding for COGs have been the state and federal governments. The state pays a regional council a flat fee for each county that is a member and provides a per capita payment for each person residing in the COG. At one time, the regional councils relied extensively on federal grants-in-aid, but there was a 70 percent decrease in direct federal funding of COGs during the 1980s. Several COGs have expanded their technical support, training, and management services for which they charge fees to offset lost revenues.[49]

SOLUTIONS TO THE PROBLEMS OF LOCAL GOVERNMENT

Privatization of Functions As local governments have sought to balance diminishing revenues with increased demands for public services, they have tended to contract out certain services to private companies. Many governments believe **privatization** can reduce costs through businesslike efficiency, and they consider it an attractive alternative in the face of voter hostility toward higher taxes. Cities, for example, are contracting for garbage pickup, waste disposal, towing, food services, security, and a variety of other services. Privatization also provides a way for cities that have reached their limit on bonded indebtedness to make new capital improvements by leasing a facility from a private contractor. A civic center or school facility can be constructed by a private contractor and leased back to the government for an extended period.

Annexation and Extraterritorial Jurisdiction Population growth in the areas surrounding most large Texas cities has forced municipalities and counties to wrestle with urban sprawl. El Paso covered 26 square miles in 1950 but had expanded to 239 square miles by 1990. Houston grew from 160 square miles in 1950 to 540 square miles in 1990, and similar expansions have occurred in most of the state's other metropolitan areas.

The cities' ability to expand their boundaries beyond suburban development derives from their **annexation powers** and **extraterritorial jurisdiction** over neighboring areas. With the Municipal Annexation Act of 1963, the legislature granted cities considerable discretionary authority over nearby unincorporated areas. Specific annexation powers and extraterritorial jurisdiction vary with the size and charter of a city. Generally, cities have extraterritorial jurisdiction over unincorporated areas within one-half mile to five miles of the city limits,

privatization The contracting by government with private companies to provide some public services.

annexation powers The authority of cities to add territory, subject to restrictions set by state law.

extraterritorial jurisdiction The power of an incorporated city to control development within nearby unincorporated areas.

Circle C Ranch: A Subdivision's Fight against Austin

For years, developers building subdivisions on the scenic western outskirts of Austin have been fighting environmentalists and Austin city officials over environmental restrictions. That war reached new intensity in 1995, when the developer of Circle C Ranch, a planned community in southwest Travis County, went to the Texas legislature to win unprecedented independence for his subdivision.

In a major departure from traditional public policy that gave cities strong control over development around them, developer Gary Bradley convinced lawmakers to enact a special law freeing Circle C Ranch from Austin's control and future annexation, although the subdivision was within the city's extraterritorial jurisdiction. The law created a new super water district to govern Circle C development, subject to approval by state environmental officials. The district was headed by a nine-member board appointed by the governor.

Bradley and other supporters of the bill, including many Circle C residents, argued that the new law was necessary to allow for a more complete development of the community, which at the time was entirely residential. Construction of offices, retail stores, and apartment houses had been blocked by Austin's strict water and development regulations. Austin officials said the regulations were necessary to control development in the environmentally sensitive area and protect the city's water supply and quality of life. But Bradley and his supporters argued it was unfair for Austin to impose such restrictions on non-Austin residents, who could not participate in city council elections. Some Circle C residents also believed more development would ease their property tax burden because it would bring in more taxpayers to help pay off the subdivision's debt on utilities and other capital necessities.

But the bill was criticized as an anti-environmental, special-interest piece of legislation made all the more suspect by the fact that Bradley, according to an analysis by the *Austin American-Statesman*, had contributed $20,355 to twenty-one legislators. And

Houses in the Circle C Ranch development.

although the state representative who represented Circle C cosponsored Bradley's bill, most other legislators from Austin and Travis County opposed it. State Senator Gonzalo Barrientos, who represented both Circle C and the city of Austin, filibustered for more than twenty-one hours on two occasions against it. "Sam Houston must be rolling over in his grave," Barrientos said. "We are creating a governmental body that is the antithesis of democracy. The board of this district is unelected."[*]

Over the objections of Austin officials, Governor George W. Bush let the bill become law without his signature and appointed nine people to the new Circle C board. But continuing the fight, Austin challenged the new law in court and, in 1997, a state district judge declared the law unconstitutional because it was designed to benefit a special class of landowners. Austin annexed Circle C in December 1997, but several legal issues remained unresolved. One was a suit brought by minority plaintiffs, who argued that the annexation of the predominantly white subdivision violated the federal Voting Rights Act because it diluted minority voting strength in the city of Austin.

In another challenge of city annexation powers, residents of suburban Kingwood asked the Texas legislature in 1997 to overturn their annexation by the city of Houston. The legislature refused to intervene, but the annexation disputes prompted a legislative study of cities' annexation powers.

---

[*]Quoted in *Austin American-Statesman*, May 25, 1995.

making development in those areas subject to the city's building codes, zoning and land use restrictions, utility easement requirements, and road and street specifications. This authority restricts the use of unincorporated land and requires those building outside the city to build according to minimal standards. Later, when those areas are annexed by the city, they are less likely to quickly degenerate into suburban slums that will require a high infusion of city dollars for basic services.

Cities can annex areas equivalent to 10 percent of their existing territory in a given year, and if this authority is not exercised in one year, it can be carried over to subsequent years. Annexation does not usually require a vote by those slated to be incorporated into the city (see *What Do You Think?* "Circle C Ranch: A Subdivision's Fight against Austin"). However, within three years, a city is required to provide annexed areas with services comparable to those provided in its older neighborhoods. Otherwise, individuals living in these newly annexed areas can exercise an option to be deannexed, a situation that rarely occurs.

Aggressive use of annexation has permitted several large cities to expand geographically as their population grows, sometimes limiting the development of small suburban towns that would potentially limit future expansion. Cities have even annexed thin strips of land, miles from urban development, along major roads and highways leading into them. Because a city's extraterritorial jurisdiction extended as far as five miles on either side of the strip that was annexed, this practice has allowed a city to control future development in a large area. In San Antonio, these annexation policies have often been referred to as "spoke annexation," and it has taken more than thirty years for much of the territory brought under the city's jurisdiction to be developed and annexed by the city.[50]

Modernization of County Government   City governments provide most basic public services in urban areas, and as cities expand to county boundaries and beyond, there is increased overlapping jurisdiction of county and city governments and a reduction of county services in the annexed areas. Counties, nevertheless, still play an important role in Texas. Rural Texans, in particular, continue to rely on counties to provide a number of services, and demands on many counties will increase. Recommendations to modernize county government include another attempt at county home rule, granting counties some legislative or ordinance-making authority, and creating an office of county administrator, appointed by the commissioners court to run the departments now assigned to commissioners. Another recommendation is to extend the civil service system to smaller counties and to all county employees.[51]

Economic Development   Historically, cities have collaborated with the private sector to stimulate local economies. Private sector initiatives have come from chambers of commerce or economic development foundations, and local governments have participated. Cities are also using a variety of new financing techniques to assist in economic development, including development impact taxes and fees, user charges, creation of special district assessments, tax increment financing, and privatization of governmental functions.[52] A state law was enacted in 1989 to permit cities, with the approval of local voters, to impose a 0.5 percent sales tax for local economic development. By 1995 voters in 229 Texas cities had approved this tax option.[53]

Texas cities, as well as some counties, aggressively court U.S. and foreign companies to relocate or develop new plants or operations in their communities. Cities and local chambers of commerce sponsor public relations campaigns touting local benefits and attractions. Local governments offer **tax abatements**—exemptions from prop-

tax abatements Exemptions from property taxes granted to certain businesses, usually to encourage them to move to or expand their operations in a city or county. The exemptions are granted for specific periods.

Up Close

Expensive Tax Breaks

As the Texas economy diversified in the 1990s, economic development was very important to many communities. Texas towns and cities competed with one another and with municipalities in other states for industries that would provide jobs and help their communities grow. They offered incentives for companies to build new plants or expand existing facilities. One popular incentive was a form of tax break called a tax abatement: companies receiving tax abatements from local governments did not have to pay property taxes on their new facilities for a designated number of years. Proponents defended such breaks as an important economic development tool and argued that abatements eventually paid for themselves in the form of an expanded tax base. But some

legislators and other critics believed school districts and other local governments were giving away too much potential tax revenue.

According to a staff report prepared for the Senate Economic Development Committee in 1996, 186 of the state's 1,050 school districts had given tax abatements since 1985. The state comptroller's office said those abatements had cost $480 million in lost property tax revenue. "Our children's future should not be traded for new jobs now," said Senator David Sibley of Waco, the committee chairman.[*] The lost money, he said, could have been spent on supplies, teacher salaries, and other educational needs. The legislature, however, chose not to enact any reforms on tax abatements during its 1997 session.

---

[*]Quoted in *Austin American-Statesman*, October 31, 1996.

---

erty taxes on a business for a specified period—to encourage a company to locate or expand in a community (see *Up Close*: "Expensive Tax Breaks"). Other financial incentives include lowered utility bills and assistance in obtaining housing for employees.

The legislature has permitted counties to form industrial development corporations or enterprise zones and to relax state regulatory policies to encourage the redevelopment of depressed areas. Portions of a county may be designated as reinvestment zones, in which tax abatements can be offered to attract new businesses. Counties also can create county boards of development, civic centers, foreign trade zones, and research and development authorities.[54]

Interlocal Contracting   Because many small governments have limited tax bases and staffs, they enter into contracts with larger governments for various public services. In 1971 the legislature, following a constitutional amendment, enacted the Interlocal Cooperation Act, which gave cities, counties, and other political subdivisions rather broad authority for such contracts.[55] The law has been amended several times to expand the scope of these agreements, and local governments are now contracting with each other for services in twenty-five functional areas, ranging from aviation to water and wastewater management.[56] Contracting is not an alternative to consolidation of local governments, but it does hold some promise for improving the quality of local services and reducing their costs.

Metro Government and Consolidation   In the metropolitan areas of Houston, Dallas, and San Antonio, literally hundreds of cities and special districts provide public services. In Harris County (Houston) alone, there are 518 separate governmental units (see Table 25-4). Legislators, scholars, and reform groups have conducted extensive studies of the duplication and other problems produced by such proliferation and fragmentation and have made numerous recommendations over the years. One proposed solution is a consolidation of city and county governments known as **metro government**, which has been tried in a dozen or so areas outside Texas. Efforts initiated by San Antonio and Bexar County to obtain constitutional authority to propose city-county consolidation to voters in the county failed in the 1997 legislative session. But in 1998, Bexar County and San Antonio were joined by several other metropolitan areas in an expanded effort to obtain this authority from the Texas legislature in the 1999 session. Without such authority, county-city collaboration is more likely to take the form of increased intergovernmental contracting and the informal cooperation that local governments develop out of necessity and mutual self-interest.[57]

Public Improvement Districts   Under one state law, property owners in a specific area of a city or its extraterritorial jurisdiction can petition the city to create a special **public improvement district**. These districts can undertake a wide range of improvements—landscaping, lighting, signs, sidewalks, streets, pedestrian malls, libraries, parking, and facilities for water, wastewater, and drainage. Public improvement districts do not have the same autonomy as other special districts. They are created solely through the discretionary powers of a city and are funded by assessments on property within their boundaries.[58] Although their budgets and assessments must be approved by the city, they can be operated and managed by private management companies or by the citizens themselves. Fort Worth created a public improvement district for its downtown area in 1986, and other cities have considered the option.

metro government   Local government in which city and county governments consolidate to avoid duplication of public services.

public improvement district   Specific area of a city in which property owners pay special taxes in return for improvements to streets and other public facilities in their neighborhood.

TABLE 25-4	Local Governments in the Ten Largest and Ten Smallest Texas Counties, 1992				
	Total	*County*	*Municipal*	*School Districts*	*Special Districts*
State	4,791	254	1,171	1,100	2,266
Harris	518	1	28	24	465
Dallas	70	1	26	16	27
Tarrant	69	1	34	18	16
Bexar	51	1	22	16	12
El Paso	35	1	6	10	18
Travis	84	1	14	8	61
Hidalgo	75	1	18	15	41
Denton	56	1	33	11	11
Collin	51	1	24	15	11
Nueces	38	1	7	13	17
Glasscock	4	1		1	2
Sterling	5	1	1	1	2
Terrell	4	1		1	2
Roberts	4	1	1	1	1
Kent	5	1	1	1	2
McMullen	5	1		1	3
Borden	2	1		1	
Kenedy	2	1		1	
King	3	1		1	1
Loving	2	1			1

Source: U.S. Department of Commerce, Bureau of the Census, *1992 Census of Governments, Government Organization*, vol. 1, table 28.

Politics in Cyberspace

Local Government in Texas

With more than 4,700 local governments in Texas, it is often difficult to determine which jurisdiction has the authority and responsibility for specific public functions or services. Outdated structures, limited powers, and overlapping jurisdictions often restrict local governments in their efforts to deal with local issues or problems.

State of Texas
http://www.state.tx.us

This site permits access to Web sites for all counties in Texas as well as the Councils of Government. Select cities have developed Web pages that can be accessed through this site. Information varies, with some sites producing more comprehensive data than others.

Texas Association of Counties
http://www.county.org

This association serves county governments throughout the state. Its site provides extensive information on recent legislation and laws pertaining to counties,

support services, news releases, and educational programs for county officials.

Texas Municipal League
http://www.tml.org

The purpose of this organization is to provide services to Texas cities. This site provides information on the association's publications, programs, and services, including its legislative policy program.

Texas Association of School Boards
http://www.tasb.org

The Texas Association of School Boards serves the 1,000-plus state school districts through policy advocacy and support services. The site includes links to many school districts as well as information pertaining to services, programs, and publications.

U.S. Bureau of the Census
http://www.census.gov

Population data are available for local geographical areas from the Bureau of the Census. Use the "Other Official Stats/FedStats" to access this information.

SUMMARY NOTES

- Local governments in Texas are the creations of the state and have only those powers granted to them by the Texas Constitution and statutes. With limited discretionary authority but with a great deal of responsibility, local governments often find it difficult to respond effectively to the needs of their citizens.

- More than 80 percent of the state's population lives in urban areas. Texas cities have highly diverse social structures, economies, and historical traditions, and, subsequently, urban politics differ markedly across the state. Five of the ten largest cities have more than 50 percent minority populations, contributing to longstanding controversies over urban electoral systems.

- Texas cities with fewer than 5,000 people are designated general law cities and can opt only for certain forms of government. Cities with more than 5,000 residents can function as home rule cities, choosing a form of government that satisfies community needs as long as it does not conflict with the state constitution or statutes.

- Texas cities have experimented with three forms of government—mayor-council, city commission, and council-manager.

- A notable feature of city politics in Texas is the widespread use of nonpartisan, at-large elections. Prompted by legal attacks under the Voting Rights Act, many cities, as well as special purpose districts, have adopted single-member districts, thus increasing minority representation on local governing bodies.

- County governments, initially created to serve a rural population, function primarily as administrative subdivisions of the state. Much like state government, county government is highly fragmented, with administrative powers shared by a variety of elected officials.

- Hundreds of special purpose districts provide numerous public services and add to the fragmentation of local government. Most people know little about their jurisdiction, structure, functions, and leadership, making them the "invisible governments" of Texas. Texas has approximately 1,050 independent school districts, which are working to improve the quality of education against a backdrop of social, cultural, and financial problems.

- Texas cities are now experiencing many of the same problems as the older cities of the East and Midwest. Populations are aging, and there is some evidence of "white flight" from the core urban centers. A disproportionately larger share of the population in the central cities is low income and least able to pay taxes to support municipal services or the improvement of deteriorating infrastructures. Federal and state governments have imposed additional requirements, or mandates, on the cities that are increasingly difficult to meet.

- Local governments are experimenting with a variety of techniques to deal with their problems. Cities have used their annexation powers and extraterritorial jurisdiction to expand their tax bases and exercise limited controls over development in adjacent areas. Cities are also using public improvement districts to permit targeted areas to impose additional taxes for needed services. Both counties and cities are privatizing governmental functions to decrease costs and increase efficiency. Interlocal contracting permits governments to provide services to each other on a contractual basis, and many counties and cities are engaged in aggressive economic development programs.

SELECTED READINGS

BRIDGES, AMY. *Morning Glories: Municipal Reform in the Southwest.* Princeton, N.J.: Princeton University Press, 1997.

BROOKS, DAVID B. *Texas Practice: County and Special District Law,* Vols. 35 and 36. St. Paul, Minn.: West, 1989.

BULLARD, ROBERT D. *Invisible Houston: The Black Experience in Boom and Bust.* College Station: Texas A&M University Press, 1987.

BURNS, NANCY. *The Formation of American Local Governments: Private Values in Public Institutions.* New York: Oxford University Press, 1994.

DELEON, ARNOLDO. *Ethnicity in the Sunbelt: A History of Mexican Americans in Houston.* Houston: University of Houston Press, 1989.

FEAGIN, JOE R. *Free Enterprise City: Houston in Political-Economic Perspective.* New Brunswick, N.J.: Rutgers University Press, 1988.

GOSWAMI, NIRMAL. "The Impact of Electoral Structure on School District Students with Special Reference to Minority Students." *Texas Journal of Political Studies* 14 (Spring/Summer 1992): 1134.

HERZOG, LAWRENCE A. *Where North Meets South: Cities, Space and Politics on the United States–Mexico Border.* Austin: University of Texas Press, 1990.

JOHNSON, DAVID R., JOHN A. BOOTH, and RICHARD J. HARRIS, eds. *The Politics of San Antonio: Community, Progress, and Power.* Lincoln: University of Nebraska Press, 1983.

JONES, LAWRENCE, and DELBERT A. TAEBEL. "Hispanic Representational Change in Texas County Government." *Texas Journal of Political Studies* 16 (Fall 1993): 321.

MCCOMB, DAVID G. *Houston: A History.* Austin: University of Texas Press, 1981.

MILLER, CHAR, and HEYWOOD T. SANDERS, EDS. *Urban Texas.* College Station: Texas A&M University Press, 1990.

NORWOOD, ROBERT E., and SABRINA STRAWN. *Texas County Government: Let the People Choose.* 2nd ed. Austin: Texas Research League, 1984.

ORUM, ANTHONY M. *Power, Money and the People: The Making of Modern Austin.* Austin: Texas Monthly Press, 1987.

PERRENOD, VIRGINIA MARION. *Special Districts, Special Purposes: Fringe Governments and Urban Problems in the Houston Area.* College Station: Texas A&M University Press, 1984.

PERRY, DAVID C., and ALFRED J. WATKINS, EDS. *The Rise of the Sunbelt Cities.* Beverly Hills, Calif.: Sage, 1977.

SMITH, KEVIN. "Texas Municipalities' Thirst for Water: Acquisition Methods for Water Planning." *Baylor Law Review* 45 (Summer 1993): 685–722.

APPENDIX

THE DECLARATION OF INDEPENDENCE

Drafted mainly by Thomas Jefferson, this document adopted by the Second Continental Congress, and signed by John Hancock and fifty-five others, outlined the rights of man and the rights to rebellion and self-government. It declared the independence of the colonies from Great Britain, justified rebellion, and listed the grievances against George the III and his government. What is memorable about this famous document is not only that it declared the birth of a new nation, but that it set forth, with eloquence, our basic philosophy of liberty and representative democracy.

IN CONGRESS, JULY 4, 1776
(The unanimous Declaration of the Thirteen United States of America)

Preamble
When, in the course of human events, it becomes necessary for one people to dissolve the political bands which have connected them with another, and to assume, among the powers of the earth, the separate and equal station to which the laws of nature and of nature's God entitle them, a decent respect to the opinions of mankind requires that they should declare the causes which impel them to the separation.

New Principles of Government

We hold these truths to be self-evident; that all men are created equal, that they are endowed by their Creator with certain unalienable rights, that among these are life, liberty, and the pursuit of happiness.

That, to secure these rights, governments are instituted among men, deriving their just powers from the consent of the governed.

That whenever any form of government becomes destructive of these ends, it is the right of the people to alter or to abolish it, and to institute new government, laying its foundation on such principles, and organizing its powers in such form, as to them shall seem most likely to effect their safety and happiness. Prudence, indeed will dictate that governments long established should not be changed for light and transient causes; and accordingly all experience hath shown that mankind are more disposed to suffer while evils are sufferable, than to right themselves by abolishing the forms to which they are accustomed. But when a long train of abuses and usurpations, pursuing invariably the same object, evinces a design to reduce them under absolute despotism, it is their right, it is their duty, to throw off such government, and to provide new guards for their future security.

Reasons for Separation

Such has been the patient sufferance of these colonies; and such is now the necessity which constrains them to alter their former systems of government. The history of the present king of Great Britain is a history of repeated injuries and usurpations, all having in direct object the establishment of an absolute tyranny over these states. To prove this, let facts be submitted to a candid world.

He has refused his assent to laws, the most wholesome and necessary for the public good.

He has forbidden his governors to pass laws of immediate and pressing importance unless suspended in their operation till his assent should be obtained; and when so suspended, he has utterly neglected to attend to them.

He has refused to pass other laws for the accommodation of large districts of people, unless those people would relinquish the right of representation in the legislature, a right inestimable to them, and formidable to tyrants only.

He has called together legislative bodies at places unusual, uncomfortable, and distant for the depository of their public records, for the sole purpose of fatiguing them into compliance with his measures.

He has dissolved representative houses repeatedly, for opposing, with manly firmness, his invasions on the rights of people.

He has refused, for a long time after such dissolutions, to cause others to be elected; whereby the legislative powers incapable of annihilation, have returned to the people at large for their exercise; the state remaining, in the meantime, exposed to all the dangers of invasion from without and convulsions within.

He has endeavored to prevent the population of these states; for that purpose obstructing the laws of naturalization of foreigners, refusing to pass others to encourage their migration hither, and raising the conditions of new appropriations of lands.

He has obstructed the administration of justice, by refusing his assent to laws for establishing judiciary powers.

He has made judges dependent on his will alone for the tenure of their offices, and the amount and payment of their salaries.

He has erected a multitude of new offices, and sent hither swarms of officers to harass our people and eat out their substance.

He has kept among us, in times of peace, standing armies, without the consent of our legislature.

He has affected to render the military independent of, and superior to, the civil power.

He has combined with others to subject us to jurisdiction foreign to our constitution and unacknowledged by our laws, giving his assent to their acts of pretended legislation:

For quartering large bodies of armed troops among us;

For protecting them, by a mock trial, from punishment for any murders which they should commit on the inhabitants of these states;

For cutting off our trade with all parts of the world;

For imposing taxes on us without our consent;

For depriving us, in many cases, of the benefits of trial by jury;

For transporting us beyond seas, to be tried for pretended offenses;

For abolishing the free system of English laws in a neighboring province, establishing therein an arbitrary government, and enlarging its boundaries, so as to render it at once an example and fit instrument for introducing the same absolute rule into these colonies;

For taking away our charters, abolishing our most valuable laws, and altering, fundamentally, the forms of our governments;

For suspending our own legislatures, and declaring themselves invented with power to legislate for us in all cases whatsoever.

He has abdicated government here, by declaring us out of his protection and waging war against us.

He has plundered our seas, ravaged our coasts, burned our towns, and destroyed the lives of our people.

He is at this time transporting large armies of foreign mercenaries to complete the works of death, desolation, and tyranny already begun with circumstances of cruelty and perfidy scarcely paralleled in the most barbarous ages and totally unworthy of the head of a civilized nation.

He has constrained our fellow-citizens, taken captive on the high seas, to bear arms against their country, to become the executioners of their friends and brethren, or to fall themselves by their hands.

He has excited domestic insurrections among us, and has endeavored to bring on the inhabitants of our frontiers the merciless Indian savages, whose known rule of warfare is an undistinguished destruction of all ages, sexes, and conditions.

In every stage of these oppressions we have petitioned for redress in the most humble terms; our repeated petitions have been answered only by repeated injury. A prince whose character is thus marked by every act which may define a tyrant is unfit to be the ruler of a free people.

Nor have we been wanting in attention to our British brethren. We have warned them, from time to time, of attempts by their legislature to extend an unwarrantable jurisdiction over us. We have reminded them of the circumstances of our emigration and settlement here. We have appealed to their native justice and magnanimity; and we have conjured them, by the ties of our common kindred, to disavow these usurpations, which would inevitably interrupt our connections and correspondence. They, too, have been deaf to the voice of justice and of consanguinity. We must, therefore, acquiesce in the necessity which denounces our separation, and hold them, as we hold the rest of mankind, enemies in war, in peace, friends.

We, therefore, the representatives of the United States of America, in General Congress assembled, appealing to the Supreme Judge of the world for the rectitude of our intentions, do, in the name and by authority of the good people of these colonies, solemnly publish and declare, that these united colonies are, and of right ought to be, free and independent states; that they are absolved from all allegiance to the British crown, and that all political connection between them and the state of Great Britain is, and ought to be, totally dissolved; and that, as free and independent states, they have full power to levy war, conclude peace, contract alliances, establish commerce, and do all other acts and things which independent states may of a right do. And, for the support of this declaration, with a firm reliance on the protection of Divine Providence, we mutually pledge to each other our lives, our fortunes, and our sacred honor.

THE FEDERALIST, NO. 10, JAMES MADISON

To the People of the State of New York: Among the numerous advantages promised by a well-constructed union, none deserves to be more accurately developed than its tendency to break and control the violence of faction. The friend of popular governments, never finds himself so much alarmed for their character and fate, as when he contemplates their propensity to this dangerous vice. He will not fail, therefore, to set a due value on any plan which, without violating the principles to which he is attached, provides a proper cure for it. The instability, injustice, and confusion introduced into the public councils, have, in truth, been the mortal diseases under which popular governments have everywhere perished; as they continue to be the favourite and fruitful topics from which the adversaries to liberty derive their most specious declamations. The valuable improvements made by the American constitutions on the popular models, both ancient and modern, cannot certainly be too much admired; but it would be an unwarrantable partiality, to contend that they have as effectually obviated the danger on this side, as was wished and expected. Complaints are everywhere heard from our most considerate and virtuous citizens, equally the friends of public and private faith, and of public and personal liberty, that our governments are too unstable; that the public good is disregarded in the conflicts of rival parties; and that measures are too often decided, not according to the rules of justice, and the rights of the minor party, but by the superior force of an interested and overbearing majority. However anxiously we may wish that these complaints had no foundation, the evidence of known facts will not permit us to deny that they are in some degree true. It will be found, indeed, on a candid review of our situation, that some of the distresses under which we labour have been erroneously charged on the operation of our governments; but it will be found, at the same time, that other causes will not alone account for many of our heaviest misfortunes; and, particularly, for that prevailing and increasing distrust of public engagements, and alarm for private rights, which are echoed from one end of the continent to the other. These must be chiefly, if not wholly, effects of the unsteadiness and injustice, with which a factious spirit has tainted our public administrations.

By a faction, I understand a number of citizens, whether amounting to a majority or minority of the whole, who are united and actuated by some common impulse of passion, or of interest, adverse to the rights of other citizens, or to the permanent and aggregate interests of the community.

There are two methods of curing the mischiefs of faction: the one, by removing its causes; the other, by controlling its effects.

There are again two methods of removing the causes of faction: the one, by destroying the liberty which is essential to its existence; the other, by giving to every citizen the same opinions, the same passions, and the same interests.

It could never be more truly said, than of the first remedy, that it was worse than the disease. Liberty is to faction what air is to fire, an aliment without which it instantly expires. But it could not be a less folly to abolish liberty, which is essential to political life, because it nourishes faction, than it would be to wish the annihilation of air, which is essential to animal life, because it imparts to fire its destructive agency.

The second expedient is as impracticable, as the first would be unwise. As long as the reason of man continues fallible, and he is at liberty to exercise it, different opinions will be formed. As long as the connection subsists between his reason and his self-love, his opinions and his passions will have a reciprocal influence on each other; and the former will be objects to which the latter will attach themselves. The diversity in the faculties of men, from which the rights of property originate, is not less an insuperable obstacle to an uniformity of interests. The protection of these faculties is the first object of government. From the protection of different and unequal faculties of acquiring property, the possession of different degrees and kinds of property immediately results; and from the influence of these on the sentiments and views of the respective proprietors, ensues a division of the society into different interests and parties.

The latent causes of faction are thus sown in the nature of man; and we see them everywhere brought into different degrees of activity, according to the different circumstances of civil society. A zeal for different opinions concerning religion, concerning government, and many other points, as well of speculation as of practice; an attachment to different leaders ambitiously contending for preeminence and power; or to persons of other descriptions whose fortunes have been interesting to the human passions, have, in turn, divided mankind into parties, inflamed them with mutual animosity, and rendered them much more disposed to vex and oppress each other, than to cooperate for their common good. So strong is this propensity of mankind, to fall into mutual animosities, that where no substantial occasion presents itself, the most frivolous and fanciful distinctions have been sufficient to kindle their unfriendly passions and excite their most violent conflicts. But the most common and durable source of factions, has been the various and unequal distribution of property. Those who hold, and those who are without property, have ever formed distinct interests in society. Those who are creditors, and those who are debtors, fall under a like discrimination. A landed interest, a manufacturing interest, a mercantile interest, a moneyed interest, with many lesser interests, grow up of necessity in civilized nations, and divide them into different classes, actuated by different sentiments and views. The regulation of these various and interfering interests forms the principal task of modern legislation, and involves the spirit of the party and faction in the necessary and ordinary operations of the government.

No man is allowed to be a judge in his own cause; because his interest will certainly bias his judgment, and, not improbably, corrupt his integrity. With equal, nay, with greater reason, a body of men are unfit to be both judges and parties at the same time; yet what are many of the most important acts of legislation, but so many judicial determinations, not indeed concerning the right of single persons, but concerning the rights of large bodies of citizens? And what are the different classes of legislators, but advocates and parties to the causes which they determine? Is a law proposed concerning private debts? It is a question to which the creditors are parties on one side, and the debtors on the other. Justice ought to hold the balance between them. Yet the parties are, and must be, themselves the judges; and the most numerous party, or, in other words, the most powerful faction, must be expected to prevail. Shall domestic manufacturers be encouraged, and in what degree, by restrictions on foreign manufacturers are questions which would be differently decided by the landed and the manufacturing classes; and probably by neither with a sole regard to justice and the public good. The apportionment of taxes, on the various descriptions of property, is an act which seems to require the most exact impartiality; yet there is, perhaps, no legislative act, in which greater opportunity and temptation are given to a predominant party to trample on the rules of justice. Every shilling, with which they overburden the inferior number, is a shilling saved to their own pockets.

It is in vain to say, that enlightened statesmen will be able to adjust these clashing interests, and render them all subservient to the public good. Enlightened statesmen will not always be at the helm; nor, in many cases, can such an adjustment be made at all, without taking into view indirect and remote considerations, which will rarely prevail over the immediate interest which one party may find in disregarding the rights of another, or the good of the whole.

The inference to which we are brought is, that the *causes* of faction cannot be removed; and that relief is only to be sought in the means of controlling its *effects.*

If a faction consists of less than a majority, relief is supplied by the republican principle, which enables the majority to defeat its sinister views, by regular vote. It may clog the administration, it may convulse the society; but it will be unable to execute and mask its violence under the forms of the Constitution. When a majority is included in a faction, the form of popular government, on the other hand, enables it to sacrifice to its ruling passion or interest, both the public good and the rights of other citizens.

To secure the public good, and private rights, against the danger of such a faction, and at the same time to preserve the spirit and the form of popular government, is then the great object to which our inquiries are directed. Let me add, that it is the great desideratum, by which alone this form of government can be rescued from the opprobrium under which it has so long laboured, and be recommended to the esteem and adoption of mankind.

By what means is this object attainable? Evidently by one of two only. Either the existence of the same passion or interest in a majority, at the same time, must be prevented; or the majority, having such coexistent passion or interest, must be rendered, by their number and local situation, unable to concert and carry into effect schemes of oppression. If the impulse and the opportunity be suffered to coincide, we well know that neither moral nor religious motives can be relied on as an adequate control. They are not found to be such on the injustice and violence of individuals, and lose their efficacy in proportion to the number combined together; that is, in proportion as their efficacy becomes needful.

From this view of the subject, it may be concluded, that a pure democracy, by which I mean a society consisting of a small number of citizens, who assemble and administer the government in person, can admit of no cure for the mischiefs of faction. A common passion or interest will, in almost every case, be felt by a majority of the whole; a communication and concert, results from the form of government itself; and there is nothing to check the inducements to sacrifice the weaker party, or an obnoxious individual. Hence, it is, that such democracies have ever been spectacles of turbulence and contention; have ever been found incompatible with personal security, or the rights of property; and have in general been as short in their lives, as they have been violent in their deaths. Theoretic politicians, who have patronized this species of government, have erroneously supposed, that by reducing mankind to a perfect equality in their political rights, they would, at the same time, be perfectly equalized and assimilated in their possessions, their opinions, and their passions.

A republic, by which I mean a government in which the scheme of representation takes place, opens a different prospect, and promises the cure for which we are seeking. Let us examine the points in which it varies from pure democracy, and we shall comprehend both the nature of the cure and the efficacy which it must derive from the union.

The two great points of difference, between a democracy and a republic, are, first, the delegation of the government, in the latter, to a small number of citizens, elected by the rest; secondly, the greater number of citizens, and greater sphere of country, over which the latter may be extended.

The effect of the first difference is, on the one hand, to refine and enlarge the public views, by passing them through the medium of a chosen body of citizens, whose wisdom may best discern the true interest of their country, and whose patriotism and love of justice, will be least likely to sacrifice it to temporary or partial considerations. Under such a regulation, it may well happen, that the public voice, pronounced by the representatives of the people, will be more consonant to the public good, than if pronounced by the people themselves, convened for the purpose. On the other hand the effect may be inverted. Men of factious tempers, of local prejudices, or of sinister designs, may by intrigue, by corruption, or by other means, first obtain the suffrages, and then betray the interest of the people. The question resulting is, whether small or extensive republics are most favourable to the election of proper guardians of the public weal; and it is clearly decided in favour of the latter by two obvious considerations.

In the first place, it is to be remarked that, however small the republic may be, the representatives must be raised to a certain number, in order to guard against the cabals of a few; and that however large it may be, they must be limited to a certain number, in order to guard against the confusion of a multitude. Hence, the number of representatives in the two cases not being in proportion to that of the constituents, and being proportionally greatest in the small republic, it follows, that if the proportion of fit characters be not less in the large than in the small republic, the former will present a greater option, and consequently a greater probability of a fit choice.

In the next place, as each representative will be chosen by a greater number of citizens in the large than in the small republic, it will be more difficult for unworthy candidates to practice with success the vicious arts, by which elections are too often carried; and the suffrages of the people being more free, will be more likely to centre in men who possess the most attractive merit, and the most diffusive and established characters.

It must be confessed, that in this, as in most other cases, there is a mean, on both sides of which inconveniences will be found to lie. By enlarging too much the number of electors, you render the representatives too little acquainted with all their local circumstances and lesser interests; as by reducing it too much, you render him unduly attached to these, and too little fit to comprehend and pursue great and national objects. The federal constitution forms a happy combination in this respect; the great and aggregate interests being referred to the national, the local and particular to the state legislatures.

The other point of difference is, the greater number of citizens, and extent of territory, which may be brought within the compass of republican, than of democratic government; and it is this circumstance principally which renders factious combinations less to be dreaded in the former, than in the latter. The smaller the society, the fewer probably will

be the distinct parties and interests composing it; the fewer the distinct parties and interests, the more frequently will a majority be found of the same party; and the smaller the number of individuals composing a majority, and the smaller the compass within which they are placed, the more easily will they concert and execute their plans of oppression. Extend the sphere, and you take in a greater variety of parties and interests; you make it less probable that a majority of the whole will have a common motive to invade the rights of other citizens; or if such a common motive exists, it will be more difficult for all who feel it to discover their own strength, and to act in unison with each other. Besides other impediments, it may be remarked, that where there is a consciousness of unjust or dishonourable purposes, communication is always checked by distrust, in proportion to the number whose concurrence is necessary.

Hence, it clearly appears, that the same advantage, which a republic has over a democracy, in controlling the effects of faction, is enjoyed by a large over a small republic—is enjoyed by the union over the states composing it. Does this advantage consist in the substitution of representatives, whose enlightened views and virtuous sentiments render them superior to local prejudices, and to schemes of injustice? It will not be denied that the representation of the union will be most likely to possess these requisite endowments. Does it consist in the greater security afforded by a greater variety of parties, against the event of any one party being able to outnumber and oppress the rest? In an equal degree does the increased variety of parties, comprised within the union, increase the security? Does it, in fine, consist in the greater obstacles opposed to the concert and accomplishment of the secret wishes of an unjust and interested majority? Here, again, the extent of the union gives it the most palpable advantage.

The influence of factious leaders may kindle a flame within their particular states, but will be unable to spread a general conflagration through the other states; a religious sect may degenerate into a political faction in a part of the confederacy; but the variety of sects dispersed over the entire face of it, must secure the national councils against any danger from that source; a rage for paper money, for an abolition of debts, for an equal division of property, or for any other improper or wicked project, will be less apt to pervade the whole body of the union than a particular member of it; in the same proportion as such a malady is more likely to taint a particular county or district, than an entire state.

In the extent and proper structure of the union, therefore, we behold a republican remedy for the diseases most incident to republican government. And according to the degree of pleasure and pride we feel in being republicans, ought to be our zeal in cherishing the spirit, and supporting the character of federalists.

THE FEDERALIST, NO. 51, JAMES MADISON

To what expedient, then, shall we finally resort, for maintaining in practice the necessary partition of power among the several departments as laid down in the Constitution? The only answer that can be given is that as all these exterior provisions are found to be inadequate the defect must be supplied, by so contriving the interior structure of the government as that its several constituent parts may, by their mutual relations, be the means of keeping each other in their proper places. Without presuming to undertake a full development of this important idea I will hazard a few general observations which may perhaps place it in a clearer light, and enable us to form a more correct judgment of the principles and structure of the government planned by the convention.

In order to lay a due foundation for that separate and distinct exercise of the different powers of government, which to a certain extent is admitted on all hands to be essential to the preservation of liberty, it is evident that each department should have a will of its own; and consequently should be so constituted that the members of each should have as little agency as possible in the appointment of the members of the others. Were this principle rigorously adhered to, it would require that all the appointments for the supreme executive, legislative, and judiciary magistracies should be drawn from the same fountain of authority, the people, through channels having no communication whatever with one another. Perhaps such a plan of constructing the several departments would be less difficult in practice than it may in contemplation appear. Some difficulties, however, and some additional expense would attend the execution of it. Some deviations, therefore, from the principle must be admitted. In the constitution of the judiciary department in particular, it might be inexpedient to insist rigorously on the principle: first, because peculiar qualifications being essential in the members, the primary consideration ought to be to select that mode of choice which best secures these qualifications; second, because the permanent tenure by which the appointments are held in that department must soon destroy all sense of dependence on the authority conferring them.

It is equally evident that the members of each department should be as little dependent as possible on those of the others for the emoluments annexed to their offices. Were the executive magistrate, or the judges, not independent of the legislature in this particular, their independence in every other would be merely nominal.

But the great security against a gradual concentration of the several powers in the same department consists in giving to those who administer each department the necessary constitutional means and personal motives to resist encroachments of the others. The

provision for defense must in this, as in all other cases, be made commensurate to the danger of attack. Ambition must be made to counteract ambition. The interest of the man must be connected with the constitutional rights of the place. It may be a reflection on human nature that such devices should be necessary to control the abuses of government. But what is government itself but the greatest of all reflections on human nature? If men were angels, no government would be necessary. If angels were to govern men, neither external nor internal controls on government would be necessary. In framing a government which is to be administered by men over men, the great difficulty lies in this: you must first enable the government to control the governed; and in the next place oblige it to control itself. A dependence on the people is, no doubt, the primary control on the government; but experience has taught mankind the necessity of auxiliary precautions.

This policy of supplying, by opposite and rival interests, the defect of better motives, might be traced through the whole system of human affairs, private as well as public. We see it particularly displayed in all the subordinate distributions of power, where the constant aim is to divide and arrange the several offices in such a manner as that each may be a check on the other—that the private interest of every individual may be a sentinel over the public rights. These inventions of prudence cannot be less requisite in the distribution of the supreme powers of the State.

But it is not possible to give to each department an equal power of self-defense. In republican government, the legislative authority necessarily predominates. The remedy for this inconveniency is to divide the legislature into different branches; and to render them, by modes of election and different principles of action, as little connected with each other as the nature of their common functions and their common dependence on the society will admit. It may even be necessary to guard against dangerous encroachments by still further precautions. As the weight of the legislative authority requires that it should be thus divided, the weakness of the executive may require, on the other hand, that it should be fortified. An absolute negative on the legislature appears, at first view, to be the natural defense with which the executive magistrate should be armed. But perhaps it would be neither altogether safe nor alone sufficient. On ordinary occasions it might not be exerted with the requisite firmness, and on extraordinary occasions it might be perfidiously abused. May not this defect of an absolute negative be supplied by some qualified connection between this weaker department and the weaker branch of the stronger department, by which the latter may be led to support the constitutional rights of the former, without being too much detached from the rights of its own department?

If the principles on which these observations are founded be just, as I persuade myself they are, and they be applied as a criterion to the several State constitutions, and to the federal Constitution, it will be found that if the latter does not perfectly correspond with them, the former are infinitely less able to bear such a test.

There are, moreover, two considerations particularly applicable to the federal system of America, which place that system in a very interesting point of view.

First. In a single republic, all the power surrendered by the people is submitted to the administration of a single government; and the usurpations are guarded against by a division of the government into distinct and separate departments. In the compound republic of America, the power surrendered by the people is first divided between two distinct governments, and then the portion allotted to each subdivided among distinct and separate departments. Hence a double security arises to the rights of the people. The different governments will control each other, at the same time that each will be controlled by itself.

Second. It is of great importance in a republic not only to guard the society against the oppression of its rulers, but to guard one part of the society against the injustice of the other part. Different interests necessarily exist in different classes of citizens. If a majority be united by a common interest, the rights of the minority will be insecure. There are but two methods of providing against this evil: the one by creating a will in the community independent of the majority—that is, of the society itself; the other, by comprehending in the society so many separate descriptions of citizens as will render an unjust combination of a majority of the whole very improbable, if not impracticable. The first method prevails in all governments possessing an hereditary or self-appointed authority. This, at best, is but a precarious security; because a power independent of the society may as well espouse the unjust views of the major as the rightful interests of the minor party, and may possibly be turned against both parties. The second method will be exemplified in the federal republic of the United States. Whilst all authority in it will be derived from and dependent on the society, the society itself will be broken into so many parts, interests and classes of citizens, that the rights of individuals, or of the minority, will be in little danger from interested combinations of the majority. In a free government the security for civil rights must be the same as that for religious rights. It consists in the one case in the multiplicity of interests, and in the other in the multiplicity of sects. The degree of security in both cases will depend on the number of

interests and sects; and this may be presumed to depend on the extent of country and number of people comprehended under the same government. This view of the subject must particularly recommend a proper federal system to all the sincere and considerate friends of republican government, since it shows that in exact proportion as the territory of the Union may be formed into more circumscribed Confederacies, or States, oppressive combinations of a majority will be facilitated; the best security, under the republican forms, for the rights of every class of citizen, will be diminished; and consequently the stability and independence of some member of the government, the only other security, must be proportionally increased. Justice is the end of government. It is the end of civil society. It ever has been and ever will be pursued until it be obtained, or until liberty be lost in the pursuit. In a society under the forms of which the stronger faction can readily unite and oppress the weaker, anarchy may as truly be said to reign as in a state of nature, where the weaker individual is not secured against the violence of the stronger; and as, in the latter state, even the stronger individuals are prompted, by the uncertainty of their condition, to submit to a government which may protect the weak as well as themselves; so, in the former state, will the more powerful factions or parties be gradually induced, by a like motive, to wish for a government which will protect all parties, the weaker as well as the more powerful. It can be little doubted that if the State of Rhode Island was separated from the Confederacy and left to itself, the insecurity of rights under the popular form of government within such narrow limits would be displayed by such reiterated oppressions of factious majorities that some power altogether independent of the people would soon be called for by the voice of the very factions whose misrule had proved the necessity of it. In the extended republic of the United States, and among the great variety of interests, parties, and sects which it embraces, a coalition of a majority of the whole society could seldom take place on any other principles than those of justice and the general good; whilst there being thus less danger to a minor from the will of a major party, there must be less pretext, also, to provide for the security of the former, by introducing into the government a will not dependent on the latter, or, in other words, a will independent of the society itself. It is no less certain that it is important, notwithstanding the contrary opinions which have been entertained that the larger the society, provided it lie within a practicable sphere, the more duly capable it will be of self-government. And happily for the *republican cause,* the practicable sphere may be carried to a very great extent by a judicious modification and mixture of the *federal principle*.

PRESIDENTIAL VOTING

Year	Candidates	Party	Electoral Vote	Popular Vote Percentage
1789	**George Washington**	Federalist	69	—
	John Adams	Federalist	34	
	Others		35	
1792	**George Washington**	Federalist	132	—
	John Adams	Federalist	77	
	Others		55	
1796	**John Adams**	Federalist	71	—
	Thomas Jefferson	Democratic-Republican	68	
	Thomas Pinckney	Federalist	59	
	Aaron Burr	Anti-Federalist	30	
	Others		48	
1800	**Thomas Jefferson**	Democratic-Republican	73	—
	Aaron Burr	Democratic-Republican	73	
	John Adams	Federalist	65	
	C. C. Pinckney	Federalist	64	
	John Jay	Federalist	1	
1804	**Thomas Jefferson**	Democratic-Republican	162	—
	C. C. Pinckney	Federalist	14	
1808	**James Madison**	Democratic-Republican	122	—
	C. C. Pinckney	Federalist	47	
	George Clinton	Independent-Republican	6	
1812	**James Madison**	Democratic-Republican	128	—
	De Witt Clinton	Fusion	89	
1816	**James Monroe**	Democratic-Republican	183	—
	Rufus King	Federalist	34	
1820	**James Monroe**	Democratic-Republican	231	—
	John Q. Adams	Independent-Republican	1	
1824	**John Q. Adams**	National Republican	84	—
	Andrew Jackson	Democratic	99	
	Henry Clay	Democratic-Republican	37	
	W. H. Crawford	Democratic-Republican	41	
1828	**Andrew Jackson**	Democratic	178	56.1
	John Q. Adams	National Republican	83	43.6
1832	**Andrew Jackson**	Democratic	219	54.2
	Henry Clay	National Republican	49	37.4
	William Wirt	Anti-Masonic	7	
	John Floyd	Nullifiers	11	
1836	**Martin Van Buren**	Democratic	170	50.8
	William H. Harrison	Whig	73	36.6
	Hugh L. White	Whig	26	
	Daniel Webster	Whig	14	
1840	**William H. Harrison**	Whig	234	52.9
	Martin Van Buren	Democratic	60	46.8
	(**John Tyler,** 1841)			

(*continued on page 916*)

Year	Candidates	Party	Electoral Vote	Popular Vote Percentage
1844	**James K. Polk**	Democratic	170	49.5
	Henry Clay	Whig	105	48.1
1848	**Zachary Taylor**	Whig	163	47.3
	Lewis Cass	Democratic	127	42.5
	(**Millard Fillmore,** 1850)			
1852	**Franklin Pierce**	Democratic	254	50.8
	Winfield Scott	Whig	42	43.9
1856	**James Buchanan**	Democratic	174	45.3
	John C. Fremont	Republican	114	33.1
	Millard Fillmore	American	8	
1860	**Abraham Lincoln**	Republican	180	39.8
	J. C. Breckinridge	Democratic	72	29.5
	Stephen A. Douglas	Democratic	12	
	John Bell	Constitutional Union	39	
1864	**Abraham Lincoln**	Republican	212	55.0
	George B. McClellan	Democratic	21	45.0
	(**Andrew Johnson,** 1865)			
1868	**Ulysses S. Grant**	Republican	214	52.7
	Horatio Seymour	Democratic	80	47.3
1872	**Ulysses S. Grant**	Republican	286	55.6
	Horace Greeley	Democratic	**	43.8
1876	**Rutherford B. Hayes**	Republican	185	47.9
	Samuel J. Tilden	Democratic	184	51.0
1880	**James A. Garfield**	Republican	214	48.3
	Winfield S. Hancock	Democratic	155	48.2
	(**Chester A. Arthur,** 1881)			
1884	**Grover Cleveland**	Democratic	219	48.5
	James G. Blaine	Republican	182	48.2
1888	**Benjamin Harrison**	Republican	233	48.6
	Grover Cleveland	Democratic	168	47.8
1892	**Grover Cleveland**	Democratic	277	46.1
	Benjamin Harrison	Republican	145	43.0
	James B. Weaver	People's	22	
1896	**William McKinley**	Republican	271	51.0
	William J. Bryan	Democratic	176	46.7
1900	**William McKinley**	Republican	292	51.7
	William J. Bryan	Democratic	155	45.5
	(**Theodore Roosevelt,** 1901)			
1904	**Theodore Roosevelt**	Republican	336	56.4
	Alton B. Parker	Democratic	140	37.6
1908	**William H. Taft**	Republican	321	51.6
	William J. Bryan	Democratic	162	43.0
1912	**Woodrow Wilson**	Democratic	435	41.8
	Theodore Roosevelt	Progressive	88	23.2
	William H. Taft	Republican	8	23.2
1916	**Woodrow Wilson**	Democratic	277	49.2
	Charles E. Hughes	Republican	254	46.1

Year	Candidates	Party	Electoral Vote	Popular Vote Percentage
1920	**Warren G. Harding**	Republican	404	60.3
	James M. Cox	Democratic	127	34.2
	(**Calvin Coolidge,** 1923)			
1924	**Calvin Coolidge**	Republican	382	54.1
	John W. Davis	Democratic	136	28.8
	Robert M. LaFollette	Progressive	13	
1928	**Herbert C. Hoover**	Republican	444	58.2
	Alfred E. Smith	Democratic	87	40.8
1932	**Franklin D. Roosevelt**	Democratic	472	57.4
	Herbert C. Hoover	Republican	59	39.6
1936	**Franklin D. Roosevelt**	Democratic	523	60.8
	Alfred M. Landon	Republican	8	36.5
1940	**Franklin D. Roosevelt**	Democratic	449	54.7
	Wendell L. Willkie	Republican	82	44.8
1944	**Franklin D. Roosevelt**	Democratic	432	53.4
	Thomas E. Dewey	Republican	99	45.9
	(**Harry S Truman,** 1945)			
1948	**Harry S Truman**	Democratic	303	49.5
	Thomas E. Dewey	Republican	189	45.1
	J. Strom Thurmond	States' Rights	39	
1952	**Dwight D. Eisenhower**	Republican	442	55.1
	Adlai E. Stevenson	Democratic	89	44.4
1956	**Dwight D. Eisenhower**	Republican	457	57.4
	Adlai E. Stevenson	Democratic	73	42.0
1960	**John F. Kennedy**	Democratic	303	49.7
	Richard M. Nixon	Republican	219	49.5
	(**Lyndon B. Johnson,** 1963)			
1964	**Lyndon B. Johnson**	Democratic	486	61.0
	Barry M. Goldwater	Republican	52	38.5
1968	**Richard M. Nixon**	Republican	301	43.4
	Hubert H. Humphrey	Democratic	191	42.7
	George C. Wallace	American Independent	46	
1972	**Richard M. Nixon**	Republican	520	60.7
	George S. McGovern	Democratic	17	37.5
	(**Gerald R. Ford,** 1974)			
1976	**Jimmy Carter**	Democratic	297	50.1
	Gerald R. Ford	Republican	240	48.0
1980	**Ronald Reagan**	Republican	489	50.7
	Jimmy Carter	Democratic	49	41.0
	John Anderson	Independent	—	
1984	**Ronald Reagan**	Republican	525	58.8
	Walter Mondale	Democratic	13	40.6
1988	**George Bush**	Republican	426	53.4
	Michael Dukakis	Democratic	112	45.6
1992	**Bill Clinton**	Democratic	370	43.2
	George Bush	Republican	168	37.7
	Ross Perot	Independent	0	19.0
1996	**Bill Clinton**	Democratic	379	49
	Robert Dole	Republican	159	41
	Ross Perot	Reform	0	8

PARTY CONTROL OF CONGRESS 1901–2001

Congress	Years	Party and President		Senate DEM.	REP.	OTHER	House DEM.	REP.	OTHER
57th	1901–03	R	T. Roosevelt	29	56	3	153	198	5
58th	1903–05	R	T. Roosevelt	32	58	—	178	207	—
59th	1905–07	R	T. Roosevelt	32	58	—	136	250	—
60th	1907–09	R	T. Roosevelt	29	61	—	164	222	—
61st	1909–11	R	Taft	32	59	—	172	219	—
62d	1911–13	R	Taft	42	49	—	228	162	1
63d	1913–15	D	Wilson	51	44	1	290	127	18
64th	1915–17	D	Wilson	56	39	1	230	193	8
65th	1917–19	D	Wilson	53	42	1	200	216	9
66th	1919–21	D	Wilson	48	48	1	191	237	7
67th	1921–23	R	Harding	37	59	—	132	300	1
68th	1923–25	R	Coolidge	43	51	2	207	225	3
69th	1925–27	R	Coolidge	40	54	1	183	247	5
70th	1927–29	R	Coolidge	47	48	1	195	237	3
71st	1929–31	R	Hoover	39	56	1	163	267	1
72d	1931–33	R	Hoover	47	48	1	216	218	1
73d	1933–35	D	F. Roosevelt	59	36	1	313	117	5
74th	1935–37	D	F. Roosevelt	69	25	2	322	103	10
75th	1937–39	D	F. Roosevelt	75	17	4	333	89	13
76th	1939–41	D	F. Roosevelt	69	23	4	262	169	4
77th	1941–43	D	F. Roosevelt	66	28	2	267	162	6
78th	1943–45	D	F. Roosevelt	57	38	1	222	209	4
79th	1945–47	D	Truman	57	38	1	243	190	2
80th	1947–49	D	Truman	45	51	—	188	246	1
81st	1949–51	D	Truman	54	42	—	263	171	1
82d	1951–53	D	Truman	48	47	1	234	199	2
83d	1953–55	R	Eisenhower	47	48	1	213	221	1
84th	1955–57	R	Eisenhower	48	47	1	232	203	—
85th	1957–59	R	Eisenhower	49	47	—	234	201	—
86th	1959–61	R	Eisenhower	64	34	—	283	154	—
87th	1961–63	D	Kennedy	64	36	—	263	174	—
88th	1963–65	D	Kennedy Johnson	67	33	—	258	176	—
89th	1965–67	D	Johnson	68	32	—	295	140	—
90th	1967–69	D	Johnson	64	36	—	248	187	—
91st	1969–71	R	Nixon	58	42	—	243	192	—
92d	1971–73	R	Nixon	55	45	—	255	180	—
93d	1973–75	R	Nixon Ford	57	43	—	243	192	—
94th	1975–77	R	Ford	61	38	—	291	144	—
95th	1977–79	D	Carter	62	38	—	292	143	—
96th	1979–81	D	Carter	59	41	—	277	158	—
97th	1981–83	R	Reagan	47	53	—	243	192	—
98th	1983–85	R	Reagan	46	54	—	269	166	—
99th	1985–87	R	Reagan	47	53	—	253	182	—
100th	1987–89	R	Reagan	55	45	—	258	177	—
101st	1989–91	R	Bush	55	45	—	260	175	—
102d	1991–93	R	Bush	57	43	—	267	167	1
103d	1993–95	D	Clinton	59	43	—	258	176	1
104th	1995–97	D	Clinton	46	54	—	204	230	1
105th	1997–99	D	Clinton	45	55	—	207	227	1
106th	1999–2001	D	Clinton			—			

SUPREME COURT MEMBERSHIP 1900–1998

Justice*	Age at Nomination	President Who Nominated	Years on Court
John M. Harlan	44	Hayes	1877–1911
Horace Gray	53	Arthur	1882–1902
Melville W. Fuller	55	Cleveland	1888–1910
David J. Brewer	52	Harrison	1890–1910
Henry B. Brown	54	Harrison	1890–1906
George Shiras, Jr.	60	Harrison	1892–1903
Edward D. White	48	Cleveland	1894–1910
Rufus W. Peckham	57	Cleveland	1895–1909
Joseph McKenna	54	McKinley	1898–1925
Oliver W. Holmes	61	T. Roosevelt	1902–1932
William R. Day	53	T. Roosevelt	1903–1922
William H. Moody	52	T. Roosevelt	1906–1910
Horace H. Lurton	65	Taft	1910–1914
Edward D. White	65	Taft	1910–1921
Charles E. Hughes	48	Taft	1910–1916
Willis Van Devanter	51	Taft	1911–1937
Joseph R. Lamar	53	Taft	1911–1916
Mahlon Pitney	54	Taft	1912–1922
James C. McReynolds	52	Wilson	1914–1941
Louis D. Brandeis	59	Wilson	1916–1939
John H. Clarke	59	Wilson	1916–1922
William H. Taft	63	Harding	1921–1930
George Sutherland	60	Harding	1922–1938
Pierce Butler	56	Harding	1922–1939
Edward T. Sanford	57	Harding	1923–1930
Harlan F. Stone	52	Coolidge	1925–1941
Charles E. Hughes	67	Hoover	1930–1941
Owen J. Roberts	55	Hoover	1930–1945
Benjamin N. Cardozo	61	Hoover	1932–1938
Hugo L. Black	51	F. Roosevelt	1937–1971
Stanley F. Reed	53	F. Roosevelt	1938–1957
Felix Frankfurter	56	F. Roosevelt	1939–1962
William O. Douglas	40	F. Roosevelt	1939–1975
Frank Murphy	49	F. Roosevelt	1940–1949
Harlan F. Stone	68	F. Roosevelt	1941–1946
James F. Byrnes	62	F. Roosevelt	1941–1942
Robert H. Jackson	49	F. Roosevelt	1941–1954
Wiley B. Rutledge	48	F. Roosevelt	1943–1949
Harold H. Burton	57	Truman	1945–1958
Fred M. Vinson	56	Truman	1946–1953
Tom C. Clark	49	Truman	1949–1967
Sherman Minton	58	Truman	1949–1956
Earl Warren	62	Eisenhower	1953–1969
John M. Harlan	55	Eisenhower	1955–1971
William J. Brennan, Jr.	50	Eisenhower	1956–1990
Charles E. Whittaker	56	Eisenhower	1957–1962
Potter Stewart	43	Eisenhower	1958–1981

(continued on page 920)

APPENDIX **919**

SUPREME COURT MEMBERSHIP 1900–1998(*continued*)

Justice*	Age at Nomination	President Who Nominated	Years on Court
Byron R. White	44	Kennedy	1962–1993
Arthur J. Goldberg	54	Kennedy	1962–1965
Abe Fortas	55	Johnson	1965–1969
Thurgood Marshall	59	Johnson	1967–1991
Warren E. Burger	61	Nixon	1969–1986
Harry A. Blackmun	61	Nixon	1970–
Lewis F. Powell, Jr.	64	Nixon	1971–1987
William H. Rehnquist	47	Nixon	1971–1986
John Paul Stevens	55	Ford	1975–
Sandra Day O'Connor	51	Reagan	1981–
William H. Rehnquist	61	Reagan	1986–
Antonin Scalia	50	Reagan	1986–
Anthony M. Kennedy	51	Reagan	1988–
David H. Souter	50	Bush	1990–
Clarence Thomas		Bush	1991–
Ruth Bader Ginsburg	60	Clinton	1993–
Stephen G. Breyer	55	Clinton	1994–

*Chief justices in boldface.

PARTY IDENTIFICATION

	1952	1954	1956	1958	1960	1962	1964	1966	1968	1970	1972
Strong Democrat	22%	22%	21%	27%	20%	23%	27%	18%	20%	20%	15%
Weak Democrat	25	25	23	22	25	23	25	28	25	24	26
Independent Democrat	10	9	6	7	6	7	9	9	10	10	11
Independent	6	7	9	7	10	8	8	12	11	13	13
Independent Republican	7	6	8	5	7	6	6	7	9	8	10
Weak Republican	14	14	14	17	14	16	14	15	15	15	13
Strong Republican	14	13	15	11	16	12	11	10	10	9	10
Apolitical	3	4	4	4	2	4	1	1	1	1	1
Number of interviews	1,784	1,130	1,757	1,808	1,911	1,287	1,550	1,278	1,553	1,501	2,694

	1974	1976	1978	1980	1982	1984	1986	1988	1990	1992	1994	1996
Strong Democrat	17%	15%	15%	18%	20%	17%	18%	17%	20%	17%	15%	19%
Weak Democrat	21	25	24	23	24	20	22	18	19	18	19	20
Independent Democrat	13	12	14	11	11	11	10	12	12	14	13	14
Independent	15	15	14	13	11	11	12	11	11	12	10	9
Independent Republican	9	10	10	10	8	12	11	13	12	13	12	11
Weak Republican	14	14	13	14	14	15	15	14	15	15	15	15
Strong Republican	8	9	8	9	10	12	10	14	10	11	16	13
Apolitical	3	1	3	2	2	2	2	2	2	1	1	0
Number of interviews	2,505	2,850	2,283	1,613	1,418	2,236	2,166	2,032	1,991	2,487	1,795	1,695

Questions: "Generally speaking, do you consider yourself a Republican, a Democrat, an Independent, or what?"
If Republican or Democrat: "Would you call yourself a strong (R/D) or a not very strong (R/D)?"
If Independent or other: "Do you think of yourself as closer to the Republican or Democratic party?"
Source: National Election Studies data, Center for Political Studies, University of Michigan.

GOVERNMENT AND THE ECONOMY

Year	President	Gross Domestic Product ($ billion)	Total Government Spending ($ billion)	Federal Government Spending ($ billion)	Annual Federal Deficits ($ billion)	Gross Federal Debt ($ billion)
1960	Eisenhower	513.4	135.2	93.4	.5	290.5
1961	Kennedy	531.8	147.1	101.7	−3.8	292.6
1962	Kennedy	571.6	158.7	110.6	−5.9	302.9
1963	Kennedy	603.1	165.9	114.4	−4.0	310.3
1964	Johnson	648.0	174.5	118.8	−6.5	316.1
1965	Johnson	702.7	185.8	124.6	−1.6	322.3
1966	Johnson	769.8	211.6	144.9	−3.1	328.5
1967	Johnson	814.3	240.2	165.2	−12.6	340.4
1968	Johnson	889.3	265.5	181.5	−27.7	368.7
1969	Nixon	959.5	284.0	191.0	−.5	365.8
1970	Nixon	1,010.7	311.2	208.5	−8.7	380.9
1971	Nixon	1,097.2	338.1	224.3	−26.1	408.2
1972	Nixon	1,207.0	368.1	249.3	−26.4	435.9
1973	Nixon	1,349.6	401.6	270.3	−15.4	466.3
1974	Ford	1,458.6	455.2	305.6	−8.0	483.9
1975	Ford	1,585.9	530.6	364.2	−55.3	541.9
1976	Ford	1,768.4	570.9	392.7	−70.5	629.0
1977	Carter	1,974.1	615.2	426.4	−49.8	706.4
1978	Carter	2,232.7	670.3	469.3	−54.9	776.6
1979	Carter	2,488.6	745.3	520.3	−38.2	828.9
1980	Carter	2,708.0	861.0	613.1	−72.7	908.5
1981	Reagan	3,030.6	972.3	697.8	−74.0	994.3
1982	Reagan	3,149.6	1,069.1	770.9	−120.1	1,136.8
1983	Reagan	3,405.0	1,156.2	840.0	−208.0	1,371.2
1984	Reagan	3,777.2	1,232.4	892.7	−185.7	1,564.1
1985	Reagan	4,038.7	1,342.2	969.9	−221.7	1,817.0
1986	Reagan	4,268.6	1,437.5	1,028.2	−238.0	2,120.1
1987	Reagan	4,539.9	1,516.9	1,065.6	−169.3	2,345.6
1988	Reagan	4,900.4	1,590.7	1,109.0	−194.0	2,600.8
1989	Bush	5,250.8	1,700.1	1,181.6	−205.2	2,867.5
1990	Bush	5,546.1	1,840.5	1,252.7	−221.4	3,206.3
1991	Bush	5,724.8	1,940.1	1,323.4	−269.2	3,599.0
1992	Bush	6,020.2	2,094.9	1,380.8	−290.4	4,002.7
1993	Clinton	6,343.3	2,261.8	1,408.6	−255.1	4,351.7
1994	Clinton	6,726.9	2,381.0	1,460.9	−203.2	4,643.7
1995	Clinton	7,254.0	2,553.0	1,538.9	−192.5	4,974.0
1996	Clinton	7,636.0	2,705.0	1,560.3	−145.6	5,224.0
1997	Clinton	8,079.9	2,727.0	1,642.8	−120.6	5,413.1
1998	Clinton	8,344.9	2,800.9	1,687.3	−10.0	5,499.5
1999	Clinton (est)	8,579.4	2,906.5	1,750.9	+9.5	5,990.0

GROUP VOTING IN PRESIDENTIAL ELECTIONS

	1952 D	1952 R	1956 D	1956 R	1960 D	1960 R	1964 D	1964 R	1968 D	1968 R	1972 I	1972 D	1972 R
Sex													
Male	47%	53%	45%	55%	52%	48%	60%	40%	41%	43%	16%	37%	63%
Female	42	58	39	61	49	51	62	38	45	43	12	38	62
Race/ethnicity													
White	43	57	41	59	49	51	59	41	38	47	15	32	68
Nonwhite	79	21	61	39	68	32	94	6	85	12	3	87	13
Education													
Grade school	52	48	50	50	55	45	66	34	52	33	15	49	51
High School	45	55	42	58	52	48	62	38	42	43	15	34	66
College	34	66	31	69	39	61	52	48	37	54	9	37	63
Age													
Under 30	51	49	43	57	54	45	64	36	47	38	15	48	52
30–49	47	53	45	55	54	46	63	37	44	41	15	33	67
50 and older	39	61	39	61	46	54	59	41	41	47	12	36	64
Religion													
Protestant	37	63	37	63	38	62	55	45	35	49	16	30	70
Catholic	56	44	51	49	78	22	76	24	59	33	8	48	52
Political affiliation													
Democrat	77	23	85	15	84	16	87	13	74	12	14	67	33
Independent	35	65	30	70	43	57	56	44	31	44	25	31	69
Republican	8	92	4	96	5	95	20	80	9	86	5	5	95
Region													
East	45	55	40	60	53	47	68	32	50	43	7	42	58
Midwest	42	58	41	59	48	52	61	39	44	47	9	40	60
South	51	49	49	51	51	49	52	48	31	36	33	29	71
West	42	58	43	57	49	51	60	40	44	49	7	41	59
Union family	61	39	57	43	65	35	73	27	56	29	15	46	54
Total	**45**	**55**	**42**	**58**	**50**	**50**	**61**	**39**	**43**	**43**	**14**	**38**	**62**

	1976			1980			1984		1988		1992			1996		
	D	R	I	D	R	I	D	R	D	R	D	R	I	D	R	I
Sex																
Male	53%	45%	1%	38%	53%	7%	36%	64%	44%	56%	41%	38%	21%	43%	44%	10%
Female	48	51	—	44	49	6	45	55	48	52	46	37	17	54	38	7
Race/ethnicity																
White	46	52	1	36	56	7	34	66	41	59	39	41	20	43	46	9
Nonwhite	85	15	—	86	10	2	87	13	82	18	82	11	7	84	12	4
Education																
Grade school	58	41	1	54	42	3	51	49	55	45	56	28	17	44	45	8
High School	54	46	—	43	51	5	43	57	46	54	43	36	20	51	35	13
College	42	55	2	35	53	10	39	61	42	58	44	39	18	59	21	11
Age																
Under 30	53	45	1	47	41	11	40	60	37	63	44	34	22	54	30	16
30–49	48	49	2	38	52	8	40	60	45	55	42	38	20	49	41	10
50 and older	52	48	—	41	54	4	41	59	49	51	50	38	12	50	45	5
Religion																
Protestant	46	53	—	39	54	6	39	61	42	58	33	46	21	45	46	9
Catholic	57	41	1	46	47	6	39	61	51	49	44	36	20	54	33	13
Political affiliation																
Democrat	82	18	—	69	26	4	79	21	85	15	77	10	13	90	6	4
Independent	38	57	4	29	55	14	33	67	43	57	38	32	30	48	33	19
Republican	9	91	—	8	86	5	4	96	7	93	10	73	17	10	85	5
Region																
East	51	47	1	43	47	9	46	54	51	49	47	35	18	60	31	9
Midwest	48	50	1	41	51	7	42	58	47	53	42	37	21	46	45	9
South	54	45	—	44	52	3	37	63	40	60	42	43	16	44	46	10
West	46	51	1	35	54	9	40	60	46	54	44	34	22	51	43	6
Union family	63	36	1	50	43	5	52	48	63	37	55	24	21			
Total	**50**	**48**	**1**	**41**	**51**	**7**	**41**	**59**	**46**	**54**	**43**	**39**	**19**	**59**	**30**	**3**

NOTES

CHAPTER ONE

1. For a discussion of various aspects of legitimacy and its measurement in public opinion polls, see M. Stephen Weatherford, "Measuring Political Legitimacy," *American Political Science Review* 86 (March 1992): 140–55.
2. Thomas Hobbes, *Leviathan* (1651).
3. For an explanation of the worldwide growth of democracy, see John Mueller, "Democracy and Ralph's Pretty Good Grocery Store," *American Journal of Political Science* 36 (November 1992): 983–1003.
4. John Locke, *Treatise on Government* (1688).
5. James Madison, Alexander Hamilton, and John Jay, *The Federalist Papers* (New York: Mentor Books, 1961), No. 10, p. 81. Madison's *Federalist Papers*, No. 10 and No. 51, are reprinted in the Appendix.
6. E. E. Shattschneider, *Two Hundred Million Americans in Search of a Government* (New York: Holt, Rinehart and Winston, 1969), p. 63.
7. Harold Lasswell and Daniel Lerner, *The Comparative Study of Elites* (Stanford, Calif.: Stanford University Press, 1952), p. 7.
8. C. Wright Mills's classic study, *The Power Elite* (New York: Oxford University Press, 1956), is widely cited by Marxist critics of American democracy, but it can be read profitably by anyone concerned with the effects of large bureaucracies——corporate, governmental, or military— on democratic government.

9. In *Who Rules America?* (New York: Prentice-Hall, 1967) and its sequel, *Who Rules America Now?* (New York: Prentice-Hall, 1983), sociologist G. William Domhoff argues that America is ruled by an "upper class" who attend the same prestigious private schools, intermarry among themselves, and join the same exclusive clubs. In *Who's Running America?* (New York: Prentice-Hall, 1976) and *Who's Running America? The Clinton Years* (New York: Prentice-Hall, 1995), political scientist Thomas R. Dye documents the concentration of power and the control of assets in the hands of officers and directors of the nation's largest corporations, banks, law firms, networks, foundations, and so forth. Dye argues, however, that most of these "institutional elites" were not born into the upper class but instead climbed the ladder to success.
10. Yale political scientist Robert A. Dahl is an important contributor to the development of pluralist theory, beginning with his *Preface to Democratic Theory* (Chicago: University of Chicago Press, 1956). He often refers to a pluralist system as a *polyarchy*—literally, a system with many centers of power. See his *Polyarchy* (New Haven, Conn.: Yale University Press, 1971); and for a revised defense of pluralism, see his *Democracy and Its Critics* (New Haven, Conn.: Yale University Press, 1989).

CHAPTER TWO

1. Gunnar Myrdal, *An American Dilemma* (New York: Harper, 1944).
2. See Martin Luther King, Jr., "Letter from Birmingham City Jail," April 16, 1963.
3. For a discussion of the sources and consequences of intolerance in the general public, see James L. Gibson, "The Political Consequences of Intolerance: Cultural Conformity and Political Freedom," *American Political Science Review* 86 (June 1992): 338–52.
4. Quoted in *The Idea of Equality*, ed. George Abernathy (Richmond, Va.: John Knox Press, 1959), p. 185; also in Herbert McClosky and John Zaller, *The American Ethos: Public Attitudes toward Capitalism and Democracy* (Cambridge, Mass.: Harvard University Press, 1984), p. 72.
5. Quoted in Richard Hofstadter, *The American Political Tradition* (New York: Knopf, 1948), p. 45. Historian Hofstadter describes the thinking of American political leaders from Jefferson and the Founders to Franklin D. Roosevelt.
6. For a discussion of how people balance the values of individualism and opposition to big government with humanitarianism and the desire to help others, see Stanley Feldman and John Zaller, "The Political Culture of Ambivalence: Ideological Responses to the Welfare State," *American Journal of Political Science* 36 (February 1992): 268–307.
7. Robert E. Lane, "Market Justice, Political Justice," *American Political Science Review* 80 (June 1986):383–402.

8. Greg J. Duncan, *Years of Poverty, Years of Plenty* (Ann Arbor: University of Michigan Press, 1984).
9. American Security Council, *The Illegal Immigration Crisis* (Washington, D.C.: ASC, 1994).
10. *Sale v. Haitian Centers Council*, 125 L. Ed. 2d 128 (1993).
11. See Peter Brimelow, *Alien Nation* (New York: Random House, 1995).
12. For a summary of recent studies, see *America's Newcomers* (Denver: National Conference of State Legislatures, 1993).
13. See Stephen Earl Bennett, "Americans' Knowledge of Ideology, 1980–92," *American Politics Quarterly* 23 (July 1995): 259–78.
14. For evidence that ideological consistency increases with educational level, see William G. Jacoby, "Ideological Identification and Issue Attitude," *American Journal of Political Science* 35 (February 1991): 178–205.
15. Richard Hofstadter, *The Paranoid Style in American Politics* (New York: Knopf, 1965).
16. Francis Fukuyama, *The End of History and the Last Man* (New York: Free Press, 1992).
17. See Roger Kimball, *Tenured Radicals* (New York: Harper & Row, 1990).
18. Herbert Marcuse, *One-Dimensional Man* (Boston: Beacon Press, 1964).
19. Allan Bloom, *The Closing of the American Mind* (New York: Simon & Schuster, 1987), p. 15.

CHAPTER THREE

1. In *Federalist Papers*, No. 53, James Madison distinguishes a "constitution" from a law: a constitution is "established by the people and unalterable by the government, and a law established by the government and alterable by the government."
2. Another important decision on opening day of the Constitutional Convention was to keep the proceedings secret. James Madison made his own notes on the convention proceedings, and they were published many years later. See Max Ferrand, ed., *The Records of the Federal Convention of 1787* (New Haven, Conn.: Yale University Press, 1911).

3. See Edward Millican, *One United People: The Federalist Papers and the National Idea* (Lexington: University Press of Kentucky, 1990).
4. Charles A. Beard, *An Economic Interpretation of the Constitution* (New York: Macmillan, 1913).
5. Robert E. Brown, *Charles Beard and the Constitution* (Princeton, N.J.: Princeton University Press, 1956).
6. James Madison, *Federalist Papers*, No. 10; reprinted in the Appendix.
7. Alexander Hamilton, *Federalist Papers*, No. 78.

CHAPTER FOUR

1. The states are listed in the order in which their legislatures voted to secede. While occupied by Confederate troops, secessionist legislators in Missouri and Kentucky also voted to secede, but Unionist representatives from these states remained in Congress.
2. *Texas v. White*, 7 Wallace 700 (1869).
3. James Madison, *Federalist Papers*, No. 51, reprinted in the Appendix.
4. Ibid.
5. The arguments for "competitive federalism" are developed at length in Thomas R. Dye, *American Federalism: Competition among Governments* (Lexington, Mass.: Lexington Books, 1990).
6. David Osborne, *Laboratories of Democracy* (Cambridge, Mass.: Harvard Business School, 1988).
7. Morton Grodzins, *The American System* (Chicago: Rand McNally, 1966), pp. 8–9.

8. Ibid., p. 265.
9. Charles Press, *State and Community Governments in the Federal System* (New York: Wiley, 1979), p. 78.
10. *Garcia v. San Antonio Metropolitan Transit Authority*, 469 U.S. 528 (1985).
11. *McCulloch v. Maryland*, 4 Wheaton 316 (1819).
12. Civil Rights Acts of 1866, 1871, and 1875.
13. Civil Rights Acts of 1883, 100 U.S. 3 (1883).
14. *National Labor Relations Board v. Jones and Laughlin Steel Corporation*, 301 U.S. 1 (1937).
15. *Wickard v. Filburn*, 317 U.S. 128 (1938).
16. *Massachusetts v. Mellers, Frothingham v. Mellon*, 262 U.S. 447 (1923).
17. *Federal-State-Local Relations: Federal Grants in Aid*, House Committee on Government Operations, 85th Cong., 2d sess., p. 7.

CHAPTER FIVE

1. See James A. Stimson, Michael B. Mackuen, and Robert S. Erikson, "Dynamic Representation," *American Political Science Review* 89 (September 1995): 543–61.
2. Robert S. Erikson, Norman R. Luttbeg, and Kent L. Tedin, *American Public Opinion*, 3rd ed. (New York: Macmillan, 1988).
3. *Public Opinion* 9 (September/October 1986): 32, also cited by Erikson et al., *American Public Opinion*, p. 55.
4. For a summary of recent literature on public opinion, see James Stimson, "Opinion and Representation," *American Political Science Review* 89 (March 1995): 179–83.
5. Sandra K. Schwartz, "Preschoolers and Politics," in *New Directions in Political Socialization*, eds. David C. Schwartz and Sandra K. Schwartz (New York: Free Press, 1975), p. 242.
6. M. Kent Jennings and Richard G. Niemi, *The Political Character of Adolescence* (Princeton, N.J.: Princeton University Press, 1974), p. 41.
7. Robert D. Hess and Judith V. Torney, *The Development of Political Attitudes in Children* (Chicago: Aldine, 1977), p. 42.
8. See also Ted G. Jelen, "The Political Consequences of Religious Group Attitudes," *Journal of Politics* 55 (February 1993): 178–90.
9. See M. Kent Jennings, "Residues of a Movement: The Aging of the American Protest Generation," *American Political Science Review* 81 (June 1987): 370–72; M. Kent Jennings and Richard G. Niemi, *Generational Politics* (Princeton, N.J.: Princeton University Press, 1982).
10. See also James A. Stimson, *Public Opinion in America: Moods, Cycles, and Swings* (Boulder, Colo.: Westview Press, 1991).
11. V. O. Key, Jr., *Public Opinion and American Democracy* (New York: Knopf, 1967), p. 537.
12. *Harper v. Virginia State Board of Elections*, 383 U.S. 663 (1966).
13. Congress had earlier passed the Voting Rights Act of 1970, which (1) extended the vote to eighteen-year-olds regardless of state law; (2) abolished residency requirements in excess of thirty days; and (3) prohibited literacy tests. However, there was some constitutional debate about the power of Congress to change state laws on voting age. Although

Congress could end racial discrimination, extending the vote to eighteen-year-olds was a different matter. All previous extensions of the vote had come by constitutional amendment. Hence Congress quickly passed the Twenty-sixth Amendment.

14. Staci L. Rhine, "Registration Reform and Turnout," *American Politics Quarterly* 23 (October 1995): 409–26: Stephen Knack, "Does 'Motor Voter' Work?" *Journal of Politics* 57 (August 1995): 796–811.
15. *General Social Survey, 1994* (Chicago: National Opinion Research Center, 1990).
16. Raymond E. Wolfinger and Steven J. Rosenstove, *Who Votes?* (New Haven, Conn.: Yale University Press, 1980).
17. John E. Filer, Lawrence W. Kenny, and Rebecca B. Morton, "Redistribution, Income, and Voting," *American Journal of Political Science* 37 (February 1993): 63–87.
18. Sidney Verba, Kay Schlozman, Henry Brady, and Norman Nie, "Citizen Activity: Who Participates? What Do They Say?" *American Political Science Review* 87 (June 1993): 303–18.
19. For a full discussion of the factors influencing black voter participation, see Katherine Tate, "Black Political Participation in the 1984 and 1988 Presidential Elections," *American Political Science Review* 85 (December 1991): 1159–76.
20. John Stuart Mill, *Considerations on Representative Government* (Chicago: Regnery, Gateway, 1962; original publication 1859), p. 144.
21. Ibid., p. 130.
22. Attributed to Arthur Hadley by Austin Ranney in "Non-Voting Is Not a Social Disease," *Public Opinion* 6 (November/December 1983): 17.
23. Quoted in ibid., p. 18.
24. Francis Fox Piven and Richard Cloward, *Why Americans Don't Vote* (New York: Pantheon, 1987).
25. Verba et al., "Citizen Activity."
26. Martin Luther King, Jr., "Letter from Birmingham City Jail," April 16, 1963.

CHAPTER SIX

1. E. E. Schartschneider, *The Semisovereign People* (New York: Holt, Rinehart & Winston, 1961), p. 68.
2. William A. Henry, "News as Entertainment," in *What's News*, ed. Elie Abel (San Francisco: Institute for Contemporary Studies, 1981), p. 133.
3. Shanto Iyengar, *Is Anyone Responsible? How Television Frames Political Issues* (Chicago: University of Chicago Press, 1991).
4. Michael Jay Robinson, "Just How Liberal Is the News?" *Public Opinion* 38 (February/March 1983): 55–60.

5. Ben J. Wattenberg, *The Good News Is the Bad News Is Wrong* (New York: Simon & Schuster, 1984).
6. Ted Smith, "The Watchdog's Bite," *American Enterprise* 2 (January/February 1990): 66.
7. Doris A. Graber, *Mass Media and American Politics* (Washington, D.C.: Congressional Quarterly Press, 1980), p. 49.
8. S. Robert Lichter, Stanley Rothman, and Linda S. Lichter, *The Media Elite* (Bethesda, Md.: Adler and Adler, 1986).

9. See David S. Castle, "Media Coverage of Presidential Primaries," *American Politics Quarterly* 19 (January 1991): 13–42; Christine F. Ridout, "The Role of Media Coverage of Iowa and New Hampshire," *American Politics Quarterly* 19 (January 1991): 43–58.

10. Michael Robinson and Margaret Sheehan, *Over the Wire and on TV* (New York: Sage, 1983). See also S. Robert Lichter, Daniel Amundson, and Richard Noyes, *The Video Campaign* (Washington, D.C.: American Enterprise Institute, 1988).

11. Robinson and Sheehan, *Over the Wire and on TV*, p. 138.

12. *New York Times v. U.S.*, 376 U.S. 713 (1971).

13. *New York Times v. Sullivan*, 376 U.S. 254 (1964).

14. For details, see "Anatomy of a Smear," *TV Guide*, May 1982.

15. Bernard Cohen, *The Press and Foreign Policy* (Princeton, N.J.: Princeton University Press, 1963), p. 16.

16. Austin Ranney, *Channels of Power* (New York: Basic Books, 1983), p. 81.

17. Benjamin I. Page, Robert Y. Shapiro, and Glen R. Dempsey, "What Moves Public Opinion," *American Political Science Review* 81 (March 1987): 23–43.

18. National Institute of Mental Health, *Television and Behavior* (Washington, D.C.: Government Printing Office, 1982).

19. Brandon Centerwall, "Exposure to Television as a Risk Factor for Violence," *American Journal of Epidemiology* 129 (April 1989): 643–52.

CHAPTER SEVEN

1. Gaetano Mosca, *The Ruling Class* (New York: McGraw-Hill, 1939), p. 51.

2. James Madison, *Federalist Papers*, No. 10, reprinted in the Appendix.

3. George Washington, Farewell Address, September 17, 1796, in *Documents on American History*, 10th ed., eds. Henry Steele Commager and Milton Cantor, Englewood Cliffs, N.J.: Prentice Hall, 1988), 1: 172.

4. E. E. Schattschneider, *Party Government* (New York: Holt, Rinehart, and Winston, 1942), p. 1.

5. Conventions continue to play a modest role in nominations in some states:

   • Colorado: Parties may hold a preprimary convention to designate a candidate to be listed first on the primary ballot. All candidates receiving at least 30 percent of the delegate vote will be listed on the primary ballot.

   • Connecticut: Party conventions are held to endorse candidates. If no one challenges the endorsed candidate, no primary election is held. If a challenger receives 20 percent of the delegate vote, a primary election will be held to determine the party's nominee in the general election.

   • New York: Party conventions choose the party's "designated" candidate in primary elections. Anyone receiving 25 percent of the delegates also appears on the ballot.

   • Utah: Party conventions select party's nominees.

   • Illinois, Indiana, Michigan, and South Carolina: Party conventions nominate candidates for some minor state offices.

6. For an argument that primary elections force parties to be more responsive to voters, see John G. Geer and Mark E. Shere, "Party Competition and the Prisoner's Dilemma: An Argument for the Direct Primary," *Journal of Politics* 54 (August 1992): 365–74.

7. For an up-to-date listing of state primaries and relevant information about them, see *The Book of the States*, published biannually by the Council of State Governments, Lexington, Kentucky.

8. Louisiana is unique in its nonpartisan statewide primary and general elections. All candidates, regardless of party affiliation, run in the same primary election. If a candidate gets more than 50 percent of the vote, he or she wins the office outright; otherwise the top two vote-getters, regardless of party affiliation, face off in the second election.

9. See John M. Bruce, John A. Clark, and John H. Kessel, "Advocacy Politics in Presidential Parties," *American Political Science Review* 85 (December 1991): 1115–25.

10. For evidence that the national party conventions raise the poll standings of their presidential nominees, see James E. Campbell, Lynna L. Cherry, and Kenneth A. Wink, "The Convention Bump," *American Politics Quarterly* 20 (July 1992): 287–307.

11. *Gallup Poll Monthly*, November 1994.

12. See John A. Clark, John M. Bruce, John H. Kessel, and William G. Jacoby, "I'd Rather Switch Than Fight: Lifelong Democrats and Converts to Republicanism among Campaign Activists," *American Journal of Political Science* 35 (August 1991): 577–97.

13. For a scholarly debate over realignment, see Byron E. Schafer, ed., *The End of Realignment: Interpreting American Election Eras* (Madison: University of Wisconsin Press, 1991).

14. See Harold W. Stanley and Richard G. Niemi, "Partisanship and Group Support, 1952–1988," *American Politics Quarterly* 19 (April 1991): 189–210; Patricia Hurley, "Partisan Realignment in the 1980's," *Journal of Politics* 53 (February 1919): 55–63.

15. Yankelovich survey, reported in *American Enterprise* 6 (May/June 1995): 105.

16. Quoted in *Newsweek*, August 29, 1995, p. 37.

CHAPTER EIGHT

1. Gerald Pomper, *Elections in America* (New York: Dodd, Mead, 1968).

2. Morris P. Fiorina, *Retrospective Voting in American National Elections* (New Haven, Conn.: Yale University Press, 1988).

3. Quoted in *Congressional Quarterly Almanac*, 1965 (Washington, D.C.: Congressional Quarterly, Inc., 1966), p. 267.

4. Alan Ehrenhalt, *The United States of Ambition: Politicians, Power and the Pursuit of Office* (New York: Random House, 1991), p. 22.

5. Alan I. Abramowitz, "Incumbency, Campaign Spending, and the Decline of Competition in U.S. House Elections," *Journal of Politics* 53 (February 1991): 55–70.

6. In the important U.S. Supreme Court decision in *Buckley v. Valeo* in 1976, James L. Buckley, former U.S. senator from New York, and his brother, William F. Buckley, the well-known conservative commentator, argued successfully that the laws limiting an individual's right to participate in political campaigns—financially or otherwise—violated First Amendment freedoms. Specifically, the U.S. Supreme Court held that no government could limit individuals' rights to spend money or publish or broadcast their own views on issues or elections. Candidates can spend as much of their own money as they wish on their own campaigns. Private individuals can spend as much as they wish to circulate their own views on an election, although their contributions to candidates and parties can still be limited. The Court, however, permitted governmental limitations on parties and campaign organizations and allowed the use of federal funds for financing campaigns. *Buckley v. Valeo*, 424 U.S. 1 (1976).

7. David J. Lanoue and Peter R. Schrott, *The Joint Press Conference: History, Impact, and Prospects of American Presidential Debates* (Westport, Conn.: Greenwood Press, 1991).

8. University-based political scientists rely heavily on a series of National Election Studies, originated at the Survey Research Center at the University of Michigan, which have surveyed the voting-age population in every presidential election and most congressional elections since 1952.

9. For an assessment of gender issues in Clinton's victory, see Marian Lief Palley, "Elections 1992 and the Thomas Appointment," *P. S.: Political Science and Politics* 26 (March 1993): 28–31.

10. See Martin P. Wattenberg, *The Rise of Candidate-Centered Politics* (Cambridge, Mass.: Harvard University Press, 1991).

11. For an argument that voters look ahead to the economic future and reward or punish the president based on rational expectations, see Michael B. MacKuen, Robert S. Erickson, and James A. Stimson, "Peasants or Bankers? The American Electorate and the U.S. Economy," *American Political Science Review* 86 (September 1992): 680–95.

CHAPTER NINE

1. Political scientist David Truman defined an interest group as "any group that is based on one or more shared attitudes and makes certain demands upon other groups or organizations in society." See *The Governmental Process* (New York: Knopf, 1971), p. 33.

2. Quoted in *Los Angeles Times*, January 19, 1981, and in Jay M. Shafritz, ed., *The HarperCollins Dictionary of American Politics* (New York: HarperCollins, 1992), p. 299.

3. James Madison, *Federalist Papers*, No. 10, reprinted in the Appendix.

4. Ibid.

5. Gale Research Company, *Encyclopedia of Associations*. 29th ed. (Detroit: Gale Research, 1995).

6. For both theory and survey data on the sources of interest-group mobilization, see Jack L. Walker, *Mobilizing Interest Groups in America: Patrons, Professions, and Social Movements* (Ann Arbor: University of Michigan Press, 1991).

7. Kay Lehman Scholzman, "What Accent the Heavenly Chorus? Political Equality and the American Pressure System," *Journal of Politics* 46 (November 1984): 1006–32; see also Jeffrey M. Berry, Kent E. Portney, and Ken Thomson, *The Case for Participatory Democracy* (Washington, D.C.: Brookings, 1994).

8. For evidence that vote buying on congressional roll calls is rare, see Janet M. Grenzke, "Shopping in the Congressional Supermarket: The Currency Is Complex," *American Journal of Political Science* 33 (February 1989): 1–24. But for evidence that committee participation by members of Congress is influenced by political action committee money, see Richard L. Hall and Frank W. Wayman, "Buying Time: Moneyed Interests and the Mobilization of Bias in Congressional Committees," *American Political Science Review* 84 (September 1990): 797–819.

9. See, for example, Mark E. Patterson, "The Presidency and Organized Interests: White House Patterns of Interest Group Liaison," *American Political Science Review* 86 (September 1992): 612–22.

10. Paul Starobin, "Merchant Marine: Too Close to Its Clients," *National Journal*, June 11, 1988.

11. *Brown v. Board of Education of Topeka*, 349 U.S. 294 (1955).

12. Samuel Huntington, *Political Order in Changing Societies* (New Haven, Conn.: Yale University Press, 1965), p. 28.

13. Mancur Olson, *The Rise and Decline of Nations* (New Haven, Conn.: Yale University Press, 1982).

CHAPTER TEN

1. James Madison, *Federalist Papers*, No. 10, reprinted in the Appendix.

2. Ibid.

3. Quoted in Jay M. Schafritz, *The HarperCollins Dictionary of American Government and Politics* (New York: HarperCollins, 1992), p. 56.

4. *McGrain v. Dougherty*, 273 U.S. 13J (1927).

5. *Baker v. Carr*, 369 U.S. 186 (1962); *Wesberry v. Sanders*, 370 U.S. 1 (1964).

6. *Gray v. Sanders*, 322 U.S. 368 (1963).

7. *Gaffney v. Cummings*, 412 U.S. 763 (1973).

8. *Davis v. Bandemer*, 478 U.S. 109 (1986).

9. *Thornburg v. Gingles*, 478 U.S. 30 (1986).

10. *Shaw v. Reno*, 125 L Ed 2d 511 (1993).

11. *Miller v. Johnson*, June 29, 1995.

12. For an in-depth analysis of who decides to run for Congress and who does not, see Linda L. Fowler and Robert D. McClure, *Political Ambition: Who Decides to Run for Congress* (New Haven, Conn.: Yale University Press, 1990).

13. See Robert A. Bernstein, *Elections, Representation, and Congressional Voting Behavior* (Englewood Cliffs, N.J.: Prentice Hall, 1989).

14. See Gary Jacobson, *The Politics of Congressional Elections*, 3rd ed. (New York: HarperCollins, 1992).

15. See David Epstein and Peter Zemsky, "Money Talks: Deterring Quality Challengers in Congressional Elections," *American Political Science Review* 89 (June 1995): 295–322.

16. See Thomas E. Mann and Raymond Wolfinger, "Candidates and Parties in Congressional Elections," *American Political Science Review* 84 (September 1990): 545–64.

17. See Mary T. Hanna, "Political Science Caught Flat-Footed by Midterm Elections," *Chronicle of Higher Education*, November 30, 1994, pp. B1–2.

18. See Michael Malbin, *Unelected Representatives* (New York: Basic Books, 1980).

19. U.S. House of Representatives, Commission on Administrative Review, *Administrative Reorganization and Legislative Management*, 95th Cong., 1st sess., H. Doc. 95-232, pp. 17–19.

20. Richard F. Fenno, *Home Style* (Boston: Little, Brown, 1978).

21. John R. Johannes, "Casework in the House," in *The House at Work*, ed. Joseph Cooper (Austin: University of Texas Press, 1981).

22. Glenn R. Parker, *Characteristics of Congress* (Englewood Cliffs, N.J.: Prentice Hall, 1989), p. 30.

23. See David W. Rohde, *Parties and Leaders in the Postreform House* (Chicago: University of Chicago Press, 1991).

24. Barbara Sinclair, "The Emergence of Strong Leadership in the House of Representatives," *Journal of Politics* 54 (August 1992): 657–84.

25. Roger H. Davidson and Walter J. Oleszek, *Congress and Its Members* (Washington, D.C.: CQ Press, 1981), p. 170.

26. John R. Hibbing, *Congressional Careers* (Chapel Hill: University of North Carolina Press, 1991).

27. See John W. Kingdon, *Congressmen's Voting Decisions*, 3rd ed. (Ann Arbor: University of Michigan Press, 1989).

28. Ibid., p. 41.

29. Larry Markinson, *The Cash Constituents of Congress* (Washington, D.C.: CQ Press, 1992).

30. Kingdon, *Congressmen's Voting Decisions*, pp. 31–32.

31. Donald Matthews, *U.S. Senators and Their World* (New York: Vintage Books, 1960).

32. David Rohde, Norman J. Ornstein, and Robert L. Peabody, "Political Change and Legislative Norms," in *Studies of Congress*, ed. Glenn R. Parker (Washington, D.C.: CQ Press, 1985), p. 175.

33. See John R. Hibbing, "Contours of the Modern Congressional Career," *American Political Science Review* 85 (June 1991): 405–28.

34. Parker, *Characteristics of Congress*, p. 12.

35. Richard Fenno, *Power of the Purse* (Boston: Little, Brown, 1965), p. 620.

36. Ibid., p. 73.

CHAPTER ELEVEN

1. For an argument that presidents encourage people to think of them as "the single head of government and moral leader of the nation who speaks for all of the people," see Barbara Hinckley, *The Symbolic Presidency: How Presidents Portray Themselves* (New York: Routledge, 1991).

2. See Theodore Lowi, *The Personal President* (Ithaca, N.Y.: Cornell University Press, 1987).

3. See Michael Less Benedict, *The Impeachment and Trial of Andrew Johnson* (New York: Norton, 1973).

4. William Howard Taft, *Our Chief Magistrate and His Powers* (New York: Columbia University Press, 1938), p. 138, reprinted in *The Presidency*, ed. John P. Roche (New York: Harcourt Brace Jovanovich, 1964), p. 23.

5. Quoted in Arthur B. Tourtellot, *Presidents on the Presidency* (New York: Doubleday, 1964), pp. 55–56.

6. Quoted in James MacGregor Burns, *John Kennedy: A Political Profile* (New York: Harcourt Brace, 1959), p. 275.

7. Quoted in Richard Neustadt, *Presidential Power* (New York: Wiley, 1960), p. 9.

8. See George C. Edwards, *The Public Presidency* (New York: St. Martin's Press, 1983). See also Richard A. Brody, *Assessing Presidents: The Media, Elite Opinion, and Public Support* (Stanford, Calif.: Stanford University Press, 1991).

9. See Paul Brace and Barbara Hinckley, "The Structure of Presidential Approval," *Journal of Politics* 53 (November 1991): 993–1017.

10. See Charles Ostrom and Dennis Simon, "The President's Public," *American Journal of Political Science* 32 (November 1988): 1096–1119; and Ostrow and Simon, "The President and the Political Use of Force," *American Political Science Review* 80 (June 1986): 541–66.

11. John Mueller, *War, Presidents, and Public Opinion* (New York: Wiley, 1973).

12. For an irreverent description of White House reporting, see Sam Donaldson, *Hold On, Mr. President* (New York: Random House, 1987).

13. See Congressional Quarterly, *Powers of the Presidency* (Washington, D.C.: CQ Press, 1989), p. 87.

14. See also Jeffrey E. Cohen, *The Politics of the U.S. Cabinet* (Pittsburgh: University of Pittsburgh Press, 1988).

15. See Stanley Rothman and S. Robert Lichter, "How Liberal Are Bureaucrats?" *Regulation,* November–December 1983, pp. 16–22, for survey data on the voting behavior and political ideology of federal bureaucrats. Earlier studies asserted that the party identification of bureaucrats reflected that of the general public; see Steven Thomas Seitz, *Bureaucracy, Policy and the Public* (St. Louis: Mosby, 1978).

16. See Bradley H. Patterson, Jr., *The Ring of Power* (New York: Basic Books, 1988).

17. John Kingdon, *Agenda, Alternatives, and Public Policies* (Boston: Little, Brown, 1984), p. 25.

18. See Daniel E. Ingberman and Dennis A. Yao, "Presidential Commitment and the Veto," *American Journal of Political Science* 35 (May 1991): 357–89.

19. See also Samuel B. Hoff, "Saying No," *American Politics Quarterly* 19 (July 1991): 310–23.

20. For a discussion of the factors affecting the use of the presidential veto, see John T. Woolley, "Institutions, the Election Cycle, and the Presidential Veto," *American Journal of Political Science* 35 (May 1991): 279–304.

21. G. J. A. O'Toole, *Honorable Treachery: A History of U.S. Intelligence from the American Revolution to the CIA* (New York: Atlantic Monthly Press, 1991).

22. *Mora v. McNamara*, 389 U.S. 934 (1964); *Massachusetts v. Laird*, 400 U.S. 886 (1970). The Court specifically refused to intervene in the conduct of the Vietnam War by Presidents Johnson and Nixon.

23. Jules Witcover, *Crap Shoot: Rolling the Dice on the Vice Presidency* (New York: Crow Publishing, 1992).

CHAPTER TWELVE

1. "Red tape" derives its meaning from the use of reddish tape by seventeenth-century English courts to bind legal documents. Unwrapping court orders entangled one in "red tape." See Herbert Kaufman, *Red Tape: Its Uses and Abuses* (Washington, D.C.: Brookings Institution, 1977).

2. H. H. Gerth and C. Wright Mills, *From Max Weber* (New York: Oxford Press, 1958).

3. James Q. Wilson, *Bureaucracy: What Government Agencies Do and Why They Do It* (New York: Basic Books, 1989).

4. William Niskanen, *Bureaucracy and Representative Government* (Chicago: Aldine, 1971).

5. The constitutional question of whether Congress can establish an executive branch commission and protect its members from dismissal by the president was settled in *Humphrey's Executor v. United States* (1935). Franklin Roosevelt fired Humphrey from the Federal Trade Commission despite a fixed term set by Congress. Humphrey died shortly afterward, and when the executors of his estate sued for his back pay, the Supreme Court ruled that his firing was illegal.

6. See Nicholas Henry, *Public Administration and Public Affairs*, 6th ed. (Englewood Cliffs, N.J.: Prentice Hall, 1996), Chapter 11.

7. See Michael Nelson, "The Short Ironic History of American National Bureaucracy," *Journal of Politics* 44 (August 1982): 747–78.

8. Quoted in U.S. Civil Service Commission, *Biography of an Ideal: A History of the Civil Service System* (Washington, D.C.: Government Printing Office, 1973), p. 16.

9. Congress sought to further protect federal employees from partisan politics in the Hatch Act of 1939, which bans federal civil servants from partisan political activity, including running for public office, soliciting campaign funds, or campaigning for or against a party or a candidate. In the cases of *United States v. Mitchell* (1979) and *Civil Service Commission v. Letter Carriers* (1973), the Supreme Court upheld the Hatch Act against charges that it unconstitutionally denied federal employees their political rights.

10. Quoted in David Rosenbloom, "Public Personnel Reforms," *Policy Studies Journal*, November 1981, p. 1232.

11. See U.S. House of Representatives Committee on Post Office and Civil Service, *The Senior Executive Service* (Washington, D.C.: Government Printing Office, 1984).

12. See Stanley Rothman and S. Robert Lichter, "How Liberal Are the Bureaucrats?" *Regulation*, November–December 1983.

13. Aaron Wildavsky, *The New Politics of the Budgetary Process* (Glenview, Ill.: Scott, Foresman, 1988), p. 8.

14. See also Lance T. LeLoup, *Budgetary Politics*, 4th ed. (Brunswick, Ohio: Kings Court, 1988).

15. See Lawrence J. White, *Reforming Regulation* (Englewood Cliffs, N.J.: Prentice-Hall, 1981).

16. *Statistical Abstract of the United States, 1992*, p. 629.

17. For research suggesting that the appointive power is a more important instrument of political control of the bureaucracy than budgets or legislation, see B. Dan Wood and Richard W. Waterman, "The Dynamics of Political Control of the Bureaucracy," *American Political Science Review* 83 (September 1991): 801–28.

18. See Joel D. Aberbach, *Keeping a Watchful Eye: The Politics of Congressional Oversight* (Washington, D.C.: Brookings Institution, 1990).

19. Evidence of the effectiveness of interventions by members of Congress in local offices of federal agencies is provided by John T. Scholz, Jim Twombly, and Barbara Headrick, "Street-Level Political Controls over Federal Bureaucracy," *American Political Science Review* 85 (September 1991): 829–50.

20. Bradley Cannon and Michael Giles, "Recurring Litigants: Federal Agencies before the Supreme Court," *Western Political Quarterly* 15 (September 1972): 183–91.

21. Reginald S. Sheehan, "Federal Agencies and the Supreme Court," *American Politics Quarterly* 20 (October 1992): 478–500.

CHAPTER THIRTEEN

1. Alexis de Tocqueville, *Democracy in America* (1835; New York: Mentor Books, 1956), p. 75.
2. Felix Frankfurter, "The Supreme Court and the Public," *Forum* 83 (June 1930): 332.
3. Alexander Hamilton, *Federalist Papers,* No. 78 (New York: Modern Library, 1937), p. 505.
4. *Marbury v. Madison,* 1 Cranch 137 (1803).
5. *Dred Scott v. Sandford,* 19 Howard 393 (1857).
6. *National Labor Relations Board v. Jones and Laughlin Steel Corp.,* 301 U.S. 1 (1937).
7. *Buckley v. Valeo,* 424 U.S. 1 (1976).
8. *Ex parte Milligan,* 4 Wallace 2 (1866).
9. *Youngstown Sheet and Tube Co. v. Sawyer,* 343 U.S. 579 (1952).
10. *United States v. Nixon,* 418 U.S. 683 (1974).
11. *Brown v. Board of Education of Topeka,* 347 U.S. 483 (1954).
12. *Roe v. Wade,* 410 U.S. 113 (1973).
13. Lawrence Baum, *The Supreme Court,* 4th ed. (Washington, D.C.: CQ Press, 1992).
14. *West Virginia Board of Education v. Barnette,* 319 U.S. 624 (1943).
15. Quoted in Henry J. Abraham, *Justices and Presidents,* 3rd ed. (New York: Oxford University Press, 1992), p. 7.
16. Quoted in Charles P. Curtis, *Lions under the Throne* (Boston: Houghton Mifflin, 1947), p. 281.
17. William O. Douglas, "Stare Decisis," *Record,* April 1947, cited in Henry J. Abraham, *The Judicial Process* (New York: Oxford University Press, 1968), p. 58.
18. *Flast v. Cohen,* 392 U.S. 83 (1968).
19. *Gideon v. Wainwright,* 372 U.S. 335 (1963).
20. *Missouri v. Jenkins,* 110 S. C.1651 (1990).
21. Robert Scigliano, *The Supreme Court and the Presidency* (New York: Free Press, 1971), pp. 147–48.
22. At one time the U.S. Supreme Court was legally required to accept certain "writs of appeal," but today very few cases come to the Court in this fashion.
23. *University of California Regents v. Bakke,* 438 U.S. 265 (1978).
24. *Abington School District v. Schempp,* 374 U.S. 203 (1963).
25. President Andrew Jackson's comments came in response to the Court's ruling in the case of *Cherokee Nation v. Georgia* (1831) and *Worcester v. Georgia* (1832), which forbade the federal or state governments from seizing Native American lands and forcing the people to move. Refusal by Jackson, an old "Indian fighter," to enforce the Court's decisions resulted in the infamous "Trail of Tears," the forced march of the Georgia Cherokees that left one-quarter of them dead along the path west.
26. See Baum, *Supreme Court,* p. 233.
27. *Grove City College v. Bell,* 465 U.S. 555 (1984).
28. *Pollock v. Farmer's Loan,* 158 U.S. 601 (1895).

CHAPTER FOURTEEN

1. James Madison, *Federalist Papers,* No. 10, reprinted in the Appendix.
2. *West Virginia Board of Education v. Barnette,* 319 U.S. 624 (1943).
3. *Barron v. Baltimore,* 7 Peters 243 (1833).
4. *Slaughter-House Cases,* 16 Wallace 36 (1873).
5. *Hurtado v. California,* 110 U.S. 516 (1884).
6. *Gitlow v. New York,* 268 U.S. 652 (1925).
7. For an argument that Madison and some other framers not only were concerned with lessening religious conflict but also were hostile to religion generally, see Thomas Lindsay, "James Madison on Religion and Politics," *American Political Science Review* 85 (December 1991): 1051–65.
8. *Reynolds v. United States,* 98 U.S. 145 (1879).
9. *Pierce v. Society of Sisters,* 268 U.S. 510 (1925).
10. *Cantwell v. Connecticut,* 310 U.S. 296 (1940).
11. *Employment Division v. Smith,* 494 U.S. 872 (1990).
12. *Wisconsin v. Yoder,* 406 U.S. 295 (1972).
13. *Bob Jones University v. United States,* 461 U.S. 574 (1983).
14. *Lukumi Babalu Aye v. Hialeah,* 125 L.Ed. 472 (1993).
15. *Everson v. Board of Education,* 330 U.S. 1, 15, 16 (1947).
16. Ibid.
17. *Zorach v. Clausen,* 343 U.S. 306 (1952).
18. Opening public meetings with prayer was ruled constitutional as "a tolerable acknowledgment of beliefs widely held among the people of this country." *Marsh v. Chambers,* 463 U.S. 783 (1983).
19. *Lemon v. Kurtzman,* 403 U.S. 602 (1971).
20. *Muebler v. Adams,* 463 U.S. 388 (1983).
21. *Tilton v. Richardson,* 403 U.S. 672 (1971).
22. *Walz v. Tax Commission,* 397 U.S. 664 (1970).
23. *Board of Education v. Mergens,* 497 U.S. 111 (1990).
24. *McGowan v. Maryland,* 366 U.S. 429 (1961), and *Braunfeld v. Brown,* 366 U.S. 599 (1961).
25. *Allegheny County v. American Civil Liberties Union,* Greater Pittsburgh Chapter, 492 U.S. 573 (1989).
26. *Engle v. Vitale,* 370 U.S. 421 (1962).
27. *Abington School District v. Schempp,* 374 U.S. 203 (1963).
28. *Wallace v. Jaffree,* 472 U.S. 38 (1985).
29. *Wisconsin v. Yoder,* 406 U.S. 295 (1972).
30. *Employment Division v. Smith,* 494 U.S. 872 (1990).
31. *Schenck v. United States,* 249 U.S. 47 (1919).
32. *Gitlow v. New York,* 268 U.S. 652 (1925).
33. *Schenck v. United States,* 249 U.S. 47, 52 (1919).
34. *Whitney v. California,* 274 U.S. 357, 377 (1927), concurring opinion.
35. *Thomas v. Collins,* 323 U.S. 516 (1945).
36. *Dennis v. United States,* 341 U.S. 494 (1951).
37. *Yates v. United States,* 354 U.S. 298 (1957).
38. *Albertson v. Subversive Activities Control Board,* 382 U.S. 70 (1965).
39. *Whitehill v. Elkins,* 389 U.S. 54 (1967).
40. *United States v. Robel,* 389 U.S. 258 (1967).
41. *Aptheker v. Secretary of State,* 378 U.S. 500 (1964).
42. *Tinker v. Des Moines Independent Community School District,* 393 U.S. 503 (1969).
43. *Brandenburg v. Ohio,* 395 U.S. 444 (1969).
44. *Texas v. Johnson,* 491 U.S. 397 (1989).
45. *United States v. O'Brien,* 391 U.S. 367 (1968).
46. *Texas v. Johnson,* 491 U.S. 397 (1989).
47. *Chaplinsky v. New Hampshire,* 315 U.S. 568 (1942).
48. *Terminiello v. Chicago,* 337 U.S. 1 (1949).
49. *Virginia State Board of Pharmacy v. Virginia Consumer Council, Inc.,* 425 U.S. 748 (1976).
50. *Bates v. Arizona State Bar,* 433 U.S. 350 (1977).
51. *Linmark Associates, Inc. v. Township of Willingboro,* 431 U.S. 85 (1977).
52. *Bigelow v. Virginia,* 421 U.S. 809 (1975).
53. *New York Times v. Sullivan,* 376 U.S. 254 (1964).
54. *Gertz v. Robert Welch, Inc.,* 418 U.S. 323 (1974).
55. *Roth v. United States,* 354 U.S. 476 (1957).
56. *Jacobellis v. Ohio,* 378 U.S. 184 (1964).
57. *Roth v. United States,* 354 U.S. 476 (1957).
58. *Jacobellis v. Ohio,* 378 U.S. 184 (1964).
59. *Roth v. United States,* 354 U.S. 476 (1957).
60. Bob Woodward and Scott Armstrong, *The Brethren* (New York: Avon, 1979), p. 233.
61. *Miller v. California,* 5413 U.S. 15 (1973).

62. Joseph F. Kobylka, *The Politics of Obscenity* (Westport, Conn.: Greenwood Press, 1991).

63. *New York v. Ferber*, 458 U.S. 747 (1982).

64. William Blackstone, *Blackstone's Commentaries on the Law*, ed. Bernard C. Gavit (Washington, D.C.: Washington Law Book Co., 1941), p. 814.

65. *Near v. Minnesota*, 283 U.S. 697 (1931).

66. *New York Times v. United States*, 403 U.S. 713 (1971).

67. *Mutual Film Corp. v. Industrial Commission*, 236 U.S. 230 (1915).

68. *Times Film Corporation v. Chicago*, 365 U.S. 43 (1961).

69. *Freedman v. Maryland*, 380 U.S. 51 (1965).

70. *Young v. American Mini Theaters, Inc.*, 427 U.S. 50 (1976).

71. *Red Lion Broadcasting Co. v. Federal Communications Commission*, 395 U.S. 367 (1969).

72. *Miami Herald Publishing Co. v. Tornillo*, 418 U.S. 241 (1974).

73. *Branzburg v. Hayes*, 408 U.S. 665 (1972).

74. *Zurcher v. Stanford Daily*, 436 U.S. 547 (1978).

75. *NAACP v. Alabama ex rel. Patterson*, 357 U.S. 449 (1958).

76. *Healy v. James*, 408 U.S. 169 (1972).

77. *National Socialist Party of America v. Skokie*, 432 U.S. 43 (1977).

78. *Frisby v. Schultz*, 487 U.S. 474 (1988).

79. James Madison, *Federalist Papers*, No. 46.

80. U.S. Department of Justice, *Criminal Victimization in the United States* (Washington, D.C.: Bureau of Justice Statistics, published annually).

81. See Wesley G. Skogan, "The Validity of Official Crime Statistics: Empirical Investigation," *Social Science Quarterly* 55 (June 1974): 25–38.

82. *Ex parte Milligan*, 4 Wallace 2 (1866).

83. *Duncan v. Kahanamosby*, 327 U.S. 304 (1946).

84. *Illinois v. Gates*, 462 U.S. 213 (1983).

85. *Arizona v. Hicks*, 480 U.S. 321 (1987).

86. *United States v. Watson*, 423 U.S. 411 (1976).

87. *Payton v. New York*, 445 U.S. 573 (1980).

88. *Spano v. New York*, 360 U.S. 315 (1959).

89. *Gideon v. Wainwright*, 372 U.S. 335 (1963).

90. *Escobedo v. Illinois*, 378 U.S. 478 (1964).

91. *Miranda v. Arizona*, 384 U.S. 436 (1966).

92. Stephen Wasby, *The Impact of the United States Supreme Court* (Homewood, Ill.: Dorsey Press, 1970).

93. *Mapp v. Ohio*, 367 U.S. 643 (1961).

94. *United States v. Leon*, 468 U.S. 897 (1984).

95. *United States v. Salerno*, 481 U.S. 739 (1987).

96. *Illinois v. Allen*, 397 U.S. 337 (1970).

97. *Maryland v. Craig*, 497 U.S. 1 (1990).

98. *Brady v. Maryland*, 373 U.S. 83 (1963).

99. *Batson v. Kentucky*, 476 U.S. 79 (1986).

100. *Sheppard v. Maxwell*, 384 U.S. 333 (1966).

101. *Williams v. Florida*, 399 U.S. 78 (1970).

102. *Johnson v. Louisiana*, 406 U.S. 356 (1972); *Apodaca v. Oregon*, 406 U.S. 404 (1972).

103. U.S. Department of Justice, *The Prevalence of Guilty Pleas* (Washington, D.C.: Government Printing Office, 1984).

104. *Furman v. Georgia*, 408 U.S. 238 (1972).

105. *Gregg v. Georgia*, 428 U.S. 153 (1976); *Proffitt v. Florida*, 428 U.S. 242 (1976); *Jurek v. Texas*, 428 U.S. 262 (1976).

106. *McCleskey v. Kemp*, 481 U.S. 279 (1987).

CHAPTER FIFTEEN

1. See Sidney Verba and Gary R. Orren, *Equality in America* (Cambridge, Mass.: Harvard University Press, 1985).

2. *Dred Scott v. Sandford*, 19 How. 393 (1857).

3. See C. Vann Woodward, *Reunion and Reaction* (Boston: Little, Brown, 1951), and Woodward, *The Strange Career of Jim Crow* (New York: Oxford University Press, 1957).

4. *Civil Rights Cases*, 100 U.S. 3 (1883).

5. *Plessy v. Ferguson*, 163 U.S. 537 (1896).

6. *Sweatt v. Painter*, 339 U.S. 629 (1950).

7. *Brown v. Board of Education of Topeka*, 347 U.S. 483 (1954).

8. Kenneth Clark, *Dark Ghetto* (New York: Harper & Row, 1965), p. 75.

9. The Supreme Court ruled that Congress was bound to respect the Equal Protection Clause of the Fourteenth Amendment even though the amendment is directed at states, because equal protection is a liberty guaranteed by the Fifth Amendment. *Bolling v. Sharpe*, 347 U.S. 497 (1954).

10. *Brown v. Board of Education of Topeka (II)*, 349 U.S. 294 (1955).

11. *Alexander v. Holmes Board of Education*, 396 U.S. 19 (1969).

12. *Swann v. Charlotte-Mecklenburg County Board of Education*, 402 U.S. 1 (1971).

13. *Milliken v. Bradley*, 418 U.S. 717 (1974).

14. *Board of Education v. Dowell*, 498 U.S. 550 (1991).

15. Martin Luther King, Jr., "Letter from Birmingham City Jail," April 16, 1963.

16. *University of California Regents v. Bakke*, 438 U.S. 265 (1978).

17. Bakke's overall grade point average was 3.46, and the average for special admissions students was 2.62. Bakke's MCAT scores were verbal, 96; quantitative, 94; science, 97; general information, 72. The average MCAT scores for special admissions students were verbal, 34; quantitative, 30; science, 37; general information, 18.

18. *United Steelworkers of America v. Weber*, 443 U.S. 193 (1979).

19. *United States v. Paradise*, 480 U.S. 149 (1987).

20. *Firefighters Local Union 1784 v. Stotts*, 467 U.S. 561 (1984).

21. *City of Richmond v. Crosen Co.*, 488 U.S. 469 (1989).

22. See Justice Antonin Scalia's dissenting opinion in *Johnson v. Transportation Agency of Santa Clara County*, 480 U.S. 616 (1987).

23. *Adarand Construction v. Pena*, 132 L Ed 2d 158 (1995).

24. *Hopwood v. Texas*, 135 L. Ed. 1095 (1996).

25. *Wards Cove Packing Co., Inc., v. Antonio*, 490 U.S. 642 (1989).

26. *Congressional Quarterly Weekly Report*, June 8, 1991, p. 1501.

27. *Coalition for Economic Equity v. Pete Wilson*, Ninth Circuit Court of Appeals, April 1997.

28. *Bradwell v. Illinois*, 16 Wall 130 (1873).

29. *Reed v. Reed*, 404 U.S. 71 (1971).

30. *Stanton v. Stanton*, 421 U.S. 7 (1975).

31. *Craig v. Boren*, 429 U.S. 190 (1976).

32. *Dothard v. Rawlinson*, 433 U.S. 321 (1977).

33. *Arizona v. Norris*, 103 S. Ct. 3492 (1983).

34. *EEOC v. Madison Community School District*, 55 U.S.L.W. 2644 (1987).

35. *Michael M. v. Superior Court of Sonoma County*, 450 U.S. 464 (1981).

36. *Rostker v. Goldberg*, 453 U.S. 57 (1981).

37. *Statistical Abstract of the United States, 1995*, p. 403.

38. National Research Council, National Academy of Sciences, *Women's Work, Men's Work* (Washington, D.C.: National Academy Press, 1985).

39. See Thomas R. Dye, *Who's Running America?* 6th ed. (Englewood Cliffs, N.J.: Prentice Hall, 1994).

40. Susan Fraker, "Why Women Aren't Getting to the Top," *Fortune*, April 16, 1984, pp. 40–45.

41. Rudolpho O. dela Garza et al., *Latino Voices: Mexican, Puerto Rican, and Cuban Perspectives on American Politics* (Boulder, Colo.: Westview Press, 1992).

42. See F. Luis Garcia, *Latinos in the Political System* (Notre Dame, Ind.: Notre Dame University Press, 1988).

43. Linda Chavez, "Tequila Sunrise: The Slow But Steady Progress of Hispanic Immigrants," *Policy Review* (Spring 1989): 64–67.

44. *Morton v. Mancari*, 417 U.S. 535 (1974).

45. See Joseph P. Shapiro, *No Pity: People with Disabilities Forging a New Civil Rights Movement* (New York: Times Books/Random House, 1993).

46. *San Antonio Independent School District v. Rodriquez*, 411 U.S. 1 (1973).
47. *Williamson v. Lee Optical of Oklahoma*, 348 U.S. 483 (1955).
48. *Gideon v. Wainwright*, 372 U.S. 335 (1963).
49. *Harper v. Virginia State Board of Elections*, 383 U.S. 663 (1966).

50. *Harris v. McRae*, 448 U.S. 297 (1980).
51. *Rodriguez v. San Antonio Independent School District*, 411 U.S. 1 (1973).
52. *Serrano v. Priest*, 5 Cal. 3d 584 (1971).

CHAPTER SIXTEEN

1. Paul Samuelson, *Economics,* 12th ed. (New York: McGraw-Hill, 1985), p. 5.
2. For an argument that the money supply expands in election years in most democracies, see Edward R. Tufte, *Political Control of the Economy* (Princeton, N.J.: Princeton University Press, 1978).
3. GDP differs very little from gross national product, GNP, which is often used to compare the performance of national economies.

4. For a revealing case study of interest-group efforts to maintain tax breaks during the struggle over the Tax Reform Act of 1986, see Jeffrey H. Birnbaum and Alan S. Murray, *Showdown at Gucci Gulch* (New York: Random House, 1986).
5. Dan Rostenkowski, speech, May 28, 1985, *Congressional Quarterly Weekly Report,* June 1, 1985, p. 1077.
6. Joseph A. Pechman, *Federal Tax Policy,* 5th ed. (Washington, D.C.: Brookings Institution, 1987).

CHAPTER SEVENTEEN

1. U.S. Bureau of the Census, *Statistical Abstract of the United States, 1995,* p. 481.
2. Christopher Jenks and Paul E. Peterson, eds., *The Urban Underclass* (Washington, D.C.: Brookings Institution, 1991). See also William A. Kelso, *Poverty and the Underclass* (New York: New York University Press, 1994).

3. See Barbara Dafoe Whitehead, "Dan Quayle Was Right," *Atlantic Monthly,* April 1993, pp. 47–80.
4. See William Julius Wilson, *The Truly Disadvantaged* (Chicago: University of Chicago Press, 1987).
5. David Ellwood, *Poor Support: Poverty in the American Family* (New York: Basic Books, 1988), p. 6.

CHAPTER EIGHTEEN

1. Hans Morgenthau, *Politics Among Nations*, 5th ed. (New York: Knopf, 1973), p. 27.
2. George F. Kennan, writing under the pseudonym "X," "Sources of Soviet Conduct," *Foreign Affairs* 25 (July 1947): 25.
3. Frank Snepp, *Decent Interval* (New York: Random House, 1977).
4. George C. Herring, *America's Longest War* (New York: Random House, 1979), p. 262.

5. General Colin Powell, testimony, Committee on the Budget, U.S. Senate, February 3, 1992.
6. See Caspar W. Weinberger, "The Uses of Military Force," *Defense* (Arlington, Va.: American Forces Information Services Survey, 1985), pp. 2–11.
7. Morgenthau, *Politics Among Nations*, p. 80.

CHAPTER NINETEEN

1. *New York Times*, November 11, 1997.
2. Harold Lasswell, *Who Gets What, When, How* (New York: Meridian Books, 1958).
3. Texas Comptroller of Public Accounts, *Fiscal Notes*, June 1998, p. 6.
4. David Easton, *A Framework For Political Analysis* (Englewood Cliffs, N.J.: Prentice Hall, 1965), Chapter 5.
5. Louise Cowan, "Myth in the Modern World," in *Texas Myths*, ed. Robert F. O'Connor (College Station: Texas A&M University Press, 1986), p. 4.
6. Ibid., p. 14. For an excellent analysis of the concept of the "myth of origin" as integrated into the American mythology, see Robert N. Bellah, *The Broken Covenant: American Civil Religion in Time of Trial* (New York: Seabury Press, 1975).
7. T. R. Fehrenbach, "Texas Mythology: Now and Forever," in *Texas Myths*, pp. 210–17.
8. Robin Doughty, "From Wilderness to Garden: Conquering the Texas Landscape," in *Texas Myths*, p. 105.
9. Lucian W. Pye, "Political Culture," *International Encyclopedia of the Social Sciences*, Vol. 12 (New York: Crowell, Collier and Macmillan, 1968), p. 218.
10. Ellen M. Dran, Robert B. Albritton, and Mikel Wyckoff, "Surrogate versus Direct Measures of Political Culture: Explaining Participation and Policy Attitudes in Illinois," *Publius* 21 (Spring 1991): 17.
11. Daniel Elazar, *American Federalism: A View from the States* (New York: Thomas Y. Crowell, 1966), p. 86.
12. Ibid., pp. 86–89.
13. Ibid., pp. 90–92.
14. Ibid., pp. 92–94.

15. Ibid., pp. 97, 102, 108.
16. Ellen N. Murray, "Sorrow Whispers in the Winds," *Texas Journal* 14 (Spring/Summer 1992): 16.
17. Terry G. Jordan with John L. Bean, Jr., and William M. Holmes, *Texas: A Geography* (Boulder, Colo.: Westview Press, 1984), pp. 79–86.
18. David Montejano, *Anglos and Mexicans in the Making of Texas, 1836–1986* (Austin: University of Texas Press, 1987), p. 38.
19. Jordan et al., *Texas*, pp. 71–77.
20. V. O. Key, *Southern Politics in State and Nation* (New York: Vintage Books, 1949), p. 261.
21. For an excellent analysis of Key's projections for political change in Texas, see Chandler Davidson, *Race and Class in Texas Politics* (Princeton, N.J.: Princeton University Press, 1990).
22. Office of the Governor, Texas 2000 Commission, *Texas Trends*, p. 5.
23. Ibid., p. 9.
24. Office of the Governor, Texas 2000 Commission, *Texas Past and Future: A Survey*, p. 6.
25. Steve H. Murdock, Nazrul Hoque, Martha Michael, Steve White, and Beverly Pecotte, *The Texas Challenge: Population Change and the Future of Texas* (College Station: Texas A&M University Press, 1997), p. 29.
26. *Forbes*, October 13, 1997.
27. U.S. Bureau of the Census, *Statistical Abstract of the United States: 1997*, 117th ed. (Washington, D.C.: Government Publication Office, 1997).
28. Elanor Baugher and Lentha Lamison-White, Bureau of the Census, *Current Population Reports: Poverty in the U.S.: 1995* (Washington, D.C.: Government Printing Office, 1996).

29. Murdock et al., *The Texas Challenge*, pp. 64–65.

30. Betsey Bishop and Terry Heller, "Education Reform: Preparing Our Children for the Future," *Fiscal Notes* (March 1991): 10.

31. For an expanded analysis of the Texas economy and the dominant role played by larger corporations, see James W. Lamare, *Texas Politics: Economics, Power and Policy*, 5th ed. (St. Paul: West, 1994), Chapter 2.

32. "Boom, Bust and Back Again: Bullock Tenure Covers Tumultuous Era," *Fiscal Notes* (December 1990): 6–7.

33. Ibid.

34. "Road to Recovery Long and Bumpy, But Positive Signs Begin to Appear," *Fiscal Notes* (March 1989): 4.

35. "Boom, Bust and Back Again," p. 7.

36. "Texas Economic Outlook," *Texas Economic Quarterly* (December 1996): 2.

37. Augustin Redwine, Fran Sawyer, and Sandra Martin, "Boom Time for Texas Metros," *Fiscal Notes* (May 1995): pp. 1, 3–6.

38. Augustin Redwine, "Back in Business: Once Beleaguered Financial Industry Riding the Waves of Texas Economic Development," *Fiscal Notes* (August 1994): 1, 10.

39. "Brac'95 Round of Base Closures Will Have a Minor Effect on the Texas Economy," *Texas Economic Quarterly* (September 1995): 12.

40. Ibid., p. 8; "Texas Economic History and Outlook, for Calendar Years: 1994 to 2001," *Texas Economic Update* (March 1998): 2.

41. Harry Hurt, "Birth of a New Frontier," *Texas Monthly* (April 1984): 130–35.

42. "Biotechnology: New Science Brings Jobs to Texas as Biotech-related Efforts Blossom," *Fiscal Notes* (April 1990): 1–8.

43. Texas Department of Economic Development, April 1998.

44. The following discussion of the ten economic regions of Texas is based on reports produced by John Sharp, Texas Comptroller of Public Accounts, in the series *Texas Regional Outlook* (Austin: Reports of the Comptroller's Forces of Change Project, 1992): *High Plains; Northwest Texas; Metroplex; Upper East Texas; Southeast Texas; Gulf Coast; Central Texas; South Texas; West Texas; Upper Rio Grande.*

45. M. Delal Baer, "North American Free Trade," *Foreign Affairs* 70 (Fall 1991): 138.

46. Joan B. Anderson, "Maquiladoras and Border Industrialization: Impact on Economic Development in Mexico," *Journal of Borderland Studies* V (Spring 1990): 5.

47. Michael Patrick, "Maquiladoras and South Texas Border Economic Development," *Journal of Borderland Studies* IV (Spring 1989): 90.

48. Martin E. Rosenfeldt, "Mexico's in Bond Export Industries and U.S. Legislation: Conflictive Issues," *Journal of Borderland Studies* V (Spring 1990): 57.

49. Patrick, "Maquiladoras and South Texas Border Economic Development," p. 90.

50. Baer, "North American Free Trade," pp. 132–149.

51. Central Intelligence Agency, *The World Factbook* (Washington, D.C.: CIA), 1997.

52. Chandler Stolp and Jon Hockenyos, "Free Trade over Texas," *San Antonio Light*, September 15, 1991, p. E-1.

53. Associated Press, published in the *Dallas Morning News*, January 4, 1998.

54. Ibid.

55. Robert S. Chose, Emily B. Hill and Paul Kennedy, "Pivotal States and U.S. Strategy," *Foreign Affairs* 75 (January/February 1996): 39.

56. Augustin Redwine, "A Bureaucracy Is Born: International Departments Being Organized to Oversee NAFTA," *Fiscal Notes* (April 1994): 12.

57. Ibid.

58. Mickey Wright, "The Year of NAFTA: Texas's New Trade Connection," *Fiscal Notes* (April 1994): 4.

59. Joan Anderson and Martin de la Rosa, "Economic Survival Strategies of Poor Families on the Mexican Border," *Journal of Borderland Studies* VI (Spring 1991): 51.

60. Howard G. Applegate, C. Richard Bath, and Jeffery T. Trannon, "Binational Emissions Trading in an International Air Shed: The Case of El Paso, Texas and Ciudad Juarez," *Journal of Borderland Studies* IV (Fall 1989): 1–25.

61. *San Antonio Express News*, January 26, 1996, p. A-9.

62. *San Antonio Express News*, February 18, 1991, p. A-1.

63. United States General Accounting Office, *Illegal Aliens* (Washington, D.C.: GAO, 1995), p. 1.

64. James F. Pearce and Jeffery W. Gunther, "Illegal Immigration from Mexico: Effects on the Texas Economy," *Federal Reserve Bank of Dallas Economic Review* (September 1985): 4.

65. Robert W. Gardner and Leon F. Bouvier, "The United States," in *Handbook on International Migration*, eds. William J. Serow, Charles B. Nam, David F. Sly, and Robert H. Weller (New York: Greenwood Press, 1990), p. 342.

66. "Congress Clears Overhaul of Immigration Law," *Congressional Quarterly Almanac, 1986* (Washington, D.C.: Congressional Quarterly, 1987), pp. 61–67.

67. Pearce and Gunther, "Illegal Immigration from Mexico: Effects on the Texas Economy," p. 2.

68. Dan Carney, "Law Restricts Illegal Immigration," *Congressional Quarterly Weekly Report* 54 (November 16, 1996): 3287.

CHAPTER TWENTY

1. David Saffell, *State Politics* (Reading, Mass.: Addison-Wesley, 1984), pp. 23–24.

2. T. R. Fehrenbach, *Lone Star: A History of Texas and the Texans* (New York: Macmillan, 1968), pp. 152–73.

3. Richard Gambitta, Robert A. Milne, and Carol R. Davis, "The Politics of Unequal Educational Opportunity," in *The Politics of San Antonio*, eds. David R. Johnson, John A. Booth, and Richard J. Harris (Lincoln: University of Nebraska Press, 1983), p. 135.

4. Joe B. Frantz, *Texas: A Bicentennial History* (New York: W. W. Norton, 1976), pp. 73, 76.

5. Fehrenbach, *Lone Star: A History of Texas and the Texans*, p. 265.

6. Frantz, *Texas*, p. 92.

7. Fehrenbach, *Lone Star*, p. 396.

8. Ibid., pp. 398–99, 401.

9. J. E. Ericson, "The Delegates to the Convention of 1875: A Reappraisal," *Southwestern Historical Quarterly* 67 (July 1963), p. 22.

10. Ibid., p. 23.

11. Ibid.

12. Ibid., pp. 25–26.

13. Fehrenbach, *Lone Star*, pp. 374, 431, 434.

14. Ericson, "The Delegates to the Convention of 1875," pp. 24–25.

15. Fehrenbach, *Lone Star*, p. 435.

16. Janice May, "Constitutional Revision in Texas," in *The Texas Constitution: Problems and Prospects for Revision* (Arlington, Tex.: Urban Development Commission, 1971), p. 82.

17. David Berman, *State and Local Politics*, 6th ed. (Dubuque, Iowa: Wm. C. Brown, 1991), p. 61.

18. May, "Constitutional Revision in Texas," p. 76.

19. John E. Bebout, "The Problem of the Texas Constitution," in *The Texas Constitution: Problems and Prospects for Revision*, pp. 9, 11.

20. Bill Hobby, quoted in the *Houston Chronicle*, January 8, 1974.

21. Greater San Antonio Chamber of Commerce, "Position Statements to Constitutional Convention Delegates," January 1974, pp. 1–2.

22. Jim Mattox, quoted in the *Houston Chronicle*, July 31, 1974.

23. Quoted in Nelson Wolff, *Challenge of Change* (San Antonio: Naylor, 1975), p. 170.

24. Abner McCall, quoted in the *Houston Chronicle*, September 20, 1973.

25. Dolph Briscoe, reported in the *Houston Chronicle*, October 15, 1975.

26. Lewis A. Froman, Jr., "Some Effects of Interest Group Strength in State Politics," *American Political Science Review* 60 (December 1966): 952–63.

27. "California's Constitutional Amendomania," *Stanford Law Review* 1 (1949), 279–88.

CHAPTER TWENTY-ONE

1. Belle Zeller, *American State Legislatures* (New York: Thomas Y. Crowell, 1954), p. 603; and Sarah McCally, *State Politics, Parties and Policy* (New York: Holt, Rinehart and Winston, 1981), p. 5.

2. Harmon L. Zeigler and Hendrik van Dalen, "Interest Groups in State Politics," in *Politics in the Americans States* (3rd ed.), eds. Herbert Jacob and Kenneth N. Vines (Boston: Little, Brown, 1976), pp. 93–136.

3. George Norris Green, *The Establishment in Texas Politics: 1938–1957* (Westport, Conn.: Greenwood Press, 1979), pp. 1,17.

4. Ibid., p. 30.

5. Chandler Davidson, *Race and Class in Texas Politics* (Princeton N.J.: Princeton University Press, 1990), p. 54, Chapters 4 and 5.

6. *Fort Worth Star-Telegram*, September 8, 1991.

7. See Green, *The Establishment in Texas Politics*, for an excellent analysis of the labor-bashing techniques used by Texas business in the 1940s and 1950s.

8. Ibid., Chapter 5.

9. See Davidson, *Race and Class in Texas Politics*, Chapter 10.

10. V. O. Key, *Southern Politics* (New York: Vintage Books, 1949), p. 255.

11. Davidson, *Race and Class in Texas Politics*, p. 21.

12. Alexander P. Lamis, *The Two-Party South*, expanded ed. (New York: Oxford University Press, 1988), p. 23.

13. Key, *Southern Politics*, pp. 302–10.

14. Green, *The Establishment in Texas Politics*, pp. 142–48.

15. Lamis, *The Two-Party South*, p. 195.

16. John R. Knaggs, *Two-Party Texas: The John Tower Era, 1961–1984* (Austin: Eakin Press, 1986), p. 15.

17. Davidson, *Race and Class in Texas Politics*, p. 199.

18. For an excellent summary of realignment theory and conditions under which realignment is likely to take place, see James L. Sundquist, *Dynamics of the Party System* (Washington, D.C.: The Brookings Institution, 1973).

19. James A. Dyer, Arnold Vedlitz, and David Hill, "New Voters, Switchers, and Political Party Realignment in Texas," *Western Political Quarterly* 41 (March 1988): 156.

20. Ibid., pp. 165–66; *Texas Poll*, Winter 1996, Spring, 1996, Summer 1996, Fall 1996.

21. V.O. Key, Jr., *Parties, Politics, and Pressure Groups*, 4th ed. (New York: Thomas Y. Crowell, 1958), p. 347.

22. Wilbourn E. Benton, *Texas Politics: Constraints and Opportunities*, 5th ed. (Chicago: Nelson-Hall, 1984), pp. 72–73.

23. *Smith v. Allwright*, 321 U.S. 649 (1944).

24. *John Terry et al., Petitioners v. A. J. Adams et al.*, 345 U.S. 461.

25. Beryl E. Pettus and Randall W. Bland, *Texas Government Today: Structures, Functions, Political Processes*, 3rd ed. (Homewood, Ill.: Dorsey, 1984), pp. 85–86.

26. *Beare et al. v. Preston Smith, Governor of Texas*, 321 F. Supp. 1100 (1971).

27. *Miller v. Johnson*, 115 S.Ct 2475 (1995); *Bush v. Vera*, 116 S.Ct. 1941 (1996).

28. Robert R. Brischetto, Southwest Voter Research Institute, Inc., San Antonio, telephone conversations, November 1, 1991.

29. Ibid.; Robert Brischetto, *The Political Empowerment of Texas Mexicans, 1974–1988* (San Antonio: Southwest Voter Research Institute, Latino Electorate Series, 1988), pp. 1–19.

30. *Texas Municipal League Directory of City Officials, 1995* (Austin: Texas Municipal League, 1995); survey conducted by the A.G. Young Institute of County Government, Texas A&M University, 1993.

31. Davidson, *Race and Class in Texas Politics*, p. 24.

32. Ibid.

33. Secretary of State, Elections Division.

34. *Houston Chronicle*, December 2, 1997.

35. *Dallas Morning News*, June 3, 1994.

CHAPTER TWENTY-TWO

1. For an extended discussion of legislative functions, see William J. Keefe and Morris S. Ogul, *The American Legislative Process*, 8th ed. (Englewood Cliffs, N.J.: Prentice Hall, 1993), pp. 16–37.

2. On the general concept of institutionalization, see Nelson W. Polsby, "The Institutionalization of the U.S. House of Representatives," *American Political Science Review* 62 (March 1968), pp. 144–68.

3. Thomas R. Dye, *Politics in States and Communities*, 8th ed. (Englewood Cliffs, N.J.: 1994), pp. 179–83.

4. Council of State Governments, *Book of the States, 1996–1997* (Lexington, Ky.: The Council of State Governments, 1996), p. 68.

5. Ibid., pp. 78–81.

6. For a comprehensive analysis of the literature on legislative recruitment and careers, see Donald R. Matthews, "Legislative Recruitment and Legislative Careers," *Legislative Studies Quarterly* IX (November 1984): 547–85.

7. *Baker v. Carr*, 369 U.S. 186 (1992); *Reynolds v. Simms*, 377 U.S. 533 (1964); *Kilgarlin v. Martin*, 252 F.Supp 404 (S.D. Tex. 1966).

8. Fred Gantt, Jr., *The Chief Executive in Texas: A Study of Gubernatorial Leadership* (Austin: University of Texas Press, 1964), p. 238.

9. *Houston Chronicle*, January 6, 1993.

10. For a good summary of the scholarly work on legislative committees, see Heinz Eulau and Vera McCluggage, "Standing Committees in Legislatures: Three Decades of Research," *Legislative Studies Quarterly* IX (May 1984): 195–270.

11. See Malcolm E. Jewell and Samuel C. Patterson, *The Legislative Process in the United States* (New York: Random House, 1966), Chapter 11, for a good summary of the function of legislative rules and procedures.

12. *Dallas Morning News*, May 26, 1991.

13. John Leedom, quoted in *Dallas Morning News*, May 27, 1991.

14. For a brief overview of the representative problem, see Neil Reimer, ed., *The Representative: Trustee? Delegate? Partisan? Politico?* (Boston: D.C. Heath 1967). For a more comprehensive treatment of the subject, see Hanna F. Pitkin, *The Concept of Representation* (Berkeley: University of California Press, 1967).

15. For an excellent treatment of the relationship of U.S. legislators to their districts and constituencies, see Richard F. Fenno, Jr., *Home Style: House Members in Their Districts* (Boston: Little, Brown, 1978).

16. There have been a considerable number of studies of these informal norms within the legislative process. One is Donald R. Matthews, *U.S. Senators and Their World* (New York: Vintage Books, 1960). For the adaptation of this concept to state legislatures, see Alan Rosenthal, *Legislative Life: People, Process, and Performance of the States* (New York: Harper & Row, 1981), pp. 123–27.

17. The general concepts for this discussion are based on John W. Kingdon, *Congressmen's Voting Decisions*, 2nd ed. (New York: Harper & Row, 1981).

18. For a general discussion of staff in state legislatures, see Rosenthal, *Legislative Life: People, Process, and Performance in the States*, Chapter 10.

19. *Fort Worth Star-Telegram*, December 4, 1990.

20. *Houston Chronicle*, December 12, 1990.

21. *Houston Chronicle*, January 1, 1991.

22. Statement issued by Governor Ann Richards, May 1991.

CHAPTER TWENTY-THREE

1. State Comptroller's Office, *Breaking the Mold: A Report of the Texas Performance Review*, vol. 1 (Austin: Texas Comptroller's Office, 1991), p. 1.
2. Joseph A. Schlesinger, "The Politics of the Executive," in Herbert Jacob and Kenneth N. Vines, eds., *Politics in the American States*, 2nd ed. (Boston: Little, Brown, 1971), Chapter 6; Thad L. Beyle, "The Governors, 1988–89," in *The Book of the States, 1990–1991* (Lexington, Ky.: The Council of State Governments, 1990), p. 54.
3. Charles F. Cnudde and Robert E. Crew, *Constitutional Democracy in Texas* (St. Paul: West, 1989), p. 90.
4. Fred Gantt, Jr., *The Chief Executive in Texas* (Austin: University of Texas Press, 1964), p. 116.
5. See James E. Anderson, Richard W. Murray, and Edward L. Farley, *Texas Politics*, 6th ed. (New York: HarperCollins, 1992), pp. 166–91, for an excellent analysis of the leadership styles of Governors Allan Shivers, Price Daniel, John Connally, Preston Smith, and Dolphe Briscoe.
6. Gantt, *Chief Executive in Texas*, pp. 229–30.
7. *Dallas Morning News*, April 1987, p. H-2.
8. *Fort Worth Star-Telegram*, August 21, 1995.
9. Wilbourn E. Benton, *Texas Politics: Constraints and Opportunities*, 5th ed. (Chicago: Nelson-Hall, 1984), pp. 164–67.
10. Gantt, *Chief Executive in Texas*, pp. 90–107.
11. *San Antonio Express-News*, November 26, 1995.
12. Robert S. Lorch, *State and Local Politics*, 3rd ed. (Englewood Cliffs, N.J.: Prentice Hall, 1989), pp. 115–19.
13. Daniel Elazar, "The Principles and Traditions Underlying State Constitutions," *Publius* 12 (Winter 1982): 17.
14. Texas Comptroller of Public Accounts, *Fiscal Notes*, December 1990, pp. 8–9.
15. Texas Comptroller of Public Accounts.
16. Ibid.
17. Theodore J. Lowi, *The End of Liberalism*, 2nd ed. (New York: W. W. Norton, 1979), p. 274.
18. Texas Sunset Advisory Commission, *Sunset Review in Texas: Summary of Process and Procedures* (Austin: Texas Sunset Advisory Commission, 1991).
19. *Dallas Morning News*, October 24, 1991.
20. Robert Lineberry, *American Public Policy* (New York: Harper & Row, 1977), pp. 84–85.
21. Bill Wells, quoted in Associated Press Story, *Dallas Times Herald*, August 14, 1983.
22. *Austin American-Statesman*, June 14, 1993.

CHAPTER TWENTY-FOUR

1. *Smith v. Allwright*, 321 U.S. 649 (1944).
2. *Miranda v. Arizona*, 384 U.S. 436 (1966).
3. Texas Research League, *The Texas Judiciary: A Structural-Functional Overview*, Report 1 (Austin: Texas Research League, August 1990).
4. Allen E. Smith, *The Impact of the Texas Constitution on the Judiciary* (Houston: University of Houston, Institute for Urban Studies, 1973), p. 45.
5. Ibid., pp. 28–31.
6. Anthony Champagne, "The Selection and Retention of Judges in Texas," *Southwestern Law Journal* 40 (May 1986): 79–80.
7. Texas Judicial Council, Office of Court Administrator. *Texas Judicial System, 67th Annual Report* (Austin: Texas Judicial Council, 1995).
8. Texas Research League, *Texas Courts: A Proposal for Structural-Functional Reform*, Report 2 (Austin: Texas Research League, May 1991), pp. 1–15.
9. *Fort Worth Star-Telegram*, September 4, 1983.
10. *Houston Chronicle*, April 12, 1986.
11. *Houston Post*, May 18, 1986.
12. Anthony Champagne, "Campaign Contributions in Texas Supreme Court Races," *Crime, Law and Social Change* 17 (1992): 91–106.
13. Kim Ross, quoted in the *Houston Post*, November 10, 1988.
14. *Houston Chronicle*, March 1, 1987.
15. *Texas Lawyer*, September 17, 1990.
16. *Austin American-Statesman*, December 9, 1993.
17. *Associated Press*, July 24, 1997.
18. *Texas Lawyer*, July 28, 1997.
19. *Texas Lawyer*, May 23, 1994.
20. Samuel Issacharoff, *The Texas Judiciary and the Voting Rights Act: Background and Options* (Austin: Texas Policy Research Forum, 1989), pp. 2, 13.
21. *Texas Lawyer*, September 18, 1989.
22. *Houston Chronicle*, December 24, 1989.
23. *Texas Lawyer*, September 18, 1989.
24. *League of United Latin American citizens et al. v. Mattox et al.*, 501 U.S. 419 (1991); *Chisom v. Roemer*, 501 U.S. 380 (1991).
25. *League of United Latin American Citizens v. Clements*, 999 F2d 831 (1993).
26. *Houston Chronicle*, January 19, 1994.
27. *Miranda v. Arizona*, 384 U.S. 436 (1966).
28. *Texas Lawyer*, November 11, 1991.
29. *Furman v. Georgia*, 408 U.S. 238 (1972).
30. *Texas Lawyer*, June 3, 1991.
31. Paul Burka, "Trial by Technicality," *Texas Monthly* (April 1982), pp. 126–31, 210–18, 241.
32. *Texas Lawyer*, July 16, 1990.
33. *William Randolph Heitman v. State*, 815 S.W.2d 681 (1991).
34. *Texas Lawyer*, July 8, 1991.
35. *Texas Lawyer*, July 10, 1995.
36. *Edgewood v. Kirby*, 777 S.W.2d 391 (1989).
37. *Fort Worth Star-Telegram*, October 4, 1982; *Brown v. Board of Education of Topeka*, 347 U.S. 483 (1954).
38. *Edgewood v. Meno*, 893 S.W.2d 450 (1995).
39. *Richards v. LULAC*, 868 S.W.2d 306 (1993); *Houston Chronicle* June 16, 1994.
40. *Texas Education Agency v. Leeper*, 893 S.W. 2d 432 (1994).
41. *Ex Parte Tucci*, 859 S.W. 2d 1 (1993). *See also Houston Chronicle*, July 1, 1993.
42. *Madsen v. Women's Health Clinic, Inc.*, 512 U.S. (1994).
43. *Republican Party of Texas v. Dietz*, 924 S.W.2d 932 (1996).

CHAPTER TWENTY-FIVE

1. Anwar Hussain Syed, *The Political Theory of American Local Government* (New York: Random House, 1966), p. 27.
2. Ibid., pp. 38–52. Syed presents an excellent analysis of Jefferson's theory of local government.
3. Roscoe C. Martin, *Grass Roots* (Tuscaloosa: University of Alabama Press, 1957), p. 5; Robert C. Wood, *Suburbia* (New York: Houghton Mifflin, 1958), p. 18.
4. *City of Clinton v. The Cedar Rapids and Missouri River Railroad Co.*, 24 Iowa 455 (1868).
5. Roscoe C. Martin, *The Cities in the Federal System* (New York: Atherton Press, 1965), pp. 28–35.
6. David B. Brooks, *Texas Practice: County and Special District Law*, vol. 35 (St. Paul, Minn.: West, 1989), pp. 41–46. A good part of the materials presented on county government rely on this comprehensive work by Brooks.

7. Advisory Commission on Inter-governmental Relations, *Measuring Local Government Discretionary Authority*, Report M-131 (Washington, D.C.: ACIR, 1981).

8. Advisory Commission on Inter-governmental Relations, *State and Local Roles in the Federal System* (Washington, D.C.: ACIR, 1982), pp. 32–33.

9. For an excellent overview of urban development in Texas, see Char Miller and David R. Johnson, "The Rise of Urban Texas," in *Urban Texas: Politics and Development*, eds. Char Miller and Heywood T. Sanders (College Station: Texas A&M University Press, 1990), pp. 3–29.

10. See Richard L. Cole, Ann Crowley Smith, and Delbert A. Taebel, *Urban Life in Texas: A Statistical Profile and Assessment of the Largest Cities* (Austin: University of Texas Press, 1986), for an example of rankings of larger Texas cities on various dimensions measuring aspects of urban "quality of life."

11. U.S. Department of Commerce, Bureau of the Census, *1992 Census of Governments, Popularly Elected Officials*, vol. 2, no. 1 (Washington, D.C.: U.S. Government Printing Office, 1995), Table 9.

12. Murray S. Stedman, *Urban Politics*, 2nd ed. (Cambridge, Mass.: Winthrop, 1975), p. 51.

13. Beryl E. Pettus and Randall W. Bland, *Texas Government Today*, 3rd ed. (Homewood, Ill.: Dorsey, 1984), p. 347.

14. Wilbourn E. Benton, *Texas Politics*, 5th ed. (Chicago: Nelson-Hall, 1984), p. 260.

15. Bureau of the Census, *1992 Census of Governments, Popularly Elected Officials*, vol. 2, no. 1, Table 11.

16. Frank J. Sturzl, "Survey Shows Municipal Fiscal Conditions Improving," *Texas Town and City* 82 (March 1995): 10–11, 36.

17. "Texas Cities Continue to Face Fiscal Squeeze," *Texas Town and City* 79 (March 1991): 26, 32–34.

18. Lawrence E. Jordan, "Municipal Bond Issuance in Texas: The New Realities," *Texas Town and City* 79 (December 1991): 12, 25.

19. Sturzl, "Survey Shows Municipal Fiscal Conditions Improving," p. 11.

20. Miller and Sanders, eds., *Urban Texas*, p. xiv.

21. Frank J. Sturzl, "The Tyranny of Environmental Mandates," *Texas Town and City* 79 (September 1991): 14.

22. Robert E. Norwood and Sabrina Strawn, *Texas County Government: Let the People Choose*, 2nd ed. (Austin: The Texas Research League, 1984), p. 9. For a sample of Texas court decisions which affirm the general principle of the Dillon rule that the county can perform only those functions allocated to it by law, see pp. 11–12.

23. The Texas Association of Counties, *1998 County Officials Salary Survey* (Austin: Texas Association of Counties, 1998).

24. *Avery v. Midland*, 88 S.Ct. 1114 (1968).

25. Norwood and Strawn, *Texas County Government*, p. 22.

26. Brooks, *Texas Practice*, 35: 331.

27. Texas Commission on Inter-governmental Relations, *An Introduction to Texas County Government* (Austin: TCIR, 1980), p. 10.

28. Brooks, *Texas Practice*, 35: 392–393.

29. Ibid., 36: pp. 104–105.

30. Texas Association of Counties, *1994 County Officials Salary Survey*.

31. Brooks, *Texas Practice*, 36: 49–50.

32. Ibid., pp. 18–49.

33. Norwood and Strawn, *Texas County Government*, p. 24.

34. Brooks, *Texas Practice*, 35: 495.

35. Ibid., 36: 122–123.

36. Texas Commission on Inter-governmental Relations, *An Introduction to County Government*, p. 22.

37. Norwood and Strawn, *Texas County Government*, p. 27.

38. Brooks, *Texas Practice*, 35: 273–274.

39. Virginia Marion Perrenod, *Special Districts, Special Purposes: Fringe Governments and Urban Problems in the Houston Area* (College Station: Texas A&M University Press, 1984), p. 4.

40. Ibid, p. 34.

41. Woodworth G. Thrombley, *Special Districts and Authorities in Texas* (Austin: Institute of Public Affairs, University of Texas, 1959), p. 13.

42. Robert S. Lorch, *State and Local Politics*, 3rd ed. (Englewood Cliffs, N.J.: Prentice Hall, 1989), p. 246.

43. Ibid., p. 247.

44. Texas Education Agency, *Snapshot '98: 1997–1998 School District Profiles* (Austin: Texas Education Agency, 1998).

45. Texas Association of School Boards, *Special Tabulation of Election Systems Used by Texas Public Schools*, August 22, 1997.

46. Governor's Planning and Budget Office, *Regional Councils in Texas: A Status Report and Directory*, 1980–1981 (Austin: Governor's Budget and Planning Office, 1981), p. 9.

47. Governor's Budget and Planning Office, *Regional Councils in Texas: Annual Report and Directory*, 1990–1991 (Austin: Governor's Budget and Planning Office, 1991), p. 8.

48. Ibid.

49. Brooks, *Texas Practice*, 36: 380–384.

50. For a more detailed discussion of annexation authority, see Benton, *Texas Politics*, pp. 264–266.

51. Norwood and Strawn, *Texas County Government*, pp. 75–81.

52. Joel B. Goldsteen and Russell Fricano, *Municipal Finance Practices and Preferences for New Development: Survey of Texas Cities* (Arlington: Institute of Urban Studies, University of Texas at Arlington, 1988), pp. 3–11.

53. Bill R. Shelton and Nancy Ratcliff, "How Cities Organize and Administer Sales Tax Revenues Dedicated to Economic Development," *Texas Town and City* 82 (December 1995): 26–27.

54. Brooks, *Texas Practice*, 36: 229–42.

55. Tom Adams, "Introduction and Recent Experience with the Interlocal Contract," in *Interlocal Contract in Texas*, eds. Richard W. Tees, Richard L. Cole, and Jay G. Stanford (Arlington: Institute of Urban Studies, University of Texas at Arlington, 1990), p. 1.

56. Tees et al., Eds, *Interlocal Contract in Texas*, pp. B1–B7.

57. Vincent Ostrom, *The Meaning of American Federalism* (San Francisco: Institute for Contemporary Studies, 1991), p. 161. Ostrom suggests that advocates of metropolitan government often overlook the "rich and intricate 'framework' for negotiating, adjudicating, and deciding questions" that is now in place in many urbanized areas with multiple governmental units.

58. Ann Long Diveley and Dwight A. Shupe, "Public Improvement Districts: An Alternative for Financing Public Improvements and Services," *Texas Town and City* 79 (September 1991): 16–10, 30, 66.

Chapter 1: **1** Jerome Friar/Impact Visuals Photo and Graphics, Inc. **2** (top left) Trippet/SIPA Press, (top right) Joe Marquette/AP/Wide World Photos, (bottom left) Richard Sheinwald/AP/Wide World Photos, (bottom right) UPI/Corbis-Bettmann **7** *Peanuts* reprinted by permission of UFS, Inc. **8** © Flip Schulke **9** Library of Congress **16** W. Wellstood/Library of Congress **17** Corbis-Bettmann **18** Reuters/Corbis-Bettmann **19** Don Hebib/Concord Monitor/Impact Visuals Photo & Graphics, Inc.

Chapter 2: **26** Frank Weise/AP/Wide World Photos **29** (left) Fred Prousaer/Reuters/Archive Photos, (right) Rose Prouser/Reuters/Archive Photos **34** (left) Smith/Monkmeyer Press, (right) Rob Crandall/Stock Boston **39** John R. Stanmeyer/AP/Wide World Photos **45** Jon Levy/Liaison Agency, Inc. **46** Barbara Boxer **49** (right) Nina Berman/SIPA Press (left) Bob Daemmrich/Stock Boston, **55** (left) Henry Abrams/UPI/Corbis-Bettmann, (right) M. Richards/PhotoEdit

Chapter 3: **60** The Granger Collection **63** The Granger Collection **65** The Granger Collection **68** Library of Congress **72** London Illustrated News/Library of Congress **75** Corbis-Bettmann **76** Amel Emric/AP/Wide World Photo **84** John van der Lyn/White House Historical Association

Chapter 4: **96** Bob Daemmrich/Stock Boston **105** AP/Wide World Photos **108** The New Yorker **109** AP/Wide World Photos **110** J. Chenet/Woodfin Camp & Associates **112** Wm. Birch & Son/Library of Congress **113** Thomas C. Roche/Library of Congress **116** Stephen Ferry/Liaison Agency, Inc. **123** Governor's Office, New Jersey

Chapter 5: **126** Steve Liss/Liaison, Agency Inc. **135** *Peanuts* reprinted by permission of UFS, Inc. **146** Larry Fisher/Quad-City Times/AP/Wide World Photos **149** UPI/Corbis-Bettmann **150** Corbis-Bettman **153** Donna Binder/Impact Visuals Photo & Graphics, Inc. **159** UPI/Corbis-Bettmann

Chapter 6: **164** Greg Gibson/AP/Wide World Photos **169** Tom Prettyman/PhotoEdit **171** UPI/Corbis-Bettmann **172** Marty Lederhandler/AP/Wide World Photos **174** Peter Morgan/Reuters/Archive Photo **177** Jeff Christensen/Liaison, Agency, Inc. **180** AP/Wide World Photos **186** AP/Wide World Photos **191** UPI/Corbis-Bettmann

Chapter 7: **194** Reuters/Joe Skipper/Archive Photos **200** The Granger Collection **210** UPI/Corbis-Bettmann **204** UPI/Corbis-Bettmann **206** Denis Paquin/AP/Wide World Photos **207** J. C. Watts, Jr. **213** Bob Daemmrich/Stock Boston **214** (top left) Culver Pictures, Inc., (top right) Jim Bourg/Liaison, Agency Inc., (bottom left) Jean-Marc Giboux/Liaison, Agency Inc.,

(bottom right) Dirck Halstead/Liaison, Agency Inc. **224** (left) B. Mahoney/The Image Works, (right) Donna Binder/Impact Visuals Photo & Graphics, Inc. **233** R.Y. Young/Library of Congress

Chapter 8: **236** Bob Daemmrich/The Image Works **238** Reuters/Gary Cameron/Archive Photos **239** Reuters/Luc Novovitch/Archive Photos **241** AP/Wide World Photos **242** Consolidated News Pictures/Archive Photos **245** Kenneth Jarecke/Contact Press Images Inc. **247** University of Oklahoma **253** Alden Pellett/AP/Wide World Photos **255** Jeffrey Markowitz/Sygma **257** National Geographic Society/AP/Wide World Photos **264** Jeffrey MacMillan/*U.S. News and World Report* **265** Porter Gifford Liaison, Agency Inc. **277** Brooks Kraft/Sygma

Chapter 9: **282** Nina Berman/SIPA Press **285** (top left) Culver Pictures Inc., (top right) Stock Montage Inc.,/Historical Pictures Collection, (center left) UPI/Corbis-Bettmann, (center right) Corbis-Bettmann, (bottom left) UPI/Corbis-Bettmann, (bottom right) LeDuc/Monkmeyer Press **288** UPI/Corbis-Bettmann **296** AP/Wide World Photos **304** Reprinted, with permission, from the April 1997 isssue of *Reason* Magazine, © 1998 by the Reason Foundation, 3415 S. Sepulveda Blvd, Suite 400, Los Angeles, CA 90034, www.reason.com **306** Porter Gifford Liaison, Agency Inc. **309** Dennis Cook/ AP/Wide World Photos

Chapter 10: **320** Terry Ashe/Liaison, Agency Inc. **323** Joe Marquette/AP/Wide World Photos **342** Jeff Greenberg/The Image Works **343** Ron Edwards/AP/Wide World Photos **346** Donna Bagby/SABA Press Photos, Inc. **350** UPI/Corbis-Bettmann **351** Rick Reinhard/ Impact/Visuals Photo & Graphics, Inc. **354** Reuters/ Mark Wilson/Archive Photos **366** Terry Ashe/ Gamma Liaison, Inc. **370** Reuters/Mike Theiler/ Archive Photos

Chapter 11: **376** Dennis Cook/AP/Wide World Photos **378** Greg Gibson/AP/Wide World Photos **380** The White House/SIPA Press **382** Mookie/Liaison, Agency, Inc. **384** AP/Wide World Photos **394** Wilfredo Lee/AP/Wide World Photos **396** Reuters/Corbis-Bettmann **407** Sasa Kralj/AP/Wide World Photos **408** U.S. Army Photo **413** Brian J. Hoosack, U.S. Navy/AP/Wide World Photos **414** AP/Wide World Photos **415** Michael Caulfield/AP/Wide World Photos **416** Bill Burke/Impact Visuals Photo & Graphics, Inc.

Chapter 12: **422** Stephen Marks/The Image Bank **429** Louie Psihoyos/Matrix International, Inc. **437** AP/Wide Photo **439** David Youngwolf/PhotoEdit **440** Corbis-Bettmann **443** J. Scott Applewhite/AP/Wide World Photos **447** Robert Giroux/Fox Sunday News/ AP/Wide

World Photos **455** Bob Daemmrich/ Stock Boston **457** Robert Trippett/SIPA Press **459** Harvey Finkle/Impact Visuals Photo & Graphics, Inc.

Chapter 13: **464** Kenneth Lambert/Washington Times/Liaison, Agency Inc. **468** Corbis-Bettmann **471** Reuters/Win McNames Corbis-Bettmann **477** J. Scott Applewhite/AP/Wide World Photos **482** Tyler Mallory/AP/Wide World Photos **489** Reuters/Rick Wilking/Corbis-Bettmann **493** Supreme Court Historical Society **497** Marcy Nighswander/AP/Wide World Photos

Chapter 14: **504** The Granger Collection **510** Rick Bower/AP/Wide World Photos **512** AP/Wide World Photos **515** Jeff Lowenthal/Woodfin Camp & Associates **517** Pat Sullivan/AP/Wide World Photos **522** T. Crosby/Liaison, Agency Inc. **524** Photofest **527** L. Kolvoord/The Image Works **528** Rod Aydelotte/Waco Tribune Herald/Sygma **535** Bob Daemmrich/The Image Works **539** Liaison, Agency Inc.

Chapter 15: **544** Todd Bigelow/Black Star **548** Culver Pictures, Inc. **550** Library of Congress **551** The New York Public Library, Schomburg Center for Research in Black Culture **553** Theo Westenberger/Liaison, Agency, Inc. **555** Patricia Hollander Gross/Stock Boston **556** Mike Smith/FPG International LLC **558** Flip Schulke/Black Star **563** Raynor/SIPA Press **569** Corbis-Bettmann **570** Reuters/Ogrocki/Archive Photos **581** Bob Child/AP/Wide World Photos **582** Johnson/Liaison, Agency Inc.

Chapter 16: **588** Doug Mills/AP/Wide World Photos **590** North Wind Picture Archives **591** Reuters/Mark Cardwel/Corbis-Bettmann **593** UPI/Corbis-Bettmann **595** Joe Marquette/ AP/Wide World Photos **599** Topham/The Image Works **605** Peter Morgan/Reuters/ Archive Photos **609** *U.S. News and World Report*/ Archive Photo **612** Ken Hawkins/Sygma

Chapter 17: **616** Steven Rubin/The Image Works **623** Wilfredo Lee/AP/Wide World Photos **626** UPI/Corbis-Bettmann **627** Bill Burke/Impact Visuals Photo & Graphics, Inc. **629** The New Yorker **633** Regan/Liaison, Agency Inc. **638** Reed Saxon/AP/Wide World Photos **640** Reuters/Mike Theiler/ Corbis-Bettmann **641** Goddard*Claussen/First Tuesday, Malibu, California

Chapter 18: **644** Christopher Smith/Impact Visuals Photo & Graphics, Inc. **647** Joe Marquette/ AP/Wide World Photos **650** UPI/Corbis-Bettmann **652** Bohdan Hrynewych/Stock Boston **654** Reuters/David Brauchli/Corbis-Bettmann **657** F.E. Zip Zimmerman/U.S. Department of Defense **662** Ahn Young-ioon/AP/Wide World Photos **664** Bruno Barbey/Magnum Photos, Inc.

INDEX

Constitution, U.S. (*continued*)
    separation of powers in, 78–79, 82
    slavery provisions, 71–72, 546–48
    structure of government and, 76–78
    voting rights and, 31
Constitutional Action Party, 234
Constitutional Conventions:
    Texas, 726–29
    U.S. (1787), 62, 66–76, 81, 334
Constitutional county courts, in Texas, 844
Constitutional government, 17–18
Constitutionalism, 62
Constitution of 1845, Texas, 712, 713,
    716–17
Constitution of 1866, Texas, 712, 713,
    717–18
Constitution of Coahuila y Texas (1827),
    712–14
Constitution of the Republic of Texas
    (1836), 713–16
Constitutions, 17, 62, 88. *See also*
    Constitution, U.S.; Texas constitutions
Consultants, 440
Consumer Federation of America, 292
Consumer Products Safety Commission
    (CPSC), 438, 453
Containment policy, 648–49
Contingency fees, 482
Continuing resolution, 450
"Contract with America," 208, 323
Contractors, 440
Contributions, political:
    candidate self-financing, 253
    Congress and, 338
    incumbents and, 244
    interest group, 306–7
    large individual donors, 252
    Political Action Committees (PACs),
        252–53, 307–10
    primary elections and, 263
    small donations, 251–52
    soft money, 253, 254, 261
Convention delegates, 218–19
Conventions. *See* Party conventions
Cook, Vernon H., 726
Coolidge, Calvin, 379, 382, 419
Cooperative federalism, 108–9
Cooptation, 828–29
Cornell University Law School, 500
Cornyn, John, 870
Corporate PACs, 308, 309, 338
Corpus Christi, Texas, 878
Cost-of-living increases (COLAs), 628
Council-manager government, in Texas,
    883–84
Council of Economic Advisers (CEA),
    399, 591, 592, 594, 613
Council on Competitive Government,
    Texas, 833–34
Council on Foreign Relations, 673
Council of State Governments, The, 124
Councils of government (COGs), in
    Texas, 900–901
County attorney, in Texas, 894
County auditor, in Texas, 895
County chair, in Texas, 754, 755
County clerk, in Texas, 893
County committees, 218
County conventions, in Texas, 756
County courts, in Texas, 843–44
County executive committee, in Texas,
    754, 755
County government, in Texas, 877,
    891–96, 903
County judge, in Texas, 892–93
County treasurer, in Texas, 895
Courts, 465–503
    constitutional powers of, 466
    federal court system, 474–80
    independent counsel investigations,
        485–86
    judicial power, 465–70
    judicial review, 466–70
    judicial self-restraint vs. judicial
        activism, 470–73
    lobbying of, 314
    politics of selecting judges, 483, 486–88

specialized rules in judicial decision
    making, 480–83
state, appeals from, 477
Supreme Court. *See* Supreme Court
in Texas. *See* Texas judiciary
Courts of Appeals, 474–76
    in Texas, 845–46
Covert action, 409
Cox, Archibald, 484
Cracking, 758
Craddick, Tom, 792
Crane, Daniel B., 373
Cranston, Alan, 371
Crime, 530–42
    in Texas cities, 890
Crime rates, 530–31
Criminal defendants, rights of, 533–40, 864
Criminal justice, in Texas, 864–69
Cuban Americans, 575–77
Cuban missile crisis, 649–50
Cultural conflict, 41–43
Culver, Barbara, 862
Cuomo, Andrew M., 436
Custom duties, 609

Daley, William, 436
Dallas, Texas, 878, 885, 902
Daniel, Price, Jr., 727–29, 749, 779
Daschle, Tom, 349
Davis, Edmund J., 711, 718–20, 745
Dawes Act (1887), 580
Dealignment, 222
Dean, John, 384, 385
Death, causes of, 634–35
Death penalty, 540–42
Debates, presidential, 268, 272, 276–77
Deceptive Trade Practices-Consumer
    Protection Act (1973), Texas, 853
Decision making:
    participation in, 15
    in Texas legislature, 795–97
Declaration of Independence, 16, 63–64,
    67
DeConcini, Dennis, 371
Deductibles, 636
De facto segregation, 554–55
Default, 603
Defendants, 481
Defense, Department of, 433, 434, 435,
    458
Defenselink, 673
Defense policy, 324–26, 407
Defense spending, 672–73
Deferrals, 388
Deficits, 603, 605
Deinstitutionalization, 622
DeLay, Tom, 349
Delegated powers. *See* Enumerated powers
Delegates:
    convention, 218–19
    representatives as, 365
Dell, Michael, 692
Democracy:
    in America, 22–23
    bureaucracy and, 440–44
    direct vs. representative, 18–19
    meaning of, 12, 15
    national rankings, 14
    paradox of, 15, 17–18
    personal liberty and, 506
Democratic ideals, 12
Democratic Leadership Council (DLC),
    49, 51, 205–6
Democratic National Committee (DNC),
    217, 234
Democratic Party, 21, 49
    emergence of, 199–201
    historic dominance of Congress, 338–40
    liberal vs. conservative views of
        activists, 219
    national conventions, 202–4, 218
    New Deal, 201–2
    "New" Democrats, 205–6
    operations in Congress, 347
    party identification and, 221–24, 272
    party voting and, 361–62

platform positions, 1996, 220
    political arenas of, 215–18
    popular images of, 210
    presidential voting and, 203
    during Reagan Coalition, 205
    social group support for, 226
    strength by state, 227
    of Texas, 739, 745, 747–52, 754–57,
        762, 764, 790–92, 818–19
Democratic-Republican Party, 93–94,
    198–99
Demonstrations:
    by interest groups, 305–6
    as protest, 157–58
    rights and, 525
Dennis, Eugene V., 517
Dennis v. United States (1951), 517
De novo cases, in Texas, 843
Dependency ratio, 627–28
Deregulation, 455–56
Desegregation, 553–54
Détente, 651
Deterrence, 655, 657
Devolution revolution, 122–23
Dignity, individual, 12, 15
Dillon rule, 876
Diplomatic recognition, 407
Direct democracy, 19, 80
Direct discrimination, 571
Direct primary elections, 762
Disabled Americans, rights of, 582–83
Discharge petition, 356
Discretionary funds, 429
Discretionary spending, 602–3
Dissent, 54–58
Dissenting opinion, 494
District attorney, in Texas, 894
District clerk, in Texas, 894
District courts, 474, 475
    in Texas, 844–45
Division of labor, 424
Division votes, in Texas legislature, 789
Doggett, Lloyd, 870
Dole, Robert, 184, 191, 208, 225, 247,
    254, 267, 269, 272–75, 277, 340,
    416
Domestic affairs, presidential use of
    military force in, 414
Domestic policy, 324–26
Douglas, Stephen A., 199
Douglas, William O., 473, 495, 523
Drafting a bill, 356
Dred Scott v. Sandford (1857), 469, 501,
    547–48
Drinking age, national, 116
Drug Enforcement Administration
    (DEA), 479, 532
Drugs, legalization of, 532
Dual federalism, 108
Dual labor market, 571
Du Bois, W. E. B., 550–51
Due Process Clause, 491, 509
Dukakis, Michael, 205, 247, 269, 272,
    274, 277, 415
Duncan, M. P. "Rusty," 861

Earle, Ronnie, 800, 801
Early voting, in Texas, 763
Earnings gap, 571–73
Easton, David, 680
Economic diversification, in Texas, 697
Economic freedom, 30
Economic growth, 590, 597–98
Economic interests, 286–87
Economic regions of Texas, 698–700
Economics, 589–614
    American performance, 596–99
    debt burden, 603–5
    decision making, 592–96
    government spending, 599–603
    taxes. *See* Taxes
    in Texas, 694–97
    theories, 590–92
Edelman, Marian Wright, 288
Edgewood v. Kirby (Texas, 1989), 733–34,
    743

Education:
    media bias and, 178
    support for political parties and, 226
    in Texas, 693, 722–23, 869–71,
        898–900
    tolerance and, 137
    voter turnout and, 154, 156
    voting behavior in presidential
        elections and, 272, 275, 278
    voting behavior in Texas and, 753
Education, Department of, 434, 435
Education Act Amendment (1972), 570–71
Education groups, in Texas, 741–43
Edwards, Al, 793
Ehrlichman, John, 384, 385
Eighteenth Amendment, 91, 292, 534
Eighth Amendment, 87, 472, 508, 509, 540
Eisenhower, Dwight D., 114, 190, 202,
    379, 382, 386, 406, 414, 416, 483,
    498, 649, 748
Elazar, Daniel, 682
Elected office, running for, 160–61
Elections, 19
    advantages of incumbency, 243–45
    campaign finance. *See* Campaign finance
    campaign strategies, 245–49
    careerism and, 242
    congressional, 337–41
    constitutional requirements for office,
        240
    as mandates, 238–39
    mass media and, 179–84
    personal ambition and, 239–40
    presidential. *See* Presidential
        campaigns; Presidential elections
    professionalism and, 242
    protection of rights, 239
    qualifications for candidates, 240, 242
    retrospective judgment, 239
    in Texas, 761–63, 885–86
Electoral College, 268–71
Electoral system, 229
Eleventh Amendment, 91
Elite, 683, 733
Elitism, 20–22, 739–40
Ellis, Rodney, 860
Ellwood, David, 629
El Paso, Texas, 878, 881, 882, 901
Emancipation Proclamation, 548
EMILY's List, 280, 309
Employer-based health plans, 638–39
End of history, 56
Energy, Department of, 435
Engels, Frederick, 55
Engle v. Vitale (1962), 512
Enoch, Craig, 870
Enterprise Institute, 50–51
Entitlement programs, 599–601, 625
Enumerated powers, 84–85, 104, 106,
    107, 115–17
Environmental Defense Fund, 314, 459
Environmental Protection Agency (EPA),
    312, 426, 434, 438, 439, 453–55,
    459–60
Equal Employment Opportunity
    Commission (EEOC), 438, 453,
    455, 460, 561, 574, 584
Equality, 15. *See also* Civil rights
    of opportunity, 30–32
    political, 31, 33–34
    politics of, 546
    of results, 31–32
Equal Protection Clause, 491, 549,
    561–63, 568, 583
Equal protection of the laws, 552–55
Equal Rights Amendment (ERA), 91–92,
    570
Equal-time rule, 185
Ervin, Sam, 157
Escobedo v. Illinois (1964), 537
Establishment, The, in Texas, 740
Estate tax, 609
Ethics:
    congressional, 369–71, 373
    Texas legislature and, 798–801
Ethics in Government Act (1978), 313, 484
Ethnic issues, in Texas, 688

Social welfare (*continued*)
power and, 617–18
reform, 122–23, 629–30, 632, 633, 706
senior citizens, 627–29
Social Security, 11, 600, 602–3, 617, 618, 624, 625, 627
Supplemental Security Income (SSI), 624, 625, 631
unemployment compensation, 624, 625
welfare policy, 618
Soft money, 253, 254, 261
Solicitor general, 492
Somalia, 665
Sorauf, Frank, 261
Sound bites, 248
Souter, David, 115, 487, 490, 495, 497
Southern Christian Leadership Conference (SCLC), 556–58
Southwest Voter Registration Education Project, 759, 760, 886
Sovereign immunity, 481
Soviet Union, 646–50, 652–56
Spanish-American War (1898), 76, 325
Sparkman, John, 415
Speaker of the House, 347, 349
in Texas legislature, 778–80, 782
Spears, Franklin, 870
Special committees, in Texas legislature, 785–86
Special districts, in Texas, 877, 896–98
Special prosecutors, 485–86
Special sessions, of Texas legislature, 771–72, 811
Specification of authority, 424
Spector, Rose, 862
Speech, freedom of, 513–14, 517–20
Spin doctors, 264
Splintering, 330
Splinter parties, 233
Spoils system, 440, 896
Stagflation, 591
Staggered terms, in Texas bureaucracy, 814
Stalin, Josef, 646
Standard partial preemption, 120
Standing, 481
Standing committees, 352–53
in Texas legislature, 783–85
Standing subcommittees, in Texas legislature, 783–85
Stanton, Elizabeth Cady, 292, 568
Stare decisis, 473
Starr, Ken, 484
START I, 656
START II, 656
"Star Wars," 658
State, Department of, 434, 435
State Board of Education, Texas, 825
State-centered federalism, 108
State chair, 754, 755
State conventions, 756
State courts:
appeals from, 477
in Texas. *See* Texas judiciary
State executive committee, 754, 755
State governments, 11, 101
constitutional amendments and, 89, 91–92
under federalism, 98
grant-in-aid programs and, 117–19
mandates and, 120, 122
powers denied to, 106, 107
preemptions and, 120
role in national government, 107
Texas. *See* Texas executive; Texas judiciary; Texas legislature.
vs. tobacco companies, 102–3
State militias, 528
State of Texas Web site, 707, 906
State party conventions, 218
State party organizations, 217
States' rights, 105
States' Rights (Dixiecrat) Party, 233
State treasurer, of Texas, 824
Statutory county courts, in Texas, 844
Statutory laws, 470, 713, 841
Stevens, John Paul, 115, 487, 490, 495, 497
Stevenson, Adlai, 221, 415

Stevenson, Coke, 821
Stewart, Potter, 487, 495
Stone, Harlan, 472
Stone, Lucy, 292, 568
Strategic Defense Initiative (SDI), 658–59
Strong mayor government, in Texas, 880–82
Studds, Gerry E., 373
Sturns, Louis, 861
Subcommittees:
congressional, 353–54
in Texas legislature, 783
Subcultures, 28
Subpoenas, 895
Succession, presidential, 382–83
Suffrage, 150, 292, 724
Sullivan rule, 186
Sunset Advisory Commission (Texas), 798, 829
Sunset legislation, in Texas, 832–33
Superdelegates, 219
Superpowers, 647
Super Tuesday, 265
Supplemental Security Income (SSI), 624, 625, 631
Supply-side economics, 591–92
Supreme Court, 78, 410, 465, 474, 476–77
characteristics of justices, 488–91
checking power of, 498–501
checks and balances and, 79, 82
conferences, 492
decision making, 491–92, 496–98
hearing of arguments by, 491–92
judicial review power of, 79, 92, 466–70
judicial self-restraint vs. judicial activism, 470–73
litmus test and candidates, 483, 486
lobbyists and, 314
nationalization of Bill of Rights and, 506, 509
policy agenda of, 491
presidential selection of candidates for, 483
public confidence in, 337
Senate confirmations of candidates, 486–88
size of, 477
structure of, 79
voting blocs, 494–95, 498
written opinions, 492, 494
Supreme Court building, 492
Supreme Court decisions:
abortion, 92, 470, 473, 496–97
affirmative action, 491–92, 561–63, 565–66
apportionment and redistricting issues, 328–29, 332, 776–77
arms, right to bear, 529
bureaucrats' success with, 461
compliance with, 499–500
congressional spending, 593
criminal defendants, 533, 535–42, 864
death penalty, 540–42
desegregation, 92, 105, 114, 314, 414, 469–70
executive privilege, 388
federalism issues, 109, 110, 112, 114, 115, 117
First Amendment issues, 184–86, 188, 498–99, 509–14, 516–19, 521–25, 527
gender equality, 568–70
gun-related school violence and, 115
independent counsel law, 484
Native Americans and, 581
obscenity, 521–22
original intent and, 472
physician-assisted suicide, 518
policy agenda, 470
presidential powers, 385, 387–89, 406
right to privacy, 496
segregation, 105, 114, 549, 552–55
sexual harassment, 574
slavery, 547–48
term limits, 334
voting rights, 148, 149, 860
Watergate scandal, 385
wisdom vs. constitutionality and, 472

Supreme Court of Texas. *See* Texas Supreme Court
Survey research, 129–34
Swann v. Charlotte-Mecklenburg County Board of Education (1971), 554
Swinford, David, 716
Swing states, 268
Symbolic speech, 517
Syria, 662

Taft, William Howard, 201, 233, 379, 385
Tag, in Texas Senate, 788
Talk radio, 168
Taney, Roger, 547–48
Tariffs, 73
Tax abatements, in Texas, 903–4
Tax assessor-collector, in Texas, 894
Taxes, 605–14
capital gains, 613–14
estate, 609
excise, 609
flat tax issue, 610–11
gift, 609
income, 114, 117, 220, 606–8
levying of, 73, 91, 322, 326
poll, 149, 723, 757
Tax expenditures, 607–8
Tax Reform Act (1986), 608, 614
Taylor, Zachary, 379
Teague, Marvin O., 861
Teen pregnancy, 621–22
Tejeda, Frank, 763
Television:
cable, 168
campaign strategies and, 245–49
candidate-voter linkage and, 179–80
influence on public opinion, 187
interpretation of news, 174
network news, 166–68
news anchors, 172
political innovations, 190–91
power of, 167
presidential campaign coverage by, 1996, 184
public confidence in, 337
public opinion on power of, 425
usage by age, 170
Television censorship, 524
Television malaise, 189
Temporary Assistance to Needy Families, 123, 630, 633
Tennessee Valley Authority (TVA), 439
Tenth Amendment, 87, 109, 508
Term limits, 334
Terrorism, 657–58, 663
Texaco, Inc., 855
Texas:
African Americans, 681–82, 685–86, 688, 690, 692, 693, 716, 718, 723, 743, 747, 749, 757–61, 774–77, 780, 793, 847, 857–61, 878, 886
Anglos, 686–87
Asian Americans, 687, 690, 692, 693
campaign finance, 763–66
challenges of the 1990s, 678–80
compared with other states, 694
demographics, 680, 684–93
economic regions, 698–700
economic and social interdependence with Mexico, 701–7
economy, 694–97
education, 693, 722–23, 869–71, 898–900
elections, 761–63
Hispanics, 681, 682, 684–85, 688, 690, 692, 693, 749, 759–60, 774–77, 793, 847, 857–61, 878, 886
individual rights, 723
interest groups, 731–32, 738–45, 797, 820, 828–29
Native Americans, 684, 692, 693
political culture, 682–84
political environment, 680–708
political gains by minorities and women, 758–61
political myths, 680–82

political participation and minorities, 757–58
political parties, 745, 747–57
racial and ethnic composition, 685
racial and ethnic issues, 688
size of, 691
transnational regionalism, 701–7
voting rights, 724
Texas Assessment of Academic Skills (TAAS), 743
Texas Association of Counties Web site, 906
Texas Association of School Boards Web site, 906
Texas bureaucracy, 825–35
appointments, 813–15
growth of, 825–27
public policy and, 827–29
strategies for controlling, 829–35
Texas cities:
characteristics, 878
crime and urban violence, 890
declining infrastructures, 889–90
general categories, 879
government. *See* Texas municipal governments
graying of, 889
ten largest, 689
urbanization, 589–90
"white flight" from, 889
Texas Citizen Action, 857
Texas Civil Rights Project, 777
Texas Conservative Coalition, 790
Texas Constitution of 1876:
ability to govern and restraints of, 734
amendments, 724–26, 729–34
change through court interpretation, 733–34
in comparative perspective, 713–14
constitutional convention, 726–29
general principles, 721
prospects for future change, 734
reform efforts, 727–31
weaknesses and criticisms of, 722–24
Texas constitutions, 711–35
Civil War Constitution (1861), 712, 713, 717
of Coahuila y Texas (1827), 712–14
of 1845, 712, 713, 716–17
of 1866, 712, 713, 717–18
of 1876. *See* Texas Constitution of 1876
Reconstruction Constitution (1869), 712, 713, 718–19
of the Republic of Texas (1836), 713–16
Texas Court of Criminal Appeals, 721, 761, 842, 843, 846, 847, 850, 851, 864–68
Texas Department of Criminal Justice Web site, 872
Texas Education Agency (TEA), 898–900
Texas Ethics Commission, 763, 764, 766
Texas executive, 805–25
agriculture commissioner, 824
attorney general, 822
bureaucracy, 825
comptroller of public accounts, 822–23
elected boards and commissions, 824–25
governor. *See* Texas governors
land commissioner, 823
lieutenant governor, 780–82, 821–22
secretary of state, 824
state treasurer, 824
structure, 807–8
Texas Farm Bureau, 744
Texas governors. *See also* names of governors
appointive and removal powers, 813–15
backgrounds, 809
budgetary powers, 813
constitutional powers granted to, 721, 722
impeachment of, 809–10
informal resources, 815–16
interest groups and, 820
judicial power, 815
legislative powers of, 787, 796, 811–13
list of, 810
mass media and, 818

Thomas R. Dye, formerly McKenzie Professor of Government and Policy Sciences at Florida State University, regularly taught large introductory classes in American politics and was University Teacher of the Year in 1987. He received his B.A. and M.A. degrees from Pennsylvania State University and his Ph.D. degree from the University of Pennsylvania. He is the author of numerous books and articles on American government and public policy, including *The Irony of Democracy*; *Politics in States and Communities*; *Understanding Public Policy*; *Who's Running America*; *Politics in Florida*; *Power in Society*; *Politics, Economics, and the Public*; and *American Federalism: Competition among Governments*. His books have been translated into many languages, including Russian and Chinese, and published abroad. He has served as president of the Southern Political Science Association, president of the Policy Studies Organization, and secretary of the American Political Science Association. He has taught at the University of Pennsylvania, the University of Wisconsin, and the University of Georgia, and served as a visiting scholar at Bar-Ilan University, Israel, the Brookings Institution, Washington, and elsewhere. He is a member of Phi Beta Kappa, Omicron Delta Kappa, and Phi Kappa Phi, and is listed in most major biographical directories.

L. Tucker Gibson, Jr., is chair and professor of political science at Trinity University, where he teaches introductory courses in American national and state government as well as courses on U.S. legislatures, political parties, and interest groups. He has served on the Civil Service Commission of the city of San Antonio, assisted local governments across central and south Texas in redistricting their government bodies, and conducted public opinion research for political candidates, businesses, and corporations. Gibson is the coauthor of *Government and Politics in the Lone Star State: Theory and Practice*.

Clay Robison has covered state government and politics in Texas for more than 25 years as a journalist, first for the *San Antonio Light*, and then, since 1982, for the *Houston Chronicle*. He is the *Houston Chronicle*'s Austin bureau chief, and in addition to covering daily news events, he writes a weekly column that appears on the newspaper's Sunday editorial page. He has covered many of the personalities and events that are incorporated in the chapters on Texas government. Robison is the coauthor of *Government and Politics in the Lone Star State: Theory and Practice*.

948